THE SUBSTANTIVE LAW OF THE EEC

AUSTRALIA
The Law Book Company
Sydney

CANADA
The Carswell Company
Toronto, Ontario

INDIA
N. M. Tripathi (Private) Ltd
Bombay

Eastern Law House (Private) Ltd
Calcutta

M.P.P. House
Bangalore

Universal Book Traders
Delhi

ISRAEL
Steimatzky's Agency Ltd
Tel Aviv

PAKISTAN
Pakistan Law House
Karachi

The Substantive Law of the EEC

by

DERRICK WYATT

M.A., LL.B. (Cantab), J.D. (Chicago)
of Lincoln's Inn, Barrister,
Fellow of St. Edmund Hall,
Oxford

and

ALAN DASHWOOD

B.A. (Rhodes), M.A. (Oxon)
of the Inner Temple, Barrister,
Director in the Legal Service of the Council
of the European Communities,
Visiting Professor of Law in the University of Leicester

LONDON
SWEET & MAXWELL
1987

First Edition 1980
Second Impression 1981
Third Impression 1986
Second Edition 1987
Second Impression 1990
Third Impression 1991

Published in 1987 by
Sweet & Maxwell Limited now of
South Quay Plaza
183 Marsh Wall, London.
Computerset by Promenade Graphics Ltd., Cheltenham
Printed in England by Clays Ltd, St Ives plc

ISBN Hardback   0 421 34870
        Paperback   0 421 34880

PREFACE

In our Preface to the first edition of this work, we noted that institutional and jurisdictional matters had loomed rather larger than substantive law in the legal literature on the European Communities then available in English and declared that we had attempted to produce a book in which that emphasis was reversed. Eight years on, with the appearance of a number of text books and monographs, dedicated to the substantive law of the European Communities, the approach seems much more conventional. However, at the risk of exchanging the mantle of the avant garde for that of the conventionally wise, we offer our readers a second edition essentially identical in conception to the original one.

Our book is aimed first and foremost at students pursuing a degree course in European Community law which contains a major element of substantive law. Thus the emphasis remains on the "core" subjects of such courses, namely the free movement of goods, persons and services, the common agricultural policy, competition and intellectual property. At the same time, we are hopeful (encouraged by the occasional sight of our first edition at the elbow of counsel in the law courts) that the book will continue to be of use to legal practitioners, particularly when guidance is needed on the principles underlying the often intricate rules of the Community system.

A significant change is the addition of a chapter on "Sex Discrimination" which reflects the major developments in this field of law over recent years. The "Introduction to the Rules on Competition" has been amplified and the Chapter on "Restrictive Practices" and "Intellectual Property" have been completely rewritten. There is also now a separate chapter on the application of Article 85 and Article 86 by the Community and national authorities.

Since our book is concerned with substantive law, we include no treatment of institutional matters beyond an examination of the composition and procedure of the Court of Justice and an outline of its various heads of jurisdiction. This seemed necessary because the Court plays such a vital part in the development of the law both in direct actions and in the preliminary ruling procedure. As before, and for the same obvious reasons, what we describe as "the Community legal order" (comprising, *inter alia*, the supremacy of Community law, direct applicability, and the general principles of Community law) is covered in some detail. Compromises have been inevitable, within the constraints of a single volume intended to be of manageable size and reasonable price. Thus the chapters in the first edition on Article 177 EEC, and on the treaty-making powers of the Community, have given way to what we believe to be higher priorities. We have also adhered to our original decision to omit the free movement of capital, transport policy and the harmonisation of laws (including company law and products liability). We note that the body of Directives comprising "European company law" is increasingly and inevitably being treated as an element of the domestic company law syllabus; and early signs are that "European products liability law" is moving in the same direction, towards incorporation in the tort syllabus.

As in our first edition, we have confined our attention to the EEC Treaty which from the breadth of its ambit dominates the field of European Community Law. The ECSC and Euratom Treaties are only referred to incidentally, by way of comparison or where their provisions cast light on those of the EEC Treaty.

The book was jointly planned but individually written. Derrick Wyatt wrote chapters 1 to 3 and 5 to 12. Alan Dashwood wrote chapters 4 and 13 to 19.

To the following we express warm thanks and appreciation: Philippa Watson, sometime Legal Secretary at the Court of Justice and official of the Commission's Directorate General for Competition, for her comments on the chapter on the social security rights of migrants; Kathleen Lee of the Solicitor's Office of the Department of Health and Social Security, who was kind enough to consider the same chapter in draft; D. Grant Lawrence of the Legal Service of the Commission who read the draft chapter on Agriculture and made helpful suggestions; Angus Murray of the Solicitor's Office of the Ministry of Agriculture, Fisheries and Food who also read that chapter; Jonathan Faull of DG IV who was generous with advice on procedure in competition matters; Malcolm Ross of the Department of Law at the University of Leicester for his assistance with the chapters on "State Aids" and "Public Undertakings" and Fiona Cownie, also of Leicester, for hers with the chapter on "Restrictive Practices"; Joan Wyatt and Julie Dashwood for their work on the galley and page proofs which enabled us to meet a tight schedule in the run up to publication; and Barbara Goodman and Christine Driver for prodigious feats of typing. Our thanks go in addition to the colleagues and friends—too numerous to mention individually—who have given us advice and encouragement; and to our publishers but for whom this edition, like its predecessor, would never have seen the light.

Alan Dashwood is now an official of the Council of the European Communities but all views expressed in this book are purely personal.

Derrick Wyatt
Alan Dashwood

June 1987

CONTENTS

TABLE OF COMMUNITY TREATIES

TABLE OF COMMUNITY SECONDARY LEGISLATION

REGULATIONS

DECISIONS AND DIRECTIVES

COMMISSION DECISIONS

TABLE OF INTERNATIONAL AGREEMENTS

TABLE OF UNITED KINGDOM STATUTES

TABLE OF CASES

TABLE OF CASES IN NATIONAL COURTS

PART I: INTRODUCTION

CHAPTER 1

HISTORICAL ORIGINS AND DEVELOPMENT

The Schuman Plan and the establishment of the European Coal and Steel Community

Although there was a certain ideological groundswell in favour of a "United Europe" shortly after the War[1]—as evidenced by the call of the 1948 Hague Congress for Western European economic and political union—the first concrete steps towards integration were prompted by the spectre of Soviet expansion. Within days of the signature by France and the United Kingdom of the Dunkirk Treaty, providing for mutual assistance in the event of a renewal of hostilities with Germany, the breakdown of the Moscow Conference over the future of occupied Germany was to set the pattern for future strained relations between the U.S.S.R. on the one side, and the United States, Great Britain and France on the other.[2] Despite the indispensable United States defence commitment affirmed in the North Atlantic Treaty, Western Europe stood divided and vulnerable in the face of a Soviet Union whose wartime military potential had been scarcely diminished by demobilisation, and whose political influence had been enhanced by successful Communist Party coups in Bulgaria, Rumania, Poland and Czechoslovakia.[2] It was in this context that M. Robert Schuman, the French Foreign Minister, made an historic proposal to a ministerial meeting in London on May 9, 1950.[3] His proposal was for no less than the fusion of the coal and steel industries of France and Germany, and any other countries wishing to participate, under a supranational high authority. Not only would such a pooling of production make future conflict between France and Germany impossible, it would provide a sound basis for economic expansion. The implications of the scheme were clearly far-reaching, constituting, as M. Schuman explained, "the first concrete foundation for a European Federation which is so indispensable for the preservation of peace."

The Schuman Plan was enthusiastically endorsed by the Benelux countries, France, Germany and Italy, but the United Kingdom declined to participate, refusing to accept the role of the projected High Authority. The Treaty Establishing the European Coal and Steel Community was signed in Paris on April 18, 1951, and came into force on July 20, of the following year.

The Treaty of Paris defines the task of the Community as that of estab-

---

[1] See generally, Michael Palmer *et al.*, *European Unity* (1968), Introduction; Gladwyn, *The European Idea* (1967), Chap. 4, A. H. Robertson, *European Institutions* (1973), pp. 5–17; Kapteyn and Van Themaat, *Introduction to the Law of the European Communities* (1973), Chap. I.

[2] *NATO—Facts and Figures* (Brussels, 1971), Chap. 1.

[3] For the French text, see *Documents on International Affairs* (1949–1950), pp. 315–317. An English translation (from which the quotations in the text are extracted) appears in 22 *Department of State Bulletin* at pp. 936, 937.

3

lishing a common market in coal and steel products, and prohibits the following as being incompatible with that aim[4]:

(a) import and export duties, or charges having equivalent effect, and quantitative restrictions on the movement of products;

(b) measures or practices which discriminate between producers, between purchasers or between consumers, especially in prices and delivery terms or transport rates and conditions; and measures or practices which interfere with the purchaser's free choice of supplier;

(c) subsidies or aids granted by States, or special charges imposed by States, in any form whatsoever;

(d) restrictive practices which tend towards the sharing or exploiting of markets.

In order to carry out its allotted task, the Community enjoys a limited power of intervention in the economies of the Member States, and is empowered, *inter alia*, to place financial resources at the disposal of undertakings for investment. Only if circumstances require is it authorised to exert direct influence upon production or the play of market forces.[5]

The Preamble to the Treaty of Paris emphasises its political inspiration, recording the resolve of the signatory powers to "substitute for age-old rivalries the merging of their essential interests; to create, by establishing an economic community, the basis of a broader and deeper Community among peoples long divided by bloody conflicts; and to lay the foundations for institutions which will give direction to a destiny henceforth shared." The reference to common institutions is particularly significant, for as Mr. Schuman had pointed out, the Coal and Steel Community was to constitute the first stage of European Federation. In accordance with this aim, the Treaty establishes four major institutions: a High Authority, a Special Council of Ministers, a Common Assembly and a Court of Justice.[6]

The High Authority, a body of independent individuals rather than government representatives, is entrusted with the duty of ensuring the realisation of Community objectives. To this end, it is empowered to take legally binding decisions,[7] and is authorised, *inter alia*, to procure funds,[8] to fix maximum and minimum prices for certain products,[9] and to fine undertakings in breach of the Treaty's competition rules.[10]

The function of the Council of Ministers, a body composed of representatives of the Member States, is primarily "to harmonise the action of the High Authority and that of Governments, which are responsible for the general economic policies of their countries."[11] With limited exceptions,[12]

---

[4] Art. 4.
[5] Art. 5.
[6] Art. 7.
[7] Art. 4. The functions of the High Authority are now carried out by the Commission of the European Communities.
[8] Art. 49.
[9] Arts. 61 and 64.
[10] Arts. 65 and 66.
[11] Art. 26. Compare the central role of the Council in the European Economic Community. The functions of the Special Council are now carried out by the Council of the European Communities.
[12] Arts. 58 and 59.

the role of the Council is confined to consultation with the High Authority, and the giving or withholding of consent to the action of the latter.

An element of public accountability is ensured by the Common Assembly, composed of delegates appointed by their respective parliaments from among their Members.[13] It is endowed with certain supervisory powers, the most potent being that of removal of the High Authority on a motion of censure.[14]

Judicial control is the responsibility of the Court of Justice, which has jurisdiction, *inter alia*, to review the legality of acts of the High Authority at the suit of Member States or the Council, or, in more limited circumstances, undertakings or associations of undertakings.[15]

Faltering steps towards European Federation

Significant as the founding of the European Coal and Steel Community may have been, it contributed little of itself to the increasingly pressing problem of incorporating West Germany into the defence network established by the Brussels and North Atlantic Treaties. While the United States was enthusiastic for German participation, France was naturally chary of seeing her recently vanquished enemy so soon rearmed. At the instigation of Sir Winston Churchill and M. Paul Reynaud[16] the Consultative Assembly of the Council of Europe[17] called for the "immediate creation of a unified European Army, under the authority of a European Minister of Defence, subject to proper European democratic control and acting in full co-operation with the United States and Canada."[18]

After a French initiative known as the "Pleven Plan," the Treaty Establishing the European Defence Community was signed—subject to ratification—by the Benelux countries, France, Germany and Italy.[19] Once again the United Kingdom, seeing herself as a Great Power in her own right, held aloof. If the Coal and Steel Community had been calculated to bind Germany to France industrially, the European Defence Community was to provide the framework for German rearmament.

The projected Defence Community had two significant characteristics. First, it was to be endowed with a supranational institutional structure not unlike that of the Coal and Steel Community. Secondly, its statute assumed that it would be of a *transitional* nature, and would give way to some more comprehensive form of Federal or Confederal European Union.

---

[13] Art. 21.
[14] Art. 24.
[15] Art. 33.
[16] Robertson, *op. cit.* p. 18.
[17] The Council of Europe is an intergovernmental organisation established in 1949. Its aim is to achieve greater unity among its members, and to this end it seeks agreement on common action "in economic, social, cultural, scientific, legal and administrative matters and in the maintenance and further realisation of human rights and fundamental freedoms." See Bowett, *The Law of International Institutions* (1975), p. 149; Robertson, *op. cit.*, p. 36.
[18] Resolution of the Consultative Assembly of the Council of Europe, August 11, 1950; *Documents on International Affairs* (1949–1950), p. 331. As is clear from the quotation cited in the text, the Council at times interprets the terms of its statute with some liberality. Robertson, *op. cit.* p. 19.
[19] May 27, 1952. See *Documents on International Affairs* (1952), pp. 116–162.

The Defence Community Treaty provided for a European Army, composed of units placed at the disposal of the Council of Ministers by the Member States. A Common Budget would be drawn up, and an executive body, the "Commissariat," would lay down common programmes in the field of armaments, provisioning and military infrastructure. The objects of the Community were to be purely defensive, within the context of the North Atlantic Treaty.

The transitional nature of the proposed Defence Community was evidenced by the terms of Article 8(2), which provided that the institutional structure laid down in the Treaty would remain in force until displaced by the establishment of the Federal or Confederal organisation envisaged by Article 38.

This latter Article required the Assembly of the European Defence Community to make proposals to the Governments of the Member States on the establishment of a *directly elected* Assembly, and the powers it should exercise. Particular regard was to be had to the principle that such a modified Parliamentary body should be able to constitute one of the elements in a subsequent federal or confederal structure.

These proposals were to be presented to the Governments of the Six after the Assembly of the Defence Community assumed its functions, but within days of the signature of the Treaty the Consultative Assembly of the Council of Europe resolved that it would be "of great advantage if the basic principles of a European supranational political authority and the nature and limits of its powers were defined within the next few months, without waiting for the entry into force of the Treaty instituting the European Defence Community."[20] Despite the fact that the Assembly provided for in Article 38 of the EDC Treaty was not yet in existence, and that the Article only referred to the constitution of a future Parliamentary body, the Foreign Ministers of the Member States of the Coal and Steel Community requested the Members of the Coal and Steel Community Assembly to co-opt additional Members, reorganise the distribution of seats laid down in the Paris Treaty in accordance with that prescribed for the Assembly of the proposed Defence Community, and draw up a draft Treaty for a European Political Community. On March 10, 1953, the "Ad Hoc Assembly" presented the requested draft.[21]

The "European Community" proposed by the Ad Hoc Assembly provided for the extensive political and economic integration of its Members. Its aims were as follows:

— to contribute towards the protection of human rights and fundamental freedoms in Member States;
— to co-operate with the other free nations in ensuring the security of Member States against all aggression;
— to ensure the co-ordination of the foreign policy of Member States in

---

[20] Resolution of May 30, 1952, *Texts Adopted* (1952), and see *Report of the Constitutional Committee instituted to work out a Draft Treaty setting up a European Political Community* (Paris, December 20, 1952), p. 8.
[21] See *Information and Official Documents of the Constitutional Committee of the Ad Hoc Assembly* (Paris, 1953), pp. 53 *et seq.*

questions likely to involve the existence, the security or the prosperity of the Community;

— to promote . . . the development of employment and the improvement of the standard of living in Member States, by means, in particular, of the progressive establishment of a common market . . .

To ensure the protection of human rights in the proposed Community, provision was made for the application—as part of the Community Statute—of the provisions of section I of the European Convention on Human Rights, along with the first Protocol to that Convention, signed in Paris on March 20, 1952.

The Institutions of the Political Community would comprise a bicameral legislature, a European Executive Council, a Council of National Ministers, Court of Justice, and an Economic and Social Council. Financial resources would be derived from a combination of Community taxation and contributions from the Member States.

The hopes of those who saw the future of Western Europe in immediate Federation were dashed when the French Parliament voted against ratification of the Defence Community Treaty. A change of Government in France, and an easing of tension between East and West,[22] contributed to the rejection of the Treaty by the combined votes of Gaullists, Communists, Socialists and Radicals.[23]

The participation of German forces in the defence of Western Europe was to be achieved by other means. The Paris Agreements of October 23, 1954 provided for the recognition of the Federal Republic of Germany as a sovereign state, and for its subsequent accession to the North Atlantic Treaty.[24]

A more modest proposal—the Spaak Report

Despite the setback to plans for Political Federation represented by the rejection of the Defence Community Treaty, the Six were still convinced of the need for closer integration. At the Messina Conference in 1955 the Foreign Ministers of the Coal and Steel Community countries expressed the belief that the time had come to make "a fresh advance towards the building of Europe," but that this must be achieved "first of all, in the economic field."[25] The twin objectives were agreed of developing atomic energy for peaceful purposes, and establishing a European common market. An Intergovernmental Committee under the Chairmanship of the Belgian Foreign Minister, M. Paul-Henri Spaak, was entrusted with the task of making proposals to this end. The United Kingdom was invited to participate in the work of the committee, but although a Board of Trade official was initially dispatched, he was recalled after a few weeks.

---

[22] Robertson, *op. cit.* p. 21.
[23] Palmer, *loc cit.*
[24] *NATO—Facts and Figures* (Brussels, 1971), p. 35. For the Protocol to the North Atlantic Treaty on the Accession of the Federal Republic of Germany, and the texts known collectively as the "Paris Agreements," see Apps. 9 and 10.
[25] *Documents on International Affairs* (1955), p. 163; Cmnd. 9525.

The Spaak Report was published on April 21, 1956.[26] It noted that the individual national markets in Europe were incapable of achieving the economies of scale achieved in the United States, citing three examples; car manufacturing, aviation, and atomic energy. It defined the object of a common market as the establishment of a large area with a common economic policy, establishing a powerful unit of production, which would allow continuous economic expansion, and the development of harmonious relations between the Member States. The Report examined, *inter alia*,

— the establishment of a customs union;
— the free movement of persons, services and capital;
— the establishment of a common agricultural policy;
— the establishment of a Community competition regime, embracing both agreements in restraint of trade, and government subsidy to industry;
— the correction of market distortions arising out of divergent national legislation.

In the committee's view it was impossible to establish a Common Market without institutional supervision, since it would be impracticable to exhaustively enumerate the procedures and mechanisms required to achieve the desired end. Four governing principles were considered to be determinative in the choice of institutional structure. First, the need to distinguish between matters of general economic policy, which remained within the domain of national governments, and problems concerning the day to day functioning of the Common Market. Secondly, the need to allow undertakings direct and speedy access to the authorities entrusted with the operation of the Community competition regime, and to ensure that the application of the Treaty rules to Member States was impartial and free from government veto. Thirdly, since certain matters of general policy were fundamental to the functioning of the common market, it would be necessary to provide for majority voting in certain areas, after the expiry of a transitional period. Finally, the committee took the view that judicial and parliamentary control would be indispensable.

Application of these principles led to the conclusion that there should be established a Council of Ministers and a European Commission. The former would take decisions on general matters of policy, usually by a unanimous vote, but exceptionally by a weighted majority. The latter would be composed of individuals chosen by common accord of the Governments of the Member States. It would act by a simple majority, and be entrusted with the task of supervising the application of the Treaty, and making proposals to the Council.

Judicial and parliamentary control would be ensured by the existing Court and Assembly of the Coal and Steel Community. In the case of the Court, it would have jurisdiction over actions concerning the legality of

---

[26] *Rapport des chefs de délégation aux ministres des affaires etrangères* (Brussels), April 21, 1956. A summarised translation of Part I of the Spaak Report—"The Common Market" was published by Political and Economic Planning as Broadsheet No. 405 of December 17, 1956.

acts of the Commission, and violations of the Treaty by the Member States and business enterprises. In the case of the Assembly, the respective sizes of national delegations would be adjusted in favour of the three largest Member States.

The Committee, it will be recalled, had also been instructed to consider the peaceful development of nuclear energy. It took the view that it would be impossible for the individual European countries to match the then current research and development effort of the United States and Great Britain, and concluded that a common approach and a common organisation was necessary.[27] The organisation would have its functions, *inter alia*, the development of research and the dissemination of its results, the establishment of safety standards for workforce and general population, the creation of a common market in nuclear materials and equipment, and the free movement of specialists. The institutional structure of such a common organisation would be identical to that proposed for the Common Market.

The European Economic Community—establishment and enlargement

After the negotiations which followed the endorsement of the Spaak Report by the Governments of the Six, two Treaties were signed at Rome on March 25, 1957, providing for the establishment of a European Economic Community, and a European Atomic Energy Community. Both Treaties came into force on January 1, 1958. Their content, and the institutional structure of the respective Communities, followed closely the recommendations of the Spaak Report. In order to minimise the resulting mushrooming of institutions, a convention signed contemporaneously with the founding treaties provided for a single Assembly and Court of Justice for the EEC and Euratom, which would also carry out the functions of the Assembly and Court of Justice of the Coal and Steel Community.[28] The institutional structure of the Communities was still rather unwieldy, since each had its own Council of Ministers and Commission—or High Authority, in the case of the Coal and Steel Community. The process of rationalisation was taken a stage further with the ratification in 1967 of a treaty providing for a single Commission and Council which would carry out institutional functions in all three Communities.[29]

Largely in response to the creation of the EEC, Austria, Denmark, Norway, Sweden, Switzerland, Portugal and the United Kingdom signed the Stockholm Convention on January 4, 1960, and the European Free Trade Association came into being in May of that year. The primary object of the "Outer Seven" was to offset any detrimental effects to their trade resulting from the progressive elimination of tariffs inside the Community by a similar reduction within EFTA. To a certain extent, EFTA was regarded as a

[27] See *Rapport des chefs de délégation, op. cit. deuxième partie*; "Euratom."
[28] Convention on Certain Institutions Common to the European Communities, March 25, 1957; see Sweet and Maxwell's *Encyclopedia of European Community Law*, Vol. 13, Part B8, B8–029.
[29] Treaty Establishing a Single Council and a Single Commission of the European Communities; see Sweet and Maxwell's *Encyclopedia*, B8–034.

stepping stone to possible future membership of the EEC. As the White
Paper of July 1971 explains: "From the outset . . . it was recognised that
some members of the EFTA might eventually wish to join, and others to
seek closer trading arrangements with, the European Communities."[30]
Indeed, barely 14 months after the Stockholm Convention entered into
force, the Macmillan Government applied for EEC membership. This was
to be the first of two applications thwarted by the opposition of President
de Gaulle. After lengthy negotiations had taken place with the Six, the
French President made it clear, in January 1963 that he would not consent
to British accession.

Applications in 1967 by the United Kingdom, Denmark, Ireland and
Norway met with a similar rebuff. Nevertheless, these four countries left
their applications "lying on the table," and at the Hague Summit Conference of the Six in December 1969 summoned on the initiative of the new
President of France, M. Pompidou, it was agreed that "The entry of other
countries of the continent to the Communities . . . could undoubtedly help
the Communities to grow to dimensions more in conformity with the present state of world economy and technology. . . . In so far as the applicant
States accept the Treaties and their political objective . . . the Heads of
State or Government have indicated their agreement to the opening of
negotiations between the Community on the one hand and the applicant
States on the other."[31]

Negotiations formally opened on June 30, 1970, and in July the following
year the British Government set out in a White Paper the terms agreed for
membership and the economic and political case for going ahead.[32] In the
section entitled "The Economic Case" can be found passages reminiscent
of the Spaak Report. "Growth and prosperity in any country," states the
White Paper, " . . . depend first and foremost upon the size and effective
use of its resources of manpower, plant, equipment and managerial
skill. . . . It is generally agreed that for advanced industrial countries the
most favourable environment is one where markets are large, and are free
from barriers to trade. These conditions favour specialisation, the exploitation of economies of scale, the developing and marketing of new products, and a high level of investment in the most modern and up-to-date
equipment. . . . In particular, the development and exploitation of
modern industrial technology, upon which so much of our employment and
income increasingly depends, requires greater resources for research and
development and wider markets than any one Western European nation
can provide."[33]

The negotiations between the applicant States and the Six resulted in
agreement on:

[30] *The United Kingdom and the European Communities*, Cmnd. 4715. After the Accession of
the U.K., Denmark and Ireland to the European Communities, Austria, Finland, Norway,
Sweden, Switzerland and Portugal entered into free trade agreements with the Nine. See
Seventh General Report on the Activities of the European Communities (1973), p. 400.
[31] *Third General Report on the Activities of the Communities* (1969), Annex—Documents on
the Summit Conference, pp. 487, 489.
[32] Cmnd. 4715. See also *The Enlarged Community—Outcome of the Negotiations with the
Applicant States*, Supplement 1.
[33] Cmnd. 4715, extracts from paras. 46 and 47.

— institutional changes;
— transitional arrangements for industry and agriculture;
— contributions to the Community Budget; and
— the position of the Commonwealth.

In the case of the institutions, the only changes required were those resulting from the need to accommodate the additional Member States. The elimination of customs duties and quotas between the prospective Member and the Six, and the adoption of the Common External Tariff, were to be phased in between April 1973 and July 1977. A transitional period was also to be allowed for the adoption of the Common Agricultural Policy, and contributions to the Community Budget. Although the United Kingdom would be compelled to forgo Commonwealth preference as such, special arrangements were agreed for the access of New Zealand dairy products and lamb, and the import of sugar from Commonwealth suppliers. It was understood that association arrangements comparable with those already accorded to developing countries enjoying traditional relations with the original Six would be made with developing countries in the Commonwealth.

On January 1, 1973, the Treaty of Accession entered into force, and Denmark, Ireland and the United Kingdom became Members of the three Communities. Norway, which had signed the Treaty on January 22, 1972, did not proceed to ratification, following an adverse result in a national referendum held on the issue of Membership.

United Kingdom referendum on continued EEC membership

The election of a Labour Government in February 1974 was to place in considerable doubt continued United Kingdom membership of the European Communities. Although the negotiations commenced by the Conservative administration in 1970 had been set in train by their predecessors, Labour in opposition declared themselves unable to accept the terms of entry which were finally agreed. When Labour returned to power in February 1974 it proceeded to "renegotiate" the agreed terms in respect of agriculture, contributions to the Community Budget, economic and monetary union, state aids to industry, movement of capital, the Commonwealth and developing countries, and value added tax. On January 23, 1975, the Prime Minister announced that a national referendum would be held on the results of renegotiation. After 12 months of negotiations with their Common Market partners the Government stated[34] that agreement had been reached on substantial changes in the original terms of entry, and that it felt able to recommend to the British people that they cast their votes in favour of continued Membership of the European Communities. This view was endorsed by an overwhelming majority of the votes cast in the referendum which followed on June 5, 1975.[35]

---

[34] *Membership of the European Community*, Cmnd. 5999, and *Membership of the European Community: Report on Renegotiation*, Cmnd. 6003.
[35] See R. E. M. Irving, "The United Kingdom Referendum" (1975–76) 1 E.L.Rev. 1.

Direct elections to the European Parliament

In December 1974, the Council finally declared itself in favour of the election of the European Assembly by universal suffrage, as contemplated by the EEC Treaty. The United Kingdom and Denmark felt unable to commit themselves at that stage, but following the completion of "renegotiations," and the British referendum result, the Council determined[36] that direct elections, to a 410 member chamber, should be held on a single date within the period May/June 1978.[37] In the event it proved impracticable to hold the elections at that time, and they were in fact held between June 7 and 10, 1979. The overall turnout of the Community electorate was a respectable 62 per cent., but in the United Kingdom only 32 per cent. of those eligible to do so cast their votes. In the elections of 1984 the overall turnout in the Community was 60 per cent., with again a turnout of approximately 32 per cent. in the United Kingdom.

Accession of Greece to the Communities

The transitional period for the accession of the new Member States was barely half spent when a further application for membership was received—that of Greece.[38] In its Opinion of January 28, 1976,[39] the Commission recommended that the Communities give an affirmative answer to this request. The Council acted upon this recommendation, and negotiations commenced on July 27, 1976. After long, and sometimes difficult negotiations, agreement was reached, and the Acts relating to Greece's accession were signed in Athens on May 28, 1979. Greece became the tenth Member State on January 1, 1981.

Accession of Spain and Portugal to the Communities

Even before agreement had been reached for the accession of Greece, Spain and Portugal had also applied for membership. The Commission's Opinion in each case was favourable.[40] After negotiations lasting six years, the instruments of Accession were signed in Lisbon and Madrid on June 12, 1985 at ceremonies attended by Prime Ministers and Foreign Ministers of the present and future Member States.[41] Spain and Portugal joined the Communities on January 1, 1986, the Act of Accession laying down the applicable transitional measures. In little more than a decade, the six had become twelve.

---

[36] Dec. 76/787, O.J. 1976 L278/1.
[37] For an examination of the form, legal basis, and content of the Council's Decision, and the Act annexed, see Forman (1977) 2 E.L.Rev. 35. Pending the establishment of a Community procedure, each Member State drew up appropriate national legislation to implement the Council's Decision. For the U.K. legislation, see the European Assembly Elections Act 1978.
[38] On January 12, 1975, E.C.Bull. 1975, No. 6, points 1201 to 1212.
[39] E.C.Bull 1976, No. 1, points 1101 to 1111, and Supplement 2/76.
[40] E.C.Bull 1978, No. 5, points 111 et seq.; E.C.Bull. 1978, No. 11, points 111 et seq.
[41] E.C.Bull 1985, No. 6, points 111 et seq.

CHAPTER 2

AIMS OF THE COMMON MARKET

THE COMMON MARKET

The Common Market[1] is apparently exclusively concerned with economic matters, inasmuch as it seeks to promote the free exchange of goods, services and capital between the Member States in the material interests of their inhabitants. In reality, of course, it is difficult to draw any hard and fast line between matters "economic" and "political," not least because the Treaty assumes the existence of a market economy in the Member States.[2] But the "political" element runs deeper than this. It results inevitably from the provisions of the Treaty requiring common policy-making and the harmonisation of national laws, and from the establishment of supranational institutions exercising jurisdiction throughout the territory of the Member States. As was indicated in the opening chapter, the economic integration contemplated by the Treaty was intended to advance the long term aim of political union. Views differ as to the future for Western European integration, whether economic or political, but it is important to appreciate the underlying assumptions of the Treaty at the outset, in order to understand its legal framework, and the approach adopted by the Court of Justice in interpreting Community Law.

Allocation of resources in the Market economy[3]

The traditional argument adduced by economists in favour of the market economy is that the forces of supply and demand lead to a more efficient allocation of resources than a system where the State directs investment, production, and pricing policy. The argument runs as follows.

A country's trade is transacted in goods and services, which are in turn produced by a combination of natural resources, labour and capital. These latter are described in the terminology of economists as the "factors of production." When trade takes place, goods are allocated to those who are able and willing to pay for them. Undertakings producing goods or supply-

---

[1] For the reason stated in the Preface, this book does not concern itself with the legal regimes governing the European Coal and Steel Community and the European Atomic Energy Community. References to "the Treaty" are references to the Treaty establishing the European Economic Community.

[2] This is probably the better view, though one can go a long way with the argument that the Treaty is essentially "neutral." As Professor Mitchell pointed out, it is possible to be "neutral" for, or "neutral" against; see 1975 CDE, at p. 474.

[3] See, in general, Lipsey, *An Introduction to Positive Economics* (1983); Samuelson, *Economics* (1979); F. W. Paish and A. J. Culyer, *Benham's Economics* (1973); Stonier and Hague, *A Textbook of Economic Theory* (1972); Fusfeld, *Economics* (1972).

ing services which people are prepared to pay for will make profits, while those which fail to do so will not. Capital and labour will be diverted to profitable ventures, and undertakings will be constrained, so far as they are able, to cut their costs and to innovate, in order to keep abreast with their competitors. The market will penalise inefficiency, and enable the consumer to choose the cheapest available goods of appropriate quality.

Practice, of course, is a somewhat pale reflection of theory, and most industrialised societies are loath to entrust their destinies entirely to the vicissitudes of laissez-faire. Government will often intervene with the express purpose of countering the effect of the market. Where, for example, industry becomes concentrated in particular regions rather than others, reflecting relative economic advantage, Government may discourage the building of factories or office buildings in one area,[4] and provide financial aids to undertakings prepared to invest in another less economically favoured.[5] Such intervention clearly has an economic cost, but this may be outweighed, in the view of Government, by the social advantages of providing jobs in depressed areas, rather than confronting a portion of the workforce with the choice between long term unemployment and migration.

Whereas the allocation of resources within a single country may be governed to a significant extent by market forces, since goods and services, labour and capital, may move fairly freely, this is less true in the international context.

Obstacles to the free movement of goods between States[6]

1. *Customs duties*

States often impose tariffs, or customs duties, on imported goods. They may do this in order to raise revenue, but more often their primary purpose will be to make imported goods more expensive than the domestic product, in order to favour the latter. The purpose of discriminating against imported products may be the short term one of allowing a domestic industry to "get on its feet" before being subjected to the rigours of international competition, or it may be the more long term one of safeguarding employment in industries in the importing state. Although it is true that discrimination against imported goods can maintain a level of employment in particular industries that might otherwise be impossible, protectionism of this sort is often criticised for two reasons. First, because consumers in

---

[4] For the use of planning permission and Industrial Development Certificates in the U.K., to prevent industrial development in over-favoured areas, see Daintith, *The Economic Law of the United Kingdom* (1975) (prepared under the auspices of the Europa Instituut, Utrecht, and the Commission of the European Communities, in connection with the International Conference on the Economic Law of the Member States in an Economic Union, held in Utrecht, May 1975), pp. 129 *et seq.*

[5] For Government assistance in the U.K. to stimulate industrial investment in areas of high unemployment or declining basic industries, see Terence C. Daintith *op. cit.*, pp. 50 *et seq.*

[6] See, in general, H. Katrak, *International Trade and the Balance of Payments* (1971); D. Swann, *The Economics of the Common Market* (1984); Sidney J. Wells, *International Economics* (1973).

the importing state are prevented from buying cheaper imported goods, thus being compelled to accept a reduced standard of living, and secondly, because insulating domestic manufacturers from foreign competition reduces their incentive to increase their efficiency.

2. *Quantitative restrictions*

An alternative, or additional, method by which a State may seek to restrict the extent to which domestic industries are subject to competition from imports is to impose import quotas, or quantitative restrictions, whereby the import of certain products is limited to a fixed volume per annum. Importers may be required to obtain a licence to import these products, and the volume of imports licensed will be limited to the size of the quota.

Quantitative restrictions are generally regarded as being more damaging to international trade than customs duties. As the United States Government argued at the first session preparatory to the drawing up of the General Agreement on Tariffs and Trade:

"In the case of a tariff the total volume of imports can expand with the expansion of trade. There is flexibility in the volume of trade. Under a quota system the volume of trade is rigidly restricted, and no matter how much more people may wish to buy or consume, not one single more unit will be admitted than the controlling authority thinks fit.

In the case of tariffs, the direction of trade and the sources of import can shift with changes in quality and cost and price. Under a quota system the direction of trade and the sources of imports are rigidly fixed by public authority without regard to quality, cost or price. Under a tariff, equality of treatment of all other states can be assured. Under a quota system, no matter how detailed our rules, no matter how carefully we police them, there must almost inevitably be discrimination as amongst other states."[7]

A further non-economic reason was given by the United States for its disapproval of the quota as a protectionist device: its tendency to make international commerce a matter of continuous political negotiation. "Goods move," it was argued, "not on the basis of quality, service and trade, but on the basis of deals completed country by country, product by product, day by day between public officials. All economic relations between countries are moved into the area of political conflict."[8]

3. *State subsidies*

It will be noted that the object of tariffs and quantitative restrictions is to place domestic products at a competitive advantage in relation to imports. A similar result can be achieved by paying government subsidies to dom-

---

[7] U.N.Doc. EPCT/A/PV. 221 at 16–17 (1947), cited Jackson, *World Trade and the Law of GATT* (1969), pp. 309, 310. And see Clair Wilcox, *A Charter for World Trade* (1949), pp. 81, 82.

[8] Jackson, *ibid.*

estic industries, with the result that their products can be sold more cheaply than would otherwise be possible. Not only do subsidies place the products of the subsidised industry in an advantageous position in the home market, but if granted with respect to exports they can give the subsidised goods a price advantage abroad.[9]

4. *State monopolies and public purchasing*

Even in the absence of tariffs or quantitative restrictions, imported products may be placed at a disadvantage *vis-à-vis* the domestic article as a result of either a state monopoly, or the exercise of discretionary purchasing powers by public bodies.

Suppose that in a particular state a government monopoly has the exclusive right to import, manufacture and sell a certain product. Obviously the monopoly may choose not to import at all, basing its judgment not on the cost or quality of foreign products, but simply on a desire to favour the domestic article. Discrimination will be inevitable where the monopoly also manufactures the goods in question. Even if a foreign manufacturer succeeds in selling to the government monopoly, it will be open to the monopoly to charge selling prices for the imported goods that place them at a competitive disadvantage compared with the domestic product. The same aim can be achieved through the machinery of a state monopoly as can be achieved through the imposition of tariffs and quotas.[10]

Again, in the modern state large sums are expended annually by public authorities in the exercise of their functions. Publicly owned industries buy computers, public hospitals buy drugs and sophisticated equipment, local authorities buy vehicles for their police forces, and so on. If a decision is taken to buy a domestically manufactured product wherever possible, the result can be to prevent imports that might otherwise have taken place had the choice of product been made solely on the grounds of price and quality.[10]

5. *Barriers arising from the diversity of national legislation*

Not only can tax rates within a single country have a distortive effect on resource allocation (if a 100 per cent. purchase tax was imposed on motor cars people would buy fewer cars than they presently do, hence "not enough" resources would be allocated to their manufacture), but differing rates of indirect taxation in different countries can constitute an obstacle to international trade. Suppose State X and State Y tax a product at the rate of 5 per cent. and 10 per cent. respectively. Assume further (a) that the tax is repaid in neither country when goods are exported, but (b) imported goods are exempt from the tax. Clearly products manufactured in State X will be at a considerable advantage both in State X and State Y. If, in the

---

[9] For Government assistance to exports in the U.K., and to specific economic sectors, *e.g.* shipbuilding and aerospace, see Terence C. Daintith, *op. cit.* pp. 61 *et seq.*; and see Jackson *op cit.* pp. 331, 332; Wilcox, *op. cit.* p. 126.

[10] Jackson, *op cit.* p. 331; Wilcox, *op. cit.* p. 95.

example given, imported goods were not exempt from tax, imports from either country into the other would be subject to double taxation, and the domestic product in the domestic market would always have the advantage.

One method of minimising the distortive effect of different tax rates is to provide (a) that taxes are repaid when goods are exported, and (b) subjected to the prevailing tax in the country of importation. Application of this principle, however, the "destination" principle, gives rise to what is known as a "fiscal frontier," inasmuch as procedures have to be adopted in the exporting state for the purposes of refunding the tax paid, and in the country of destination for levying taxes on imports.[11]

Obviously national legislation differs in many areas other than that of taxation. In the interests of public safety, most countries lay down specifications for the manufacture of everything from light bulbs to combine harvesters. Suppose that an undertaking in State X sells 200,000 cars a year on the home market, and is in a position to sell 100,000 cars a year to dealers in State Y. Producing 300,000 cars a year in the manufacturer's existing plant might lead to a significant reduction in cost per car. But suppose that State X's legislation provides that car doors must open from the front, while State Y's provides that they must open from the rear. The manufacturer in State X will not be able to use his existing production line, but will be compelled to modify it to cater for State Y's requirements. Thus diverse national legislation can make production more costly than it would otherwise be.

6. *Behaviour of private persons*

Few would contest the proposition that allocation of resources via the market may be distorted either by agreements in restraint of trade, or by the business policy of enterprises occupying a market dominating position. Let us assume that a dozen firms compete in price and quality in the manufacture of a particular article. The play of market forces will be blunted considerably if the firms agree (a) not to charge less than a certain price for the product in question, and (b) to restrict their sales effort to defined territorial areas of the country in question.[12] Similarly, an enterprise whose market share and financial resources gives it considerable room for manoeuvre may be in a position to insulate itself from competition by predatory practices such as buying out competitors, or selling its products in particular areas below cost with the object of putting competitors out of business.[13] Not only are such practices capable of distorting competition at

---

[11] For the destination principles and Art. III of the GATT, see Jackson, *op cit.* pp. 294 *et seq.* Fiscal frontiers may be abolished by harmonisation of tax rates, and rules defining taxable transactions, which enables the "origin principle" to be applied; *i.e.* the principle that taxable events are taxed in the country in which they occur, without reimbursement on exportation.

[12] For a brief outline of the economic issues, see Valentine Korah, *Competition Law of Britain and the Common Market* (1975), pp. 3 *et seq.*

[13] For examples revealed by the investigations of the Monopolies Commission, see Wyatt, "The British Monopolies Commission and the Dominant Firm" (1974) J.W.T.L. 492, at pp. 517, 518.

the national level, they are capable of distorting trade between states. Removal of tariffs and quotas on trade between State X and State Y will be a futile exercise if manufacturers in each agree to sell only in the home market.

Restrictions on the movement of labour and capital between states

The present discussion is concerned with the movement of goods and resources between states. So far consideration has been confined to restrictions on the former, though it was suggested earlier that a key advantage of the market economy was the diversion of labour and capital to efficient, profit-making ventures.

Even within a single state, there are limits to the mobility of labour between undertakings in different parts of the country. Individuals become attached to people and places, and do not lightly discard long associations for the sake of economic advantage. On the other hand, people *do* move for the sake of a better job, or simply for a job, if they are unemployed. Thus people travel thousands of miles in the United States to settle in California, and on a rather less grandiose scale, workers leave depressed areas of Scotland and the north-west, and seek opportunity in the Midlands and south-east.

The natural reluctance of workers to move from their homes in search of economic advantage is the greater when a move to a foreign country is involved. To the inevitable dislocation of settling into a new environment are added linguistic and cultural problems. But that is not the end of the matter. Substantial legal obstacles are likely to lie in the way of a national of one State seeking work in another. He will often be required to hold a work permit, which may be granted only for a limited period. He may be subject to discrimination in fact, in that he may be dismissed before national workers at a time of recession, and discrimination in law, in that he may be denied political and economic rights accorded to national workers. Linguistic, cultural and legal disincentives to immigration will often deter all but the most determined.

Capital, of course, is a different matter. Here the principal restrictions on transfers between states are legal. A country suffering from a balance of payments deficit may limit its imports by means of exchange control, *i.e.* undertakings wishing to import goods will require permission from the Government to acquire the necessary foreign exchange. Individuals or enterprises may wish to invest capital in another country where it will bring a higher return. The philosophy of the market economy might regard this as an efficient allocation of resources, but as in the case of unrestricted imports, governments often see such transfers as conflicting with domestic economic policy. As a result, most countries insist on vetting any transfers of capital above a certain limit.[14]

---

[14] Exchange control in the United Kingdom is now a reserve power, see *Halsbury's Laws*, Vol. 32, para. 272, and Supplement.

Eliminating obstacles to inter-state trade

1. *The General Agreement on Tariffs and Trade (GATT)*[15]

The bitter experience of the 1930s, when the imposition of increased tariffs and quotas exacerbated a deepening recession, lent momentum to a post-War American initiative favouring world-wide free trade. Although an original ambitious scheme for an International Trade Organisation came to nothing, 1947 saw the signature of the General Agreement on Tariffs and Trade, a multilateral treaty intended to provide the framework for the progressive elimination of tariff barriers. Salient features of the GATT are as follows. First, the agreement embodies the "most favoured nation" principle, whereby any privilege or favour granted by a contracting party to the products of any other country in respect of customs duties or charges shall be accorded immediately and unconditionally to similar products originating in the territory of any other contracting party.[16] The General Agreement contains no timetable for tariff cuts, but it does provide that any concessions negotiated between one contracting party and another shall be granted to all other contracting parties.[17] Several negotiating "rounds" have resulted in significant reductions in world tariff levels.

Quantitative restrictions were prohibited outright by the General Agreement,[18] but this prohibition is subject to wide-ranging exceptions in the case of balance of payments difficulties,[19] agriculture,[20] and the particular problems arising in connection with trade with the developing countries.[21]

Certain measures, such as imposing internal taxation at a higher rate on imports than on the domestic product,[22] and charging fees in excess of cost for customs services,[23] are also subject to restriction, since their effect is equivalent to that of a tariff.

The following observations may be made concerning the GATT. First, although the General Agreement has provided a framework within which tariffs have in fact been reduced, the existence of different rates of tariff at the outset, coupled with the principle of reciprocity in tariff negotiations, has led to the maintenance of tariffs at differing levels throughout the world. Secondly, it has had little impact in respect of non-tariff barriers such as state monopolies, and the existence of diverse national trading rules. However, the "Tokyo Round" of multilateral trade negotiations, which was concluded in April 1979, seems to have produced some agreement on limiting certain non-tariff barriers, including rules for customs valuation, and public procurement.

Although the most favoured nation principle would seem to preclude states from dismantling tariffs to trade on a regional basis, without granting

[15] See K. Dam, *The GATT* (1969); Jackson, *op cit.*
[16] Art. I.
[17] Art. II.
[18] Art. XI.
[19] Arts. XII–XIV.
[20] Art. XI.
[21] Art. XVIII.
[22] Art. III.
[23] Art. VIII.

similar concessions to other members of the GATT, the General Agreement in fact makes exceptions in the case of free trade areas, and customs unions.[24]

2. *The free trade area*

Article XXIV(8) of the General Agreement defines a free trade area as a "group of two or more customs territories in which the duties and other restrictive regulations of commerce . . . are eliminated on substantially all the trade between the constituent territories in products originating in such territories." An excellent example of such an arrangement is the European Free Trade Association,[25] whose founding Convention was signed in Stockholm on January 4, 1960, in response to the establishment of the European Economic Community. The possibilities for trade liberalisation on a regional basis are well illustrated by the broad scope of the Convention. Both customs duties and quantitative restrictions are subjected to a strict timetable for abolition,[26] and these provisions are reinforced by the prohibition of discriminatory indirect taxation on imported goods.[27] The signatory states were clearly conscious of the possibly distortive effects of differing rates of taxation, and the Convention provides accordingly that corrective measures may be taken in the event of an increase in imports of particular goods resulting from a combination of reduced tariffs and quotas *and* the incidence of higher taxation on component materials of the goods in question in the importing state.[28]

Three principal forms of non-tariff barrier are prohibited when their effect is to frustrate the benefits flowing from the abolition of customs duties and quotas; government subsidies, discrimination by public undertakings, and agreements in restraint of trade.

Unlike the EEC Treaty, the Stockholm Convention does not extend to agricultural products, apart from providing for bilateral agreements between members.[29]

The main drawback of the free trade area, from the point of view of trade liberalisation, is that since each Member State remains free to fix tariffs at a level of its own choosing *vis-à-vis* the outside world, the benefits of free trade are restricted in principle to goods originating within the territory of a member. Any other solution would lead to products from third countries avoiding the tariff of one Member State by import via another imposing a lower tariff. The Stockholm Convention provides that goods eligible for "area tariff treatment," *i.e.* free trade, must either have been wholly produced within the territory of a member, or, at any rate, must not contain materials imported from third countries representing more than 50 per cent. of the export price of the goods.[30] The application of "origin"

---

[24] Art. XXIV.
[25] See A. H. Robertson, *European Institutions* (1973), p. 227. The Stockholm Convention is set out at pp. 384 *et seq.* For an empirical study of the EFTA, see Curzon, *The Essentials of Economic Integration* (1973).
[26] Arts. 3, 8, 10 and 11.
[27] Art. 6.
[28] Art. 5.
[29] Art. 23.
[30] Art. 3.

rules—inevitable in the free trade area—can lead to administrative procedures at the frontiers of Member States which themselves constitute a barrier to interstate trade.

3. *Economic integration—customs union and Common Market*

The customs union[31] represents a further stage of economic integration, inasmuch as the problems of origin intrinsic in the free trade area are eliminated by the establishment of a common external tariff. Such a common policy presupposes a high degree of economic and political co-operation, since it precludes such special relationships with third countries as "Commonwealth Preference," which was expressly excluded from the application of the General Agreement, and largely unaffected by the provisions of the Stockholm Convention.

The Treaty establishing the European Economic Community, signed in Rome on March 25, 1957, creates first and foremost a customs union, but it goes further than that. It founds a "common market." The distinction is that whereas both free trade area and customs union are in their nature concerned with eliminating tariff and non-tariff barriers to trade between their members, a common market has two additional features. First, it seeks to remove obstacles to the free movement of the factors of production; at any rate labour and capital. Secondly, the common market adopts an extended notion of the non-tariff barrier to trade. Where diverse national legislation and policy making tends to burden inter-state trade, the common market contemplates common standards and common policies.

The "common market" philosophy explains in large part the substantive provisions of the EEC Treaty. A customs union is established, inasmuch as customs duties and quantitative restrictions are subjected to a timetable for abolition,[32] and a common external tariff is phased in over a period of years.[33] Non-tariff barriers, such as state monopolies of a commercial character, government subsidies, and agreements in restraint of trade, are either subjected to a timetable for adjustment,[34] or prohibited outright subject to exceptions.[35] The Treaty contains provisions for the harmonisation of such legislation as directly affects the establishment or functioning of the Common Market,[36] and Member States undertake to regard their short term economic policy as a matter of common concern.[37] Unlike the Stockholm Convention, the EEC Treaty provides for a common policy for agriculture, and seeks to liberalise the movement of persons, services and capital between the Member States.[38]

Since government intervention is a familiar feature of the contemporary

---

[31] For a definition, see Art. XXIV(8)(*a*) of the General Agreement.
[32] Arts. 12–17, 30–37, and see Art. 95.
[33] Arts. 18–29.
[34] Art. 37.
[35] Arts. 85, 92, 93.
[36] Art. 100. For progress, *e.g.* on harmonisation of safety provisions with respect to motor vehicles and tractors, see E.C.Bull. 1977, No. 6, p. 28.
[37] Art. 103.
[38] Arts. 48–73.

mixed economy, the Treaty is drafted accordingly. The provisions relating to state aids contain wide-ranging exceptions, and are administered with considerable flexibility.[39] The Treaty expressly reserves to Member States the right to take industries into public ownership.[40]

The economic aim of the Treaty is far-reaching. It amounts to assimilating economic activity between individuals and undertakings in different Member States to economic activities within a single state. The legal implications are clearly considerable, though the titles of the various sections of the Treaty, reminiscent of the sub-headings in an economics text-book, hint only obliquely at the impact of the Treaty in the national legal order. It is hardly obvious from a scrutiny of the "Table of Contents" that the section on "Right of Establishment" might be concerned with company law,[41] or that national measures of price control might raise legal problems under the diverse headings of "Elimination of Quantitative Restrictions between Member States,"[42] and "Agriculture."[43] In other areas the legal implications of the Treaty are more obvious. Thus the prohibition of agreements likely to distort competition has a clear impact on the validity of contract,[44] while the principle that men and women should receive equal pay for equal work is reflected in national legislation throughout the Community.[45]

At this point matters "economic" and "political" again converge. This is hardly surprising, since the genesis of the common market is to be found in the political aspiration for a United Europe. Economic integration was to be the chosen means, rather than the ultimate end.

---

[39] And national measures are supplemented by a Community Regional Fund. See *Encyclopedia of European Community Law*, Vol. C, Pt. C. 11.
[40] Art. 222 EEC.
[41] See *infra*, pp. 213 *et seq.*
[42] See *infra*, pp. 133 *et seq.*
[43] See *infra*, p. 336.
[44] See *infra*, at p. 352.
[45] See, *e.g. Garland* v. *British Rail Engineering Ltd.* [1983] 2 A.C. 751, in which the HL held that the Sex Discrimination Act 1975 was to be construed, if it was reasonably capable of bearing such a meaning, as being intended to carry out the obligation to observe the provisions of Art. 119 of the EEC Treaty (on equal pay) and not to be inconsistent with it.

PART II: THE COMMUNITY LEGAL SYSTEM

Chapter 3

THE COMMUNITY LEGAL ORDER

Sources of Community Law

The sources of Community law are as follows:
— the Treaties establishing the three Communities, and the secondary legislation made thereunder;
— related treaties concluded between Member States;
— treaties concluded between the Member States and third countries[1];
— international treaties binding upon all the Member States, where the responsibilities of the latter have been assumed by the Community[2];
— decisions of the Member States having legal effect within the sphere of operation of the Treaties[3];
— decisions of the European Court of Justice[4];
— the general principles of law and the fundamental rights upon which the constitutional law of the Member States is based.[5]

For the purposes of simplicity, where consideration of the abovementioned sources requires reference to the Treaties and to the secondary legislation made thereunder, discussion will be limited to the legal effects of the Treaty establishing the European Economic Community, and the secondary legislation—regulations, directives and decisions—made thereunder.

Member States are bound in international law to carry out the obligations imposed by the Treaty and secondary legislation. Breach of these obligations may give rise to an action before the Court of Justice at the suit of either the Commission, or another Member State.[6] The legal impact of Community law in the Member States, however, springs from its capacity, even its tendency to give rise to rights in individuals which national courts are bound to safeguard. The position is complicated by a rather confusing terminology, which describes provisions of Community law as being either "directly applicable," or "directly effective." The latter expression describes a provision endowed with sufficient clarity and precision to bestow a legal right on a natural or legal person, as against another natural or legal

---

[1] Appropriately worded provisions of such agreements may be invoked before the courts of Member States, see, *e.g.* Case 104/81, *Kupferberg* [1982] E.C.R. 3641 *infra*, p. 48.
[2] Cases 21–24/72, *International Fruit* [1972] E.C.R. 1219 *infra*, at p. 50.
[3] *e.g.* the "acceleration" decisions of May 12, 1960, and May 15, 1962, see *infra*, p. 102. See Case 22/70, E.R.T.A. [1971] E.C.R. 263.
[4] Decisions of the Court under Article 177 EEC are binding on the referring Court; see Case 29/68, *Milchkontor* [1969] E.C.R. 165; Case 52/76, *Benedetti* [1977] E.C.R. 163. *Stare decisis* applies in the United Kingdom by virtue of s. 3(1) of the European Communities Act 1972. A ruling of the Court under Article 177 on the invalidity of a Community act is binding *erga omnes*; see Case 66/80, *International Chemical Corporation* [1981] E.C.R. 1191.
[5] See *infra*, at p. 59.
[6] Arts. 169, 170, *infra*, at p. 74.

person, or a Member State. Establishing direct effect is a matter of interpretation, and it is clear that specific provisions of the Treaty, as well as
specific provisions of regulations, directives or decisions, may be endowed
with this quality. It has been argued that direct effect, in the sense of practical operation for all concerned, is to be presumed unless established to
the contrary.[7] Direct applicability, on the other hand, is that attribute of a
regulation which ensures its access, in its entirety, to the national legal
order, without the need for specific incorporation. National reproduction
of the text of a regulation is not only otiose, but impermissible, and its status as direct Community legislation allows it to pre-empt national legislative competence.

Confusion arises because the expressions "directly applicable" and
"directly effective" are sometimes used interchangeably, even by the
Court.[8] While specific provisions of the Treaty, and of directives and
decisions, may be directly effective, these instruments as a whole lack the
unique pre-emptive quality of regulations.

Nature of the Community legal order

The European Community is a developed form of international organisation which displays characteristics of an embryonic federation. Analysis of
the nature of the Community legal system is of intrinsic interest, and may
facilitate the solution of practical problems. The debt owed by Community
law to public international law is considerable, and usually understated.[9]
The twin pillars of the Community legal system are the doctrines of direct
applicability/direct effect, and the supremacy of Community law. Both
doctrines are derived from international law.[10] Equally, however, the relationship between Community law and national law clearly lends itself to
comparison with the relationship between state and federal law in a federal
system. In *Simmenthal* the Court of Justice held that Community law was
competent to "preclude the valid adoption"[11] of inconsistent national
legislation. This is a controversial formulation, and seems to equate the
relationship between Community law and national law to a constitutional
relationship, thereby distancing Community law from international law.
As one learned writer on international law has put it: "International tribunals cannot declare the internal invalidity of rules of national law since
the international legal order must respect the reserved domain of domestic

---

[7] Pescatore, "The Doctrine of 'Direct Effect': An Infant Disease of Community Law" (1983)
8 E.L.Rev. 155.
[8] See the ruling in Case 2/74, *Reyners* [1974] E.C.R. 631, to the effect that Article 52 of the
Treaty is directly applicable. In similar vein, see Case 17/81, *Pabst* [1982] E.C.R. 1331;
Case 104/81, *Kupferberg* [1982] E.C.R. 3641.
[9] Wyatt, "New legal Order or Old?" (1982) 7 E.L.Rev. 147; De Witte, "Retour à 'Costa': La
primauté du droit communautaire à la lumière du droit international" (1984) 20 R.T.D.E.
425.
[10] For direct applicability, see "Jurisdiction of the Courts of Danzig" (1928) P.C.I.J.Ser. B.,
No. 15. For the principle that treaty obligations take priority over national law, see Vienna
Convention on the Law of Treaties, Art. 27: "Treatment of Polish Nationals in Danzig"
(1932) P.C.I.J. Rep.Ser. A/B, No. 44, p. 24.
[11] Case 106/77 [1978] E.C.R. 629 at 643, para. [17].

jurisdiction."[12] Nevertheless, the International Court of Justice has pronounced certain official acts of South Africa in Namibia to be "illegal and invalid,"[13] and there appears to be no difference in principle between the demands of public international law and Community law in this regard.

For its own part, the European Court of Justice has contrasted the EEC Treaty with "ordinary international treaties,"[14] and even before the establishment of the EEC Advocate General Lagrange, in the *Fédéchar* case,[14] had floated the argument that the Court of Justice was not "an international court but the court of a Community created by six States as a model which is more closely related to a federal than to an international organisation," though he then dismissed the international court versus federal court argument as an "academic discussion." The Court of Justice referred in the event to a "rule of interpretation generally accepted in both international and national law."[15] More significantly, in *Commission* v. *Luxembourg & Belgium*,[16] the Court rejected an argument based on international law, that a default by the Commission in its obligations to a Member State had the effect of suspending the reciprocal obligations of the latter.[17] The Court has subsequently rejected the proposition that a default by one Member State suspends the reciprocal obligations of other Member States.[18] Yet this conclusion is perfectly consistent with the public international law basis of the Community legal system; the International Court of Justice has similarly denied that the "self-contained regime" established by the Vienna Convention on Diplomatic Relations leaves any room for self-help.[19] The principle affirmed by the International Court of Justice is that the provision of procedures capable of providing a remedy for the breach of an international obligation may be held to oust the customary law right of self-help.

The truth is that there are certain legal characteristics which may be encountered both in international organisations and in federal systems. Thus the principles of direct applicability/direct effect, the supremacy of Community law, and the predominance of judicial remedies over self-help, allow analogies to be drawn with both federal constitutional and international law. At the present stage of development of Community law, the international organisation model is in some respects still appropriate. First, a federal state is characterised by the central government's legal monopoly

---

[12] Brownlie, *Principles of Public International Law* (3rd ed.), p. 43, citing "Interpretation of the Statute of the Memel Territory" (1932) P.C.I.J.Ser. A/B, No. 49, p. 236. Yet the Permanent Court's judgment makes it clear that it confined itself to interpreting the statute because that was the intention of the Four Powers when they submitted the point in question to the Court.

[13] *Namibia Case* (1971) I.C.J.Rep., p. 16, at p. 56, para. 125.

[14] Case 8/55 [1954–6] E.C.R. 245.

[15] [1954–6] E.C.R. 292 at p. 299. For consideration of internationalist, federalist, and functionalist theories of the Community legal order, see Dagtoglou, "The legal nature of the European Community" in *Thirty Years of Community Law* (E.C. Publication, 1983) Chapter II.

[16] Cases 90 and 91/63, [1964] E.C.R. 625.

[17] For the doctrine in international law, see *Tacna-Arica Arbitration* 2 R.I.A.A. 921 (1925); *US-France Air Services Arbitration* 54 I.L.R. 303; Vienna Convention on the Law of Treaties, Art. 60.

[18] Case 43/75 *Defrenne* [1976] E.C.R. 455; Case 232/78 *Commission* v. *France* [1979] E.C.R. 2729.

[19] *Hostages* (1980) I.C.J.Rep., p. 3 at p. 28, para. 83.

over foreign relations. In the Community, the Commission and Council as yet enjoy no such monopoly, though the potential exists for an increase in Community competence in this field.[20] Secondly, the Community is based upon international treaties concluded between states, and the efficacy of Community law is in some Member States still dependent upon its status as international law. In a federal system, state courts resolve conflicts upon the basis of federal "conflict," or supremacy rules. In the Community, national courts still resolve conflicts between national law and Community law upon the basis of national law. Community law is applied to the extent that it has been incorporated into national law in accordance with national constitutional requirements. For the most part, the response of national courts to Community law remains as much the response of state courts to a treaty, as the response of state courts to a federal constitution. However, while the international organisation model may provide a more or less plausible analysis of the history of the Community legal order to date, we doubt that it will provide either the Court of Justice, or the national courts in the Member States, with their inspiration for the future.

The Supremacy of Community Law

International law by its nature binds the State in its executive, legislative and judicial activities, and no international tribunal would permit a respondent State to plead provisions of its own law or constitution as a defence to an alleged infringement of an international obligation.[21] The same is true of European Community law, "over which no appeal to provisions of internal law of any kind whatever can prevail,"[22] and the Court has always declined to accept a plea of *force majeure* where a Member State has attempted to comply with Community obligations, but failed as a result of delays in the constitutional process. The Court's decision in *Commission* v. *Belgium*[23] is illustrative. Belgian indirect taxation of home grown and imported timber discriminated against the latter, contrary to Article 95 of the Treaty. In its defence to an action by the Commission under Article 169 of the Treaty, the Belgian Government argued that it had introduced draft legislation to the Chamber of Representatives two years previously, to remedy the situation, but that it had yet to be passed. Under the principle of the separation of powers prevailing in Belgium, pointed out the Government, it could do no more. The Court was unmoved. "The obligations arising from Article 95 of the Treaty," it observed, "devolve upon States as such and the liability of a Member State under Article 169 arises whatever the agency of the State whose action or inaction is the cause of the failure

---

[20] Case 22/70 *E.R.T.A.* [1971] E.C.R. 263; Cases 3, 4 and 6/76 *Kramer* [1976] E.C.R. 1279.
[21] *Treatment of Polish Nationals in Danzig* (1932) P.C.I.J.Rep., Ser. A/B, No. 44, at p. 24. Vienna Convention on the Law of Treaties 1969, Art. 27.
[22] Case 48/71 *Commission* v. *Italy* [1972] E.C.R. 527 at 535.
[23] Case 77/69 [1970] E.C.R. 237. The Court has taken the same position in a consistent line of cases, see, *e.g.* Case 254/83, *Commission* v. *Italy* [1984] E.C.R. 3395.

to fulfil its obligations, even in the case of a constitutionally independent institution."[24]

The duty of Member States to take all appropriate measures to ensure the fulfilment of obligations arising under the Treaty or secondary legislation is laid down explicitly in Article 5, and this duty devolves directly upon national courts where directly effective provisions of Community law are involved.[25] This factor was emphasised in *Costa* v. *ENEL*,[26] in which it was argued that the Court's ruling would be irrelevant to the solution of the main suit, since the national tribunal which had made the reference would be bound to apply national law in any event. The Court responded with an analysis of the Community legal system, and an affirmation of its supremacy over national law:

> "By contrast with ordinary international treaties, the EEC Treaty has created its own legal system which, on the entry into force of the Treaty, became an integral part of the legal systems of the Member States and which their courts are bound to apply.
>
> By creating a Community of unlimited duration, having . . . powers stemming from a limitation of sovereignty, or a transfer of powers from the States to the Community, the Member States have limited their sovereign rights, albeit within limited fields, and have thus created a body of law which binds both their nationals and themselves."[27]

As the Court acknowledged in *Costa*, the supremacy of Community regulations is implicit in the legal characteristics ascribed to them in Article 189 of the Treaty.[28] Not only does direct applicability require their access to the national legal order without the favour of specific incorporation, but they have the capacity to pre-empt national legislative competence.[29] Their very nature precludes their modification by inconsistent measures of national law.

The supremacy principle is especially significant to individuals seeking to invoke directly effective provisions of Community law in national courts, for it is only when national law fails to protect the right in issue, or positively impedes its enjoyment, that they resort to Community law. When individuals do invoke such rights, the duty of national courts is clear. As the Court said of Regulation 1612/68, Directive 68/360 and Directive 64/221, all three being instruments concerned with the rights of migrant workers:

> "The effect of all these provisions, without exception, is to impose duties on Member States and it is, accordingly, for the courts to give the rules of Community law which may be pleaded before them precedence over the provisions of national law if legislative measures adopted by a Member State in order to limit within its territory free-

---

[24] [1970] E.C.R. 237 at 243, para. 15.
[25] See, *e.g.* Case 45/76 *Comet* [1976] E.C.R. 2043 at 2053, para. 12.
[26] Case 6/64 [1964] E.C.R. 585. And see Case 17/67 *Neumann* [1967] E.C.R. 441 at 453.
[27] [1964] E.C.R. 585 at 593.
[28] "The precedence of Community law is confirmed by Article 189, whereby a regulation 'shall be binding' and 'directly applicable in all Member States.'" [1964] E.C.R. 585 at 594.
[29] *Infra*, p. 40.

dom of movement or residence for nationals of other Member States prove to be incompatible with any of those duties."[30]

That the duty of national courts to give precedence to Community law over national law extends to national legislation adopted after the incorporation of the relevant Community rules into the national legal order was made clear in *Simmenthal*[31]:

"Furthermore, in accordance with the principle of the precedence of Community law, the relationship between provisions of the Treaty and directly applicable measures of the institutions on the one hand and the national law of the Member States on the other is such that those provisions and measures not only by their entry into force render automatically inapplicable any conflicting provision of current national law but—in so far as they are an integral part of, and take precedence in, the legal order applicable in the territory of each of the Member States—also preclude the valid adoption of new national legislative measures to the extent to which they would be incompatible with Community provisions . . . . It follows from the foregoing that every national court must, in a case within its jurisdiction, apply Community law in its entirety and protect rights which the latter confers on individuals and must accordingly set aside any provision of national law which may conflict with it, whether prior or subsequent to the Community rule."

The principle of the supremacy of Community law, well-established as it is in the jurisprudence of the Court, may be denied its full effect by national tribunals. Although as a matter of Community law it is impermissible to condition the effects of its provisions on the requirements of national law, however fundamental,[32] national courts may nevertheless feel constrained to temper the rigour of the Treaty's requirements, for national courts are instituted under national law, and are entrusted first and foremost with maintaining the integrity of the national legal order.

The legal effect of Treaty provisions in national courts

1. *Rights of the individual against the state*

The judicial *fons et origo* of the principle that certain provisions of the Treaty may be invoked by individuals in national courts is the decision in *Van Gend en Loos* v. *Nederlandse Administratie der Belastingen*.[33] Dutch importers challenged the rate of import duty charged on a chemical product imported from the Federal Republic of Germany, alleging that reclassifying it under a different heading of the Dutch customs tariff had

---

[30] Case 36/75 *Rutili* [1975] 1219 at 1229, para. 16.
[31] Case 106/77 [1978] E.C.R. 629 at pp. 643, 644.
[32] Case 11/70 *Internationale Handelsgesellschaft* [1970] E.C.R. 1125.
[33] Case 26/62 [1963] E.C.R. 1.

resulted in an increase in duty prohibited under Article 12 of the Treaty, which provides that: "Member States shall refrain from introducing between themselves any new customs duties on imports . . . or any charges having equivalent effect, and from increasing those which they already apply in their trade with each other." The Tarief-commissie, an administrative tribunal having final jurisdiction in revenue cases, asked the Court whether the Article in question had "direct application within the territory of a Member State, in other words, whether nationals of such a State can, on the basis of the Article in question, lay claim to individual rights which the courts must protect." The Dutch Government, in its submissions to the Court, argued that an infringement of the Treaty by a Member State could be submitted to the Court only under the procedure laid down by Articles 169 and 170, *i.e.* at the suit of the Commission or another Member State.[34] This view, to the effect that the provisions of the Treaty simply give rise to rights and obligations between Member States in international law, was rejected by Advocate General Roemer, who argued that anyone "familiar with Community law" knew that "in fact it does not just consist of contractual relations between a number of States considered as subjects of the law of nations."[35] This followed from the fact that the Community was authorised to make rules of law capable of bestowing rights and imposing obligations on private individuals as well as on Member States.[36] The Court, in a landmark judgment, upheld the Advocate General's reasoning:

> "The objective of the EEC Treaty, which is to establish a Common Market, the functioning of which is of direct concern to interested parties in the Community, implies that this Treaty is more than an agreement which merely creates mutual obligations between the contracting States.
>
> The task assigned to the Court of Justice under Article 177, the object of which is to ensure uniform interpretation of the Treaty by national courts and tribunals, confirms that the States have acknowledged that Community law has an authority which can be invoked by their nationals before those courts and tribunals.
>
> The conclusion to be drawn from this is that the Community constitutes a new legal order of international law for the benefit of which the States have limited their sovereign rights, albeit within limited fields, and the subjects of which comprise not only Member States but also their nationals. Independently of the legislation of Member States, Community law therefore not only imposes obligations on individuals but is also intended to confer upon them rights which become part of their legal heritage. These rights arise not only where they are expressly granted by the Treaty, but also by reason of obligations which the Treaty imposes in a clearly defined way upon individuals as

---

[34] [1963] E.C.R. 1 at p. 6.
[35] [1963] E.C.R. 1 at p. 20.
[36] The Adv. Gen. cited in support of this proposition Arts. 187, 189, 191 and 192 of the Treaty.

well as upon the Member States and the institutions of the Community."[37]

Although the Advocate General had taken the view that certain Treaty provisions were "clearly intended to be incorporated into national law and to modify or supplement it,"[38] he had not numbered among them Article 12, since its application required the resolution of complex issues of interpretation. To hold such a provision directly applicable, he pointed out, would create uncertainty in the law: enterprises would be far more likely to rely upon national customs legislation than upon the text of the Treaty. The Court's approach was less cautious. "The wording of Article 12," it argued, "contains a clear and unconditional prohibition which is not a positive but a negative obligation. This obligation, moreover, is not qualified by any reservation on the part of states which would make its implementation conditional upon a positive legislative measure enacted under national law. The very nature of this prohibition makes it ideally adapted to produce direct effects in the legal relationship between Member States and their subjects."[39]

The *Van Gend en Loos* judgment affirms the existence of the "new legal order" in which individuals, as well as Member States, may have rights and obligations, and it lays down the criteria to be applied in deciding whether or not a particular provision may be invoked by individuals in national courts. These criteria were to be applied subsequently in numerous cases,[40] and were summed up as follows by Advocate General Mayras in *Reyners* v. *Belgian State*:

— the provision in question must be sufficiently clear and precise for judicial application[41];
— it must establish an unconditional obligation[42];
— the obligation must be completed and legally perfect, and its implementation must not depend on measures being subsequently taken by Community institutions or Member States with discretionary power in the matter.[43]

The second requirement, that the obligation be unconditional, was of

---

[37] [1963] E.C.R. 1 at p. 12.
[38] He cited Arts. 85, 86, 88, 177 and 192.
[39] [1963] E.C.R. 1 at p. 13.
[40] *e.g.* provisions of the Treaty were held directly effective in the following cases: Case 6/64 *Costa* [1964] E.C.R. 585 (Arts. 53 and 37(2)); Case 57/65 *Lütticke* [1966] E.C.R. 205 (Arts. 95(1) and 95(3)); Case 28/67 *Molkerie-Zentrale* [1968] E.C.R. 143 (Art. 95(1)); Case 27/67 *Fink-Frucht* [1968] E.C.R. 223 (Art. 95(2)); Case 13/68 *Salgoil* [1968] E.C.R. 453 (Arts. 31 and 32(1)); Case 33/70 *SACE* [1970] E.C.R. 1213 (Art. 13(2)); Case 18/71 *Eunomia* [1971] E.C.R. 811 (Art. 16); Case 127/73 *SABAM* [1974] E.C.R. 51 (Arts. 85 and 86).
[41] See, *e.g.* Case 26/62 *Van Gend en Loos*: Case 6/64 *Costa*; Case 33/70 *SACE*; Case 18/71 *Eunomia*; for references, see note 40; Case 41/74 *Van Duyn* [1974] E.C.R. 1337 (Art. 48).
[42] See, *e.g.* Case 26/62 *Van Gend en Loos*; Case 6/64 *Costa*; Case 57/65 *Lütticke*; for references, see note 40.
[43] See, *e.g.* Case 26/62 *Van Gend en Loos*; Case 57/65 *Lütticke*; Case 33/70 *SACE*; Case 18/71 *Eunomia*; for references, see note 40; Case 41/74 *Van Duyn*, note 41. Nevertheless, in Case 2/74 *Reyners* [1974] E.C.R. 631, the Court held that Art. 52 of the Treaty was directly effective, despite the fact that restrictions on freedom of establishment were to be abolished within the framework of a General Programme, and Council Directive. The fulfilment of the obligation in question was to be facilitated by, but not made dependent upon, the measures in question. See *infra*, p. 204. *Cf.* Case 10/71 *Muller* [1971] E.C.R. 723 (Art. 90(2)).

considerable importance in the transitional period, during which national restrictions on the free movement of goods, persons and services were to be progressively abolished.[44] These conditional prohibitions in the Treaty become unconditional on the expiration of the transitional period, and national measures in force when the Treaty came into effect could be challenged in national courts.[45]

The first and third requirements, that a legal provision be clear and precise, and be independent of measures to be taken subsequently by the Community institutions or the Member States, may be illustrated by reference to *Salgoil* v. *Italian Ministry for Foreign Trade*,[46] in which the Court denied direct effect to Article 32(1), last sentence, and Article 33, of the Treaty. These provisions required Member States to phase out quantitative restrictions on imports, by converting bilateral quotas into global quotas, and by progressively increasing their total value. The rate of liberalisation was prescribed for products where "the global quotas amounted to less than three per cent. of the national production of the State concerned." The Court conceded that these provisions laid down obligations which were not subject to the adoption of measures by the institutions of the Community, but pointed out that: "Some discretion does fall to be exercised by the Member States from the obligation to 'convert any bilateral quotas . . . into global quotas' and from the concepts of 'total value' and 'national production.' In fact, since the Treaty gives no indication as to the data . . . or as to the methods applicable, several solutions may be envisaged."[47] It followed, in the Court's view, that the provisions in question were insufficiently precise to be considered directly effective.

It must be emphasised that the fact that provisions of Community law may require the appreciation of complex economic issues does not preclude their being directly effective, providing the requisite conditions are satisfied. Thus Article 95(1) of the Treaty prohibits the imposition "on the products of other Member States" of "any internal taxation of any kind in excess of that imposed directly or indirectly on similar domestic products." The second paragraph of that Article adds that: "no Member State shall impose on the products of other Member States any internal taxation of such a nature as to afford indirect protection to other productions." In *Fink-Frucht* v. *Hauptzollamt München*,[48] the Court considered whether or not this latter provision was directly effective. It decided that it was, in face of the arguments of the Federal Republic that the paragraph was "vague and incomplete" and that the "value-judgments" it required should not be forced on national courts.[49] In the Court's view, the provision contained a

---

[44] See, *e.g.* Arts. 13(1), (2); Arts. 30, 32(1); Art. 48(1); Art. 52; Art. 59.
[45] Ranbow, "The End of the Transitional period" (1969) 6 C.M.L.Rev. 434. For obligations directly effective as of the end of the transitional period, see, *e.g.* Case 77/72 *Capolongo* [1973] E.C.R. 611 (Art. 13(2)); Case 74/76 *Ianelli & Volpi* [1977] E.C.R. 557 (Art. 30); Case 59/75, *Manghera* [1976] E.C.R. 91 (Art. 37(1)); Case 41/74 *Van Duyn* [1974] E.C.R. 1337 (Art. 48); Case 2/74 *Reyners* [1974] E.C.R. 631 (Art. 52); Case 33/74 *Van Binsbergen* [1974] E.C.R. 1299 (Art. 59).
[46] Case 33/68 [1968] E.C.R. 453.
[47] [1968] E.C.R. 453 at p. 461.
[48] Case 27/767 [1968] E.C.R. 223.
[49] [1968] E.C.R. 223 at p. 229.

straightforward prohibition against protection; it established an unconditional obligation, and no action was required on the part of the institutions of the Community or the Member States for its implementation." Although this provision involves the evaluation of economic factors," observed the Court, "this does not exclude the right and duty of national courts to ensure that the rules of the Treaty are observed whenever they can ascertain . . . and the conditions necessary for the application of the article are fulfilled."[50]

2. *The rights and obligations of individuals inter se*

In the cases discussed above, the Court of Justice was called upon to consider whether or not a provision of the Treaty had modified the legal position of individuals *vis-à-vis* the State. Beginning with the decision in *Belgische Radio en Televisie* v. *SABAM*,[51] we see a new development; the acknowledgment that provisions of the Treaty are capable of modifying the rights of individuals *inter se*. Thus in *SABAM* the Court observed that the prohibitions of Articles 85(1) and 86 "tend by their very nature to produce direct effects in relations between individuals," and "create direct rights in respect of the individuals concerned with the national courts must safeguard."[52] It might have been arguable that Articles 85 and 86, being explicitly concerned with private action, could be treated as special cases, but the Court's later decision in *Walrave and Koch* v. *Association union cycliste internationale*[53] suggested a more general principle. Motorcyclists who earned their living "pacing" pedal cyclists in international events asked the Arrondissementsrechtsbank, Utrecht, for a declaration that certain rules of the defendant association infringed the Treaty's prohibition of discrimination on grounds of nationality. Doubts were expressed by the Commission[54] as to whether the prohibition in question applied to *private* action, and the Court, although the issue was not explicitly before it, addressed itself to the question as follows:

> "It has been alleged that the prohibitions in these Articles refer only to restrictions which have their origin in acts of an authority and not to those resulting from legal acts of persons or associations who do not come under public law.
>
> Articles 7, 48, 59 have in common the prohibition, in their respective spheres of application, of any discrimination on grounds of nationality.
>
> Prohibition of such discrimination does not only apply to the acts of public authorities, but extends likewise to rules of any other nature aimed at regulating in a collective manner gainful employment and the provision of services."[55]

It followed, in the Court's view, that the provisions of Articles 7, 48 and

---

[50] [1968] E.C.R. 223 at p. 232.
[51] Case 127/73 [1974] E.C.R. 51.
[52] [1974] E.C.R. 51 at p. 62.
[53] Case 36/74 [1974] E.C.R. 1405.
[54] [1974] E.C.R. 1405 at p. 1410.
[55] [1974] E.C.R. 1405 at p. 1418, paras. 15, 16, 17.

59 of the Treaty could be taken into account in judging the validity and the effects of the rules of a sporting association.

The extent to which the Treaty may impose obligations on individuals was once again raised in *Defrenne* v. *Sabena*,[56] a reference from the Belgian Tribunal du Travail. The national suit arose from proceedings brought by a former air-hostess against her former employer, Sabena, in which she alleged infringement of Article 119 of the Treaty. The latter Article provides that during the first stage "Each Member States shall . . . ensure and subsequently maintain the application of the principle that men and women should receive equal pay for equal work." The original Six had not complied with this obligation by January 1, 1973, nor had the new Member States been in a position to do so on accession. The Tribunal du Travail asked the Court of Justice whether the Article in question entitled workers to undertake proceedings before national courts in order to ensure its observance. The Court replied in the affirmative; even though the complete implementation of the equal pay principle could not be achieved without legislative elaboration at the Community or national level, the requirement was nevertheless apt for national judicial application in cases of "direct and overt discrimination which may be identified solely with the aid of the criteria based on equal work and equal pay referred to by the article in question."[57] The Court went on to reject the argument that the Article could not be applied to the activities of private parties. "In fact," declared the Court, "since Article 119 is mandatory in nature, the prohibition on discrimination between men and women applies not only to an action of public authorities, but also extends to all agreements which are intended to regulate paid labour collectively, as well as to contracts between individuals."[58] The Treaty's prohibition on discrimination, whether it be on the grounds of nationality or sex (at any rate as far as pay is concerned) may, it seems, be invoked against natural and legal persons, as well as against Member States.

3. *The exceptional case—the prospective effect of a holding of direct applicability*

Although the Court in *Defrenne* held that Article 119 of the Treaty was directly applicable—at least in part—it also held that the Article could not be relied upon to support claims in respect of pay periods prior to the date of its judgment, except as regards workers who had already brought legal proceedings or made equivalent claims. The Court seems to have been moved by the pleas of Ireland and the United Kingdom that claims to back pay based on Article 119 could have disastrous economic effects in these countries. It responded as follows:

"Although the practical consequences of any judicial decision must be

---

[56] Case 43/75 [1976] E.C.R. 455. The decision provoked a great deal of discussion, see Wyatt, (1975–6) 1 E.L.Rev. 399–402, 418, 419; Crisham (1977) 14 C.M.L.Rev. 102, and references cited at pp. 108, 109, note 1. Allott [1977] C.L.J. 7.

[57] [1976] E.C.R. 455 at p. 473, para. 18, *e.g.* discrimination in national legislation or in collective labour agreements, which could be detected on the basis of a purely legal analysis of the situation, [1976] E.C.R. 455 at p. 473, para. 21.

[58] [1976] E.C.R. 455 at p. 476, para. 39.

carefully taken into account, it would be impossible to go so far as to diminish the objectivity of the law and compromise its future application on the ground of the possible repercussions which might result, as regards the past, from such a judicial decision.

However, in the light of the conduct of several of the Member States and the views adopted by the Commission and repeatedly brought to the notice of the circles concerned, it is appropriate to take exceptionally into account the fact that, over a prolonged period, the parties concerned have been led to continue with practices which were contrary to Article 119, although not yet prohibited under their national law.

The fact that, in spite of the warnings given, the Commission did not initiate proceedings under Article 169 against the Member States concerned on grounds of failure to fulfil an obligation was likely to consolidate the incorrect impression as to the effects of Article 119.

In these circumstances, it is appropriate to determine that, as the general level at which pay would have been fixed cannot be known, important considerations of legal certainty affecting all the interests involved, both public and private, make it impossible to reopen the question as regards the past."[59]

In other words, the *unexpectedness* of the Court's ruling militated against its retrospective application. The legal basis of the decision is the principle of "legal certainty," which embraces the notion that parties acting reasonably on the basis of the law as it stands ought not to have their expectations frustrated by subsequent legislative action.[60] Analogous principles underlie the practice of the Supreme Court of the United States, which has declared in certain cases that constitutional rulings shall have only prospective effect.[61] In so doing, it has emphasised three criteria: (i) the purpose to be served by the new rule; (ii) the extent of reliance by law enforcement authorities on the old rule; and (iii) the effect on the administration of justice of a retrospective application of the new rule.[62] Application of these criteria to the equal pay situation before the Court in *Defrenne* is instructive. Commission, State authorities and private individuals had certainly relied in good faith on the fact that Article 119 did not have direct effect as of the end of the first stage. Again, there can be little doubt that a retroactive ruling in *Defrenne* could have created insuperable problems for the "administration of justice," for, as the Court pointed out, it would have been impossible to have ascertained the wage patterns that would have emerged had the requirement of the Treaty been observed at the proper time.[63] Nor would a retroactive ruling have accorded with the "purpose of the rule"—its social aims might well have been frustrated by national

---

[59] [1976] E.C.R. 455 at pp. 480, 481, paras. 71–74.
[60] For the relationship between "legal certainty" and "legitimate expectation," see Usher, "The Influence of National Concepts on Decisions of the European Court" (1975–76) 1 E.L.Rev. 359, at 363. For these concepts as general principles of Community Law, see *infra*, at p. 61.
[61] See Wilson, 42 Fordham L.Rev. 653.
[62] *Stovall* v. *Denno* 388 U.S. 293, at p. 297; L.Ed. 2d 1199; 87 S.Ct. 1967.
[63] It is fanciful to suppose that the increased cost of equal pay would have had no impact on the level of earnings.

courts giving judgments against employers resulting in unemployment or even bankruptcy.[64]

The Court's ruling that Article 119 should have direct effect only prospectively is novel, and clearly exceptional,[65] but that is not to deny that it is firmly founded in principles affirmed consistently by the Court in its previous jurisprudence, unexceptionable in themselves, and essential to a Court exercising a quasi-constitutional function in the legal order established by the founding Treaties.

4. *Direct application of rules of the Treaty which do not give rise to rights in individuals*

The law is not exclusively concerned with bestowing rights, or imposing obligations, on individuals; it may, for instance, authorise public authorities to take action which they would not otherwise be authorised to take. Treaty provisions which fall into this category are not "directly effective," as that expression has been defined by the Court in the cases discussed above, but they may nevertheless be susceptible to direct application in national courts. It will be recalled that the Advocate-General in *Van Gend en Loos* referred to Treaty provisions being "clearly intended to be incorporated into national law and to modify or supplement it,"[66] and this approach is echoed in the words of the Court of Justice in *Costa* v. *ENEL* to the effect that the "EEC Treaty has created its own legal system which, on the entry into force of the Treaty, became an integral part of the legal systems of the Member States and which their courts are bound to apply."[67]

Whether or not a Treaty provision is to be applied by a national court, independently of national implementation, depends on the interpretation of the provision in question. If, on its proper construction, it is intended to have legal effect, then English courts are bound to give it such, under the appropriately worded text of section 2(1) of the European Communities Act 1972.[68] Thus Article 177 of the Treaty directly bestows on national courts the competence to refer questions to the Court of Justice for a preliminary ruling. National provisions may establish the relevant details of procedure,[69] but they neither create, nor may they condition, the capacity to make the reference. The provision is not directly effective, in that it does not give rise to rights in individuals which national courts are bound to safeguard (apart, perhaps, from the third paragraph of Article 177), but is

---

[64] "Levelling down" is not a permissible method of complying with Art. 119, see [1976] E.C.R. 455 at p. 472, para. 15.
[65] Case 61/79 *Denkavit* [1980] E.C.R. 1200 (prospective effect ruling for Court of Justice alone); Case 69/80 *Worringham & Humphreys* [1981] E.C.R. 767; Cases 142 and 143/80 *Essevi and Salengo* [1981] E.C.R. 1413; (Case 811/79 *Ariete* [1980] E.C.R. 2545; Case 826/79 *Mireco* [1980] 2559.) Rulings on the invalidity of Community legislation are more readily given prospective effect: see, *e.g.* Case 4/79 *Providence Agricole* [1980] E.C.R. 2823, p. 2853; Case 109/79 *Maiseries de Beauce* [1985] E.C.R. 2883 at 2913; Case 145/79 *Roquette* [1985] E.C.R. 2917, at p. 2946; Case 41/84 *Pinna* [1986] E.C.R. 66 [1963] E.C.R. 1 at p. 20.
[66] [1963] E.C.R. 1 at p. 20.
[67] [1964] E.C.R. 585 at p. 593. And see Case 17/67 *Neumann* [1967] E.C.R. 441 at p. 453.
[68] See Mitchell *et al.* (1972) 9 C.M.L.Rev. 134, 137.
[69] See, *e.g.* R.S.C., Ord. 114.

nevertheless directly applicable, in the sense that it has direct application, in the national legal order.

THE LEGAL EFFECTS OF COMMUNITY ACTS

One of the most striking characteristics of the legal order established by the Treaty is the competence vested in the Council, and to a lesser extent in the Commission, to enact legislation for the purpose of attaining the objectives of the Treaty. Thus Article 189 provides that: "In order to carry out their task the Council and the Commission shall, in accordance with the provisions of this Treaty, make regulations, issue directives, take decisions, make recommendations, or deliver opinions." Since "recommendations and opinions have no binding force," emphasis will be placed on regulations, directives and decisions.

Regulations

Article 189 of the Treaty provides that: "A regulation shall have general application. It shall be binding in its entirety and directly applicable in all Member States." At first sight, this description of regulations appears to attribute to them the characteristics of those Treaty provisions capable of giving rise to rights in individuals which national courts are bound to safeguard. Even a cursory scrutiny of the *Official Journal*, however, reveals that each and every provision of each and every regulation does not give rise to rights in individuals as against other individuals or as against Member States. Various explanations have been offered for this unsurprising phenomenon. On the one hand, it has been suggested[70] that since characterisation as a regulation *vel non* is a matter of substance, not form,[71] the provisions of a regulation which do not satisfy the conditions for direct applicability are not regulations in the true sense at all. "In such an instance," the argument runs, "the merely formal regulations could be denied direct application."[72] This view is not without difficulty. It seems to discount the possibility that Community law may empower national courts to apply rules which do not actually bestow rights on individuals. Again, it leads to the conclusion that if the Treaty authorises the Council to legislate on certain matters by regulation and regulation only, each and every provision of such a regulation must give to rights in individuals which national courts are bound to safeguard; any such provision which does not have this quality is not part of the regulation, in law, is unauthorised by the Treaty Article in question, and therefore invalid.[73]

Another view[74] is that the reference to direct applicability in Article 189

[70] Bebr, [1970] I.C.L.Q. 257 at pp. 290 *et seq.*
[71] Cases 16, 17, 19–22/62, *Confederation nationale* [1962] E.C.R. 471; Case 30/67, *Industria Molitoria* [1968] E.C.R. 115; Case 6/68 *Zuckerfabrik* [1968] E.C.R. 409.
[72] [1970] I.C.L.Q. 257 at p. 290.
[73] Art. 94 of the Treaty authorises only regulations.
[74] J. A. Winter, (1972) 9 C.M.L. Rev. 425.

concerns the *process of incorporation* of regulations into the national legal order. This description emphasises that national courts must take cognisance of regulations as legal instruments whose validity and recognition by national courts must not be conditioned on national procedures of incorporation into the national legal order. Whether or not *particular provisions* of such an instrument in fact give rise to rights in individuals which national courts must safeguard is a matter of interpretation of the provisions concerned, in light of the criteria established by the Court of Justice with respect to the direct application of provisions of the Treaty. This is the better view, and is quite consistent with the decided cases, though the Court has gone out of its way to clarify the matter. Thus in *Politi* v. *Italian Ministry of Finance*,[75] the Turin Tribunale asked the Court whether certain provisions of an agricultural regulation were (i) directly applicable, and (ii) if so, whether they created rights for individuals which national courts were bound to safeguard. The question presented to the Court reflects neatly the distinction indicated above; the Court's response does not. "Under the terms of the second paragraph of Article 189," it declared, "regulations 'shall have general application' and 'shall be . . . directly applicable in all Member States.' Therefore, by reason of their nature and their function in the system of the sources of Community law, regulations have direct effect and are as such capable of creating individual rights which national courts must protect."[76] Similar reasoning appears in *Leonesio* v. *Italian Ministry of Agriculture and Forestry*,[77] in which the Pretore of Lonato posed questions which again separated the issues of direct applicability and direct effect. The Court ruled that: "A Community regulation has direct effect and is, as such capable of creating individual rights which national courts must protect." Advocate-General Roemer, on the other hand, pointed out that simply to acknowledge the status of the instrument in question did not solve the problem before the Court, *i.e.* whether certain of its provisions bestowed enforceable rights on individual farmers as against the Italian State "wherefore an answer to the question of the legal effects," he argued, "depends on the questions whether an area of discretion was left to the national authorities in the matter of implementation and in what manner the national provisions were to supplement the measures adopted."[78]

Although the Court of Justice had not explicitly acknowledged that the direct applicability of regulations does not require the automatic effect of their provisions at the suit of individuals, such is clearly the case, and it is always possible that the Court's reticence results from the conviction that the distinction is either obvious, or of little practical importance. If the question were raised before the Court that on its true construction a particular provision of a regulation was incapable of giving rise to rights in individuals because it was conditioned on national implementation, the Court would no doubt construe the provision in question, to see if it were apt for judicial enforcement. Thus in *Caisse commune d'assurances "la pré-*

[75] Case 43/71 [1971] E.C.R. 1039.
[76] [1971] E.C.R. 1039 at p. 1048, para. 9.
[77] Case 93/71 [1972] E.C.R. 287.
[78] [1972] E.C.R. 287 at p. 300.

voyance sociale" v. *Bertholet*,[79] the Court was asked whether Article 52 of Regulation 3 was applicable in national courts before the bilateral agreements referred to therein had been concluded between the Member States concerned. The Court answered in the affirmative, on the grounds that the first paragraph of that Article was couched in unequivocal terms, while its provisions were clear and could be applied without difficulty. Obviously the mere status of the instrument in which the provision was found could not determine a question dependent on the true construction of the provision itself.

A corollary of the proposition that regulations must be recognised as legal instruments without the need for national implementation is that such implementation, unless authorised in a particular case,[80] is impermissible, inasmuch as it tends to disguise from those subject to the law the Community source of their rights and obligations. That the legislative duplication of regulations might in itself be inconsistent with Community law was made clear in *Commission* v. *Italy*,[81] in which the Italian Government had failed to implement certain regulations concerning slaughter premia and the withholding of milk supplied from the market, resulting in an action by the Commission under Article 169 of the Treaty. Not only did the Commission complain of the delay of the Italian Government in instituting the scheme, but also of the technique of reproducing the texts of regulations in Italian legislation. This, said the Court, itself constituted a default, since by adopting this procedure, the Italian Government had brought into doubt both the legal nature of the applicable provisions and the date of their coming into force. The Court reiterated its position in *Fratelli Variola* v. *Amministrazione italiana delle Finanze*. "No procedure is permissible," it emphasised, "whereby the Community nature of a legal rule is concealed from those subject to it."[82] Member States are *a fortiori* prohibited from adopting national measures designed to alter the scope of regulations, or amend their provisions.[83] Nevertheless, the Court has acknowledged that where Community regulations require implementation by national measures, the incorporation of the texts of such regulations may be justified for the sake of coherence and in order to make them comprehensible to the persons to whom they apply.[84]

Since regulations constitute direct legislations by the Community, not only may individuals rely on specific provisions as against other individuals and Member States, they may invoke the *general objective and purpose* of regulations as against national legal provisions. This pre-emptive quality of regulations has become most obviously apparent in the context of the common agricultural policy, where the Court has ruled on several occasions that national measures have been incompatible with the legal regime established by a Community regulation (as opposed to specific provisions vest-

---

[79] Case 31/64 [1965] E.C.R. 81.
[80] Case 31/78 *Bussone* [1978] E.C.R. 2429; Case 230/78 *Zuccheri* [1979] E.C.R. 2749.
[81] Case 39/72 [1973] E.C.R. 101.
[82] Case 34/73 [1973] E.C.R. 981 at p. 991, para. 11.
[83] Case 74/69 *Krohn* [1970] E.C.R. 451; Case 40/69 *Bollmann* [1970] E.C.R. 69 at p. 79; Case 18/72 *Granaria* [1972] E.C.R. 1163.
[84] Case 272/83 *Commission* v. *Italy* [1985] E.C.R. at p. 1074, para. 27.

ing rights in individuals)[85] Thus national measures which hinder agricultural producers from selling on the market at a price equal to the target
price may be challenged by individuals concerned in national courts,
although producers have no "right" to sell at that price. In effect, they are
allowed to invoke the encroachment by national legislation on an area of
Community competence. As the Court explained in *Amsterdam Bulb BV*
v. *Produktschap voor Siergewassen*:

> "From the moment that the Community adopts regulations under
> Article 40 of the Treaty establishing a common organisation of the
> market in a specific sector the Member States are under a duty not to
> take any measure which might create exemptions from them or affect
> them adversely.
> The compatibility with the Community regulations of the provisions
> referred to by the national court must be considered in the light not
> only of the express provisions of the regulations but also of their *aims
> and objectives*."[86] (emphasis added)

In certain cases, it seems that the subject-matter of a regulation may preclude the enactment of national legislation entirely in the field in question.
Thus in *Hauptzollamt Bremen* v. *Krohn*, the Court declared: "In so far as
the Member States have conferred on the Community legislative powers in
tariff matters, in order to ensure the proper functioning of the common
market in agriculture, they no longer have the power to issue independent
provisions in this field."[87]

Regulations, in short, are to be treated as "law" in every sense of the
word. National courts must take judicial notice of them in their entirety;
specific provisions contained therein may bestow on individuals rights as
against other individuals or Member States; and their effect in a particular
area may be to pre-empt national legislative competence.

2. Directives and decisions

(a) *General*

Article 189 says of directives and decisions:
> "A directive shall be binding, as to the result to be achieved, upon
> each Member State to which it is addressed, but shall leave to the
> national authorities the choice of form and methods.
> A decision shall be binding in its entirety upon those to whom it is
> addressed."

Whereas a directive may be addressed only to a state, a decision may
also be addressed to a natural or legal person. An example of an individual
decision would be a Commission ruling that a firm or firms had acted in
breach of Articles 85 and 86 of the Treaty. Such a decision might include

---

[85] See, *e.g.* Case 60/75 *Russo* [1976] E.C.R. 45; Case 77/76 *Fratelli Cucchi* [1977] E.C.R. 987;
see Wyatt [1977] C.L.J. 216 at p. 217.
[86] Case 50/76 [1977] E.C.R. 137 at p. 147, para. 8. See further in chapter on Agriculture,
infra, pp. 335 *et seq.*
[87] Case 74/69 [1970] E.C.R. 451 at p. 458. And see Case 40/69 *Bollmann* [1970] E.C.R. 69 at
p. 79.

the imposition of a fine.[88] An example of a decision addressed to a Member State, by contrast, would be an act of the Commission requiring a Member State to abolish or amend measures of aid to national undertakings.[89] The choice of form and methods for the implementation of directives left to Member States allows a Member State to choose the legislative format which it considers appropriate.[90]

Mere administrative practices, which by their nature may be altered at the whim of the authorities and lack the appropriate publicity cannot be regarded as a valid fulfilment of the obligation imposed by Article 189 on Member States to which directives are addressed.[91] However, the Court has held that directives do not require legislative implementation where there exist general principles of constitutional or administrative law which render specific legislation superfluous, provided that these principles guarantee the application of the directive, are clear and precise, are made known to those subject to the law, and are capable of being invoked in the courts.[92] It follows that legislation is also superfluous where national legislative provisions in force afford similar guarantees that a directive will be effectively implemented.

(b) *Rights of individuals against the state*

It was initially believed that directives and decisions gave rise exclusively to rights and obligations as between their addressees on the one hand, and the Community institutions and Member States on the other.[93]

A series of decisions of the Court of Justice, beginning with that in *Franz Grad* v. *Finanzamt Traunstein*,[94] necessitated a radical reappraisal of the traditional view. In the *Grad* case, the Finanzgericht, München, asked the Court of Justice whether the obligation imposed upon Member States by Article 4 of Council Decision 65/271,[95] coupled with the deadline for its fulfilment contained in Article 1 of Directive 67/227[96] were capable of vesting rights in individuals which national courts were bound to safeguard.

The Court of Justice held that directives and decisions might contain directly effective provisions. "Although it is true," declared the Court, "that by virtue of Article 189, regulations are directly applicable and therefore by virtue of their nature capable of producing direct effects, it does not follow from this that other categories of legal measures mentioned in that

---

[88] See Arts. 85–87; Reg. 17, O.J. Sp.Ed. 1959–62, p. 87, Arts. 15, 16. See *infra*, p. 444.

[89] Art. 93(2) EEC; see *infra*, p. 467.

[90] Case 163/82 *Commission* v. *Italy*, [1983] E.C.R. 3723, at pp. 3286, 3287.

[91] Case 102/79 *Commission* v. *Belgium* [1980] E.C.R. 1473; Case 96/81 *Commission* v. *Netherlands* [1982] E.C.R. 1791; Case 145/82 *Commission* v. *Italy* [1982] E.C.R. 1791; Case 145/82 *Commission* v. *Italy* [1983] E.C.R. 711.

[92] Case 29/84 *Commission* v. *Germany* [1986] 3 C.M.L.R. 579.

[93] See, *e.g. Joseph Aim* [1972] C.M.L.R. 901 (Cour d'Appel de Paris); *Firma Baer Getreide GmbH* [1972] C.M.L.R. 539 (Hessischer Verwaltungsgerichtschof); and more recently, *Cohn-Bendit* [1979] Dalloz Jur. 155 (Conseil d'Etat); and *Kloppenburg*, Judgment of April 25, 1985 (Bundesfinanzhof) see (1985) 10 E.L.Rev. 303.

[94] Case 9/70 [1970] E.C.R. 825; see also Case 20/70 *Transports Lesage* [1970] E.C.R. 861; and Case 23/70 *Haselhorst* [1970] E.C.R. 881.

[95] O.J.Sp.Ed. 1965–1966, p. 67, providing for the application of the common value added tax system to transport of goods by road, rail and inland waterway.

[96] O.J.Sp.Ed. 1967, p. 14 on the harmonisation of legislation of Member States concerning turnover taxes.

Article can never produce similar effects. In particular, the provision according to which decisions are binding in their entirety on those to whom they are addressed enables the question to be put whether the obligation created by the decisions can only be invoked by the Community institutions against the addressee or whether such a right may possibly be exercised by all those who have an interest in the fulfilment of this obligation."[97] In the Court's view to adopt the alternative solution would call in question the binding nature of decisions, and diminish their useful effect. While the effects of a decision might not be identical with those of a provision contained in a regulation, this difference did not preclude the possibility that the end result, namely the right of the individual to invoke the measure before the courts, might be the same as that of a directly applicable provision of a regulation. This conclusion was reinforced by the wording of Article 177 of the Treaty:

"Article 177, whereby the national courts are empowered to refer to the Court all questions regarding the validity and interpretation of *all acts of the institutions without distinction*, also implies that individuals may invoke *such acts* before the national courts. Therefore, in each particular case, it must be ascertained whether the nature, background and wording of the provision in question are capable of producing direct effects in the legal relationships between the addressee of the act and third parties." (emphasis added)[98]

The reasoning of the Court has been reiterated in subsequent cases. Thus in *Van Duyn* v. *Home Office*[99] the Court held that Article 3(1) of Directive 64/221[1] gave rise to rights in individuals which national courts were bound to safeguard, and in *Rutili* v. *French Minister of the Interior* went so far as to hold that the directive in question was directly effective in its entirety.[2] Again, in *Verbond van Nederlandse Ondernemingen* v. *Inspecteur der Invoerrechten en Accijnzen*,[3] the Court held that one of the provisions of the Council's Second Directive on Value Added Tax vested rights in individuals which national courts were bound to safeguard. Although the decisions are based on virtually identical reasoning, the cases represent a certain progression, at least with respect to directives. The decision in *Grad* concerned merely a time-limit in a directive,[4] the substantive obligation was to be found elsewhere, in a decision. The decision in *Van Duyn* admittedly concerned a substantive provision of a directive, but that directive, according to the Court in *Procureur du Roi* v. *Royer*[5] gave rise to no new rights in favour of persons protected by Community law, but simply determined the scope and detailed rules for the exercise of rights conferred directly by the Treaty. *Verbond*, on the other hand, concerned a

---

[97] [1970] E.C.R. 825 at p. 837, para. 5.
[98] [1970] E.C.R. 825 at p. 837, para. 6.
[99] Case 41/74 [1974] E.C.R. 1337.
[1] O.J.Sp.Ed. 1963–64, p. 117.
[2] This conclusion applies equally to Dir. 68/360, O.J.Sp.Ed. 1968 (II), p. 485; and to Dir. 73/148, O.J. 1973, L172/14. Case 36/75 [1975] E.C.R. 1219 at p. 1229, para. 16.
[3] Case 51/76 [1977] E.C.R. 113.
[4] And see Case 33/70 *SACE* (1970] E.C.R. 1213.
[5] Case 48/75 [1976] E.C.R. 497.

substantive provision contained in a harmonisation directive based on Articles 99 and 100 of the Treaty, Articles which, unlike Article 48, do not of themselves vest rights directly in individuals. The Court has upheld the direct effect of appropriately worded provisions of directives in a consistent line of cases.[6]

The provisions of a directive may only have direct effect where they have not been correctly implemented by the Member State in question before the end of the period prescribed for that purpose.[7] Where a directive has been properly implemented by national measures, its effects extend to individuals through the medium of those implementing measures,[8] though the directive may be invoked before national courts as an aid to the construction of national statutes,[9] and national courts are obliged to construe national law, whether specifically introduced to implement the directive or not, in the light of the wording and purpose of the directive in order to achieve the result referred to in the third paragraph of Article 189.[10] Again, where a directive has been properly implemented by national measures, it is not open to a litigant to side-step the appropriate provisions of national law and rely upon the directive effect of the provisions of the directive.[11] This follows from the terms of Article 189 EEC, which provides that directives, while binding as to the result to be achieved, "shall leave to the national authorities the choice of form and methods." National legislative implementation of a directive constitutes both the due performance of a Community obligation, and the exercise of a sovereign choice to exclude the direct application of the directive itself by the national courts.

While the appropriate test for the direct effect of a directive is said to be the clarity and precision of its terms,[12] it must be added that even the precise and unconditional terms of a directive will not be directly effective (as far as judicial application is concerned) unless intended to be given effect by the national judicial authorities, rather than national administrative authorities.[13]

Irrespective of the direct effect of the substantive provisions of a directive, its terms may lack an unconditional and precise obligation as to the specific remedies to be made available in national courts,[14] though if a Member State chooses to penalise the breach of an obligation required to

---

[6] See, e.g. Case 38/77 *Enka* [1977] E.C.R. 2203; Case 148/78 *Ratti* [1979] E.C.R. 1629; Case 8/81 *Becker* [1982] E.C.R. 53; Case 255/81 *Grendel* [1982] E.C.R. 2301; Case 70/83 *Kloppenburg* [1984] E.C.R. 1075; Case 5/84 *Direct Cosmetics* [1985] 2 C.M.L.R. 145; Case 152/84 *Marshall* [1986] 1 C.ML.R. 688.

[7] Case 148/78 *Ratti* [1979] E.C.R. 1629; Case 8/81 *Becker* [1982] E.C.R. 53; Case 126/82 *D. J. Smit* [1983] E.C.R. 73.

[8] Case 102/79 *Commission* v. *Belgium* [1980] E.C.R. 1473; Case 8/81 *Becker* [1982] E.C.R. 53.

[9] Case 32/74 *Haaga* [1974] E.C.R. 1201; Case 11/75 *Mazzalai* [1976] E.C.R. 657; Case 270/81 *Felicitas* [1982] E.C.R. 2771.

[10] Case 14/83 *Von Colson* [1984] E.C.R. 1891 at p. 1909, para. 26; Case 79/83 *Harz* [1984] E.C.R. 1921 at p. 1942, para. 26.

[11] Case 270/81 *Felicitas* [1980] E.C.R. 2771.

[12] Case 126/82 *D.J. Smit* [1983] E.C.R. 73.

[13] Case 815/79 *Cremonini & Vrankovich* [1980] E.C.R. 3583.

[14] Case 14/83 *Von Colson* [1984] E.C.R. 1891; Case 79/83 *Harz* [1984] 1921; it is clear that the substantive obligations of Dir. 76/207 are directly effective, see Case 152/84 *Marshall* [1986] 1 C.M.L.R. 688.

be imposed under a directive by the award of compensation, that compensation must be adequate in relation to the damage sustained.[14]

(c) *Rights of individuals inter se*

The Court has held that while directives may be invoked against the State, both in its private law and public law capacities, they can never be invoked against private individuals.[15] The legal effects of directives (and presumably decisions addressed to Member States) thus differ from those of both treaty provisions and regulations, and the reasons for this merit consideration.

Before the judgment in the *Ratti* case,[16] there was nothing in the Court's case law to suggest that the legal effects of a directly effective provision in a directive would be any different from those of a directly effective treaty provision. Since the Court had held that treaty provisions were capable of binding individuals, as well as States,[17] it would have followed that directives could have similar effects. There were several arguments, however, which could be marshalled against this conclusion.[18] First, since there was no legal requirement to publish directives, it might seem to be implied that directives could only bind those to whom they were addressed. Secondly, it was arguable that to allow directives to be pleaded against individuals would assimilate directives to regulations, which would run counter to Article 189 of the Treaty. Thirdly, there was the argument that to allow directives to be pleaded against individuals would be contrary to the principle of legal certainty, since those subject to obligations contained in directives might be unsure whether to rely upon national implementing legislation, or upon the underlying directives. While none of these arguments were conclusive, there *was* a further argument, of a political, rather than legal nature: the courts in some Member States were having difficulty in accepting that directives could have direct effect at *all*[19]; to go further and to allow "horizontal" effect to directives might further diminish the credibility of the Court of Justice in such Member States, and lead to the uneven enforceability of directives in the Community.

The Court laid the conceptual foundations for its later compromise solution in a judgment of April 5, 1979. In the *Ratti* case[20] the Court of Justice declared that:

> "a Member State which has not adopted the implementing measures required by the directive in the prescribed period may not rely, as against individuals, *on its own failure to perform the obligations which the directive entails.*"[21]

The italicised words indicated that the legal basis for the direct effect of directives was that a State could not rely upon its own wrong as a defence to an action based upon a directive before its own courts. This doctrine

---

[15] Case 152/84 *Marshall* [1986] 1 C.M.L.R. 688.
[16] Case 148/78 *Ratti* [1979] E.C.R. 1629.
[17] See *supra*, p. 34.
[18] See, in general, Easson, (1979) 4 E.L.Rev. 67, at pp. 70–73.
[19] Pescatore, (1983) 8 E.L.Rev. 155, at pp. 169–170.
[20] Case 148/78 [1979] E.C.R. 1629.
[21] [1979] E.C.R. 1629, at para. 22. Emphasis added.

seemed to restrict the application of directives by national courts to actions against defaulting Member States, and to rule out actions against individuals. The Court's case-law following *Ratti* incorporated the above-mentioned formulation.[22]

The Court's decision in *Marshall*[23] finally laid speculation to rest. The appellant in the national proceedings, Miss. M. H. Marshall, was an employee of an Area Health Authority in the United Kingdom. She had been dismissed at the age of 62, since she had passed "the normal retirement age" (of 60) applied by the Authority to women employees.

An exception had in fact been made for Miss Marshall to work until the age of 62. The normal retiring age for men was 65. Miss Marshall instituted proceedings against the Authority alleging sex discrimination contrary to the principle of equality of treatment laid down in Directive 76/207.[24] The Area Health Authority argued before the Court of Justice: (1) that the directive could not be relied upon against individuals; (2) that the Authority, although a public authority emanating from the central government, had acted *qua* employer in dismissing Miss Marshall, rather than *qua* State. The Court held that since a directive was binding under Article 189 EEC only upon "each Member State to which it was addressed," it could not of itself impose obligations upon an individual. However, this did not preclude an individual relying upon a directive against the State, regardless of the capacity in which the latter was acting, whether as an employer or as a public authority. The United Kingdom had argued that the possibility of relying on provisions of the directive against the Authority would give rise to arbitrary and unfair distinctions between the rights of state employees and those of private employees. The Court of Justice did not find this argument convincing. On the contrary, such a distinction might easily be avoided if the Member State concerned correctly implemented the directive in national law.

The *Marshall* decision allows the invocation of the "private law" directives against the State, but rules out such actions against private parties. While the compromise may be justifiable on policy grounds, the Court's reasoning seems less than compelling. The Court avers that directives bind the State, and therefore cannot be invoked against individuals. Yet this very argument failed in *Defrenne*[25] to prevent Article 119 of the Treaty being held to bind private parties as well as the State. What is true of the Treaty should also, it might be thought, be true of directives, for the obligation to comply with a directive is itself a treaty obligation, and the Court has held that directives have an effect no less binding than that of any other rule of Community law.[26]

That is not to say that the Court's ruling in *Marshall* cannot be justified on legal grounds; on the contrary, there has always been a strong case against the horizontal effect of directives based on the principle of legal

[22] See, *e.g.* Case 8/81 *Becker* [1982] E.C.R. 53.
[23] Case 152/84 *Marshall* [1986] 1 C.M.L.R. 688.
[24] O.J. 1976, L39/40.
[25] Case 43/75, [1976] E.C.R. 455.
[26] Case 79/72, *Commission* v. *Italy* [1972] E.C.R. 667; Case 52/75, *Commission* v. *Italy* [1976] E.C.R. 277.

certainty.[27] Private individuals should clearly not be placed in unreasonable doubt as to their obligations by requiring the scrutiny of overlapping texts at both the national and Community level as a prerequisite to a complete appreciation of the law. The fact that individuals may be bound by treaty provisions and regulations does not give rise to the same risk of uncertainty. The Treaty is a finite document; the threat to legal certainty posed by the fact that its provisions may create obligations for individuals as well as rights is insignificant. Regulations, again, constitute direct Community legislation; they are as capable of binding individuals as any provision of national law, and are only subject to national implementation where they so provide. In this respect they must be distinguished from directives, and decisions addressed to Member States, which must be implemented by national legislation, resulting in the duplication of the substance of Community texts, and possible legal insecurity for individuals. For obvious reasons, the principle of legal certainty can hardly be invoked by a national authority as a ground for denying the legal efficacy of a directive, irrespective of the capacity in which the authority is alleged to be bound.

The disadvantage of the Court's approach in *Marshall* however, is that it rules out horizontal direct effect for directives even in cases where such effect could not prejudice the legal security of individuals, *e.g.* in cases where the direct effect of provisions of a "private law" directive have already been established in proceedings against the authorities of a Member State. The advantage of a case by case approach, allowing the principle of legal certainty to be pleaded as a complete defence to private individuals in some cases, and as justifying prospective effect for the Court's rulings in others, has apparently been foregone.

The legal effect of ancillary treaties[28]

It is established that international agreements between the Community and third countries constitute part of the Community legal order, and that appropriately worded provisions of such agreements may be invoked before national courts in the Member States. The true position was for some time unclear. In *Haegeman*[29] the Court of Justice held that the EEC-Greece Association Agreement of September 25, 1961, inasmuch as it was concluded by the Council under Articles 228 and 238 of the EEC Treaty, constituted an act of the institutions of the Community within the meaning of Article 177(1)(*b*) of the Treaty. It followed that the Court was competent to interpret the Agreement on a reference from a national court. In *Bresciani*[30] the Court took a further step, and held that Article 2(1) of the Convention of Association signed at Youndé on July 20, 1963, was directly effective. This Convention established an unequal association, inasmuch as the Community assumed greater obligations towards the undeveloped

---

[27] See the first edition of this book, pp. 40, 41.
[28] See Pescatore, (1983) 8 E.L.Rev. 155, at p. 171.
[29] Case 181/73 [1974] E.C.R. 449.
[30] Case 87/75 [1976] E.C.R. 129.

associated states than vice versa. The Court of Justice held that this factor did not preclude recognition by the Community that some of the provisions of the Convention had direct effect. By expressly referring, in Article 2(1) of the Convention, to Article 13 of the EEC Treaty, the Court held that the Community had undertaken precisely the same obligations towards the Associated States as in the Treaty the Member States had assumed towards each other.

What remained unclear was the extent to which the Court's conclusion in *Bresciani* could be extended to all treaties concluded between the Community and third countries. In *Polydor*[31] the Court of Appeal asked the Court of Justice for an interpretation of certain articles of the Association Agreement between the EEC and Portugal, and whether one of those articles was enforceable by individuals. The Court of Justice did not find it necessary to answer the latter question. Advocate General Rozes, however,[32] took the view that the direct effect of Treaty provisions was based on the premise that the Treaty had established a common market, with its own institutions, and a trading system based on reciprocity. These facts were lacking in the EEC-Portuguese agreement.[33] There could be no guarantee that the Portuguese courts would enforce the Agreement. The *Bresciani* case was distinguishable because the Yaoundé Convention was designed to establish an association lacking in reciprocity, and because it incorporated by reference an obligation from the EEC Treaty.

There can be no doubt that the Rozes thesis, had it been upheld by the Court, would have placed substantial restrictions upon the direct effect of third country agreements in the Community legal order.

In the *Pabst* case,[34] the Court of Justice held that Article 53(1) of the EEC-Greece Association Agreement was directly applicable. Advocate General Rozes did not oppose this conclusion, since in her view the Agreement constituted much more than a free trade agreement of the classical type with other non-Member countries. The Contracting Parties had declared themselves determined "to establish ever closer bonds between the Greek people and the peoples brought together in the European Economic Community with a view to the subsequent accession of Greece to the Community. These objectives were reflected in the agreement's structure and content, which was based on the EEC Treaty.

Some six months later the Court of Justice found it necessary to decide whether the distinctive quality of direct effect was limited to such agreements as aforesaid, or whether it extended to agreements with third countries in general.

In *Kupferberg*[35] the Court was asked whether Article 21 of the EEC-Portuguese Association Agreement was directly applicable. No fewer than

---

[31] Case 270/80 [1982] E.C.R. 329.
[32] [1982] E.C.R. 329 at 353 *et seq.*
[33] The argument of Adv. Gen. Rozes is a striking example of the erroneous conclusions that can follow from the premise that direct effect is unique to the "new legal order" of Community law, rather than a consequence of the treaty obligations of Member States. See Wyatt, "New Legal Order or Old?" (1982) 7 E.L.Rev. 147 at pp. 148–150.
[34] Case 17/81 [1982] E.C.R. 1331.
[35] Case 104/81 [1982] E.C.R. 3641.

four Member States opposed this conclusion in argument before the Court. Advocate General Rozes recalled her opinion in *Polydor*.[36] The differences in content, structure and objectives between the EEC Treaty and the EEC-Portuguese Association Agreement in her view militated against the direct effect of the latter.[37] The learned Advocate General in particular thought the existence of the "political procedure" of the "Joint Committee" (Articles 32 *et seq.* of the Agreement) to be incompatible with the judicial implementation of the Agreement.[38] The Court however held the provisions in issue to be directly applicable, justifying its conclusion at some length, and in terms applicable to all third country agreements. In ensuring respect for commitments arising from an agreement concluded by the Community institutions, declared the Court, the Member States fulfilled an obligation not only in relation to the non-member country concerned but also and above all in relation to the Community which had assumed responsibility for the due performance of the agreement. It followed from the Community nature of such provisions that their effect in the Community could not be allowed to vary according to whether their application was in practice the responsibility of the Community institutions or of the Member States, and, in the latter case, according to the effects in the internal legal order of each Member State which the law of that State assigns to international agreements concluded by it. Furthermore, the possibility that the courts of third countries might not accord direct effect to Association Agreements was not incompatible with the direct applicability of appropriately worded provisions of such agreements. The international legal obligations of states to fulfil their treaty commitments left them freedom to determine the legal means for attaining that end in their own legal system, unless the agreement itself specified such means. Thus the fact that the courts of one country might accord a provision direct effect while the courts of another might not would not of itself constitute a lack of reciprocity in the implementation of the agreement. Again, the existence of joint committees designed to secure the proper implementation of the agreements did not exclude their judicial implementation. Application by a national court of an unconditional treaty obligation could not adversely affect the powers that the agreement conferred upon a joint committee.

The decision of the Court in *Kupferberg* is of considerable significance, providing as it does for the justiciability before the national courts of Member States of the world-wide trading relations of European countries, their residents, and their overseas trading partners.

The Court of Justice has held that it is competent to review the validity of Community acts for consistency with rules of international law which are both binding on the Community and directly effective.[39] The General Agreement on Tariffs and Trade is binding on the Community, since under the EEC Treaty the Community has assumed the powers previously exer-

---

[36] Case 270/80 [1982] E.C.R. 329.
[37] [1982] E.C.R. 3641 at p. 3674.
[38] [1982] E.C.R. 3641 at p. 3674.
[39] Cases 21–24/72 *International Fruit* [1972] E.C.R. 1219; Case 9/73 *Schluter* [1973] E.C.R. 1135; Cases 267–269/81 *Societa Petrolifera Italiana* [1983] E.C.R. 801; Cases 290–291/81 *Compagnia Singer* [1983] E.C.R. 847.

cised by Member States with respect to the GATT.[39] However, the Court has rejected arguments that direct effect can be attributed to the GATT as regards Article II, Article XI, the Protocols concluded within the framework of the GATT, and those provisions of the GATT which determine the effect of such Protocols.[39] These conclusions are based on the general scheme of the GATT, and the flexibility of its provisions, in particular those concerning the possibilities for derogation by Contracting States.

Rights and remedies

1. *Introduction*

In the main, the Community system is administered by national authorities,[40] with the result that national agencies, courts, and tribunals are entrusted with the application of sometimes subtle combinations of Community law and national law, based on variations of the following:
— rules of Community law incapable of direct application incorporated into national law in discharge of Community obligations;
— directly applicable rules of Community law, supplemented by directly applicable Community procedural rules [supplemented by national procedural rules and national remedies];
— directly applicable rules of Community law, supplemented by national procedural rules and national remedies.

2. *Rules of Community law incapable of direct application*

Where non-directly applicable rules of Community law are incorporated into national law, the Community source of the national rules in question will only be relevant for purposes of interpretation.[41]

The validity *vel non* of a national measure implementing an invalid act raises questions, not of Community law, but of national law.[42] In the United Kingdom, an order made under section 2(2) of the European Communities Act 1972, implementing such an act, would almost certainly be *ultra vires*.[43]

3. *Directly applicable provisions of Community law supplemented by directly applicable Community procedural rules*

Community regulations may not only vest rights in individuals as against national authorities; they may also provide detailed procedural rules for the enjoyment of these rights, including the standard and burden of proof necessary to sustain a claim to the payment of money. Such provisions are

---

[40] Though obviously not entirely, for the Commission and the Court of Justice play a significant role.
[41] References from national courts under Art. 177 for the purpose of simply ensuring the consistent interpretation of national law with Community law are not infrequent, see p. 44, note 9, *supra*.
[42] Case 23/75 *Rey Soda* [1975] E.C.R. 1279.
[43] Collins, *European Community Law in the United Kingdom*, (3rd ed., 1984), p. 95.

a commonplace in the sphere of agriculture and the reader is referred accordingly to Chapter 8 in particular to the sections on Buying-In, Export Refunds, and Import and Export Licences.[44]

It is important to establish whether or not a regulation lays down comprehensive procedural rules in a specific area, since if it does not, the national authorities are free to supplement Community law with the rules of the forum.[45] For the sake of the uniform application of Community law, however, resort to provisions of internal law is permissible only to the extent necessary to give effect to the regulation in question.[46]

4. Directly applicable provisions of Community law supplemented by national procedural rules and remedies

While regulations may, and sometimes do, provide detailed procedural rules for the vindication of Community rights, Community law more often than not vests rights in individuals (either against the State, or against other individuals), without prescribing explicitly the procedural rules applicable in national tribunals, or providing the remedies for infringement of these rights. In these cases, it is for national law to specify the appropriate court or tribunal in which an individual alleging violation of his rights is to present his claim,[47] and for such court or tribunal to choose an appropriate remedy from those available under national law.[48] As the Court observed in *Comet* v. *Produktschap*,[49] a decision in which it upheld the rights of Member States to apply national statutes of limitation to proceedings in national courts based on directly applicable provisions of Community law:

" . . . in the absence of any relevant Community rules, it is for the national legal order of each Member State to designate the competent courts and to lay down the procedural rules for proceedings designed to ensure the protection of the rights which individuals acquire through the direct effect of Community law, provided that such rules are not less favourable than those governing the same right of action on an internal matter . . . . The position would be different only if those rules and time-limits made it impossible in practice to exercise rights which the national courts have a duty to protect."[50]

While it is incumbent upon national courts to deploy all available national remedies to secure the implementation of Community law, the courts cannot be expected to forge new remedies for this purpose. As the Court of Justice explained in *Rewe* v. *Haupzollamt Kiel*:

" . . . although the Treaty has made it possible in a number of instances for private persons to bring a direct action, where appropriate, before the Court of Justice, it was not intended to create new rem-

---

[44] *Infra*, at pp. 313 *et seq.*
[45] Case 31/69 *Commission* v. *Italy* [1970] E.C.R. 25.
[46] Case 39/70 *Norddeutsches Vieh-und Fleischkontor* [1971] E.C.R. 49.
[47] Case 13/68 *Salgoil* [1968] E.C.R. 453.
[48] See, *e.g.* Case 28/67, *Mokerei-Zentrale* [1968] E.C.R. 143; Case 34/67, *Luck* [1968] 245.
[49] Case 45/76 [1976] E.C.R. 2043; and see Case 33/76 *Rewe-Zentralfinanz* [1976] E.C.R. 1989.
[50] [1976] E.C.R. 2043 at p. 2053, paras. 13, 16.

edies in national courts to ensure the observance of Community law other than those already laid down by national law. On the other hand the system of legal protection established by the Treaty, as set out in Article 177 in particular, implies that it must be possible for every type of action provided for by national law to be available for the purpose of ensuring observance of Community provisions having direct effect, on the same conditions concerning the admissibility and procedure as would apply were it a question of ensuring observance of national law."[51]

There can be no doubt that it is for national law to specify the appropriate court, and the appropriate remedy, to enable an individual to pursue his rights under Community law, but this principle cannot preclude a national court from applying directly effective rules of Community law in all cases falling within its jurisdiction. This problem arose in stark form in *Simmenthal*.[52] Should an Italian court refuse to apply national legislation already held by the Court of Justice to be incompatible with Community law, or should the Italian court only do so after first referring the question to the Italian Constitutional Court? The Court of Justice ruled that:

> "A national court which is called upon, within the limits of its jurisdiction, to apply provisions of community law is under a duty to give full effect to those provisions, if necessary refusing of its own motion to apply any conflicting provisions of national legislation, even if adopted subsequently, and it is not necessary for the court to request or await the prior setting aside of such provisions by legislative or other constitutional means."[53]

5. *Recovery of money levied contrary to Community law*

That the distinction between Community rights and national remedies may be less than clear cut is well illustrated by the cases on the recovery of money levied by Member States contrary to Community law. In *Pigs and Bacon Commission* v. *McCarren*[54] the Court considered the case of a trader who had paid a levy demanded, contrary to Community rules, within the framework of a national marketing system for pork. The court declared that:

> "In principle any trader who is required to pay the levy has therefore the right to claim the reimbursement of that part of the levy which is then devoted to purposes incompatible with Community law. However, it is for the national court to assess, according to its national law, in each individual case, whether and to what extent the levy paid may be recovered and whether there may be set off against such a debt the sums paid to a trader by way of export bonus."[55]

This formulation is not without difficulty. In particular, the words

[51] [1981] E.C.R. 1805 at p. 1838.
[52] Case 196/77 [1978] E.C.R. 629.
[53] [1978] E.C.R. 629 at p. 644. For the acceptance in Italian constitutional law of the European Court's position, see Petriccione, (1986) 11 E.L.Rev. 320.
[54] Case 177/78 [1979] E.C.R. 2161.
[55] [1979] E.C.R. 2161, at p. 2192.

"*whether* and to what extent . . . " (emphasis added) imply that there may be circumstances in which a trader's right in principle to reimbursement may fail to be upheld for want of an appropriate national remedy. What, for instance, would be the position where national rules provide no general right to restitution for monies paid under a mistake of law?

In *Just*,[56] an importer of spirits had sought recovery before a national court of taxes levied contrary to Article 95 of the Treaty by the Danish authorities. The Court acknowledged that the consequences of a rule of Community law prohibiting national charges would have different consequences in national law in the different Member States.

"A comparison of the national systems shows that the problem of disputed charges which have been unlawfully claimed or the refunding of charges paid but not owed is settled in the various Member States, and even within a single Member State, in different ways, according to the various kinds of taxes or charges in question. In certain cases objections or claims of this type are subject to specific procedural conditions and time-limits under the law with regard both to complaints submitted to the tax authorities and to legal proceedings . . . .

In other cases claims for repayment of charges which were paid but not owed must be brought before the ordinary courts, mainly in the form of claims for the refunding of sums paid but not owed. Such claims are available for varying lengths of time, in some cases for the limitation period laid down under the general law, with the result that Member States involved may be faced with a heavy accumulation of claims when certain national tax provisions have been found to be incompatible with the requirements of Community law."[57]

The Court referred to its decisions in *Rewe*[58] and *Comet*[59] for the proposition that, while it was for national law to designate the courts having jurisdiction to uphold Community rights, and to determine the applicable procedural conditions, such conditions could not be less favourable than those relating to similar actions of domestic nature, and must not be "so adapted as to make it impossible in practice to exercise the rights" which the national courts were bound to protect.[60]

The Court in *Just*, however, regarded as legitimate a national rule precluding the recovery of charges levied contrary to law in circumstances where the charges had been passed on to purchasers of the goods on which the charges had been levied. Recovery in such a case would amount to unjust enrichment.[61]

In *San Giorgio*,[62] the Court of Justice again considered a national rule which precluded the repayment of duties or taxes unduly paid where such

[56] Case 68/79 [1980] E.C.R. 501; see also Case 61/79 *Denkavit Italiana* [1980] E.C.R. 1205; Case 826/79 *Ariete* [1980] E.C.R. 2545; Case 826/79 *Mireco* [1980] E.C.R. 2559.
[57] [1980] E.C.R. at p. 522.
[58] Case 33/76 [1976] E.C.R. 1989.
[59] Case 45/76 [1976] E.C.R. 2043.
[60] [1980] E.C.R. at p. 523.
[61] [1980] E.C.R. at p. 523.
[62] Case 199/82 [1983] E.C.R. 3595.

duties or taxes had been passed on to third parties. However, under the national rule in question, duties or taxes were presumed to have been passed on whenever the goods in respect of which a charge had been levied had been transferred to third parties, in the absence of documentary proof to the contrary. The Court of Justice confirmed that national courts might legitimately take into account the fact that unduly levied charges had been incorporated in the price of goods and thus passed on to purchasers. However, any requirement of proof which had the effect of making it "virtually impossible or excessively difficult" to secure the repayment of charges levied contrary to Community law would be incompatible with Community law. That was particularly so in the case of presumptions or rules of evidence placing upon the taxpayer the burden of establishing that the charges had not been passed on to other persons, or in the case of special limitations concerning the form of evidence to be adduced, such as the exclusion of any kind of evidence other than documentary evidence. Once it was established that the levying of the charge was incompatible with Community law, the national court must be free to decide whether or not the burden of the charge had been passed on, wholly or in part, to other persons. Furthermore, the court emphasised that national rules rendering recovery virtually impossible could not be justified on the basis that they were not discriminatory, inasmuch as recovery of taxes paid unduly under national law was also virtually impossible.

> "It must be pointed out in that regard that the requirement of non-discrimination laid down by the court cannot be construed as justifying legislative measures intended to render any repayment of charges levied contrary to Community law virtually impossible, even if the same treatment is extended to taxpayers who have similar claims arising from an infringement of national tax law. The fact that rules of evidence which have been found to be incompatible with the rules of Community law are extended, by law, to a substantial number of national taxes, charges and duties or even to all of them is not therefore a reason for withholding the repayment of charges levied contrary to Community law."[63]

National procedural conditions which may lawfully be taken into account in relation to the repayment of taxes levied contrary to Community law include time limitations[64]; unjust enrichment resulting from the taxes having been passed on to third parties[65]; damage to the trade of taxpayers resulting from the imposition of the unlawful tax[66]; and any benefits accruing to a person paying unlawful taxes by virtue of the payment.[67] Again, if national authorities exact money payments in contravention of

---

[63] [1983] E.C.R. at p. 3614.
[64] Case 33/76 *Rewe* [1976] E.C.R. 1989; Case 45/76 *Comet* [1976] E.C.R. 2043.
[65] Case 68/79 *Just* [1980] E.C.R. 501; Case 61/79 *Denkavit Italiana* [1980] E.C.R. 1205; Cases 142 and 143/80 *Essevi and Salengo* [1981] E.C.R. 1413; Case 199/82 *San Giorgio* [1983] E.C.R. 3595.
[66] Case 68/69 *Just* [1980] E.C.R. 501.
[67] Case 177/78 *Pigs and Bacon Commission* [1979] E.C.R. 2161.

Community law, the question whether interest is payable on repayment is one for national, not Community law.[68]

6. *The extent to which national courts must adapt national remedies in aid of Community law*

The Court of Justice held in *Rewe* v. *Hauptzollamt Kiel*[69] that national courts are under a duty to deploy all available national remedies in aid of Community law, but that they are not bound to create new remedies. This is logical, since the creation of a new remedy is a legislative, rather than a judicial act. On the other hand, however, the Court in *San Giorgio*[70] has affirmed that a Member State cannot subject the repayment of national charges levied contrary to Community law to procedural requirements which make recovery virtually impossible. There are two ways of reconciling these principles. One is by stressing the fact that the Court uses the phrase "Member States" in *San Giorgio*, while in *Rewe* it stresses the duty of national *courts*. In other words, the effect of the ruling in *San Giorgio* would be to put the legislature on notice that amendment of national remedial rules was necessary in order to comply with the Treaty; all that the national *court* in question could be required to do by Community law would be to deploy the presently available Italian remedies according to the application procedural rules of Italian law. Yet this explanation is hardly satisfactory, for in *San Giorgio* the Court pointed out:

" . . . that entitlement to the repayment of charges levied by a Member State contrary to the rules of Community law is a consequence of, and an adjunct to, the rights conferred on individuals by the Community provisions prohibiting charges having an effect equivalent to customs duties or, as the case may be, the discriminatory application of internal taxes."[71]

If the right to repayment is an adjunct to directly effective provisions of the Treaty, it seems hard to deny that the right to repayment itself has direct effect. While such a right would not be sufficient to create a *new* national remedy, it would certainly impose upon a national court a right to grant an existing remedy, *e.g.* restitution, shorn of any restrictive national conditions incompatible with Community law. For example, if national law allowed in principle an action for restitution against public authorities, a national rule precluding recovery of taxes paid under a mistake of law[72] could not be applied to bar recovery of taxes levied contrary to the requirements of Community law.[73] On the other hand, if national law allowed restitution actions against private individuals but not against the

---

[68] Case 6/60 *Humblet* [1960] E.C.R. 559; Case 26/74 *Roquette* [1976] E.C.R. 677.
[69] Case 158/80 [1981] E.C.R. 1805, at p. 1838.
[70] Case 199/82 [1983] E.C.R. 3595.
[71] [1983] E.C.R. 3595, at p. 3612.
[72] Still the orthodox position in the U.K., see Birks, *An Introduction to the Law of Restitution*, pp. 295 *et seq.*
[73] If national legislation authorises discretionary payments in such cases, national public law remedies may provide the basis for securing payment in accordance with Community law, see, *e.g.* s. 17(5)(*b*) of the Customs and Excise Management Act 1979.

administration, would it be creating a new remedy for a national court to
grant such relief against the administration in aid of Community law? In
Rewe v. *Hauptzollamt Kiel*,[74] the Court's statement that Community law
did not require the creation of new remedies by national courts was made
in connection with the alleged "right of a trader to request the courts to
require the authorities of a Member State to compel a third party to comply with obligations arising from Community rules in a given legal situation
in which that trader is not involved but economically adversely affected by
the failure to observe Community law."[75] In other words, in order for
Community law to apply directly to a national *remedy* an affirmative
answer must be given to the question: could that category of plaintiff claim
that relief against that category of defendant? As Advocate General Capotorti put it:

> "In order to be entitled to institute proceedings before the courts (for
> example for an injunction requiring another person to fulfil certain
> obligations) the plaintiff must be personally entitled to the right which
> the proceedings are specifically intended to uphold."[76]

If the above analysis is correct, it is not open to a litigant in a national
court to claim a form of relief in aid of Community law unless national law
allows that relief to be granted between the parties in proceedings before
the court in question. Any conflict with Community law which results from
the application of this principle must be remedied by the legislature, and
not by national courts. Yet if national law does allow the relief claimed to
be granted between the parties by the court before which proceedings are
instituted, it is the duty of that court to make that relief available in aid of
Community law, and to disregard any substantive restrictions or procedural conditions of national law which are either discriminatory, or deprive
the Community right of useful effect.

7. *Damages as a remedy for breach of Community law*

It has been demonstrated[77] that Community law requires restitution in
certain cases as an adjunct to the directly effective Community right to
resist the application of customs duties, discriminatory internal taxation,
etc. Are there any directly effective provisions of Community law which
have as their adjunct the right to damages for breach? There are suggestions in the Court's case-law that this may indeed be the case. In *Humblet*[78]
the Court declared:

> "In fact if the Court rules in a judgment that a legislative or adminis-
> trative measure adopted by the authorities of a Member State is con-
> trary to Community law, that Member State is obliged, by virtue of
> Article 86 of the ECSC Treaty[79] to rescind the measure in question

---

[74] Case 158/80 [1981] E.C.R. 1805.
[75] [1981] E.C.R. 1805 at p. 1838.
[76] [1980] E.C.R. 1805 at p. 1850.
[77] *Supra*, at p. 52.
[78] Case 6/60 [1960] E.C.R. 559.
[79] Art. 86 provides, that "Member States undertake to take all appropriate measures,
whether general or particular, to ensure fulfilment of the obligations resulting from
decisions and recommendations of the institutions of the Community and to facilitate the
performance of the Community's tasks." *Cf.* Art. 5 EEC.

and to make reparation for any unlawful consequences which may have ensued . . . "[80]

The above statement is of significance in two respects. First, it suggests that a duty upon the authorities to make reparation might be a consequence of an adverse decision of the Court of Justice in a direct action. Secondly, it suggests that national courts (themselves addressees of obligations under Article 5 of the Treaty in conjunction with directly effective provisions of the Treaty) might be under a duty to award damages in actions brought before them to establish breach of the Community rules by national authorities. This latter conclusion is reinforced by the Court's dictum in *Russo*[81]:

> "If an individual producer has suffered damage as a result of the intervention of a Member State in violation of Community law it will be for the State, as regards the injured party, to take the consequences upon itself in the context of the provisions of national law relating to the liability of the State."[82]

It would seem to follow that in some cases at least a right to compensation in accordance with national law constitutes an adjunct to the direct effect of rules of Community law. For example, suppose the national authorities of a Member State, contrary to Article 30 of the Treaty,[83] seize imported goods. The direct effect of Article 30 would seem to require that the competent national courts grant appropriate relief. Such relief would surely have to include the restitution of the detained goods. This follows in principle and from the cases on the restitution of charges unduly paid.[84] Indeed, the contrary seems unarguable. Equally, if the national authorities had seized and destroyed the goods in question, the national courts would be bound to award damages, and their failure to do so would amount to a breach of Article 5 and 30 of the Treaty by the Member State concerned. This latter breach could be established by action before the Court of Justice under Article 169 or 170 of the Treaty. An adverse ruling by the Court of Justice would give rise to an obligation under Article 171[85] to make appropriate reparation to the importers whose goods had been destroyed.

8. *National procedures subject to Community standards*

Member States are under an obligation to take all "appropriate" measures to ensure the fulfilment of the obligations arising out of the Treaty or resulting from action taken by the institutions of the Com-

---

[80] [1960] E.C.R. 559, at p. 569.
[81] Case 60/75 [1976] E.C.R. 45, at p. 57.
[82] [1976] E.C.R. 45, at p. 57.
[83] As to which, see *infra* at p. 123.
[84] As to which, see *supra*, p. 52. The Court has held that Dir. 76/207 on sex discrimination does not contain any sufficiently precise obligation to enable an individual to obtain the specific remedy of damages when that remedy is not provided for or permitted by national law, see *infra*, at p. 280.
[85] Art. 171 provides that "If the Court of Justice finds that a Member State has failed to fulfil an obligation under this Treaty, the State shall be required to take the necessary measures to comply with the judgment of the Court of Justice."

munity.[86] Although the Court has suggested on occasion that what is "appropriate" is for the Member State in question to decide,[87] this would render the obligation nugatory, and an objective interpretation is more in accordance with principle.[88] It follows that national procedural rules and remedies are subject in principle to Community minimum standards, and support for this proposition may be found in *Rheinmühlen-Düsseldorf* v. *EVSt*,[89] in which the Court acknowledged the competence of national authorities to adopt the standard of proof they thought fit for the purpose of assessing claims of export refunds, but added that complete reliance on shipment without a Community transit document as proof of exportation might nevertheless constitute an abuse of their discretion.

Whether or not Community law provides implicit procedural rules may often be difficult to establish without the benefit of a reference to the Court of Justice. The Court's decision in *Officier van Justitie* v. *de Peijper*[90] suggests that in certain cases a party alleging the consistency of national measures with Article 36 of the Treaty must prove the proportionality of such measures to the desired end, rather than the burden passing to the other party to prove the contrary. The intrusion of Community law into the question of the burden, and the standard, of proof, will clearly only be necessary in those cases where the application of diverse rules is likely to prejudice the uniform application of Community law. The Court will no doubt be slow to reach such a conclusion; it certainly did not think that the application of different periods of limitation in the various Member States was itself likely to lead to such a result.[91]

9. Penal sanctions

The possibility of having to compensate the legally wronged may not always provide sufficient encouragement to those subject to the law to comply with its terms. Again, the infringement of certain rules may damage the public interest rather than infringe individual rights. Exceptionally, Community law resorts to coercion to secure compliance with its norms. One example is the authority of the Commission to fine undertakings for conduct prohibited under Articles 85 and 86 of the Treaty.[92] Milder forms of encouragement are encountered in the field of agriculture, deposits subject to forfeiture being especially favoured.[93] For the rest, Community law relies upon the enforcement procedures of the Member States. "Article 5 of the Treaty . . . " commented the Court in one case, " . . . allows the various Member States to choose the measures which they

---

[86] Art. 5 EEC.
[87] Case 50/76 *Amsterdam Bulb* [1977] E.C.R. 137, at p. 150, para. 32.
[88] The Court has held that although the "choice of form and methods" in implementing directives is left to the Member States, they are nevertheless obliged to choose the most appropriate form and method to ensure the effective functioning of directives, account being taken of their aims; Case 48/75, *Royer* [1976] E.C.R. 497, at p. 518, para. 73.
[89] Case 6/71 [1971] E.C.R. 823.
[90] Case 104/75 [1976] E.C.R. 613.
[91] Case 33/76 *Rewe* [1976] E.C.R. 1989; Case 45/76 *Comet* [1976] E.C.R. 2043.
[92] See *infra*, p. 444.
[93] *e.g.* in the case of import and export licences for trade with third countries, see *infra*, p. 324.

consider appropriate, including sanctions which may be criminal in nature."[94]

THE GENERAL PRINCIPLES OF COMMUNITY LAW

1. A judicial development

In addition to the explicit rules laid down in the Treaty and secondary legislation, the Court of Justice has developed certain general principles of law, inspired by the national laws of the Member States, in accordance with which it interprets the express provisions of Community law, and evaluates the legality of acts of the institutions. Although a distinction may be drawn between "general principles" on the one hand, and "fundamental rights" on the other, the latter rights have been declared by the Court of Justice to constitute an integral part of the general principles of law which it is bound to uphold.[95]

2. Juridical basis

The Court can hardly be said to have exceeded its jurisdiction by its recourse to the general principles of law. No treaty regime, let alone the "new legal order" of the Community, could be interpreted in a legal vacuum. International tribunals have long been regarded as competent to draw upon the general principles of municipal law as a source of international law,[96] and the competence of the Court of Justice in the interpretation and application of Community law could surely be no less. The Treaty itself implies as much. Article 164 states: "The Court of Justice shall ensure that in the interpretation and application of this Treaty the law is observed."

This exhortation is not merely tautologous. The words "the law" render the French phrase "respect du droit," which suggests a *corpus juris* transcending the treaty texts.[97] Other provisions of the Treaty are consistent with the proposition that the general principles of law constitute a source of Community law.

Article 173 includes among the grounds of invalidity of Community acts infringement of "any rule of law" relating to the Treaty's application, an expression wide enough to encompass the principles under consideration. Furthermore, Article 215 of the Treaty provides that the non-contractual liability of the Community shall be determined "in accordance with the general principles common to the laws of the Member States," which

---

[94] Case 50/76 *Amsterdam Bulb* [1977] E.C.R. 137, at p. 150, para. 32.
[95] Case 4/73 *Nold* v. *Commission* [1974] E.C.R. 491.
[96] See Wyatt, "New Legal Order, or Old?" (1982) 7 E.L.Rev. 147 at p. 157. *Cf.* Art. 38 of the Statute of the International Court of Justice, which lists as a source of international law, "the general principles of law recognised by civilised nations."
[97] See Pescatore, "Fundamental Rights and Freedoms in the System of the European Communities" [1970] A.J.I.L. 343, at p. 348.

amounts to express recognition of the role of the general principles of national law as a source of Community law.

3. Particular principles

(a) *Proportionality*

One of the most oft-invoked of the general principles of law developed by the Court of Justice[98] is that of proportionality. This principle holds that "the individual should not have his freedom of action limited beyond the degree necessary for the public interest."[99]

This principle finds explicit expression in the Treaty as a constraint on Community action. Thus Article 40(3), which authorises the establishment of a common organisation of the market, declares that such organisation "may include all measures *required* to attain the objectives set out in Article 39" (emphasis added).[1] On the other hand, the wording of the Treaty does not seem to be a decisive factor. The Court examined the proportionality of Regulation 974/71 in *Balkan-Import-Export* v. *Hauptzollamt Berlin-Packhof*,[2] a regulation which was at that time based on Article 103(2) of the Treaty which provides that the Council may take "appropriate" measures. The Court observed that: "In exercising their powers, the Institutions must ensure that the amounts which commercial operators are charged are no greater than is *required* to achieve the aim which the authorities are to accomplish" (emphasis added).[3] There can be little doubt that the principle is applicable in its own right as a criterion of the validity of Community action.

The principle has operated to invalidate a provision of a regulation providing for the forfeiture of a security for any failure to perform a contractual undertaking, irrespective of the gravity of the breach.[4] The Court held that the

> "absolute nature . . . of the above-mentioned regulation is contrary to the principle of proportionality in that it does not permit the penalty for which it provides to be made commensurate with the degree of failure to implement the contractual obligations or with the seriousness of the breach of those obligations."[5]

As well as constituting a constraint upon Community legislative activities, the principle of proportionality may be resorted to in assessing the legitimacy of State action otherwise authorised under the Treaty. Thus in

---

[98] See in general Usher, "The Influence of National Concepts in Decisions of the European Court" (1975–76) 1 E.L.Rev. 359.

[99] Case 11/70, *Internationale Handelsgesellschaft* [1970] E.C.R. 1125, at p. 1127, *per* Adv. Gen. Dutheillet de Lamothe.

[1] For the application of the principle of proportionality in the agricultural context, see *infra* at p. 302.

[2] Case 5/73 [1973] E.C.R. 1091.

[3] [1973] E.C.R. 1091 at pp. 1111–1112, para. 22. Though as the Court acknowledges, it does not necessarily follow that the obligation to respect the principle of proportionality must be measured in relation to the individual situation of any one particular group of operators. See also Cases 26 and 86/79 *Furges* [1980] E.C.R. 1083, at p. 1093.

[4] Case 240/78 *Atalanta* [1979] E.C.R. 2137.

[5] [1979] E.C.R. 2137, at p. 2151.

Rivoira[6] the Court held that it was disproportionate for a Member State to apply a criminal penalty provided under national law for false declarations in connection with prohibited imports to an import which could not be subjected to prohibition or restriction. The principle applies in particular to State action in the context of those Treaty provisions allowing limited derogation from basic Treaty rules, such as Articles 36, 48(3) and (4), 55 and 56. Thus, while Article 48 provides for the free movement of workers between Member States, Article 48(3) allows for exceptions justified on grounds, *inter alia*, of public policy. The court has made it clear that this provision only allows derogations from the fundamental rule of Article 48 in case of a *genuine and sufficiently serious threat to the requirements of public policy*.[7]

(b) *Legal certainty and legitimate expectation*

The principle of legal certainty requires that those subject to the law should not be placed in a situation of uncertainty as to their rights and obligations. The related concept of legitimate expectation constitutes an important corollary to this principle: those who act in good faith on the basis of the law as it is or seems to be should not be frustrated in their expectations.

The Court of Justice held in *Goudrand Freres*[8] that the principle of legal certainty requires that ambiguity or lack of clarity in measures imposing charges should be resolved in favour of the taxpayer. The Court declared:

"The principle of legal certainty requires that rules imposing charges on the taxpayer must be clear and precise so that he may know without ambiguity what are his rights and obligations and may take steps accordingly.

The rules in question are obviously unclear as is apparent *inter alia* from the fact that even the competent customs authorities originally interpreted them in the same way as the respondent in the main action and it was not until three years after the date of the first imports that they sought to recover the monetary compensatory amounts which would have been due in respect of the exports in question."[9]

The principle is capable of operating in favour of Member States. In *Germany* v. *Commission*[10] the court held that the principle of legal certainty:

" . . . requires that a provision laying down a preclusive period, particularly one which may have the effect of depriving a Member State of the payment of financial aid its application for which has been approved and on the basis of which it has already incurred considerable expenditure, should be clearly and precisely drafted so that the Member States may be made fully aware of the importance of their complying with the time limit."[11]

---

[6] Case 179/78 [1979] E.C.R. 1147.
[7] Case 36/75 *Rutili* [1975] E.C.R. 1219; Case 30/77 *Bouchereau* [1977] E.C.R. 1999.
[8] Case 169/80 [1981] E.C.R. 1931.
[9] [1981] E.C.R. 1931, at p. 1942.
[10] Case 44/81 [1982] E.C.R. 1855.
[11] [1982] E.C.R. 1855, at p. 1877.

The Court has held that Member States are bound to implement directives in a way which meets the requirements of clarity and certainty, and
that mere administrative practices will be inadequate for this purpose.[12]

The principle of legal certainty militates against administrative and legislative measures taking effect without adequate notice to persons concerned. As the Court declared in *Racke*[13]:

> "A fundamental principle in the Community legal order requires that
> a measure adopted by the public authorities shall not be applicable to
> those concerned before they have the opportunity to make themselves
> acquainted with it."[14]

The Court explained the implications of the principle for the retroactive
effect of Community measures in *Decker*[15]:

> "Although in general the principle of legal certainty precludes a Com-
> munity measure from taking effect from a point in time before its pub-
> lication, it may exceptionally be otherwise where the purpose to be
> achieved so demands and where the legitimate expectations of those
> concerned are duly respected."[16]

The above principles have implications for both the *vires* of Community
measures, and their interpretation. In *Salumi*[17] the court stated:

> "Although procedural rules are generally held to apply to all proceed-
> ings pending at the time when they enter into force, this is not the case
> with substantive rules. On the contrary, the latter are usually inter-
> preted as applying to situations existing before their entry into force
> only in so far as it clearly follows from the terms, objectives or general
> scheme that such an effect must be given to them.
>
>   This interpretation ensures respect for the principles of legal cer-
> tainty and the protection of legitimate expectation, by virtue of which
> the effect of Community legislation must be clear and predictable for
> those who are subject to it."[18]

Measures taken by the Commission under powers delegated by the Council may be precluded from having retroactive effect at all.[19] If retroactive
effect for administrative and legislative measures is the exception, it is for
judicial decisions the rule. Yet, exceptionally, in *Defrenne* v. *Sabena*[20] the
Court held that legal certainty precluded the retroactive effect of its ruling
that Article 119 of the Treaty was directly effective. In *Defrenne*, the Court
took into account "the conduct of several of the Member States and the
views adopted by the Commission and repeatedly brought to the notice of
the circles concerned" and noted that "the fact that, in spite of the warnings
given, the Commission did not initiate proceedings under Article 169

---

[12] Case 102/79 *Commission* v. *Belgium* [1980] E.C.R. 1473, at p. 1486.
[13] Case 98/78 [1979] E.C.R. 69.
[14] [1979] E.C.R. 69, at p. 84. And see Case 84/81 *Staple Dairy Products* [1982] E.C.R. 1763,
at p. 1777; Case 108/81 *Amylum* [1982] E.C.R. 3107, at p. 3130.
[15] Case 99/78 [1979] E.C.R. 101.
[16] [1979] E.C.R. 101, at p. 111. See also Case 276/80 *Pedana* [1982] E.C.R. 517, at p. 541;
Case 258/80 *Rumi* [1982] E.C.R. 487, at p. 503.
[17] Cases 212–217/80 [1981] E.C.R. 2735.
[18] [1981] E.C.R. 2735, at p. 2751.
[19] Case 77/71 *Gervais-Danone* [1971] E.C.R. 1127; Case 158/78, *Biegi* [1979] E.C.R. 1103;
Case 196/80, *Anglo-Irish Meat* [1981] E.C.R. 2263.
[20] Case 43/75 *Defrenne* [1976] E.C.R. 455. See *supra*, p. 35.

against the Member States concerned . . . was likely to consolidate the incorrect impression as to the effects of Article 119."[21] Yet in *Maizena*[22] the Court rejected the argument that inaction by the Commission in the face of conduct of the Federal Republic of Germany contrary to Community law could give rise to legitimate expectation in a trader as follows:

"A practice of a Member State which does not conform to Community rules may never give rise to legal situations protected by Community law and this is so even where the Commission has failed to take the necessary action to ensure that the State in question correctly applies the Community rules."[23]

Whether the above statement represents a retreat from the principles underlying *Defrenne* or not, the court has subsequently stressed the exceptional nature of a ruling on the interpretation of Community law having only prospective effect, and has never since ruled to similar effect.[24]

The Court has nevertheless been ready to modify the temporal effect of judgments determining the invalidity of regulations, where legal certainty is so required. It is the principle of legal certainty which underlies Article 174 of the Treaty, which allows the Court of Justice to determine which of the legal effects of a regulation declared to be void by the Court shall be considered as definitive. On the basis of this same principle, the Court of Justice has in a number of cases applied Article 174 by analogy in preliminary rulings on invalidity under Article 177 of the Treaty, denying retroactivity to its decisions.[25] The application of the principle in a direct action for annulment is strikingly illustrated in *Simmenthal*,[26] in which the Court annulled a Commission decision fixing the minimum selling prices for frozen beef put up for sale by intervention agencies. However, "for reasons of legal certainty and taking special account of the established rights of the participants in the invitation to tender whose tenders have been accepted"[27] the Court ruled that the annulment must be restricted to the specific decision to reject the applicant's tender which stemmed from the decision in question.

Respect for vested rights is itself an aspect of the principles of legal certainty and legitimate expectation. In *Rossi*[28] the Court stressed that:

"The Community rules could not, in the absence of an express exception consistent with the aims of the Treaty, be applied in such a way as to deprive a migrant worker or his dependents of the benefit of a part of the legislation of a Member State."[29]

---

[21] [1976] E.C.R. 455, at p. 473.

[22] Case 5/82 [1982] E.C.R. 4601.

[23] [1982] E.C.R. 4601, at p. 4615. However, if the authorities of a Member State make *ultra vires* payments under the CAP as the result of a good faith misinterpretation of the law induced by the Community authorities, the cost will be borne by the EAGGF, see *infra*, p. 333.

[24] See, *e.g.* Case 61/79 *Dankavit Italiana* [1980] E.C.R. 1205, at p. 1223. Case 826/79 *Mireco* 2559, at p. 2573; see *supra* at p. 35.

[25] Case 4/79, *Providence Agricole* [1980] E.C.R. 2823, at p. 2853; Case 109/79, *Maizeries de Beauce* [1980] E.C.R. 2883, at p. 2913; Case 145/79, *Roquette* [1980] E.C.R. 2917, at p. 2946; Case 41/84, *Pinna*.

[26] Case 92/78 [1979] E.C.R. 777.

[27] [1979] E.C.R. 777 at p. 811.

[28] Case 100/78 [1979] E.C.R. 831.

[29] [1979] E.C.R. 831 at p. 844.

Yet the principle cannot be stretched too far. Vested interests are not to be equated with vested rights, and cannot insulate traders from changes in the law. As the Court explained in *Eridania*[30]:

> " . . . an undertaking cannot claim a vested right to the maintenance of an advantage which it obtained from the establishment of a common organisation of the market and which it enjoyed at a given time."[31]

The principle of legitimate expectation operates to protect individuals where they have acted in reliance upon measures taken by the Community institutions. Thus if an undertaking purchases grain for denaturing with a view to qualifying for a Community subsidy, it is not permissible to discontinue or reduce the subsidy without giving the interested party a reasonable opportunity of denaturing the grain in question at the old rate.[32] Again, if the Community induces prudent traders to omit to cover their transactions against exchange risks, by establishing a system of compensatory amounts which in practice eliminate such risks, it must not withdraw such payments with immediate effect, without providing appropriate transitional measures.[33] Similar reasoning protected certain former Community officials in receipt of pensions which had increased in value over a number of years as a result of the Council's failure to adjust the exchange rates used to calculate the amounts due. The Council sought to rectify the situation and phase out the advantages which had accrued over a ten month period. The Court held that respect for the legitimate expectations of those concerned required a transitional period twice as long as that laid down by the Council.[34]

(c) *Equality*

A further principle binding upon the Community in its administrative and legislative activities is the principle of equality, whereby differentiation between comparable situations must be based on objective factors.

The principle applies in the relationship between the Community institutions and its officials. As the Court has stated:

> "According to the Court's consistent case law the general principle of equality is one of the fundamental principles of the law of the Community civil service."[35]

On this basis the Court has invalidated differentiation between Community officials on grounds of sex in the payment of expatriation allowances.[36] However, the Community cannot be called to account for inequality in the treatment of its officials for which it is not itself responsible. In *Souasio*[37] it was alleged that a Community dependent child tax

---

[30] Case 230/78 [1979] E.C.R. 2749.
[31] [1979] E.C.R. 2749 at p. 2768.
[32] Case 48/74 *Deuka* [1975] E.C.R. 421; Case 5/75 *Deuka* [1975] E.C.R. 759. For the operation of this principle in the agricultural context, see *infra*, at p. 304.
[33] Case 74/74 *C.N.T.A.* [1975] E.C.R. 533.
[34] Case 127/80 *Grogan* [1982] E.C.R. 869; Case 164/80, *De Pascale* [1982] E.C.R. 909; Case 167/80 *Curtis* [1982] E.C.R. 931.
[35] Cases 152, etc./81, *Ferrario* [1983] E.C.R. 2357 at p. 2367.
[36] Case 20/71 *Sabbatini* [1972] E.C.R. 345; Case 21/74, *Airola* [1972] E.C.R. 221; see also *Razzouk and Beydoun* [1984] E.C.R. 1509.
[37] Cases 81, 82 and 146/79, [1980] E.C.R. 3557.

allowance paid only once in respect of each child, even where both parents were employed by the Community, was contrary to the principle of equality, since it did not take into account tax allowances which might be claimed by a spouse who did not work for the Community, under national law. The Court rejected this argument:

"The principle of equality does not require account to be taken of possible inequalities which may become apparent because the Community and national systems overlap."[38]

The principle of equality provides a basis for the judicial review of measures adopted by the Community in all its various activities. Thus the Court has invalidated a Regulation which provided substantially more severe criteria for the determination of the origin of cotton yarn than for the determination of the origin of cloth and fabrics.[39] The Court has also required consistency in the Commission's policy of imposing fines upon undertakings for the infringement of production quotas for steel.[40]

The principle of equality has been held to add a gloss to Article 40(3) of the Treaty, which provides that the common organisations of the agricultural markets "shall exclude any discrimination between producers or consumers within the Community." In *Ruckdeschel*[41] and *Moulins*[42] proceedings arose from challenges in national courts to the validity of the Council's action in abolishing production refunds on maize used to make quallmehl and gritz, while continuing to pay refunds on maize used to make starch, a product in competition with both quellmehl and gritz. Producers of the latter product argued that they had been placed at a competitive disadvantage by the Council's discriminatory, and hence unlawful action. Their pleas were upheld. Referring to Article 40(3) of the Treaty, the Court observed:

"Whilst this wording undoubtedly prohibits any discrimination between producers of the same product it does not refer in such clear terms to the relationship between different industrial or trade sectors in the sphere of processed agricultural products. This does not alter the fact that the prohibition of discrimination laid down in the aforesaid provision is merely a specific enunciation of the general principle of equality which is one of the fundamental principles of Community law. This principle requires that similar situations shall not be treated differently unless differentiation is objectively justified."[43]

The principle of equality has also been invoked in the budgetary context,[44] and the "equality of states" has been resorted to as a general principle for the interpretation of the Treaties.[45] It seems that in the Community legal order, the notion of "equality before the law," far from constituting merely an appeal to the better judgment of the legislator, pro-

---

[38] [1980] E.C.R. 3557, at p. 3572.
[39] Case 162/82 *Cousin* [1983] E.C.R. 1101.
[40] Case 234/82 *Ferriere di roe Volciano* [1983] E.C.R. 3921.
[41] Cases 117/76 and 16/77 [1977] E.C.R. 1753.
[42] Cases 124/76 and 20/77 [1977] E..R. 1795.
[43] [1977] E.C.R. 1753 at p. 1769; [1971] E.C.R. 1795 at p. 1811.
[44] Case 265/78 *Ferwerda* [1980] E.C.R. 617.
[45] Case 128/78 *Commission* v. *United Kingdom* [1979] E.C.R. 419, at p. 429; Case 231/78 *Commission* v. *United Kingdom* [1979] E.C.R. 1447, at p. 1462.

vides a ground for invalidating administrative or legislative action adjudged by the Court to differentiate arbitrarily between persons in comparable circumstances.

(d) *Fundamental rights*

Unlike the abortive Treaty for the establishment of a European Political Community, which provided explicitly for the application of section I of the European Convention on Human Rights,[46] the Treaty establishing the European Economic Community makes no provision in this regard. Although the circumstances in which Community activities are likely to encroach upon rights generally regarded as fundamental will be rare,[47] the Court has made it clear that there are such rights enshrined in Community law, and that they are capable of limiting the legislative competence of the Community. Thus in *Stauder* v. *City of Ulm*,[48] the Court was asked by the Verwaltungsgericht, Stuttgart, whether a Commission Decision which conditioned the distribution of butter at reduced prices on the disclosure of the name of the recipient was compatible "with the general principles of Community law in force." The Court replied that on its true construction the Decision in question did not require the disclosure of the names of beneficiaries to retailers, and added that: "Interpreted in this way the provision at issue contains nothing capable of prejudicing the fundamental human rights . . . protected by the Court."[49] The existence of fundamental Community principles (albeit in the main unspecified) was confirmed in *Internationale Handelsgesellschaft* v. *EVSt*,[50] a request for a ruling on the validity of the import and export licensing system established under the common organisation of the grain market. The grant of licences was conditioned on the lodging of a deposit, which was forfeited in the event of the licence being unused in whole or in part during its period of validity. The Verwaltüngsgericht, Frankfurt-am-Main sought the ruling in question because of doubts as to the compatibility of such arrangements with the principles of German constitutional law. The Court denied that the validity of a Community act could be impugned for inconsistency with principles of national constitutional law, however fundamental, but added:

"However, an examination should be made as to whether or not any analogous guarantee inherent in Community law has been disregarded. In fact, respect for fundamental rights forms an integral part of the general principles of law protected by the Court of Justice. The protection of such rights, whilst inspired by the constitutional traditions common to the Member States, must be ensured within the framework of the structure and objectives of the Community. It must therefore be ascertained . . . whether the system of deposits has

---

[46] See *supra*, p. 27.
[47] *Pescatore*, (1970) A.J.I.L. 343, at p. 348.
[48] Case 29/69 [1969] E.C.R. 419.
[49] [1969] E.C.R. 419, at p. 425, para. 7.
[50] Case 11/70 [1970] E.C.R. 1125.

infringed rights of a fundamental nature, respect for which must be ensured in the Community legal system."[51]

If *Stauder* confirmed the existence of fundamental rights in Community law, and *Internationale Handelsgesellschaft* identified their primary source as the national constitutions of the Member States, *Nold* v. *Commission* introduced a secondary source: "international treaties for the protection of human rights on which the Member States have collaborated or of which they are signatories."[52]

The Court's case law was endorsed by the Parliament, the Council and the Commission in their Joint Declaration of April 5, 1977.[53] The Declaration notes that the Treaties are based on the principle of respect for the law, and acknowledges that "law" comprises, over and above the rules embodied in the treaties and secondary Community legislation, the general principles of law and in particular the fundamental rights, on which the constitutional law of the Member States is based. The Institutions stress in the Declaration that they attach prime importance to the protection of fundamental rights, as derived in particular from the constitutions of the Member States and the European Convention on Human Rights, and commit themselves to respect for those rights.

In *Hauer*[54] the court held that the right to property is guaranteed in the Community legal order in accordance with the ideas common to the constitutions of the Member States, which are reflected in the First Protocol to the European Convention on Human rights. However, the Court upheld a Community imposed restriction on the planting of vines to constitute as a legitimate exception to the principle of a type recognised in the constitutional systems of the Member States.[55] The Court has denied that the guarantee afforded to the ownership of property can be extended to protect commercial interests, and uncertainties of which are part of the very essence of economic activity.[56]

The Court has referred to specific provisions of the European Convention on Human Rights in a number of judgments. In *National Panasonic*[57] the Court relied upon an exception to the guarantee of respect for private and family life to be found in Article 8 of the European Convention on Human Rights. In *Kirk*[58] the Court held that the retroactivity of a Community regulation could not have the effect of validating *ex post facto* national measures of a penal nature which imposed penalties for an act which was not punishable at the time it was committed. The Court declared:

"The principle that penal provisions may not have retroactive effect is one which is common to all the legal orders of the Member States and is enshrined in Article 7 of the European Convention . . . as a funda-

[51] [1970] E.C.R. 1125, at p. 1134, para. 4.
[52] Case 4/73 [1974] E.C.R. 491, at p. 507, para. 13.
[53] O.J. 1977 C103/1.
[54] Case 44/79 [1979] E.C.R. 3727.
[55] [1979] E.C.R. 3727, at p. 3747.
[56] Case 4/73 *Nold* [1974] E.C.R. 491; Cases 154, etc./78, and 39, etc./79, *Valsabbia* [1980] E.C.R. 907.
[57] Case 136/79 [1980] E.C.R. 2033 at p. 2057.
[58] Case 63/83 [1984] E.C.R. 2689.

mental right; it takes its place among the general principles of law whose observance is ensured by the court of Justice."[59]

The above cases support the following propositions. First, for the purpose of applying Article 173 of the Treaty,[60] which provides for the judicial review of Community legislation, and Article 215, which provides for the tortious liability of the Community, certain fundamental rights will be taken into account as part of Community law. Secondly, these rights are to be deduced from the common constitutional principles of the Member States, and from international treaties on which the Member States have collaborated or of which they are signatories. It will be noted that these propositions are exclusively concerned with constraints on *Community* legislative or executive action, not with restrictions on the activities of *Member States*, and it is for this reason that *Rutili* v. *French Minister of the Interior*[61] is of interest. In this case the Court observed that the criterion of proportionality amounted to a specific manifestation of a general principle referred to in various provisions of the European Convention on Human Rights. Apart from highlighting the European Convention as a potential source of the general principles to which the Court will resort, the observation is significant in that the *Rutili* case concerned the legitimacy of *State* action under Article 48(3) of the Treaty, and it inevitably raises the question whether provisions such as Article 48(3) of the Treaty must be interpreted in the light of the substantive guarantees provided in the European Convention on Human Rights. On this view, the latter Article could not justify the deportation of a national of a Member State on the ground that his activities amounted to the exercise of a right guaranteed in the European Convention, even if nationals of the offended Member State were themselves denied the right in question.

The extent to which the general principles of Community law, including those safeguarding fundamental rights, may be binding on the activities of Member States, merits further considerations. First, it is arguable that the same general principles of law which bind the Community in its activities bind the Member States in the fulfilment of their obligation not to discriminate on grounds of nationality. Since Community law can hardly require Member States to derogate from the fundamental principles of its own legal order, it can hardly require one Member State to treat nationals of another on a par with its own, if par falls below the minimum standards required by the general principles of Community law. Suppose a national of one Member State works in another where the standard of trade union rights accorded to national workers falls below the standard required under the European Convention on Human Rights, can it be the case that Community law, since it prohibits discrimination, in such circumstances, requires the host State to accord to the migrant worker treatment which is inconsistent with the fundamental principles of the Community legal

---

[59] [1984] E.C.R. 2689, at p. 2718.
[60] And of course Arts. 177 and 184.
[61] Case 36/75 [1975] E.C.R. 1219.

order? An affirmative reply would amount to condoning Community complicity in conduct which would be unlawful if carried out by the Community itself. If this argument is correct, it suggests that the general principles of Community law are binding on Member States in all areas of economic activity in which they are prohibited from discrimination on grounds of nationality.

A second argument would sustain a more extensive application of the general principles of Community law to the activities of Member States. Article 5 of the Treaty requires Member States to take all "appropriate" measures to fulfil the obligations arising out of the Treaty or the acts of the institutions. As indicated earlier, the better view is that such a formulation imposes an objective obligation on Member States.[62] It would seem to follow that whenever a Member State takes action in fulfilment of a Community obligation, its action must be proportional, it must respect the principle of legal certainty, and it must conform with those fundamental rights which find expression in the general principles of Community law. The Court has certainly held that in implementing directives, the Member States are obliged to use the *most appropriate* means.[63]

The Court has hinted that this obligation entails respect for the general principles of law.[64] It would seem to follow that a similar obligation existed in respect of regulations, decisions, and provisions of the Treaty. Indeed, in *Zuckerfabrik*, the Court examined whether national rules implementing a regulating laying down common rules for the denaturing of sugar for animal feed were consistent with "superior rules of Community law, in particular with the principles of legal certainty and proportionality . . . ."[65] It will be recalled that in *Stauder* v. *City of Ulm*[66] the Court held that the decision in question did not require the disclosure to retailers of the name of recipients of butter at reduced prices, but that the decision did permit such disclosure. Is it not arguable that although the text of the decision permitted Member States to condition the benefit in question on such disclosure, the general principles of Community law did not, since to attach such a condition would not be a "necessary" or "appropriate" way of implementing the decision?

Again, it may be argued that States are bound by the general principles of Community law where their infringement would be likely to constitute an obstacle to the free movement of persons between Member States. In *Criminal Proceedings against Lynne Watson and Alessandro Belmann*,[67] the Court held that Member States were entitled to take measures to ascertain the movement of nationals of other Member States within their borders, providing that the penalties for failure to comply with these requirements were comparable with penalties for offences of similar gravity committed by the nationals of the host State, and were proportional to the offence in question. Otherwise, pointed out the Court, such penal-

---

[62] *Supra*, p. 58.
[63] Case 48/75 *Royer* [1976] E.C.R. 497.
[64] Case 5/83 *Rienks* [1983] E.C.R. 4233, at p. 4245.
[65] Case 77/81 [1982] E.C.R. 681, at pp. 694, 695.
[66] Case 29/69 [1969] E.C.R. 419.
[67] Case 118/75 [1976] E.C.R. 1185.

ties might constitute an obstacle to the free movement of persons. Certainly, derogations from the fundamental principles of European Community law, at least derogations founded in national law, or consistent administrative practice, would seem to be capable in principle of constituting such an obstacle.

Other principles

The categories of general principles which the Court will uphold do not appear to be closed. In *Transocean Marine Paint*[68] the Court resorted to the general principle that a person whose interests are affected by a decision taken by a public authority must be given an opportunity to make his point of view known. In a subsequent staff case,[69] the Court referred to

" . . . a general principle of good administration to the effect that an administration which has to take decisions, even legally, which cause serious detriment to the person concerned, must allow the latter to make known their point of view, unless there is a serious reason for not doing so."[70]

With respect to the relations between the Community and its officials, the Court may take it upon itself to *urge* consultation, even where this is not legally required. In one case,[71] the Court acknowledged that there was no duty to consult, but added:

"Nevertheless, it is in accordance with the requirements of good faith and mutual confidence, which should characterise the relationship between officials and the administration, that the latter should, as far as possible, put the official in a position to make his point of view on the projected decision known. Such a practice is also likely to prevent legal disputes."[72]

The right to be assisted by counsel has been recognised by the Court as a general principle of law. In a staff case[73] the Court held that the refusal of the Commission to allow the applicant's counsel, as well as the applicant, access to the disciplinary file in the course of proceedings which resulted in a disciplinary measure being taken, amounted to a breach of a fundamental legal principle which the Court would uphold. The Court emphasised that respect for the rights of the defence was all the more important when the disciplinary proceedings were likely to result in particularly severe disciplinary measures.[74]

In a landmark decision,[75] the Court held that Article 14 of Regulation

---

[68] Case 17/74 [1974] E.C.R. 1063.
[69] Cases 33 and 75/79 *Kuhner* [1980] E.C.R. 1671.
[70] [1980] E.C.R. 1671, at p. 1698.
[71] Case 125/80 *Arning* [1981] E.C.R. 2539.
[72] [1981] E.C.R. 2439, at p. 2554.
[73] Case 115/80 *Demont* [1981] E.C.R. 3147.
[74] [1981] E.C.R. 3147, at p. 3158.
[75] Case 155/79 *A.M. & S.* [1982] E.C.R. 1575.

17,[76] empowering the Commission to require the production of the business records of an undertaking, was subject to the principle that the confidentiality of certain communications between a lawyer and his client was to be protected.[77]

The general principles of "good administration" clearly provide fertile ground for judicial development. For example, the Court has stigmatised the failure to respond to a communication as a "neglect of the rules of good administration," and reduced a fine accordingly.[78]

A further principle which has been invoked by the Court as a guide to the construction of secondary legislation is that of Community preference.[79]

---

[76] Reg. 17 deals with the power of the Commission to establish violations of Arts. 85 and 86 EEC. See *infra* at p. 440.

[77] Communications between a lawyer and his client are protected providing they are made for the purposes of and in the interests of the client's rights of defence, and that they emanate from independent lawyers, that is, lawyers who are not bound to the client by a relationship of employment.

[78] Case 179/82 *Lucchini* [1983] E.C.R. 3083, at p. 3095.

[79] Case 6/78 *Union Francaise* [1978] E.C.R. 1695.

CHAPTER 4

THE EUROPEAN COURT

The legal framework

A single Court of Justice of the European Communities (or "European Court") was created pursuant to the Convention of 1957 on Certain Institutions Common to the European Communities.[1] The Court exercises the jurisdiction conferred on the courts for which separate provision was made in the ECSC, EEC and Euratom Treaties.[2]

The primary sources of law on the European Court are the Treaties themselves and the Statutes of the Court annexed as a Protocol to each of them.[3] The Statutes have been given detailed effect in the Rules of Procedure of the Court.[4] The Rules are adopted by the Court itself but they require the unanimous approval of the Council.[5]

There is a constantly evolving body of case law and practice on matters of organisation and procedure.

Members of the Court

The European Court has two kinds of Member—Judges and Advocates General. The distinctive role of the Advocate General in the judicial process of the Court is considered below.

The number of Judges was raised to 13 and that of Advocates General to six on the accession of Portugal and Spain to the Communities in January 1986.[6] The power to decide on an increase belongs to the Council, acting unanimously at the request of the Court.[7] It is a moot point whether such a request should come from all of the Court's existing Members or from the Judges alone. The relevant provisions of the Treaties refer to a request from "the Court of Justice," a phrase which elsewhere in the same provisions plainly excludes the Advocates General. Here, in our submission, it should be interpreted as including them, since they have as much interest in a possible enlargement of the Court as the Judges do.

The rules on appointment are the same for the Judges and the Advocate General. They must be "persons whose independence is beyond doubt and who possess the qualifications required for appointment to the highest judicial offices in their respective countries or who are jurisconsults of

---

[1] The institutions in question were, besides the Court, the European Parliament and the Economic and Social Committee.
[2] Convention, Art. 3.
[3] The Statutes are practically identical. Unless the context indicates otherwise, references hereinafter are to the EEC Statute.
[4] Hereinafter "Rules."
[5] See Art. 188 EEC and Statute, Art. 44; Art. 161 Euratom and Statute, Art. 45. There is no corresponding provision in the ECSC Treaty but see ECSC Statute, Art. 44.
[6] See Art. 32 ECSC, Art. 165 EEC and Art. 137 Euratom, as amended (Judges); Art. 32(*a*) ECSC, Art. 166 EEC and Art. 138 Euratom, as amended (Advocates General).
[7] *Ibid.*

recognised competence."[8] The term "jurisconsult" is wide enough to cover lawyers in private practice and academic lawyers in Member States where access to the Bench is not normally open to those branches of the legal profession. The method of appointment is "by common accord of the Governments of the Member States" for a period of six years, which is renewable.[9] A partial replacement, of either seven or six Judges and three Advocates General, occurs every three years.[10]

There is nothing in the Treaties about the national composition of the Court. In practice however, one Judge is appointed from each Member State and the additional post is held by nationals of different Members States in turn. Before the enlargement of 1986, the practice was for there to be one Advocate General from each of the bigger Member States (Germany, France, Italy and the United Kingdom), while a fifth post rotated among the smaller ones. On that basis it might have been expected that the sixth Advocate General would be from Spain but in the event a Portuguese national was chosen.[11] Whether this marks a breach with the practice of reserving posts for the bigger Member States remains to be seen.

It is important that the Judges and Advocates General should represent between them the full range of national jurisdictions. This is because, in refining and developing the law of the Communities, the Court draws upon the legal traditions and institutions of the Member States. For the United Kingdom the representation of its two national jurisdictions has been achieved hitherto by the appointment of an English Advocate General[12] and a Scottish Judge.[13]

The jurisdiction of the Court

The nature of the jurisdiction

The European Court has, in French parlance, a "competence d'attribution," *i.e.* it has jurisdiction only in the specific cases in which this is given by the Treaties.[14] The Court's general duty under Article 164 EEC to ensure that in the interpretation and application of the Treaty the law that is observed does not connote a general power to determine any case that may be submitted to it. In *CFDT* v. *Council*[15] it was argued that, although Article 38 ECSC restricts to Member States and the Commission the right to seek the annulment of acts of the Council, an action could be brought for this purpose by a trade union on the basis of Article 31 ECSC (which corresponds to Article 164 EEC) and the duty of any court to avoid a denial of justice. The Court said that, while those considerations might militate in favour of a wide interpretation of the provisions concerning the

---

[8] Art. 32(*b*) ECSC; Art. 167 EEC; Art. 139 Euratom.
[9] *Ibid.*
[10] *Ibid.*
[11] Mr. J. L. da Cruz Vilaça.
[12] Mr. J.-P. Warner (as he then was) January 1973–March 1981; Sir Gordon Slynn since April 1981.
[13] Lord Mackenzie Stuart since 1973.
[14] See Waelbroeck *et al.*, *Le droit de la CEE* Vol. 10, pp. 6–8.
[15] Case 66/76 [1977] E.C.R. 305.

institution of proceedings, "they do not permit the Court on its own authority to amend the actual terms of its jurisdiction."[16]

The main heads of jurisdiction[17]

The main kinds of proceedings that may be brought in the Court of Justice are:

(i) *An infringement action* (Articles 169–171 EEC). Legal proceedings may be brought against a Member State which fails to fulfil an obligation under the EEC Treaty or the law derived therefrom. The initiative may be taken either by the Commission under Article 169 or by another Member State under Article 170.[18]

The proceedings fall into two distinct phases. In the "administrative" phase the Commission receives observations on the allegation of non-compliance from the Member State (or in proceedings under Article 170, the Member States) concerned and defines its own position in a reasoned opinion. An attempt is made to reach a satisfactory settlement without resorting to litigation and in the great majority of cases this has proved possible.[19] Where it is not, an action is brought by the Commission or by the complaining Member State in the European Court. The aim of the action is to obtain a declaration by the Court that the defendant Member State has failed in a specified manner to fulfil its obligations under specified provisions of EEC law. A Member State found to be in default is required by Article 171 EEC to take the necessary measures to comply with the judgment. There is, however, no provision under the EEC Treaty for sanctions to be imposed in the event of non-compliance.[20] The only legal resort for the Commission is fresh proceedings under Article 169, this time for the infringement of Article 171.[21]

Individuals or firms whose interests have been harmed by a Member State's failure to fulfil Community obligations are given no direct remedy in the Court of Justice. Courses open to a private party in such circumstances would be to lodge a complaint with the Commission, which might lead to the initiation of Article 169 proceedings, or to bring an action in the courts of the Member State concerned and, where appropriate, ask for a reference to be made to the European Court for a preliminary ruling on the interpretation of the Community provision alleged to have been infringed.

(ii) *An action for annulment* (Articles 173, 174 and 176 EEC). The Court of Justice has jurisdiction to review the legality of acts of the Community

---

[16] [1977] E.C.R. at p. 310.

[17] The discussion that follows merely sketches the broad lines of the court's jurisdiction. For a fuller treatment, see Vandersanden and Barav, *Contentieux Communautaire*, Bruylant (1977); Hartley, *The Foundations of European Community Law*, Clarendon Press (1981); Brown and Jacobs, *The Court of Justice of the European Communities*, Sweet & Maxwell (1983); Waelbroeck *et al. op cit.* note 14, *supra*.

[18] See the equivalent provisions of Arts. 141 and 142 Euratom. The ECSC Treaty deals with Member State violations somewhat differently: see Art. 88 ECSC.

[19] See Audretsch, *Supervision in European Community Law*, Amsterdam (1978); Ehlermann in *Feschtschrift für Hans Kutscher* (1981); Everling (1984) 9 E.L.Rev. 215.

[20] *Cf.* Art. 88 ECSC.

[21] See, *e.g.* Case 7/68 *Commission* v. *Italy (Art Treasures No. 1)* [1968] E.C.R. 423; [1969] C.M.L.R. 1; Case 48/71 *Commission* v. *Italy (Art Treasures No. 2)* [1972] E.C.R. 527; [1972] C.M.L.R. 699.

institutions on the grounds set out in Article 173 and, if the act is found wanting, to declare it void under Article 174. The institution concerned is required under Article 176 to take the measures necessary to comply with such a judgment.[22]

Review under Article 173 is not confined to regulations, directives and decisions as defined by Article 189 EEC but extends to all acts that are intended to have legal consequences.[23] This includes legally effective action taken by the European Parliament.[24]

Member States, the Council and the Commission are privileged applicants, in the sense that they are able to challenge any act falling within the scope of Article 173, regardless of its legal character and without showing that an interest of their own has been affected.[25] They are assumed to have an interest in the strict observance of the limits and conditions governing powers of decision conferred by the Treaty, whatever the purpose for which the powers may have been exercised in a given case. On the other hand, a private party may only bring proceedings "against a decision addressed to that person or against a decision which, although in the form of a regulation or a decision addressed to another person, is of direct and individual concern to the former." The policy of that provision, as interpreted by the European Court, is to limit *locus standi* to cases where the disputed act is either a decision addressed to the applicant himself or an act affecting the applicant in a similar way to such a decision. The requirement of "direct and individual concern" highlights different aspects of the effects a decision has on the person addressed. Direct concern means that the position of the applicant must be immediately determined by the act itself and not by some intervening factor such as a discretionary decision by national authorities.[26] Individual concern means that the act must appear to single out the applicant as a target.[27] The case law suggests it will rarely be possible to persuade the Court that an act in the form of a regulation affects the applicant otherwise than in a general way. An exception to this rule is found in the case of regulations imposing anti-dumping duties. Exporters whose pricing behaviour has been taken into account in the determination of dumping,[28] and complainants whose evidence of the difficulties encountered by the local industry have been taken into account in the determination of injury,[29] will normally have *locus standi* to challenge such regulations. In the field of competition it is now well settled that a complainant will be directly and individually concerned by a decision of the Commission, addressed to the parties to a restrictive agreement, which exempts the agreement pursuant to Article 85(3) EEC from the prohibition in Article 85(1)[30]; or by one addressed to a Member State which auth-

---

[22] See the equivalent provisions of Arts. 146, 147 and 149 Euratom. *Cf.* Art. 33 ECSC.
[23] Case 22/70 *Commission* v. *Council (ERTA)* [1971] E.C.R. 263; [1971] C.M.L.R. 335.
[24] Case 294/83 *Les Verts-Parti Ecologiste* v. *European Parliament* (not yet reported).
[25] See, *e.g.* Case 41/83 *Italy* v. *Commission (British Telecom)* (1985) 2 C.M.L.R. 368.
[26] Case 69/69 *Alcan* v. *Commission* [1970] E.C.R. 385; [1970] C.M.L.R. 337.
[27] Case 25/62 *Plaumann* v. *Commission* [1963] E.C.R. 95; [1964] C.M.L.R. 29.
[28] See Joined Cases 239/82 and 175/82 *Allied Corporation* v. *Commission* [1984] E.C.R. 1005; [1985] C.M.L.R. 572.
[29] Case 264/82 *Timex* v. *Commission* [1985] 3 C.M.L.R. 550.
[30] Case 27/76 *Metro* v. *Commission (No. 1)* [1977] E.C.R. 1875; [1978] 2 C.M.L.R. 1.

orises the granting of aid pursuant to Article 93 EEC.[31] The time limit for bringing an action under Article 173 is two months.[32]

The grounds of review specified in the Article are: lack of competence; infringement of an essential procedural requirement; infringement of the Treaty or of any rule of law relating to its application; and misuse of powers. Failure to observe the right to a hearing of a respondent undertaking in competition proceedings would be an example of a procedural infringement meriting the annulment of the act in question.[33] Infringement of the Treaty includes any infringement of the general principles of law which the Court of Justice upholds.[34]

(iii) *An action for a failure to act* (Articles 175 and 176 EEC). This complements the action for annulment. Where a failure to act has been established in proceedings under Article 175, the institution concerned is required by Article 176 to take any necessary measures of compliance.

The institution alleged to be in default must first be called upon to act. If within two months it has not "defined its position," the action can be brought within a further period of two months. Defining a position need not involve the adoption of an act attackable under Article 173. In Case 48/65 *Lutticke* v. *Commission*[35] for example, the applicant argued, *inter alia*, that the Commission was guilty of having failed to take action against the Federal Republic of Germany in respect of a turnover equalisation tax allegedly in breach of Article 95. It was held that a letter from the Commission informing the applicant that it did not consider the tax incompatible with Article 95 was sufficient protection against proceedings under Article 175.

The action is expressed to be available to Member States and to "the other institutions of the Community" (*i.e.* other than the one whose failure to act is being questioned), which includes the European Parliament. An important instance of the use of this remedy by the Parliament was in the *Transport* case[36] against the Council. A private party may only bring the action in respect of a failure to address an act to himself. The conditions of *locus standi* for individuals are thus even more restrictive than under Article 173.

(iv) *An action for damages in respect of the non-contractual liability of the Community* (Articles 178 and 215, second paragraph EEC). The Community is required pursuant to Article 215, second paragraph to make good, in accordance with the general principles common to the laws of the Member States "any damage caused by its institutions or by its servants in the performance of their duties." Jurisdiction in such proceedings is given

---

[31] Case 169/84 *COFAZ* v. *Commission* (not yet reported).
[32] See also Rules, Art. 81(1).
[33] See, *e.g.* Case 17/74 *Transocean Marine Paint Association* v. *Commission* [1974] E.C.R. 1063; [1974] 2 C.M.L.R. 459.
[34] See, *e.g.* Joined Cases 119 and 120/76 *Olmuhle and Becher* v. *HZA Hamburg and HZA Bremen-Nord (Skimmed Milk Powder)* [1977] E.C.R. 1269; [1979] 2 C.M.L.R. 83.
[35] [1966] E.C.R. 19; [1966] C.M.L.R. 378. See also Case 125/78 *GEMA* v. *Commission* [1979] E.C.R. 3173.
[36] Case 13/83 *European Parliament* v. *Council* [1985] 1 C.M.L.R. 138.

to the Court of Justice by Article 178. A five-year limitation period is fixed by Article 43 of the Court's EEC Statute.

The notion of non-contractual liability broadly covers liability for acts of maladministration and in tort. The basic ingredients are an unlawful act by a community institution, harm to the applicant and a causal connection between the two.[37] Where the damage complained of results from "a legislative measure which involves choices of economic policy" liability will only arise if there has been "a sufficiently serious breach of a superior rule of law for the protection of the individual."[38] To satisfy that requirement in circumstances where a wide discretion is essential for the implementation of the Common Agricultural Policy the institutions must be shown to have "manifestly and gravely disregarded the limits on the exercise of its powers."[39] These stringent requirements developed by the Court in the light of the general principles applicable in the various national laws mean that actions in respect of normative acts are seldom winnable.[40] The prospects are much better where the complaint is one of a wrongful administrative act, such as a breach of the duty of confidentiality where information is provided in the context of competition proceedings.[41]

Where the national authorities responsible for the implementation of a Community policy are concurrently liable, the Court of Justice may insist that an applicant pursue any available remedy in the courts of the Member State concerned before he can be awarded damages against the Community.[42]

(v) *A reference for a preliminary ruling* (Article 177 EEC). The preliminary ruling procedure was designed to meet the danger that divergent lines of authority on points of Community law would develop in the various Member States, reflecting disparities in their legal traditions and their economic and social circumstances.[43] The procedure enables a national court, faced with the necessity of deciding a question of the interpretation or validity of a Community provision, to obtain authoritative guidance from the Court of Justice. The national proceedings are suspended and the Community point is encapsulated in one or more questions on which the

---

[37] Joined Cases 5, 7 and 13–24/66 *Kampffmeyer* v. *Commission* [1967] E.C.R. 245; Case 4/69 *Lütticke* v. *Commission* [1971] E.C.R. 325.

[38] See Case 5/71 *Zuckerfabrik Schöppenstedt* v. *Council* [1971] E.C.R. 975; Case 74/74 *CNTA* v. *Commission* [1976] E.C.R. 797; Joined Cases 83 and 94/76 and 4, 15 and 40/77 *HNL* v. *Council and Commission* [1978] E.C.R. 1209; [1978] 3 C.M.L.R. 566; Case 143/77 *Koninklijke Scholten Honig* v. *Council and Commission* [1979] E.C.R. 3583. The citations are from *Koninklijke Scholten Honig* [1979] E.C.R. at pp. 3625–3626.

[39] [1979] E.C.R. at p. 3636.

[40] The applicants were successful in the *Quellmehl* and *Gritz* cases: see Joined Cases 64 and 113/76, 167 and 239/78 and 27, 28 and 45/79 *Dumortier* v. *Council* [1979] E.C.R. 3091; Case 238/78 *Ireks-Arkady* [1979] E.C.R. 2955; Joined Cases 141, 242 and 245–250/78 *DGV* v. *Commission and Council* [1979] E.C.R. 3017; Joined Cases 261 and 262/78 *Interquell* [1979] E.C.R. 3045. Contrast Joined Cases 116 and 124/77 *Amylum and Tunnel Refineries* v. *Council and Commission* [1979] E.C.R. 3497; Case 143/77 *Koninklijke Scholten Honig* v. *Council and Commission loc. cit.* note 38, *supra*.

[41] Case 145/83 *Stanley Adams* v. *Commission* (not yet reported).

[42] See Joined Cases 5, 7 and 13–24/66 *Kampffmeyer* v. *Commission loc. cit.* note 37, *supra*; Case 96/71 *Haegerman* v. *Commission* [1972] E.C.R. 1015; Case 99/74 *Grands Moulins des Antilles* v. *Commission* [1975] E.C.R. 1531; Case 26/74 *Roquette* v. *Commission* [1976] E.C.R. 677.

[43] See Case 166/73 *Rheinmuhlen* v. *EVG (No. 1)* [1974] E.C.R. 33; [1974] 1 C.M.L.R. 523.

European Court is invited to rule. After the Court has done so, it will be for the national court to apply the ruling in the concrete circumstances of the case before it. The ruling is "preliminary" in the sense that it does not form part of the decision that disposes of the case. The proceedings in the European Court represent a stage in proceedings which begin and end in another court.

Power to make a reference for a preliminary ruling is given by Article 177 to "any court or tribunal of a Member State." A body may constitute a "court or tribunal" for this purpose although it is not so regarded in national law. The characteristics for which the Court of Justice looks are, notably: the establishment of the body in question on a permanent footing with the task of resolving disputes through the application of rules of law; the appointment of its chairman and members (or some of them) by public authorities; an adversarial procedure similar to that of an ordinary court; and the compulsory nature of its jurisdiction, especially where this means there is effectively no other forum for the enforcement of certain Community rights.[44] The Court has refused to rule on a question referred to it by an arbitrator in a commercial dispute, on the grounds that the insertion into the disputed contract of a compulsory arbitration clause had been the free choice of the parties and that the German authorities were not involved at any stage in the arbitration proceedings.[45] In *Borker*[46] the Court rejected a reference by the Council of the Paris Bar arising out of a request by one of its members, who had been refused audience by a court in Germany, for a declaration that he was entitled to provide legal services in other Member States pursuant to Articles 59 *et seq.* EEC and Directive 77/249. The Court said a preliminary ruling could only be requested under Article 177 by a body "called upon to give judgment in proceedings intended to lead to a decision of a judicial nature."[47] This implied that a professional body may constitute a "court or tribunal" when it acts, for example, in a disciplinary capacity; but only, it is thought, if the body is subject, at least indirectly to some form of public authorisation and its jurisdiction is compulsory.

The exercise of the power to make a reference for a preliminary ruling is subject to conditions. First, a question which is genuinely one of Community law must have been raised before the national court.[48] This may have been done by either of the parties or by the court of its own motion.[49] A question is not regarded as having been properly raised if the dispute underlying the national proceedings was fabricated by the parties for the

---

[44] Case 61/65 *Vaassen* v. *Beamptenfonds Mijnbedrijf* [1966] E.C.R. 261; [1966] C.M.L.R. 508; Case 36/73 *Nederlandse Spoorwegen* v. *Minister van Verkeer en Waterstaat* [1973] E.C.R. 1299; [1974] 2 C.M.L.R. 148; Case 246/80 *Broekmeulen* v. *Huisarts Registratie Commissie* [1981] E.C.R. 2311; [1982] 1 C.M.L.R. 91.
[45] Case 102/81 *Nordsee* v. *Reederei Mond* [1982] E.C.R. 1095.
[46] Case 138/80, [1980] E.C.R. 1975; [1980] 3 C.M.L.R. 638.
[47] [1980] E.C.R. at p. 1977.
[48] The Court twice rejected references made by the Acting Judge at Hayange in Lorraine because they concerned general social issues outwith the scope of the EEC Treaty: Case 105/79, [1979] E.C.R. 2257; Case 68/80, [1980] E.C.R. 771.
[49] Case 126/80 *Salonia* v. *Poidomani* [1981] E.C.R. 1563.

specific purpose of obtaining a ruling on it by the Court of Justice.[50] This is because the Court's duty under Article 177 is "not that of delivering advisory opinions on general or hypothetical questions but of assisting in the administration of justice in the Member States."[51] Secondly, the national court must consider that a decision on the Community point is necessary to enable it to give judgment. A decision should count as "necessary," it is submitted, if it is perceived by the national court as a step, which need not be the final one, in its strategy for disposing of the case.[52] The European Court has repeatedly stressed that it will not interfere with the national court's discretion in this matter[53]; but it shows no compunction about reformulating questions, so as to provide an answer that will be really useful.[54] Nor will it always deal with all the questions referred, if answers given to other questions in the same reference are considered sufficient for the ultimate disposal of the case.

Where the national court is one "against whose decisions there is no judicial remedy under national law" the power of referral is coupled with a duty. The better view is that the duty attaches to the court which is the highest for the purpose of the proceedings in question, although it may not be the highest in the legal system of the Member State concerned.[55] The duty is not absolute. In *CILFIT*[56] the Court of Justice acknowledged that a national court of final resort might properly refrain from making a reference for a preliminary ruling in three situations: where it does not consider a decision on the question that has arisen to be necessary to enable it to give judgment; where the question has already been decided by the European Court; and where the correct application of Community law is so obvious as to leave no scope for any reasonable doubt as to the manner in which the question should be resolved. Before coming to the last conclusion, the national court must be convinced that the matter would seem equally obvious to other national courts and to the Court of Justice itself. That has to be assessed "on the basis of the characteristic features of Community law and the particular difficulties to which its interpretation gives rise,"[57] namely the existence of texts in different language versions, the use of concepts and of terminology in a sense different from their sense in their national laws and the need to interpret Community provisions in their con-

---

[50] Case 104/79 *Foglia* v. *Novello (No. 1)* [1980] E.C.R. 745; [1981] 1 C.M.L.R. 45; Case 244/80 *Foglia* v. *Novello (No. 2)* [1981] E.C.R. 3045; [1982] 1 C.M.L.R. 585. For critical commentaries, see Barav, (1980) 5 E.L. Rev. 443; Bebr, (1980) 17 C.M.L. Rev. 525 and (1982) 19 C.M.L. Rev. 428. *Cf.* Wyatt, (1981) 6 E.L. Rev. 447; (1982) 7 E.L. Rev. 186.

[51] [1981] E.C.R. at p. 3062.

[52] A narrower view, that the Community point must be conclusive of the case, was espoused by Lord Denning M.R. in *Bulmer* v. *Bollinger* [1974] Ch. 401. This seems incompatible with the view of the Court of Justice that it is for the national court to decide at what stage in the proceedings a reference for a preliminary ruling should be made: see Joined Cases 36 and 71/80 *Irish Creamery Milk Suppliers Association* v. *Ireland* [1981] E.C.R. 735.

[53] See the classic statement of this position in Case 6/64 *Costa* v. *ENEL* [1964] E.C.R. 585; [1964] C.M.L.R. 425. Other references can be found in Jacobs and Durand, *References to the European Court*, Butterworths (1975).

[54] For a remarkable recent example, see Case 137/74 *Ministère Public* v. *Mutsch* (not yet reported).

[55] See Case 6/64 *Costa* v. *ENEL loc. cit.* note 63, *supra* where the Court of Justice treated a small claims court in Milan (*judice conciliatore*) as one with a duty to refer.

[56] Case 283/81 [1982] E.C.R. 3415.

[57] [1982] E.C.R. at p. 3430.

text and with regard to the objectives of the system as a whole and its state of evolution at the relevant date.

A ruling by the Court of Justice under Article 177 is binding on the national court deciding the case to which it relates.[58] Courts faced with the same question in future cases should either apply the ruling or make a fresh reference to the Court, in the hope that it may be persuaded to take a different view.[59]

Other heads of jurisdiction

Among the European Court's various other heads of jurisdiction brief mention may be made of the following:

(i) *Penalties provided for in Council regulations* (Article 172 EEC). A regulation of the Council that creates a power to impose a penalty may give the European Court unlimited jurisdiction in cases arising out of the exercise of the power. Thus Regulation 17, the chief implementing measure of the rules on competition, provides in its Article 17 that the Court may cancel, reduce or increase fines or periodic penalty payments imposed by the Commission for infringements of the rules.

(ii) *Staff cases* (Article 179 EEC). The European Court has the task of resolving disputes between institutions of the Community and their employees. Staff cases account for a significant proportion of the Court's work load. The jurisdiction is a "minor" one only in the sense that the cases do not often involve issues of general concern.

(iii) *Contractual liability of the Community* (Articles 181 and 215 EEC). A contract concluded by or on behalf of the Community may contain a clause giving the European Court jurisdiction in disputes that may arise.[60] If the parties to the contract do not stipulate the law to be applied, the Court will have to decide this on the basis of principles of private international law common to the Member States.[61]

(iv) *Opinions pursuant to Article 228(1) EEC*. Where it is proposed to conclude an agreement between the Community and a third state or an international organisation, the opinion of the European Court may be sought by the Council, the Commission or a Member State as to whether the agreement is compatible with the EEC Treaty.[62] In the face of an adverse opinion of the Court, the agreement may only enter into force if the Treaty is amended in accordance with Article 236 EEC. The procedure may be used for, *inter alia*, the

---

[58] Case 29/68 *Milch-Fett-und Eierkontor* v. *HZA Saarbrucken* [1969] E.C.R. 165; [1969] C.M.L.R. 390.

[59] The principle that a national court is always free to request a fresh interpretation was stated by the Court in Joined Cases 28–30/62 *Da Costa* [1963] E.C.R. 31; [1963] C.M.L.R. 224. This, it seems, does not extend to the reconsideration of rulings on validity. See Case 66/80 *International Chemical Corporation* v. *Italian Financial Administration* [1981] E.C.R. 1191. See the note by Usher, (1981) 6 E.L. Rev. 284.

[60] See, *e.g.* Case 23/76 *Pellegrini* v. *Commission* [1976] E.C.R. 1807.

[61] The Court may obtain assistance from the Convention of 1980 on the Law Applicable to Contractual Obligations: see J.O. 1980 L 266/1. See the discussion in Hartley at pp. 476–480; Waelbroeck *et al.*, Vol. 10 at pp. 348–350.

[62] *Cf.* the somewhat similar procedure under Art. 103 Euratom which provided the basis for Ruling 1/78, [1978] E.C.R. 2151 relating to the draft Convention on the Physical Protection of Nuclear Materials, Facilities and Transports.

resolution of a difference of opinion between the Commission and the Member States as to how far a particular agreement falls within the exclusive jurisdiction of the Community.[63]

Organisation of the Court

The President

The President of the Court is elected by the Judges from among their own number for a term of three years and may be re-elected.[64] It may seem odd that the Advocates General do not take part in the election but there is a good reason for this. The most important task of a President is to chair the deliberations over the judgment to be given in cases heard by the full Court and he must, therefore, be a person who enjoys the confidence of a majority of the Judges. That might not be so, if it were possible for the votes of the Advocates General to tip the scales in an election.

The President directs the judicial business and the administration of the Court.[65] Apart from presiding at hearings and deliberations of the full Court and at administrative meetings, his functions include appointing a Judge Rapporteur in each case, fixing or extending the time limits for the lodging of pleadings and dealing with most applications for interlocutory relief.

Chambers

The European Court may decide cases either in plenary session (where the quorum is seven Judges)[66] or in Chambers of three or five Judges.[67] Under present arrangements there are four three-member Chambers and two five-member Chambers. These are reconstituted, and their Presidents elected,[68] on a yearly basis.

The Treaties provide that cases brought by a Member State or a Community institution must be decided by the Court in plenary session.[69] The kinds of case that may be assigned to Chambers are identified in Article 95 of the Rules. They include references for preliminary rulings, as well as actions for annulment, for a failure to act or for damages, where the applicant is a private party. However, a Member State or a Community institution which is a party to such a case has a right to insist upon trial by the full Court.[70] Staff cases go automatically to Chambers of three Judges. In other cases the choice between assignment to the full Court or to a three- or five-member Chamber is made in the light of the difficulty and importance of the issues involved and any special circumstances.[71]

---

[63] See, *e.g.* Opinion 1/78 [1979] E.C.R. 2871.
[64] Art. 32(*b*) ECSC; Art. 167 EEC; Art. 139 Euratom. See also Rules, Art. 7.
[65] Rules, Art. 8.
[66] Statute, Art. 15.
[67] Art. 32 ECSC; Art. 165 EEC; Art. 137 Euratom.
[68] Rules, Art. 10.
[69] Art. 32 ECSC; Art. 165 EEC; Art. 137 Euratom.
[70] Rules, Art. 95(2). A Member State or Community institution counts as a "party" for this purpose where it intervenes in a direct action or submits written observations in a reference for a preliminary ruling.
[71] Rules, Art. 95(1).

The Judge Rapporteur

A Judge Rapporteur is nominated by the President in each case before the European Court.[72] It is his responsibility generally to manage the case as it progresses through the various stages of the Court's procedure. At the close of pleadings he submits a Preliminary Report on the basis of which the Court decides whether to assign the case to a Chamber and whether it is necessary to order any "measures of inquiry."[73] He is also required to produce a "Report for the Hearing," which summarises the facts found and the arguments of the parties, presenting a picture of the case as it stands at the moment when the oral procedure begins. After the Advocate General has delivered his opinion in the case, the Judge Rapporteur performs his major duty, the drafting of the judgment. The Judges then deliberate on the draft, which may go through a number of versions before a decision is finally taken.[74]

The Advocate General

The model before the minds of those who decided to endow the European Court with Advocates General is believed to have been the *commissaire du gouvernement* in the procedure of the French Conseil d'Etat.[75] However, commentators are agreed that the office, as it has developed in the unique context provided by the European Community Treaties, must be regarded as *sui generis*.[76]

An Advocate General is not a Judge but his role is, in a broad sense, judicial. After the parties have concluded their written and oral submissions, and before the Judges begin their deliberation, the Advocate General presents in open court his own independent and impartial opinion on the case. The opinion is fully reasoned, in the manner of a reserved judgment in the higher English courts. It sets out any relevant facts and legislation, discusses the issues that have been raised, situating them in the evolving pattern of the Court's case law, and recommends a decision to the Judges. There is good reason to believe that a persuasive opinion will strongly influence the subsequent deliberation.[77] Certainly, in the great majority of cases the judgment and its rationale follow the Advocate General fairly closely. Nor is the impact of an opinion limited to the case in which it is given. It will be published alongside the judgment in the *European Court Reports* and may be cited as an authority by counsel or Advo-

---

[72] Rules, Art. 9(2).

[73] See pp. 85–86, *infra*.

[74] For a fuller discussion of the role of the Advocate General, see Dashwood, (1982) 2 *Legal Studies* 202; Brown and Jacobs, Chap. 4.

[75] See the helpful discussion of the parallels between the offices of *commissaire du gouvernement* and Advocate General by Barav, (1974) *Revue internationale de droit comparé* 809. See also Gori, (1976) C.D.E. 375; Condorelli-Braun in (Rideau *et al.*, eds.), *La France et les Communautés europeennés* at pp. 457–458.

[76] This was the view taken by Adv. Gen. Warner (as he then was) in an unpublished lecture on "The role of the Advocate General at the European Court of Justice," delivered in Luxembourg on November 19, 1976. The same conclusion is reached by Gori, *op. cit.* note 43, *supra* at p. 393. See also Vandersanden and Barav at p. 16.

[77] An important witness is Mr. Robert Lecourt, a former President of the European Court, whose speech of farewell on the occasion of the retirement of Advocate General Roemer includes this passage:

"Pour avoir une idée vraie du rôle des conclusions, c'est au délibére qu'il faut avoir

cates General in future cases, or in legal literature. The analogy with the role of a judge of first instance is tempting, but there are significant differences. First, the Advocate General does not sit alone but hears the case with the Judges. Secondly, the opinion only contains a recommendation: the Judges decide the case for the first and only time. Thirdly, counsel are not given an opportunity to make submissions by way of an "appeal" against the opinion. Nevertheless, it is an important safeguard that, although the European Court is (for the time being) a court of first and last resort, all cases are, in effect, judicially considered twice over.

The office of First Advocate General rotates annually among the Advocates General, like the Presidency of Chambers among the Judges. The main duty of the First Advocate General is that of assigning one of his colleagues to each case that reaches the Court.[78]

The Registrar

The European Court appoints its Registrar for a term of six years, which is renewable.[79] The Registrar is responsible for the reception, transmission and custody of documents relating to cases before the Court.[80] In addition, he acts as the head of the Court's administration, under the authority of the President.[81]

The proposal for a Court of First Instance

The Single European Act of 1986 empowered the Council, at the request of the Court of Justice and after consulting the Commission and the European Parliament, to create a court of first instance with jurisdiction to hear and determine "certain classes of action or proceeding brought by national or legal persons." Actions brought by Member States or Community institutions and references for preliminary rulings are expressly excluded. At the time of writing a proposal for the creation of such a court had been put forward by the Court of Justice and was being considered by the Council. Under the Court's proposal the first instance jurisdiction would be confined to staff cases, to actions brought by individuals under Article 173 or 175 EEC relating to competition or anti-dumping matters and to actions under Article 33 ECSC against individual acts relating to the application of Articles 57 to 66 ECSC.

---

acces. On y decouvrirait l'intérêt de cet ultime répit entre le débat de l'audience et la médiation de juge et l'utile décantation de conflit judiciare qui en résulte. On y apprecierait qu'une voix autorisée et libre, s'élevant au-dessus des parties, ait pu analyser avec le recul nécessaire l'argumentation de chacune et pris le risque de porter sur le litige un premier jugement. On relèverait, enfin, l'importance de cette tension de l'ésprit que provoque, en chaque juge, des orientations qui alimenteront les éventuelles confrontations du délibéré, en l'absence de votre personne, mais non dans le silence de votre voix."

The speech was delivered at the ceremonial sitting of the Court held on October 9, 1973.

[78] See Rules, Art. 10.
[79] Art. 32(c) ECSC; Art. 168 EEC; Art. 140 Euratom. See also Rules, Art. 12.
[80] Rules, Art. 17(1).
[81] Statute, Art. 11.

Practice and procedure[82]

The written procedure

The opening phase in an action before the European Court is known as "the written procedure."

(i) *Direct actions.* There are actions which start and finish in the European Court itself, as opposed to references for preliminary rulings which represent an episode in national proceedings. Direct actions are commenced by an application in writing addressed to the President and Members of the Court and submitted to the Registrar. The application does not have to be in any particular form but must contain certain detailed information, which is listed in Article 38 of the Rules. It must, for instance, give an address for service of documents in Luxembourg and the name of an authorised person who has expressed willingness to accept service. However, the main function of the application is to define the issues between the parties. The subject matter of the dispute and the grounds on which the application is based must be set out. There must also be a statement as to the form of order sought and the nature of any evidence relied upon. The original copy of the application, and of all other pleadings, must be signed by the party's agent or lawyer and must be lodged together with five copies for the Court and a copy for every other party to the proceedings.

Service of documents is effected by the Registrar.[83] Under Article 40 of the Rules the defendant must lodge his defence within one month after the application has been served on him. If no defence is lodged in time, a procedure is available to the applicant under Article 94 of the Rules for obtaining judgment in default. The time limit for lodging the defence is subject to the extensions laid down on account of distance[84] and may also be extended by decision of the President, on a reasoned application by the defendant.[85] However, such application must be made before the time limit expires. If the defendant contests the admissibility of the action he may choose to raise this as a preliminary objection. The objection will be dealt with under the procedure laid down by Article 91 of the Rules. A separate application must be made, stating the grounds of fact and law relied on and the form of order sought. The opposite party must be given an opportunity to make written submissions. The Court, after hearing the Advocate General, either decides on the application or reserves its decision for the final judgment.

After the application and defence there is a further degree of pleading, which is optional, consisting of a reply by the applicant and a rejoinder by the defendant.[86] The time limits for lodging these pleadings are fixed by the President.[87]

---

[82] Two excellent monographs on the procedure of the European Court have recently been published. See Usher, *European Court Practice*, Sweet & Maxwell (1983); K. P. Lasok, *The European Court of Justice: Practice and Procedure*.
[83] Rules, Art. 17.
[84] See Rules, Annex II.
[85] Rules, Art. 40(2).
[86] Rules, Art. 41(1).
[87] Rules, Art. 41(2).

Article 42(1) of the Rules allows a party to indicate further evidence in his reply or rejoinder but he must give reasons for not having indicated it earlier. On the other hand, Article 42(2) provides that:

> "No fresh issue may be raised in the course of proceedings unless it is based on matters of law or of fact which come to light in the course of the written procedure."

Where a fresh issue is so based, the other party may be given an opportunity to answer it, even after the expiry of the normal time limits.

The rule against raising fresh issues is applied by the Court with some severity.[88] It is, therefore, essential for parties to set out their case fully in the initial pleadings.

(ii) *References for preliminary rulings.* In cases under Article 177 EEC the procedure commences with the notification to the European Court of the Order for Reference made by the national court. Since the Court is not here concerned with the merits of the case, there is no need for the area of dispute between the parties to be defined by means of formal pleadings. Instead, provision is made by Article 20 of the Statute and Article 103 of the Rules for notification to be given to, and written observations submitted by, the parties, any Member State, the Commission and the Council (the last-named only if the case concerns a measure of which it is the source). However, it must be stressed that there is no compulsion on those notified to submit written observations; failure to do so does not constitute a bar to appearing at the hearing.

Fact-finding

In the light of the Preliminary Report presented by the Judge Rapporteur, and after hearing from the Advocate General, the Court may decide that a preparatory inquiry is necessary to clarify issues of fact in the case. For this purpose it will order a "preparatory inquiry," which will normally be conducted by a Chamber. It is one of the unfamiliar features of the Court's procedure that fact-finding should be separated in this way from the hearing. Various "measures of inquiry" are provided for in Article 45 of the Rules: appearance by the parties in person; a request for information or for the production of documents; oral testimony; experts' reports; and an inspection of the place or thing in question. At one time questions could only be put to witnesses through the Court but direct questioning by the representatives of the parties is now permitted. Nevertheless, the cutting edge of cross-examination is liable to be blunted when it cannot be guaranteed that witnesses will speak the same language as counsel. In practice, the Court does not often find it necessary to order measures of inquiry, other than in the form of written questions addressed to the parties and requiring written answers.

In references for preliminary rulings it is not for the European Court to

---

[88] *e.g.* in Joined Cases 54 to 60/76 *Compagnie Industrielle du Comte de Loheac and Others* v. *Council and Commission* [1977] E.C.R. 645, the Court ruled that a plea of inadmissibility raised by the Council in its rejoinder was out of time.

find the facts lying behind the national proceedings. These are taken from the Order for Reference, as well as from the national file on the case, if it is made available to the Court.[89]

The oral procedure

The oral procedure is formally divided into two parts. The first part consists of the public hearing of oral submissions by representatives of the parties. In direct actions counsel for the plaintiff speaks first, followed by counsel for the defendant and for any interveners, and an opportunity is provided to reply to points made by opponents. In cases referred under Article 177 the usual order of speaking is: counsel for the plaintiff in the main action; counsel for the defendant in the main action; counsel for any Member State that may be represented; and finally, counsel for the Commission. Members of the Bench will sometimes interrupt counsels' speeches, although for the most part they reserve their questions until everyone has been heard. Because the issues in a case will have been so thoroughly aired in the written procedure, hearings are relatively short. Most are completed in a morning.

The second part of the oral procedure is the delivery of his opinion by the Advocate General. In straightforward cases the opinion may be *ex tempore*. However, the Advocate General will usually reserve his opinion and deliver it at a sitting of the Court some weeks after the hearing.

In principle, once the Advocate General has delivered his opinion the oral procedure is closed. However, after hearing the Advocate General, the Court may order that the procedure be re-opened.[90] The Court has resisted attempts by parties to have the proceedings re-opened in order to enable them to comment on points made in the opinion, on the ground that this would interfere with the independence of the Advocate General.

Deliberation and judgment

The draft judgment presented by the Judge Rapporteur forms the starting point for the Court's deliberations. The latter take place in secrecy, which is strictly observed. If necessary, the decision can be taken by a majority, but all the Judges sign the final text. There are no dissenting judgments and it is impossible to find out which Judges, if any, may have been in a minority.[91]

Two reasons are usually put forward to justify the collegiate nature of the Court's judgments. The first is that, as a young judicial institution, the Court needed to build up its authority by presenting a united front to the world. The second is that anonymity preserves the Judges from the various forms of political pressure to which they might otherwise be subject. Those

---

[89] Issues of fact may, nevertheless, arise in references for preliminary rulings, concerning the Community provision which is the subject of the reference: see Case 51/75 *EMI* v. *CBS* [1976] E.C.R. 811 at p. 854 (Adv. Gen. Warner); Case 131/77 *Milac* v. *HZA Saabrücken* [1978] E.C.R. 1041. See the discussion in Usher, *op. cit.* note 50, *supra* at pp. 188–189.

[90] Rules, Art. 61.

[91] Statute, Art. 32; Rules, Art. 64(2).

seem to be good and sufficient reasons. The resulting judgment may perhaps have the look of a "committee" document, lacking in elegance and occasionally even in coherence, but the opinion of the Advocate General will always be available to provide a deeper and clearer factual and legal perspective on the case.

Article 64(1) of the Rules requires that judgments be delivered in open court. However, to save time it is only the short operative part of the judgment that is read out.

Interlocutory relief

The European Court has jurisdiction under Article 185 EEC, if it considers that circumstances so require, to order that the application of a contested measure be suspended. In addition, Article 186 provides that the Court may in any case before it prescribe any necessary interim measures.[92]

Interlocutory relief might typically be sought by an undertaking which is challenging a decision of the Commission finding it guilty of an infringement of the EEC rules on competition and requiring some action to be taken to rectify the position. For example, in the *United Brands* case[93] suppliers of bananas were given dispensation, pending the outcome of the main action, from a requirement that they cease to apply a prohibition against the resale of green fruit, which the Commission regarded as a device for isolating high-price from low-price markets.[94]

Interim measures can only be granted in respect of a case pending before the Court.[95] The application must be made separately from the application in the main proceedings[96] and must establish that the order requested is urgently necessary because, without it, the applicant would be liable to suffer serious and irreparable harm.[97] It must also be shown that the claim in the main proceedings is not manifestly unfounded.[98] For his part, the defendant may argue that he would be seriously and irreparably harmed by the granting of the order.[99]

Because of the urgent nature of such applications the President of the Court has been given power to decide on them himself,[1] and generally does

---

[92] See the discussion of interim measures by Usher, *op. cit.* note 50, *supra* at pp. 269–286; Lasok, *op. cit.* note 50, *supra* at pp. 145–176.

[93] Case 27/76 R *United Brands* v. *Commission* [1976] E.C.R. 425. For discussion of the main proceedings in the case, see Chap. 15, *infra*.

[94] Other interesting cases on interim measures in the field of competition are Case 71/74 R and RR *FRUBO* v. *Commission* [1974] E.C.R. 1031; Case 3175 R *Johnson and Firth Brown* v. *Commission* [1975] E.C.R. 1; Case 729/79 R *Camera Care* v. *Commission* [1980] E.C.R. 119; Joined Cases 225 and 229/82 R *Ford AG and Ford of Europe* v. *Commission* [1982] E.C.R. 3091.

[95] Rules, Art. 83(1).

[96] Rules, Art. 83(3).

[97] Case 31/59 *Acciaieria de Brescia* v. *High Authority* [1960] E.C.R. 98; Case 61/76 R II *Geist* v. *Commission* [1976] E.C.R. 2075; Case 113/77 R and 113/77 R-Int. *NTN Toyo* v. *Council (Ballbearings)* [1977] E.C.R. 1721; Case 121/77 R *Nachi Fujikoshi* v. *Council (Ballbearings)* [1977] E.C.R. 2107; Joined Cases 225 and 229/82 R *Ford AG and Ford of Europe* v. *Commission, loc. cit.* note 94, *supra*.

[98] Case 3/75 R *Johnson and Firth Brown* v. *Commission, loc. cit.* note 62, *supra*.

[99] *Ibid.* See also Case 26/76 R *Metro* v. *Commission* [1977] E.C.R. 1875.

[1] Rules, Art. 85.

so. However, where a case is difficult or important he may refer it to the Court.[2]

Intervention

A right to intervene in proceedings between other parties is given by Article 37 of the Statute[3] to Member States and to "institutions of the Community." It was established in the *Isoglucose* case[4] that the latter phrase encompasses the European Parliament.

Intervention by private parties is also allowed, subject to two limitations.[5] First, the case must not be one between Member States, between Community institutions or between a Member State and a Community institution or, to put the matter positively, a private party may intervene in an action brought by another private party for annulment, for a failure to act or for damages.[6] Secondly, a private intervener must be able to establish an interest in the result of the case. A distinction is drawn between having an interest in the acceptance by the Court of a certain set of aruguments and having an interest in the outcome of the case itself. Only the latter will justify intervention.[7] For example, in the *Amylum* case[8] an application was made by associations of sugar producers to intervene on the side of the Community in an action for damages brought by producers of isoglucose. While the sugar producers were obviously interested in the view the Court might take as to the alleged wrong underlying the claim (the imposition of a discriminatory production levy that eliminated the competitive advantage of isoglucose as a sweetner), they had no interest in the specific order being sought (for the payment of damages). Their application was accordingly rejected.

An application to intervene must be lodged within three months of the publication of the notice relating to the case in the *Official Journal*.[9] The third paragraph of Article 37 of the Statute provides that "submissions made in an application to intervene shall be limited to supporting the submissions of one of the parties." This must be taken to mean that the prospective intervener must support the *claim* of one side or other in the case, making no additional claim: the particular arguments put forward in furtherance of the claim need not be the same as, or even consistent with,

---

[2] *Ibid.*
[3] Art. 38 of the Euratom Statute is in identical terms. *Cf.* Art. 34 of the ECSC Statute.
[4] Case 138/79 *Roquette Frères* v. *Council* [1980] E.C.R. 3333.
[5] See Statute, Art. 37, second para.
[6] A typical case would be that of a party who sets in motion competition or anti-dumping proceedings by a complaint to the Commission. If proceedings are brought under Art. 173 EEC to challenge the action taken, the complainant may intervene in support of the Commission (or, as the case may be, of the Council): see, *e.g.* Joined Cases 56 and 58/64 *Consten and Grundig* v. *Commission* [1966] E.C.R. 299; Cases 113 and 118–121/77 *NTN Toyo Bearing Co. and Others* v. *Council (Ballbearings)* [1979] E.C.R. 1185. Intervention is also common in staff cases.
[7] See Case 111/63 *Lemmerz-Werke GmbH* v. *High Authority* [1965] E.C.R. 716; Joined Cases 41, 43 and 44/73 *Générale Sucrière and Others* v. *Commission* [1973] E.C.R. 1465; Joined Cases 116, 124 and 143/77 *Amylum NV and Others* v. *Council and Commission* [1978] E.C.R. 893; Case 155/79 *AM & S Europe Limited* v. *Commission* [1982] E.C.R. 1575.
[8] *Loc. cit.* note 74, *supra.*
[9] Rules, Art. 93(1).

those put forward by the party to whom support is given.[10] The application will be served on the original parties and they will be given an opportunity of making submissions on it. After hearing the opinion of the Advocate General, the Court will issue an order either allowing or refusing the intervention.[11] If it is allowed, the intervener will have a right to receive a copy of every document served on the parties. However, the Court may, on application by a party, omit confidential documents,[12] *e.g.* where this would involve the disclosure of business secrets to a competitor. Within a time limit fixed by the President, the intervener will be given an opportunity of making known in writing the grounds of his submissions[13] and he may also be represented at the hearing.

Article 37 of the Statute only applies to direct actions. The provision made by Article 20 of the Statute for the submission of observations in references for preliminary rulings was considered above.[14]

Language

The language in which a case is conducted may be any one of the Communities' nine official languages as well as Irish.[15] The general rule is that the choice of language lies with the applicant.[16] However, where an action is brought against a Member State, the language of the case is the official language of that State.[17] In references for preliminary rulings, it is the language of the referring court.[18]

The submissions of the parties, both written and oral, must be made in the language of the case and supporting documents must be either in that language or accompanied by a translation.[19] The Court may, on application, allow one of the other official languages to be used for the whole or part of the proceedings, but this concession does not apply to the Community institutions, which are expected to be able to operate in all the official languages.[20] A change in the Rules for the benefit of Member States now enables the latter to use their own official languages when intervening in a case or taking part in a reference for a preliminary ruling.[21]

Inside the Court itself French remains the working language, although English is now used a great deal. The Advocates General draft and deliver their Opinions in their own languages.[22] On the other hand, Judgments are always drafted and deliberated upon in French, so the authentic version of

---

[10] See, *e.g.*, Case 155/79 *AM & S Europe Limited* v. *Commission, loc. cit.* note 74, *supra*, where the French Government intervened on the side of the Commission but on the basis of a completely different understanding of the law of legal professional privilege. The point is discussed by Usher, *op. cit.* note 50, *supra* at pp. 294–295.
[11] Rules, Art. 93(3).
[12] Rules, Art. 93(4).
[13] Rules, Art. 93(5).
[14] At p. 85.
[15] Rules, Art. 29(1).
[16] Rules, Art. 29(2).
[17] *Ibid.* at (a).
[18] *Ibid.* at (b).
[19] Rules, Art. 29(3).
[20] Rules, Art. 29(2)(*c*).
[21] Rules, Art. 29(3).
[22] Rules, Art. 29(5) allows Advocates General to use any of the Court's languages.

the Judgment in the language of the case, if it is one other than French, will, in fact, be a translation.

Representation

Article 17 of the Statute lays down the rules on representation of parties before the Court. Member States and Community institutions are represented by an agent appointed for the case, who may be assisted by an adviser or by a lawyer entitled to practise before a court of a Member State. For instance, in a case involving the United Kingdom, the agent will normally be a member of the Treasury Solicitor's Department, who may be "assisted by" a barrister. Other parties must be represented by a lawyer entitled to practise before a court of a Member State. In direct actions they may not appear in person.

The position is different as regards references for preliminary rulings, where the Court is required to take account of the rules of procedure of the national court making the reference.[23] An example of a case in which the plaintiff appeared in person was the *Coenen* case[24] on freedom to provide services, a reference from a specialised tribunal in the Netherlands dealing with social matters.

Costs

In direct actions the general principle, according to Article 69(2) of the Rules, is that the unsuccessful party shall be ordered to pay costs, if they have been asked for in the successful party's pleadings. In one of the *Japanese Ballbearing* cases[25] counsel for a party that was ultimately successful forgot to ask for costs. He pointed out at the hearing that the wording of Article 69(2) did not preclude an award of costs in such circumstances; and in the end he did obtain his costs. Under Article 69(3) even a successful party may be ordered to pay costs which the Court considers to have been unreasonably or vexatiously caused to the other side.

According to Article 73 of the Rules, recoverable costs consist of:
> "(a) sums payable to witnesses and experts;
> (b) expenses necessarily incurred by the parties for the purpose of the proceedings, in particular the travel and subsistence expenses and the remuneration of agents, advisers or lawyers."

Disputes about costs are settled by a Chamber, on application by the party concerned, and after hearing the opposite party and the Advocate General. There is no appeal from the Order of the Chamber.[26]

In *Dietz* v. *Commission*[27] the Court refused the Commission costs in respect of the conduct of a case by its agent, who was a member of the Commission's own legal service. The ground of the refusal was that such an official is under a duty to advise and assist his institution and to perform the tasks entrusted to him within his sphere of action, and the consideration for

---

[23] Rules, Art. 104(2).
[24] Case 39/75 *Coenen* v. *Sociaal-Economische Raad* [1975] E.C.R. 1547.
[25] See Case 113/77 *NTN Toyo Bearing Company* v. *Council* [1979] E.C.R. 1185 at p. 1274 (Adv. Gen. Warner).
[26] Rules, Art. 74.
[27] Case 126/76 *Dietz* v. *Commission* [1979] E.C.R. 2131.

that overall performance is to be found in the salary which he receives under the relevant Staff Regulations. So all the Commission could recover was the derisory sum representing the agent's travel expenses between Brussels and Luxembourg and his daily allowance. Similar reasoning would presumably apply to salaried lawyers in government service or in the service of private companies.

In references for preliminary rulings the question of costs is left for determination by the national court or tribunal concerned.[28] Costs incurred by Member States or Community institutions which take advantage of their right to submit observations in such casts are not recoverable.

Legal aid

The European Court is empowered by Article 76 of the Rules to grant legal aid to a party to a direct action "who is wholly or in part unable to meet the costs of the proceedings." Applications for legal aid are considered by a Chamber, which makes an order without giving reasons. In the decision as to costs at the end of the case the Court may order the payment to its cashier of amounts advanced by way of legal aid. Such an order might seem appropriate if the recipient of the aid won his case and costs were awarded against the other party.

In references for a preliminary ruling, parties to the national proceedings may be eligible under national rules for legal aid in respect of the proceedings before the European Court.[29] It is also possible for the Court itself in exceptional circumstances to grant legal aid to enable a party to submit written observations or attend the hearing.[30] The non-availability of national aid is not a sufficient condition for obtaining such assistance.[31] There is no express provision for the recovery by the European Court, when a decision on costs has been taken at the conclusion of the national proceedings, of any legal aid it may have advanced.

Methods of interpretation[32]

A court adopts the methods of interpretation suited to the legal texts it is called upon to apply. The characteristic approach of the European Court is to give weight, in varying degrees depending on the circumstances, to three things: the wording of the provision in question; the place of the provision within the scheme of the instrument to which it belongs, and of that instru-

---

[28] Rules, Art. 104(3).
[29] The reference counts as a step in the national proceedings: see Case 62/72 *Bollmann* v. *HZA Hamburg-Waltershof* [1973] E.C.R. 269 at p. 275. In *R.* v. *Marlborough Street Stipendiary Magistrate, ex p. Bouchereau* [1977] E.C.R. 1999 an existing legal aid certificate was held to extend to a reference made in the proceedings to which it applied. See now regulation 6(2)(*d*) of the Legal Aid (General) Regulations 1971 (S.I. 1971 No. 62) as amended by the Legal Aid (General) Amendment Regulations 1977 (S.I. 1977 No. 1293).
[30] Rules, Art. 104(3).
[31] In Case 96/80 *Jenkins* v. *Kingsgate (Clothing Productions) Ltd.* [1981] E.C.R. 911, a case on the right to equal pay under Art. 119 EEC (see Chap. 11, *infra*, the employing company applied to the Court for legal aid on the ground that, without it, the company would not be able to put in submissions. The application was rejected. See the opinion of Adv. Gen. Warner at p. 932.
[32] For fuller discussion of the methods of interpretation used by the European Court, see Brown and Jacobs, pp. 237–259; Waelbroeck *et al.*, Vol. 10, pp. 8–18.

ment in the Community order ("contextual interpretation"); and the objects of that provision, that instrument and the Community order ("teleological interpretation").

A literal method of interpretation under which the "plain" or "ordinary" meaning of words and phrases is treated as decisive cannot be used where texts exist in multiple language versions, all of them equally authentic. The Court has said that interpreting a provision in a Community text involves a comparison between the different versions.[33] Such a comparison in the *Schwarze* case[34] helped to resolve an ambiguity in the German phrase *stammend aus* ("coming from") in an agricultural regulation.[35] It was clear from the Dutch, French and Italian versions of the relevant provisions[36] that the phrase was intended to cover both products harvested in the exporting Member State and products in free circulation there. Where the meaning of the different versions conflicts, the Court opts for the one best adapted to the objects of the measure in question. In *Stauder*,[37] it will be remembered, the question was whether a scheme for the distribution of cut-price butter made it a condition that beneficiaries produce a coupon stating their names. The Dutch and German texts of the relevant Decision appeared to impose this condition, while the French and Italian texts merely required the coupon to be in a form that made a check on entitlement possible. It was held by the Court that in such cases the more liberal interpretation must prevail provided that, as here, it was sufficient to achieve the objects being pursued.[38]

An example of contextual interpretation can be seen in the priority the Court gives to the principles identified in Part Two of the EEC Treaty as representing the "Foundations of the Community." It has repeatedly been stated by the Court that provisions such as those of Article 36 EEC, which derogate from fundamental principles, have to be strictly construed.[39]

Teleological interpretation of the Treaties is facilitated by the specification of objects in their preambles and in many of their provisions,[40] and similar indications are to be found in the statements of reasons the Community institutions are required to include in the preambles to law-making acts.[41] The method has been extensively used by the Court, both to confirm interpretations suggested by the wording and context of provisions and to fill in gaps in the legal framework. The latter have become especially apparent since the EEC entered its definitive phase in 1970 with the legislative programme for the establishment of a genuinely common market still far from complete.[42]

In cases where little or no assistance can be obtained from the relevant

[33] Case 283/81 *CILFIT* v. *Italian Ministry of Heath* [1982] E.C.R. 3415.
[34] Case 16/65 *Schwarze* v. *EVF* [1965] E.C.R. 877 at p. 889.
[35] Reg. 19 on the progressive establishment of a common organisation of the market in cereals, O.J. 1962, 933.
[36] Reg. 19, Arts. 2 and 3.
[37] Case 29/69 *Stauder* v. *Ulm* [1969] E.C.R. 419.
[38] [1969] E.C.R. at pp. 424–425.
[39] See, *e.g.* Case 47/76 *Bauhuis* v. *Netherlands* [1977] E.C.R. 5; Case 113/80 *Commission* v. *Ireland (Irish Souvenirs)* [1981] E.C.R. 1625.
[40] See, *e.g.* Arts. 2, 3, 39, 110 and 117 EEC.
[41] Art. 15 ECSC; Art. 190 EEC; Art. 162 Euratom.
[42] See the chapters below relating to the free movement of goods, persons and services.

texts an appeal to the broad aims of the Communities is often associated with two other techniques the Court has made its own. One of these is an adaptation of the principle of effectiveness (*l'effet utile*) in international law. As applied by the Court, the principle means that a provision must be interpreted in the way that enables it to achieve its object as effectively as possible.[43] A notable illustration of the principle at work can be found in the line of cases on the right of an individual to invoke the provisions of a directive against the authorities of a Member State which has failed, wholly or in part, to implement the directive. In judgment after judgment it has been explained that the right is recognised because, without it, the effectiveness of the measure would be diminished.[44] The other technique is the comparative analysis of national provisions to discover the solution to a problem that will best serve the purposes of Community law. The detailed comparison is usually to be found in the opinion of the Advocate General, the Court merely recording its own conclusions in the judgment. A recent example was the judgment in *AM & S*[45] where it was accepted, in the light of successive opinions by Advocate General Warner and Advocate General Slynn, that a limited doctrine of legal professional privilege applies in EEC competition matters.

The Court makes little use of *travaux préparatoires* (preparatory documents) as an aid to discovering the intentions of the authors of a measure, although this is a popular method of interpretation in international law. In fact, the *travaux préparatoires* of the Treaties themselves have never been made public, but in a few early cases there were references to explanations given by signatory Governments in the course of ratification debates.[46] Resort to *travaux préparatories* seems inappropriate in respect of the Treaties, because their authors set in motion a process of economic and political integration whose course and outcome could not be foreseen in detail. In respect of legislative measures, formal expressions of view, such as an amendment to a proposal on an agricultural matter, put forward by the Management Committee of the relevant market organisation,[47] may be indicative of the position it was agreed finally to accept or reject. On the other hand, the views of individual participants in a decision are not a reliable guide to its objective meaning.[48]

It has been said of the European Court, by admirers as well as by critics, that its approach to the interpretation of the Treaties and of acts of the Community institutions is tantamount in some cases to legislating. This, in

---

[43] See Kutscher, *Methods of Interpretation as seen by a Judge of the Court of Justice* (1976), p. 41; Brown and Jacobs, p. 258; Waelbroeck *et al.*, Vol. 10, p. 15.

[44] See, *e.g.* Case 8/81 *Becker* v. *FZA Münster-Innenstadt* [1982] E.C.R. 53.

[45] Case 155/79 *AM & S Europe Ltd.* v. *Commission* [1982] E.C.R. 1575.

[46] See Case 6/54 *Netherlands* v. *High Authority* [1954–1956] E.C.R. 103 at pp. 125–126 (Adv. Gen. Roemer); Case 6/60 *Humblet* [1960] E.C.R. 559 at pp. 575–576.

[47] Case 29/69 *Stauder* v. *Ulm* [1969] E.C.R. at p. 425. Another example cited by Brown and Jacobs at p. 248 and by Waelbroeck *et al.*, Vol. 10 at p. 11, is the acceptance by the Court, as the basis of the Common Customs Tariff, of the so-called "Brussels Nomenclature" which was established by the Convention of 1950 on Nomenclature for the Classification of Goods in Customs Tariffs: see Case 14/70 *Bakels* v. *Oberfinanzdirektion München* [1970] E.C.R. 1001 at 1009.

[48] See Case 28/76 *Milac* v. *HZA Freiburg* [1976] E.C.R. 1639 at p. 1664 (Adv. Gen. Warner): Case 136/79 *National Panasonic* v. *Commission* [1980] E.C.R. 2033 at p. 2066 (Adv. Gen. Warner).

our submission, is misconceived. The Court does not purport to enjoy a legislator's freedom to impose its own view as to how the Community should develop. Like any other court, it makes new law by drawing out the consequences of what has been established in legal texts and in earlier decisions. If its jurisprudence seems unusually bold and creative, that is because of the unusual challenge it faces, as the judicial organ of a new and dynamic order, whose legislative organs have so far proved unequal to their task.

PART III: THE FREE MOVEMENT OF GOODS

CHAPTER 5

CUSTOMS DUTIES AND DISCRIMINATORY
INTERNAL TAXATION

Establishment of a customs union

It was pointed out in Chapter 2 that whereas a free trade area comprises a group of customs territories in which duties are eliminated on trade in goods originating in such territories, a customs union represents a further step in economic integration, since a common tariff is adopted in trade relations with the outside world.

Article 9 of the Treaty[1] provides that the Community "shall be based upon a customs union which shall cover all trade in goods and which shall involve the prohibition between Member States of custom duties on imports and exports and all charges having equivalent effect, and the adoption of a common customs tariff in their relations with third countries." The "goods" referred to are all products which have a monetary value and may be the object of commercial transactions. The Court rejected an argument adduced by the Italian Government that the free movement provisions of the Treaty could have no application to a charge levied on the export of goods of historic or artistic interest. The products covered by the Italian law in issue, said the Court, regardless of any other qualities which might distinguish them from other commercial goods, resembled such goods in that they had a monetary value and could constitute the object of commercial transactions—indeed, the Italian law recognised as much by fixing the charge in relation to the value of the object in question.[2]

The reason why the abolition of duties between the constituent territories of a free trade area is normally restricted to goods *originating* in such territories, in that otherwise members of the area maintaining high tariffs against non Member countries would find their markets open to imports from such countries via the territory of low tariff neighbours. The problem is obviated if all members adopt the same tariffs in their trade with third countries. Thus the Treaty provides[3] that its free movement provisions[4] apply not only to goods originating in Member States, but also to products coming from third countries which are in free circulation in Member States.

---

[1] Directly applicable in conjunction with other Treaty Articles; Cases 2 & 3/69 *Sociaal Fonds etc.* v. *Brachfeld and Chougol Diamond Co.* [1969] E.C.R. 211, (Arts. 9 and 12); Case 33/70 *SACE* v. *Italian Ministry of Finance* [1970] E.C.R. 1213, (Arts. 9 and 13(2); Case 18/71 *Eunomia* v. *Italian Ministry of Education* [1971] E.C.R. 811, (Arts. 9 and 16).
[2] Case 7/68 *Commission* v. *Italy* [1968] E.C.R. 423. It is open to Member States to *prohibit* the export of national treasures under Art. 36. Coins may constitute "goods" if they do not constitute a means of payment in the Member States, see Case 7/78 *R.* v. *Johnson* [1978] E.C.R. 2247.
[3] Art. 9(2).
[4] Arts. 12–17, 31–37.

97

Goods originating in Member States

Although products from third countries in free circulation benefit in equal measure from the provisions guaranteeing the free movement of goods, it is nevertheless necessary to differentiate between products according to origin in several circumstances:

— for the purposes of the application of the Common Customs Tariff, in the case of imports from third countries;
— where Member States have to certify the origin of goods exported to third countries, because required to do so by the authorities in such countries;
— where the Commission, acting under Article 115 of the Treaty, authorises Member State A to take protective measures against the import of a certain product, originating in a third country, which has been imported into Member State B, and is in free circulation therein.

Rules for determining the origin of goods in such circumstances are contained in Regulation 802/68.[5] Under the latter Regulation, a product is considered to have originated in a particular country if it has been wholly obtained or produced in that country.[6] Goods in the production of which two or more countries have been concerned are considered to have originated in the country in which the last economically justifiable process was performed, provided that such operation was carried out in an undertaking equipped for the purpose, and resulted in the manufacture of a new product or represented an important stage of manufacture.[7] The Court has held[8] that the stage of manufacture referred to must bring about a "significant qualitative change" in the properties of the original product. Special rules for determining the origin of particular products have been made under the parent Regulation (*e.g.* regarding the origin of tape-recorders, and spare parts).[9] Provision is made for the issue of certificates of origin by authorised national agencies.[10]

Goods in free circulation in the Member States

Article 10 of the Treaty provides that products coming from a third country shall be considered to be in free circulation in a Member State:

— if import formalities have been complied with;
— if customs duties or charges having equivalent effect have been levied; and
— if there has been no reimbursement of such duties or charges.

The reimbursement referred to is possible in the case of "inward process-

---

[5] O.J. English Sp.Ed. 1968 (I), p. 165. See in general, Forrester, (1980) 5 E.L.Rev. 167.
[6] Art. 4. On origin of fish under Art. 4(2)(*f*), see Case 100/84 *Commission* v. *United Kingdom* [1985] 2 C.M.L.R. 199.
[7] Art. 5.
[8] Case 49/76 *Uberseehandel* [1977] E.C.R. 41. See also Case 95/83 *ZENTRAG* [1984] E.C.R. 1095.
[9] The Court has held two such Regulations invalid: Reg. 2067/77 (zip-fasteners) in Case 34/78 *Yoshida* [1979] E.C.R. 115, and Case 114/78 *Yoshida* [1979] E.C.R. 151; and Reg. 749/78 (textile products), in Case 162/82 *Cousin* (1983) E.C.R. 1101.
[10] Reg. 802/68, Art. 10.

ing," when goods are imported simply for the purposes of processing followed by re-export.[11]

Evidence of entitlement to freedom of movement—Community transit

Article 10(2) provides for administrative co-operation to facilitate the application of the free movement of goods provisions to all products qualifying under Article 9(2). An early Commission Decision laid down that such products should be admitted to the benefit of the relevant Treaty provisions on the presentation of documentary evidence, which would be issued by the customs authorities of the Member State of export, at the request of the exporter.[12] Two certificates were specified in the Decision; Form DD1, issued in respect of goods transported directly from the Member State of export to that of import, and Form DD3, issued in other cases. This requirement simplified customs clearance, but it did not obviate the necessity of a succession of customs formalities in the case of goods traversing several Member States. It was to minimalise such formalities that the Community transit system was instituted. Regulation 222/77[13] establishes two procedures: one for external Community transit, and one for internal Community transit. The first procedure applies, essentially, to goods which neither originate in a Member State nor are in free circulation (*i.e.* goods from third countries on which duty has not been paid), while the second applies to goods which either do originate in a Member State, or, if not, are in free circulation.

An example of the external transit procedure would be as follows. Suppose that eligible goods are to be transported between Member States A and D, via Member States B and C. The exporter must make a "T1" declaration in the customs office in State A.[14] The office will register the T1 declaration, prescribe the period within which the goods must be produced at the requisite customs office in State D, retain a copy of the T1 declaration, and return copies to the exporter.[15] Identification of the goods will in general be secured by sealing.[16] Transit through Member States B and C will be accomplished simply by presentation of the T1 declaration, and customs inspection to ensure that the seals are not broken.[17]

The procedure is similar for internal Community transit, except that the relevant document is a "T2" declaration.

The Community transit procedure is mandatory for all movement of goods between two points situated in the Community,[18] with certain limited exceptions.[19] Even when the exceptions apply, the Community

---

[11] See Reg. 1999/85, J.O. 1985, L188/1.
[12] Dec. December 5, 1960, J.O. 1961, 29.
[13] O.J. 1977, L38/1, superseding Reg. 542/69, O.J. 1969, L77/1, and consolidating its amending texts. Reg. 222/77 has been the subject of amendment, latterly by Reg. 3617/82, O.J. 1982 L382/6, and Reg. 1901/85, O.J. 1985 L179/6.
[14] Art. 12.
[15] Art. 17.
[16] Art. 18.
[17] Art. 20.
[18] Art. 1.
[19] Arts. 2–8, 42–49.

nature of goods is certified, for the purposes of the free movement provisions of the Treaty, by Community transit documents. In these cases a
slight modification of the form T2 is specified, and termed T2L.[20]

The EEC Treaty does not expressly prohibit transit charges. In *Societa
Italiana per l'Oleodotto Transalpino*[21] an Italian undertaking challenged
before an Italian court charges imposed upon oil landed at Trieste for consignment via the transalpine oil pipe-line to Germany. The court asked the
Court of Justice whether such transit charges were compatible with Community law. The Court held that it was a necessary consequence of the Customs Union and the mutual interest of the Member States that there be
recognised a general principle of freedom of transit of goods within the
Community. The imposition of transit charges was incompatible with this
principle, unless the charges in question represented the costs of transportation or of other services connected with transit, including general benefits derived from the use of harbour works or installations, for the
navigability and maintenance of which public authorities were responsible.

Elimination of customs duties and measures having equivalent effect on imports and exports—the framework of articles 12 to 17 of the treaty

Articles 12 to 17 EEC provide for the abolition of customs duties and
similar charges, calling for:
— a standstill on customs duties and measures having equivalent effect
   on imports and exports (Article 12);
— the progressive elimination of customs duties on imports during the
   transitional period (Articles 13(1), 14 and 15);
— the progressive elimination of charges having an effect equivalent to
   customs duties on imports during the transitional period (Article
   13(2));
— the abolition of customs duties and charges having equivalent effect
   on exports by the end of the first stage (Article 16).

The "Standstill"

Article 12 provides that Member States shall refrain from introducing
between themselves any new customs duties on imports and exports or any
charges having equivalent effect, and from increasing those which they
already apply in their trade with each other. The Article, which applies
equally to agricultural goods,[22] is directly applicable.[23]

The Court emphasised the central role of the prohibition of customs
duties and similar charges, contained in Articles 9 and 12, in *Commission*

---

[20] Reg. 223/77, O.J. 1977, L38/20, Arts. 69–74. Reg. 223/77 has been frequently amended,
   latterly by Reg. 1482/83, O.J. L151/29 and Reg. 1709185, O.J. 1985 L124/19.
[21] Case 266/81 [1983] E.C.R. 731.
[22] Cases 90 and 91/63 *Commission* v. *Luxembourg and Belgium* [1964] E.C.R. 65.
[23] Case 26/62 *Van Gend en Loos* v. *Nederlandse Administratie der Belastingen* [1963] E.C.R.
   1; Cases 2 & 3/69 *Sociaal Fonds etc.* v. *Brachfeld and Chougol Diamond Co.* [1969] E.C.R.
   211.

v. *Luxembourg and Belgium*,[24] basing its view on the respective provisions of these Articles in the scheme of the Treaty, "Article 9 being placed at the beginning of the Title relating to 'Free Movement of Goods' and Article 12 at the beginning of the section dealing with the 'Elimination of Customs Duties.' "[25] Any exception to such an essential rule would require to be clearly stated, and would receive a narrow construction.[26] Thus, to the extent that a Council Regulation concerning the common organisation of the market in wine authorised Member States to impose charges on intra-Community trade, it was held to be invalid by the Court of Justice.[27] The Court's rigorous approach is reflected in its subsequent case law. In *Social Fonds voor de Diamantarbeiders* v. *Brachfeld and Chougol Diamond Co.*,[28] the Court was faced with a reference from an Antwerp magistrate, concerning a levy imposed under Belgian law on imported diamonds. The Belgian Government submitted that the levy could not be regarded as infringing Articles 9 and 12, since it was devoid of protectionist purpose in the first place, Belgium did not even produce diamonds, and in the second place, the purpose of the levy was to provide social security benefits for workers in the diamond industry. The following statement of the Court emphasises that the achievement of a single market between Member States requires more than the elimination of protection:

"In prohibiting the imposition of customs duties, the Treaty does not distinguish between goods according to whether or not they enter into competition with the products of the importing country. Thus, the purpose of the abolition of customs barriers is not merely to eliminate their protective nature, as the Treaty sought on the contrary to give general scope and effect to the rule on elimination of customs duties and charges having equivalent effect in order to ensure the free movement of goods. It follows from the system as a whole and from the general and absolute nature of the prohibition of any customs duty applicable to goods moving between Member States that customs duties are prohibited independently of any consideration of the purpose for which they were introduced and the destination of the revenue obtained therefrom. The justification for this prohibition is based on the fact that any pecuniary charge—however small—imposed on goods by reason of the fact that they cross a frontier constitutes an obstacle to the movement of such goods."[29]

Whether or not a customs duty is a "new" customs duty, or whether or not it represents an increase in one already applied, must be determined in relation to the duties actually applied at the date the Treaty entered into force, rather than those which in strict law ought to have been applicable.

---

[24] Cases 2 and 3/62 [1962] E.C.R. 425.
[25] [1962] E.C.R. 425 at p. 431.
[26] Art. 115 permitted unilateral derogation from the free movement provisions of the Treaty, in cases of urgency, during the transitional period. Now a Commission authorisation is necessary.
[27] Cases 80 & 8/77 *Société Les Commissionaires Reunis Sarl* v. *Receveurs des Douanes* [1978] E.C.R. 927.
[28] Note 23.
[29] Note that there is no "de minimis" defence; *cf.* the position under Art. 95, *infra*, p. 108 and the interpretation given to Art. 85, *infra*, p. 377.

The significance of the point is illustrated in *Commission* v. *Italy*,[30] arising out of proceedings instituted under Article 169 of the Treaty. As the result of legislative oversight, two different duties became applicable in Italy to imported radio parts as of July 14, 1956: one of 35 per cent. and one of 30 per cent. coupled with a specific minimum of 150 lira. In these circumstances the Italian customs authorities were instructed to apply to each particular case the duty more favourable to the importer. In its application of Articles 12 and 14 of the Treaty, the Italian Government treated the 35 per cent. duty as being without lawful effect, and applied the Treaty on the basis of the alternative charge. The Court held that the provisions of the Treaty in question must be given effect on the basis of the duties actually applied in each case. Any other solution would leave the Commission the task of inquiring into the validity of domestic administrative measures with respect to the law of the Member States. This view was reiterated in *Van Gend en Loos* v. *Netherlands Inland Revenue Administration*,[31] the Court adding that a reclassification of a particular product under a tariff heading attracting a higher duty was no more consistent with Article 12 than a straightforward increase in the original rate.

The progressive elimination of customs duties on imports during the transitional period—Articles 13(1), 14 and 15

The Original Six

Article 13(1) EEC provided for the progressive abolition of customs duties on imports in force between Member States during the transitional period, in accordance with Articles 14 and 15. Article 14 contained a detailed timetable for the reduction of customs duties between the original six Member states during the 12 year transitional period provided for in Article 8.

Article 15, contemplating the possibility that the Member States might wish to reduce tariffs more speedily than required by the timetable of Article 14, expressly provided for this eventuality. The effect of the Article was simply declaratory of powers retained by the Member States. The economic climate being favourable, they in fact agreed on May 12, 1960,[32] and May 15, 1962[32] to reduce duties by 30 per cent. as of July 1, 1960, and by 50 per cent. as of July 1, 1962.

These decisions in no way prejudiced the continued application of the timetable prescribed by the Treaty,[33] with the result that by January 1, 1966 basic duties had been reduced by 80 per cent. as against the 60 per cent. required.

On July 26, 1966, the Council, acting under Article 235 of the Treaty,

---

[30] Case 10/61 (1962) E.C.R. 1, (1962) C.M.L.R. 187.
[31] Note 23.
[32] J.O. 1960, 1217, J.O. 1962, 1284. As the exercise of powers retained by the Member States, these decisions are not based on Art. 15, nor are they decisions within the meaning of Art. 189.
[33] That is, a reduction of at least ten per cent. was required on the dates specified, regardless of the additional reductions.

decided[34] to reduce duties to 15 per cent. of the basic duties on July 1, 1967 and to eliminate them entirely from July 1, 1968—18 months before the end of the transitional period.

The first and second Accessions

Denmark, Ireland and the United Kingdom acceded to the European Communities on January 1, 1973. Customs duties were abolished in the enlarged Community by July 1, 1977. Greece acceded to the European Communities on January 1, 1981. Customs duties were abolished in trade between Greece and the other Member States by January 1, 1986.

The accessions of Spain and Portugal

Under the Third Act of Accession, customs duties in trade between the Community and Spain and Portugal are to be progressively abolished between March 1, 1986 and January 1, 1993.[35]

Definition of "charges having equivalent effect"

Article 13(2) EEC provides for the progressive abolition of charges having an effect equivalent to customs duties on imports. This requirement has been described by the Court as the "logical and necessary complement"[36] to the first paragraph of the Article in question, which calls for the elimination of customs duties proper. The prohibition of charges having equivalent effect, like the prohibition on customs duties, constitutes a basic Treaty norm, and any exceptions must be clearly and unambiguously provided for.[37]

The concept of charges having equivalent effect must be interpreted in the light of the objects and purposes of the Treaty, in particular the provisions dealing with the free movement of goods.[38] "Consequently," the Court has declared, "any pecuniary charge, however small and whatever its designation and mode of application, which is imposed unilaterally on domestic or foreign goods by reason of the fact that they cross a frontier, and which is not a customs duty in the strict sense, constitutes a charge having equivalent effect within the meaning of Articles 9, 12, 13 and 16 of the Treaty, even if it is not imposed for the benefit of the State, is not discrimi-

---

[34] Dec. 66/532, J.O. 1966, 2971. Being based on Art. 235, this is a Decision within the meaning of Art. 189, having been taken by the Council as a Community institution, rather than as a group of Governmental representatives, as to which see Case 38/69 *Commission* v. *Italy* [1970] E.C.R. 47. The decision did not bring forward the date of expiry of the transitional period, see Case 27/78 *Italian Finance Administration* v. *Rasham* [1978] E.C.R. 1761.

[35] Third Act of Accession, see in particular, Arts. 31 and 190.

[36] Cases 52 & 55/65, *Germany* v. *Commission* [1966] E.C.R. 159; and see, *e.g.*, Cases 2 & 3/69, *Chougol Diamond* [1969] E.C.R. 211; Case 24/68, *Commission* v. *Italy* [1969] E.C.R. 193.

[37] Cases 52 & 55/65 note 36.

[38] See, *e.g.* Cases 2 & 3/69; Case 24/68 note 36. A prohibition on charges having equivalent effect often appears in secondary legislation. Such a provision is invariably given the same meaning as the similar provision in the Treaty: Case 25/67 *Milch-, Fett- und Eirkontor* v. *Hauptzollamt Saarbrucken* [1968] E.C.R. 207; Case 34/73 *Variola* v. *Italian Ministry of Finance* [1973] E.C.R. 981; Case 21/75 *Schroeder* v. *Oberstadtdirektor Cologne* [1975] E.C.R. 905. This may not be the case, however, in the case of imports from a third country: Case 70/77 *Simmenthal* v. *Italian Ministry of Finance* [1978] E.C.R. 1453; see *infra*, at p. 121.

natory or protective in effect and if the product on which the charge is imposed is not in competition with any domestic product."[39]

On several occasions the Court has been confronted with the argument that a charge levied on the crossing of a frontier was not a charge having equivalent effect to a customs duty, but a fee for a service rendered. This argument has been adduced in the case of a "fee" charged by a national agricultural intervention agency for the issue of import licences,[40] a "fee" levied on all imports and exports to defray the costs of compiling statistical data, the availability of which allegedly benefited traders,[41] and "fees" to offset the costs of compulsory health and sanitary inspections.[42] The Court has taken the view that "a charge may escape prohibition as a charge having equivalent effect if the charge in question is the consideration for a service actually rendered to the importer and is of an amount commensurate with that service."[43] The Court has rejected the "consideration for services" argument in the case of unilateral measures, either because the services in question were rendered in the general interest (*e.g.* health inspections), rather than in the interests of traders themselves, or, if the services did benefit traders, because they benefited them as a class in a way which was impossible to quantify in a particular case (*e.g.* compilation of statistical data). Charges imposed by a Member State to cover the cost of complying with Community measures will not however amount to measures having equivalent effect, at any rate where the Community measures reduce obstacles to intra-Community trade which would otherwise result from divergent national measures.[44] It is not necessary in such a case to establish whether or not the service is of direct benefit to importers or exporters.[45] Measures taken by a Member State under an international treaty to which all Member States are parties, and which encourage the free movement of goods, may be assimilated to Community measures, and fees covering costs may be charged accordingly.[46]

A case neatly illustrating the difficulties of establishing whether or not national charges may be regarded as charges having equivalent effect was *Commission* v. *Belgium*.[47] The development of Community transit[48] enabled importers to convey their goods from the frontier to public warehouses situated in the interior of the country without paying duties and taxes. In these warehouses, importers could have customs clearance oper-

---

[39] Case 24/68 *Commission* v. *Italy* [1969] E.C.R. 193, at p. 201.
[40] Cases 52 & 55/65 note 36. Note that even if Art. 36 permitted a quantitative restriction or measure having equivalent effect, it would not justify a fee charged in connection with such a measure, Case 29/72 *Marimex* v. *Italian Finance Administration* [1972] E.C.R. 1309. But *cf.* Case 46/76 *Bauhuis* v. *Netherlands State* [1977] E.C.R. 5, where Community rules justified the restriction in question.
[41] Case 24/68 note 36.
[42] Case 39/73 *Rewe-Zentralfinanz* v. *Landwirtschaftskammer* [1973] E.C.R. 1039; Case 87/75 *Bresciani* v. *Italian Finance Administration* [1976] E.C.R. 129; Case 35/76 *Simmenthal* v. *Italian Minister of Finance* [1976] E.C.R. 1871; Case 251/78 *Firma Denkavit Futtermittel Gmbh* v. *Minister for Food* [1979] E.C.R. 3369.
[43] Case 132/82 *Commission* v. *Belgium* [1983] E.C.R. 1649.
[44] Case 46/76 *Bauhuis* v. *Netherlands State* [1977] E.C.R. 5.
[45] *Ibid.*
[46] Case 89/76 *Commission* v. *Netherlands* [1977] E.C.R. 1355.
[47] Case 132/82 [1983] E.C.R. 1649.
[48] See *supra* at p. 99.

ations carried out, and they also had the opportunity of placing their goods in temporary storage, pending their consignment to a particular customs procedure. The Belgian Government levied storage charges on goods deposited in such public warehouses in the interior of the Community. The Court held that these charges were charges having equivalent effect when they were imposed solely in connexion with the completion of customs formalities, but that they were justified in cases where the trader elected to place his goods in storage. In the latter case, the Court accepted that the storage represented a service rendered to traders. A decision to deposit the goods could only be taken at the request of the trader concerned, and ensured storage of the goods without payment of duties. The Belgian Government argued that also in the former case—where the goods were cleared through customs without storage—a service was rendered to the importer. It was always open to the latter to avoid payment by choosing to have his goods cleared through customs at the frontier, where such a procedure was free of charge. By using a public warehouse, the importer could have the goods declared through customs near the places for which his products were bound. The Court acknowledged that the use of a public warehouse in the interior of the country offered certain advantages, but noted that such advantages were linked solely with the completion of customs formalities which, whatever the place, was always compulsory. Furthermore, the advantages in question resulted from the scheme of Community transit, not in the interest of individual traders, but in order to encourage the free movement of goods and facilitate transport in the Community. "There can therefore," concluded the Court, "be no question of levying charges for customs clearance facilities accorded in the interests of the Common Market."[49]

Article 13(2) EEC was held to be directly applicable as of the end of the transitional period in *SACE* v. *Italian Ministry of Finance*, and *Capolongo* v. *Azienda Agricola Maya*.[50]

Charges having equivalent effect—timetable for abolition

The original six

The provisions of Article 13(2) EEC require the progressive abolition of charges having equivalent effect during the transitional period. No specific timetable was specified in the Treaty, but the Commission was empowered to establish such a timetable by means of Directives, taking into account the rules contained in Article 14(2) and (3), governing the elimination of customs duties proper. The Commission issued a number of such Directives.

---

[49] It is not clear whether or not this represents a retreat from Case 46/76 *Bauhuis* [1977] E.C.R. 5, and Case 89/76 *Commission* v. *Netherlands* [1977] E.C.R. 1355, which allow national charges for the completion of procedures established in the general interests of the Community. These latter cases were referred to by the Court with approval in Case 1/83 *IFG Intercontinetale* [1984] E.C.R. 349.

[50] Case 33/70 [1970] E.C.R. 1213 and Case 77/72 [1973] E.C.R. 611. But not *before* the end of the transitional period; the Council's "acceleration" Decision of July 26, 1966, J.O. 1966, 2971, applied only to customs duties, not to charges having equivalent effect, *infra*, p. 103.

The first and second accessions

The first Act of Accession provided for the abolition of charges having equivalent effect on imports by July 1, 1977.[51] The second Act of Accession provided for the abolition of charges having equivalent effect on imports between Greece and the rest of the Community by January 1, 1980.[52]

The accession of Spain and Portugal

Under the Third Act of Accession, any charges having equivalent effect to a customs duty on imports between the Community and Spain and Portugal were abolished on March 1, 1986.[53]

Customs duties and charges having equivalent effect on exports—Article 16 EEC

The fact that the achievement of a single market between Member States is dependent on more than the suppression of measures calculated to protect domestic industry is well illustrated by the prohibition of customs duties and charges having equivalent effect on exports as well as imports. As Advocate General Gand pointed out in *Commission* v. *Italy*, "What distinguishes customs duties on exports is not that they protect the national industry but that they increase the price of goods and thus tend to hinder their exportation and, without prohibiting trade in goods, to make it more difficult."[54]

Article 16 requires the abolition of all duties and charges having equivalent effect by the end of the first stage at the latest (December 31, 1961), and the Court held in *Eunomia di Porro & Co.* v. *Italian Ministry of Education*[55] that this Article, in conjunction with Article 9, produced direct effects in the Member States. In the case of Denmark, Ireland and the United Kingdom, Article 37 of the Act of Accession provides for the abolition of all charges between the Community as originally constituted and the new Member States and between the new Member States themselves by January 1, 1974 at the latest.

Customs duties on exports and charges having equivalent effect were abolished between Greece and the other Member States on January 1, 1981.[56]

Under the Third Act of Accession, customs duties on exports and charges having equivalent effect in trade between the Community and Spain and Portugal were abolished on March 1, 1986.[57] The Court has held that an internal duty which falls more heavily on exports than on domestic sales amounts to a charge having equivalent effect to a customs duty.[58]

---

[51] Art. 36(1).
[52] Art. 29.
[53] Third Act of Accession, Arts. 35 and 193.
[54] Case 7/68 [1968] E.C.R. 423 at p. 434. And see the *Chougol Diamond* case, *supra*, p. 101.
[55] Case 18/71 [1971] E.C.R. 811.
[56] Second Act of Accession, Art. 30.
[57] Third Act of Accession, Arts. 36 and 195.
[58] Cases 36 & 71/80 *Irish Creamery Milk Suppliers Assn.* v. *Govt. of Ireland* [1981] E.C.R. 735.

The prohibition on discriminatory fiscal charges on imports

Article 95

The first paragraph of Article 95 of the Treaty provides that no Member State shall impose, directly or indirectly, on the product of any other Member State any internal taxation of any kind in excess of that imposed directly or indirectly on similar domestic products. Paragraph 2 adds that Member States shall furthermore impose no taxation of such a kind as to afford indirect protection to other products.

Purpose of Article 95

The Court has stated that the Article is calculated to close any loopholes which internal taxation might open in the prohibition on customs duties and charges having equivalent effect.[59] Advocate General Gand explained its rationale as follows in *Lutticke* v. *Hauptzollamt Saarlouis*:

> "The rules of Chapter 2, 'Tax Provisions,' have as their purpose the prevention of the distortion of competition arising from differences amongst taxes in the Member States. From this point of view, they have the same purpose as the provisions relating to customs duties between Member States. The system applied is as follows: in trade between Member States, the imported product is exempted from taxes in the country of origin and on the other hand is liable to the taxes in force in the 'country of delivery,'[60] subject to the reservation that Article 95 prohibits the heavier taxation of that product than of similar domestic products."[61]

The rule prohibiting discriminatory internal taxation on imported goods constitutes an essential basic principle of the common market,[62] and has produced direct effects in the Member States from January 1, 1962.[63]

Member States free to choose system of internal taxation, providing its advantages are extended to imported products

Article 95, first paragraph, prohibits discrimination against imported products, with respect to the rate of taxation, basis of assessment,[64] or detailed rules.[65]

Article 95 leaves each Member State free to establish the system of taxation which it considers the most suitable in relation to each product, provided that the system is treated as a point of reference for determining whether the tax applied to a similar product of another Member State complies with the requirements of the first paragraph of that article.[66] It mat-

---

[59] Cases 2 & 3/62 *Commission* v. *Belgium and Luxembourg* [1962] E.C.R. 425 at p. 431.
[60] The expression "country of destination" is more usual.
[61] Case 57/65 [1966] E.C.R. 205, at p. 214.
[62] Case 57/65 *Lutticke*, note 61.
[63] Case 57/65 note 61; Case 28/67 *Mokerei-Zentrale* v. *Hauptzollampt Paderborn* [1968] E.C.R. 143; Case 45/75 *Rewe-Zentrale etc.* v. *Hauptzollampt Landau/Pfalz* [1976] E.C.R. 181; Case 74/76 *Iannelli & Voloi* v. *Paolo Meroni* [1977] E.C.R. 557.
[64] Case 54/72 *F.O.R.* v. *V.K.S.* [1973] E.C.R. 193; Case 20/76 *Schottle & Sohne* v. *Finanzamt Freudenstadt* [1977] E.C.R. 247; Case 74/76 *Iannelli & Volpi* v. *Paolo Meroni* [1977] E.C.R. 557.
[65] Case 169/78 *Commission* v. *Italy* [1980] E.C.R. 385; Case 55/79 *Commission* v. *Ireland* [1980] E.C.R. 385.
[66] Case 127/75 *Bobie-Getrankevertrieb* v. *Hauptzollampt Aachen-Nord* [1976] E.C.R. 1079.

ters not that tax concessions for domestic products rest, not directly upon national law, but on administrative instructions to the authorities.[67]

In the *Hansen* case[68] the question arose whether an importer of spirits into Germany was entitled to take advantage of tax relief available, *inter alia*, in respect of spirits made from fruit by small businesses and collective farms. The Court acknowledged that tax advantages of this kind could serve legitimate ecomomic or social purposes, such as the use of certain raw materials, the continued production of particular spirits of high quality, or the continuance of certain classes of undertakings such as agricultural distilleries. However, Article 95 required that such preferential systems must be extended without discrimination to spirits coming from other Member States.[69]

The above principle was applied to the Republic of Italy when that country charged lower taxes on regenerated oil than on ordinary oil, on ecological grounds, while refusing to extend this advantage to imported regenerated oil. Italy argued that it was impossible to distinguish whether oil was of primary distillation, or regenerated. The Court of Justice[70] refused to accept this argument as a justification. It was for importers to establish that their oil qualified for the relief in question, while the Italian authorities were to set standards of proof no higher than was necessary to prevent tax evasion. The Court of Justice observed that certificates from the authorities of exporting Member States could provide one means of identifying oil which had been regenerated.

The Court seemed to retreat from the strict requirements established in the *Hansen* case[71] in the *Schneider Import case*.[72] The plaintiff had imported cognac into Germany, and paid duty therein. The importer claimed the benefit of certain tax advantages accruing to small businesses, *e.g.* he pointed out that production limits could be carried over under the German tax rules, and that fruit growers' quotas could be aggregated, permitting an increase in the established limits for small businesses. The Court noted that the tax advantages in the national proceedings were closely linked to the methods of taxation and fiscal supervision under German law, and that it was accordingly difficult to apply them to spirits produced in accordance with different legislative arrangements. The Court nevertheless held that Article 95 could be complied with where the taxation applied to imports was equivalent in practical effect to that applied to domestic products. In a case such as that in issue none of the advantages brought about a "considerable" reduction in the level of taxation in respect of domestic products as compared to imports.

The above case must be treated with caution. When an importer of light rum into Germany claimed the advantages extended to small scale farmer cooperatives under German law, a German court, influenced by the

[67] Case 17/81 *Pabst & Richarz* [1982] E.C.R. 1331.
[68] Case 148/77 *H. Hansen* v. *Hauptzollampt Flensburg* [1978] E.C.R. 1787.
[69] *Ibid.*
[70] Case 21/79 *Commission* v. *Italy* [1980] E.C.R. 1. See also Case 140/79 *Chemial* v. *DAF* [1981] E.C.R. 1; Case 46/80 *Vinal* v. *Orbat* [1981] E.C.R. 77.
[71] Case 148/77 [1978] E.C.R. 1787.
[72] Case 26/80 *Schneider-Import* v. *Hauptzollamt Mainz* [1980] E.C.R. 3469.

Schneider-Import case, asked the Court of Justice whether all or only some of the conditions for tax concessions under German law must be satisfied by German importers, before they could claim such concessions. The Court of Justice held[73] that all such conditions must be satisfied before the concessions could be claimed, as long as the conditions were applicable without discrimination to imported and domestic products alike. In a later case the Court held that "even a tax relief the discriminatory effect of which is slight falls within the prohibition in Article 95."[74]

While it is open to Member States to differentiate between like products on objective grounds consistent with the Treaty, they are not permitted to discriminate by conditioning tax concessions on requirements which can only be, or in fact only are, satisfied by national products. Examples of such discrimination would be charging lower tax rates on those products which could be inspected on national territory at the manufacturing stage,[75] and charging lower rates on products without a designation of origin or provenance where no such protection was available for domestic products and the higher rate applied in practice only to imports.[76]

It would seem that the decision of the three-Judge Chamber in *Schneider-Import*[77] must either be regarded as being somewhat anomalous, since it contemplates tax concessions, albeit minor ones, being enjoyed exclusively by national producers, or as a rare example of the principle "de minimis non curat lex."[78]

National taxes applicable in practice only to imports

The principle that Article 95 allows each Member State to establish the system of taxation which it considers the most suitable in relation to each product, provided that the system is treated as the point of reference for determining whether the same tax is applied to a similar product of another Member State, may be subject to qualification in another important respect. In *Commission* v. *Italy (Wool Imports)*[79] the Italian Republic had imposed turnover tax on imported skin wool (*i.e.* wool obtained from stripping raw pelts) at a rate corresponding to that payable by domestic enterprises when the stripping firm sold domestic skin wool to other processing enterprises. But in fact, such sales were rare because of the widespread integration of the Italian wool processing industry. The Commission argued that discrimination could not be ruled out, despite the fact that imports and domestic goods were taxed at the same rate and the same tax base was used. Although judgment was not given by the Court on the merits (as a result of the Commission's failure to comply strictly with the Article 169 procedure), Advocate General Roemer considered the questions and concluded that "if an examination of a national tax system shows

---

[73] Case 38/82 *Hauptzollamt Flensburg* v. *Hansen Gmbh & Co.* [1983] 1271.
[74] Case 277/83 *Commission* v. *Italy*, Judgment of July 3, 1985, at para. 17.
[75] Case 142 & 143/80 *Italian Finance Administration* v. *Essevi Sp.A* [1981] E.C.R. 1413.
[76] Case 319/81 *Commission* v. *Italy* [1983] E.C.R. 601.
[77] Note 70.
[78] The Court acknowledged the application of the *de minimis* principle in the application of Article 95(2) EEC in Case 27/67 *Fink-Frucht* v. *Hauptzollamt Munchen-Landbergstrasse* [1968] E.C.R. 223.
[79] Case 7/69 [1970] E.C.R. 111.

that, taking into account the legal structure of the economic sector to which it applies, a particular rate is practically never applied, this fiscal charge is in fact non-existent for the national sector."[80] He reasoned that it would be more logical for the normal national situation to be determinative for a comparison of taxes under Article 95, resulting in the imported goods in the case at hand being tax-exempt.[81] Advocate General Roemer repeated his reasoning in the later case of *F.O.R.* v. *V.K.S.*,[82] but once again, the Court did not address itself to the point.

In *Humblot*[83] the question arose squarely for decision. France imposed two types of annual tax on motor vehicles: a differential tax on cars with a fiscal rating equal to or less than 16 CV and a special tax imposed on private cars more powerful than 16 CV. The special tax was set at a single fixed rate, considerably higher than the highest point of the differential tax. No cars more powerful than 16 CV were manufactured in France. The Court of Justice held that a system of internal taxation was only consistent with Article 95 in so far as it was free from any discriminatory or protective effect. The system in question did not fulfil that condition. Although it did not establish a formal distinction based on the origin of cars, such a system obviously had discriminatory or protective effects. The threshhold which determined the applicability of the special tax had been fixed at such a level that only imported cars, and in particular those imported from other Member States, were subject to that tax, while all cars made in France were subject to the considerably less burdensome differential tax.

Article 95(1)—taxation in excess of that imposed "indirectly" on domestic products

It will be recalled that Article 95 first paragraph, prohibits internal taxation of any kind in excess of that imposed directly or indirectly on similar domestic products. In *Molkerei-Zentrale* v. *Hauptzollamt Paderborn*[84] the Court was asked for a definition of the "indirect" taxation in question. Advocate General Gand suggested that the charges in question must include all those imposed on raw materials and component goods and services. The Court agreed that the words "directly or indirectly" were to be construed broadly, and defined them as embracing all taxation which was actually and specifically imposed on the domestic product at earlier stages of the manufacturing and marketing process. This formulation might suggest that taxes on components, not being actually and specifically imposed on the product, might be excluded. This is not the case. As the Court's interpretation of the words "directly or indirectly" in Article 96 indicated,[85] "indirect" taxation indeed includes charges levied on raw materials and semi-finished products incorporated in the goods in question.

---

[80] [1970] E.C.R. 111, at p. 121.
[81] Adv. Gen. Roemer regarded the Court's reasoning in Case 10/61 *Commission* v. *Italy* [1962] E.C.R. 1, on the duty *applied* when the Treaty entered into force, as providing an appropriate parallel, see *supra*, p. 102.
[82] Case 54/72 [1973] E.C.R. 193.
[83] Case 112/84 [1986] 2 C.M.L.R. 338.
[84] Case 28/67 note 63.
[85] Case 45/64 *Commission* v. *Italy* [1965] E.C.R. 857.

Nevertheless, the Court entered a caveat in *Molkerei-Zentrale*: the effect of these charges diminished with the incidence of stages of production and distribution and tended rapidly to become negligible, and that fact ought to be taken into account by Member States when calculating the indirect charges applied to domestic products.

Although the taxation of undertakings manufacturing products will not in general be regarded as constituting taxation of the products themselves, the taxation of specific activities of an undertaking which has an "immediate effect" on the cost of the national imported product must by virtue of Article 95 be applied in a manner which is not discriminatory to imported products. Thus taxation imposed indirectly upon products within the meaning of Article 95 must be interpreted as including charges imposed on the international transport of goods by road according to the distance covered on the national territory and the weight of the goods in question.[86]

The object of Article 95 is to abolish direct or indirect discrimination against imported products, but not to place them in a privileged tax position.[87] Internal taxation may therefore be imposed on imported products, even in the absence of a domestically produced counterpart, where the charge in question applies to whole classes of domestic or foreign products which are all in the same position no matter what their origin.[88] However, the Court has held that such a limited number of products as "groundnuts, groundnut products and Brazil nuts" cannot fall within the concept of such whole classes of products, a concept which implies a much larger number of products determined by general and objective criteria.[89]

Domestic products may not claim equality with imports

However, Article 95 does not prohibit the imposition on national products of internal taxation in excess of that on imported products.[90] It has been noted that Member States may differentiate for tax purposes between products, provided that discrimination against imports does not result. What if national law imposes a higher rate of tax on product X than on competing product Y, where product X is largely, but not entirely, imported? It seems that importers of product X may claim the protection of Article 95, while domestic producers may legitimately be taxed at the higher rate! Thus Danish revenue laws imposed a lower rate of tax on aquavit than on other spirits, which other spirits were mainly, but not entirely, imported. In proceedings instituted by the Commission under Article 169 EEC the Court held that these rules were contrary to Article 95,[91] and in later proceedings the Court emphasised that only importers

---

[86] Case 20/76 *Schottle & Sohne* v. *Finanzamt Freudenstadt* [1977] E.C.R. 247.
[87] Case 153/80 *Rumhaus Hansen* [1981] E.C.R. 1165; Case 253/83 *Kupferberg* [1985] E.C.R. 157.
[88] Case 78/76 *Steinike und Weinlig* v. *Federal Republic of Germany* [1977] E.C.R. 595; Case 27/67 *Fink-Frucht* v. *Hauptzollamt Munchen-Landsbergstrasse* [1968] E.C.R. 223; Case 90/79 *Commission* v. *France* [1981] E.C.R. 283.
[89] Case 158/82 *Commission* v. *Denmark* [1983] E.C.R. 3573.
[90] Case 86/78 *Grandes Distilleries Peureux* v. *Directeur des Services Fisceaux* [1979] E.C.R. 89.
[91] Case 171/78 *Commission* v. *Denmark* [1980] E.C.R. 447. And see Case 168/78 *Commission* v. *France* [1980] E.C.R. 347.

could rely on Aritlce 95, and not domestic producers of those spirits subject to the "discriminatory" tax.[92]

In *Commission* v. *United Kingdom*[93] the Commission, arguing (successfully in the event) that United Kingdom law imposed a discriminatory tax on wine as compared to beer, nevertheless conceded that if a State produced both wine and beer, and taxed the former more heavily, the tax on imported wine would be judged, not by reference to domestic beer, but domestic wine. This was not the case in the United Kingdom, whose domestic production of wine was negligible. But if this approach is correct, it may prove difficult to decide when domestic production of a highly taxed product X which is largely but not entirely imported and in competition with a less highly taxed domestic product Y, becomes sufficiently substantial to establish the tax rate on product X (rather than that on product Y) as the appropriate comparator for the purposes of Article 95. The Court has acknowledged that an internal tax system cannot be said to favour domestic fruit liqueur wine over imported whisky, bearing a higher rate of tax, where all spirits, and the majority of those domestically produced bear the higher rate of tax. Such a system will be consistent with Article 95 where a significant proportion of domestic production of alcoholic beverages falls within each of the relevant tax categories.[94]

Scope of Article 95(1) and (2)

Whereas Article 95, first paragraph, prohibits internal taxation in excess of that imposed on similar domestic products, paragraph 2 adds that Member States shall furthermore impose no taxation of such a kind as to afford indirect protection to other products.

The respective scope of these two paragraphs is as follows. Under Article 95(1) it is necessary to consider as similar products those which have similar characteristics and which meet the same needs from the point of view of consumers. The appropriate criterion is not the strictly identical nature of the products but their similar and comparable use.[95] The Court at one stage held that "similarity" within Article 95(1) existed when the products were normally, for tax, tariff or statistical purposes, placed in the same classification.[96] In a later case the Court confirmed that classification under the same heading in the Common Customs Tariff was an important consideration in assessing similarity under Article 95.[97] But the Court has stressed that the fact that rum and whisky are given separate subdivisions under the CCT is not conclusive on the question of "similarity" under Article 95(1),[98] and when asked by an Italian court whether it should apply the "tariff classification" test, or the broader economic approach referred to above, the Court reiterated the latter criterion, without adverting to the

[92] Case 68/79 [1980] E.C.R. 501.
[93] Case 170/78 [1983] E.C.R. 417.
[94] Case 243/83 *John Walker*, Judgment of March 4, 1986.
[95] Case 169/78 *Commission* v. *Italy* [1980] E.C.R. 385.
[96] Case 27/67 *Fink-Frucht* v. *Hauptzollamt Munchen-Landsbergstrasse* [1968] E.C.R. 223. Case 28/69 *Commission* v. *Italy* [1979] E.C.R. 187.
[97] Case 45/75 *Rewe-Zentrale etc.* v. *Hauptzollamt Landau/Pfalz* [1976] E.C.R. 181.
[98] Case 169/78 *Commission* v. *Italy* [1980] E.C.R. 385; Case 168/78 *Commission* v. *France* [1980] E.C.R. 347; Case 106/84 *Commission* v. *Denmark*, Judgment of March 4, 1986.

former.[99] Nevertheless, it would seem that CCT classification constitutes at least evidence one way or the other of "similarity" within the meaning of Article 95(1).

In *John Walker*,[1] the Court held that in order to determine whether the products in question (fruit liqueur wines and whisky) were "similar" within the meaning of Article 95(1), it was first necessary to consider objective characteristics of the respective products, such as their origin, method of manufacture, and their organoleptic qualities, in particular taste and alcohol content, and secondly necessary to consider whether both categories of beverages were capable of meeting the same needs from the point of view of consumers. Applying the first test, it was not sufficient that the same raw material, alcohol, was to be found in both products. For the products to be regarded as similar that raw material would have to be present in more or less equal proportions in both products. Since whisky contained twice the alcoholic content of fruit liqueur wines, the products could not be regarded as "similar" within the meaning of Article 95(1).

Article 95(2) covers all forms of indirect tax protection in the case of products which, without being similar within the meaning of Article 95(1), are nevertheless in competition, even partial, indirect or potential, with products of the importing country. It is sufficient for the imported product to be in competition with the protected domestic product by reason of one or several economic uses to which it may be put, even though the conditions of similarity for the purposes of Article 95(1) are not fulfilled.[2]

To illustrate the inter-relation between Article 95(1) and (2), reference may be made to the great range of spirit drinks; aquavit, geneva, grappa, whisky, etc. While these drinks have common generic factors (distillation, high alcohol level), there are different types of spirits, characterised by the raw material used, their flavour, and processes of manufacture.[3] Furthermore, spirits may be consumed in different forms: neat, diluted, or in mixtures.[4] They may also be consumed on different occasions, as aperitifs or digestifs, at meal times, or on other occasions.[5] The Court of Justice has held that among spirit drinks there exists an indeterminate number which can be regarded as similar products within the meaning of Article 95(1), and that where it is impossible to identify a sufficient degree of similarity between the products concerned for the purposes of Article 95(1), there exist nevertheless characteristics common to all spirits which are sufficiently marked for it to be said that they are all at least partly, indirectly or potentially in competition for the purposes of Article 95(2).[6] The result is that in a case involving alleged discrimination between domestic spirits and imported spirits, it is not necessary to distinguish between the application of Article 95(1) and that of Article 95(2), since it cannot reasonably

---

[99] Case 216/81 *Cogis SpA* v. *Italian Finance Ministry* [1982] E.C.R. 2701.
[1] Case 243/83 *John Walker*, Judgment of March 4, 1986.
[2] Case 169/78 note 98.
[3] See Case 168/78 note 98; Case 169/78 note 98; and Case 171/78 *Commission* v. *Denmark* [1980] E.C.R. 447.
[4] Case 169/78 note 98.
[5] Case 168/78 note 98.
[6] Case 319/81 *Commission* v. *Italy* [1983] E.C.R. 601; referring to Case 168/78 note 98; Case 169/78 note 98; Case 171/78, note 3.

be denied that the products are in at least partial, indirect or potential competition.[7]

The fact that Article 95(2) embraces potential as well as actual competition significantly widens its ambit. In *Commission* v. *United Kingdom*,[8] the United Kingdom argued that wine and beer could not be considered to be competing beverages, since beer was a popular drink consumed generally in public houses, while wine was generally consumed on special occasions. The Court of Justice stressed that it was necessary to examine not only the present state of the market in the United Kingdom but also possible developments in the free movement of goods within the Community and the further potential for the substitution of products for one another which might result from an intensification of trade. Consumer habits varied in time and space, and the tax policy of a Member State must not crystallise given consumer habits so as to consolidate an advantage acquired by the national industries concerned. The Court held that to a certain extent at least wine and beer were capable of meeting identical needs and that there was a degree of substitution one for another.

While Article 95(1) prohibits a higher tax on imported products than similar domestic products, Article 95(2), because of the difficulty of making a sufficiently precise comparison between the products in question, employs a more general criterion, *i.e.* the indirect protection afforded by a domestic tax system. Protective effect need not, however, be shown statistically. It is sufficient for the purposes of Article 95(2) for it to be shown that a given system of taxation is likely, in view of its inherent characteristics, to bring about the protective effect referred to by the Treaty.[9] Furthermore, statistics showing import penetration by products allegedly discriminated against cannot rebut the inference of protective effect to be drawn from the inherent characteristics of a national tax system.[10] However, statistics are admissible to show that a tax system which is apparently neutral in fact burdens imports to a greater extent than domestic products.[11]

The Court in one case, noting that Article 95(2) lacked the precise reference point for comparisons between domestic and imported goods contained in Article 95(1), accepted that it was open to national courts to accept a *de minimis* argument in cases where a charge ceases to have the protective effects prohibited by the Treaty.[12] And it must be admitted that in the case of some products found to have a competitive relationship it may be extremely difficult to establish the tax ratio. A striking illustration is afforded by the Court's decision in *Commission* v. *United Kingdom*,[13] in which the Court attempted to establish the degree of indirect protection afforded beer by the excessive taxation of wine. On the basis of tax per unit of volume, wine bore an overall tax burden equal to 400 per cent. that on

---

[7] Case 168/78 note 98.
[8] Case 170/78 [1980] E.C.R. 417, [1983] E.C.R. 2265.
[9] Case 170/78 *Commission* v. *U.K.* [1980] E.C.R. 417.
[10] Case 168/78 note 98; Case 319/81 note 6.
[11] Case 319/81 note 6.
[12] Case 27/67 *Fink-Frucht* [1968] E.C.R. 223.
[13] Case 170/78 note 8.

beer. On the basis of alcoholic strength per unit of volume, wine was subject to a tax burden 100 per cent. in excess of that on beer. On the basis of tax as a proportion of the net price of the beverage free of tax, the court admitted that the evidence was difficult to assess, suggesting additional tax burdens of between 58 per cent. and 286 per cent.! The Court concluded that whichever criterion for comparison was used, the tax system offered indirect protection to national production, and that there was no need to express a preference for one or other of the criteria discussed! Though Article 95(2) was long ago held to be directly effective,[14] in such a case one might well sympathise with an importer challenging a national tax claim who seeks to quantify the amount by which his national tax demand offends Article 95(2) EEC!

Only true fiscal charges subject to Article 95

It must be emphasised that while Article 95 permits the imposition of internal taxation on imports to the extent that domestic goods bear similar charges, it cannot justify any charges imposed with a view to assimilating the *prices* of imports to those of domestic goods. The point arose in *Commission* v. *Luxembourg and Belgium*,[15] a proceeding under Article 169 in which the Commission alleged infringement of Articles 9 and 12 in respect of charges levied on the issue of import licences for gingerbread. The defendants argued that the charges compensated for the effect of measures of price support for domestically produced rye, and were accordingly justified under Article 95. The purpose of the disputed charge, said the Court, was not to equalise charges which would otherwise unevenly burden domestic and imported products, but to equalise the very *prices* of such products.[16] A similar point arose in *Hauptzollamt Flensburg* v. *Hermann C. Andresen & Co. KG.*[17] A charge was imposed on spirits imported into Germany, being a charge also applicable to domestic spirits, and calculated to defray (in the case of domestic spirits) the administrative and operating costs of the Federal Spirits Monopoly. The Court held that a charge such as this was not a true fiscal charge, and that Article 95 only permitted the imposition on imports of such elements of the price of domestic spirits which the monopoly was required by law to remit to the State Treasury.

Prohibition of customs duties and charges having equivalent effect and prohibition of discriminatory internal taxation mutually exclusive

The prohibitions of Articles 12 and 13 on the one hand, and Article 95 on the other, have often been contrasted by the Court. The former applies to all charges exacted at the time of or by reason of importation which are imposed specifically on an imported product to the exclusion of the similar domestic product; the latter embraces financial charges levied within a general system of internal taxation applying systematically to domestic and

[14] Case 27/67 note 12.
[15] Cases 2 & 3/62 [1965] E.C.R. 425.
[16] See also Case 45/75 *Rewe-Zentrale* [1976] E.C.R. 181.
[17] Case 4/81 [1981] E.C.R. 2835.

imported goods.[18] The application of these respective prohibitions has been held to be mutually exclusive, not only because one and the same charge could not have been both removed during the transitional period (Articles 13 and 14), and by no later than the beginning of the second stage (Article 95),[19] but also because customs duties and charges having equivalent effect are required to be simply abolished, while Article 95 provides solely for the elimination of any form of discrimination between domestic products and products originating in other Member States.[20] The Court has explicitly rejected the argument that an equalisation tax on an imported product which exceeds the charges applied to similar domestic products takes on the character of a "charge having equivalent effect" as to the difference.[21] Again, since the respective fields of application of the Treaty's prohibition on obstacles to the free movement of goods are to be distinguished, obstacles which are of a fiscal nature or have equivalent effect and are covered by Articles 9 to 16 or 95 of the Treaty cannot fall within the prohibition of Article 30, on quantitative restrictions and measures having equivalent effect.[22]

Charges on imports falling within Article 95, rather than Articles 12 and 13, are all those which are imposed in the same way within the State on similar or comparable products, or, where there are no comparable products, charges that in any event come within the framework of a general internal charge or are intended to offset such charges.[23] But charges must be levied at the same marketing stage on both domestic goods and imports to fall within the ambit of Article 95,[24] and if there is an insufficiently close connexion between the charges levied on domestic goods, and those levied on imports, in that they are determined on the basis of different criteria, they will fall to be classified under Article 12 EEC, rather than Article 95.[25]

The Court held in *Wohrmann* v. *Hauptzollamt Bad Reichenhall*,[26] that, *in the absence of any protective purpose*, an internal tax could not be regarded as a charge having equivalent effect to a customs duty. This seems at first sight surprising, since the Court has often emphasised that a charge may have an effect equivalent to a customs duty under Articles 12 and 13 independently of either its purpose or the destination of its revenue.[27] The significance of protective purpose in this context is that a charge applicable equally to domestic and imported products—and therefore ostensibly

---

[18] Case 77/82 *Capolongo* v. *Azienda Agricola Maya* [1973] E.C.R. 611.

[19] Case 10/65 *Deutschmann* v. *Federal Republic of Germany* [1965] E.C.R. 469. And see Case 57/65 *Lutticke* v. *Hauptzollamt Saarlouis* [1966] E.C.R. 205; Case 27/74 *Demaq* v. *Finanzamt Duisburg-Sud* [1974] E.C.R. 1037.

[20] Case 94/74 *IGAV* v. *ENCC* [1975] E.C.R. 699.

[21] Case 25/67 *Milch- Fett- und Eierkontor* v. *Hauptzollamt Saarbrucken* [1968] E.C.R. 207; Case 32/80 *Officier van Justitie* v. *Kortmann* [1981] E.C.R. 251.

[22] Case 74/76 *Iannelli & Volpi* v. *Paolo Meroni* [1977] E.C.R. 557 at para. 9.

[23] Cases 2 & 3/69 *Chougol Diamond Co.* [1969] E.C.R. 211.

[24] Case 132/78 *Denkavit Loire Sarl* v. *France* [1979] E.C.R. 1923. But VAT levied on imports does not amount to a charge having equivalent effect, Case 249/84 *Prefant* [1986] 2 C.M.L.R. 378.

[25] Case 132/80 *United Foods* [1981] E.C.R. 995.

[26] Case 7/67 [1968] E.C.R. 177.

[27] *e.g.* Case 63/74 *Cadskey* [1975] E.C.R. 281; Cases 2 & 3 *Chougol Diamond Co.* [1969] E.C.R. 211.

"internal taxation" under Article 95—may nevertheless fall to be classified as a charge having equivalent effect, if the revenue from the charge is devoted exclusively to benefit domestic producers. In *Interzuccheri* v. *Ditta Rezzano e Cassava*,[28] the Court considered a charge imposed on sales of sugar, whether home produced or imported, the proceeds of which were used for the exclusive benefit of national sugar refineries and sugar beet producers. The Court held that such a charge, on the face of it internal taxation, could only be considered a charge having equivalent effect if:

— it had the sole purpose of financing activities for the specific advantage of the taxed domestic product;
— the taxed product and the domestic product benefiting from it were the same;
— the charges imposed on the domestic product were made good in full.

Since the charge in issue in the national proceedings financed sugar beet producers, as well as sugar refiners, it would not seem to constitute a charge having equivalent effect, according to the Court's stringent criterion.

In the later case of *Commission* v. *Italy*,[29] the Commission challenged the same Italian charge in contentious proceedings, arguing that if the charge were *entirely* offset by reimbursements in the form of aid, it amounted to a charge having an equivalent effect to a customs duty, while if it were only partly offset, it infringed Article 95. Somewhat puzzlingly, the Court held that Italy had violated Article 95, and that internal taxation would be regarded as indirectly discriminatory within the meaning of that Article if its proceeds were used *exclusively* or principally to finance aids for the sole benefit of domestic products. Yet in the later case of *Officier van Justitie* v. *Kortmann*,[30] the Court confirmed the *Interzuccheri* proposition that an internal tax amounted to a charge having equivalent effect to a customs duty when in fact it was imposed solely on imported products to the exclusion of domestic products. The explanation for the apparent inconsistency seems to be that *Commission* v. *Italy*[31] concerned a charge on one product (imported sugar) which was used to benefit sugar beet as well as sugar. Indeed, this was why it is clear from the Court's ruling in *Interzuccheri*[32] that the charge in question could not be regarded as a charge having equivalent effect. Thus the ruling in *Commission* v. *Italy* that an equal charge imposed on both imported and domestic products may amount to discriminatory internal taxation if used *exclusively* to finance aids for the sole benefit of domestic products (which appears to be categorising as discriminatory internal taxation that which is a charge having equivalent effect to a customs duty) would seem to be confined to cases where the domestic products benefited are not identical to the imported products subject to the charge. The proposition is of course unexception-

---

[28] Case 195/76 [1977] E.C.R. 1029; Case 77/72 *Capolongo* [1973] E.C.R. 611; Case 94/74 *IGAV* [1975] E.C.R. 699; Case 77/76 *Fratelli Cucchi* [1977] E.C.R. 987; Case 222/78 *ICAP* v. *Walter Beneventi* [1979] E.C.R. 1163.
[29] Case 73/79 [1980] E.C.R. 1533.
[30] Case 32/80 [1981] E.C.R. 251.
[31] Case 73/79 note 29.
[32] Case 105/76 [1977] E.C.R. 1029.

able insofar as it refers to the proceeds of a charge used principally (or indeed at all) to benefit domestic products alone. Where the products are identical, and the *Interzuccheri*[33] criteria are satisfied, the ostensible internal tax is to be categorised as a charge having equivalent effect to a customs duty. It will be noted that these problems only arise if a Member State has resort to ear-marked taxes, as Italy pointed out to the Court during the proceedings in *Commission* v. *Italy*.[34]

Discriminatory tax treatment of exports

As indicated above,[35] the system adopted for taxing products in intra-Community trade is based on the "destination principle," *i.e.* goods exported from a Member State receive a rebate of internal taxation paid, and are in turn subjected to internal taxation in the country of destination. The purpose of Article 95 is to prevent this process being used to place a heavier burden on imports than on domestic goods, but the system is vulnerable to another, equally damaging abuse: the repayment to exporters of an amount exceeding the internal taxation in fact paid, which would amount to an export subsidy for domestic production. It is to counteract this possibility that Article 96 provides that where products are exported to the territory of any Member State, any repayment of internal taxation shall not exceed the internal taxation imposed on them, whether directly or indirectly.

The Court laid down decisive guidelines as to the extent of repayments permissible under this Article in *Commission* v. *Italy*,[36] a case arising from proceedings under Article 169 alleging excessive repayment of taxes levied on certain engineering products. The Commission claimed that the repayment of duties paid on licenses, concessions, motor vehicles and advertising, in connection with the production and marketing of the products in question, were ineligible for repayment under Article 96. The court ruled that the words "directly or indirectly" referred to the distinction between taxes which had been levied on the products themselves (directly), and taxes levied on the raw materials and semi-finished goods used in their manufacture (indirectly).[37] It followed that the charges referred to by the Commission could not be repaid consistently with Article 96, for the simple reason that they were not taxes imposed on the products at all, but "upon the producer undertaking in the very varied aspects of its general commercial and financial activity."[38]

But whereas Article 12 applies to customs duties and charges having equivalent effect on both imports and exports, Article 95, on its face, applies only to tax discrimination against imports. Nevertheless, in *Staten Kontrol* v. *Larsen*,[39] the Court held that the rule against discrimination

---

[33] Note 28.
[34] Note 29.
[35] See Adv. Gen. Gand in Case 57/65 *Lutticke, supra*, p. 107.
[36] Case 45/64 [1965] E.C.R. 857.
[37] On a similar wording in Art. 95(1), see Case 28/67 *supra*, p. 110 and note 61.
[38] [1965] E.C.R. 857, at p. 866.
[39] [1978] E.C.R. 1787.

underlying Article 95 also applied when the export, rather than import, of a product constituted, within the context of a system of internal taxation, the chargeable event giving rise to a fiscal charge. It would be incompatible with the system of tax provisions laid down in the Treaty to acknowledge that a Member State, in the absence of an express prohibition laid down in the Treaty, were free to apply in a discriminatory manner a system of internal taxation to products intended for export to another Member State. Article 95, it seems, prohibits internal taxation which either discriminates against imports or exports, as compared to domestic products.[40]

Furthermore, in *Hulst* v. *Produktschap voor Siergewassen*,[41] the Court held that an internal levy applying to domestic sales and exports could have an effect equivalent to a customs duty when either its application fell more heavily on export sales than on sales within the country, or when the levy was intended to finance activities likely to give preferential treatment to the product intended for marketing within the country, to the detriment of that intended for export.

The relationship between Articles 12 and 95, and other provisions of the Treaty

Where national measures are financed by a discriminatory internal tax, Article 95 is applicable to the latter, despite the fact that it forms part of a national aid, subject to scrutiny under Articles 92 and 93 EEC.[42] Equally, Article 12 and Articles 92 and 93, would seem to be cumulatively applicable in such circumstances.

Articles 9–16 and Article 95 do not however overlap with Article 30. The Court held in *Ianelli & Volpi* v. *Paolo Meroni*[43] that:

"However wide the field of application of Article 30 may be, it nevertheless does not include obstacles to trade covered by other provisions of the Treaty. Thus obstacles which are of a fiscal nature or have equivalent effect and are covered by Articles 9 to 16 and 95 of the Treaty do not fall within the prohibition of Article 30."

The relationship between Article 37 on state monopolies, and Article 95, was considered by the Court in *Grandes Distilleries Peureux*.[44] Whereas Article 37 was acknowledged to have provided an exception to certain rules of the Treaty—*in casu* Article 95—during the transitional period, this was declared to be no longer the case. Where internal taxation is concerned, Article 95 apparently constitutes a *lex specialis*, even it seems in the case of activities which would otherwise qualify for scrutiny under Article 37.

It will be recalled that in *Staten Kontrol* v. *Larsen*,[45] the Court held that, while a Member State was precluded under Article 95 from taxing exports

---

[40] *Cf.* Case 27/74 *Demag* [1974] E.C.R. 1037.
[41] Case 51/74 [1975] E.C.R. 79, [1975] 1 C.M.L.R. 236.
[42] Case 47/69 *France* v. *Commission* [1970] E.C.R. 487; Case 73/79 *Commission* v. *Italy* [1980] E.C.R. 1547; Case 17/81 *Pabst and Richarz* v. *Hauptzollamt Oldenburg* [1982] E.C.R. 1331; Case 277/83 *Commission* v. *Italy*, Judgment of July 3, 1985.
[43] Case 74/76 [1977] E.C.R. 557.
[44] Case 86/78 [1979] E.C.R. 897.
[45] Case 142/77 [1978] E.C.R. 1787. *supra*, p. 118.

more heavily than domestically traded goods, it was open to a Member State to tax exports in the same way as domestic goods, even if this led to taxes overlapping with those imposed in the country of destination: this latter problem would fall to be solved by harmonisation of national legislation under Articles 99 or 100 of the Treaty. However, in *Gaston Schul*,[46] the Court held that a member State was required by Article 95, when imposing value added tax on imports, to take into account value added tax paid but not refunded (and not refundable under the applicable VAT Directive) in the country of export. So far from the harmonisation of national tax provisions ousting Article 95, the Court held that the applicable VAT Directive must be construed in accordance with the terms of Article 95, which were mandatory and binding upon the Community institutions in the enactment of such legislation.

Common customs tariff and external relations

The preceding exposition has been concerned with the elimination of customs duties and other financial charges on trade between the Member States, but brief mention must be made of imports and exports between the Community and third countries.

In the case of the original six, Articles 18 to 29 of the Treaty provided for the establishment of a Common Customs Tariff during the transitional period. In accordance with the "acceleration" decisions referred to earlier,[47] the Common Customs Tariff, or CCT as it is usually called, was in fact established on July 1, 1968. The first Act of Accession[48] provided for the progressive adoption of the CCT by Denmark, Ireland and the United Kingdom by July 1, 1977. The second Act of Accession provided for the adoption of the CCT by Greece by January 1, 1986.[49] The third Act of Accession provided for the progressive adoption of the CCT by Spain and Portugal by January 1, 1993.[50]

Neither the relevant Articles of the Treaty, nor Regulation 950/68 on the Common Customs Tariff,[51] explicitly provide for the regulation of charges having an equivalent effect in trade relations between the Member States and third countries. Nevertheless, the Court held in *Sociaal Fonds voor de Dimantarbeiders* v. *Indiamex*[52] that the unilateral imposition of such charges after the adoption of the Common Customs Tariff was inconsistent with the aim of the Treaty that Member States adopt a common policy in their trade relations with the outside world.

But the Treaty itself has no provision analogous to Article 95 applying to imports from non member countries.[53] Agreements between the EEC and third countries, and the provisions of agricultural regulations, may prohibit customs duties, charges having equivalent effect, and discriminatory inter-

---

[46] Case 15/81 *Gaston Schul* (1982) E.C.R. 1409.
[47] *Supra*, p. 102.
[48] Art. 39.
[49] Art. 31.
[50] Arts. 37 and 197.
[51] O.J.Sp.Ed. 1968 (1), p. 275.
[52] Cases 37 & 38/73 [1973] E.C.R. 1609.
[53] Case 148/77 *Hansen* [1978] E.C.R. 1787.

nal taxation, on trade between the EEC and third countries. It cannot be assumed without more that such provisions as these are to be construed as strictly as analogous provisions governing intra Community trade. Even where a provision of a regulation prohibits charges having equivalent effect on trade with third countries, and the Court takes the view that the concept is the same as that embodied in Article 9 *et seq.* of the EEC Treaty, the requirement may be subject to derogation authorised by the Community institutions in a way that would not be possible were intra-Community trade involved.[54] And where health inspections are permitted by Community regulations on imports from third countries, the inspections may be more strict, and the fees charged higher, than in intra-Community trade, since Community law does not require Member States to show the same degree of confidence towards non member countries as they are required to show other Member States.[55]

Where a treaty prohibits discriminatory internal taxation on imports from third countries, it will be a matter of interpretation whether or not the provision in question is intended to fulfil the same purpose in relations between the EEC and third countries as Article 95 fulfils in respect of intra-Community trade. Thus a three-Judge Chamber held in *Pabst & Richarz* v. *HZ Oldenburg*[56] that Article 53 of the Association Agreement between the EEC and Greece fulfilled, within the framework of the Association between the Community and Greece, the same function as that of Article 95. A full Court in *HZ Mainz* v. *Kupferberg*[57] however, considering Article 21 of the EEC-Portugal free trade agreement, also prohibiting discriminatory internal taxation, observed that although Article 21 of the Agreement and Article 95 of the EEC Treaty had the same object, they were nevertheless worded differently, and must be considered and interpreted in their own context. The Court concluded that interpretation given to Article 95 of the Treaty could not be applied by way of simple analogy to the agreement on free trade.

Since the Court has held that Conventions concluded by the Council pursuant to Article 228 and 238 (conclusion of agreements with third countries) constitute an integral part of Community law,[58] and that appropriately worded provisions of such agreements are capable of giving rise to rights in individuals which national courts are bound to safeguard,[59] it is clear that the principles discussed above have a significance extending far beyond the confines of intra-Community trade.

Customs duties on trade with third countries are established by the Common Customs Tariff,[60] which the Court has held must be interpreted in such a way as to give effect to a single trading system with third countries, and not in such a way that products are treated differently according to the

---

[54] Case 70/77 *Simmenthal* [1978] E.C.R. 1543.
[55] Case 30/79 *Land Berlin* v. *Wigei* [1980] E.C.R. 151.
[56] Case 17/71 [1982] E.C.R. 1331.
[57] Case 104/81 [1982] E.C.R. 3641.
[58] Case 181/73 *Haegeman* v. *Belgian State* [1974] E.C.R. 449.
[59] Case 87/75 *Bresciani* [1976] E.C.R. 129; Case 17/81 *Pabst & Richarz* [1982] E.C.R. 1331; Case 104/78 *Kupferberg* [1982] E.C.R. 3641.
[60] Note 48.

country by which they enter the Community.[61] But customs duties are only chargeable under the CCT upon goods capable of being lawfully traded within the Community, and not, for example, upon smuggled narcotic drugs.[62]

[61] Case 135/79 *Gedelfi* [1980] E.C.R. 1713.
[62] Case 50/80 *Horvath* [1981] E.C.R. 385; Case 221/81 *Wolf* [1982] E.C.R. 3681; Case 240/81 *Einberger* [1982] E.C.R. 3699.

CHAPTER 6

QUANTITATIVE RESTRICTIONS AND MEASURES HAVING EQUIVALENT EFFECT

Introduction

A quantitative restriction, or a quota, is a measure restricting the import of a given product by amount or by value. In order to obviate the risk of importers ordering goods, only to have them excluded at the frontier because the quota has been filled, a licensing system may be adopted, whereby a government agency formally authorises particular importers to import stated quantities, or money's worth, of goods.[1] Since quotas are capable of disturbing the flow of international trade to a greater extent than tariffs,[2] and indeed found favour during the 1930s as a means of restricting imports without infringing international agreements prohibiting the introduction of customs duties,[3] it is hardly surprising that the authors of the Spaak Report considered their elimination as a "fundamental element" in the creation of a common market.[4] Accordingly, the Treaty provided for the abolition of quantitative restrictions and measures having equivalent effect on imports and exports,[5] in the former case by the end of the transitional period,[6] and in the case of exports by the end of the first stage.[7] "Standstill"[8] provisions prevented Member States from introducing new quantitative restrictions or measures having equivalent effect,[9] or making more restrictive those measures already in existence when the Treaty entered into force,[10] As in the case of customs duties,[11] the Member States were able to achieve liberalisation in advance of the date specified in the Treaty, and the Council's Decision of May 12, 1960—the first "acceleration" decision referred to previously in the context of customs duties[12]—provided for the elimination of all quantitative restrictions on imports of

---

[1] Jackson, *World Trade and the Law of GATT* (1969), p. 305.
[2] The volume of imports cannot expand to meet increased demand, nor can the improvement of efficiency of manufacturers in exporting countries secure their access to the protected markets, Wilcox, *A Charter for World Trade* (1949), pp. 81 *et seq.*; K. Dam. *The GATT* (1970), p. 148; Jackson, *op. cit.* pp. 309–310.
[3] Jackson, *op. cit.* p. 306.
[4] *Rapport des Chefs de Délégation aux Ministres des Affaires etrangères* (1956), p. 35.
[5] The Spaak Report points out that one result of the removal of restrictions on imports would be increased interdependence of the Member States. This would require, as a necessary corollary, that importing countries be able to rely on continuity of supplies from exporting countries. *Rapport* p. 38.
[6] Arts. 30, 32, 33.
[7] Art. 34. For detailed treatment of Arts. 30–36, see Oliver, *Free Movement of Goods in the EEC*, 1982, with supplements; Gormley, *Prohibiting Restrictions on Trade within the EEC*, 1985.
[8] *Cf. supra*, p. 100.
[9] Art. 31.
[10] Art. 32. There is no explicit standstill for quantitative restrictions and measures having equivalent effect on *exports*, but Art. 34(1) prohibits such measures outright.
[11] *Supra*, p. 102.
[12] J.O. 1960, 1217, *supra*, p. 102.

industrial products of the Member States by December 31, 1961.[13] When the Community was first enlarged, Article 42 of the First Act of Accession provided for the immediate abolition of quantitative restrictions on imports and exports between the original six and the new Member States, subject to exceptions for two years in the case of exports of waste and scrap iron and steel.

Measures having an effect equivalent to quantitative restrictions were unaffected by the terms of the acceleration decision of May 12, 1960 and were accordingly required to be abolished by the end of the transitional period. Whereas Article 33 of the Treaty provided for the annual increase of quotas as a means of liberalising quantitative restrictions proper, in the case of measures having equivalent effect, the Article placed the responsibility for establishing an appropriate timetable on the Commission, empowering it to issue directives to this end.[14] In the enlarged Community, Article 42 of the Act of Accession provided for the elimination of measures having equivalent effect by January 1975 at the latest. When Greece became a Member of the Community quantitative restrictions and measures having equivalent effect were abolished from the date of accession between the Community and Greece, with certain exceptions expiring on December 31, 1985.[15] When Spain and Portugal became Members of the Community quantitative restrictions and measures having equivalent effect were abolished from the date of accession, subject to certain transitional provisions.[16]

The prohibition on quantitative restrictions and measures having equivalent effect is applicable without distinction to products originating in Member States and to those coming from non-member countries which are in free circulation.[17]

Quantitative Restrictions

The notion of a quantitative restriction is well understood, and definition poses little difficulty. As the Court explained in *Geddo* v. *Ente Nazionale Risi*, "The prohibition on quantitative restrictions covers measures which amount to a total or partial restraint of, according to the circumstances, imports, exports, or goods in transit."[18] Thus, when the Italian authorities suspended imports of pork into Italy from other Member States in June 1960, the Court ruled that such a measure amounted to an infringement of the "standstill" provision of Article 31, first paragraph, of the Treaty.[19] Again, a prohibition on the import of pornographic material amounts to a

[13] Art. 4, J.O. 1960, 1218.
[14] Art. 33(7). See Dir. 64/486, J.O. 1964, 2253 Dirs. 66/682 and 66/683, J.O. 1966, 3745, 3748; Dir. 70/32, J.O. 1970, L13/1; and Dir. 70/50, J.O. 1970, L13/29.
[15] Second Act of Accession, Arts. 35 to 39.
[16] Third Act of Accession, Arts. 42–44, Arts. 202–207.
[17] Case 41/76 *Donckerwolcke* [1976] E.C.R. 1921; Case 288/83 *Commission* v. *Ireland* [1985] 3 C.M.L.R. 152.
[18] Case 2/73 [1973] E.C.R. 865, at p. 879.
[19] Case 7/61 *Commission* v. *Italy* [1961] E.C.R. 317.

quantitative restriction contrary to Article 30, subject to possible justification under Article 36.[20]

Measures having equivalent effect to quantitative restrictions on imports—Directive 70/50

The concept of measures having equivalent effect to quantitative restrictions is rather more complex. Article 2(1) of Directive 70/50[21] prohibits measures, other than those applicable equally to domestic or imported products, which hinder imports which could otherwise take place, including those "which make importation more difficult or costly than the disposal of domestic production." This provision was relied upon by the Court in terms in *Ianelli & Volpi*[22]. In other cases the Court has relied upon the principle involved without reference to the Directive. Thus in *Commission v. Italy*[23] the Court held that an import deposit scheme was contrary to Article 30 because its effect was to render imports "more difficult or burdensome" than internal transactions, and thereby produced restrictive effects on the free movement of goods. With respect to imports, Article 2(2) of Directive 70/50 provides that measures having equivalent effect include those which "make imports or the disposal, at any marketing stage, of imported products subject to a condition—other than a formality—which is required in respect of imported products only, or a condition differing from that required from domestic products and more difficult to satisfy." This provision was cited with approval in *Rewe-Zentralfinanz v. Landwirtschaftskammer*,[24] in which the Court declared that health inspections of plant products at national frontiers constituted a measure having equivalent effect, where similar domestic products were not subject to a similar examination. Although the Article refers to measures other than formalities, the Court has held that national measures requiring import or export licences in intra-Community trade—even though such licences are granted automatically—infringe the prohibition of Articles 30 and 34(1).[25]

Article 2(3) lists examples of the national measures covered by the definitions contained in Articles 2(1) and 2(2). Thus Article 2(3)(g) refers to measures which make the access of imported products to the domestic market conditional upon having an agent or representative in the territory of the importing Member State. This provision was relied upon by the Com-

---

[20] Case 34/79 *Henn and Darby* [1979] E.C.R. 3795. For exemptions under Article 36, see *infra* at p. 138. United Kingdom restrictions on imports of main crop potatoes amounted to quantitative restrictions, see Case 118/78 *Meijer* [1979] E.C.R. 1387; Case 231/78 *Commission* v. *United Kingdom* [1979] E.C.R. 1447.
[21] O.J.Sp.Ed. 1970(I), p. 17. Technically applicable only to measures in force at the end of the transitional period, it provides valuable guidance on the meaning of measures having equivalent effect.
[22] Case 74/76 [1977] E.C.R. 557.
[23] Case 95/81 [1982] E.C.R. 2187.
[24] Case 4/75 [1975] E.C.R. 843.
[25] Cases 51–54/71 *International Fruit* [1971] E.C.R. 1107; Case 53/76 *Bouhelier* [1977] E.C.R. 197; Case 68/76 *Commission* v. *French Republic* [1977] E.C.R. 515; Case 124/81 *Commission* v. *United Kingdom* [1983] E.C.R. 203.

mission in an action against the Federal Republic of Germany.[26] German legislation provided that pharmaceutical products could be placed on the market only by a pharmaceutical undertaking having its headquarters in the area in which that legislation was applicable. The Court held—without reference to the Directive—that the legislation in question was likely to involve additional costs for undertakings which found no good reason for having a representative of their own established in Germany, and which sold directly to customers. The legislation was therefore likely to hinder trade within the Community and amounted to a measure having equivalent effect. Again, Article 2(3)(s) refers to national measures which "confine names which are not indicative of origin or source to domestic products only."[27] However, even names which are indicative of origin or source may only be confined to domestic products if the geographical area of origin of a product confers upon it a specific quality and characteristic of such a nature as to distinguish it from all other products.[28] It follows that making the application of a designation of quality which is neither an indication of origin or source conditional upon one or more stages of the production process taking place on national territory, amounts to a measure having equivalent effect.[29]

Article 3 of Directive 70/50 covers measures governing the marketing of products which deal in particular with the presentation or identification of products and which apply equally to domestic and imported products, where the restrictive effect of such measures on the free movement of goods exceed the effects intrinsic to trade rules. This is stated to be the case, in particular, where the restrictive effects on the free movement of goods are out of proportion to their purpose, or where the same objective can be attained by other means which are less of a hindrance to trade. This provision has been cited by the Court of Justice.[30] Although the tenth recital to the preamble of Directive 70/50 might suggest that Article 3, despite referring to measures which "are equally applicable" to domestic and imported products, only covers national measures which are indirectly *discriminatory*, since the recital refers to imports which are "either precluded or made more difficult or costly than the disposal of domestic production," the better view is probably that Article 3 also applies to national measures which are simply capable of restricting the volume of imports, by, *e.g.* affecting marketing opportunities for both domestic products and imports.[31]

---

[26] Case 247/81 *Commission* v. *Germany* [1984] E.C.R. 1111. See also Case 87/85 *Laboratoires de Pharmacie Legia*, Judgment of May 27, 1986. Art. 2(3) contains a list of examples and cannot be pleaded to defeat the purpose of Art. 30; Case 103/84 *Commission* v. *Italy*, Judgment of June 5, 1986.

[27] Case 12/74 *Commission* v. *Germany* [1975] E.C.R. 181; Case 13/78 *Eggers* [1978] E.C.R. 1935.

[28] Case 12/74 note 27; Case 13/78 note 27.

[29] Case 13/78 note 27.

[30] Case 75/81 *Blesgen* [1982] E.C.R. 1211. A decision which is probably correct in result yet unsupported by cogent reasoning.

[31] This view is supported by the reasoning in Case 286/81 *Oosthoek* [1982] E.C.R. 4575, at para. 15; and Cases 60 and 61/84 *Cinétheque* [1986] 1 C.M.L.R. 365.

Measures having equivalent effect to quantitative restrictions—jurisprudence of the Court

General scope of the prohibition on measures having equivalent effect

The Court has adopted a broad definition of measures having equivalent effect to quantitative restrictions on imports, defining them as "all trading rules enacted by Member States which are capable of hindering, directly or indirectly, actually or potentially, intra-Community trade."[32] The prohibition in question has direct effect and creates individual rights which national courts must protect.[33]

It is *not* necessary for a national measure to have an *appreciable* effect on trade for it to fall within the prohibition of Article 30.[34] Indeed, the Court has stressed that Article 30:

" . . . does not distinguish between measures . . . according to the degree to which trade between Member States is affected. If a national measure is capable of hindering imports it must be regarded as a measure having an effect equivalent to a quantitative restriction, even though the hindrance is slight and even though it is possible for imported products to be marketed in other ways."[35]

In one case the Court referred to a "national measure which has, or *may* have, a restrictive effect on trade."[36] The position appears to be that even the possibility of a slight effect on intra-Community trade is sufficient to bring a national measure within the ambit of Article 30.

The fact that Article 30 extends to indirect as well as direct restrictions on imports is of considerable significance. It extends the reach of Community law beyond frontier restrictions and the formalities of import transactions to the whole range of commercial and marketing rules applied in the Member States. Thus, *e.g.* national rules on advertising and promotion are capable of amounting to measures having equivalent effect if there is a possibility that they may affect the prospects of importing products from other Member States.[37] As the Court explained in *Oosthoek's Uitgeversmaatschappij BV*[38]:

---

[32] Case 8/74 *Dassonville* [1974] E.C.R. 837, at 852, para. 5; Case 4/75 *Rewe-Zentralfinanz* [1975] E.C.R. 843; Case 65/75 *Tasca* [1976] E.C.R. 291; Cases 88–90/75 *SADAM* [1976] E.C.R. 323. The formulation has been confirmed on numerous occasions, either in identical, or similar terms. See, *e.g.* more recently, Case 174/82 *Sandoz* [1983] E.C.R. 2445, at para. 7; Case 229/83 *Leclerc* [1985] 2 C.M.L.R. 286, at para. 23; Cases 87 & 88/85 *Laboratoires de Pharmacie de Legia*, Judgment of May 27, 1986, at para. 12.

[33] Case 74/76 *Ianelli & Volpi* [1977] E.C.R. 557, at para. 13.

[34] Case 16/83 *Prantl* [1984] E.C.R. 1299.

[35] Cases 177 & 178/82 *Jan van de Haar* [1984] E.C.R. 1797, at para. 13. Case 155/80 *Oebel* [1981] E.C.R. 1993 is to be reconciled with this principle on the basis that there was apparently no reason to suppose that fewer imports would be effected via warehouses and intermediaries than would have been effected had deliveries directly to retailers been possible during the night. Case 75/81 *Blesgen* [1982] E.C.R. 1211, is anomalous in reasoning, if not in result. See Oliver, *Free Movement of Goods*, Annex I. It may perhaps be distinguished on the somewhat specious ground that statistics before the Court indicated that consumption of strong spirits in Belgium was static, but that imports were on a rising trend. There was thus in Adv. Gen. Reishl's view no disadvantage to imports, see [1982] E.C.R. at p. 1239. In our view, the outcome could be supported on the ground that the national measure amounted to a measure having equivalent effect, but was justifiable on public health grounds.

[36] Case 97/83 *Melkunie* [1984] E.C.R. 2367, at para. 12. Emphasis added.

[37] Case 152/78 *Commission* v. *France* [1980] E.C.R. 2299.

[38] Case 286/81 [1982] E.C.R. 4575, at p. 4587, para. 15.

"Legislation which restricts or prohibits certain forms of advertising and certain means of sales promotions may, although it does not directly affect imports, be such as to restrict their volume because it affects marketing opportunities for the imported products."

On the other hand, the Court in the *Kramer*[39] case contrasted the production stage of the economic process with the marketing stage, and indicated that Article 30 *et seq.* applied to the latter but not to the former. Furthermore, Article 30 would not seem capable, in principle, of extending to the general powers of economic management vested in the Member States. For example, restrictions on the availability of credit are capable of reducing the volume of imports, but would not, it is submitted, fall foul of Article 30 in the absence of some element of discrimination.[40]

A common defence advanced by national authorities has been that although a particular measure is apparently contrary to Article 30 *et seq.* it is in fact administered with flexibility, and exceptions may be made. The Court has consistently rejected this argument.[41] As the Court explained in *Kelderman*[42]:

" . . . a measure caught by the prohibition provided for in Article 30 . . . does not escape that prohibition simply because the competent authority is empowered to grant exemptions, even if that power is freely applied to imported products. Freedom of movement is a right whose enjoyment may not be dependent upon a discretionary power or on a concession granted by the national administration."

The measures defined by the Court as infringing Article 30 *et seq.* are invariably described as "national" measures, or trading rules "of the Member States" or "enacted by Member States." This would seem to exclude the conduct of private individuals and undertakings unsupported by State action of a legislative, executive or judicial character. The Court has condemned as a measure having equivalent effect a campaign funded by a Member State to promote the sale of domestic goods with a view to limiting imports, despite the fact that the campaign was conducted by a private company limited by guarantee. The management committee of the company was appointed by the national authorities, and the aims and outlines of the campaign were decided upon by those authorities. The Court held that the Member State in question could neither rely upon the fact that the campaign was conducted by a private company, nor upon the fact that the campaign was based upon decisions which were not binding upon undertakings, to avoid liability under Article 30.[43] The Court observed in another case that a body established and funded by Government with a view, *inter alia*, to promoting the sale of domestic products could not under Community law enjoy the same freedom as regards methods of advertising

---

[39] Cases 3, 4 & 6/76, [1976] E.C.R. 1279, at para. 27.
[40] This may be an explanation of the Court's reasoning in Case 238/82 *Duphar* [1984] E.C.R. 523. See *infra*, at p. 145.
[41] Case 82/77 *Van Tiggele* [1978] E.C.R. 25; Case 251/78 *Denkavit* [1979] E.C.R. 3369; Case 27/80 *Fietje* [1980] E.C.R. 3839. It is of course otherwise if the restrictions are capable of being justified in accordance with the Treaty, as to which, see *infra*, at p. 138.
[42] Case 130/80 [1981] E.C.R. 517 at para. 14. See also Case 124/81 *Commission* v. *United Kingdom* [1983] E.C.R. 203, at para. 10.
[43] Case 249/81 *Commission* v. *Ireland* [1982] E.C.R. 4005.

as that enjoyed by producers themselves or producer's associations of a voluntary character.[44]

It is clear that many barriers to intra-Community trade are capable of elimination through the technique of harmonisation of national laws under Article 100 of the EEC Treaty, which provides that:

"The Council shall . . . issue directives for the approximation of such provisions laid down by law, regulation or administrative action in Member States as directly affect the establishment or functioning of the common market."

The possibility of harmonisation however, cannot justify derogation from the requirements of Article 30. In *Commission* v. *Republic of Italy*[45] the defendant Member State argued that the Commission should have sought harmonisation before resorting to Articles 30 to 36 of the Treaty. The Court rejected the argument as follows:

"The fundamental principle of a unified market and its corollary, the free movement of goods, must not under any circumstances be made subject to the condition that there should first be an approximation of national laws for if that condition had to be fulfilled the principle would be reduced to a mere cipher."[46]

Articles 30 to 36 apply to trade in all goods, subject only to the exceptions provided in the Treaty itself.[47] In *Campus Oil*[48] the Irish Government argued unsuccessfully that oil, being of vital national importance, should be regarded as impliedly exempt from Article 30. The Court held that goods could not be considered to be exempt merely because they were of particular importance for the life or economy of a Member State.[49] Coins which constitute legal tender do not fall within Articles 30 to 36; coins which no longer constitute legal tender do.[50]

Where national procedures are contrary to Articles 30 to 36, any charge made by the national authorities for completion of such procedures is likewise unlawful.[51]

It should be noted that the inconsistency of national rules with Articles 30 to 36 is a point which can only be taken in respect of goods imported or to be imported from another Member State.[52]

Measures having equivalent effect to quantitative restrictions on exports

Article 34(1) of the EEC Treaty provides that quantitative restrictions on exports, and all measures having equivalent effect, shall be prohibited between Member States. The notion of measures having equivalent effect clearly embraces measures which formally differentiate between domestic

---

[44] Case 222/82 *Apple and Pear Development Council* [1983] E.C.R. 4083.
[45] Case 193/80 [1981] E.C.R. 3019.
[46] *Ibid.* at para. 17.
[47] See Art. 36, *infra*, at p. 138; and Art. 223, dealing with trade in arms, munitions and war materials. Case 72/83 *Campus Oil* [1984] E.C.R. 2727.
[48] Case 72/83 note 47.
[49] Case 72/83 note 47, para. 17.
[50] Case 7/78 *Thompson* [1978] E.C.R. 2247.
[51] Case 50/85 *Schloh*, Judgment of June 12, 1986.
[52] Cases 314–316/82 *Waterkeyn* [1982] E.C.R. 4337.

trade on the one hand, and the export trade on the other, as the *Bouhelier* case illustrates.[53] In order to ensure quality control, French legislation authorised a public authority to inspect pressed lever watches and watch movements made in France and destined for export to other Member States. If the watches or movements complied with the relevant quality standards, a certificate was issued to that effect. The export of such watches and movements was subject to the grant of a licence, except in the case of consignments in respect of which a standards certificate had been issued. The Court held that Article 34 of the Treaty precluded both export licensing and the imposition of quality controls on exports. Since the latter controls were not required in the case of products for the domestic market, their imposition amounted to arbitrary discrimination and constituted an obstacle to intra-Community trade.

In the case of quantitative restrictions on *imports* the Court's case law has developed to the stage where it is not necessary to establish discrimination in order to invoke the terms of Article 30. The Court takes judicial notice of the "protective effect" of national trading rules which, while applying to domestic products and imports alike, exclude or discourage imports from other Member States.[54]

It seems that the concept of measures having equivalent effect to quantitative restrictions on exports is not as broad as the same concept applicable to imports. Discrimination, either formal or material, still seems to be an essential element in the former case. As the Court explained in *Groenveld*[55]:

> "That provision [*i.e.* Art. 34(1)] concerns the national measures which have as their specific object or effect the restriction of patterns of exports and thereby the establishment of a difference in treatment between the domestic trade of a Member State and its export trade in such a way as to provide a particular advantage for national production or for the domestic market of the State in question at the expense of the production or of the trade of other Member States. This is not so in the case of a prohibition like that in question which is applied objectively to the production of goods of a certain kind without drawing a distinction depending on whether such goods are intended for the national market or for export."

The Court has repeated this formulation on numerous occasions.[56]

The prohibition in question binds the Community institutions as well as the Member States, and the traditional formulation has been held to be satisfied where Community rules made equivalent but not identical provision for administrative supervision both for exports in bulk of compound feedingstuffs and for the marketing thereof within the Community.[57]

---

[53] Case 53/76 [1977] E.C.R. 197.
[54] For the *Cassis* decision, Case 120/78 *Rewe* [1979] E.C.R. 649, and its progeny, see *infra* at p. 134.
[55] Case 15/79 [1979] E.C.R. 3409, at para. 7.
[56] See *e.g.* Case 155/80 *Oebel* [1981] E.C.R. 1993, at para. 15; Case 286/81 *Oosthoek's* [1982] E.C.R. 4575, at para. 13; Case 172/82 *Inter-Huiles* [1983] E.C.R. 555, at para. 12.
[57] Case 15/83 *Denkavit* [1984] E.C.R. 2171.

Import licences, declarations, etc.

Apart from the exceptions for which provision is made by Community law itself,[58] Articles 30 and 34 of the EEC Treaty preclude the application to intra-Community trade of a national provision which requires, even purely as a formality, import or export licences or any other similar procedure.[59]

An obligation imposed by an importing Member State to produce a certificate of fitness issued by an exporting Member State in connexion with the import of a product amounts to a measure having equivalent effect.[60]

However, requiring declarations from importers concerning the origin of goods for the purpose of monitoring the movement of goods does not amount to a measure having equivalent effect provided that the importer is not required to declare more than he knows or can reasonably be expected to know, and provided that penalties for failure to comply are not disproportionate.[61]

Specific preference for domestic products

National measures which express a preference for domestic products or confer some advantage on domestic products alone will amount to measures having equivalent effect to quantitative restrictions. The Court of Justice has so ruled in the case of a quality designation reserved for alcoholic drinks containing 85 per cent. spirits distilled on national territory.[62] Similarly, in *Campus Oil* the Court held that Irish rules requiring importers of petroleum products to purchase a certain proportion of their requirements at prices fixed by the competent minister from a state-owned company operating a refinery in Ireland amounted to a measure having equivalent effect.[63] In *Commission v. Hellenic Republic*[64] it was conceded by the defendant Member State that requiring the Agricultural Bank of Greece not to finance purchases of imported agricultural machinery except upon proof that machinery of that kind was not manufactured in Greece amounted to a measure having equivalent effect. The Court held that the concession was rightly made. It has even been held that state financed publicity campaigns promoting the purchase of national products on the grounds of national origin and disparaging products from other Member States infringe Article 30.[65]

---

[58] Note that import licences may in principle be excused in appropriate cases under Article 36 (as to which see *infra* at p. 000), Case 124/81 *Commission* v. *United Kingdom* [1983] E.C.R. 203; Case 74/82 *Commission* v. *Ireland* [1984] E.C.R. 317; Case 40/82 *Commission* v. *United Kingdom* [1984] E.C.R. 283.

[59] Cases 51–54/71 *International Fruit* [1971] E.C.R. 1107; Case 68/76 *Commission* v. *French Republic* [1977] E.C.R. 515; Case 41/76 *Donckerwolcke* [1976] E.C.R. 1921; Case 124/81 *Commission* v. *United Kingdom* [1983] E.C.R. 203.

[60] Case 251/78 *Denkavit* [1979] E.C.R. 3369, at para. 11.

[61] Case 41/76 *Donckerwolcke* [1976] E.C.R. 1921; Case 179/78 *Rivoira* [1979] E.C.R. 1147.

[62] Case 13/78 *Eggers* [1978] E.C.R. 1935.

[63] Case 72/83 [1984] E.C.R. 2727. But the Court held that such a measure might in principle be excused under Art. 36 on grounds of national security.

[64] Case 192/84 Judgment of December 11, 1985.

[65] Case 249/81 *Commission* v. *Ireland* [1982] E.C.R. 4005; Case 222/82 *Apple and Pear Development Council* [1983] E.C.R. 4083.

Conditions imposed in respect of imported products only

One of the most easily detected infringements of the Treaty's prohibition on measures having equivalent effect to quantitative restrictions is a national rule imposing conditions on imported products which are not imposed on their domestic counterparts. Thus phytosanitary inspections on imports of plant products where no compulsory examination is made of domestic products amounts to a measure having equivalent effect.[66] Again, a national requirement that imported drinks be at least of the alcohol content specified as the minimum in the country of origin, where no minimum alcoholic content was specified for similar domestic products, has been held to be contrary to Article 30.[67] In *Commission* v. *Italy* the Court condemned an Italian measure prohibiting the testing, for the purposes of registration, of buses which were more than seven years old and came from other Member States, where no such prohibition applied to Italian buses.[68]

Measures making imports more difficult or more costly

A ground advanced by the Court for holding frontier checks of imported products to amount to measures having equivalent effect is that such checks make imports more difficult or costly.[69] Examples of national measures which have been held to be contrary to Article 30 (subject to appropriate justification in accordance with the Treaty)[70] on this ground are an import deposit scheme for imports for which payment was made in advance[71]; the extension to imported products of national rules which prohibited the sales of silver goods without hallmarking[72]; the extension to imported products of a national rule which required that margarine be sold in cube shaped packs[73]; the extension to imported products of a requirement that certain information be *not* provided on the packaging of certain products[74]; the extension to imported products of a national rule which prohibited the sale of goods by retail unless they bore an indication of their country of origin[75]; and the roadworthiness testing of imported vehicles.[76]

Impeding access to certain channels of distribution

The definition of measures having equivalent effect which the Court has adopted has led it to conclude that measures are forbidden which "favour, within the Community, particular trade channels or particular commercial operators in relation to others."[77] An example of such a measure is provided by the proceedings in *Procureur du Roi* v. *Dassonville*.[78] The defend-

---

[66] Case 4/75 *Rewe* [1975] E.C.R. 843. In this case the measures were justified under Art. 36.
[67] Case 59/82 *Schutzverband* [1983] E.C.R. 1217.
[68] Case 50/83 [1984] E.C.R. 1633.
[69] Case 4/75 *Rewe* [1975] E.C.R. 843, at para. 11; Case 42/82 *Commission* v. *French Republic* [1983] E.C.R. 1013, at para. 50.
[70] As to which, see *infra* at p. 138.
[71] Case 95/81 *Commission* v. *Italy* [1982] E.C.R. 2187.
[72] Case 220/81 *Robertson* [1982] E.C.R. 2349.
[73] Case 261/81 *Rau* [1982] E.C.R. 3961.
[74] Case 94/82 *De Kikvorsch* [1983] E.C.R. 947.
[75] Case 207/83 *Commission* v. *United Kingdom* [1985] 2 C.M.L.R. 259.
[76] Case 50/85 *Schloh* [1987] 1 C.M.L.R. 450.
[77] Case 155/73 *Sacchi* [1974] E.C.R. 409 at p. 427, para. 8.
[78] Case 8/74 [1974] E.C.R. 837.

ants in the national suit imported into Belgium Scotch whisky which they had purchased from French distributors. Belgian legislation required such goods to be accompanied by a British certificate of origin made out in the name of the Belgian importers, and the goods in question were without such certificates, which could have been obtained only with the greatest difficulty once the goods had been imported previously into France. The Court of Justice held that a requirement such as that laid down by the Belgian legislation in issue constituted a measure having equivalent effect, inasmuch as it favoured direct imports from the country of origin over imports from a Member State where the goods were in free circulation.

The Court reiterated its view that there must be no discrimination between channels of trade in *de Peijper*.[79] Dutch legislation laid down certain safety requirements in the case of imports of medicinal preparations. The importer was bound to present certain documentation, verified by the manufacturer, to the Dutch public health authorities. Centrafarm purchased quantities of Valium, manufactured by Hoffmann-La Roche in England, from a British wholesaler, packed the tablets in packages bearing the name Centrafarm and marked with the generic name of the product in question, and distributed them to pharmacies in the Netherlands. Centrafarm could not rely on Hoffmann-La Roche's co-operation with regard to the relevant documentation, and was charged under Dutch law. On a reference from the Kantongerecht, Rotterdam, the Court ruled that national practices which resulted in imports being channelled in such a way that certain traders could effect these imports, while others could not, constituted measures having equivalent effect.

Price restrictions

The Court has considered on a number of occasions the compatibility with Article 30 of national measures fixing the selling prices of products.

Selective price measures taken by national authorities to restrict importation of products from other Member States will clearly be incompatible with Article 30.[80]

Where a maximum selling price applies without distinction to domestic and imported products it does not of itself amount to a measure having equivalent effect. It will only do so when it is fixed at such a low level that the sale of imported products becomes, if not impossible, at any rate more difficult than that of domestic products.[81] This would be the case where imports could only be effected at a loss,[82] or where traders were impelled by the disparity between the lower cost of domestic goods and imports to give preference to the latter.[83] Imports would equally be impeded if the minimum prices which could be charged by traders were fixed at such a

---

[79] Case 104/75 [1976] E.C.R. 613. See also Case 261/81 *Rau* [1982] E.C.R. 3961, at para. 13.
[80] Case 90/82 *Commission* v. *France* [1983] E.C.R. 2011, at para. 27.
[81] See, *e.g.* Case 65/75 *Tasca* [1976] E.C.R. 291, at para. 13; Cases 88–90/75 *SADAM* [1976] E.C.R. 323, at para. 15; Case 5/79 *Hans Buijs* [1979] E.C.R. 3203, at para. 26; Cases 16–20/79 *Danis* [1979] E.C.R. 3327.
[82] Case 65/75 and Cases 88–90/75, note 81.
[83] Case 5/79 *Hans Buijs* [1979] E.C.R. 3203, at para. 26; Cases 16–20/79 *Danis* [1979] E.C.R. 3327.

high level that the price advantage enjoyed by imports over domestic goods were cancelled out.[84]

Even if national rules establish different criteria for fixing the selling prices of imports than are established for fixing the selling prices of domestic goods, there will only be a violation of Article 30 if imports are actually put at some disadvantage. This follows from the *Roussel* case,[85] in which the Court held that:

> "Legislation . . . which differentiates between the two groups of products, must be regarded as a measure having an effect equivalent to a quantitative restriction where it is capable of making more difficult, in any manner whatever, the sale of imported products."[86]

That separate rules for the price fixing of imports do not of themselves infringe Article 30 is confirmed in *Leclerc*, in which the Court condemned separate price fixing rules for imported books *which were liable to impede trade between Member States*.[87] Nevertheless, if price-fixing rules applied exclusively to imported products, this would violate Article 30 without more since it would of itself place imported products at some disadvantage.

Discrimination may be either formal or material

Where it is alleged that a national measure amounts to a measure having equivalent effect to a quantitative restriction on imports it will invariably be sufficient—whether or not it is also necessary[88]—to show that it discriminates against imports. Discrimination exists not only when a national measure treats similar situations in different ways—so called "formal" discrimination (*e.g.* prohibiting the testing of imported buses more than seven years old while allowing it in the case of similar buses of domestic manufacture),[89] but also when a national measure treats different situations in the same way[90]—so called "material" discrimination (*e.g.* applying the same maximum selling price to imported goods as to domestic goods where the former cost more than the latter).[91]

Disparities between national laws as measures having equivalent effect

Prior to the landmark decision of the Court of Justice in the *Cassis* case[92] it was generally assumed—and the Court's case law was consistent with this assumption—that Article 30 had no application to a national measure unless it could be proved that the measure in question discriminated in some way, formally or materially, between either imports and domestic products, or between channels of intra-Community trade.

The *Cassis* case involved the intended importation into Germany of a

---

[84] Case 82/77 *Van Tiggele* [1978] E.C.R. 25.
[85] Case 181/82 [1983] E.C.R. 3849.
[86] Case 181/82 at para. 19.
[87] Case 229/83 [1985] E.C.R. 2.
[88] For discrimination as an element in establishing infringement of Article 30, see *infra* at p. 144.
[89] Case 50/83 [1984] E.C.R. 1633.
[90] Case 13/63 *Republic of Italy* v. *Commission* [1963] E.C.R. 165.
[91] Case 65/75 *Tasca* [1976] E.C.R. 291; Cases 88–90/75 *SADAM* [1976] E.C.R. 323. See *supra* at p. 133.
[92] Case 120/78 *Rewe* [1979] E.C.R. 649.

consignment of the alcoholic beverage "Cassis de Dijon." Under German legislation fruit liqueurs such as "Cassis" could only be marketed if they contained a minimum alcohol content of 25 per cent., whereas the alcohol content of the product in question was between 15 per cent. and 20 per cent. A German court asked the Court of Justice whether legislation such as that in issue was consistent with Article 30 of the Treaty. Before the Court of Justice the Federal Republic of Germany argued that the legislation in question was discriminatory in neither a formal nor a material sense; any obstacles to trade resulted simply from the fact that France and Germany contained different rules for the minimum alcohol contents of certain drinks. The Court's judgment makes no reference at all to the issue of discrimination. Rather it regards incompatibility with Article 30 as flowing from the very fact that the "Cassis" could not be placed lawfully on the German market, and addresses itself at once to the question whether there existed any *justification* for the restriction.

"In the absence of common rules relating to the production and marketing of alcohol . . . it is for the Member States to regulate all matters relating to the production and marketing of alcohol and alcoholic beverages on their own territory.

Obstacles to movement within the Community resulting from disparities between the national laws relating to the marketing of the products in question must be accepted in so far as those provisions may be recognized as being necessary in order to satisfy mandatory requirements relating in particular to the effectiveness of fiscal supervision, the protection of public health, the fairness of commercial transactions and the defence of the consumer."[93]

The Court rejected the arguments of the Federal Republic of Germany relating to the protection of public health and to the protection of the consumer against unfair commercial practices, and continued:

"It is clear from the foregoing that the requirements relating to the minimum alcohol content of alcoholic beverages do not serve a purpose which is in the general interest and such as to take precedence over the requirements of the free movement of goods, which constitutes one of the fundamental rules of the Community."[94]

In the paragraphs which follow the Court describes the restrictive effect of national rules such as those in issue in terms which either make the existence of an element of discrimination irrelevant in establishing violation of Article 30, or *presume* it to exist from the very fact of exclusion of products lawfully produced and marketed in one of the Member States.

"In practice, the principal effect of requirements of this nature is to promote alcoholic beverages having a high alcohol content by excluding from the national market products of other Member States which do not answer that description.

It therefore appears that the unilateral requirement imposed by the rules of a Member State of a minimum alcohol content for the pur-

---

[93] Case 120/78, note 92, at paras. 8, 9.
[94] *Ibid.* at para. 14.

poses of the sale of alcoholic beverages constitutes an obstacle to trade which is incompatible with the provisions of Article 30 of the Treaty.

There is therefore no valid reason why, provided that they have been lawfully produced and marketed in one of the Member States, alcoholic beverages should not be introduced into any other Member State; the sale of such products may not be subject to a legal prohibition on the marketing of beverages with an alcohol content lower than the limit set by the national rules."[95]

The Court was soon to confirm the approach it had adopted in *Cassis* in *Gilli & Andres*,[96] a case concerning national legislation prohibiting the marketing of vinegar containing acetic acid derived otherwise than from the acetic fermentation of wine. In this case the Court slightly modified one of its observations in *Cassis*:

"In practice, the principal effect of provisions of this nature is to protect domestic production by prohibiting the putting on to the market of products from other Member States which do not answer the descriptions laid down by the national rules."[97]

If discrimination was the distinguishing feature of national measures prima facie contrary to Article 30 before the *Cassis* decision, emphasis after that case was placed upon the protective effect of national rules which excluded from the market of one Member State goods lawfully produced and marketed in the territory of another. As the Commission stated in its Communication of October 3, 1980 concerning the consequences of the *Cassis* case:

"Any product imported from another Member State must in principle be admitted to the territory of the importing Member State if it has been lawfully produced, that is, conforms to rules and processes of manufacture that are customarily and traditionally accepted in the exporting country, and is marketed in the territory of another."[98]

Examples of measures held by the Court to fall foul of the *Cassis* formulation (subject to justification in accordance with the Treaty[99]) are national rules imposing a labelling requirement[1]: national rules prohibiting use of the additive nisin in cheese[2]; national rules regulating the dry matter content of bread[3]; national rules requiring silver products to be hall-marked[4]; national rules requiring margarine to be sold in cube-shaped packets[5]; national rules restricting or prohibiting certain forms of advertising[6]; and national rules prohibiting the retail sale of certain products unless marked with their country of origin.[7]

There can be no doubt that the *Cassis* formulation may cover national

[95] *Ibid.* at para. 14.
[96] Case 788/79 [1980] E.C.R. 2071.
[97] Case 788/79, note 96, at para. 10.
[98] O.J. 1980 C256/2.
[99] As to which, see *infra* at p. 138.
[1] Case 27/80 *Fietje* [1980] E.C.R. 3839; Case 94/82 *De Kikvorsch* [1983] E.C.R. 947.
[2] Case 53/80 *Eyssen* [1981] E.C.R. 409.
[3] Case 30/80 *Kelderman* [1981] E.C.R. 517.
[4] Case 220/81 *Robertson* [1982] E.C.R. 2349.
[5] Case 261/81 *Rau* [1982] E.C.R. 3961.
[6] Case 286/81 *Oosthoek's etc.* [1982] E.C.R. 4575.
[7] Case 207/83 *Commission* v. *United Kingdom* [1985] 2 C.M.L.R. 259.

measures which are discriminatory and which are capable of infringing Article 30 on that ground. At times the new notion of protective effect and the old notion of discrimination appear to coalesce. Thus in *Prantl* the Court declared:

" . . . even national legislation on the marketing of a product which applies to national and imported products alike falls under the prohibition laid down in Article 30 . . . if in practice it produces protective effects by favouring typical national products and, by the same token, operating to the detriment of certain types of products from other Member States."[8]

Nevertheless, the Court made it clear in the *Cinétheque* case[9] that the *Cassis* formulation is not limited in its application to national measures which are proved to have or assumed to have some discriminatory purpose or effect. The case concerned French rules which provided that video-cassettes of films could not be distributed within one year of the release of the films in question at the cinema. The Court made the following observations:

" . . . such a system, if it applies without distinction to both video-cassettes manufactured in the national territory and to imported video-cassettes, does not have the purpose of regulating trade patterns; its effect is not to favour national production as against the production of other Member States, but to encourage cinematograph production as such.

Nevertheless, the application of such a system may create barriers to intra-community trade in video-cassettes because of the disparities between the systems operated in the different Member States and between the conditions for the release of cinematographic works in the cinemas of those States. In those circumstances a prohibition of exploitation laid down by such a system is not compatible with the principle of the free movement of goods provided for in the Treaty unless any obstacle to intra-Community trade thereby created does not exceed what is necessary in order to ensure the attainment of the objective in view and unless that objective is justified with regard to Community law."[10]

While the existence of the non-discriminatory trade restriction has been unequivocally confirmed by the Court, it does not follow that establishing discrimination is no longer appropriate where infringement of Article 30 is alleged. First, even if not a necessary ingredient in all Article 30 cases, the existence of discrimination against imported products will invariably give rise to the presumption that a national rule amounts to a measure having equivalent effect. Secondly, there are clearly certain cases where discrimination remains a necessary element in establishing violation of Article 30.[11] Thirdly, the existence of discrimination may be crucial in determining

---

[8] Case 16/83 [1984] E.C.R. 1299, at para. 21.
[9] Cases 60 & 61/84, [1986] 1 C.M.L.R. 365.
[10] Cases 60 & 61/84, note 9, paras. 21, 22.
[11] For example, the price control cases, and cases where a Member State takes steps to promote the financial stability of a national social security scheme, see *infra* at p. 144.

whether a measure having equivalent effect may be *justified* on the grounds recognised under Community law.[12]

Derogation from Articles 30 to 34

Article 36 of the EEC Treaty

Article 36 of the Treaty provides:
> "The provisions of Articles 30 to 34 shall not preclude prohibitions or restrictions on imports, exports or goods in transit justified on grounds of public morality, public policy or public security; the protection of health and life of humans, animals or plants; the protection of national treasures possessing artistic, historic or archaeological value; or the protection of industrial and commercial property. Such prohibitions or restrictions shall not however, constitute a means of arbitrary discrimination or a disguised restriction on trade between Member States."

The grounds of derogation. Article 36 constitutes an exception to the fundamental rule that all obstacles to the free movement of goods between Member States shall be abolished and the Article must be interpreted strictly.[13] It follows that the list of exceptions is exhaustive.[14] Thus the Court has held that Article 36 does not justify derogation from Article 30 on the grounds of the protection of consumers or the fairness of commercial transactions,[15] economic policy,[16] or the protection of creativity and cultural diversity,[17] since none of the foregoing are referred to in the Article.

While the Court has accepted that the expression "public policy" is capable of embracing a national ban on the export of coins no longer constituting legal tender,[18] it has refused to accept that the expression includes the protection of consumers.[19]

In the absence of harmonised rules at the Community level, recourse to Article 36 may entail the application of different standards in different Member States, as a result of different national value-judgments, and different factual circumstances. Thus the Court has emphasised that:
> "In principle, it is for each Member State to determine in accord-

---

[12] See *infra* at pp. 142 and 143.
[13] Case 46/76 [1977] E.C.R. 5; Case 113/80 *Commission* v. *Ireland* [1981] E.C.R. 1625; Case 95/81 *Commission* v. *Italy* [1982] E.C.R. 2187.
[14] Case 95/81 *Commission* v. *Italy* [1982] E.C.R. 2187.
[15] Case 95/81 *Commission* v. *Italy* [1982] E.C.R. 2187; Case 220/81 *Robertson* [1982] E.C.R. 2349; Case 229/83 *Leclerc* [1985] E.C.R. 2. Such considerations may however, in the case of non-discriminatory restrictions, amount to mandatory requirements justifying reasonable restrictions on the free movement of goods in the general interest, see *infra* at p. 142.
[16] Case 7/61 *Commission* v. *Italy* [1961] E.C.R. 317; Case 95/81, note 13; Case 238/82 *Duphar* [1984] E.C.R. 523; Case 72/83 *Campus Oil* [1984] E.C.R. 2727; Case 288/83 *Commission* v. *Ireland* [1985] 3 C.M.L.R. 152. Such considerations may however, in the case of non-discriminatory restrictions, amount to mandatory requirements justifying reasonable restrictions on the free movement of goods in the general interest, see Case 238/82 *Duphar* E.C.R. 523 *infra* at p. 145.
[17] Case 229/83 *Leclerc* [1985] E.C.R. 2.
[18] Case 7/78 *Thompson* [1978] E.C.R. 2247.
[19] Case 177/83 *Kohl* [1984] E.C.R. 3651.

ance with its own scale of values and in the form selected by it the requirements of public morality in its territory."[20]

Again, in connexion with the protection of public health, it has stated:

"In so far as the relevant Community rules do not cover certain pesticides, Member States may regulate the presence of residues of those pesticides in a way which may vary from one country to another according to the climatic conditions, the normal diet of the population and their state of health."[21]

While Article 36 leaves a margin of discretion in the national authorities as to the extent to which they wish to protect the interests listed therein, the discretion is limited by two important principles. First, that any discrimination between imports and domestic products must not be arbitrary. Secondly, that national measures must not restrict trade any more than is necessary to protect the interest in question.

Arbitrary discrimination or a disguised restriction on trade. Article 36 provides that prohibitions or restrictions permitted under that Article shall not however constitute a means of arbitrary discrimination or a disguised restriction on trade between Member States. The purpose of this formulation has been said by the Court to be to:

" . . . prevent restrictions on trade based on the grounds mentioned in the first sentence of Article 36 from being diverted from their proper purpose and used in such a way as either to create discrimination in respect of goods originating in other Member States or indirectly to protect certain national products."[22]

In determining whether or not discrimination against imported goods is arbitrary, the crucial test will be a comparison with measures taken *vis-à-vis* domestic goods: *Rewe-Zentralfinanz* v. *Landwirtschaftskammer*.[23] As a precaution against transmission of the destructive San José Scale insect, German legislation provided for the phyto-sanitary examination of certain imported fruit and vegetables at point of entry. On a reference from the Verwaltungsgericht Cologne, the Court held that such measures must be considered to be justified in principle under Article 36, provided that they did not constitute a means of arbitrary discrimination. This would not be the case where effective measures were taken to prevent the distribution of contaminated domestic products, and where there was reason to believe that there would be a risk of the harmful organism spreading if no inspections were held on importation.

National measures only justified if they are no more restrictive than is strictly necessary. The Court has emphasised that Article 36 is not designed to reserve certain matters to the exclusive jurisdiction of Member States, but only permits national laws to derogate from the principle of the free movement of goods to the extent to which such derogation is and continues to be justified for the attainment of the objectives referred to in that

[20] Case 34/79 *Henn & Darby* [1979] E.C.R. 3795.
[21] Case 94/83 *Heijn* [1984] E.C.R. 3263.
[22] Case 34/79 *Henn & Darby* [1979] E.C.R. 3795, at para. 21; Case 40/82 *Commission* v. *United Kingdom* [1984] E.C.R. 283, at para. 36.
[23] Case 4/75 [1975] E.C.R. 843.

article.[24] The word "justified" is to be construed as meaning "necessary."[25] Application of the Article is thus to be conditioned upon compliance with the principle of proportionality.[26] As the Court explained in
Commission v. *Belgium*:

> "However [public health] measures are justified only if it is estab-
> lished that they are necessary in order to attain the objective of protec-
> tion referred to in Article 36 and that such protection cannot be
> achieved by means which place less of a restriction on the free move-
> ment of goods within the Community."[27]

Thus, in *de Peijper*,[28] the Court considered the argument that restrictive
provisions of Netherlands legislation which favoured imports by dealers
securing the cooperation of the manufacturer were justified on the basis
that they were necessary for the protection of the health and life of
humans. While the Court acknowledged that this interest ranked first
among the interests protected by Article 36 of the Treaty, it emphasised
that national measures did not fall within the exception if the health or life
of humans could be as effectively protected by means less restrictive of
intra-Community trade. In particular, Article 36 did not justify restrictions
motivated primarily by a concern to facilitate the task of the authorities, or
reduce public expenditure, unless alternative arrangements would impose
unreasonable burdens on the administration.

As long as the rules relating to health protection in a particular sector
have not been harmonised, it is open to the Member States to carry out any
necessary inspections at national frontiers.[29] However, the free movement
of goods is facilitated by the carrying out of health inspections in the
country of production and the health authorities of the importing Member
State should co-operate in order to avoid the repetition, in the importing
country, of checks which have already been carried out in the country of
production.[30] Similar considerations apply to approval by national authorities of products which have been approved on health grounds in other
Member States. Whilst a Member State is free to require such products to
undergo a fresh procedure of examination and approval, the authorities of
that Member State are bound to assist in bringing about a relaxation of the
controls applied in intra-Community trade,[31] and are not entitled unnecessarily to require technical or chemical analyses or tests where those analyses or tests have already been carried out in another Member State and
their results are available to those authorities, or may at their request be
placed at their disposal.[32]

---

[24] Case 5/77 *Tedeschi* [1977] E.C.R. 1556; Case 251/78 *Denkavit* [1979] E.C.R. 3327.
[25] Case 153/78 *Commission* v. *Germany* 2555, at para. 8; Case 251/78 *Denkavit* [1979] E.C.R.
3327, at para. 21.
[26] As to which, see *supra* at p. 60.
[27] Case 155/82 [1983] E.C.R. 531. See also Case 97/83 *Melkunie* [1984] E.C.R. 2367, at
para. 12.
[28] Case 104/75 [1976] E.C.R. 613.
[29] Case 73/84 *Denkavit* [1986] 2 C.M.L.R. 482.
[30] Case 251/78 *Denkavit* [1979] E.C.R. 3327. Case 73/84 *Denkavit* [1986] 2 C.M.L.R. 482.
[31] Case 104/75 *de Peijper* [1976] E.C.R. 613; Case 272/80 *Frans-Nederlandse* [1981] E.C.R.
3277.
[32] Case 272/80 *Frans-Nederlandse* [1981] E.C.R. 3277.

Disguised restrictions, arbitrary discrimination, and proportionality. The requirements that measures taken by Member States under Article 36 must not constitute a means of arbitrary discrimination, nor a disguised restriction on trade, and must comply with the principle of proportionality, overlap, and should not be considered in isolation. Thus, infringement of the principle of proportionality may lead to a measure being categorised as a disguised restriction on trade.[33] Again, in deciding in *Commission* v. *France*[34] whether or not the frequency of French frontier tests of Italian wine complied with the principle of proportionality, the Court took into account not only the fact that similar checks on Italian wine were carried out by the Italian authorities, but also the fact that the frequency of the French frontier inspections was distinctly higher than the occasional checks carried out on the transportation of French wine within France.

The effect of harmonisation directives and other Community measures on recourse to Article 36. Recourse to Article 36 is no longer justified if Community rules provide for the necessary measures to ensure protection of the interests set out in that article.[35] This may be the case, *e.g.* when directives enacted under Article 100 of the EEC Treaty provide for the full harmonisation of the measures necessary for the protection of animal and human health, and establish the procedures to check that they are observed.[36] Thus, if such a directive places the responsibility for public health inspections of a product upon the Member State of export, the national authorities of the importing Member State will no longer be entitled to subject the product to systematic inspection upon importation; only occasional inspections to check compliance with the Community standards will be permissible.[37]

Burden of proof lies on the national authorities. It is for the national authorities of the Member States to prove that their restrictive trading rules may be justified under Article 36. As the Court stated in *Leendert van Bennekom*[38]:

" . . . it is for the national authorities to demonstrate in each case that their rules are necessary to give effective protection to the interests referred to in Article 36 of the Treaty."

Thus in *Cullet* the French Government defended national rules fixing retail selling prices for fuel on grounds of public order and security represented by the violent reactions which would have to be anticipated on the part of retailers affected by unrestricted competition. The Court rejected this argument summarily:

"In that regard, it is sufficient to state that the French Government

---

[33] Case 272/80 *Frans-Nederlandse* [1981] E.C.R. 3277, paras. 13, 14; Cases 2–4/82 *Le Lion* [1983] E.C.R. 2973, at para. 12.
[34] Case 42/82 [1983] E.C.R. 1013, at paras. 51 to 57.
[35] Case 72/83 *Campus Oil* [1984] E.C.R. 2727, at para. 27.
[36] Case 251/78 *Denkavit* [1979] E.C.R. 3369, at para. 14; Case 227/82 *Leendert* [1983] E.C.R. 3883, at para. 35.
[37] Case 35/76 *Simmenthal* [1976] E.C.R. 1871; Cases 2–4/82 *Le Lion* [1983] E.C.R. 2973.
[38] Case 227/82 [1983] E.C.R. 3883, at para. 40; see also Case 104/75 *de Peijper* [1976] E.C.R. 613; Case 251/78 *Denkavit* [1979] E.C.R. 3369, at para. 24; Case 174/82 *Sandoz* [1983] E.C.R. 2445, at para. 22.

has not shown that it would be unable, using the means at its disposal, to deal with the consequences which an amendment of the rules in question . . . would have upon public order and security."[39]

The burden of proving that Article 36 applies accordingly entails: (i) showing that the national measures in question fall within one of the categories (*e.g.* public health, public policy or public morality) referred to in Article 36[40]; (ii) establishing that the measure does not constitute a means of arbitrary discrimination, that is to say, that if it differentiates between domestic products and imports, it does so on objective and justifiable grounds[41]; (iii) establishing that the measure does not constitute a disguised restriction on trade, that is to say, that any restrictive effect on the free movement of goods is limited to what is necessary to protect the interest in question.[42]

Mandatory requirements in the general interest

Although the Court has stated repeatedly that the exceptions listed in Article 36 are exhaustive,[43] it in effect established further grounds upon which Member States may derogate from Article 30 in the *Cassis* case, in which it held that obstacles to the free movement of goods in the Community resulting from disparities between national marketing rules must be accepted in so far as they were necessary to satisfy mandatory requirements relating in particular to the effectiveness of fiscal supervision, the protection of public health, the fairness of commercial transactions, and the defence of the consumer.[44] The theoretical explanation for this apparent inconsistency is that the *Cassis* list does not so much provide grounds for derogating from Article 30 as define the circumstances in which national measures fall within Article 30 in the first place.

The categories of justification under the *Cassis* formulation are not closed, as appears from the formulation itself, which refers to four categories "in particular." The Court has added to the list environmental protection,[45] and the encouragement of film-making, upholding on this latter ground national rules providing that video-cassettes of films could not be distributed until one year after the release of the films at the cinema.[46] In one case the Court hinted that legitimate interests of economic and social policy, consistent with the Treaty, might similarly justify impediments to the free movement of goods.[47]

A useful example of mandatory requirements justifying national measures is provided in *Oosthoek's Uitgeversmaatschaapij B.V.*[48] The national measures in question restricted the giving of free gifts as a means of sales promotion. The Court took the view that to compel a producer

---

[39] Case 231/83 [1985] E.C.R. 000, at paras. 32, 33.
[40] *Supra* at p. 138.
[41] *Supra* at p. 139.
[42] *Supra* at p. 139.
[43] See *supra* at p. 138.
[44] Case 120/78 *Rewe* [1979] E.C.R. 649. See *supra* at p. 134.
[45] Case 240/83 *Brûleurs d'Huiles Usagées* [1985] E.C.R. 532.
[46] Cases 60 & 61/84 *Cinétheque* [1986] 1 C.M.L.R. 365.
[47] Case 155/80 *Oebel* [1981] E.C.R. 1993, at para. 12.
[48] Case 286/81 [1982] E.C.R. 4575.

either to adopt advertising or sales promotion schemes which differed from one Member State to another or to discontinue a scheme which he considered to be particularly effective might constitute an obstacle to imports even if the legislation in question applied to domestic goods and to imports without distinction. Nevertheless, the Court upheld such rules on the grounds of the fairness of commercial transactions and the defence of the consumer:

> "It is undeniable that the offering of free gifts as a means of sales promotion may mislead consumers as to the rule prices of certain products and distort the conditions on which genuine competition is based. Legislation which restricts or even prohibits such commercial practices for that reason is therefore capable of contributing to consumer protection and fair trading."[49]

Consumer protection and fair trading however raise issues which extend beyond the market of the importing Member State. In *Prantl*[50] the Court considered trading rules reserving to national wine producers the use of the characteristically shaped "Bocksbeutel" bottle. Consumer protection and fair trading were pleaded in support of the national rules. The Court noted however that in the common market consumer protection and fair trading as regards the presentation of wines must be guaranteed "with regard on all sides for the fair and traditional practices observed in the various Member States."[51] It followed that an exclusive right to use a certain type of bottle granted by national legislation in a Member State could not be used to bar imports of wines originating in another Member State put up in bottles of the same or similar shape in accordance with a fair and traditional practice in that Member State.

Recourse to mandatory requirements is subject to the principle of proportionality, as the Court made clear in the *Rau* case:

> "It is also necessary for such rules to be proportionate to the aim in view. If a Member State has a choice between various measures to attain the same objective it should choose the means which least restrict the free movement of goods."[52]

A further limitation on recourse to mandatory requirements is that they may only be invoked in the case of national rules which apply without discrimination to both domestic and imported products.[53] Thus in the case of national rules requiring certain imported products but not their domestically produced counterparts to bear an indication of country of origin, the Court held that considerations of consumer protection and the fairness of commercial transactions could have no application.[54] In the case of national rules requiring both domestic goods and imports to bear an indication of country of origin, the Court again refused to consider arguments based on considerations of consumer protection on the grounds that the national rules were in fact discriminatory:

---

[49] Case 286/81, at para. 18.
[50] Case 16/83 [1984] E.C.R. 1299.
[51] Case 16/83 [1984] E.C.R. 1299, at para. 27.
[52] Case 261/81 [1982] E.C.R. 3961, at para. 12.
[53] Case 113/80 *Commission* v. *Ireland* [1981] E.C.R. 1625.
[54] Case 113/80 *Commission* v. *Ireland* [1981] E.C.R. 1625.

> "The requirements relating to the indication of origin of goods are applicable without distinction to domestic and imported products only in form because, by their very nature, they are intended to enable the consumer to distinguish between those two categories of products, which may thus prompt him to give his preference to national products."[55]

It seems that recourse to mandatory requirements is impermissible if national rules are discriminatory, either in a formal[56] or material sense,[57] from the point of view of their effect on trade,[58] or if national rules are applied in a similarly discriminatory manner.[59] However, care must be taken to differentiate discrimination, which ousts the application of mandatory requirements, from the "protective effect" characteristic of *Cassis* restrictions.[60]

Colourable transactions

In *Leclerc* the Court held that a national price-fixing measure amounting to a measure having equivalent effect was not to be so regarded *vis-à-vis* products exported for the sole purpose of reimportation in order to circumvent the national legislation in question.[61] This conclusion is to be supported, not on the basis of the theory of "abuse of rights," but on the basis that the so-called "imports" were in commercial reality purely internal transactions.

Cases in which discrimination is a necessary element in establishing a measure having equivalent effect

It has been noted that prior to the *Cassis*[62] decision it was generally assumed that discrimination was a necessary element in establishing a measure having equivalent effect.[63] Since that decision two things have become clear. First, that national rules may amount to measures having equivalent effect despite applying equally and without any discrimination to domestic products and to imports.[64] Secondly, that there nevertheless remain cases where discrimination is an indispensable element in establishing the existence of a measure having equivalent effect. The principle example is that of the price-control cases.[65] There are several possible

---

[55] Case 207/83 *Commission* v. *United Kingdom* [1985] 2 C.M.L.R. 259. ·

[56] For the distinction between formal and material discrimination, see *supra*, at p. 134. Cases of formal discrimination ousting mandatory requirements are Case 113/80 *Commission* v. *Ireland* [1981] E.C.R. 1625; Case 59/82 *Shutzverband* [1983] E.C.R. 1217.

[57] Case 177/83 *Kohl* [1984] E.C.R. 3651; Case 207/83 *Commission* v. *United Kingdom* [1985] 2 C.M.L.R. 259.

[58] Case 177/83 *Kohl* [1984] E.C.R. 3651, at para. 14.

[59] Case 177/83 *Kohl* [1984] E.C.R. 3651, at para. 14.

[60] See *supra* at p. 135, in particular the definition of protective effect in Case 16/83 *Prantl* [1984] E.C.R. 1299, at para. 21.

[61] Case 229/83 [1985] 2 C.M.L.R. 286. For the view that this is an example of "abuse of imports," see Oliver, (1986) 23 C.M.C.Rev. 325, at 327. ·

[62] As to which, see *supra*, at p. 134.

[63] As to which, see *supra*, at p. 134. See Wyatt, "Article 30 and non-discriminatory trade restrictions," (1981) 6 E.L.Rev. 185.

[64] Case 286/81 *Oosthoek's* [1982] E.C.R. 4575; Cases 60 & 61/84 *Cinétheque* [1986] 1 C.M.L.R. 365 see *supra* at p. 137.

[65] As to which, see *supra*, at p. 133.

explanations for the continuing requirement of discrimination in these cases. One is simply that the first cases were decided before *Cassis*, they were followed thereafter, and the resulting case law is *sui generis* and anomalous. However, in a more recent case, *Duphar*,[66] the Court made it clear that a national measure excluding certain types of drugs from reimbursement under a state social security scheme would only fall foul of Article 30 if it were discriminatory. The decision is to be welcomed. To have eschewed the requirement of discrimination and to have applied the principle of proportionality would have been tantamount to subjecting the public expenditure policy of the Member State concerned to judicial review. There can be no doubt that many of the public expenditure decisions of public authorities have an indirect effect upon imports, as indeed do many of the fiscal and monetary measures adopted with a view to the general management of the economy. It may be that measures of this type either do not in their nature amount to measures having equivalent effect, or do not constitute such measures unless they discriminate against imports. This view would explain the price control cases as well as *Duphar*, because price-fixing legislation is an instrument of general economic management; indeed it constitutes an alternative or supplementary policy instrument to fiscal and monetary measures in times of inflation.

The relationship between Articles 30 to 36 and other provisions of the Treaty

However wide the field of application of Articles 30 and 34 may be, it does not include obstacles to trade covered by other provisions of the Treaty, such as Articles 9 to 16 (customs duties and charges having equivalent effect), 95 (discriminatory internal taxation), and 92 and 93 (state aids).[67]

National measures which fail to be scrutinised by the Commission under Articles 92 and 93 cannot be categorised as measures having equivalent effect simply by virtue of their effects upon trade, unless the aid in question produces "restrictive effects which exceed what is necessary to enable it to attain the objectives permitted by the Treaty."[68] This may be the case where aid is granted to traders who obtain supplies of imported products through a state agency but is withheld when the products are imported direct, if this distinction is not clearly necessary for the attainment of the objectives of the said aid or for its proper functioning.[69] Furthermore, the Court has held that the possibility that state subsidies to a campaign designed to favour domestic products might fall within Articles 92 and 93 does not mean that the campaign itself thereby escapes the prohibitions laid down in Article 30.[70]

Other provisions of the Treaty may at times affect the application of

---

[66] Case 238/82 [1984] E.C.R. 523.
[67] Case 74/76 *Iannelli & Volpi* [1977] E.C.R. 557; Case 222/82 *Apple and Pear Development Council* [1983] E.C.R. 4083, at para. 30.
[68] Case 74/76 *Iannelli & Volpi* [1977] E.C.R. 557.
[69] Case 74/76 *Iannelli & Volpi* [1977] E.C.R. 557.
[70] Case 249/81 *Commission* v. *Ireland* [1982] E.C.R. 4005, at para. 18.

Articles 30 to 36, in particular Articles 39 to 46 (common agricultural policy),[71] Article 103 (conjunctural policy), Articles 108–109 (measures to combat balance of payments problems), Articles 115, and Articles 223 to 225 (safeguard measures).[72]

[71] As to which, see *infra* at pp. 305 *et seq*.
[72] See Vaughan, *Law of the European Communities*, 12.113, to 12.116. For the relationship between Art. 30 and 37, see the following chapter.

CHAPTER 7

STATE MONOPOLIES OF A COMMERCIAL CHARACTER

Commercial monopolies as a barrier to intra-Community trade

The Spaak Report pointed out that the exercise by State agencies of exclusive import rights raised particular problems for the opening of national markets, since in each case the prospective purchaser of foreign products and the body controlling the level of imports would be one and the same.[1] Applying a similar scheme to that proposed for the progressive abolition of quotas would be out of the question, since it could result in obliging a state agency to purchase goods which it did not need.[2] The Report suggested that by the end of the transitional period such national organisations must either be eliminated, be adapted to the requirements of the Common Market, or be replaced by a common organisation. Necessary adjustments would be made gradually during the transitional period, subject to the guidance of the European Commission.[3]

An instructive example of the type of organisation in question is that of the Italian cigarette lighter monopoly, whose powers and practices were described in Recommendations addressed by the Commission to the Republic of Italy in November 1969.[4] An association of private interests, the Consorzio Industrie Fiammiferi, enjoyed the exclusive right to manufacture, import and sell cigarette lighters in Italy. The Consorzio purchased lighters from manufacturers at home and abroad, re-sold them to retailers (in most cases fixing the retail prices), and undertook to provide after-sales service. Customs clearance for imported lighters was the exclusive preserve of the Consorzio.

The Commission made the following findings:
— that the right of the Consorzio to decide the type and quantity of lighters it bought allowed it to arbitrarily limit imports;
— that being exclusively authorised to arrange customs clearance, the Consorzio was in a position to delay the distribution of imported goods;
— that being solely authorised to carry stocks, the Consorzio could cause delays in the supply of imported lighters to retailers;
— that the power to fix retail prices allowed the Consorzio to price imported goods excessively in relation to the domestic product;
— that the exclusive right to provide after-sales service was capable of

---

[1] *Rapport des Chefs de Délégation aux Ministres des Affairs etrangéres*, p. 37; *The Spaak Report* (PEP 1956), p. 229.
[2] The Report proposed percentage increases in quotas, see *Rapport*, p. 36, *Spaak*, p. 228. Despite the strictures of the Spaak Committee, it will be noted that the Commission did in fact ask State monopolies to increase their purchases by an annual percentage amount, see, *e.g.* Recommendations on the French tobacco monopoly, described *infra*, p. 149.
[3] *Rapport*, p. 37, *Spaak*, p. 229.
[4] O.J. Sp. Ed., Second Series, Vol. VI, p. 6.

discriminatory application, and that delay in servicing imported products could cause damage to the reputation of imported brands.

On the basis of the information at its disposal, the Commission took the view that discrimination had in fact occurred in three respects: (i) a failure to import certain types of lighter; (ii) the differential pricing of domestic and imported goods; (iii) the incomplete filling of retailer's orders for imported lighters, and consequential refusal by the Consorzio to grant the time to pay customary in the case of bulk orders.

Since the discriminatory application of exclusive rights as extensive as those described above would clearly be capable of rendering nugatory the elimination of customs duties and quotas on the goods in question, it is hardly surprising that the representatives of the Six considered that the problem posed by the existence of the State monopolies justified specific provision in the Treaty.

Article 37—direct applicability

Article 37 of the Treaty provides, in part:

"1. Member States shall progressively adjust any State monopolies of a commercial character so as to ensure that when the transitional period has ended no discrimination regarding the conditions under which goods are procured and marketed exists between nationals of Member of States.

The provisions of this Article shall apply to any body through which a Member of State, in law or in fact, either directly or indirectly supervises, determines or appreciably influences imports or exports between Member States. These provisions shall likewise apply to monopolies delegated by the State to others.

2. Member States shall refrain from introducing any new measure which is contrary to the principles laid down in paragraph 1 or which restricts the scope of the Articles dealing with the abolition of customs duties and quantitative restrictions between Member States."

The provisions of paragraph 2 were held to be directly applicable from the date of entry into force of the Treaty in *Costa* v. *ENEL*.[5] Paragraph 1 was held to have similar effect from the end of the transitional period in *Pubblico Ministero* v. *Flavia Manghera*[6] and *Rewe-Zentrale des Lebensmittel-Grosshandels* v. *Hauptzollamt Landau/Pfalz*.[7] The State monopolies in question are those enjoying exclusive rights in the procurement and distribution of *goods*, not services.[8]

Adjustment during the transitional period

It will be noted that the Article imposes both a duty to "adjust" and a "standstill" provision for new measures. The process of adjustment must

---

[5] Case 6/64 [1964] E.C.R. 585.
[6] Case 59/75 [1976] E.C.R. 91.
[7] Case 45/75 [1976] E.C.R. 181.
[8] Case 155/73 Sacchi [1974] E.C.R. 409; Case 271/81 *Société d'Insémination Artificielle* [1983] E.C.R. 2057. In the latter case the Court recognised the possibility that a monopoly over the provision of services might have an indirect influence on trade in goods.

be "harmonised with the abolition of quantitative restrictions on the same products provided for in Articles 30–34."[9] Article 37 is indeed the final Article in the Chapter entitled "Elimination of Quantitative Restrictions between Member States," but whereas Article 33(7) empowers the Commission to issue Directives establishing the procedure and timetable for the abolition of measures having an effect equivalent to quotas, the Commission's competence under Article 37(6) is limited to making "recommendations as to the manner in which and the timetable according to which the adjustment provided for in this Article shall be carried out," no doubt reflecting the sensitivity of Member States to trade in products covered by State monopolies at the time the Treaty was drafted.

An example of the approach of the Commission to the problem of adjustment is provided by its Recommendations of April 1962 concerning the French tobacco monopoly,[10] in which it first isolates the characteristics of the monopoly giving rise to discrimination and then makes appropriate proposals. Three types of discrimination, in the view of the Commission, would require elimination if the aim of the Article was to be achieved: the use of discretion to limit imports; the differential pricing of imports and domestic goods in favour of the latter; and discrimination in the conditions of distribution of products, in particular regarding the supply of goods to retailers, and advertising. The Commission recommended that the monopoly (i) make an annual percentage increase in the volume of tobacco products imported from other Member States; (ii) establish pricing criteria on the basis of percentage margins and apply such criteria to imports and domestic products alike; and (iii) allow advertising of imports on the same basis as domestic products.

Comparison of the above with the Commission's analysis of the Italian cigarette lighter monopoly reveals the occurrence of similar "patterns" of discrimination. This is confirmed by other Commission Recommendations to Member States on the adjustment of State monopolies, which are in large part reasoned in "standard form."[11]

Prohibition *per se* of exclusive import rights

Whether or not exclusive import rights enjoyed by State monopolies would be prohibited *per se* from the end of the transitional period was long the subject of controversy.[12] One view had it that although theoretically it was possible to conceive of a State monopoly exercising its exclusive rights under conditions providing equal opportunity for domestic and imported goods, in practice discrimination would be inevitable—certainly where the national monopoly manufactured or processed the goods in question.[13]

---

[9] Art. 37(3).

[10] J.O. 1962, 1500.

[11] See, *e.g.* J.O. 1962, 1502 (French match monopoly), J.O. 1962, 1505 (Italian match monopoly), J.O. 1962, 1506 (French potash monopoly).

[12] See, *e.g.* Van Hecke (1965–66) 3 C.M.L.Rev. 450, Kapteyn and VerLoren van Themaat, *Introduction to the Law of the European Communities* (1973), p. 205.

[13] Opinion of the Advocate General in Case 82/71 *Public Prosecutor v. SAIL* [1972] E.C.R. 119, at p. 146. The Commission's observations, at least on the latter point, were in a similar vein.

Another view conceded the likelihood of discrimination by national agencies enjoying exclusive import rights, but denied that the exclusive rights were *per se* prohibited. Adherents of this latter view referred to the requirement in Article 37(1) that State monopolies be "adjusted." This wording was said to be inconsistent with the notion that exclusive import rights could be prohibited *per se*, since this would result in the abolition, rather than the adjustment, of the State monopoly.

The Commission invariably took the latter view, albeit with a certain reluctance. In its recommendations to Member States during the transitional period, it made it clear that if its proposals did not result in imports from the Member States subject to the monopoly being placed in a situation comparable to that resulting from the abolition of tariffs and quantitative restrictions, the exclusive import rights would be considered incompatible with the provisions of the Treaty concerning the free movement of goods.[14] Recommendations made in anticipation of the end of the transitional period, while not going so far as to characterise exclusive import rights as being *per se* incompatible with Article 37, suggested their abolition as being the most effective means of complying with that Article.[15] Observations expressed by the Commission before the Court of Justice were in similar vein.[16]

The question was posed squarely to the Court in *Pubblico Ministero* v. *Flavia Manghera et al.*[17] The case arose from criminal proceedings instituted before the Investigating Judge at the Tribunale di Como, alleging importation into Italy of tobacco manufactured abroad, in violation of legislation reserving to the State a monopoly in the manufacture, preparation, import and sale of that product. The investigating Judge sought a preliminary ruling from the Court of Justice on the question, *inter alia*, whether, as of the end of the transitional period, commercial monopolies should have been reorganised in such a way as to eliminate even the possibility of discrimination being practised against Community exporters, with the consequential restriction, as of January 1, 1970, of the exclusive right to import from other Member States. The Court replied in the affirmative. Taking into account the position of Article 37 under the Title on the Free Movement of Goods and in particular under Chapter II on the abolition of quantitative restrictions between Member States,[18] in the Court's view it followed

> " . . . that the obligation laid down in paragraph (1) aims at ensuring compliance with fundamental rule of the free movement of goods throughout the common market, in particular by the abolition of quantitative restrictions and measures having equivalent effect in trade between Member States. This objective would not be attained if,

---

[14] See, *e.g.* J.O. 1962, 1502 (French match monopoly), J.O. 1962, 1505 (Italian match monopoly), J.O. 1962, 506 (French potash monopoly).
[15] See, *e.g.* J.O. 1970, L6/13 (French potash monopoly), J.O. 1970, L6/16 (Italian lighter monopoly), J.O. 1970, L31/1 (Italian match monopoly).
[16] *Costa* v. *ENEL*, note 5, *Public Prosecutor* v. *SAIL*, note 13, *Sacchi*, note 8.
[17] Note 6.
[18] See also *Costa* v. *ENEL* [1964] E.C.R. 585 at p. 598, and the Commission Recommendations cited in note 14.

in a Member State where a commercial monopoly exists, the free movement of goods from other Member States similar to those with which the national monopoly is concerned were not ensured. . . . The exclusive right to import manufactured products of the monopoly in question thus constitutes, in respect of Community exporters, discrimination prohibited by Article 37(1). The answer to the first question should therefore be that Article 37(1) of the EEC Treaty must be interpreted as meaning that as from December 31, 1969 every national monopoly of a commercial character must be adjusted so as to eliminate the exclusive right to import from other Member States."[19]

Although the Court could have restricted its finding to national agencies enjoying the exclusive right to import goods which they themselves manufactured, it did not do so. The Advocate General agreed with the Commission[20] that where this was the case the exclusive right itself amounted to discrimination, but was prepared, like the Court, to go further. First, since Article 37 completed the preceding Articles dealing with the elimination of quantitative restrictions and measures having equivalent effect, it would be inconsistent to apply a different test to that enunciated by the Court of Justice in *Procureur du Roi* v. *Dassonville*,[21] to the effect that Article 30 embraced trading rules whose effect on trade was merely potential. Secondly Advocate General Warner saw confirmation of this reasoning in the requirement in Article 37(1) that abolition of discrimination be "ensured." The abolition of something could not be ensured if the possibility of the occurrence remained.[22]

The early case law—Article 37 held to apply to measures indirectly connected with the existence of a state monopoly

In the case of a State monopoly enjoying an exclusive right of import, discrimination flows directly from the existence, or the exercise, of the exclusive right itself, but the Court held in the *Cinzano*[23] case that Article 37 also extended to measures merely *connected* with a state monopoly. The national proceedings concerned a challenge to the imposition of the *monopolausqleich*, or monopoly equalisation charge, on a consignment of vermouth imported into the Federal Republic of Germany. The charge was imposed on imported alcoholic drinks of those types *not* subject to the German alcohol monopoly, in order to burden imported drinks to the same degree as similar domestic alcoholic drinks marketed independently of the monopoly. The competent German court asked the Court of Justice whether a charge such as that in issue, imposed after the Treaty came into force, was consistent with Article 37(2). The Federal Rupublic argued in its

---

[19] [1976] E.C.R. 91 at pp. 100, 101.
[20] Their reasons differed. The Commission took the view that the manufacturer with exclusive import rights could not fail to favour its own products, the Advocate General saw discrimination in the manufacturer being free to sell in other Member States but having an exclusive right to import into its own.
[21] Case 8/74 [1974] E.C.R. 837. See *supra*, at p. 132.
[22] [1976] E.C.R. 91, at p. 108.
[23] Case 13/70, E.C.R. 1089.

submissions to the Court that although the German alcohol monopoly was indeed a state monopoly within the meaning of Article 37(1), it did not cover vermouths, which were simply subjected to a charge on import. Accordingly, Article 37 was inapplicable.

The Court did not accept this contention, interpreting the word "measure" in Article 37(2) by reference to the "definition" of monopolies subject to the Article contained in the second sentence of Article 37(1):

> "This definition is worded in deliberately general terms so as to include activities by which the State concerned acts only '*de facto*' or 'indirectly' in trade between Member States as well as activities by which, far from 'supervising' or 'determining' such trade, it is satisfied merely by 'influencing' it. It follows from this that the application of Article 37 is not limited to imports or exports which are directly subject to the monopoly but covers all measures which are connected with its existence and affect trade between Member States in certain products, whether or not subject to the monopoly."[24]

In two subsequent cases, *Miritz*,[25] and *Rewe-Zentrale*,[26] the Court reiterated its view that Article 37 applies to all measures which are connected with a State monopoly and effect trade between Member States, reasoning, rather more obliquely, that this follows from the fact that:

> "Article 37(1) is not concerned exclusively with quantitative restrictions but prohibits any discrimination, when the transitional period has ended, regarding the conditions under which goods are procured and marketed, between nationals of Member States."[27]

The early case law—the relationship between Article 37 and the other provisions of the Treaty

In the *Cinzano* case, the Court considered the interpretation of Article 37 in relation to a charge such as that in issue in the main suit, and took the view that if the new duty placed no greater burden on imported products than on the domestic article, there could be no question of infringing either Article 37(1) or 37(2).[28] Although the Court systematically examined paragraphs (1) and (2), considering firstly the general notion of discrimination, and secondly, the more specific prohibition of measures restricting the scope of the articles dealing with the abolition of customs duties and quantitative restrictions, the former will usually[29] embrace the latter. The wording of the respective paragraphs is perhaps explicable on the grounds that the draftsman intended the "discrimination" of paragraph (1) to be discrimination other than customs duties and quantitative restrictions *simpliciter*, which would be subjected to the specific provisions of Articles 12 to

---

[24] [1970] E.C.R. 1089, at p. 1095.
[25] Case 91/75, [1976] E.C.R. 217.
[26] Case 45/75, [1976] E.C.R. 181.
[27] [1976] E.C.R. 217, at pp. 229, 230.
[28] [1970] E.C.R. 1089, at p. 1096.
[29] But not always, *e.g.* customs duties are prohibited even if there is no domestically produced counterpart: Cases 2 and 3/69 *Chougol Diamond* [1969] E.C.R. 211.

17, and 30 to 34. But this view did not initially commend itself to the Court.[30]

The truth is that the relationship between Article 37 and the Articles preceding it was not made immediately clear. In *Albatros* v. *SOPECO*[31] the Court found it unnecessary to decide whether or not the application of Article 37 to national monopolies precluded the application of the other provisions of the Chapter concerning the abolition of quantitative restrictions between Member States. After some hesitation, the Advocate General took the view that Article 37 was exclusively applicable to commercial monopolies,[32] and this view was upheld by the Court in *Hauptzollamt Göttingen* v. *Wolfgang Miritz*,[33] a case arising from proceedings before the Bundesfinanzhof concerning the German alcohol monopoly. After relinquishing exclusive import rights, the Federal Republic imposed the *Preisausgleich*, or "special equalisation charge," on imports of alcohol, equal to the difference between the normal selling price in Germany, and the lowest price at which it was possible, in another Member State of the European Community, to buy alcohol intended for consumption. Wolfgang Miritz challenged a demand for payment of the *Preisausgleich* in the German courts, resulting in a request from the Bundesfinanzhof for a preliminary ruling on the compatibility of such a charge with Article 12 and/or Article 37(2) of the Treaty. Since in the Court's view, the structure and character of the equalisation charge linked it to the system of the German alcohol monopoly, it confined its attention to the text of Article 37, which dealt specifically with the adjustment of such monopolies. Where Article 37 applied, it seemed that it did so exclusively of Articles 12 to 17, and 30 to 36.[34] The Court held that since Article 37(1) aimed at ensuring compliance with the fundamental rule of the free movement of goods throughout the common market, *in casu* by the abolition of customs duties and charges having equivalent effect, a levy of the type in issue, introduced after the entry into force of the Treaty, was contrary to Article 37(2).

If *Miritz* clarified the relationship between Article 37 on the one hand, and Articles 12 to 17, and 30 to 36 on the other, the decision in *Rewe-Zentrale des Lebensmittel-Grosshandels*[35] was instructive on the relationship between that Article and the other provisions of the Treaty—*in casu* Article 95. The case concerned the *monopolausgleich*, or monopoly equalisation charge, imposed under the German alcohol monopoly. A German court asked the Court of Justice whether the charge infringed Article 37(1) and/or Article 95(1) (on discriminatory internal taxation[36]) The Court of Justice considered the compatibility of the charge first under Article 37, and then under Article 95. In *Miritz*, Article 37 was regarded as a *lex spe-*

---

[30] It is inconsistent with the Court's reasoning in Case 59/75 *Manqhera* [1976] E.C.R. 91, and Case 91/75 *Miritz* [1976] E.C.R. 217.

[31] Case 20/64 [1965] E.C.R. 29, at p. 45.

[32] [1965] E.C.R. 29, at p. 45.

[33] Case 91/75 [1976] E.C.R. 217.

[34] The Advocate General in *SAIL* thought Art. 36 would apply to measures relating to a state monopoly, see Case 82/71 [1972] E.C.R. 119, at p. 147.

[35] Case 45/75 [1976] E.C.R. 181.

[36] As to which, see, *supra* at p. 107.

cialis, precluding the necessity of considering individually Articles 12 to 17 and 30 to 36, but in *Rewe-Zentrale* the court seems to refute any suggestion that this might also be the case as regards other provisions of the Treaty, by considering first Article 95, and then Article 37. Having emphasised that compatibility with Article 95 could in no way prejudge a finding under other Articles, including Article 37, the Court proceeded to interpret Article 37(1) in identical terms to its interpretation of Article 95.

The latter case law—a modified theory emerges

In its submissions in the first *Hansen* case[37] the Commission advanced a new argument. An argument which, if correct, would require a reformulation of the by then conventional wisdom. According to the Commission, by the end of the transitional period, all State monopolies should have been adjusted so as to comply with the requirements of Article 37(1). Since the article abolished the exclusive right of importation, and with it the exclusive right to market products subject to the monopoly, such monopolies could no longer be regarded as state monopolies of a commercial character within the meaning of Article 37. In short, the article was largely spent. It was applicable only to the extent that exclusive rights to import, export or market goods, remained unadjusted. In relation to all other measures, the general provisions of the Treaty were applicable, in particular, Articles 12, 30, 34 and 95.

The national proceedings in the first *Hansen* case concerned an allegedly discriminatory rate of taxation levied on imported spirits by the Federal Monopoly Administration (the plaintiff had been refused a tax exemption extended to certain collective farms, small enterprises, etc.). The national court had sought a preliminary ruling on the interpretation of Articles 37 and 95. The Court of Justice did not address the problem in quite the terms suggested by the Commission. But it noted that preferential arrangements comparable to those provided for under German law existed in several Member States, in different forms, and that such arrangements were capable of existence quite independently of any connection with a commercial monopoly, within the framework of national fiscal legislation. The Court concluded that it seemed *preferable* to examine the problem from the point of view of the general requirements of Article 95 EEC, rather than from the point of view of Article 37, which was specifically applicable to State monopolies. In any event, added the Court, Articles 37 and 95 were based on the same principle, *i.e.* the elimination of all discrimination in trade between Member States. While the Court does not adopt the Commission's reasons for addressing itself solely to the text of Article 95, the result is the same. Article 37 is not consulted, even *pro forma*, in contrast with the Court's earlier approach in *Rewe-Zentrale*, in which it considered first Article 95, and then Article 37.

---

[37] Case 148/77 [1978] E.C.R. 1787.

The plaintiff in the *Cassis* case[38] wished to import Cassis into Germany, but was refused an import authorisation on the ground that the Cassis was of insufficient alcoholic strength. The competent German court asked for a preliminary ruling on the interpretation of Articles 30 and 37, but the Court of Justice confined its attention to Article 30, noting that Article 37 related specifically to state monopolies of a commercial character. In the Court's view:

> "That provision is therefore irrelevant with regard to national provisions which do not concern the exercise by a public monopoly of its specific function—namely, its exclusive right—but apply in a general manner to the production and marketing of alcoholic beverages, whether or not the latter are covered by the monopoly in question."[39]

The above statement of the Court is certainly consistent with the Commission's "new view" of the role of Article 37 after the end of the transitional period.

The Court again considered the ambit of Article 37, and its relationship with Article 95 of the Treaty, in the first *Grandes Distilleries* cases,[40] a reference arising from national proceedings concerning the operation of the French alcohol monopoly. The plaintiff in the national proceedings had paid a charge on domestically produced alcohol, equal to the charge imposed on imported alcohol. However, he claimed that since the latter charge was not legally payable, inasmuch as it had been prohibited under Article 37, he had been discriminated against, contrary to Article 37. The Court of Justice held: (i) that Article 37 only applied to activities intrinsically connected with the specific business of the monopoly and was irrelevant to national provisions which had no connection with such specific business: (ii) that while during the transitional period, Article 37 suspended the operation of Article 95, as of the end of the transitional period, the position of internal taxes was subject exclusively to Article 95: (iii) that it was not necessary to decide whether Article 37 prohibited discrimination against national products, because Article 95 did not, and Article 95 was exclusively applicable.

The Court's emphasis that only activities intrinsically connected with specific business of the monopoly fall within the ambit of Article 37 clearly signalled a departure from its previous jurisprudence, and came close to acceptance of the view of the Commission referred to above.[41]

In the second *Grandes Distilleries case*[42] the Court applied both Articles 30 and 37 to the operation of the French alcohol monopoly, under which producers were required to deliver certain alcohol to the national monopoly (reserved alcohol), but were entitled to sell other alcohol (freed alcohol) directly to purchasers. The plaintiff in the national proceedings had sought to import from Italy into France oranges steeped in alcohol for the purposes of distillation. The French authorities had informed the plaintiff

---

[38] Case 120/78 [1979] E.C.R. 649.
[39] Case 120/78 note 38, at para. 7.
[40] Case 86/78 [1979] E.C.R. 897.
[41] *Supra* at p. 154.
[42] Case 119/78 [1979] E.C.R. 975.

that importation was permissible but that imported raw materials could not be used for the production of reserved alcohol, only freed alcohol. The matter was referred to the Court of Justice, which held: (i) that Article 37 required the adjustment, but not the abolition of state monopolies[43]: (ii) that it followed that the obligation to deliver to the monopoly and the corresponding obligation on it to purchase national alcohol was compatible with Article 37(1) and (2): but (iii) that a distinction drawn between nationally produced alcohol obtained from the distillation of national raw materials and nationally produced alcohol obtained from the distillation of raw materials originating in another Member State was inconsistent with both Articles 30 and 37 EEC.[44]

The legal position before the *Grandes Distilleries* cases seems to have been: (a) that Article 37 and Article 95 might be cumulatively applicable to a charge connected with a state monopoly of a commercial character having the character of internal taxation[45] and (b) that Article 37, where it applied, did so exclusively of the foregoing provisions on the free movement of goods.[46] After these cases the position is that Article 95 displaces Article 37 where internal charges are concerned, and Article 37 is cumulatively applicable with the earlier provisions of the chapter on the elimination of quantitative restrictions, and perhaps the provisions on customs duties and charges having equivalent effect.

In the second *Hansen* case,[47] arising once again from the operation of the German alcohol monopoly, the Court held: (i) that after the end of the transitional period, Article 37 remained applicable wherever the exercise by a state monopoly of its exclusive rights entailed a discrimination or restriction prohibited by that Article; (ii) that Article 37 prohibited a monopoly's right to purchase and re-sell national alcohol from being exercised so as to undercut imported products with publicly subsidised domestic products; and (iii) that Articles 37 and 92/93 were capable of cumulative application to one and the same fact situation.

In *Pigs and Bacon Commission* v. *McCarren*[48] the Court held that Article 38(2) of the Treaty[49] gave priority to the rules for the organisation of the agricultural markets over the application of Article 37. The better view is that this means merely that Article 37 cannot be pleaded by way of derogation from rules imposed by a common organisation: the positive obligations of that Article are surely to be implied into the framework of a common organisation and it is trite law that common organisations can derogate only in exceptional circumstances from the free movement provisions of the Treaty.[50]

---

[43] See also Case 59/75 *Manghera* [1976] E.C.R. 91: Case 91/78 *Hansen* [1979] E.C.R. 935: Case 78/82 *Commission* v. *Italy* [1983] E.C.R. 1955.
[44] The Court applies Art. 37 and Art. 30 cumulatively in case 90/82 *Commission* v. *France* [1983] E.C.R. 2011.
[45] Case 45/75 *Rewe-Zentrale* [1986] E.C.R. 181.
[46] Case 91/75 *Miritz* [1976] E.C.R. 217.
[47] Case 91/78 [1979] E.C.R. 935.
[48] Case 177/78 [1979] E.C.R. 2161.
[49] As to which see *infra*, at p. 305.
[50] See *infra*, at p. 307.

Adjustment of agricultural monopolies

A further question posed to the Court in *Miritz*[51] was whether, in the event of a charge such as that in issue infringing Article 12 or Article 37(2), the imposition of the charge could nevertheless be justified under Article 37(4), which provides, in the case of agricultural products, that steps should be taken in applying the rules contained in the Article to ensure equivalent safeguards for the employment and standard of living of the producers concerned.

It is appropriate at this point to advert to the background to the German legislation imposing the *Preisausgleich*, and to the decision of the Court of Justice in *Charmasson* v. *Minister for Economic Affairs*.[52] Shortly before the expiry of the transitional period, the Commission addressed Recommendations to the Federal Republic on the adjustment of the alcohol monopoly. The Commission took the position,[53] citing Article 37(4), that the German alcohol monopoly constituted a national organisation of the market in an agricultural product and that, pending the entry into force of rules establishing a common organisation in the alcohol sector, the interests of German producers could be legitimately safeguarded, beyond the expiry of the transitional period, by national measures. One such measure proposed by the Commission was the levy of a special tax on spirit for consumption, at a level not exceeding the difference between the price of alcohol in the Federal Republic intended for manufacture into alcohol for consumption, and the lowest price available to a producer of spirit for consumption in the Member State of export. The Commission's view of the legitimacy of such a measure was based on its understanding of Articles 43(3) and 45 of the Treaty, on the common agricultural policy. The effect of these provisions, in the Commission's view, was that pending the establishment of a common organisation of the market within the meaning of Article 40(2) of the Treaty, it was permissible to maintain in force *national* market organisations, beyond the end of the transitional period, and that such organisations would be exempt from the provisions of the Treaty concerning the free movement of goods, *in casu*, Article 37. In *Charmasson*, however, the Court of Justice ruled that the derogation allowed to national market organisations under Articles 43 and 45 extended only until the end of the transitional period. This ruling clearly undermined the reasoning favouring the legitimacy of national measures such as the *Preisausgleich* after December 31, 1969. Accordingly, the Commission notified the Member States in July 1975 that they were, in view of the Court's decision, under a duty to abolish all the derogations from the obligation to adjust laid down in Article 37 which had until then been granted to them pursuant to Article 37(4).

The train of events outlined above explains the unprecedented suggestion by the Commission to the Court that despite the ruling in *Charmasson*, there should be a "final period of time during which the national market

---

[51] Case 91/75 [1976] E.C.R. 217.
[52] Case 48/74 [1974] E.C.R. 1383.
[53] J.O. 1970, L31/20 at 22, 23.

could be kept in existence pending its replacement by the general rules of the Treaty." The Court, evidencing little sympathy with the predicament of the Federal Republic, held that Article 37(4), far from allowing any derogation beyond the transitional period, had never allowed any derogation at all. The "equivalent safeguards" referred to in Article 37(4) must themselves be compatible with the provisions of Article 37(1) and (2).

State monopolies in the enlarged community

When the Community was enlarged in 1973, Article 44 of the Act of Accession provided that the new Member States should progressively adjust their state monopolies of a commercial character so as to ensure the elimination of discrimination in the conditions under which goods are procured and marketed. Adjustment was to be completed by December 31, 1977, and an equivalent obligation was imposed on the original Six *vis-à-vis* the new Member States. The Commission was entrusted with the responsibility of making recommendations as to the mode and timing of appropriate adjustments.

At the time of enlargement, it was the Commission's view that the French monopolies for alcohol, manufactured tobacco, and petroleum, and the Italian monopolies for matches and manufactured tobacco, had yet to be adjusted to meet the requirements of Article 37 *vis-à-vis* the original Member States. The new Member States having declared that they had no monopolies of the type subject to Article 37, the Commission addressed recommendations to France and Italy to make appropriate adjustments in their respective monopolies, where such monopolies differentiated between the original and the new Member States.

The French alcohol monopoly was adjusted in September 1985 following recourse by the Commission to the procedure under Article 169 of the Treaty, and the imposition of countervailing charges on exports of French alcohol of agricultural origin under Article 46 of the Treaty.[54]

Under the second Act of Accession Greece was bound to adjust her State monopolies so as to ensure that by December 31, 1985 no discrimination regarding the conditions under which goods are procured and marketed existed between nationals of the Member States, and the Member States were under equivalent obligations.[55]

Under the Third Act of Accession the kingdom of Spain shall progressively adjust her State monopolies so as to ensure that by December 31, 1991 at the latest no discrimination regarding the conditions under which goods are procured and marketed exists between nationals of the Member States.[56] The Member States have equivalent obligations.[57] The position is similar for Portugal, though the final date for adjustment is January 1, 1993.[58]

---

[54] For Article 46, see *infra*, at p. 297.
[55] Art. 40.
[56] Art. 48(1).
[57] Art. 48(1).
[58] Third Act of Accession, Art. 208(1).

PART IV: THE FREE MOVEMENT OF PERSONS AND FREEDOM TO PROVIDE SERVICES

CHAPTER 8

FREE MOVEMENT OF WORKERS

GENERAL

THE Treaties establishing the European Communities each contain provisions designed to facilitate the movement of workers between the Member States. The signatories to the Treaty establishing the European Coal and Steel Community undertook in Article 69 to remove any restrictions based on nationality upon the employment in the coal and steel industries of workers holding the nationality of one of the Member States and having recognised qualifications in coalmining or steelmaking, and a similar provision appears in Article 96 of the Treaty establishing the European Atomic Energy Community, declaring the right of nationals of the Member States to take skilled employment in the field of nuclear energy. Acting under this latter Article the Council issued a Directive in 1962[1] defining the scope of skilled employment and requiring that Member States adopt all necessary measures to ensure that any authorisation required for taking up employment in the field specified should be automatically granted.

As Treaties concerned only with limited economic integration, the ECSC and Euratom Treaties naturally only dealt with workers in their respective sectors. The EEC Treaty, on the other hand, seeks to promote comprehensive economic integration, and its provisions requiring that "freedom of movement for workers shall be secured within the Community by the end of the transitional period at the latest" are applicable to all "workers of the Member States" regardless of occupation.[2] It is with the provision of the EEC Treaty, and the implementing legislation made thereunder, that we shall be hereafter concerned.

Since a common market requires the removal of all obstacles to the free movement of the factors of production, as well as of goods and services, the free movement of workers in the Community may be seen simply as a prerequisite to the achievement of an economic objective. Support for this view may be found in the Spaak Report,[3] and in the texts of Articles 48, 49 and 51 of the Treaty. Under Article 48, workers of the Member States are to be free to accept offers of employment actually made, and to remain in a Member State for the purposes of carrying on employment. Article 49 authorises legislation by the Council to eliminate administrative procedures likely to impede the movement of workers, and to set up machinery for matching offers of employment in one Member State with available candidates in another. The provisions of Article 51 of the Treaty,

---

[1] J.O. 1962, 1650.
[2] Art. 48. But the EEC Treaty does not "affect" the provisions of the ECSC Treaty, nor "derogate" from those of the Euratom Treaty; see Art. 232 EEC.
[3] *Rapport des chefs de délégation aux ministres des affaires etrangères* (Brussels, April 21, 1956), pp. 18, 88.

empowering the Council to take legislative action in the field of social security, appears to extend this authorisation only to measures necessary for safeguarding the rights of the migrant worker *stricto sensu*.

Yet such a functional economic approach to the interpretation of the free movement provisions is likely to be inadequate for two reasons. First, in the graphic words of Article 6 of the Clayton Anti-Trust Act, because of the notion that "the labour of a human being is not a commodity or article of commerce," or, as Advocate General Trabucchi has put it: "The migrant worker is not regarded by Community law—nor is he by the internal legal systems—as a mere source of labour but is viewed as a human being."[4] A similar sentiment may be discerned in the fifth recital to the preamble to Regulation 1612/68 of the Council,[5] which speaks of the exercise of workers' rights in "freedom and dignity,' and describes freedom of movement for workers as a "fundamental right" and "one of the means by which the worker is guaranteed the possibility of improving his living and working conditions and promoting his social advancement, while helping to satisfy the requirements of the economies of the Member States." It is significant that the macroeconomic objectives of the Community are placed second to the personal right of the Community worker to improve his standard of life by the exercise of the rights guaranteed by Article 48.

But for another reason a purely economic approach is likely to be deficient. The EEC was established after the failure of rather more grandiose attempts to institute a Western European military and political union, and it represented an attempt to achieve a similar political aim by means of economic integration. Thus the first recital to the preamble of the Treaty of Rome records the determination of the signatories to lay the foundation of an ever closer union among the peoples of Europe, and the eighth records their resolve to strengthen peace and liberty by a pooling of their respective resources. The last sentence of Article 2 of the Treaty lays down as one of the Community's allotted tasks that of promoting closer relations between the Member States. To this extent, there may be said to be a political objective enshrined in the provisions relating to the free movement of persons. The halting steps of the Member States towards "European Union" are apparently taken in the belief that they are taking the Community concept to its logical conclusion. It is significant that the Declaration issued after the Summit Conference of October 1972 included the words: "The Member States re-affirm their resolve to base their Community's development on democracy, freedom of opinion, *free movement of men and ideas* and participation by the people through their elected representatives."[6]

The Court of Justice has sometimes interpreted the provisions of

---

[4] Case 7/75 *Mr. and Mrs. F.* v. *Belgian State* [1975] E.C.R. 679, at p. 696, [1975] 2 C.M.L.R. 442 at p. 450.
[5] J.O. 1968, L257/2. The Court has referred to the fifth recital both as a guide to the interpretation of the Regulation, and as an indication of the scope of application of the Treaty: Case 76/72 *Michel S* [1973] E.C.R. 457, Case 9/74 *Casagrande* [1974] E.C.R. 773, (interpretation of Reg. 1612/68); Case 152/81 *Forcheri* [1983] ECR 2323, (scope of application of the Treaty).
[6] Emphasis added. Bull. E.C. 10/72 at p. 15.

Articles 48 to 51 of the Treaty, and the implementing legislation made thereunder, in a rather more liberal manner than would be dictated by a purely functional view of the Treaty based on its economic objectives. In *Hessische Knappschaft* v. *Maison Singer*[7] a German national on holiday in France had been killed in a road accident. His dependents were paid benefit by a German social security institution, which then brought an action in France against the employer of the driver of the other vehicle, claiming that the French court was bound to recognise the subrogation that German law allowed, by virtue of Article 52 of Regulation 3.[8] In the course of the proceedings before the Court of Justice, it was argued that to apply Article 52 of the Regulation in circumstances such as those before the national court would be incompatible with Article 51 of the Treaty, inasmuch as that provision only allowed the Council to adopt such measures as were necessary to provide freedom of movement for workers *qua* workers, not *qua* holidaymakers. The Court responded:

> "Since the establishment of as complete as possible a freedom of movement of labour is among the "foundations" of the Community, it is the ultimate goal of Article 51 and, therefore, governs the exercise of the power it confers upon the Council. It would not be in keeping with such a concept to limit the idea of "worker" to migrant workers strictly speaking or to travel connected with their employment. Nothing in Article 51 requires such a distinction; moreover, such a distinction would make the application of the contemplated rules unfeasible. On the other hand, the system adopted for Regulation No. 3, which consists in removing, as much as possible, the territorial limitations for applying the various social security systems, is quite in keeping with the objectives of Article 51 of the Treaty."[9]

In his Opinion in *Mr. and Mrs. F.* v. *Belgian State*, Advocate General Trabucchi explicitly eschewed a functional economic approach to the interpretation of the Community social security Regulations:

> "If we want Community law to be more than a mere mechanical system of economics and to constitute instead a system commensurate with the society which it has to govern, if we wish to be a legal system corresponding to the concept of social justice and to the requirements of European integration, not only of the economy but of the people, we cannot disappoint the Belgian court's expectations, which are more than those of legal form."[10]

The Court of Justice was able to make the effort required of it.

THE AMBIT OF ARTICLE 48 OF THE TREATY

Article 48 aims to secure freedom of movement for workers. While this provision may require Member States to amend their legislation, even with

[7] Case 44/65 [1965] E.C.R. 965, [1966] C.M.L.R. 82.
[8] J.O. 1958, 561.
[9] [1965] E.C.R. 965 at p. 971, [1966] C.M.L.R. 82 at p. 94.
[10] [1975] E.C.R. at p. 697, [1975] 2 C.M.L.R. at p. 452.

respect to their own nationals (*e.g.* to allow them to leave their own Member State to seek work in another[11]), it does not extend to situations wholly internal to a Member State,[12] for example the binding over of a person charged with theft on condition that she proceed to Northern Ireland and not return to England or Wales for three years.[12] A worker cannot rely upon Article 48 unless he or she has exercised the right to freedom of movement within the Community,[13] or is seeking to exercise that right, and the purely hypothetical possibility that an individual may at some time in the future seek work in another Member State is not sufficient.[14]

The application of Article 48 is not conditional upon all conduct pertaining to an economic relationship or activity occurring within the territory of the Member States: it applies in judging all legal relationships which can be localised within the Community, by reason either of the place where they were entered into, or the place where they take effect.[15]

The Concept of "Worker"

Article 48 refers to freedom of movement for "workers." Article 1 of Regulation 1612/68 on freedom of movement for workers within the Community refers to the right to "take up an activity as an employed person." Neither formulation is defined,[16] but the concepts must be interpreted according to their ordinary meaning, and in the light of the objectives of the Treaty.[17] The terms cannot be defined according to the national laws of the Member States,[18] but have a Community meaning.[19] Since these concepts define the field of application of one of the fundamental freedoms guaranteed by the Treaty, they must not be interpreted restrictively.[20] A person may be a "worker," or person pursuing an "activity as an employed person" even if engaged in only part-time work, and in receipt of pay below the minimum guaranteed wage in the sector in question.[20] However, the concepts cover only the pursuit of effective and genuine activities, and not activities on such a small scale as to regarded as "marginal and ancillary."[20] Furthermore, the motives which may have prompted a "worker" to seek employment in another Member State are of no account as regards his right to enter and reside in the territory of that State, provided that he pursues or wishes to pursue an effective and genuine activity.[20]

A person who has never been employed, and who goes to another Member State to study, is not to be regarded as a "worker," at any rate where

---

[11] See, *e.g.* Art. 2(1) of Dir. 68/360; see *infra*, at p. 166.
[12] Case 175/78 *Saunders* [1979] E.C.R. 1129. Case 298/84, *Iorio* [1986] 3 C.M.L.R. 665.
[13] Cases 35, 36/82 *Morson* [1982] E.C.R. 3723.
[14] Case 180/83, *Moser* [1984] E.C.R. 2539.
[15] Case 36/74 *Walrave* [1974] E.C.R. 1405; Case 237/83 *Prodest* [1984] E.C.R. 3153.
[16] Except for the purposes of Reg. 1408/71, on Social Security; see Art. 1(*a*).
[17] Case 53/81, *Levin* [1982] E.C.R. 1035.
[18] Though to some extent they are: in the context of the social security rules; see Reg. 1408/71, Art. 1(*a*); *infra*, p. 231.
[19] Case 75/63 *Hoekstra (née Unger)* [1964] E.C.R. 177. Case 53/81 *Levin* [1982] E.C.R. 1035.
[20] Case 53/81 *Levin* [1982] E.C.R. 1035. Case 139/85, *Kempf* Judgment of June 3, 1986.

he is not during his sojourn in the latter Member State subject to a social security scheme designed to benefit employed persons.[21]

The definition of "worker" in the Community sense rarely causes difficulty because if an economically active claimant under Article 48 is not a worker, he is as like as not self-employed, in which case Articles 52 or 59 EEC come into play. The Court has held that Articles 48, 52 and 59 are based on the same principles both as far as entry and residence and non-discrimination on grounds of nationality are concerned,[22] and so categorisation under Article 48, as opposed to Articles 52 or 59, will rarely be crucial.[23]

REMOVAL OF RESTRICTIONS ON MOVEMENT AND RESIDENCE IN THE MEMBER STATES

The Treaty provides that freedom of movement for workers shall entail the right to move freely within the Member States for the purpose of accepting offers of employment actually made and empowers the Council to implement this object by legislation. Acting under this authority the Council issued Directive 68/360 of October 15, 1968, on the abolition of restrictions on movement and residence for workers of the Member States and their families.[24] The provisions of Article 48 of the Treaty have been held to be directly applicable,[25] as have those of Directive 68/360.[26] As the Court explained in *Procureur du Roi* v. *Royer*,[27] "the directives concerned [including 68/360] determined the scope and detailed rules for the exercise of rights conferred directly by the Treaty."

Persons to whom Directive 68/360 is applicable

The Directive applies to nationals of the Member States and those members of their families to whom Regulation 1612/68 is applicable.[28] In Article 10(1) of the latter Regulation we find members of the worker's family defined as:

(a) his spouse and their descendant who are under the age of 21 years or are dependants;

(b) dependent relatives in the ascending line of the worker and his spouse.

The Article declares that these members of the family, irrespective of nationality, have the right to "install" themselves with a worker who is a national of one Member State employed in the territory of another. In the

---

[21] Case 66/77 *Kuyken* [1977] E.C.R. 2311; Case 238/83 *Meade* [1984] E.C.R. 2631.
[22] Case 48/75 *Royer* [1976] E.C.R. 497; see *infra*, p. 205.
[23] See *infra*, p. 205.
[24] J.O. 1968, L257/13.
[25] Case 167/73 *Commission* v. *French Republic* [1974] E.C.R. 359, [1974] 2 C.M.L.R. 216; Case 41/74 *Van Duyn* v. *Home Office* [1974] E.C.R. 1337, [1975] 1 C.M.L.R. 1.
[26] Case 36/75 *Rutili* v. *French Minister of the Interior* [1975] E.C.R. 1219, [1976] 1 C.M.L.R. 140.
[27] Case 48/75 *Procureur du Roi* v. *Royer* [1976] E.C.R. 497, [1976] 2 C.M.L.R. 619.
[28] Art. 1.

Morson case[29] the Court held that Article 10(1) does not cover the relatives of a worker who is a national of the host State, and has never exercised the right of free movement.[30] The members of the family referred to need not actually reside under the same roof as the worker, in order to claim the benefit of Article 10(1), and a spouse retains that status until the formal dissolution of the marriage.[31]

Article 10(2) of the Regulation provides that Member States shall "facilitate the admission" of dependent members of a worker's family other than children or those in the ascending line, and any members of the family living under the worker's roof in the country whence he came.

The right of the worker and members of his family to leave their home country in order to pursue employment in another Member State

The Directive deals not only with the right to enter other Member States, it also grants the right to leave one's own.[32] Member States are obliged to grant workers the right to leave their territory for the purpose of taking up activities as employed persons and pursuing such activities in the territory of another Member State. Members of their family enjoy the same right as the national on whom they are dependent. The exercise of this right is conditioned simply on the production of a valid identity card or passport, which Member States are under a duty both to issue, and to renew. Passports must be valid for all Member States and for countries through which the holder must pass when travelling between Member States. Where a passport is the only document on which the holder may lawfully leave the country, its period of validity shall be at least five years. Member States may not demand exit visas or equivalent documents from workers or members of their families.

The right of a worker and members of his family to enter another Member State

Member States are required to allow the persons to whom Directive 68/360 applies to enter their territory simply on production of a valid identity card or passport.[33] No entry visas or equivalent documents may be demanded save from members of the family who are not EEC nationals. Member States must accord to such persons every facility for obtaining the necessary visas.[34] The Court has construed "entry visa or equivalent docu-

---

[29] Cases 35 and 36/82 *Morson* [1982] E.C.R. 3723.
[30] The qualification is important: there seems to be no reason why Arts. 7 and 48 could not be invoked by the relatives of a worker against his State of nationality, *e.g.* where he had married in another EEC country, and was returning home to work, accompanied by his new family.
[31] Case 267/83 *Diatta* [1985] E.C.R. 567. In referring to "spouse," Art. 10(1) refers to a relationship based on marriage, see Case 59/85 *Reed* Judgment of April 17, 1986.
[32] Art. 2. In the U.K. passports are issued by virtue of the royal prerogative. Prior to January 1, 1973, passports could not be claimed as of right, and a passport, once granted, could be impounded or cancelled at any time. The position is modified *pro tanto* by the terms of Art. 48 EEC and Dir. 64/221. See David W. Williams, "British Passports and the Right to Travel" (1974) 23 I.C.L.Q. 642, at pp. 647, 648, and 652, 653.
[33] Art. 3(1).
[34] Art. 3(2).

ment" as covering any formality for the purpose of granting leave to enter the territory of a Member State which is coupled with a passport check at the frontier, whatever the place or time at which leave is granted, and in whatever form it may be granted.[35]

Article 48(3)(*b*) of the Treaty envisages free movement of workers for the purpose of accepting offers of employment actually made, but makes no mention of a right to move freely *in search of* employment. It would seem to follow that Member States are only bound to apply Article 3 of the Directive in the case of workers who have already been offered a job, but the Court of Justice in *Procureur du Roi* v. *Royer*[36] referred to the right of workers to enter the territory of a Member State and reside there for the purposes intended by the Treaty, in particular to *look for* or pursue an activity as an employed person. Such a construction of Article 48 is clearly consistent with its purpose and wording. Freedom of movement entails the abolition of any discrimination based on nationality between workers of the Member States as regards, *inter alia*, employment. In Article 7 of Regulation 1612/68 the notion of equality in matters of employment is construed by the Council as involving *re*-instatement and *re*-employment. Preventing a national of a Member State who has lost his job from entering another Member State to seek employment could be said to amount to discrimination based on nationality, since he would be restricted to seeking employment in that Member State via the postal services and his own local labour exchange. Article 69 of Regulation 1408/71[37] on the social security rights of migrant workers, in providing unemployment benefit to a national of one Member State seeking employment in another, certainly assumes that he will be admitted for such a purpose.

When the Council of Ministers was drafting Directive 68/360, it was understood that a worker entering a Member State for employment could stay for three months to find a job and thus qualify for residence, but no specific provision was made.[38] Consistently with this view, Regulation 1408/71 Article 69(1)(*c*) provides that entitlement to unemployment benefit under that Article should continue for no more than three months.

The right of residence

The worker, the worker's spouse, and children under the age of 21 years[39]: In accordance with Article 48(3)(*c*) of the Treaty, Directive 68/360 provides that Member States shall grant the right of residence to workers able to produce:

(a) the document with which they entered the Member State's territory, and

(b) a confirmation of engagement from an employer, or a certificate of employment.

---

[35] Case 157/79 *Pieck* [1980] E.C.R. 2171.
[36] Case 48/75 [1976] E.C.R. 497.
[37] J.O. 1971 L149/2; consolidated in Reg. 2001/83, O.J. 1983, L230/6.
[38] H. Ter Heide, 6 C.M.L. Rev. 466, 476. The U.K. allows a stay of six months; see *Statement of Changes in Immigration Rules* H.C. Papers (1982–83) 169, paras. 67, 70.
[39] Dir. 68/360, Art. 4(3)(*c*), (*d*).

In the case of a worker's spouse and children under the age of 21 years, the right of residence is acquired upon production of:
  (a) the document with which they entered the territory, and
  (b) a document proving their relationship, issued either by their State of origin, or the State whence they came.

Dependent children over the age of 21 years, and other dependent relatives in the ascending line of the worker and the worker's spouse.[40] In the case of the aforementioned, there is required in addition to the document with which they entered the territory a document testifying to their dependence, issued either by the State of origin or the State whence they came.

Dependent relatives other than children or those in the ascending line, and relatives living under the worker's roof in the country whence they came: According to Article 10(2) of Regulation 1612/68, such members of the family do not have a right of entry, much less of residence, merely on account of their relationship to the worker, and Member States are simply under an obligation to "facilitate" their admission. Directive 68/360, however, provides in Article 4(1) that Member States shall grant the right of residence to those persons: (a) referred to in Article 1 of the Directive; (b) who are able to produce the documents specified in Article 4(3). As to (a), Article 1 of the Directive refers to members of the worker's family to whom Regulation 1612/68 is applicable. Article 10(2) of that Regulation, as has been pointed out, indeed makes provision for the relatives in question, albeit to a limited extent. As to (b), Article 4(3)(e), in specifying those documents production of which gives rise to a right of residence, provides in pertinent part: "in the cases referred to in Article 10(1) and (2) of Regulation (EEC) No. 1612/68, a document issued by the competent authority . . . testifying that they are dependent on the worker or that they live under his roof in such country." Just as Article 4 assumes that the members of the family in question may claim a right of residence, so Article 3 suggests that they are entitled to enter a Member State simply on production of a valid identity card or passport, as "persons referred to in Article 1 . . . "

The contrary argument is that Article 4(1) of the Directive, in requiring Member States to grant a right of residence to members of worker's family to whom Regulation 1612/68 is applicable, contemplates that this right of residence will be co-extensive with the right of "installation" granted by Article 10(1) of Regulation 1612/68 to spouse, children under 21 years or over that age and dependent, and dependent relatives in the ascending line, but not to the other relatives in question. A legislative intent to ensure the conformity of the Directive with the Regulation may be discerned in the first recital to the preamble to the former, which states: " . . . whereas, measures should be adopted . . . which conform to the rights and privileges accorded by the said Regulation to nationals of any Member States . . . and to members of their families."

British practice is to take a restrictive view,[41] admitting as of right only

---

[40] Dir. 68/360, Art. 4(3)(*e*).
[41] *Statement of Changes in Immigration Rules*, H.C. Papers (1982–83) 169, para. 68.

the relatives specified in Article 10(1) of Regulation 1612/68, but it is submitted that the liberal interpretation would accord more closely to the aim of the relevant Articles of the Treaty. One cannot imagine a more potent disincentive to migration than the inability to provide a home for a dependent relative for whom one has assumed responsibility. It is unlikely that the Court would uphold the somewhat arbitrary distinctions necessitated by a restrictive interpretation.

The residence permit

Article 4 of Directive 68/360 provides that a residence permit shall be issued to the worker and members of his family who are nationals of Member States of the EEC, as proof of the right of residence. This document must include a statement that it has been issued pursuant to Regulation 1612/68 and to the measures taken by the Member States for the implementation of the Directive. The text of the statement is given in the Annex to the Directive.

A member of a worker's family who is not a national of a Member State must be issued with a residence document having the same validity as that issued to the worker on whom he or she is dependent.[42]

The drafting of the provisions of the Directive relating to the issue, validity, expiry and renewal of residence permits is not entirely satisfactory. Whereas Article 4(2) provides that a residence permit is issued as proof of the right of residence, subsequent provisions define the extent of the migrant's rights in terms of the validity of his or her permit. The conceptual confusion led the Tribunal de Première Instance of Liège in *Procureur du Roi* v. *Royer*[43] to seek a preliminary ruling from the Court of Justice on the question, *inter alia*, whether a worker's right of residence was conferred directly by the Treaty and the terms of Directive 68/360, or was conditional on the issue of a document drawn up by national authorities. The Court held that Article 48 vested rights directly in all persons falling within its ambit. Implementing legislation gave rise to no new rights in favour of persons protected by Community law, but simply determined the scope and detailed rules for the exercise of rights conferred directly by the Treaty. The grant of a permit was to be regarded "not as a measure giving rise to rights but as a measure by a Member State serving to prove the individual position of a national of another Member State with regard to provisions of Community law."[44] It followed that Member States were under a duty to grant the right of residence to any person who was able to prove, by producing the documents specified in Article 4(3) of the Directive, that he or she fell within one of the categories referred to in Article 1.

The Directive provides that completion of the formalities for obtaining a residence permit shall not hinder the immediate commencement of employment under a concluded contract.[45]

[42] Art. 4(4).
[43] Case 48/75 [1976] E.C.R. 497.
[44] [1976] E.C.R. 497 at 513. No other permit may be required of workers of the Member States, Case 8/77 *Sagulo* [1977] E.C.R. 1495; Case 157/79 *Pieck* [1980] E.C.R. 2171.
[45] Art. 5.

The residence documents granted to nationals of the Member States must be issued and renewed free of charge or on payment of an amount not exceeding the dues and taxes charged for the issue of identity cards to nationals. The visa which may be demanded of members of a worker's family who are not nationals of a Member State of the EEC shall be free of charge.[46]

Expiry and renewal of the residence permit

Although *Royer* makes it clear that a right of residence arises independently of the issue of a residence permit, the Directive defines the substantive rights of migrants in terms of the validity of their permits. The transference of thought is confusing, but it is proposed to adopt it for the sake of consistency with the terms of the Directive.

A residence permit, issued when the worker or member of his family satisfies the conditions stated in Article 4 of the Directive, must be valid throughout the territory of the Member States which issued it for a period of at least five years from the date of issue, and be automatically renewable.[47] Although original acquisition of the residence permit requires a certification of employment, it must be noted that a valid residence permit may not be withdrawn from a worker solely on the grounds that he is involuntarily unemployed, this being duly confirmed by the competent unemployment office.[48] It would seem to follow that a worker who is voluntarily unemployed may have his permit withdrawn, *i.e.* lose his right of residence in the territory. This is certainly in accord with the scheme of Article 48 of the Treaty which guarantees residence for the purpose of seeking or engaging in activities as an employed person. An individual who is voluntarily unemployed can no longer be considered a "worker" within the meaning of Article 48.[49]

If a Member State wishes to terminate a residence permit valid for five years for any other reason apart from voluntary unemployment or prolonged absence, it must have resort to the proviso contained in Article 48(3) of the Treaty, to the effect that the rights defined therein are subject to limitations justified on grounds of public policy, public security or public health.[50]

At the end of a five year period, a Member State is obliged to renew the document automatically for a further five years. The only exception to this, apart from cases of voluntary unemployment, prolonged absence, or the public policy proviso, is on the occasion of renewal of a residence permit for the first time. In this case, the period of residence may be restricted to a period of not less than 12 months, if the worker has been involuntarily unemployed for more than 12 consecutive months.[51] When this second, curtailed period of residence expires, it would seem that the worker has no

---

[46] Art. 9.
[47] Art. 6.
[48] Art. 7(1).
[49] This follows from the reasoning in Case 53/81 *Levin* [1982] E.C.R. 1035.
[50] See *infra*, pp. 186 *et seq*.
[51] Art. 7(2).

right to an automatic renewal of his permit, and must acquire his right of residence afresh, by producing the documents referred to in Article 4 of the Directive, *i.e.* an entry document and a declaration of employment.

The validity of a residence permit is stated to be unaffected by either breaks in residence not exceeding six consecutive months, or absence on military service.[52] It would seem to follow that breaks in residence lasting longer than six consecutive months may provide grounds for withdrawal of a residence permit, and loss of the right of residence, pending compliance once again with the provisions of Article 4 of the Directive.

Temporary residence permit

Workers employed for periods exceeding three months but not exceeding a year must be issued with a temporary residence permit, the validity of which may be limited to the expected period of their employment.[53] Such a permit is not stated to be automatically renewable, and on expiry the worker would be obliged to present anew the documents referred to in Article 4 of the Directive. Temporary residence permits are similarly issued to seasonal workers employed for more than three months. The period of employment must be indicated in the certificate of employment required, along with their entry document, for the acquisition of the residence permit.[54]

Recognition of the right of residence without the issue of permits

In three cases the Directive requires Member States to recognise the right of workers to reside in their territory without the issue of residence permits.[55] The first category comprises workers pursuing activities expected to last not more than three months. Presentation of the worker's entry document coupled with a certification from his employer stating the expected duration of his employment is sufficient to cover his stay.

The Directive makes similar provision for frontier workers, *i.e.* workers who, having their residence in one Member State to which they return in principle once a day or at least once a week, work in another Member State.[56] Although such a worker would prima facie be entitled to a full residence permit under Article 4 of the Directive (although, of course, he is not really "resident" at all), Article 8(1)(*b*) relieves the State where he is employed of any duty to provide such a permit, and provides that it *may* issue such a worker with a special permit valid for five years and automatically renewable.

The final category of workers, seasonal workers, have already been considered in the context of workers who must be issued with temporary residence permits. Such workers holding contracts of employment stamped by

---

[52] Art. 6(2).
[53] Art. 6(3).
[54] *Ibid.*
[55] Art. 8.
[56] Dir. 68/360 does not use the term "frontier worker," but see Art. 1(*b*) of Reg. 1408/71. Does Art. 8(1)(*b*) intend to confer a right of "residence" in both the state of employment *and* the state of residence? The final sentence of the provision suggests only the former.

the competent authority of the Member State on whose territory they have come to work need not be issued with residence permits, where they are employed for less than three months.[57]

In all three cases cited, *supra*, the Member State may require the worker to report his presence in its territory.

The three "degrees" of residence

It will be appreciated that several groups of workers falling within Article 4 of the Directive enjoy varying degrees of "security of tenure" in the State of employment.

The first group, those who find a job of an expected duration of more than 12 months, receive a permit entitling them to at least six years residence in the host State, providing, of course, that they do not become voluntarily unemployed or conduct themselves in such a way as to fall within the scope of the "public policy proviso" of Article 48(3) of the Treaty.

The second group of workers comprises those who take up employment for a period of between three and 12 months, and seasonal workers who are employed for more than three months. Here security of residence is restricted by means of a temporary residence permit to the expected duration of the employment in question. Should such a worker become involuntarily unemployed, he would seem to retain his right of residence—by virtue of Article 7(1) of the Directive—until expiry of the temporary residence permit.

The final group of workers contemplated by Directive 68/360 have the most precarious right of all—the right to reside in a Member State only for the actual duration of their employment. This group comprises workers who expect to pursue employment for less than three months, seasonal workers employed for less than three months holding stamped employment contracts, and frontier workers. In the case of the latter, a "special residence permit" may be issued at the option of the host State. Such a permit must be valid for five years and be renewable automatically. On this occasion the context suggests that the Directive's reference to renewal of the permit is a reference to its formal validity rather than to the rights of its holder.

A right bestowed by the Treaty

The rights of workers may be rather less clear cut than the above scheme suggests, since their rights stem directly from the Treaty, and it is the function of secondary legislation merely to define their scope and provide the detailed rules for their enjoyment. For instance, suppose a worker enters a Member State in search of a job. After three months he finds a job of an expected duration of six months. He is issued with a temporary residence permit for that period. After six months permit and employment expire. Is the worker entitled to remain in the Member State concerned for a reason-

---

[57] Art. 6(3), second paragraph, and Art. 8(1)(*c*).

able time in order to seek further employment? The spirit of Article 48 suggests an affirmative answer; the text of the Directive the contrary. Other problems arise; how often is a worker entitled to enter the same Member State in search of employment? The answer to such questions may turn less on the interpretation of the detailed provisions of Community secondary legislation, than on the Court's view of the ambit of Article 48 itself. It is arguable that the latter Article requires absolute freedom of movement and residence for all nationals of the Member States engaged in employment or genuinely in search of it. On the other hand, Article 48 does not preclude a Member State from drawing distinctions between workers on the basis of the length and continuity of their relationship with that State.[58] A worker is entitled to remain in a Member State for a reasonable time seeking employment, but if it becomes apparent that he is unlikely to find a job, he may be required to return to his country of origin, or to the Member State where he was last employed. An extended period of employment in a Member State, however, entitles an unemployed worker to the same opportunities as a member of the indigenous workforce, *i.e.* indefinite equal access to the host State's employment exchanges and unemployment benefits. On this view, the provisions of secondary legislation such as Directive 68/360 will be applicable to the extent that they regulate the modalities of the exercise of rights enjoyed directly under the Treaty, but ineffective to restrict their scope.

EQUALITY OF TREATMENT

Article 48(2) of the Treaty provides that freedom of movement for workers shall entail the abolition of any discrimination based on nationality between workers of the Member States as regards employment, remuneration and other conditions of work and employment. Although, as we shall see later, this prohibition is not restricted to national measures which directly relate to the employment context, it *is* restricted to discrimination which may impede the free movement of persons. Thus, for instance, Article 48 does not exclude the right of Member States to adopt reasonable measures to keep track of the movement of aliens within their territory.[59] On the other hand, while Member States may impose penalties to compel compliance with the requirements of Community law relating to migrants, such penalties must be comparable to those attaching to the infringement of provisions of equal importance by nationals,[60] and such punishment must be proportional[61] to the gravity of the offences involved. However, where Community law permits differentiation between migrants and national workers, for instance in allowing Member States to require the possession of residence permits by aliens,[62] Member States may impose

[58] *Cf.* Case 20/75 *D'Amico* v. *Landesversicherungsanstalt* [1975] E.C.R. 891.
[59] Case 118/75 *The State* v. *Watson and Belmann* [1976] E.C.R. 1185, discussed (1975–76) 1 E.L. Rev. 556.
[60] Case 118/75, note 59.
[61] For the concept of "proportionality," see *supra*, p. 60.
[62] As to which, see *supra*, p. 169.

more serious penalties for infractions of such requirements than would be imposed in the case of the commission by nationals of comparable offences, for instance the failure to comply with the requirement that nationals possess identity cards.[63]

Whereas Directive 68/360 ensures entry and residence for Community workers, the right to equal treatment in respect of job opportunity and conditions of employment is governed by Regulation 1612/68 of October 15, 1968 on freedom of movement for workers within the Community.[64] Part I of the Regulation is divided into three Titles:

— Eligibility for employment;
— Employment and equality of treatment; and
— Workers' families.

It is convenient to adopt the scheme of the Regulation for the purposes of exposition of its terms and discussion of the case law of the Court.

Eligibility for employment

The Regulation guarantees to workers the right to take up employment in the territory of a Member State with the same priority as the nationals of the State in question.[65] Employees and employers are entitled to exchange their applications for and offers of employment, and to conclude and perform contracts in accordance with "the provisions in force laid down by law, regulation or administrative action, without any discrimination resulting therefrom."[66]

National provisions, whether the result of legal regulation or administrative action, are stated to be inapplicable if they limit explicitly or implicitly the right of workers to take up and pursue employment. An exception is made in the case of linguistic requirements necessitated by the nature of the post to be filled. Article 3 of the Regulation itemises, as particular instances of the provisions declared inapplicable by the foregoing, those which:

"(a) prescribe a special recruitment procedure for foreign nationals;
 (b) limit or restrict the advertising of vacancies in the press or through any other medium or subject it to conditions other than those applicable in respect of employers pursuing their activities in the territory of that Member State;
 (c) subject eligibility for employment to conditions of registration with employment offices or impede recruitment of individual workers where persons who do not reside in the territory of that State are concerned."

Article 4 of the Regulation provides that national rules restricting by number of percentage the employment of foreign nationals are to be inapplicable to nationals of the Member States. Alleged infringement of this

---

[63] Case 8/77 *The State* v. *Sagulo* [1977] E.C.R. 1495, discussed (1977) 2 E.L. Rev. 445.
[64] J.O. 1968 L257/2.
[65] Art. 1(2).
[66] Art. 2.

requirement by the Republic of France gave rise to proceedings before the Court of Justice at the suit of the Commission.[67] Article 3(2) of the Code du Travail Maritime of 1926 provided that such proportion of the crew of a ship as was laid down by order of the Minister for the Merchant Fleet must be French nationals. Ministerial Orders of November 1960 and June 1969 provided that certain employments on board ship were restricted exclusively to French nationals, and an overall ratio was imposed of three French to one non-French. The Commission took the view that such legislation contravened Article 48 of the Treaty and Article 4 of Regulation 1612/68. The French Government argued that Article 48 of the Treaty had no application to sea transport, but nevertheless proceeded to lay a draft amendment before the French Parliament. No legislation was in the event forthcoming, and the Commission referred the matter to the Court of Justice under Article 169 of the Treaty, claiming a declaration that the failure of the French Republic to amend Article 3(2) of the Code insofar as it applied to nationals of the Member States amounted to a breach of Community law.

In order to appreciate the significance of the Court's ruling, it must be noted that the French Government insisted that no discrimination had in fact taken place, since oral instructions had been given not to apply Article 3(2) of the Code to Community nationals, and that no finding was made on this issue. The Court (holding that Article 48 indeed applied to sea transport) acknowledged that the objective legal situation was clear—namely, that Article 48 of the Treaty and Regulation 1612/68 were directly applicable in France—yet found that by failing to amend Article 3(2) of the Code du Travail Maritime insofar as it applied to nationals of the Member States, France was in breach of her legal obligations. In view of the position adopted by the French Government to the effect that the nondiscriminatory application of the offending Article was a matter of grace, not of law, she had thereby brought about *an ambiguous situation creating uncertainty for those subject to the law*. Such an admittedly "secondary" obstacle to equal access to employment was nevertheless caught by the general prohibition of Article 48, and the specific provisions of Article 4 of Regulation 1612/68.

Since covert discrimination can be as effective in excluding foreign workers as express legal provisions or administrative measures, the Regulation further provides that the engagement or recruitment of a national of one Member State for a post in another shall not depend on medical, vocational or other criteria which are discriminatory by comparison with those applied in the case of national workers.[68] Nevertheless, when an employer actually offers a job to a national of another Member State he may expressly condition this offer on the candidate undergoing a vocational test.[69]

A worker seeking employment in a Member State other than his own is

[67] Case 167/73 *Commission* v. *French Republic* [1974] E.C.R. 359, [1974] 2 C.M.L.R. 216.
[68] Art. 6(1).
[69] Art. 6(2).

entitled to receive from its employment services the same assistance as that afforded to national workers.[70]

Equality in employment

Article 48(2) of the Treaty provides for the abolition of discrimination based on nationality in terms and conditions of employment and this prohibition is reiterated and expanded in Article 7(1) of the Regulation, as follows:

> "A worker who is a national of a Member State may not, in the territory of another Member State, be treated differently from national workers by reason of his nationality in respect of any conditions of employment and work, in particular as regards remuneration, dismissal, and should he become unemployed, re-instatement or re-employment."

Infringement of the principle of equality will occur where national legislation expressly attaches different terms to the conditions of employment of national workers and workers from other Community countries. In *Marsman* v. *Rosskamp*,[71] a Dutch national resident in the Netherlands was employed in Gronau, in the Federal Republic. After becoming incapacitated as the result of an accident at work, he was dismissed by his employer. German legislation provided that seriously disabled workers could not be dismissed without the approval of the main public assistance office. While this protection extended to nationals resident outside Germany, it applied only to non-nationals within the jurisdiction. Mr. Marsman challenged the legality of his dismissal before the Arbeitsgericht, which sought a ruling from the Court of Justice as to whether a Community national in the position of Mr. Marsmann was entitled to the same protection against dismissal as that afforded to German nationals. The Court replied in the affirmative, emphasising that the social law of the Community was based on the principle that the laws of every Member State were obliged to grant nationals of the other Member States employed in its territory all the legal advantages that it provided for its own citizens.

A slightly more complex situation arises when legislation conditions certain advantages on criteria which, although theoretically applicable to nationals and non-nationals alike, will in practice be fulfilled only by nationals. The point is illustrated in *Württembergische Milchverwertung-Südmilch* v. *Ugliola*.[72] The respondent in the main suit was an Italian national employed by the appellant concern in the Federal Republic. He performed his military service in Italy between May 1965 and August 1966, and claimed the right to have this period taken into account in calculating his seniority with his employer. German legislation provided that military service in the Bundeswehr was to be taken into account for such purposes, but made no similar provision for services in the forces of other States. The Bundesarbeitsgericht sought a preliminary ruling from the Court of Justice

---

[70] Art. 5.
[71] Case 44/72 [1972] E.C.R. 1243.
[72] Case 15/69 [1969] E.C.R. 363.

on the question whether Article 7 of Regulation 1612/68 entitled a Community national in the position of Mr. Ugliola to have his military service in his home country taken into account for the purposes of the German legislation in question. In its observations to the Court, the German Government argued that the Job-protection Law was not discriminatory, since (a) it did not apply to nationals who served in the forces of other States, and (b) it did not apply to non-nationals who served in the Bundeswehr. Advocate General Gand regarded such an argument as tempting, but was not convinced, since performance of military service in the Army of a Member State other than the one whose nationality one possessed was a hypothesis which the German Government agreed was quite theoretical. The Court agreed. The provisions of Community law in question prohibited Member States from *indirectly* establishing discrimination in favour of their own nationals. The Court's decision may be explained as follows. First, by recourse to the notion of discrimination itself, which comprises not only differentiation between the like, but also the failure to differentiate between the unlike.[73] Thus to treat non-nationals in the same way as nationals, where this results in disadvantage in view of objective difference between their respective situations, is discriminatory. The principle is identical to that discussed in the context of measures having an equivalent effect to quantitative restrictions: fixing the same prices for domestic and imported goods can amount to discrimination against the latter where differing costs hinder their competitive disposal on the market.[74] Secondly, the prohibition on discrimination contained in Article 48 must be considered in the light of the preamble to the Treaty, which calls for the elimination of the barriers which divide Europe, and the words of Article 3(c), which prescribe the "abolition, as between Member States, of obstacles to freedom of movement for persons, services and capital." Realisation of these aims calls for no less than the assimilation of the several legal orders of the Member States to a single legal order within the sphere of operation of the Treaty. It follows that if the performance of military duties is to be taken into account in the employment context, it can amount to discrimination to differentiate between the flags of the Member States.

The Court was faced with the problem of allegedly indirect discrimination once more in *Sotgiu* v. *Deutsche Bundespost*.[75] The plaintiff, an Italian whose family lived in Italy, was employed by the German postal service. He received a separation allowance at 7·50 DM per day, on the same basis as workers of German nationality. In accordance with a Government circular the allowance paid to workers residing within Germany at the time of their recruitment was increased to 10 DM per day, while those workers residing abroad at the time of their recruitment—German and foreign alike—continued to receive the allowance at the old rate. Sotgiu invoked Regulation 1612/68 in the German courts, and the Bundesarbeitsgericht sought a ruling, *inter alia*, on whether Article 7(1) of the Regulation could be interpreted as prohibited discrimination on the basis of *residence* as well

---

[73] Case 13/63 *Italy* v. *Commission* [1963] E.C.R. 165.
[74] See *supra*, p. 133.
[75] Case 152/73 *Sotgiu* v. *Deutsche Bundespost* [1974] E.C.R. 153.

as on the basis of nationality. In the course of the arguments before the Court it became apparent that although workers residing within Germany at the time of their recruitment indeed received a larger allowance, it was conditional on their willingness to move to their place of work, and in any event was no longer paid after two years. No such conditions were attached to payment of the allowance to workers residing abroad at the time of recruitment.

The Court affirmed that Article 7 prohibited all covert forms of discrimination which, by the application of criteria other than nationality, nevertheless led to the same result. Such an interpretation was consonant with the fifth recital to the Regulation, which required that equality of treatment for workers be established in fact as well as in law. Application of criteria such as place of origin or residence, argued the Court, could, in appropriate circumstances, have a discriminatory effect in practice that would be prohibited by the Treaty and the Regulation. This would not, however, be the case where the payment of a separation allowance was made on conditions which took account of objective differences in the situation of workers, which differences could involve the place of residence of a worker when recruited. Similarly, the fact that in the case of one group of workers allowances were only temporary while in the case of another they were of unlimited duration, could be a valid reason for differentiating between the amounts paid. A factual assessment of the situation would of course be a matter for the national court.

In order to ensure equality for Community workers in the employment context, the Regulation provides that they shall have "by virtue of the same right and under the same conditions as national workers . . . access to training in vocational schools and retraining centres."[76] Similarly, they are entitled to equality of treatment as regards membership of trades unions and the exercise of rights attaching thereto, including the right to vote.[77]

Freedom from discrimination for Community workers, although limited explicitly to the employment context in the Treaty, could not be achieved without requiring appropriate adjustments to all fields of national law and practice which might be likely to have an effect on the conditions under which migrants take up and pursue employment. Thus Article 7(2) of the Regulation provides that a national of one Member State employed in another "shall enjoy the same social and tax advantages as national workers." The wording and context of the Article suggest that it might be restricted to social and tax advantages conferred by national law *qua* worker, but the Court of Justice has taken a more liberal view, as its judgment in *Fiorini* v. *SNCF*[78] illustrates. French legislation provided that in families of three or more children under the age of 18 years, the father, mother, and each child under 18 years should receive a personal identity card entitling them to a reduction of between 30 and 75 per cent. in the

---

[76] Art. 7(3).
[77] Art. 8, as amended by Reg. 312/76, O.J. 1976 L39/2.
[78] Case 32/75 [1975] E.C.R. 1085, [1976] 1 C.M.L.R. 573.

scheduled fare charged by the Société Nationale des Chemins de Fer Français (SNCF). The Cour d'Appel of Paris sought a preliminary ruling from the Court of Justice on the question whether the reduction card issued by the SNCF to large families constituted for the workers of the Member States a "social advantage" within the meaning of Article 7(2) of the Regulation. The SNCF, in its observations to the Court, argued that Article 7(2) referred exclusively to advantages attaching to the nationals of Member States by virtue of their status as workers, and accordingly had no application to a benefit such as the reduction card issued by the SNCF. The Court rejected this view, reasoning as follows:

"Although it is true that certain provisions in this article refer to relationships deriving from the contract of employment, there are others, such as those concerning reinstatement and re-employment should a worker become unemployed, which have nothing to do with such relationships and even imply the termination of a previous employment.

It therefore follows that, in view of the equality of treatment which the provision seeks to achieve, the substantive area of application must be delineated so as to include all social and tax advantages, whether or not attached to the contract of employment, such as reductions in fares for large families."[79]

The Court has subsequently held that Article 7(2) applies to any benefit payable by virtue of an individual's status as a worker, or residence on national territory, where the extension of the benefit to nationals of other Member States seems suitable to facilitate the free movement of workers.[80] Applying this test, the Court has excluded from the ambit of Article 7(2) early retirement on full pension for those in receipt of an invalidity pension granted by an Allied Power in respect of war service.[81] The abovementioned formulation has on the other hand been held to cover seven year interest-free means-tested loans to families in respect of newly-born children, even though the loans were of a discretionary nature.[82] Benefits held to fall within the ambit of the Article include an allowance to handicapped adults covered by Regulation 1408/71 on Social Security[83]; a guaranteed minimum subsistence allowance[84]; the possibility of using one's own language in court proceedings[85]; a special unemployment benefit for young persons falling outside the ambit of Regulation 1408/71[86]; an old age benefit for those lacking entitlement to a pension under the national social security system[87]; and a guaranteed minimum income for old persons.[88]

The Regulation recognises the importance of freely available housing to the migrant worker when it provides that he shall "enjoy all the rights and benefits accorded to national workers in matters of housing, including

[79] [1975] E.C.R. 1085 at p. 1094, 1095, [1976] 1 C.M.L.R. 582.
[80] Case 107/78 *Even* [1979] E.C.R. 2019.
[81] *Ibid.*
[82] Case 65/81 *Reina* [1982] E.C.R. 33.
[83] Case 63/76 *Inzirillo* [1976] E.C.R. 2057.
[84] Case 249/83 *Hoeckx* [1985] E.C.R. 973; Case 122/84 *Scrivner* [1985] E.C.R. 1027.
[85] Case 137/84 *Mutsch* [1986] 1 C.M.L.R. 648.
[86] Case 94/84 *Deak* Judgment of June 20, 1985.
[87] Case 157/84 *Frascogna* Judgment of June 6, 1985.
[88] Case 261/83 *Castelli* [1984] E.C.R. 3199.

ownership of the housing he needs."[89] He may also, "with the same right as nationals, put his name down on the housing lists in the region in which he is employed, where such lists exist; he shall enjoy the resultant benefits and priorities." If the worker's family have remained in the country whence he came, they must be considered, for the purposes of priority on housing lists, as residing in the area where the worker is employed, where national workers benefit from a similar presumption.[90]

Workers' families

Under Article 10 of Regulation 1612/68, the following members of a worker's family are entitled to install themselves with the worker in the host state:

> "(a) his spouse and their descendants who are under the age of 21 years or are dependants;
> (b) dependent relatives in the ascending line of the worker and his spouse."

In the case of other members of the family who are dependent on the worker, or who were living under his roof in the country whence he came, Article 10(2) requires merely that Member States shall "facilitate" their admission.

The migrant is obliged to provide housing for his family that is considered normal for national workers in the region where he is employed. This requirement must not, however, give rise to discrimination between national workers and workers from other Member States.[91] Since discrimination must not occur in fact or in law, housing must be "considered normal" when it attains a standard equivalent to that actually enjoyed by workers in the region, even though such a standard may not accord with officially recommended levels of occupancy, or even legal requirements. The discriminatory application of national rules in themselves non-discriminatory could clearly amount to a breach of the Treaty.

Although the protection of the Regulation is limited to workers who are nationals of the Member State, their spouses and children under 21 years or dependent, regardless of nationality, are entitled to take up employment throughout the territory in which the worker is employed.[92]

The third recital of the preamble to Regulation 1612/68 describes freedom of movement as a fundamental right of workers *and their families*, and indeed, genuine equality for the worker would be a chimera if the members of his family could be deprived of social advantages in the host State on account of their nationality. Thus Article 12 provides that the children of a worker residing in the territory of a Member State shall be admitted to that State's general educational, apprenticeship and vocational training courses under the same conditions as nationals of that State. This provision clearly bestows rights directly upon such children, although the second paragraph

---

[89] Art. 9(1).
[90] Art. 9(2).
[91] Art. 10(3).
[92] Art. 11. See Case 131/85 *Gül* [1987] 1 C.M.L.R. 501.

of Article 12, to the effect that "Member States shall encourage all efforts to enable such children to attend these courses under the best possible conditions," is not directly effective, and provides merely an admonition to Member States as to the spirit in which they should apply the first paragraph of that Article, and a guide to courts in its interpretation.

The Court of Justice has had cause to interpret Article 12 on several occasions. In *Michel S.* v. *Fonds national de reclassement social des handicapés*,[93] the plaintiff in the main suit was the mentally handicapped son of a deceased Italian national who had worked as a wage-earner in Belgium. He was refused benefit from a national fund established to assist persons of Belgian nationality whose chances of employment had been seriously diminished by physical or mental handicap. The Court, having declared that Article 7 of the Regulation protected workers, but not their families, went on to consider Article 12, drawing on the wording of the fifth recital of the preamble as an aid to its interpretation. According to the Court, the "integration" contemplated by the preamble presupposed that the handicapped child of a foreign worker would be entitled to take advantage of benefits provided by the law of the host country for rehabilitation of the handicapped on the same basis as nationals in a similar position. No conclusion to the contrary could be drawn from the failure of the Council explicitly to mention such benefits in the text of the Article; rather, this omission could be explained by the difficulty of including all possible hypotheses.

The Court's liberal approach to the text of Article 12 in *Michel S.* was followed in *Casagrande* v. *Landeshauptstadt München*,[94] in which the son of a deceased Italian national who had worked as a wage-earner in the Federal Republic was refused, on grounds of nationality, a means-tested educational grant under a Bavarian Statute. The Bayerisches Verwaltungsgericht sought a ruling from the Court of Justice on the consistency of such discriminatory provisions with Article 12. The Court resorted once again to the fifth recital of the Regulation's preamble. Read with the words of the second paragraph of Article 12, it became apparent that the Article guaranteed not simply *access* to educational courses, but all benefits intended to facilitate educational attendance.

The Court has retreated from its position in *Michel S.* that Article 7 of the Regulation protects workers but not their families. This will not be the case where the survivors of a worker living in the State where he was last employed claim a social advantage granted to the dependants of survivors of national workers in similar circumstances. In *Fiorini*, it will be recalled that the widow of a deceased Italian national applied for a reduced fare card on French national railways. The Court of Justice held that Article 7(2) must be interpreted as meaning "that the social advantages referred to by that provision include fares reduction cards issued by a national railway authority to large families and that this applies, even if the said advantage is only sought after the worker's death, to the benefit of his family remain-

---

[93] Case 76/72 [1973] E.C.R. 457.
[94] Case 9/74 [1974] E.C.R. 773, and see Case 68/74 *Alaimo* v. *Prefect of the Rhone* [1975] E.C.R. 109.

ing in the same Member State."[95] In *Inzirillo*,[96] the Court, dealing with a reference on the scope of Regulation 1408/71 observed that the protection of Article 7(2) of Regulation 1612/68 extended to handicapped, dependent adult children of a worker who have installed themselves with the worker in accordance with Article 10 of Regulation 1612/68. More recently, in *Castelli*,[97] and *Frascogna*,[98] the Court has held that Article 7(2) is intended to protect, as well as workers themselves, their dependent relatives in the ascending line who have installed themselves with the worker. It follows from the above cases that any member of a worker's family who is entitled to, and does, install himself with the worker, is also entitled to equal treatment with nationals of the host State in the grant of all social and tax advantages. The rationale of this proposition would seem to be the deterrent effect upon free movement for workers which would result from the possibility of discriminating against dependent members of his family.[99] The Treaty basis of this right to equality *in the relatives* (as opposed to rights vested in the worker) is to be found in Article 7 EEC. Indeed, the Commission argued as much in *Fiorini*. Support for this view is to be found in the *Forcheri*[1] case, which held that discrimination against a national of one Member State lawfully established in another in the provision of vocational training, infringed Article 7 EEC. The plaintiffs in the national proceedings were a Commission official, and his wife (the latter being the victim of the alleged discrimination). The Court's reasoning appears to be based both on Article 48 EEC (of which the Commission Official was a beneficiary), and upon Article 7 EEC, the Court being of the opinion that vocational training fell squarely within the "scope of application of the Treaty."

RESIDENCE AFTER RETIREMENT OR INCAPACITY

The preamble to Regulation 1251/70 of June 29, 1970,[2] describes the right of workers to remain in the territory of a Member State after having been employed there as a corollary to the freedom of movement secured by Regulation 1612/68 and Directive 68/360. The Regulation applies to nationals of one Member State who have worked in the territory of another, and to the Members of their family referred to in Article 10 of Regulation 1612/68.

The right of workers to remain in a Member State after having been employed there

The Regulation grants a right of residence after termination of employment to two classes of workers—the retired and the incapacitated. A worker acquires a right of residence on retirement provided; (i) that he has

[95] [1975] E.C.R. 1085 at 1095.
[96] Case 63/76 [1976] E.C.R. 2057.
[97] Case 261/83 [1984] E.C.R. 3199.
[98] Case 157/84 Judgment of June 6, 1985.
[99] Case 63/76 *Inzirillo* [1976] E.C.R. 2057, para. (17) of the Court's judgment.
[1] Case 152/82 [1983] E.C.R. 2323. See also Case 293/83, *Gravier* [1985] E.C.R. 593.
[2] J.O. 1970 L142/24.

reached the age laid down by the law of the host State for entitlement of an old age pension; (ii) that he has been employed in the host State for at least 12 months; and (iii) that he has resided continuously in the host State for more than three years.[3]

A worker who ceases employment as a result of permanent incapacity acquires a right to remain if he has resided in the host State for at least two years. If the permanent incapacity is the result of an accident at work, or an occupational disease entitling him to a pension for which an institution of the host state is entirely or partially responsible, he is entitled to remain regardless of the length of his previous residence.[4]

The above rules assume that a worker is employed and resident in the same Member State, but Regulation 1251/70 also makes limited provision for workers who live in one State while working in another. In the case of a worker who has completed three years continuous employment and residence in the territory of one Member State, and then takes up employment in the territory of another, periods of employment completed in the latter are taken into account for the purposes of establishing a right to remain in the former State on retirement or in the event of incapacity, providing that the worker retains his residence in the former State, to which he returns, as a rule, each day, or at least once a week.[5] The preamble to the Regulation, after rehearsing the importance of guaranteeing to workers who have been resident and employed in a Member State the right to remain after ceasing work through retirement or incapacity, continues: "it is equally important to ensure that right for a worker who, after a period of employment or residence in the territory of a Member State, works as an employed person in the territory of another Member State, while still retaining his residence in the territory of the first State." It is difficult to see why this general consideration should be limited in its application to "frontier workers." Suppose a national of Member State X works and resides in Member State Y, and then takes up a job in Member State Z, returning to his home and family in Member State Y every two weeks. On retirement, Regulation 1251/70 apparently gives him no right of residence in Member State Y, where his home and family are located. Such differentiation between workers residing in a State than that of employment would seem to be arbitrary, and unjustified by the object and purpose of Article 48 of the Treaty.

In order to establish the requisite periods of residence, on which the right to remain in a Member State may be conditioned, retiring or incapacitated workers are entitled to adduce any evidence normally accepted in the country of residence. Continuity is not affected by temporary absences totalling up to three months per year, nor by longer absences due to military service.[6] Periods of involuntary unemployment, duly recorded by the competent employment office, and absences due to illness or accident, are treated as equivalent to periods of employment.[7]

[3] Art. 2(1)(*a*).
[4] Art. 2(1)(*b*).
[5] Art. 2(1)(*c*).
[6] Art. 4(1).
[7] Art. 4(2).

A retiring or incapacitated worker is not bound to fulfil the requisite periods of employment or residence if his spouse is a national of the Member State in question, or lost that nationality as a result of marriage to the worker.[8]

Once a worker has acquired a right to remain in a Member State under the terms of Regulation 1251/70, he has two years in which to decide whether or not to exercise it. During this period he is free to leave the territory of the State in question without prejudice to his right of permanent residence, which may be exercised without formality.[9]

Rights of workers' families

If a retiring or incapacitated worker has acquired a right of residence in a Member State, the members of his family to whom the Regulation applies are entitled to remain in the host State after his death.[10]

If however, a worker dies during his working life and before having acquired a right of residence, members of his family are nevertheless entitled to remain, provided that: (a) the worker, at the date of his death, has resided continuously in the territory of that Member State for at least two years; or (b) his death resulted from an accident at work or an occupational disease; or (c) the surviving spouse is a national of the State of residence or lost the nationality of that State by marriage to the worker.[11]

Equality of treatment

The right to equality of treatment provided by Regulation 1612/68 is also enjoyed by the beneficiaries of Regulation 1251/70.[12] As far as the survivors of workers are concerned, this seems at first sight to provide but a slender guarantee, since the provisions apparently applicable are those contained in Title III of that Regulation, headed *Workers' Families*, and covering: (a) the right to take up employment in a Member State (Art. 11); and (b) the right to equal access to educational and vocational facilities (Art. 12). Social security rights would be safeguarded by Regulation 1408/71, but what of rights classified as "social assistance," excluded from the ambit of Regulation 1408/71, by Article 4(4) of that Regulation? Article 7(2) of Regulation 1612/68 would seem to provide a right to such benefits *qua* "social . . . advantages," but in *Michel S*[13] the Court held that Article 7(3) of the Regulation had no application to the families of workers, only to workers themselves. However, it will be recalled that in *Fiorini*,[14] the Court countenanced a claim founded on Article 7(2) being brought by the survivors of a worker. Thus the survivors of a deceased worker who enjoy

---

[8] Art. 2(2).
[9] Art. 5.
[10] Art. 3(1).
[11] Art. 3(2).
[12] Art. 7.
[13] Case 9/74 [1974] E.C.R. 773.
[14] Case 32/75 [1975] E.C.R. 1085. See also Case 261/83 *Castelli* [1984] E.C.R. 3199, and Case 157/84 *Frascogna* Judgment of June 6, 1985.

the right to remain in a Member State are entitled to the same "social and tax advantages" as the survivors of national workers.

Residence permits

Persons who have acquired a right to remain in the territory of a Member State are entitled to receive a residence permit which must be valid throughout the territory of the issuing State for a period of at least five years, and be automatically renewable. Any charge made must not exceed the amount charged to nationals for the issue or renewal of identity documents.[15]

Periods of non-residence not exceeding six consecutive months may not affect the validity of a residence permit, but it would seem to follow that periods exceeding six months may affect such validity.[16] Whether absence exceeding six months is capable of prejudicing a person's substantive right to remain is unclear, since the function of the permit is not made explicit. It will be recalled that Article 4(2) of Directive 68/360 provides that the residence permit therein described be issued as proof of the right of residence,[17] but subsequent provisions, in particular Article 7, suggest that withdrawal of the residence permit has substantive implications. The better view would seem to be that Article 6 of Regulation 1251/70 provides for the possible forfeiture of the right to remain in a Member State in the event of non-residence exceeding six months. It is difficult to discern any other purpose in the provision.

Derogation from national rules

The provision of the Regulation in no way derogate from national rules more favourable to Community workers.[18] An express provision to this effect is probably unnecessary, since the Court has often expressed the view that the free movement provisions of the Treaty authorise legislative action only to improve the legal situation in which the worker would have found himself but for the Community rules.[19]

Admittance of workers without a strict right to residence

The Regulation places a duty on Member States to "facilitate re-admission" to their territories of workers who have left after a long period of residence and employment and wish to return when they have reached retirement, or become incapacitated.[20] The legal effect of such a genera-

---

[15] Art. 6(1).
[16] Art. 6(2).
[17] *Supra*, p. 169.
[18] Art. 8(1).
[19] See, *e.g.* Case 191/73 *Niemann* v. *Bundesversicherungsanstalt für Angestellte* [1974] E.C.R. 571, Case 27/75 *Bonaffini* v. *INPS* [1975] E.C.R. 971.
[20] Art. 8(2).

lised provision is unclear. It can hardly be said to provide a right of re-entry; its terms are far too vague for that, nor can it be said to provide a principle in light of which related provisions must be interpreted.[21] At best it would seem to provide a principle account of which must be taken by national authorities when considering whether or not a person falling within the relevant category ought to be re-admitted to national territory.

LIMITATIONS JUSTIFIED ON GROUNDS OF PUBLIC POLICY, PUBLIC SECURITY OR PUBLIC HEALTH

1. General

Article 48(3) of the Treaty subjects the free movement of workers to limitations justified on grounds of public policy, public security or public health. The text makes it clear that the exception limits the rights itemised in the third paragraph of the Article, but not the right to equality in terms and conditions of employment guaranteed in Article 48(2). As Advocate General Gand explained in *Ugliola*, "on grounds of public policy or public security a foreigner may not be permitted to enter a country and take up employment there, but those considerations have no bearing on conditions of work once employment has been taken up in an authorised manner."[22] The Court agreed; the proviso applied only to "the cases expressly referred to in paragraph 3."[23]

Since Article 48(3) can be invoked to exclude a worker from the territory of a Member State, it would seem to follow that the exception could justify a *partial* restriction on residence, but this is not the case. In *Rutili* v. *French Minister of the Interior*,[24] an Italian national resident in France was issued with a residence permit subject to a prohibition on residence in certain French departments. The Court of Justice held that the reservation contained in Article 48(3) had the same scope as the right subject to limitation. It followed that any prohibition on residence could be imposed only in respect of the whole of the national territory. In the case of partial prohibitions on residence. Article 7 of the Treaty required that persons covered by Community law must be treated on a footing of equality with nationals of the host State.

The Court held in the *Pieck* case[25] that the public policy proviso in Article 48(3) did not amount to a condition precedent to the acquisition of a right of entry and residence, but provided a possibility, in individual cases where there was sufficient justification, of imposing restrictions on the exercise of a right derived directly from the Treaty. It did not therefore jus-

[21] *Cf. Casagrande*, in which the second paragraph of Art. 12 of Reg. 1612/68 was resorted to as an aid to interpretation of the first, *supra*, p. 181.
[22] Case 15/69 [1969] E.C.R. 363, at p. 365, [1970] C.M.L.R. 194, at p. 200.
[23] [1969] E.C.R. 363 at p. 369, [1970] C.M.L.R. 194 at p. 202. This suggests that the right to enter a Member State in search of work must be founded on Art. 48(3), rather than upon 48(2).
[24] Case 36/75 [1975] E.C.R. 1219, [1976] 1 C.M.L.R. 140.
[25] Case 157/79, [1980] E.C.R. 2171.

tify general formalities at the frontier other than the simple production of a valid identity card or passport.

2. Directive 64/221

The scope of Article 48(3) may be clarified by reference to Directive 64/221 of February 25, 1964, on the co-ordination of special measures concerning the movement and residence of foreign nationals which are justified on grounds of public policy, public security or public health.[26] The Directive *in toto* gives rise to rights in individuals which national courts are bound to safeguard.[27]

The Directive applies to workers of one Member State travelling to or residing in another for the purpose of employment, and to members of their families.[28] It declares that the proviso may not be invoked to serve economic ends.[29] All measures relating to entry, the issue and renewal of residence permits, and expulsion, which are taken by Member States on grounds of public policy, public security or public health, are subject to its terms,[30] and must be based on the personal conduct of the individual concerned.[31] Previous criminal convictions, while no doubt relevant to the assessment of an individual's conduct, do not in themselves constitute grounds for applying the proviso.[32] These requirements are central to the protection afforded to individuals by Article 48(3) and Directive 64/221, as *Bonsignore* v. *Oberstadt-direktor Cologne*[33] illustrates. Carmelo Bonsignore, an Italian worker resident in the Federal Republic, unlawfully acquired a Beretta pistol, with which he accidentally shot his younger brother Angelo. He was fined for unlawful possession of a firearm, and deportation was ordered by the Chief Administrative Office of the City of Cologne. A reference to the Court of Justice sought a ruling on the question whether Article 3(1) and (2) of the Directive were to be interpreted as excluding deportation of a national of a Member State for the purpose of deterring other foreign nationals for such offences, or whether expulsion was only permissible when there were clear indications that an EEC national, who had been convicted of an offence, would *himself* commit further offences or in some other way disregard public security or public policy. "As departures from the rules concerning the free movement of persons consistute exceptions which must be strictly construed," declared the Court, "the concept of 'personal conduct' expresses the requirement that a deportation order may only be made for breaches of the peace and public security which might be committed by the individual affected."[34] In

---

[26] J.O. 1964, 850.
[27] Case 36/75, *Rutili* [1975] E.C.R. 1219.
[28] Art. 1.
[29] Art. 2(2).
[30] Art. 2(1).
[31] Art. 3(1).
[32] Art. 3(2). The word "measure" in Art. 3(1) and 3(2) includes a recommendation for deportation under the Immigration Act 1971; Case 30/77 *R.* v. *Bouchereau* [1977] E.C.R. 1999.
[33] Case 67/74 [1975] E.C.R. 297.
[34] [1975] E.C.R. 297 at p. 307.

R. v. *Bouchereau,*[35] however, Advocate General Warner expressed agreement with the Government of the United Kingdom that "cases do arise, exceptionally, where the present conduct of an alien has been such that, whilst not necessarily evincing any clear propensity on his part [to indulge in future misbehaviour], it has caused such deep public revulsion that public policy requires his departure."[36] The Court apparently took a similar view. While emphasising that "The existence of a previous criminal conviction can therefore only be taken into account in so far as the circumstances which gave rise to that conviction are evidence of personal conduct constituting a present threat to the requirements of public policy," and admitting that, "in general, a finding that such a threat exists implies the existence in the individual concerned of a propensity to act in the same way in the future,' the Court added that "it is possible that past conduct alone may constitute such a threat to the requirements of public policy."[37] It was for the national authorities, and, where appropriate, national courts, to consider each individual case in the light of the legal position of persons subject to Community law and the fundamental nature of the principle of the free movement of persons. It seems clear, as Advocate General Warner notes, that it will only be in the most exceptional cases that past conduct will of itself be capable of justifying deportation.

The Directive explicitly provides that expiry of an identity card or passport used to enter the host country and obtain a residence permit shall not justify expulsion, and furthermore, that the State which issued such travel documents should allow the holder to re-enter its territory without formality even if the document is no longer valid, or the nationality of the holder is in dispute.[38]

Grounds of "public health" as well as "public policy" and "public security," justify recourse to the proviso. The fourth recital to the preamble of the Directive declares that it would be of little practical use to compile a list of diseases and disabilities which might endanger public health, public policy or public security, and that it is sufficient to classify such diseases and disabilities in groups. The result is an Annex to the Directive, comprising a Group A—diseases and disabilities which might threaten public health (infectious diseases), and a Group B—diseases and disabilities which might threaten public policy or public security (such as drug addiction or mental illness). Article 4 of the Directive provides that the only diseases or disabilities justifying refusal of entry into a territory or refusal to issue a first residence permit are those listed in the Annex. Diseases or disabilities occurring after a first residence permit has been issued do not justify refusal to renew the residence permit or expulsion from the territory.[39]

In addition to the substantive safeguards referred to above, the Directive also provides a number of procedural safeguards.

Decisions to grant or refuse a first residence permit must be taken as

---

[35] Case 30/77 [1977] E.C.R. 1999.
[36] [1977] E.C.R. 1999 at p. 2022.
[37] [1977] E.C.R. 1999 at p. 2012. For possible circumstances when *past* conduct may justify deportation, see Wyatt (1978) 15 C.M.L. Rev. 221 at pp. 224, 225.
[38] Art. 3(3), (4).
[39] Art. 4(2).

soon as possible and in any event not less than six months after the date of application for the permit, and the worker is entitled to remain in the territory of the host State pending a decision in his particular case.[40] Although a Member State may, if it thinks it essential, request the Member State of origin of the applicant for details of any criminal record, and the latter State is obliged to respond within two months, such enquiries must not be made as a matter of routine.

The individual concerned must always be officially notified of any decision to[41] refuse the issue of renewal of a residence permit, or to expel him from the territory, and of the time allowed him to leave. Save in cases of urgency, this period must not be less than 15 days where the person has not yet been granted a residence permit, and not less than a month in all other cases.[42]

In order to allow workers an opportunity to safeguard their rights, Article 6 of the Directive provides that in all cases the individual concerned is entitled to be informed of the grounds of public policy, public security or public health upon which the decision taken in his case was based, unless to do so would be contrary to the interests of the security of the State involved.

With respect to decisions relating to entry, the refusal to issue or renew a residence permit, or expulsion, the person concerned is entitled to the same legal remedies as are available to nationals of the State concerned in respect of acts of the Administration.[43]

There are three types of case in which a decision refusing renewal of a residence permit or ordering the expulsion of the holder of a residence permit must not be taken—save in cases or urgency—until an opinion has been obtained from a competent authority of the host country before which the person concerned enjoys such rights of defence and representation as are provided by domestic law.[44] These three types of case are: (i) where there is no right of appeal to a court of law; (ii) where such an appeal lies only in respect of the legal validity of the decision; (iii) where the appeal cannot have suspensory effect. The purpose of recourse to the "competent authority"[45] is, in the first case, to compensate for the absence of a right of appeal to the courts; in the second case to enable a detailed examination to be made of the situation of the person concerned, including the appropriateness of the measure contemplated, before the decision is finally taken; and in the third case to permit the person concerned to request and to obtain, if appropriate, a stay of the execution of the measure envisaged in such a way as to compensate for the absence of a right to obtain a stay of execution from the courts.

The "competent authority" referred to in Article 9 of Directive 64/221 must not be the same as that empowered to take the decision refusing

[40] Art. 5.
[41] Art. 5.
[42] Art. 7.
[43] Art. 8. The Article is directly effective: Case 131/79, *Santillo* [1980] E.C.R. 1585.
[44] Art. 9(1). Art. 9 is directly effective; Case 131/79 *Santillo* [1980] E.C.R. 1585.
[45] Case 98/79 *Pecastaing* [1980] E.C.R. 691.

renewal of the residence permit or ordering expulsion.[46] It must be independent of the administration, but Member States are given a margin of discretion as to the nature of the authority.[47] Thus it has been held that a recommendation for deportation made by a criminal court at the time of conviction may constitute an opinion of competent authority within the meaning of Article 9 of the Directive.[48] However, such an opinion must be sufficiently proximate in time to the decision ordering expulsion to ensure that there are no new factors to be taken into account occurring between the opinion and the decision, liable to deprive the opinion of its useful effect.[49]

Where a decision is taken refusing the issue of a first residence permit, or ordering expulsion of the person concerned before the issue of the permit, the worker must be entitled to refer the decision for reconsideration by the competent authority referred to above, where he can submit his defence in person.[50]

The Court of Justice considered Articles 6, 8 and 9 of the Directive in *Rutili* v. *French Minister of the Interior*,[51] and concluded that any person enjoying the protection of these provisions was entitled to a double safeguard comprising notification to him of the grounds on which any restrictive measure had been adopted and the availability of a right of appeal. The Court added that all steps should be taken by Member States to ensure that the double safeguard was in fact available to anyone against whom a restrictive measure had been adopted. "In particular," declared the Court, "this requirement means that the State concerned must, when notifying an individual of a restrictive measure adopted in his case, give him a precise and comprehensive statement of the grounds for the decision to enable him to take effective steps to prepare his defence."[52]

The question of the relationship between Articles 8 and 9 of the Directive arose in *Procureur du Roi* v. *Royer*,[53] in which the Tribunal de Première Instance of Liège sought a ruling from the Court of Justice on the question, *inter alia*, whether a decision ordering expulsion or a refusal to issue a residence permit could give rise to immediate measures of execution or whether such a decision could only take effect after the exhaustion of national remedies. The Court held that in the case of the remedies referred to in Article 8 of Directive 64/221, the person concerned must at least have the opportunity of lodging an appeal and thus obtaining a stay of execution before the expulsion order was carried out. If no remedy was available, or if it was available, but did not have suspensive effect, the decision could not be taken—save in cases of urgency which had been properly justified—until the party concerned had had the opportunity of appealing to the competent authority referred to in Article 9 of the Direct-

---

[46] Art. 9(1).
[47] Case 131/79 *Santillo* [1980] E.C.R. 1585, para. (15) of Judgment. Cases 115 and 116/81 *Adoui* [1982] E.C.R. 1665.
[48] *Santillo*, para. (17) of Judgment.
[49] *Santillo*; but see [1981] 2 All E.R. 897, C.A.
[50] Art. 9(2).
[51] Case 36/75 [1975] E.C.R. 1219.
[52] [1975] E.C.R. 1219 at 1233.
[53] Case 48/75 [1976] E.C.R. 497.

ive, and until this authority had reached a decision. Referring to the right of appeal provided for in Articles 8 and 9 of the Directive, the Court declared that "this guarantee would become illusory if the Member State could, by the immediate execution of a decision ordering expulsion, deprive the person concerned of the opportunity of effectively making use of the remedies which he is guaranteed by Directive No. 64/221."[54]

The Court returned to the relationship between Articles 8 and 9 in *Pecastaing*.[55] In its view Article 9 would be rendered nugatory unless expulsion were suspended pending the giving of the opinion of the competent authority (save that is, in cases of urgency). But there was no analogous requirement in the case of Article 8. While a decision ordering expulsion could not be executed (save in cases of urgency) before the party concerned was able to complete the formalities necessary to avail himself of the national remedy contemplated by Article 8, it could not be inferred from that provision that the person concerned was entitled to remain on the territory of the state concerned throughout the proceedings initiated by him.

In the case of decisions concerning *entry*, it will be noted that Article 8 is applicable, but that Article 9 is not, since the latter provision conspicuously omits such decisions.

3. The area of discretion left to national authorities under Article 48(3).

The area of discretion left to national authorities in the application of Article 48(3) has been clarified in a number of decisions of the Court of Justice, in particular *Van Duyn*,[56] *Rutili*,[57] *Bouchereau*,[58] and *Adoui*.[59]

Miss Van Duyn was a Dutch national who had been offered employment as a secretary with the Church of Scientology at its College at East Grinstead. Since the United Kingdom Government regarded Scientology as objectionable, socially harmful, and damaging to the health of its practitioners, it had announced its intention in 1968 of taking all steps within its power—short of legal prohibition—to curb its growth. Accordingly, Miss Van Duyn was refused leave to enter the United Kingdom. Alleging violation of her rights as a Community national under Article 4 of the Treaty, and Article 3 of Directive 64/221, she sought a declaration in the High Court to the effect that she was entitled to enter the United Kingdom to take up her employment at East Grinstead. The High Court posed the question, *inter alia*, whether

"a Member State, in the performance of its duty to base a measure taken on grounds of public policy exclusively on the personal conduct of the individual concerned is entitled to take into account as a matter of personal conduct:
(a) the fact that the individual is or has been associated with some

---

[54] [1976] E.C.R. 497 at p. 516.
[55] Case 98/79 [1980] E.C.R. 691
[56] Case 41/74 [1974] E.C.R. 1337.
[57] Case 36/75 [1975] E.C.R. 1219.
[58] Case 30/77 [1977] E.C.R. 1999.
[59] Cases 115 & 116/81 [1982] E.C.R. 1665.

body or organisation whose activities the Member State considers contrary to the public good but which are not unlawful in that State;

(b) the fact that the individual intends to take employment in the Member State with such body or organisation, it being the case that no restrictions are placed upon nationals of the Member State who wish to take similar employment with such body or organisation."

On the first point the Court, acknowledging that a person's past association could not, in general, justify refusal of entry, declared that nevertheless present association, reflecting participation in the activities of the organisation as well as identification with its aims or designs, could be considered as a voluntary act of the person concerned and, consequently, as part of his personal conduct within the meaning of the Article cited. As to the fact that the United Kingdom authorities had not prohibited the practice of Scientology, the Court took the view that although Article 48(3), as an exception to a fundamental freedom under the Treaty, must be interpreted strictly, nevertheless the Member States were allowed a margin of discretion, inasmuch as the particular circumstances justifying recourse to the concept of public policy might vary from one country to another and from one period to another. "It follows," the Court said, " . . . that where the competent authorities of a Member State have clearly defined their standpoint as regards the activities of a particular organisation and where, considering it to be socially harmful, they have taken administrative measures to counteract these activities, the Member State cannot be required, before it can rely on the concept of public policy, to make such activities unlawful, if recourse to such a measure is not thought appropriate in the circumstances."[60] The fact that the result of the policy of the United Kingdom authorities was to bar employment to non-national Community workers while allowing similar employment to United Kingdom nationals seemed to raise no further issue of principle for the Court. The very essence of the exception was that it enabled national authorities to treaty non-nationals in a discriminatory fashion. "It follows," declared the Court, "that a Member State . . . can, where it *deems necessary* [emphasis added], refuse a national of another Member State the benefit of the principle of freedom of movement for workers . . . where such a national proposes to take up a particular offer of employment even though the Member State does not place a similar restriction upon its own nationals."[61]

The Court's decision in *Van Duyn* introduces a subjective element into the application of Article 48(3) that is apparently at odds with its statement that "its scope cannot be determined unilaterally by each Member State without being subject to control by the institutions of the Community."[62] But it must be remembered that the Court was faced with a very limited question—whether or not, *in principle*, a State was entitled to take into account the factors indicated. This question is answered in the affirmative.

---

[60] [1974] E.C.R. 1337 at p. 1350.
[61] [1974] E.C.R. 1337 at p. 1351.
[62] [1974] E.C.R. 1337 at p. 1350.

It did not have to examine the circumstances in which such factors could *justify* an exclusion in a particular case. Such a question was posed to the Court in *Rutili* v. *French Minister of the Interior*.

The plaintiff in the main suit was an Italian resident in France, who had incurred the displeasure of the French authorities as a result of political, and allegedly subversive activities. He was issued with a residence permit subject to a prohibition on residence in certain departments. Mr. Rutili brought proceedings before the Tribunal Administratif for the annulment of the decision limiting the territorial validity of his residence permit. During the proceedings before the Tribunal, the argument was advanced that Mr. Rutili's presence in the departments prohibited to him was "likely to disturb public policy." Two questions were referred to the Court for a preliminary ruling. The first asked whether the expression "subject to limitations justified on grounds of public policy" in Article 48(3) of the Treaty concerned merely legislative decisions of the Member States, or whether it concerned also individual decisions taken in application of such legislative decisions. The second question sought the precise meaning to be attributed to the word "justified."

On the first question, the Court held that inasmuch as the object of the provisions of the Treaty and of secondary legislation was to regulate the situation of individuals and to ensure their protection, it was also for the national courts to examine whether individual decisions were compatible with the relevant provisions of Community Law.

The Court then considered the meaning to be given to the word "justified" in Article 48(3). Since the exception was a derogation from a fundamental freedom granted by the Treaty, and must be interpreted strictly, it followed, argued the Court, that "restrictions cannot be imposed on the right of a national of any Member State to enter the territory of another Member State, to stay there and to move within it unless his presence or conduct constitutes a *genuine and sufficiently serious threat to public policy* (emphasis added)."[63] The Court concludes:

> "Taken as a whole, these limitations placed on the powers of Member States in respect of control of aliens are a specific manifestation of the more general principle, enshrined in Articles 8, 9 10 and 11 of the Convention for the Protection of Human Rights and Fundamental Freedoms, signed in Rome on November 4, 1950, and ratified by all the Member States, and in Article 2 of the Protocol No. 4 of the same Convention, signed in Strasbourg on 16 September 1963, which provide, in identical terms, that no restrictions in the interests of national security or public safety shall be placed on the rights secured by the above-quoted articles other than such as are necessary for the protection of those interests in a democratic society."[64]

The Court thus makes explicit the test of "proportionality" in the judicial review of individual decisions taken on the basis of Article 48(3). The principle of "proportionality"—whereby legal authorisation of legisla-

---

[63] [1975] E.C.R. 1219 at p. 1231.
[64] [1975] E.C.R. 1219 at p. 1232.

tive or administrative action to a particular end extends only to those measures which, being apt to achieve the permitted end are, objectively speaking, least burdensome to those subject to the law—is well established in the jurisprudence of the Court of Justice. The principle may be invoked as a result of the express wording of the Treaty or implementing legislation, or as one of the basic principles of law which the Court of Justice is bound to safeguard.[65]

In *R. v. Bouchereau*, the Court added a gloss to its statement in *Rutili*. Not only must the threat to the requirements of public policy be "genuine and sufficiently serious," but the requirements invoked must affect "one of the fundamental interests of society."[66]

The *Van Duyn*[67] decision seems in retrospect to have formulated somewhat generous criteria for the exercise of national discretion under Article 48(3). In *Adoui*[68] the Court stressed that while Article 48(3) allowed different treatment for aliens than for its own nationals (since Member States could not expel their own nationals), it did not authorise measures which discriminated against nationals of other Member States on arbitrary grounds. The Court amplified its reference in *Bouchereau*[69] to "a genuine and sufficiently serious threat affecting one of the fundamental interests of society," as follows:

> "Although Community law does not impose upon the Member States a uniform scale of values as regards the assessment of conduct which may be considered as contrary to public policy, it should nevertheless be stated that conduct may not be considered as being of a sufficiently serious nature to justify restrictions on the admission to or residence within the territory of a national of another Member State in a case where the former Member State does not adopt, with respect to the same conduct on the part of its own nationals, repressive measures or other genuine and effective measures to combat such conduct."[70]

It is clear that the national judge, in assessing the legality of action by national authorities under Article 48(3), must decide whether such action is "excessive" with regard to the threat to public policy posed by the individual concerned. In making such an assessment, he must take as his yardstick the view which the national authorities take of such conduct when engaged in by nationals, for although Article 48(3) by its nature permits discrimination, such discrimination must not be arbitrary.

It is interesting to note that the Court refers in *Rutili* to the European Convention on Human Rights, ratified, as the Court points out, by all the Member States. The Court's concern for the maintenance of basic rights within the sphere of operation of the Treaty has been expressed on several occasions, but always as a constraint of Community action.[71] The Court's

---

[65] Case 11/70 *Internationale Handelsgesellschaft* [1970] E.C.R. 1125.
[66] Case 30/77 [1977] E.C.R. 1999 at 2014, para. (35).
[67] Case 41/74 [1974] E.C.R. 1337.
[68] Cases 115 & 116/81 [1982] E.C.R. 1665.
[69] Case 30/77 [1977] E.C.R. 1999.
[70] Cases 115 & 116/81 [1982] E.C.R. 1665, para. (8) of Judgment.
[71] See, *e.g.* Case 11/70, *Internationale Handelsgesellschaft* [1970] E.C.R. 1125; Case 4/73 *Nold* [1974] E.C.R. 491.

judgment in *Rutili* suggests that Treaty provisions binding on the Member States will be interpreted by the Court in the light of the fundamental freedoms guaranteed by the European Convention.

If *Van Duyn* supports the proposition that the "categories" of national interest which are eligible for protection under the proviso may vary in time and space[72] without prejudicing the uniform application of Community law, *Rutili* and subsequent cases emphasise that the *extent* to which such interests may be safeguarded will be subject to strict judicial control.

Naturally, each Member State has its own rules for controlling the entry of aliens and their residence in national territory. The decision of the Court in *Royer*[73] makes it clear that failure to comply with national immigration formalities cannot of itself provide grounds for expulsion under Article 48(3). Mr. Royer, a Frenchman, had been expelled from Belgium for failing to comply with national formalities concerning the residence of aliens. He returned to Belgium, and was tried for the offence of illegal residence in the Kingdom. The Tribunal de Première Instance of Liège sought a ruling from the Court on the question, *inter alia*, whether the mere failure of an EEC national to comply with local entry formalities could provide a ground for expulsion under Article 48(3). The Court replied in the negative. While Community law did not prevent Member States providing sanctions for breaches of national law relating to the control of aliens, such sanctions could not include expulsion. "Since it is a question of the exercise of a right acquired under the Treaty itself," said the Court, "such conduct cannot be regarded as constituting in itself a breach of public policy or public security."[74] The view of the Court accords with the principle enunciated in *Schlüter & Maack* v. *Hauptzollamt Hamburg-Jonas*[75]—national requirements may be attached to rights arising under Community law, but not as a precondition to their exercise. Any other solution would prejudice the uniform application of Community law. From another perspective, it could simply be said that such minor infringements as those in issue could never amount to the genuinely and sufficiently serious threat to public policy required by the terms of Article 48(3).

The Public Service Proviso

Article 48(4) of the Treaty declares that the "provisions of this Article shall not apply to employment in the public service." The provision does not apply to *all* employment in the public service, nor does it allow discrimination in the terms and conditions of employment once appointed. This much is clear from the Judgment of the Court in *Sotgiu* v. *Deutsche Bundespost*,[76] in which the Bundesarbeitsgericht sought a ruling from the Court

[72] *Adoui* reaffirms this proposition; see note 70.
[73] Case 48/75 [1976] E.C.R. 497.
[74] [1976] E.C.R. 497 at 513.
[75] Case 94/71 [1972] E.C.R. 307.
[76] Case 152/73 [1974] E.C.R. 153.

on the question whether or not Article 7 of Regulation 1612/68 was applicable to employees in the German postal service in view of this proviso. The Court replied that since the exception contained in Article 48(4) could not be allowed a scope extending beyond the object for which it was included, the provision could be invoked to restrict the *admission* of foreign nationals to *certain activities* in the public service, but not to justify discrimination once they had been admitted.

The Court further clarified the scope of Article 48(4) in *Commission* v. *Belgium* (Case 149/79, No. 1), holding that that Article:

" . . . removes from the ambit of Article 48(1)–(3) a series of posts which involve direct or indirect participation in the exercise of powers conferred by public law and duties designed to safeguard the general interests of the State or of other public authorities. Such posts in fact presume on the part of those occupying them the existence of a special relationship of allegiance to the State and reciprocity of rights and duties which form the foundation of the bond of nationality."[77]

Thus not all posts in the public service fall within the public service proviso. In the Court's view, to extend Article 48(4) to posts which, while coming under the State or other organisations governed by public law, still do not involve any association with tasks belonging to the public service properly so called, would be to remove a considerable number of posts from the ambit of the principles set out in the Treaty and to create inequalities between the Member States according to the different ways in which the State and certain sectors of economic life are organised.

Nevertheless, classification of particular posts can cause difficulty. In *Commission* v. *Belgium* (Case 149/79, No. 2),[78] the Court approved the Commission's concession that the following posts fell within the ambit of Article 48(4): head technical office supervisor, principal supervisor, works supervisor, stock controller, and nightwatchman, with the Municipalities of Brussels and Auderghem. The Court also upheld the Commission's view that a number of other jobs with Belgian National Railways, Belgian Local Railways, the City of Brussels, and the Commune of Auderghem, fell outside Article 48(4). These jobs included railway shunters, drivers, platelayers, signalmen and nightwatchmen, and nurses, electricians, joiners and plumbers employed by the Municipalities of Brussels and Auderghem.

Whereas access to the posts in question will often be direct, it might also be by promotion from other posts which could not be classified along with those "certain activities" to which access may be limited. It would seem to follow that Article 48(4) should be read as permitting discrimination against Community nationals already holding posts in the public service, insofar as promotion to "sensitive" posts is concerned. This consideration was argued by the German Government in *Commission* v. *Belgium*[79] to militate against construing Article 48(4) as only applying to certain posts within the public service, rather than to the public service at large. The

---

[77] Case 149/79 [1980] E.C.R. 3881.
[78] Case 149/79 [1982] E.C.R. 1845. And see Case 307/84, *Commission* v. *France* Judgment of June 3, 1986, Case 66/85 *Lawrie-Blum* Judgment of July 3, 1986.
[79] Case 149/79 [1980] E.C.R. 3881.

Court's reply was that applying Article 48(4) to all posts in the public service would impose a restriction on the rights of nationals of other Member States which went further than was necessary to achieve the aims of the proviso.

CHAPTER 9

THE RIGHT OF ESTABLISHMENT AND THE FREEDOM TO PROVIDE SERVICES

INTRODUCTION

As well as ensuring the free movement of workers, the Treaty guarantees the right of establishment, and the freedom to provide services between Member States: what Article 48 provides for the employee, Articles 52 and 59 provide for the employer, the entrepreneur and the professional.

The right of establishment is the right of a natural person or a company to settle in a Member State and to pursue economic activities therein.[1] It includes the right to take up and pursue an occupation in a self-employed capacity, and to set up and manage undertakings.[2]

The right of establishment is to be contrasted with the freedom to provide services. The former entails settlement in a Member State for economic purposes, and connotes permanent integration into the host State's economy. The latter entails a person established in one Member State providing services in another, as in the case of a doctor established in France visiting a client in Belgium. The distinction may not always be clear-cut, because the provision of services may involve temporary residence in the host State, as in the case of a German firm of business consultants which advises undertakings in France, or a construction company which erects buildings in a neighbouring country. As long as such residence is temporary, the activities in question will fall within the ambit of Articles 59–66, on freedom to provide services[3]; if it is of a more permanent character, they will be regulated by the provisions governing the right of establishment. It is evident that the provision of services from one State to another on a regular basis, accompanied by temporary residence in the host State, may shade imperceptibly into establishment. The separate legal treatment of these related concepts has been criticised. Not only is it somewhat arbitrary from an economic standpoint, but it may lead to unnecessary difficulties of classification.[4]

---

[1] Brita Sundberg-Weitman, *Discrimination on Grounds of Nationality* (1977), p. 179; W. van Gerven (1966) 3 C.M.L.Rev. 344.

[2] Art. 52, second para. Case 182/83 *Fearon* [1984] E.C.R. 3677.

[3] Art. 60, third para., provides: "Without prejudice to the provisions of the Chapter relating to the right of establishment, the person providing a service may, in order to do so, temporarily pursue his activity in the State where the service is provided, under the same conditions as are imposed by that State on its own nationals." Where the activities of a person established in one Member State are directed principally towards the territory of another, the rules relating to establishment rather than services may apply: Case 33/74 *Van Binsbergen* [1974] E.C.R. 1299, at p. 1309, para. 13.

[4] Dr. Ulrich Everling, *The Right of Establishment in the Common Market* (1964), p. 51; Kapteyn and VerLoren van Themaat, *Introduction to the Law of the European Communities* [1973], p. 213. See Case 39/75 *Coenen* (1975) E.C.R. 1547, decided on the basis of Art. 59, concerned an individual apparently established in the same State as the recipients of the services in question; it was his personal residence outside that State that was held against him.

Certain occupational activities, on the other hand, appear to fall within the ambit of neither Article 52 nor Article 59. How, for instance, would one classify the activities of a British camera crew filming scenes in France and Germany? On a strict construction of Articles 52 and 59, taking each Article individually, the crew would seem to be neither establishing themselves, nor providing or receiving services. Such a conclusion—that there may be "gaps" between the scope of Article 52 and Article 59—would seem to conflict with the object of the Treaty to create a single market between the Member States. A more satisfactory solution would be to consider Articles 52 and 59 as a whole, and in the light of the object and purpose of the Treaty. On this view, the chapters on establishment and freedom to provide services would be interpreted as requiring the fullest possible freedom of movement for self-employed persons wishing to engage in economic activities, *regardless of the stage of provision or distribution of the service involved*. The British film crew would be entitled to entry into and residence in France and Germany on the basis of Article 59 of the Treaty, since their activities would be a step in the provision of services.[5] Articles 52 and 59 are intended to safeguard the rights of self-employed persons to pursue occupational activities throughout the Community regardless of the location of their place of business—not to differentiate between various stages of the economic process. Signs of a broad approach on the part of the Court may be detected in the *Coenen*[6] and *Koestler*[7] cases.

The Right of Establishment

Establishment of natural persons

Article 52 draws a distinction between nationals[8] of Member States *simpliciter*, and those *already established* in the territory of a Member State. The former are entitled to establish *themselves* in any Member State, the latter are entitled to set up agencies and branches.

The right to set up agencies and branches has been described by the Court as a specific statement of a general principle, applicable equally to the liberal professions, according to which the right of establishment includes the freedom to set up and maintain, subject to observance of the professional rules of conduct, more than one place of work within the Community.[9] Thus Article 52 *et seq.* of the Treaty have been held to preclude the denial to a national of another Member State the right to enter

---

[5] Everling, *op. cit.* pp. 51, 52 and 165, 166. Art. 48 would not provide an independent ground for such activity, even if the camera crew in the hypothetical situation postulated in the text were employed persons: what is in issue is not the right of the worker to take up or maintain an employment relationship, but the right of the employer to carry on economic activities in the host State. *Cf.* Cases 262 and 263/81 *Seco* [1982] E.C.R. 223.

[6] Case 39/75 [1975] E.C.R. 1547.

[7] Case 15/78 [1978] E.C.R. 1971; see *infra* at p. 218.

[8] For the position of nationals of the countries and territories listed in Annex IV of the Treaty, see Sundberg-Weitman, *op. cit.* p. 186.

[9] Case 107/83 *Klopp* [1984] E.C.R. 2971.

and to exercise the profession of advocate solely on the ground that he maintains chambers in another Member State.[10]

The distinction between the right to establish oneself, and the right, once initially established in the territory of a Member State, to establish agencies, branches and subsidiaries, is significant in relation to the establishment of companies, and will be considered later.[11]

The Treaty provides for the abolition of restrictions on freedom of establishment in progressive stages during the transitional period. Such abolition was to be facilitated by secondary legislation prohibiting discrimination on grounds of nationality, ensuring the mutual recognition of "diplomas and certificates, and other evidence of formal qualifications,"[12] and co-ordinating national requirements governing the pursuit of non-wage-earning activities.[13] Legislation on the abolition of restrictions was to be preceded by a General Programme, which was to be drawn up by the Council before the end of the first stage. The Programme[14] was adopted in December 1961,[15] and provided the basis for the Council's subsequent legislative activities in this area.

Entry and residence

Title II of the Council's General Programme sought the adjustment of the legislative and administrative requirements in the Member States governing entry and residence, to the extent that such requirements might impair the access of nationals of other Member States to non-wage-earning activities. Directive 64/220 of February 25, 1964 followed,[16] providing for the abolition of restrictions on movement and residence within the Community, and applied, like many other instruments in this area, to the provision of services as well as to the right of establishment. It was superseded by Directive 73/148,[17] which brought the law governing the entry and residence of the self-employed into line with that applying to employees, and indeed, it follows closely the pattern of Directive 68/360,[18] which has been considered in detail in the context of the free movement of workers.[19]

Directive 73/148, like its predecessor, applies to both the right of establishment and to the provision of services. Its beneficiaries are described in Article 1(1) as:

"(a) nationals of a Member State who are established or who wish to

---

[10] *Ibid.* Similarly, it is not permissible to make practice as a doctor or dentist in one Member State conditional on cancellation of registration in another, see Case 96/85 *Commission* v. *French Republic* [1986] 3 C.M.L.R. 57.

[11] *Infra*, p. 214.

[12] Art. 57(1).

[13] Art. 57(2).

[14] It constitutes neither a Regulation, Directive nor Decision within the meaning of Art. 189 of the Treaty. For the view that it bound the Community institutions, but not the Member States, see van Gerven (1966) 3 C.M.L. Rev. 344, at p. 354. There seems to be no reason why it could not bind the Member States, see Case 22/70 *ERTA* [1971] E.C.R. 263.

[15] O.J. 1974, Sp. Ed., Second Series, IX, p. 7. The Court has referred to the General Programme in Case 7/76 *Thieffry* [1977] E.C.R. 765; case 136/78 *Auer* [1979] E.C.R. 452; Case 182/83 *Fearon* [1984] E.C.R. 3677; Case 107/83 *Klopp* [1984] E.C.R. 2971.

[16] J.O. 1964, 845.

[17] O.J. 1973 L172/14.

[18] J.O. 1968, L257/13.

[19] *Supra*, p. 165.

establish themselves in another Member State in order to pursue activities as self-employed persons, or who wish to provide services in that State;

(b) nationals of Member States wishing to go to another Member State as recipients of services;

(c) the spouse and the children under 21 years of age of such nationals, irrespective of their nationality;

(d) the relatives in the ascending and descending lines of such nationals and of the spouse of such nationals, which relatives are dependent on them, irrespective of their nationality."

Following the pattern of Directive 68/360, Directive 73/148 bestows the following rights on the above persons:

— the right to be allowed to leave national territory, and to be issued with an identity card or passport (Art. 2);

— the right to be allowed to enter the territory of the Member States merely on production of a valid identity card or passport (Art. 3).

A distinction is drawn between the right of residence of a person exercising the right of establishment, and the right of a person providing services. In the former case, Article 4(1) applies, requiring each Member State to "grant the right of permanent residence to nationals of other Member States who establish themselves within its territory in order to pursue activities as self-employed persons." This right is evidenced by a "residence Permit for a National of a Member State of the European Communities," which must be valid for not less than five years and be automatically renewable.[20] In the case of the provision of services, the Directive declares that "the right of residence for persons providing and receiving services shall be of equal duration with the period during which the services are provided."[21] Where such periods exceed three months, the Member State in whose territory the services are performed must issue a "right of abode" as proof of residence.[22] An applicant for a residence permit or right of abode is only required to produce: (a) the identity card or passport with which he or she entered the territory in question; and (b) proof that he or she comes within the protection of the Directive.[23]

Whereas Directive 68/360 is ambiguous as to the rights of entry and residence of dependent relatives other than children or those in the ascending line, and relatives living under the worker's roof in the country whence they came,[24] Directive 73/148 contains no such ambiguity in the case of the relatives of the self-employed. Article 1 of the Directive makes it clear that such persons do not enter and reside as of right, though Member States "shall favour" their admission. As indicated earlier,[24] it is believed that such differentiation between dependent relatives is capable of constituting an obstacle to the free movement of persons, and is accordingly contrary to Articles 7, 48, 52 and 59 of the Treaty.

[20] Art. 4(1), second sub-para.
[21] Art. 4(2), first sub-para.
[22] Art. 4(2), second sub-para.
[23] Art. 6.
[24] *Supra*, p. 168.

The right to remain in the territory of a Member State after having been self-employed there

The Court has on several occasions stressed the parallels between Articles 48, 52 and 59,[25] and indeed, they comprise an integrated whole embracing all economic activities,[26] whether carried on by the employed or the self-employed, regardless of the stage of production, distribution or provision of services concerned, and, apart from the case of activities confined to a single Member State, irrespective of the place of business of a supplier undertaking relative to that of its customers. Nevertheless, there are substantial differences in the scheme and text of these various provisions, not least in the omission of any explicit authority in Articles 52–58: (i) to make provision for the social security rights of the self-employed,[27] and (ii) to safeguard the position of self-employed persons who may wish to remain in the territory of the Member States after terminating their business activities. It is as a result of the latter omission that Directive 75/34[28] on the right of self-employed persons to remain in Member States, *inter alia*, after retirement is based on Article 235, the third recital to its preamble acknowledging the absence of authority in Article 54(2). The rights of the self-employed enumerated in the Directive are identical to those bestowed upon workers in Regulation 1251/70,[29] and permit retired and incapacitated persons to remain in a Member State where they have previously been self-employed. For the details of these provisions, the reader is referred to the treatment of Regulation 1251/70 in the Chapter on the free movement of workers.[29]

Oddly enough, in the case of the self-employed, the Council proceeded by Directive, although a Regulation could have been adopted under Article 235, which authorises "appropriate measures." This is somewhat puzzling, since the Council adopts an almost identical text to that of Regulation 1251/70. Workers may clearly rely on the latter instrument; its provisions are directly applicable and hence capable by their very nature of producing direct effects. Article 8(2) in both the Regulation and the Directive may lack the clarity and the precision characteristic of a directly effective provision, but this cannot be said of the principal rights enumerated in each instrument: they clearly give rise to rights in individuals which national courts are bound to safeguard.[30] This being the case, it would seem that both employed and self-employed persons may invoke in national courts the right to remain in a Member State after having pursued economic activities therein. Nevertheless, the adoption of a Regulation in one case renders otiose and impermissible in principle any national legislative duplication of the provisions in question,[31] while the adoption of a Directive in the other invites national implementation, notwithstanding the

---

[25] See *infra*, p. 205.
[26] Subject to Arts. 60 and 61 of the Treaty.
[27] Reg. 1408/71 on the application of social security schemes to employed persons, is extended to self employed persons by Reg. 3795/81, O.J. 1981 L378/1. See *infra*, at p. 230.
[28] O.J. 1975, L14/10.
[29] *Supra*, p. 182.
[30] For direct effect, see *supra*, p. 30.
[31] *Supra*, p. 40.

apparent direct effect of its provisions. Such legislative inconsistency on the part of the Council can only give rise to needless difficulty.

Abolition of discriminatory restrictions

Title III of the General Programme called for the abolition of discriminatory measures which might impair access to the non-wage-earning activities of nationals of the Member States, such as measures which:

— conditioned the access to or exercise of a non-wage-earning activity on an authorisation or on the issuance of a document, such as a foreign merchant's card or a foreign professional's card;

— made the access to or exercise of a non-wage-earning activity more costly through the imposition of taxes or other charges such as a deposit or surety bond paid to the receiving country;

— barred or limited membership in companies, particularly with regard to the activities of their members.

In addition to measures primarily likely to discriminate against nationals of the Member States with respect of *access* to non-wage-earning activities, the General Programme condemned specific national practices discriminating against such persons in the *exercise* of these activities, such as those limiting the opportunity:

— to enter into certain types of transactions, such as contracts for the hire of services or commercial and farm leases;

— to tender bids or to participate as a co-contractor or sub-contractor in public contracts or contracts with public bodies[32];

— to borrow and to have access to various forms of credit;

— to benefit from aids granted by the State.

Subsequently, the Council issued a series of Directives implementing the General Programme, and dealing with the right of establishment in a wide variety of commercial callings, from the wholesale trade to the provision of electricity, gas, water and sanitary services![33] Many such Directives are applicable to both establishment and the provision of services, emphasising again the close practical relationship between the two. Directive 64/223,[34] concerning the attainment of freedom of establishment and freedom to provide services in respect of activities in the wholesale trade, may be considered for illustrative purposes. Under the Directive Member States are required to abolish the restrictions itemised in Title III of the General Programmes with respect to the commercial activities concerned. Specific legislative provisions in effect in the Member States are singled out for prohibition, such as the obligation under French law to hold a carte d'identité d'etrangère commerçant,[35] while Member States are obliged to ensure that

---

[32] See in particular Dir. 71/305, O.J. 1971, L185/5, as amended, on the coordination of procedures for the award of public works contracts; and Dir. 77/62, O.J. 1977, L13/1, as amended, coordinating procedures for the award of public supply contracts. The Court has held that the criteria in Dir. 71/305 for the eligibility of contractors are exhaustive, and cannot be supplemented by national requirements; Case 76/81 *Transporoute* [1982] E.C.R. 417. See also Case 274/83 *Commission* v. *Italian Republic* [1987] 1 C.M.L.R. 345.

[33] The Directives are too numerous to list. For the collected texts, see the *Encyclopaedia of European Community Law*, Vol. CIV, Part C12.

[34] J.O. 1964, 863.

[35] Art. 3.

beneficiaries of the Directive have the right to join professional or trade organisations under the same conditions, and with the same rights and obligations as their own nationals.[36] Where a host State requires evidence of good character in respect of its own nationals taking up the commercial activities concerned, provision is made for accepting appropriate proof from other Member States, and for the taking of a solemn declaration by self-employed persons from such States, where the State in question does not issue the appropriate documentation.[37]

Although Article 53 of the Treaty, prohibiting Member States from introducing any *new* restrictions on the right of establishment of nationals of other Member States, was held by the Court to be directly applicable in *Costa* v. *ENEL*,[38] the Council's extensive legislative scheme, based on the General Programme, was clearly adopted on the basis that the prohibition of discrimination contained in Article 52 was ineffective in the absence of implementation. That this was not the case was made clear by the Court of Justice in *Reyners* v. *Belgian State*.[39] The plaintiff in the main suit was a Dutch national resident in Belgium. He had been born in Belgium, educated there, and taken his docteur en droit belge, only to be finally refused admission to the Belgian bar on the ground of his Dutch nationality. On a reference for a preliminary ruling, the Court held that the prohibition on discrimination contained in Article 52 was directly applicable as of the end of the transitional period, despite the opening words of the text of that Article, which referred to the abolition of restrictions "within the framework of the provisions set out below." These provisions—the General Programme and the Directives provided for in Article 54—were of significance "only during the transitional period, since the freedom of establishment was fully attained at the end of it." According to the Court, the aim of Article 52 was intended to be facilitated by the Council's legislative programme, but not made dependent upon it.

The Court's decision had immediate repercussions. The Commission undertook, at a meeting of the Permanent Representatives, to report to the Council its view of the implications of the *Reyners* case for the implementation of the right of establishment. In its promised memorandum,[40] the Commission expressed the view that all the rules and formalities cited in the Directives on the abolition of restrictions were no longer applicable to nationals of the Member States, though, in the interests of legal security, the Member States should formally bring their legislation into line with the requirements of Article 52. In view of this, the Commission considered that it was no longer necessary to adopt Directives on the abolition of restrictions, and furthermore, since Directives were by their nature constitutive, that the adoption of such instruments having only declaratory effect

---

[36] Art. 4.
[37] Art. 6, amended by the first Act of Accession, Annex I(III)(D)(1).
[38] Case 6/64 [1964] E.C.R. 585.
[39] Case 2/74 [1974] E.C.R. 631. For a discriminatory provision remaining on the statute book contrary to Art. 52, see Case 159/78, *Commission* v. *Italy* [1979] E.C.R. 3247. For discriminatory conditions of tender contrary to Art. 52, see Case 197/84 *Steinhauser* [1986] 1 C.M.L.R. 53.
[40] Commission Communication, SEC (74) Final, Brussels.

would create confusion and protract the work of the Council unnecessarily. With respect, the latter view is open to question. Several Directives in the field of free movement of persons have been stated by the Court to give rise to no new rights, but merely to give closer articulation to rights bestowed directly by the Treaty.[41] This would also appear to be the case with Directive 75/117 on equal pay, which clarifies but does not add to the material scope of Article 119. It was on this ground that Advocate General VerLoren van Themaat urged the Court to hold a Member State in breach of Article 119, rather than the Directive, in proceedings brought by the Commission under Article 169 EEC. The Court nonetheless held the Member State in default for failing to implement the Directive.[42] As the Court commented in *Reyners* itself, Directives already issued under Article 54(2) would not lose all interest, since they would "preserve an important scope in the field of measures intended to make easier the effective exercise of the right of freedom of establishment."[43] The Court was no doubt mindful of the value to the individual litigant before a national tribunal of some more precise formulation of his rights than the general prohibitions of the Treaty. In any event, the Commission formally withdrew a large number of proposed Directives on abolition of restrictions on freedom of establishment.

Parallel interpretation of Articles 48, 52 and 59

Theoretically, problems may arise in differentiating between the employed and the self-employed, and between instances of establishment and provision of services, but it will in many cases be unnecessary to make any hard and fast classification, because the applicable principles will be the same in any event. Thus, in *Procureur du Roi* v. *Royer*,[44] the Court of Justice, considering a request for a preliminary ruling from a national court which was uncertain whether the subject of the proceedings before it was to be considered as falling within Article 48, Article 52 or Article 59, observed:

> " . . . comparison of these different provisions shows that they are based on the same principles both in so far as they concern the entry into and residence in the territory of Member States of persons covered by Community law and the prohibition of all discrimination between them on grounds of nationality."[45]

An important corollary is that Article 52, like Article 48, must be construed as prohibiting discrimination by private parties as well as by public authorities.[46] In *Walrave* v. *Union cycliste internationale*,[47] the Court expressed the opinion that Article 48 of the Treaty extended to agreements and rules other than those emanating from public authorities, citing in support of its view the text of Article 7(4) of Regulation 1612/68, which nulli-

---

[41] Case 48/75 *Royer* [1976] E.C.R. 497.
[42] Case 58/81 *Commission* v. *Luxembourg* [1982] E.C.R. 2175.
[43] [1974] E.C.R. 631, at 652.
[44] Case 48/75 [1976] E.C.R. 497. And see Case 118/75, *Watson & Belmann* [1976] E.C.R. 1185.
[45] [1976] E.C.R. 497 at 509.
[46] Sundberg-Weitman, *op. cit.*, p. 203.
[47] Case 36/74 [1974] E.C.R. 1405.

fies discriminatory clauses in individual or collective employment agreements. A similar conclusion was justified in the case of Article 59, since the activities referred to therein were "not to be distinguished by their nature from those in Article 48, but only by the fact that they are performed outside the ties of a contract of employment."[48] It follows that Article 52 has a similar ambit.

Reference has already been made to the similarity between the legislative provisions governing both the entry and residence of employed and self-employed persons, and the right to remain in the territory of a Member State having been employed therein.[49] On the other hand, drafting differences between the articles do seem to lead to anomalies. In the *Choquet* case,[50] the Court held that for a Member State to require of a national of another Member State that he pass a driving test which in substance duplicated a test taken in another Member State, and attested by a current driving licence, could amount to an impediment to the free movement of persons, contrary to Articles 48, 52 and 59 of the Treaty. To what extent could the benefit of this principle be successfully invoked by a national of the Member State requiring the test? There would seem to be no obstacle to such a plea under Article 59, which guarantees freedom to provide services to nationals of Member States established in a State of the Community other than that of the person for whom the services are intended. The Article is in no way limited to restrictions imposed upon nationals of other Member States, and indeed the *locus classicus* on its interpretation involved a plea raised in a Netherlands court by a Netherlands national challenging the compatibility of Netherlands law with the Treaty.[51] Again, since Article 48 safeguards both freedom of movement (thus granting nationals the right to leave their own Member States) and freedom from discrimination, its terms could seemingly be invoked by a national against his own Member State if action such as that castigated in *Choquet* inhibited his freedom of movement. Only Article 52 causes difficulty. Its guarantee is framed in terms of Member States abolishing restrictions on the establishment of nationals of one Member State in the territory of another. This formulation is apt to cover restrictions imposed by the Member State of origin on its own nationals seeking to establish themselves in other Member States, and restrictions by the host State on nationals of other Member States. But it is not apt to cover restrictions imposed by the host State on the establishment therein of its own nationals. Thus, in the *Auer* case,[52] in which a French national alleged that the refusal of the French authorities to recognise an Italian veterinary qualification amounted to an obstacle to his

---

[48] [1974] E.C.R. 1405 at 1419.
[49] *Supra*, pp. 200, 202.
[50] Case 16/78 *Choquet* [1978] E.C.R. 2293.
[51] Case 33/74 [1974] E.C.R. 1299. Para. (10) of the Judgment shows clearly that the final sentence of Art. 60 in no way limits the broad prohibition contained in Art. 59(1). Similarly, Case 39/75 *Coenen* [1975] E.C.R. 1547, arose from national proceedings in which an individual invoked Art. 59 against his own State.
[52] Case 136/78 *Auer* [1979] E.C.R. 437. But Art. 52 does prevent one Member State discriminating against nationals of another in refusing to recognise qualifications as equivalent to its own solely on the ground that they have been acquired in another Member State; see *infra* p. 212.

freedom of establishment, contrary to Article 52, the Court declared that the latter Article could, by virtue of its wording, concern only, in each Member State, nationals of other Member States. The *Choquet* principle would thus seem capable of being invoked by a national against his own Member State, only if he can bring himself within the ambit of either Article 48 or Article 59, but not if his activities fall to be categorised within Article 52. In such a case, he must await the enactment of harmonisation directives under Article 57. Such directives can be invoked by individuals, regardless of their nationality.[53] This conclusion supports the view that separate legal treatment of establishment and services if of questionable value. An apt solution would be to supplement the deficiencies of Article 52 by resort to Article 7 of the Treaty. The "discrimination on grounds of nationality" referred to therein should arguably be construed as referring to all arbitrary differentiation between persons based on factors connecting them with one Member State rather than another. This construction would give effect to the central aim of the Treaty: the establishment of a single market between the Member States. The Treaty's prohibition on discrimination is not imposed for its own sake—it is calculated to ensure the fullest possible freedom on inter-State economic activity within the Community.

There can be no doubt that Articles 48, 52 and 59 have one feature in common—they prohibit discrimination which is indirect, as well as that which is direct. However, indirect differentiation on *objective* grounds consistent with the Treaty does not amount to prohibited discrimination. Although residence requirements may amount in certain cases to indirect discrimination,[54] the Court has held that a national law exempting rural land from compulsory acquisition if the owners have lived on or near the land for a specified period, is consistent with Article 52, where the purpose of the law is to ensure as far as possible that rural land belongs to those who work it, and where the law applies equally to its own nationals and to the nationals of other Member States.[55] Similarly, an insurance scheme in the Federal Republic of Germany under which no-claims bonuses were not granted to owners of vehicles bearing customs registration plates has been held to be compatible with Articles 7, 48, 59 and 65, where it was based exclusively on objective actuarial factors and the objective criterion of registration under customs plates. The fact that it affected mainly the nationals of other Member States did not condemn the scheme, since it was also capable of affecting nationals of the Federal Republic in certain circumstances.[56]

Exception in the case of activities connected with the exercise of official authority

Article 55 provides that the provisions of Chapter 2 shall not apply, "so far as any given Member State is concerned, to activities which in that State

[53] Case 115/78 *Knoors* [1979] E.C.R. 399.
[54] Case 152/73 *Sotgiu* [1974] E.C.R. 153.
[55] Case 182/83 *Fearon* [1984] E.C.R. 3677.
[56] Case 251/83 *Eberhard Haug-Adrion* [1984] E.C.R. 4277.

are connected, even occasionally, with the exercise of official authority."
This exception constitutes a derogation from a fundamental Treaty rule,
and must be interpreted strictly, so as not to exceed the purpose for which
is was inserted.[57]

The notion of "official authority" is not defined in the Treaty. In *Reyners*
v. *Belgian State*,[58] it was argued that the profession of avocat was exempted
from the chapter on establishment because it involved the exercise of
official authority. The Court, while tacitly acknowledging that the
occasional exercise of *judicial* power by an avocat would amount to the
exercise of official authority, declared that this would not be the case with
respect to the avocat's other responsibilities:

> "Professional activities involving contacts, even regular and
> organic, with the courts, including even compulsory cooperation in
> their functioning, do not constitute, as such, connexion with the exer-
> cise of official authority.
>
> The most typical activities of the profession of *avocat*, in particular,
> such as consultation and legal assistance and also representation and
> the defence of parties in court, even when the intervention or assist-
> ance of the *avocat* is compulsory or is a legal monopoly, cannot be
> considered as connected with the exercise of official authority."[59]

The Commission argued in its observations that the exercise of official
authority involved the exercise of "prerogatives outside the general law,"[60]
and the Advocate-General agreed, describing official authority as "that
which arises from the sovereignty and majesty of the State; for him who
exercises it, it implies the power of enjoying the [*sic*] prerogatives outside
the general law, privileges of official power and powers of coercion over
citizens."[61] This definition is consistent with the views of commentators,
and would include the exercise of law-making or judicial authority.[62]

Reference by analogy to *Commission* v. *Belgium*,[63] on the ambit of
Article 48(4) would seem to be permissible, since that Article pursues the
same aim as Article 55. Possible examples of activities falling within Article
55 would be the carrying out of certain functions by notaries public,[64] or
the issuing of death certificates by doctors.[65]

Article 55 refers to "activities" connected with the exercise of official
authority, rather than to "professions." The Court in *Reyners* made it clear
that while certain "activities" forming part of a particular profession might
fall within Article 55, the profession as a *whole* might nevertheless be subject to the right of establishment. This would be the case wherever the
activities could be "severed" from the profession concerned, as they could
be so severed, it seems, in the case of the avocat called upon to perform

---

[57] Case 2/74 *Reyners* [1974] E.C.R. 631. *Cf.* Case 152/73 *Sotgiu* [1974] E.C.R. 153.
[58] *Ibid.*
[59] [1974] E.C.R. 631 at 655.
[60] [1974] E.C.R. 631 at 640.
[61] [1974] E.C.R. 631 at 664.
[62] Everling, *op. cit.*, 85, 86; Sundberg-Weitman, *op. cit.*, 206, 207; Smiot and Herzog, 2–605.
[63] Case 149/79 [1980] E.C.R. 3881. On Article 48(4), see pp. 195, *supra*.
[64] Everling, *op. cit.*, 86, note 20; Sundberg-Weitman, *op. cit.*, p. 207; Smit and Herzog,
    2–608; Lipstein, *The Law of the European Economic Community*, pp. 132, 133.
[65] Sundberg-Weitman, *op. cit.*, p. 207; Smit and Herzog, *op. cit.*, p. 209.

occasional judicial functions. The Court took the view that the exception allowed by Article 55 could only be extended to a whole profession where the activities in question "were linked with that profession in such a way that freedom of establishment would result in imposing on the Member State concerned the obligation to allow the exercise, even occasionally, by non-nationals of functions appertaining to official authority."[66] In the final analysis the relevant question must be whether it is reasonable to regard particular activities as constituting an essential aspect of a particular profession considered as a whole.[67]

In view of the Court's decision in *Sotgiu* v. *Deutsche Bundespost*,[68] it would seem that Article 55 should be interpreted as applying only to *access* to activities connected with the exercise of official authority; not as authorising discriminatory conditions of work once a person had been allowed to take up such activities.

The second paragraph of Article 55 provides that the Council may rule "that the provisions of this Chapter shall not apply to certain activities." It seems that these words must be construed subject to the text of the previous paragraph, *i.e.* as involving activities connected with the exercise of official authority. The authority bestowed thereby upon the Council is extremely limited, and has not, so far, been exercised. In applying Article 55 to a particular profession, it will be necessary to establish the ambit of the "activities" which "taken on their own, constitute a direct and specific connexion with the exercise of official authority."[69] While the "exercise of official authority" is a concept of Community *law*, the question of "direct and specific connexion" with such exercise is one of fact which, unresolved, can lead to uncertainty on the part of those subject to the law. It is submitted that the Council's function is limited to finding, as a fact, that certain activities do indeed have a "direct and specific connexion" with the exercise of official authority.

Article 56—the public policy proviso

Article 56 declares that "The provision of this Chapter and measures taken in pursuance thereof shall not prejudice the applicability of provisions . . . providing for special treatment for foreign nationals on grounds of public policy, public security or public health." The integrated scheme of Articles 48 to 66, the parallel interpretation given to these provisions in relation to discrimination, entry and residence,[70] and the fact that the public policy provisos of Article 48(3) and Article 56 are given "closer articulation" in one and the same Directive—Directive 64/221 of February 25, 1964[71]—compels the conclusion that the text of Article 56 is

---

[66] [1974] E.C.R. 631 at p. 654.
[67] See Everling, *op. cit.*, p. 87, " . . . a substantial part of the economic activity which cannot be separated from its other parts."
[68] Case 152/73 [1974] E.C.R. 153.
[69] [1974] E.C.R. 631 at p. 654.
[70] *Supra*, p. 205.
[71] J.O. 1964, 850, as amended by Dir. 75/35, O.J. 1975, L14/14, which provides that Dir. 64/221 shall apply to nationals of Member States and members of their families benefiting from the provisions of Dir. 75/34, see *supra*, p. 187.

to be interpreted in an identical manner to that of Article 48(3). Thus, for instance, Article 56 must be interpreted as permitting derogation from the chapter on establishment only in respect of entry and residence—not in respect of the terms and conditions under which occupational activities are carried on.[72] For a detailed analysis of the terms of Directive 64/221, and an examination of the Court's jurisprudence on the public policy proviso in Article 48(3), the reader is referred to the chapter on freedom of movement for workers.[73]

Article 56 permits derogation from the right of establishment in the case of foreign nationals. The chapter may be subject to further implicit requirements of national law (*cf.* Articles 30 and 59) which can be invoked also against a State's own nationals seeking to establish themselves in another Member State.[74]

Mutual recognition of diplomas and the co-ordination of national qualifications

Paragraphs (1) and (2) of Article 57 provide, respectively, for the "mutual recognition of diplomas, certificates, and other evidence of formal qualifications,' and for "the coordination of the provisions laid down by law, regulation or administrative action in Member States concerning the taking up and pursuit of activities as self-employed persons."

The General Programme contemplated transitional measures, whereby access to non-wage-earning activities might be allowed on proof of "actual and legitimate exercise of the activity in the country of origin."[75] An example of such a transitional regime is provided by Directive 75/369, dealing with the activities of itinerant tradespeople, such as fairground operators.[76] The Directive provides that where, in the case of its own nationals, a Member State requires documentary evidence of good repute, or of never having been declared bankrupt, it must accept, in the case of nationals of other Member States, appropriate equivalent documentation issued in their country of origin.[77] Where no such documentation is issued, the host State must accept a declaration on oath, or a solemn declaration, made before, and duly certified by, a competent judicial or executive authority in the appropriate country of origin.[78] Where in a Member State the pursuit of the activities in question is subject to the possession of "general, commercial or professional knowledge and ability,' that Member State must accept as sufficient evidence of such knowledge and ability the fact that the activity in question has been previously carried on in another Member State.[79] The period required is either two or three years, depending on whether it was completed in an employed or self-employed capacity,

---

[72] Case 152/73 *Sotgiu* [1974] E.C.R. 153; Case 15/69 *Ugliola* [1969] E.C.R. 363, *supra*, p. 177.
[73] *Supra*, p. 186.
[74] See *supra*, at p. 142, and *infra*, at p. 222. However, the risk of tax evasion cannot justify discrimination contrary to Art. 52; Case 270/83, *Commission* v. *French Republic* [1987] 1 C.M.L.R. 401.
[75] Title IV, O.J. 1974, Sp. Ed., Second Series, IX, p. 10
[76] O.J. 1975, L167/29.
[77] Art. 3(1), (2).
[78] Art. 3(3).
[79] Art. 5(1).

and on whether or not the relevant experience was preceded by a course of training.[80]

The Directive applies also to employees,[81] no doubt because differences in national vocational requirements are as capable of constituting an obstacle to the free movement of workers as they are of hindering the peregrinations of the self-employed.

Progress under Article 57 in ensuring freedom of establishment for the learned professions has predictably been slow. Nevertheless, the adoption of Directives 75/362 and 75/363[82] of June 16, 1975, on the mutual recognition of medical diplomas and the co-ordination of national medical qualifications, must be regarded as a breakthrough. In the case of non-specialist medicine, the Directives require[83] that each Member State recognise diplomas awarded to nationals of the Member States by other Member States[84] on condition that the diplomas comply with the requirements specified in Article 1 of Directive 75/363. This Article provides that diplomas awarded in the Member States must guarantee that a doctor, during his training period, has acquired:

"(a) adequate knowledge of the sciences on which medicine is based and a good understanding of the scientific methods including the principles of measuring biological functions, the evaluation of scientifically established facts and the analysis of data;

(b) sufficient understanding of the structure, functions and behaviour of healthy and sick persons, as well as relations between the state of health and the physical and social surroundings of the human being;

(c) adequate knowledge of clinical disciplines and practices, providing him with a coherent picture of mental and physical diseases, of medicine from the point of view of prophylaxis, diagnosis and therapy and of human reproduction;

(d) suitable clinical experience in hospital under appropriate supervision."

In addition, a course in medical training must comprise at least a six-year course or 5,500 hours of theoretical or practical instruction given in a university or under the supervision of a university.[85]

The requirements specified above are of a somewhat general nature, and no doubt reflect the conviction that standards of medical education in the Member States are, on the whole, comparable. That is not to say that the various qualifications are *equivalent*, and Directive 75/362 admits as much.[86] Thus a doctor of one Member State established in another may use the professional title customary therein, but the host State may require

---

[80] Art. 5(1).
[81] Art. 1(2).
[82] O.J. 1975, L167/1, 14. Dir. 75/362 was supplemented by Dir. 81/1057, O.J. 1981 L385/25, and amended by Dir. 82/76, O.J. 1982, L43/21. Dir. 75/363 was also amended by Dir. 82/76.
[83] Dir. 75/362, Arts. 2 and 3; Dir. 75/363, Art. 1.
[84] Note that the Directive does not cover qualifications awarded in third countries and recognised in Member States.
[85] Dir. 75/63, Art. 1(2).
[86] Second recital to the preamble to Dir. 75/362.

that his academic title be expressed in the language of his country of origin,[87] and be followed by the "name and location of the establishment or examining board which awarded it.'[88]

Even in the case of medical diplomas which do not conform with the requirements specified in Article 1 of Directive 75/362, recognition will still be accorded if they were awarded by a Member State before the implementation of Directive 75/363, and they are accompanied by a certificate stating that the doctor in question has been "effectively and lawfully" engaged in his profession for at least three consecutive years during the five years prior to the date of the issue of the certificate.[89]

Similar provision is made with respect to qualifications in specialist medicine.[90] Both Directives apply to employed persons, as well as to the self-employed.[91] In the event of difficulties arising in the implementation of the Directives, two Committees, established by Council Decision, have the responsibility of considering such matters, and making recommendations as to, e.g. the necessity for amending the present arrangements.[92]

Whereas under the above mentioned directives additional requirements may be imposed in the case of specialists, this is not permitted in the case of general practitioners. General practitioners came to be regarded as specialists in their own right in the Netherlands, and in that country a year's professional training after qualification was laid down for all nationals. The requirement was not made of nationals of other EEC countries, since the Netherlands authorities accepted that such persons were entitled to rely on the directives. The Court of Justice held that a Netherlands national, who had qualified in Belgium, was equally entitled to rely on the directives, and to avoid the additional year's professional training.[93] This situation—that a Member State may impose additional requirements upon the holders of its own general medical qualifications, but not upon the holders of those of other Member States—is clearly anomalous. Directive 85/432 on the free movement of pharmacists was amended in draft to avoid the difficulty by providing that a Member State may, where appropriate, require "additional professional experience" of practitioners.[94]

Even in the absence of directives under Article 57, recognition of foreign diplomas may be required under Article 52, prohibiting discrimination on grounds of nationality, as *Thieffry* v. *Paris Bar Council*[95] shows. A Belgian national held a Belgian law degree recognised by the University of Paris as equivalent to a French law degree. He acquired the qualifying certificate

---

[87] Dir. 75/362, Art. 10(1), is ambiguous on this point, but the seventh recital to the preamble is not.
[88] Art. 10(1).
[89] Art. 9. And see Dir. 81/1057, O.J. 1981 L385/25, by virtue of which the provision also applies to training commenced before implementation, and finishing afterwards.
[90] Dir. 75/362, Chaps. III and IV; Dir. 75/363, Art. 6.
[91] Dir. 75/362, Art. 24; Dir. 75/363, Art. 6.
[92] See Council Dec. 75/364 and 75/365, establishing, respectively, an Advisory Committee on Medical Training, and a Committee of Senior Officials on Public Health, and defining their functions, see Dir. 75/362, Art. 26; Dir. 75/363, Art. 12.
[93] Case 246/80 *Broekmulen* [1981] E.C.R. 2311. See Dir. 86/457 on specific training in general medical practice, O.J. 1986 L267/26.
[94] Watson, (1983) 20 C.M.L. Rev. 767, 784.
[95] Case 71/76 [1977] E.C.R. 765. See Case 11/77 *Patrick* [1977] E.C.R. 1199; and Case 65/77 *Razanatsimba* [1977] E.C.R. 2229 (Lomé Convention, Art. 62).

for the profession of advocate, but the Paris Bar Council refused to allow him to undergo practical training on the ground that he did not possess a French law degree. The Court of Justice held that such a refusal could amount to *indirect* discrimination prohibited by Article 52 of the Treaty. As the General Programme for the abolition of restrictions on freedom of establishment made clear in Title III(B), the Council proposed to eliminate not only overt discrimination, but also any form of *disguised* discrimination, including "Any requirements imposed . . . in respect of the taking up or pursuit of an activity as a self-employed person where, although applicable irrespective of nationality, their effect is exclusively or principally to hinder the taking up or pursuit of such activity by foreign nationals."[96] It would be for the competent national authorities, taking account of the requirements of Community law, to judge whether a recognition granted by a university authority could, in addition to its academic effect, constitute valid evidence of a professional qualification.

Establishment of companies

The right of establishment is enjoyed by companies and firms, as well as by natural persons. Article 58 provides:

"Companies or firms formed in accordance with the law of a Member State and having their registered office, central administration or principal place of business within the Community shall, for the purposes of this Chapter, be treated in the same way as natural persons who are nationals of Member States

'Companies or firms' means companies or firms constituted under civil or commercial law, including co-operative societies, and other legal persons governed by public or private law, save for those which are non-profit making."

The Court has held that to allow a Member State in which a company carried on its business to treat that company in a different manner solely because its registered office was in another Member State would render Article 58 nugatory.[97]

The definition of "companies or firms" is framed so as to encompass the widest possible circle of beneficiaries.[98] The reference to "other legal persons" might suggest that the entities concerned must possess full "legal personality," *i.e.* must, in addition to the capacity to bring and defend actions, enjoy the capacity to possess goods and to enter into other legal transactions.[99] On the other hand, the (as yet unratified) Convention on the Mutual Recognition of Companies and Legal Persons, drawn up to provide for the mutual recognition of "companies or firms within the meaning of the second paragraph of Article 58," declares in its opening Article that "Companies . . . established in accordance with the law of a

---

[96] O.J. 1974, English Special Edition, Second Series, IX, p. 8.
[97] Case 79/85 *Segers* Judgment of July 10, 1986.
[98] Everling, *op. cit.* p. 69. Sundberg-Weitman, p. 189.
[99] Goldman, 6 C.M.L. Rev. 1969 at p. 116.

Contracting State which grants them the *capacity of persons having rights and duties* . . . should be recognised as of right." Goldman concludes that "[i]t follows . . . that if a company is given by the law under which it was formed the capacity to bring or defend actions in its own name, but not that of being owner . . . that will suffice for it to be recognised."[1] Other commentators take a similar view.[2] Thus a partnership under English law, capable of suing and being sued in its own name, is included in the definition contained in the second paragraph of Article 58.

The exclusion of non-profit-making companies from the bodies entitled to claim the right of establishment is not intended to exclude subsidised public enterprise,[3] and the purpose of the clause seems to be to exclude organisations of a political, cultural religious, social or charitable nature, which are unconnected with the economic objectives of the Treaty.[4]

A company formed in accordance with the law of a Member State is entitled to exercise the right of establishment if it has either its registered office, its central administration, or its principal place of business within the Community. As indicated at the beginning of the present chapter, Article 52 draws a distinction between transferring a primary establishment to another Member State, and setting up a secondary establishment, in the form of a branch or a subsidiary. In the former case the only qualifying characteristic is the nationality of a Member State, while in the latter there must be an existing establishment in one of the Member States. The General Programme construed this qualification as requiring a 'real and continuous link with the economy of a Member State."[5]

Article 54(3)(*f*) of the Treaty provides for the abolition of restrictions on the transfer of personnel from the main establishment to managerial or supervisory posts in its branches or subsidiaries.[6] In the event of such personnel holding the nationality of a Member State, they will, of course, be entitled to assert an independent right of entry and residence under the provisions of the Treaty guaranteeing freedom of movement for workers.[7]

A change of primary establishment involving a transfer of company headquarters may be hindered by national legal provisions to the effect: (a) that a company transferring its executive offices out of the jurisdiction loses it corporate personality; or (b) that a company wishing to establish its executive offices within the jurisdiction must be newly constituted there.[8] These requirements amount to a refusal to recognise the legal personality of a company incorporated in a Member State other than where its central administration is located. It may be that to deny recognition to a company satisfying the requirements of the first paragraph of Article 58 amounts to a denial of that company's right of establishment,[9] though the matter is not

---

[1] Goldman, *loc. cit.* p. 113.
[2] Everling, *op. cit.* p. 68; Sundberg-Weitman, p. 190.
[3] Smit and Herzog, 2–642.
[4] Everling, *op. cit.* p. 69.
[5] Title I, O.J. 1974, Sp.Ed., Second Series, IX, p. 7.
[6] And see the General Programme, Title III, A, final paragraph, *loc. cit.*, p. 8.
[7] *Supra*, p. 161.
[8] Smit and Herzog, 2–647.
[9] Everling, *op. cit.* p. 71.

free from doubt.[10] The position will be clarified when the Member States ratify the 1968 Convention on the Mutual Recognition of Companies and Legal Persons, which seeks to resolve the difficulties which arise from the existence of different national rules relating to the recognition of foreign companies. Of the legal systems of the original six, Dutch law, like English law, adhered to the "law of incorporation" rule, whereby a company would be recognised if formed in accordance with the law of the State of incorporation. The other Member States favoured the law of the "real seat" (*siège réel*), whereby a company would be recognised if incorporated in accordance with the law of the place of its central management.[11]

The 1968 Convention grants recognition as of right to the following:

— companies established in accordance with the law of a Member State[12] which grants them the capacity of persons having rights and duties, and having their statutory registered office in the territory of a Member State (Article 1);
— bodies corporate—other than "companies"—which fulfil the conditions stipulated above, and have as their main or accessory object an economic activity normally carried on for reward, and which, without infringing the law under which they were established, do in fact continuously carry on such an activity (Article 2).

Recognition entails the exercise in the recognising State, by the above entities, of the capacity accorded by the law under which they were established.[13]

It will be noted that whereas in the case of "bodies corporate" the need for having as object the pursuit of an activity "normally exercised for reward" is explicit, the pursuit of such an activity is presumed in the case of "companies," including co-operatives.[14]

The text of Articles 1 and 8[15] might suggest that whereas "companies" are entitled to recognition despite the absence of full legal personality, this is not so of the "bodies corporate" referred to in Article 2. Such a conclusion would however, be inconsistent with the reference in Article 2 to the "conditions" stipulated in Article 1, which include possessing merely "the capacity of persons having rights and duties.[16]

One might conclude that partnerships under English law were covered by Article 1 of the Convention, were it not for the fact that they do not have a "Statutory registered office."[17] Nevertheless, a literal interpretation would seem to be appropriate, in order to secure consistency with Article 58 of the Treaty. The desired result might be attained by a Joint Declar-

[10] Smit and Herzog, 2–640.
[11] Stein, *Harmonisation of European Company Laws*, p. 399; G. K. Morse, (1972) J.B.L. 195, at pp. 198, 199; Schmitthoff, *European Company Texts*, pp. 44, 45.
[12] References to Member States and their territory have been substituted for references to the Contracting States and the territories to which the Convention applies.
[13] Art. 6. And see Art. 7.
[14] Art. 1. See Goldman, 6 C.M.L. Rev. p. 115.
[15] Art. 8 provides that "the capacity, rights and powers of a company recognised by virtue of the Convention may not be denied or restricted for the sole reason that the law in accordance with which it was established does not grant it the legal status of a body corporate."
[16] Goldman, *loc. cit.* pp. 117, 118.
[17] G. K. Morse, (1972) J.B.L. 195 at p. 220.

ation upon ratification,[18] and would be consistent with the object and purpose of the Convention, which is essentially to adopt the incorporation theory of recognition, subject to certain qualifications.

An exception to the incorporation theory may be invoked where the central management of a company or body corporate is situated outside the territory of the Member States. In such a case, unless the entity concerned has a "genuine link" with the economy of one of the Member States, application of the Convention may be withheld.[19] As Stein points out, the provision is designed to "prevent a non-Community enterprise from claiming recognition within the Community on the basis of nothing more than a 'post-office-box address.' "[20]

Where a company or body corporate is established under the law of one Member State, but its central management is situated in another, the latter State may, despite its obligation to recognise the entity in question, require compliance with "any provisions of its own legislation which it deems essential."[21] Should Member States take advantage of this provision, the advantages of recognition could be significantly reduced.[22]

As one might expect, the Convention is subject to a public policy proviso. Article 9 provides for the waiver of the Convention "when the company or body corporate invoking it contravenes by its object, its purpose or the activity which it actually exercises the principles or rules which the said State considers as being a matter of public policy as defined in private international law." This formulation would apparently leave Member States free to invoke the concept of public policy normally applied by them in the conflict of laws.

Although the implementation of the Convention would not be free from difficulty, it would certainly provide an important corollary both to the right of establishment and the freedom to provide services.

The prospect of firms incorporated under the law of one Member State being free to establish themselves in another led the drafters of the Treaty to insert Article 54(3)(g), which requires the co-ordination of the provisions of national company law which safeguard the position of investors and creditors. A number of Directives have been adopted under this provision. The First Directive, 68/151,[23] deals with the public disclosure of certain matters such as the company's memorandum and articles, and the names of those from time to time authorised to represent the company; the validity of acts of such persons which are *ultra vires* the company, or beyond their authority,[24] and the conditions for a judicial declaration of nullity of a company—a procedure unknown in English law. The Second

---

[18] *Cf.* Joint Declaration No. 1, made on signature, to the effect that Art. 1 of the Convention applies to the societa semplice in Italian law and the vennootschap onder firma in Netherlands law. For the relevant principle of interpretation in international law, see Art. 31(2)(*a*) of the Vienna Convention on the Law of Treaties.

[19] Art. 3.

[20] Stein, *op. cit.* p. 429.

[21] Art. 4.

[22] Goldman, *loc. cit.* pp. 123 *et seq.*

[23] O.J. 1974, Sp.Ed., I, p. 8.

[24] Implemented in s.9 of the European Communities Act 1972. See Wyatt, [1978] L.Q.R. 182.

Directive, 77/91, deals with the raising and maintenance of capital.[25] The Third Directive, 78/885, deals with mergers of public companies.[26] The Fourth Directive, 78/660, deals with the annual accounts of certain types of companies.[27] The Sixth Directive, 82/891, deals with the division of public limited liability companies.[28] The Seventh Directive, 83/349, deals with consolidated accounts.[29] The Eighth Directive, 84/253, deals with the approval of persons responsible for carrying out statutory audits of accounting documents.[30] Work continues on the draft Fifth Directive dealing, more controversially, with the structure of companies and employee participation.[31]

THE FREEDOM TO PROVIDE SERVICES

Article 59 of the Treaty provides that "[w]ithin the framework of the provisions set out below, restrictions on freedom to provide services within the Community shall be progressively abolished during the transitional period in respect of nationals of Member States who are established in a State of the Community other than that of the person for whom the services are intended." It will be noted that in order to invoke this provision, nationals must be "established" in a Member State. In the case of companies whose registered office is situated inside the Community, but whose central management or principal place of business is not, this requirement is satisfied by their activities having "a real and continuous link with the economy of a Member State, excluding the possibility that this link might depend on nationality, particularly the nationality of the partners or the members of the managing or supervisory bodies, or of persons holding the capital stock."[32]

"Services" are defined in Article 60, and are considered as such when they are "normally provided for remuneration." One would expect the remuneration to be normally provided by the receiver of services, but this may not be essential. In the *Debauve* and *Coditel* cases,[33] Advocate General Warner expressed the opinion that the purpose of the definition of "services" in Article 60 was to exclude those that are normally provided gratuitously. Television broadcasting thus in his view fell within the definition whether it was financed by licence fees, or by advertising. The decisive factor was that the broadcasting was remunerated in one way or another.

A non-exhaustive list of services in Article 60 specifies activities of an industrial character, activities of a commercial character, activities of

---

[25] O.J. 1977, L26/1. For a commentary on the Directive, see G. K. Morse, (1977) 2 E.L. Rev. 126.
[26] O.J. 1978, L295/36; annotated by G. K. Morse, (1978) 3 E.L. Rev. 795.
[27] O.J. 1978 L222/11. Van Hulle, (1981) 18 C.M.L. Rev. 121.
[28] O.J. 1982, L378/47.
[29] O.J. 1983, L193/1. See Van Hulle, *op. cit.*; Petite, (1984) 21 C.M.L. Rev. 81.
[30] O.J. 1984, L126/20.
[31] Seventeenth General Report on the Activities of the E.C., p. 87.
[32] General Programme (Services), O.J. 1974, Sp.Ed., 2nd Series, IX, p. 3.
[33] Case 52/79 *Debauve* [1980] E.C.R. 833, Case 62/79 *Coditel* [1980] E.C.R. 881, Opinion at p. 876.

craftsmen, and activities of the professions. Where a particular activity falls within the provisions of the Treaty relating to the free movement of goods, capital or persons, however, these latter provisions govern. The Court has held that tourism, medical treatment, and education, are covered by the freedom to provide services.[34]

Without prejudice to the right of establishment, a person providing a service may, in order to do so, "temporarily pursue his activity in the State where the service is provided, under the same conditions as are imposed by that State on its own nationals."[35] As observed above, the pursuit of economic activities on a more permanent basis would amount to establishment in the host State.[36]

A literal interpretation of Articles 59 and 60 would guarantee freedom to provide services in the following circumstances:

— freedom to provide services "across State lines," where provider and recipient remain in their respective Member States, as in the case of financial advice from United Kingdom advisers to French clients;

— freedom to provide services *in situ*, where the provider of a service visits temporarily the recipient in the latter's Member State, as in the case of a United Kingdom doctor visiting a French patient.

As indicated at the beginning of the Chapter, however,[37] it is important to consider the provisions of Articles 52 and 59 as a whole, and in the light of the object and purpose of the Treaty, which is to ensure the fullest possible freedom to engage in economic activities in the territory of the Member States, regardless of the stage of provision or distribution of the services involved.

The Court's case law leaves scope for such an approach. In *Coenen*,[38] the Court held that Article 59 applied to a Netherlands national resident in Belgium who was providing services as an insurance intermediary through an office in the Netherlands, on the ground that the precise object of that Article was to abolish restrictions on freedom to provide services imposed on persons "who do not reside in the State where the service is to be provided." It will be recalled that Article 59 contemplates *establishment* in a state different from that of the receiver of the services. It is not clear whether Mr. Coenen was established in his own right in Belgium or not, and the Court does not seem to think it material. In truth, Mr. Coenen does seem to have been established in the Netherlands, and the Court's ruling prevented his personal residence in Belgium from being held against him in the former country. In *Koestler*[39] contractual relations between a French bank and a German national resident in France were held to fall within Article 59 because the German national returned to Germany without having paid his debts. If the latter case decides that the residence of the recipient and the establishment of the provider in different states need not be contemporaneous with the actual provision of services, and *Coenen*

[34] Cases 286/82 and 26/83 *Luisi* [1984] E.C.R. 377, at p. 403, para. 16.
[35] Art. 60, third para.
[36] *Supra*, p. 198.
[37] *Supra*, p. 198.
[38] Case 39/75 [1975] E.C.R. 1555.
[39] Case 15/78 [1978] E.C.R. 1971.

decides that the personal residence of the provider may be an equivalent disability to that of establishment for the purposes of defining the mischief at which Article 59 is aimed, the way is open to the Court to hold that a visit by an English journalist to France to write a news story on a French election for an English newspaper is a step in the provision of services which falls within the ambit of Article 59.

The entry and residence of self-employed persons under Article 59 of the Treaty is governed by the same secondary legislation as entry and residence under Article 52, on the right of establishment, and the reader is referred accordingly to the treatment of Directive 73/148 found earlier in this chapter.[40]

Although Article 59 only explicitly refers to the freedom to *provide* services, it will be recalled that Article 1(1)(*b*) of Directive 73/148 includes among its beneficiaries "nationals of Member States wishing to go to another Member State as recipients of services." In *Luisi*,[41] the Court held that the freedom to provide services included the freedom, for the recipients of services, to go to another Member State in order to receive a service there, without being obstructed by restrictions, and that tourists, persons receiving medical treatment and persons travelling for the purpose of education or business were to be regarded as recipients of services. The application of Article 59 is supplemented in this context by Article 7 EEC. In *Gravier*[42] the Court held that a discriminatory registration fee imposed as a condition of access to vocational training courses infringed the latter Article. The Court did not deal with Article 59, although the Commission's observations were based principally upon this provision. This may be because the national court's questions referred only to Article 7. Or it may be because, since the right of *recipients* of services under Article 59 is, strictly, derivative of the rights of *providers* expressly guaranteed in that Article, and discrimination *by a provider against a recipient* was in issue in *Gravier*, Article 7 provided a more logical basis for the Court's ruling than Article 59. Again, recourse to Article 7 side-steps difficulties as to when educational services are "normally provided for remuneration."

Abolition of restrictions

Like Article 54, Article 63 provides for the drawing up of a General Programme for the abolition of restrictions on freedom to provide services within the Community. The Programme was adopted in December 1961,[43] and closely resembles the General Programme for the abolition of restrictions on the right of establishment. Thus, *e.g.* Title III calls for the abolition of restrictions such as those which "condition the provision of services on an authorisation or on the issuance of a document, such as a foreign merchant's card or a foreign professional's card."[44] As indicated earlier,

[40] *Supra*, p. 200.
[41] Cases 286/82 and 26/83 [1984] E.C.R. 377.
[42] Case 293/83 [1985] E.C.R. 593.
[43] O.J. 1974, Sp.Ed., 2nd Series IX, p. 3. The programme has been referred to by the Court in Case 15/78 *Koestler* [1978] E.C.R. 1971; Case 136/78 *Auer* [1979] E.C.R. 452; Cases 286/82 and 26/83 *Luisi* [1984] E.C.R. 377.
[44] O.J. 1974, *loc. cit.*, p. 4.

most of the Directives issued to abolish restrictions on the right of establishment apply in addition to freedom to provide services. Thus Directive 64/223, used for illustrative purposes in the context of establishment,[45] also applies, in relation to the wholesale trade, to freedom to provide services.

Just as the Court's decision in *Reyners* v. *Belgian State*[46] on the direct applicability of Article 52 reduced significantly the importance of Directives requiring the abolition of particular discriminatory restrictions, so its later decision in *Van Binsbergen* v. *Bedrijfsvereniging Metaalnijverheid*,[47] upholding the direct effect of Articles 59, first paragraph and 60, third paragraph entailed similar consequences for the provisions of Directives concerned with the abolition of restrictions on the supply of services.[48] Thus where discrimination is concerned, individuals and enterprises alike are entitled to rely directly on the Treaty, irrespective of national implementation of particular Directives, and regardless of whether or not Directives have even been adopted in the field in question.

Though individuals may be entitled to rely upon the Treaty in national courts, not every act of differentiation on grounds of nationality will amount to prohibited discrimination. In *Dona* v. *Mantero*,[49] the Chairman of Rovigo Football Club, Mr. Mantero, asked a Mr. Dona to make enquiries abroad to discover whether any foreign players might be willing to play for Mr. Mantero's team. When Mr. Dona claimed the expenses of certain advertisements placed in Belgian newspapers, Mr. Mantero argued that Mr. Dona had acted prematurely, in view of the Rules of the Italian Football Federation, which excluded non-Italian players. The Guidice Conciliatore, Rovigo, sought a preliminary ruling on the question, *inter alia*, whether football players enjoyed rights under Article 59 of the Treaty on the grounds that their services were in the nature of a gainful occupation. The Court replied as follows:

> "Having regard to the objectives of the Community, the practice of sport is subject to Community law only in so far as it constitutes an economic activity within the meaning of Article 2 of the Treaty.
>
> This applies to the activities of professional or semi-professional players, which are in the nature of gainful employment or remunerated service.
>
> Where such players are nationals of a Member State they benefit in all the other Member States from the provisions of Community law concerning freedom of movement of persons and of provision of services.
>
> However, those provisions do not prevent the adoption of rules or of a practice excluding foreign players from participation in certain matches for reasons which are not of an economic nature, which relate to the particular nature and context of such matches and are thus of

---

[45] *Supra*, p. 203.
[46] Case 2/74 [1974] E.C.R. 631.
[47] Case 33/74 [1974] E.C.R. 1299; and see Case 36/74 *Walrave* [1974] E.C.R. 1405; Case 13/76 *Dona* v. *Mantero* [1976] E.C.R. 133; Cases 110 and 111/78, *Van Wesemael* [1979] E.C.R. 35.
[48] See Commission Communication to the Council, SEC(74) 4024 Final, Brussels.
[49] See note 45.

sporting interest only, such as, for example, matches between national teams from different countries."[50]

The true explanation of the Court's reasoning is that Article 7 of the Treaty prohibits differentiation on grounds of nationality where to permit it would hinder the creation of a single market between Member States and the achievement of an "ever closer union among the peoples of Europe"[51]; it does not prohibit such differentiation on non-economic grounds in furtherance of interests consistent with the object and purpose of the Treaty.

Since the essence of the right granted by Article 59 is that a person established in one Member State should be permitted to provide services in another, a requirement that those providing certain services within the jurisdiction must be established or resident therein would be prima facie contrary to its provisions.

The Court has held that the restrictions to be abolished under Articles 59 and 60 include:

"all requirements imposed on the person providing the service in particular by reason of his nationality or the fact that he does not habitually reside in the State where the service is provided, which do not apply to persons established within the national territory or which prevent or otherwise obstruct the activities of the person providing the service."[52]

Requiring an undertaking already licensed in the Member State of establishment to take out a similar licence in the State where the services are provided has been held to constitute a restriction contrary to Articles 59 and 60.[53] As has a provision of national law requiring the employers of short-stay workers to pay social security contributions in respect of workers still affiliated to the scheme of another Member State and accordingly themselves exempted from the scope of the rules of the temporary host State.[54]

It seems, however, that a national restriction need not be discriminatory to fall foul of Article 59. The Court has condemned as incompatible with Article 59 restrictions which create discrimination against persons established in other Member States *or* raise obstacles to access to the profession in question which go beyond what is necessary.[55]

It may be that Articles 59 and 60 catch not only national rules which directly impede the provision of services, but also those which indirectly have that effect. On this view, television broadcasts from one Member State picked up in another and relayed to cable users, would fall within these Articles to the extent that interference with the cable users' receipt of

---

[50] [1976] E.C.R. 1333 at p. 1040, and see Case 36/74 *Walrave* [1974] E.C.R. 1405 at 1417, 1418.
[51] Preamble to the Treaty, first recital.
[52] Case 33/74 *Van Binsbergen* [1974] E.C.R. 1299, at p. 1309. The Court condemned rules imposed by Member States requiring insurance undertakings to do business in those States through persons established in those States, in Case 205/84 *Commission* v. *Germany*; Case 206/84 *Commission* v. *Ireland*; Case 220/83 *Commission* v. *France*; Case 252/83 *Commission* v. *Denmark*; Judgments of December 4, 1986.
[53] Cases 110 and 11/78 *Van Wesemael* [1979] E.C.R. 35; Case 249/80 *Webb* [1981] E.C.R. 3305.
[54] Cases 62 and 63/81 *Seco* [1982] E.C.R. 223.
[55] Case 96/85, *Commission* v. *French Republic* [1986] 3 C.M.L.R. 57 at paras. 11, 13.

the programmes indirectly affected the provision of services across a State line.[56]

REASONABLE RESTRICTIONS IN THE GENERAL INTEREST

A State may impose a residence requirement if it is strictly necessary to do so in order to prevent the evasion, by those resident outside its borders, of professional rules applicable to the pursuit of a particular activity.[57] Needless to say, such a requirement cannot be considered necessary if the provision of certain services in a Member State is "not subject to any sort of qualification or professional regulation and when the requirement of habitual residence is fixed by reference to the territory of the State in question."[58] Even if professional rules are appliable to a particular activity, a requirement that practitioners maintain a personal residence within the jurisdiction will not normally be justified in the case of those who maintain a *bona fide* place of business therein.[59] An example of a permissible residence requirement given by the Court was the rule that "persons whose functions are to assist in the administration of justice must be permanently established for professional purposes within the jurisdiction of certain courts or tribunals,"[60] though this statement must now be read in the light of Article 4(1) of Directive 77/249, on the freedom to provide legal services.[61]

The Court has held that Article 59 does not preclude the enforcement of national rules for the protection of intellectual property, save where such application constitutes a means of arbitrary discrimination or a disguised restriction on trade between Member States.[62] Likewise, it does not preclude national rules prohibiting the transmission of advertisements by cable television, if those rules are applied without distinction as regards the origin, whether national or foreign, of those advertisements, the nationality of the person providing the service, or the place where he is established.[63]

Transport, banking and insurance

The scope of Articles 59–66 on the provision of services is subject to certain derogations and exceptions in favour of other Articles of the Treaty, such as the provisions relating to the movement of goods, capital and persons.[64] Similarly, freedom to provide services in the field of transport is governed by the provisions of Title IV of Part Two of the Treaty, relating

---

[56] Adv.Gen. Warner in Case 52/79 *Debauve* [1980] E.C.R. 833, and Case 62/79 *Coditel* [1980] E.C.R. 881; Opinion at pp. 874, 876. For the application of Articles 59 and 60 to television broadcasts, see Case 155/73 *Sacchi* [1974] E.C.R. 490.
[57] Case 33/74 *Van Binsbergen* [1974] E.C.R. 1299; Case 39/75 *Coenen* [1975] E.C.R. 1547.
[58] Case 33/74 *Van Binsbergen* [1974] E.C.R. 1299 at p. 1310.
[59] Case 39/75 *Coenen* [1975] E.C.R. 1547.
[60] Case 33/74 *Van Binsbergen* [1974] E.C.R. 1299 at p. 1310.
[61] O.J. 1977, L18/17.
[62] Case 62/79 *Coditel* [1980] E.C.R. 881.
[63] Case 52/79 *Debauve* [1980] E.C.R. 833.
[64] Art. 60, first para.

thereto,[65] while the liberalisation of banking[66] and insurance[67] services connected with the movement of capital is to be effected in step with the progressive liberalisation of the latter.[68]

Exercise of official authority, and the public policy proviso

Article 66 of the Treaty provides that Articles 55 to 58 shall apply to the provision of services as they do to the right of establishment, and the reader is referred accordingly to the treatment of these Articles earlier in the present chapter.[69]

The Court has so far had recourse to the concept of reasonable restrictions in the public interest as an exception implicit in Article 59, rather than to the terms of Article 56(1). This may be because Article 56(1) is limited to restrictions on foreign nationals, while the implicit exceptions to Article 59 may be invoked against one's own nationals.[70]

---

[65] Art. 61(1). For Transport, see Arts. 74–84, and for secondary legislation, see *Encyclopedia of Community Law* Vol. C, Part C16.

[66] For legislation on banks and credit institutions, see Dir. 73/183, O.J. 1973 L194/1; Dir. 77/80, O.J. 1977 L322/30; Dir. 83/350, O.J. 1983 L193/18.

[67] For legislation on insurance, see Dir. 64/225, O.J. Sp.Ed. 1963–1964 p. 131; Dir. 73/229, O.J. 1973, L227/3, amended by Dir. 76/580, O.J. 1976 L189/13, and Dir. 84/641, O.J. 1984 L339/21; Dir. 73/240, O.J. 1973, L228/20; Dir. 77/92, O.J. 1977 L26/14; Dir. 78/473, O.J. 1978 L151/25; Dir. 79/267, O.J. 1979 L63/1. See Poole, (1984) 21 C.M.L. Rev. 123; Chappatte (1984) 9 E.L. Rev. 3.

[68] Art. 61(2). For the free movement of capital, see Arts. 67–73; First Directive for implementation of Art. 67, O.J. Sp.Ed. 1959–1962, p. 49; Second Council Directive, O.J. Sp.Ed. 1963–64, p. 5. Oliver, (1984) 9 E.L. Rev. 401.

[69] See *supra*, pp. 207 *et seq.*

[70] This was the case in Case 33/74 *Van Binsbergen* [1974] E.C.R. 1299, and Case 39/75 *Coenen* [1975] E.C.R. 1547.

PART V: SOCIAL POLICY

CHAPTER 10

SOCIAL SECURITY FOR MIGRANTS

The territorial limitations of national social security law

Articles 48 and 49 of the Treaty, and the secondary legislation made thereunder, grant to employed persons the right to seek and to take up employment throughout the Community, without discrimination on grounds of nationality. Articles 52 and 59 of the Treaty, implemented by the applicable secondary legislation, make analogous provision for the self-employed. Such rights, while of the utmost importance, cannot of themselves secure genuine freedom of movement, in view of the territorial limitations of the national social security systems. Such limitations are capable of constituting an obstacle to the free movement of employed and self-employed persons in several respects. First, both entitlement to benefit, and the amount of benefit payable, may depend on the claimant's having paid, or having been credited with, social security contributions. And yet contributions in one Member State will not give rise to a right to benefit under the national law of another. A hypothetical example is illustrative. Suppose an employed or self-employed person works for five years, paying social security contributions, in one Member State, and then moves to another, where he takes up wage-earning or self-employed activities. Suppose that after six months he becomes ill, and claims sickness benefit from the social security authorities of his State of residence. Although our employed or self-employed person has insured continuously for five and a half years, he will receive benefit exclusively on the basis of his contributions in the State where he is now employed, *i.e.*, on the basis of six months' contributions. The reasons for this are perfectly understandable, but the practical effect is that he has forfeited his insurance contribution record in one State by taking up employed or self-employed activities in another.

National social security schemes may place the migrant at a further disadvantage if his wife and family have remained for the time being in his country of origin. Although the law of the host State may provide for an increased rate of benefit to be payable in respect of a claimant's dependants, it may also condition such increased payment on the presence of said dependants in national territory. Although not the object of formal discrimination on grounds of nationality, the migrant is undoubtedly placed at a disadvantage compared to the indigenous wage-earning or self-employed worker.

Again, national authorities may refuse to pay benefit to a claimant outside the jurisdiction, even if he otherwise satisfies the contribution conditions required under national law. Thus a migrant who has acquired a right to an old age pension under the law of the host State, but returns to his country of origin on retirement, may find himself denied advantages accorded to workers remaining within the territory of the host State. Although an employed or self-employed person who has acquired a right to a pension under national law may be allowed to "export" the right abroad, he may thereby disentitle himself to any subsequent cost-of-living increases which would be payable were he to remain within the jurisdiction.

The solution prescribed by community law

It was with these problems in mind that the signatories of the Treaty declared, in Article 51, that the Council should adopt such measures in the field of social security as would be necessary to provide freedom of movement for workers. To this end, the Council was instructed to make arrangements to secure for migrant workers and their dependants:

"(a) aggregation, for the purpose of acquiring and retaining the right to benefit and of calculating the amount of benefit, of all periods taken into account under the laws of the several countries;

(b) payment of benefits to persons resident in the territories of Member States."

These aims are realised in the text of Regulation 1408/71,[1] which, *inter alia*, remedies for the employed person the territorial limitations of national law described above. The process of aggregation ensures for the worker who pursues employment in several Member States a continuous contribution record. Thus, in the case of sickness and maternity benefits, the Regulation requires that the authorities of a Member State whose legislation makes the "acquisition, retention or recovery of the right to benefits" conditional upon the completion of insurance periods "take account of periods of insurance . . . completed under the legislation of any other Member State as if they were periods completed under the legislation which it administers."[2] Similar provisions ensure aggregation in the case of invalidity, old age and death pensions, death grants, unemployment benefits, and family benefits and allowances.[3]

Whereas a claimant may only be entitled to a higher rate of benefit under national law in respect of members of his family that are to be found within the jurisdiction, the Regulation requires that national authorities "take into account the members of the family of the person concerned who are resident in the territory of another Member State as if they were resident in

---

[1] J.O. 1971, L149/1, O.J.Sp.Ed., 1971 (II), p. 416: as amended and updated, (and in effect consolidated) in Reg. 2001/83, O.J. 1983, L230/6. Reg. 1408/71 is implemented by Reg. 574/72, J.O. 1972, L74/1, also amended and updated and consolidated in Reg. 2001/83, *supra*. With respect to Spain and Portugal, see Arts. 60 and 220 respectively of the 1985 Act of Accession, and Annex I, VIII, 1. For a comprehensive treatise, see Watson, *Social Security Law of the European Communities*, 2nd. ed.
[2] Reg. 1408/71, Art. 18(1).
[3] Arts. 38, 45, 64, 67, 72. But it should be noted that aggregation can only be relied upon to establish qualifying periods; not to establish *affiliation* to a national system, Case 70/80 *Vigier* [1981] E.C.R. 229.

the territory of the competent State."[4] Furthermore, in accordance with paragraph (b) of Article 51 of the Treaty, provision is made for the payment of cash benefits to claimants absent from the territory of the competent State. Thus in the case, *inter alia*, of old age pensions, Member States are precluded from withdrawing or reducing benefit on the ground that the recipient is resident in a Member State other than that whose institution is responsible for payment.[5]

Whereas Article 51 of the Treaty provides for Community measures designed to safeguard the social security rights of *employed* persons, the Treaty makes no specific provision for the social security rights of the *self-employed*. In the first instance, Regulation 1408/71, based on Articles 2, 7 and 51 of the Treaty, was limited in its application to the social security rights of employed persons. Regulation 1390/81,[6] based on Articles 2, 7, 51 and 235[7] of the Treaty, extended the provisions of Regulation 1408/71 to the self-employed.

Although Regulation 1408/71 superseded its predecessor, Regulation 3,[8] on October 1, 1972, the latter Regulation may still be applicable to persons who acquired rights thereunder. Thus Article 94(5) of Regulation 1408/71 provides that persons whose pension rights[9] were determined before the entry into force of this Regulation . . . may apply for such pension rights to be reviewed, taking account of the provisions of this Regulation." The Court explained in *Alfonsa Reale* v. *Caisse de compensation des allocations familiales* that the paragraph was based on the principle "that benefits awarded under Regulation No. 3 which are more favourable than those payable under the new regulation shall not be reduced."[10]

It has been noted that Regulation 1390/81 extended the application of Regulation 1408/71 to the self-employed. The former Regulation, however, does not affect any rights acquired, prior to its entry into force, under Regulation 1408/71.[11] With respect to self-employed persons, no right may be acquired under Regulation 1408/71, as amended by Regulation 1390/81, in respect of a period prior to July 1, 1982.[12] All insurance periods and, where appropriate, all periods of employment, of self-employment or of residence completed under the legislation of a Member State before July 1,

---

[4] Art. 23(3), relating to sickness and maternity benefit. Arts. 68(2) and 73, 74 make similar provision in respect of unemployment and family benefits respectively. Art. 39(4) provides for the taking into account of members of the family other than children in the case of invalidity pensions; for the position of children in the case of old age, invalidity and occupational pensions, see Chap. 8 of the Regulation.

[5] Art. 10(1).

[6] O.J. 1981 L143/1.

[7] Art. 235 provides: "If action by the Community should prove necessary to attain, in the course of the operation of the common market, one of the objectives of the Community and this Treaty has not provided the necessary powers, the Council shall, acting unanimously on a proposal from the Commission and after consulting the Assembly, take the appropriate measures."

[8] J.O. 1958, 561. Implemented by Reg. 4, J.O. 1958, 597.

[9] See Art. 1(*t*) of Reg. 1408/71. The pensions referred to are not simply those in respect of old age, but include invalidity and survivors' benefits, and benefits payable in respect of accidents at work.

[10] Case 32/76 [1976] E.C.R. 1523, at p. 1531.

[11] Reg. 3795/81 O.J. 1981 L378/1, Art. 3. And see Case 32/76 *Reale* [1976] E.C.R. 1523.

[12] Reg. 1408/71, Art. 95. This date is the date of the entry into force of Reg. 1390/81; see Reg. 1390/81, Art. 4, and Reg. 3795/81, O.J. 1981 L378/1, Art. 5.

1982 shall be taken into consideration for the determination of the rights of the self-employed to benefits under Regulation 1408/71.[13] Subject to the exclusion of rights arising before July 1, 1982, rights may nevertheless be acquired relating to contingencies which materialised prior to that date.[14] The rights of a self-employed person to whom a pension was awarded prior to July 1, 1982 may, on the application of the person concerned, be reviewed, taking into account the provisions Regulation 1408/71, as amended.[15]

Persons to whom Regulation 1408/71 applies

Article 2(1) of Regulation 1408/71 provides that it shall apply to "employed or self-employed persons who are or have been subject to the legislation of one or more Member States and who are nationals[16] of one of the Member States . . . also to the members of their families and their survivors."[17]

Employed and self-employed persons

One might expect that the "employed persons" (formerly "workers" before Reg. 1408/71 was extended to cover the self-employed) referred to in Article 2(1) of Regulation 1408/71 would be none other than the "workers" referred to in Article 48 of the Treaty, but this is not precisely the case. The discrepancy is best understood in the light of the provisions of Regulation 3, predecessor of Regulation 1408/71, and the case law of the Court thereon. Article 4(1) of the latter Regulation declared it to be applicable to "wage-earners and comparable workers."[18] The Court held in *Hoekstra (née Unger)*[19] that this category included persons compulsorily insured in the first place as workers who continued to make contributions on a voluntary basis after ceasing employment. In the Court's view it was the intention of the Treaty and the Regulation to protect those who had terminated their employment as well as those actually employed—this followed from the text of Article 48(3) of the Treaty, which referred to persons likely "to remain in the territory of a Member State after having been employed in that State," and from the definition in Article 4 of Regulation 3, which embraced wage-earners who were or *had been* subject to the legislation of one or more of the Member States.

Although the Court in *Hoekstra* defined the ambit of Regulation 3 primarily by reference to Article 48 of the Treaty, later decisions were to define the concept of "travailleurs assimilés" by reference to the national

---

[13] Reg. 1408/71, Art. 95(2).

[14] Reg. 1408/71, Art. 93(3).

[15] Reg. 1408/71, Art. 95(5). NB Reg. 3795/81, Art. 3; and Case 32/76 *Reale* [1976] E.C.R. 1523.

[16] Nationality of a Member State at the time of the completion of insurance periods has been held to be decisive, even if such nationality was lacking at the time the claim was made, Case 10/78 *Belbouab* [1978] E.C.R. 1915, see Watson, (1979) 4 E.L.Rev. 106.

[17] Stateless persons and refugees resident within the territory are also covered, as are civil servants. But see Art. 4(4) of Reg. 1408/71, which excludes special schemes for civil servants from the ambit of the Community rules.

[18] "Travailleurs salariés ou assimilés."

[19] Case 75/63 [1964] E.C.R. 177.

social security systems. In *De Cicco*,[20] an Italian, resident in Italy, claimed a German pension on the basis of German insurance contributions made as an employed person, and Italian insurance contributions made as a self-employed artisan. The question referred to the Court was whether such a self-employed artisan could be regarded as a "comparable worker" within the meaning of Regulation 3. The Court noted that the terms of Article 4 of that Regulation were consistent with the general tendency of the social law of the Member States, which was to extend the benefits of social security beyond employees *stricto sensu* and in favour of new categories of persons exposed to similar risks. The extent of such assimilation could only be determined by reference to the national legislations to which the Regulation refer. In the case of craftsmen, they were to be considered as assimilated to wage-earners "to the extent to which, by virtue of the provisions of national legislation, they are protected against one or more risks by extension of a scheme organised for the benefit of the generality of workers."[21]

The fourth recital to the preamble to Regulation 1408/71 recorded that considerable differences in the categories of persons to whom the national legislations applied made it preferable to establish the principle that the Regulation applied to all nationals of Member States insured under social security schemes for employed persons. The same principle was applied to extend the application of Regulation 1408/71 to the self-employed. Article 1(*a*) of the Regulation classifies employed and self-employed persons, not by reference to Articles 48, 52 and 59 of the Treaty, but according to the character of the social security schemes applicable to them. Thus, under subparagraph (i) an employed or self-employed person is so classified because he is insured under a scheme established to benefit employed or self-employed persons.[22] Under subparagraph (ii) a claimant who is affiliated to a scheme established to benefit the whole working population, or all residents, may be classified as an employed or self-employed person, *inter alia*, (a) by virtue of the method by which the scheme is administered or financed, or (b) as a result of simultaneous affiliation to a scheme for employed or self-employed persons, albeit in respect of risks other than those covered by Regulation 1408/71.[23]

The Regulation itself is silent as to the modes of administration or financing ((a) above) which permit the identification as "employed or self-employed persons" of claimants covered by general schemes. In the *Brack*

---

[20] Case 19/68 [1968] E.C.R. 473.

[21] [1968] E.C.R. 473 at p. 481.

[22] Art. 1(*a*)(i) provides that "employed person" and "self-employed person" mean respectively "any person who is insured, compulsorily or on an optional continued basis, for one or more of the contingencies covered by the branches of a social security scheme for employed or self-employed persons." It will be noted that a person is covered by this provision even if he is not in fact insured, as long as he *ought* to be insured, see Case 39/76 *Mouthaan* [1976] E.C.R. 1901. The formulation covers those who are no longer economically active: Case 182/78 *Pierik* [1978] E.C.R. 1971.

[23] Art. 1(*a*)(ii) refers to "any person who is compulsorily insured for one or more of the contingencies covered by the branches of social security dealt with in this Regulation, under a social security scheme for all residents or for the whole working population, if such person:—can be identified as an employed or self-employed person by virtue of the manner in which such scheme is administered or financed, or—failing such criteria, is insured for some other contingency specified in Annex I under a scheme for employed or self-employed persons, or a scheme referred to in (iii), either compulsorily or on an optional

case[24] the Court held that a person insured as an employed person for nine years, and then insured as a self-employed person for 17 years, could still be identified as a "worker" (in current terminology an "employed person") by virtue of his earlier contributions, where such contributions were to be taken into account for the purpose of establishing entitlement to benefit at the full rate under national law. The Court acknowledged that Article 1(a)(ii) of Regulation 1408/71 (at that time applicable only to "workers") might cover both self-employed persons who had formerly been employed persons, and those self-employed persons who were nevertheless treated as employed persons by the national social security systems. Thus even before Regulation 1408/71 was extended to the self-employed, it already covered certain categories of such persons, as was acknowledged by the sixth recital to Regulation 1390/81.

Annex I, J, entitled Employed persons and/or self employed persons (Art. 1(a)(ii) and (iii) of the Regulation), states under heading L, United Kingdom,

> "Any person who is an 'employed earner' or a 'self-employed earner' within the meaning of the legislation of Great Britain or of the legislation of Northern Ireland shall be regarded respectively as an employed person or a self-employed person within the meaning of Article 1(a)(ii) of the Regulation"[25]

The Court held in *Walsh*[26] that a person who is entitled under the legislation of a Member State to benefits covered by Regulation 1408/71 by virtue of contributions paid compulsorily does not lose his status as a "worker" under Article 1(a)(ii) by reason only of the fact that at the time when the contingency occurred he was no longer paying contributions and was not bound to do so. At the time of this decision, made on a reference from the National Insurance Commissioner, Part I of Annex V (the then applicable Annex) provided that as regards the United Kingdom:

> "All persons required to pay contributions as employed workers shall be regarded as workers for the purposes of Article 1(a)(ii) of the Regulation."

The Court held[27] that this provision in Annex V did not restrict the term "worker" in Article 1(a)(ii), but had the sole purpose of clarifying the scope of that Article *vis-à-vis* British legislation so that persons covered by the definition in the regulation could be identified as such by the way in which the British system was administered or financed.

---

continued basis or, where no such scheme exists in the Member State concerned, complies with the definition given in Annex I."

Art. 1(a)(iii) refers to a person "who is compulsorily insured for several of the contingencies covered by the branches dealt with in this Regulation, under a standard social security scheme for the whole rural population in accordance with the criteria laid down in Annex I."

[24] Case 17/76 [1976] E.C.R. 1429.

[25] It is also provided that "Any person in respect of whom contributions are payable as an 'employed person' or a 'self-employed person' in accordance with the legislation of Gibraltar shall be regarded respectively as an employed person or a self-employed person within the meaning of Article 1(a)(ii) of the Regulation."

[26] Case 143/79 [1980] E.C.R. 1639. On the definition of "worker" under Article 1(a)(ii) see also Case 84/77 *Tessier* [1978] E.C.R. 7, Wyatt, (1978) 3 E.L.Rev. 391; Case 99/80 *Galinsky* [1981] E.C.R. 941.

[27] Confirming Case 17/76 *Brack* [1976] E.C.R. 1429 on the same point.

Article 1 of Regulation 1408/71 includes in the categories of "employed person" and "self-employed person" any one who is *voluntarily* insured for one or more of the contingencies covered by the branches of social security dealt with in the Regulation, under a social security scheme of a Member State for employed or self-employed persons, or for all residents, or for certain categories of residents, provided that certain conditions are satisfied. These are that such a person carries on an activity as an employed or self-employed person, or has previously been compulsorily insured for the same contingency under a scheme for employed or self-employed persons of the same Member State.[28]

Who are or have been subject to the law of one or more Member States

An employed or self-employed person may be entitled to rely on Regulation 1408/71, although he pursues his occupation in his country of origin, always has done, and has never been subject to the legislation of another Member State. This results from the wording of Article 2(1), which provides that the Regulation shall apply to workers who are or have been subject to the legislation of *one* or more Member States. Considering the interpretation of the similar terms of Article 4(1) of Regulation 3, the Court observed that:

> "The general wording of this provision shows that the application of the Regulation is limited neither to workers who have been employed in several States nor to workers who are or have been employed in one State while residing or having resided in another."[29]

Thus a worker subject to Netherlands social security legislation who fell ill during a visit to her parents in Germany, was entitled to claim for the cost of treatment received in that country on her return.[30] Furthermore, in the *Laumann*[31] case, the Court held that the right to orphans' benefits in respect of the children of a worker who had never moved between Member States fell within the ambit of Regulation 1408/71 as a result of the *children's* change of residence to another Member State.

The scope of Regulation 1408/71 ratione personae and the governing Treaty provisions

It is apparent from the foregoing that Regulation 1408/71 is applicable, not only to migrants subject to the legislation of several Member States, but also to persons who have never pursued occupational activities in more than one country nor been subject to the social security legislation of more than one Member State. This may seem surprising, since Article 51 of the Treaty, the legal basis for Regulations 3 and 1408/71, merely authorises the Council to adopt such measures in the field of social security as are necessary to provide freedom of *movement for workers*. Article 235, one of the Treaty Articles upon which Regulation 1390/81 is based, is invoked in conjunction with Article 51, and apparently to similar effect with respect to the

---

[28] Art. 1(*a*)(iv). On "self-employed person," see case 300/84 *Roosmalen*, Judgment of October 23, 1986.
[29] Case 31/64 *Bertholet* [1965] E.C.R. 81, at p. 87.
[30] Case 75/63 *Hoekstra (née Unger)* [1964] E.C.R. 177.
[31] Case 115/77 [1978] E.C.R. 805, (1979) 4 E.L.Rev. 371.

self-employed. The purpose of the latter Articles, read in conjunction with the texts of Articles 48, 52 and 59, would seem to suggest that the only persons entitled to take advantage of the Community provisions co-ordinating the national social security systems are migrants seeking employment or self-employment, engaged in employment or self-employment, or remaining in a Member State after cessation of employment or self-employment under the conditions specified in Regulation 1251/70[32] or Directive 75/34.[33] The Court however, recognising the practical difficulties of co-ordinating diverse systems of social security legislation, has allowed the Council a margin of discretion in its implementation of Article 51 of the Treaty. The *Maison Singer*[34] case is illustrative. A German national holidaying in France was killed in a collision between his motorcycle and a livestock van belonging to Maison Singer and driven by one of its employees. The Hessische Knappschaft paid benefits to the dependants of the deceased, and sued in a French court for reimbursement from Maison Singer on the ground that, under French law and Article 52 of Regulation 3, it was subrogated to the rights of the dependents. The Court dealt in its judgment with the argument that Regulation 3, and in particular Article 52 thereof, was incompatible with the limitations set forth in Article 51 of the Treaty. This argument the Court rejected, as follows:

"The establishment of as complete freedom of movement for workers as possible, which thus forms part of the 'foundations' of the Community, therefore constitutes the ultimate objective of Article 51 and thereby conditions the exercise of the power which it confers upon the Council.

It would not be in conformity with that spirit to limit the concept of 'worker' solely to migrant workers *stricto sensu* or solely to workers required to move for the purpose of their employment. Nothing in Article 51 imposes such distinctions, which would in any case tend to make the application of the rules in question impracticable.

On the other hand, the system adopted by Regulation No. 3, which consists in abolishing as far as possible the territorial limitations on the application of the different social security schemes, certainly corresponds to the objectives of Article 51 of the Treaty."[35]

The Court's reasoning is based on two propositions: the first is that freedom of movement for workers is a right which is not strictly limited by the economic requirements of a common market[36]; the second is that a permissible method of facilitating such freedom of movement is the removal of territorial limitations on the application of the various social security systems. This reasoning is equally applicable to sustain the amendments to Regulation 1408/71 made to extend its operation to the self-employed. In the process of removing the territorial limitations on the application of the national social security systems, benefits will inevitably accrue to employed

---

[32] O.J.Sp.Ed. 1970 (II), p. 42, see *supra*, p. 182.
[33] O.J. 1975, L14/10, *supra*, at p. 202.
[34] Case 44/65 [1965] E.C.R. 965.
[35] [1965] E.C.R. 965 at p. 971.
[36] See *supra* at p. 162.

and self-employed persons who are not migrants, and to members of their families, and may even accrue to persons who are not employed or self-employed persons at all, but are treated as such by the applicable social security systems.

Members of workers' families, and survivors

Article 51 of the Treaty refers to the need to ensure social security coverage for workers' dependants, and Regulation 1408/71 provides accordingly for the families of employed persons, and, more latterly, for the families of the self-employed. A "member of the family" is any person defined or recognised as a member of the family or designated as a member of the household by the legislation under which benefits are provided.[37] Members of the family may only claim such rights as are derived under national law from the family relationship with the employed or self-employed person.[38] Where national law regards as a member of the family only a person living under the same roof as the employed or self-employed person, this condition is considered satisfied if the person in question is mainly dependent on that person.[39] Regulation 1408/71 vests rights to sickness and maternity benefits directly in members of the family of an employed or self-employed person visiting another Member State.[40] In such a case the classification of members of the family is in accordance with the law of the Member State of residence of the person in question.[41] Furthermore, it is not necessary in this case that the applicable national legislation provides benefits derived from the family relationship with the employed or self-employed person.[42]

Regulation 1408/71 applies also to the survivors of employed or self-employed persons.[43] A "survivor" means any person defined or recognised as such by the legislation under which the benefits are granted.[44] Where that legislation regards as a survivor only a person who was living under the same roof as the deceased, this condition shall be considered satisfied if such person was mainly dependent on the deceased.[45]

Social security benefits falling within the ambit of Regulation 1408/71

National legislation concerning the following branches of social security falls within the ambit of the Regulation[46]:

— sickness and maternity benefits;

---

[37] Reg. 1408/71, Art. 1(f).
[38] Case 40/76 *Kermaschek* [1976] E.C.R. 1669; Case 157/84 *Frascogna*, Judgment of June 6, 1985; Case 94/84 *Deak*, Judgment of June 20, 1985; Case 7/75 *Mr. and Mrs. F.* [1975] E.C.R. 679, which allows the dependent child of a worker to claim a benefit for the handicapped in his own right under Reg. 1408/71, is inconsistent with the above cases. The deficiencies of Reg. 1408/71 are largely remedied by Art. 7(2) of Reg. 1612/68, see *supra* at p. 179.
[39] Reg. 1408/71, Art. 1(f).
[40] Art. 22(3).
[41] Reg. 1408/71, Art. 1(f).
[42] The Court's case law referred to in note 38 would seem to have no relevance to a case where the Reg. vests rights directly in members of the family.
[43] Art. 2(1). See, *e.g.* Art. 44(1).
[44] Art. 1(g).
[45] Reg. 1408/71, Art. 1(g).
[46] Art. 4(1).

10(1) of the Regulation, which prohibits the reduction of benefit for the sole reason that the beneficiary has transferred his residence to another Member State.[56]

The exclusion of benefit schemes for victims of war or its consequences has been held to apply to a scheme for early payment of old-age pensions at full rate to former prisoners of war,[57] and to a scheme for early retirement on full pension for those in receipt of war service invalidity pensions.[58]

The Member States are obliged to specify the legislation and schemes referred to in Article 4(1) in declarations which are to be notified to the Council and published in the Official Journal.[59] Failure of a Member State to specify particular benefits is not of itself conclusive evidence that the law or regulation in question does not fall within the application of Regulation 1408/71, but the fact that a Member State has specified particular benefits in a declaration is conclusive.[60]

Prohibition of discrimination on grounds of nationality

Persons to whom Regulation 1408/71 applies who are resident in the territory of one of the Member States "shall be subject to the same obligations and enjoy the same benefits under the legislation of any Member State as the nationals of that State,"[61] subject only to the special provisions of the Regulation itself. This guarantee prohibits indirect or covert discrimination as well as direct or overt discrimination. The point is well illustrated in the *Palermo* case,[62] which concerned a claim by an Italian woman to an allowance payable under the French Social Security Code to French women of at least 65 years and insufficient means, who were married and who had brought up at least five dependant children of French nationality during a period of at least nine years before their sixteenth birthday. The French authorities waived the nationality requirement in the case of the woman herself, but refused to benefit on the ground that five of her seven children were Italian, and not French. In the view of the Court of Justice, the French authorities had been quite right to waive the nationality requirement in the case of the claimant. But Article 3(1) went further than that. It not only prohibited patent discrimination based on the nationality of the beneficiaries of social security schemes, but also all disguised forms of discrimination which, by the application of other distinguishing criteria,

---

[56] Case 24/74 *Biason*, note 49.

[57] Case 9/78 *Gillard* [1978] E.C.R. 1661, Wyatt, (1979) 4 E.L.Rev. 369. It was not argued that Art. 7(2) of Reg. 1612/68 applied to such a benefit as one of the "social and tax advantages" which must be accorded to workers without discrimination on grounds of nationality.

[58] Case 207/78 *Even* [1979] E.C.R. 2019, Wyatt, (1981) 6 E.L.Rev. 42. The Court held that such a benefit did not amount to a social or tax advantage within the meaning of Art. 7(2) of Reg. 1612/68. A German scheme providing for reparation to victims of Nazi persecution by allowing the retroactive payment of social security contributions, and which supplemented the general provisions of German social security law, has been held to fall within Reg. 1408/71: Case 70/80 *Vigier* [1981] E.C.R. 229.

[59] Arts. 5 & 97.

[60] Case 35/77 *Beerens* [1977] E.C.R. 2249; Case 237/78 *Palermo* [1979] E.C.R. 2645; Case 70/80 *Vigier* [1981] R.C.R. 229.

[61] Art. 3(1).

[62] Case 237/78 [1979] E.C.R. 2645, Wyatt, (1981) 6 E.L.Rev. 42, 44.

led in fact to the same result. A condition concerning the nationality of the children, such as that imposed by the applicable French legislation, was capable of leading in fact to the result that a mother of foreign nationality could benefit from the allowance only in exceptional cases. In particular she would be at a disadvantage in relation to mothers who were nationals of the State of residence when the nationality of the children depended in principle on that of the parents under the legislation of the country of residence, as in the case of French legislation in this regard.

It will be recalled that "indirect" or "covert" discrimination was condemned by the Court in the *Sotqiu* case.[63] But the Court added the rider that differentiation based on objective factors did not amount to prohibited discrimination. The French authorities in *Palermo* argued that the furtherance of demographic policy, *viz.*, the expansion of the French population, amounted to an objective feature justifying differentiation based on the nationality of the children of the claimant of the benefit in issue. The Court held that Regulation 1408/71 did not make any distinction between social security schemes to which it applied according to whether those schemes did or did not pursue objectives of demographic policy.

Despite the prohibition on discrimination referred to above, if the law of a Member State requires insurance periods to be completed in that State as a condition of *affiliation* to a social security scheme, an employed or self-employed person cannot rely upon the concept of indirect discrimination in order to qualify for affiliation on the basis of insurance periods completed in another Member State.[64]

It is not entirely clear whether the effect of Article 3(1) of Regulation 1408/71, in conjunction with Articles 7, 48, 52 and 59 of the Treaty, prohibits reverse discrimination, that is to say, discrimination by national authorities against their own nationals and in favour of migrants. The question arose in the *Kenny*[65] case, in which an Irish national had claimed sickness benefit in the United Kingdom for a period during which he was serving a prison sentence in Ireland. Under the applicable British rules, he would have been disqualified for benefit had he served a prison sentence in the United Kingdom. The social security authorities refused benefit, arguing that the British rules on their true construction also applied to imprisonment outside the United Kingdom, and that Articles 7 and 48 of the EEC Treaty in any event required that they be so construed, since otherwise they would have the effect of discriminating against British nationals. This discrimination would result from the fact that migrants would be more likely than British nationals to serve prison sentences outside the United Kingdom. The Court's judgment does not clearly indicate whether reverse discrimination of the kind alleged is consistent with the Treaty or not. On the one hand, the Court asserts that the laws of the various Member States "must affect all persons subject to them in accordance with objective criteria and without regard to their nationality."[66] On the other hand, the

---

[63] Case 152/73 [1974] E.C.R. 153; see *supra*, p. 177.
[64] Case 110/79 *Coonan* [1980] E.C.R. 1145; Case 70/80 *Vigier* [1981] E.C.R. 229.
[65] Case 1/78 [1978] E.C.R. 1489, Wyatt, (1978) 3 E.L.Rev. 488.
[66] Judgment, para. 18.

Court refers to discrimination against nationals of "the *other* Member States,"[67] though the Court goes on to say that its reply applies "to the same extent to cases in which the worker concerned is a national of the Member State to which the competent institution belongs."[68] The circumstances in which Articles 48, 52 and 59 of the Treaty may be invoked by an employed or self-employed person against his own State has already been considered.[69] In our view, since discrimination on grounds of nationality is prohibited primarily in order to remove obstacles to the free movement of persons, it would seem to follow that Articles 7, 48, 51, 52 and 59, and Regulation 1408/71, are intended to ensure that workers be free to move as they please between the Member States, without being either advantaged or disadvantaged by the territorial application of the national social security systems. It is the aim of the Treaty that national rules, supplemented by Community regulations, be *neutral* in their effect on free movement. It need hardly be added that freedom of movement includes the freedom *not* to migrate, as well as the right so to do. Reverse discrimination in the administration of national social security rules should in our view be regarded as incompatible with the Treaty.

The principle of non-discrimination operates as a constraint not only upon national authorities in the formulation and implementation of national rules, but upon the Council in framing the Community rules which coordinate the national social security systems, as the *Pinna* case[70] demonstrates.

Article 73(1) of Regulation 1408/71 provides that family benefits are to be provided under the law of the Member State of employment. Article 73(2) provided that where the Member State of employment was France, however, the level of available allowances was determined by the law of the State in which the members of the family resided. Mr. Pinna, an Italian national resident in France, was refused family allowances under French law for periods when his two children were visiting Italy. He challenged Article 73(2) of Regulation 1408/71 before a French court, arguing that its effect was to discriminate in two respects against non-French nationals subject to French legislation. First, such workers were treated less favourably than French workers; and secondly, they were treated less favourably than workers subject to the legislation of any Member State other than France. Article 73(2) therefore infringed Articles 7, 48 and 51 of the EEC Treaty.

The Court of Justice considered first the alleged discrimination in Article 73 between migrant workers employed in France, and migrant workers employed in the other Member States. The Court acknowledged that Article 51 of the Treaty provided for the coordination of the legislation of the Member States, rather than for their harmonisation, thus leaving intact the differences between the national social security systems. This resulted in migrants enjoying different social security rights according to the law of their State of employment.

---

[67] Judgment, para. 20.
[68] Judgment, para. 21.
[69] *Supra*, at p. 206.
[70] Case 41/84 Judgment of January 15, 1986.

However, in the Court's view securing freedom of movement for workers would be made more difficult if avoidable differences between the social security entitlements of migrants were actually introduced by Community law. It followed that Community social security rules made under Article 51 of the Treaty must not add to those differences which already resulted from the lack of harmonisation of the national systems.

Article 73, held the Court, created two different systems for migrant workers, one for migrant workers subject to the law of France, and one for workers subject to the legislation of the other Member States. In this way it added to the disparities intrinsic in the existence of the different national systems, and impeded the purposes of Articles 48 to 51 of the Treaty.

The Court next considered the allegation that Article 73(2) discriminated between migrant workers employed in France, and French workers employed in France. The Court recalled that the principle of non-discrimination prohibited not only overt discrimination, based on nationality, but also all forms of covert discrimination which, by the application of criteria other than nationality, led in fact to the same result. Yet this was the very effect of the criterion—residence of members of the family in a Member State other than France—adopted in Article 73(2) to determine the legislation under which family benefits were payable. Although French workers employed in France whose families were resident in other Member States were treated no more favourably than migrant workers employed in France whose families were resident in other Member States, it was likely to be migrant workers, rather than French workers, who had families resident in other Member States. Thus the criterion of residence of members of the family in a Member State other than France was not appropriate to secure the equality of treatment prescribed by Article 48 of the Treaty and it could not properly be used as a means of coordinating the national social security systems for the purpose of promoting the free movement of workers in the Community.

Payment of benefit to recipients in other Member States

It is not uncommon for an employed or self-employed migrant to return with his family to his country of origin at the end of his working life, or if an accident incapacitates him for work. It would cause grave hardship to migrants and their dependants if such a person or the members of his family were forced to forego the right to benefits acquired under the law of the Member State (or Member States) where he had been employed, simply because of such a change of residence. Article 10(1) of Regulation 1408/71 provides accordingly:

"Save as otherwise provided in this Regulation, invalidity, old-age or survivors' cash benefits, pensions for accidents at work or occupational diseases and death grants acquired under the legislation of one or more Member States shall not be subject to any reduction, modification, suspension, withdrawal or confiscation by reason of the fact that the recipient resides in the territory of a Member State other than that in which the institution responsible for payment is situated."

One effect of this provision is to allow beneficiaries to "export" benefits when they cease to reside in the State responsible for payment. Thus an Italian national resident in France in receipt of both an invalidity pension and a means-tested supplementary allowance, awarded independently of periods of work or contributions, would be entitled to continue to receive both benefits on her return to her country of origin.[71] This conclusion illustrates a possible anomaly of classifying means-tested supplementary allowances such as that in issue as social *security* rather than social *assistance*: benefits awarded to ensure a minimum income to members of a national community are treated as transferable deferred earnings.[72]

The "legislation" under which the right to benefits is acquired under Article 10(1) is national legislation *modified by the provisions of Community law*. As the Court explained in *Smieja*:

"The aim of this provision is to guarantee the party concerned his right to have the benefit of such payments even after taking up residence in a different Member country, *e.g.* his country of origin.

The rights under discussion often derive, not from national legislation alone, but from that legislation combined with the principle of non-discrimination on the basis of nationality set out in Article 8 of Reg. 3 and Article 3(1) of Regulation No. 1408/71.

In the event of the party's rights deriving from the legislation of several Member States—a possibility expressly foreseen in Article 10—payment is always made according to the provisions in the regulation.

It may therefore be concluded that the phrase 'legislation of one or more Member States' in Article 10(1) must be interpreted as embracing the relevant provisions of Community law."[73]

The text of Article 10 suggests that rights once acquired cannot be reduced simply because of a transfer of residence, but makes no explicit provision for a situation where national law conditions the *acquisition* of rights on residence. It seems, however, from the Court's judgment in *Smieja* that this is also forbidden. A German worker who had been employed in Holland returned to his country of origin, and claimed a supplement to his Dutch pension. A person in his position was entitled to such a supplement, provided only (a) that he was of Dutch nationality, and (b) resident within the Kingdom. The Court held that "to the extent that a national law . . . imposes a condition of residence on *would-be recipients* (emphasis added) of some of the benefits of the type mentioned in Article 10, the fact that the person concerned resides in the territory of a different Member State is no ground for modification . . . of such benefit."[74] The effect of the Court's ruling was that the claimant would acquire a right to

---

[71] Case 24/74 *Biason* [1974] E.C.R. 999.

[72] See the comments of the Commission and the Advocate General, [1974] E.C.R. 999, at p. 1004 and 1015. On the other hand, can one draw a hard and fast line between the "revalorisation increases" of Art. 1(*t*), and means-tested benefits payable to ensure minimum earnings, especially in time of inflation?

[73] Case 51/73 [1973] E.C.R. 1213, at pp. 1221, 1222.

[74] [1973] E.C.R. 1213, at p. 1222. And see the reasoning of the Court in Case 32/77 *Giuliani* [1977] E.C.R. 1857. Note that what is forbidden is conditioning entitlement on present residence; the Article cannot obviate the need for completion of periods of residence as a condition of entitlement.

benefit under Dutch legislation (incorporating the no-discrimination rule of Article 3(1) of Regulation 1408/71) which could not be conditioned on residence within national territory (Article 10(1)).

This principle was confirmed in *Carraciolo*,[75] in which a claim to invalidity benefit under Belgian law was made by a person resident in Italy. Benefit was refused because the claimant was not present in Belgium. The Court of Justice, referring to *Smieja*, declared that:

" . . . the aim of the provision contained in Article 10 is to promote the free movement of workers by insulating those concerned from the harmful consequences which might result when they transfer their residence from one Member State to another. It is clear from that principle not only that the person concerned retains the right to receive pensions and benefits acquired under the legislation of one or more Member States even after taking up residence in another Member State, but also that he may not be prevented from acquiring such a right merely because he does not reside in the territory of the State in which the institution responsible for payment is situated."[76]

Selection of national legislation applicable to migrants[77]

Articles 13 and 14 of Regulation 1408/71 lay down rules for determining which national social security system applies to an employed or self-employed person at any given time. However, these choice of law rules are subject to the special provisions regarding the various categories of benefits laid down in title III of the Regulation.[78] The fact that a national system is applicable in principle in accordance with the choice of law rules does not of itself secure affiliation to a national scheme otherwise than under the conditions laid down for affiliation under national law.[79] However, if the Community choice rules specify a national social security regime as being applicable, it would be incompatible with the Regulation for the national system to deny affiliation to an employed or self-employed person on the ground that the migrant is insured under the law of another Member State.[80] A contrary conclusion would allow the substitution of national choice rules for those laid down in the Regulation.

Where an employed person is resident in one Member State and employed in another—Article 13(2)(a) of Regulation 1408/71

A worker resident[81] in one Member State and employed in another is subject to the social security legislation of the latter, even if the registered office or place of business of his employer is situated in the territory of another Member State. The aim of this provision was described by the

---

[75] Case 92/81 [1982] E.C.R. 2213, Watson, (1984) 9 E.L.Rev. 113.
[76] Judgment, para. 14.
[77] Arts. 13 and 14 of Reg. 1408/71, some of the provisions of which are discussed in the text, are applicable to schemes of compulsory insurance. For optional insurance, see Art. 15.
[78] Case 227/81 *Aubin* [1982] E.C.R. 1991.
[79] Case 275/81 *Koks* [1982] E.C.R. 3013, referring to Case 110/79 *Coonan* [1980] E.C.R. 1445. See Watson, (1984) 9 E.L.Rev. 428.
[80] Case 276/81 *Kuijpers* [1982] E.C.R. 3027, Watson, (1984) 9 E.L.Rev. 428.
[81] Art. 1(h) of Reg. 1408/71 provides that "residence" means "habitual residence." See Case 13/73 *Hakenberg* [1973] E.C.R. 935.

Court in *Massonet* as being "to avoid any plurality or purposeless overlapping of contributions and liabilities which would result from the simultaneous or alternate application of several legislative systems and, moreover, preventing those concerned, in the absence of legislation applying to them, from remaining without protection in the matter of social security."[82] This explanation of the principle underlying Article 13(2)(*a*) is in fact the justification for including choice rules in Regulation 1408/71 in the first place. The normal subject of national social security legislation is the worker both employed and resident in national territory. When workers take to residing in one Member State and working in another—or several others—they run a two-fold risk: on the one hand they may find themselves unprotected by any scheme at all, and on the other hand they may find themselves bound to contribute to several systems simultaneously.

Where a self-employed person is resident in one Member State and self-employed in another—Article 13(2)(b)

What Article 13(2)(*a*) provides for the employed worker, Article 13(2)(*b*) provides for the self-employed: a person who is self-employed in the territory of one Member State is subject to the legislation of that State even if he resides in the territory of another.

Logical as the general rule may be, to the effect that the governing legislation is that of the Member State of employment or self-employment, its invariable application would itself give rise to anomalies. The subsequent provisions of the Regulation thus contain certain exceptions.[83]

Where a worker normally engaged in one Member State is posted temporarily to another—Article 14(1)(a)

Article 14(1)(*a*) of the Regulation provides as follows:
"(i) a person employed in the territory of a Member State by an undertaking to which he is normally attached who is posted by that undertaking to the territory of another Member State to perform work there for that undertaking shall continue to be subject to the legislation of the first Member State, provided that the anticipated duration of that work does not exceed twelve months and that he is not sent to replace another worker who has completed his term of posting."[84]

In the absence of such an exception, application of the general rule would require an undertaking established in the territory of one Member State to register its workers, usually subject to the social security legislation of that State, with the social security system of the Member State where

---

[82] Case 50/75 [1975] E.C.R. 1473, at p. 1482. The concept of a worker employed in a Member State includes a worker *last* employed in that State: Case 150/82 *Coppola* [1983] E.C.R. 43.
[83] In addition to the exceptions in the text, special provision is made in the case of those employed in international transport, as diplomats, etc.
[84] Art. 14(1)(*b*) provides for an extension of the application of the law of the original state for a further 12 months, subject to the consent of the authorities of the state of temporary employment.

they were sent to perform short-term jobs of work; the result would be administrative complications for workers, undertakings, and social security institutions.[85]

The scope of this provision is well illustrated by two decisions of the Court of Justice on the analogous terms of Article 13(1)(a) of Regulation 3[86]:

Manpower[87] and Hakenberg[88]

Manpower, an employment agency specialising in short term placements, posted a French skilled worker to Germany for three days in 1969. On arrival, he sustained an accident on the site, received medical treatment, and later sought reimbursement of the cost from the French social security authorities. The Court of Justice rejected the argument that a posting such as that in issue fell outside the ambit of Article 13(1)(c) of Regulation 3 merely because the object of Manpower was not to perform work, but to place workers at the disposal of other undertakings. The crucial factors in such a case were (a) whether or not the worker in question was attached to an undertaking established in one Member State, and (b) whether or not he remained in the employment of such undertaking for the duration of his posting. This latter requirement would be satisfied at any rate where the undertaking paid the worker's wages and retained the right of dismissal.

It seems that the terms of the provisions in question cannot be applied to the case of a commercial traveller, paid by commission, who represents undertakings established in one Member State, and spends nine months of each year canvassing for orders in another. Such was the view of the Court in the *Hakenberg* case, reasoning that Article 13(1)(a) applied to wage-earners employed on a regular basis rather than business representatives paid by commission, and that "the strict time limits laid down . . . are not compatible with working activities which involve making regular business-canvassing tours in the territory of a Member State, in the interests of undertakings situated in another Member State."[89]

Where a person normally self-employed in one Member State performs work in another

A person who is normally self-employed in the territory of one Member State who performs work in the territory of another shall continue to be subject to the legislation of the former Member State, provided that the anticipated duration of the work does not exceed 12 months.[90]

---

[85] Case 35/70 [1970] E.C.R. 1251.
[86] As amended by Art. 1 of Reg. 24/64, J.O. 1964, 746.
[87] Case 35/70 [1970] E.C.R. 1251.
[88] Case 13/73 [1973] E.C.R. 935.
[89] [1973] E.C.R. 935, at p. 948.
[90] Art. 14a(1)(a). Art. 14a(1)(b) provides for an extension of the application of the law of the original state for a further twelve months, subject to the consent of the authorities of the state of temporary self-employment.

Where a worker is normally employed in several Member States—Article 14(2)

Article 14(2) of the Regulation provides as follows:

"A person normally employed in the territory of two or more Member States shall be subject to the legislation determined as follows:

(b) . . .

(i) to the legislation of the Member State in whose territory he resides, if he pursues his activity partly in that territory or if he is attached to several undertakings or several employers who have their registered offices or places of business in the territory of different Member States[91];

(ii) to the legislation of the Member State in whose territory is situated the registered office or place of business of the undertaking or individual employing him, if he does not reside in the territory of any of the Member States where he is pursuing his activity.[92]

The purpose of these exceptions to the general rule is to avoid the simultaneous application of the laws of the several Member States where the worker is employed. Since this is the case, the Court has held that it is a prerequisite for the application of Article 13(1)(c), first sentence, of Regulation 3 (the sense of which provision is incorporated into the text of Article 14(1)(c)(i)) that the worker be indeed affiliated to a social security institution in the State where he has his permanent residence. Otherwise, the general rule is applicable, and the law of the State of employment applies.[93]

Although the text of Article 14 refers to workers who *normally* carry out their activities on the territory of several Member States, the Court has made it clear that a worker who is *occasionally* employed in a Member State other than that of his permanent residence is not thereby excluded.[94]

Where a person is normally self-employed in several Member States—Article 14a(2)

Once again, a similar choice rule is applicable to the self-employed as to the employed in analogous circumstances. A person normally self-employed in the territory of two or more Member States is subject to the legislation of the Member State in whose territory he resides if he pursues any part of his activity in the territory of that Member State. If he does not pursue any activity in the territory of the Member State in which he resides, he is subject to the legislation of the Member State in whose territory he pursues his main activity.[95]

---

[91] Reproducing the sense of the first and third sentences of Art. 13(c) of Reg. 3, as amended by Reg. 24/64.

[92] Reproducing the sense of the second sentence of Art. 13(c) of Reg. 3.

[93] Case 8/75 *Association du foot-ball club d'Andlau* [1975] E.C.R. 739.

[94] Case 8/75 note 93.

[95] Art. 14a(2). The criteria used to determine the principal activity are laid down in Art. 12a(5)(d) of Reg. 547/72, according to which account shall be taken first and foremost of the locality in which the fixed and permanent premises from which the person concerned pursues his activity is situated, and failing that, account shall be taken of criteria such as the usual nature or the duration of the activities pursued, the number of services rendered and the income arising from those activities.

Whether national law applicable under Articles 13 and 14 of Regulation 1408/71 is exclusively so

The foundation of the choice rules of Regulation 1408/71 is the rule that the applicable law is that of the State of employment; this general rule is only modified where its application would lead to administrative inconvenience, or to the cumulative application of the legislation of several Member States. Thus Community law at any given time requires the application of the law of a single State.

But it will be recalled that the Community system of choice rules was adopted to ensure not only that at any given time at least one national legal system would be applicable, but also to prevent the *purposeless* cumulation of national social security legislation.

The Court, in its decision on the interpretation of Regulation 3, has been somewhat ambivalent as to the extent to which the law required by the Community choice rules is *exclusively* applicable. In two decisions, *Nonnenmacher*[96] and *Van der Vecht*,[97] the Court held that Article 12 of Regulation 3 (equivalent to Article 13(2)(*a*) of Regulation 1408/71) only prohibited Member States other than that in whose territory the worker was carrying out his duties from applying their social security legislation if this would lead to additional contributions on the part of the worker or his employer without a corresponding increase in social security benefits. The basis of these decisions was the objective of Articles 48 to 51 of the Treaty; to protect migrant workers from legal detriments, without withdrawing from them the protection of national rules which would be in any event applicable. Such reasoning suggests that although the choice rules of Regulation 3 require the application of at least one national system at any given time, they do not rule out the concurrent application of other systems, providing that workers are entitled to additional benefits for any additional contributions which they are required to make. On the other hand, if this is so, what is one to make of the Court's observation in *Manpower* to the effect that the purpose of Article 13(1)(*c*) of Regulation 3 was to obviate the need for short-term registration of workers who were posted to other Member States?[98] If the reasoning in *Nonnenmacher* is correct, one cannot rule out *a priori* the necessity for short term registration. The Court in *Manpower* certainly does not base its reasoning on the assumption that short term affiliation can never provide benefits, observing merely that "more often than not" the worker would suffer, because national legislation "generally" does not provide benefits to workers affiliated for short periods. The reasoning in *Nonnenmacher* and *Van der Vecht* suggests that the "short-term-posting" rule grants a worker the right to remain affiliated to a social security scheme in the State where he is normally employed, but only releases him from his obligation to contribute to the applicable scheme in the State where he is actually employed, if his period of affiliation is to be so short as to preclude his receiving any benefits in return.

It is now clear that these difficulties need no longer trouble us, since

[96] Case 92/63 [1964] E.C.R. 281.
[97] Case 19/67 [1967] E.C.R. 345.
[98] *Supra*, at p. 245 [1970] E.C.R. 1251, at p. 1257.

Article 13(1) of Regulation 1408/71 provides that "A worker to whom this Regulation applies shall be subject to the legislation of a *single Member State only*. That legislation *shall be determined in accordance with the provisions of this Title*." (Emphasis added.) However, the Court in *Nonnenmacher* based its reasoning in part on Articles 48 to 51 of the Treaty, holding that these Articles, being calculated to protect the worker, were inconsistent with an interpretation of Regulation 3 whereby a State would be prohibited from extending supplementary social protection to members of its population employed in another Member State. This reading of the Treaty underlies the Court's oft repeated view that the Community's social security rules should only be applied so as to *improve* the lot of the migrant, not so as to diminish rights acquired under national legislation independently of Community law.[99] The argument could thus be adduced that Article 13(1) of Regulation 1408/71 is inconsistent with the Treaty to the extent that it excludes the concurrent application of the legislation of a Member State other than that applicable under the Regulation's choice rules, where such legislation provides additional protection in return for additional contributions.

In the *Perenboom*[1] and *Kuijpers*[2] cases, the Court applied Article 13(1) of Regulation 1408/71, but without excluding the possibility that national legislation other than that applicable by virtue of the Community choice of law rules might also be applicable where that legislation provided additional social protection for workers.

In the *Ten Holder*[3] case, the Court placed the matter beyond dispute, holding that the provisions of Title II of Regulation 1408/71 constitute a complete system of conflict rules the effect of which is to divest the legislature of each Member State of the power to determine the ambit and the conditions for the application of its national legislation so far as the persons who are subject thereto and the territory within which the provisions of national law take effect are concerned.[4] The Court stressed that the rule is not at variance with its decisions[5] to the effect that the application of Regulation 1408/71 cannot entail the loss of rights acquired exclusively under national legislation; that principle applies not to the rules for determining the legislation applicable but to the rules of Community law on the overlapping of benefits provided for by different national legislative systems.[6] The Court's judgment is to be welcomed, but the distinction it draws between the immunity of rights acquired under national law from the operation of the Community rules against overlapping, and the ousting of rights which would be enjoyed under national law but for the Community choice of law rules, is, it is submitted, a distinction without substance. Indeed, the

---

[99] See, *e.g.* Case 191/73 *Niemann* [1974] E.C.R. 571, on Reg. 3, Arts. 27 and 28; Case 24/75 *Petroni* [1975] E.C.R. 1149, on Reg. 1408/71, Art. 46(3); Case 27/75 *Bonaffini* [1975] E.C.R. 971, on Reg. 1408/71, Art. 69; Case 69/79 *Jordens-Vasters* [1980] E.C.R. 75.

[1] Case 102/76 [1977] E.C.R. 815.

[2] Case 276/81 [1982] E.C.R. 3027.

[3] Case 302/84 Judgment of June 12, 1986. See also Case 60/85 *Vermoolen*, Judgment of July 7, 1986.

[4] *Ibid.*, para. 21 of judgment.

[5] The Court cites Case 24/75 *Petroni* [1975] E.C.R. 1149. And see cases at note 99, and *infra* at p. 258.

[6] *Ibid.*, at para. 22 of judgment.

principle which protects rights acquired under national law alone from the operation of the Community rules against overlapping is itself anomalous, and ripe for reconsideration by the Court.

Exceptions to the normal choice rules by agreement between Member States—Article 17

It is provided in Regulation 1408/71 that two or more Member States or the competent authorities of those States may, by common agreement, provide for exceptions to the choice rules normally applicable under the provisions discussed above, in the interest of certain workers or categories of workers.[7]

The *Brusse case*[8] is illustrative. The proceedings in the national court involved a Netherlands national who had originally worked in the Netherlands, but been employed and resident in the United Kingdom since 1964. Under the applicable choice of law rule he should have been subject to the social security legislation of the United Kingdom, but in fact he had remained affiliated to, and paid, voluntary contributions to the Netherlands scheme. The irregularity was discovered in 1977. The competent authorities decided to conclude an agreement under Article 17, whereby the person concerned was to be regarded as subject to the Netherlands social security scheme for the period ending on December 31, 1977, and thereafter regarded as being subject to the legislation of the United Kingdom.

On the basis of this agreement, the person concerned claimed family allowances under the law of the Netherlands for periods prior to December 31, 1977. Benefits were refused on the ground that it was not open to Member States to specify by agreement, with retroactive effect, the application of national legislation other than that stated to be applicable under the Community choice rules.

The Court of Justice held however that it was indeed open to the national authorities to derogate by agreement from the normally applicable choice rules, provided that the agreement was in the interest of the worker concerned. Furthermore, it followed in the court's view from the spirit and scheme of Article 17 that an agreement made thereunder must be capable of covering past periods, in order to remedy an existing situation the injustice of which appeared only after it had arisen. In view of the time needed for two or more Member States to reach agreement as to whether it was appropriate to derogate from the normal rules, Article 17 would be deprived of much of its meaning if the agreement could have only prospective effect.

Title III of Regulation 1408/71—special provisions relating to the various categories of benefits

Title III of Regulation 1408/71 contains eight chapters which lay down the special provisions applicable to the various categories of benefits listed

---

[7] Art. 17.
[8] Case 101/83. *Brusse* [1984] E.C.R. 2223.

in Article 4. The rules are somewhat complex, and must be read in the light of the implementing provisions of Regulation 574/72.[9] It is proposed to illustrate the operation of the Community rules by reference to three categories of benefits: sickness and maternity benefits, unemployment benefits, and old age pensions.

Chapter I of Title III (Article 18 to 36)—sickness and maternity benefits

Although the provisions of Chapter 1 are detailed, certain governing principles may be identified. The first is that of aggregation, whereby, according to Article 18(1) of the Regulation: "The competent institution of a Member State whose legislation makes the acquisition, retention or recovery of the right to benefits conditional upon the completion of insurance periods . . . shall, to the extent necessary, take account of insurance periods . . . completed under the legislation of any other Member State as if they were periods completed under the legislation which it administers."[10] The worker who is employed in several Member States may thus retain a continuous contribution record.

A further principle is that the provision of health and welfare services, for reasons of practicality, must be undertaken by the social security authorities of the country of residence of the worker, despite the fact that he may be affiliated to a social security institution in another Member State, where he is employed.

A third principle is that a worker should not be precluded from making claims for cash benefits against an insurance institution simply because he is resident in another Member State, and a fourth that the social security institution to which a worker is presently affiliated is in general liable for the costs of benefits provided to that worker, even if such benefits are in fact provided on its behalf by the social security authorities of another Member State.

Residence in a Member State other than that of social insurance affiliation

The application of the rules of Chapter 1 may be illustrated by reference to a hypothetical situation. Suppose a worker, a citizen of the United Kingdom and Colonies, is employed in the United Kingdom, and insured there as an employed person. He takes up permanent residence in Belgium, but is employed in France, returning home, on average, less than once a week (were he to return home every day, or on average once a week, he would be known as a "frontier worker")[11] In accordance with Article 13(2)(c) of the Regulation, he is subject to the social security legislation of France, and is insured thereunder as an employed person. The social security institution with which he is insured is termed, for the purposes of the Regulation, the "competent institution,"[12] and France, as the Member State in

---

[9] J.O. 1983 L230/6.
[10] See Art. 16 of Reg. 574/72, providing for certification of insurance periods by relevant social security institutions.
[11] Art. 1(b) of Reg. 1408/71.
[12] Art. 1(o) of Reg. 1408/71.

whose territory the competent institution is situated, is termed the "competent State."[13]

Suppose our hypothetical worker becomes ill, and is unable to work. He consults a doctor in Belgium, and is shortly afterwards admitted to hospital for a minor operation. His legal position under Regulation 1408/71 is as follows. His entitlement to benefit is governed by the legislation of the competent State (France). In the application of this legislation the competent institution will be obliged to take into account, to the extent necessary, any insurance periods completed under the legislation of any other Member State (the United Kingdom) as if they were periods completed under its own legislation. If the claimant satisfies the conditions imposed by French legislation to qualify for benefit, he will be entitled to receive, in the State in which he is resident (Belgium) the following[14]

> "(a) benefits in kind provided on behalf of the competent institution by the institution of the place of residence in accordance with the provisions of the legislation administered by that institution as though he were insured with it;
>
> (b) cash benefits provided by the competent institution in accordance with the legislation which it administers. However, by agreement between the competent institution and the institution of the place of residence, such benefits may be provided by the latter institution on behalf of the former, in accordance with the legislation of the competent State."

The distinction between benefits "in kind" and "cash benefits" requires explanation. The former benefits comprise not only health and welfare services administered under the terms of the relevant legislation, but also cash payments payable to reimburse the cost of such services for which the claimant has already been charged. "Cash benefits" are benefits payable to compensate for loss of earnings resulting from incapacity.[15]

The result of the application of the terms of Article 19 of the Regulation is thus that the claimant is entitled to such cash benefits as are provided under French law, from the institution of the competent State (France),[16] and to reimbursement, from the relevant Belgian institution, of the costs of medical care received. Such benefits "in kind" awarded by the Belgian institution must in turn be reimbursed by the competent French institution, unless there exists a reciprocal agreement between France and Belgium to waive such refunds.[17] Members of the worker's family resident in Belgium

---

[13] Art. 1(q) of Reg. 1408/71.

[14] Art. 19(1) of Reg. 1408/71.

[15] Case 61/65 *Vaassen* [1966] E.C.R. 261, at p. 278. Health benefits in kind calculated to improve or restore capacity to work have been classified as sickness benefits, rather than invalidity benefits: Case 69/79 *Jordens-Vosters* [1980] E.C.R. 75.

[16] Art. 18(8) of Reg. 574/72 provides: The competent institution shall pay cash benefits by the appropriate method, in particular by international money order, and shall inform the institution of the place of residence and the person concerned accordingly. Where cash benefits are paid by the institution of the place of residence on behalf of the competent institution the latter shall inform the person concerned of his rights and shall notify the institution of the place of residence of the amount of the cash benefits, the dates of payment, and the maximum period during which they should be granted, in accordance with the legislation of the competent State.

[17] Art. 36 of Reg. 1408/71.

would have an equal right to claim reimbursement of medical costs against the relevant Belgian institution,[18] again subject to reimbursement by the French institution.

It will be recalled that our hypothetical worker was accustomed to return home, on average, less than once a week. Were he to return daily, he would be classed as a frontier worker, and would have the right, in urgent cases, to claim benefits in the territory of the competent State, as would members of his family.[19]

The above legal position would be identical if our hypothetical migrant were self-employed.

Medical care and benefits during a visit to another Member State and visits for the purpose of medical treatment

In two cases sickness and maternity benefits may be claimed by an employed or self-employed person or a member of his family during a visit to a Member State other than the competent State or State of residence. First, where the condition of such a person or a member of his family necessitates immediate benefits during a stay in the territory of another Member State.[20] Secondly, where an employed or self-employed person or a member of his family is authorised by the competent institution to go to the territory of another Member State to receive treatment appropriate to his condition.[21]

It is the first provision which enables employed and self-employed persons and members of their families to claim the benefit of the various health services of the Member States while on holiday, despite the fact that their travel is quite unconnected with the employment of a worker or the professional or trade activities of a self-employed person.

Further consideration is necessary of the circumstances in which a person may be authorised to go to another Member State to seek medical treatment. Article 22(1) provides that an employed or self-employed person who satisfies the conditions of the legislation of the competent State for entitlement to benefits, taking into account where appropriate the provisions of Article 18 (which deals with the aggregation of insurance periods) and

"(c) who is authorised by the competent institution to go to the territory of another Member State to receive there treatment appropriate to his condition, shall be entitled:
(i) to benefits in kind provided on behalf of the competent institution by the institution of the place of stay or residence in accordance with the provisions of the legislation which it administers, as though he were insured with it; the length of the period during which benefits are provided shall be governed, however, by the legislation of the competent State;
(ii) to cash benefits provided by the competent institution in

---

[18] Art. 19(2) of Reg. 1408/71.
[19] Art. 20 of Reg. 1408/71. An odd result. Our worker's connection with the competent State is closer.
[20] Art. 22(1)(*a*); Art. 22(3). Benefits in kind and cash benefits are covered.
[21] Art. 22(1)(*c*); Art. 22(3). Benefits in kind and cash benefits are covered.

accordance with the provisions of the legislation which it administers. However, by agreement between the competent institution and the institution of the place of stay or residence, such benefits may be provided by the latter institution on behalf of the former, in accordance with the provisions of the legislation of the competent State."

The Court has had occasion to rule on the scope of Article 22(1)(c) in the two *Pierik* cases.[22] In the first case the Court described Article 22 as "one of the measures intended to permit a worker [self-employed persons are of course now included] who is a national of a Member State of the Community, without regard to the national institution to which he is affiliated or the place of his residence, to receive benefits in kind provided in any other Member State."

The Court in the first *Pierik* case clarified the scope of Article 22(1)(c) as follows:

— the benefits in kind referred to covered all treatment calculated to be effective for the sickness or disease from which the person concerned suffered;
— a person was not restricted to those benefits in the State to which he went for treatment to which he was entitled in the State in which he was insured;
— the costs relating to benefits in kind provided on behalf of the competent institution by the institution of the place of stay were to be fully refunded, in accordance with Article 36(1) of Regulation 1408/71.[23]

At the time of the first *Pierik* ruling, Article 22(2) provided that the authorisation referred to above might not be refused where the treatment in question could not be provided for the person concerned within the territory of the Member State in which he resided. Also in issue in the *Pierik* case were the circumstances in which authorisation might be refused by the competent institution.

The Court held that the power to refuse authorisation to a worker to receive treatment abroad was limited by the requirement that the person concerned should be guaranteed the opportunity of receiving treatment appropriate to his state of health provided in any Member State, whatever the place of his residence or the Member State to which the social security institution to which he was affiliated belonged. Thus the provision that authorisation be not refused where the treatment in question was unavailable in the State of residence implied that the authorisation might similarly not be refused in cases in which the treatment was *less effective* than that which the person concerned could receive in another Member State. This principle is reinforced by the current text of Article 22(2) second subparagraph which provides that the authorisation required under paragraph (1)(c):

---

[22] Case 117/77 [1978] E.C.R. 825, Wyatt, (1978) 3 E.L.Rev. 394; Case 182/78 [1979] E.C.R. 1977, Wyatt, (1981) 6 E.L.Rev. 47.
[23] Art. 36(1) provides that "benefits in kind provided in accordance with the provisions of this Chapter by the institution of one Member State on behalf of the institution of another Member State shall be fully refunded."

"may not be refused where the treatment in question is among the benefits provided for by the legislation of the Member State on whose territory the person concerned resides and where he cannot be given such treatment within the time normally necessary for obtaining the treatment in question in the Member State of residence taking account of his current state of health and the probable course of the disease."

In the second *Pierik* case the Court was asked whether Article 22(1)(*c*) also covered cases in which the treatment requested was excluded from the scheme of benefits in kind available under the legislation of the competent State on medical, medical-ethical or financial grounds. The Court noted that its decision in the first *Pierik* case implicitly acknowledged that it was for the competent institution objectively to assess the medical grounds for granting or refusing authorisation, having regard *inter alia* to the state of health of the person concerned, the seriousness of his sickness or disease and the effectiveness of the treatment in question. Financial considerations, it seems, do not enter into the equation.

The court was also asked in the second *Pierik* case whether the right to an authorisation by the competent State, and the right to treatment in the Member State of ensuing temporary residence, only applied to benefits to which there was a *right* under the latter State's social security rules, or if it was enough that there was a discretion to grant it. The Court emphasised that the competent institution was bound to refund the costs of treatment in the Member State of stay. Since the costs relating to the treatment in question were chargeable to the competent institution which granted the authorisation, the institution of the Member State to which the person concerned went to receive the treatment was required to provide it upon presentation of such an authorisation, even if, under the legislation which it administered, it did not have a duty, but only a power to grant it.

The Court's ruling on this final point is clearly open to some implicit qualification. The United Kingdom Government, in the course of proceedings before the European Court, observed that Article 22(1)(*c*) did extend to discretionary benefits in the second State, but argued that the institution in question would have the discretion to grant or withhold the treatment in question, so long as it acted on the same basis as it would in deciding whether or not to grant such treatment to a national of its own Member State insured with that institution. The Commission concurred, expressing the view that the institution must apply the same criteria to workers and their families from other Member States as to workers insured with it, *e.g.* the criteria of urgency, or placing on a waiting list.

These observations are in our view correct. Regulation 1408/71 seeks to coordinate national social security systems, and eliminate discrimination on grounds of nationality. Thus, Article 22 may allow the institution of one Member State (the competent State) to take a financial decision binding upon the institution of another Member State (the State of subsequent temporary residence). Again, neither financial decision nor medical decisions can be taken on the basis of the nationality of the claimant/patient. What Article 22 does not and cannot do, is bind the State of temporary residence to provide medical treatment to a patient in circumstances where the responsible medical staff of that State would not give such treatment to a national in analogous circumstances, on medical grounds, on ethical grounds, on the ground that more urgent cases of that type demanded priority, or on the ground that the time of medical staff ought not, for some fixed or indeterminate period, be devoted to certain kinds of medical treatment at all, *e.g.* heart transplants.

Calculation of cash benefits

The social security authorities of the competent State, in applying its legislation, are required to take into account insurance periods completed under the legislation of other Member States.[24] However, if its legislation provides for the calculation of cash benefits on the basis of average earnings or average contributions, such average earnings or contributions shall be determined exclusively by reference to earnings or contributions under *its* legislation.[25] Again, if its legislation provides that the calculation of cash benefits shall be based on standard earnings, it must take account exclusively of the standard earnings, or where appropriate, the average of standard earnings for the periods completed under its legislation.[26]

Where cash benefits vary with the number of members of the family, the social security authorities of the competent State must take into account members of the employed or self-employed person's family resident in the territory of other Member States.[27]

Chapter 3 of Title III (Articles 44 to 51)—old age and death pensions

Aggregation and apportionment

The provisions of Regulation 1408/71 dealing with pension entitlement are based on the principle of aggregation and apportionment. The principle of aggregation is by now familiar, and requires the social security authorities of one Member State to take into account periods of insurance completed under the legislation of another.[28] Apportionment is the other side of the coin: the rights acquired under successive social security schemes are rights against the social security institutions under whose law insurance periods were in fact completed. The rationale of aggregation is that without it the migrant's contribution record might be inadequate to sustain a right to a pension; the rationale of apportionment that the cost of pensions be borne proportionately to contributions received.

Once again, a hypothetical example is illustrative. Suppose a migrant is employed in France, and then in Germany, where he retires, having completed insurance periods in both countries. He presents a claim to the relevant social security institution in each country, and each institution

---

[24] Art. 18 of Reg. 1408/71.
[25] Art. 23(1).
[26] Art. 23(2).
[27] Art. 23(3).
[28] Art. 45 contemplates aggregation of insurance periods only for the purpose of the acquisition, retention or recovery of the right to benefits. As such it does not deal with affiliation to social security schemes, which is governed by national law. Case 266/78 *Brunori* [1979] E.C.R. 2705, Wyatt, (1981) 6 E.L.Rev. 41; Case 110/79 *Coonan* [1980] E.C.R. 1445, Watson, (1980) 5 E.L.Rev. 220.

proceeds as follows.[29] First, it calculates the total number of insurance periods completed by the worker in France and Germany, and estimates the amount of benefit to which he would have been entitled had he completed all such periods under its law. Secondly, it determines what proportion of the total insurance periods completed in both Member States constituted insurance periods completed under its legislation. Finally, it awards a pension equal to the proportion so determined of the total benefit which would have been payable had all periods in fact been completed under its legislation. To put the most simple case, suppose our migrant had been employed for ten years in France, and for ten years in Germany. The relevant institution in each Member State would calculate the pension payable under its law to a claimant who had contributed for 20 years, and award a pension equal to half that amount.

Sanctity of pension rights acquired under national law

Although the object of aggregation and apportionment is to improve the lot of the migrant, it could on occasion lead to his receiving a smaller pension from a particular institution than would in any event be payable under national law alone, independently of Community rules. This can happen, *e.g.* when a pension is calculated on the basis of a basic rate plus a sliding scale graduated according to contributions paid. The Court, in a series of decision on the application of Regulation 3,[30] held the process of aggregation and apportionment to be impermissible in such circumstances. The *Niemann* case[31] is illustrative. The claimant had completed periods of insurance under French and German legislation. Under German law alone, Mr. Niemann would have been entitled to a monthly pension of DM 1142.77, but the Germany authorities applied the process of aggregation and apportionment laid down in Articles 27 and 28 of Regulation 3, and awarded a monthly pension of DM 1001.11. The Court held that the aim of Articles 48–51 of the Treaty would not be attained if, as a consequence of the exercise of their right of freedom of movement, workers were to lose advantages in the field of social security guaranteed to them in any event by the laws of a single Member State. "The aggregation and apportionment provided for by Articles 27 and 28 . . . ," declared the Court, "cannot therefore be carried out if their effect is to diminish the benefits which the person concerned may claim by virtue of the laws of a single Member State on the basis solely of the insurance periods completed under these laws, always provided, that this methods cannot lead to a duplication of benefits for one and the same period."[32]

The detailed scheme of Regulation 1408/71

The procedure for apportionment laid down in Article 46 of Regulation 1408/71 is as follows:

---

[29] Arts. 27 and 28 of Reg. 3, and Arts. 45 and 46 of Reg. 1408/71. All claims may be submitted via the institution of the place of residence, see Art. 36 of Reg. 574/72.
[30] See, *e.g.* Case 1/67 *Ciechelski* [1967] E.C.R. 181; Case 2/67 *de Moor* [1967] E.C.R. 197; Case 22/67 *Goffart* [1967] E.C.R. 321; Case 140/73 *Mancuso* [1973] E.C.R. 1449.
[31] Case 191/73 [1974] E.C.R. 571.
[32] [1974] E.C.R. 571, at p. 579.

1. where a worker is entitled to benefits under the law of a Member State without recourse to Community law, the institution of that State shall so calculate his benefits (Article 46(1), first sub-paragraph);

2. where a worker is entitled to benefits under the law of a Member State, but his entitlement is less than the maximum, aggregation and apportionment may enable him to claim a higher rate of benefit. Where this is the case, the institution shall take into consideration the higher rate (Articles 46(1), second sub-paragraph, and Article 46(2)(a) and (b));

3. where a worker is entitled to no benefits at all under the law of a Member State, without recourse to Community law, the institution of the State concerned shall aggregate all insurance periods, and apportion the pension which would have been payable had all such periods been completed under its law (Article 46(2)(a) and (b)).[33]

National legislation may contain rules which reduce the pension payable under national law, to take account of a pension payable under the legislation of another country (these are known as rules against overlapping). The calculation to be undertaken under Article 46(1) of Regulation 1408/71, referred to above, is undertaken *without regard to such national rules against overlapping*.[34] The Court has held that "the amount referred to in Article 46(1) is the amount to which worker would be entitled under national legislation if he were not in receipt of a pension by virtue of the legislation of another Member State."[35]

Just as application of the process of aggregation and apportionment can in some cases lead to reduction of a pension payable in any event under national law, so it has the effect in others of entitling a migrant to several pensions, payable by the institutions of several Member States, which exceed in total the amount which would have been payable had the worker spent his entire working life in any one of the countries concerned! It was to counter this "new discrimination" that the Council adopted Article 46(3) of Regulation 1408/71, which provides that the total sum payable under the terms of Article 46(1) and (2) must not exceed the highest amount of pension that would have been payable had all insurance periods been payable under the laws of a single Member State. In the event of this ceiling being exceeded, the paragraph provides that any institution applying Article 46(1), *i.e.* any institution receiving a claim from a worker who is entitled to benefit without the need for aggregation (even if such entitlement is to less than the maximum amount available), must make a deduction from the pension payable. Reasonable as this limitation may seem, it is clear that on occasion its application can lead to a reduction of rights acquired under national law independently of Community rules—a reduction which would arguably conflict with Articles 48 and 51 of the Treaty.

---

[33] Special national rules designed to reduce the theoretical amount determined under Article 46(2) of Reg. 1408/71 are incompatible with that provision, Case 274/81 *Besem* [1982] E.C.R. 2995.

[34] See Art. 12(2) of Reg. 1408/71; Cases 116, etc./80, *Celestre* [1981] E.C.R. 1737; Case 58/84, *Romano* Judgment of June 4, 1985; Case 117/84 *Ruzzu* Judgment of June 4, 1985; *Sinatra* Judgment of March 13, 1986.

[35] See Cases 116, etc./80, *Celestre*; Case 58/84 *Romano*; Case 117/84 *Ruzzu*; note 34.

The point was argued before the Court in *Petroni*.[36] The claimant was entitled, under Belgian law, to a pension, and he was also entitled, after aggregation and apportionment, to an Italian pension. The total of the Belgian and Italian pensions was, however, in excess of the pension which would have been payable had Mr. Petroni completed all his insurance periods in Belgium. Applying Article 46(3) of the Regulation, the Belgian authorities reduced the pension which was otherwise payable under Article 46(1), and entitlement to which arose exclusively under Belgian law. The Court of Justice, repeating its reasoning in the *Niemann* case, held that Article 46(3), to the extent to which it operated to reduce rights acquired independently of Community rules, was incompatible with Article 51 of the Treaty. Article 46(3) will still have some effect, but only to the extent to which it provides for the limitation of rights acquired under Community law.

In some circumstances a migrant might be better off renouncing the protection of Article 46 (along with its rule against overlapping contained in Article 46(3)), and claiming a pension exclusively on the basis of national law, *including its rules against overlapping* (*i.e.*, including national rules providing for the reduction of the claimant's pension to take account of pension rights arising under the law of other Member States). The Court has held that such a course is always open to the migrant.[37]

The Court has on several times affirmed its reasoning in *Petroni*,[38] and has denied that limiting the effect of Article 46(3) can lead to discrimination in *favour* of migrants, arguing as follows:

> "The charge that migrant workers obtain an advantage over workers who have left their country cannot be accepted, since no discrimination can arise in legal situations which are not comparable."[39]

This view is open to criticism. It hardly seems consistent with the Court's ruling in the *Pinna* case,[40] in which one ground on which the Court annulled Article 73(2) of Regulation 1408/71 was that it discriminated between migrants working in France on the one hand, and French workers working in France on the other, by selecting the law governing the availability of family allowances by reference to the Member State of residence of their families. Furthermore, the purpose of the Treaty is to provide a single market between the Member States, to assimilate economic activity within the 12 to economic activity within one, and to neutralise the effect of national frontiers. Freedom of movement entails the right to move or not to move. A legal regime which favours one over the other no more furthers free movement than export subsidies favour free trade. However, the Court seems set in its view.

---

[36] Case 24/75 [1975] E.C.R. 1149. Note that a pension arising under national law plus Article 10(1) of Regulation 1408/71 nevertheless arises under national law alone for the purposes of the *Petroni* rule; Case 32/77 *Guiliani* [1977] E.C.R. 1857.

[37] Case 236/78 *Mura* [1979] E.C.R. 1819; Case 238/81 *Van der Bunt-Craig* [1983] E.C.R. 1385; Case 296/84 *Sinatra* Judgment of March 13, 1986.

[38] Case 62/76 *Strehl* [1977] E.C.R. 211; Case 112/76 *Manzoni* [1977] E.C.R. 1647.

[39] Case 22/77 *Mura* 1699, at p. 1707.

[40] Case 41/84 Judgment of January 15, 1986.

Supplement payable to ensure minimum payable in State of residence

The Regulation places an additional responsibility on the authorities of the State of residence, over and above that to pay an apportioned pension under the provisions of Articles 45 and 46. If a migrant resides in the territory of a Member State, and is in receipt of a pension under its legislation, the social security authorities of that State must ensure that the total benefits received under the provisions of Articles 45 and 46 amount to no less than the minimum pension prescribed by national law for insurance periods equal to all the insurance periods taken into account for the purposes of aggregation. The social security authorities must pay, if necessary, a supplement equal to the difference between the total of the benefits due under Articles 45 and 46, and the amount of the minimum benefit.[41]

The minimum pension referred to is a benefit which amounts to a specific guarantee the object of which is to ensure for recipients of social security benefits a minimum income which is in excess of the amount of benefit which they may claim solely on the basis of their periods of insurance and contributions.[42]

Revalorisation and recalculation of pension

If, in a Member State paying a pension under Articles 45 and 46, the rules governing the method of calculating pension entitlement are changed, a recalculation of the pension payable must be made on the basis of Article 46.[43] However, if benefits are simply increased by a fixed percentage or amount, to compensate for cost of living increases or changes in the level of wages or salaries or the like, this increase must be applied directly to the benefits determined under Article 46, without the need for a recalculation.[44]

The purpose of these provisions is to exclude a fresh calculation (and thereby reduce the burden upon the administration) when the alterations in benefits result from events which are unconnected with the personal circumstances of the insured person and are the consequences of the "general evolution of the economic and social situation."[45] But such exclusion may not be extended to changes in the *personal circumstances* of the insured person, such as the fact that his spouse is now earning, so as to require reduction of his pension to the "single" rather than "household" rate.[46]

By the same token, a recalculation of a pension payable in one Member State is not necessary in order to take account of a cost of living increase in a benefit—even of a different type—in another Member State, the level of which influenced the amount at which the pension was originally fixed, by virtue of the application of the national rules against overlapping.[47]

---

[41] Art. 50 of Reg. 1408/71. See Case 64/77 *Torri* [1977] E.C.R. 2299.
[42] Case 22/81 *Browning* [1981] E.C.R. 3357.
[43] Art. 51(2) of Reg. 1408/71.
[44] Art. 51(1) of Reg. 1408/71.
[45] Case 7/81 *Sinatra* [1982] E.C.R. 137, para. 10.
[46] Case 7/81, note 45.
[47] Case 104/83 *Cinciuolo* [1984] E.C.R. 1286.

Chapter 6 of Title III (Articles 67 to 71)—unemployment

Aggregation

Where the law of the competent State conditions benefits on the completion of periods of insurance, the competent institution shall take into account:

— periods of insurance completed under the law of any other Member State;

— periods of *employment* completed under the legislation of any other Member State and treated as periods of *insurance* under that legislation;

— periods of *employment* completed under the legislation of any other Member State, and treated *as such* under that legislation, provided that such periods are recognised as insurance periods under the law of the competent State.[48]

Where the legislation of the competent State conditions benefits on the completion of periods of employment, it shall take into account periods of insurance or employment completed as an employed person under the legislation of any other Member State, as though they were periods of employment completed under the legislation which it administers.[49]

Unemployed persons going to a Member State other than the competent State

Articles 69 and 70 of the Regulation provide an invaluable corollary to the right of a worker to enter the territory of a Member State in order to seek employment therein: the right to receive employment benefit during his stay.

A worker who is wholly unemployed and who satisfies the conditions of the legislation of a Member State for entitlement to benefits, and who goes to one or more other Member States seeking employment, retains his right to benefit, providing that he complies with certain requirements. Before leaving the competent State, he must have been registered with the employment services therein, and have remained available for work for at least four weeks after becoming unemployed.[50] Upon registration with the employment services of another Member State, in which he is seeking employment, the worker is entitled to receive benefits from the relevant social security authorities.[51] These benefits must be reimbursed by the authorities of the State where the worker was last employed, unless the State providing benefits waives such reimbursement.[52] Benefit is payable for a period of three months from the date when the worker concerned ceased to be available to the employment services of the State under the law of which he was originally entitled to benefit, provided that he does not

---

[48] Art. 67(1) of Reg. 1408/71; Case 126/77 *Frangiamore* [1978] E.C.R. 725.
[49] Art. 67(2) of Reg. 1408/71.
[50] Unless this requirement is waived by the authorities of the competent State; Art. 69(1)(*a*).
[51] Art. 69(1)(*b*). The worker is considered registered for the period prior to registration provided he registers within seven days of his ceasing to be available to the employment services of the State which he left.
[52] Art. 70(1), (3), of Regulation 1408/71.

receive benefits for a longer period than that during which he would have been entitled had he remained in that State.[53] If a worker returns to the competent State within three months, he maintains his entitlement in that State.[54]

The Court has held that these provisions have no application to an unemployed person who has never been in employment and never been treated as an unemployed person under the relevant national legislation.[55]

The State to which an unemployed worker goes seeking work, and where he is entitled to unemployment benefits under national law alone, independently of the Community rules, may not deny him benefit on the ground that he has not complied with the procedures referred to above.[56]

An unemployed worker who fails to return to the competent State before the expiry of the period during which he is entitled to benefits "shall lose all entitlement to benefits under the legislation of the competent State. . . . In exceptional cases, the time limit may be extended by the competent services or institution."[57]

In *Coccioli*[58] the Court held that "exceptional cases" might be of such a nature as to prevent not only the return of the worker but also the lodging of a request for benefit. In the Court's view national authorities were free to take into account all relevant factors in assessing "exceptional cases," and it was quite permissible to consider a request for an extension made after the expiry of the period referred to above.

It will be recalled that the Court has held in a number of cases, notably the *Petroni* case,[59] that it would be inconsistent with Articles 48 to 51 of the Treaty for Regulation 1408/71 to diminish rights acquired under national law and independently of the Community rules. In *Testa*,[60] the question arose whether Article 69(2) was on this ground inconsistent with the Treaty. Workers in receipt of unemployment benefit in Germany went to Italy to seek work, but returned to Germany after the expiry of the applicable three month period. Under German law they were still entitled to benefit, but benefit was refused on the basis of Article 69(2) of Regulation 1408/71. In reply to a question concerning the validity of Article 69(2), the Court of Justice upheld that provision, and distinguished the *Petroni* case. Article 69, held the Court, conferred on a person availing himself of that provision an advantage as compared with a person who remains in the competent State. He is freed for a period of three months of the duty to make himself available to the employment services of the competent State and be subject to the control procedure organised therein, even though he must register with the employment services of the Member State to which he goes. The Court concluded:

"As part of a special system of rules which gives rights to workers

[53] Art. 69(1)(c) of Reg. 1408/71.
[54] Art. 69(2).
[55] Case 66/7 *Kuyken* [1977] E.C.R. 2311; cited in Case 238/83 *Meade* [1984] E.C.R. 2631, para. 9 of Judgment.
[56] Case 27/75 *Bonaffini* [1975] E.C.R. 971.
[57] Art. 69(2) of Reg. 1408/71.
[58] Case 139/78 [1979] E.C.R. 991, Watson, (1979) 4 E.L.Rev. 367.
[59] Case 24/75 [1975] E.C.R. 1149, see *supra*, at p. 258.
[60] Cases 41/79, 121/79, 769/79, [1980] E.C.R. 1979.

which they would not otherwise have, Article 69(2) cannot therefore be equated with the provisions held invalid by the Court in . . . *Petroni* . . . to the extent to which their effect was to cause workers to lose advantages in the field of social security guaranteed to them in any event by the legislation of a single Member State."[61]

In our view the *Testa* decision is a reasonable one, and its reasoning persuasive. It is surely open to the Community legislature to limit rights under national law in return for the grant of rights under Community law; in particular where the person concerned may choose whether or not to avail himself of his rights under Community law at the outset. But are the provisions dealt with in the *Petroni* case really so very different? Could not analogous reasoning justify a literal construction and lawful application of Article 46(3) of Regulation 1408/71? A claimant could always enjoy rights under national law alone unless he sought to supplement those rights by recourse to aggregation and apportionment in order to secure parallel pension rights in other Member States, in which case he would be obliged in appropriate circumstances to accept the application of Article 46(3) even to a pension acquired under national law alone. *Petroni* however, may be too long established to be undermined by contrary argument.

Unemployed persons resident in the territory of a Member State other than the competent State during last employment

A wholly unemployed worker who is resident in a State other than the competent State has an option open to him. If he remains available to the employment services in the competent State, he is entitled to receive unemployment benefit in accordance with its law, at its expense, as though he were residing there.[62] If, on the other hand, he makes himself available for work to the employment services of the State in which he resides, he is entitled to receive benefits in accordance with the legislation of that State, at its expense, as if he had last been employed there.[63] However, if such a worker has acquired a right to benefits in the competent State, his rights in the State of residence are governed by Article 69 of the Regulation, and any right to benefit under the legislation of the State of residence is suspended as long as he is so entitled.[64]

The Court has held that Article 71(1)(*b*)(ii) of Regulation 1408/71, which allows workers to claim benefits in their State of residence rather than of last employment, must be interpreted strictly, as an exception to the general rule that workers are entitled to claim unemployment benefit exclusively from the authorities of the Member State in which they were last employed. Transfer of liability to the Member State of residence is justified only where the worker has retained close ties with the country where he is settled and habitually resident. For the purpose of applying the pro-

---

[61] Cases 41/79, etc. [1980] E.C.R. 1979, at para. [15] of Judgment.
[62] Art. 71(1)(*b*)(i) of Reg. 1408/71.
[63] Art. 71(1)(*b*)(ii) of Reg. 1408/71. The worker is bound by this election and may not claim benefit in the competent State on the basis of registration as an employed person in the State of residence; Case 227/81 *Aubin* [1982] E.C.R. 1991.
[64] Art. 71(1)(*b*)(ii).

vision in question, account must be taken of the length and continuity of a worker's residence, the length and purpose of his absence in the State of employment, the nature of his occupation and "the intention of the person concerned as it appears from all the circumstances." Whenever a worker has a stable employment in a Member State there is a presumption that he resides there, even if he has left his family in another State. It is for the national authorities concerned to locate the "habitual centre of his interests."[65]

Frontier workers, it will be recalled, are those employed in one Member State and reside in another, returning as a rule daily, or at least once a week. If such a worker is wholly unemployed, he is entitled to receive benefits in accordance with the legislation of the State where he resides, at its expense, as though he had been subject to that legislation while last employed.[66]

An unemployed worker entitled to benefits under Article 71 in the State of residence may not rely on Article 69 of Regulation 1408/71 so as to claim unemployment benefit in the State where he was last employed. Article 69 only applies to persons going to a Member State *other than the competent State*, and the Member State of last employment is still the competent State in this context, despite the entitlement of the unemployed person to benefit in the State of residence.[67]

Calculation of benefits

If the legislation of a Member State provides that benefits should be calculated on the basis of a worker's previous earnings, the previous earnings which must be taken into account are those received by the person concerned in respect of his last employment in that State. If the worker has been employed there for less than four weeks, benefits must be calculated on the basis of the normal wage in the place of residence for work similar to that of his last employment in another Member State.[68]

The abovementioned provisions have no application to a frontier worker, in whose case the competent institution should take into account the salary earned in the Member State where he was last employed.[69]

Where the legislation of a Member State provides that the amount of benefits should vary with the number of members of the family, the social security authorities must take into account any members of the family who are residing in other Member States. An exception is made where another person is entitled to unemployment benefits in respect of the same members of the family in their country of residence.[70]

---

[65] Case 76/76 *Di Paolo* [1977] E.C.R. 315.
[66] Art. 71(1)(*a*)(ii) of Reg. 1408/71. The unemployed person may claim only in the Member State of residence even if entitled under the legislation of the Member State of last employment. However, if he has maintained links favouring his employment prospects in the Member State where he was last employed, he must not be regarded as a frontier worker, and Art. 71(1)(*b*) applies: Case 1/85 *Miethe*, Judgment of June 12, 1986.
[67] Case 145/84 *Cochet* [1985] E.C.R. 2801.
[68] Art. 68(1) of Reg. 1408/71.
[69] Case 67/79 *Fellinger* [1980] E.C.R. 535.
[70] Art. 68(2) of Reg. 1408/71.

Overlapping of benefits

The purpose of Regulation 1408/71 is to ensure that employed and self-employed persons are not prejudiced by exercising their right of free movement; it is not to ensure that they are placed in a more favourable position. Accordingly, Article 12(1) of the Regulation provides:

> "This Regulation can neither confer nor maintain the right to several benefits of the same kind for one and the same period of compulsory insurance. However, this provision shall not apply to benefits in respect of invalidity, old-age, death (pensions) or occupational disease which are awarded by the institutions of two or more Member States, in accordance with the provisions of Arts. . . . 46 etc."

In the case of pensions, the overlapping which would arise from simple aggregation is qualified by apportionment, though the migrant may nevertheless acquire a right to several pensions under the laws of several Member States, which exceed in sum the total pension which would have been payable had he spent his entire working life in any one Member State. This is a form of "overlapping"; the migrant is in effect being credited with fictional insurance periods under one legislation while actual periods were in fact completed under another.[71] It was to counter such overlapping that the Council adopted Article 46(3) of Regulation 1408/71. As we have seen, however, it is only applicable to the extent that it operates to diminish rights acquired under the Regulation—not to diminish rights acquired under national law independently of the Community rules.[72]

National legislation may contain rules designed to reduce benefits paid under national law to take account of (a) other benefits paid under national law (so-called internal rules against overlapping), or (b) benefits paid under the laws of other countries (so-called external rules against overlapping). Article 12(2) of Regulation 1408/71 accordingly provides:

> "The provisions of the legislation of a Member State for reduction, suspension or withdrawal of benefit in cases of overlapping with other social security benefits or other income may be invoked even though the right to such benefits was acquired under the legislation of another Member State or such income arises in the territory of another Member State. However, this provision shall not apply when the person concerned receives benefits of the same kind in respect of invalidity, old-age, death (pensions) or occupational disease which are awarded by the institutions of two or more Member States in accordance with the provisions of Arts. 46 . . . etc."[73]

It follows from the second sentence of Article 12(2) that in calculating the amount of pension payable under national law for the purposes of Article 46(1) of Regulation 1408/71, national rules for the reduction of a

---

[71] On the assumption that a full pension represents a life-time's deferred earnings which may, for reasons of equity, be paid to a worker who has completed insurance periods for only a fraction of his working life.

[72] See *supra*, at p. 258.

[73] Art. 11(2) of Reg. 3 was in similar terms. For a limiting provision of national law falling outside the scope of Art. 12(2), see Case 79/81 *Baccini* [1982] E.C.R. 1063.

pension to take account of a pension arising in another Member State are to be left out of account.[74]

The Court has held that a national provision which reduces notional additional years of employment normally accredited to a worker by the number of years in respect of which he may claim a pension in another Member State constitutes a provision for the reduction of benefit within the meaning of Article 12(2) which, by virtue of the second sentence of that Article, must not be applied when the amount of pension is calculated under Article 46(1) of Regulation 1408/71.[75]

It is always open to a migrant, however, to opt for a pension payable under national law alone, including national rules against overlapping, where that pension is greater than that which would be payable under the provisions of Article 46 of Regulation 1408/71.[76] Thus it may be advantageous to a migrant to opt for pension payable under national law alone, and subject to a deduction under national overlapping rules, rather than for a higher pension payable under the rules for aggregation and apportionment, the advantage of which in the particular case is eliminated by the application of Article 46(3) of Regulation 1408/71.

It may sometimes be a matter of some difficulty to determine whether benefits are indeed of the *same kind* for the purposes of the second sentence of Article 12(2).[77]

The first sentence of Article 12(2) has the effect of allowing the national authorities of a Member State to rely on an *internal* rule against overlapping (that is to say, a rule calculated to suspend or reduce one national benefit to take account of another) in a case where the second benefit arises under the law of another Member State. However, Article 12(2) can only be invoked to "transform" an internal overlapping rule into an external rule (that is to say, a rule calculated to suspend or reduce a national benefit to take account of a benefit arising under the law of another country) where the benefit to be suspended or reduced arises as a result of the operation of the Community rules.[78] In cases where the benefit to be suspended or reduced arises under national law independently of the Community rules, Article 12(2) cannot be relied upon to transform an internal rule against overlapping into an external rule.[79] This is because, according to the Court in *Jerzak*, Article 12(2) constitutes:

> " . . . the counterpart of the advantages which Community law affords workers in enabling them to require the social security legislation of more than one Member State to be applied simultaneously.

---

[74] See, *e.g.* Cases 116, etc./80, *Celestre* [1981] E.C.R. 1737. See *supra* at p. 257.

[75] Case 58/84 *Romano* Judgment of June 4, 1985

[76] See, *e.g.* Case 236/78 *Mura* E.C.R. 1819; *supra* at p. 258.

[77] Case 4/80 *D'Amico* [1980] E.C.R. 2951 (invalidity benefits converted into old-age pensions and unconverted invalidity benefits of same kind); Case 171/81 *Valentini* [1983] E.C.R. 2157 (guaranteed income allowance not of same kind as old-age pension, and national rules against overlapping apply).

[78] Case 184/73 *Kaufmann* [1974] E.C.R. 517. A decision on the scope of Art. 11(2) of Reg. 3. It is immaterial whether the benefit of which account is taken arises under national law or under the Community rules, *per* Advocate General Warner, at p. 531.

[79] Case 34/69 *Duffy* [1969] E.C.R. 597 (a decision on Art. 11(2) of Reg. 3); Case 279/82 *Jerzak* [1983] E.C.R. 2603.

Its purpose is to prevent them from deriving advantages from that possibility which in national law are considered excessive.

However, although the Court has consistently held that limitations may be imposed on migrant workers to balance the social security advantages which they derive from the Community regulations and which they could not obtain without them, the aim of Articles 48 to 51 of the Treaty would not be attained if the social security advantages which a worker may derive from the legislation of a single Member State were to be withdrawn or reduced as a result of the application of those regulations."[80]

However, where a national *external* overlapping rule is concerned, a benefit acquired under national law alone may, consistently with the first sentence of Article 12(2) of Regulation 1408/71, be suspended or reduced to take account of benefits arising under the laws of other Member States.[81]

Social security authorities are furthermore entitled to invoke provisions of national law for the reduction, suspension or withdrawal of benefit in the case of persons in receipt of invalidity benefits or anticipatory old age benefits who are pursuing a professional or trade activity, even though they are pursuing such activity in another Member State.[82]

Subrogation

Article 93(1) of Regulation 1408/71[83] provides that if a person is in receipt of benefit under the legislation of one Member State in respect of an injury in another, and is entitled to claim compensation for that injury from a third party in the latter State's territory, any right of subrogation vested in the institution[84] liable for payment of benefit under the law applicable to it shall be recognised in the other Member States. Thus if a worker is killed in France by the negligence of a third party, and as a result his widow receives a pension from a German social security institution, the latter may be subrogated, in accordance with German law, to the widow's rights against the tortfeasor in France. These were indeed the facts of the *Töpfer* case,[85] in which the widow received a pension from the German social security institution, and was subsequently successful in her claim in France against the tortfeasor and his insurance company. The German social security institution claimed from Mrs. Töpfer's damages a sum equivalent to *all* the pension payments to which Mrs. Töpfer had become entitled, including payments in respect of periods after Mr. Töpfer would

---

[80] Case 279/82 [1983] E.C.R. 2603, at paras. 10 to 12 of the Judgment.
[81] Case 171/82 *Valentini* [1983] E.C.R. 2157.
[82] Art. 12(3) of Reg. 1408/71.
[83] Superseding Art. 52 of Reg. 3. On the interpretation of Art. 52, see Case 31/64 *Bertholet* [1965] E.C.R. 81; Case 33/64 *van Dijk* [1965] E.C.R. 97; Case 44/65 *Maison Singer* [1965] E.C.R. 965; Case 27/69 *Assurance generale* [1969] E.C.R. 405; Case 78/82 *de Waal* [1973] E.C.R. 499.
[84] The term "institution" in Art. 93 means the body or social security authority responsible for administering all or part of a Member State's social security legislation, and it does not include a private insurance company which has indemnified an assured under an ordinary insurance policy; Case 313/82 *NV Tiel Utrecht* [1984] E.C.R. 1389.
[85] Case 72/76 [1977] E.C.R. 271.

have attained pensionable age, and received a pension in any event. This claim was based on German law, which permitted such recovery by way of subrogation in order to prevent an injured party recovering both a pension *and* full damages in respect of the same loss. French law, less concerned with the prospect of unjust enrichment of the injured party, only allowed recovery by way of subrogation of such pension payments as had been made as a result of the action of the tortfeasor. Thus payments made to a claimant after the date on which the insured person would have attained pensionable age would be irrecoverable.

The Court of Justice held that subrogation under Article 52 of Regulation 3 (the predecessor of Article 93(1) of Regulation 1408/71) was governed by the law applicable to the institution liable to pay benefits, with the result that German law was applicable in Mrs. Töpfer's case. The Court added, however, that Article 52 only allowed recovery against a third party in respect of damage compensated by the claimant institution. This latter point may be illustrated by reference to the proceedings in the French courts in the case in issue. Mrs. Töpfer was awarded damages under French law in respect of grief at her bereavement, financial loss, and funeral expenses. Since, "in the eyes of German law, a widow's pension was compensation for her loss of her husband's obligation to maintain her,"[86] the rights of the German institution by way of subrogation would be limited to damages payable under French law in respect of financial loss resulting from the death of a husband.

The Department of Health and Social Security enjoys no general right of subrogation under English law, but Article 93 may well be invoked by the social security authorities of other Member States against tortfeasors in English courts.

---

[86] Advocate General Warner, [1977] E.C.R. 271, at p. 288.

CHAPTER 11

SEX DISCRIMINATION

Article 119—rationale

Article 119 EEC provides that each Member State shall during the first stage ensure and subsequently maintain the application of the principle that men and women should receive equal pay for equal work. According to the Court of Justice, this article pursues a double aim.[1] First, it seeks to avoid a situation in which undertakings established in States which implement the principle of equal pay suffer a competitive disadvantage as compared with undertakings established in States which fail to do so. Secondly, the provision forms part of the social objectives of the Community, which is not merely an economic union, but is intended to ensure social progress and seeks the improvement of the living and working conditions of its peoples. The principle of equal pay thus forms part of "foundations of the Community," and requires the "levelling up" of women's salaries, rather than the "levelling down" of men's.[2] Fundamental as the principle is, it is limited, as its terms suggest, to pay, and does not extend to securing equality in other terms and conditions of employment. The ingenious argument that the guarantee of equality in pay presumed, and therefore secured implicitly, equality in all conditions of employment, has been rejected by the Court.[3]

Direct effect of Article 119

In the landmark judgment of *Defrenne* v. *Sabena*,[4] the Court of Justice upheld the direct effect of Article 119. Miss Gabrielle Defrenne, an air hostess formerly employed by the airline Sabena, had sued her former employer before a Belgian court, claiming compensation for discrimination in terms of the pay she received as compared with male colleagues doing the same work as "cabin stewards." The Belgian court asked the Court of Justice whether Article 119 could be relied upon before national courts, independently of national legal provisions. The Court's answer was a qualified affirmative. The article could be relied upon, at least to the extent that the discrimination alleged was "direct and overt discrimination" which could be identified "solely with the aid of the criteria based on equal work and equal pay referred to by the article in question." In such cases, Article 119 was described as directly applicable and as giving rise to individual rights which national courts must protect. In other cases—described by the

---

[1] Case 43/75 *Defrenne* [1976] E.C.R. 455.
[2] *Ibid.* at p. 472, paras. 8–15.
[3] Case 148/77 *Defrenne (No. 2)* [1978] E.C.R. 1365.
[4] See note 1.

Court as cases of "indirect and disguised discrimination"—judicial implementation of Article 119 would have to await the passage of appropriate legislative measures at the Community and national level.

The terminology of "indirect and disguised discrimination" is potentially misleading. It refers in this context only to discrimination which cannot be detected by judicial enquiry in ordinary legal proceedings. It does not refer, e.g. to pay structures which can be established to the satisfaction of a judge to be discriminatory in fact, but which apparently provide for equal pay regardless of sex. This latter variety of "indirect" discrimination is certainly caught by directly effective provisions of the Treaty prohibiting discrimination on grounds of nationality,[5] and Article 119 has a similar scope.[6] Thus if an employer pays full-time workers more per hour than part-time workers, and the full-time workers are men, and the part-time workers are women, Article 119 would be directly effective if the employer were unable to establish that the difference in pay was attributable to factors other than sex. This would be a case of indirect discrimination in the more normal sense of the term.[7] If, however, a woman claims that she is being discriminated against by comparison, not with a man actually employed in the undertaking, or even previously employed in the undertaking, but by comparison with what a man would be paid were he in her position, the alleged discrimination is indirect and disguised in the sense that that term is used in *Defrenne*, and while there may indeed be a violation of Article 119, that provision cannot be directly invoked before national courts in such a case.[8]

The Court of Justice gave as examples of direct discrimination which might be identified solely by reference to the criteria laid down in Article 119 "those which have their origin in legislative provisions or in collective agreements and which may be detected on the basis of a purely legal analysis of the situation." This would be the case where men and women received unequal pay for equal work carried out in the same establishment or service, whether public or private.[9] This latter principle will sustain the direct effect of Article 119 in cases where a woman receives less pay than a formerly, but not contemporaneously, employed man doing the same job[10]; where male employees receive an increment to their salary to fund a retirement scheme, which is non-contributory in the case of women[11]; and where part-time workers are paid a lower hourly rate than full-time workers because of their sex.[12] Similarly, where recourse to the criteria of equal work and equal pay, without the operation of Community or national measures, enables a court to establish that the grant of concessionary transport facilities for the families of retired male employees but not

---

[5] Case 152/73 *Sotgiu* [1974] E.C.R. 153.
[6] The point is made by Adv. Gen. Warner in Case 96/80 *Jenkins Kingsgate (Clothing Productions) Ltd.* [1981] E.C.R. 911, at p. 937.
[7] Case 96/80 note 6.
[8] Case 129/79 *McCarthys* v. *Wendy Smith* [1980] E.C.R. 1288 at p. 1289, para. 15.
[9] Case 43/75 *Defrenne* [1976] E.C.R. 455, at p. 473, paras. 21, 22.
[10] Case 129/79 *McCarthys* v. *Wendy Smith*, [1980] E.C.R. 1288.
[11] Case 69/80 *Worringham & Humphreys* v. *Lloyds Bank* [1981] E.C.R. 767.
[12] Case 96/80 *Jenkins* v. *Kingsgate (Clothing Productions) Ltd.* [1981] E.C.R. 911.

for the families of retired female employees amounts to discrimination on grounds of sex, the provisions of Article 119 are directly applicable.[13]

Article 119 provides that each Member State shall "during the first stage" ensure sex equality in matters of pay. Thus, for the original six, the equal pay principle was to be "fully secured and irreversible . . . by 1 January 1962."[14] The Resolution of the Member States of December 31, 1961 calling for the phasing out of discrimination in pay by December 31, 1964, was incapable of modifying the time-limit fixed by the Treaty, since, apart from any specific provisions, the Treaty can only be modified by means of the amendment procedure carried out in accordance with Article 236 EEC.[15] Nor could Directive 75/117, designed to eliminate in particular indirect discrimination in pay, modify either the content of Article 119 or the time-limit specified therein.[16]

In the course of the proceedings before the Court in *Defrenne*, both the United Kingdom Government and the Commission argued that Article 119, even if directly effective, could only be invoked as between individuals and the State; it could not be invoked in relations between individuals. The Court rejected this distinction, declaring that:

> "since Article 119 is mandatory in nature, the prohibition on discrimination between men and women applies not only to the action of public authorities but also extends to all agreements which are intended to regulate paid labour collectively, as well as to contracts between individuals."[17]

The way was now clear for individuals to challenge their employers directly on the basis of the EEC Treaty in national courts in cases where they believed themselves victims of sex discrimination in matters of pay.

Despite the applicability of Article 119 from January 1, 1962, objections were raised to its direct effect from that date before the Court in *Defrenne*. The Court held for a number of reasons, discussed elsewhere,[18] that the direct effect of Article 119 could not be relied on in order to support claims concerning pay periods prior to the date of its judgment, except as regards workers who had already brought legal proceedings or made an equivalent claim.[19] The Court declined to give similar limited effect to its ruling in the later case of *Worringham & Humphreys* v. *Lloyds Bank*,[20] since the essential features brought to its attention in *Defrenne* were lacking in the later case.

Equal pay for equal work

Article 119 requires that men and women receive equal pay for equal work. This guarantee extends to both the private and public sectors.[21] The

---

[13] Case 12/81 *Garland* v. *BREL* [1981] E.C.R. 359.
[14] Case 43/75 *Defrenne* [1976] E.C.R. 455, at p. 478, para. 56.
[15] *Ibid.* at para. 58.
[16] *Ibid.*, at para. 68.
[17] *Ibid.*, at para. 39.
[18] See *supra*, at p. 35.
[19] Case 43/75 *Defrenne* (1976) E.C.R. 455, at p. 481, para. 75.
[20] note 11.
[21] Case 43/75 *Defrenne* (1976) E.C.R. 455; Case 58/81 *Commission* v. *Luxembourg* (1982) E.C.R. 2175.

Court of Justice has confirmed in *MacCarthys* v. *Wendy Smith*[22] that a
requirement of contemporaneity of employment is not to be read into the
Article. Wendy Smith was employed at a salary of £50 per week in a job in
which her male predecessor had received £60. The Court of Appeal[23] took
the view that the Equal Pay Act 1970 only contemplated comparison
between men and women doing the same job at the same time, and asked
the Court of Justice for an interpretation of Article 119 EEC in order to
establish whether or not it was to be so construed. The Court held that it
was not. The only relevant issue was whether or not the work was "equal,"
and it did not matter whether or not the man and woman whose work and
pay were to be compared were employed at the same time in the undertaking or not. The Court also implied in this case that Article 119 extended to
cases where a woman alleged discrimination inasmuch as she received less
pay than she would have received had she been a man; but stressed that
this must be classed as "indirect and disguised discrimination" and that
accordingly it fell outwith the direct application of Article 119.

A problem of "indirect discrimination" in the conventional sense[24] was
confronted by the Court in *Jenkins* v. *Kingsgate (Clothing Productions)
Ltd.*[25] Suppose that all or most part-time workers are women, and part-
time workers receive a lower rate of pay than full-time workers. On the
face of it, all workers are paid according to criteria which apply independently of sex. But is the indirect effect of the full-time/part-time differential
to discriminate on grounds of sex? In the course of the proceedings before
the Court of Justice, the Advocate General observed that in the Community as a whole, about 90 per cent. of part-time workers were women,
being mostly married women with family responsibilities. The Court of
Justice held that lower rates of pay for part-time workers did not *per se*
offend the principle of equal pay in so far as the difference in pay between
part-time and full-time work was attributable to factors which were objectively justified and in no way related to discrimination based on sex. Thus,
differentiation could be justified when an employer, on objective economic
grounds, was seeking to encourage full-time work irrespective of the sex of
the worker. On the other hand, if considerably fewer women than men
could manage full-time working, the inequality in pay would be contrary to
Article 119 where, regard being had to the difficulties encountered by
women in arranging to work the maximum number of hours per week, the
pay policy of the undertaking in question could not be explained by factors
other than discrimination based on sex. It would of course be for the
national courts to decide whether there was discrimination or not, in the
light of all the "facts of the case, its history, and the employer's intention."
It would seem to follow from the Court's judgment that in such circumstances an employer might be guilty of discrimination contrary to Article
119 even if he thought there were objective economic grounds for his pay
differentials, if it were established that no such objective factors existed,

[22] Case 129/79 [1980] E.C.R. 1288.
[23] [1979] 3 All E.R. 325.
[24] See *supra* at p. 268 for the confusing terminology adopted by the court.
[25] Case 96/80 [1981] E.C.R. 911.

e.g. if as a matter of fact the differential was not effective in encouraging full-time working, or if full-time working did not in fact contribute to the efficiency of his operation.[26] Indeed, the Court has held that the employer must demonstrate to the competent national court that his apparently discriminatory measures are appropriate and necessary to satisfy a real need on the part of the undertaking.[27]

The definition of "pay"

Article 119 EEC provides the following definition of "pay":
"For the purpose of this Article, "pay" means the ordinary basic or minimum wage or salary and any other consideration, whether in cash or in kind, which the worker receives, directly or indirectly, in respect of his employment from his employer."

The word "consideration" is not used in its English technical contractual sense,[28] and payments in cash or kind in fact made to employees in respect of their employment will amount to "pay" whether such payments are legally obligatory or not.[29]

The Court has held that a retirement pension granted under a social security scheme did not amount to "consideration" received indirectly by a worker in respect of his employment, because under such schemes the employee normally receives the benefits not by reason of his employer's contributions, but simply because he fulfils the conditions established by law for the benefits to be granted.[30] On the other hand, a supplement paid by the employer to employees to fund the provision of a private pension scheme has been held to be "pay" to the extent that it was included in the calculation of the gross salary payable to the employee and that it directly determined the calculation of other advantages linked to the salary, such as redundancy payments, unemployment benefits, family allowances, and credit facilities.[31] It seems that the above analysis is applicable to schemes which substitute for social security arrangements under "contracting out" provisions.[32]

Directive 75/117 on equal pay for work of equal value

Article 119 was described by Advocate General Warner in *Worringham & Humphreys* as the "translation" into Community law of the International Labour Organisation's Convention No. 100 dated June 29, 1951 "Concerning equal remuneration for men and women workers for work of

---

[26] See *Jenkins* v. *Kingsgate*, E.A.T. [1981] I.R.L.R. 391.
[27] Case 170/84 *Bilka-Kaufhaus* [1982] 2 C.M.L.R. 701, at p. 721, paras. 36, 37.
[28] Adv. Gen. Warner in Case 69/80 *Worringham & Humphreys* v. *Lloyds Bank* [1981] E.C.R. 767, at p. 804.
[29] Case 69/80 *Worringham & Humphreys* [1981] E.C.R. 767; Case 12/81 *Garland* [1982] E.C.R. 359.
[30] Case 80/70 *Defrenne* v. *Belgian State* [1971] E.C.R. 445.
[31] Case 69/80 *Worringham & Humphreys* [1981] E.C.R. 767; Case 23/83 *Liefting* [1984] E.C.R. 5225; Case 170/84 *Bilka-Kaufhaus* [1986] 2 C.M.L.R. 701.
[32] Case 69/80 *Worringham & Humphreys*, note 30; see Snaith, (1981) E.L.Rev. 193.

equal value."[33] Article 119 provides for equal pay for equal work, irrespective of sex. Article 2 of the ILO Convention provides that "Each Member shall . . . promote and . . . ensure the application to all workers of the principle of equal remuneration for men and women workers for work of equal value." In accordance with this requirement[34] Article 1 of Directive 75/117 provides in part as follows:

> "The principle of equal pay for men and women outlined in Article 119 of the Treaty, hereinafter called "principle of equal pay," means, for the same work or for work to which equal value is attributed, the elimination of all discrimination on grounds of. sex with regard to all aspects and conditions of remuneration."

The principal purposes of Directive 75/117 are to make it clear that Article 119 extends to work of equal value as well as the same work, and to facilitate the operation of Article 119 in the field of indirect discrimination, *i.e.* in those situations in which discrimination on grounds of sex cannot be directly determined by national courts without elaboration of further criteria at the legislative level.[35] It would seem to follow that Article 119, properly construed, itself requires equal pay for the same work or work of equal value.[36] Ensuring equal pay for work of equal value will sometimes involve the direct effect of Article 119, where the discrimination is "direct and overt," that is to say, capable of being identified by reference to Article 119 alone, *e.g.* where a collective agreement ascribes equal value to categories of work, but men and women do not receive equal pay for doing work within these categories. On other occasions, securing equal pay for work of equal value will involve eliminating indirect and disguised discrimination, that is to say, discrimination which cannot be detected solely by reference to Article 119, *e.g.* by the use of a job classification scheme as provided by national law.[37] In such cases, Article 119 is not of course directly effective, but can only secure equality with the assistance of national implementing rules.

While Article 1 of Directive 75/117 declares that the concept of "same work" contained in the first paragraph of Article 119 EEC includes cases of "work to which equal value is attributed," it does not affect the concept of "pay" contained in the second paragraph of Article 119, but refers by implication to it.[38]

The second paragraph of Article 1 of Directive 75/117 provides:

> "In particular, where a job classification system is used for determining pay, it must be based on the same criteria for both men and women and so drawn up as to exclude any discrimination on grounds of sex."

[33] The Convention entered into force on May 23, 1953, and has been ratified by 107 states. See Brownlie, Basic Documents on Human Rights, p. 200. UNTS Vol. 1651, p. 304. Bowman & Harris, *Multilateral Treaties*, p. 1951, and Supplements. All Member States have ratified.
[34] Case 43/75 *Defrenne*, [1976] E.C.R. 455, at p. 473, para. 20.
[35] Case 43/75 *Defrenne*, note 33; Case 61/81 *Commission* v. *United Kingdom* [1982] E.C.R. 2601, at p. 2621, *per* Adv. Gen. VerLoren van Themaat.
[36] Case 69/80 *Worringham & Humphreys*, (1981) E.C.R. 767, at p. 792, para. 23.
[37] See, *e.g.* S.I. 1983 No. 1794, The Equal Pay (Amendment) Regulations.
[38] Case 69/80 *Worringham & Humphreys*, [1981] E.C.R. 767, at p. 791, para. 21.

It was this provision which lay at the heart of a dispute as to the effect of Directive 75/117 between the Commission and the United Kingdom, culminating in legal proceedings before the Court of Justice.[39]

When the terms of the Directive were adopted the United Kingdom secured the inclusion in the minutes of the Council meeting a statement on the interpretation of the words "work to which equal value is attributed" which read:

> "The circumstances in which work is considered in the United Kingdom to have equal value attributed to it are where the work is broadly similar or where pay is based on the results of job evaluation."

Under the British legislation giving effect to Directive 75/117[40] equal pay was required in cases both of a man and woman employed on "like work," and of a man and woman employed on work "rated as equivalent" on the basis of a job evaluation scheme undertaken with the consent of the employer. The Commission took the view that since "like work" did not extend to "work of equal value," and since the latter could only be established if the employer consented to a job evaluation scheme, the United Kingdom had failed to implement Directive 75/117. The matter came before the Court of Justice in proceedings instituted under Article 169 of the Treaty. The United Kingdom denied that Article 1 of the Directive gave a right to job evaluation, stressing that the provision referred to work to which "equal value is attributed," which is plainly not the same as work "of equal value." The Court of Justice took the view that the United Kingdom's interpretation amounted to a denial of the very existence of a right to equal pay for work of equal value where no job classification has been undertaken. Where there was disagreement as to the application of the concept of work of equal value the general scheme and provisions of Directive 75/117 required that the worker be entitled to claim before an appropriate authority that his work had the same value as the other work in issue. Such a right had not been secured in the United Kingdom, which had accordingly failed to comply with its obligation to implement the Directive. The response to the Court's judgment was the promulgation of the Equal Pay (Amendment) Regulations 1983, which entered into force on January 1, 1984.[41] These Regulations provided, *inter alia*, that an industrial tribunal be empowered to require a member of a panel of independent experts to prepare a report with respect to the question whether or not any work were of equal value to that of a man in the same employment.[42]

There can be no doubt that Directive 75/117 in substance reiterates the obligations contained in Article 119, without modifying either the content of that Article, or its temporal effect.[43] In *Commission* v. *Luxembourg*,[44] Advocate General VerLoren van Themaat objected that the Commission's

---

[39] Case 61/81 *Commission* v. *United Kingdom* [1982] E.C.R. 2601. See also on job classification, Case 237/85 *Rummler*, Judgment of July 1, 1986.
[40] The Equal Pay Act, as amended by the Sex Discrimination Act 1975.
[41] S.I. 1983 No. 1794.
[42] Regulations 2 and 3.
[43] Case 43/75 *Defrenne* [1976] E.C.R. 455; Case 58/81 *Commission* v. *Luxembourg* [1982] E.C.R. 2175 at p. 2186, *per* Adv. Gen. VerLoren van Themaat.
[44] Note 42.

action against Luxembourg for failing to comply with Directive 75/117 by February 12, 1976 could not be upheld. He argued that the conduct in question was caught by Article 119 EEC, which had been binding on Luxembourg since January 1, 1962. To the extent that Article 3 of Directive 75/117, which required that "Member States shall abolish all discrimination between men and women arising from laws, regulations, or administrative provisions which is contrary to the principle of equal pay," duplicated Article 119, it could serve no purpose with respect to the implementation of the latter. He concluded that the Court should uphold the Commission's action upon the basis of Article 119 and Article 119 alone. The Court, without commenting on the Advocate General's objections, held that Luxembourg's failure to implement Directive 75/117 amounted to a violation of its obligations under the Treaty. It is submitted that the Advocate General's misgivings were groundless. The fact that Directive 75/117 might either wholly or in part duplicate obligations arising under the Treaty cannot rob it of either efficacy or validity. A parallel situation arises in the relationship between Article 48 EEC, and the implementing legislation made under Article 49. As the Court stated in *Procureur du Roi* v. *Royer*[45] "the directives concerned determined the scope and detailed rules for the exercise of rights conferred directly by the Treaty."

Directive 75/117 requires Member States to introduce into their national legal systems such measures as are necessary to enable all employees who consider themselves to have been wronged by failure to apply the principle of equal pay to pursue their claims by judicial process after possible recourse to other competent authorities.[46] This provision clearly duplicates the requirements of Article 119, as does the requirement that Member States abolish all discrimination between men and women arising from laws, regulations or administrative provisions which is contrary to the principle of equal pay.[47]

Article 4 of the Directive states:

"Member States shall take the necessary measures to ensure that provisions appearing in collective agreements, wage scales, wage agreements or individual contracts of employment which are contrary to the principle of equal pay shall be, or may be declared, null or void or may be amended."

This mode of implementation of a non-discrimination guarantee is not unique. Article 7(4) of Regulation 1612/68 provides that classes of collective or individual agreements which discriminate against workers who are nationals of other Member States shall be null and void. Directive 76/207 on equal treatment for men and women in access to employment, etc., has similar provisions.[48] In the case of Article 4 of Directive 75/117 and Article 7(4) of Regulation 1612/68, it is submitted that the provisions in question merely restate guarantees implicit in Article 119 and Article 48 EEC respectively. If discriminatory clauses in agreements are given effect, they are clearly

---

[45] Case 48/75 [1976] E.C.R. 497, at p. 512, para. 28.
[46] Art. 2.
[47] Art. 3.
[48] Art. 3(2)(*b*); Art. 4(*b*); Art. 5(2)(*b*).

incompatible with the Treaty. If they are not actually enforced, but are nominally in force, or even stand unamended in non-binding agreements, they are capable of misleading those subject to the law and this is in turn at odds with the non-discriminatory guarantees of the Treaty.[49]

The requirement that Member States take "the necessary measures to protect employees against dismissal by the employer as a reaction to a complaint within the undertaking or to any legal proceedings aimed at enforcing compliance with the principle of equal pay"[50] reiterates a duty inherent in Article 119 itself, as do the terms of Article 6 of the Directive, which enjoins Member States to "take the measures necessary to ensure that the principle of equal pay is applied (and to) see that effective means are available to take care that this principle is observed." Only in its final substantive article does Directive 75/117 appear to go beyond the requirements of Article 119. Member States are to:

> "take care that the provisions adopted pursuant to this Directive, together with the relevant provisions already in force, are brought to the attention of employees by all appropriate means, for example at their place of employment."

It is submitted that the principle of legal certainty combined with Article 119 requires both the amendment of misleading provisions of national laws, regulations, collective agreements, etc.,[51] and the formal publication of national laws clearly implementing Community obligations.[52] But more than this is not required by the Treaty itself in combination with the general principles of Community law, in the absence of a provision of secondary legislation such as Article 7 of Directive 75/117.

Directive 76/207 on equal treatment in employment

Article 117 EEC states:

> "Member States agree upon the need to promote improved working conditions and an improved standard of living for workers, so as to make possible their harmonisation while the improvement is being maintained.
>
> They believe that such a development will ensue not only from the functioning of the common market, which will favour the harmonisation of social systems, but also from the procedures provided for in this Treaty and from the approximation of provisions laid down by law, regulation or administrative action."

The Council of Ministers has concluded that the principle of harmonisation of living and working conditions while maintaining their improvement entails the principle that male and female workers receive equal

---

[49] Case 167/73 Commission v. French Republic [1974] E.C.R. 359; Case 165/82 Commission v. United Kingdom [1983] E.C.R. 3431.
[50] Art. 5.
[51] Case 167/73 Commission v. French Republic [1974] E.C.R. 359.
[52] Case 143/83 Commission v. Kingdom of Denmark [1985] E.C.R. 427, at p. 435, paras. 10, 11.

treatment in access to employment, vocational training, and promotion, and in respect of working conditions.[53] Since the Treaty does not confer the necessary specific powers for this purpose, the Council resorted to Article 235 EEC as the basis of Directive 76/207 on the implementation of the principle of equal treatment for men and women as regards access to employment, vocational training and promotion, and working conditions.[54] The "core" of the Directive constitutes the guarantee of equal treatment in three areas:

— access to all jobs or posts, whatever the sector or branch of activity, and to all levels of the occupational hierarchy (Art. 3);
— access to all types and levels of vocational guidance, vocational training, advanced vocational training and retraining (Art. 4);
— working conditions, including the conditions governing dismissal (Art. 5).

The principle of "equal treatment" is defined as meaning "that there shall be no discrimination whatsoever on grounds of sex either directly or indirectly by reference in particular to marital or family status."

Application of the principle of equal treatment in the three areas referred to above—access to employment, vocational training, and working conditions—is to be secured in each case by Member States taking the measures necessary to ensure that

— any laws, regulations and administrative provisions contrary to the principle of equal treatment shall be abolished (Arts. 3(2)(*a*); 4(*a*); 5(2)(*a*));
— any provisions contrary to the principle of equal treatment which are included in collective agreements, individual contracts of employment, internal rules of undertakings or in rules governing the independent occupations and professions shall be, or may be declared, null and void or may be amended (Arts. 3(2)(*b*); 4(*b*); 5(2)(*b*));

The Court has held[55] that in order to comply with the above requirement, it is not enough that national law ordains the invalidity of binding agreements containing offending clauses. National rules must go further and secure that where such clauses are to be found in non-binding agreements (as are most collective agreements in the United Kingdom) they can be "rendered inoperative, eliminated or amended by appropriate means." The reasoning of the Court was to the effect that even non-binding collective agreements have important *de facto* consequences for the employment relationships to which they refer.

With respect to equal treatment in access to employment, and in working conditions, Member States are required to take the measures necessary to ensure that:

"those laws, regulations and administrative provisions contrary to the principle of equal treatment when the concern for protection which

---

[53] Directive 76/207, preamble.
[54] O.J. 1976, L39/40. Art. 2(1), in conjunction with Arts. 3(1), 4(1), and 5(1), may be relied on in national courts, at least as against public authorities, Case 152/84 *Marshall* [1986] 1 C.M.L.R. 688; Case 222/84 *Johnston* [1986] 3 C.M.L.R. 240; as may Art. 6, Case 222/84.
[55] Case 165/82 *Commission* v. *United Kingdom* [1983] E.C.R. 3431.

originally inspired them is no longer well founded shall be revised; and that where similar provisions are included in collective agreements labour and management shall be requested to undertake the desired revision." (Arts. 3(2)(c); 5(2)(c)).

In the case of vocational training, this provision is not appropriate, and it is instead the duty of Member States to take measures to ensure that, without prejudice to the freedom granted in certain Member States to certain private training establishments, vocational guidance, training and retraining shall be accessible without discrimination on grounds of sex (Art. 4(c)).

Article 2(2) of Directive 76/207 provides that the Directive shall be "without prejudice to the right of Member States to exclude from its field of application those occupational activities and, where appropriate, the training leading thereto, for which, by reason of their nature or the context in which they are carried out, the sex of the worker constitutes a determining factor." The Court was called upon to define the ambit of this provision in *Commission* v. *United Kingdom*.[56] The Sex Discrimination Act 1975 provided for exceptions to the principle of equal treatment: (i) where employment was in a private household[57]; (ii) where the number of persons employed by an employer did not exceed five[57] and (iii) where the employment, promotion and training of midwives was concerned[58] In the first two cases, the Court held the British legislation to be incompatible with Directive 76/207. It observed that the "private household" exception was designed to reconcile the principle of equality of treatment with the principle of respect for family life, which was also fundamental, and acknowledged that, for certain kinds of employment in private households, that consideration might be decisive. However, that could not be the case for all the kinds of employment in question. As far as the "small business" exception was concerned, the Court noted that the United Kingdom had not put forward any argument to show that in such undertakings the sex of the worker could be a determining factor by reason of the nature of his activities or the context in which they were carried out. It followed that the "private household" and "small business" exceptions contained in s.6(3) of the 1975 Act, by their very generality, went further than was necessary to secure the objectives of Article 2(2) of the Directive. The Court took a different view of the restrictions imposed in the United Kingdom upon the entry of men into the midwifery profession. Under the 1975 Act,[59] until a day to be specified by order of the Secretary of State, men were granted access to the occupation in question and could be trained for that purpose only in certain specific places. It was argued that this situation was due to the fact that in the United Kingdom the occupation in question was not traditionally engaged in by men. Fears were expressed in particular that women from ethnic minorities might refuse medical services provided by male midwives. Since patients' sensitivities were of particular importance, the United Kingdom argued that the restrictions in issue were consistent

---

[56] Note 55.
[57] S.6(3).
[58] S.20.
[59] Sched. 4, para. 3.

with Article 2(2) of the Directive. Advocate General Rozes did not think that a restriction on entry for men was justified, and expressed the view that the guarantee of a free choice for patients, while admittedly necessary, would also be sufficient to allay the fears expressed by the United Kingdom Government. The Court upheld the position of the latter. It recognised that at the present time personal sensibilities played an important role in relations between midwife and patient, and that accordingly the United Kingdom had not exceeded the limits of the power granted to Member States under Article 2(2) of the Directive. It is interesting to note that the United Kingdom had, before judgment was given, issued orders under the 1975 Act bringing to an end the restrictions on access by men to the profession of midwifery. To meet the difficulties voiced by the Government during the proceedings, Health Authorities were to be asked to ensure that women were always given the opportunity to be attended by a female midwife if they chose and to ensure that, where a male midwife was provided, adequate chaperoning was also provided.

The Court has held that a policy of not recruiting women for armed police duties on the grounds that women would make easy targets for terrorists, who might then acquire their firearms, was capable of justification under Article 2(2) of the Directive.[60]

It is clear that the Court will construe broadly the guarantees of equality contained in the Directive, and narrowly the exceptions referred to therein. Thus the question arose in *Burton* v. *BRB*[61] whether or not the word "dismissal" in Article 5(1) of the Directive could be construed to include termination of the employment relationship between a worker and his employer even as part of a voluntary redundancy scheme. The Court held that the "dismissal" was to be broadly construed, and did indeed extend to access to a voluntary redundancy scheme. By contrast, the Court's approach to the exception contained in Article 2(2) in *Commission* v. *United Kingdom*[62] evidences a strict construction in accordance with Advocate General Rozes' exhortation to that effect.

The Directive is stated to be "without prejudice" to: (i) provisions concerning the protection of women, particularly as regards pregnancy and maternity[63]; (ii) measures to promote equal opportunities, in particular by removing existing inequalities which affect women's opportunities.[64] Without referring expressly to the Directive's proviso for measures concerning the protection of women, the Court has upheld "maternity" leave for women, but not for men, immediately after a child under six years of age is adopted into the family. This differentiation between men and women was said to be justified "by the legitimate concern to assimilate as far as possible the conditions of entry of the child into the adoptive family to those of the arrival of a newborn child in the family during the very delicate initial

---

[60] Case 222/84 *Johnston* [1986] 3 C.M.L.R. 240.
[61] Case 19/81 [1982] E.C.R. 555. For the broad construction to be given to "dismissal" in Art. 5(1) of Dir. 76/707, see also Case 267/84, *Beets-Proper*, Judgment of February 26, 1986, [1986] I.C.R. 706.
[62] Note 55.
[63] Art. 2(3).
[64] Art. 2(4).

period."[65] The case may turn on the protection of women proviso, or on the Court's concern for the integrity of family life,[66] or on the broader principle that differentiation on objective grounds compatible with the Treaty is not unlawful discrimination.[67] The Court has upheld maternity leave after childbirth for women, on the basis of the Directive's proviso for measures concerning the protection of women, and confirmed that such leave may be denied to men, even if such leave is claimed as an alternative to leave by the mother.[67a]

The directive's proviso for the protection of women is to be construed strictly. It is intended to protect a woman's biological condition and the special relationship which exists between a woman and her child. It does not allow women to be excluded from a certain type of employment on the ground that public opinion demands that women be given greater protection than men against risks which affect men and women in the same way and which are distinct from women's specific needs of protection.[68]

Although Directive 76/207 conditions the interpretation and application of legislation adopted to give effect to its terms, it does not contain any sufficiently precise obligation to enable an individual to obtain a specific remedy under the directive when that is not provided for or permitted by national law.[69]

Directive 79/7 on equal treatment in social security matters

The Commission's first draft of what was to become Directive 76/207 applied also to equality in social security matters.[70] But the Member States objected, and it was excluded from the draft directive in 1976.[71] Article 1(2) Directive 76/207 provided only that "with a view to ensuring the progressive implementation of the principle of equal treatment in matters of social security, the Council, acting on a proposal from the Commission, will adopt provisions defining its substance, its scope and the arrangements for its application." In accordance with this mandate, the Council promulgated Directive 79/7 of 19 December on the progressive implementation of the principle of equal treatment for men and women in matters of social security.[72] The Member States were obliged to bring their laws into line with the Directive by December 19, 1984.

It is necessary to consider in what respects national social security laws may be said to discriminate on grounds of sex.[73] A few examples will suf-

---

[65] Case 163/82 *Commission* v. *Italian Republic* [1983] E.C.R. 3273.
[66] *Commission* v. *United Kingdom*, note 55.
[67] Case 152/73, *Sotgiu* [1974] E.C.R. 153.
[67a] Case 184/83 *Hofmann* [1984] E.C.R. 3042.
[68] Case 222/84 *Johnston* [1986] 3 C.M.L.R. 240.
[69] Case 14/83 *Von Colson* [1984] E.C.R. 1891; Case 79/83 *Harz* [1984] E.C.R. 1921.
[70] Com (75) 36 Final, 12/2/75.
[71] O'Donovan, "The Impact of Entry into the European Community on Sex Discrimination in British Social Security Law," in "Essays for Clive Schmitthoff" (ed. J. Adams) p. 87. The "social security" exception to Dir. 76/707 is to be strictly construed, Case 157/84 *Marshall* [1986] 3 C.M.L.R. 688; Case 151/84 *Roberts* [1986] 1 C.M.L.R. 714; Case 262/84 *Beets-Proper*; in Judgment of February 26, 1986, [1986] I.C.R. 706.
[72] O.J. 1979, L6/24.
[73] See in general O'Donovan, note 71.

fice. First, the retirement age for women may be lower than that for men. If a lower pension is payable, this is disadvantageous to women. On the other hand, the later date could be disadvantageous to men wishing to retire. Secondly, women tend to be treated by social security systems as dependants rather than breadwinners, even if this is not actually so in individual cases. Thus, when a man receives unemployment benefit, he may well receive supplements for his children, his status as "head of household" being taken for granted. Yet a woman may only be recognised as "head of household" if her husband is physically incapable of work—even if he is unemployed while she is supporting the family. Again, certain kinds of benefits may only ever be claimed by the "head of the household" and not by his "dependent" married or co-habiting partner.[74]

The purpose of Directive 79/7 is the progressive implementation of the principle of equal treatment for men and women in matters of social security.[75] It applies to the working population, employed and self-employed alike, and includes those whose work has been interrupted by illness, accident or involuntary unemployment. It also applies to persons seeking employment, and to retired and invalided workers.[76]

Article 3(1) provides that the Directive shall apply to:
"(a) Statutory schemes which provide protection against the following risks:
— sickness,
— invalidity,
— old age,
— accidents at work and occupational diseases,
— unemployment.
(b) social assistance, in so far as it is intended to supplement or replace the schemes referred to in (a)."

Article 3(2) adds that:
"This Directive shall not apply to the provisions concerning survivors' benefits nor to those concerning family benefits, except in the case of family benefits granted by way of increases in benefits due in respect of the risks referred to in paragraph 1(a)."

The principle of equal treatment means that there shall be no discrimination whatsoever on grounds of sex either directly, or indirectly, by reference in particular to marital or family status.[77] This guarantee of equal treatment applies in particular to the scope of social security schemes, and the conditions of access thereto, to the obligations to contribute and the calculation of contributions, and to the calculation of benefits, including increases due in respect of a spouse and dependants, and the conditions governing the duration and retention of entitlement to benefits.[78] The prin-

---

[74] For a synopsis of then prevalent discrimination in social security systems in the Member States, see Com (75) 36 Final, 12/2/75.

[75] Art. 1.

[76] Art. 2.

[77] Art. 4(1).

[78] Art. 4(1). Art. 4(1) may be invoked before national courts against incompatible national legislation, see Case 71/85 *Federatie Nederlandse Vakbeweging*, Judgment of December 4, 1986.

ciple of equal treatment, however, shall be without prejudice to provisions relating to the protection of women on grounds of maternity.[79]

The Directive has brought changes in Social Security law in the United Kingdom.[80] For example, the Social Security Act 1980 made women eligible for the same benefit increases or additions for their children as men in a number of cases, including unemployment, sickness and retirement.[81] And women may now be "nominated breadwinners" for the purpose of collecting Supplementary Benefits. Previously only the male breadwinner could claim for his wife or co-habiting partner.[82]

In *Drake* the Court held that the Directive applied to an invalid care allowance payable to a person caring for an invalid, where the allowance was not payable to a married woman living with her husband and maintained by him, but was payable to a married man in similar circumstances.[83]

The Directive has a number of exceptions, *e.g.* it is "without prejudice to the right of Member States to exclude from its scope . . . the determination of pensionable age for the purposes of granting old-age and retirement pensions and the possible consequences thereof for other benefits."[84] The effect of this proviso was illustrated in *Burton* v. *BRB*.[85] British Rail had offered voluntary early retirement for workers whose jobs had been the subject of reorganisation. The qualifying age was 55 years for women, but 60 years for men. Mr. Burton, aged 58 years, applied for voluntary early retirement, but was rejected as being ineligible. He claimed that he had been discriminated against on grounds of sex. The Court of Justice held that access to the voluntary early retirement scheme fell within the scope of Directive 76/207, but that the differential qualifying ages were justified in Community law because they were linked to the differential minimum qualifying ages for a state retirement pension—60 for women and 65 for men. The link was established by the availability of a number of social security benefits for those taking advantage of the early retirement scheme, provided they retired within five years of the normal retirement age. Since Directive 79/7 excluded retirement age from the principle of equal treatment, an early retirement scheme linked to pensionable age fell outside the ambit of Directive 76/207. However, the Court has held that the proviso cannot justify compulsory *retirement* at a discriminatory pensionable age.[86]

Directive 86/378 on equal treatment in occupational social security schemes

In the first *Defrenne* case the Court held that Article 119 does not apply to statutory social security schemes.[87] For certain such schemes the prin-

---

[79] Art. 4(2).
[80] See O'Donovan, note 71.
[81] Social Security Act 1980, Sched. 1, paras. 1(1) and (2). O'Donovan, *op. cit.* p. 97.
[82] O'Donovan, *op. cit.*, pp. 93, 95.
[83] Case 150/85 [1986] 3 C.M.L.R. 43.
[84] Art. 7(1)(*a*).
[85] Case 19/81 [1982] E.C.R. 555.
[86] Case 152/84 *Marshall* 1 C.M.L.R. 688; Case 262/84 *Beets-Proper*, Judgment of February 26, 1986.
[87] *Supra* at p. 272.

ciple of equal treatment is however applicable by virtue of Directive 79/7.[88] But this Directive does not apply to occupational schemes based on private law. These latter schemes will fall within the scope of Article 119 to the extent that the benefits can be regarded as deferred earnings, and hence "pay." To the extent that the discrimination in question is "direct and overt,"[89] Article 119 can be relied upon before national courts, but in the case of "indirect and disguised" discrimination[90] the adoption of additonal measures is required to secure implementation of the principle of equal pay. Directive 86/378[91] is calculated to provide such an additional measure, and thus to apply the principle of equal treatment to occupational social security schemes which fall outside the scope of Directive 79/7.

"Occupational social security schemes" are schemes which are not governed by Directive 79/7, and whose purpose is to provide employed or self-employed persons with benefits intended to supplement the benefits provided by statutory social security schemes or to replace them, whether membership of such schemes is compulsory or optional.[92] The Directive does not however apply to: (a) individual contracts; (b) schemes having only one member; and (c) in the case of salaried workers, insurance schemes offered to participants individually to guarantee them either additional benefits, or a choice of date on which the normal benefits will start, or a choice between several benefits.[93] The Directive applies to members of the working population, including self-employed persons, persons whose activity is interrupted by illness, maternity, accident or involuntary unemployment, and persons seeking employment, and to retired and disabled workers.[94]

The following schemes are covered by the Directive:

(a) occupational schemes which provide protection against the following risks:

— sickness,
— invalidity,
— old age, including early retirement,
— industrial accidents and occupational diseases,
— unemployment;

(b) occupational schemes which provide for other social benefits, in cash or in kind, and in particular survivors' benefits and family allowances, if such benefits are accorded to employed persons and thus constitute a consideration paid by the employer to the worker by reason of the latter's employment.[95]

Under the conditions laid down in the Directive, the principle of equal treatment requires that there shall be no discrimination on the basis of sex,

---

[88] *Supra.*
[89] *Supra* at p. 268.
[90] *Supra* at p. 269.
[91] O.J. 1986 L225/40.
[92] Art. 2(1).
[93] Art. 2(2).
[94] Art. 3.
[95] Art. 4.

either directly or indirectly, by reference in particular to marital or family status, especially as regards:
— the scope of the schemes and the conditions of access to them;
— the obligation to contribute and the calculation of contributions;
— the calculation of benefits, including supplementary benefits due in respect of a spouse or dependants, and the conditions governing the duration and retention of entitlement to benefits.[96]

Examples of provisions of schemes covered by the principle of equal treatment are listed,[97] and include:
— setting different conditions for the granting of benefits or restricting such benefits to workers of one or other of the sexes[98];
— fixing different retirement ages[99];
— suspending the retention or acquisition of rights during periods of maternity leave or leave for family reasons which are granted by law or agreement and are paid by the employer[1];
— setting different levels of benefit, except insofar as may be necessary to take account of actuarial calculation factors which differ according to sex in the case of benefits designated as contribution-defined.[2]

Where the granting of benefits within the scope of this Directive is left to the discretion of the scheme's management bodies, the latter must take account of the principle of equal treatment.[3]

Member States are obliged to take all necessary steps to ensure that:

(a) provisions contrary to the principle of equal treatment in legally compulsory collective agreements, staff rules or undertakings or any other arrangements relating to occupational schemes are null and void, or may be declared null and void or amended;

(b) schemes containing such provisions may not be approved or extended by administrative measures.[4]

All necessary steps are to be taken by Member States to ensure that the provisions of occupational schemes contrary to the principle of equal treatment are revised by January 1, 1993.[5] However, the Directive does not preclude rights and obligations relating to a period of membership of an occupational scheme prior to revision of that scheme from remaining subject to the provisions of the scheme in force during that period.[6] Application of the principle of equal treatment may be deferred in several cases, in particular with respect to the determination of pensionable age for the purposes of granting old-age or retirement pensions.[7] Member States are obliged to introduce measures to comply with the Directive by July 30, 1989.[8]

---

[96] Art. 5(1). The principle of equal treatment shall not however prejudice the provisions relating to the protection of women by reason of maternity.
[97] Art. 6.
[98] Art. 6(1)(e).
[99] Art. 6(1)(f).
[1] Art. 6(1)(g).
[2] Art. 6(1)(h).
[3] Art. 6(2).
[4] Art. 7.
[5] Art. 8(1).
[6] Art. 8(2).
[7] Art. 9.
[8] Art. 12(1).

Directive 86/613 on equal treatment in self-employment

The purposes of Directive 86/613[9] are to extend the application of Directive 76/207 to self-employed persons, and to secure application of the principle of equal treatment in cases where the self-employed person and his or her spouse are engaged together in the same work.

The Directive applies to self-employed workers, *i.e.* to all persons pursuing a gainful activity on their own account, including farmers and members of the liberal professions, and to their spouses, not being employees or partners, where they habitually participate in the activities of the self-employed worker and perform the same tasks or ancillary tasks.[10]

For the purposes of the Directive the principle of equal treatment requires the absence of all discrimination on grounds of sex, either directly or indirectly, by reference in particular to marital or family status.[11]

As regards self-employed persons, Member States are obliged to take all necessary measures to ensure the elimination of all provisions which are contrary to the principle of equal treatment as defined in Directive 76/207, especially in respect of the establishment, equipment or extension of a business or the launching or extension of any other form of self-employed activity including financial facilities.[12]

Without prejudice to the specific conditions for access to certain activities which apply equally to both sexes, Member States shall take the measures necessary to ensure that the conditions for the formation of a company between spouses are not more restrictive than the conditions for the formation of a company between unmarried persons.[13]

Where a contributory social security system for self-employed workers exists in a Member State, that Member State shall take the necessary measures to enable those spouses who participate in the work of the self-employed worker and who are not protected under the self-employed worker's social security scheme to join a contributory social security scheme voluntarily.[14]

Member States are obliged to bring into force the measures necessary to comply with the Directive by June 30, 1989.[15]

Sex equality as a general principle of community law

It is ironic that the first "head of household" provision to be condemned by the Court of Justice was contained in the Community's own Staff Regulations! Under those Regulations expatriation allowances were payable to officials of the Community in appropriate circumstances. An official who married a person who did not qualify for the allowance forfeited the allow-

[9] O.J. 1986, L 359/56.
[10] Art. 2.
[11] Art. 3.
[12] Art. 4.
[13] Art. 5.
[14] Art. 6.
[15] Art. 12(1). If a Member State has to amend its legislation on matrimonial rights and obligations in order to secure the principle of equal treatment in the formation of companies, the final date for compliance is June 30, 1991.

ance unless that official became by virtue of the marriage a "head of household."[16] This provision was not, as far as it went, discriminatory, but "head of household" was defined as normally referring to a married male official, whereas a married female official was considered to be a head of household only in exceptional circumstances, in particular in cases of the invalidity or serious illness of the husband.[17] To put the matter simply, if an Italian male official working in Belgium married a Belgian girl, he retained his expatriation allowance, being regarded without more as a "head of household." If on the other hand an Italian female official married a Belgian man, she lost her expatriation allowance; she was regarded as being economically and socially dependent upon her husband, and no longer an expatriate—even if she in fact earned more than her husband, or her husband was unemployed. The Court of Justice in *Sabbatini* v. *European Parliament*[18] held that this definition of "head of household" created an arbitrary difference of treatment between officials. The withdrawal of allowance following the marriage of the recipient might be justified in cases in which this change in family situation was such as to bring an end to the state of expatriation which was the justification for the benefit in question. What was impermissible was the Staff Regulations treating officials differently according to whether they were male or female. According to the Court, "termination of the status of expatriate must be dependent for both male and female officials on uniform criteria, irrespective of sex." The Court does not rely directly upon Article 119 EEC, which is of course addressed to the Member States, but does refer to it formally in its statement of reasons. The Court appears to apply Article 119 by analogy, relying upon the principle of equal treatment, irrespective of sex, as a general principle of Community law.

The principle of equal treatment, as a general principle of Community law, prohibits indirect, as well as direct discrimination. The Court in *Airola* v. *Commission*[19] considered the case of a Belgian woman who had acquired dual Italian nationality by virtue of her marriage to an Italian. Upon appointment as a Commission official at Ispra in Italy, the woman in question was denied the expatriation allowance she would have received had she not acquired Italian nationality by marriage. The Staff Regulations conditioned payment of expatriation allowances upon a combination of nationality and residence criteria. The Court noted that under the national law of none of the Member States did a man acquire the nationality of his wife. To take into account a nationality acquired by a woman as a result of marriage where she had no choice in the matter (as under Italian law she did not) would be to discriminate against the woman. It followed that the Staff Regulations should not be so construed. The Court awarded the allowance accordingly. However, the Court has held that it is not discriminatory to withdraw an expatriation allowance where a woman acquires the

---

[16] Annex vii, Art. 4(3).
[17] Annex vii, Art. 1(3).
[18] Case 20/71 [1972] E.C.R. 345. See also Cases 75 and 117/82 *Razzouk and Beydoun* [1984] E.C.R. 1509.
[19] Case 21/74 [1975] E.C.R. 221.

nationality of the State where she is working in circumstances where she is entitled to renounce that nationality, whether she actually does so or not.[20] In such a case her change of status results from her own voluntary act, and not from unlawful discrimination on the part of the Community.

It must be stressed that, while the principle of equal treatment is a general principle of Community law, the primary addressee of such general principles is the Community itself, rather than the Member States. When dealing with the obligations of the Member States, the Court has confined its attention to Article 119 EEC, and to the Directives referred to in this Chapter.[21]

---

[20] Case 37/74 *Van den Broeck* [1975] E.C.R. 235; Case 257/78 *Devred* [1979] E.C.R. 3767.
[21] Case 149/77 *Defrenne (No. 2)* [1978] E.C.R. 1365; Case 275/81 *Koks* [1982] E.C.R. 3013.

PART VI: THE COMMON AGRICULTURAL POLICY

Chapter 12

AGRICULTURE

Introduction

The Treaty subjects agricultural products and industrial goods to different legal regimes. In the case of the latter it is assumed that consumer demand is potentially infinite, and that in seeking to satisfy such demand, a policy of free trade will encourage the efficient allocation of resources, economic expansion, stable prices, and full employment. While such an assumption may be made in principle where industrial goods are concerned, this is not so with respect to agricultural products.[1] Demand is inelastic. Agriculture is subject to the vicissitudes of the climate, making it difficult for producers to match supply to demand. Price fluctuations, influenced by the volume of world production from year to year, can, in a "good" year for the consumer, beggar the producer. These inescapable economic factors, combined with concern for the disparity between urban and agricultural incomes, and a desire to increase domestic production for balance of payments and security reasons, led to the present Member States of the EEC, even prior to membership, to adopt interventionist policies in the agricultural sector, in order to ensure increased production, and a stable income for producers. Measures taken in Germany between 1952 and 1962, and in the United Kingdom prior to Accession, with respect to cereals, illustrate two contrasting approaches. The Federal Republic[2] fixed maximum and minimum prices annually, and obliged a national agency to purchase grain at the minimum price wherever it could not be sold at this price on the open market. This ensured a guaranteed price for the producer, and encouraged production. If the consumer was unable to buy at the maximum price on the market, the national agency released grain in order to depress the prevailing market price. A system of authorised imports had the effect of imposing a charge on products likely to undercut domestic price levels, and thus insulated the domestic market from world price fluctuations. The system applied in the United Kingdom was quite different.[3] British policy was to allow imports of food at world prices, but to subsidise the producers when sales at such prices would result in his suffering a loss. Subsidies were calculated on the basis of the costs of an efficient farmer, so that the less efficient were obliged to improve their

---

[1] See Jaconelli, "The Law of the Common Agricultural Policy," Chap. XII in *The Law of the Common Market* (Wortley ed., 1974), pp. 149 *et seq.*; Kapteyn and Van Themaat, *Introduction to the Law of the European Communities* (1973) p. 302; Mathijsen, *A Guide to European Community Law* (1985), p. 143; L. B. Krause, *European Economic Intergration and the United States* (1968), pp. 77–79, reprinted in part in Stein, Hay, Walbroeck, *European Community Law and Institutions* (1976), p. 429; *Rapport des chefs de délégation aux ministres des affaires étrangères* (1956), p. 44. For an excellent monograph, see Snyder, *Law of the Common Agricultural Policy* (1986).

[2] Smit and Herzog, *The Law of the European Economic Community*, 2–187.

[3] Jaconelli, *op. cit.*, p. 15.

methods, or go out of business. It will be noted that the German method was characterised by price-support, and protection, with the result that the consumer paid directly the difference between the price of the domestic product and that of a possible substitute bought on the world market. The British method was characterised by free trade and subsidies, with the result that the consumer paid the "going rate," influenced by world market prices, while any shortfall from the producer was made up by the taxpayer, rather than the consumer.

The Spaak Report rehearses the particular problems of the agricultural sector, and stresses the difficulties which arise from a large agricultural population farming on smallholdings.[4] It is the latter factor which no doubt encouraged the original Six to adopt an agricultural policy analogous to the German model described above, rather than one along British lines; the latter is administratively suited to a small agricultural population farming relatively large holdings.

The Treaty provides for the establishment of a common agricultural policy, after a transitional period, during which the national market organisations would be phased out.[5] Such a common policy was established in large part by 1967, when Regulations providing for common organisations of the market for most major agricultural products were adopted. Thus the common organisation of the cereals market[6] is characterised by: (i) price support; (ii) external protection; and (iii) export refunds. Producers are assured a minimum return by the obligation of intervention agencies to buy in grain at a specified price. Where such price (as is usually the case[7]) exceeds the price of grain on the world market, a system of levies ensures that imports do not undercut Community prices. In the event of a surplus of Community grain, intervention agencies pay a subsidy on grain exported to countries outside the Common Market.

Intervention agencies are bodies established under national law and charged with the duty of carrying out the common agricultural policy.[8] It should be noted that national intervention agencies do not act as agents of the Community in the implementation of the common agricultural policy, and that their contractual and non contractual liability may not be attributed to the Community.[9] This remains the case where the Commission advises the national intervention agencies as to what it considers to be the appropriate way in which to proceed.[10]

Integration of the United Kingdom into the common agricultural policy was achieved by a five year transitional period between 1973 and 1978, during which time deficiency payments were phased out, and British agricultural producers relied increasingly on the price-support system of the

---

[4] *Op. cit.*, pp. 44, 47.
[5] Arts. 40 and 43(3) EEC.
[6] For a detailed account, see *infra*, pp. 309 *et seq.*
[7] But not always; where Community prices are lower than world prices levies are imposed on exports to ensure supplies to the Community. As to export levies, see *infra*, p. 328.
[8] For the establishment in the U.K. of the Intervention Board for Agricultural Produce, see the European Communities Act 1982, s.6.
[9] Case 109/83 *Eurico* [1984] E.C.R. 3581.
[10] Case 133/79 *Sucrimex* [1980] E.C.R. 1299; Case 217/81 *Interagra* [1982] E.C.R. 2233; Case 109/83 *Eurico* [1984] E.C.R. 3581.

Community.[11] More recently, problems of over-production of cereals in the Community have led to the imposition of levies designed to limit production, and to the grant of direct aid to small producers to compensate them for loss of income resulting from these levies.[12]

So accustomed are we to considering the economic and political implications of the common agricultural policy that we are inclined to forget that it gives rise to *legal* issues of considerable practical importance; this is inevitable since the common organisations of the market established under Community law bestow rights and impose obligations on agricultural producers. The point may be simply illustrated. Prior to August 1973,[13] a premium was payable in certain circumstances to producers of common wheat and rye of breadmaking quality for quantities denatured, *i.e.* rendered unfit for human consumption (thus limiting the use of the wheat and rye concerned to use as animal feed). In order to qualify for the premium, denaturing had to be effected in agreement with an intervention agency, and under its supervision.[14] It was further provided in Article 4(3) of Regulation 1403/69[15] that: "The duration of the denaturing process shall not exceed one day per 40 metric tons of cereals processed." In August 1971, Firma Joseph Aimer, of Rotthalmünster, applied for and received authorisation to denature up to 200 metric tons of wheat. On August 24 and 25 it denatured, respectively, 74 and 71 metric tons, and on the August 26 another 27 metric tons. The German intervention agency refused a premium for the grain denatured on August 26, since on that day less than 40 tons had been processed. Joseph Aimer brought an action for the premium, and the Verwaltungsgericht sought a preliminary ruling from the Court on the question whether Article 4(3) of Regulation 1403/69 precluded a producer from claiming a premium even where the total amount of denatured grain was such that the rate of denaturation *averaged* 40 tons a day. The Court replied in the negative.[16] While the fact that the denaturing operations entailed considerable supervisory costs justified the requirement that at least 40 tons of wheat be denatured per day, if the denaturing operation extended over several days, "the objectives sought are attained if the total duration of the process does not exceed a period which is equivalent to a daily average of 40 denatured tonnes, provided that the undertaking's capacity has been used in a rational way."[17] Any narrower interpretation of Article 4(3), observed the Court, would exceed the objective sought and must therefore be objected.

The subject-matter of the main suit in *Aimer*, and the reasoning of the Court, illustrate two features of the common agricultural policy. First,

[11] See 1973 Act of Accession, Arts. 50–64. For provisions relating to particular organisations of the market, see Arts. 65–103.
[12] See Reg. 1579/86, O.J. 1986, L139/29; and Reg. 1983/86, O.J. 1986, L171/1. For details, see *infra*, at p. 319.
[13] Reg. 2727/75, O.J. 1975, L281/1, Art. 7(1) provided for denaturation. Reg. 1143/76, O.J. 1976, L130/1, modified the intervention price system for common wheat and rye of breadmaking quality, making denaturation unnecessary, and the provision in Art. 7(3) was deleted accordingly.
[14] Reg. 172/67, J.O. 1967, 2602, superseded by Reg. 2739/75, O.J. 1975, L281/51, Art. 8.
[15] J.O. 1969, L180/4.
[16] Case 27/72 *Aimer* [1972] E.C.R. 1091.
[17] [1972] E.C.R. 1091 at p. 1098.

much of the law relating to agriculture is concerned with granting legal rights to producers in return for their fulfilling specified conditions; it is thus hardly surprising that legal disputes arise. Secondly, agricultural legislation, as in the case of Community law in general, must be interpreted in light of its object and purpose,[18] while in its application, national courts may be confronted with arguments involving an appreciation of economic factors, such as the "rational use" of an entrepreneur's capacity.

The difficulties that may arise in interpreting the Community legislation which implements the common agricultural policy should not be underestimated. Thus, the purposive rule of interpretation has required that a premium payable for the non-marketing of cow's milk be applied also to ewe's milk.[19] Furthermore, the Court has held that the meaning to be given to the same words or phrases used in Community legislation may not be uniform, and may vary according to the objective pursued by the rules in question.[20] While in general a Community term is to be given a single Community meaning, Community rules do, exceptionally, contemplate a variable construction in the different Member States; thus the meaning of "thin flank" of beef has been held to vary according to local methods of boning and cutting.[21]

Products subject to Articles 39 to 46 of the Treaty

The common agricultural policy applies to "products of the soil, of stockfarming and of fisheries and products of first-stage processing directly related to these products."[22] The relevant products are listed in Annex II of the Treaty.[23] The Council took advantage of the authorisation contained in Article 38(3) to add to the list within two years of entry into force of the Treaty, and adopted Regulation 7a/59.[24] This Regulation was in fact issued on January 30, 1961, though dated December 18, 1959. Its legality was upheld by the Court[25] on the basis that although it was *issued* after the lapse of the two year deadline, its contents had in fact been *settled* in good time. The derogations allowed in the case of agricultural products from the rules establishing the common market constitute exceptional measures, and must be given a strict construction.[26] Thus any products unspecified in either Annex II or Regulation 7a/59 fall outside the common agricultural policy and are subject to the general rules of the Treaty.[26] The words "products of *first-stage* processing" on the other hand were given a broad construction by the Court in *König*,[27] in which the Bundesfinanzhof asked the Court whether the inclusion of ethyl alcohol for human consumption in

---

[18] See, *e.g.* Case 292/82 *Merck* [1983] E.C.R. 3781, para. 12.
[19] Case 109/84 *Menges* [1985] E.C.R. 2.5.85.
[20] Case 85/77 *Azienda Agricola* [1978] E.C.R. 527 at p. 540.
[21] Case 327/82 *EKRO* [1984] E.C.R. 107.
[22] Art. 38(1) EEC.
[23] Art. 38(3).
[24] J.O. 1961, 71.
[25] Case 185/73 *König* [1974] E.C.R. 507.
[26] Cases 2 & 3/62 *Commission* v. *Luxembourg and Belgium* [1962] E.C.R. 425. The proposition in the text holds good even if the products in question fall within the general scope of Article 38(1) EEC, see Case 77/83 *CILFIT* [1984] E.C.R. 1257.
[27] Case 185/73 [1974] E.C.R. 607.

Regulation 7a/59 was consistent with Article 38 of the Treaty, inasmuch as it was subject, after distillation (first-stage processing), to a further process, namely, dilution with water. The Court responded that Article 38(3) was to be construed in the light of the aim of the agricultural policy, and of the list of products to be found in Annex II. Many of these latter could not be described as products of first-stage processing in the strict sense, but were characterised by their close economic relationship with basic agricultural products. It followed that "products of first-stage processing directly related" to basic products must be interpreted as implying "a clear economic interdependence between basic products and products resulting from a productive process, *irrespective of the number of operations* involved therein."[28] Where the cost of processing a product rendered the price of its agricultural raw material merely marginal, the product would be excluded from the ambit of Article 38(1), but this could not be said to be so in the case of ethyl alcohol.

Objectives of the common agricultural policy

The objectives of the common agricultural policy are stated in Article 39 of the Treaty as:

"(a) to increase agricultural productivity by promoting technical progress and by ensuring the rational development of agricultural production and the optimum utilisation of the factors of production, in particular labour;

(b) thus to ensure a fair standard of living for the agricultural community, in particular by increasing the individual earnings of persons engaged in agriculture;

(c) to stabilise markets;

(d) to assure the availability of supplies;

(e) to ensure that supplies reach consumers at reasonable prices."

While the objectives of the common agricultural policy are binding on the Community legislator, they must be construed as a whole, and it will be difficult to challenge legislation successfully on the ground that it conflicts with any single objective itemised in Article 39. Thus when the Commission refused Germany permission to import duty free oranges, on the ground that to do so would disturb the market in apples, pears and peaches, Germany failed in her contention that the Commission's action was inconsistent with Article 39(1)(*e*). The Commission conceded that consumers could acquire most agricultural products more cheaply if it pursued an "open door" policy, but pointed out that this would involve an abandonment of other agricultural objectives, *in casu* the requirement that a stable market[29] be maintained for apples, pears and peaches. The Court took the view that there had been no infringement of Article 39 since the

---

[28] Emphasis added.

[29] By a stable market is meant a market in which violent price fluctuations are minimised. This requires in practice insulation from world markets by levies on imports when world prices are falling, and levies on exports when (exceptionally) they are rising. Even significant changes in the patterns of established trade resulting from the creation of a single market will not conflict with Art. 3(1)(*c*), see Cases 63–69/72 *Werhahn* [1973] E.C.R. 1229.

expression "reasonable prices" had to be interpreted in the light of the agricultural policy taken as a whole, and could not be taken to mean the lowest possible prices.[30] On the other hand, the Court has upheld co-responsibility levies on milk as a measure designed to stabilise the market in question.[31]

The Court has made it clear that the task of balancing the various objectives of the common agricultural policy must be undertaken in the light of the overriding principle of "Community preference."[32] German importers had challenged the validity of Regulation 144/65, which introduced a compensatory tax on imports of grapes from Bulgaria and Rumania, in order to reduce their competitive advantage *vis-à-vis* Community grapes. The importers alleged that this automatic levy gave unilateral preference to the interests of the Community fruit and vegetable producers and that this violated Article 39(1)(*d*) and (*e*). They were unsuccessful. "These objectives," declared the Court, "which are intended to safeguard the interests of both farmers and consumers, may not all be simultaneously and fully attained. In balancing these interests, the Council must take into account, where necessary, in favour of the farmers, the principle known as 'Community preference,' which is one of the principles of the Treaty and which in agricultural matters is laid down in Article 44(2)."[33]

Fundamental as the principle of Community preference may be, it cannot prevent the granting of less favourable treatment to importers from Community countries than to importers from third countries where their respective situations are not truly comparable. During the transitional period, Article 17(2) of Regulation 19/62,[34] on the common organisation of the grain market, provided for the possibility of having the levy on imports from third countries set in advance, but not the levy from other Community countries. A German enterprise imported oats from the Netherlands which were allegedly delayed in transit to the Federal Republic because the canals were frozen over. The German importer accordingly had to pay a higher levy than he would have had to pay on the date originally scheduled for importation. While in the case of imports from third countries a plea of *force majeure* would have been available, and the levy set in advance for the *scheduled* date of import applicable, in the case of imports from other Member States no such facility was available. The Court denied[35] any infringement of the principle of Community preference, emphasising: (i) that levies on intra-Community trade and those on trade with third countries fulfilled different purposes; and (ii) that price fluctuations in the Common Market were much smaller than on the world

---

[30] Case 34/62 *Germany* v. *Commission* [1963] E.C.R. 131; Case 59/83 *Biovilac* [1984] E.C.R. 4057. For the temporary priority of any one of these objectives, see Case 5/73 *Balkan-Import-Export* [1973] E.C.R. 1091 at 1112, para. 24; Case 29/77 *Roquette* [1977] E.C.R. 1835. But *quaere* whether long term imbalance is permissible. Surely increasing support prices for products in structural surplus, in the absence of effective measures to reduce production, could be successfully challenged under Article 39?
[31] Case 138/78 *Stolting* [1979] E.C.R. 713.
[32] Case 5/67 *Beus* [1968] E.C.R. 83.
[33] [1968] E.C.R. 83 at p. 98. Art. 44(2) refers to "the development of a natural preference between Member States."
[34] J.O. 1962, 933.
[35] Case 73/69 *Dehlmann* [1970] E.C.R. 467.

market, precisely because of the Community rules, while the lines of communication with the principal exporting third countries were generally longer than the intra-Community routes. Since the two legal regimes were not strictly comparable, differentiation between them could not amount to discrimination.

The Court has held that since a single trading system with non-member countries constitutes one of the fundamental objectives of the common market, it will be regarded as one of the essential aims of a Regulation establishing a common organisation of the market.[36]

Article 39(2) of the Treaty provides:

"In working out the common agricultural policy and the special methods for its application, account shall be taken of:

(a) the particular nature of agricultural activity, which results from the social structure of agriculture and from structural and natural disparities between the various agricultural regions;

(b) the need to effect the appropriate adjustments by degrees;

(c) the fact that in the Member States agriculture constitutes a sector closely linked with the economy as a whole."

In the *Kind* case, the Court upheld different reference prices for sheepmeat in different Member States, alleged by the applicant to be discriminatory, in part on the basis of Article 39(2)(*a*) and (*c*) of the Treaty. As the Court said:

" . . . far from precluding any form of gradual approach in achieving the common organisation of agricultural markets Article 39(2) of the Treaty provides *inter alia* that 'in working out the Common Agricultural Policy and the special methods for its application, account shall be taken of . . . structural and natural disparities between the various agricultural regions' and of 'the need to effect the appropriate adjustments by degrees'."[37]

In *Faust*,[38] the Court invoked the principle that agriculture constitutes a sector closely linked with the economy as a whole to justify the pursuit of objectives of external commercial policy within the framework of a common organisation of the market,[39] and in *Samvirkande Dansk*[40] the Court relied upon the same principle to refute the argument that the common agricultural policy was intended to shield the agricultural population from the impact of a national income policy implemented by a tax on agricultural land.

Countervailing charges

Agricultural products which have not yet been subjected to a common organisation of the market (and the only two products of any note falling within this category are potatoes and ethyl alcohol of agricultural origin), may remain subject to a national organisation of the market, though from

[36] Case 135/79 *Gedelfi* [1980] E.C.R. 1713.
[37] Case 186/81 [1982] E.C.R. 2885, para. 19.
[38] Case 52/81 [1982] E.C.R. 3745.
[39] Case 52/81 [1982] E.C.R. 374.
[40] Case 297/82 [1983] E.C.R. 3199.

the end of the transitional period, the free movement provisions of the
Treaty also apply to such products.[41] If an agricultural product in one
Member State is subject to the free play of competition, while in another
Member State it enjoys the support of a national market organisation, the
unqualified application of the free movement provisions of the Treaty
would subject the produce of the first Member State to unfair competition
from the produce of the second Member State. Moreover, in the absence
of a common organisation of the market providing to the contrary, the provisions of the Treaty on State aids have no application.[42] To meet such
eventualities, Article 46 of the Treaty provides as follows:

> "Where in a Member State a product is subject to a national market
> organisation or to internal rules having equivalent effect which affect
> the competitive position of similar production in another Member
> State, a countervailing charge shall be applied by Member States to
> imports of this product coming from the Member State where such
> organisation or rules exist, unless that State applies a countervailing
> charge on export.
>
> The Commission shall fix the amount of these charges at the level
> required to redress the balance; it may also authorise other measures,
> the conditions and details of which it shall determine."

The Commission has in recent years had occasion to impose countervailing charges under this Article on excessively low priced exports of French
ethyl alcohol of agricultural origin to other Member States.[43]

In the *St. Nikolaus* case[44] the Court rejected arguments to the effect: (1)
that Article 46 had no application after the end of the transitional period;
and (2) that it could only be invoked with regard to *lawful* national
measures, Article 169 of the Treaty being available to combat *unlawful*
national support measures. Furthermore, the Court made the following
observations:

> "Article 46 constitutes for the Commission a useful instrument which
> allows it to adopt immediate safeguards against distortions of compe-
> tition created by a Member State. The introduction of a countervailing
> charge pursuant to that Article thus facilitates the achievement—by
> the maintenance of normal trade patters in the exceptional and tem-
> porary circumstances which justify the measure—of the aims of
> Article 39 of the Treaty, which seeks *inter alia* to stabilize the markets
> and to ensure a fair standard of living for the agricultural population
> concerned.
>
> Moreover, although such a countervailing charge appears to be an
> impediment to intra-Community trade, it cannot be compared to a
> charge having an effect equivalent to a customs duty. It is a charge
> imposed in the general interest, the amount of which is fixed by the

[41] See *infra*, p. 305.
[42] See *infra*, at p. 309.
[43] See Reg. 851/76, O.J. 1976 L96/41, considered by the Court in Case 337/82 *St. Nikolaus*
[1984] E.C.R. 1051; Reg. 1407/78, O.J. 1978 L170/4; Reg. 2541/84, O.J. 1984 L238/16;
Reg. 644/85, O.J. 1985 L73/15, considered by the Court in Case 181/85 *France* v.. *Commission* Judgment of February 12, 1987.
[44] Case 337/82 note 43.

Commission and not unilaterally by a Member State. It enables products from States where aids are granted to be exported to other Member States without disturbing their markets and thus prevents artificial differences between prices in the exporting Member State and those in the importing Member State, resulting from disparities in the national markets before the establishment of a common organisation, from creating imbalances in trade. In each case it is for the Commission to ensure that the duration and the amount of the charge remain within the limits circumscribed by the need to re-establish equilibrium."

There can be no doubt that Article 46 remains an important tool in the hands of the Commission in those limited circumstances in which it may be invoked.

Common organisations of the market—mechanisms

The Treaty provides that in order to attain the objectives of the agricultural policy common organisations of agricultural markets shall be established, and that such organisations may include "all measures required to attain the objectives set out in Article 39, in particular regulation of prices, aids for the production and marketing of the various products, storage and carry-over arrangements and common machinery for stabilising imports or exports."[45] The choice of means placed at the disposal of the Council is large, and its range may be illustrated by reference to Regulation 804/68 on the milk and milk products market,[46] which provides for: (i) the setting of a target price for milk, and an intervention price for butter and skimmed milk powder (regulation of prices)[47]; (ii) the granting of aid for skimmed milk and skimmed milk powder for use as feedingstuffs, and for skimmed milk processed into casein (aids for production); (iii) aid for the private storage of butter and cream (storage arrangements)[48]; (iv) measures to prevent market disturbance as a result of price alterations at the time of change-over from one milk year to the next, including, in certain circumstances, the taxation of milk stocks (carry-over arrangements)[49]; and (v) levies on imports into the Community of milk, butter, cheese, cream, etc. (common machinery for stabilising imports). Since 1977, a co-responsibility levy has been applied to milk, in order to curb excess production.[50] In 1984, persistent problems of over-production in the dairy sector led to the introduction of milk production quotas and an additional levy on surplus production.[51]

---

[45] Art. 40(3), first sub-para.
[46] J.O. 1968, L148/13.
[47] For target and intervention prices, see the survey of the common organisation of the grain market, *infra*, at p. 311.
[48] Aid to private storage keeps produce off the market, and hence amounts to a measure of price support.
[49] *Cf.* the carry-over payments which may be made under Reg. 2727/75, *infra*, at p. 311.
[50] Reg. 1079/77, O.J. 1977, L131/6.
[51] See Reg. 856/84, O.J. 1984, L90/10, amending Reg. 804/68, and Reg. 857/84, O.J. 1984 L90/13, as amended, on general rules for the application of the additional levy. For controls on surplus production under the common agricultural policy, see Snyder, *op. cit.*, note 1, pp. 122 *et seq.*

The Court has construed the Council's authority broadly. In *Neumann* v. *Hauptzollamt Hof/Saale*[52] it was alleged that levies on imports on poultry from Poland constituted customs duties which could not be justified under Article 40(3) of the Treaty. The Court observed that levy systems such as those in issue[53] constituted methods of regulating prices and common machinery for stabilising the import of agricultural products, but that in any event the list of intervention mechanisms itemised in Article 40(3) was not exhaustive. The breadth of this provision was illustrated graphically in a later case[54] in which the legality of "compensatory amounts" was called in question.[55] When the currencies of Germany and the Netherlands relinquished their fixed parities and floated upwards as against the currencies of the other Member States, the former countries were authorised to charge compensatory amounts on imports, and to grant them on exports, in order to offset their *de facto* revaluation, and maintain intact the common agricultural policy's single price system. At first authorised under Article 103 EEC, this mechanism was later incorporated into the common agricultural policy under, *inter alia*, Article 43.[56] The Court rejected the argument that such measures were *ultra vires* the latter Article, insisting that "the powers conferred for implementing the common agricultural policy do not relate merely to possible structural measures but extend equally to any immediate short-term economic intervention required in this area of production . . . ."[57]

Constraints on the legislative competence of the Council and the Commission

Article 43(2) of the Treaty provides that the Council, on a proposal from the Commission, and after consulting the Assembly, shall make Regulations, issue Directives, or take Decisions, to implement the common agricultural policy. It is customary for the Council to lay down basic Regulations which contain provisions for further implementation under the "Management Committee" procedure. The Court has upheld the validity of agricultural Management Committees, ruling that the Council need not draw up all the details of the common policy, it being sufficient for the purposes of Article 43 "that the basic elements of the matter to be dealt with have been adopted in accordance with the procedure laid down by that provision."[58]

Both the Council and the Commission enjoy wide discretionary powers in fulfilling their functions under the common agricultural policy. The Court has stressed that the Council must be recognised as having a discretionary power in this area which corresponds to the political responsi-

---

[52] Case 17/67 [1967] E.C.R. 441.
[53] Under Regs. 22, 109, and 135/62, J.O. 1962, 959, 1939 and 2621.
[54] Case 5/73 *Balkan-Import-Export* [1973] E.C.R. 1091.
[55] For a brief account of monetary compensatory amounts, see *infra*, at pp. 354 *et seq.*
[56] Art. 43(3) authorises the Council to enact Regulations, Directives or Decisions to implement the common agricultural policy.
[57] [1973] E.C.R. 1091 at p. 1108.
[58] Case 30/80 *Scheer* [1970] E.C.R. 1197 at p. 1208.

bilities which Articles 40 and 43 impose upon it.[59] In the case of both the Commission and the Council, this discretion extends to assessment of the factual basis of the measures they adopt, as well as to the purpose and scope of those measures. As the court declared in *Ludwigschafener*:

> "It should be remembered that, in their determining their policy in this area, the competent Community institutions enjoy wide discretionary powers regarding not only establishment of the factual basis of their action, but also definition of the objectives to be pursued, within the framework of the provisions of the Treaty, and the choice of the appropriate means of action."[60]

The Court has held that where the Commission is charged with evaluation of a complex economic situation, it enjoys a wide measure of discretion, and that in reviewing the legality of such discretion, the Court must confine itself to examining whether it contains a manifest error or constitutes a misuse or power or whether the administration has clearly exceeded the bounds of its discretion.[61]

While the responsibilities of the Council and the Commission are not identical, it seems that the same principles govern the review of the exercise of discretionary powers by both institutions. Thus the Court has held that the "legality of a measure can only be adversely affected if the measure is manifestly unsuitable for achieving the aim pursued by the competent Community institution"[62] and in the *Sermide* case[63] the Court concluded that the Council's choice of dates for the commencement of the marketing year could only be challenged if it constituted a misuse of powers.

The principal constraints on the competence of the Council are the principles of non-discrimination and proportionality. The first results from the wording of Article 40(3), which provides that common organisations shall "exclude any discrimination between producers or consumers within the Community." The principle of proportionality, whereby measures must be no more burdensome than is strictly necessary to achieve their desired end, constitutes a general principle of Community law,[64] and is mentioned explicitly in this context in Article 40(3), which provides that common organisations "may include all measures *required* [emphasis added] to attain the objectives set out in Article 39." Both principles have been invoked on numerous occasions by litigants before the Court.

The Court has defined the principle of non-discrimination as follows in *Sermide*:

> "It is appropriate in the first place to point out that under the principle of non-discrimination between Community producers or consumers, which is enshrined in the second subparagraph of Article 40(3) . . .

---

[59] Case 138/78 *Stölting* [1979] E.C.R. 713; Case 179/84 *Bozzetti* [1986] 2 C.M.L.R. 246.
[60] Cases 197–200, etc./80, [1981] E.C.R. 3211, at p. 3251, para. 37; see also Case 160/78 *Italy v. Council* [1979] E.C.R. 2575.
[61] Case 78/74 *Deuka* [1975] E.C.R. 421; Case 98/78 *Racke* [1979] E.C.R. 69.
[62] Case 59/73 *Biovilac* [1984] E.C.R. 4057, at para. 17.
[63] Case 106/83 [1984] E.C.R. 4209.
[64] Case 11/70 *Internationale Handellsgesellschaft* [1970] E.C.R. 1125; Case 5/73 *Balkan-Import-Export* [1973] E.C.R. 1091.

and which includes the prohibition of discrimination on grounds of nationality laid down in the first paragraph of Article 7 of the EEC Treaty, comparable situations must not be treated differently and different situations must not be treated in the same way unless such treatment is objectively justified. It follows that the various elements in the common organisation of the markets, such as protective measures, subsidies, aid and so on, may not be differentiated according to region or according to other factors affecting production or consumption except by reference to objective criteria which ensure a proportionate division of the advantages and disadvantages for those concerned without distinction between the territories of the Member States."[65]

The *Wagner* case[66] affords a helpful illustration of objective criteria justifying differentiation between apparently similar situations. Community rules provided for reimbursement of storage costs in respect of sugar in transit between two approved warehouses situated in the *same* Member State, but not in respect of sugar in transit between two approved warehouses in *different* Member States. The Court rejected the argument that this was discriminatory, since the difference in treatment was based on requirements of supervision which could be objectively justified. The Court's ruling is a reminder that the principle of non-discrimination is only infringed where the Community legislator treats *comparable* situations in different ways.[67] It follows that an allegation of discrimination cannot be based on differences in treatment of products subject to different market organisations which are not in competition with each other.[68]

The Court has held that the prohibition of non-discrimination contained in Article 40(3) is but a specific enunciation of the general principle of equality recognised in Community law.[69] However, the Article is not concerned with "discrimination" between producers and consumers, for this is a matter for Article 39 of the Treaty.[70] Furthermore, there is no requirement of equal treatment for non-member countries in the external relations of the Community.[71]

The Court has defined the principle of proportionality as follows:

"In order to establish whether a provision of Community law is consonant with the principle of proportionality it is necessary to establish, in the first place, whether the means it employs to achieve the aim correspond to the importance of the aim and, in the second place, whether they are necessary for its achievement."[72]

A common device employed by the Community legislator to secure fulfilment by traders of their obligations is the lodging of a security which will

---

[65] Case 106/83 [1984] E.C.R. 4209 at p. 4231, para. 28; see also Case 139/77 *Denkavit* [1978] E.C.R. 1317; Case 106/81 *Kind* [1982] E.C.R. 2885.

[66] Case 8/82 [1983] E.C.R. 271.

[67] See, *e.g.* Case 6/71 *Rheinmulen Dusseldorf* [1971] E.C.R. 719; Case 283/83 *Racke* [1984] E.C.R. 3791.

[68] Cases 292 and 293/81 *Jean Lion* [1982] E.C.R. 3887.

[69] Cases 117/76 and 16/77 *Ruckdeschel* [1977] E.C.R. 1753; Case 125/77 *KSH* [1978] E.C.R. 1991; Cases 103 and 145/77 *RSH* v. *IBAP* [1978] E.C.R. 2037; Case 245/81 *Edeka* [1982] E.C.R. 2745; Case 282/82 *Unifrex* [1984] E.C.R. 1969.

[70] Case 5/73 *Balkan-Import-Export* [1973] E.C.R. 1091.

[71] Case 52/81 *Faust* [1982] E.C.R. 3745.

[72] Case 66/82 *Fromancais* [1983] E.C.R. 395.

be forfeit in the event of default. Such deposits have been subject to numerous challenges on the grounds that they infringe the principle of proportionality. The court has upheld such deposits in principle, provided that they are not excessive in amount.[73] Thus in *Beste Boter*[74] the Court upheld a deposit system whereby an undertaking which tendered for cheap butter for processing would be liable to forfeit his deposit if a subsequent purchaser failed to process the butter as required. The amount of the deposit was set to cover the difference between the market price of the butter and the minimum selling price fixed by tender. The effect of forfeiture of the deposit where the butter was not processed was therefore to make the successful tenderer pay a total amount equivalent to the market price of the butter in accordance with a contractual obligation which he had freely entered into. In these circumstances the forfeiture of the deposit for the default of a third party could not be regarded as a disproportionate burden upon the traders in question.

More successful objections have been raised to the entire forfeiture of a security for failure to comply with any of several obligations of varying degrees of importance. Thus in *Buitoni*[75] the forfeiture of the entire deposit on an import/export licence in the case both of failure to import/export *and* failure merely to provide proof within a specified period was held to be disproportionate.[76] However, the Court has denied that the Community legislator is obliged to mitigate forfeiture of a deposit for minor breach of the principal obligation with which the deposit seeks to secure compliance.[77] In *E. D. & F. Man*[78] the Court emphasised the distinction between principal and secondary obligations secured by the lodging of a security. In that case Community rules provided for export refunds on surplus sugar, for the lodging of a security against export, and the forfeiture of the entire security in the event of either a failure to export, or a failure to make a timely application for an export licence. Man applied for an export licence four hours late and the security was forfeit! The Court held that where the Community legislator drew a distinction between a primary obligation, compliance with which was necessary in order to attain the objective sought, and a secondary obligation, essentially of an administrative nature, it could not, without breaching the principle of proportionality, penalise failure to comply with the secondary obligation as severely as failure to comply with the primary obligation. In the case in question, the obligation to export was the primary obligation, and the obligation to apply for a licence was of secondary importance. It follows that automatic forfeiture of the entire security for breach of the latter obligation offended the principle of proportionality.

A challenge to the legality of a Council Regulation based on the prin-

---

[73] Case 11/70 *Internationale Handellsgesellschaft* [1970] E.C.R. 1125.
[74] Cases 99 & 100/76 [1977] E.C.R. 861.
[75] Case 122/78 [1979] E.C.R. 677.
[76] See also Case 240/78 *Atalanta Amsterdam* [1979] E.C.R. 2137.
[77] Case 272/81 *RU-MI* [1982] E.C.R. 4167.
[78] Case 181/84 [1985] 3 C.M.L.R. 759. The *Man* case may represent an extension of the *Buitoni* principle since in *Buitoni* the primary obligation had already been fulfilled, yet in *Man* the primary obligation could not arise until the export licence was applied for.

ciples of non-discrimination and proportionality was successful in *Bela-Mühle Josef Bergmann* v. *Grows-Farm*.[79] Regulation 563/76[80] had been adopted with a view to reducing surpluses of skimmed milk powder by making its use compulsory in the feeding of livestock. Thus the Council had conditioned the grant of aids under Community law for certain vegetable feedingstuffs,[81] as well as the free circulation within the Community of similar imported products,[82] on the purchase from intervention agencies of quantities of skimmed milk powder. The granting of aids and the free circulation of imports were conditioned on the deposit of a surety, or alternatively, on presentation of proof that certain quantities of skimmed milk powder had been purchased and denatured.[83] The cost to users of skimmed milk powder they were compelled to buy was three times that of the equivalent amount, in nutritional terms, of vegetable feedingstuffs, while forfeiture of the surety was even more expensive than buying the skimmed milk powder. On references from German and Dutch courts, the Court held, in a brief judgment, that the scheme in question had placed an economic burden not only on milk producers (who presumably were the only producers to benefit from the arrangements) but also, and even mainly, on producers *in other fields of agricultural production*. Compulsory purchase at a price so disproportionate had resulted in allocating the burden between agricultural producers in a quite discriminatory fashion. Furthermore, such measures went above and beyond what was *necessary* to attain the objective of diminishing the surpluses of skimmed milk powder. Consequently, the Regulation in question could not be justified within the framework of the common agricultural policy and its objectives.

A third principle which may condition the interpretation and validity of Community legislation is that of legal certainty.[84] This principle requires that traders should be able to act with confidence on the basis of the law as it stands, and that the legislator will respect their legitimate expectations. Thus if Community rules provide for a premium for denaturing grain, and the premium is reduced for grain denatured after a certain date, the rules will be construed so as to allow traders who have purchased grain for denaturation before the amendment and offered it for denaturation before the date in question, to claim the premium at the old rate, even if denaturation actually takes place after that date.[85] That is not to say that undertakings acquire a vested right in the continuance of any particular regime established under the common agricultural policy.[86] Thus, there can be no guarantee of continuous application of the system of monetary compensatory amounts.[87] However, when agricultural rules are amended, protection of legitimate expectation is required where, under the previous system,

---

[79] Case 114/76 [1977] E.C.R. 1211, and Case 116/76 *Granaria* [1977] E.C.R. 1247, and Cases 119 and 120/76 *Olmühle Hamburg* [1977] E.C.R. 1269.
[80] O.J. 1976, L67/18.
[81] Art. 2.
[82] Art. 3.
[83] Arts. 2, 3 & 4.
[84] See *supra* at p. 61.
[85] Case 78/74 *Deuka* [1975] E.C.R. 421.
[86] Case 26/77 *Balkan-Import-Export* [1977] E.C.R. 2031.
[87] Case 74/74 *CNTA* [1975] E.C.R. 533; Case 96/77 *Bauche* [1978] E.C.R. 383.

traders had already informed the competent authorities of their intention to carry out specific transactions over a period extending beyond the time of the introduction of the new system and have irrevocably committed themselves thereto by the lodging of a security.[88] The Court has stressed the importance of the distinction, for the purpose of applying the principle of the protection of legitimate expectation, to be drawn between cases where traders commit themselves to the public authorities to carry out certain transactions, and those in which they do not. The principle "cannot be extended to the point of generally preventing new rules from applying to the future effects of situations which arose under the earlier rules in the absence of obligations entered into with the public authorities."[89]

Application of the general rules of the Treaty to agricultural products

Article 38(2) provides: "Save as otherwise provided in Articles 39 to 46, the rules laid down for the establishment of the common market shall apply to agricultural products." The Articles in question "otherwise provide" in that:

— during the transitional period the Member States were authorised to apply non-discriminatory minimum export prices (Article 44) and bilateral trading agreements *inter se* (Article 45);
— Articles 40 and 43 authorise the establishment of common organisations of the market whose mechanism (such as levies) may derogate from the general rules of the Treaty (such as the common customs tariff);
— the provisions of the Treaty relating to competition and state aids are applicable to the production of and trade in agricultural products only to the extent determined by the Council (Article 42).

Since exceptions to the rules of the Treaty on the free movement of goods must be clearly provided for, even during the transitional period standstill provisions, such as Article 12, were otherwise applicable to trade in agricultural goods.[90]

As of the end of the transitional period, trade in agricultural products in sectors lacking a common organisation of the market became subject to the free movement provisions of the Treaty[91] even if the goods in question were subject at the time to a national organisation of the market. The contrary was generally thought to be the case prior to the Court's decision in *Charmasson* v. *Minister for Economic Affairs and Finance*,[92] a reference

---

[88] Case 74/74 *CNTA* [1975] E.C.R. 533; Case 90/77 *Stimming* [1978] E.C.R. 995.

[89] Case 84/78 *Tomadini* [1979] E.C.R. 1801.

[90] Cases 90 and 91/63 *Commission* v. *Luxembourg & Belgium* [1964] E.C.R. 625. Art. 226 applied to agricultural goods during the transitional period, see Case 72/72 *Baer-Getreide* [1973] E.C.R. 377.

[91] For the rules on competition and state aids, see *infra* at p. 309. Art. 26 has been applied to agricultural products, see Smit & Herzog, *The Law of the European Economic Community*, 2–211, as has Art. 115, see Case 62/70 *Bock* [1971] E.C.R. 897. For state monopolies applicable to agricultural products, see *supra*, at p. 157.

[92] Case 48/74 [1974] E.C.R. 1383. Art. 43 EEC authorises the Council to replace national organisations of the market by common organisations. It was thought that if the Council had not done so, the national organisations were entitled to derogate from the general rules of the Treaty. For the views of commentators, see the references of Adv. Gen. Warner to van der Meersch and Mégrét in support of his arguments, [1974] E.C.R. 1383 at p. 401.

from the French Conseil d'Etat on the question whether the existence in a Member State of a national market organisation within the meaning of Articles 43, 45 and 46 of the Treaty precluded the application of the Treaty's prohibition on quantitative restrictions to quotas on imported bananas.[93] In their submissions to the Court, the Commission, the French Government and the Advocate-General unanimously suggested an affirmative reply: while Article 43 of the Treaty authorised the Council to replace national organisations of the market by common organisations, in the absence of Council action, such national organisations were entitled to derogate from the general rules of the Treaty. The Court, however, took a different view:

"Under the provisions of Article 40(1) Member States shall, by the end of the transitional period at the latest, bring the common agricultural policy into force.

Under the provisions of Articles 43 and 46 of the Treaty, the national market organisations may provisionally be kept in existence pending the establishment of a common organisation within the meaning of Article 40(2) under the conditions defined in Article 43(3).

Nevertheless Article 45 of the Treaty provides that during the first stage 'trade shall be developed' by the conclusion of long term agreements or contracts between importing and exporting Member States.

Paragraph (2) of this Article provides for an 'increase' in the volume of imports based upon a specified period of reference.

It would be contrary to the letter and spirit of these provisions to admit that in the absence of agreements or long term contracts national organisations remain permanently excluded from the rules relating to the elimination of quantitative restrictions and may therefore thwart the development of trade expressed in paragraphs (1) and (2) of that Article."[94]

The Court affirmed its position in *Commission* v. *French Republic*,[95] in which France argued that the absence of a common organisation of the market necessitated recognition of the competence of Member States to take appropriate action in the event of a crisis. The Court disagreed, insisting that from the end of the transitional period the provisions of Articles 39 to 46 could not be relied upon to justify a unilateral derogation from the provisions of Article 34 of the Treaty, even in respect of an agricultural product for which no common organisation of the market had been established. The Court rejected the argument that the absence of such an organisation resulted in a "legal vacuum which the Member States are entitled to fill," since Articles 39 to 46 of the Treaty remained applicable. "It is precisely because of the transfer of powers to a Community," declared the Court, "and of the fundamental purposes of the transfer that, following the

[93] From Zaire, Somaliland, and Surinam. The Treaty's provisions were applicable under Art. 5 of the first Yaounde Convention of July 20, 1963, J.O. 1964, 1431, and Art. 4 of Council Dec. 64/349, J.O. 1964, 1472.

[94] [1974] E.C.R. 1383, at pp. 1393, 1394. The Court in fact found that the simple application of quotas could not in any event amount to a "national marketing organisation" within the meaning of the Treaty.

[95] Case 68/76 [1977] E.C.R. 515.

end of the transitional period, problems such as those with which this case is concerned may be solved solely by Community measures drawn up in the interests of all producers and consumers within the Community."[96]

The Community measures to which the Court refers may derogate in certain respects from the general rules of the Treaty.

In *Neumann* v. *Hauptzollamt Hof/Saale*,[97] the Court considered an objection that import levies on Polish poultry constituted customs duties on imports, and were inconsistent with Article 18 of the Treaty, on the establishment of the common customs tariff. The Court upheld the Council's authority to establish common organisations of the market whose machinery derogates from the general rules of the Treaty as follows:

"Under Article 38(2) of the Treaty, save as otherwise provided in Articles 39 to 46, the rules laid down for the establishment of the Common Market shall apply to agricultural products. These provisions as a whole may constitute a derogation from any of the said rules, including those set out in Article 18 *et seq.* . . . . By establishing . . . a system regulating prices and stabilising the market, the system of levies constitutes one of the bases of the 'common organisation of agricultural productions' prescribed by Article 40(2)."[98]

However, this general statement must be treated with caution. While the Council has a wide range of options at its disposal in the establishment of a common organisation of the market, it does not have the power to introduce measures calculated to impede trade between Member States. The Court has ruled that Articles 38–46 contain no provisions which either expressly or by implication authorise, after the end of the transitional period, charges having equivalent effect to customs duties. It followed that a provision in a Community regulation authorising a levy on goods from other Member States, since it amounted to such a charge, was incompatible with Article 13 of the Treaty, and accordingly with Articles 38–46 of the Treaty.[99] Furthermore, the provisions of the Treaty relating to the abolition of tariff and commercial barriers to intra-Community trade are to be regarded as an integral part of a common organisation.[1]

The Court has held that the provisions of the Treaty relating to the common agricultural policy take precedence, in case of any discrepancy, over other rules relating to the establishment of the common market, and concluded that the specific provisions creating a common organisation thus take precedence over the rules laid down in Article 37 of the Treaty for the adjustment of state monopolies.[1] However, that is to say, that any permissive general provisions of the Treaty should not be construed as derogating from the specific requirements of a common organisation, rather than that a common organisation may include measures incompatible with the free movement of goods provisions of the Treaty.

While a common organisation may not derogate from the provisions of

---

[96] [1977] E.C.R. 515 at p. 531.
[97] Case 17/67, [1967] E.C.R. 441.
[98] [1967] E.C.R. at p. 452.
[99] Cases 80 & 81/77, *Commissionaires Réunis* [1978] E.C.R. 927.
[1] Case 83/78 *Redmond* [1978] E.C.R. 2347; Case 231/78 *McCarren* [1979] E.C.R. 2161.

the Treaty requiring the free movement of goods between Member States, it may be possible to classify measures which appear to amount to, *e.g.* charges having equivalent effect to customs duties, as something quite different, if the purpose of such measures is actually to safeguard intra-Community trade. To the extent that monetary compensatory amounts have an effect analogous to customs duties, this has been held to be justifiable on the ground that the overall aim of the Community legislator is to preserve a single market.[2] This approach to Community measures is in stark contrast to the Court's approach to unilateral measures by Member States,[3] and analogous to the Court's classification of countervailing charges imposed by the Commission under Article 46 of the Treaty to products which remain subject to a national organisation of the market.[4]

The attainment of a single market is the fundamental purpose of the Treaty, and the Council's authority must be construed accordingly. Thus, in *Werhahn* v. *Council and Commission*,[5] the Court rejected the argument that discrimination against German millers with respect to access to supplies of durum wheat could be countered by fixing a lower threshold price for that product in Member States which did not produce it, on the ground that such a solution would conflict with the realisation of a single market, which was the aim of Regulation 120/67, and would jeopardise the principle of free movement of goods.

In the case of competition and state aids Article 42 provides that the provisions of the relevant chapter of the Treaty shall apply to production of and trade in agricultural products only to the extent determined by the Council within the framework of Article 43(2) and (3) and in accordance with the procedure laid down therein, account being taken of Article 39. The Council may, in particular, authorise the granting of aid:

(a) for the protection of enterprises handicapped by structural or national conditions;

(b) within the framework of economic development programmes.

With respect to the rules of competition between enterprises, Regulation 26[6] provides that Articles 85 to 90 of the Treaty shall apply to the production of and trade in the products listed in Annex II to the Treaty,[7] but that Article 85(1) shall "not apply to such of the agreements, decisions and practices referred to in the preceding Article as form an integral part of a national market organisation or are necessary for attainment of the objectives set out in Article 39 of the Treaty." In particular, adds the Regulation, Article 85(1) shall not apply "to agreements, decisions and practices of farmers, farmers' associations, or associations of such associations belonging to a single Member State which concern the production or sale of agricultural products or the use of joint facilities for the storage, treatment or processing of agricultural products, and under which there is no

---

[2] Case 5/73 *Balkan-Import-Export* [1973] E.C.R. 1091; Case 136/77 *Racke* [1978] E.C.R. 1245.
[3] As to which see, *e.g. supra* at p. 101.
[4] See *supra* at p. 298.
[5] Cases 63–69/72 [1973] E.C.R. 1229.
[6] O.J.Sp.Ed. 1959–62, p. 129. See further Snyder, *op. cit.*, pp. 32–38.
[7] Art. 1.

obligation to charge identical prices, unless the Commission finds that competition is thereby excluded or that the objectives of Article 39 of the
Treaty are jeopardised."[8]

In order to qualify for exemption on the ground that an agreement or
practice is necessary for attainment of the objectives set out in Article 39 of
the Treaty, it must be shown that *all* such objectives are furthered—thus an
agreement between Dutch wholesalers and importers of citrus fruit from
third countries fell outside the ambit of Regulation 26 since the marketing
of such produce was necessary neither "to increase agricultural productivity" nor to "ensure a fair standard of living for the agricultural community," though admittedly it did contribute to ensuring market stability,
and the availability of supplies to consumers at reasonable prices.[9]

In order to appreciate the scope of application of the competition rules
to agricultural products, it is necessary to take into account the provisions
of particular organisations of the market.[10] Thus, Regulation 1035/72, on
the fruit and vegetables market, provides for the withdrawal of goods from
the market by producers' organisations if their members' produce fails to
fetch a specified price.[11]

With respect to Articles 92 to 94 of the Treaty on state aids, Regulation
26 makes no provision, so that they are in principle inapplicable to agricultural products under Article 42 of the Treaty. In practice, however, most
organisations of the market provide specifically that the rules on state aids
are applicable, unless excluded in particular cases by the relevant basic
Regulation. Thus Regulation 1035/72 on the fruit and vegetables market,
provides that: "Save as otherwise provided in this Regulation, Articles 92,
93 and 94 of the Treaty shall apply to the production of and trade in [fruit
and vegetables]."[12] In fact, Member States are specifically authorised to
grant aids, under certain circumstances, to national producers' organisations.[13] Such aids are thus exempt from scrutiny under Article 92. Community aids to producers are of course a familiar feature of common
organisations of the market. Thus Regulation 2727/75 on the market in cereals provides for the payment of aid for the production of durum wheat,
the aid to be paid per hectare, and differentiated region by region if appropriate.[14]

The common organisation of the cereals market

Profile of a common organisation

The law relating to agriculture cannot be examined solely, or even
mainly, by reference to the framework of Articles 38 to 46; rather, it is

---

[8] Art. 2.
[9] Case 71/74 *FRUBO* [1975] E.C.R. 563; see also Cases 40–48, etc./73, *Suiker Unie* [1975]
E.C.R. 1663; Case 258/78 *Nungesser* [1982] E.C.R. 2015.
[10] Smit & Herzog, *op. cit.*, 2–138.
[11] Arts. 13–15, 18.
[12] Art. 31. Where Arts. 92–94 applied to a sector covered by a covered by a common organisation of the market, Art. 92 clearly cannot excuse an aid incompatible with the governing
regulation, see Case 177/78 *McCarren* [1979] E.C.R. 2161, para. 11.
[13] Art. 14.
[14] Art. 10.

necessary to examine the operation of the common organisations of the
market applicable in all major sectors. It is proposed to examine as a model
the cereals market, beginning with a general survey of the basic Regulation—2727/75[15]—and continuing with a more detailed consideration of the
implementing legislation and caselaw applicable to particular specialist
areas, such as buying-in, the co-responsibility levy, and the import and
export system. While some of the legal provisions in question (such as
those relating to the price system, and buying-in), relate specifically to the
cereals sector, other provisions, (such as those relating to import and
export licences establish common rules applicable to most organisations of
the market.[16]

1. *General Survey.* The common organisation of the cereals market comprises a "price and trading system" and covers, principally, common
wheat, rye, barley, oats, maize, sorghum and durum wheat.[17] The "price
and trading system" is characterised by:
   — price support, coupled with selective Community aids to agriculture
     producers;
   — a co-responsibility levy to combat over-production; and
   — protection from competition by producers in third countries.
The price support system is based on the annual fixing of *intervention
prices*, prices at which national agencies entrusted with the task of carrying
out the common agricultural policy will buy in grain, at Community
expense, which producers are unable to dispose of on the market. Intervention prices for the various products are set before the beginning of the
marketing year, which commences on July 1 and ends the following June
30.[18] An intervention price is set for common wheat, durum wheat, rye,
barley, maize and sorghum.[19] In the case of common wheat and rye of
breadmaking quality a *special premium* is also fixed.[20] In the event of producers of the above grains being unable to dispose of their produce on the
market, they have the right to sell at the intervention price to intervention
agencies in the Member States during a specified period in the year.[21] In
the case of all the grains mentioned, the prices are established for standard
qualities, and are subject to appropriate variation.[22]

---

[15] O.J. 1975 L281/1, as amended.
[16] For example, Reg. 3183/80, O.J. 1980, L338/1, as amended, lays down common detailed
rules for the application of the system of import and export licences which applies also,
inter alia, to the milk, beef, wine and poultry sectors; particular rules on this matter are laid
down for cereals in Reg. 2042/75, O.J. 1975, L213/5, as amended. Again, Reg. 2746/75,
O.J. 1975, L281/78, as amended, lays down rules for granting export refunds in the cereals
market, while Reg. 2730/79, O.J. 1979, L317/1, as amended, lays down common detailed
rules for the application of export refunds in most agricultural sectors.
[17] Reg. 2727/75, Art. 1 and Annex A.
[18] Reg. 2727/75, Art. 2. The marketing year was formerly August 1 to July 31. The change
was made to accommodate Spain and Portugal, whose harvests are earlier than elsewhere.
[19] Reg. 2727/75, Art. 3(1). *E.g.* see Reg. 1584/86, O.J. 1986, L139/41, fixing the intervention
price for common wheat and maize at 179,44 ECU/tonne, the intervention price for rye,
sorghum and barley at 170,47 ECU/tonne, and the intervention price for durum wheat at
299,60 ECU/tonne, for the 1987/88 marketing year.
[20] Reg. 2727/75, Art. 3(1). Thus for the 1986–87 marketing year, the premium was 3,59 ECU/
tonne for common wheat, and 8, 97 ECU/tonne for rye, see Reg. 1564/86, O.J. 1986, L139/
41.
[21] Reg. 2727/75, Art. 7.
[22] Reg. 1629/77, O.J. 1977, L181/26, Art. 3(2), 7(5).

Since the cost of storage tends to exert an upward influence on market prices during the course of the marketing year, provision is made for monthly increases in intervention prices.[23] At the onset of the new marketing year, intervention prices are offered which may be below the level of the previous years' end increased intervention prices. When this is the case, producers tend to offer for intervention their grain from the old harvest before the end of the marketing year, even though the market may be capable of absorbing it later. To prevent this, provision is made for granting a *carry-over* payment[24] for grain from the old harvest, to assure producers that grain can be kept in storage without financial disadvantage until the end of the marketing year.

To counter structural surpluses in the cereals market, a co-responsibility levy was introduced in the 1986/87 marketing year, to be collected on cereals undergoing first processing, intervention buying, or export in the form of grain. To offset the adverse social effects of this measure, a direct aid system for small producers was also introduced.[25]

The system of price support outlined above would prove quite unworkable if any substantial amounts of grain imported from third countries were allowed access to the Community market at below Community prices; the result would be massive buying-in by intervention agencies. For this reason, provision is made to insulate the Community market from price fluctuations on the world market. To establish such protection, two prices are fixed: the *target price*, and the *threshold price*. The former is crucial, for it determines the level of protection of the Community market. It is set at a level sufficiently above the intervention price (and the reference price) to assure market fluidity and to balance excess production in surplus areas and shortages in deficit areas. Thus, to establish the target price, there are added to the intervention prices, elements reflecting the cost of transport between surplus and deficit areas, and a market element which takes into account the respective market behaviour of the different products involved. The target price is calculated for Duisburg, which is the centre having the greatest deficit for all cereals, and the transport element referred to above is calculated on the basis of transport to Duisburg from Ormes, the centre in largest surplus.[26]

Insulation of the Community market is achieved by ensuring that imports of grain from third countries are subject to a *levy on importation* which makes it impossible to sell them for less than the target price at Duisburg. This is where the *threshold price* comes in. This price is fixed for the Community "in such a way that the selling price for the imported product on the Duisburg market shall be the same as the target price, differences in quality being taken into account."[27] The threshold price is, of course, fixed

---

[23] Reg. 2727/75, Art. 6. For the monthly increases for the 1986/87 marketing year, see Reg. 1585/86, O.J. 1986, L139/43.

[24] Reg. 2727/75, Art. 9. See the lucid explanation of Adv. Gen. Roemer in Case 52/72 *Walzenmuhle Magstadt Kienle* [1972] E.C.R. 1267 at p. 1276.

[25] Reg. 1579/86, O.J. 1986 L.139/29, amending Reg. 2727/75.

[26] Reg. 2727/75, art. 3(4)(*a*). Thus for the 1986/87 marketing year there was a common target price of 233,86 ECU/tonne for maize, rye, sorghum and barley, and target prices of 256,16 for common wheat, and 357,70 for durum wheat, see Reg. 1584/86, O.J. 1986, L139/41.

[27] Reg. 2727/75, Art. 5.

for the same standard qualities as the target price,[28] and equals the latter price reduced by the transport costs between the port of Rotterdam and Duisburg.[29] It follows that any grain imported into Rotterdam at a c.i.f. price equivalent to the threshold price has no competitive advantage over Community grain selling at the target price or below. That all third country grain *is* in effect imported at a c.i.f. price equivalent to the threshold price is ensured by a system of *import levies*, which are equivalent to the threshold price less the c.i.f. price calculated for Rotterdam on the basis of the most favourable purchasing opportunities on the world market, and are charged on all imports of the product concerned.[30] The levy to be charged is that applicable on the day of importation,[31] though the levy may—in order to facilitate forward planning by dealers—be set in advance, in which case the levy is that applicable on the day application is made for an import licence (necessary for all third country trade) adjusted on the basis of the threshold price which will be in force during the month when the import is to be effected.[32]

The object of price support is to assure a minimum income to producers, and to this end, the common organisation of the cereals market also makes provision for *export refunds*, and *production aids*.

Where there is a surplus of grain in the Community, yet the price on the world market is such that producers can only export to third countries at a loss, provision may be made for the granting of an *export refund*, which is uniform throughout the whole Community, but may be varied according to use or destination.[33] As in the case of levies, the amount of the refund applicable may be that fixed for the day of exportation, or it may be fixed in advance, adjusted for the threshold price which will be in force during the month when the import will be effected.[34]

Production aids supplement the price system where the latter is inadequate to attain particular policy objectives. It has long been Community policy to encourage production of durum wheat. Since durum wheat and common wheat are interchangeable on the market, their respective intervention prices are bound to reflect the normal ratio between their respective prices. This level of price support being inadequate to provide the required incentive to durum wheat production, the original price system of Regulation 120/67 provided for a *guaranteed minimum price* for durum wheat, and for an aid to be paid to producers at the level of the difference between that price and the intervention price.[35] Thus the producers of durum wheat received part of their income from a price-supported market, and part, where necessary, in the form of direct aid. By 1976, the level of production of durum wheat was such that a "blanket" aid was no longer

[28] Art. 5(1).
[29] Art. 5(4).
[30] Art. 13(2).
[31] Art. 15(1).
[32] Art. 15(2).
[33] Art. 16(1), (2).
[34] Art. 16(3), (4). For the purpose of advance fixing, see Cases 44–51/77 *Union Malt* [1978] E.C.R. 57.
[35] Reg. 2727/75, Art. 10, reproducing Reg. 120/67, Art. 10, until amended by Reg. 1143/76, Art. 5.

justifiable; henceforth it could be confined to certain regions, and its rate—payable per hectare of land sown and harvested—varied.[36] Provision was made for aid to be granted "only for durum wheat having qualitative and technical characteristics to be determined." This reflected a desire to favour durum wheat suitable for the manufacture of pasta products.[37] It follows from the provision of a uniform Community aid system for durum wheat that it is not open to Member States to grant additional production aids for this product.[38]

In the case of *production refunds* granted for maize and common wheat used in the Community for the manufacture of starch, the reason for the producer receiving a subsidy is to reduce his price to a user industry who might otherwise resort to chemical substitutes.[39]

While maintenance of the price system necessitates the imposition of levies on imports, to prevent grain imported from third countries at lower prices disrupting the Community market, similar disruption is also possible when world prices are higher than Community prices. "When the quotations or prices on the world market . . . reach the level of Community prices," declares the basic Regulation, "appropriate measures may be taken." These measures may take the form of *export levies*, which prevent Community producers from exporting at high prices and thus jeopardising the stability of the Community market.[40]

2. *Buying-in.* The lynch-pin of the price support system is the right vested in producers[41] to sell grain to intervention agencies if they are unable to dispose of it on the market. The basic Regulation provides:

> "The intervention agencies designated by the Member States shall buy in, during the period from 1 October to 30 April, cereals . . . which have been harvested in the Community and which are offered to them, provided that the offers comply with conditions, in particular in respect of quality and quantity . . . ."[42]

Furthermore,

> "intervention agencies shall buy in the cereals offered to them from 1 September on deferred payment terms, and, in Portugal, Italy, France and Spain from 1 August, for cereals harvested in those countries."[42]

Holders of grain may submit offers to any intervention agency.[43] The locations of national intervention centres are decided by the Management Committee procedure in accordance with rules laid down by the Council,[44]

---

[36] Reg. 2727/75, Art. 10. For the regions, see Reg. 3103/76, O.J. 1976, L351/1, as amended. For aid for the 1986/87 marketing year, see Reg. 1586/86, O.J. 1986, 1139/45.
[37] Reg. 2727/75, Art. 10(2).
[38] Case 169/82 *Commission* v. *Italy* [1984] E.C.R. 1603.
[39] Reg. 2727/75, Art. 11. See Case 2/77 *Hoffman's Starkefabrieken* [1977] E.C.R. 1375; Cases 117/76 and 16/77 *Ruckdeschel* [1977] E.C.R. 1753; Cases 124/76 and 20/77 *Moulins* E.C.R. 1795. Art. 11 is to be repealed with effect from the first day of the 1989/90 marketing year, see Reg. 1006/86, O.J. 1986, L94/1.
[40] Reg. 2727/75, Art. 19.
[41] Or anybody else, for that matter.
[42] Reg. 2727/75, Art. 7(1).
[43] Reg. 1581/86, O.J. 1986 L139/36, replacing Reg. 2738/75, Art. 1; Reg. 1569/77, O.J. 1977, L174/15, Art. 1.
[44] Reg. 2727/75, Art. 3(7)

and these rules require that centres must meet one of the following conditions:

    (a) location in regions having an appreciable production of cereals which substantially exceeds local demand either regularly or occasionally, taking account of agricultural and market structures in that region;

    (b) existence of substantial storage facilities;

    (c) special importance as a market for the goods inside and outside the Community.[45]

In order to take advantage of the centres' legal obligation to buy grain, a holder must offer, during the appropriate period of the marketing year, at least 80 tonnes of common wheat, rye, barley, maize or sorghum or ten tonnes of durum wheat, all of which must have been harvested in the Community.[46] Acceptance is subject to the cereal being "sound, fair and of marketable quality,"[47] and detailed quality criteria are laid down in the Annex to Regulation 1569/77.[48] In the event of disagreement about the quality and characteristics of the grain offered, samples taken by both parties are submitted for analysis to a laboratory approved by the competent authorities, and the results of such analysis are final.[49]

Providing the holder of grain makes an offer in writing, or by telegram or telex,[50] to an appropriate centre, in respect of a quantity of grain of at least the minimum amount, and the quality of which complies with the standards referred to above, "acceptance of the offer by the intervention agency shall be given with the least possible delay, together with the necessary particulars of the conditions under which the goods will be taken over."[51] The relevant "conditions" concern primarily the *place* where the cereals are to be taken over, which is for the intervention agency to specify.[52] Should the offeror wish to object to the conditions specified by the intervention agency, he must do so within 48 hours of the receipt of the agency's acceptance,[53] in which case neither holder nor intervention agency is obliged to go ahead on the basis of the original offer. While an agency is obliged to accept all offers made in proper form, an offer is only effective from the time it actually reaches the agency, and on condition that it specifies, *inter alia*, the location of the grain in question. This appears from the Court's decision in *Hagen G* v. *EVSt*.[54] Anticipation of the devaluation of the French franc in 1969 led to sales of French currency at a discount, and dealers used such cheaply acquired francs to buy grain at the intervention price in France, which they then sold to the German intervention agency. The Commission took safeguard measures under Article 226 EEC, with

---

[45] Reg. 1145/76, O.J. 1976, L130/8, Art. 1, and see Art. 2.
[46] Reg. 1569/77, Art. 1.
[47] Reg. 1569/77, Art. 2.
[48] Prices are increased or reduced in appropriate cases, see reg. 1570/77, O.J. 1977, O.J. 1977, L174/18, on price increases and reductions applicable to interventions in cereals.
[49] Reg. 1569/77, Art. 4(3), (4).
[50] Reg. 1569/77, Art. 3(1).
[51] Reg. 1569/77, Art. 3(2).
[52] Reg. 1581/86, O.J. 1986, L139/36, superseding Reg. 2738/75, O.J. 1975 L281/49.
[53] Reg. 1569/77, Art. 3(2).
[54] Case 49/71 [1972] E.C.R. 23; and Case 50/71 *Wunsche* [1972] E.C.R. 53.

the effect that after May 8, 1969, the German intervention agency was bound to buy in only grain harvested in Germany. The Hagen firm bought grain in France, and offered it in Germany, making an offer on May 5, 1969, which reached the Germany agency on the 6th. The offer did not state the location of the grain, which was still in transit. Hagen informed the Germany agency of the location of the grain on May 12 at which time the agency refused the offer on the ground that it had been made out of time. It was Hagen's contention, essentially, that their original offer, even if incomplete, could be subsequently completed with retrospective effect. The Court of Justice held that since an offer in proper form imposes a legal obligation on an intervention agency, it could not be regarded as effective until the latter had notice of it. Furthermore, an offer must specify the location of the grain at the time the offer was made, in order to enable the intervention agency to establish whether or not the offer was binding upon it; whether, for instance, it was made to one of the three "nearest centres." This was important, emphasised the Court, because precautions must exist to ensure that no incentive exists to transport grain simply in order to obtain a better intervention price at a different centre. This aspect of the Court's judgment refers to the system of regionalised intervention prices, which no longer exists, but the Court also refers to the agency's duty to designate the place at which the grain is to be taken over.

While transport costs from the place where the grain is in store when the offer is made to the intervention centre to which they can be transported at least expense are borne by the offeror, any additional transport costs resulting from the agency taking over the grain at a place other than the above-mentioned intervention centre are borne by the agency.[55] It is thus clearly essential for the agency to be told where the grain is situated at the time the offer is made, in order for it to make the most rational choice of place of takeover. For this reason, the *Hagen* case still seems to be good law.

The price to be paid to the seller is the price valid for the month specified as the month of delivery at the time of the acceptance of the offer, account being taken of appropriate increases and reductions. Payment shall be made between the 90th and 120th day following takeover for grain offered for intervention from October 1. However, for cereals offered for intervention in August in Greece, Spain, Italy and Portugal, and in September in the Community as a whole, payment shall be made between the 120th and 150th day following takeover.[56]

Grain bought in by intervention agencies is stored pending disposal, at Community expense. Products must be stored within national jurisdiction, unless an agency receives Community authorisation for storage elsewhere.[57] Such authorisation "shall be granted" if such storage is essential in light of the following factors: "(a) storage possibilities and storage requirements in the Member States within whose jurisdiction the interven-

---

[55] Reg. 1581/86, Art. 1. For storage after takeover at the warehouse of the offeror, see Art. 2.
[56] Reg. 1569/77, as amended, Art. 3(4).
[57] Reg. 1055/77, O.J. 1977, L128/1, Art. 1(1).

tion agency falls and in other Member States; (b) any additional costs resulting from storage in the Member States within whose jurisdiction the intervention agency falls and from transportation."[58] While authorisation for storage in a third country may be granted, this is only the case if storage in another Member State creates significant difficulties.[59] Transportation across state lines resulting from an authorisation referred to above does not, of course, attract customs duties or other levies usually payable under the common policy.[60] Although products held by an intervention agency outside national territory are disposed of under conditions applicable at the place of storage, failing their return to the former agency, it is the former agency which remains responsible for such products pending disposal.[61]

Intervention agencies holding grain are required by the basic Regulation to offer it for sale either for supply on the internal market, or for export to third countries.[62] Re-sale on the internal market is undertaken by invitation to tender, subject to specified rules.[63] Invitation to tender is defined by Regulation 1836/82 as "offering for sale by inviting tenders, the contract being awarded to the person or persons tendering the best price and conditions in conformity with this Regulation."[64]

All invitations to tender must be made public.[65] Member States communicate to the Commission the quantity and description of the cereal to be offered for tender. The announcement of the call for tenders is published in the Official Journal not later than five working days after receipt of the above communication. A period of at least ten days must elapse between the date of the Official Journal notice and the first closing date for the submission of tenders fixed by the Member State. Intervention agencies are obliged to draw up, at least 12 days before the first closing date for the submission of tenders,[66] a notice of invitation to tender in prescribed form, indicating, *inter alia*, the characteristics of the various lots and their places of storage and the name and address of the storer, and to publicise it, in particular by displaying it on their premises.[67]

The notice of invitation to tender, which must be forwarded immediately to the Commission, must specify the maximum quantities to which tenders may relate,[68] and intervention agencies are further required to take all necessary steps to enable interested parties to assess the quality of cereals put up for sale before submitting their tenders.[69]

Successful tenderers must offer a price at least equivalent to the market price for a similar quantity recorded on the market for the place of storage, or failing such a price, the price on the nearest market taking account of

---

[58] Reg. 1055/77, Art. 1(2).
[59] Reg. 1055/77, Art. 1(3).
[60] Reg. 1055/77, Art. 2.
[61] Reg. 1055/77, Art. 3.
[62] Reg. 2727/75, Art. 7(3).
[63] Reg. 1836/82, O.J. 1982, L202/23, as amended.
[64] Art. 1(2).
[65] Reg. 1836/82, Art. 2.
[66] Reg. 1836/82, Art. 12.
[67] Reg. 1836/82, Art. 12.
[68] Reg. 1836/82, Art. 3.
[69] Reg. 1836/82, Art. 14.

transport costs. The tender price must not, in any circumstances, be lower than the intervention prices applicable on the closing date for the submission of tenders.[70]

Invitations to tender may also be made with a view to the export of grain held in storage.[71] Interested parties are to be informed of a decision to invite tenders by publication in the Official Journal. At least 15 days must elapse between the date of such publication and the first closing date for the submission of tenders. In the notice of invitation to tender proposed by the intervention agencies, there is specified for each lot the port or point of exit which involves the lowest transport costs and which has adequate technical facilities for exporting the cereals put up for tender.[72] The lowest transport costs between the place of storage and the place of landing at the port or point of exit referred to above shall be reimbursed to the successful tenderer by the intervention agency for the quantities exported. In particular cases transport may be undertaken by the intervention agency under the same conditions. Once again, intervention agencies must take all necessary steps to enable interested parties to assess the quality of cereals put up for sale.[73]

Tenders for grain for export may be refused if they relate to lots of less than 500 tonnes,[74] and are only valid if they are accompanied by an application for an export licence, together with an application for the advance fixing of the export refund or levy for the relevant destination, and an application for the advance fixing of the applicable monetary compensatory amount.[75]

In all cases tenders are valid only if they are accompanied by proof that the tenderer has provided a security for 5 ECU per tonne,[76] and in the case of tenders for export, where the price is less than the intervention price, they are accompanied by an undertaking by the tenderer, endorsed by a credit institution, to provide a security covering the difference between the two prices not later than two working days after receiving notification of award of a contract.[77]

Intervention agencies are required to inform all tenderers immediately of the outcome of their tender.[78] The successful tenderer is obliged to pay for the cereals before they are removed and at the latest one month after notification of the outcome of the tender. The successful tenderer bears all risks and storage costs in respect of cereals not removed within the period of payment. In the case of export, the price to be paid is that shown in the tender plus a monthly increase where the cereals are removed during the month following that in which the contract was awarded, except for contracts awarded in the 11th month of the marketing year, in which case the

---

[70] Reg. 1836/82, Art. 5(1). These price rules may not be modified by the national authorities, see Case 61/82 *Italy* v. *Commission* [1983] E.C.R. 655.
[71] Reg. 1836/82, Art. 7.
[72] Reg. 1836/82, Art. 7(2).
[73] Reg. 1836/82, Art. 14.
[74] Reg. 1836/82, Art. 8(1).
[75] Reg. 1836/82, Art. 8(2).
[76] Reg. 1836/82, Art. 13(2).
[77] Reg. 1836/82, Art. 8(2)(c).
[78] Reg. 1836/82, Art. 15.

tender price governs.[79] If cereals are not paid for within the period referred to above, the intervention agency shall terminate the contract in respect of the quantities for which payment has not been received.[80]

The security of five ECU per tonne on all tenders is released in respect of quantities for which no contract has been awarded, and for which the selling price has been paid within the period specified.[81] The security payable is respect of tenders for export below the intervention price is released, *inter alia*, when proof is furnished under Article 20 of Regulation 2730/79[82] that customs entry formalities for home used in the third country concerned have been completed, or proof is furnished that the goods have become unfit for human or animal consumption.[83] This latter security is forfeited, except in cases of *force majeure*, where payment is not made within the period specified,[84] or where proof of completion of customs entry formalities is not provided within 12 months.[85] In the case of both the takeover of grain by intervention agencies and its disposal, agencies may be entitled, under the Regulations from time to time in force, to adopt additional provisions and conditions, compatible with the Regulations in question.

Such an authorisation does not permit national intervention agencies to restrict in any way the category of persons entitled to participation in the intervention process under Community law. This appears clearly from the Court's decision in *Syndicat national des céréales* v. *Office national des céréales*[86] In 1968 the French intervention agency increased the minimum quantity of cereals which could at that time be offered for buying-in (50 tonnes) to 500 tonnes, as authorised under Article 1 of Regulation 1028/68,[87] and further provided that only *authorised collecting agencies*—cooperatives and dealers fulfilling certain conditions, and who were alone allowed to purchase direct from producers—should be entitled to offer cereals for intervention. On a reference for a preliminary ruling from the Conseil d'Etat, the Court held that the conditions that the intervention agency were permitted to add to those imposed by Community law related only to the quality and minimum quantities of cereals which could practicably be offered,[88] but not to the definition of "holder" who "shall be entitled to offer . . . cereals to the intervention agency." "Whilst including measures of price support," declared the Court, "the intervention machinery does not aim to derogate from the normal conditions of the market beyond what is strictly necessary to achieve its objective. It appears both from the

---

[79] Reg. 1836/82, Art. 16.
[80] Reg. 1836/82, Art. 16.
[81] Reg. 1836/82, Art. 17(1).
[82] O.J. 1979, L317/1, as amended.
[83] Reg. 1836/82, Art. 17(3).
[84] Reg. 1836/82, Art. 17(4).
[85] Reg. 1836/82, Art. 17(5), referring to Art. 31 of Reg. 2730/79, as amended by Reg. 1663/81, O.J. 1981, L166/9.
[86] Case 34/70 [1970] E.C.R. 1233.
[87] J.O. 1968, L176/1, equivalent to Reg. 1569/77, Art. 1, prior to its amendment by Reg. 2134/86, O.J. 1986, L187/23.
[88] See Reg. 1569/77, fifth recital, referring to Member States applying, "concurrently with the provisions of this Regulation, certain provisions of their own which are suited to their own climatic and commercial practices."

general objectives and those of the common organisation of the market in cereals that the intervention machinery requires the widest possible access for all those concerned in the functioning of the market."[89] Different national definitions of the class of persons entitled to offer into intervention would burden the market with quantities excluded from intervention, argued the Court, and prejudice the uniform application of the Community system. It followed that the "conditions" which Member States might add under Article 5 of Regulation 1028/68 did not extend to modification of the word "holder" in Article 1 thereof.[90] Similar reasoning militates against the adoption of national qualifications to the Community tendering procedure which could in any way narrow the circle of potential purchasers.

The losses of national intervention agencies on their purchases and sales of grain under Article 7 of the basic Regulation are borne by the guarantee section of the European Agricultural Guidance and Guarantee Fund, which forms part of the Community budget.[91] To this end, intervention agencies establish, for each marketing year and for each product for which an intervention price is fixed, an account, which must be debited and credited in accordance with Community rules.[92]

3. *The co-responsibility levy and direct aid to small producers.* An inevitable consequence of price support measures in agriculture is increased production. When that production persistently exceeds demand, urgent remedial measures are necessary. Such measures have become necessary in the cereals market, a market "characterized by structural surpluses resulting from the imbalance between the supply of, and demand for, the products covered by Regulation 2727/75."[93] The Council has acknowledged that "production has outstripped both consumption in the Community and outlets on world markets" and that "the resulting costs and market management problems could, if that trend is not checked, jeopardise the future of the common agricultural policy."[93] The solution adopted is a co-responsibility levy, collected on all cereals produced in the Community which undergo first stage processing, or are bought in by intervention agencies, or are exported in the form of grain.[94] The levy, to apply for the 1986/87 to the 1990/91 marketing year,[95] is to be regarded as one of the intervention measures designed to stabilize agricultural markets and is to be allocated to financing the cost of cereal market support measures.[96] It can be collected only once in respect of any quantity of cereals,[97] and in the case of resale of

[89] [1970] E.C.R. 1233 at p. 1239, paras. 7, 8.
[90] *Cf.* Case 39/70 *Fleischkontor* [1971] E.C.R. 49, in which German legislation purported to attach a criterion of "trustworthiness" to those entitled to claim suspension of import levies under Reg. 888/68, J.O. 1968, 156/7.
[91] Reg. 1883/78, O.J. 1978, L216/1; Reg. 3247/81, as amended, O.J. 1981, L327/1. For the EAGGF, see Reg. 729/70, O.J. 1970 L94/13, as amended.
[92] Reg. 1883/78, and Reg. 3247/81. For the consequences of the national agencies financing intervention measures otherwise than in accordance with Community law, see *Disallowance, infra* at p. 330.
[93] Reg. 1579/86, O.J. 1986, L139/29, preamble.
[94] Reg. 2727/75, Art. 4, inserted by Reg. 1579/86.
[95] Reg. 2727/75, Art. 4(1).
[96] Reg. 2727/75, Art. 4(4). For the 1986/87 marketing year the co-responsibility levy was set at 5,38 ECU/tonne, see Reg. 1584/86, O.J. 1986, L139/41.
[97] Reg. 2040/86, O.J. 1986, L73/65, Art. 3.

intervention stocks, the intervention agency shall issue a certificate of eligibility for exemption from the co-responsibility levy for given quantities.[97] It is provided that operators who process, or sell into intervention, or export, and thereby pay the levy, shall pass it back to their suppliers, and that they in turn, if not themselves producers, will pass it back up the chain to the producer.[98] To this end, supporting documents for each of the transactions in the sales chain shall indicate separately the amount of the levy deducted.[98] The levy is even to be passed on in contracts concluded or executed prior to the marketing year during which the co-responsibility levy is collected.[99]

Operators who undertake first-stage processing (meaning any treatment of grain such that the product may no longer be classified under Chapter 10 of the Common Customs Tariff)[1] are obliged to keep accounts at the disposal of the competent national authorities, indicating in particular:

  (a) the names and addresses of the producers or operators who delivered cereal to them as grain;
  (b) the quantities involved in the above-mentioned deliveries;
  (c) the amount of the co-responsibility levy deducted;
  (d) the quantities of cereals processed, subject to and exempt from the levy.[2]

Furthermore, Member States are required to take any additional measures required to ensure that the co-responsibility levy is collected in accordance with the applicable Regulation, and to that end may draw up a list giving the names of the operators undertaking first stage processing of grain.[3]

To offset the effect of the levy on the income of small producers, a system of direct aid has been introduced to supplement their incomes.[4] The global amount of aid to be made available must not exceed the total estimated amount produced by the co-responsibility levy on producers marketing not more than 25 tonnes,[5] and in no individual case may the amount of aid exceed, for a producer, the equivalent of a levy for 25 tonnes of cereals.[6]

4. *Import levies and export refunds.* As indicated earlier, insulation of the Community market from world price fluctuations is ensured primarily by means of import levies and export refunds. Import levies, equal to the "threshold price less the c.i.f. price,"[7] are charged on all products subject

---

[98] Reg. 2040/86, Art. 5(1).
[99] Reg. 2040/86, Art. 5(2).
[1] Reg. 2040/86, Art. 1(2). Note that processing of cereals delivered or placed at the disposal of an undertaking by a producer with a view to subsequent utilisation on his holding shall be considered first stage processing. However, processing operations carried out by a producer on his agricultural holding shall be exempt from the co-responsibility levy where the product obtained is used on that holding for animal feed. *Ibid.*
[2] Reg. 2040/86, Art. 6.
[3] Reg. 2040/86, Art. 7.
[4] Reg. 2727/75, Art. 4a, inserted by Reg. 1579/86.
[5] Reg. 2727/75, Art. 4a(1).
[6] Reg. 1983/86, Art. 2.
[7] The Commission is not required to reply to individual requests for disclosure of the technical data relied upon in calculating these levies, such data would, however, have to be produced to a court of competent jurisdiction. Case 64/82 *Tradex* [1984] E.C.R. 1359.

to the basic Regulation.[8] The levy to be charged is that applicable on the "day of importation,"[9] or, if the levy is fixed in advance, is that applicable on the day on which application for a licence is made, adjusted on the basis of the threshold price which will be in force during the month of importation.[10] Since the levies are "intended to protect and stabilise the Community market, in particular by preventing fluctuations in world market prices from having repercussions within the Community . . . the levy is fixed on the basis of the day from which the imported goods exercise an influence on the internal market of the Community, that is to say, the date on which they finally reach this market and enter into competition with domestic goods."[11] Thus goods stored after customs clearance in a deferred duty warehouse under customs supervision in the State of destination are nevertheless not "imported" until their release.[12] In other cases, the "day of importation" is to be construed as the date of customs clearance, *i.e.* the date on which customs officials accept the importer's declaration of intention to put the goods into free circulation.[13]

Export refunds are paid to enable the products subject to the basic Regulation to be sold on third country markets, and are fixed so as to cover the difference between the price on the world market, and prices in the Community.[14] More specifically, they are fixed with reference to: (a) cereal prices on various representative Community markets; (b) the most favourable quotations on the various markets of importing third countries; and (c) marketing costs and the most favourable transport charges from the Community markets referred to in (a) to ports or other points of export in the Community serving those markets, as well as cost incurred in placing the goods on the world market.[15] The refund may be supplemented by a "carry-over" element in the case of grain on hand at the end of the marketing year, and this compensatory amount is equal to the difference between the target price valid for the last month of the marketing year and that valid for the first month of the next marketing year.[16]

For the purpose of determining the applicable rate of refund, the date of exportation is the day on which the customs authorities accept the document by which the declarant states his intention to export the product in question and qualify for a refund. At this time the product must be placed under customs control and remain so until it leaves the Community.[17]

Certain non-export transactions, such as supplies for ships and aircraft, and international organisations established within the Community, are

---

[8] Reg. 2727/75, Art. 13(1).
[9] Reg. 2727/75, Art. 15(1).
[10] Reg. 2727/75, Art. 15(2). See Case 6/77 *Schouten* [1977] E.C.R. 1291; Case 85/78 *Hirsch* [1978] E.C.R. 2517.
[11] Case 35/71 *Schleswig-Holsteinische Hauptgenossenschaft* [1971] E.C.R. 1083 at p. 1093, para. 3.
[12] *Ibid.*
[13] Case 113/75 *Frecassetti* [1976] E.C.R. 983. And see Case 113/78 *Schouten* [1979] E.C.R. 695.
[14] Reg. 2727/75, Art. 16(1).
[15] Reg. 2746/75, O.J. 1975, L281/78, Art. 3. For "marketing costs," see Cases 131 & 150/78 *Becker* [1979] E.C.R. 1421, at para. 6.
[16] Reg. 2746/75, Art. 6.
[17] Reg. 2730/79, O.J. 1979, L317/1, Art. 3.

treated as exports for the purpose of eligibility for refunds, providing that like products imported from third countries for these uses are exempt from duty on importation into the Member State in question.[18]

Refunds are paid on written application to the Member State in whose customs territory formalities are completed.[19] Proof must be provided that the product in question left the geographical territory of the Community in unaltered form (or, in the case of international organisations, etc., reached its destination) within 60 days of completion of export formalities.[20] "Unaltered" means that any alteration in the presentation of the goods, where it is such as to render customs control more difficult, entails forfeiture of the refund.[21] Where *force majeure* prevents a claimant complying with this time limit, it may be extended by the competent authorities of the Member State in question.[22] Where there is "serious doubt as to the true destination of the product," or where it is possible that the product may be reintroduced into the Community, having regard to the difference between the rate of refund and the charges which would be applicable to such a product on importation from a third country, the payment of a refund is conditional not only on the product leaving the Community, but also on its importation into an appropriate third country.[23]

Since different conditions apply in different export markets, and different distances (and hence transport costs) separate them from the Community, export refunds may be varied according to destination.[24] Where this is the case, a refund is only payable if the product has actually been imported into a third country or countries in respect of which the refund has is prescribed.[25] A product is considered to have been imported when the customs formalities for entry into free circulation in the third country concerned have been completed, and proof must be furnished by production of the relevant documentation, or a copy thereof.[26] If, on the other hand, owing to circumstances beyond the control of the importer, adequate proof cannot be furnished in this way, the competent authorities must accept documentary proof that the goods have at least been unloaded in the appropriate country.[27]

In all cases the exporter must produce a copy or photocopy of the transport document.[28] Where a transaction gives rise to an entitlement for an export refund of less than either 500 ECUs or 2,500 ECUs (according to product and destination) and adequate assurances are offered that the products in question will reach their destination, the competent authorities of

---

[18] Reg. 2730/79, Art. 5.
[19] Reg. 2730/79, Art. 30(1). Refunds of less than 12 ECU may be refused, Art. 18.
[20] Reg. 2730/79, Art. 9.
[21] Case 276/84 *Gebrüder Metelmann* Judgment of December 12, 1985.
[22] Reg. 2730/79, Art. 9.
[23] Reg. 2730/79, Art. 10(1).
[24] Reg. 2746/75, Art. 7.
[25] Reg. 2730/79, Art. 20(1).
[26] Reg. 2730/79, Art. 20(2), (3). And see Case 125/75 *Milch-Fett.* [1976] E.C.R. 771; Case 820/79 *Belgium* v. *Commission* [1980] E.C.R. 3537; Case 89/83 *Dimex* [1984] E.C.R. 2815. And national authorities may require additional proof that the product has been placed on the markets, Art. 20(1), last sub-para.
[27] Reg. 2730/79, Art. 20(4).
[28] Reg. 2730/79, Art. 20(5).

Member States may exempt the exporter concerned from furnishing the proof normally required.[29] In derogation from the rule that export refunds varying according to the country of destination are only payable on import into the latter, in certain circumstances Member States may advance to the exporter that part of the refund equal to the refund payable at the lowest applicable rate.[30]

Export refunds will not be granted for goods which are not "of sound and fair marketable quality, or for products intended for human consumption whose characteristics or condition exclude or substantially impair their use for that purpose."[31] The relevant date for determining the characteristics of the product is the day on which export formalities are completed.[32] The Court considered the quality criteria for export refunds in *Muras* v. *Hauptzollamt Hamburg-Jonas*,[33] a reference from the Finanzgericht, Hamburg. A German merchant purchased Rohwürste (a type of sausage) for export to Yugoslavia. He was initially granted an export refund, which the German authorities later sought to recover, on the ground that the sausage in question could not be properly so described, in that it contained no meat, and that it was unfit for human consumption. The Finanzgericht asked the Court of Justice whether the quality criteria applicable to the grant of export refunds should be assessed by reference to standards pertaining in the Community, or in the country of destination. The Court upheld the former view; the alternative solution would render the export refunds mechanism uncertain in its application, and impossible to administer.

The level of refund payable may be fixed, where appropriate, by tender.[34] The decision whether or not to open an invitation to tender is taken in accordance with the Management Committee procedure,[35] and the decision specifies the terms of the invitation. The terms must guarantee equal access to all persons established within the Community.[36] The opening of an invitation to tender is accompanied by notice to that effect prepared by the Commission. The notice shall include *inter alia* particulars of the various dates for the submissions of tenders and of the competent authorities of Member States to which tenders must be addressed.[37] It may also indicate the total quantity in respect of which a maximum export refund may be fixed.[38]

A tender must be in writing, must contain certain specified information, and is only valid if: (a) before the expiry of the time limit for the submission of tenders proof is furnished that the tenderer has lodged an appro-

---

[29] Reg. 2730/79, Art. 23.
[30] Reg. 2730/79, Art. 21.
[31] Reg. 2730/79, Art. 15.
[32] Reg. 2730/79, Art. 4(2).
[33] Case 12/73 [1973] E.C.R. 963, on the interpretation of reg. 1041/67, J.O. 1967, 23, Art. 6, reg. 1041/67, as amended, was consolidated in reg. 192/75, Art. 6 of the former being reproduced in Art. 8 of the latter. Art. 15 of reg. 2730/79 now governs.
[34] Reg. 2746/75, Art. 5(1).
[35] Reg. 279/75, O.J. 1975, L31/8, as amended by Reg. 2944/78, O.J. 1978 L351/16, Art. 1.
[36] Reg. 279/75, Art. 1(1).
[37] Reg. 279/75, Art. 1(2).
[38] *Ibid.*

priate security; and (b) it is accompanied by a written undertaking to
lodge, within two days of the receipt of notification of the award of a contract, an application for an export licence in respect of the quantity
awarded, together with an application for advance fixing of an export
refund equal to that indicated in the tender.[39] Tenders are examined in private session by the competent authorities of the Member States, and are
communicated, without names, to the Commission[40] which decides
whether to fix a maximum export refund, or to make no award. If a maximum export refund is fixed a contract must be awarded to any tenderer
whose tender indicated a rate of refund equal to or less than the maximum.[41] Except in case of *force majeure*, the security lodged by a tenderer
is released only if the tender is rejected, or if he furnishes proof that the
export has taken place so as to entitle him to release of the security for the
export licence issued following acceptance of his tender.[42]

5. *Import and export licences.* The basic Regulation subjects imports from,
and exports to, third countries to the submission of licences, which are
issued as of right[43] to all applicants. The purpose of the licensing system is
to monitor third country trade, so as to use the more effectively the
assorted intervention mechanisms available to the Community authorities
under the common organisation of the grain market.[44] A secondary function of import and export licences is as supporting documents for the
advanced fixing of levies and refunds, the amounts being endorsed on the
documents in question.

Applications for licences must be sent or delivered direct to the competent authorities, in the specified form.[45] Telex applications containing the
requisite information must be accepted, though Member States may
require an application in the appropriate form to follow (without prejudice
to the validity of the original communication).[46] All applications must be
accompanied by a deposit, either in cash, or in the form of a guarantee
issued by an institution approved by the authorities of the Member State
concerned.[47]

The security is at the rate of 0.50 ECU per tonne for import and export
licences where the levy or refund is not fixed in advance; 16 ECU per tonne
for import licences for cereals where the levy is fixed in advance (3,67 ECU
per tonne for other products); and either eight or ten ECU per tonne,
according to the product concerned, for export licences where the levy or
refund is fixed in advance.[48]

The issue of an import or export licence establishes the right and creates
the obligation to import or export during the period of its validity the quan-

[39] Reg. 279/75, Art. 2.
[40] Reg. 279/75, Art. 4.
[41] Reg. 279/75, Art. 5(2).
[42] Reg. 279/75, Art. 7.
[43] Reg. 2727/75, Art. 12; Case 158/73 *Kampffmeyer* [1974] E.C.R. 101, at p. 109, para. 5.
[44] Reg. 2727/75, 12th recital.
[45] Reg. 3183/80, O.J. 1980, L338/1, as amended; Arts. 12, 16 and Annex I.
[46] Reg. 3183/80, Art. 12(1).
[47] Reg. 3183/80, Art. 5(2), (4).
[48] Reg. 2042/75, Art. 12.

tity of grain specified therein.[49] Where appropriate, the licence will include provision for the advance fixing of the levy or refund.[50] The obligation deriving from a licence is not transferable, but the right is, at least by the original holder.[51] The transfer is effective from the time the competent authorities endorse on the licence the name and address of the transferee, and the date of the entry.[52]

For the purpose of determining its period of validity, a licence is considered to have been issued on the day on which the application for it was lodged, that day being included in the calculation of the period in question.[53] The duration of licences for grain varies according to the product concerned, and according to whether import or export is involved.

Import licences are valid either for 45 days (common wheat, rye, barley, oats, maize, and durum wheat), or 60 days (flour).[54] Export licences are valid until the end of the fourth month following that of the issue of the licence.[55]

Licences are drawn up at least in duplicate, one copy, the "holder's copy," marked "No. 1," being issued to the applicant, and the second, the issuing agency's copy," marked "No. 2," being retained by the issuing agency.[56] The No. 1 Copy is submitted to the officers responsible for completing the customs formalities in the case of imports or exports, is endorsed, and returned to the party concerned.[57]

As regards complying with the obligation to import or export *during the period of validity of the licence*, the obligation to import is considered to have been fulfilled when customs formalities have been completed (providing always that the grain in question is actually put into free circulation),[58] while the obligation to export is discharged simply on completion of customs formalities.[59] Import formalities are considered to have been completed on the day on which the customs authorities accept the document by which a party states his intention to put the products in question into free circulation, or, the day on which occurs any other act having the same effect in law as such acceptance.[60]

In the case of exports, formalities are completed on the day on which the customs authorities accept the document by which the exporter states his intention to export the goods in question, and on which the products are placed under customs control pending departure from the Community.[61] Release of the security deposited upon application for a licence is subject to *proving* completion of import or export formalities.[62] In the case of

---

[49] Subject to seven per cent. tolerance either way, Reg. 2042/75, Art. 2.
[50] Reg. 3183/80, Art. 8.
[51] Reg. 3183/80, Art. 9(1).
[52] Reg. 3183/80, Art. 9(2), (3).
[53] Reg. 3183/80, Art. 21(1).
[54] Reg. 2042/75, Art. 8 and Annex I, as amended.
[55] Reg. 2042/75, Art. 8 and Annex II, as amended.
[56] Reg. 3183/80, Art. 19.
[57] Reg. 3183/80, Art. 32.
[58] Reg. 3183/80, Art. 29(a); see Case 186/73 *Fleischkontor* [1974] E.C.R. 533.
[59] Reg. 3183/80, Art. 29(b).
[60] Reg. 3183/80, Art. 32(a).
[61] Reg. 3183/80, Art. 32(b).
[62] Reg. 3183/80, Art. 30.

imports, this is accomplished simply by producing the No. 1 Copy of the licence,[63] but in the case of exports, further proof is required. This is at the discretion of the Member State concerned where the issue of the licence and the completion of export formalities took place in the same State, but in other cases is provided by a Community transit document.[64]

The deposit system was challenged before the Court in *Internationale Handelsgesellschaft* v. *EVSt*[65] on the ground that it was disproportionate to the desired end. Less burdensome means of monitoring imports and exports could have been adopted, it was argued, such as simply requesting importers and exporters to report their transaction, or perhaps providing penalties, after the event, for failure to report such transactions. The Court considered that the knowledge of import and export transactions—present and future—was essential if the competent authorities were to make proper use of the intervention mechanisms available to them, such as buying-in, storage, removal from storage, and the setting of export refunds. This was particularly necessary in view of the financial burdens placed on the Community and the Member States by the implementation of the common policy. Since a purely voluntary system would be unlikely to provide adequate data, while a system of fines after the event would cause great administrative difficulties, it could not be said that the deposit system was disproportionate to the result it sought to achieve—neither in principle, nor with respect to the level of deposits required. The Court also held in the *Internationale Handellsgesellschaft* that the deposits involved did not amount to penalties, and this reasoning supported the conclusion in a later case—*Könecke*[66]—that deposits wrongly released by the competent authorities could not be recovered.

Special rules regarding the issue, and period of validity, of export licences, apply in certain circumstances. In "special cases," the period of validity of licences for common wheat, rye, barley, maize and certain other products may be longer than that specified in Annex II of Regulation 2042/75.[67] Such applications may only be made in respect of quantities of at least 75,000 tonnes.[68]

Where an application for an export licence is submitted in connection with an invitation to tender for products in storage, a licence is only issued for the quantities in respect of which the applicant obtains a contract, and the security on the balance of the application is released.[69] If, under an invitation to tender offered by an intervention agency, a tender is only valid if accompanied by an application for an export licence, and for an advance fixing of the export levy or refund for the relevant destination, the country or destination must be specified in the licence as the compulsory destination, and it shall be obligatory to export thereto.[70]

[63] Reg. 3183/80, Art. 31(1)(*a*).
[64] Reg. 3183/80, Art. 31(2).
[65] Case 11/70 [1970] E.C.R. 1125.
[66] Case 117/83 [1984] E.C.R. 3297.
[67] Reg. 2042/75, Art. 11(1).
[68] Reg. 2042/75, Art. 11(2).
[69] Reg. 2042/75, Art. 3(1); reg. 3183/80, Art. 19(2).
[70] Reg. 2042/75, Art. 3(2). However, a group of countries for which the same export refund or levy rate applies shall be considered to constitute a single destination; *ibid.*

A further concession is made in the case of invitations to tender opened in third countries. In such cases an export licence for common wheat, rye, barley, maize and certain other products is valid from the time of issue until the date when the contract in question is to be performed, providing this period does not exceed eight months following the month of issue of the licence.[71]

The obligation to import or export during the validity of a licence is not absolute. Where importation or exportation cannot be effected during this period, as a result of *force majeure*, the competent agency of the relevant Member State may decide either to cancel the obligation completely, and release the security, or to extend the period of validity as it considers necessary in the circumstances. Such an extension may be granted after the licence has expired.[72]

The concept of *force majeure* differs in content in different areas of the law, and its precise meaning must be decided by reference to the legal context in which it is intended to operate. *Kampffmeyer* v. *EVSt*[73] is illustrative. The main action concerned an appeal against the forfeiture of a deposit on a licence, the full amount specified therein not having been imported. The importer claimed to have lost his import licence in the post, precluding him from importing the amount outstanding thereon, and that this amounted to *force majeure*. It defined the notion in the following terms:

> "The public interest, which requires as accurate a forecast as possible of import trends in each Member State and justifies the deposit of security against the grant of authorisation to import, must be reconciled to the necessity of not hampering trade between Member States by too rigid obligations, a necessity which also derives from the public interest.
>
> The threat of forfeiture of security is intended to encourage the fulfilment of the obligation to import by importers enjoying the authorisation and thus to ensure the accurate forecasting of import trends required by the general interest mentioned above.
>
> It follows that, in principle, an importer who has exercised all reasonable care is released from the obligation to import when external circumstances render it impossible for him to complete the importation within the period of validity.
>
> The answer . . . should therefore be that the loss of such an import licence constitutes a case of *force majeure* . . . when such loss occurs despite the fact that the titular holder of the licence has taken all the precautions which could reasonably be expected of a prudent and diligent trader."[74]

The decision to cancel or extend a licence must be confined to that quantity of the product which could not be imported or exported by reason of

[71] Reg. 2042/75, Art. 10(1).
[72] Case 71/82 *Brüggen* [1982] E.C.R. 4647. Reg. 3183/80, Arts. 36, 37.
[73] Case 158/73 [1974] E.C.R. 101. See also Case 4/68 *Schwarzwaldmilch* [1968] E.C.R. 377; Case 11/70 *Internationale Handelsgesellschaft* [1970] E.C.R. 1125; Case 3/74 *Pfützenreuter* [1974] E.C.R. 589; Case 808/79 *Pardini* [1980] E.C.R. 2103.
[74] [1974] E.C.R. 101, at p. 110, paras. 9, 10.

force majeure,[75] and where a Member State accepts a case as such, it must notify the Commission, which will notify the other Member States, with a view to ensuring the uniform application of the exception throughout the Community.[76]

6. *Safeguard measures in trade with third countries.* Articles 19 and 20 of the basic Regulation provide for measures to be taken to ensure that world price fluctuations do not disrupt the Community price mechanism. The Articles at first sight overlap, but they are in fact calculated to deal with rather different problems; the first seeks to prevent Community producers from exporting to third countries when the prices here rise to a higher level than that of Community prices (thus leading to price increases on the Community market), while the second seeks to limit trade with third countries when prices rise or fall excessively on the community market as a result of the defective operation of the Community price mechanism.

Article 19 provides for "appropriate measures" when "prices on the world market . . . reach the level of Community prices, and when that situation is likely to continue and to deteriorate, thereby disturbing or threatening to disturb the Community market." Prices are regarded as having reached the level of Community prices "when they approach or exceed the threshold price,"[77] and the situation is regarded as being likely to continue "when the imbalance between supply and demand is established and where this imbalance is likely to persist, having regard to foreseeable production and market price trends."[78] The Community market is regarded as being disturbed or threatened with disturbance as a result of this situation when either "international trade prices are so high as to impede the importation" of products subject to the basic Regulation, or as to "provoke the exportation of such products from the Community, so as to put at risk the stability of the market or the security of supplies."[79] When these conditions are present, export levies may be applied, or export licences may be suspended in whole or in part.[80] The decision as to whether or not to take such measures is in principle taken under the Management Committee procedure, though, if necessary, the Commission may introduce or modify the export levy, and in an emergency, the Commission may, for a period not exceeding seven days, suspend import licences.[81]

Export levies are collected by the Member States in whose territory customs export formalities are completed,[82] and the rate applicable—except where the levy is fixed in advance or fixed under a tendering procedure[83]— is that in force on the day on which the customs authority accepts the exporter's declaration of intention to export the products in question. At the time of such acceptance the products concerned must be placed under

---

[75] Reg. 3183/80, Art. 37(2).
[76] Reg. 3183/80, Art. 37(5).
[77] Reg. 2747/75, O.J. 1975, L281/82, Art. 1.
[78] Reg. 2747/75, Art. 1(2).
[79] Reg. 2747/75, Art. 1(3).
[80] Reg. 2747/75, Art. 2(1).
[81] Reg. 2747/75, Art. 4(2), (3), 5(1).
[82] Reg. 645/75, O.J. 1975, L67/16, Art. 5.
[83] See *infra*.

customs control and remain so until they leave the Community.[84] It is the latter date which is determinative for ascertaining the quantity, nature and characteristics of the product exported.[85]

Where the rate of levy varies according to destination, the levy fixed for the destination specified in the exporter's declaration of intention to export is charged, but in addition the exporter must lodge a security to cover the difference between that amount and the amount of the highest levy chargeable on the relevant date. Save for cases of *force majeure*, the person liable to the levy must, within six months of the completion of export formalities, furnish proof that the product has arrived at the appropriate destination, such proof being that provided for in the case of export refunds payable upon proof of importation into a specified third country.[86] If the required proof is not furnished within the time limit prescribed, then, apart from cases of *force majeure*, the product exported is regarded as having reached a third country in respect of which the highest rate of levy is chargeable, and the security is forfeited or treated as a levy.[87]

The export levy is fixed at regular intervals[88] under the Management Committee procedure, but it may also be fixed by tender.[89] Where this is the case, the tendering procedure is similar to that applied where the rate of export refund is determined by tender.[90]

Export levies are not applicable to exports in respect of which a refund has already been fixed in advance, or under a tendering procedure, nor are they applicable in certain specified cases, such as products for victualling purposes on seagoing vessels or aircraft serving on continental routes, or products for the armed forces of a Member State stationed outside the Community.[91] Again, exporters may cancel outstanding licences rather than pay a levy, if no levy was applicable on the day the licence was applied for, and are entitled to the return of their security.[92]

Article 20 of the basic Regulation provides that: "If by reason of imports or exports the Community market . . . experiences or is threatened with serious disturbances which may endanger the objectives set out in Article 39 of the Treaty," appropriate measures may be applied. In order to assess whether such a situation has come about, account is taken of:

(a) the quantities of products for which import or export licences have been issued or applied for;

(b) the quantities of products available on the Community market;

(c) the prices recorded on the Community market or the foreseeable trend of these prices and in particular any excessive upward trend thereof, or in the case of products for which no intervention price has been fixed, any excessive downward trend thereof;

---

[84] Reg. 645/75, Art. 4(1).
[85] Reg. 645/75, Art. 4(3).
[86] *i.e.* provided in Reg. 2730/79, Art. 20, see *supra*, p. 322; Reg. 645/75, Art. 5(2).
[87] Reg. 645/75, Art. 5(2)(c).
[88] Reg. 2747/75, Art. 4(2).
[89] Reg. 2747/75, Art. 2(1).
[90] Reg. 3130/73, L319/10; for the tendering procedure for export refunds, see *supra*, at p. 323.
[91] Reg. 645/75, Art. 3(1) (2).
[92] Reg. 645/75, Art. 10.

(d) the quantities of products for which intervention measures have been taken or may need to be taken if the above mentioned situation arises as a result of imports.[93]

If, after a summary examination of the situation based on these factors, the Commission determines that the market is either experiencing, or threatened by, serious disturbances, it must suspend the advance fixing of levies and refunds, and the issue of import and export licences, for a period not exceeding 48 hours.[94] Such a decision may be appealed to the Council by a Member State within three working days,[95] and the Council may amend or repeal the measure in question. It is open to Member States to take, on their own initiative, interim measures of protection, but the Commission must be notified, and such a notification constitutes a request to the Commission to take a decision on the suspension of levies, refunds, and licences. Such measures may only be taken to such extent and for such length of time as is strictly necessary.[96]

Disallowance

The European Agricultural Guidance and Guarantee Fund forms part of the budget of the Communities.[97] It comprises two sections, the Guidance Section, and the Guarantee Section. The latter section finances: (a) refunds on exports to third countries; and (b) intervention intended to stabilise the agricultural markets.[98] It is provided that refunds on exports to third countries, granted in accordance with the Community rules within the framework of the common organisation of agricultural markets, shall be financed by the Guarantee Section, as shall intervention intended to stabilise the agricultural markets, undertaken according to Community rules within the framework of the common organisation of agricultural markets.[99] It falls to the Commission to clear the accounts presented by each Member State each year in respect of expenditure qualifying for reimbursement from the Guarantee Section of the EAGGF.[1] Although it is the duty of the Commission to make up the accounts for one year before the end of the following year, it in fact carries out its duties several years in arrears. Naturally, the Commission will refuse to clear, or will "disallow" expenditure which either has not been "granted in accordance with the Community rules within the framework of the common organisation of the agricultural markets," or has not been "undertaken according to Community rules within the framework of the common organisation of agricultural markets."[2] Vis-à-vis the Community, such expenditure is ultra vires, and cannot be reimbursed from Community funds.

The role of the Commission in clearing the accounts presented by the

---

[93] Reg. 2748/75, O.J. 1975, L281/85, Art. 1.
[94] Reg. 2727/75, Art. 20(2); Reg. 2748/75, Art. 3(1).
[95] Reg. 2727/75, Art. 20(3).
[96] Reg. 2748, Art. 4, 2(2).
[97] Reg. 729/70, O.J. 1970, L94/13, as amended, Art. 1(1).
[98] Reg. 729/70, Art. 2(1).
[99] Reg. 729/70, Art. 3(1).
[1] Reg. 729/70, Art. 5.
[2] See Reg. 729/70, Art. 2(1), 3(1).

Member States, that is to say, agreeing or not with the Member States' assessment of which money expended qualifies for reimbursement, constitutes an important control mechanism for securing compliance by Member States with the rules laying down the common agricultural policy. If a Member State does not agree with the Commission's assessment, it can of course challenge it under Article 173 of the Treaty, and such actions have become fairly common. However, Member States do not relish litigation, and the possibility of disallowance by the Commission of expenditure means that the competent authorities of the Member States will attach particular weight to the advice of the Commission as to the interpretation of Community rules governing intervention measures and export refunds.[3]

The Court of Justice has endorsed the twin principles: (a) that only expenditure properly incurred can be charged to the EAGGF; and (b) that Regulations conferring financial benefits on traders from Community funds are to be construed strictly.[4] Examples of items of expenditure disallowed by the Commission on the *ultra vires* principle, and confirmed by the Court of Justice when challenged, are as follows:

— *Netherlands* v. *Commission*,[5] expenditure on the sale of butter for export at reduced prices disallowed because the butter was not exported within the 30 day time limit specified in the Community rules;

— *France* v. *Commission*,[6] disallowance of denaturing aids since unsupported by the required documentation;

— *Belgium* v. *Commission*,[7] disallowance of import refunds paid without proper proof that the goods had reached their destination;

— *Italy* v. *Commission*,[8] disallowance of expenditure on wine storage contracts entered into after permissible date;

— *Italy* v. *Commission*,[9] disallowance of costs of sale of intervention cereals where Italian agency sold below the local market price, contrary to Community rules; disallowance of aids for skimmed milk used in animal feed, to the extent that Italy paid out two per cent. excess in respect of "processing waste"; disallowance of aid for the storage of cheese without the conclusion of the required storage contracts;

— *Luxembourg* v. *Commission*,[10] disallowance of private storage aid to the extent that it was paid in respect of "table wine" later classified as quality wine;

---

[3] See, *e.g.* Case 272/81 *RU-MI* [1982] E.C.R. 4167. An intervention agency refused to pay an aid for what it regarded as an improperly conducted denaturation. The trader objected. The intervention agency consulted the Commission, which stated that in its view the EAGGF would be unable to finance the aid in quesion. The trader brought an action before a national court, which referred a question to the European Court, which confirmed the view of the Commission that the trader was not entitled to the aid.

[4] Cases 146, 192 and 193/81 *Baywa* [1980] E.C.R. 1503; Case 55/83 *Italy* v. *Commission* [1985] E.C.R. 27.2.85.

[5] Case 11/76 [1979] E.C.R. 245.

[6] Cases 15 & 16/76 [1979] E.C.R. 321.

[7] Case 820/79 [1980] E.C.R. 3537.

[8] Case 1251/79 [1981] E.C.R. 205.

[9] Case 61/82 [1983] E.C.R. 655.

[10] Case 49/83 [1984] E.C.R. 2931.

— *United Kingdom* v. *Commission*,[11] disallowance of cumulative payment of seed and feed aid contrary to Community rules.

On a number of occasions, Member States have successfully challenged disallowance decisions by the Commission on the ground that their interpretation of the Community rules was correct, and that of the Commission was wrong, with the consequence that expenditure alleged by the Commission to be *ultra vires* was in fact *intra vires*.[12]

Not all the costs of *ultra vires* expenditure must be borne by the Member States which mistakenly authorise the expenditure. Article 8 of Regulation 729/70 provides:

"1. The Member States in accordance with national provisions laid down by law, regulation or administrative action shall take the measures necessary to:

—satisfy themselves that transactions financed by the Fund are actually carried out and executed correctly;

—prevent and deal with irregularities;

—recover sums lost as a result of irregularities or negligence."

If payment is made by the national authorities, under colour of Community rules, where the fraud or mistake of the beneficiary prevents compliance with the relevant Community requirements, the Member State is under a duty to recover back the money.[13] The basis for such actions is the national law of the Member State concerned, not Community law.[14] However, while national rules apply, they must not make recovery impossible, they must not be discriminatory as compared with like actions in a purely national context, and interest may be chargeable under applicable national rules.[15]

If a Member State, in the circumstances referred to in the previous paragraph, fails to recover all the money involved, the loss is charged to the EAGGF, with the exception of the consequences of irregularities or negligence attributable to the administrative authorities or other bodies of the Member State.[16]

If payment is made by the national authorities, under colour of Community rules, but, as a result of a good faith misinterpretation of Community law by those authorities, essential Community requirements are not complied with, the cost of payment cannot be charged to the EAGGF.[17] In these circumstances, where the beneficiary is innocent of fraud or negligence, it seems that money paid is generally irrecoverable. As the Court has explained:

"In cases where, viewed objectively, Community law has been incor-

---

[11] Case 133/84 [1987] 1 C.M.L.R. 294.

[12] See, *e.g.* Case 18/76 *Germany* v. *Commission* [1979] E.C.R. 343; Case 46/82 *Germany* v. *Commission* [1983] E.C.R. 3549; Case 49/83 *Luxembourg* v. *Commission* [1984] E.C.R. 2931; Case 133/84 *United Kingdom* v. *Commission* [1987] 1 C.M.L.R. 294.

[13] Case 11/76 *Netherlands* v. *Commission* [1979] E.C.R. 245; Cases 146, 192 and 193/81 *Baywa* [1982] E.C.R. 1503.

[14] Cases 205–215/82 *Deutsche Milchkontor* [1983] E.C.R. 2633.

[15] Case 54/81 *Fromme* [1982] E.C.R. 1449.

[16] Reg. 729/70, Art. 8(2).

[17] Case 11/76 *Netherlands* v. *Commission* [1979] E.C.R. 245.

rectly applied on the basis of an interpretation adopted in good faith by the national authorities it is not possible as a general rule, either under Community law or under most of the national legal systems, to recover sums paid in error from the recipients and it is not possible to undertake administrative or judicial procedures against those responsible."[18]

It is established that if the authorities of a Member State make *ultra vires* payments as a result of a good faith misinterpretation of the law induced by the Community authorities, the cost will be borne by the EAGGF.[19]

A further problem of some difficulty may arise in connection with disallowance proceedings. What if a Member State incurs *intra vires* expenditure at an excessive rate as a result of a collateral wrongful act by the national authorities of that Member State in connection with its administration of the common agricultural policy? May the Commission disallow *intra vires* expenditure in such circumstances? There is some support in the Court's caselaw for this proposition. In *France* v. *Commission*[20] Community aid was payable in respect of wine purchased for distillation at not less than FF6.10. The French authorities paid a Community aid plus a national aid in respect of wine purchased for distillation at not less than FF7.10. The Court upheld the Commission's disallowance of *all* expenditure incurred by France in respect of wine for distillation under these arrangements. The Court held that the procedure for the discharge of accounts was not only intended to determine that expenditure was properly incurred, but that the costs of the common agricultural policy were correctly apportioned between the Community and the Member States. In this respect the Commission had no discretionary power to derogate from the rules governing the allocation of expenses. It was impossible to establish with certainty what quantities of wine would have been distilled in France if the national measure had not been adopted, and in the circumstances the Commission had no choice but to refuse to charge to the EAGGF the expenditure incurred by the French authorities.

The above decision certainly broke new ground. The expenditure was not disallowed because it was *ultra vires*. The French did not claim reimbursement of the national aid, only the pro rata amount of the Community aid. This was unacceptable to the Court because of the probability that the national aid had increased the volume of Community aid above the level which would have prevailed but for the national aid, and it was impossible to establish what that level would have been. It would seem to follow from this decision that lawful expenditure (lawful in the sense that national authorities would have no defence to a claim by putative beneficiaries based on the applicable Community Regulations) may be disallowed to the extent that it is incurred at a higher level than would have been the case but for a breach of Community law by the Member State in question.

Whether the French wine aids case reasoning is based on the wording of

[18] Case 11/76 [1979] E.C.R. 245 at p. 278, para. 8.
[19] Case 1251/79 *Italy* v. *Commission* [1981] E.C.R. 205.
[20] Cases 15 and 16/76 [1979] E.C.R. 321.

Articles 2 and 3 of Regulation 729/70 or not,[21] it is clear that it is based upon a different principle from the other disallowance cases endorsed by the Court and referred to above. The basis of disallowing the cost of lawful but excessive expenditure resulting from the unlawful act of a Member State can only be that the Member State's default releases the Community from the obligation which it would otherwise incur to make payment of Community money to that Member State. This principle of reciprocity of obligations has not been recognised by the Court when invoked by Member States against the Community[22] or against other Member States.[23] Indeed, applied in this context, it would allow the Commission to, in effect, collect "damages" against Member States for the consequences of their mismanagement of the common agricultural policy, subject to appeal by the Member State concerned to the Court of Justice.[24]

Monetary compensatory amounts

Prices under the common agricultural policy are fixed in terms of a unit of account known as the European Currency Unit, or ECU, which is defined as the sum of specified amounts of the currencies of the Member States other than Spain and Portugal.[25] Problems for the single market can arise if the exchange rate of a national currency deviates substantially from the rate applicable *vis-à-vis* the ECU in which the agricultural prices are fixed. If a national currency is revalued, intervention prices in terms of that currency go down, imports of agricultural products become cheaper, and exports more expensive. If the national currency is devalued, the reverse happens. Two devices have been adopted to mitigate these consequences of parity changes. First, the adoption of a "green" or representative rate of exchange, whereby a parity other than the market rate for the currency in question is maintained or imposed for the purposes of conversion into the ECU in which agricultural prices are fixed.[26] The second device is the monetary compensatory amount, or MCA, which is either charged, or granted, on imports and exports of agricultural products, in order to bridge the gap between the prices of those products as defined in national currency valued according to its market rate against the ECU, and their prices defined in national currency according to its representative conversion rate against

---

[21] See *supra* at p. 330.

[22] Cases 90 and 91/63 *Commission* v. *Luxembourg and Belgium* [1964] E.C.R. 625, at p. 631.

[23] Case 43/75 *Defrenne* [1976] E.C.R. 475, at para. 33; Case 232/78 *Commission* v. *France* [1979] E.C.R. 2729, at p. 2739, para. 9.

[24] Note that Art. 88 of the ECSC Treaty authorises the High Authority to withhold payments due to a Member State in default of its obligations. Other Member States may be authorised to derogate from their obligations *vis-à-vis* the defaulter. Yet safeguards exist: recourse to the Court is available before the High Authority acts, and the High Authority's action is subject to the assent of the Council. No similar provisions appear in the EEC Treaty.

[25] Reg. 3180/78, O.J. 1978, L379/1; Reg. 2626/84, O.J. 1984, L247/1; see also the Joint Declaration on the inclusion of the peseta and the escudo in the ECU in the Final Act of the Treaty of Accession of Spain and Portugal.

[26] This device was upheld by the Court of Justice in Case 138/78 *Stölting* [1979] E.C.R. 713; and Case 49/79 *Pool* [1980] E.C.R. 569.

the ECU.[27] For example, suppose the Community price for market organisation product X has been fixed at 100 ECU. At the time this corresponded in national currencies to DM235 or FF670. Suppose however that revaluation of the German Mark and devaluation of the French Franc change these amounts to DM225 and FF690. The effect is that guaranteed producer prices fall by DM10 in Germany and rise by FF20 in France! To mitigate the effects of these national price changes, representative green rates of DM230 and FF680 could be fixed for the remainder of the marketing year. It would follow that in cross border trade in this agricultural product there would have to be positive compensation of DM5, and negative compensation of FF10. That is to say, MCAs of DM5 would be granted on exports of the product from Germany, and imposed on imports into Germany, and MCAs of FF10 would be charged on exports from France, and granted on imports into France.[28]

MCAs are also granted and charged in trade with third countries. Those granted on imports will be deducted from the import duties payable, and in general, those charged on exports are deducted from export refunds.[29]

The system for calculating and imposing MCAs is complex. It is currently laid down in Regulation 1677/85.[30] In practice Member States are often reluctant to align green rates, for domestic economic and political reasons. Nevertheless, the Council has acknowledged the need to dismantle MCAs,[31] and has to this end amended both the method for calculating MCAs and the method for calculating the agricultural conversion rates.[32]

The co-existence of national measures with common organisations of the market

Where the Community has established a common organisation of the market in a particular sector, Member States are under an obligation to refrain from taking any measure which might undermine or create exceptions to it.[33] It is often a matter of some difficulty to determine whether national rules which determine or influence the pricing, production, presentation or marketing of products subject to a common organisation are or are not consistent with that common organisation.

National measures calculated to support producer prices will inevitably

---

[27] MCAs were first introduced in 1971, see Reg. 974/71, O.J. 1971 L106/1, as consolidated and republished in Reg. 1677/85, O.J. 1985, L164/6. The Court has considered the legality and application of the MCA in a number of cases, see, *e.g.* Case 5/73 *Balkan-Import-Export* [1973] E.C.R. 1091; Case 9/73 *Schlüter* [1973] E.C.R. 1135; Case 10/73, *Rewe-Zentral* [1973] E.C.R. 1175; Case 97/76 *Merkur* [1977] E.C.R. 1063; Case 29/77 *Roquette* [1977] E.C.R. 1835; Case 6/78 *Union Francaise* [1978] E.C.R. 1675 (accession MCAs); Case 127/78 *Spitta* [1979] E.C.R. 171; Case 151/77 *Peiser* [1979] E.C.R. 1469; Case 4/79 *Providence Agricole* [1980] E.C.R. 2823; Case 250/80 *Topfer* [1981] E.C.R. 2465 (accession MCAs). For a lucid treatment of units of account, "green money" and MCAs, see Snyder, *op. cit.* pp. 105–121.

[28] The example is that given in the EC publication, *The European Community's Budget* (4th ed., 1986) pp. 35, 36.

[29] Reg. 1677/85, Art. 11.

[30] O.J. 1985, L164/6, consolidating and republishing Reg. 974/71.

[31] Reg. 1677/85, 15th recital.

[32] Reg. 1677/85.

[33] See, *e.g.* Case 51/74 *Hulst* [1975] E.C.R. 79; Case 11/76 *Van den Hazel* [1977] E.C.R. 901; Case 177/78 *McCarren* [1979] E.C.R. 2161; Case 83/78 *Redmond* [1978] E.C.R. 2347.

fall foul of common organisations of the market which provide for Community intervention to the same end. Thus the Court has condemned national legislation fixing a uniform regional producer price for cow's milk,[34] and legislation providing for production aids for durum wheat.[35] National measures which directly or indirectly fix prices at the retail or consumption level will not be inconsistent with a common organisation of the market providing for a price system unless they interfere with that system.[36] Price restrictions at the retail level are capable of depressing prices at the wholesale and producer level, and this would be inconsistent with a common organisation if it precluded sales by traders at the target price, or the intervention price, according to circumstances. Where a common organisation provides for methods of supervision, it seems that national charges which do not exceed the costs involved may be made.[37]

The Court in the *Cucchi* case condemned fiscal measures which appropriated to the national treasury an increase in the value of sugar stocks resulting from the devaluation of a representative exchange rate.[38] However, in a later case, *Irish Creamery*, it upheld a temporary excise duty on certain agricultural products as part of an incomes policy designed to divide the tax burden between the various sectors of the working population, observing that the community price mechanism was not intended to guarantee certain prices net of tax.[39] In *Samvirkande Dasnke*,[40] the Court considered the argument that a tax on agricultural land, constituting a part of an incomes policy designed to apportion the tax burden among the various sectors of the working population, was intended to neutralise the intended effect on farmer's incomes of a devaluation of a national currency against the ECU, and was accordingly incompatible with Community law. The Court rejected this argument, since the purpose of the devaluation was not to ensure a higher net income for farmers, but to avoid the introduction of monetary compensatory amounts. However, the Court added that the new tax would be incompatible with Community law to the extent that it exerted an appreciable influence on price formation, or on the nature and volume of supplies on the market.

Whether or not national restrictions on production, or national quality standards, will be consistent with a common organisation, will depend in large part on the structure of the organisation in question.

In *Officier van Justitie* v. *Beert van den Hazel*,[41] the Gerechtshof, Amsterdam, asked the Court of Justice whether national quotas on the number of chickens to be slaughtered within a certain reference period was

[34] Case 10/79 *Toffoli* [1979] E.C.R. 3301.
[35] Case 169/82 *Commission* v. *Italy* [1984] E.C.R. 1603.
[36] See, *e.g.* Case 31/74 *Galli* [1975] E.C.R. 47; Case 60/75 *Russo* [1976] E.C.R. 45; Case 65/75 *Tasca* [1976] E.C.R. 291; Cases 88–90/75 *SADAM* [1976] E.C.R. 323; Case 50/76 *Amsterdam Bulb* [1977] E.C.R. 137; Case 52/76 *Benedetti* [1977] E.C.R. 163; Case 154/77 *Dechmann* [1978] E.C.R. 1573; Case 223/78 *Grosoli* [1979] E.C.R. 2621; Case 5/79 *Buys* [1979] E.C.R. 3203; Cases 16–20/79 *Danis* [1979] E.C.R. 3327; Cases 95 and 96/79 *Kefer and Delmelle* [1980] E.C.R. 103.
[37] Case 31/78 *Bussone* [1978] E.C.R. 2429; Case 233/81 *Denkavit* [1982] E.C.R. 2933.
[38] Case 77/76 [1977] E.C.R. 987.
[39] Cases 36 and 37/80 [1981] E.C.R. 735.
[40] Case 297/82 [1983] E.C.R. 3299.
[41] Case 111/76 [1977] E.C.R. 901.

compatible with Regulation 123/67 on the common organisation of the market in poultrymeat, Article 2 of which expressly precluded—at the Community level—withdrawal from the market. The Court declared that in its view the absence of provision for withdrawal from the market did not disclose an intention to leave such withdrawal to the discretion of Member States, but constituted a positive economic policy—confirmed not only in Article 2 of the Regulation, but also in Article 13, prohibiting customs duties and quantitative restrictions, to rely "essentially on market forces to obtain the desired balance." This being the case national measures of the type in question were capable of affecting the system of trade as it had been established under Regulation 123/67, and were accordingly prohibited.

By contrast, in *Jongeneel Kaas*,[42] the Court considered whether national rules laying down exhaustively the types and specification of cheeses which might be produced in the Member State in question were compatible with the applicable common organisation of the market. The Community rules made no mention of the designation and quality of cheeses subject to the common organisation, but in this case the Court refused to deduce from this the inference that Member States were obliged to accord absolute freedom to producers. The Commission argued to no avail that the national measures in question limited the possibility for intervention, and hindered the Community policy of increasing demand through diversity of production. In the first place intervention measures were extremely limited in the cheese sector, and in the second place a policy of furthering demand could be equally be furthered by high quality of a limited range, as by widening the range of products available.

Where a common organisation, such as that for fruit and vegetables, lays down an exhaustive system of quality standards applicable to the products in question, the national authorities are prohibited from imposing unilateral quality standards upon national producers.[43] However, where a common organisation provides for the establishment of quality standards at the Community level, but the Community fails to act, national measures to the same effect may be taken pending the introduction of Community measures, providing that the access of products lawfully marketed in other Member States is not impeded.[44]

It is not in any event open to Member States, in the name of quality control, to condition the freedom of commercial transactions, in particular the freedom to import and export, upon affiliation to a supervisory body designated by the authorities of a Member State.[45]

Once the provisions of Community law governing a common organisation may be regarded as forming a "complete system," especially as regards prices and intervention, trade with non-member countries, and rules on production and designation, Member States no longer have any powers in the field in question, subject to any special Community pro-

---

[42] [1984] E.C.R. 483.
[43] Case 222/82 *Apple and Pear Development Council* [1983] E.C.R. 2933.
[44] Cases 47 and 48/83 *Van Miert* [1984] E.C.R. 1721. See also Case 804/79 *Commission* v. *United Kingdom* [1981] E.C.R. 1045.
[45] Case 94/79 *Vriend* [1980] E.C.R. 327; Case 29/82 *Van Luipen* [1983] E.C.R. 151.

visions to the contrary.[46] Since the common organisation of the wine market constitutes such a system, the Court has held that it is not open to a
Member State to limit the designation rosé wine to wines produced in
accordance with traditional national practices.[47] In contrast, the Court has
held that it is consistent with the above-mentioned Community rules for a
Member State to restrict a traditional bottle shape to a designated national
wine. This conclusion followed from the fact that the market organisation
in question authorised the Council to adopt rules governing the designation
and presentation of wines, and authorised Member States in the meantime
to adopt measures to the same end. Since the Court took the view—
deduced in part from draft legislation considered by the Council—that the
latter body had not exhausted its competence in this regard, it followed
that the national measure in issue was compatible with the common organisation of the wine market.[48]

In the *Holdijk* case,[49] the Court emphasised that the establishment of a
common organisation does not have the effect of exempting agricultural
producers from national provisions intended to attain objectives other than
those covered by the common organisation, even though such provisions
may, by affecting the conditions of production, have an impact on the
volume or the cost of national production and therefore on the operation
of the common market in the sector concerned. On this basis, national
measures requiring enclosures for fattening calves allowing the animals to
lie down unhindered were held consistent with the applicable common
organisation of the market, which contained no provisions on the subject
of animal health.

[46] Case 16/83 *Prantl* [1984] E.C.R. 1299 (market in wine); Case 89/84 *Ramel* [1985] E.C.R.
14.5.85 (market in wine).
[47] Case 89/84 *Ramel* [1985] E.C.R.
[48] Case 16/83 *Prantl* [1984] E.C.R. 1299; but the national measure infringed Art. 30 of the
Treaty.
[49] Cases 141–143/81 [1982] E.C.R. 1299.

PART VII: COMPETITION

CHAPTER 13

INTRODUCTION TO THE RULES ON COMPETITION

Competition and the common market

The list of "activities of the Community" in Article 3 EEC includes under (*f*) "the institution of a system ensuring that competition in the common market is not distorted."[1] There are two main reasons why competition policy was singled out in this way as a key factor in the pursuit of the broad objectives laid down for the Community in Article 2.

In the first place, a conscious choice was made by the authors of the Treaty, and by those who have since adhered to it, not only of an economic life in common but of a way of life in which the market plays a central, though not necessarily an exclusive, role. Competition is an essential aspect of the market mechanism because the availability of choice between goods and services establishes a link between the success of an undertaking and its ability to satisfy customers' wishes. The phrasing of Article 3(*f*) is, perhaps, not altogether happy, since the idea of "distortion" implies deviation from a state of perfect competition. That, of course, is unrealistic. What is needed is the preservation of *effective* competition, *i.e.* a level of challenge from other operators sufficient to make efficiency and innovation a condition of ultimate survival as a market participant. In the introduction to its *First Report on Competition Policy* the Commission wrote:

> "Competition is the best stimulant of economic activity since it guarantees the widest possible freedom of action to all. An active competition policy pursued in accordance with the provisions of the Treaties establishing the Communities makes it easier for the supply and demand structure continually to adjust to technological development. Through the interplay of decentralized decision-making machinery, competition enables enterprises continuously to improve their efficiency, which is the *sine qua non* for a steady improvement in living standards and employment prospects within the countries of the Community. From this point of view, competition policy is an essential means for satisfying to a great extent the individual and collective needs of our society."[2]

Thus competition policy is seen as ensuring that the common market envisaged by the Treaty functions as a genuine *market*.

Secondly, competition policy contributes to the creation and preservation of a market that is *common*, since it reinforces the provisions of the Treaty aiming at the removal of barriers between the economies of the Member States. It would be futile to require the abolition of customs duties

---

[1] For an account of EEC competition policy and its relationship with industrial policy in the strategy for the creation of a genuine internal market in goods and services, see Dennis Swann, *Competition and Industrial Policy in the European Community* (1983).

[2] Comp. Rep. 1971, p. 11.

and charges having equivalent effect and of quantitative restrictions and measures having equivalent effect if the isolation of national markets could effectively be maintained by restrictive practices on the part of undertakings, or by State aid policies giving competitive advantages to the national industries. As we shall see, for an agreement or practice to have the object or effect of dividing the common market involves a particularly serious infringement of the rules on competition. Those rules, accordingly, by opening up possibilities for competition on a Community-wide scale, both supplement the provisions of Part Two of the Treaty and assist in the attainment of the greater prosperity mentioned in Article 2 through the operation of economies of scale.

The EEC Treaty provisions on competition

The preamble to the Treaty and the general provisions of Articles 2 and 3 have played a significant part in the development of the case-law on competition.[3] However, the primary Treaty provisions in which the substantive law on the topic is to be found are Articles 85 to 94.

So far as the behaviour of undertakings is concerned, the Treaty adopts a distinction which is familiar in competition law (or, to use the American term, "anti-trust law") between two types of problem that may arise.[4] The first concerns restrictive agreements or practices involving a degree of collusion between undertakings that are economically independent of each other. Such combinations in restraint of trade are sometimes referred to as "cartels." An example would be an agreement between trade associations representing French and German manufacturers of garden gnomes that each group would refrain from selling its products on the other's market. Article 85 of the Treaty is designed to deal with such a situation. It is considered in Chapter 14, *infra*. The second type of problem arises where a single undertaking or a group of undertakings has reached a position of such strength on a given market that the normal constraints of the competitive process no longer apply to it. Community law calls that a "dominant position" and English law a "monopoly situation." Dominant undertakings represent a danger to other operators on the same market and to their customers or suppliers. They may, for example, drive the remaining participants in the same market out of business or charge unreasonably high prices for their products. One way of averting this danger is to attack the fact of dominance itself, by seeking to prevent the growth of undertakings beyond a certain point, and by taking power to break up any that may succeed in doing so. An alternative approach is to attempt to regulate the behaviour of dominant undertakings. Here public power is used as a constraining influence, to compensate for the absence of effective competition.

---

[3] See, *e.g.* Case 32/65 *Italy* v. *Council and Commission* [1966] E.C.R. 389 at p. 405; Case 6/72 *Europemballage and Continental Can* v. *Commission* [1973] E.C.R. 215 at pp. 243–244.

[4] On the nature of the problems, and the different solutions adopted in United Kingdom and Community law, see Korah, *Competition Law of Britain and the Common Market* (3rd revised ed., 1982).

The latter was the approach adopted by the EEC Treaty which in Article 86 outlaws the "abuse" of dominant positions.[5] However, it will be seen in Chapter 15, *infra*, that the European Court has held that, in certain circumstances, a further accretion of market power to a dominant undertaking may, in itself, constitute an abuse.

Provision for the application of the substantive rules in Articles 85 and 86 is made by Articles 87 to 89 of the Treaty. Article 87 empowers the Council, acting by a qualified majority on a proposal from the Commission and after consulting the European Parliament, to adopt implementing regulations or directives. This power has been used for the enactment of, *inter alia*, Regulation 17, which established the basic machinery for the execution of EEC competition policy, giving primary responsibility to the Commission.[6] Articles 88 and 89 contain transitional provisions applicable in the absence of such special machinery. The only economic sectors still subject to the transitional regime are air and sea transport.[7]

Problems arising from the relationships between governments, on the one hand, and public undertakings or undertakings which have been entrusted with the performance of certain tasks in the public interest, on the other, are the subject of Article 90. This relationship, although clearly liable to affect the conditions of competition, has a wider significance for the operation of the common market. It is discussed in Chapter 19, *infra*.

Article 91 laid down procedures to be followed if dumping should take place within the common market during the transitional period of the Community as originally constituted.[8] "Dumping" is a species of unfair competition which consists of selling goods on an export market below their "normal value." There are various ways of establishing the normal value of a product, the most straightforward being the price charged on the domestic market. The provision was limited to the transitional period since, once barriers to internal trade had come down, dumped products could be re-exported to the country of origin, where they could be sold at a price that would undercut the price prevailing there. The Article itself is, therefore, of mainly historical interest, though equivalent provisions are found in the accession arrangements with new Member States.[9]

Under Articles 92 to 94 the Community institutions, and in particular the Commission, have supervisory powers over the granting of aids to industry in the various Member States. The general principle is that aid must not be granted if it distorts or threatens to distort competition by favouring certain undertakings or forms of production, in so far as trade between Member States may be affected. However, wide exceptions are permitted, enabling the Commission to take account of the economic and social pressures to

---

[5] On the variety of approaches adopted by national authorities, see Van Damme, *Regulating the behaviour of monopolies and dominant undertakings in Community Law* (1977).
[6] J.O. 1962, 204; O.J. 1959–1962, 87.
[7] On the application of the competition rules to air transport, see Joined Cases 209 to 213/84 *Ministère Public* v. *Asjès and Others* (not yet reported).
[8] Anti-dumping measures against third countries are an aspect of the Common Commercial Policy. See Art. 113 EEC and Reg. 2176/84, O.J. 1984 L 201/1.
[9] See Act of Accession, Denmark, Ireland and United Kingdom, Art. 136; Greece, Art. 131; Spain and Portugal, Art. 380.

which the Member States are subject. These provisions are discussed in Chapter 17, *infra*.

Other sources of EEC competition law

Besides the EEC Treaty itself, the principal sources of EEC competition law are regulations pursuant to Article 87, the case law of the Court of Justice and the administrative practice of the Commission.

Regulations on competition have been adopted by both the Council and the Commission, the latter acting under delegated powers. Regulation 17,[10] the general implementing measure, has already been mentioned. This is supplemented by various measures governing more detailed matters, such as Regulation 99[11] on the the conduct of hearings and Regulation 2988/74[12] on periods of limitation. There is also a growing body of regulations granting "block" exemptions under Article 85(3) in respect of categories of agreements (*e.g.* exclusive distribution agreements, exclusive purchasing agreements, specialisation agreements) which would otherwise be liable to prohibition under Article 85(1).[13]

The Court of Justice has played a vital part in the development of the rules on competition, as of other areas of Community law. Competition matters normally come to the Court by way of proceedings under Article 173 EEC for the review of decisions of the Commission applying the rules; or of references under Article 177 from national courts before which the rules have been invoked. In addition, Regulation 17 has conferred on the Court unlimited jurisdiction as provided by Article 172 EEC, to hear appeals against the imposition by the Commission of fines for infringements of the rules.[14] In interpreting the competition provisions of the Treaty and of regulations the Court has followed its usual approach of giving weight, as appropriate, to their wording, their legal content and their objectives, as well as to the wider objectives of the Community. A bold example of the application of the principle of effectiveness was the decision in *Camera Care*[15] that the Commission has power to adopt interim measures in competition proceedings, despite the silence of Regulation 17 on this point. The technique of comparative analysis of national laws, including United States anti-trust law, has also proved fruitful.[16]

As we have seen, the Commission is the authority charged with the administration of the competition system at Community level. For this purpose it has been empowered to take decisions, *inter alia*, ordering the ter-

---

[10] *Loc. cit.* note 6, *supra*.
[11] J.O. 1963, 2268; O.J. 1963–1964, 47.
[12] O.J. 1974 L 319/1.
[13] See the discussion, pp. 387 *et seq.*, *infra*.
[14] See Reg. 17, Art. 17.
[15] Case 792/79R *Camera Care* v. *Commission* [1980] E.C.R. 119; [1980] 1 C.M.L.R. 334.
[16] The actual analysis is normally to be found in the opinion of the Advocate General in the case. See, *e.g.* Case 48/69 *ICI* v. *Commission (Dyestuffs)* [1972] E.C.R. 619; [1972] C.M.L.R. 557; Case 155/79 *A.M. & S. Europe* v. *Commission* [1982] E.C.R. 1575; [1982] 2 C.M.L.R. 264.

mination of infringements,[17] granting exemption under Article 85(3)[18] and imposing fines[19] or periodic penalty payments.[20] The competition decisions of the Commission are the best guide to the practical working of the rules. Further guidance may be obtained from the press releases the Commission issues when it terminates a proceeding without a formal decision and from the annual Reports on Competition Policy annexed to its General Report to the European Parliament. The Commission has also published a series of Notices setting forth its views on a variety of issues.[21] The Notices have made a useful contribution to general understanding of the law but they may not give reliable guidance in individual cases.

Finally, it may be noted, the directly effective provisions of Article 85 and Article 86 are being applied with increasing frequency by the courts of the Member States. The resulting case law is an additional source of persuasive authority on the interpretation of those provisions.

The scope of the EEC rules on competition

Personal scope

The rules in Article 85 and Article 86 apply to "undertakings." No definition of this concept for the purposes of competition law is provided by the EEC Treaty.[22] It has been described as much wider and looser than the concept of "persons"[23] and seems to extend to any entity carrying on economic activities.[24] A rough synonym would be a "business concern."

The requirement of participation in economic activities must be understood in a wide sense. It covers not only the production and distribution of goods but also the provision of services.[25] A body that exists for a non-economic purpose but engages in certain operations of a commercial nature will be, to that extent, an undertaking[26]: *e.g.* a public service broadcasting establishment when it licenses the manufacture of toys based on a popular children's series.[27] Nor is there any need for the body in question to be motivated by the pursuit of profits. Thus societies that manage the

---

[17] Reg. 17, Art. 3(1).
[18] Reg. 17, Art. 9(1).
[19] Reg. 17, Art. 15.
[20] Reg. 17, Art. 16.
[21] Notices have been issued on the following subjects: agreements with commercial agents, J.O. 1962, 2921; patent licensing, O.J. 1922, 2922 (withdrawn after the enactment of the block exemption measure for patent licensing agreements, Reg. 2349/84, see Chap. 18, *infra*); cooperation agreements, J.O. 1968 C 75/3; imports of Japanese products, J.O 1972 C111/13; agreements of minor importance, O.J. 1986 C231/2 (replacing a Notice of 1977); subcontracting agreements, O.J. 1979, C 1/2.
[22] *Cf.* the definitions in Art. 80 ECSC and Art. 196 Euratom. See also the partial definition in Art. 52 EEC for the purposes of the provisions on freedom of establishment.
[23] By Ad. Gen. Warner in Joined Cases 6 and 7/73 *Commercial Solvents Corporation* v. *Commission* [1974] E.C.R. 223 at p. 263.
[24] See the definition offered by Ad. Gen. Roemer in Case 32/65 *Italy* v. *Council and Commission* [1966] E.C.R. at p. 418.
[25] Case 155/73 *Sacchi* [1974] E.C.R. 409; [1974] 2 C.M.L.R. 177.
[26] *Ibid.*
[27] *Re BBC* [1976] 1 C.M.L.R. D89. The same would be true of sports clubs: see *Re English Football League* Comp. Rep. 1979, points 116–117.

rights of authors and performing artists on a non-profit making basis qualify as undertakings because they provide a commercial service.[28]

The entities accepted as undertakings by the Court of Justice and the
Commission exhibit a wide range of legal forms. They include companies,
partnerships,[29] co-operatives[30] and even the mutual marine insurance
associations known as "P and I Clubs."[31] Individuals may be undertakings,
e.g. an inventor who grants licences for the use of patents he has taken
out[32] or opera stars who contract to perform for a television company.[33] At
the opposite end of the spectrum are nationalised industries and the other
kinds of public corporation.[34] The Commission regards as undertakings the
foreign trade organisations of Eastern Bloc countries, even if under their
domestic law they have no identity separate from the state.[35] A similar
view would, it is submitted, be taken of a Member State, or of a subdivision of the state such as a local authority, engaging directly in commercial activity.[36]

In applying the rules on competition to groups of companies the Court of
Justice does not hesitate to go behind the facade of separate corporate
identity. This pragmatic approach is illustrated by the *Hydrotherm* case[37]
which concerned the block exemption granted by Regulation 67/67[38] to
certain categories of exclusive dealing agreements. The exemption was
expressly limited to agreements "to which only two undertakings are
party."[39] That condition was held to be fulfilled where the parties to a contract were, on the distribution side, a German company, and on the manufacturing side, the Italian developer of a product and two legally
independent firms controlled by him. The Court explained that "In competition law, the term 'undertaking' must be understood as designating an
economic unit for the purpose of the subject-matter of the agreement in
question even if in law that economic unit consists of several persons, natural or legal."[40] In practice, the main impact of the "enterprise entity" doc-

[28] Case 127/73 *BRT* v. *SABAM* [1974] ECR 51 and 313; [1974] 2 C.M.L.R. 238; Case 7/82
    GVL v. *Commission* [1983] E.C.R. 483; [1983] 3 C.M.L.R. 645.
[29] *e.g.* Re *William Prym-Werke* J.O 1973 L 296/24; [1973] C.M.L.R. D 250.
[30] *e.g.* Re *Rennet* O.J. 1980 L51/19; [1980] 2 C.M.L.R. 402. The decision was upheld by the
    Court in Case 61/80 *Cooperatieve Stremsel-en-Kleurselfabriek* v. *Commission* [1981]
    E.C.R. 851; [1982] 1 C.M.L.R. 240. See also Re *Milchförderungsfonds* O.J. 1985 L 35/35;
    [1985] 3 C.M.L.R. 101.
[31] See Re *P and I Clubs* O.J. 1985 C 9/11. The Clubs are groupings of shipowners, charterers,
    and operators who agree to share certain liabilities, in particular contractual and third party
    liabilities, on a non-profit making basis. Risks in excess of certain agreed thresholds are
    often shared between 'pools' of P and I Clubs.
[32] See, *e.g.* Re *AOIP/Beyrard* O.J. 1976 L 6/8; [1976] 1 C.M.L.R. D14; *Re Vaessen/Moris*
    O.J. 1979 L19/32; [1979] 1 C.M.L.R. 511.
[33] *Re Unitel* O.J. 1978 L 157/39; [1978] 3 C.M.L.R. 306.
[34] *e.g.* Re *British Telecom* O.J. 1982 L 360/36; [1983] 1 C.M.L.R. 457. The decision was
    upheld by the Court in Case 41/83 *Italy* v. *Commission* [1985] 2 C.M.L.R. 368. See also *Re
    Federacion Nacional de Cafeteros de Colombia* O.J. 1982 L 360/31; [1983] 1 C.M.L.R. 703.
[35] *Re Aluminium Imports from Eastern Europe* O.J. 1985 L 92/1.
[36] But see Bellamy and Child, *Common Market Law of Competition* (3rd ed., 1987) at para.
    2–011 where it is argued that a clear distinction is drawn throughout the Treaty between
    Member States and undertakings.
[37] Case 170/83 *Hydrotherm Gerätebau* v. *Andreoli* [1984] E.C.R. 2999.
[38] J.O. 1967, 849; O.J. 1967, 10. This was replaced by Reg. 1983/83 (exclusive distribution)
    O.J. 1983 L 173/1 and Reg. 1984/83 (exclusive purchasing) O.J. 1983 L 173/5: see Chap. 14,
    infra.
[39] Reg. 67/67, Art. 1(1).
[40] [1984] E.C.R. at p. 3016.

trine has been on two issues: the assertion of jurisdiction against a parent company established in a third country which has subsidiaries within the common market; and the application of Article 85 to agreements and practices between parent companies and subsidiaries. These issues are further examined below.[41]

Material scope

The EEC rules on competition apply generally, to all sectors of the economy, except where express derogations are provided in other Articles of the Treaty.[42]

The main sectors falling outside the rules are coal and steel, which are governed by the ECSC Treaty.[43] However, where an ECSC undertaking deals in goods other than those defined in Annex I to the ECSC Treaty, the EEC rules will apply to it.[44]

By Article 42 EEC the extent to which the competition provisions should apply to agricultural products was made a matter for the discretion of the Council. In exercising its discretion the Council differentiated between the rules applicable to undertakings in Articles 85 to 90 and the rules on state aids in Articles 92 to 94. The former Articles were extended to agricultural products by Regulation 26,[45] subject to an exemption from the prohibition in Article 85(1) for the benefit of agreements that form an integral part of a national market organisation or that are necessary for the attainment of the objectives of the Common Agricultural Policy set out in Article 39 EEC. The exception has been narrowly interpreted and is of limited practical significance.[46] In the case of state aids, effect has been given to the relevant provisions of the EEC Treaty by the basic regulations of the various common organisations of national markets.

One other economic sector that should perhaps be mentioned is that of transport. The Court of Justice has held that the Treaty provisions on competition apply to transport.[47] However, separate arrangements have been made for the implementation of the rules in this sector. The Council excluded transport from the scope of Regulation 17[48] and adopted a special implementing measure, Regulations 1017/68,[49] in relation to transport by road, rail and inland waterway. As we have noted, air and sea transport remain subject to the transitional regime of Articles 88 and 89.

---

[41] See, respectively, pp. 348 et seq. and pp. 353–354, infra.
[42] Joined Cases 209 to 213/84 Ministère Public v. Asjès and Others (not yet reported).
[43] See Art. 232 EEC.
[44] Case 1/59 Macchiorlatti Dalmas v. High Authority [1959] E.C.R. 199.
[45] J.O. 1962, 993; O.J. 1959–1962, 129.
[46] The first limb of the exception ceases to be available once a common organisation of the market has been established in respect of the product in question: Case 83/78 Pigs Marketing Board v. Redmond [1978] E.C.R. 2347 at pp. 2369–2370; [1979] 1 C.M.L.R. 177. To satisfy the second limb of the exception, an agreement must be shown to be necessary for the attainment of all five of the objectives in Art. 39 EEC: Case 71/74 FRUBO v. Commission [1975] E.C.R. 563 at pp. 582–583. See also Decs. of the Commission in Groupement d'Exportation de Léon v. Soc. d'Investissements et de Co-opération Agricoles O.J. 1978 L 21/23; [1978] 1 C.M.L.R. D 66; Re Milchföderungsfonds, loc. cit. note 30, supra.
[47] Joined Cases 209 to 213/84 Ministère Public v. Asjès and Others (not yet reported).
[48] By Reg. 141, J.O. 1962, 2751; O.J. 1959–62, 291.
[49] J.O. 1968 L 175/1; O.J. 1968, 302.

Territorial scope[50]

The prohibition in Article 85 applies to arrangements between undertakings "which may affect trade between Member States and which have as their object or effect the prevention, restriction or distortion of competition within the common market"; and that in Article 86 to any abuse of a dominant position "within the common market or in a substantial part of it . . . in so far as it may affect trade between Member States." This wording makes it clear that the target of the prohibitions is behaviour having an actual or intended impact on the conditions of competition in the territory over which the common market extends, *i.e.* the territory of the Community as defined by Article 227 EEC.

It follows that undertakings carrying on business in the Community are free under the EEC rules on competition to participate in agreements or practices that may interfere with the functioning of the market mechanism in third countries, so long as the consequences are unlikely to spill back into the common market.[51] Thus in its *VVVF* Decision[52] the Commission allowed a Dutch association of paint and varnish manufacturers to continue a system of minimum prices and uniform conditions of sale in respect of exports by its members outside the common market, after securing the abolition of the system in respect of intra-Community trade.

The converse case is where undertakings not physically present on Community territory behave in ways that are liable to affect competition on the common market. How far does the Community claim extraterritorial jurisdiction in competition matters? In addressing this question it is useful to bear in mind the distinction drawn by international lawyers between "prescriptive jurisdiction" (the power to make rules and to take decisions under them) and "enforcement jurisdiction" (the power to give effect to such rules or decisions through executive action).[53] The assertion of either form of jurisdiction, but especially the latter, against an undertaking located on another state's territory raises legal and political issues of some delicacy. Three possible bases for the application of the EEC rules in such cases fall to be considered.

First, it is generally accepted in international law that a state is entitled to jurisdiction where activity which was commenced abroad is brought to consummation on its territory. This is known as the "objective territorial principle."[54] It would, for example, allow the Commission to apply Article

---

[50] For a detailed examination of this topic, see Barack, *The Application of the Competition Rules (Antitrust Law) of the European Economic Community to Enterprises and Arrangements External to the Common Market* (1981). There are excellent shorter accounts in Kerse, *EEC Antitrust Procedure*, pp. 196 *et seq.*, and Whish, *Competition Law*, pp. 264 *et seq.*

[51] Community law is not alone in tolerating anti-competitive behaviour when its effects are limited to export markets. *Cf.* the Webb-Pomerene Act in the United States and the approach adopted under the Restrictive Trade Practices Act 1976 in the United Kingdom. See Whish, *op. cit.* note 50, *supra*, pp. 264–265.

[52] J.O. 1969 L 168/22; [1970] C.M.L.R. D 1.

[53] See Ch. XIV, "Jurisdictional Competence," in Brownlie, *Principles of Public International Law* (3rd ed., 1979).

[54] *Ibid.* pp. 300–301. Under the "subjective territorial principle" jurisdiction may be asserted where activity commenced in the state in question is consummated abroad.

85 to a contract made in a third country but substantially performed, at least on one side, within the Community.

Secondly, and more controversially, the Court of Justice has developed the doctrine of enterprise entity as a basis of jurisdiction against a parent company which has subsidiaries inside the Community, though situated itself on the outside. Under the doctrine, where material aspects of the subsidiary's commercial policy are controlled by the parent company, behaviour of the former in contravention of the rules on competition may be imputed to the latter. The leading case is *Dyestuffs*,[55] which concerned a decision by the Commission that a group of major manufacturers of aniline dyes had been guilty on three separate occasions of concerted price fixing. The addressees of the decision included ICI (this was prior to British accession) and certain Swiss companies. Objections by these companies to the jurisdiction of the Commission were dismissed by the Court on the ground that all of them had subsidiaries within the common market for whose decisions on pricing they could be held responsible.[56] In a later case, *Commercial Solvents Corporation*,[57] Advocate General Warner suggested that a subsidiary should be presumed to act in accordance with its parent's wishes; and that the assumption should be rebuttable only by affirmative proof that the subsidiary carried on its business autonomously.[58] The Court did not adopt this suggestion but it seems willing to infer from fairly slender evidence that a sufficient degree of practical control is exercised by the parent company.[59] The main indicators of control are a majority (or larger) shareholding in the subsidiary, representation on its board of directors and other organs, general ability to influence its business decisions and any evidence of specific instructions having been given to it.[60]

The enterprise entity doctrine has been used by the Court and the Commission to found not only prescriptive but also enforcement jurisdiction. Thus competition proceedings may be validly initiated against the foreign parent of a Community subsidiary by sending it a statement of objectives through the post[61]; and the final decision finding the company guilty of an infringement of the rules may be similarly served.[62] A fine may be imposed on the parent company for the infringement, and it may be ordered to take

---

[55] There was, in fact, a group of cases brought by different addressees of the decision in question, to which this collective designation is given. See, in particular, Case 48/69 *ICI* v. *Commission loc. cit.* note 16, *supra*.

[56] See, besides the *ICI* case, *supra*, Case 52/69 *Geigy* v. *Commission* [1972] E.C.R. 787 and Case 53/69 *Sandoz* v. *Commission* [1972] E.C.R. 845.

[57] Joined Cases 6 and 7/73 *Commercial Solvents Corporation* v. *Commission, loc. cit,* note 23, *supra*.

[58] [1974] E.C.R. at p. 264.

[59] See, *e.g.* the *ICI* case, *loc. cit.* note 16, *supra* and *Commercial Solvents Corporation loc. cit.* note 23, *supra*. See the critical comments by Mann (1973) 22 I.C.L.Q 35. Kerse, *op. cit.* note 50, *supra* at p. 200, note 23 remarks on the paucity of the evidence adduced against the parent company in the Commission's *Johnson & Johnson* Dec. (O.J. 1980 L 377/16; [1981] 2 C.M.L.R. 287).

[60] Barack, *op. cit.* note 50, *supra*, pp. 53 *et seq*.

[61] See, *e.g.* Case 52/69 *Geigy* v. *Commission loc. cit.* note 56, *supra*.

[62] Case 6/72 *Europemballage and Continental Can* v. *Commission, loc. cit.* note 3, *supra*. An alternative would be to serve the decision on the Community subsidiary, as the Commission did in *Dyestuffs*.

remedial action. In *Commercial Solvents Corporation*,[63] for example, an American multi-national company was found to have infringed Article 86 by refusing, through its Italian subsidiary, to supply a customer with a product in which it held the world monopoly. The Court did not question the power of the Commission, besides fining Commercial Solvents, to require it to make an immediate delivery of a specified quantity of the product in question to the customer and to submit proposals for longer term supply arrangements.[64] Of course, if fines are not paid, they can only be enforced by levying execution on property of the parent or subsidiary which is on the territory of a Member State.[65]

A third, and still more controversial, basis for the extra-territorial application of competition law is the so-called "effects doctrine." Broadly, the doctrine holds that a state is entitled to assert jurisdiction in respect of activities by non-nationals abroad, where these produce effects felt within the state's own territory. A strong lead in asserting jurisdiction on the ground of the anti-competitive effects of conduct in other countries has been given by courts in the United States.[66] Their readiness not only to find that such conduct infringes United States anti-trust law but to issue orders requiring, for example, the production of documents or the disposal of patent rights held by foreign companies,[67] has provoked some states, including the United Kingdom, into taking defensive measures.[68]

How far the effects doctrine has been received into the competition law of the EEC remains uncertain. In the *Dyestuffs* case Advocate General Mayras gave his support to a moderate form of the doctrine according to which the EEC rules may be applied where agreements or practices outside the Community have effects inside its territory that are direct, reasonably forseeable and substantial.[69] The Commission also accepts, and has acted on, the doctrine.[70] On the other hand it has never yet been applied by the Court of Justice. Thus in *Dyestuffs*, contrary to the opinion of its Advocate General, the Court opted for enterprise entity as the basis of jurisdiction against the British and Swiss addressees of the decision. In the *Béguelin*

---

[63] Joined Cases 6 and 7/73 *loc. cit.* note 23, *supra*.

[64] *Cf* the narrower view taken by Adv. Gen. Mayras in *Dyestuffs* as to the scope of enforcement jurisdiction based on the "effects doctrine": [1972] E.C.R. at pp. 694–695.

[65] See Art. 192 EEC.

[66] See the statement of Judge Learned Hard in *United States* v. *Aluminium Company of America* that " . . . it is settled law . . . that any state may impose liabililities, even upon persons not within its allegiance, for conduct outside its borders that has consequences within its borders:" 148 F. 2d. 416 (2d Cir. 1945) at p. 444. For a critical view, see Jennings (1957) BYBIL 146.

[67] For notorious examples of the assertion of enforcement jurisdiction, see *United States* v. *ICI* 145 F. Supp 215 (S.D. N.Y. 1952); *United States* v. *The Watchmakers of Switzerland Information Centre* 1963 Trade Cases para. 70.600 (S.D. N.Y. 1962). In more recent decisions there is recognition of the constraints imposed on the effects doctrine by international law and comity. See, in particular, *Timberlane Lumber Company* v. *Bank of America* 49 F. 2d. 597 (9th Cir. 1976); *Mannington Mills* v. *Congoleum Corporation* 595 F. 2d. 1287 (3d. Cir. 1979).

[68] *e.g.*. Protection of Trading Interests Act, 1980.

[69] Case 48/69 [1972] E.C.R. at pp. 687–697.

[70] See, *e.g.*, Decs. of the Commission in *Re Aniline Dyes Cartel* J.O. 1969 L 195/11; [1969] C.M.L.R. D 23; *Re Wood Pulp* O.J. 1985 L 85/1. See also the statement in Comp. Rep. EC 1981, points 34–42. The Commission's approach is fully analysed by Barack, *op. cit.* note 50, *supra* at p. 98 *et seq*.

case,[71] which arose out of the appointment of a Belgian firm by a Japanese manufacturer as the exclusive distributor of its products in Belgium and France, the Court said "The fact that one of the undertakings which are parties to the agreement is situate in a third country does not prevent application of that provision *since the agreement is operative in the territory of the common market*" (emphasis added).[72] The italicised phrase has sometimes been taken as indicating acceptance of the effects doctrine, but this seems misconceived. The Court was surely making the point that the actual performance of the contract was to take place within the Community.

Further light may be shed on the status of the effects doctrine in Community law by the *Wood Pulp* case which is currently before the Court.[73] In the decision under challenge the Commission found that a concerted practice had existed for a number of years between North American and Scandinavian producers of wood pulp as to the prices at which they supplied the paper industry in the common market. The activities regarded by the Commission as amounting to concertation took place in the producers' home countries, and several of those allegedly implicated have no establishment and no subsidiaries within the Community. The case is, therefore, one in which it seems the Court will have to resolve the issue of jurisdiction without resorting to the objective territorial principle or to enterprise entity.

Temporal scope

The rules on competition came into force under the EEC Treaty with effect from January 1, 1958. An agreement completely performed before that date would not be caught by the rules; but if the objects of the agreement were still being pursued by means of a concerted practice, the latter might fall within Article 85.[74]

Each time the Community has been enlarged, a new range of agreements and practices has been brought within the purview of the competition rules from the date of accession. It must, however, be remembered that undertakings established on the territory of a new Member State may have been subject to the rules even prior to accession, *e.g.* as parties to an agreement to be performed in the EEC or because they had subsidiaries there.[75]

The prohibitions in Article 85(1) and Article 86 began to have direct effect for the general class of agreements and practices from the date when Regulation 17 with its implementing machinery came into force, *viz.* March 13, 1962.[76] In the air and sea transport sectors, where, as we have seen, such machinery is still lacking, they are not yet directly effective.[77]

---

[71] Case 22/71 *Béguelin Import* v. *GL Import Export* [1971] E.C.R. 949; [1972] C.M.L.R. 81.
[72] [1971] E.C.R. at p. 959.
[73] Cases 125–129/85.
[74] Case 51/75 *EMI* v. *CBS United Kingdom* [1976] E.C.R. 811 at pp. 848–849. In Case 40/70 *Sirena* v. *Eda* [1971] E.C.R. 69 at p. 83 the Court had used language which might have been taken to imply that Art. 85 could be invoked where the effects of an agreement were still being felt, even in the abscence of a continuing understanding between the parties. See Chap. 18 *infra*.
[75] As in the *Dyestuffs* case.
[76] Case 13/61 *Bosch* v. *de Geus* [1962] E.C.R. 45; [1962] C.M.L.R. 1.
[77] Joined Cases 209 to 213/84 *Ministère Public* v. *Asjès and Others* (not yet reported).

Chapter 14

RESTRICTIVE PRACTICES

Article 85 EEC

Article 85 addresses the problem of interference with the play of competition on the common market resulting from collusion between market participants over their business decisions. The strategy of the Article is to prohibit such interference prima facie, while providing an avenue of escape for arrangements which, in spite of their anti-competitive character, are found to be, on balance, economically beneficial.

The Article provides:

"1. The following shall be prohibited as incompatible with the common market: all agreements between undertakings, decisions by associations of undertakings and concerted practices which may affect trade between Member States and which have as their object or effect the prevention, restriction or distortion of competition within the common market, and in particular those which:

    (a) directly or indirectly fix purchase or selling prices or any other trading conditions;

    (b) limit or control production, markets, technical development, or investment;

    (c) share markets or sources of supply;

    (d) apply dissimilar conditions to equivalent transactions with other trading parties, thereby placing them at a competitive disadvantage;

    (e) make the conclusion of contracts subject to acceptance by the other parties of supplementary obligations which, by their nature or according to commercial usage, have no connection with the subject of such contracts.

2. Any agreements or decisions prohibited pursuant to this Article shall be automatically void.

3. The provisions of paragraph 1 may, however, be declared inapplicable in the case of:

    — any agreement or category of agreements between undertakings;

    — any decision or category of decisions by associations of undertakings;

    — any concerted practice or category of concerted practices; which contributes to improving the production or distribution of goods or to promoting technical or economic progress, while allowing consumers a fair share of the resulting benefit, and which does not:

    (a) impose on the undertakings concerned restrictions which are not indispensable to the attainment of these objectives;

(b) afford such undertakings the possibility of eliminating competition in respect of a substantial part of the products in question."

The generality of the prohibition in paragraph (1) has been remarked upon.[1] Some guidance is given as to the kinds of arrangement that are liable to fall within the paragraph, but the list of examples has proved to be of limited practical importance. Paragraph (2) withdraws the support of national law from arrangements intended to have binding effect which are caught by the prohibition. Paragraph (3) sets out the criteria that must be met by arrangements prima facie within paragraph (1), in order to benefit from a declaration of the inapplicability of the paragraph. As we shall see, power to grant exemption under Article 85(3) has been reserved by Regulation 17 to the Commission.[2]

CRITERIA OF PROHIBITION

Co-operative market behaviour

The target of the prohibition in Article 85(1) is co-operative market behaviour. The EEC Treaty assumes that an undertaking acting unilaterally cannot threaten competition, unless it occupies a dominant position within the meaning of Article 86.

Acts in furtherance of a contract do not escape prohibition under Article 85(1) merely because they are performed by a single party. In the *AEG* case[3] the Court of Justice was called upon to assess the compatibility with Article 85 of a system of selective distribution. Under such a system the resale of goods is limited to a network of "approved" dealers.[4] One of the arguments put forward by AEG was that refusal to admit prospective dealers to its network was a unilateral act and therefore not within the scope of the prohibition. The argument was rejected by the Court on the ground that refusals of approval were acts performed in the context of AEG's contractual relations with approved dealers.[5]

It is settled law that Article 85 does not apply to an agreement between a parent company and a subsidiary where the latter enjoys no real freedom to determine its course of action on the market.[6] Nor does the Article

---

[1] See Korah, *Competition Law of Britain and the Common Market* (3rd ed., 1982), Marthinus Nijhoff, p. 198.
[2] The machinery for the implementation of Art. 85 is discussed in Chap. 16 *infra*.
[3] Case 107/82 *AEG* v. *Commission* [1983] E.C.R. 3151; [1984] 3 C.M.L.R. 325.
[4] On the application of Art. 85 to selective distribution systems, see pp. 370–372, *infra*.
[5] See also Joined Cases 25 and 26/84 *Ford* v. *Commission* (not yet reported).
[6] Case 22/71 *Béguelin Import* v. *G.L. Import Export* [1971] E.C.R. 949 at p. 959; [1972] C.M.L.R. 81; Case 15/74 *Centrafarm* v. *Sterling Drug* [1974] E.C.R. 1147 at p. 1167; [1974] 2 C.M.L.R. 480; Case 16/74 *Centrafarm* v. *Winthrop* [1974] E.C.R. 1183 at p. 1198. For an example of an agreement of a classic anti-competitive type (market sharing) which the Commission found unobjectionable because the parties were a parent company and its subsidiary, see *Re Christiani & Nielsen* J.O. 1969 L165/12; [1969] C.M.L.R. D36. The corollary is the imputation to parent companies of infringements of the competition rules by subsidiaries: see the discussion at pp. 349–350, *supra*. Cf. *Re Peroxygen Products*, where the Commission was not willing to regard the Interox grouping as an undertaking with an identity sufficiently distinct from its parent companies, Solvay and Laporte, to absolve them from liability under Art. 85: O.J. 1985 L35/1; [1985] 1 C.M.L.R. 481.

apply to the relationship *inter se* of a group of subsidiaries which operate under the tight control of their parent.[7] In such cases the element of consensus between independent market participants (in the language of the Article, "undertakings") is missing.[8] The "agreement" amounts in effect to a "distribution of tasks within a single economic entity."[9]

A similar analysis has been adopted in the case of agreements within a pure agency relationship, where the agent acts in the name and for the account of his principal, taking none of the risks of a transaction upon himself.[10] Such an agent, the Court of Justice has said, when working for his principal can be regarded "as an auxiliary organ forming an integral part of the latter's undertaking bound to carry out the principal's instructions and thus, like a commercial employee, forms an economic unit with this undertaking."[11] An agreement by the agent not to trade in goods competing with the products of his principal would not in these circumstances fall within Article 85(1).[12]

Forms of co-operation

Article 85(1) refers to three forms of co-operation on which the prohibition may bite—agreements between undertakings, decisions of associations of undertakings and concerted practices. Something will be said about each of these forms, although the lines of demarcation between them are of mainly theoretical interest.[13] The Commission will sometimes leave open the classification of an arrangement, saying that it amounts "if not to an agreement properly so called, at least to a concerted practice."[14]

Agreements between undertakings

Must agreements for the purposes of Article 85(1) be intended by the parties to have binding legal force? The Commission considers

[7] See *Re Kodak* J.O. 1970 L147/24; [1970] C.M.L.R. D19.
[8] There was formerly some doubt as to the correctness of this rationale because of references in Case 15/74 *Centrafarm* v. *Sterling Drug* and Case 16/74 *Centrafarm* v. *Winthrop* to both the parent company and the subsidiary as "undertakings." That doubt has been put to rest by the clear statement in Case 170/83 *Hydrotherm Geraetebau* v. *Andreoli* [1984] E.C.R. 2999 at p. 3016, cited at p. 346, *supra*. An alternative rationale, adopted by the Commission in *Re Christiani & Nielsen*, *loc.cit* note 4, *supra*, and by the Court in Case 22/71, *Béguelin Import* v. *G.L. Import Export*, *loc. cit.* note 4, *supra*, is that, as between a parent company and a subsidiary, there can be no competition for any agreement to restrict. The rationale is less satisfactory, because it does not cover the possibility that an agreement may restrict competition between one of the parties *and a third party* (see *infra*).
[9] This was the Commission's description in *Re Christiani & Nielsen*, [1969] C.M.L.R. at p. D39.
[10] Joined Cases 40–48, 50, 54–56, 111, 113 and 114/73 *Suiker Unie and Others* v. *Commission (Sugar)* [1975] E.C.R. 1163; [1976] 1 C.M.L.R. 295.
[11] [1975] E.C.R. at p. 2007.
[12] *Ibid.* In the instant case the relationship between a German sugar producer and its trade representatives was found not to be such as to escape the prohibition in Art. 85(1).
[13] The view of some commentators that, unlike an agreement, a concerted practice is only caught by Art. 85(1) once the anti-competitive object has been put into effect does not seem compatible with the definitions in the *Sugar* and *Bank Charges* cases which are discussed *infra*, pp. 357–359. A similar point is made by Bellamy and Child, *Common Market Law of Competition* at paras. 2–033 *et seq.*, (3rd ed., 1987 Sweet & Maxwell) and by Whish, *Competition Law*, Butterworths (1985) at p. 167.
[14] See, *e.g. Re Peroxygen Products* O.J. 1985 at L35/14.

that they need not,[15] and the Court of Justice appears to share this view.

In the *Quinine* cases,[16] for instance, the Court had to consider the application of Article 85(1) to arrangements between European producers of quinine and quinidine contained in an "export agreement" and a "gentlemen's agreement": the former, which was signed and made public, purported to apply only to trade with third countries but its provisions were extended by the latter, which remained unsigned and secret, to trade within the EEC. In view of its clandestine character, let alone its name, the gentlemen's agreement cannot have been intended to be legally enforceable. The parties had, however, made clear that it faithfully expressed their joint intention as to their conduct on the common market and that they considered themselves no less bound by it than by the export agreement. The Court, therefore, accepted it as an agreement within Article 85(1).

A further illustration can be found in the *BMW* case.[17] This concerned an attempt by BMW's subsidiary in Belgium to discourage dealers in that country from selling cars for export to other Member States. A circular condemning such sales had been sent by BMW Belgium to the dealers, who were asked to indicate assent by returning a signed copy, and this was accompanied by a circular in similar vein from a representative body, the "Dealers' Advisory Committee." BMW Belgium, the Advisory Committee and dealers who had given their consent were held to have entered into an "agreement" the detailed content of which was determined by the two circulars, though it is clear there was no intention to create binding legal relations.

It is submitted, therefore, that "agreements" in Article 85(1) covers any kind of arrangement under which an intention to co-ordinate market behaviour is manifested in the explicit acceptance of obligations, whether legal or moral, by one or more of the parties.

Decisions of associations of undertakings

A typical example would be a resolution of a trade association laying down standard terms on which its members are required to do business. An express reference to "decisions of associations of undertakings" in Article 85(1) may not have been strictly necessary.[18] Such decisions, if they fulfil the other criteria in the paragraph, are likely to be caught by the prohibition, either as representing the consequence of an agreement (the association's constitution) or as providing the basis for a concerted practice between the members. The reference, however, enhances legal certainty

---

[15] See, *e.g. Re Quinine* J.O. 1969 L 192/5; [1969] C.M.L.R. D41; *Re Franco-Japanese Ball-bearings Agreement* O.J. 1974 L34/19; [1975] 1 C.M.L.R. D8; *Re Preserved Mushrooms* O.J. 1975 L29/26; [1975] 1 C.M.L.R. D83; *Re Stichting Sigarettenindustrie Agreements* O.J. 1982 L232/1; [1982] 3 C.M.L.R. 702.

[16] See Cases 41, 44 and 45/69 *ACF Chemiefarma and Others* v. *Commission* [1970] E.C.R. 661.

[17] Joined Cases 32/78 and 36–82/78 *BMW Belgium and Others* v. *Commission* [1979] E.C.R. 2435; [1980] 1 C.M.L.R. 370.

[18] Whish, *op. cit.* note 13, *supra*, discusses the point at pp. 168–169.

and makes it possible, in an appropriate case, for the Commission to impose a fine on the trade association itself.[19]

The Court of Justice is inclined to brush aside technical arguments about the precise legal character of acts of trade associations. Its attitude is summed up by the remark in the *FRUBO* judgment[20] that "Article 85(1) applies to associations in so far as their own activities or those of the undertakings belonging to them are calculated to produce the results to which it refers."[21] For instance, the constitution of an association has sometimes been treated as a decision[22] and sometimes as an agreement.[23]

There is no more need for "decisions" than for "agreements" to be legally binding. In *Re Fire Insurance*[24] the Commission applied Article 85 to a "recommendation" by an association of insurers in Germany that premiums for various classes of policy be raised by a stipulated percentage. Although described in its title as "non-binding" the recommendation was found to constitute a decision within the meaning of the first paragraph. "It is sufficient for this purpose," the Commission said, "that the recommendation was brought to the notice of members as a statement of the association's policy provided for, and issued in accordance with, its rules."[25] In other cases a pattern of past compliance with recommendations has been emphasised.[26] The conclusive factor, it is submitted, is the ability of the association, in fact if not in law, to determine its members' conduct.

It is common for a number of trade associations to be grouped together in a wider association, *e.g.* the national associations of manufacturers of textile machinery belonging to CEMATEX, which existed for the purpose of organising periodic trade fairs.[27] The decisions of such groupings count as decisions of associations of undertakings for the purposes of Article 85(1).

The fact that an association has its chairman and members appointed by a government minister and that it is entrusted with certain public functions will not prevent its decisions on commercial policy from being caught by Article 85(1).[28] Similarly, a decision fixing minimum prices for a product will not escape prohibition merely because its binding effect has been extended to non-members of the association by an official act.[29]

---

[19] See, *e.g. Re AROW/BNIC* O.J. 1982 L379/1; [1983] 2 C.M.L.R. 240.
[20] Case 71/74 *FRUBO* v. *Commission* [1975] E.C.R. 563; [1975] 2 C.M.L.R. 123.
[21] [1975] E.C.R. at p. 583.
[22] *Re ASPA* [1970] J.O. L148/9; [1970] C.M.L.R. D25. A similar view was taken of an association's general regulations in *Re Centraal Bureau voor de Rijwielhandel* O.J. 1978 L20/18; [1978] 2 C.M.L.R. 194.
[23] *Re Nuovo CEGAM* O.J. 1984 L99/29; [1984] 2 C.M.L.R. 484.
[24] O.J. 1985 L35/20. The Dec. was upheld by the Court of Justice in Case 45/85, (not yet reported).
[25] O.J. 1985 at L35/24.
[26] See, in particular, Joined Cases 209–215 and 218–78 *Van Landewyck* v. *Commission* (FEDETAB) [1980] E.C.R. 3125; [1981] 3 C.M.L.R. 134; Joined Cases 96–102, 104, 105, 108 and 110/82, *IAZ* v. *Commission* [1983] E.C.R. 3369; [1984] 3 C.M.L.R. 276.
[27] *Re CEMATEX (No. 1)* J.O. 1971 L227/26; [1973] C.M.L.R. D135; (No. 2) O.J. 1983 L140/27; [1984] 3 C.M.L.R. 69. See also *Re CECIMO* J.O. 1969 L69/13; [1969] C.M.L.R. D1; *Re AROW/BNIC loc. cit.* note 19, *supra*; *Re Milchförderungsfonds* O.J. 195 L35/35; [1985] 3 C.M.L.R.
[28] *Re Pabst and Richarz/BNIA* O.J. 1976 L231/24; [1976] 2 C.M.R. D63.
[29] *Re AROW/BNIC loc. cit.* note 19, *supra*.

Concerted practices

The concept of a concerted practice

The Court of Justice has defined a concerted practice as "a form of co-ordination between undertakings which, without having reached the stage when an agreement properly so called has been concluded, knowingly substitutes practical co-operation between them for the risks of competition."[30] That definition was first offered in the *Dyestuffs* case, where the Court upheld a Decision of the Commission that concertation had taken place between the principal suppliers of aniline dyes in the EEC over price rises effected in 1964, 1965 and 1967. The adequacy of the evidence of "practical co-operation" accepted by the Court on that occasion is considered below.

Further light was shed on the concept in the *Sugar* case[31] where one of the infringements found by the Commission related to a concerted practice protecting sugar producers in the Netherlands against imports from Belgium.[32] The finding was contested by the Belgian and Dutch producers on the ground, *inter alia*, that a concerted practice presupposes a plan and the aim of removing any doubt as to the future conduct of competitors, which the evidence produced against them did not support. The Court responded that the criteria of co-ordination and co-operation did not require the working out of an actual plan. The key to understanding the criteria was the principle underlying the EEC rules on competition that "each economic operator must determine independently the policy which he intends to adopt on the common market . . . "[33] The Court went on:

> "Although it is correct to say that this requirement of independence does not deprive economic operators of the right to adapt themselves intelligently to the existing and anticipated conduct of their competitors, it does however strictly preclude any direct or indirect contact between such operators, the object of effect whereof is either to influence the conduct on the market of an actual or potential competitor or to disclose to such a competitor the course of conduct which they themselves have decided to adopt or contemplate adopting on the market."[34]

The definition in *Dyestuffs* and the gloss put on it in *Sugar* were quoted in the *Bank Charges* judgment[35] as part of the advice given to a German

---

[30] Case 48/69 *ICI* v. *Commission* [1972] E.C.R. 619 at p. 655; [1972] C.M.L.R. 557. See the identical definitions in Cases 49 and 51–57/79, [1972] E.C.R. at pp. 733, 773, 828, 875, 915 and 952. See also Joined Cases 40–48, 50, 54–56, 111, 113 and 114/73 *Suiker Unie and Others* v. *Commission (Sugar) loc. cit.* note 8, *supra*, at p. 1916; Case 172/80 *Zuchner* v. *Bayerische Vereinsbank (Bank Charges)* [1981] E.C.R. 2021 at p. 2031; [1982] 1 C.M.L.R. 313.

[31] *Loc. cit.* note 10, *supra*.

[32] *Ibid.*, Chap. 2.

[33] [1975] E.C.R. at p. 1942.

[34] *Ibid.* The view expressed here was foreshadowed in *Dyestuffs*: see [1972] E.C.R. at p. 660.

[35] [1981] E.C.R. at pp. 2031–2032. The passage from *Sugar* was reformulated by the Court in terms relating less specifically to the context of that case. The Court spoke of "contact . . . the object or effect of which is to create conditions of competition which do not correspond to the normal conditions of the market in question, regard being had to the nature of the product or services offered, the size and number of the undertakings and the volume of the said market."

court in proceedings under Article 177 EEC concerning the application of Article 85 to the uniform service charges imposed by banks in respect of transfers of funds by cheque from one Member State to another. Together they form a coherent statement of the Court's considered view as to the nature of a concerted practice.

On that view, the subjective content of the concept falls well short of agreement even in the extended sense discussed above. A meeting of minds must take place but nothing need be put into words.[36] Nor need there be any guarantee, however loose or informal, as to future conduct. The minimum of mutuality that will bring a relationship within the purview of Article 85(1) is "contact," which would normally connote a conscious act of communication. If that is the sense of "contact" in *Sugar* and *Bank Charges* it would not be sufficient that a course of conduct voluntarily undertaken was likely to increase the transparency of dealings between the parties: one of them must be shown to have intended specifically to impart information to the other, who must have been aware that the information was aimed at him. There would be contact in the required sense if X notified a business decision to Y, an individual competitor, or to their trade association; and perhaps also if he were identifiable as the source of information published in a specialised trade journal.[37] On the other hand, the fact that X and Y have a number of common customers may mean that each will quickly get to know, in the course of bargaining, what terms the other one is offering. This, it is submitted, would not amount to "contact" between X and Y, unless positive proof could be found that they were using their customers as a conduit for the exchange of information.

It is not altogether clear whether the Commission regards an intention to communicate as an essential ingredient of "contact." One aspect of the concerted practice condemned in the *Wood Pulp* Decision[38] was found to consist of the "system" of calendar quarterly price quotation which was an old established custom of the pulp trade. Prices were fixed on a quarterly basis and customers were notified of those applicable during a given quarter some little time before the end of the previous one. The timing of the notifications was considered by the Commission to be an important cause of the rapid spread of information about prices among the producers. The Decision states that "The system of quarterly price announcements, which the firms voluntarily chose, constituted in itself, at the very least, an indirect exchange of information on future market conduct."[39] This suggests the Commission may have taken the view that, by its very nature, a practice of the kind in question involved "contact" between the parties, irrespective of their motives for adopting it.[40] However, an alternative interpretation is possible—that the Commission concluded, in the light of

---

[36] Whish, *op. cit.* note 13, *supra*, makes this point at p. 171.
[37] See *Re. Wood Pulp* which refers to the giving of prices to the trade press as a form of indirect exchange of information: O.J. 1985 L85/1 at para. 108.
[38] *Ibid.*
[39] *Ibid.*
[40] See also para. 86 of the Dec. where calendar quarterly price quotation is said not to be "necessitated by objective market conditions."

all the circumstances, that the price announcement "system" was consciously exploited by the producers as a medium of communication.[41]

Evidence of concertation

Proving that a concerted practice exists may be a delicate task. Care has to be taken to preserve the distinction, which we have seen may be a fine one, between co-ordinated market behaviour and parallel behaviour resulting from decisions by traders which have been independently arrived at. Such innocent parallelism may, in particular, entail the exercise of the right, acknowledged by the Court in *Sugar* and *Bank Charges*, to "adapt intelligently" to the decisions of competitors, of which a trader has become aware in the ordinary course of his business.

Direct evidence of relevant contact between the parties may be available in the form of letters, telexes or records of telephone conversations or meetings. For instance, the concerted practice between the Belgian and Dutch sugar producers dealt with in Chapter 2 of the *Sugar* judgment was proved by a wealth of documentation discovered during the Commission's investigation.[42] This consisted in the main of correspondence between a major Belgian producer and a Belgian sugar dealer, and the Dutch producers contested its admissibility as evidence against them. The Court, however, agreed with Advocate General Mayers that such evidence must be treated on its merits. In case any misgivings may be felt about the use of hearsay evidence in competition proceedings, it is worth pointing out that the fines that may be imposed are expressly declared by Regulation 17 "not to be of criminal law nature."[43]

Where direct evidence of concertation is lacking or inconclusive, the Commission has to rely on circumstantial evidence, *i.e.* on the inferences that can be drawn from the behaviour of the alleged parties, in the light of an analysis of conditions on the market in question.[44] In such cases the Commission, and ultimately the Court, must be satisfied that there can be no reasonable explanation of the parties' behaviour other than the existence of a concerted practice between them.

The point is well illustrated by the *Zinc Products* case.[45] The concerted practice in issue was allegedly designed to protect the German market for rolled zinc products, where prices were higher than elsewhere in the Community, against parallel imports. A French producer, CRAM,[46] and a German producer, Reheinzink, had delivered quantities of zinc products to a Belgian dealer, Schiltz, under contracts which stipulated that the products be exported to Egypt. Schiltz, however, relabelled them and sent them back to Germany, where they were sold below the normal price. It was common ground that employees of Rheinzink found out about the reim-

---

[41] There is support for this interpretation in the allegation that common selling agents, as well as the trade press, were used by the producers to transmit information: see para. 108.

[42] *Loc. cit.* note 10, *supra*, at pp. 1924 *et seq.*

[43] J.O. 1962, 204; O.J. 1959–1969, 87. See Art. 15(3).

[44] Case 48/69 *ICI* v. *Commission* [1972] E.C.R. at p. 655; Joined Cases 40–48, 50, 54–56, 111, 113 and 114/73, *Suiker Unie and Others* v. *Commission (Sugar)* [1975] E.C.R. at p. 1916.

[45] Joined Cases 29 and 35/83 *CRAM and Rheinzink* v. *Commission* [1984] E.C.R. 1679; [1985] C.M.L.R. 688.

[46] Compagnie Royale Asturienne des Mines SA.

ports towards the end of October 1976 and that CRAM and Rheinzink discontinued their deliveries to Schiltz on, respectively, 21st and 29th of that month. In its Decision[47] the Commission had taken the view that the cessation of deliveries by CRAM and Rheinzink could only be explained as the result of an exchange of information for the purpose of preventing imports into Germany. "Faced with such an argument," the Court said, "it is sufficient for the applicants to prove circumstances which cast the facts established by the Commission in a different light and which thus allow another explanation of the facts to be substituted for the one adopted by the contested decision."[48] In the event, CRAM was able to point to two such circumstances: the fact that, when it ceased deliveries on October 21, it had completed a particular order from Schiltz; and the fact that there had been difficulties over obtaining payment for products supplied to Schiltz in September (and there were to be similar difficulties in respect of the October delivery). The Court concluded that the Commission had failed to provide "sufficiently precise and coherent proof" of a concerted practice.[49]

Whether the Commission has discharged its burden of proof is sometimes a matter of nice judgment over which lawyers, not to mention economists, may differ. A leading example is the *Dyestuffs* case,[50] long the subject of controversy.[51] The case arose, it will be remembered, out of the imposition on three separate occasions of uniform price rises in respect of a range of aniline dyes. The first price rise was announced in January 1964 (with immediate effect) the announcements by different producers following each other on the various national markets at very short intervals. In the case of the second price rise announcements were made in advance, between October and December 1964, to take effect on January 1, 1965. Similarly, in 1967 announcements were made in August and September and came into effect on October 16. The producers sought to explain their behaviour as conscious parallelism typical of a market comprising a small number of large firms, which is known as an "oligopoly." In such a market any significant increase in a firm's sales is liable to be made at the expense of the other participants.[52] This results in a situation where, in the words of Advocate General Mayras, "the producers are closely interdependent so that none can take a decision concerning competition, particularly as regards prices, without the others' being immediately affected, being aware that this is the case and being bound to do something about it."[53] Thus if one oligopolist lowers his prices, the others may be compelled to lower theirs; while no one may feel able to raise his prices unless he is reasonably sure that his competitors are ready to make a similar move. That line of argument was rejected by the Court in a very few words. The dyestuffs market, it held, was not in the strict sense an oligopoly in which

[47] *Re Rolled Zinc Products and Zinc Alloys* O.J. 1982 L362/40; [1983] 2 C.M.L.R. 285. Another aspect of the case is discussed at pp. 362–363, *infra*.
[48] [1984] E.C.R. at p. 1702.
[49] *Ibid.*
[50] *Loc. cit.* note 30, *supra*.
[51] For critical comments, see Mann (1973) 22 I.C.L.Q. 35; Korah (1973) 36 M.L.R. 220 and *op. cit.* note 1, *supra*, at pp. 201 *et seq.*
[52] The notion is clearly explained by Korah, *op. cit.* note 1, *supra*, at p. 8.
[53] [1972] E.C.R. at p. 677.

price competition could no longer play a substantial role. The producers
were sufficiently powerful and numerous for there to be a real possibility
that some might resist the pressure to follow prices upwards and try instead
to increase their market share. For the Court, the main indicator of concertation between the dye producers seems to have been the fact that the
increases of 1965 and 1967 were made public well in advance of the date
when they were to be applied.[54] "By means of these advance announcements," the Court said, "the various undertakings eliminated all uncertainty between them as to their future conduct and, in doing so, also
eliminated a large part of the risk usually inherent in any independent
change of conduct on one or several markets."[55] A further consideration
was the division of the common market, in practice, into five national markets which had different price levels and structures. The Court found it
hardly conceivable "that the same action could be taken spontaneously at
the same time on the same national markets and for the same range of products."[56] On the other hand, curiously little is made in the judgment of the
direct evidence of concertation that was before the Court. This included
evidence of a meeting of producers in Basle in August 1967 where one of
the firms announced an intention to increase its prices, apparently by the
precise amount, and on the precise date, of the rise that subsequently took
place.[57] There was also the fact that notification of the price rise in 1964
had been given by several of the producers to their subsidiaries and agents
in language so similar as to suggest a common origin.[58] The Court's almost
total reliance on general economic arguments, stated in a summary way
that makes it hard to assess their force, helps to explain why some commentators have found the judgment unsatisfactory.

Parallel behaviour may be the outcome of collusion between certain
traders and of independent adaptation by others to that state of affairs,
which they encounter as an objective condition of the market. It follows
that direct evidence of concertation between X and Y will not serve as cor-
roboration that Z, whose conduct was parallel to theirs, colluded with
them. Any explanation offered by Z must be examined by the Commission
on its individual merits. If this were not so, the concept of a concerted practice would be deprived of even the vestigial element of mutuality surviving
in the requirement that "contact" must have taken place between the
undertakings in question.[59]

Where, however, a contractual network, such as a distribution system,
already exists, and some of the members can be shown to have taken part
in a concerted practice, not much evidence may be needed to convince the
Court that other members were involved. This is especially true of the dis-

---

[54] *Cf.* the situation in *Re Wood Pulp*, *loc. cit.* note 37, *supra*, where the timing of price
announcements could be explained as a custom of the trade.
[55] [1972] E.C.R. at p. 659.
[56] *Ibid.*
[57] Described by A. G. Mayras at [1972] E.C.R. pp. 679–680.
[58] *Ibid.* at p. 681.
[59] In *Re Wood Pulp*, *loc. cit.* note 37, *supra*, the Commission treated direct evidence against
certain of the producers as confirming the existence of a concerted practice involving all
those whose pricing was parallel. Whether it was right to do so may become clear in Cases
125–129/85 *Westar Timber and Others* v. *Commission*, pending before the Court of Justice.

tributor himself, since he stands at the heart of the network. In *Musique Diffusion Française* v. *Commission*[60] the annulment was sought of a Decision that the European subsidiary of the Japanese Pioneer company and the exclusive distributors of Pioneer hi-fi equipment in France, Germany and the United Kingdom had collaborated in attempts to prevent parallel imports from reaching the French market on which prices were relatively high. In confirming that Pioneer (Europe) had been implicated in the prohibited conduct, the Court said that "on account of its central position, it was obliged to display particular vigilance in order to prevent concerted efforts of that kind from giving rise to practices contrary to the competition rules."[61]

Competition

Article 85(1) refers to agreements, etc.[62] "which have as their object or effect the prevention, restriction or distortion of competition within the common market."

Object or effect

The phrase "object or effect" must be read disjunctively.[63] The precise purpose of the agreement must first be ascertained by examining its terms in the particular context in which they will have to be performed. Where it can be seen that the purpose, if achieved, will entail the prevention, restriction or distortion of competition to an appreciable degree,[64] there will be no need to go on and show that such has in fact been the outcome. Where, however, the implications an agreement may have for competition are less clear-cut, it will be necessary to undertake an analysis of economic conditions on the relevant market to assess the actual extent of any adverse impact.[65]

An example of contractual terms found by the Court of Justice to be anti-competitive in their object can be seen in the *Zinc Products* case.[66] It will be remembered that the Belgian dealer, Schiltz, was put under an obligation to export to Egypt the rolled zinc products delivered under its contracts with CRAM and Rheinzink. The obligation had been accepted by Schiltz after CRAM had queried its first order on the ground that products with the dimensions in question, although widely sold in France and Germany, were not in demand in Belgium. However, despite the purported

---

[60] Joined Cases 100–103/80 *Musique Diffusion Française* v. *Commission (Pioneer)* [1983] E.C.R. 1825; [1983] 3 C.M.L.R. 221.

[61] [1983] E.C.R. at p. 1898. See also Case 86/82 *Hasselblad* v. *Commission* [1984] E.C.R. 883; [1984] 1 C.M.L.R. 559.

[62] References hereinafter to "agreements" should be understood as applying also to decisions and concerted practices unless the context indicates otherwise.

[63] Case 56/65 *Société Technique Minière* v. *Maschinenbau Ulm* [1966] E.C.R. 235; [1966] 1 C.M.L.R. 357.

[64] On the *de minimis* rule, see pp. 377–379, *infra*.

[65] [1966] E.C.R. at p. 249.

[66] *Loc. cit.* note 45, *supra*. For another well known example, see Joined Cases 56 and 58/64 *Consten and Grundig* v. *Commission* [1966] E.C.R. 299; [1966] C.M.L.R. 418.

destination of the goods, the prices at which they were supplied to Schiltz by CRAM and Rheinzink were identical with, or closely similar to, those charged for goods intended for the Belgian market. "In those circumstances," the Court said, "the conclusion cannot be avoided that the export clauses were essentially designed to prevent the re-export of the goods to the country of production so as to maintain a system of dual prices and restrict competition within the common market."[67]

The case showed that an agreement may have as its object the restriction of competition without this necessarily representing the common intention of the parties. In the words of the Court, "It is rather a question of examining the aims pursued by the agreement as such, in the light of the economic context in which the agreement is to be applied."[68] Regard must also be had to the legal context. In *Consten and Grundig* v. *Commission*[69] certain of the terms of an agreement creating an exclusive distributorship were held to have the object of restricting competition. Consten had been given the sole right to sell Grundig products in France and an attempt had been made to provide it with "absolute territorial protection," *i.e.* to prevent the contract products from being brought into the country by any other importer. The desired level of protection was to be achieved in two ways. First, Grundig undertook not to deliver the contract products, even indirectly, to other traders for export to France. Secondly, Consten was authorised to register in France the trademark GINT which was affixed to all Grundig products. This would enable it to oppose the sale of any parallel imports reaching the French market, as an infringement of its trademark right.[70] The point that concerns us here was that the contract with Consten was one of a network of contracts with Grundig customers and exclusive distributors in other territories, all prohibiting the exportation of the products to be supplied. Those agreements were not themselves in issue in the case but they were relevant to an assessment of the aims of the Grundig/Consten agreement, since they contributed to the isolation of the French market for Grundig products. The legal context may be similarly relevant when it is not the object but the practical effects of an agreement that are being considered.[71]

Prevention, restriction or distortion

Nothing turns on the distinction between "prevention," "restriction" and "distortion" of competition. The *Consten and Grundig* judgment, for instance, describes the agreement in question as being "such as to *distort* competition in the common market," while a few lines later it refers to "the above-mentioned *restrictions*"[72] (emphasis added). The three terms

[67] [1984] E.C.R. at p. 1704.
[68] *Ibid.*
[69] *Loc. cit.* note 66, *supra.*
[70] The use of rights of intellectual property so as to impede the movements of goods between Member States is discussed in Chap. 18, *infra.*
[71] See, *e.g.* Case 23/67 *Brasserie de Haecht* v. *Wilkin (No. 1)* [1967] E.C.R. 407; [1968] C.M.L.R. 26.
[72] [1966] E.C.R. at p. 343.

express, with varying emphasis, the basic idea of a change for the worse in the state of competition.

No competition to restrict

The starting point for an enquiry on the implications of an agreement for competition is the situation as it would have been if the agreement did not exist.[73] Without some competition capable of being restricted by the agreement, there can be no infringement of Article 85. In *Re Cement Makers Agreement*,[74] for example, the Commission gave negative clearance to an agreement between an association of manufacturers of Portland cement in Belgium and a number of lime burning companies which produced "natural" cement. In consideration of the payment to them of an indemnity the lime burners had undertaken, *inter alia*, to refrain from manufacturing Portland cement; but the Commission found they would not have been able, anyway, to finance a change in their production. Lack of competition in a market may also be the result of government intervention. In Chapter 2 of the *Sugar* judgment[75] the Court of Justice held that measures taken to regulate the market in Italy had fundamentally restricted the scope for competition between sugar producers. The Commission's finding of an infringement of Article 85 was, therefore, quashed, although it was manifest that concertation had taken place between the Italian producers and exporters from other Member States.

Where, however, despite intervention by the public authorities, some room remains for competitive pressures to influence the decisions of market participants, further restriction of competition through an agreement between undertakings is liable to fall foul of Article 85(1). Indeed, the Commission contends that in such circumstances the anti-competitive effects of private arrangements are all the more significant.[76] A central issue in the *Van Landewyck* case was whether competition had effectively been banished from the Belgian market for tobacco products as a result of the system of levying excise duties on those products, combined with legislation imposing price controls.[77] The Court of Justice accepted that in the circumstances it was practically impossible for manufacturers and importers to compete in such a way as to affect the level of retail selling prices. However, there did still appear to be a possibility of competition in respect of the profit margins allowed to wholesalers, which could have provided an incentive for the latter to pursue a sales policy beneficial to the producers or importers willing to treat them more generously. That kind of competition had been prevented from developing because of the agreement between the tobacco manufacturers and importers relating to the size

---

[73] Case 56/65 *Société Technique Minière* v. *Maschinenbau Ulm* [1966] E.C.R. at p. 250.
[74] [1969] C.M.L.R. D15.
[75] Joined Cases 40–48, 50, 54–56, 111, 113 and 114/73 *Suiker Unie and Others* v. *Commission loc. cit.* note 10, *supra*, at pp. 1916 *et seq.*
[76] See, *e.g. Re Stichting Sigarettenindustrie Agreements loc. cit.* note 15, *supra*. The point is mentioned in Joined Cases 209–215 and 218–78, *Van Landewyck* v. *Commission loc. cit.* note 26, *supra* at p. 3261.
[77] *Loc. cit.* note 24, *supra*, at pp. 3251–3265.

of the margins and bonuses allowed to traders, which accordingly amounted to a restriction within the meaning of Article 85(1).

Horizontal and vertical agreements

Article 85 applies both to agreements between undertakings operating at the same level in the process of production and distribution, which are known as "horizontal" agreements, and to agreements between undertakings operating at different levels, known as "vertical" agreements.

The classic forms of cartel are horizontal agreements restricting actual or potential competition between the parties themselves. Examples can be seen in the first three items on the list in Article 85(1), *viz.* agreements whereby traders co-ordinate the prices and other conditions they will apply in purchasing or selling goods or services, agreements to limit production, markets, technical development or investment and agreements sharing out markets or sources of supply. In some of the major cartels dealt with under Article 85 several of these objectionable features have been present together. One such agreement was the subject of the Decision of the Commission in *Re Zinc Producer Group*.[78] The Group comprised the main Western zinc mining and smelting companies, apart from those based in Japan. The members agreed to establish a common "producer price" for zinc and to apply it instead of the price on the London Metal Exchange, where they would no longer sell their zinc. They also agreed to support the zinc price on the London Metal Exchange by intervention buying and, where necessary, to limit their production and sales. Zinc was to be supplied only to bona fide customers for their own consumption and subject to a prohibition against resale. Regular exchanges of information took place, including information about individual firms' investment plans. Finally, there was an agreement to sell only specified quantities of zinc in fellow producers' traditional markets. Price fixing, limitation of output and investment and the sharing of markets were just some of the ways in which, it was found, the parties had sought to manipulate competition in the EEC.[79]

It used to be argued by some commentators that the prohibition in Article 85(1) did not apply to vertical agreements.[80] That view was firmly rejected by the Court in its *Consten and Grundig* judgment[81] and in another judgment delivered the same day in a case brought by Italy for the annulment of Regulation 19/65, which authorised the Commission to grant block exemptions pursuant to Article 85(3) in respect of certain types of agreement, among them exclusive dealing agreements.[82] The Court pointed out that there was nothing in the wording of Article 85 to limit its

---

[78] O.J. 1984 L220/27; [1985] 2 C.M.L.R. 108.
[79] See also, among many examples, the *Quinine* cases *loc. cit.* note 16, *supra* (price fixing, market sharing, export quotas, limitation of production of quinidine); *Re Flat Glass* O.J. 1984 L212/13; 1985 2 C.M.L. 350 (price fixing, market sharing, exchange of information); *Re Peroxygen Products loc. cit.* note 6, *supra* (price fixing, market sharing).
[80] See, *e.g.* Morera, (1964) *Rivista di Diritto Industriale* 52.
[81] *Loc. cit.* note 66, *supra*.
[82] Case 32/65 *Italy* v. *Council and Commission* [1966] E.C.R. 389.

scope to horizontal restraints.[83] Nor was it an argument against applying the Article to exclusive dealing agreements that the parties to such agreements were not themselves competitors. "Competition," the Court said, "may be distorted within the meaning of Article 85(1) not only by agreements which limit it as between the parties, but also by agreements which prevent or restrict the competition which might take place between one of them and third parties."[84] A related point, which *Consten and Grundig* also makes clear, is that the "competition" referred to includes, as well as competition between products of different brands ("inter-brand competition"), that between distributors of products of the same brand ("intra-brand competition"). The Court considered the absolute territorial protection aimed at by the parties unacceptable, because some competition from parallel imports was needed to spur dealers on to greater efforts and to prevent them from charging unduly high prices.[85]

Consten and Grundig laid the foundation of what has become an extensive structure of case law and legislation on the application of Article 85 to various kinds of vertical agreements, notably systems of exclusive and selective distribution.[86] In recent years, however, there has been criticism of the Community authorities for exaggerating the anti-competitive effects of such agreements. The current orthodoxy in the United States appears to be that vertical restraints, such as the limitation of outlets for a product to a number of specialised wholesale and retail traders, are normally imposed by businessmen not in order to fetter competition but in the hope of competing more effectively, thereby increasing their sales—and that they are in the best position to make a judgment about this. Competition authorities are, accordingly, only justified in taking action where vertical restraints are the consequence of *horizontal* agreements between either producers or distributors.[87] This analysis may be persuasive in relation to the American market, but its extension to the common market seems to us to be misconceived. It was grasped by the Commission and the Court of Justice at an early stage that vertical agreements represent a serious threat to the unification of the market, because they often involve limiting distribution rights to a particular territory. As the Court remarked in the case on Regulation 19/65, "An agreement between producer and distributor intended to restore national partitioning in trade between Member States would be such as to run counter to the most fundamental objectives of the Community."[88] This is a valid concern in the application of Article 85, since continuing compartmentalisation of the market is a major cause of the distortion of competition in the EEC.

---

[83] Korah, *op. cit.* note 1, *supra*, p. 207, points out that the last two items on the list in Art. 85(1) presuppose more than one level of trade.
[84] [1966] E.C.R. at p. 339.
[85] See the discussion at [1966] E.C.R. 343.
[86] On selective distribution agreements, see pp. 370–372, *infra*.
[87] See, in particular, Bork, *The Anti-Trust Paradox* (1978); Chard, (1980) *Anti-Trust Bulletin* 405; Posner, (1981) 48 *University of Chicago Law Review* 6; Baxter, *Journal of Reprints for Antitrust Law and Economics*, Vol. XV, No. 2.
[88] Case 32/65 *Italy* v. *Council and Commission* [1966] E.C.R. at p. 408. See the equivalent passage in *Consten and Grundig* where, however, "objectives" is misprinted "objections": [1966] E.C.R. at p. 340.

The rule of reason

In the United States the rigour of the prohibition in section 1 of the Sherman Act against contracts in restraint of trade has been mitigated by the development in the case law of the so-called "rule of reason."[89] The rule applies to agreements other than those, such as horizontal price-fixing agreements, which are treated by the American courts as illegal *per se*. Essentially, a court is required under the rule to consider the overall impact of the agreement in question on competition within the relevant market. This involves, in particular, identifying any pro-competitive effects the agreement may have and weighing them against its anti-competitive effects. A straightforward example would be a promise by the seller of a business not to compete with the buyer for a reasonable period. Without protection of this kind for the buyer, the goodwill of the business might have been worth a great deal less, or have been unsaleable. The pro-competitive effect of permitting the disposal of a going concern may be regarded as outweighing the temporary restriction of competition between the buyer and the seller.[90] However, it must be emphasised that the rule of reason cannot be used to *justify* behaviour that restricts competition.[91] Its importance in American anti-trust law is, indeed, explained by the absence of any "gateway" through which a restrictive agreement which is felt, nevertheless, to be economically beneficial may escape prohibition. Where application of the rule leads to a favourable assessment of an agreement under the Sherman Act, that will be because the agreement is judged, on balance, not to be restrictive of competition.

In EEC law, on the other hand, an agreement that restricts competition within the meaning of Article 85(1) may still qualify for exemption under Article 85(3). Where pro-competitive aspects of an agreement are not regarded as tipping the scales against a finding that it is restrictive, they may be taken into account in assessing the economic benefits that may justify a grant of exemption. Does it then matter under which paragraph of the Article such aspects fall to be considered? The answer is that it does matter because, while Article 85(1) may be applied by courts in the Member States, the power to grant exemption under Article 85(3) is reserved exclusively to the Commission. If a national court finds that a contract falls within Article 85(1), its only options are to hold the contract void or to adjourn the proceedings pending a decision by the Commission. Proponents of the rule of reason point out that the Commission has found it impossible in practice to deal on an individual basis with more than a fraction of the notifications made with a view to obtaining exemption and that uncertainty as to the status of agreements may last for years. Thorough-going application of the rule would widen the range of cases that could be

---

[89] For a fuller account of the rule of reason in American anti-trust law, see Neale and Goyder, *The Antitrust Laws of the USA*, (3rd ed., 1980). The rule is nicely epitomised by Steindorff (1984) 21 C.M.L.R. 639 at pp. 639–641.

[90] See *National Society of Professional Engineers* v. *United States* 435 U.S. 679 at p. 689. The example is cited by Steindorff, *op. cit.* note 89, *supra*, at p. 643. On the position in EEC law, see *infra*.

[91] See Steindorff, *op. cit.* note 89, *supra*, at pp. 640–641.

disposed of under Article 85(1). This, it is argued, would enable national courts to play a more active part in the application of EEC competition law, leaving the Commission free to concentrate its limited resources on cases of strategic importance.[92]

There is evidence of cautious acceptance by the Court of Justice of the utility of a rule of reason approach to the analysis of cases under Article 85, though within rather narrow limits. The Commission has shown some reluctance to follow the Court down this road.[93] The rule can be seen at work in the case law in three ways.

First, in a growing number of cases the Court has held that contractual provisions giving a measure of protection against competition do not fall within Article 85(1) if they are genuinely necessary to enable a partner to be found in a business transaction.[94] The earliest reference to this "indispensable inducement" rationale is in *Société Technique Minière* v. *Maschinenbau Ulm*[95] which concerned an exclusive distribution agreement. Under the agreement the supplier promised not to appoint another distributor in the concession territory or to sell the goods there himself, but no protection was provided against parallel imports. The Court said that "it may be doubted whether there is an interference with competition if the said agreement seems really necessary for the penetration of a new area by an undertaking."[96] The case is distinguishable from *Consten and Grundig*,[97] where the absolute territorial protection sought by the parties could not be regarded as "really necessary" to secure access for Grundig products to the French market.[98] In the *Maize Seeds* case[99] the analysis was applied to a licensing agreement for the exploitation of plant breeders' rights. An "open" exclusive licence, which would not impede parallel imports, was held compatible with Article 85(1), since without some protection against competition no one might have been willing to take the risk of introducing previously unknown crop varieties onto the market in question.[1] In *Pronuptia*,[2] on the other hand, exclusivity provisions in a franchising agreement were found to be within Article 85(1) because the franchisor's

---

[92] On the need for a rule of reason in EEC competition law see, in particular, Joliet, *The Rule of Reason in Antitrust Law* (1967); Korah, (1981) 3 *New Journal of International Law and Business* 320; Schechter, (1982/2) LIEI 1; Joliet, (1984) 20 RTDE 1; Forrester and Norrall (1984) 21 C.M.L. Rev.11. More qualified support is given by Steindorff, *op. cit.* note 89, *supra*. Whish, *op. cit.* note 13, *supra*, at p. 180 points out that the pressure on the Commission has been eased by the adoption of a number of block exemptions and by procedural changes.

[93] On the contrasting approaches of the Court and the Commission, see Whish *op. cit.* note 13, *supra*, at pp. 179–180. The contrast comes out especially clearly in respect of agreements for the exclusive licensing of intellectual property rights: see Chap. 18, *infra*.

[94] See Steindorff, *op. cit.* note 89, *supra*, at p. 646.

[95] Case 56/65 *loc. cit.* note 63, *supra*.

[96] [1966] E.C.R. at p. 250. The lack of further authority on "indispensable inducement" in respect of exclusive distribution agreements is due, presumably, to the enactment of a block exemption regulation soon afterwards: see Reg. 67/67, O.J. 1967, 10.

[97] Joined cases 56 and 58/64, *loc. cit.* note 66, *supra*.

[98] A similar point is made in Halsbury, *Laws of England*, Vol. 52, p. 889.

[99] Case 258/78 *Nungesser* v. *Commission* [1982] E.C.R. 2105; [1983] 1 C.M.L.R. 278. The case is more fully discussed in Chap. 18, *infra*.

[1] See also Case 262/81 *Coditel* v. *Cine Vog Films* [1982] E.C.R. 3381; [1983] 1 C.M.L.R. 49. The case concerned an exclusive licence of the performing rights in a film. See Chap. 18, *infra*.

[2] Case 161/84 *Pronuptia de Paris* v. *Schillgalis* [1986] 1 C.M.L.R. 414.

trademark was already widely known.[3] The novelty of the product, or at least of the brand, may thus be of crucial significance where the territorial protection of distributors is in issue. A last example to mention is *Remia*[4] where the Court accepted that the seller of a business could be put under an obligation not to compete with the buyer, while emphasising that "such clauses must be necessary to the transfer of the undertaking concerned and their duration and scope must be strictly limited to that purpose."[5] The Court refused to interfere with the Commission's finding that four years' protection for the buyer of a sauce-manufacturing business would have been enough to cover the introduction of a new trademark and to win customer loyalty, instead of the ten-year period which had been agreed.

Secondly, in its *Pronuptia*[6] judgment the Court held that various provisions in an agreement forming part of a distribution franchise system did not restrict competition within the meaning of Article 85(1) because they were necessary to the successful functioning of the system. Its approach has been described as amounting to the application of a doctrine of "ancillary restraints" similar to that developed in American anti-trust law.[7] This goes beyond the simple "but for" analysis of the cases referred to in the previous paragraph: the issue is not whether, apart from the provisions in question, a bargain could have been struck but whether the essential aims of the transaction (considered to be one that competition law ought not to disfavour) could have been realised. As applied by the Court the analysis comprises four logical steps: (i) definition of the salient features of the transaction; (ii) finding that the transaction is not in itself restrictive of competition; (iii) identification of the conditions that have to be met to enable such a transaction to be satisfactorily performed; (iv) identification of the contractual terms indispensable to the fulfilment of those conditions. Distribution franchising,[8] the Court explained, is a marketing system under which an established distributor whose success is associated with a certain trademark and certain commercial methods (the franchisor) puts his mark and methods at the disposal of independent traders (the franchisees) in return for the payment of a royalty. This has the advantage to the franchisor of enabling him to exploit his know-how without having to commit his own capital; and to the franchisees of giving them access to methods they could otherwise only have acquired through prolonged effort and research, while also allowing them to profit from the reputation of the mark. The success of such a system depended on two things: the franchisor must be able to communicate his know-how to the franchisees and help them in putting his methods into practice without running the risk that his competitors might benefit, even indirectly; and he must be able to take

---

[3] The relevant passage of the judgment is far from clear. However, the court appears to have contemplated that absolute territorial protection of the members of the network might have been acceptable, if the franchisor had been a new market entrant. On this, see Venit, (1986) 11 E.L.Rev. 213 at p. 218.

[4] Case 42/84 *Remia* v. *Commission* (not yet reported).

[5] See para. 20 of the judgment.

[6] Case 161/84, *loc. cit.* note 2, p. 368, *supra.*

[7] The suggestion was made by Venit, *op. cit.* note 3, *supra*, at p. 217.

[8] The case was confined to this form of franchise agreement. Other forms are service franchise agreements and production franchise agreements: see [1986] 1 C.M.L.R. at p. 442.

appropriate measures to preserve the identity and reputation of the network symbolised by the mark. Under the agreement in question the franchisee had undertaken not to open a shop selling competing goods and not to dispose of the franchise premises except with the prior consent of the franchisor. These terms imposed quite severe restraints on the running of the franchisee's business but they were found to be indispensable to the fulfilment of the first condition and so outwith Article 85(1). Among the terms excluded from Article 85(1) by the second condition was the franchisee's obligation to obtain stock only from the franchisor or from suppliers chosen by him. This helped to protect the reputation of the network by ensuring that the public would find goods of uniform quality in all Pronuptia shops. Given the character of the franchise products (wedding dresses and formal wear) it would, in the Court's view, have been impossible to achieve that result by formulating a set of objective quality specifications. The Court has been criticised, however, for holding that terms in the agreement giving members of the network a measure of territorial protection were contrary to Article 85(1).[9] In a system of uniform business-format franchising like that of Pronuptia a particular area may, in practice, be able to support no more than one outlet. Depending on the size of territories, exclusivity could, it is argued, be an indispensable element in a well-functioning franchise system.

Thirdly, it is well established that a system of selective distribution based on objective qualitative criteria which are applied in a non-discriminatory way may be compatible with Article 85(1).[10] Under such a system, for example, a manufacturer may limit the outlets for a product which is expensive and technically complex to dealers able and willing to promote it effectively and to provide pre-sales advice, and an after-sales maintenance and repair service, for customers.[11] Selectivity is likely, on the one hand, to result in higher prices. As the Court itself has pointed out, "prices charged by specialist traders necessarily remain within a much narrower span than that which might be envisaged in the case of competition between specialist and non-specialist traders."[12] On the other hand, opportunities are created for competition between manufacturers in respect of the customer services associated with their brands. The issue was first addressed by the Court in Metro v. Commission (No. 1)[13] The background to the case was the refusal

---

[9] See Venit, op. cit. note 3, p. 369, supra, at pp. 220–221. The relevant provisions were given exemption under Art. 85(3): see Re Pronuptia O.J. 1987 L13/39.

[10] See, in particular, Case 26/76 Metro v. Commission (No. 1) [1977] E.C.R. 1875; [1978] 2 C.M.L.R. 1; Joined Cases 253/78 and 1–3/79 Guerlain, Rochas, Lanvin and Nina Ricci (Perfumes) [1980] E.C.R. 2327; [1981] 2 C.M.L.R. 99; Case 99/79 Lancôme v. Etos (Perfumes) [1980] E.C.R. 2511; [1981] 2 C.M.L.R. 164; Case 31/80, L'Oreal v. De Nieuwe AMCK (Perfumes) [1980] E.C.R. 3775; [1981] 2 C.M.L.R. 235; Case 86/82 Hasselblad v. Commission [1984] E.C.R. 883; 3 C.M.L.R. 325; Case 107/82 AEG v. Commission [1983] E.C.R. 3151; [1984] 2 C.M.L.R. 325; Case 243/83 Binon v. Agence et Messageries de la Presse [1985] 3 C.M.L.R. 800; Case 75/84 Metro v. Commission (No. 2) (not yet reported). See also, among numerous Decs. of the Commission, Re Omega J.O. 1970 L242/22; [1970] C.M.L.R. D49; Re BMW J.O. 1975 L29/1; [1975] 1 C.M.L.R. D44; Re Junghans J.O. 1977 L30/10; [1977] 1 C.M.L.R. D82; Re Murat J.O. 1983 L348/20; [1984] 1 C.M.L.R. 219.

[11] The Perfumes cases, loc. cit. supra, illustrate selective distribution of another kind of product thought to require special handling, viz. luxury items.

[12] Case 107/82 AEG v. Commission [1983] E.C.R. at pp. 3196–3197.

[13] Case 26/76 loc. cit., supra.

by SABA, a manufacturer of electronic goods such as television sets, radios and tape recorders, to admit the cash and carry wholesalers, Metro, to its distribution network. The Court upheld the decision of the Commission that the central features of the Metro system of selective distribution did not infringe Article 85(1), whilst other features were eligible for exemption under Article 85(3).[14] The starting point of the Court's analysis was the concept of "workable competition" defined as "the degree of competition necessary to ensure the observance of the basic requirements and the attainment of the objectives of the Treaty, in particular the creation of a single market achieving conditions similar to those of a domestic market."[15] In accordance with that concept, the nature and intensity of competition might vary to an extent dictated by the products and services in question and the economic structure of the market. The Court went on:

"In the sector covering the production of high quality and technically advanced consumer durables, where a relatively small number of large and medium-scale producers offer a varied range of items which, or so consumers may consider, are readily interchangeable, the structure of the market does not preclude the existence of a variety of channels of distribution adapted to the peculiar characteristics of the various producers and to the requirements of the various categories of consumers.

On this view the Commission was justified in recognizing that selective distribution systems constituted, together with others, an aspect of competition which accords with Article 85(1), provided that resellers are chosen on the basis of objective criteria of a qualitative nature relating to the technical qualifications of the reseller and his staff and the suitability of his trading premises and that such conditions are laid down uniformly for all potential resellers and are not applied in a discriminatory fashion."[16]

The rationale was spelt out even more clearly in the subsequent *AEG* case[17] which also concerned a system of selective distribution for electronic equipment. The Court said:

" . . . there are legitimate requirements, such as the maintenance of a specialist trade capable of providing specific services as regards high-quality and high-technology products, which may justify a reduction of price competition in favour of competition relating to factors other than price. Systems of selective distribution, in so far as they aim at the attainment of a legitimate goal capable of improving competition in relation to factors other than price, therefore constitute an element of competition which is in conformity with Article 85(1)."[17]

The analytical method in such cases consists of weighing the pros and cons of different forms of competition against each other. This rather sophisticated application of the rule of reason has not been extended to other

---

[14] The Dec. of the Commission to similar effect in respect of a subsequent version of the SABA system was upheld by the Court in *Metro* v. *Commission (No. 2)* (not yet reported).
[15] [1977] E.C.R. at p. 1904.
[16] *Ibid.*
[17] Case 107/82 [1983] E.C.R. at p. 3194.

terms that may be found in selective distribution agreements, *e.g.* the limitation of outlets on a *quantitative* basis, resale price maintenance and export bans.[18] The unwillingness of the Court and the Commission to recognise such terms as being "capable of improving competition," thus eluding Article 85(1), has brought accusations of inconsistency, since the purpose of their inclusion in the agreement may be to ensure a sufficient turnover for the dealer to support the desired range of customer services.[19] They might, in other words, constitute "ancillary restraints," indispensable to the selective method of marketing judged appropriate for goods of the kind in question.

Some critics of the approach adopted by the Court and the Commission to Article 85(1) may be guilty of neglecting the definition of "workable competition" in *Metro* v. *SABA (No. 1)*[20] with its stress on the objective of creating a single internal market. An Ariadne thread running through the case law is a very strong presumption that contractual provisions tending to preserve or reinforce the division of the market along national lines are anti-competitive. This explains, for example, the difference in the treatment of qualitative criteria of selective distribution, as compared with quantitative criteria, resale price maintenance terms and export bans: the latter, but not the former, are all liable, in their different ways, to have market-splitting effects. Although lines are sometimes difficult to draw, the presumption has been applied with reasonable consistency, the Court showing more readiness than the Commission to accept evidence in rebuttal.[21] The practical consequence has been that, to escape prohibition, any agreement that might have an adverse impact on the unity of the market, has had to be brought specifically to the attention of the Commission under the procedure for obtaining exemption. That a presumption of this kind was thoroughly justified in the economic, political and legal circumstances of a common market in the course of evolution seems undeniable. The only question is whether the EEC has now reached a stage in its development where some relaxation of the presumption, allowing further devolution of enforcement to the national level, has become desirable.

Permissible co-operation

There are many forms of co-operation between undertakings that offer no threat to the maintenance of effective competition, while they may bring a variety of economic benefits such as the pooling of experience or the reduction of costs. It would be unfortunate if undertakings, especially small and medium sized ones, were to be deterred from such activities by ungrounded fears of infringing Article 85. To avoid this, the Commission

---

[18] Quantitative criteria, though not resale price maintenance provisions or export bans, have a good prospect of exemption under Art. 85(3): see *Re Omega loc. cit.* note 10, p. 370, *supra*.

[19] See the very full analysis by Chard, (1982) 7 E.L.Rev. 83. See also Whish, *op. cit.* note 13, p. 354, *supra*, at pp. 443–448.

[20] Case 26/76, *loc. cit.* note 10, p. 370, *supra*.

[21] See the cases discussed at p. 368, *supra*.

issued in 1968 a "Notice on Co-operation Agreements" setting out the considerations by which it would be guided in applying Article 85(1) to such agreements and identifying the categories it considered did not fall within the provisions of the paragraph.[22]

Eight categories of co-operative activity are listed in the Notice:
— exchanges of information and joint information gathering, *e.g.* through market research, comparative studies of enterprises or industries and preparation of statistics and calculation models, but not where these lead to co-ordination of market behaviour[23];
— financial co-operation (in accountancy, the provision of credit guarantees, debt collection and consultancy facilities on business and tax matters);
— joint research and development up to the stage of industrial application, but not where the partners enter into commitments which restrict their own research and development activity or the exploitation of the results of their joint efforts[24];
— sharing of production, storage and transport facilities;
— co-operation in the execution of orders, where either the parties are not in competition with each other or, although competitors, they would not be able individually to execute a given order;
— joint selling or the joint provision of after-sales services, where the partners are not competitors[25];
— joint advertising, but not where the partners are prevented from advertising individually[26];
— use of a common label indicating a certain quality, where the label is available to all competitors on the same conditions.[27]

The Notice is useful but undertakings relying on it need to be warned that its terms are narrowly construed by the Commission. This has been seen especially in relation to research and development agreements. In *Re Henkel/Colgate*[28] the Commission found that an agreement between two major manufacturers of detergents setting up a joint subsidiary to carry out research fell within Article 85(1). Under the agreement the partners were free to continue their independent research but were required to make the results known to the joint subsidiary. This, in the view of the Commission, made it very unlikely in practice that such research would take place, since the party concerned could obtain no competitive advantage from it. Thus the effect of the agreement, though not its express provisions, took it out-

---

[22] Notice of July 29, 1968 on Co-operation Agreements, J.O. 1968 C75/3; [1968] C.M.L.R. D5.
[23] For an example of an exchange of information considered acceptable by the Commission, see *Re Department Stores* Comp.Rep. 1979, p. 62. For references showing the limits of acceptability, see note 38, *infra*.
[24] See the discussion of the block exemption Reg., *infra*, pp. 394–396.
[25] *e.g. Re Wild/Leitz* J.O. 1972 L61/21; [1972] C.M.L.R. D36. For examples of joint sales agencies outside the Notice, see note 37, *infra*.
[26] *e.g. Re Association pour la promotion du tube d'acier soundé electriquement* J.O. 1970 L153/14; [1970] C.M.L.R. D31.
[27] *Ibid.*
[28] J.O. 1972 L14/14.

side the scope of the Notice.[29] It must be added that the Notice is without prejudice to the interpretation of Article 85(1) by the Court of Justice.

An Article 85(1) checklist

Examples of agreements especially likely to restrict competition are given in Article 85(1) itself. However, it will be clear from the discussion so far that, depending on the circumstances and the particular combination of terms, many agreements other than those expressly mentioned may be caught by the paragraph. A list of such agreements, which does not purport to be exhaustive, is given below. The items on the list are commercially important transactions which, experience shows, are liable, either in themselves or because of terms commonly associated with them, to attract the unwelcome attention of the Commission. Before entering into one of these transactions firms should consider carefully any possible incompatibility with Article 85(1), the relevance of any of the block exemption regulations and the advisability of seeking individual exemption.

The list comprises:
— exclusive distribution agreements[30];
— exclusive purchasing agreements (including "tied house" and garage "solus" agreements)[31];
— exclusive licences of intellectual property rights (patents, trademarks, copyright, etc.)[32];
— selective distribution agreements[33];
— franchise agreements[34];
— research and development agreements[35];
— joint ventures (firms collaborating on a particular project, often one they would not have had the financial or technical resources to undertake individually)[36];
— joint sales and buying agencies[37];
— information agreements (concerning matters normally kept confidential from competitors)[38];

---

[29] See also *Re Research and Development* [1971] C.M.L.R. D31; *Re Beecham/Parke Davis* O.J. 1979 L70/11; [1979] 2 C.M.L.R. 157.

[30] See the discussion of the block exemption Reg., *infra*, pp. 388–389.

[31] See the discussion of the block exemption Reg., *infra*, pp. 389–391.

[32] See Chap. 18, *infra*.

[33] See the discussion, *supra*.

[34] See the discussion, *supra*.

[35] See the Notice on Co-operation Agreements, *supra*, and the discussion of the block exemption Reg., *infra*, pp. 394–396.

[36] For recent examples, see *Re BP/Kellogg* O.J. 1986 L369/6; [1986] 2 C.M.L.R. 619; *Re Optical Fibres* O.J. 1986 L236/30; See the analysis by Korah, (1987) 12 E.L.Rev. 18. See also the statements of the Commission's policy in relation to joint ventures, Comp.Rep. 1974, pp. 25–27; Comp.Rep. 1976, pp. 38–41; Comp.Rep. 1983, pp. 50–52.

[37] See, *e.g. Re CFA* J.O. 1968 L276/29 [1968] C.M.L.R. D57; *Re Supexie* J.O. 1971 L10/12; [1971] C.M.L.R. D1; *Re Centraal Stikstof Verkoopkantoor* O.J. 1978 L242/15; [1979] 1 C.M.L.R. 11; *Re Floral* O.J. 1980 L39/51; [1980] 2 C.M.L.R. 285; *Re Italian Flat Glass* O.J. 1981 L326/32; [1982] 3 C.M.L.R. 366. See also Comp.Rep. 1971 pp. 31–35 and 52–53.

[38] See *Re COBELPA/VNP* O.J. 1977 L242/10; [1977] 2 C.M.L.R. D28; *Re Italian Cast Glass* O.J. 1982 L383/19; [1982] 2 C.M.L.R. 61; *Re Zinc Producer Group loc. cit.* note 78, *supra*.

— trade fairs (where participation is often conditional or not exhibiting at other fairs in a given period).[39]

Effect on trade between Member States

The purpose of the condition in Article 85(1) relating to the effect of an agreement on trade between Member States is, in the words of the Court of Justice, "to define, in the context of the law governing competition, the boundary between the areas respectively covered by Community law and the law of the Member States."[40] Where behaviour may have implications for competition in more than one of the Member States, the EEC rules apply: where its effects are confined to a single Member State, the matter is one exclusively for national law. The line of demarcation is the same under both Article 85 and Article 86.[41]

The concept of the common market determines where that line is to be drawn. "Community law," the Court has said, "covers any agreement or any practice which is capable of constituting a threat to freedom of trade between Member States in a manner which might harm the attainment of a single market between the Member States, in particular by partitioning the national markets or by affecting the structure of competition within the common market."[42] As the passage indicates, the question whether an agreement represents a threat to the unity of the market may be approached in more than one way.

The approach normally adopted by the Court and the Commission is to examine the effect of an agreement on the flow of goods and services between Member States.[43] The test, first formulated in *Société Technique Minière*, is that "it must be possible to foresee with a sufficient degree of probability on the basis of a set of objective factors of law or of fact that the agreement in question may have an influence, direct or indirect, actual or potential, on the pattern of trade between Member States."[44] The crucial element is the diversion of trade flows from the pattern they would naturally follow in a unified market. Where trade has been so diverted, it is immaterial that the agreement may have led to an increase in the volume of goods or services reaching the market in other Member States. Thus in *Consten and Grundig*[45] trade was held to be affected in the necessary sense, regardless of any increase in imports of Grundig products into France, because not only were all such imports to be channelled through Consten but their re-exportation to other Member States was prohibited.

In practice, the requirement of a direct or indirect, actual or potential influence on the pattern of trade does not usually present a serious obstacle to establishing an infringement of Article 85(1). Trade is liable to be affec-

---

[39] See, *e.g.*, *Re CECIMO* J.O. 1969 L69/13; [1969] C.M.L.R. D1; *Re CEMATEX loc. cit.* note 27, p. 356, *supra*; *Re UNIDI (No. 1)* O.J. 1975 L228/14; [1975] 2 C.M.L.R. D51; (No. 2) O.J. 1984 L322/10; [1985] 2 C.M.L.R. 38.
[40] Case 22/78 *Hugin* v. *Commission* [1979] E.C.R. 1869 at p. 1899; [1979] 3 C.M.L.R. 345.
[41] [1979] E.C.R. at p. 1899.
[42] *Ibid.*
[43] See Bellamy and Child at para. 2–116, *op. cit.* note 13, p. 354, *supra*; Whish, *op. cit.*, *ibid.*, pp. 184–187.
[44] Case 56/65 [1966] E.C.R. at p. 249.

ted directly by, for instance, the grant of an exclusive distributorship or an exclusive patent licence in respect of a Member State's territory. An example of indirect effect would be where the product covered by an agreement is not itself exported to other Member States but a product derived from it is exported. Thus in *BNIC* v. *Clair*[46] it was pointed out that the product in question, potable spirits used in the manufacture of cognac, was not normally sent outside the Cognac region of France. The Court responded that "any agreement whose object or effect is to restrict competition by fixing minimum prices for an intermediate product is capable of affecting intra-Community trade, even if there is no trade in that intermediate product between the Member States, where the product constitutes the raw material for another product marketed elsewhere in the Community."[47] An agreement between parties in the same Member State and relating to sales of domestic products within that State may affect trade indirectly, *e.g.* by making it harder for imports to penetrate the market, especially where it extends over the whole national territory. For example, in *Cementhandelaren* v. *Commission*[48] an agreement setting target prices for cement throughout the Netherlands was found capable of affecting trade, although it did not apply to imports or exports. Such an agreement, the Court said, "by its very nature has the effect of reinforcing the compartmentalisation of markets on a national basis, thereby holding up the economic interpenetration which the Treaty is designed to bring about and protecting domestic production."[49] Since a potential effect on trade will suffice, there is no need for the Commission to produce statistical evidence showing that, as a result of the agreement, trade has actually begun to flow through different channels. Nor does the absence for the time being of concrete effects necessarily provide an answer to objections raised against an agreement, if there is a reasonable expectation that things may be different in the future. In *AEG* v. *Commission*[50] it was argued, *inter alia*, by the company that the operation of its selective distribution system could not create appreciable obstacles to trade between Member States because the dealers concerned did not, in fact, engage in such trade or were not in a position to do so. Citing its *Miller* judgment,[51] the Court remarked;

"... the mere fact at a certain time traders applying for admission to a distribution network or who have already been admitted are not engaged in intra-Community trade cannot suffice to exclude the possibility that restrictions on their freedom of action may impede intra-Community trade, since the situation may change from one year to another in terms of alterations in the conditions or composition of the market both in the common market as a whole and in the individual national markets."[52]

[45] Joined Cases 56 and 58/64 *loc. cit.* note 66, *supra*.
[46] Case 123/83 *BNIC* v. *Clair* [1985] E.C.R. 402; [1985] 2 C.M.L.R. 430.
[47] [1985] E.C.R. at p. 425.
[48] Case 8/72 [1972] E.C.R. 977; [1973] C.M.L.R. 7.
[49] [1977] E.C.R. at p. 991. See also Case 126/80 *Salonia* v. *Poidomani* [1981] E.C.R. 1563; [1982] 1 C.M.L.R. 64; Case 42/84 *Remia* v. *Commission* (not yet reported).
[50] Case 107/82 *loc. cit.* note 10, p. 370, *supra*.
[51] Case 19/77 *Miller* v. *Commission* [1978] E.C.R. 131; [1978] 2 C.M.L.R. 334.
[52] [1983] E.C.R. at p. 3201.

An alternative approach has been adopted by the Court of Justice in some cases under Article 86. Attention is focused not on any change in the pattern of imports or exports but on the consequences of the behaviour in question for the structure of competition within the common market. The leading case is *Commercial Solvents Corporation* v. *Commission*.[53] Commercial Solvents was found to have abused its dominant position (amounting to a world monopoly) in respect of a product used as a raw material in the manufacture of a medicinal drug, by refusing to supply the product to an Italian company, Zoja. Since there was no other source of supply, Zoja was liable to be driven out of business as a manufacturer of the drug. The argument that trade between Member States could not be affected, since Zoja sold almost all of its production outside the common market, was rejected by the Court. The requirement of an effect on trade would, it was held, be satisfied by the impairment of the competitive structure caused by the elimination of a major EEC producer. This structural test is less likely to be relevant in cases under Article 85, where the starting point is not, as it is under Article 86, the existence of a dominant position.[54] However, the Court considers the test to be available in such cases,[55] and it has occasionally been applied by the Commission. Thus in *Re Wood Pulp*[56] trade between Member States was said to have been affected owing to the impairment of competition throughout the Community by the creation of an artificially uniform price level.

The de minimis rule

For Article 85(1) to apply, the agreement in question must have the object or effect of restricting competition, and an actual or potential impact on trade between Member States, to a degree that is appreciable. This *de minimis* rule is a specialised aspect of the rule of reason. It was laid down by the Court of Justice in *Völk* v. *Vervaecke*[57] where the agreement in question was for the grant of an exclusive distributorship with absolute territorial protection. Such an agreement would, following *Grundig and Consten*,[58] normally be considered to be restrictive in its object. However, in the instant case the manufacturer had a minute share of the market in the contract products.[59] The Court said that the conditions in Article 85(1)

---

[53] Joined Cases 6 and 7/73 [1974] E.C.R. 223; [1974] 1 C.M.L.R. 309. See also Case 22/79, *Greenwich Film Production* v. *SACEM* [1979] E.C.R. 3275; [1980] 1 C.M.L.R. 629, Case 7/82 *GVL* v. *Commission* [1983] E.C.R. 483; [1983] 3 C.M.L.R. 645.

[54] See, in the same sense, Bellamy and Child at para. 2–118, *op. cit.* note 13, p. 354, *supra*; Whish, *op. cit. ibid.*, p. 187.

[55] This is clear from the reference to Arts. 85 and 86 in the passage in the *Hugin* judgment concerning the purpose of the requirements of an effect on inter-Member State trade: Case 22/78 [1979] E.C.R. at p. 1899.

[56] *Loc. cit.* note 37, p. 358, *supra*, at para. 137. See also *Re Vacuum Interrupters (No. 1)* O.J. 1977 L48/32; [1977] 1 C.M.L.R. D67.

[57] Case 5/69 *Völk* v. *Vervaecke* [1969] E.C.R. 295; [1969] C.M.L.R. 273.

[58] Joined Cases 56 and 58/64, *loc. cit.* note 66, *supra*.

[59] The agreement was for the supply of washing machines manufactured in Germany to a Belgian dealer. The manufacturer's share of the German market was between 0·2 and 0·5 per cent. The volume represented by this share was also very small—between 2361 and 861 units.

relating to competition and inter-State trade must be understood by reference to the actual circumstances of the agreement. "Consequently an agreement falls outside the prohibition in Article 85 when it has only an insignificant effect on the market, taking into account the weak position which the persons concerned have on the market of the product in question."[60]

Guidance as to whether an agreement is capable of having an appreciable impact on market conditions was provided by the Commission's Notice Concerning Agreements of Minor Importance, the most recent version of which was published in 1986.[61] The test of appreciability offered in the Notice consists of two criteria: the products which are the subject of the agreement and other products of the participating undertakings[62] considered by users to be equivalent in view of their characteristics, price or use must not represent in the affected part of the common market more than 5 per cent. of the total market for such products; and the aggregate annual turnover of the participating undertakings must not exceed 200 million ECUs. As Advocate General Warner pointed out in the *Miller* case,[63] the test appears to have been formulated with horizontal agreements in mind: it is difficult to see how the criterion relating to aggregate annual turnover can be applied to vertical agreements. At all events, the Notice stresses that the test is purely indicative and it is, again, without prejudice to the interpretation of Article 85 by the Court of Justice.[64]

The *de minimis* argument appears to have swayed the Commission in a number of cases relating to joint sales or buying agencies formed by very small undertakings to enable them to compete more effectively. In *Re SAFCO*,[65] for example, an agency in France for the exportation of vegetable preserves, accounting for only 1 to 2 per cent. on average of consumption of those products in Germany, its principal export market, was found not to constitute a restriction of competition.[66] This may be contrasted with *Re Floral*[67] which concerned an agency set up by three French fertiliser manufacturers to handle their exports to Germany. The quantities exported through the agency represented only 2 per cent. of the German fertiliser market but the Commission decided that the case fell within Article 85(1) owing to the size of the undertakings concerned (their combined share of the EEC market was 10 per cent.) and the fact that the

---

[60] [1969] E.C.R. at p. 302. See also Case 1/71 *Cadillon* v. *Hoss* [1971] E.C.R. 351; [1971] C.M.L.R. 420.

[61] O.J. 1986, C231/2. This replaced a Notice of 1977, itself replacing one of 1970.

[62] The Notice defines "participating undertakings" so as to cover, as well as the parties themselves, undertakings controlling or controlled by them.

[63] Case 19/77 *Miller* v. *Commission* [1978] E.C.R. at pp. 157–158.

[64] On two occasions when the Notice had been cited to the Court, Adv. Gen. Dutheillet de Lamothe made the point that, because of peculiarities in the market in question, even an agreement meeting the criteria laid down by the Commission might be caught by Art. 85(1): see Case 1/71 *Cadillon* v. *Hoss* [1971] E.C.R. at p. 361; Case 22/71 *Béguelin Import* v. *GL Import Export* [1971] E.C.R. 949 at p. 968; [1972] C.M.L.R. 81.

[65] J.O. 1972 L13/14; [1972] C.M.L.R. D83.

[66] See also *Re Alliance de Constructeurs Français de Machines-Outils* J.O. 1968 L201/1; [1968] C.M.L.R. D23; *Re SOCEMAS* J.O. 1968 L201/4; [1968] C.M.L.R. D28; *Re Intergroup Trading (Spar)* O.J. 1975 L212/23; [1975] 2 C.M.L.R. D14.

[67] *Loc. cit.* note 37, p. 374, *supra.*

uniform supply terms made an already oligopolistic market structure even tighter.[68]

In applying the rule, the Court of Justice has regard, in particular, to the size of the parties to the agreement, their market shares and those of their competitors, their absolute turnover figures and any effect on the structure of the market. In *Distillers Company* v. *Commission*,[69] for example, it was held that an agreement concerning the terms of supply of Pimms was not covered by the rule, although sales of the drink outside the United Kingdom were minimal as compared with those of other spirits. This was due to the importance of Distillers, the sole producer of Pimms, on the market for alcoholic drinks.[70] In *Pioneer*[71] the Court found that the market in hi-fi products in the Member States where a concerted practice had occurred was extremely fragmented. The fact that the shares held by the parties, though small, exceeded those of most of their competitors, taken together with their absolute turnover figures, made it impossible to regard the practice as insignificant.[72]

A necessary step in assessing the significance of an agreement is the definition of the relevant market. This was an issue between the parties in *Pioneer* where the Court admitted that there was no generally agreed conception of "hi-fi products." It was, however, unnecessary on that occasion to resolve the issue, since the estimates of their market shares put forward by the parties to the concerted practice themselves were sufficient for the purposes of Article 85(1).[73] In the *Hasselblad* case[74] the Court accepted the view of the Commission that the relevant market was that of medium format reflex cameras, which excluded all 35 mm cameras. Because of their particular characteristics (format, quality of reproduction, handiness and range of accessories) Hasselblad cameras were found to be "virtually indispensable for a large number of users in the various Member States of the Community."[75]

CRITERIA OF EXEMPTION

Agreements that appreciably restrict competition may nevertheless bring significant economic advantages. Some systems of competition law, accordingly, provide "gateways" through which a restrictive agreement serving certain important objectives of public policy may escape prohibi-

---

[68] See also *Re Toltecs and Dorcet (Trade Marks)* O.J. 1982 L379/19; [1983] 1 C.M.L.R. 412. This was the Dec. reviewed in Case 35/83 *BAT Cigaretten-Fabriken* v. *Commission* [1985] 2 C.M.L.R. 470 where, however, the *de minimis* issue was not addressed by the Court.

[69] Case 30/78 [1980] E.C.R. 2229; [1980] 3 C.M.L.R. 121.

[70] [1980] E.C.R. at p. 2265. See also Case 19/77 *Miller* v. *Commission loc. cit.* note 51, p. 376, *supra*; Joined Cases 29 and 30/83, *CRAM and Rheinzink* v. *Commission loc. cit.* note 45, p. 359, *supra*.

[71] Joined Cases 100–103/80 *Musique Diffusion Française* v. *Commission loc. cit.* note 60, p. 362, *supra*.

[72] [1983] E.C.R. at pp. 1899–1901. See also the Opinion of Adv. Gen. Sir Gordon Slynn in that case: (1983) E.C.R. at pp. 1942–1944.

[73] [1983] E.C.R. at p. 1900.

[74] Case 86/82 *Hasselblad* v. *Commission* [1984] E.C.R. 883; [1984] 1 C.M.L.R. 559.

[75] [1984] E.C.R. at p. 902. See the definition of the relevant product and geographic market in the 1986 Notice.

tion.[76] The function of Article 85(3) is to enable a balance to be struck between the maintenance of effective competition and other aspects of the Community's task as defined in Article 2 EEC.

Pursuant to Article 85(3) the provisions of Article 85(1) may be declared inapplicable to "any agreement or category of agreements." It has already been noted that the power to grant exemption in respect of individual agreements is reserved by Regulation 17 to the Commission. The procedure for obtaining individual exemption by notification of the agreement in question is described in Chapter 16, below. "Block" exemption of categories of agreements is given by regulations of the Commission which are adopted under powers delegated by the Council in accordance with Article 87 EEC. The block exemption regulations so far enacted relate to exclusive distribution agreements, exclusive purchasing agreements, patent licensing agreements, motor vehicle distribution and servicing agreements, specialisation agreements and research and development agreements.[77] Their scope and effect are examined in the final section of this chapter.

In the present section we consider the criteria in Article 85(3) that must be met by agreements in order to qualify for exemption. There are two positive criteria and two negative ones.

Economic benefit

The first of the positive criteria identifies in broad terms a number of economic benefits that provide the rationale for refraining from applying Article 85(1). The agreement must contribute "to improving the production or distribution of goods or to promoting technical or economic progress." It may be found that a given agreement helps to further more than one, or even all, of these objects.

The basic target of the Commission in applying the criterion of economic benefit is that the gain to welfare must exceed what could have been achieved without any restriction of competition. As the Commission has stated:

> "For the agreements to contribute to the improvement of production or distribution, or to promote technical or economic progress, they must objectively constitute an improvement on the situation that would otherwise exist. The fundamental principle in this respect, established at the time the Common Market was formed, lays down that fair and undistorted competition is the best guarantee of regular supply on the best terms. Thus the question of a contribution to economic progress within the meaning of Article 85(3) can only arise in those exceptional cases where the free play of competition is unable to produce the best result economically speaking."[78]

---

[76] Cf. the provisions of ss.10 and 19 of the Restrictive Trade Practices Act 1976. See the discussion in Whish, op. cit. note 13, p. 354, supra, at pp. 132 et seq.

[77] The first four of these Regs. were adopted by the Commission pursuant to Council Reg. 19/65 (J.O. 1965, 533; O.J. 1965–1966) and the last two pursuant to Council Reg. 2821/71 (J.O. 1971, L285/46; O.J. 1971, 1032).

[78] Re Bayer/Gist-Brocades O.J. 1976 L30/13; [1976] 1 C.M.L.R. D98. See para. 57 of the Dec.

The matter is to be judged in the light of the general interest in a well functioning market. It is not sufficient merely that the parties themselves may secure advantages in their production and distribution activities.[79]

Re VBBB/VBVB[80] provides an example of an agreement which was found not to have objective advantages outweighing the disadvantage of its restrictive effect on competition. The agreement, which was between associations of booksellers and publishers in the Netherlands and in Belgium, established a system of collective resale price maintenance for trade between the two countries in books in the Dutch language. The main grounds relied on to justify this system were that it made possible the cross-subsidisation of less popular titles by more popular ones and also helped to ensure the survival of small book shops. The Commission did not deny the worthiness of these objectives but took the view that their dependence on the disputed system had not been demonstrated. Cross-subsidisation could have been achieved by individual publishers' decisions on pricing, while the number of specialised booksellers had declined sharply, despite resale price maintenance, owing in part to the rise of self-service shops and the activities of book clubs. On the debit side, by excluding price competition in respect of a given title, the agreement removed an important means of rationalising and improving the system of book distribution.[81]

The balance of advantage and disadvantage may go against an agreement because of the way in which it is applied in practice. In *Re Ford Werke*[82] the Commission considered the compatibility with Article 85 of the standard form agreement concluded between Ford Germany and its main dealers. Essentially, a dealer would be given an exclusive right to distribute and service Ford vehicles within an allotted territory, while undertaking not to sell vehicles of other makes. The agreement was caught by Article 85(1), since it affected the intensity of competition within the distribution network, as well as limiting the outlets available to other car manufacturers, but might have been expected, on its terms, to qualify for exemption under Article 85(3). Exemption was, however, refused by the Commission on the ground that Ford Germany had cut off supplies of right hand drive vehicles to its dealers. The purpose of this action was to staunch the flow of parallel imports into the United Kingdom where local Ford prices were significantly higher than in Germany. Ford's argument that it had acted purely unilaterally, and therefore outside Article 85, was rejected by the Commission and subsequently by the Court of Justice.[83] The Court held that the refusal to supply formed part of the contractual relationship between Ford and its dealers, whose admission to the network implied acceptance of the company's policy regarding the models to be delivered to the German market. It could, therefore, properly be taken into account in assessing the eligibility of the agreement for exemption.

In preserving the delicate balance between the benefits claimed to flow

---

[79] Joined Cases 56 and 58/64 *Consten and Grundig* v. *Commission* [1966] E.C.R. at p. 348.
[80] O.J. 1982 L54/36; [1982] 2 C.M.L.R. 344.
[81] The Dec. was upheld by the Court of Justice in Joined Cases 43 and 63/82 [1984] E.C.R. 19; [1985] 1 C.M.L.R. 87.
[82] O.J. 1983 L327/31; [1984] 1 C.M.L.R. 596.
[83] Joined Cases 25 and 26/84 *Ford* v. *Commission* (not yet reported).

from an agreement and the need to maintain effective competition, an important part is played by the time limits and conditions imposed pursuant to Article 8(1) of Regulation 17. Time limits are at the discretion of the Commission. Agreements are generally given a period of five to ten years to produce the hoped-for result but, in the case of research and development agreements and manufacturing joint ventures relating to products not yet established on the market, 15 years may be judged appropriate.[84] Despite their limited period of validity, many exemptions will produce permanent changes in the structure of the market concerned: thus specialisation agreements by their very nature entail a decisive shift in the business activities of the parties. In addition, where a period of exemption has elapsed it may be renewed by the Commission, although not necessarily on the same terms.[85] The conditions attached to a grant of exemption will be designed to ensure that benefits really are obtained and competition is not unduly prejudiced. An example would be an obligation to report from time to time on the progress made in implementing the agreement.[86]

As might be expected, improvements in production have frequently been found to result from agreements which enable the parties to specialise in particular areas of production[87] or which provide for collaboration in research and development.[88] Typical of such improvements would be: a reduction in costs or an increase in productivity, thanks to economies of scale; enhancement of output or of the quality and range of goods, through the modernisation of plant or the centralisation of production and planning; and avoidance of duplication in research and development projects, giving a better chance of obtaining a useful result and reducing the time needed to do so. Patent and know-how licensing agreements[89] and manufacturing joint ventures[90] may contribute to improving production by allowing inventions and processes to be more widely exploited. A consideration of particular importance may be the facilitation of the transfer of new technology to EEC companies.[91] Distribution agreements have also on occasion been seen as beneficial to production, e.g. where there was provision for exchanges of information between the manufacturer and the distributors, which might lead to improvements in design.[92]

Common examples of arrangements bringing improvements in distribu-

---

[84] See, e.g. Re United Reprocessors O.J. 1976 L51/7; [1976] 2 C.M.L.R. D1.
[85] See, e.g. Re Transocean Marine Paint Association (No. 2) O.J. 1974 L19/18; [1974] 1 C.M.L.R. D11; Re Jaz/Peter (No. 2) O.J. 1978 L61/17; [1978] 2 C.M.L.R. 186; Re Vacuum Interrupters (No. 2) O.J. 1980 L383/1; [1981] 2 C.M.L.R. 217.
[86] See, e.g. Re Bayer/Gist-Brocades loc. cit. note 78, p. 380, supra.
[87] See, e.g. Re Jaz/Peter (No. 1) J.O. 1969 L195/5; [1970] C.M.L.R. 129; Re Lightweight Paper J.O. 1972 L182/24; [1972] C.M.L.R. D94; Re Prym/Beka O.J. 1973 L296/24; [1973] C.M.L.R. D250; Re Bayer/Gist-Brocades loc. cit., supra. See also the discussion of Reg. 417/85, infra.
[88] See, e.g. Re United Reprocessors loc. cit., supra; Re Vacuum Interrupters (No. 1) loc. cit. note 56, p. 377, supra; [1977] 1 C.M.L.R. D67; Re Beecham/Parke Davis loc. cit. note 29, p. 374 supra; Re BP/Kellogg loc. cit. note 36, p. 374, supra. See also the discussion of Reg. 418/85, infra.
[89] See Chap. 18, infra.
[90] See, e.g. Re Optical Fibres loc. cit. note 36, p. 374, supra.
[91] Ibid., para. 59.
[92] Re BMW loc. cit. note 10, p. 370, supra. See also Re Pronuptia loc. cit. note 9, p. 370, supra.

tion are exclusive distributorships,[93] selective dealer networks[94] and trade fairs.[95] In the case of exclusive distribution agreements, recognised advantages are the easier penetration of markets (especially foreign ones), continuity of supply, more effective promotion of the goods, maintenance of adequate stocks and the organisation of after-sales services.[96] These factors have also been cited in justification for limiting the outlets for certain types of product on a quantitative basis under systems of selective distribution.[97] Rationalisation of participation in trade fairs may improve distribution by periodically bringing together the complete range of products on offer in a given sector, thereby providing an overview and saving manufacturers the heavy costs involved in exhibiting at a series of smaller events.[98] Despite the wording of Article 85(3), account is taken of improvements in the distribution of *services*. Thus in *Re ABI*[99] agreements restricting competition in respect of the charges imposed for their services by banks in Italy were given exemption because they made possible the standardisation and simplification of banking procedures. Exceptionally, a market sharing agreement has been regarded as improving distribution, where it allowed a number of small or medium sized undertakings to compete with much larger rivals in the supply of marine paint, through the establishment of a worldwide network.[1]

The promotion of technical progress is often linked by the Commission with improvements in production, and the range of agreements it may be invoked to justify is similar. Instances of technical progress mentioned in the Decisions include the discovery and application of new technology, the development of new products and the improvement of existing ones, better standards of safety for consumers and the public and the saving of energy.[2] In *Re X/Open Group*[3] exemption was granted in respect of an agreement between a number of substantial computer manufacturers having as its object the establishment of a standard interface for an operating system which it was possible to use on a wide variety of machines. An "open industry standard" would extend the availability of software and increase the opportunities for users to switch between hardware and software from different sources. This, it was found, would contribute to promoting technical progress by enabling software houses, and conceivably members of the Group as well, to develop application programmes for which there might not otherwise have been a market.

"Economic progress" *might* be viewed as a "catch-all" term, to fall back on when it is desired to exempt an agreement which does not clearly fulfil any other positive requirement. It has been invoked in the case of

[93] See the discussion of Reg. 1983/83, *infra*.
[94] See the cases cited in note 10, p. 370, *supra*.
[95] See, *e.g. Re CECIMO loc. cit.* note 27, p. 356, *supra*; *Re CEMATEX ibid.*; *Re UNIDI* O.J. 1975 L228/14; [1975] 2 C.M.L.R. D51.
[96] See the 6th recital to Reg. 1983/83.
[97] *Re Omega loc. cit.* note 10, p. 370, *supra*; *Re BMW ibid.*
[98] See, *e.g.* the reasoning in *Re CECIMO loc. cit.*, *supra*.
[99] O.J. 1987 L43/51.
[1] *Re Transocean Marine Paint Association (No. 1)* J.O. 1967, 163; [1967] C.M.L.R. D9.
[2] See the cases cited in note 88, p. 382, *supra*.
[3] O.J. 1987 L35/36.

trade fairs, where the co-ordination of supply and demand was improved.[4] From these decisions, however, it can be deduced that the Commission is here looking at improvements in the way the *market operates*. In other cases economic progress has been found because of improvements in the *structure* of a particular industry. Thus in *Davidson Rubber Company*,[5] a patent licence agreement led to economies of scale; and in *Kabelmetal*,[6] which again concerned a patent licence, the agreement was justified because it brought a better return on investment. The introduction of new goods or processes might amount to "economic progress."[7] This is also the heading that seems most apt for dealing with "crisis cartels," formed to enable an industry to adapt in an orderly way to adverse economic conditions such as a decline in the overall market for its products. There is a long-running controversy as to whether Article 85(3) can be used to sanction such cartels.[8] The view of the Commission is that it can be, where the purpose is to achieve a co-ordinated reduction of overcapacity and the commercial freedom of the participants is not restricted.[9] Thus in *Re Synthetic Fibres*[10] an agreement providing for joint measures to cut capacity, in an industry where the trend in demand had not kept pace with increased output resulting from rapid technical advances, was considered eligible for exemption. The advantages identified by the Commission included the shedding of the financial burden of keeping underutilised capacity open, the achievement of optimum plant size and specialisation in the development of products adapted to user's requirements. "The eventual result," the Commission said, "should be to raise the profitability and restore the competitiveness of each party."[11]

Another controversial issue is whether it is proper for the Commission to take social advantages, into account in applying Article 85(3). Among the factors mentioned in support of the *Synthetic Fibres* exemption was the possibility of cushioning the social effects of restructuring by making suitable arrangements for the retraining and redeployment of redundant workers. In our submission, the right approach in such cases is that indicated by the Court of Justice in *Metro (No. 1)*[12] concerning the obligation of SABA distributors to enter into six-monthly supply contracts based on forecasts of the probable growth of the market. The establishment of such forecasts, the Court said, "constitutes a stabilising factor with regard to the provision of employment which, *since it improves the general conditions of production*, especially when market conditions are unfavourable, comes within the framework of the objectives to which reference may be had pursuant to Article 85(3)" (emphasis added).[13] As the italicised phrase makes clear, the Court was here treating stability of employment not as a purely

---

[4] *Re CECIMO loc. cit.* note 27, p. 356, *supra*.

[5] J.O. 1972 L143/31; [1972] C.M.L.R. D52.

[6] *Re Kabelmetal/Luchaire* O.J. 1975 L272/34; [1975] 2 C.M.L.R. D40.

[7] *Re Bronbemaling/Heidemaatschappij* O.J. 1975 L249/27; [1975] 2 C.M.L.R. D67.

[8] See the references cited by Faull at (1986) 11 E.L.Rev. 64.

[9] See Comp.Rep. 1982, pp. 43–45; Comp.Rep. 1983, pp. 53–54; Comp.Rep. 1984, pp. 69–72.

[10] O.J. 1984 L207/17; [1985] 1 C.M.L.R. 787.

[11] *Ibid.*, para. 36.

[12] *Loc. cit.* note 10, p. 370, *supra*.

[13] [1977] E.C.R. at p. 1916.

social objective but as a matter going to the economic well being of the sector in question.

Benefit to consumers

The second positive criterion is that consumers must receive a fair share of the benefit resulting from the restriction of competition. At first sight, the use of the term "consumer" suggests that only the consuming public, or end consumer, is meant. Such a construction, however, would have the effect of severely limiting the scope of possible exemptions, because in many cases the parties to the agreement cannot by themselves do anything to ensure that the condition is met. For instance, manufacturers often, and if small usually, sell through middlemen; they could not guarantee that these middlemen will pass on the benefits of the agreement, even if they themselves do so. It is not therefore surprising that the Commission has taken the view that consumers include persons at intermediate stages in the marketing process. For example, in *Re ACEC/Berliet*[14] the agreement in question was one concerning the development and ultimate marketing of buses equipped with an electrical transmission system invented by one of the parties. Here the consumers likely to benefit were operators of bus companies. The term "consumer" in English may, besides, have a narrower connotation than the term used in other language texts: the French text uses the term *utilisateur*.

The requirement of a "fair share of the resulting benefit" involves two considerations: what is a benefit, so far as the consumer is concerned; and how can the Commission be sure that the consumer will receive it? The first consideration is closely related to the type of improvement at which the agreement is aiming. Improvements in production or the promotion of technical progress will usually result in a cheaper and/or better product. Improvements in distribution and the promotion of economic progress will usually result in better supply and greater choice of product. The second consideration depends on the pressures on the undertakings to pass on the benefits. The Commission has generally been content to establish that the parties will continue to be subject to lively competition from other competitors.[15] Where the agreement concerns research and development there may be no other likely competition than that between the parties once the project is completed, but here the Commission may have regard to the power of purchasers[16] or to its own conditions.[17]

No restrictions that are not indispensable

The first negative criterion is that exemption cannot be given to restrictions of competition going beyond what is absolutely necessary to achieve the objectives regarded as beneficial.

[14] J.O. 1968 L201/7; [1968] C.M.L.R. D35.
[15] See, *e.g. Re Rank/Sopelem* O.J. 1975 L29/20; [1975] 1 C.M.L.R. D72.
[16] In *Re United Reprocessors loc. cit.* note 84, p. 382, *supra*, the primary consumers of reprocessing services were the electricity monopolies in the Member States. See also the *Davidson Rubber Company, loc. cit.* note 5, p. 384, *supra*.
[17] *Re KEWA* O.J. 1976 L51/15; [1976] 2 C.M.L.R. D15; *Re United Reprocessors loc. cit.* note 84, p. 382, *supra*.

For the commoner forms of restrictive agreement it has long been clear whether a given term is likely to be considered essential or non-essential. The protection against direct competition from the supplier himself or from other distributors appointed within the concession territory is accepted as the price for securing the wholehearted performance of his obligations by an exclusive distributor. On the other hand, since *Consten and Grundig*[18] the chances of establishing the indispensability of absolute territorial protection have been minimal. Quantitative criteria in a selective distribution system may be recognised as indispensable where, without the guarantee of a minimum turnover, dealers would not be in a position to provide the pre- and post-sales service appropriate to the marketing of certain classes of goods.[19] In a specialisation agreement an obligation to purchase exclusively from the other party will normally only pass the test if it is open to the purchaser to accept more favourable offers from third parties.[20] As for research and development agreements, the delicacy of the relationship between the partners may justify a wide variety of restrictions, including the obligation not to carry on the activity in question either independently or with a third party.[21]

The indispensability requirement is of great practical significance, since the Commission is in a position to insist that certain of the provisions in an agreement be dropped before it will grant exemption. Revision of an agreement carried out under the threat of a refusal of exemption, and hence of automatic nullity, may sometimes be far-reaching. For example, under the joint venture arrangements in *Re Optical Fibres*,[22] as they were originally conceived, the technology provider (the American firm, Corning) had a share of the equity giving it effective control over production and marketing policies. This, it was feared, might enable Corning to prevent the joint ventures from competing actively with each other. The Commission, therefore, persuaded the parties to reduce Corning's voting rights to below the level that could give it a veto over decisions at shareholder's meetings, while also curbing its influence over day-to-day management. It has been argued[23] that intervention by the Commission in cases of this kind may compel parties to renegotiate an agreement after there has been a shift in their relative bargaining power. The risk of such an outcome may deter overseas providers of technology from entering into arrangements particularly beneficial to the European economy.

No possibility of eliminating competition

The final criterion is that the agreement must not afford the parties the possibility of eliminating competition in respect of a substantial part of the product in question. There is thus, in principle, a limit beyond which con-

---

[18] Joined Cases 56 and 58/64, *loc. cit.* note 66, p. 362, *supra.*
[19] *Re Omega loc. cit.* note 10, p. 370, *supra.*
[20] *Re Clima Chappée* J.O. 1969 L195/1; [1970] C.M.L.R. D7. See also Reg. 417/85, Art. 2(1)(*a*), *infra.*
[21] See the cases cited in note 88, p. 382, *supra.* See also Reg. 418/85, Arts. 2 and 4, *infra.*
[22] *Loc. cit.* note 36, p. 374, *supra.*
[23] By Korah, *op. cit.*, *ibid.*

siderations of general economic policy cannot be allowed to prevail over the maintenance of effective competition in the common market.

Here, as in the application of the *de minimis* rule, the Commission has the task of defining the relevant markert.[24] This is done by identifying the range of products competing with those affected by the contract, taking into account the geographic scope of offers, and on occasion also their timing. In *Kali und Salz*[25] a Decision of the Commission refusing exemption to an agreement for the exclusive sale of "straight" potash fertiliser was annulled by the Court on the ground, *inter alia*, that the relevant product market had been wrongly defined. The Commission had taken the view that the agreement was liable to result in the substantial elimination of competition because between them the parties accounted for the whole production of "straight" potash fertiliser in the Federal Republic of Germany. However, the Commission's own reasoning showed there was competition between the product and "compound" potash fertiliser, which ought therefore to have been regarded as belonging to the same market. In some cases, especially where a vertical agreement is in question, it may be appropriate to limit consideration to the territory of the Member State in which the performance takes place,[26] while in other cases the Commission may have regard to the existence of lively competition on the common market as a whole,[27] or even on the world market.[28] The time factor may be relevant where, for example, it is anticipated that the parties to a research and development agreement will become competitors when the stage of exploiting their final product is reached.[29]

Experience suggests that an agreement which clearly satisfies the other criteria in Article 85(3) is unlikely to fail under this one.

BLOCK EXEMPTION

An agreement that would otherwise be liable to prohibition under Article 85(1) will automatically escape this fate if it fulfils the terms of a block exemption regulation. The parties to qualifying agreements are saved the uncertainty and delay of seeking individual exemption, although that route would remain open where none of the regulations applied. The gain in terms of legal certainty, it has been pointed out,[30] is paid for in the acceptance of a degree of dirigisme, since the parties to a prospective agreement are inevitably under pressure to order their affairs so as to attract block exemption, if it should be available.

A standard approach is discernible in the drafting of the regulations. The category of agreements to which the regulation applies is identified in

---

[24] See p. 379, *supra*. See also the discussion of this issue in the context of Art. 86.
[25] Joined Cases 19 and 20/74 *Kali und Salz* v. *Commission* [1975] E.C.R. 499; [1975] 2 C.M.L.R. 154.
[26] *e.g.* Joined Cases 209–215 and 218/78 *Van Landewyck* v. *Commission loc. cit.* note 26, p. 356, *supra*.
[27] *e.g.*, *Re Lightweight Paper loc. cit.* note 87, p. 382, *supra*.
[28] *e.g.*, *Re Vacuum Interrupters (No. 1) loc. cit.* note 56, p. 377, *supra*.
[29] *Re United Reprocessors loc. cit.* note 84, p. 382, *supra*.
[30] By Whish, *op. cit.* note 13, p. 354, *supra*, at pp. 179 and 202–205.

broad terms and lists are then give of specific obligations which may or may not be included without forfeiting the benefit of the block exemption. These are sometimes referred to as, respectively, the "white" and "black" lists. Provision will be made for the withdrawal of the exemption by the Commission if it finds that, despite compliance with the regulation, an agreement has certain effects that do not satisfy the criteria in Article 85(3). There will also be transitional provisions, and the duration of the regulation will be specified. Some of the regulations have introduced an "opposition procedure" which expedites the process of obtaining exemption on an individual basis. An agreement not covered by the regulation may be notified to the Commission which is given a period (normally six months) to express its opposition. If the agreement is not opposed by the Commission within the prescribed period, it is brought within the scope of the block exemption.

In the remainder of this section we examine the main features of the block exemption regulations in force at the time of writing, with the exception of the regulation on patent licensing agreements which is treated in Chapter 18, below.

Exclusive distribution agreements

The earliest of the block exemption measures was Regulation 67/67[31] which covered exclusive distribution, exclusive purchasing and combinations of the two. This has been replaced by two regulations, which came into force on July 1, 1983. Exclusive distribution agreements are dealt with in Regulation 1983/84.[32] Its companion, Regulation 1984/84,[33] which deals with exclusive purchasing, is considered below.

Under an exclusive distribution agreement one party (the supplier) allocates to the other party (the distributor) a defined territory in which the distributor is required to concentrate his sales effort. In return, the supplier undertakes not to deliver the contract products to other resellers within the concession territory. We have seen in the discussion of Article 85(3) what advantages marketing systems of this kind may bring. However, like its predecessor, Regulation 1983/83 reflects the view in the case law that absolute territorial protection cannot be regarded as essential to enable the distributor to work the market intensively.[34]

The general class of agreements to which Regulation 1983/83 applies is defined in Article 1 as "agreements to which only two undertakings are party and whereby one party agrees with the other to supply certain goods for resale within the whole or a defined area of the common market only to the other." Although the block exemption is thus confined to bilateral

---

[31] J.O. 1967, 849; O.J. 1967, 10. This was amended, and its period of validity was extended, by Reg. 2591/72 (O.J. 1982 L276/15) and Reg. 3577/82 (O.J. 1982 L373/58). It expired on June 30, 1983.

[32] O.J. 1983 L173/1. The Reg. and its companion were the subject of an explanatory Notice: O.J. 1984 L101/2.

[33] O.J. 1983 L173/5.

[34] The leading authority is Joined Cases 56 and 58/64 *Consten and Grundig* v. *Commission loc. cit.* note 66, p. 362, *supra*.

agreements,[35] it can be seen from the case law on Regulation 67/67 that agreements in a distribution network will be covered.[36] On the other hand, an agreement between two trade associations, both of which have a large membership, will not be.[37] The contract product must be supplied "for resale" and not, for instance, for further processing or consumption. The Article makes clear, as the equivalent provision of Regulation 67/67 did not, that a concession territory consisting of the whole of the common market may qualify for exemption.[38]

The Regulation's "white" list of contractual provisions is found in Article 2. Apart from his obligation pursuant to Article 1 not to appoint other distributors in the concession territory, the only restriction on competition that may be imposed on the supplier is the obligation not to sell the contract product there himself. Allowable restrictions on the distributor are listed in the second paragraph. He may be required to refrain from manufacturing or distributing competing products, to purchase the contract products exclusively from the supplier and to refrain from pursuing an active sales policy outside the concession territory (though not from responding to orders). The third paragraph sets out a number of positive obligations, designed to ensure the effective marketing of a contract product, that may be accepted by the reseller, such as the purchasing of complete ranges of goods, advertising or the provision of customer and guarantee services.

Article 3 excludes the block exemption in two important kinds of case. The first is that of exclusive distribution agreements, whether reciprocal or otherwise, between competing manufacturers. However, for the sake of small manufacturers, who may be dependent on agreements with larger competitors to increase distribution of their products, the block exemption may apply to non-reciprocal agreements, where one of the parties has a total annual turnover of no more than 100 million ECUs.[39] The second kind of case involves absolute territorial protection. Particular attention is drawn to the use of industrial property rights in order to prevent parallel imports. However, the Article makes clear that the benefit of the block exemption will be lost even where absolute territorial protection is not the result of active steps taken by either party. Action to prevent imports from third countries will cause loss of the exemption, if there is no alternative source of supply within the common market. The Regulation expires at the end of 1997.

Exclusive purchasing agreements

Under an exclusive purchasing agreement goods are supplied to a reseller who undertakes to obtain his requirements exclusively from the

[35] On the meaning of "agreements to which only two undertakings are party," see Case 170/ 83 *Hydrotherm Geraetebau* v. *Andreoli loc. cit.* note 8, p. 354, *supra*.
[36] Case 1/70 *Parfums Marcel Rochas* v. *Bitsch* [1970] E.C.R. 515; [1971] C.M.L.R. 104.
[37] Case 126/80 *Salonia* v. *Poidomani* [1981] E.C.R. 1563; [1982] 1 C.M.L.R. 64.
[38] For an example of an agreement relating to the whole common market, see *Re Duro-Dyne/ Europair* O.J. 1975 L29/11; [1975] 1 C.M.L.R. D62.
[39] The turnover threshold is further defined by Art. 5.

supplier. In contrast to exclusive distribution agreements, there is no obligation on the supplier to refrain from delivering the contract product to
other resellers in the same area and at the same level of distribution. The
incentive for the reseller lies in security of supply, which may be reinforced
with various forms of help in equipping or running his business. Arrangements of this kind may streamline distribution, though they carry a danger
of shutting other suppliers who are potential competitors out of the market. The approach adopted by the Commission in Regulation 1984/83 was
to lay down conditions for the block exemption of exclusive purchasing
agreements in general, while making specific provision, in the light of
investigations of the sectors concerned, in relation to beer supply (or "tied
house") agreements and service station (or "solus") agreements.

The general provisions of the Regulation are found in Title I. Under
Article 1, block exemption is granted in respect of "agreements to which
only two undertakings are party and whereby one party, the reseller,
agrees with the other, the supplier, to purchase certain goods specified in
the agreement for resale only from the supplier or from a connected undertaking or from another undertaking which the supplier has entrusted with
the sale of his goods." The only restriction of competition Article 2 allows
to be imposed on the supplier without loss of exemption is the obligation
not to compete directly with the reseller in his principal sales area: the supplier cannot be prevented from appointing other resellers in that area. The
reseller may be required not to manufacture or sell goods competing with
the contract goods and he may accept marketing obligations similar to
those allowed under the exclusive distribution Regulation. Article 3
excludes the block exemption in the case of agreements between competing manufacturers (subject again to the turnover threshold of 100 million
ECUs if the agreement is non-reciprocal) and of agreements that involve
"tying."[40] It also imposes a limit of five years on the duration of agreements qualifying for exemption.

Title II contains the special provisions for beer supply agreements.
These are defined by Article 6(1) as "agreements to which only two undertakings are party and whereby one party, the reseller, agrees with the
other, the supplier, in consideration for according special commercial or
financial advantages, to purchase only from the supplier . . . certain beers,
or certain beers and certain other drinks, specified in the agreement for
resale in premises used for the sale and consumption of drinks and designated in the agreement." The subject-matter of agreements eligible for
exemption may, therefore, either be beers, specified by brand or type in
the agreement, or beers together with other specified drinks: exclusive purchasing agreements relating, e.g., to spirits but not to beer are not covered.
Examples of "special commercial or financial advantages" accorded in consideration of an exclusive purchasing obligation would be a loan on favourable terms, or the provision of business premises, equipment or fittings.[41]
The description of the resale premises would cover a public house, club or

---

[40] The language of Art. 3(c) reflects that of Art. 85(1)(e) EEC. See the discussion of tying in
the context of Art. 86, infra.
[41] See the 13th recital to the Reg.

restaurant but an agreement between a supplier and an off-licence retailer would fall under Title I. Article 6(2) extends the scope of the exemption to, *inter alia*, agreements providing for the transmission of an exclusive purchasing obligation from the owner of licensed premises to his tenant or from an owner or tenant to his successor in title. Restrictions on competition additional to the exclusive purchasing obligation, which may be imposed on the reseller without loss of the block exemption, are set out in Article 7. He may, in particular, be put under an obligation not to sell beers or other drinks supplied by other undertakings which are of the same type as those supplied under the agreement. The sale of draught beers of a different type to those specified in the agreement may also be restricted, but not where the sale of such beers in draught form is customary or where there is sufficient consumer demand for it. Any other curb on the freedom of the reseller to choose his suppliers will bring denial of exemption under Article 8. The Article places a limit of five years on the duration of qualifying agreements where the exclusive purchasing obligation relates to specified beers and other drinks and of ten years where it relates to beers only. However, where the reseller occupies the designated premises under a lease or licence from the supplier, the time limit is extended for as long as he carries on business there. Because of the reseller's special vulnerability to pressure in such circumstances, in order to qualify for exemption the agreement must expressly preserve his right to obtain drinks other than beer from other sources, where the supplier does not match the terms or deal in the brands that are on offer.

Title III provides in a similar way for solus agreements. According to Article 10, the subject-matter of the agreement in question may be either "certain petroleum-based motor vehicle fuels," such as petrol, diesel and LPG, or those fuels together with "other fuels," such as heating oil, bottled gas and paraffin. Article 11 permits a ban on the sale of competing fuels, and also on the use of competing lubricants, though as to the latter only where the supplier has made available or financed a lubrication bay or other equipment. In Article 12, as in Article 8, an attempt is made to preserve the freedom of the reseller, apart from the exclusive purchasing obligation and any ban on dealing in competing products, to obtain goods and services where he chooses. The maximum duration of exempted agreements is ten years, except that, once again, the time limit does not apply where the designated premises are operated by the reseller under a lease or licence from the supplier. This regulation, too, expires at the end of 1997.

Motor vehicle distribution and servicing agreements

Exclusive dealing agreements in the motor vehicle sector may be eligible for exemption under the general regulations on exclusive distribution and exclusive purchasing agreements. However, the Commission took the view that certain restrictions not covered by those Regulations may be acceptable in the special circumstances of the motor trade. In particular, given the nature of motor vehicles as consumer durables requiring expert maintenance, not always in the same location, throughout their useful lives, consumers may benefit from close co-operation between a manufacturer and his dealers, which guarantees specialised servicing. Regulation 123/85[42] on motor vehicle distribution and servicing agreements was accordingly adopted, though it is expressly provided that the Regulation shall not apply where the scope of the block exemption in Regulation 1983/83 or Regulation 1984/83 is wider.

The class of agreements to which the new block exemption applies is defined in Article 1 of the Regulation. It consists of bilateral agreements under which one party undertakes to supply exclusively to the other party (or to that party and a specified number of other undertakings within the distribution system) for resale "certain motor vehicles intended for use on public roads and having three or more road wheels, together with spare parts therefor." Article 2 allows the supplier to be put under an additional obligation not to sell contract goods to final consumers or to provide them with servicing for such goods within the contract territory.

The various restrictions and obligations that may be imposed on dealers in a distribution network are set out in Articles 3 and 4. Dealers may be required, *inter alia*: not to sell new vehicles or spare parts from another manufacturer which compete with contract goods; not to conclude with third parties distribution or servicing agreements for competing goods; to impose similar conditions on their subcontractors; not to maintain a branch or depot or to seek customers for contract goods outside the contract territory nor to subcontract distribution or servicing outside the territory; not to supply contract goods to dealers outside the network. Obligations to ensure the provision of customer services and active exploitation of the market include: observance of minimum standards with regard to equipment, technical facilities, staff training, advertising and the collection, storage, delivery and servicing of contract goods; endeavouring to meet a minimum sales quota; keeping stocks at an appropriate level; and performing guarantee work.

Of considerable interest are the conditions in Article 5 which have to be satisfied before the benefit of the Regulation can be claimed. These are designed to prevent competition from being unduly restricted and, more especially, to avoid compartmentalisation of the common market. Dealers are required to undertake to honour guarantees and carry out servicing on contract goods supplied anywhere in the common market by or with the consent of the manufacturer.[43] The Decision in *Re Ford Werke*[44] is reflected in the requirement that the manufacturer "supply to the dealer, for the purpose of performance of a contract of sale concluded between the dealer and a final consumer in the common market, any passenger car which corresponds to a model within the contract programme and which is marketed by the manufacturer or with the manufacturer's consent in the Member State in which the vehicle is to be registered." This should serve

---

[42] O.J. 1984 L15/16. An explanatory Notice was provided: O.J. 1985 L17/4.
[43] *Cf. Re Fiat* [1984] 2 C.M.L.R. 497 (Press Release). To obtain a refund under Fiat's guarantee system, the vehicle had to be presented for examination by the dealer who originally supplied it. This obviously created difficulties for customers who bought vehicles in other Member States. The system was changed, following intervention by the Commission.
[44] *Loc. cit.* note 82, p. 381, *supra*.

as a deterrent to refusals to supply by manufacturers wishing to protect their dealers in high priced markets against competition from individual imports. To ensure the effectiveness of the provision, while the consent of the manufacturer to the modification of the contract goods may generally be required, a dealer may not be prevented from modifying a particular vehicle (*e.g.* from left hand to right hand drive) which has been purchased by a final consumer.[45]

Article 6 denies block exemption where the parties to the agreement are both motor vehicle manufacturers; as also where a dealer is under an obligation to apply minimum resale prices or maximum trade discounts.

Circumstances in which the benefit of the Regulation may be withdrawn from otherwise qualified agreements are identified in Article 10. Two such circumstances deserve special mention: where a manufacturer or dealer makes strenuous efforts, by means not allowed under the Regulation, to hinder final consumers from purchasing, or obtaining servicing for, contract goods within the common market; and where, over a considerable period, prices and conditions of sale vary substantially between different Member States, and this is chiefly due to obligations covered by the block exemption.[46] The Regulation expires on June 30, 1995.

Specialisation agreements

Under a typical specialisation agreement each party will give up the manufacture of specified products, leaving the other to concentrate his efforts in that field. Mutual renunciation of activities is often accompanied by arrangements for mutual exclusive dealing, so that the parties will have an assured outlet for, and an assured supply of, their respective specialities. The likely benefits of specialisation in terms of improved efficiency have to be weighed against the consequences of the agreed cessation of competition between the parties. The more powerful the parties, and the larger the share of the market affected, the more serious those consequences are liable to be. The broad policy of Regulation 417/85,[47] like that of the original measure which it replaces,[48] is to grant block exemption to specialisation agreements on terms that are fairly generous, subject to specified thresholds designed to prevent the elimination of competition in respect of a substantial part of the products in question.

According to Article 1, the block exemption applies to agreements under which the parties "accept reciprocal obligations: (a) not to manufacture certain products or to have them manufactured, but to leave it to other parties to manufacture the products or have them manufactured; or (b) to manufacture certain products or have them manufactured only jointly." A

---

[45] Art. 3(1).
[46] In its Notice the Commission announced that it did not intend to take action where the difference in list prices for similar vehicles did not exceed 12 per cent. of the lower price over a period of a year or 18 per cent. over a lesser period; where the difference affected an insignificant number of the vehicles covered by the agreement; or where it was attributable to the levels of national taxation or price controls.
[47] O.J. 1985 L53/1.
[48] Reg. 2779/72, O.J. 1972 L292/23. Amended and extended by Reg. 2903/77, O.J. 1977 L338/14.

non-reciprocal obligation to cease production is not within the Regulation.[49] A line may have to be drawn between specialisation and market sharing. In *Re Italian Cast Glass*[50] arrangements fixing quotas for sales in Italy of certain types of cast glass were found not to constitute genuine specialisation. The Commission noted, *inter alia*, that the arrangements could not be justified with reference to objective criteria such as the parties' production facilities or the intrinsic characteristics of the product; and they applied only to output destined for the Italian market.

Article 2 allows the inclusion of an obligation not to enter into specialisation agreements with third parties relating to identical or competing products, and of exclusive purchasing and exclusive distribution provisions.[51] It is also permissible to require one of the parties to supply the others with products which are the subject of specialisation and to maintain minimum stocks of, and provide customer and guarantee services for, such products.

The thresholds governing the availability of the block exemption are found in Article 3. In the first place, the products which are the subject of specialisation, and other competing products of the participating undertakings, must not represent more than 20 per cent. of the market for such products in a substantial part of the common market. Secondly, the aggregate annual turnover of all the participating undertakings must not exceed 500 million ECUs. The thresholds may be exceeded by up to 10 per cent. in any two consecutive financial years without the loss of exemption.

An opposition procedure is provided under Article 4, where the turnover threshold (but not the market share threshold) is exceeded. The Regulation expires at the end of 1997.

Research and development agreements

Agreements on joint research and development up to, but not including, the stage of industrial application are among the forms of permissible co-operation recognised by the Commission's Notice of 1968.[52] However, as we have seen, the Notice is narrow in scope and does not apply, for example, where the object or effect of an agreement is to prevent the parties from carrying on independent research. In practice, the Commission has usually found that research and development agreements are liable to restrict competition and affect trade between Member States, at least potentially, but has been willing to grant them exemption in view of their expected contribution towards improving production and promoting technical and economic progress. Experience gained over the years in dealing with individual notifications have now made possible the grant of a block exemption by Regulation 418/85.[53]

Article 1 of the Regulation confers exemption on three classes of agree-

---

[49] *Re Prym/Beka loc. cit.* note 87, p. 382, *supra*.
[50] Loc. cit. note 38, p. 374, *supra*.
[51] Exemption in the case of an exclusive purchasing obligation is subject to the proviso that the purchaser must be free to accept more favourable terms offered by a third party which the party charged with manufacturing the contract product is unwilling to match: see Art. 2(1)(*b*).
[52] Discussed at pp. 372–374, *supra*.
[53] O.J. 1985 L53/5.

ments: those for joint research and development of products or processes and joint exploitation of the result; those for joint exploitation of the results of research and development jointly carried out under a prior agreement between the parties; and those for joint research and development, without subsequent exploitation (in so far as they fall within Article 85(1)).[54] As defined in the Article, "exploitation" includes the manufacture of products, the application of processes and the assignment or licensing of intellectual property rights but not, it seems, distribution or selling. This is consistent with the practice of the Commission, which has been ready to acknowledge the advantages of joint production, such as the possibility of achieving economies of scale, while treating collaboration at the marketing stage with much greater reserve.[55]

Article 2 lays down conditions that must be satisfied if the exemption is to apply. The joint research and development work must be carried out under a programme defining its objectives and the relative field. All parties must have access to the results of the work and, if there is not to be joint exploitation, each of them must be free to exploit the results independently. Any joint exploitation must be limited to results which are protected by intellectual property rights or which constitute know-how; and the result must be decisive for the manufacture of the contract product or the application of the contract processes. Finally, any joint venture or third party charged with manufacture of the products must be required to supply them exclusively to the parties, while undertakings charged with manufacture by way of specialisation must be required to fulfil orders from all of the parties.

The provisions of Article 3 aim to prevent the substantial elimination of competition as a result of the agreement. Where two or more of the parties are competing manufacturers of products which may be improved or replaced by the contract products, block exemption is only available if their combined share of the market does not exceed 20 per cent. The Article also seeks to limit the duration of joint exploitation. Whether the parties are competitors or not, exemption will be lost five years after the contract products are first put on to the common market, if by then output of those products, together with the parties' combined output of competing products, exceeds 20 per cent. of the total market for such products in a substantial part of the common market.

The "white" list of restrictions in Article 4 includes an obligation not to carry out independent research and development in the field to which the programme relates and an obligation to procure the contract product exclusively from other parties, a joint venture or third parties. This is supplemented by the list in Article 5 containing obligations not thought to fall within Article 85(1), but which are mentioned in case exceptionally they should require exemption, e.g. an obligation to protect intellectual property rights and know-how. The "black" list in Article 6 of terms that

---

[54] In Re BP/Kellog loc. cit. note 36, p. 374, supra, an agreement was found not to be within the block exemption because the restrictions imposed on the parties extended to products and processes they had not developed together. However, individual exemption was granted.

[55] e.g. Re Henkel/Colgate loc. cit. note 28, p. 373, supra.

exclude the block exemption reflect two main preoccupations of the Commission: that restrictions should not be allowed to extend into fields unconnected with the programme, or beyond the date of its completion; and that the parties should be free to compete at the marketing stage.

Article 7 provides an opposition procedure for agreements within Article 1, which fulfil the conditions in Articles 2 and 3 and are not caught by Article 6.

Under Article 10 the Commission has the usual power to withdraw exemption in respect of individual agreements, *e.g.* where, without any objectively valid reason, the parties do not exploit the results of the joint research and development. The Regulation expires at the end of 1997.

CHAPTER 15

ABUSE OF A DOMINANT POSITION

Introduction

The Court of Justice has said that "Articles 85 and 86 seek to achieve the same aim on different levels, *viz.* the maintenance of effective competition within the common market."[1] The "level" at which Article 86 operates is that of seeking to neutralise the adverse consequences of an absence of effective competition.

Dominant undertakings may conduct their business efficiently, keeping down prices and maintaining or improving the quality of their product; indeed, the existence of a dominant position may have positive economic advantages, *e.g.* enabling the undertaking in question to pursue an adventurous research and development policy. On the other hand, insulation from competitive pressure is liable to encourage bad habits: *e.g.* an undertaking may choose to limit its output and charge high prices rather than to increase its output and charge lower prices. The function of Article 86 is to ensure that the market conduct of dominant undertakings remains consistent with the objectives of the EEC Treaty. As the Court explained in the *Michelin* case:

"A finding that an undertaking has a dominant position is not in itself a recrimination but simply means that, irrespective of the reasons for which it has such a dominant position, the undertaking concerned has a special responsibility not to allow its conduct to impair genuine undistorted competition on the common market."[2]

Article 86 provides:

"Any abuse by one or more undertakings of a dominant position within the common market or in a substantial part of it shall be prohibited as incompatible with the common market in so far as it may affect trade between Member States. Such abuse may, in particular, consist in:

(a) directly or indirectly imposing unfair purchase or selling prices or other unfair trading conditions;

(b) limiting production, markets or technical development to the prejudice of consumers;

(c) applying dissimilar conditions to equivalent transactions with other trading parties, thereby placing them at a competitive disadvantage;

(d) making the conclusion of contracts subject to acceptance by the other parties of supplementary obligations which, by their

---

[1] Case 6/72 *Europemballage and Continental Can* v. *Commission* [1973] E.C.R. 215 at p. 244; [1973] C.M.L.R. 199.
[2] Case 322/81 *NV Nederlandsche Banden-Industrie Michelin* v. *Commission* [1983] E.C.R. 3461 at p. 3511.

nature or according to commercial usage, have no connection
with the subject of such contracts."

The concept of a dominant position

The EEC Treaty does not define a dominant position,[3] but the meaning
and scope of the concept have been clarified by the practice of the Commission and the case law of the Court of Justice.

In a famous passage of its *Continental Can* Decision the Commission
identified as the hallmark of dominance overall independence of behaviour
on the market. The Commission stated:

> "Undertakings are in a dominant position when they have the power
> to behave independently, which puts them in a position to act without
> taking into account their competitors, purchasers or suppliers. That is
> the position when, because of their share of the market, or of their
> share of the market combined with the availability of technical knowl-
> edge, raw materials or capital, they have the power to determine
> prices or to control production or distribution for a significant part of
> the products in question. This power does not necessarily have to
> derive from an absolute domination permitting the undertakings
> which hold it to eliminate all will on the part of their economic
> partners, but it is enough that they be strong enough as a whole to
> ensure to those undertakings an overall independence of behaviour,
> even if there are differences in intensity in their influence on the differ-
> ent partial markets."[4]

This formulation was described by Advocate-General Roemer in his
Opinion relating to the *Continental Can* case as being "obviously in agreement with the prevailing opinion and with tests legally laid down."[5]

The definition of a dominant position which has become the standard
one was first put forward by the European Court in *United Brands*.[6]
According to this definition, as formulated in the Court's *Michelin* judgment, a dominant position consists of

> "a position of economic strength enjoyed by an undertaking which
> enables it to hinder the maintenance of effective competition on the
> relevant market by allowing it to behave to an appreciable extent inde-

---

[3] *Cf.* Art. 66(7) ECSC which speaks of undertakings holding or acquiring in the market for
one of the products within the jurisdiction of the High Authority (now the Commission) "a
dominant position shielding them against effective competition in a substantial part of the
common market." The importance not only of this provision, but of Arts. 65 and 66 ECSC
as a whole, in the interpretation of Art. 86 has been stressed by Schröter in Van Damme,
Regulating the behaviour of monopolies and dominant undertakings in Community law, at
pp. 446 *et seq.*

[4] J.O. 1972 L 7/25 at L/35. Tr. from [1972] C.M.L.R. D11 at D35. In a Memorandum published on December 1, 1965, the Commission had put forward a wider definition of a dominant position, emphasising the ability of the undertaking or undertakings concerned to
influence the behaviour of other operators in a substantial and foreseeable way: see EEC,
Serie Concurrence 3, *Le problème de la concentration dans le marché commun* (Brussels
1966). *Cf.* the definition suggested by the group of professors which the Commission had
appointed in 1963 to advise it on the interpretation of Art. 86, *ibid.* .

[5] [1973] E.C.R. at p. 257.

[6] Case 27/76 *United Brands Company* v. *Commission* [1978] E.C.R. 207 at p. 277; [1978] 1
C.M.L.R. 429.

pendently of its competitors and customers and ultimately of consumers."[7]

The concept, therefore, refers to the economic power of the undertaking concerned, which frees it from the constraints normally imposed by dealing at arms length on a competitive market. This liberation is qualified: in *Continental Can* the Commission used the phrase "*overall* independence of behaviour,"[8] while the Court speaks of "power to behave *to an appreciable extent* independently" (emphasis added). So understood, a dominant position is compatible with the survival of some competition.[9] It will be sufficient if the undertaking in question is able "at least to have an appreciable influence on the conditions under which that competition will develop, and in any case to act largely in disregard of it so long as such conduct does not operate to its detriment."[10]

Thus in the *United Brands* case it was admitted that UBC encountered very lively competition in Denmark and Germany during 1973 when other banana suppliers had mounted advertising and promotional campaigns and had cut their prices; while in the Netherlands competition had pushed banana prices below those in Germany, which was traditionally a lower priced market. Indeed, the European Court seems to have accepted, for the sake of argument, UBC's claim that its banana division had made a loss over several years. However, not only was the competition limited in its duration and its geographical scope, it was also finally ineffective: UBC had suffered no significant reduction of its market share, while remaining the highest priced supplier. Of course, if UBC had been forced by the tactics of its competitors to sustain continuing losses over a long period, at some point its "overall independence of behaviour" would have been put in question.[11]

Although dominant positions more often relate to the supply of goods or services, it must not be forgotten that they may also exist on the demand side. For instance Eurofima,[12] an agency set up by a number of national railway administrations to supply them with rolling stock of standard design, was regarded by the Commission as a dominant customer for a new form of passenger carriage for which tenders had been invited. The terms offered by Eurofima, which appeared to the Commission to be extremely

---

[7] [1984] E.C.R. at p. 3503. See also Case 85/76 *Hoffmann-La Roche* v. *Commission* [1979] 461 at p. 520; Case 31/80 *NV L'Oreal und SA L'Oreal* v. *PVBA De Nieuwe AMCK* [1980] E.C.R. 3775 at p. 3793; Case 311/84 *Centre Belge d'Etudes de Marché—Télé-marketing SA* v. *Commission* (not yet reported). The definition echoes references in earlier judgments of the Court to "the power to impede the maintenance of effective competition," see Case 40/70 *Sirena* v. *Eda* [1979] E.C.R. 69 at p. 83; [1971] C.M.L.R. 260; Case 78/70 *Deutsche Grammophon* v. *Metro* [1971] E.C.R. 487 at p. 501; [1971] C.M.L.R. 631; Joined Cases 40–48, 50, 54 to 56, 111, 113 and 114/73, *Suiker Unie and Others* v. *Commission (Sugar)* [1975] E.C.R. 1663 at pp. 1978 and 1994; [1976] 1 C.M.L.R. 295.

[8] In its *BP* Decision the Commission referred to the ability of a firm "to act *fully* independently" (emphasis added): see O.J. 1977 L 117/1. However, it is thought this apparent adoption of an absolutist standard should be attributed to defective drafting.

[9] Case 85/76 *Hoffmann-La Roche* v. *Commission* [1979] E.C.R. at p. 520.

[10] *Ibid.*

[11] In the *Michelin* case the Court similarly brushed aside the argument that NBIM had been incurring losses, remarking that "*temporary* unprofitability or even losses are not inconsistent with the existence of a dominant position" (emphasis added): [1983] E.C.R. at p. 3511.

[12] [1973] C.M.L.R. D 217. See also Comp.Rep. 1973, p. 60.

harsh, were amended without a formal decision being necessary. Another example of dominance as a purchaser would be that of companies with the exclusive right to provide television services in a Member State, in respect of the market for materials for broadcasting.[13]

The existence of a dominant position[14]

It now seems to be well-established in Community law that the process of determining the existence of a dominant position in a particular case should normally comprise two distinct stages: first the definition of the relevant market; and secondly, the assessment of the strength of the undertaking in question on that market.[15]

The relevant market

This expression is used to designate the field of competitive forces within which the undertaking operates in either satisfying, or obtaining satisfaction of a certain demand. The aim of defining the relevant market is to differentiate between those performances of other undertakings which must be taken into account in evaluating the position of the undertaking subject to the investigation, and those which can safely be left out of account for this purpose. The two main questions to be answered are how wide a range of products, and what geographical distribution of offers, should be covered by the evaluation. Sometimes, in addition, the timing of the offers may be significant. These three criteria of relevance—material, geographic and temporal—will be examined separately.

(i) *The material criterion or product market.* The definition of the product market is not always an easy matter because, on the one hand, things which are physically dissimilar may be in competition with regard to a particular application (*e.g.* oil and gas domestic heating systems) while on the other hand, things which are physically similar may not be in competition (*e.g.* tyres for heavy vehicles and tyres for vans or motor cars[16]). It will usually be an advantage for the undertaking in question to have the product market defined as widely as possible, since the greater the variety of products involved, the more difficult it will be to make out the existence of a dominant position.

Various tests to help in the delineation of product markets have become part of the common currency of competition jurisdictions.[17] The funda-

---

[13] See *e.g.* the complaint that was the subject of the proceedings in Case 298/83 *C.I.C.C.E.* v. *Commission*, 1985 (not yet reported).

[14] For a critical view of the Court's analysis of the existence of a dominant position, see Baden Fuller, (1979) 4 E.L.Rev. 423. See also Gyselen and Kyriazis, (1986) 11 E.L.Rev. 134.

[15] See the structure of the judgments in Case 27/76 *United Brands, loc. cit.* note 6, *supra*; Case 85/76 *Hoffmann-La Roche, loc. cit.* note 7, *supra*; Case 322/81 *Michelin, loc. cit.* note 2, *supra.* See also the strong statement by the Court in Case 31/80 *L'Oreal, loc. cit.* note 7, *supra* at p. 3793.

[16] See Case 322/81 *Michelin, loc. cit.* note 2, *supra* and the discussion, *infra*, of the issue of the relevant product market in that case.

[17] The American experience has been particularly influential. See the useful discussion by Holley in Van Damme, *op. cit.* note 3, *supra*, p. 201.

mental test is that of the interchangeability of product X and product Y as to their end uses.[18] In the words of the European Court,

" . . . the possibilities of competition must be judged in the context of the market comprising the totality of the products which, with respect to their characteristics, are particularly suitable for satisfying constant needs and are only to a limited extent interchangeable with other products."[19]

The Court has stressed, however, that examination should not be limited to the objective characteristics of the products in question: "the competitive conditions and the structure of supply and demand on the market must also be taken into consideration."[20] A test which sometimes proves useful, since it focuses on the real reactions of consumers, is "cross-elasticity of demand." By this is meant the degree to which sales of X increase in response to an increase in the price of Y; high elasticity, *i.e.* a substantial increase in the quantity of X sold when the price of Y rises only slightly, provides a clear indication of competition between the products. There is also the narrower test of "peculiar characteristics and uses," which makes the common sense point that highly specialised products are likely to be found on a separate market.[21] It must, though, be stressed that these and similar tests are only capable of guiding analysis in a rough and ready way.

The operation of the test of limited interchangeability may be illustrated by the *United Brands*[22] case on the supply of bananas to certain of the Member States. The proceedings arose out of the condemnation of the supplier concerned, the United Brands Company (UBC), by the Commission on four counts of abusive conduct contrary to Article 86. According to the Commission, the product market consisted of "bananas of all varieties, where branded or unbranded." On the other hand, UBC argued that bananas formed part of the general market for fresh fruit: in other words, customers make their choice freely between bananas and other varieties of fruit on the basis of availability and relative prices. If this were so, even a very large supplier of bananas like UBC would not be at liberty to set prices within a wide range, since allowance would have to be made for the risk of potential customers altering their preferences (assuming of course that the same company did not control the supply of other fruits). The Court said that:

"For the banana to be regarded as forming a market which is sufficiently differentiated from other fruit markets it must be possible for it to be singled out by such special features distinguishing it from other fruits that it is only to a limited extent interchangeable with them and

---

[18] A well known example from the United States is the *Du Pont* case where there was held to be competition as to end use, and hence a single market, between cellophane and other flexible packaging materials: see *United States* v. *Du Pont de Nemours*, 1956 Trade Cases s.68, 369 (Sup.Ct.) discussed by Holley *loc. cit.* note 17, *supra*, at pp. 147–149.

[19] Case 31/80 *L'Oreal* [1980] E.C.R. at p. 3793; Case 322/81 *Michelin* [1983] E.C.R. at p. 3505.

[20] Case 322/81 *Michelin, ibid.*

[21] *e.g.* the different groups of vitamins in Case 85/76 *Hoffmann-La Roche* v. *Commission, loc. cit.* note 7, *supra*.

[22] Case 27/76 *United Brands Company* v. *Commission, loc. cit.* note 6, *supra*. See also the Dec. of the Commission (entitled *Chiquita*), O.J. 1976 L 95/1; [1976] 1 C.M.L.R. D28.

it is only exposed to their competition in a way that is hardly perceptible."[23]

In the Court's view, the test was satisfied. It noted, in particular, the year-
round excess of banana supplies over demand, which enabled marketing to
be adapted to the seasonal fluctuations of other fruits. There was no
evidence of "significant long term cross-elasticity," nor of "seasonal substi-
tutability in general between the banana and all the seasonal fruits," the
latter occurring only in Germany in respect of peaches and table grapes.
Bananas, also, had characteristics enabling them to play an important
part in the diet of a large section of the population comprising the very
old, the very young and the sick. The constant needs of such consumers,
and the limited and sporadic nature of the competition, justified recognition of the separate entity of the banana market.

The question arises whether perhaps, the relevant market in this case
ought to have been defined still more narrowly, in terms of a separate market for all branded bananas, or of a separate market for the "Chiquita"
brand of UBC. Such fragmentation of the market might be the result of
building up consumer preferences for the branded fruit by advertising and
by maintaining a consistently high quality. That some development of this
kind had taken place is suggested by the difference of 30 to 40 per cent.
between the prices of UBC's branded and unbranded bananas.[24] The
Commission, however, did not examine this possibility in its Decision (so
that there was no call for the Court to do so), presumably because it felt
sufficiently confident of proving the dominance of UBC on the general
banana market; had there been any doubt on the matter it might have
seemed worthwhile to establish the independence of the narrower market.

Interchangeability must be considered on the supply side of the market
as well as on the demand side. This was brought home by the quashing of
the Decision of the Commission in *Continental Can Company*.[25] The Commission had found that the acquisition of a Dutch packaging firm, Thomas-
sen en Drijver-Verblifa (TDV), by the Continental Can subsidiary,
Europemballage Corporation, amounted to an abuse of the dominant position which the American firm enjoyed, through its German subsidiary,
Schmalbach-Lubecke-Werke (SLW) on the market in Germany for meat
tins, fish tins and metal closures for glass jars; the abuse consisting of an
unacceptable strengthening of SLW's position on the markets concerned
since, in the Commission's view, TDV had been a potential competitor of
SLW. The main ground for the annulment of the Decision was that the
Commission had not shown convincingly why manufacturers, *e.g.* of tins
for vegetables, condensed milk, olive oil or fruit juice could not, by making
some adaptation to their product, enter the field as serious competitors to
SLW, if the latter raised its prices unduly. The Commission was also criticised for not dealing adequately with the possibility that SLW's major customers might begin to manufacture the relevant types of container
themselves. The essence of these objections was that potential competition

[23] [1978] E.C.R. at p. 272.
[24] See the note by Korah on the Dec. of the Commission, (1975–76) 1 E.L.Rev. 322 at p. 324.
[25] Case 6/72 *Europemballage and Continental Can* v. *Commission*, *loc. cit.* note 1, *supra*.

from new products or new producers ("elasticity of supply") had not been ruled out.

In the *Michelin*[26] case analysis of the structure of both supply and demand contributed crucially to the definition of the product market. The case concerned a decision of the Commission that NBIM, the Dutch subsidiary of the Michelin tyre group, was guilty of infringing Article 86 because of certain terms included in the contracts under which it supplied dealers. The Court of Justice approved the Commission's definition of the market as that in new "replacement" tyres for heavy vehicles. This market was distinguishable from: (a) the market in "original equipment" tyres; (b) the market in tyres for cars and light vans; and (c) the market in retreads. As to (a), it was common ground that the structure of demand for replacements was entirely different from that for original equipment tyres, although they were identical products: while the former were supplied to dealers for retail sale, the latter were supplied to manufacturers to be fitted to new vehicles. As to (b), besides the lack of interchangeability at user level between car and van tyres and heavy vehicle tyres, there was again a difference of demand structures. For car and van drivers the purchase of tyres was an occasional event; whereas buyers of heavy vehicle tyres were normally haulage undertakings for which tyres represented an important business cost and which expected specialised advice and services from dealers. Nor was there elasticity of supply between tyres for light and heavy vehicles: the time and expenditure needed to switch production from one to the other made this impracticable as a way of responding to fluctuations in demand.[27] As to (c), the Court acknowledged that retreads were to some extent interchangeable, and hence in competition, with new tyres, but not sufficiently to undermine a dominant position on the market for the latter. Some consumers had reservations, whether rightly or wrongly, about the safety and reliability of retreads. In addition, a significant proportion of retreads used by transport undertakings were made to order from their own tyre carcasses. These would not compete with new tyres, since their production involved the provision of a service directly by retreading firms to the tyre owners. A further consideration was the dependence of the market for retreads, with respect to price and supply, on the market for new tyres. Every retread must have started life as a new tyre; and there was a limit to the number of times retreading could be done. So a dominant supplier of new tyres would have a privileged position *vis-à-vis* retreading undertakings. On an opposite tack, NBIM had suggested that the various types and sizes of tyres for heavy vehicles could be regarded as belonging to separate markets, because from a user's point of view they were not interchangeable. That suggestion was rejected by the Court on

---

[26] Case 322/81 *loc. cit.* note 2, *supra*.

[27] The Court noted that in 1977, when there was a shortfall in the supply of heavy vehicle tyres, NBIM chose to grant an extra bonus rather than use surplus car tyre capacity to meet demand: [1983] E.C.R. at p. 3506. *Cf.* the *Continental Can* case, *loc. cit.* note 1, *supra*, where the Dec. of the Commission adverted to the barriers to market entry confronting possible competitors, notably the size of the necessary investments, but the Court did not think the burden of proof had been discharged.

the ground that dealers had to be ready to meet demand from their customers for the whole range of such tyres. Also, in the absence of specialisation on the part of the undertakings concerned, the similarity between heavy vehicle tyres of different types and sizes and the way in which they complemented one another at the technical level meant they were subject to the same conditions of competition on the market.

Prior economic choices by a consumer may narrow the range of offers from which future demands have to be met. This phenomenon is sometimes referred to as "lock-in."[28] It operates where the opportunity cost of reversing a choice is felt to outweigh the advantages in the longer term of doing so. For instance, oil, gas and other domestic fuels may form a single market from the point of view of a person contemplating the installation of a new central heating system, but not after one or other system has been installed. Similar reasoning may apply where spare parts for a consumer durable are available only from the manufacturer. In *Hugin*[29] the Court found that most of the spare parts for Hugin cash registers were not interchangeable with parts made to fit any other type of machine, so that the operator of an independent maintenance, repair or reconditioning business, was entirely dependent on Hugin for supplies. The relevant market was, accordingly, that for Hugin spare parts required by such businesses. This was a crucial issue in the case, since the share held by Hugin of the market for cash registers as such was very modest.[30]

One issue in *Commercial Solvents Corporation*[31] was whether the market for a raw material (or base or intermediate product) may be considered separately from the market for the end product. The case arose from a complaint to the Commission by the Italian pharmaceutical firm, Zoja, that CSC, through its Italian subsidiary, Istituto, had refused to supply it with aminobutanol, the base product for the manufacture of the drug ethambutol, which was used in the treatment of tuberculosis. CSC contended, *inter alia*, that the relevant market could not be that for aminobutanol, on which its dominance was relatively easy to prove, since the derivative, ethambutol, formed part of a wider market for anti-tubercular drugs. With this the Court disagreed:

> "Contrary to the arguments of the applicants it is in fact possible to distinguish the market in raw material necessary for the manufacture of a product from the market on which the product is sold. An abuse of a dominant position on the market in raw materials may thus have effects restricting competition in the market on which the derivatives

---

[28] See the discussion of lock-in by Gyselen and Kyriazis, *op. cit.* note 14, *supra* at pp. 143–144.

[29] Case 27/28 *Hugin Kassaregister AB* v. *Commission* [1979] E.C.R. 1869; [1979] 3 C.M.L.R. 345. For the Dec. of the Commission, see O.J. 1978 L22/23; [1978] 1 C.M.L.R. D 19. But see the criticism of Baden Fuller, *op. cit.* note 14, *supra* at pp. 426–427.

[30] Hugin had a market share of 12 per cent. in the common market as a whole and 13 per cent. in the U.K. Its largest competitor, the American company, National Cash Register had shares of 36 per cent. and 40 per cent. respectively.

[31] Commission: J.O. 1972 L 299/51, [1973] C.M.L.R. D50. Court: Cases 6 and 7/73 *Istituto Chemioterapico Italiano and Commercial Solvents Corporation* v. *Commission* [1974] E.C.R. 223; [1974] 1 C.M.L.R. 309. *Cf.* Case 311/84 *Télémarketing, loc. cit.* note 7, *supra,* which concerned related markets for the provision of services.

of the raw material are sold and these effects must be taken into account when considering the effects of an infringement, even if the market for the derivative does not constitute a self-contained market."[32]

Thus, according to the Court, the raw material may constitute a relevant market in its own right; but it may still be valid, in determining whether a dominant position on that market has been abused, to take into account any anti-competitive effects which may have been felt on the market for the derivative.

(ii) *The geographic criterion.* The geographic distribution of producers and consumers may prevent effective competition from taking place between goods or services which in other circumstances would be readily interchangeable. For instance, a motorway café may be able to set its prices within a very wide range, because travellers are unwilling to make a detour in search of equivalent services offered by other establishments in the neighbourhood. It is, therefore, necessary in defining a relevant market for the purpose of Article 86 to identify the specific territory within which the interplay of supply and demand is to be considered. The starting point will normally be the sales area of the undertaking concerned, and the question will be whether the geographic market is co-terminous with that area, or wider or narrower in extent.

Factors obviously tending to promote geographic isolation would be a lack of transport facilities, or the cost of transportation relative to the value of a product, giving an unchallengeable advantage to local producers. The cost factor has been mentioned by the European Court as being of particular relevance in the case of the sugar market.[33] In other cases, the separation of a market may be due to government action, *e.g.* the Dutch price controls which, according to the Commission, during the oil supply crisis of November 1973 to March 1974 helped to create a separate market for petrol refined in the Netherlands.[34] Habit and commercial convenience may also play a part. In *Michelin*[35] the Court found that tyre companies operated on the Dutch market through local subsidiaries, to which local dealers looked for their supplies. The Commission had, therefore, been right in regarding the Netherlands as the area from which the competition facing NBIM mainly came.[36]

The chosen area must be one "where the conditions of competition are

---

[32] *Ibid.* pp. 249–250.
[33] Joined Cases 40–48, 50, 54–56, 111, 113 and 114/73, *Suiker Unie and others* v. *Commission*, *loc. cit.* note 7, *supra*.
[34] The price controls made it impractical for Dutch distributors to buy motor spirit on the world market, so that they were entirely dependent on local refiners: see O.J. 1977 L 117/1. The Decision of the Commission was annulled by the European Court: see Case 77/77 *B.P.* v. *Commission* [1978] E.C.R. 1511. On the reasons for the annulment, see *infra*. For a comment on the Decision, see Williams (1977) 2 E.L.Rev. 294; and on the judgment, see Laddie (1978) 3 E.L.Rev. 501.
[35] Case 322/81 *loc. cit.* note 2, *supra*.
[36] It was, of course, open to the Commission, in assessing the position of NBIM on the Netherlands market, to take into account the strength of the Michelin group as a whole: see *infra*.

sufficiently homogeneous for the effect of the economic power of the undertaking to be able to be evaluated."[37] In *United Brands* it was held that the Commission had been right to exclude France, Italy and the United Kingdom from the relevant market because, for historical reasons, each of these Member States applied a different preferential system in respect of banana imports (*e.g.* Commonwealth preference in the United Kingdom). On the other hand, a system of free competition was common to the six Member States included in the market.[38]

The market territory must also satisfy a *de minimis* rule which is implicit in the reference in Article 86 to "a dominant position within the common market or in a substantial part of it." The test of "a substantial part" is not the geographic extent of the territory in question but the economic importance of the market situated there. This was made clear in the *Sugar* judgment where the Court said:

> "For the purpose of determining whether a specific territory is large enough to amount to 'a substantial part of the common market' within the meaning of Article 86 of the Treaty the pattern and volume of the production and consumption of the said product as well as the habits and economic opportunities of vendors and purchasers must be considered."[39]

And after mentioning figures for sugar production and consumption in Belgium and in the whole Community between the marketing years 1968–69 and 1971–72, it concluded:

> "If the other criteria mentioned above are taken into account these market shares are sufficiently large for the area covered by Belgium and Luxembourg to be considered, so far as sugar is concerned, as a substantial part of the common market in this product."[40]

From the criteria cited, it can be seen that the Court was dealing in one breath with the two separate issues of the territorial extent of the relevant market, and the substantiality of that market. In determining the latter, the crucial consideration was the relative size of the Belgo-Luxembourg sugar market, as compared with the size of the sugar market in the whole Community.

Two comments seem called for on this *de minimis* rule. In the first place, because it is based on a principle of relativity, it is capable of being satisfied by markets which are, in absolute terms, extremely small, if the common market in the product concerned is itself small. For instance, the rule provided no impediment to the Commission's Decision in *General Motors Continental*: the product market was that for inspections, to ensure conformity with technical standards, of Opel vehicles imported into Belgium, a specialised service which by definition could be offered only in that

---

[37] See Case 27/76 *United Brands* v. *Commission*, [1978] E.C.R. at p. 270.
[38] The Court noted that in the six Member States concerned it had been possible for UBC to adopt an integrated marketing policy, centred on its Dutch subsidiary, United Brands Continentaal: *ibid.* at pp. 273–276.
[39] Joined Cases 40–48, 50, 54–56, 111, 113 and 114/73 *Suiker Unie and others* v. *Commission*, [1975] E.C.R. at p. 1977.
[40] *Ibid.*

country.[41] Secondly, it may be that the importance of the market should not be assessed with regard to purely quantitative criteria. In *BP*[42] the Advocate-General, Mr. Warner, found that on the Commission's reasoning as to the existence of a dominant position between the major oil companies and their customers during the supply crisis, the relevant market must have been the market for motor spirit among BP's regular customers, or at most, among its customers generally in the Netherlands. On BP's estimate that the Dutch market represented 4.8 per cent. of the common market for motor spirit, and given that BP held ten per cent. of the Dutch market, the relevant share of the common market could not have exceeded 0.48 per cent. Could a market below 0.5 per cent. be regarded as sufficiently substantial? Mr. Warner was prepared to accept as tenable the view that it could not be, but warned against focusing attention exclusively on percentages. He went on:

"The opposite of 'substantial' is 'negligible,' and what may seem negligible when looked at in terms of a percentage may seem otherwise when looked at in absolute terms. The population of Luxembourg is, I believe, about .23 per cent. of the population of the whole Community. I would however shrink from saying that one who had a monopoly, or near monopoly, of the Luxembourg market for a particular product was exempt from the application of Article 86. Similarly I would shrink from holding that BP's share of the Dutch market for motor spirit was negligible."[43]

At one time it used to be debated whether the territories of some of the smaller Member States would be large enough to satisfy the *de minimis* rule, or whether, *e.g.* the Benelux countries should be grouped together for this purpose.[44] What has been said above, shows that this debate was misconceived: a market amounting to a substantial part of the common market may cover a number of Member States or a single Member State or parts of one of more Member States. In fact, although relevant markets have been found more often than not to coincide with the territories of States, this is a tendency which is likely to decline as the Community system develops. An issue which has not yet received the attention of the Court is whether a relevant market may extend beyond Community territory. In principle, it is thought that, if the concept of the relevant market is applied at all, it must relate to the actual supply/demand situation in which an undertaking finds itself; where this overlaps with third States, domi-

---

[41] Commission: O.J. 1975 L 29/14; [1975] 1 C.M.L.R. D20. Court: Case 26/75 *General Motors Continental* v. *Commission* [1975] E.C.R. 1367; [1976] 1 C.M.L.R. 95. Under the relevant Belgian legislation responsibility for carrying out inspections and issuing certificates of conformity was delegated to the sole authorised agent of any foreign manufacturer in the case of new cars and cars imported into Belgium after being registered abroad for less than six months. Similar arrangements in the U.K. were the subject of the Commission's *BL* Dec., O.J. 1984 L 207/11. See Case 226/84 *British Leyland* v. *Commission* (not yet reported) when the Decision of the Commission was upheld.

[42] Case 77/77 *B.P.* v. *Commission, loc. cit.* note 34, *supra*. The Commission had actually stated in its Decision that the relevant market was that for petroleum spirit in the Netherlands. However, dominance on this *general* market could not have been explained by the relationship of dependence between *particular* suppliers and their customers.

[43] [1978] E.C.R. at p. 1537.

[44] The Commission itself flirted with this idea: see the proposal sent to the Council on May 29, 1970 (J.O. 1970, C92/14).

nance under Article 86 will have to be assessed in relation to the wider area. However, this would be subject to the condition that the part of the market which is located within the Community amounted to a substantial part of the common market.

(iii) *The temporal criterion.* The market on which an undertaking operates may fluctuate from time to time with respect both to the range of products and the geographical area covered. For example, if the view had been taken in *United Brands* that the demand for bananas was seriously affected by the availability of various seasonal fruits, it might have concluded that bananas formed part of a series of different markets at different times of the year; and it would have followed that the position of UBC must be examined in relation to each of these markets. Another example is provided by *Commercial Solvents Corporation.* It had been argued by CSC that the manufacture of ethambutol was possible by processes other than that involving aminobutanol. However, the Court held that the processes in question were still of an experimental nature and incapable at the material time of being used for production on an industrial scale. They, therefore, did not constitute a realistic alternative for the customer, Zoja.[45]

Market power will only give a dominant position if it is capable of enduring for a considerable time. The prospect of substitutes becoming available in the short run limits freedom of action because of the risk of future defections by customers.[46] Thus in *BP* Mr. Warner contested the Commission's view that, because there was no petrol available from other sources, the oil companies occupied a dominant position in respect of their customers during the crisis of 1973 to 1974. He pointed out that in a *temporary* supply crisis, a trader cannot determine his distribution policy without having regard to his customers. "He must have it in mind that, once the emergency is over, they will have memories of the way in which they were treated by him during the period of scarcity."[47]

The criteria of dominance

A variety of factors may point to the conclusion that a dominant position exists on a given market. In each case it is necessary to consider whether the particular combination of factors which is found to be present confers the requisite degree of power upon the undertaking in question.

(i) *Market share.* The most important factor is the size of the undertaking's share of the relevant market. In assessing this any part of production which is transported outside the relevant market must be left out of account. The European Court has said that, allowing for exceptional circumstances, extremely large market shares may be regarded as constituting

---

[45] [1973] E.C.R. at p. 248.
[46] Gyselen and Kyriazis, *op. cit.* note 14, *supra*, stress that market power only gives cause for concern if it is a long-run phenomenon.
[47] Case 77/77 *B.P.* v. *Commission*, [1978] E.C.R. at p. 1538.

in themselves proof of the existence of a dominant position.[48] Where the share of the market held by the undertaking is smaller, other factors take on increased significance.

In a number of cases Article 86 has been applied in relation to undertakings enjoying a more or less complete monopoly. For instance, in *Commercial Solvents Corporation*[49] the Commission found that CSC had a "world monopoly" in the production and sale of the base products used in the manufacture of the anti-tubercular drug, ethambutol. The European Court, without itself adopting the Commission's phrase, appears to have been satisfied that the CSC group was the only practical source of materials for the manufacture of ethambutol on an industrial scale, alternative sources, suggested by CSC, being either of an experimental nature or of limited capacity. More recently, the Court confirmed the Commission's finding that GVL had a *de facto* monopoly on the market in Germany in services relating to the management of performing artists' rights of "secondary exploitation."[50] It makes no difference to the application of the Article that a monopoly position may have been created by statute.[51]

Even in cases where control has been less complete, market shares have normally been high. For example, according to the Commission's figures in *Continental Can Company*[52] SLW accounted for 70 to 80 per cent. of the market in Germany for meat tins, 80 to 90 per cent. of the market for fish tins and 50 to 55 per cent. of the market for metal closures for glass jars. And in *Hoffmann-La Roche* the shares held by Roche on three of the seven vitamin markets considered by the Court amounted to more than 80 per cent.[53] Comparatively low for an undertaking which has been held to occupy a dominant position was the 45 per cent. share of the banana market in six Member States attributed to UBC by the Commission. UBC contended that its share had dropped to 41 per cent. by 1975, and the European Court was content to accept the figure of "more than 40 per cent. and nearly 45 per cent." In *Michelin*[54] NBIM's share of the relevant market was somewhat higher, varying between 57 and 65 per cent. during the reference period of 1975–1980. The Commission has expressed the view that a dominant position will usually be found once a market share of

---

[48] Case 85/76 *Hoffmann-La Roche* v. *Commission* [1979] E.C.R. at p. 521. A figure of 90 per cent. was suggested by Judged Learned Hand in *United States* v. *Aluminium Co. of America* 1945 Trade Cases s.57, 342 (2d. Cir.) at s.57, 679. See the discussion in Holley, *loc. cit.* note 17, *supra* pp. 174 *et seq.*

[49] Joined Cases 6 and 7/73 *loc. cit.* note 31, *supra.*

[50] Case 7/82 *GVL* v. *Commission* [1983] E.C.R. 483. "Secondary exploitation" occurs where a performance which has previously been recorded is broadcast or disseminated to the public in some other manner. See also the Commission's *GEMA* Dec. concerning a monopoly in the management of musical authors' rights: J.O. 1971 L134/15; [1971] C.M.L.R. D35; (No. 2) J.O. 1972 L166/22.

[51] See Case 26/75 *General Motors Continental* v. *Commission, loc. cit.* note 41, *supra*; Case 13/77 *INNO* v. *ATAB* [1977] E.C.R. 2115; Case 41/83 *Italy* v. *Commission (British Telecom)* [1985] 2 C.M.L.R. 368; Case 311/84 *Télémarketing, loc. cit.* note 7, *supra.*

[52] Case 6/72 *loc. cit.* note 1, *supra.* The figures were disputed by Continental Can.

[53] Case 85/76 *loc. cit.* note 7, *supra.* The figures for the seven markets were: Vitamin A, 47 per cent.; Vitamin B2, 74.8–87 per cent.; Vitamin B3, 18.9–51 per cent.; Vitamin B6, 83.9–90 per cent.; Vitamin C, 63–66.2 per cent.; Vitamin E, 50–64 per cent.; Vitamin H. 93–100 per cent. (lowest and highest figures for value or quantity). Roche was held to be dominant, on account of its market share alone or in combination with other factors, on all the markets except that for Vitamin B3.

[54] Case 322/81 *loc. cit.* note 2, *supra.*

the order of 40 to 45 per cent. is reached; and that the existence of such a position cannot be ruled out in respect of shares between 20 and 40 per cent.[55]

The *United Brands* Judgment contained the rather surprising statement that:

> "A trader can only be in a dominant position on the market for a product if he has succeeded in winning a large part of this market."[56]

This suggests that the existence of an important market share is not only a more or less reliable indicator, but a *necessary* (though not a *sufficient*) condition of dominance. However, such a condition would not be consistent with the essentially dynamic concept of a dominant position which both the Court and the Commission employ. As the Commission has written:

> "An undertaking which is able, when it so wishes, to eliminate the other competing undertakings from the market may already enjoy a dominant position and decisively determine the behaviour of the other undertakings even if its own share of the market is still relatively weak."[57]

The impression created by the passage quoted from *United Brands* was corrected by the court in the *Hoffman-La Roche* judgment, where it said:

> "A substantial market share as evidence of the existence of a dominant position is not a constant factor and its importance varies from market to market according to the structure of these markets, especially as far as production, supply and demand are concerned."[58]

(ii) *Shares of other market participants.* It may be helpful to compare the size of the market share under investigation with the size of the shares held by other operators on the relevant market. An undertaking with a relatively low market share, *e.g.* 30 to 40 per cent., may still be in a dominant position if the rest of the market is highly fragmented, so that none of the other participants constitutes a serious threat to its independence. Thus in *United Brands* the European Court cited as a consideration affording evidence of "preponderant strength" the fact that UBC's percentage of the market was several times greater than that of Castle and Cooke (16 per cent.) which was its nearest competitor, with the remaining market participants well behind.[59] The gap in *Michelin* was even wider, the shares of NBIM's main competitors amounting only to between 4 and 8 per cent.[60] On the other hand, in an oligopoly where, for example, three operators divide a market more or less evenly between them no single undertaking will be able to act without taking the reactions of the others into account. None of them can, therefore, be regarded as individually occupying a dominant position, although they might do so as a group.[61]

---

[55] Comp.Rep. 1980, point 150.
[56] [1978] E.C.R. at p. 282.
[57] Authors' translation. See Memorandum, *loc. cit.* note 4, *supra.*
[58] [1979] E.C.R. at p. 520.
[59] [1978] E.C.R. at pp. 282–283. See also Case 85/76 *Hoffman-La Roche* v. *Commission,* where the smallness of its competitors' market shares helped to establish the dominance of Roche on the markets for Vitamins A, C and E.
[60] [1983] E.C.R. at pp. 3509–3510.
[61] On collective dominant positions see further *infra.*

(iii) *The conditions of market entry*. Even a very large market share can be rapidly eroded when the market is penetrated by lively new competitors. An example is provided by the lamentable decline in the British motor cycle industry, which in the 1950s accounted for 70 per cent. of the world market but was unable to withstand competition from Continental and Japanese manufacturers, responding to the demand for smaller motor cycles.[62] A careful analysis of a dominant position should, therefore, refer to any advantages enjoyed by the undertaking in question, or to any difficulties in the way of potential market entrants, making it unlikely that the structure of the market will change radically in the shorter run.

This might be the case, for example, because the undertaking controls essential patents or know-how; or because, like UBC, it is vertically integrated, with privileged access to supplies, means of transport and distribution outlets[63]; or because, like Michelin, it has a well developed network of commercial representatives providing continuous contact with customers[64]; or because of its technical superiority, sustained by a continuous programme of research and development and the resulting scope of its product range.[65] Another factor which may be influential is "product differentiation." By this is meant the phenomenon of consumer preference becoming attached to a particular brand of goods to an extent which cannot be justified by the specific properties of the goods as compared with available substitutes. Such a preference may have been built up by a protracted advertising campaign.

From the point of view of a potential competitor the chief difficulty in overcoming such advantages would be that of cost. Very large resources may be needed, for instance, to finance independent research or countervailing advertising. The crucial consideration will be the range within which the undertaking is free to fix its prices without making it commercially attractive for others to risk the investment required in order to mount a challenge. Also in the present context it is important to bear in mind the time factor. The possibility that, at the end of a very long period of development, another undertaking may succeed in establishing itself as a serious competitor would not normally be sufficient to impair an existing dominant position.[66]

The advantages helping to reinforce the market strength of an undertaking may be wholly attributable to its business initiative. Could it then be argued that taking them into account in deciding whether the undertaking fulfils the conditions for the application of Article 86, would be to put a premium on enterprise and efficiency? It is thought that such an objection would be misplaced. Whether or not an undertaking occupies a dominant

---

[62] The story is related in Bruce-Gardyne, *Meriden: Odyssey of a Lame Duck*, published by The Centre for Policy Studies.

[63] Case 27/76 [1978] E.C.R. at pp. 278–280.

[64] Case 322/81 [1983] E.C.R. at p. 3511. See also the reference to "a highly developed sales network" in Case 85/76 *Hoffman-La Roche* [1979] E.C.R. at p. 524.

[65] This was referred to as a relevant factor in Case 27/76 *United Brands* [1978] E.C.R. at p. 279; Case 85/76 *Hoffmann-La Roche* [1979] E.C.R. at p. 524; Case 322/81 *Michelin* [1983] E.C.R. at p. 3510.

[66] See the very full analysis of those features of UBC's banana operation which the European Court regarded as contributing to its retention of a large market share: Case 27/76 [1978] E.C.R. at pp. 278–281.

position is a question which has to be determined irrespective of the means, fair or foul, by which the position was attained. It is at a later stage, when it has to be decided whether the dominant position has been abused, that the efficiency of the undertaking may become relevant.

(iv) *Financial resources*. The ability of an undertaking to command finance is bound to enhance its freedom of action. In particular, it will allow the undertaking to keep abreast of the latest developments in technology, to adapt rapidly to changes in the pattern of demand and to expand its operation, either vertically or horizontally. Thus in *Continental Can Company*[67] the Commission drew attention to the fact that Continental Can, because of its large size, was able to resort to the international capital market; and that it had done so in 1969 to finance the acquisition of an additional 60 per cent. participation in SLW with loans in Eurodollars and Deutsche Marks. The concept of parent companies and their subsidiaries all forming part of the same undertaking is important in the present context.[68] Its consequences may be particularly striking where the undertaking concerned is a conglomerate, *i.e.* a business group having interests in a wide variety of separate economic sectors.

(v) *Conduct and performance of the undertaking*. The criteria examined so far have related to the structure of the market,[69] *i.e.* the reasonably stable features of the competitive environment within which the undertaking operates and to which accordingly its decisions must be adjusted, and of the undertaking itself, *i.e.* its general organisation and resources both for the purposes of the particular line of business in question and for any other purpose having a bearing on that business. It remains to say something about the behavioural criteria of dominance, consisting of the conduct and performance of the undertaking on the relevant market. Roughly speaking, by "conduct" is meant the activities pursued by the undertaking in the course of its business, *e.g.* its policies on pricing, output and sales promotion[70]; and by "performance" is meant the result of these activities, *e.g.* the level of profits, the efficiency of production or the quality and range of the goods produced.[71]

It might be thought that the actual conduct or performance of an undertaking would provide the best possible evidence of the existence or otherwise of a dominant position. If an undertaking is able to behave in a manner, or to achieve results, which would not be expected under conditions of effective competition, the inference is surely legitimate that competitive restraints are, in fact, absent. However, writers have warned of the equivocality of such evidence.[72] Given that in practice the competitive process works more or less imperfectly, it may be possible for an undertaking to make very large profits, to limit its output or to impose discriminatory

---

[67] *Loc. cit.* note 4, *supra*.
[68] See the discussion, *supra*, Chap. 13.
[69] This definition is culled from the definitions discussed by Joliet in *Monopolization and Abuse of Dominant Position* (Nijhoff, 1970), pp. 25–26.
[70] See *ibid.*, pp. 27–28.
[71] See *ibid.*, pp. 29–30.
[72] See *ibid.* pp. 96 *et seq.* and references. See also Gyselen and Kyriazis, *op. cit.* note 14, *supra* at pp. 135–137.

prices, although it does not enjoy market power amounting to dominance; while, on the other hand, it has been pointed out that a monopolist wishing to safeguard his long term position may treat his customers relatively benignly.[73] Predatory practices such as local price cutting may be an indication of a wish to acquire a dominant position, rather than of dominance already achieved.[74] The better view is, therefore, that behavioural evidence should not normally be treated as sufficient in itself to establish the existence of a dominant position. However, it may be invoked to corroborate the evidence resulting from a structural analysis. It will be more persuasive, the longer the conduct or performance in question is found to have continued.

In *United Brands* the European Court was faced with a choice between two performance criteria: the loss which UBC claimed that its banana division had suffered from 1951 to 1976; and the success of UBC in retaining its share of the banana market against vigorous competition. Because it accorded with the impression of overall strength gained from a structural analysis of the relevant market, the Court gave greater weight to the latter.[75]

One or more undertakings

The concept of an undertaking was examined in Chapter 13.[76] It will be remembered that legally distinct companies may be regarded as forming a single undertaking, if in practice they are subject to common control. The importance of this principle in the context of Article 86 is that, in determining whether the conduct of one member of a group constitutes an abuse of a dominant position on a relevant market within the common market, it may be possible to take into account the economic strength of other members of the group, some or all of them established in third countries. For example, in *Continental Can Company*[77] the dominant position on which the Commission relied was that of SLW on the German market, while the alleged abuse had been committed by Europemballage through its acquisition of TDV; and this conduct was attributable to the parent company, Continental Can. In the same way, in *Commercial Solvents Corporation*[78] it was CSC's control over world supplies of aminobutanol that gave Istituto a dominant position on the common market; CSC was legally answerable for Instituto's refusal to supply Zoja.[79]

In addition, Article 86 expressly recognises that a dominant position may be jointly held by undertakings which are both legally and economically independent of each other. The European Court has yet to pronounce on the nature of the conduct which will lead to the conclusion that undertak-

---

[73] By Edwards in *Maintaining Competition* (1949), p. 125, cited by Joliet, *op. cit.* (note 60), *supra*, pp. 97 to 98.
[74] See *ibid.* p. 127.
[75] [1978] E.C.R. at p. 284–285.
[76] See pp. 345–347, *supra*.
[77] *Loc. cit.* note 1, *supra*.
[78] *Loc. cit.* note 31, *supra*.
[79] See also Case 322/81 *Michelin*, *loc. cit.* note 2, *supra*.

ings are jointly dominant. It has been suggested[80] that parallel conduct pursued by undertakings operating on the same market and evidencing a mutual abstention from competition might be so regarded. This is to be distinguished from parallel conduct enforced by the actual pressure of competition on the market. Any agreement, decision or concerted practice within the meaning of Article 85 would, presumably, constitute a sufficient link between undertakings for the purposes of Article 86. However, it is submitted, actual concertation cannot be required, or the provision on joint dominance would be otiose.

In its *Sugar* Decision the Commission found that the two Dutch producers SU and CSM together occupied a dominant position on the sugar market in the Netherlands. The Commission said:

> "These two producers cooperate closely in almost all their activities, that is to say the joint purchase of raw materials, rationing of production, collaboration in the use of intermediate products, pooling of research, cooperation on market research, advertising and sales promotion and the harmonisation of ex-factory prices and conditions of sale."[81]

Assuming that collaboration of this nature had taken place, which SU and CSM denied, it would be hard to think of a clearer case for the joint assessment of market strength.

The concept of an abuse

The wording of Article 86 makes it clear that the existence of a dominant position does not in itself attract the prohibition contained in the Article. Some additional element is required, amounting to an abuse of that position. There is no definition of an abuse in the EEC Treaty, and guidance in interpreting the concept must be sought from the objects and general principles set out in the Preamble to the Treaty and in Articles 2 and 3, especially Article 3(*f*), and from the case law.

In its *Hoffmann-La Roche* judgment the Court of Justice said:

> "The concept of abuse is an objective concept relating to the behaviour of an undertaking in a dominant position which is such as to influence the structure of a market where, as a result of the very presence of the undertaking in question, the degree of competition is weakened and which, through recourse to methods different from those which condition normal competition in products or services on the basis of the transactions of commercial operators, has the effect of hindering the maintenance of the degree of competition still existing in the market or the growth of that competition."[82]

The definition confirms the answer given in *Continental Can Company*[83] to two important questions about the meaning of "abuse" in Article 86.

The first question was whether the concept was confined to unfair and

---

[80] By Bellamy and Child in *Common Market Law of Competition* (3rd ed.) at para. 8–035. *Cf.* the reference to "joint dominance" in the Oil Companies Report: Comp.Rep. 1975, p. 18.
[81] O.J. 1973 L 140/17.
[82] Case 85/76 [1979] E.C.R. at p. 541.
[83] Case 6/72 *loc. cit.* note 1, *supra.*

oppressive behaviour towards suppliers and consumers, or included behaviour towards actual or potential competitors tending to protect or reinforce the dominant position. This question reflects the distinction which is sometimes drawn between two broad approaches to the control of market power, one aiming to ensure the good behaviour of the undertaking concerned, and the other to limit the power itself by seeking to preserve effective competition.[84] It has been noted that the two approaches tend in practice to converge[85] and in this respect Community competition law has proved no exception. From the definition in *Hoffman-La Roche* it seems the Court regards anti-competitive behaviour as the primary target of Article 86; but it is equally clear that exploitative behaviour, such as imposing excessive prices or other unfair teaching conditions, may be caught by the Article.[86]

The second question was whether a causal link must exist between the dominant position and the behaviour constituting an abuse. In other words, was full value to be given to the notion of "exploiting" a dominant position, so that the undertaking in question must have used its power as the means of achieving the result which is regarded as objectionable? One of the arguments put forward by Continental Can had been precisely that that there was no causal connection between its acquisition of a controlling participation in TDV and its position on the German market which, through SLW, it was alleged to dominate. However, the Court held that, if a merger had the effect of substantially fettering competition, "the question of the link of causality raised by the applicants which in their opinion had to exist between the dominant position and its abuse, is of no consequence, for the strengthening of the position of an undertaking may be an abuse and prohibited under Article 86 of the Treaty, regardless of the means and procedure by which it is achieved . . . ."[87] A similar line of argument was rejected by the Court in *Hoffman-La Roche*.[88] The idea that abusive behaviour consists of obtaining advantages which would not have been obtainable under conditions of effective competition is thus seen to be too restrictive.[89] A dominant undertaking may be prohibited from taking action which would be possible and permissible for an undertaking having less market power, because of the adverse consequences that are liable to ensue for the competitive structure of the market.

Article 86 does not contain any provision like Article 85(3) expressly providing an escape from the broad prohibition which it imposes. However, in practice the operation of the two Articles is rather similar, owing to the flexibility of the concept of an abuse. Behaviour which might appear to be prima facie abusive *e.g.* because it falls within one of the categories mentioned in Article 86, may nevertheless escape prohibition if in the cir-

---

[84] See the clear account in Joliet, *op. cit.* note 69, *supra.* pp. 8 *et seq.*
[85] See Waelbroeck in Van Damme, *op. cit.* note 3, *supra*, pp. 111–112.
[86] See Art. 86(*a*) and the examples of abuses discussed, *infra.*
[87] Case 6/72 [1973] E.C.R. at p. 245. See the criticism by Focsaneanu in Van Damme, *op. cit.* note 3, *supra*, pp. 324 *et seq.*
[88] Case 85/76 [1979] E.C.R. at p. 541.
[89] This was the definition suggested by the group of professors appointed in 1963 to advise the Commission on the interpretation of Art. 86. It is quoted in the Memorandum cited in note 4, *supra.*

cumstances it is found to be objectively justified. This can be seen, for example, in the cases relating to refusals to deal, which are discussed *infra*.[90]

The Commission regards the occurrence of an abuse as an objective matter: there is no need for the undertaking to have intended to cause harm, nor for its behaviour to have been morally reprehensible. Thus the Commission rejected as immaterial the argument put forward by GEMA[91] that it had not been aware of the discriminatory consequences of its activities. Intention or negligence only become relevant if the Commission sees fit to impose a penalty under Article 15(2)(*a*) of Regulation 17. The definition of "abuse" in *Hoffman-La Roche* supports that view.[92]

The fact that an abuse of a dominant position may have been encouraged by national legislative provisions does not provide any justification for the undertaking concerned.[93] However, some element of free will on the part of the undertaking is required. If it acts under legal constraint there will be no direct infringement of Article 86, but the Member State responsible will be in breach of its general duty under the second paragraph of Article 5 to abstain from any measure capable of jeopardising the attainment of the objectives of the Treaty.[94]

Member States acting in the exercise of their sovereign powers may interfere with the normal functioning of the competition system, *e.g.* by imposing a parafiscal charge on certain products in order to finance an aid to the domestic industry. Article 86 (and, indeed, Article 85) will not apply in such cases, even if the task in question has been assigned to a legally autonomous public body.[95] However, this does not mean that the Member State in question will get off scot free, since a number of other Treaty provisions may be relevant.[96]

Examples of abuses

Examples of behaviour which has been, or is likely to be, held abusive under Article 86 are discussed below. The list of possible abuses contained in the Article, like that of possibly restrictive agreements in Article 85, is purely illustrative. The list will not be analysed as such, but examples appearing under its various items will be considered either individually or

---

[90] See also the part of the *United Brands* judgment dealing with the clause in UBC's sales contracts prohibiting the resale of green bananas. UBC had argued that the sole purpose of the clause was to protect the "Chiquita" brand name, and ultimately the consumer, by ensuring that bananas were of consistently high quality; and this could only be done by reserving supplies for ripeners with proper equipment and expertise. The Court took the view that, as a quality control the blanket prohibition on resales was unduly restrictive. However, it is implicit in the judgment that a clause limiting resales to approved "Chiquita" ripeners, although restrictive of competition because excluding non-approved ripeners from this activity, would have escaped censure: Case 27/76 [1978] E.C.R., pp. 285 *et seq.*

[91] *Loc. cit.* note 50, *supra.* But see Case 26/75 *General Motors Continental* v. *Commission loc. cit.* note 41, *supra* where the Court appeared to give weight to subjective factors in deciding that no abuse had been committed.

[92] Case 85/76 *loc. cit.* note 82, *supra.*

[93] Case 13/77 *INNO* v. *ATAB* [1977] E.C.R. at p. 2144.

[94] *Ibid.* If a public or privileged undertaking is concerned, there will be an infringement of Art. 90(1): see Ch. 19, *infra.*

[95] Case 94/74 *IGAV* v. *ENCC* [1975] E.C.R. 699 at p. 714; [1976] 2 C.M.L.R. 37.

[96] Those mentioned by the European Court, *ibid.* were Arts. 37, 90, 92–94, 101 and 102.

in the particular forms of behaviour in which they most frequently manifest themselves.

(i) *Unfair prices*

(a) *Excessively high prices exacted by dominant sellers.* This is probably the first example of an abuse of a dominant position which would occur to most people, because of the direct impact felt by consumers. However, it is not easy to formulate theoretically adequate and practically useful criteria for determining where the line between fair and unfair prices should be drawn in a given case.[97]

The European Court in its *United Brands*[98] judgment, echoing its earlier judgment in *General Motors Continental*,[99] spoke of a price being excessive "because it has no reasonable relation to the economic value of the product supplied." It went on to approve as one test of excess over economic value, a comparison between the selling price of a product and its cost of production, which would disclose the size of the profit margin. As the Court said, the question was "whether the difference between the costs actually incurred and the price actually charged is excessive"; and if so, "whether a price has been imposed which is either unfair in itself or when compared to competing products."[1]

Such a test may attract criticism. Thus it has been pointed out[2] that high profits may be the result of a firm's efficiency which deserves to be rewarded (although it is reasonable to require some element of cost saving to be handed on to consumers); while low profits may be the result of inefficiency, in which case prices may still be excessive. The task of assessing how efficiently a dominant undertaking employs it resources is likely to be a formidable one. There is also the question of the proportion of indirect costs and general expenditure which should be allocated to the cost of putting a particular product on the market. And the structure of the undertaking, the number of subsidiaries and their relationship with each other and with their parent company, may cause further complications. However, it is clear that the Court was aware of these problems and intended the test to be applied sensitively, with due regard to its limitations. In the case of the banana market, the Court was of the opinion that a satisfactory estimate could have been arrived at.

The Commission in its *United Brands* Decision[3] sought to avoid the pitfalls of comparing production costs and prices by offering indirect evidence of unfair pricing. This took the form of comparisons between the prices charged by UBC for "Chiquitas" destined, respectively, for the Irish and Continental markets, between UBC's prices for "Chiquitas" and the prices of other branded bananas of similar quality and between the prices of "Chiquitas" and UBC's unbranded bananas. The Court took the Commission to task for not having at least required UBC to give particulars of

---

[97] The problem is very fully analysed by Schwarz in Van Damme, *op. cit.* note 3, *supra*, pp. 381 *et seq.*
[98] Case 27/76 [1978] E.C.R. at p. 301.
[99] Case 26/75 *loc. cit.* note 41, *supra*.
[1] *Loc. cit.* note 98, *supra*.
[2] By Korah in Van Damme, *op. cit.* note 3, *supra* at p. 237.
[3] *Loc. cit.* note 22, *supra*.

its production costs, but did not dispute the relevance of the indicators actually referred to in the Decision: it was the lack of supporting evidence which led to the annulment of this head of abuse.[4]

The moral the Commission may draw from *United Brands* is that, in seeking to establish an abuse in the form of unfairly high prices, it should normally proceed by way of an analysis of the cost structure of the undertaking concerned. However, other methods of proving unfairness will continue to be acceptable, if the Court is satisfied of their appropriateness in the specific circumstances of the case.[5]

(b) *Excessively low prices exacted by dominant buyers.* A dominant buyer may be successful in obtaining the reduction of prices to an unreasonable extent. Possible objections are that the profitability of the supplier, and his capacity to expand production or improve his product, may be jeopardised; and that other operators at the same market level at the buyer may be put at a competitive disadvantage, for reasons which have nothing to do with the buyer's efficiency.

The proceedings in *CICCE* v. *Commission*[6] concerned a complaint that television companies in France would only pay very low fees for broadcasting films originally made for the cinema. The Commission, while accepting that a dominant purchaser may commit an abuse within the meaning of Article 86 by imposing an unfair price for a service, rejected the complaint on account of its generality. The reasonableness of the broadcasting fee could, in the view of the Commission, be judged only in respect of the value of individual films, which was very variable.[7]

(c) *Predatory price cutting.* A dominant seller may adopt a tactic of pricing his goods very low, or even below cost, in order to drive out of business competitors with more limited resources who cannot for long sustain the losses occasioned by matching the terms he is offering. Consumers, of course, benefit from price reductions in the short run but risk finding themselves even more at the mercy of the dominant undertaking after it has captured a larger share of the market.

The application of Article 86 to predatory price cutting is illustrated by the *AKZO* Decision of the Commission.[8] AKZO is the EEC's major supplier of a chemical substance, benzoyle peroxide, which is used in the manufacture of plastics and in the blanching of flour.[9] The Commission found that, in order to deter ECS, a small competitor in the market in flour additives, from expanding its business into the market in organic peroxides for plastics, AKZO had first threatened and later implemented a campaign

---

[4] See the reasoning of the Court at [1978] E.C.R. pp. 299–303.
[5] The Court did not question the Commission's finding in *General Motors Continental* that the fee for conformity inspections of parallel imports from other European countries was excessive, while holding on other grounds that no abuse had been committed: see Case 26/75 *loc. cit.* note 41, *supra.* See also the *BL* Dec., *loc. cit.* note 41, *supra.*
[6] Case 298/83 *Comité des Industries Cinématographiques des Communantés Européennes* v. *Commission* (not yet reported). The action was brought in respect of the Commission's Dec. not to proceed with the complaint lodged by the CICCE.
[7] The Court held that in the circumstances the Commission had been justified in not taking the matter further.
[8] O.J. 1985 L 374/1.
[9] AKZO estimated its share of the relevant market as 50 per cent. or more. It was equivalent to those of all the remaining producers together.

of price cuts aimed at important customers of ECS in the former market. If successful, the campaign would not only have eliminated ECS as a competitor in the supply of organic peroxides; it would also have discouraged other potential challenges to AKZO's established position.

(ii) *Discriminatory prices*

A dominant undertaking may fall foul of Article 86 by charging different prices in respect of equivalent transactions without objective justification. If the customers concerned are "trading parties," *i.e.* the purchase is made for the purposes of a economic activity in which they are engaged, the objectionable feature of such a pricing policy is found in the competitive disadvantage suffered by those called upon to pay the higher prices, and the case falls precisely within Article 86(*c*). However, even in transactions with ultimate consumers, discriminatory pricing may be abusive, if it is incompatible with any aims of the Treaty.

An abuse may take the form of discriminating between customers within the same market or of following different pricing policies on different markets, although in the latter case objective justification may be more readily available. It should be noted that the customers concerned need not be in competition with each other: the one paying the higher price suffers a "competitive disadvantage" simply because he is, to that extent, less well equipped to meet competition, whichever quarter it may come from.

The *United Brands* case highlighted the particular problem of how far it is permissible for dominant undertakings to adapt their pricing policies to take account of the diversity of marketing conditions in the various Member States.[10] For instance, there may be significant disparities in rates of taxation, freight charges or the wages paid to workers for assembling or finishing the product, which may influence costs; or in other factors relevant to a marketing strategy, such as consumer preferences or the intensity of competition. In addition, price differences may result from government action over which a supplier has no control, *e.g.* the alteration of exchange rates or the imposition of a price freeze. Some convergence of these conditions may be expected as the common market develops, but markets within the Community are bound to retain a degree of territorial specificity (although not necessarily along national lines) due, *e.g.* to climate, geography and cultural differences.

UBC had put forward, as objective justification for its policy of charging different prices for its bananas, depending on the Member State where the ripened fruit was to be sold, the continuing division of the market for bananas along national lines. Each of the national markets had its own internal characteristics, and accordingly different price levels; and the prices to the ripener/distributors in a given week were intended to reflect as accurately as possible the prices which ripened bananas were expected to fetch on the individual markets during the following week. The defect which the European Court found in this argument was that UBC did not operate directly

---

[10] Case 27/76 [1978] E.C.R., pp. 294 *et seq.* The Commission found that UBC's differential pricing policy amounted to a separate head of abuse, and this part of the Dec. was upheld by the Court of Justice.

on the retail markets. It was not, therefore, entitled to take account of market pressures which only made themselves felt at the retail stage.

The view of the European Court is evidently that a dominant undertaking may charge different price for the same product in different Member States, where this represents a response to real market pressures operating on it. For instance, there would have been no objection to UBC's adopting lower prices in relation to a certain national market where a price war was raging, if pressure to do so had been exerted by the relevant ripener/distributors in the course of a genuine bargaining process. On the other hand, there may be a case of abusive discrimination if the aim of the undertaking is simply to obtain maximum profits by setting its prices at the highest level which each of the markets will bear, especially since, in order for this policy to be effective, measures will probably be necessary to maintain the isolation of the markets from each other.[11]

(iii) *Unfair trading conditions*

Apart from determining the level of prices, a dominant undertaking may be able to compel its trading partners to accept other terms which are unreasonably onerous.

For instance, a number of the conditions of membership of the German copyright society, GEMA, were condemned by the Commission as unfair[12]; and subsequently in *BRT* v. *SABAM*[13] which arose out of proceedings involving GEMA's sister society in Belgium, the European Court was asked whether it might be abusive for such a body, occupying a dominant position, to demand a global assignment of copyrights, without making any distinction between specific categories of rights, and one which would apply to both present and future rights. The Court's answer was that a balance must be struck between allowing authors, composers and publishers maximum freedom, and enabling the society to manage their rights effectively. The crucial issue was whether the conditions imposed by a copyright society were absolutely necessary to enable it to carry out its task. If not, the encroachment on members' freedom could constitute an abuse.

An example of the use of purchasing power to impose unfair conditions on a seller was provided by the tender which the Commission examined in *Eurofima*.[14] The term to which the Commission took exception would have required the manufacturers of the rolling stock to cede to the purchasing organisation an unlimited right to the use of patents resulting from the development, including a right to grant licences under future patents to third parties, without consulting the manufacturers or paying compensation. The contract was revised so as to limit the use of the right to Eurofima's own needs. The granting of licences to third parties was to require the consent of the manufacturers, and further payment.

---

[11] In *United Brands* the clause prohibiting the resale of green bananas was capable of having such an effect, since the exportation of ripened bananas would be impracticable.
[12] *Loc. cit.* note 50, *supra*.
[13] Case 127/73 [1974] E.C.R. 313; [1974] 2 C.M.L.R. 238.
[14] *Loc. cit.* note 12, p. 399, *supra*.

(iv) *Exclusive rights of supply*

Purchasers may become bound to a particular supplier either by accepting a direct obligation to obtain all or most of their requirements of goods of a certain description from him[15] or through the pressure exerted by "loyalty" or "target" discounts.

A loyalty discount[16] consists of a reduction in the price of a product which is granted on condition that the purchaser obtain a specified proportion (normally very high) of his requirements of the product from the supplier granting the discount. The usual arrangement will be for the discount to be paid as a rebate at the end of, say, a year, and entitlement will be lost in respect of the whole period, if the limit agreed for procurements from third parties is exceeded. This means that a competing supplier will have to pitch his offer at a level that takes into account not only the rebate on the particular quantity ordered but also the higher price the customer will have to pay for the remainder of the goods purchased from the first supplier.[17]

In the case of a target discount the price reduction is conditional on the purchasing of an agreed quantity of products from the supplier in question during the reference period. The target is not linked to any specific proportion of the customer's requirements but is likely in practice to be set at a level that will lead to the loss of the discount if substantial purchases are made from third parties. To win orders from the customer, therefore, competing suppliers must, again, be prepared to cover that loss.[18]

Loyalty and target discounts are to be distinguished from "quantity" discounts, where the reduction in the price is determined by the actual volume of goods purchased from the supplier. Quantity discounts are not considered anti-competitive, because of the correlation between cost savings to the supplier and the lower price paid by the purchaser.[19]

On the other hand, an exclusive or preferential right of supply, whether it operates directly or through a discount system, is very likely to infringe Article 86 if the supplier enjoys a dominant position on the market in question. Such arrangements, the European Court has said,[20] are incompatible with the objective of undistorted competition because, except in circumstances of the kind that might lead to a grant of exemption under Article 85(3), they have no economic justification but are designed to deprive the customer of any choice of his sources of supply, or at least to restrict his choice, and to deny other producers access to the market. The effect will be further to strengthen the position of the dominant supplier. Another possible objection, when loyalty or target discounts are involved, is that charging two customers different net prices for the same quantity of goods, because of purchases made or not made on other occasions, amounts to discrimination contrary to Article 86(*c*).

[15] On the application of Art. 85 to exclusive supply agreements, see Chap. 14, *supra*.
[16] Also known as a "fidelity" discount.
[17] See the analysis of loyalty discounts in Case 85/76 *Hoffmann-La Roche* v. *Commission* [1979] E.C.R. at pp. 539–541.
[18] See the analysis of target discounts in Case 322/81 *Michelin* v. *Commission* [1983] E.C.R. at pp. 3514–3515.
[19] Case 85/76 *Hoffmann-La Roche* v. *Commission* [1979] E.C.R. at p. 540.
[20] *Ibid.*

In *Hoffmann-La Roche* the Commission condemned the provisions giving Roche a more or less exclusive right of supply, usually in combination with loyalty rebates, which were contained in agreements with a number of important bulk purchasers of vitamins. Under the so-called "English clause" which was generally included in the agreements, customers were required to notify Roche if they received more favourable offers from other manufacturers; and if Roche then chose not to match the offers, these could be accepted without the loss of any rebate entitlement. However, the Commission regarded the clause as mitigating the exclusive supply system only slightly, because it left the decision to Roche whether the customer in question should be free to purchase from the third party; and anyway, the clause was usually restricted to offers coming from "reputable" manufacturers in the customer's own territory, and was therefore of limited effect. The Court upheld the decision of the Commission as to the abusive nature of the contractual provisions in question.[21]

The *Michelin* case illustrates the application of Article 86 to a system of target discounts. An "annual variable discount," based on the previous year's turnover in Michelin tyres of all types, and a sales target for heavy vehicle tyres were fixed at the beginning of each year by discussion between a commercial representative of NBIM and individual dealers. The system allowed a proportion of the discount to be paid as an advance but the full amount would only be rebated if the sales target for the year was reached. The European Court found that the variation dependent on the attainment of the target was a mere 0.2 to 0.4 per cent. Nevertheless, it was held, even quite a slight variation could exert significant pressure on a dealer towards the end of a relatively long reference period, when the chance of earning the discount might turn on a single order. Other factors tending to accentuate the pressure on the dealers were: the difference between NBIM's market share and those of its main competitors, which made it hard for the latter to offer inducements sufficient to compensate dealers risking the loss of the target discount; the lack of transparency of the discount system as a whole and the fact that particular traders' discounts and sales targets were never confirmed by the company in writing, which left them in a state of uncertainty; and the existence of a network of NBIM representatives to remind dealers of their situation and encourage them to place further orders. The result was "to prevent dealers from being able to select freely at any time in the light of the market situation the most favourable of the offers made by the various competitors and to change supplier without suffering any appreciable economic disadvantage."[22] That loss of independence on the part of the dealers could not be justified by the interest of NBIM in selling more tyres and planning its production more evenly. The discount system, therefore, amounted to an abuse of NBIM's dominant position on the Dutch market.

---

[21] [1979] E.C.R. at pp. 544–546. See also *Sugar* where SZV was found guilty of an abuse for having inserted into its sales contracts a clause allowing an annual rebate of 0.30 Deutsche Marks per 100 kg to customers who had purchased exclusively from members of SZV: Joined Cases 40–48, 50, 54 to 65, 111, 113 and 114/73 *Suiker Unie and Others* v. *Commission, loc. cit.* note 7, p. 399, *supra.*

[22] Case 322/81 *Michelin* v. *Commission* [1983] E.C.R. at p. 3518.

(v) *Restrictions on distribution*

Various types of obligation which suppliers commonly impose on the distributors of their products have already been discussed in connection with Article 85.[23] If the supplier concerned is a dominant undertaking, it may also be necessary to consider whether the obligations fall within the purview of Article 86.[24]

Export bans and other devices for restricting the distribution of goods to a certain geographical area are liable to be considered serious infringements of Article 86, as of Article 85. For instance, in *Sugar*[25] the Court upheld the Commission's finding that the Belgian producer RT had abused its dominant position by bringing pressure to bear on sugar dealers in Belgium to fall in with its export policy in relation to the Netherlands and the western part of the Federal Republic. The pressure took the form of threatening to cut off supplies of sugar; and the policy, that of selling sugar only to the Dutch and German producers themselves, or selling for specified purposes, *e.g.* milk processing but not sweet manufacture. In the Court's view, the behaviour of RT in restricting the outlets of the dealers and indirectly of ulterior purchasers fell within the terms of Article 86(*b*). Similarly, in *United Brands*[26] the prohibition against the resale of green bananas which UBC imposed on its ripener/distributors was condemned as limiting markets to the prejudice of consumers. Given the perishable nature of ripened bananas, the clause had the effect, *inter alia*, of partitioning national markets.

(vi) *Refusal to deal*

There is a well developed case law on the circumstances in which a refusal by a dominant undertaking to deal, in the ordinary course of its business, with another undertaking—especially to supply goods or services or to supply them in the desired quantity—may amount to an abuse. Such conduct is liable to conflict with the objective of undistorted competition in Article 3(*f*), and more particularly to fall within the terms of Article 86(*b*) and (*c*), involving the limitation of markets and discrimination.[27] Whether it does so may require a nuanced decision, taking account of, *inter alia*, the relationship between the parties, the nature of the order which has been refused, the effect of the refusal and reasons for the refusal.

The earliest case on refusal to deal was *Commercial Solvents Corporation*.[28] The refusal from the end of 1970 to supply Zoja with aminobutanol required for the manufacture of the derivative, ethambutol, was the result of a policy decision by the CSC Group to manufacture and sell the derivative on its own account. Upholding the Decision of the Commission that CSC had been guilty of an abuse, the Court said:

" . . . an undertaking being in a dominant position as regards the production of raw material and therefore able to control the supply to

---

[23] See Ch. 14, *supra*.
[24] See Case 126/80 *Salonia* v. *Poidomani* [1981] E.C.R. 1563.
[25] Joined Cases 40–48, 50, 54 to 56, 111, 113 and 114/73, *loc. cit.* note 7, p. 399, *supra*.
[26] Case 27/76 [1978] E.C.R., pp. 285 *et seq*.
[27] Case 27/76 [1978] E.C.R. at p. 292.
[28] Joined Cases 6 and 7/73 *loc. cit.* note 31, *supra*.

manufacturers of derivatives, cannot, just because it decides to start manufacturing these derivatives (in competition with its former customers) act in such a way as to eliminate their competition which in the case in question, would amount to eliminating one of the principal manufacturers of ethambutol in the common market."[29]

Three main points emerge from this passage. In the first place, Zoja was an established customer of CSC. Admittedly, at the beginning of 1970 Zoja had cancelled its orders under the current supply contract, but the Court regarded this as irrelevant because CSC had anyway decided to cut off the supplies once deliveries under the contract had been completed. Secondly, the effect of withholding supplies of the raw material was likely to be serious, namely the elimination of a major producer from the market for the derivative. Thirdly, the reason for driving Zoja out of the market was to smooth CSC's own entry. The Court made it clear that the conduct in question could not be justified as a legitimate competitive tactic.

The *United Brands* judgment contains an even more forthright condemnation of refusal to supply:

" . . . it is advisable to assert positively from the outset that an undertaking in a dominant position for the purpose of marketing a product—which cashes in on the reputation of a brand name known to and valued by the consumers—cannot stop supplying a long standing customer who abides by regular commercial practice, if the orders placed by that customer are in no way out of the ordinary."[30]

The victim was the Danish ripener/distributor, Olesen, which UBC has refused to supply with "Chiquitas" after it had taken part in a sales campaign mounted by the rival supplier, Castle and Cooke. That collaboration was not regarded by the Court as justifying the refusal. Even a dominant undertaking may act in defence of its commercial interests, but such action must be reasonable and proportional to the threat, which that taken against Olesen had not been.

Refusal to supply a service may be illustrated by the *Tele-marketing* case.[31] "Tele-sales" or "tele-marketing" is a technique whereby an advertisement in the media includes a telephone number which the public are invited to call in order to obtain further information or to respond in some other way. The proceedings arose from the fact that the company which operates the RTL television station in Luxembourg would only sell advertising time for telephone marketing if the number used was that of an agency, Information Publicité, which belonged to the same group.[32] Such behaviour, it was held, was tantamount to a refusal to provide the services of a broadcasting station to other tele-marketing undertakings. If the purpose of the refusal were to reserve the downstream market in tele-sales operations for an affiliated agency, and the other conditions of Article 86

---

[29] [1974] E.C.R. at pp. 250–251.
[30] [1978] E.C.R. at p. 292.
[31] Case 311/84 *loc. cit.* note 7, p. 399, *supra*. For another example, see Case 7/82 *GVL* v. *Commission, loc. cit.* note 50, *supra*.
[32] The case came to the Court of Justice by way of a reference for a preliminary ruling under Art. 177. The Court was, therefore, able to rule only in general terms.

were satisfied, there would be an infringement of the Article analogous to that in *Commercial Solvents Corporation*.

The importance of distinguishing carefully between different categories of customer was highlighted by the *BP*[33] judgment, in which the Court annulled the Decision of the Commission that BP had abused the dominant position which it enjoyed in relation to its Dutch customers during the oil supply crisis of November 1973 to March 1974 by reducing deliveries of motor spirit to a particular customer, ABG, more drastically than to others. The Court found that BP had given notice of the termination of its supply contract with ABG in November 1972, and that at the time when the crisis broke, ABG's relationship with BP, so far as concerned supplies of motor spirit, was that of a casual customer. BP could not, therefore, be blamed for treating ABG less favourably than its regular customers, since the latter would have received a substantially smaller quantity than they were entitled to expect, if a standard rate of reduction had been applied.[34]

To sum up these developments,[35] it seems that a refusal by a dominant undertaking to supply a regular customer placing an unexceptional order will amount to an abuse within the meaning of Article 86 unless the refusal can be objectively justified. There would obviously be justification if the goods were not available for reasons beyond the supplier's control, *e.g.* one of its factories had burnt down; and also perhaps,if the supplier was expanding activities on a downstream market and genuinely required the whole of its own production of a raw material in order to cover these new commitments. In general though, a dominant supplier is expected to behave even towards difficult customers with consideration and restraint. It remains to be seen whether a refusal to supply a first-time customer may be abusive, given a sufficiency to meet the needs of established customers, and where the refusal has anti-competitive consequences.

(vii) *Tying*

The example in Article 86(*d*) covers all kinds of "tying" arrangements, where a person is required to accept, as a condition of entering into a contract, "supplementary obligations which, by their nature or according to commercial usage, have no connection with the subject of such contracts." For instance, the purchase of a freezer may entail an obligation to receive monthly packages of frozen food for the first year of ownership (product tied to product)[36]; or the purchase of a heating system, the obligation to enter into a five-year service contract (product tied to service). On the

---

[33] Case 77/77 *loc. cit.* note 47, *supra*.

[34] As Adv.-Gen. Warner pointed out, a legal and moral right to security of supplies is the counterpart, for a contractual customer, of his loss of freedom to seek the best available bargain at a given moment, and the loyalty of regular, though non-contractual, customers also merits special consideration: [1978] E.C.R. at p. 538.

[35] See also the Dec. of the Commission in *Hugin, loc. cit.* note 29, p. 404, *supra*. In its judgment in Case 22/78 *Hugin* v. *Commission ibid.*, the Court did not deal with the issue of whether Hugin's behaviour constituted an abuse, since it found that there could have been no effect on trade between Member States.

[36] See also the allegations of "memory bundling" and "software bundling" in the Commission's Statement of Objections against IBM, which are summarised in the account of the settlement of the case: Comp.Rep. 1984, point 94.

other hand, the inclusion of a meal in the price of an airline ticket has been cited[37] as a possible example of tying sanctioned by commercial usage.

The main objection to tying is that it enables a dominant position on market A to be used in order to gain a competitive advantage on market B, by reducing the outlets for third parties operation on that market. It may also be directly oppressive to consumers on market A.

(viii) *Mergers*

A merger takes place when two or more undertakings which were formerly independent are brought under common control.[38] There is a great variety of ways in which this may come about, most obviously where the company carrying on undertaking A acquires a controlling percentage of shares in the company carrying on undertaking B.[39] A merger between undertakings operating on totally unrelated markets may result in an accretion of economic power, through improved access to finance, entailing either the creation or the enhancement of a dominant position on one of the markets. However, the type of merger which is most likely to have an adverse effect on competition is one between undertakings which are actually or potentially competitors, or between an undertaking and its major supplier or consumer.

The EEC Treaty does not contain any explicit merger control provision equivalent to Article 66 ECSC, which requires the prior authorisation of the Commission for mergers involving coal or steel undertakings. However, *Continental Can Company*[40] established that a merger which causes a dominant position to be strengthened beyond a certain point may amount to an abuse of that position within the meaning of Article 86.

The facts of the case have been referred to several times, and a brief recapitulation should be sufficient here. The American container manufacturer, Continental Can Company, had acquired control of the German firm SLW which was an important manufacturer of certain light metal containers and other related products. Subsequently, through its subsidiary, Europemballage, Continental Can acquired the Dutch firm TDV which specialised in similar products. The Commission decided that the merger with TDV amounted to an abuse of the dominant position which Continental Can held, through SLW, on three packaging markets in Germany, because TDV had been a potential competitor of SLW and the effect of bringing it into the Continental Can group had been practically to eliminate competition in the products concerned over a substantial part of the common market.

Although the Decision was annulled on the ground that the relevant facts had not been adequately analysed, the Court confirmed the view of

---

[37] By Siragusa in Van Damme, *op. cit.* note 3, p. 398, *supra* at p. 412.
[38] Where an undertaking already exercises effective control over another, measures taken in order to integrate the undertakings more fully amount merely to an internal reorganisation. See the Commission's comments on the planned reorganisation of Kleber-Colombes within the Michelin group: Comp.Rep. 1980, point 156.
[39] For a clear discussion of the different forms mergers may take, see Korah, *Competition Law of Britain and the Common Market*.
[40] Case 6/72 *loc. cit.* note 1, p. 397, *supra*.

the Commission that, in principle, Article 86 might apply in such circumstances. Four main reasons for this were given in the judgment[41]:

(a) *The distinction between market behaviour and structural measures.* A distinction had been drawn by the applicants between practices having a direct effect on the market to the detriment of consumers and trade partners, and internal structural measures of an undertaking. In the Court's view, the distinction could not be decisive for the application of the Article because "any structural measure may influence market conditions, if it increases the size and the economic power of the undertaking."[42] In other words, the difference between the two cases is one of degree in the directness of the effect felt by other market participants.

(b) *Articles 2 and 3(f).* The Court said that it was necessary "to go back to the spirit, general scheme and wording of Article 86, as well as to the system and objectives of the Treaty."[43] In particular, the Court described the requirement in Article 3(f) of instituting a system to ensure undistorted competition in the Common Market as being "so essential that without it numerous provisions of the Treaty would be pointless."[44] This requirement corresponded with the Community's task of promoting "a harmonious development of economic activities" in Article 2. The Court reasoned *a fortiori* from Article 3(f) that the complete elimination of competition would not be permissible. The Treaty might allow competition to be restricted under certain conditions in order to achieve a balance between its various aims, but this would always be subject to the limitations implicit in Articles 2 and 3. "Going beyond this limit involves the risk that the weakening of competition would conflict with the aims of the common market."[45]

(c) *The parallel between Article 85 and Article 86.* Given that "Articles 85 and 86 seek to achieve the same aim on different levels"[46] they must not be interpreted in a contradictory way. It would put the common market system in jeopardy if undertakings could avoid the prohibition in Article 85 by forming a closer combination virtually excluding any serious possibility of competition, without bring themselves within the scope of Article 86.

(d) *The examples of abuses in Article 86.* The Court pointed out that the list was not intended to be exhaustive. Nevertheless, the examples in Article 86(c) and (d) showed that the Article was not only aimed at practices directly harmful to consumers but also at those "which are detrimental to them through their impact on an effective competitive structure."[47]

The Court concluded:

---

[41] These are set out at [1973] E.C.R., pp. 242 *et seq.*
[42] *Ibid.* p. 243.
[43] *Ibid.*
[44] *Ibid.*, p. 244.
[45] *Ibid.*, p. 245.
[46] *Ibid.*, p. 244.
[47] *Ibid.*, p. 245.

"Abuse may therefore occur if an undertaking in a dominant position strengthens such position in such a way that the degree of dominance reached substantially fetters competition, *i.e.* that only undertakings remain in the market whose behaviour depends on the dominant one."[48]

Continental Can was a landmark case because it showed that an adverse effect on the competitive structure of a market would be sufficient in itself to attract the prohibition in Article 86.[49] Nevertheless, as an instrument of merger control the Article has serious drawbacks. In the first place, there must be a pre-existing dominant position to be abused. Arguably, this may include the case where a single merger operation, *e.g.* between the two leading firms on a given market, results in the creation of a dominant position of such magnitude as substantially to fetter competition, although it may not be possible to identify separate points in time at which the dominant position was created and afterwards strengthened. However, it is clear that Article 86 cannot apply to mergers falling short of dominance, even if these seriously restrict effective competition and make further concentration inevitable. Secondly, in *Continental Can* the Court spoke of strengthening an undertaking's position to a point where all the remaining operators on the market are dependent upon it. In the light of developments in non-merger cases,[50] it seems unlikely that the Court would insist on a merger having such a drastic effect before it would qualify as abusive. Nevertheless, at the best Article 86 can only cover cases where severe damage to the competitive process has already been done.

A proposal has been put forward by the Commission for a regulation to establish more effective machinery for the control of mergers with a Community dimension. This would include a requirement that large-scale mergers be notified in advance to the Commission and a power for the latter to order the suspension of a merger during investigation of its compatibility with the common market. The proposal was first submitted to the Council in 1973 and amended versions were submitted in 1981 and 1984.[51] At the time of writing it was still being discussed by the Council's Economic Questions Working Group and agreement seemed unlikely without further significant amendments. It was not, therefore, thought appropriate to examine the provisions of the proposed regulation in detail.

Meanwhile the Commission continues to monitor, pursuant to Article 86, the more significant mergers that take place in the Community, using the general powers for the application of the rules on competition given to it by Regulation 17. In some cases its intervention has resulted either in the abandonment of merger proposals or in their modification so as to ensure

---

[48] *Ibid.*

[49] See the discussion at pp. 414–415, *supra.*

[50] See, in particular, Joined Cases 6 and 7/73 *Commercial Solvents Corporation, loc. cit.* note 31, p. 404, *supra;* Case 27/76 *United Boards, loc. cit.* note 6, p. 398, *supra;* Case 85/76 *Hoffmann-La Roche, loc. cit.* note 7, p. 399, *supra;* Case 322/81 *Michelin, loc. cit.* note 2, p. 397, *supra.* The Commission has written that "strengthening by means of merger is likely to constitute an abuse if any distortion of the resulting market structure interferes with the maintenance of remaining competition (which has already been weakened by the very existence of this dominant position) or its development": Comp.Rep. 1980, point 150. See also Siragusa in Van Damme, *op. cit.* note 3, p. 398, *supra.* pp. 402–407.

[51] See, respectively, O.J. 1973 C92/1, O.J. 1982 C36 and O.J. 1984 C51.

the maintenance of adequate competition on the market in question.[52] The power to adopt interim measures in competition matters, which was recognised by the European Court in *Camera Care*,[53] is available to the Commission to prevent the implementation of a merger plan pending a decision as to its compatibility with the common market. This is an important power, in view of the failure so far to establish special merger control machinery, since it is notoriously hard to reverse the economic consequences of a merger once it has been completed.[54]

Effect on trade between Member States

An abuse of a dominant position only attracts the prohibition in Article 86 if it is capable of affecting trade between Member States.

As we have seen, the same condition applies under Article 85, and the general principles relating to its operation were discussed in Chapter 14, *supra*,[55] including those established in cases which have arisen under Article 86.[56] It was noted, in particular, that the Court of Justice considers the purpose of the condition to be that of defining the boundary between the EEC rules on competition and the competition laws of Member States. The test is whether the agreement or practice in question constitutes a threat to freedom of trade between Member States in a way that might harm the attainment of the objectives of a single Member State. The Court has also made clear that the condition may be satisfied in different ways: through the diversion of the flow of goods or services from its normal channels; or through the modification of the structure of competition within the common market.

The leading case on the application of the condition in the context of Article 86 is *Hugin*.[57] The abuse found by the Commission against the Swedish manufacturer of cash registers, Hugin, was that it had refused to supply spare parts for its machines to a London firm, Liptons, and had prohibited its subsidiaries and distributors in the common market from selling spare parts outside its distribution network. The business of Liptons was the maintenance and repair of cash registers and the renting-out or sale of reconditioned machines. The supply of spare parts from Sweden to the United Kingdom would not entail trade between Member States, but there were two ways in which the condition might have been satisfied. One was that the withholding of the parts might have interfered with the commercial activities of Liptons in other Member States. However, the Court of Justice was satisfied that the firm had never extended its activities outside the

---

[52] See, *e.g.* the acquisition by Pilkington of BSN-Gervais-Danone's German subsidiary, Flachglas AG, Comp.Rep. 1980, points 152–155, and the proposed merger between Fortia AB and Wright Scientific Ltd., Comp.Rep. 1981, point 112.

[53] Case 792/79R *Camera Care* v. *Commission* [1980] E.C.R. 119.

[54] An application for interim measures was made by the complainant, Amicon Corporation, in relation to the proposed Fortia/Wright scientific merger. It was withdrawn when the merger negotiations were broken off.

[55] At pp. 375–377.

[56] See, in particular, Joined Cases 6 and 7/73 *Commercial Solvents Corporation*, *loc. cit.* note 31, p. 404, *supra*; Case 22/78 *Hugin*, *loc. cit.* note 29, p. 404, *supra*; Case 22/79 *Greenwich Film Production* v. *SACEM* [1979] E.C.R. 3275.

[57] Case 22/78 *loc. cit.* note 29, p. 404, *supra*. See the discussion at [1979] E.C.R., pp. 1898–1901.

United Kingdom; indeed, its business was of a kind that could only be carried on profitably within a local area. The second possibility was that Hugin's policy of not supplying spare parts outside its distribution network restricted intra-Community trade in the parts. This, too, was rejected. The Court pointed out that the value of the articles was small and that anyone needing a part which the local Hugin subsidiary could not supply would normally address its request directly to the parent company. Hugin had not, therefore, been guilty of diverting trade from channels it would otherwise have followed. The Court regarded cases like that of Liptons, which had attempted to obtain Hugin spare parts in other Member States, as exceptional and, therefore, it seems, covered by the *de minimis* principle.[58]

---

[58] See Case 56/65 *La Technique Minière* v. *Maschinenbau Ulm* [1966] E.C.R. 235; [1966] C.M.L.R. 357; Case 5/69 *Volk* v. *Vervaecke* [1969] E.C.R. 295; [1969] C.M.L.R. 273. See also the discussion of the principle in Chap. 14, *supra*.

CHAPTER 16

APPLICATION OF ARTICLES 85 AND 86

Introduction

Articles 87 to 89 EEC contain provisions relating to the implementation of the substantive rules on competition in Article 85 and Article 86. Under Article 87 the Council is empowered to enact "any appropriate regulations or directives" for this purpose. Pending the exercise by the Council of its powers under Article 87, a transitional regime is provided by Articles 88 and 89. The task of applying the competition rules in individual cases, including the granting of exemption under Article 85(3), is given by Article 88 to "the authorities in Member States." The Commission is required under Article 89 to investigate cases of suspected infringement and, where it finds an infringement has occurred, to propose measures for bringing it to an end. If this does not produce the desired result, the Commission must record the infringement in a reasoned decision, which may be published; and it may authorise Member States to take the steps needed to remedy the situation. However, it has no powers that can be used directly against offending undertakings.

The principal measure enacted by the Council under Article 87 is Regulation 17, which came into force on March 13, 1962.[1] The Regulation has been amended from time to time[2] but the legal machinery established by it remains substantially in place. This has been supplemented by further Council regulations[3] and by regulations adopted by the Commission under delegated powers.[4] On its own terms Regulation 17 is of general application but the transport sector was removed from its scope by Regulation 141.[5] A special competition measure for transport by road, rail and inland waterway, Regulation 1017/68,[6] was subsequently adopted. The transitional regime in Articles 88 and 89 has thus been superseded by regulations pursuant to Article 87, except in the case of air and sea transport.[7]

The present chapter is concerned mainly with the system for the administration of the EEC rules on competition developed on the basis of Regulation 17. Under this system the Commission wields real executive powers, subject to judicial control by the European Court. We examine the central functions of the Commission in the machinery and the ancillary role reserved for national competition authorities. We also discuss briefly the

[1] J.O. 1962, 204; O.J. 1959–62, 87.
[2] Most recently by the 1985 Act of Accession.
[3] See, in particular, those empowering the Commission to adopt block exemption regs, Chap. 14, *supra.*
[4] Notably Reg. 99/63 on the hearings provided for in Art. 19(1) and (2) of Reg. 17: (J.O. 1963 2268; O.J. 1963–64, 47).
[5] J.O. 1962, 2751.
[6] J.O. 1968 L. 175/1; O.J. 1968, 302. The machinery established by the Reg. is broadly similar to that of Reg. 17.
[7] On the implications for the direct effect of Arts. 85 and 86, see *infra.*

application of the competition rules, in so far as they are directly effective, by the ordinary courts in the Member States.[8]

First steps

Proceedings for the application of Article 85 or Article 86 may be started by the Commission on its own initiative[9] or in response to an application for negative clearance[10] and/or the notification of an agreement[11] or to a complaint.[12]

(i) *Action by the Commission*

Where the Commission itself takes the initiative in a competition matter it is said to act *ex officio*. It may be prompted to do so by various factors, *e.g.* newspaper reports, the results of studies or unofficial representations.

(ii) *Action by the parties to a possible infringement*

A feature of Regulation 17 is the encouragement given to the parties to a possible infringement of the competition rules to bring the matter themselves to the attention of the Commission, through the negative clearance and notification procedures.

The purpose of an application for negative clearance is to enable undertakings to ascertain whether the Commission considers any aspects of an agreement to which they are party, or of their business conduct, to fall within Article 85(1) or Article 86.[13] A formal grant of clearance consists of a decision by the Commission certifying that, on the basis of the facts in its possession, there are no grounds under those provisions for action to be taken in respect of the agreement or conduct in question. An application will only have point where infringement of Article 85 or Article 86 seems a genuine possibility. Undertakings that feel any doubts about an agreement should consider, in particular, whether it may be covered by a block exemption regulation or by one of the Commission's Notices.

With the adoption of Regulation 17 the national competition authorities lost their transitional power under Article 88 to declare the prohibition in Article 85(1) inapplicable to agreements which fulfil the criteria of Article 85(3). Article 9(1) of the Regulation confers that power exclusively upon the Commission. Notification of an agreement to the Commission is made for the purpose of seeking exemption, either by an individual grant or under the opposition procedure of a block exemption regulation.[14] Where there are grounds for believing that an agreement may be caught by Article 85(1), Regulation 17 provides powerful incentives for the parties to notify punctually.

---

[8] The subject-matter of this chapter is covered in greater depth by Kerse in his excellent treatise, *EEC Antitrust Procedure*, (1981) European Law Centre, with cumulative supplements.
[9] Reg. 17, Art. 3(1).
[10] Reg. 17, Art. 2. See *infra*.
[11] Reg. 17, Arts. 4(1) and 5(1). See *infra*.
[12] Reg. 17, Art. 3(1) and (2).
[13] See the Complementary Note to Commission Reg. 2526/85, O.J. 1985 L 240/1 at p. 6. The Reg. amended Reg. 27 on the form to be used in applying for negative clearance or notifying an agreement (see *infra*).
[14] *Ibid.* at p. 7. On the opposition procedure, see Chap. 14, *supra*.

In the first place, Article 4(1) of the Regulation lays down the general rule that, until agreements have been notified to the Commission, they cannot be the subject of a decision in application of Article 85(3). This is so, even if the agreement in question manifestly satisfies the criteria of exemption in the paragraph. Certain categories of agreements are, however, excused notification, as a matter of administrative convenience, because they pose no very serious threat to competition and are considered particularly likely to qualify for exemption.[15] The list, which is to be found in Article 4(2), comprises: (1) agreements between parties from the same Member State which do not relate either to imports or to exports between Member States, *e.g.* a tied house agreement with a local brewery[16]; (2) agreements between two parties which *only*: (a) restrict the freedom of one party to determine the prices or conditions of business on which goods obtained from the other party may be resold; or (b) impose restrictions on the exercise of the rights of an assignee or user of industrial property rights or of know-how[17]; (3) agreements which have as their *sole* object: (a) the development or uniform application of standards or types; or (b) joint research and development; or (c) specialisation in the manufacture of products including agreements necessary for the achievement thereof, subject to a market share threshold of 15 per cent. and an aggregate turnover threshold of 200 million units of account. The categories in Article 4(2) are narrowly drawn and the paragraph has been largely superseded by the block exemption Regulations[18] in whose provisions, it has been pointed out, there lies greater legal security.[19]

Secondly, the date of notification determines how far a grant of exemption may be made retrospective. For this purpose Regulation 17 draws a distinction between agreements which have been entered into since the date when it came into force, known as "new agreements," and agreements then already in existence, known as "old agreements." Under Article 6(1) in the case of new agreements exemption canot be granted from a date earlier than that of notification. In respect of any period which may have elapsed between its making and notification, a new agreement caught by Article 95(1) is irretrievably void pursuant to Article 85(2). Old agreements, on the other hand, benefit from transitional arrangements. If notified by the dates specified in Article 5(1) of Regulation 17,[20] they are

---

[15] Case 63/75 *Fonderies Roubaix-Wattrelos* v. *Fonderies A. Roux* [1976] E.C.R. 111; [1976] 1 C.M.L.R. 538.

[16] See Case 43/69 *Bilger* v. *Jehle* [1970] E.C.R. 127; [1974] 1 C.M.L.R. 382. The Court said in that case that the phrase "relate to imports or exports" in Art. 85(1). See also Case 63/75 *Fonderies Roubaix-Wattrelos* v. *Fonderies A. Roux, loc. cit.* note 15, *supra*, where it was held that agreements between undertakings from the same Member State granting exclusive sales concessions in that State need not be regarded as relating to imports within the meaning of Art. 4(2)(1) merely because the goods in question came originally from another Member State. *Cf.* joined Cases 209–215 and 218/78 *Van Landewyck* v. *Commission* [1980] E.C.R. 3125; [1981] 3 C.M.L.R. 134; joined Cases 96–102, 104, 105, 108 and 110/82 *IAZ* v. *Commission* [1983] E.C.R. 3369; [1984] 3 C.M.L.R. 276.

[17] Art. 4(2)(2)(*b*) has been very strictly construed by the Commission: see *Re. Vaessen/Moris* 1979 O.J. L19/32; [1970] 1 C.M.L.R. 511. On patent licensing agreements, see Chap. 18 *infra*.

[18] See Chap. 14, *supra*.

[19] By Kerse, *op. cit.* note 8, *supra*, at p. 42.

[20] February 1, 1963 for bilateral agreements, otherwise November 1, 1962.

eligible for exemption extending back to the date when Article 85(1) first applied to them. In addition, if there are clauses in a duly notified old agreement which are ineligible for exemption, the Commission has power under Article 7(1) to grant retrospective validation to the agreement as a whole, provided that the offending clauses are amended or abandoned for the future. Similar arrangements have been made to cater for agreements brought within the scope of the competition rules as a result of successive enlargements of the Community ("accession agreements").[21] The period of grace for the notification of such agreements is six months from the date of accession.[22]

Thirdly, where activity takes place under an agreement which has been notified, the parties are protected by Article 15(5) of Regulation 17 against the imposition of fines for the infringement of Article 85. However, the Commission may put an end to that immunity by informing the parties that, in the light of a preliminary examination, it has formed the view that Article 85(1) applies to the agreement and exemption under Article 85(3) is not justified.[23] The intimation of such an assessment is an act reviewable under Article 173, since it alters the legal position of the parties to the agreement.[24]

A final incentive to notify, which applies only to old agreements, is found in the doctrine of provisional validity. We return to the topic of provisional validity in the section dealing with the application of the EEC competition rules in the national courts.

For Article 86 there is, of course, no equivalent to the procedure for notifying agreements with a view to obtaining exemption under Article 85(3).

A special form, known as Form A/B, has been provided for applications for negative clearance in respect of Article 85(1) and for notifications,[25] and its use is compulsory.[26] There is no such requirement in the case of applications for negative clearance in respect of Article 86. In all cases the relevant facts must be fully and accurately disclosed to the Commission.[27] A decision granting negative clearance on the basis of incomplete or incorrect information could be without effect, and one granting exemption could be revoked. The Commission also has power under Article 15(1)(a) of Regulation 17 to impose fines on undertakings that intentionally or negligently supply incorrect or misleading information.

(iii) Complaints

Article 3(2) of Regulation 17 provides that those entitled to make application to the Commission to set infringement proceedings in motion are Member States and "natural or legal persons who claim a legitimate inter-

---

[21] Reg. 17, Art. 25.
[22] Ibid., para. (2).
[23] Reg. 17, Art. 15(6).
[24] Joined Cases 8–11/66 Cimenteries v Commission [1967] E.C.R. 75; [1967] C.M.L.R. 77.
[25] The latest version of Form A/B was annexed to Reg. 2526/85, loc. cit. note 13, supra, at pp. 3–5.
[26] Reg. 27, Art. 4. See Case 30/78 Distillers Company v. Commission [1980] E.C.R. 2229; [1980] 3 C.M.L.R. 121; Joined Cases 209–215 and 218/78, Van Landewyck v. Commission loc. cit. note 16, supra.
[27] See Complementary Note to Reg. 2526/85, loc. cit. note 13, supra. at p. 8.

est." The practice of the Commission indicates that complaints will be accepted from persons with a plausible claim to have suffered as a result of an alleged infringement of the competition rules or from a body representing such persons. There is a form for the submission of complaints (Form C) but its use is optional. To maximise the chance that action will be taken by the Commission, an attempt should be made in the complaint to demonstrate, with as much detailed information as possible, that each of the criteria of prohibition in Article 85 and/or Article 86 is satisfied and, where relevant, that exemption under Article 85(3) is not available.

A complainant has no right to insist that the Commission adopt a final decision as to the existence or otherwise of an alleged infringement.[28] On the other hand, he is entitled to have his complaint taken seriously. Where the Commission does not propose to initiate infringement proceedings, it is required by Article 6 of Regulation 99/63 to inform any complainants of its reasons and to fix a time limit within which they may submit further comments in writing. A letter sent in response to such further comments, which finally rejects the complaint, may be the subject of an action for annulment under Article 173 even if it is not signed by a member of the Commission but by the Director-General for Competition.[29] Moreover, it has been clear since *Metro (No. 1)*[30] that a complainant whose interests are affected by a grant of exemption under Article 85(3) has *locus standi* to bring annulment proceedings.

Fact-finding

Where fact-finding is necessary, the Commission has important powers under Article 11 and Article 14 of Regulation 17.

Article 11 enables the Commission to obtain "all necessary information from the Governments and competent authorities of the Member States and from undertakings and associations of undertakings." For seeking information from undertakings a two-stage procedure is laid down. The first stage consists of an informal request for specified information to be given by a certain date.[31] If the information requested is not forthcoming, the procedure enters its second, formal stage with the adoption by the Commission of a decision ordering that it be supplied.[32] Failure to comply with such a decision may result in the imposition of a fine under Article 15(1)(*b*) or of a periodic penalty payment under Article 16(1)(*c*).

Under Article 14 the Commission is empowered to enter the premises of undertakings, to examine and take copies of, or extracts from, books and business records and to ask for oral explanations on the spot. Inspections may take place on the basis of an authorisation in writing pursuant to para-

---

[28] Case 125/78 *GEMA* v. *Commission* [1979] E.C.R. 3173; [1980] 2 C.M.L.R. 177.
[29] Case 298/83 *CICCE* v. *Commission* (not yet reported). See also Case 210/81 *Demo-Studio Schmidt* v. *Commission* [1983] E.C.R. 3045; [1984] 1 C.M.L.R. 63.
[30] Case 26/76 *Metro* v. *Commission (No. 1)* [1977] E.C.R. 1875; [1978] 2 C.M.L.R. 1.
[31] Reg. 17, Art. 11(3). An incorrect response will attract a fine under Art. 15(1)(*b*) of the Reg. See, *e.g. Re Telos* O.J. 1982 L58/19; [1982] 1 C.M.L.R. 267.
[32] Reg. 17, Art. 11(5). See, *e.g.*, *Re. UNITEL* O.J. 1978 L157/39; [1978] 3 C.M.L.R. 306.

graph (2) of the Article or of a Commission decision pursuant to paragraph (3). In neither case need any advance warning be given.[33] Where the Commission's inspectors are armed merely with a written authorisation, the undertaking concerned may refuse to submit to investigation; but once it has agreed, there is an obligation to cooperate fully. Refusal of an investigation ordered by a decision may attract a fine under Article 15(1)(c) or a periodic penalty payment under Article 16(1)(d). In *National Panasonic*[34] the Court rejected the argument that Article 14 envisages a two-stage procedure, like that of Article 11, under which a binding decision may be adopted only after an attempt to carry out an investigation on the basis of a written authorisation has proved unsuccessful. The Court took the view that, on a true construction of the Article, the Commission has a choice between two possible methods of proceeding.

The Commission may be denied access to documents protected by the principle of the confidentiality of communications between lawyer and client. The principle, which is narrower in scope than the legal professional privilege of English law, was recognised by the Court of Justice in the *AM & S* case.[35] Protection of confidentiality was held to be subject, in effect, to three conditions. First, the communication must be "made for the purposes and in the interests of the client's rights of defence." That extended, in particular, to "all written communications exchanged after the initiation of the administrative procedure under Regulation No. 17 which may lead to a decision on the application of Articles 85 and 86 of the Treaty or to a decision imposing a pecuniary sanction on the undertaking,"[36] as well as to "earlier written communications which have a relationship to the subject-matter of that procedure."[37] Secondly, the communication must "emanate from independent lawyers, that is to say, lawyers who are not bound to the client by a relationship of employment."[38] Thirdly, the lawyers in question must be entitled to practise their profession in one of the Member States. Communications with two classes of lawyers are accordingly outwith the privilege, *viz* in-house lawyers, even in those Member States where they are subject to professional ethics and discipline, and lawyers from non-EEC countries.[39] Where the status of a document is disputed, the Commission may adopt a decision ordering its disclosure, which may then be challenged in proceedings under Article 173. Such proceedings would not automatically have suspensory effect, although suspension of the application of the decision, or any other interim measure, could be ordered in an appropriate case.[40]

---

[33] Case 136/79 *National Panasonic* v. *Commission* [1980] E.C.R. 2033; [1980] 3 C.M.L.R. 169.

[34] *Ibid.*

[35] Case 155/79 *A.M. & S.* v. *Commission* [1982] E.C.R. 1575; [1982] 2 C.M.L.R. 264.

[36] [1982] E.C.R. at p. 1611.

[37] *Ibid.*

[38] *Ibid.*

[39] The Commission sought unsuccessfully a mandate from the Council to negotiate agreements with certain third countries for the purpose of extending the principle of confidentiality to communications with lawyers from those countries. See Faull, (1985) 10 E.L.Rev. 119.

[40] See Arts. 185 and 186 EEC.

Positive reactions

(i) *General*

Once the relevant facts have been found, the Commission will consider the legal position and, if it seems likely that an infringement of Article 85 and/or Article 86 has occurred, proceedings may be initiated by sending the undertaking or undertakings concerned a statement of objections. Infringement proceedings are discussed in the next section of this Chapter. Where, on the other hand, Article 85(1) or Article 86 are thought not to apply, or exemption under Article 85(3) is available, a positive reaction will be prepared. To elicit such a reaction from the Commission it may have been necessary for parties to modify or abandon aspects of an agreement or business practice.[41] In some cases a decision of the Commission formally granting negative clearance or exemption may be considered necessary. Most proceedings, however, are brought to an end by a letter from the Directorate-General for Competition (DGIV) informing the parties that the file in the case is to be closed. These are known colloquially as "comfort letters."

(ii) *Negative clearance*

We have seen that negative clearance is a certification by the Commission that the facts in its possession provide no grounds under Article 85 or Article 86 for intervention. The value of the assurance given is proportional to the completeness of the disclosure made to the Commission. A decision granting negative clearance is probably not binding on national courts which derive jurisdiction to apply Article 85(1) or Article 86 from the direct effect of those provisions, though it is likely to have considerable persuasive authority. Where the Commission intends to grant negative clearance, it is required by Article 19(3) of Regulation 17 to publish in the *Official Journal* a summary of the relevant application and invite all interested third parties to submit their observations within a specified time limit, which may not be less than a month. The final decision must also be published.[42]

(iii) *Individual exemption*

A decision of the Commission granting individual exemption pursuant to Article 85(3) declares the prohibition in Article 85(1) inapplicable to the agreement in question. The extent to which exemption may be made retrospective was considered above. Under Article 8 of Regulation 17 exemption is granted for a fixed period and may be subjected to conditions. Before imposing an onerous condition the Commission must inform the parties of what it has in mind and give them an opportunity of making rep-

---

[41] See, *e.g.*, the far-reaching modifications required by the Commission in *Re Optical Fibres* O.J. 1986 L 236/30. These are discussed at p. 386, *supra*.
[42] Reg. 17, Art. 21(1).

resentations.[43] That right is not derived from the provisions of Regulation 99/63 on hearings in competition matters but from general principle. Exemption may be revoked pursuant to Article 8(3) where there has been a material change in the facts, where an obligation attached to the grant has been breached, where the decision was based upon incorrect information or induced by deceit or where the exemption has been abused by the parties. In the last three cases, the revocation may be made retroactive. As with negative clearance, the Commission must publish an Article 19(3) notice before adopting a final decision; and the latter must be published also.[44]

(iv) *Block exemption*

(a) *Conformity.* Where a notified agreement is found to be in conformity with a block exemption Regulation, the parties will be so informed by letter. Such letters merely state a view as to the applicability of directly effective provisions of Community law.

(b) *"No opposition" or "withdrawal of opposition."* Where the Commission expresses no opposition to a notified agreement within the period stipulated in a block exemption regulation (normally six months), or withdraws its opposition, the effect is to trigger the Regulation in respect of the agreement.[45] Since it alters the legal situation, the decision not to oppose or to withdraw opposition must, it is submitted, be susceptible of review under Article 173.

(v) *Comfort letters*

These are, in the phrase used by the Court of Justice in the *Perfumes* cases,[46] "merely administrative letters" signed by an official of D.G.I.V., usually of the rank of Director. Comfort letters may be used to indicate either that there are no grounds for applying Article 85(1) or Article 86 (in other words, as an informal negative clearance) or that an agreement falling within Article 85(1) is considered eligible for exemption under Article 85(3).[47] They state that the file will be closed, with the proviso that it may be re-opened if material legal or factual circumstances change. Dealing with a case in this way has the great advantage of simplifying and shortening the proceedings: a disadvantage is that the legal consequences of comfort letters remain somewhat uncertain.

For the addressee, it is submitted, a comfort letter gives rise to the legitimate expectation that, unless there is a material change of circumstances, no further action will be taken by the Commission on the file that has been

---

[43] Case 17/74 *Transocean Marine Paint* v. *Commission* [1974] E.C.R. 1063; [1974] 2 C.M.L.R. 459.

[44] Reg. 17, Art. 21(1).

[45] See D. Waelbroeck, (1986) 11 E.L.Rev. 268. *Cf.* Venit (1985) 22 C.M.L.Rev. 167.

[46] Joined Cases 253/78 and 1–3/79 *Procureur de la Republique* v. *Giry and Guerlain* [1980] E.C.R. 2327; [1981] 2 C.M.L.R. 94; Case 99/79 *Lancome* v. *Etos* [1980] E.C.R. 2511; [1981] 2 C.M.L.R. 164; Case 31/80 *L'Oreal* v. *De Nieuwe AMCK* [1980] E.C.R. 3775; [1981] 2 C.M.L.R. 235. See Korah, (1981) 6 E.L.Rev.14.

[47] On the extension of the use of comfort letters from the application of Art. 85(1) to that of Art. 85(3), see Comp.Rep. 1983 pp. 61–62.

closed.[48] If, without any change of circumstances, a decision inconsistent with a comfort letter were subsequently adopted, there would be grounds for seeking its annulment under Article 173. The Court of Justice has said that comfort letters are not binding on national courts; but a court may properly take into account the opinion contained in such a letter in reaching its own conclusion on the applicability of Article 85(1) or Article 86.[49] It has also been held that comfort letters bring to an end the provisional validity enjoyed by duly notified old agreements.[50] The Commission is not legally bound to publish a notice under Article 19(3) of Regulation 17 before disposing of a case by comfort letter but in the *Eleventh Report on Competition Policy* it announced that, where appropriate, it would do so.[51] By allowing interested third parties to make representations, a more rounded picture of a case may be obtained and the danger that facts may subsequently come to light that call for the reopening of the file is reduced. In our view, the security provided by a comfort letter following the publication of an Article 19(3) notice is not markedly inferior in practice to that provided by a decision granting negative clearance. However, where exemption is required, the use of comfort letters may be less satisfactory. The letter will state the Commission's view that the criteria in Article 85(3) are fulfilled but will do nothing to lift the prohibition in Article 85(1). Faced with evidence that an agreement falls within Article 85(1), and incapable itself of applying Article 85(3), a national court may feel justified in holding the agreement void pursuant to Article 85(2); though a better course would be to suspend proceedings and invite the Commission to adopt a formal decision granting exemption. The revised Form A/B asks notifying firms to indicate whether closure of the proceedings by a comfort letter would be acceptable to them. It seems wise advice to say no to this, if there is any risk at all that the validity of the agreement in question may be contested in proceedings before a national court.

A complainant dissatisfied with the closure of proceedings by a comfort letter faces the difficulty that the letter itself probably does not constitute an act susceptible of review under Article 173. However, from the Court's repeated statements about the need to safeguard the legitimate interests of complainants, it is impossible to believe no remedy would be available.[52] The right approach, it is submitted, is to challenge the legality of the decision rejecting the complaint.

[48] In *L'Oreal* v. *De Nieuwe AMCK* Advocate General Reischl said " . . . having regard to the principle that legitimate expectations must be upheld, the Commission may depart from the judgment arrived at by its officers only if the factual circumstances change or if its finding was reached on the basis of incorrect information": [1980] E.C.R. at p. 3803. See also the views expressed extra-judicially by Lord Mackenzie Stuart, 1983/1 LIEI 64. The crucial issue is whether a comfort letter can be regarded as an expression of intention by the Commission itself. D. Waelbroeck, *op. cit.* note 45, *supra*, recalls the strict requirements of a valid delegation of authority laid down by the Court in Case 9/56 *Meroni* v. *High Authority* [1957–58] E.C.R. 133. The Court refused in Case 71/74 *FRUBO* v. *Commission* to treat as binding upon the Commission a statement by an official that a certain amendment to an agreement would enable it to qualify for exemption: [1975] E.C.R. 563; [1975] 2 C.M.L.R. 123. That case is, in our view, distinguishable, since a comfort letter purports to dispose of the matter in question, albeit provisionally.
[49] See *Perfumes*, *loc. cit.* note 46, *supra*.
[50] Case 99/79 *Lancome* v. *Etos*, *loc. cit.* note 46, *supra*.
[51] See Comp.Rep. 1981, pp. 27–28; Comp.Rep. 1982, p. 83.
[52] See the cases cited in notes 29 and 30, *supra*.

Infringement proceedings

(i) *The right to a hearing*

(a) *Legal basis.* Before it adopts a decision applying Article 85 or Article 86 the Commission is required, pursuant to Article 19 of Regulation 17, to give the undertakings concerned the opportunity of being heard on the matters to which the Commission has taken objection. Other natural or legal persons, if they can show a sufficient interest, will also be entitled to a hearing. Detailed provisions on hearings were laid down by the Commission in Regulation 99/63.

Those provisions implement in the sphere of competition the general principle of law that a person whose interests are liable to be adversely affected by an individual decision of a public authority has a right to make his views known to the authority before the decision is taken. In cases to which Regulation 99 does not apply, it may be possible to invoke the general principle directly.[53]

(b) *The statement of objections.* In order for a person effectively to exercise his right to a hearing, he must be informed of the facts and considerations on the basis of which the responsible authority is minded to act.[54] Article 2(1) of Regulation 99 accordingly places the Commission under a duty to inform undertakings in writing of the objections raised against them. The issuing of a "statement of objections" marks the formal initiation of proceedings that may culminate in a finding that Article 85 or Article 86 has been infringed. Under Article 2(3) of the Regulation a fine or periodic penalty payment may only be imposed on an undertaking where objection has been notified in the requisite manner; while Article 4 provides that the Commission in its decisions shall deal only with objections on which undertakings have been afforded an opportunity of making their views known.

The Court of Justice has repeatedly affirmed that the statement of objections must set forth clearly all the essential facts upon which the Commission relies against the respondent undertakings.[55] A fairly succinct summary may be judged adequate for this purpose.[56] The final decision need not be an exact replica of the statement, since the Commission must take into account factors which emerge during the administrative proceedings: some objections may be abandoned altogether; and different arguments may be put forward in support of those which are maintained.[57]

---

[53] Case 17/74 *Transocean Marine Paint* v. *Commission loc. cit.* note 43, *supra*.
[54] See the principle enunciated by Advocate General Warner in Cases 113 and 118–121/77, *NTN Toyo Bearing Company and Others* v. *Council and Commission (Ballbearings)* [1979] E.C.R. 1185 at p. 1261; [1979] 2 C.M.L.R. 257. This was in the context of anti-dumping proceedings but the Advocate General clearly regarded the principle as applying generally in Community law.
[55] See Case 45/69 *Boehringer Mannheim* v. *Commission* [1970] E.C.R. 769; Case 85/76 *Hoffman La Roche* v. *Commission* [1979] E.C.R. 461; [1979] 3 C.M.L.R. 211; Joined Cases 100–103/80 *Musique Diffusion Francaise* v. *Commission (Pioneer)* [1983] E.C.R. 1825; [1983] 3 C.M.L.R. 221; Joined Cases 43 and 63/82 *VBVB and VBBB* v. *Commission* [1984] E.C.R. 19; [1985] 1 C.M.L.R. 27.
[56] *Ibid.*
[57] Joined Cases 100–103/80 *Pioneer loc. cit.* note 55, *supra*; Joined Cases 209–215 and 218/78 *Van Landewyck* v. *Commission loc. cit.* note 16, *supra*.

Where, however, the Commission wishes to introduce fresh objections, a supplementary statement should be sent to the respondents.[58]

In the *IBM* case[59] the Court upheld an objection to the admissibility of an action under Article 173 for the annulment of the decision to initiate competition proceedings against the applicants and of the statement of objections setting out the grounds on which the Commission considered they had violated Article 86. These, in the Court's view, were not acts within the meaning of the first paragraph of Article 173 but merely preparatory steps that might lead to the adoption of a reviewable act. In particular, the Court pointed out that a statement of objections does not place the undertaking concerned under any obligation to alter its business practices or deprive it of any protection it may enjoy against the imposition of fines. To review the legality of the measure in question would, the Court thought, be incompatible with the division of competences between itself and the Commission. Nevertheless, care was taken in the judgment not to exclude altogether the possibility of bringing an action under Article 173 to challenge measures still only at a preparatory stage, where the illegality is manifest.

(c) *Access to the file*. The Commission is not legally obliged to give respondent undertakings access to the whole of its file in a case.[60] In *Hoffman La-Roche* the Court said that undertakings "must have been afforded the opportunity during the administrative procedure to make known their views on the truth and relevance of the facts and circumstances alleged and on the documents used by the Commission to support its claim that there has been an infringement . . . "[61] The duty of disclosure is thus confined to documents specifically relied upon in constructing the case against a given respondent. However, the current practice of the Commission is more liberal than the law requires. Once a statement of objections has been issued, the respondent is allowed to examine and copy all the contents of the file, with the exception of "internal documents" and documents containing "business secrets."[62]

An example of an internal document would be the final assessment report of the inspectors who have conducted an investigation (as distinct from a clearly factual account of an inspection visit or a minute of statements by employees or officers of the undertaking concerned).[63] More difficult to classify are working documents produced by the Commission which constitute a vital element in the proof of the alleged infringement, *e.g.* a comparative study of the prices charged by a group of competing undertaking for which the existence of a concerted practice has been inferred. Subject to what is said below about the protection of business secrets, it is submitted that access ought to be given to such documents,

---

[58] Case 54/69 *Francolor* v. *Commission* [1972] E.C.R. 851; [1972] C.M.L.R. 557.
[59] Case 60/81 *IBM* v. *Commission* [1981] E.C.R. 2639; [1981] 3 C.M.L.R. 635.
[60] Joined Cases 56 and 58/64 *Consten and Grundig* v. *Commission* [1966] E.C.R. 299; [1966] C.M.L.R. 418; Joined Cases 43 and 63/82 *VBVB and VBBB* v. *Commission loc. cit.* note 55, *supra*.
[61] [1979] E.C.R. at p. 512.
[62] See Comp.Rep.1981, p. 30; Compt.Rep. 1982, pp. 40–41; Comp.Rep. 1983, pp. 63–64. See also Joshua, (1986) 6 E.L.Rev. 409.
[63] Comp.Rep. 1983, pp. 63–64.

where this is necessary to enable an undertaking fully to grasp the case it has to answer.

Article 20(1) provides that information required pursuant to the Commission's powers under Regulation 17 shall be used only for the purposes of the relevant investigation. This precludes its use, for instance, in civil proceedings before a national court. By Article 20(2) the Commission is forbidden to divulge information so acquired which is "of the kind covered by the obligation of professional secrecy." That duty is, however, expressed to be without prejudice to the provisions of Article 19 of the right to a hearing and of Article 21 on the publication of decisions. It follows that certain information within the protection of Article 20 may properly be disclosed to an undertaking to enable it to answer objections that have been raised against it. However, there is a duty, deriving not from Regulation 17 but from general principle, against the disclosure of business secrets.[64] What amounts to a business secret has yet to be clarified fully but the notion would presumably cover such things as turnover figures, customer lists, investment plans and technical or commercial know-how. The Commission is not allowed to use against an undertaking documents which it is prevented from disclosing because they contain other firms' business secrets, where the withholding of the documents would adversely affect the ability of the respondent to express its views on them.[65] To avoid such an outcome, the Commission may seek the permission of the undertakings concerned (which are likely to be competitors or customers of the respondent) to the disclosure of their secrets. Or it may offer the respondent an edited version of the documents.

The Commission takes the view that the complainant in a case is not automatically entitled to see the file.[66] However, it will normally provide him with at least an edited version of the reply received from the undertaking complained against; and, it may invite his comments, where relevant, on certain evidence, *e.g.* documents discovered in the course of an investigation under Article 14. If the respondent asserts that documents the Commission is proposing to hand over to the complainant contain business secrets, it must be given an opportunity to challenge the decision rejecting that claim, before the delivery takes place.[67]

(d) *Hearing the parties.* The letter under cover of which the statement of objections is sent will invite the respondent undertaking to make known in writing its views on the objections within a specified period (normally three months). The undertaking will also be informed that it may include in its written comments a request for an opportunity to put forward its arguments orally. Under Article 7 of Regulation 99/63 the Commission is bound to accede to a request for an oral hearing, where a sufficient interest

---

[64] Case 53/85 *AKZO* v. *Commission* (not yet reported).
[65] Case 85/76 *Hoffmann La Roche* v. *Commission loc. cit.* note 55, *supra.*
[66] Comp.Rep. 1983, p. 64. See also Joshua, *op. cit.* note 62, *supra*, pp. 419–423. In Joined Cases 209–215 and 218/78 *Van Landewyck* v. *Commission loc. cit.* note 16, *supra*, the Court said Art. 19(2) of Reg. 17 gives complainants "a right to be heard and not a right to receive confidential information": [1980] E.C.R. at p. 3239.
[67] Case 53/85, *AKZO.* v. *Commission* (not yet reported).

is shown or where it is proposing to impose a fine or periodic penalty payment. The complainant in a case will usually be invited to the oral hearing.

The purpose of the oral hearing is to enable the parties further to develop their written submissions. The procedure is administrative in character and parties are not allowed to question the Commission. To reassure parties that they would be given a fair opportunity to state their case and that due account would be taken of their submissions at the decision-making stage, the post of "Hearing Officer" was created in 1982.[68] The Hearing Officer has nothing to do with preparing or bringing home the allegation that the rules on competition have been infringed. He presides at the oral hearing and his views on the case are made known to the member of the Commission responsible for competition, to whom he has a right of direct access. His opinion is not disclosed to the parties. Whether its production may be obtained in proceedings before the Court of Justice, to support the argument that the rights of the defence have been violated, is an issue still to be resolved.

(ii) *Final decision*

(a) *Order to terminate infringement.* Article 3(1) of Regulation 17 provides that, where the Commission finds that there is an infringement of Article 85 or Article 86, it may by decision order this to be brought to an end. Termination may involve positive action on the part of the addressee or addressees, and the decision may specify the steps to be taken. Thus in *Commercial Solvents Corporation*[69] the Commission imposed on CSC and Istituto an obligation to deliver an initial quantity of aminobutanol to Zoja within 30 days and to submit within two months a plan for making supplies available in the longer term. The order was upheld by the Court of Justice which said of Article 3:

> "This provision must be applied in relation to the infringement which has been established and may include an order to do certain acts or provide certain advantages which have been wrongly withheld as well as prohibiting the continuation of certain action, practices or situations which are contrary to the Treaty."[70]

A periodic penalty payment may be attached to the order to ensure that it is complied with.

It was argued, *inter alia*, in the *G.V.L.*[71] case that the Commission had no power under Regulation 17 to adopt a decision recording an infringement which had already been brought to an end. The Court of Justice held that the Commission might well have a legitimate interest in taking such a decision, where it was necessary to clarify the legal position in order to prevent a repetition of the infringement.[72]

---

[68] Comp.Rep. 1982, 41–42. The Hearing Officer's terms of reference were published as an annex to the *Thirteenth Report on Competition Policy* (1983).
[69] Joined Cases 6 and 7/73 *Commercial Solvents Corporation* v. *Commission* [1974] E.C.R. 223; [1974] 1 C.M.L.R. 309.
[70] [1974] E.C.R. at p. 255.
[71] Case 7/82 *GVL* v. *Commission* [1983] E.C.R. 483; [1983] 3 C.M.L.R. 645.
[72] No dec. is necessary to bring the prohibition in Art. 85(1) or Art. 86 into force. See Reg. 17, Art. 1.

(b) *Fines*. For negligent or intentional infringements of Article 85 or Article 86 the Commission has power under Article 15(2) of Regulation 17 to impose fines of between 1000 and 1,000,000 ECUs, or a greater sum not exceeding 10 per cent of the turnover in the previous business year of each of the participating undertakings. In fixing the amount of fines regard must be had to the gravity and the duration of the infringement.

The power to fine is not only a means of punishing individual infringements: it is one of the policy instruments given to the Commission to enable it to apply in the sphere of competition the principles laid down by the EEC Treaty. An argument put forward by the applicants in the *Pioneer* case[73] was that the level of the fines imposed on them had been determined not by the gravity or duration of their particular conduct but by a change of policy on the part of the Commission. The Court of Justice held that it was open to the Commission to adopt a change of policy involving an increase in the fines imposed, where this was necessary to reinforce their deterrent effect.[74]

The gravity of an infringement is to be appraised, the Court has said, "by taking into account in particular the nature of the restrictions on competition, the number and size of the undertakings concerned, the respective proportions of the market controlled by them within the Community and the situation in the market where the infringement was committed."[75] Also relevant is the fact that agreements or conduct of the kind in question have been found in the past to be incompatible with the common market. Infringements the Commission considers particularly susceptible to heavy fines are, in respect of Article 85, export bans, market sharing and horizontal or vertical price-fixing and, in respect of Article 86, refusals to supply, price discrimination, exclusive or preferential long term supply arrangements and loyalty rebates.[76]

Where an undertaking cooperates with the Commission in the investigation of an infringement, this may be reflected in the level of the fine imposed on it. Another mitigating factor may be willingness to give certain undertakings as a guarantee against the recurrence of the infringement. In *Wood Pulp*[77] the fines on some of the respondents were reduced by 90 per cent. in consideration of an undertaking to market a proportion of their products in local EEC currencies instead of in U.S. dollars, which it was thought would make concerted price-fixing more difficult. The text of the undertakings was annexed to the decision.

The Commission will refrain from taking steps to collect a fine pending the outcome of review proceedings in the Court of Justice, if two conditions are met. These are the agreement of the undertaking concerned to pay interest in respect of any fine to which it is held liable by the Court and the provision of a bank guarantee covering the interest as well as the principal sum. The practice received the approval of the Court in the *A.E.G.*

[73] Joined Cases 100–103/80, *loc. cit.* note 55, *supra*.
[74] See the statement on the Commission's fining policy, Comp.Rep. 1983, pp. 56–58.
[75] Case 41/69 *ACF Chemiefarma* v. *Commission* [1970] E.C.R. 661 at p. 701.
[76] See Comp.Rep. 1983, p. 56.
[77] O.J. 1985 L85/1.

case.[78] The amount of interest normally charged by the Commission is the local bank rate plus 1 per cent..

The Commission's power to adopt interim measures

Regulation 17 does not expressly empower the Commission to adopt interim measures in respect of behaviour which is the subject of proceedings for the infringement of Article 85 or Article 86. The drafting of Article 3 of the Regulation in particular, seems to assume that, before a binding order is made, the Commission must have found that an infringement exists. However, in the *Camera Care* case[79] the Court of Justice held that a power to adopt interim measures is impliedly conferred on the Commission "to avoid the exercise of the power to make decisions given by Article 3 from becoming ineffectual or even illusory because of the action of certain undertakings."[80] According to the *Camera Care* judgment, the adoption of interim measures is subject to four conditions: that the case is urgent and the measures are needed to avoid a situation likely to cause serious and irreparable damage to the party seeking them, or one which is intolerable for the public interest; that the measures are of a temporary and conservatory nature and are restricted to what is necessary in the situation; that in adopting the measures the Commission maintains the essential safeguards guaranteed under Regulation 17, in particular by Article 19; and that the decision is made in a form that would enable it to be challenged before the Court.

In the *Ford* case[81] an interim decision of the Commission requiring Ford Germany to resume delivery of right hand drive vehicles to German dealers was annulled on the ground that the measure was not within the scope of the final decision that could be taken in the proceedings pending before the Commission. Those proceedings, it will be remembered, related to the standard form dealer agreement notified by Ford; and any decision under Article 3 would simply require the termination of the agreement. Even assuming (as was subsequently held)[82] that the refusal to supply right hand drive vehicles provided grounds for withholding exemption from the dealer agreement, the Commission could not by means of an interim decision adopt a separate enforceable order leaving Ford no option but to resume supplies.

Proceedings for the taking of interim measures will be suspended if satisfactory undertakings are obtained from the parties concerned.[83] For instance, in 1985 proceedings were started by the Commission in response to complaints from independent manufacturers that Ford was attempting to exclude them from the market for body panels in the United Kingdom by claiming copyright protection and refusing to grant licences on reasonable terms. The suspension of the proceedings followed an undertaking by

[78] Case 107/83 *AEG* v. *Commission* 3151; [1984] 3 C.M.L.R. 325.
[79] Case 792/79R *Camera Care* v. *Commission* [1980] E.C.R. 119; [1980] 1 C.M.L.R. 334.
[80] [1980] E.C.R. at p. 131.
[81] Joined Cases 228 and 229/82 *Ford* v. *Commission* [1984] E.C.R. 1129; [1984] 1 C.M.L.R. 649.
[82] Joined Cases 25 and 26/84 *Ford* v. *Commission* (not yet reported).
[83] See Comp.Rep. 1985, pp. 55–56.

Ford to offer licences immediately to its competitors in the United Kingdom for the manufacture and sale of the body parts of certain models and an offer to settle copyright infringement proceedings pending before the English courts.

Review by the Court of Justice

Decisions of the Commission in the exercise of its powers in connection with the application of Articles 85 and 86 are subject to review by the Court of Justice under Article 173 EEC. We have seen that an action may lie in respect of decisions on ancillary matters such as an order to produce documents,[84] as well as of final decisions ordering the termination of infringements or granting negative clearance or exemption. The parties to an agreement or to conduct which is the subject of competition proceedings, and any complainants,[85] should have no difficulty in establishing *locus standi*. The four usual grounds of review apply: lack of competence; infringement of an essential procedural requirement; infringement of the Treaty or of any rule of law relating to its application; and misuse of powers. The Court has made clear from the outset that, where complex economic evaluations are called for, it will not substitute its own discretion for that of the Commission but will confine itself to an examination of the relevance of the facts and considerations taken into account, and of the conclusions drawn, in the decision.[86]

However, in reviewing a decision to impose a fine or periodic penalty payment, the Court enjoys unlimited jurisdiction, pursuant to Article 17 of Regulation 17 and Article 172 EEC. This means that it is not required simply to quash a decision of which it disapproves but may determine for itself what the fine or penalty, if any, should be.

The role of national competition authorities

(i) *Application of the EEC rules on competition*

It was pointed out in the opening section of this Chapter that the leading role given to national authorities under the transitional regime of Article 88 was lost to the Commission with the coming into force of Regulation 17. The authorities referred to in Article 88 are those responsible in the Member States for the application of domestic competition law, including courts specifically entrusted with this function, but not the ordinary courts before which directly effective Community provisions may be invoked.[87] Under Article 9 of Regulation 17 the national authorities have no power to apply Article 85(3); and their power to apply Article 85(1) and Article 86 is lost as soon as the Commission initiates any procedure under Article 2 (negative clearance), Article 3 (termination of infringements) or Article 6 (exemption). One of the questions put to the Court of Justice in *Brasserie*

---

[84] See, *e.g.*, Case 53/85 *AKZO* v. *Commission* (not yet reported).
[85] See the cases cited in notes 28 and 29, *supra*.
[86] Joined Cases 56 and 58/64 *Consten and Grundig* v. *Commission loc. cit.* note 60, *supra*.
[87] Case 127/73 *BRT* v. *SABAM* [1974] E.C.R. 51; [1974] 2 C.M.L.R. 238.

de Haecht (No. 2)[88] was whether acknowledgement of the receipt of an application for negative clearance or of a notification amounted to the initiation of a procedure for this purpose. The Court held that it did not. The reference in Article 9(3) concerned "an authoritative act of the Commission, eivdencing its intention of taking a decision under the said Articles."[89]

The Commission is required to exercise its powers under Regulation 17 in close liaison with the national authorities.[90] They are sent all the important documents in a case and are represented on the Advisory Committee on Restrictive Practices and Monopolies which must be consulted before a decision is taken establishing an infringement of Article 85 or Article 86 or granting negative clearance or exemption. A report on the outcome of the consultation is annexed to the Commission's draft decision. The fact that the report is not made available to the undertakings concerned may represent a defect in the implementation of the right to a hearing.[91]

(ii) *Application of national competition law*

There is scope for conflict between the EEC rules of competition and the competition law of Member States but in practice this has not proved to be a serious problem. The general principle was laid down by the Court of Justice in *Wilhelm* v. *Bundeskartellamt*[92] which arose out of action by the German authorities overlapping that of the Commission in respect of the famous dyestuffs cartel. The principle is that, since their objectives are different, the national rules may be applied in parallel with those of the EEC; but not so as to prejudice the uniform application of the latter throughout the common market. The implications of the principle are not free from doubt but they may be summarised as follows. First, if behaviour is contrary to both sets of rules, it may be dealt with under both, though to avoid double jeopardy there should be a set-off of any pecuniary sanctions that may be imposed.[93] Secondly, behaviour prohibited by Article 85 or Article 86 but permissible under the competition rules of a given Member State, cannot be treated as lawful in that one State. Thirdly, behaviour which does not satisfy the criteria in Article 85(1) or Article 86, *e.g.* because trade between Member States is not appreciably affected, may nevertheless be prohibited under national competition law.[94] Fourthly, a grant of exemption pursuant to Article 85(3) probably overrides any conflicting rules of national competition law, since it represents a positive choice of policy by the Community authorities. Such would appear to be the view of the Commission,[95] though the view that exemption merely removes the Community

---

[88] Case 48/72 *Brasserie de Haecht* v. *Wilkin (No. 2)* [1973] E.C.R. 77; [1973] C.M.L.R. 287.
[89] [1973] E.C.R. at p. 88.
[90] See in particular, Reg. 17, Arts. 10, 11(2) and 14(2), (4) and (5). See also Comp.Rep.1983 pp. 66–67.
[91] See the remarks on the Advisory Committee procedure by Advocate General Warner in Case 30/78 *Distillers Company* v. *Commission* [1980] E.C.R. at p. 2292.
[92] Case 14/68, [1969] E.C.R. 1; [1969] C.M.L.R. 100.
[93] *Ibid.*
[94] The Court of Justice so held in the *Perfumes* cases, *loc. cit.* note 46, *supra.*
[95] See Comp.Rep. 1974, p. 29.

barrier to the enforcement of an agreement, leaving any national barrier in place, has had powerful advocates.[96]

The EEC rules on competition and the national courts

(i) *The direct effect of Article 85(1) and Article 86*

In *BRT* v. *SABAM* the Court of Justice said: "As the provisions of Articles 85(1) and 86 tend by their very nature to produce direct effects in relations between individuals, these Articles create direct rights in respect of the individuals concerned which the national courts must safeguard."[97] That broad statement of principle needs to be qualified in two ways. First, the provision of Articles 85(1) and Article 86 are only directly effective within the framework of implementing measures adopted under Article 87, such as Regulation 17 itself. In the economic sectors where the transitional regime still applies (*i.e.* air and sea transport), the courts of Member States have no jurisdiction to apply those provisions in the absence of a relevant ruling by national competition authorities pursuant to Article 88 or of a decision by the Commission pursuant to Article 89(2).[98] Secondly, the doctrine of provisional validity, which is discussed below, prevents the application of the prohibition in Article 85(1) to, and consequential nullity of, certain agreements pending a decision by the Commission on the availability of exemption under Article 85(3).

We are concerned in this section with the ordinary national courts to which falls the task of safeguarding the rights (including privileges and immunities in the Hohfeldian sense)[99] conferred on individuals by Article 85(1) and Article 86, as by other directly effective provisions of Community law. They are to be distinguished from courts with special responsibilities in national competition matters whose authority to apply the EEC competition rules is derived from Article 88 and is subject to the limitation imposed by Article 9(3) of Regulation 17.[1]

(ii) *Nullity of prohibited agreements*

(a) *Euro-Defences.* So-called "Euro-Defences," based on the alleged infringement of Article 85 or Article 86, may be invoked in proceedings before national courts to cast doubt on the validity of transactions of which the enforcement is being sought. In the case of Article 85 the civil consequences of infringement are spelt out by the second paragraph which provides: "Any agreements or decisions prohibited pursuant to this Article shall be automatically void." The Court of Justice has stated that Article 85(2) is directly effective.[2] Article 86 contains no equivalent provision but

---

[96] See Markert (1974) 11 C.M.L.Rev. 92; Kerse *op. cit.* note 8, *supra*, at pp. 280–282.

[97] Case 127/73, [1974] E.C.R. at p. 62.

[98] Case 209/84 *Ministere Public* v. *Asjes* (not yet reported). On the situation prior to the enactment of Reg. 17, see Case 13/61 *Bosch* v. *de Geus* [1962] E.C.R. 45; [1962] C.M.L.R. 1.

[99] Hohfeld, *Fundamental Legal Conceptions*. In Hohfeld's analysis "privilege" connotes the absence of duty (hence of a right vested in another) and "immunity" the absence of liability (hence of a power vested in another).

[1] Case 127/73 *BRT* v. *SABAM loc. cit.* note 87, *supra*.

[2] Case 48/72 *Brasserie de Haecht* v. *Wilkin (No 2) loc. cit.* note 88, *supra*.

it is clear from general principle that a national court would be required to refrain from giving effect to an agreement caught by the prohibition in the Article, *e.g.* one binding a purchaser to obtain all or most of his requirements of goods of a certain description from a dominant supplier.

(b) *Provisional validity.* We have seen that Article 9(1) of Regulation 17 empowers the Commission alone to grant exemption under Article 85(3): in other words, the paragraph is not directly effective. Where, therefore, a national court finds an agreement to be within Article 85(1), it cannot save the agreement from the automatic nullity prescribed under paragraph (2) of the Article by declaring the prohibition inapplicable pursuant to paragraph (3). This will not matter in cases where exemption is excluded in principle because the agreement is a notifiable one which has not been notified: even if it were subsequently notified and received exemption, the decision of the Commission could not be made retrospectively effective to the date of the national proceedings. It is different where the proceedings relate to an agreement which is non-notifiable or has been notified, and which may accordingly benefit from a retroactive grant of exemption at some future date. For the prohibition in Article 85(1) to be declared inapplicable to an agreement to which it has already been applied by a national court would be highly unsatisfactory.

That risk has been removed in respect of old agreements by the development of the doctrine of provisional validity. The doctrine has been explained by the Court of Justice as a compromise between the general principle of legal certainty, which underlies the power of retrospective validation in Article 7 of Regulation 17, and the intention of Article 85(2) "to attach severe sanctions to a serious prohibition."[3] In *Brasserie de Haecht (No. 2)* the Court said:

> "In the case of old agreements: the general principle of contractual certainty requires, particularly when the agreement has been notified in accordance with the provision of Regulation No. 17, that the Court may only declare it to be automatically void after the Commission has taken a decision by virtue of that Regulation.
>
> In the case of new agreements, as the Regulation assumes that so long as the Commission has not taken a decision the agreement can only be implemented at the paties' own risk, it follows that notifications in accordance with Article 4(1) of Regulation No. 17 do not have suspensive effect."[4]

An old agreement which is non-notifiable or was notified by the dates specified in Article 5(1) of Regulation 17 must, therefore, be treated as valid in proceedings before a national court unless and until the Commission has taken a decision refusing it exemption.[5] In the latter event, however, the agreement will be rendered void *ab initio*. The view has been expressed by the Commission[6] that the doctrine should be applied by ana-

---

[3] *Ibid.* at p. 86.
[4] *Ibid.* at pp. 86–87.
[5] This was confirmed in Case 59/77 *De Bloos* v. *Bouyer* [1977] E.C.R. 2359; [1978] 1 C.M.L.R. 511. See Faull and Weiler, (1978) 3 E.L.Rev. 116.
[6] Comp.Rep. 1973, p. 19.

logy to accession agreements, and that, it is submitted, is likely to be the approach taken by the Court, if the issue is ever raised before it. On the other hand, new agreements, whether notifiable or not, do not enjoy provisional validity. According to the Court of Justice in *Brasserie de Haecht (No. 2)*, "Whilst the principle of legal certainty requires that, in applying the prohibitions of Article 85, the sometimes considerable delays by the Commission in exercising its powers should be taken into account, this cannot, however, absolve the Court from the obligation of deciding on the claims of interested parties who invoke the automatic nullity."[7] In such circumstances, the choices open to the national court are: to enforce the agreement, if it has no perceptible effect on competition or trade between Member States and is, therefore, clearly outwith Article 85(1); to treat the agreement as void if the Court considers it to be caught by Article 85(1) and to have no realistic hope of exemption under Article 85(3); otherwise, to suspend proceedings until the Commission has made up its mind.[8]

(c) *Severance*. In *Societe Technique Miniere* v. *Maschinenbau Ulan*[9] the Court of Justice declared that the automatic nullity in Article 85(2) "applies to those parts of the agreement affected by the prohibition, or to the agreement as a whole if it appears that those parts are not severable from the agreement itself."[10] Whether any offending clauses can be severed, leaving the main part of the agreement intact, falls to be determined under the law of the Member State concerned. In England it is not clear whether the doctrine of severance as applied in the field of covenants in restraint of trade is to be regarded as applying in the case of Article 85(1). In the *Chemidus Wavin*[11] case Buckley L.J. in the Court of Appeal indicated that he doubted whether the question was really one "of severance in the sense in which we in these courts are accustomed to use that term in considering whether covenants contained in contract of employment and so forth are void as being in restraint of trade." It appeared rather to be "whether, after the excisions required by the Article of the Treaty have been made from the contract, the contract could be said to fail for lack of consideration or any other ground, or whether the contract could be so changed in its character as not to be the sort of contract the parties intended to enter into at all."[12]

(iii) *Civil remedies for infringements*

It seems clear in principle that the directly effective rights conferred upon individuals by Articles 85 and 86 should be exercisable offensively as well as defensively. The availability of remedies for their enforcement is, however, as normally under the EEC Treaty, a matter for national law. All Community law requires is that the conditions governing those remedies in a Community matter should be no less favourable than when they are used

---

[7] [1973] E.C.R. at p. 87.
[8] The topic of provisional validity has been much debated by commentators. See the full discussion, and references in Kerse, *op. cit.* note 8, p. 432, *supra*, at pp. 259–266.
[9] Case 56/65 [1966] E.C.R. 235; [1966] C.M.L.R. 357.
[10] [1966] E.C.R. at p. 250.
[11] *Chemidus Wavin* v. *TERI* [1978] 3 C.M.L.R. 514.
[12] [1978] 3 C.M.L.R. at p. 519.

in purely national matters; and that the conditions should not make it impossible in practice to exercise rights which the national courts are called upon to safeguard.[13]

There is now authority in English law for the granting in appropriate cases of remedies by way of an injunction or damages to the victims of infringements of the EEC competition rules.[14] It was suggested by Lord Denning M.R. some years ago that special new torts had been created by Article 85 and Article 86 entitled, respectively "undue restriction of competition within the common market" and "abuse of dominant position within the common market,"[15] but this suggestion won little support.[16] The preferred approach of English courts appears to be to treat claims in such cases as arising out of a breach of statutory duty.[17]

---

[13] See, *e.g.* Case 33/76 *Rewe* v. *Landwirtschaftskammer für das Saarland* [1976] E.C.R. 1989; [1977] 1 C.M.L.R. 533; Case 45/76, *Comet* v. *Produktschap voor Siergewassen* [1976] E.C.R. 2043; [1977] 1 C.M.L.R. 533; Case 61/79 *Denkavit* v. *Amministrazione delle Finanze* [1980] E.C.R. 1205; [1981] 3 C.M.L.R. 694; Joined Cases 66, 127 and 128/79 *Amministrazione delle Finanze* v. *Salumi* [1980] E.C.R. 1237; [1981] 1 C.M.L.R. 1; Case 826/79 *Amministrazione delle Finanze* v. *MIRECO* [1980] E.C.R. 2559.

[14] See, in particular, *Garden Cottage Foods* v. *Milk Marketing Board* [1984] A.C. 130. Noted by Jacobs, (1983) 8 E.L.Rev. 353.

[15] *Applications des Gaz S.A.* v. *Falks Veritas Ltd.* [1974] 3 All E.R. 51 at p. 58.

[16] See the reservations exposed by Roskill L.J. in *Valor International Ltd.* v. *Applications des Gaz S.A. and EPI Leisure Ltd.* [1978] 3 C.M.L.R. 87.

[17] The various possible bases for damages in English law are fully discussed by Kerse, *op. cit.* note 8, p. 432, *supra,* at pp. 267–275.

CHAPTER 17

STATE AIDS

State aids and the common market

The provision out of public funds of subsidies or other forms of aid to undertakings is generally considered a necessary instrument of government policy even in countries like the Member States of the EEC where free competition and the market mechanism continue to occupy a central place in the economic system. The purpose of such aid may be, for example, to attract investment into areas that are economically underdeveloped or where the existing industries are declining; or to enable the undertakings in a given industrial sector to improve their efficiency; or to encourage the development of new, high-technology industries requiring heavy expenditure on research and development. In particular, during a period of economic difficulty, such as that through which the Community and the other industrialised nations have been passing, there are strong social and political pressures for State aids to be used to preserve jobs, even where there is no real prospect of the undertakings in question returning to profitability.[1]

State aid is liable to cause serious difficulties in a system which has as its primary objective the creation and maintenance of a single internal market.

In the first place, by giving particular firms in a Member State an unearned competitive advantage over other providers of the goods or services in question, aid may interfere with the functioning of the market mechanism at the Community level. This may be so, whether the aided product is sold on the domestic market or exported to another Member State. In the former case, the aid may constitute an indirect barrier to trade by protecting the less efficient home industry against competition from imports. In the latter case, the aid may make it possible to penetrate an export market, threatening an industry in the State of importation which would otherwise be perfectly viable. Either situation is likely to give rise to pressure from the disadvantaged industry for its own government to provide compensatory aid, which makes no economic sense. There will also be temptation, when the threat comes from aided imports, for a government to take steps to keep them out, even at the risk of infringing Article 30 EEC. Thus massive French aid to the poultry industry in Brittany provided a spur to the illegal action by the Government of the United Kingdom in the *Turkey* case.[2]

Secondly, the dismantling of barriers between the national economies means that the aid policies of one Member State react on those of another, affecting both their cost and their prospects of success. As the Commission has written:

[1] An idea of the vast range of aids applied by the Member States can be obtained from the annual *Report on Competition Policy* produced by the Commission.
[2] Case 40/82 *Commission* v. *United Kingdom* [1982] E.C.R. 2793; [1982] 3 C.M.L.R. 497.

"Conflict between objectives and measures drawn up essentially within national contexts may very well result in a reciprocal neutralisation of national policies, or in a shifting of difficulties from one Member State to another, or even in new difficulties arising."[3]

Regional aids are a good example. Where governments bid against each other to attract investment funds, aid is liable to be fixed at a higher level than is warranted to compensate for the disadvantage of a given region; and resources may be diverted from those parts of the Community where they are needed most.

It was, therefore, inevitable that State aid should be brought within the scope of the EEC Treaty. One solution might have been for industrial policy, including policy on aid, to be taken out of national hands and made a Community responsibility. However, politically the only feasible option was to allow the Member States to continue granting aids but to establish a system of supervision by the Community institutions.

The relevant provisions of the Treaty are Articles 92 to 94.

The structure of Article 92 EEC

Article 92 EEC sets out the principles on the basis of which the compatibility of State aids with the common market is to be judged.[4]

Paragraph (1) of the Article lays down the general principle that State aids fulfilling certain broadly defined criteria are incompatible with the common market. The paragraph does not expressly declare incompatible aids to be prohibited (*cf.* the drafting of Articles 85 and 86 EEC) but the European Court has accepted that it contains an implied prohibition.[5]

The general principle in Article 92(1) is qualified by "exceptions *ipso jure*" listed in paragraph (2) and "discretionary exceptions" listed in paragraph (3). If an aid is found to be within one of the categories in paragraph (2), it must, as a matter of law, be regarded as compatible with the common market. On the other hand, the compatibility of aids falling within the categories in paragraph (3) is a discretionary matter, requiring an assessment of the positive and negative effects of the aid from the point of view of the Community as a whole. Under the machinery of Article 93 (see below) that discretion is exercised by the Commission, subject to reserve powers of the Council and the usual control by the European Court.

Article 92(1): aids incompatible with the common market

Article 92(1) provides:

"Save as otherwise provided in this Treaty, any aid granted by a Member State or through State resources in any form whatsoever which dis-

---

[3] Comp.Rep. 1971, point 133.
[4] On the interpretation of Art. 92 see further Hochbaum in Groeben *et al* (eds.), *Kommentar zum EWG-Vertrag* (1983) p. 1590; Colliard in Ganshof van der Meersch, *Droit des Communautés européennes*, 2172 *et seq.*; Mégret *et al*, *Le droit de la Communauté économique européenne*, Vol. 4, p. 379 *et seq.*; See also Schrans (1973) 10 C.M.L. Rev. 174.
[5] See the references to "an aid which is prohibited" in Case 6/69, *Commission v. France* [1969] E.C.R. 523 and "the prohibition in Article 92(1)" in Case 78/76 *Firma Steinike und Weinlig v. Germany* [1977] E.C.R. 595; [1977] 2 C.M.L.R. 688.

torts or threatens to distort competition by favouring certain undertakings or the production of certain goods shall, in so far as it affects
trade between Member States, be incompatible with the common
market."

A general definition of State aid for the purposes of the EEC Treaty was
offered by the European Court in Case 61/79 *Amministrazione delle
finanze dello stato* v. *Denkavit*,[6] where it said that paragraph (1) of the
Article:

"refers to the decisions of Member States by which the latter, in pursuit of their own economic and social objectives give, by unilateral and
autonomous decisions, undertakings or other persons resources or
procure for them advantages intended to encourage the attainment of
the economic or social objectives sought."[7]

State aid is thus to be understood in terms of its function as an instrument
of national economic and social policy involving the provision of some kind
of tangible benefit for specific undertakings or individuals.

It is immaterial what form the benefit may take or what particular goal of
policy it may be designed to serve. In Case 173/73 *Italy* v. *Commission*[8] the
measure in question was a provision in an Italian statute reducing for a
period of three years the contributions payable in respect of family allowances by employers in the textile industry. It had been argued, *inter alia*, on
behalf of the Italian Government that this measure could not constitute an
aid because it took the form of a reduction of tax liability and because the
charge to which it applied was an instrument of social policy. In rejecting
that argument, the Court said:

"The aim of Article 92 is to prevent trade between Member States
from being affected by benefits granted by the public authorities
which, in various forms, distort or threaten to distort competition by
favouring certain undertakings or the production of certain goods.

Accordingly, Article 92 does not distinguish between the measures
of State intervention concerned by reference to their causes or aims
but defines them in relation to their effects.

Consequently, the alleged fiscal or social aim of the measure in issue
cannot suffice to shield it from the application of Article 92."[9]

A useful list of forms of aid was given by the Commission in reply to a
Written Question in 1963,[10] comprising: direct subsidies; exemption from
duties and taxes; exemption from parafiscal charges; preferential interest
rates; guarantees of loans on especially favourable terms; making land or
buildings available either gratuitously or on especially favourable terms;
provision of goods or services on preferential terms; indemnities against
operating losses; or any other measure of equivalent effect. This was

---

[6] [1980] E.C.R. 1205; [1981] 3 C.M.L.R. 694.
[7] [1980] E.C.R. at p. 1228; *Cf.* the position under the ECSC Treaty, Case 30/59 *Steenkolen-
mijnen* v. *High Authority* [1961] E.C.R. 1 at p. 19; "An aid is a very similar concept [to a
subsidy], which, however, places emphasis on its purpose and seems especially devised for
a particular objective which cannot normally be achieved without outside help."
[8] [1974] E.C.R. 709; [1974] 2 C.M.L.R. 593.
[9] *Ibid.*, pp. 718–719.
[10] J.O. 1963, 2235.

further elaborated in a subsequent document[11] to include: reimbursement of costs in the event of success; State guarantees, whether direct or indirect, to credit operations; preferential rediscount rates; dividend guarantees; preferential public ordering; and deferred collection of fiscal or social contributions. The catalogue should not, of course, be regarded as exhaustive, although it covers the forms of aid most frequently granted by the Member States. In 1985 the Commission announced its intention of carrying out a comprehensive survey of State aid in the Community, the results of which would be published in a White Paper. A detailed standardised inventory of all the various aid instruments in force and of their practical application would be drawn up.[12]

An issue which has recently come to the fore is the provision of aid through the purchase by the State of shares in a company. The *Intermills* case[13] concerned action taken by the authorities in Belgium for the benefit of a paper-making firm which was in financial difficulties. Loans had been made to the firm and there had been an injection of capital into it by the Walloon Regional Executive, giving the latter a controlling interest. The European Court held that no distinction could be drawn between aid granted in the form of loans and aid granted in the form of a holding acquired in the capital of an undertaking. It is, therefore, clear in principle that State participation may amount to aid but it was unnecessary on the facts of the case for the Court to define the circumstances in which this will be so. Guidance is, however, available in the Opinion of Advocate General Sir Gordon Slynn in *Leeuwarder*[14] (also concerned with a paper-maker, though this time a Dutch one) where the test was said to be "whether the purchase of shares by the State can be regarded as an investment for the purposes of obtaining income or capital appreciation, the aim of the ordinary investor, or whether it is merely a vehicle for providing financial support for a particular company."

The increasing frequency of capital injections as a form of State aid led the Commission to address a letter on the subject to the Member States in September 1984.[15] The Commission takes as its guiding principle the provision of equity capital according to standard company practice in a market economy.

Another way in which aid may be granted indirectly is through preferential pricing of energy supplies, whether these are used as a raw material input or as an energy source.[16] The Commission has, for example, persuaded the authorities in the Netherlands to amend the tariff system for natural gas supplied to the ammonia industry. Ammonia is the base product of nitrate fertilisers and the Commission considered that the previous

---

[11] Doc. 20.502/IV/68 of December 1968, cited by Venceslai (1969) Riv.Dir.Eur. 257 at p. 258.
[12] Comp.Rep. 1985, point 172.
[13] [1984] E.C.R. 3809; [1986] 1 C.M.L.R. 614.
[14] Joined Cases 296 and 318/82, *The Netherlands and Leeuwarder Papierwarenfabriek BV v. Commission* [1985] 3 C.M.L.R. 380. This was similar in substance to the approach adopted by Adv. Gen. Verloren van Themaat in *Intermills, loc. cit.* note 13. *supra.*
[15] Bull. EC 9–1984, point 2.1.30. See also Comp.Rep. 1984, point 198. For a full discussion, see Hellingman (1986) 23 C.M.L.Rev. 111.
[16] Comp. Rep. 1985, point 182.

tariff gave a competitive advantage to Dutch fertiliser manufacturers.[17]
The Commission's approach is that, where energy tariffs do not reflect supply economies to a given sector of industry, an element of State aid may be
presumed to exist.

The "benefit" conferred by an aid must be without any real counterpart
on the side of the recipient.[18] Payment for goods or services or the
reimbursement of losses due to decisions taken in the public interest, for
example, the fixing of rail or bus fares at unremunerative levels, would not
amount to aids. However, the European Court has said that a measure
does not lose the quality of a "gratuitous advantage" merely because it is
wholly or partially financed out of contributions levied on the undertakings
concerned.[19]

Aid within the meaning of Article 92(1) must be granted "by a Member
State or through State resources." That must be taken to include grants by
regional or local authorities as well as by central government.[20] Nor is it
material whether the authorities choose to act directly or through the
agency of some public or private body. Thus in a case concerning an aid
system in Germany under which the proceeds of a levy were put at the disposal of a statutory body and used by it for market research and advertising
both at home and abroad, in order to promote the sale of products of the
German agricultural, food and forestry industries, the Court said:

> "In applying Article 92 regard must primarily be had to the effects of
> the aid on the undertakings or producers favoured and not the status
> of the institutions entrusted with the distribution and administration of
> the aid."[21]

On the other hand, the fixing of a minimum retail price for a product at the
exclusive cost of consumers would not constitute an aid granted through
State resources.[22]

The effects that render State aid incompatible with the common market
are the actual or threatened distortion of competition "by favouring certain
undertakings or the production of certain goods," where this has some
impact on intra-Community trade.

A distinction is, therefore, drawn between general measures of economic policy, such as the devaluation of a currency or the easing of credit
controls, which may very well improve the position of undertakings in the
country concerned vis-à-vis their competitors elsewhere in the Community,
and measures giving a competitive advantage to particular undertakings or
industrial sectors. In Cases 6 and 11/69 Commission v. France[23] the European Court held that a preferential discount rate for exports must be

---

[17] Comp. Rep. 1983, point 235. The decision of the Commission closing the procedure it had
initiated under Art. 93(2) was challenged in proceedings brought under Art. 173 EEC by
competitors of the Dutch fertiliser manufacturers in France. See Case 169/84 COFAZ v.
Commission (not yet reported).

[18] See Mégret et al, op. cit. (note 5, supra), p. 380.

[19] Case 78/76 Firma Steinike und Weinlig v. Germany, loc cit. note 5, supra.

[20] Cf. the terms of the Transparency Directive 80/723, discussed in more detail in Ch. 19,
infra.

[21] Case 78/76 loc. cit. note 5, supra. See also Case 173/73 Italy v. Commission, loc. cit. note 8,
supra; Case 290/83 Commission v. France [1986] 2 C.M.L.R. 546.

[22] Case 82/77 Openbaar Ministerie v. van Tiggele [1978] E.C.R. 25; [1978] 2 C.M.L.R. 528.

[23] [1969] E.C.R. 523.

regarded as an aid falling within Article 92(1), despite the fact that it applied to all national products without distinction. The explanation is that the possibility of obtaining credit more cheaply for export purposes was directly felt as a benefit by individual French manufacturers.

A case showing that the distinction may not always be easy to apply was raised by a Belgian member of the European Parliament in a Written Question in 1967.[24] It concerned press reports of a change of plan by an American company as to the location of a new chemical factory, allegedly after it was informed by the authorities of the region ultimately chosen that a sewer was to be built there which would make it unnecessary for the company itself to provide for the purification of water used in its manufacturing processes. The Commission was asked whether public works undertaken in such circumstances were not caught by Article 92 EEC. In its Answer the Commission said that the provision by public authorities of infrastructures which are traditionally paid for out of State or local authority budgets would not normally constitute an aid within the meaning of the Article, but that it may do so if works are carried out specifically in the interest of one or more undertakings or of a certain type of product.

The favoured undertakings may be public or private, subject to the exception in Article 90(2) as regards entrusted undertakings and fiscal monopolies.[25] A politically delicate matter is the financing of public undertakings, which frequently contains an element of aid. For example, the waiver of interest on capital which the State makes available to a public undertaking may constitute an aid if a private investor in a comparable situation, acting from purely economic motives, would not have waived his rights, or would only have done so to a limited extent.[26] Part of the rationale behind the adoption of the Transparency Directive[27] was to respond to problems of detection and inadequate information in this area. In addition, the Commission has refined its own policy guidelines.[28]

According to the European Court, " . . . in the application of Article 92(1) the point of departure must necessarily be the competitive position existing within the common market before the adoption of the measure in issue."[29] If the effect of the measure is to alter that position to the advantage of particular undertakings or products, there will be a distortion of competition within the meaning of the Article. It was, therefore, of no avail for the French Government in Cases 6 and 11/69 to argue that its aim was merely to approximate the discount rates for exports to the lower discount rates generally applying in the other Member States; nor for the Italian Government in Case 173/73 to argue that the social charges devolving on employers in the textile industry were heavier in Italy than elsewhere. As the Court said in the latter case:

" . . . the unilateral modification of a particular factor of the cost of

---

[24] J.O. 1967, 2311.
[25] Case 78/76 *Steinike und Weinlig* v. *Germany, loc. cit.* note 5, *supra.*
[26] *Cf.* Case 323/82 *Intermills, loc. cit.* note 13, *supra*; Joined Cases 296/82 and 318/82 *Leeuwarder, loc. cit.* note 14, *supra.*
[27] Dir. 80/723, O.J. 1980 L195/35, as amended O.J. 1985 L229. See further Ch. 19, *infra.*
[28] See note 15, *supra.*
[29] Case 173/73 *Italy* v. *Commission, loc. cit.* note 8, *supra.*

production in a given sector of the economy of a Member State may have the effect of disturbing the existing equilibrium. Consequently, there is no point in comparing the relative proportions of total production costs which a particular category of costs represents, since the decisive factor is the reduction itself and not the category of costs to which it relates."[30]

If the arguments of the French and Italian Governments had been accepted, the scope of Articles 92 to 94 would have been drastically reduced, pending the harmonisation under Articles 99 and 100 EEC of the factors influencing production costs in the Member States, since it would have been all too easy for a State to point to a particular high-cost factor as justifying a compensatory aid.

One of the questions in *Firma Steinike und Weinlig* asked, in substance, whether the effect on competition and trade of the activities of a State agency might not be mitigated by the fact that similar activities were carried on by similar bodies in other Member States. The Court replied that a breach of Article 92 by a Member State could not be justified by the fact that other Community partners were guilty of similar breaches. "The effects of more than one distortion of competition on trade between Member States do not cancel one another out but accumulate and its damaging consequences to the common market are increased."[31]

What kind of proof is needed to make out a case of actual or threatened distortion of competition affecting trade between Member States, such as to bring an aid within Article 92(1)? This was one of the issues in Case 730/79 *Philip Morris Holland* v. *Commission*.[32] The aid in question was an investment premium the Dutch authorities had been proposing to grant the cigarette manufacturer, Philip Morris, in connection with a plan to close one of its two factories in the Netherlands and to expand production at the other factory. The premium would have amounted to 3.8 per cent. of the total investment. The reorganisation meant that Philip Morris would account for 50 per cent. of the cigarettes manufactured in the Netherlands, of which 80 per cent. would be exported. The European Court said that "When financial aid strengthens the position of an undertaking as compared with other undertakings competing in intra-Community trade the latter must be regarded as affected by that aid."[33] For the Court the decisive factors were: (a) that the premium was to help Philip Morris increase its capacity to produce cigarettes for export; and (b) that it would have reduced the cost of converting the company's production facilities, thus giving Philip Morris a competitive advantage over other cigarette manufacturers, which would have to finance such a conversion privately.

The lesson of *Philip Morris Holland* is that it may be possible to infer from the circumstances in which an aid is granted that it is liable to distort

---

[30] [1974] E.C.R. at p. 720.

[31] *Loc. cit.*, note 5, *supra* at p. 612. The same point was made by the Commission in its decision on the subsidy on fuel oil given to French fishermen: see Case 93/94 *Commission* v. *France* [1985] 3 C.M.L.R. 169.

[32] [1980] E.C.R. 2671; [1981] 2 C.M.L.R. 321. Noted by Flynn (1981) 6 E.L.Rev. 208.

[33] [1980] E.C.R. at pp. 2688–2689. This echoed the words of Adv. Gen. Capotorti: *ibid.* at p. 2697. See, in a similar sense, the opinion of Adv. Gen. Warner in Case 173/73, [1974] E.C.R. at p. 728.

competition and affect inter-State trade. This will be so, in particular, when it can be shown that the ability of the recipient of the aid to compete as a producer of goods traded between Member States has been enhanced. In such a case, more elaborate analysis of the pattern of competition on the relevant market would be superfluous. However, a decision of the Commission which fails to indicate the precise circumstances allowing inferences to be drawn as to the effect of an aid on competition and trade in a given case runs the risk of annulment on the ground of inadequate reasoning.[34]

Article 92(2): exceptions *ipso jure*

Article 92(2) provides that the following categories of aid *shall* be compatible with the common market:

"(a) *aid having a social character, granted to individual consumers, provided that such aid is granted without discrimination related to the origin of the products concerned*"

An example would be the payment of a subsidy to manufacturers of a basic foodstuff, compensating them for any loss of profits resulting from a price freeze imposed in respect of sales to consumers. So long as it complied with the proviso that there must be no discrimination regarding the origin of the goods concerned, such aid would be unlikely to distort competition or affect trade at all, and so would fall outside the general principle in Article 92(1).[35] However, it might be caught by the principle if, for instance, the subsidised product were given a real competitive advantage over possible substitutes. In such a case the compatibility of the aid with the common market would be assured by the present exception.

"(b) *aid to make good the damage caused by natural disasters or exceptional occurrences*"

Aid to make good the damage caused by natural disasters is an obvious candidate for automatic exemption from the general principle in Article 92(1). Italian measures which the Commission has treated as falling under this heading were the assistance given in Liguria to repairs and reconstruction required as a result of the floods in 1977, and the provision in Friuli-Venezia Giulia of low interest loans and subsidies for the reconstruction of industrial plant destroyed by the earthquake in 1976.[36]

---

[34] See Case 323/82 *Intermills, loc. cit.* note 13, *supra*; Joined Cases 296 and 318/82, *Leeuwarder, loc. cit.* note 14, *supra*. The Commission restated its approach in Comp.Rep. 1984, point 201.

[35] *e.g.* the Italian scheme under which hard wheat purchased by AIMA (the Intervention Agency for Agricultural Markets) was resold to manufacturers of pasta at prices well below the market rate, following the imposition of a freeze on the retail prices of pasta products. The Commission was satisfied that hard wheat benefiting from the subsidy was only used in the manufacture of pasta for domestic consumption and that imports into Italy of pasta made from hard wheat were insignificant: see Comp.Rep. 1975 points 126–129. In Case 40/75 *Produits Bertrand* v. *Commission* [1976] E.C.R. 1, an action for damages brought by a French pasta manufacturer against the Commission for its failure to prevent the granting of the aid was dismissed by the European Court on the ground that a causal connection between the behaviour complained of and the alleged damage had not been established.

[36] Comp.Rep. 1978, point 164.

The notion of "exceptional occurrences" is very vague. The exception would, presumably, cover aid to repair business premises damaged by acts of political terrorism. Its applicability in the case of difficulties of an economic nature is more doubtful. The exceptional aid measures adopted by the Member States in the face of the serious recession, which began to affect the Community from the second half of 1974 onwards, were dealt with by the Commission under Article 92(3)(*b*) (see below).

> "(c) *aid granted to the economy of certain areas of the Federal Republic of Germany affected by the division of Germany, in so far as such aid is required in order to compensate for the economic disadvantages caused by that division.*"

The areas particularly affected are those bordering on East Germany (the so-called *Zonenrandgebiet*), as well as West Berlin. In the current practice of the Commission these are now dealt with under the principles applying to schemes of regional aid, which are considered further below.[37]

Article 92(3): discretionary exceptions

The discretion given to the Commission under Article 92(3) is a wide one. Advocate General Capotorti described it in *Philip Morris Holland* as "implying an assessment of an economic, technical and policy nature."[38] The Court said that the exercise of the discretion "involves economic and social assessments which must be made in a Community context."[39]

The Commission only has power to authorise aids which are necessary for the furtherance of one of the objectives listed in paragraph (3). Where action which, in fact, promotes one of those objectives would have been taken in response to normal market forces, the element of necessity is lacking. Thus in *Philip Morris Holland* the Court upheld the view of the Commission that aid as an incentive to an investment that would have been made in any event was ineligible, on that ground alone, for exemption.[40]

The categories of aid that *may* be compatible with the common market are as follows:

> "(a) *aid to promote the economic development of areas where the standard of living is abnormally low or where there is serious under-employment*"

The economic problem of the region in question must be more serious to attract this exception than to attract the general exception relating to sectoral and regional aids in subparagraph (3) (see below). The latter exception is, however, subject to the proviso that the aid "does not adversely affect trading conditions to an extent contrary to the common interest." No such limitation applies here, because the seriousness of the situation may justify exceptionally drastic measures.

---

[37] For an example of the use of Art. 92(2)(*c*), see Bull. EC 2, 65, Ch. III, point 18.
[38] [1980] E.C.R. at p. 2701.
[39] *Ibid.* at p. 2691.
[40] *Ibid.* at p. 2690. For the view of the Commission, see Comp. Rep. 1980, point 215; Comp. Rep. 1984, point 202.

The scope for invoking paragraph (a) is significantly restricted by the requirement that the assessment of socio-economic problems be made in a Community, not a national, context. In *Philip Morris Holland* it was claimed that in the Bergen-op-Zoom region, the location of the factory it was planned to enlarge, unemployment was higher, and *per capita* income lower, than the national average in the Netherlands. However, the Court supported the Commission's approach in taking the Community level as the appropriate yardstick.[41]

An example of aids authorised by the Commission under Article 92(3)(*a*) were measures to promote the economic recovery of the sulphur-mining areas of Sicily.[42]

"(b) *aid to promote the execution of an important project of common European interest or to remedy a serious disturbance in the economy of a Member State*"

The exception applies to two completely different types of aid. The first is uncontroversial.[43] As to the second, the Commission used it as a safety valve in the economic troubles besetting Member States in the period after 1974.

In an important policy statement in the *Fifth Report on Competition Policy* the Commission wrote:

"Both in the case of general aid schemes (in the form of industry programmes or individual measures for specific undertakings) and in the case of new economic recovery measures, the Commission, bearing in mind the exceptional economic and social situation confronting the Member States, has agreed to certain measures which, in this particular phase of the Community's existence, it deemed eligible for the derogation provided for under Article 92(3)(*b*) of the Treaty . . .

The Commission thus concluded that Member States, in an attempt to protect employment, were justified in boosting investment by granting firms financial benefits (in the form of tax deductions or low-interest loans) on an automatic or quasi-general basis for a limited period. Similarly, it agreed to financial aid being granted to ensure the survival of firms which have run into difficulties, thereby avoiding redundancies . . .

On the basis of the same considerations the Commission has also permitted Member States, for the duration of the present economic situation, to reimburse a part of the wage costs incurred by firms creating new jobs, for young people in particular, or refraining from staff cuts which would be justified by lower production figures . . . ."[44]

It remains necessary to examine "serious disturbances" in the light of the gravity of the recession throughout the Community as a whole. Exemption will not be available where the aid amounts to the transfer of an investment

---

[41] For other instances of failure to satisfy the stringent tests of paragraph (a), see Dec. 80/1157 *Re Investment Aids at Antwerp* O.J. 1980 L343/38; Joined Cases 296/82 and 318/82, *Leeuwarder, loc. cit.* note 14, *supra.*
[42] Comp.Rep. 1976, points 209–211.
[43] Parry & Hardy, *EEC Law*, p. 347 suggest a road tunnel under the Alps or a hydro-electric scheme in Luxembourg.
[44] Comp.Rep. 1975, point 133.

which could have been effected in other Member States in a less favourable economic situation.[45]

"(c) *aid to facilitate the development of certain economic activities or of certain economic areas, where such aid does not adversely affect trading conditions to an extent contrary to the common interest . . . .*"

This is the most important of the exceptions to the general principle in Article 92(1). It enables the Commission to authorise aids to particular industrial sectors (*e.g.* taking the headings under which national aids were discussed by the Commission in the *Fifteenth Report on Competition Policy*[46]: energy; shipbuilding and ship-repair; textiles and clothing; synthetic fibres; industrial investment; car and spare parts industries; information technologies and consumer electronics; household appliances; primary aluminium and semi-finished aluminium products; ceramics, glass, paper, wood and rubber) and aids to particular regions of a Member State.

The legal limits of the Commission's discretion are defined by the notion of facilitating the development of the industries or areas concerned and by the proviso that aid must not have an adverse effect on trading conditions "to an extent contrary to the common interest."

"Development" presupposes some improvement in economic performance or prospects. Thus aids of a purely conservatory nature, designed to prevent undertakings in a given industry or area from going out of business, thereby creating unemployment, do not fall within the exception.[47] Recipients of aid must be at least potentially competitive. It seems to follow that financial assistance to an undertaking should normally be temporary and given on a declining scale.

The purpose of the aid must be the development of the sector or region in question and not of particular undertakings within it. In the *Belgian Textile Aid* case Advocate General Sir Gordon Slynn was of the opinion that the Commission ought not to have authorised grants to certain weak undertakings, given the relative strength of the market sector as a whole.[48]

The proviso imposes a limit, albeit a flexible one, on the extent to which disruption of the market mechanism may be tolerated for the sake of the socio-economic benefit sectoral or regional aids may bring. Its operation may be illustrated by Case 47/69 *France* v. *Commission*.[49] The aid in question took the form of contributions towards research and the restructuring of French textile undertakings, and seemed prima facie to be exactly the type of sectoral aid to which Article 92(3)(*c*) was intended to apply. However, the Commission objected to the fact that the aid was financed out of a parafiscal charge imposed both on textile products manufactured in France and on imports. The European Court agreed with the Commission that the method of financing an aid system was one of the factors to be taken into

---

[45] See Case 730/79 *Philip Morris Holland* v. *Commission* [1980] E.C.R. at p. 2693. See also the Opinion of Adv. Gen. Sir Gordon Slynn in Joined Cases 296/82 and 318/82 *Leeuwarder* [1985] 3 C.M.L.R. at p. 390.

[46] Comp.Rep. 1985, points 182 to 217.

[47] See the remarks of Adv. Gen. Sir Gordon Slynn in Case 84/82 *Germany* v. *Commission (Belgian Textile Aid)* [1982] E.C.R. at p. 1505.

[48] *Ibid.* at p. 1504.

[49] [1970] E.C.R. 487.

account in assessing its compatibility with the common market. It was capable of adding to the disturbance of trading conditions, thus rendering the system as a whole contrary to the common interest. That was the case here, because of the protective effect of applying the charge to imports. The amount of aid available increased automatically in proportion to any increase in revenue, so that the more undertakings from other Member States succeeded in making sales in France, the more they would have to contribute for the benefit of their French competitors, who might not have made similar efforts.

In that case the Court seems to have assessed the extent to which trading conditions were liable to be adversely affected independently of the benefits expected to flow from the aid.[50] Its approach was that, however worthwhile the objective being pursued, disruption of the market beyond a certain point must be judged contrary to the common interest. The Commission, on the other hand, has declared that it considers itself bound "to weigh the beneficial effects of the aid on the development of certain economic activities or of certain economic areas against its adverse effects on trading conditions and the maintenance of undisturbed competition."[51] That would allow greater interference with the play of market forces, the greater the importance of the Community interest an aid was thought to serve. The possible divergence in the approaches of the Court and the Commission was noted by Advocate General Sir Gordon Slynn in the *Belgian Textile Aid* case.[52]

In applying the proviso, account must be taken of any factors that may moderate the anti-competitive impact of an aid. In its *Intermills* judgment the Court said that "the settlement of an undertaking's existing debts in order to ensure its survival does not necessarily adversely affect trading conditions to an extent contrary to the common interest, as provided in Article 92(3), where such an operation is, for example, accompanied by a restructuring plan."[53] Failure to show that the possibly mitigating effects of restructuring had been adequately considered was one of the reasons for the annulment of the decisions of the Commission in the *Intermills* and *Leeuwarder* cases.[54]

"(d) *such other categories of aid as may be specified by decision of the Council acting by a qualified majority on a proposal from the Commission*"

A series of five directives on aids to shipbuilding in the Member States has been adopted under this provision.[55] It was not possible to rely on Article 92(3)(c) because the measures included "production aids" which could not be regarded as facilitating "development."

---

[50] The Court concluded that the Commission was justified in considering the aid system as contrary to the common interest "whilst acknowledging both the useful nature of the aid properly so called and the fact that it conformed with 'the common interest' if the method whereby it was financed could be modified": see [1970] E.C.R. at p. 496.

[51] Comp.Rep. 1984, point 202.

[52] [1982] E.C.R. at pp. 1506–1507.

[53] [1984] E.C.R. at p. 3832.

[54] *Loc. cit.* notes 13 and 14, *supra*, respectively.

[55] For the fifth directive in the series, see O.J. 1981 L137; extended O.J. 1985 L2. For an illustration of its application, see Bull. EC 7/8–1985, points 2.1. 62–67.

It was assumed (correctly, it is submitted) that the term "decision" in this subparagraph is used in the general sense of Article 145 EEC to refer to a law-making act, as opposed to the sense of an "individual act" in Article 189 EEC.

The application of Article 92

We have seen that State aids meeting the criteria in Article 92(1) are not automatically to be regarded as incompatible with the common market, since they may fall within one of the excepted categories in paragraphs (2) and (3) of the Article. Moreover, the application, in particular, of Article 92(3) entails a complex appreciation of economic and social factors in the light of the overall Community interest. The approach adopted by the Treaty is, accordingly, to make the Community institutions responsible in the first instance for giving concrete effect to the principles of Article 92, and machinery has been provided for this purpose in Articles 93 and 94.

The corollary of the provision of special machinery at Community level is that courts in the Member States may not apply Article 92 independently of that machinery. In the words of the European Court, the parties concerned cannot:

" . . . simply, on the basis of Article 92 alone, challenge the compatibility of an aid with Community law before national courts or ask them to decide as to any compatibility which may be the main issue in actions before them or may arise as a subsidiary issue. There is this right however where the provisions of Article 92 have been applied by the general provisions provided for in Article 94 or by specific decisions under Article 93(2)."[56]

In that sense, Article 92 is not directly effective. However, it does not follow that national courts may not sometimes have to interpret Article 92, *e.g.* to decide whether a measure introduced by a Member State without obtaining clearance under Article 93(3) constitutes "aid."[57] And in such a case the Court could obtain assistance in interpreting the Article by seeking a preliminary ruling under Article 177 EEC.[58]

The machinery in Articles 93 and 94 EEC[59]

Different treatment is accorded to "existing aids", *i.e.* aid systems which were already established when the EEC Treaty came into force (in new Member States, on the date of their accession) or which have been lawfully introduced since that date after passing through the clearance procedure under Article 93(3), and "plans to grant or alter aid," which are also referred to as "new aids."

---

[56] Case 78/76 *Firma Steinike und Weinlig* v. *Germany* [1977] E.C.R. at p. 609.
[57] See, *e.g.* R. v. *Attorney-General, ex parte ICI* (not yet reported) C.A.; *Potato Marketing Board* v. *Robertsons* [1983] 1 C.M.L.R. 93 (Oxford County Court); and on similar facts, *Potato Marketing Board* v. *Drysdale* (not yet reported) (C.A.).
[58] Case 78/76 *Firma Steinike und Weinlig* v. *Germany, loc. cit.* note 5, *supra.*
[59] On this machinery, see further Venceslai, *op. cit.* note 11, *supra*; Dashwood (1975) C.M.L.Rev. 43; Gilmour (1981) C.M.L.Rev. 63.

The clearance procedure for new aids

Article 93(3) provides:

"The Commission shall be informed, in sufficient time to enable it to submit its comments, of any plans to grant or alter aid. If it considers that any such plan is not compatible with the common market having regard to Article 92, it shall without delay initiate the procedure provided for in paragraph 2. The Member State concerned shall not put its proposed measures into effect until this procedure has resulted in a final decision."

The paragraph establishes a system of prior control which is designed to prevent any aid incompatible with the common market from being introduced. Member States are required to notify the Commission of plans to grant or alter aid sufficiently in advance of the date set for their implementation to enable it to examine the plans and form a view as to whether the procedure under Article 93(2) should be initiated against them.

The last sentence of Article 93(3) imposes a "standstill" obligation upon the Member State proposing to introduce an aid.[60] This applies during the period of preliminary review by the Commission and, if the procedure under Article 93(2) is initiated, continues until a final decision is reached. *A fortiori*, a Member State is prohibited from putting an aid into effect without notifying it at all.

The Commission must be allowed sufficient time for its preliminary examination of a notified aid project. However, it is required to act with due expedition, bearing in mind the interest of Member States in obtaining clarification in cases where there may be an urgent need to take action. The European Court has fixed on two months as a reasonable length of time for this purpose. If at the end of this period the Commission still has not defined its attitude towards the project, the Member State concerned may implement the aid but should, in the interests of legal certainty, give notice to the Commission of its intention of doing so.[61]

The outcome of the preliminary examination may be that the Commission finds the new aid compatible with the common market. This decision must be communicated to the Member State which made the notification and implementation of the aid may then go forward.[62]

However, should the Commission be left in any serious doubt as to the compatibility of the aid with the common market, it is bound to continue its examination within the framework provided by Article 93(2). The importance of the transition from the preliminary to the definitive phase in the examination of the aid is that only in the latter phase do interested parties other than the notifying State have a legal right to make their views known.[63] The issue was considered in the *Belgian Textile Aid* case,[64] where

---

[60] Case 84/82 *Germany* v. *Commission* [1984] E.C.R. at p. 1488, which was foreshadowed in Case 120/73 *Lorenz* v. *Germany* [1973] E.C.R. 1471.

[61] *Ibid.* The two month period was chosen by analogy with Arts. 173 and 175 EEC.

[62] *Ibid.* Once the project has been implemented it will be an "existing aid" subject to constant review pursuant to Art. 93(1). See *infra*.

[63] The right is given by Art. 93(2), first sub-paragraph. See *infra*.

[64] [1984] E.C.R. at pp. 1488–1490. See the analysis of this case by Flynn at (1984) 9 E.L.Rev. 367.

a decision of the Commission granting temporary approval to a scheme which had been the subject of negotiations lasting for 16 months was annulled by the Court. The Commission, it was held, being evidently dissatisfied with the scheme as originally notified, ought immediately to have initiated the procedure under Article 93(2) and formally invited comments from Member States and the textile trade, so that it would be fully informed of all the facts of the case before making up its mind.

Where an aid proposal is altered after having been notified to the Commission, the latter must be informed of the amendment, although this may be done in the course of consultations arising from the original notification.[65] Failure to bring amendments to the attention of the Commission will cause the standstill under Article 93(3) to remain in force against a scheme which has otherwise been found compatible with the common market. The only exception would be where the amendment could properly be regarded as a separate measure, examination of which was unlikely to have a bearing on the Commission's assessment of the notified plan.[66]

The prohibition against the implementation of new aids which have not been notified or which, during the preliminary stage following notification, are being investigated by the Commission or in respect of which proceedings under Article 93(2) are in progress has been held to be directly effective.[67] The criteria here are purely procedural and have nothing to do with the incompatibility under Article 92 of the aid in question. Individuals may, therefore, take advantage of any available remedies in the legal system of the Member State concerned in order to prevent aids from being granted in such circumstances.[68]

Review of existing aids

Article 93(1) provides:

"The Commission shall, in co-operation with Member States, keep under constant review all systems of aid existing in those States. It shall propose to the latter any appropriate measures required by the progressive development or by the functioning of the common market."

The Commission, in collaboration with the national authorities, is under a duty to keep existing aid systems under constant review and has the power to make any recommendations the progressive development or functioning of the common market may require. This supervision applies to all systems of aid in force, including those covered by the exception in Article 92(2). It enables the Commission to ensure that aids previously regarded as compatible with the common market do not change their character and are not applied abusively in particular cases. If a recommendation does not suffice to rectify the situation, the Commission may resort to the enforcement procedure under Article 93(2).

---

[65] Joined Cases 91 and 127/83, *Heineken Brouwerijen* v. *Inspecteurs der Vernootschapsbelasting* [1984] E.C.R. 3435; [1985] 1 C.M.L.R. 389.
[66] *Ibid.* at p. 3454.
[67] Case 72/72 *Capolongo* v. *Maya* [1973] E.C.R. 611; [1974] 1 C.M.L.R. 230; Case 120/73 *Lorenz* v. *Germany, loc. cit.* note 57, *supra.*
[68] For an interesting example, see the *ICI* case, *loc. cit.* note 57, *supra.* See also the note by Flynn (1986) 11 E.L.Rev. 232.

The special enforcement procedure for State aids

Article 93(2) provides:

"If, after giving notice to the parties concerned to submit their comments, the Commission finds that aid granted by a State or through State resources is not compatible with the common market having regard to Article 92, or that such aid is being misused, it shall decide that the State concerned shall abolish or alter such aid within a period of time to be determined by the Commission.

If the State concerned does not comply with the decision within the prescribed time, the Commission or any other interested State may, in derogation from the provisions of Articles 169 and 170, refer the matter to the Court of Justice direct . . . ."

The first and second subparagraphs of Article 93(2) lay down a special procedure for securing the abolition or modification of an aid which is found on examination by the Commission to be incompatible with the common market.

The formal opening of the procedure is by the publication in the *Official Journal* of a notice inviting interested parties to submit their comments. The Commission is not obliged to give individual notice to firms in receipt of aid under the scheme which is being scrutinised.[69] Further examination may lead the Commission to drop its objections to the scheme; or it may do so in response to agreement by the awarding State to make substantial modifications. If, however, the Commission reaches the conclusion that the aid is incompatible with the common market or is being misused, it will adopt a decision requiring its abolition or alteration within a specified time. In the event of non-compliance with the decision, the Commission itself, or any interested Member State, may refer the matter to the European Court, by-passing the administrative phase of proceedings under Article 169 or Article 170 EEC. Direct referral to the Court is permitted because the parties have already been heard and the Commission has adopted a decision in which it has made known its views.

The procedure under Article 93(2) applies both to existing aids about which questions have been raised in the course of a review and to new aids. As to the latter, the drafting of Article 93(3) seems to assume that any plan in respect of which the Commission initiates the procedure will have been duly notified and subjected to a preliminary examination. However, the European Court has held that the procedure may also be invoked against unnotified aids, although here the Commission would have the option of taking action under Article 169 for the infringement of the standstill obligation in Article 93(3).[70]

A decision by the Commission finding an aid incompatible with the com-

---

[69] Case 323/82 *Intermills* v. *Commission, loc. cit.* note 13, *supra*. The Commission has announced various alterations in its practice under Art. 93(2) to encourage participation by interested third parties: Comp.Rep. 1985, point 171.

[70] See Case 173/73 *Italy* v. *Commission, loc. cit.* note 8, *supra*; Case 73/79, *Commission* v. *Italy* [1980] E.C.R. 1411; [1982] 1 C.M.L.R. 1. See the discussion of the latter case by Gilmour, *op. cit.* note 59, *supra*; and by Flynn (1983) 8 E.L.Rev. 297. There is no such option where the compatibility of an aid scheme with the Common Market is in issue: Case 290/83 *loc. cit.* note 21, *supra*. See the discussion of this case by Flynn (1987) 12 E.L.Rev. 124.

mon market and requiring its abolition or alteration will have a different effect in law depending on whether the aid in question is an existing or a new one. In the case of existing aids, the effect of the decision is clearly constitutive, bringing into force, from the date set for compliance by the Member State concerned, the implied prohibition in Article 92(1). Thereafter, the granting of the aid will be unlawful and it will be the duty of national courts to recognise the fact.[71] In the case of new aids, the measure will either not have been implemented at all or, if it has been implemented in breach of Article 93(3), it will already be unlawful. However, it may not be accurate to describe the effect of the decision here as purely declaratory. What it does is to transform a prohibition of a provisional nature, based on the procedural criteria of Article 93(3), into a prohibition based on Article 92(1) that will remain in force unless and until the Commission can be persuaded to revoke it, following a material change of circumstances. A practical consequence of the difference between the two cases is that when a new aid is in question the decision of the Commission does not have to specify any time-limit.[72]

Whether the procedure ends in a finding of compatibility or incompatibility with the common market, the decision of the Commission will be challengeable by an action under Article 173 EEC in the same way as any other institutional act capable of producing legal effects. Satisfying the conditions of admissibility in the second paragraph of the Article should present no problem to a direct recipient of the aid[73] or to an undertaking which responded to the Commission's invitation to submit comments and which is able to produce prima facie evidence of substantial harm to its interests resulting from the granting of the aid to a competitor.[74]

Authorisation of aid by the Council "in exceptional circumstances"

The third and fourth subparagraphs of Article 93(2) provide:

" . . . On application by a Member State, the Council may, acting unanimously, decide that aid which that State is granting or intends to grant shall be considered to be compatible with the common market, in derogation from the provisions of Article 92 or from the regulations provided for in Article 94, if such a decision is justified by exceptional circumstances. If, as regards the aid in question, the Commission has already initiated the procedure provided for in the first subparagraph of this paragraph, the fact that the State concerned has made its application to the Council shall have the effect of suspending that procedure until the Council has made its attitude known.

If, however, the Council has not made its attitude known within

---

[71] There is a passage in the judgment in Case 70/72 *Commission* v. *Germany* [1973] E.C.R. 813 suggesting that a decision taken by the Commission under Art. 93(2) may have certain retrospective effects: [1973] E.C.R. at p. 829. See Bronkhorst (1974) C.M.L.Rev. 206; Dashwood, *op. cit.* note 59, *supra.* However, in Case 177/78, *Pigs & Bacon Commission* v. *McCarren Ltd.* [1979] E.C.R. 3409, [1979] 3 C.M.L.R. 389 Adv. Gen. Warner pointed out that the Court's remark was made in the context of an aid introduced or continued in force in breach of the Treaty.
[72] Case 173/73 *Italy* v. *Commission, loc. cit.* note 8, *supra.*
[73] Case 730/79 *Philip Morris Holland* v. *Commission, loc. cit.* note 32, *supra*; Case 323/82 *Intermills* v. *Commission, loc. cit.* note 13, *supra.*
[74] Case 169/84 *COFAZ and Others* v. *Commission* (not yet reported).

three months of the said application being made, the Commission shall give its decision on the case."

On application by the aid-awarding State, the Council, acting unanimously, has the power exceptionally to authorise an aid not falling within any of the categories in Article 92(2) or (3).[75] If the procedure under Article 93(2) has already been initiated in respect of such aid, the application to the Council has the effect of suspending it. However, if the Council has not made its attitude known within three months, the Commission may proceed to adopt a decision. Given the need for unanimity, and the fact that there will nearly always be at least one Member State whose producers may be adversely affected by the granting of the aid, the possibility of such applications succeeding must generally be regarded as poor.

Implementing regulations adopted by the Council

Article 94 provides:

"The Council may, acting on a qualified majority on a proposal from the Commission, make any appropriate regulations for the application of Articles 92 and 93 and may in particular determine the conditions in which Article 93(3) shall apply and the categories of aid exempted from this procedure."

The Council's power to adopt regulations under Article 94 covers the application of Article 92 as well as Article 93. However, the power has not hitherto been exercised.[76]

The effectiveness of the State aids machinery

The surge in importance of the provisions of the EEC Treaty on State aids was summarised by the Commission in the *Fourteenth Report on Competition Policy*, comparing its two most recent four-year periods of office:

"While it should be remembered that the period 1977–80 was not one of quite such extreme economic and social difficulty as the period 1981–84, nevertheless the figures provide an interesting commentary. In the period 1977–80, Member States notified just over 500 aid proposals in the industrial field. In the period 1981–84, this number rose by over 25 per cent. However, the total number of Commission decisions in the same period rose by over 50 per cent., reflecting the increasing proportion of cases in which it opened the procedure under Art. 93(2) . . . Between the two periods, the number of Article 93(2) procedures multiplied by a factor of three. Even greater was the increase in the number of negative decisions taken by the Commission, *i.e.* those decisions in which the aid proposed was prohibited completely. This figure multiplied by 12 between the periods 1977–80 and 1981–84. If to this latter figure are added the increasing number of aid proposals withdrawn by the Member State in question after the Commission has opened the Article 93(2) procedure, which therefore

---

[75] For a recent example of the exercise of this power, see Comp.Rep. 1985, point 251.
[76] A Draft Regulation on the application of Art. 93 was submitted by the Commission to the Council in 1966 but has never been enacted. *Cf.* the powers of the Commission under Art. 90(3), discussed in Chapter 19, *infra.*

are not granted by the Member State concerned and are thus in effect
the equivalent in economic terms of a negative decision, this figure
rises considerably further. It should be underlined also that most proposals which are in the end accepted by the Commission after examination under the Article 93(2) procedure are substantially amended by
the Member State before the Commission finally raises no objection to
their implementation."[77]

The sharp increase in the notification of aids declined in 1985. However, as
the Commission has conceded,[78] decreasing notifications need to be
matched by a fall in the *volume* of aid which they represent before the controls imposed by the Community provisions can be said to be achieving a
more competitive effect.

The persistent infringement by certain Member States of their obligation
under Article 93(3) to notify new aids in advance has given cause for concern.[79] The problem has been exacerbated by the Commission's apparent
preference for dealing with unnotified aids under Article 93(2), rather than
seeking to have them withdrawn by bringing infringement proceedings
under Article 169. In 1983 the Commission wrote to the Member States
warning them that it would order the recovery from recipients of aids
granted in breach of Article 93(3).[80] A Communication to this effect was
also published in the *Official Journal*.[81] However, the effectiveness of the
threat, which depends on the availability under national law of means for
the recovery of illicit aid, remains seriously in doubt.

The practice of the Commission[82]

General aids

A general aid system may be defined as one lacking any specific sectoral
or regional orientation, its objectives being expressed broadly in terms of
"industrial modernisation," "economic expansion" or some similar for-
mula. A typical example is section 8 of the Industrial Development Act
1982[83] in the United Kingdom, sub-section (1) of which provides:

" . . . the Secretary of State may, with the consent of the Treasury,
provide financial assistance where, in his opinion—
  (a) the financial assistance is likely to benefit the economy of the
      United Kingdom, or of any part or area of the United King-
      dom; and
  (b) it is in the national interest that the financial assistance should
      be provided on the scale, and in the form and manner, pro-
      posed; and

---

[77] Comp.Rep. 1984, point 197.
[78] Comp.Rep. 1985, point 168.
[79] The point is vigorously argued by Flynn, *op. cit.* note 70, *supra*.
[80] Comp.Rep. 1983, point 220. See Flynn (1984) 9 E.L.Rev. 365.
[81] O.J. 1983 C 318/3.
[82] For a fuller account of the recent practice of the Commission, see Mortelmans (1984)
     C.M.L.Rev. 405; Cownie (1986) 11 E.L.Rev. 247.
[83] Consolidating, *inter alia*, Parts I and II of the Industry Act 1972.

(c) the financial assistance cannot, or cannot appropriately, be so provided otherwise than by the Secretary of State."[84]

Such aid systems are objectionable in a Community perspective because it is impossible for the Commission to tell from the outset what effect they will have on competition and trade. In the jargon of the subject, the aids are excessively "opaque." They would obviously not be covered by the exemption in Article 92(3)(c) and would be unlikely to qualify under any of the other categories in paragraphs (2) and (3) of the Article. However, since the Member States value the ability, which powers of a general nature give them, to react quickly and flexibly when economic difficulties arise, two practical solutions have been found by the Commission to ensure compliance with the provisions of Articles 92 and 93. One solution is for the general aid system to be implemented by means of programmes relating to specific industries or geographical areas which must be notified in advance to the Commission. The second solution is for important individual applications of the aid system to be notified in advance to the Commission.

In the case of aid under section 8 of the Industrial Development Act 1982, the solution normally adopted has been that of notifying sectoral programmes, e.g. the notification in 1984 of a proposed scheme to benefit sections of the clothing, footwear, knitting and textile industries. The stated purpose of the scheme was to enable small and medium-sized firms to invest in advanced technology equipment. The scheme, limited to £20 million, was to take the form of either grants of up to 20 per cent. of investment costs or guarantees of 80 per cent. for the first two years of loans granted by approved financial institutions for the purchase of equipment.[85] Examples of important individual applications that were notified to the Commission and received its approval were the aids granted as from 1975 to British Leyland and Chrysler (UK) Ltd.[86]

Sectoral (industry) aids

The main criteria against which the Commission examines the sectoral aid proposals notified to it were described in the *Eighth Report on Competition Policy* as follows:

(i) sectoral aid should be limited to cases where it is justified by circumstances in the industry concerned;

(ii) aid should lead to a restoration of long-term viability by resolving problems rather than preserve the status quo and put off decisions and changes which are inevitable;

(iii) nevertheless, since adjustment takes time, a limited use of resources to reduce the social and economic costs of change is admissible in certain circumstances and subject to strict conditions;

(iv) unless granted over relatively short periods, aids should be progres-

---

[84] See also the companion provision, s.7 of the Act, which is the main vehicle for regional aid in the United Kingdom. On the compatibility of the Industry Acts 1972 and 1975, and aids granted thereunder, with EEC law, see further Dashwood and Sharpe (1978) C.M.L.Rev. 9 and 115.

[85] Comp.Rep. 1984, point 228. The Commission opened the Art. 93(2) procedure.

[86] Comp.Rep. 1975, points 117–118.

sively reduced and clearly linked to the restructuring of the sector concerned;

(v) the intensity of aid should be proportionate to the problem it is designed to resolve so that distortions of competition are kept to a minimum; and

(vi) industrial problems and unemployment should not be transferred from one Member State to another.[87]

The Commission has said[88] that it does not think it wise to define the type of aid which it regards as acceptable in each industrial sector, since this might encourage the Member States to introduce aids that were not strictly necessary. However, policy guidelines have been developed for particular areas of sensitivity, such as the crisis industries of shipbuilding, steel (where the relevant law is the ECSC Treaty) and textiles.[89] The Commission has also stressed its favourable stance towards small and medium-sized firms, which it views as especially innovative and dynamic.[90]

Regional aids

In order to avoid the negative consequences which may accompany regional aids,[91] the Commission has developed a set of co-ordinating principles to measure compatibility with the Treaty.[92] Put shortly, these are based on:

(i) *differentiated ceilings of aid intensity*, according to the various regions of the Community, expressed as a percentage of initial investment or in EUA's per job created by the investment;

(ii) *transparency*, to allow the impact of aids to be assessed[93]; and

(iii) *regional specificity*, to overcome the variations in urgency and gravity of development problems.

The principles provide in general terms for a system of supervision by notification of individual cases. The details are fixed when a decision is taken under Article 93 in relation to a given scheme.[94]

Horizontal aids[95]

The Commission is also working towards the definition of its position concerning key non-sectoral problems. There are "Community Frameworks" for research and development aids[96] and for environmental protection.[97] Schemes involving aids to employment may also attract a

---

[87] Comp.Rep. 1978, point 176.
[88] *Ibid.*
[89] Textiles are no longer to be regarded as a crisis sector: see Comp.Rep. 1984, point 224; *General Report 1985*, point 392.
[90] Comp.Rep. 1985, point 16.
[91] See Comp.Rep. 1972 point 141 *et seq.* See also Pappalardo, "State aids and competition policy" in Bates (ed.) *In Memoriam J. D. B. Mitchell* (1983), p. 184.
[92] O.J. 1979 L31/9. See also the discussion of policy in Comp.Rep. 1984, points 261–263.
[93] *Cf.* the general requirements of the Transparency Directive, *loc. cit.* note 35, *supra.*
[94] For a good illustration of supervision, see the history of Regional Development Grants in the United Kingdom: Comp.Rep. 1980, point 175; Comp.Rep. 1984, point 272.
[95] The term is used by the Commission in its 15th Competition Report, 1985.
[96] Bull. EC 12–1985, point 2.1.69.
[97] See Comp.Rep. 1980 for letter of July 7, 1980 extending the transitional period for favouring aids on environmental protection to December 31, 1986. For the conditions of this, see *ibid.* points 225–226.

favourable response from the Commission. For example, the Youth Training Scheme in the United Kingdom was first authorised by the Commission in 1983 and then extended in 1985 in view of the acute problem of youth unemployment and the perceived success of the original scheme.[98]

The relationship between Articles 92 to 94 EEC and other provisions of Community law

By virtue of Article 38(2) EEC the agricultural provisions of the Treaty contained in Articles 39 to 46 take precedence over Articles 92 to 94, as they do over the other rules laid down for the establishment of the common market.[99] In particular, the rules on State aids are among those the application of which Article 42 puts at the discretion of the Council. Provision was made in Article 4 of Regulation 26 for their application in the agricultural sphere, but only to a very limited extent. However, it has become customary for the basic regulations of the various common organisations of agricultural markets established under Article 40 EEC to lay down that, "save as otherwise provided" in the regulation, Articles 92 to 94 are to apply *in toto* to the production of and trade in the products in question. Thus, in the case of goods covered by a common organisation of the market, Member States are required to observe the State aid provisions of the Treaty in the normal way, except where such observance would be incompatible with the rules of the common organisation.[1]

The European Court has had to deal with the question whether Articles 92 to 94 may have a similar pre-emptive effect to the Treaty provisions on agriculture (except, of course, in relation to those provisions). In other words, if a measure can be regarded as forming part of an aid system, does its compatibility with Community law fall to be determined exclusively on the basis of the State aid provisions? It would be convenient for the governments of Member States if this were so, because it would mean that such a measure could not be challenged before a national court unless the aid system in question had been the object of a decision under Article 93(2) or of a regulation under Article 94.[2]

The answer that emerges from the case-law is definitely negative. Thus it was made clear in Case 73/79[3] that a measure of discriminatory taxation, which may be considered at the same time as forming part of an aid system covered by Article 92, remains nonetheless subject to the prohibition in Article 95. A similar approach was taken in Case 91/78 *Hansen* v. *Hauptzollamt Flensburg*[4] where one of the questions raised concerned the relationship between the State aid rules and Article 37 on State monopolies. The Court said:

---

[98] Comp.Rep. 1985, point 226.
[99] See Case 83/78 *Pigs Marketing Board* v. *Redmond* [1978] E.C.R. 2347; [1979] 1 C.M.L.R. 177; Case 177/78 *Pigs & Bacon Commission* v. *McCarren Ltd.*, *loc. cit.* note 71, *supra.*
[1] Case 169/82 *Commission* v. *Italy* [1984] E.C.R. 1603; [1985] 3 C.M.L.R. 30; Case 114/83 *Société d'Initiatives et de Co-operation Agricoles and Others* v. *Commission* [1985] 2 C.M.L.R. 767. See also Snyder, *Law of the Common Agricultural Policy*, pp. 32–38.
[2] *e.g.* the arguments advanced in Case 177/78 *Pigs & Bacon, loc. cit.* note 71, *supra.*
[3] *Commission* v. *Italy, loc. cit.* note 70, *supra.* See also Case 17/81 *Pabst & Richarz* v. *Hauptzollamt Oldenburg* [1982] E.C.R. 1331; [1983] 3 C.M.L.R. 11.
[4] [1979] E.C.R. 935; [1980] 1 C.M.L.R. 162.

" . . . Article 37 of the Treaty constitutes in relation to Articles 92 and 93 a *lex specialis* in the sense that State measures, inherent in the exercise by a State monopoly of a commercial character of its exclusive right must, even where they are linked to grant of an aid to producers subject to the monopoly, be considered in the light of the requirements of Article 37."[5]

However, the European Court has viewed the relationship between State aids and Articles 30–34 rather differently. In *Iannelli* v. *Meroni* it held that:

"The aids referred to in Articles 92 and 93 of the Treaty do not as such fall within the field of application of the prohibition of quantitative restrictions on imports and measures having equivalent effect laid down by Article 30 . . . ."[6]

That is because, if the competitive edge that the granting of aid gives to national products were treated as a measure having equivalent effect to a quantitative restriction, the directly effective prohibition in Article 30 would render the provisions of Articles 92 and 94 totally superfluous. The Court noted in the same case that some aspects of aid contravening specific Treaty provisions other than Articles 92 to 94 may be so indissolubly linked to the object of the aid that it would be impossible to evaluate them separately; but where a particular part of an aid system could be seen as not necessary for the attainment of its object or for its proper functioning, severance would be possible to enable directly effective provisions of the Treaty to operate. However, a finding that certain elements of an aid infringe Article 30 will not permit national courts to strike down the system of aid as a whole or declare that levies raised to finance the aid are illegal.[7]

Fixing the line of demarcation may not always be easy. In *Commission* v. *Ireland ("Buy Irish")*[8] an advertising campaign inspired and financed by the Irish Government through the medium of a private company was held by the Court to fall within Article 30, contrary to the views of Advocate General Capotorti. The fact that Articles 92 and 93 might apply to the method of financing the operation did not mean that the campaign itself could escape the prohibition of Article 30.[9]

Thus, on the analysis adopted by the European Court, the EEC rules on State aids do not seem to present a serious threat to the protection against illegal action by Member States which the direct effect of much of Community law affords to the individual.

---

[5] [1979] E.C.R. at p. 953.
[6] Case 74/76 [1977] E.C.R. 557 at p. 576; [1977] 2 C.M.L.R. 688.
[7] *Ibid.* See also Gormley, *Prohibiting Restrictions on Trade within the EEC*, pp. 246–7; Schramme (1985) RTDE p. 487.
[8] Case 249/81 [1982] E.C.R. 4005; [1983] 2 C.M.L.R. 99.
[9] See also Case 18/84 *Commission* v. *France* (not yet reported); Case 103/84 *Commission* v. *Italy* (not yet reported). Dicta in those cases have been interpreted as amounting to a reversal of *Ianelli*: see Oliver (1986) 23 C.M.L.Rev. 325. Flynn, *op. cit.* note 70, *supra*, points out, however, that like *Buy Irish*, the cases were concerned with unnotified aids. The court, it is submitted, cannot have intended that the "blunt instrument" of Art. 30 should replace the "precision instrument" of Art. 92 in the assessment of an aids compatibility with the common market. See the strong statement of Adv. Gen. Warner in *Ianelli* [1977] E.L.R. at p. 588.

PART VIII: INTELLECTUAL PROPERTY

CHAPTER 18

INTELLECTUAL PROPERTY[1]

What is intellectual property?

The term "industrial property" is applied to certain valuable rights connected with the production and distribution of goods and the provision of services. A catalogue of such rights is found in the Paris Convention on the Protection of Industrial Property[2] which refers to "patents, utility models, industrial designs, trade marks, service marks, trade names, indications of source or appellations of origin, and the repression of unfair competition." Similar rights exist in relation to literary and artistic productions, the most important being copyright. "Intellectual property" is now widely accepted as a generic designation covering both industrial and artistic property, and this is the sense in which the term is used here.[3] It is not found in the EEC Treaty, where Article 36 speaks of "industrial and commercial property." As we shall see, that phrase has been widely interpreted by the Court of Justice.

A normal feature of intellectual property rights is their exclusiveness: they reserve to a particular person the enjoyment of some valuable advantage. Typically also, the rights have a territorial dimension. Thus a patentee (or his assignee or licensee) is the person solely entitled to manufacture and market the patented product within the territory of the State by which a patent is granted.[4] The sale within that State of any product covered by the patent specification would attract infringement proceedings.

The protection afforded to these rights is proprietary in nature, good against the world in general. Other exclusive rights closely associated with the main forms of intellectual property depend upon secrecy for the preservation of their commercial value. The guarantee of secrecy may be found in the law of contract or in rules on the confidentiality of information communicated by one party to another. An example of such a right is "know-how," consisting of specialised knowledge of industrial techniques and processes without which, for example, it may be impossible to exploit a patent properly.[5]

---

[1] For a full analysis of the United Kingdom law of intellectual property and its international (including its EEC) dimension, see Cornish, *Intellectual Property*, Sweet & Maxwell (1981). The impact of the EEC Treaty on intellectual property rights is treated in depth in Guy and Leigh, *The EEC and Intellectual Property*, Sweet & Maxwell (1981). See also Whish, *Competition Law*, Butterworths (1985), Chap. 13.

[2] Convention of March 20, 1883. Most recently revised, Stockholm, July 14, 1967, Art. 1(2).

[3] The term is convenient, if not wholly appropriate, and received international recognition in the title of the World Intellectual Property Organisation. See Cornish, *op. cit.* note 1, *supra*, p. 3. See also Harris (1975–76) 1 E.L.Rev. 515 at pp. 515–516.

[4] The State's legislation may make the granting of licences to work the patent compulsory in certain circumstances. The right of the patent holder will then be confined essentially to receiving a royalty. On the position in the United Kingdom, see the Patents Act 1977, ss.48–54. See Cornish, *op. cit.* note 1, *supra*, pp. 250 *et seq.*

[5] On the status of know-how in English law, see *Handley Page* v. *Butterworth* (1935) 19 T.C. 328.

Intellectual property and the common market

The main problem underlying the legal developments discussed in this chapter was neatly summarised by the European Court in the following passage from its judgment in *Parke, Davis* v. *Centrafarm*:

> "The national rules relating to the protection of industrial property have not yet been unified within the Community. In the absence of such unification, the national character of the protection of industrial property and the variations between the different legislative systems on this subject are capable of creating obstacles both to the free movement of the patented products and to competition within the common market."[6]

The co-existence of separate systems of protection for intellectual property rights in the different Member States is liable to conflict with the objective of creating a single market covering the whole Community. One aspect of the problem is that variations in the content of the rules relating to intellectual property between the Member States necessarily entail inequalities in the conditions of competition under which business is carried on. However, this is only one of a number of factors, such as differences in taxation systems or in the strictness of laws on the protection of the environment, contributing to such inequalities. More serious is the "national character" of intellectual property, the sheer fact that rights relating to the same subject-matter have an independent legal existence in each of the Member States where they are recognised. Given the exclusiveness of intellectual property rights and their territorial character, there is a danger that the market in goods or services covered by such rights may be divided up into more or less watertight national compartments. For example, X Ltd., the holder of a patent or trade mark right protected under the law of Member State A, may be entitled to oppose the importation into that State of an article manufactured under a parallel patent or bearing a parallel mark protected under the law of Member State B; and this may be so even if the holder of the patent or mark in Member State B is none other than X Ltd. itself or a subsidiary or licensee of X Ltd. It is obvious that such use of the patent or trade mark recognised by Member State A interferes with the free movement of goods and is liable to have a distorting effect on competition.

Unification of laws on intellectual property

The remedy hinted at by the Court in the passage quoted from *Parke, Davis* is that national rules on the protection of intellectual property rights should be unified.

In fact, since the judgment in that case an important step has been taken towards the goal of unification through the signing of the Convention for the European Patent for the Common Market (otherwise known as the Community Patent Convention) on December 15, 1975.[7] The general purpose of the Convention is to introduce a unitary patent for the common

[6] Case 24/67. [1968] E.C.R. 55 at p. 71.
[7] O.J. 1976 L17/1.

market, within the framework of the wider Convention on the Grant of European Patents,[8] and to lay down the "common system of law" by which this patent is to be governed. Article 2 of the Convention provides:

"1. European patents granted for the Contracting States shall be called Community patents.

2. Community patents shall have a unitary character. They shall have equal effect throughout the territories to which this Convention applies and may only be granted, transferred, revoked or allowed to lapse in respect of the whole of such territories. The same shall apply *mutatis mutandis* to applications for European patents in which the Contracting States are designated.

3. Community patents shall have an autonomous character. They shall be subject only to the provisions of this Convention and those provisions of the European Patent Convention which are binding upon every European patent and which shall consequently be deemed to be provisions of this Convention."

An examination of the detailed provisions of the Convention would fall outside the scope of this book. What concerns us is the likely effect of the Convention on the problem of the partitioning of the common market through the operation of national patents. Here the first point to notice is that national patents will continue to exist side by side with Community patents (although not in relation to the same inventions). Where an inventor chooses to take out a Community patent, he will receive protection on a Community-wide basis. There will thus be a single proprietor of the patent, whose rights will be exhausted by putting a protected product onto the market in one of the Member States. The possibility that the granting of licenses limited to certain areas might be used as a means of splitting the common market has been provided against. Where an inventor prefers to take out a national patent, the situation will be much the same as before, except that Article 81 of the Convention provides a legislative basis for the exhaustion of rights principle developed by the Court in its case law.[9] It may be concluded that the Community Patent Convention, if it can finally be brought into force, will go a considerable way towards reconciling the legitimate interests of patent holders with the requirements of a well-functioning common market; but areas of conflict will remain and the case

---

[8] Or "European Patent Convention." This came into force on October 7, 1977. The European Patent Office which processes patent applications has been established in Munich, with a branch in The Hague. An applicant for a European patent specifies the contracting States in which protection is sought. If granted, the patent will have the same effect as a national patent in each of those States. However, subject to transitional arrangements, once the Community Patent Convention is in force the only available form of European patent for EEC members will be a unitary Community patent.

[9] Art. 81(1) provides:
"The rights conferred by a national patent in a Contracting State shall not extend to acts concerning a product covered by that patent which are done within the territory of that Contracting State after that product has been put on the market in any Contracting State by the proprietor of the patent or with his express consent, unless there are grounds which, under Community law, would justify the extension to such acts of the rights conferred by the patent."
On the relevant case law, see *infra*.

law of the Court, which is discussed below, has certainly not been super-seded.[10]

As for other types of intellectual property, significant steps have been taken so far only in relation to trade marks. After earlier initiatives had come to nothing, a Memorandum on the creation of an EEC trade mark was published by the Commission in 1976.[11] This was followed in 1980 by the submission to the Council of a proposal for a directive to harmonise national trade-mark laws and a proposal for a regulation on a Community trade mark.[12] At the time of writing it was still impossible to predict when, or even whether, these measures would be adopted.

A judicial solution—existence and exercise

The stark question for the Court of Justice has been how far it is bound to recognise the rights conferred by national laws on holders of intellectual property where these allow activity, usually involving the exclusion from the market in question of imports from another Member State, which would normally be prohibited under Community law. The answer that effect must be given to all such rights might seem to follow from the pro-vision of Article 222 EEC that:

"This Treaty shall *in no way* prejudice the rules in Member States governing the system of property ownership" (emphasis added).

On the other hand, Article 36 EEC, which contains the only express dero-gation from the general rules of the Treaty for the benefit of intellectual property rights, provides in pertinent part:

"The provisions of Articles 30 to 34 shall not preclude prohibitions or restrictions on imports, exports or goods in transit justified on grounds of . . . the protection of industrial and commercial property. Such prohibitions or restrictions shall not, however, constitute a means of arbitrary discrimination or a disguised restriction on trade between Member States."

While restrictions on imports that are genuinely necessary for the protec-tion of industrial and commercial property are here exempted from the prohibition in Article 30, it is made unequivocally clear in the second sen-tence of the Article that there may be circumstances where, regardless of rights existing under national law, the prohibition will apply.

The compromise enshrined in Article 36 pointed the way to a solution which has also been applied by analogy in the fields of competition and the provision of services. This was formulated in a leading case *Terrapin* v. *Terranova*[13] as follows:

---

[10] At the time of writing the main impediment to the entry into force of the Convention was continuing unwillingness on the part of Denmark and Ireland to ratify it (or the European Patent Convention). A diplomatic conference in December 1985 failed to overcome the opposition of those Member States but did bring forth a solution to the vexed question of the enforcement of the Convention. On the proposal to establish a new court with direct appellate jurisdiction from national courts concerning the infringement or validity of Com-munity patents, see Wadlow, (1986) 11 E.L.Rev. 295.

[11] Bull. EC Supp. 8/76.

[12] O.J. 1980 C351 at, respectively, pp. 1 and 5. See Gormley (1981) 6 E.L.Rev. pp. 385 and 463.

[13] Case 119/75 [1976] E.C.R. 1039; [1976] 2 C.M.L.R. 482. The formulation is found, with small verbal differences, in numerous judgments.

" . . . whilst the Treaty does not affect the existence of rights recognized by the legislation of a Member State in matters of industrial and commercial property, yet the exercise of those rights may nevertheless, depending on the circumstances, be restricted by the prohibitions in the Treaty. Inasmuch as it provides an exception to one of the fundamental principles of the common market, Article 36 in fact admits exceptions to the free movement of goods only to the extent to which such exceptions are justified for the purposes of safeguarding the rights which constitute the specific subject-matter of that property."[14]

The distinction drawn by the Court between the existence of rights and their exercise is evidently inspired by a wish to remain at least within the letter of Article 222. It invites the criticism that a form of property *is* the bundle of rights recognised by national law under a particular designation; and if Community law prevents any rights in the bundle from being exercised, the property is to that extent diꞏinished. What the Court has done, in reality, emerges from the second sentence in the quoted passage. The derogation in Article 36 has been confined to rights which, the Court considers, constitute the essential core or "specific subject-matter" of the property in question.[15] The exercise of such rights is tolerated, even if it impedes trade or competition, because otherwise it would no longer be possible to say that the property was receiving protection. On the other hand, rights which the Court regards as merely incidental to the property are not allowed to interfere with the project of unifying the market.

The solution worked out in the Court's case law on intellectual property is the fruit of teleological interpretation of the EEC Treaty. In *Polydor* v. *Harlequin*[16] the Court was invited to extend that interpretation to provisions in a free trade agreement with a third country which were similarly worded to Articles 30 and 36 EEC, but declined to do so. That was because the purpose of such agreements was less far-reaching than the purpose of the Treaty—"to create a single market reproducing as closely as possible the conditions of a domestic market."[17]

Freedom of movement—the exhaustion of rights principle

The exclusive right of an owner of intellectual property to put into circulation for the first time goods that are subject to the property is likely to be understood in the law of the Member State concerned as applying to sales in that State's territory. Sales elsewhere will not count as an exercise of the right—in the jargon of the subject, they are considered not to "exhaust" it.[18] This means that, as a matter of national law, it will be open to the owner of the property to oppose the sale by other traders of imported products acquired in a Member State where they have been marketed by the owner himself. There would be an incentive for such "parallel" importing

---

[14] [1976] E.C.R. at p. 1061.
[15] The definitions the Court has given in its case law of the "specific subject-matter" of various important forms of intellectual property are considered, *infra*.
[16] Case 270/80 [1982] E.C.R. 329; [1982] 1 C.M.L.R. 677.
[17] [1982] E.C.R. at p. 349.
[18] On the exhaustion of patent rights in the law of the United Kingdom, see Cornish, *op. cit.* note 1, *supra*, pp. 190 *et seq*.

if, for some reason, the products in question were significantly cheaper in the State of initial distribution than in the one from which it was sought to exclude them.

On the other hand, the Court of Justice has repeatedly stated, as a general principle, that "the proprietor of an industrial or commercial property right protected by the legislation of a Member State may not rely on that legislation in order to oppose the importation of a product which has lawfully been marketed in another Member State by, or with the consent of, the proprietor of the right himself or a person legally or economically dependent on him."[19] Whatever the position in national law, the proprietor's exclusive right is deemed in Community law to be exhausted by putting products into circulation anywhere within the common market. The rationale of the principle is to be found in the limitation of the exception in Article 36 by the notion of the specific subject-matter of property. Where exhaustion occurs it is because the right to exclude imports originally marketed in another Member State is not seen as part of the essential guarantee provided by the property in question. The exercise of the right would, therefore, not be "justified" within the meaning of Article 36 as being necessary for the protection of the property.[20]

The principle has now been applied by the Court of Justice to most of the important forms of intellectual property.[21]

Patents

The leading case on the application of the exhaustion of rights principle to patents is *Centrafarm* v. *Sterling Drug*.[22] Patents for a drug used in the treatment of urinary infections were held by Sterling Drug, an American company, in the United Kingdom and the Netherlands. The case originated in the proceedings brought for the infringement of the Dutch patent against Centrafarm, a company famous in the annals of the European Court as a parallel importer of pharmaceutical products.[23] Centrafarm's alleged infringement consisted of importing into the Netherlands and offering for sale there quantities of the patented product which had been lawfully marketed by licensees of Sterling Drug in the United Kingdom. This was commercially attractive for Centrafarm, since the price of the drug on the United Kingdom market was only about half the price on the Dutch market.

The Court of Justice defined the specific subject-matter of a patent as:

" . . . the guarantee that the patentee, to reward the creative effort of the inventor, has the exclusive right to use an invention with a view to manufacturing industrial products and putting them into circulation

---

[19] See, among many instances, Case 144/81 *Keurkoop* v. *Nancy Kean Gifts* [1982] E.C.R. 2853 at p. 2873.

[20] This analysis was applied by the Court for the first time in Case 78/70 *Deutsche Grammophon* v. *Metro* [1971] E.C.R. 487; [1971] C.M.L.R. 631. It is more fully worked out in Case 15/74 *Centrafarm* v. *Sterling Drug* [1974] E.C.R. 1147; [1974] 2 C.M.L.R. 480.

[21] There is a very full review of the case law in Gormley, *Prohibiting Restrictions on Trade within the EEC*, T.M.C. Asser Instituut (1985), pp. 184 *et seq.* On the earlier cases, see Harris, *op. cit.* note 3, *supra*.

[22] *Loc. cit.* note 20, *supra*.

[23] There were parallel proceedings for the infringement of the Dutch trade mark: Case 16/74 *Centrafarm* v. *Winthrop* [1974] E.C.R. 1183; [1974] 2 C.M.L.R. 480, discussed *infra*.

for the first time, either directly or by the grant of licences to third parties as well as the right to oppose infringements."[24]
The essential function of a patent is here acknowledged to be the rewarding of (and hence encouragement to) creative effort. The reward comes from the patentee's ability to earn a monopoly profit through an exclusive right to manufacture the protected product and put it into circulation for the first time. That right may be exploited directly or by appointing licensees. It has, as a corollary, a right to oppose manufacturing or first marketing of the product by third parties.

In the light of that definition the Court went on to consider the circumstances in which the use of a patent to block the importation of protected products from another Member State might be justified. Two cases of possible justification were mentioned: where the product is not patentable in the Member State of origin and has been manufactured there by a third party without the consent of the patentee in the Member State of importation[25]; and where a patent exists in each of the Member states in question but the original proprietors of the patents are legally and economically independent. On the other hand, there could be no justification for opposing importation "where the product has been put onto the market in a legal manner, by the patentee himself or with his consent, in the Member State from which it has been imported, in particular in the case of a proprietor of parallel patents."[26] If a patent could be used in this way, the patentee would be able to cordon off national markets, thereby restricting trade between Member States, "where no such restriction was necessary to guarantee the essence of the exclusive rights flowing from the parallel patents."[27] The objection that national patents were unlikely to be truly parallel, with the result that levels of protection would vary between Member States, was brushed aside. "It should be noted here," the Court said, "that, in spite of divergences which remain in the absence of any unification of national rules concerning industrial property the identity of the protected invention is clearly the essential element of the concept of parallel patents which it is for the courts to assess."[28] The conclusion was:

" . . . that the exercise, by a patentee, of the right which he enjoys under the legislation of a Member State to prohibit the sale, in that State, of a product protected by the patent which has been marketed in another Member State by the patentee or with his consent is incompatible with the rules of the EEC Treaty concerning the free movement of goods within the common market."[29]

The basis of the ruling was not made altogether clear. On the one hand, it might be thought the existence of parallel patents was a crucial factor: a right to oppose the importation of protected products could be regarded as superfluous, because the patentee would already have received the mono-

---

[24] [1974] E.C.R. at p. 1162.
[25] This was the situation in Case 24/67 *Parke, Davis* v. *Centrafarm* [1968] E.C.R. 55; [1968] C.M.L.R. 47. The questions put to the Court were, however, formulated with reference to the competition rules.
[26] [1974] E.C.R. at p. 1163.
[27] *Ibid.*
[28] *Ibid.*
[29] *Ibid.*

poly profit, which was his due, in the Member State where the products were first put on the market. On the other hand, the general terms in which the ruling was expressed, taken with other hints in the judgment,[30] strongly suggested the principle of exhaustion would apply, even where the initial marketing occurred without the benefit of patent protection. If that were so, then the explanation could only lie in the patentee's consent to the marketing. That such was indeed the Court's meaning was shown in the later case of *Merck* v. *Stephar*.[31]

The plaintiff in the national proceedings, Merck, was the holder in the Netherlands of patents relating to a drug used mainly in the treatment of high blood pressure. The proceedings arose because Stephar had imported the drug into the Netherlands from Italy where, although it was not patentable, it had been put into circulation by Merck. On Merck's behalf it was argued that the function of rewarding an inventor's creative effort would not be fulfilled if, owing to the impossibility of patenting a product, its sale in the Member State in question did not take place under monopoly conditions. To this the Court replied:

"That right of first placing a product on a market enables the inventor, by allowing him a monopoly in exploiting his product, to obtain the reward for his creative effort without, however, guaranteeing that he will obtain such a reward in all circumstances.

It is for the proprietor of the patent to decide, in the light of all the circumstances, under what conditions he will market his product, including the possibility of marketing it in a Member State where the law does not provide patent protection for the product in question. If he decides to do so he must then accept the consequences of his choice as regards the free movement of the product within the Common Market, which is a fundamental principle forming part of the legal and economic circumstances which must be taken into account by the proprietor of the patent in determining the manner in which his exclusive right will be exercised."[32]

The owner of a national patent, therefore, has a choice. He may decide to exploit his exclusive rights to the utmost, in which case he will have to stay out of markets in Member States where he has weaker protection or none at all. Or he may go into those other markets, at the cost of accepting a lower profit in his protected market. Whether it makes sense from an economic point of view for a patentee to be confronted with such a choice may be open to question; but for the Court the unity of the market takes precedence over conflicting considerations of economic policy.[33]

It used to be debated whether an owner of parallel national patents was entitled to resist the importation into one of the Member States concerned of products manufactured under a compulsory licence issued in respect of

---

[30] See, in particular, the reference, *ibid.*, to non-patentable goods "manufactured by third parties without the consent of the patentee."
[31] Case 187/80 [1981] E.C.R. 2063; [1981] 3 C.M.L.R. 463.
[32] [1981] E.C.R. at pp. 2081–2082.
[33] See Cornish, *op. cit.* note 1 *supra*, pp. 245 *et seq.*

his patent in the other Member State.[34] The question received a clear affirmative answer in *Pharmon* v. *Hoechst*.[35] Parallel patents in a medicinal drug were owned by Hoechst in Germany, the Netherlands and the United Kingdom. A compulsory licence for the manufacture of the drug had been obtained in the United Kingdom and Pharmon had purchased a consignment from the licensee with a view to selling it on the Dutch market. This Hoechst was anxious to prevent. Pharmon rested its case on the exhaustion of rights principle, arguing that Hoechst had entered the British market with its eyes open and must be taken to have accepted all the legal consequences flowing from the registration of a parallel patent. The passage quoted above from the judgment in *Merck* seemed to give force to that argument.[36] It was, however, rejected by the Court on the ground that the compulsory character of a licence meant the holder of the patent could not be regarded as having consented to the actions of the licensee. "In fact," the Court said, "the holder of the patent is deprived by such an official act of his right to decide freely on the conditions under which he will place his product on the market."[37] The provision of the Community Patent Convention excepting from the principle of exhaustion "the case of a product put on the market under a compulsory licence" has thus been shown to reflect the law of the EEC Treaty.[38]

Trade marks

Centrafarm v. *Sterling Drug*[39] had a companion case, *Centrafarm* v. *Winthrop*,[40] relating to the infringement of the trade mark, NEGRAM, under which the imported drug was sold. The plaintiff in the national proceedings was the Dutch subsidiary of Sterling Drug, Winthrop B.V., which owned the trade mark in the Netherlands. The United Kingdom mark was held by another Sterling subsidiary, Sterling Winthrop Group Ltd.

The European Court's conclusion was similar to that in the patent case and reached by a similar process of reasoning. The specific subject-matter of a trade mark was said to be:

" . . . the guarantee that the owner of the trade mark has the exclusive right to use that trade mark, for the purpose of putting products protected by the trade mark into circulation for the first time, and is therefore intended to protect him against competitors wishing to take advantage of the status and reputation of the trade mark by selling products illegally bearing that trade mark."[41]

The emphasis here is on what makes a trade mark valuable—the reservation to the owner, through his exclusive right to put marked products into circulation, of the goodwill associated with the mark. Why such a right should be given (the question of the "essential function" of a trade mark)

---

[34] Under a system of compulsory licensing a patentee may be deprived of his monopoly by an official decision to grant licenses to third parties in return for a reasonable royalty. See note 4, *supra.*
[35] Case 19/84 [1985] 3 C.M.L.R. 775.
[36] [1981] E.C.R. at p. 2082.
[37] [1985] 3 C.M.L.R. at p. 791.
[38] Community Patent Convention, Art. 81(3).
[39] *Loc. cit.* note 20, *supra.*
[40] Case 16/74 *loc. cit.* note 23, *supra.*
[41] [1974] E.C.R. at p. 1194.

was not considered by the Court on this occasion.[42] The Court went on to find that, where goods have been marketed by a trade mark owner or with his consent in another Member State "so there can be no question of abuse or infringement of the trade mark,"[43] their exclusion could not be justified as being necessary to guarantee the "essence" of the owner's right. The Court, accordingly, ruled:

" . . . that the exercise, by the owner of a trade mark, of the right which he enjoys under the legislation of a Member State to prohibit the sale, in that State, of a product which has been marketed under the trade mark in another Member State by the trade mark owner or with his consent is incompatible with the rules of the EEC Treaty concerning the free movement of goods within the common market."[44]

This statement adopting consent to marketing as the criterion of the exhaustion of trade mark rights was seen to be in need of qualification in *Hoffmann La Roche* v. *Centrafarm*[45] and *Centrafarm* v. *American Home Products*,[45] which came to the Court of Justice by way of references under Article 177 by courts in, respectively, Germany and the Netherlands. The background was, again, the resale by Centrafarm of pharmaceutical products it had purchased at the relatively low prices prevailing on the British market; however, a new feature of the cases was that Centrafarm had played a more active role in relation to the products than that of a mere importer. The product in the German case was the tranquilliser VALIUM, which had been marketed in the United Kingdom by the British subsidiary of Hoffmann-La Roche. The VALIUM was imported into the Netherlands where its original packaging was removed and it was put up into larger packages. On these Centrafarm placed the trade mark owned by Hoffmann-La Roche in Germany as well as a notice giving its own name and address as the vendor of the product. It then re-exported the VALIUM for sale on the German market. In the Dutch case Centrafarm had gone even further. The product there was a tranquilliser which was sold by American Home Products Corporation (AHPC) in various Member States under different trade marks. In the United Kingdom the mark used by AHPC was SERENID and in the Benelux countries it was SERESTA. Quantities of the tranquilliser which AHPC had put into circulation in the United Kingdom under the mark SERENID were imported into the Netherlands by Centrafarm and sold there after the original mark had been removed and the mark SERESTA substituted. The European Court was asked, in effect, by the referring courts whether Article 36 enabled Hoffmann-La Roche and AHPC to rely on their respective trade mark rights in Germany and the Netherlands to curb these activities. In both cases the answer given by the Court was in the form of statements of general principle, deduced from the first sentence of Article 36, subject to a qualification deduced from the second sentence of the Article.

---

[42] See Case 102/77 *Hoffmann La Roche* v. *Centrafarm* [1978] E.C.R. 1139; [1978] 3 C.M.L.R. 217; Case 3/78 *Centrafarm* v. *American Home Products* [1978] E.C.R. 1823; [1978] 1 C.M.L.R. 326. The cases are discussed, *infra*.
[43] [1974] E.C.R. 1195.
[44] *Ibid.*
[45] *Loc. cit.* note 42, *supra*.

In the German case the Court held that:

"The proprietor of a trade-mark right which is protected in two Member States at the same time is justified pursuant to the first sentence of Article 36 of the EEC Treaty in preventing a product to which the trade-mark has lawfully been applied in one of those States from being marketed in the other Member State after it has been repackaged in new packaging to which the trade mark has been affixed by a third party."[46]

It reached that conclusion in the light of the "essential function of the trade mark" which, it said, was "to guarantee the identity of the trade-marked product to the consumer or ultimate user, by enabling him without any possibility of confusion to distinguish that product from products which have another origin."[47] There is a certain inelegance in juxtaposing this definition of *essential function* from the point of view of the consumer's interest in not being deceived with a definition of *specific subject-matter* from the point of view of the trade-mark holder's interest in his goodwill. In the present context the Court took the view that the guarantee of origin meant "that the consumer or ultimate user can be certain that a trade-marked product which is sold to him has not been subject at a previous stage of marketing to interference by a third person, without the authorisation of the proprietor of the trade-mark, such as to affect the original condition of the product."[48] It followed that the right to prevent any dealing with the marked product which was likely to impair this guarantee formed part of the specific subject-matter of the trade-mark right.

The Court then turned its attention to the proviso in Article 36 that the exercise of rights must not constitute "a disguised restriction on trade between Member States." It was held that such a restriction might arise if the variation of the packaging of the product in the different Member States formed part of a marketing strategy enabling the trade-mark holder to compartmentalise the market. However, he would only be prevented from exercising his right against the seller of the imported product if three further conditions were satisfied. In the first place, the repackaging must have been carried out in a way which did not affect the original condition of the product. This might be the case, for example, where the product was marketed by the proprietor of the trade mark in a double packaging and the repackaging only affected the outer layer; or where the repackaging was inspected by a public authority. Secondly, the proprietor of the mark must be given prior notice of the marketing of the repackaged product. And thirdly, the new packaging must indicate the person by whom the operation has been performed. In this way the Court sought to reconcile, on the one hand, the legitimate interests of consumers and of the trade-mark holder and, on the other hand, the principle of free internal trade, requiring that the seller of the imported goods be given "a certain licence which in normal circumstances is reserved to the proprietor himself."[49]

---

[46] [1978] E.C.R. at p. 1167.
[47] [1978] E.C.R. at p. 1164.
[48] *Ibid.*
[49] See [1978] E.C.R. at pp. 1165–1166.

In the Dutch case the Court ruled that, in principle, the proprietor of a trade mark in one Member State was justified in opposing the sale by a third party of a product bearing that mark, even if the product had previously been marketed in another Member State under a different mark held by the same proprietor. Here too, the emphasis was on the essential function of a trade mark in providing a guarantee of a product's origin. The Court said that this guarantee would be compromised if anyone other than the trade mark owner were allowed to place the mark on the product. It was, therefore, consistent with the essential function of this type of property that, where a person held two or more trade marks in respect of the same product, national law should prevent any unauthorised third party from taking it upon himself to place one or other of the marks on any part of the production in question or to alter the marks placed by the holder on different parts of such production; the same would apply where the different parts of the production, bearing different marks, came from two different Member States.

As to the proviso in Article 36, the Court pointed out that there might be perfectly good reasons for using different trade marks in respect of the same products in different Member States. (An obvious case would be where it was impossible for the holder of a trade mark in State A to obtain registration of the mark in State B owing to its similarity to a mark of independent origin already protected in that State.) On the other hand, the proviso might apply if the trade mark rights were exploited for the purposes of a market-splitting strategy. It is, of course, for the national court to determine whether or not, in fact, the right is being legitimately exercised. Thus the derogation in Article 36 will not apply to a right the protection of which would otherwise be justified because it belongs to the specific subject-matter of the property in question, if the right is being exploited for an anti-competitive purpose.[50]

An ingenious parallel importer may find a way of repackaging marked products that does not compromise the guarantee of origin the trade mark represents to consumers. There was a good example in *Pfizer* v. *Eurim-Pharm*,[51] another case of alleged infringement of a German trade mark through the importation of pharmaceutical products first marketed in the United Kingdom. The packaging for the British market consisted of "blister strips," each containing five tablets, which were enclosed in an outer wrapping. The trade mark "VIBRAMYCIN PFIZER" was printed on the strips. After removing the outer wrapping, the importer, Eurim-Pharm, placed each strip in its own box, with an information leaflet as required by German legislation. The boxes had transparent windows through which the trade mark on the strip was plainly visible. On the back of the boxes the names and addresses of the manufacturer and the importer were given, and it was stated that the latter had been responsible for the packaging. Advance warning of its intentions had been given by Eurim-Pharm to

[50] See the analysis by Judge Pescatore in a paper "Libre circulation des marchandises et droits de protection industrielle dans le marché commun" at the Institut Universitaire International, Luxembourg in July 1978.
[51] Case 1/81 [1981] E.C.R. 2913; [1982] 1 C.M.L.R. 406.

Pfizer, the owner of the German mark and parent of the British company which had put the products into circulation.

Here, in contrast to *Hoffmann-La Roche* v. *Centrafarm*, nothing was done that might carry a risk of interference with the original condition of the products or of consumers' being misled as to their origin. The sealed inner packaging was left intact. The importer merely replaced the outer wrapping, exposing the mark affixed by the manufacturer himself. All the information needed by consumers was made available to them. In those circumstances, it was held, Article 36 could not be relied upon to prevent the sale of the imported products. The ruling was based on lack of justification—a right of the kind being claimed by Pfizer would not form part of the specific subject-matter of the trade mark. There was no need for Eurim-Pharm to fall back on the argument that the variation in packaging amounted to a market-splitting strategy, restricting trade between Member States contrary to the second sentence of the Article.

Copyright

The phrase "industrial and commercial property" in Article 36, while it clearly applies to patents and trade marks, is less apt as a description of artistic property.[52] Nevertheless, after some initial hesitation by the Court of Justice,[53] it is now beyond doubt that copyright and other rights protecting literary and artistic work are covered.

A right akin to copyright was the subject of *Deutsche Grammophon* v. *Metro*,[54] the earliest case in which the exhaustion of rights principle can be seen at work. Deutsche Grammophon (DG), the plaintiff in the national proceedings, supplied the records it manufactured to retailers in Germany under a retail price maintenance arrangement. It also exported records to France where they were marketed by its subsidiary, Polydor. Metro, the defendant, had succeeded in obtaining records originally sold in France by Polydor, which it then resold in Germany at prices well below the controlled price. DG sought to prevent these sales by invoking against Metro the exclusive right of distribution, akin to copyright, which manufacturers of sound recordings enjoy under German legislation. On a reference from the German court to which the case went on appeal, the European Court held that:

" . . . it would be in conflict with the provisions prescribing the free movement of products within the common market for a manufacturer of sound recordings to exercise the exclusive right to distribute the protected articles, conferred upon him by the legislation of a Member State, in such a way as to prohibit the sale in that State of products placed on the market by him or with his consent in another Member state solely because such distribution did not occur within the territory of the first Member State."[55]

---

[52] See the remarks by Advocate General Warner in his opinion relating to case 62/79 *Coditel* v. *Ciné Vog Films (No. 1)* [1980] E.C.R. at pp. 878–879.

[53] In the *Deutsche Grammophon* case, *infra*, the Court left open the question whether a record manufacturer's right analogous to copyright came within the scope of Art. 36.

[54] Case 78/70 [1971] E.C.R. 487; [1971] C.M.L.R. 631.

[55] [1971] E.C.R. at p. 500.

The conclusion is clear but the steps by which it was reached are less so. The judgment contains the first mention of the limitation of the derogation in Article 36 to measures justified for the safeguarding of rights which constitute the specific subject-matter of a form of intellectual property. However, the Court did not go on to define the specific subject-matter of a record manufacturer's exclusive right of distribution; nor did it rule that a right to oppose the sale of records marketed by a manufacturer or with his consent in another Member State could not be included in such subject-matter. It simply reasoned that the purpose of unifying the market could not be attained "if, under the various legal systems of the Member States, nationals of those States were able to partition the market and bring about arbitrary discrimination or disguised restrictions on trade between Member States."[56]

A decade later the fully-fledged principle was applied by the Court in *Musik-Vetrieb Membran* v. *GEMA*.[57] The case concerned the importation of records and cassettes into Germany from other Member States, one being the United Kingdom, where they had been manufactured and put on the market with the consent of the copyright owners. The copyright management society, GEMA, claimed the importation was in breach of the owners' rights in Germany. However, it did not seek to exclude the recordings from the German market but only to recover a sum representing any difference between the royalties payable in Germany and those paid in respect of the initial distribution. Three points in the case are of particular interest.

First, an attempt was made to establish a special status for copyright beyond the reach of the case law on the exhaustion of rights. The French Government, which intervened on the side of GEMA, stressed the moral aspect of the protection given to authors, such as their right to object to any distortion, mutilation or alteration of their work or to any other action in relation to it that might prejudice their honour or reputation.[58] The Court of Justice readily conceded the special character of copyright but pointed out it was not the moral but the economic aspect of protection that was in issue. From the point of view of commercial exploitation, and the threat this might pose to the unity of the market, copyright was on all fours with other forms of intellectual property.

Secondly, GEMA relied on the fact that it was not actually opposing the importation of the records. That, in the Court's view, was immaterial, since the society's royalty claim was based on the infringement of its members' exclusive rights of exploitation, which enabled it to interfere with the free movement of recordings. A further consideration was that individuals could not be allowed, in effect, to impose import levies on goods already in free circulation in the common market.[59]

Thirdly, it was argued that lower royalties in the United Kingdom, which

---

[56] *Ibid.*
[57] Joined Cases 55 and 57/80 [1981] E.C.R. 147; [1981] 2 C.M.L.R. 44.
[58] On the moral aspect of copyright, see Cornish, *op. cit.* note 1, *supra*, pp. 392–396.
[59] The point is only touched on briefly. However, it is clear the prohibition relates to the national legislation enabling private parties to levy charges on imports. This is, therefore, an Art. 30 not an Art. 9 matter.

encouraged exportation to Germany, were the product not of competition but of statutory intervention. Effectively, there was a ceiling on the remuneration a copyright owner could secure from a licensee, since anyone was entitled to reproduce a recording, once it had been put on the market with the author's consent, on payment of a royalty of 6.25 per cent.[60] This was, in substance, the old argument that traders should be protected against distortions of competition resulting from continuing disparities between the legislation of Member States, and inevitably it failed.[61] The ground given by the Court for its ruling was that the exploitation of a copyright in a given market was a matter for the free choice of the owner. "He may," the Court said, "make that choice according to his best interests, which involve not only the level of remuneration provided in the Member State in question but other factors such as, for example, the opportunities for distributing his work and the marketing facilities which are further enhanced by virtue of the free movement of goods within the Community."[62] As a trader within the common market he must, in other words, abide by the consequences of his decisions.

Copyright is a complex form of property, reflecting the diversity of the works to which it relates.[63] *Deutsche Grammophon* and *GEMA* concerned the aspect of copyright which protects an owner's interest in the reproduction and sale of material objects incorporating creative work, *in casu* sound recordings. That kind of interest is adequately served by the control the copyright owner enjoys over the initial marketing of protected products. There is, however, another aspect of copyright, namely the "performing rights" in a work such as a film or play, where exploitation takes place through public exhibitions which may be repeated an indefinite number of times. The principle of exhaustion obviously cannot apply to performing rights in the same way as it does to the marketing of goods. This was brought home in the earlier of two successive references to the Court of Justice arising out of copyright infringement proceedings in Belgium against the cable television undertaking, Coditel.[64]

The background to the case was as follows. The copyright in a film called "Le Boucher" was owned by a French company, Les Films la Boétie. The company granted Ciné Vog films an exclusive licence to exhibit "Le Boucher" in Belgium for a period of seven years. One of the conditions of the licence was that the film should not be broadcast on Belgian television until 40 months after its first cinema showing. A different licensee was appointed in Germany on terms which, it seems, allowed the television

---

[60] Pursuant to Copyright Act 1956, s.8.
[61] *Cf.* the treatment of a similar argument relating to the price of pharmaceutical products in Case 15/74 *Centrafarm* v. *Sterling Drug* [1974] E.C.R. at pp. 1164–1165.
[62] [1981] E.C.R. at p. 165.
[63] See the discussion in Cornish, *op. cit.* note 1, *supra* at pp. 318 *et seq.*
[64] Case 62/79 *Coditel* v. *Ciné Vog Films (No. 1)* [1980] E.C.R. 881; [1981] 2 C.M.L.R. 362. The reference was made by the Cour d'Appel of Brussels. On further appeal to the Cour de Cassation the need was felt for a reference on a different question of Community law: see Case 262/81 *Coditel* v. *Ciné Vog Films (No. 2)* [1982] E.C.R. 3381; [1983] 1 C.M.L.R. 49. As to the latter, see *infra*, p. 506, note 38. *Coditel* v. *Ciné Vog Films (No. 1)* was joined for the purposes of the oral procedure with another case involving Coditel companies, though originating in different proceedings, namely a prosecution for the infringement of the ban then in force on television advertising in Belgium. This was Case 52/79 *Procureur du Roi* v. *Debauve* [1980] E.C.R. 833; [1981] 1 C.M.L.R. 362.

rights in the film to be exploited immediately. "Le Boucher" was accordingly shown in a dubbed version on German television more than two and a half years before it could have been broadcast in Belgium. That broadcast was picked up by Coditel on Belgian territory and relayed over its cable diffusion network. Under Belgian copyright law Coditel's action amounted to a "communication to the public" requiring the authorisation of the national licensee, Ciné Vog. In its defence Coditel argued, *inter alia*, that to prohibit the cable diffusion of a broadcast emanating from another Member State where it had been made with the consent of the copyright owner would be incompatible with Article 59 EEC on the freedom to provide services.

The EEC Treaty does not expressly exempt from the provisions of Article 59 restrictions on the provision of services justified for the protection of rights of intellectual property. Advocate General Warner, however, took the view that Article 36 applied by analogy in the present context and the Court, though it did not refer to the Article, seems to have agreed. The relevant passage of the judgment reads:

> "Whilst Article 59 of the Treaty prohibits restrictions upon freedom to provide services, it does not thereby encompass limits upon the exercise of certain economic activities which have their origin in the application of national legislation for the protection of intellectual property, save where such application constitutes a means of arbitrary discrimination or a disguised restriction on trade between Member States. Such would be the case if that application enabled parties to create artificial barriers to trade between Member States."[65]

The Court and the Advocate General were also at one as to the specific subject-matter of the performing right in a film. This consisted of the right of authorities to forbid each and every performance of the film, including the possibility of its being televised. The point is not fully developed in the judgment but its significance is apparent. Cable diffusion of a television broadcast constitutes a "performance" separate from the broadcast itself. The intervention by Coditel could not, therefore, be regarded as merely extending the performance covered by the German licence.[66] It was a fresh performance within the territory where Ciné Vog had been granted an exclusive right to exhibit "Le Boucher"; and the restriction claimed was necessary to guarantee the essence of that exclusive right. The only question was whether the strategy followed by Les Films la Boétie of appointing different licensees in different Member States might amount to an artificial barrier to trade. The Court decided in the circumstances it would not, since the strategy was objectively justifiable, owing to the organisation of television services on the basis of legal broadcasting monopolies. It, therefore, held:

> " . . . that the provisions of the Treaty relating to the freedom to provide services did not preclude an assignee of the performing right in a cinematographic film in a Member State from relying upon his right to

---

[65] [1980] E.C.R. at p. 903.
[66] It was assumed by the Court that Ciné Vog would have been bound by any authorisation given by the licensor, Les Films la Boétie, to its fellow licensee in Germany.

prohibit the exhibition of that film in that State, without his authority, by means of cable diffusion if the film so exhibited is picked up and transmitted after being broadcast in another Member State by a third party with the consent of the original owner of the right."[67]

Other property forms

In *Keurkoop* v. *Nancy Kean Gifts*[68] the Court of Justice had its first opportunity of considering the application of Article 36 to industrial designs. The case concerned the design of a ladies' handbag which had been registered under the Uniform Benelux Law on Designs by Nancy Kean Gifts. The registration had been effected without the consent of the American author of the design but this had no bearing on its validity in the Netherlands.[69] The reference to the Court was made in proceedings brought by Nancy Kean Gifts to prevent the sale on the Dutch market of handbags of the same design which had been imported by Keurkoop. It was held by the Court that industrial designs came within the protection afforded by Article 36 to "industrial and commercial property" since they had the aim of defining exclusive rights which was characteristic of such property. That protection enabled the owner of the right to a design in a Member State to prevent the sale of identical products imported from another Member State where they had been legally acquired by a third party—the situation described in the reference. However, the Court made it clear that the principle of the exhaustion of rights would apply if the products in question had been put on the market in the Member State of origin by or with the consent of the design owner in the Member State of importation or by a person legally or economically dependent on him.[70]

The leading case on plant breeders' rights, *Nungesser* v. *Commission (Maize Seeds)*[71] involved an attempt to obtain the annulment of a Decision applying Article 85 to a licensing agreement. However, underlying part of the applicant's case was the claim that breeders' rights enjoy a special status in Community law because of the role the owner is called upon to play in maintaining the stability of the plant variety.[72] Rejecting that argument, the Court said the object of such rights was not to substitute control by the owner for control by national authorities but to protect private interests. The owner's position was similar to that of a patentee or trade mark owner in respect of a product subject to strict public control, such as a medicinal drug.[73] "It is, therefore, not correct," the Court said, "to consider that breeders' rights are a species of commercial or industrial property right with characteristics of so special a nature as to require, in relation

---

[67] [1980] E.C.R. at p. 904.
[68] Case 144/81 [1982] E.C.R. 2853; [1983] 2 C.M.L.R. 47.
[69] One of the questions put by the referring court to the Court of Justice was whether a rule giving an exclusive right to the first person to register a design, irrespective of its authorship, was compatible with Art. 36. The Court's response was that, in the absence of standardisation or harmonisation of laws on industrial designs, it was for national law to lay down the necessary conditions and procedures.
[70] [1982] E.C.R. at p. 2871.
[71] Case 258/78 [1982] E.C.R. 2015; [1983] 1 C.M.L.R. 278. See the discussion *infra*.
[72] See [1982] E.C.R. at pp. 2060–2065.
[73] See Case 15/74 *Centrafarm* v. *Sterling Drug* and Case 16/74 *Centrafarm* v. *Winthrop* [1974] E.C.R. at, respectively, p. 1165 and p. 1196.

to the competition rules, a different treatment from other commercial or industrial property rights."[74] Though expressed in relation to the competition rules that conclusion would, it is submitted, apply equally in the sphere of freedom of movement, including the limitation imposed on the exception in Article 36 by the exhaustion of rights principle.

Unfair competition laws, on the other hand, do not seem to be regarded by the Court as a species of intellectual property. Where such rules are invoked against imports, justification has to be sought in the public interest criteria of the *Cassis de Dijon* doctrine.[75] This can be seen in the *Beele*[76] case where the Court was asked, in effect, whether a product imported from Germany could be excluded from the Dutch market on the ground that, for no compelling reason, it was practically identical to, and thus liable to be confused with, a product which had long been sold in the Netherlands. Article 36 was specifically mentioned in the reference but was ignored by the Court. The judgment cited *Cassis de Dijon*[77] and *Irish Souvenirs*,[78] and the exclusion of imports in circumstances such as those of *Beele* was found to be justifiable, as meeting the "mandatory requirements" of consumer protection and the promotion of fair trading.[79]

What of the exhaustion of rights principle in such cases? The Court in *Beele* referred to the fact that there was no "dependence" between the producers involved,[80] implying that, if the manufacturer of the original product had consented to the marketing of the alleged imitation in Germany, he would not have been able to prevent its importation. It would, however, be misleading to attribute this outcome to the exhaustion of a private right belonging to the manufacturer, since it is not the function of the *Cassis de Dijon* doctrine to protect such rights. The explanation would lie in the absence of objective justification in the general public interest for keeping out authorised "imitations".

Freedom of movement—the common origin principle

A more controversial restriction on the use of intellectual property rights as a defence against parallel imports is the common origin principle. To date, the principle has only been directly applied in a case concerning a trade mark, and its scope remains uncertain. According to the principle, when trade marks held by different persons in different Member States have a common origin, the sale in a Member State of goods lawfully bear-

---

[74] [1982] E.C.R. at p. 2065.

[75] The doctrine is examined *supra*, Chap. 6.

[76] Case 6/81 *Industrie Diensten Groep* v. *Beele* [1982] E.C.R. 707; [1982] 3 C.M.L.R. 102. See the discussion of the case by Gormley, *op. cit.* note 21, *supra* at p. 210. See also Whish, *op. cit.* note 1, *supra* at p. 381.

[77] Case 120/78 *Rewe-Zentralfinanz* v. *Bundesmonopolverwaltung für Branntwein* [1979] E.C.R. 649; [1979] 3 C.M.L.R. 337.

[78] Case 113/80 *Commission* v. *Ireland* [1981] E.C.R. 1625; [1982] 2 C.M.L.R. 706.

[79] The Court adopted a similar approach to the unfair competition point in Case 58/80 *Dansk Supermarked* v. *Imerco* [1981] E.C.R. 181; [1981] 3 C.M.L.R. 590. *Cf.* Case 144/81 *Keurkoop* v. *Nancy Kean Gifts, loc. cit.* note 68, *supra*, where the claim was also for the exclusion of an identical product but was based upon a proprietary right arising from registration. *Cf.* also Case 119/85, *Terrapin* v. *Terranova*, discussed *infra*, where the issue was the similarity of trade marks.

[80] [1982] E.C.R. at p. 717.

ing one of the national marks cannot be prevented merely because another of the marks is protected by the law of that State. It makes no difference whether the imported goods are sold by the proprietor of the mark himself or by some third party who has duly acquired them in the State of origin; or whether the fragmentation of the original trade mark was due to a voluntary act of parties or to an act of a public authority.

The source of the common origin principle was the decision of the European Court in *Van Zuylen* v. *Hag*.[81] The proceedings before the national court arose as a result of the importation into Luxembourg of decaffeinated coffee bearing the HAG trade mark which had been manufactured in Germany by Hag AG. In 1927 Hag AG had established a Belgian subsidiary to which it subsequently assigned its rights in the HAG trade mark for Belgium and Luxembourg. After the Second World War the subsidiary was sequestrated by the Belgian authorities as enemy property and was ultimately sold to the Van Oevelen family, who assigned the trade mark in 1971 to Van Zuylen Frères (VZ), the proprietor at the time when Hag AG commenced its deliveries to the Luxembourg market. The case, therefore, concerned a trade mark which was still held by the original common proprietor in the country from which the product was exported but which had come into the hands of an unrelated company through an act of the authorities in the country where it was sold.

The Court of Justice substantially repeated the statement it had made in *Deutsche Grammophon*[82] about the scope of the derogation in Article 36, adding that "the application of the legislation relating to the protection of trade marks at any rate protects the legitimate holder of the trade mark against infringement on the part of persons who lack any legal title." It then went on:

"The exercise of a trade mark right tends to contribute to the partitioning off of the markets and thus to affect the free movement of goods between Member States, and all the more so since—unlike other rights of industrial and commercial property—it is not subject to limitations in point of time.

Accordingly, one cannot allow the holder of a trade mark to rely upon the exclusiveness of a trade mark right—which may be the consequence of the territorial limitation of national legislations—with a view to prohibiting the marketing in a Member State of goods legally produced in another Member State under an identical trade mark having the same origin. Such a prohibition, which would legitimize the isolation of national markets, would collide with one of the essential objects of the Treaty, which is to unite national markets in a single market.

Whilst in such a market the identification of origin of a product covered by a trade mark is useful, information to consumers on this

---

[81] Case 192/73 [1974] E.C.R. 731; [1974] 2 C.M.L.R. 127. The principle was foreshadowed in Case 40/70 *Sirena* v. *Eda* [1971] E.C.R. 69; [1971] C.M.L.R. 260. In that case, however, the reference was made and dealt with by the Court on the basis of the rules on competition. The facts of the case are given at p. 501, *infra*.

[82] *Loc. cit.* note 54, *supra*.

point may be ensured by means other than such as would affect the free movement of goods."[83]

Three arguments are put forward in the quoted passage: that the exercise of the right claimed by VZ would have the effect of partitioning the market, thereby conflicting with one of the fundamental aims of the Treaty; that the effect would be all the more serious because of the indefinite duration of trade mark rights; and that the interests of consumers can be adequately safeguarded by means of supplementary designations of origin. These are powerful enough arguments in favour of the general proposition that a narrow view must be taken of the derogation in Article 36 so far as concerns trade marks. They do not, however, provide any clue as to why the Court attached special significance to the factor of a common origin. Thus it has been pointed out that the reasoning of the Court with regard to indefinite duration and the partitioning of the market would apply equally in the case of trade marks which were identical or similar although not of common origin.[84] Not surprisingly, therefore, the implications of the *Hag* decision became the subject of anxious debate which was only quietened by the judgments of the Court in *EMI* v. *CBS*[85] and in *Terrapin* v. *Terranova*.[86]

The three *EMI cases*[87] originated in trade mark infringement proceedings before courts in the United Kingdom, Denmark and Germany to restrain the importation and sale of records manufactured by CBS in the United States and bearing the trade mark COLUMBIA. The plaintiff in the proceedings was EMI, the proprietor of the trade mark in all the Member States of the EEC, and the defendants were subsidiaries of CBS, the proprietor of the mark in the United States. The European Court was invited by the referring courts to consider, in effect, whether this use by EMI of its trade mark rights was compatible with the EEC rules on the free movement of goods and on competition.

Until 1917 the COLUMBIA trade mark in Europe and the United States had been the property of the same company. A series of assignments then took place which resulted in EMI acquiring the European trade marks in 1931 and CBS the American mark in 1938. The trade marks, therefore, had a common origin, although they had been under separate control since 1931. Taking advantage of this fact, CBS sought the protection of the principle enunciated by the Court in *Van Zuylen* v. *Hag*, arguing that the exclusion of its records from the markets in question amounted to an unjustifiable restriction upon the free movement of goods. The obvious flaw in this argument was that the rules of the Treaty on the free movement of goods apply to trade *between Member States*, whereas CBS was attempting to gain access to the internal market for goods originating outside the Community. The Court accordingly held that:

---

[83] [1974] E.C.R. at p. 744.
[84] See Johannes and Wright, (1975–76) 1 E.L.Rev. 230 at pp. 234–235.
[85] See note 87, *infra*.
[86] See note 90, *infra*.
[87] Case 51/75 *EMI Records* v. *CBS United Kingdom* [1976] E.C.R. 811; [1976] 2 C.M.L.R. 235; Case 86/75 *EMI Records* v. *CBS Grammofon* [1976] E.C.R. 871; Case 96/75, *EMI Records* v. *CBS Schalplatten* [1976] E.C.R. 913.

" . . . the exercise of a trade-mark right in order to prevent the marketing of products coming from a third country under an identical mark, even if this constitutes a measure having an effect equivalent to a quantitative restriction, does not affect the free movement of goods between Member States and thus does not come under the prohibitions set out in Article 30 *et seq.* of the Treaty."[88]

The common origin of the COLUMBIA marks was irrelevant, because no question of partitioning the common market between the proprietor of the mark in all the Member States and the proprietor in a third State could arise. Nor would the position be any different if the marked product were manufactured within the Community by the holder of the trade mark in a third country or by one of its subsidiaries, instead of being imported. The Court said:

"In fact the protection of industrial and commercial property established by Article 36 would be rendered meaningless if an undertaking other than the proprietor of a mark in the Member States could be allowed there to manufacture and market products bearing the same mark since such conduct would amount to an actual infringement of the protected mark."[89]

Of course, if CBS had held the COLUMBIA mark in any one of the Member States, it would have been able to market its records there lawfully, irrespective of whether they were locally manufactured or imported from the United States, thereby obtaining entry to the common market as a whole.

The decision in *Terrapin* v. *Terranova*[90] has been described as a "landmark."[91] The Court treated the case as an opportunity for summing up its views on the interpretation of Article 36 as regards industrial property in general and, more particularly, for clarifying the scope of the principle enunciated in *Van Zuylen* v. *Hag*.

The case arose out of an attempt to prevent the marketing in Germany of a British-manufactured product bearing the trade mark TERRAPIN, on account of an alleged risk of confusion with a similar product bearing the locally protected mark TERRANOVA, which was also used as a business name. It was, of course, a matter for the national court whether any confusion between the names was likely to occur in practice. However, the European Court pointed out that in deciding this issue the national court must bear in mind that the protection which is accorded to industrial property rights cannot be permitted to constitute "a means of arbitrary discrimination or a disguised restriction on trade between Member States." It should, therefore, ascertain "whether the rights in question are in fact exercised by the proprietor with the same strictness whatever the national origin of any possible infringer."[92]

---

[88] [1976] E.C.R. at p. 845.
[89] [1976] E.C.R. at p. 847.
[90] Case 119/75 [1976] E.C.R. 1039; [1976] 2 C.M.L.R. 482.
[91] By Harris, *op. cit.* note 3, *supra*, p. 527.
[92] [1976] E.C.R. at p. 1060.

Three situations were identified by the Court where the derogation under Article 36 would not apply to the use of an industrial property right to prevent goods from being sold in the State protecting the right. The first was where the product had been lawfully marketed in another Member state by the holder of the right or with his consent—the exhaustion of rights principle; the second, where the right relied on was "the result of the sub-division, either by voluntary act or as a result of public constraint, of a trade mark right which originally belonged to one and the same proprie-tor"—the common origin principle[93]; and the third, where the rights in question belonged to different persons but their exercise was "the purpose, the means or the result of an agreement prohibited by the Treaty."[94] It is interesting to note the rationale which the Court provided for the common origin principle: "the basic function of the trade mark to guarantee to con-sumers that the product has the same origin is already undermined by the subdivision of the original right."[95] This completes the reasoning in the *Hag* case and serves as a basis for distinguishing it from the present case where marks of separate origin happened to possess a certain similarity.

The Court was quite clear that:

" . . . in the present state of Community law an industrial or commer-cial property right legally acquired in a Member State may legally be used to prevent under the first sentence of Article 36 of the Treaty the import of products marketed under a name giving rise to confusion where the rights in question have been acquired by different and inde-pendent proprietors under different national laws. If in such a case the principle of the free movement of goods were to prevail over the pro-tection given by the respective national laws, the specific objective of industrial and commercial property rights would be undermined. In the particular situation the requirements of the free movement of goods and the safeguarding of industrial and commercial property rights must be so reconciled that protection is ensured for the legit-imate use of the rights conferred by national laws, coming within the prohibitions on imports 'justified' within the meaning of Article 36 of the Treaty, but denied on the other hand in respect of any improper exercise of the same rights of such a nature as to maintain or effect artificial partitions within the common market."[96]

The reference to "the present state of Community law" suggests that a less lenient view may perhaps be taken once the national laws on industrial property have been brought into closer harmony with each other. For the moment, however, the avoidance of confusion between products may be regarded as forming part of the specific subject-matter of the protection accorded by trade mark laws, provided there is no restrictive agreement or relationship of dependence between the undertakings concerned and their respective rights have been created separately.

---

[93] [1976] E.C.R. at p. 1061.
[94] *Ibid.*
[95] *Ibid.*
[96] *Ibid.* at pp. 1061–1062.

Terrapin v. *Terranova* confirmed and explained the application of the common origin principle to trademarks but gave no guidance as to whether it applies to other forms of intellectual property. There are good reasons for believing that it does not. First, the rationale of the principle given in *Terrapin* v. *Terranova*—that the subdivision of a trade mark defeats the essential purpose of providing a guarantee of origin to consumers—cannot easily be adapted to property forms such as patents or copyright whose function is to reward creativity. Secondly, as the Court itself pointed out in the *Hag* case, partitioning of the market through the subdivision of a trade mark is an especially serious matter owing to the permanent character of the rights in question; whereas other property forms entail purely temporary monopolies. Thirdly, the Court has indicated that it considers trade marks to be, on the whole, less important, and less deserving of protection in derogation from the EEC rules on freedom of movement, than other intellectual property rights.[97] Fourthly, if the common origin principle were capable of applying to copyright, one would expect it to have been considered, and if necessary distinguished, in *Coditel* v. *Ciné Vog Films (No. 1)*; however, both the Advocate General and the Court approached the case from the point of view of the exhaustion of rights principle.[98] Finally, a principle which allows parallel imports without any previous marketing in another Member State is simply too wide for general application. It has been said that: "If the doctrine is sound, it is hard to see where the exhaustion principle can be used, since the owner of an intellectual property right could never impede the import of goods produced or marketed under a related right."[99]

One qualification is, perhaps, necessary. In *Keurkoop* v. *Nancy Kean Gifts*[1] the Court mentioned as one of the conditions enabling a design owner to oppose the importation of identical products "that the respective rights of the proprietors of the right to the design in the various Member States were created independently of one another."[2] This suggests that the common origin principle applies, at least, to registered industrial designs, a view which Advocate General Reischl appeared to share.[3] If that is so, the explanation would presumably be that the essential function of rights to industrial designs is considered, like that of trade mark rights, to be the provision of a guarantee of origin.

---

[97] See Case 40/70 *Sirena* v. *Eda*, *loc. cit.* note 81, *supra*, at p. 82. The point is not a strong one since there are trade marks, like the HAG mark itself, which are of vastly greater value than many of the gadgets for which patents can be obtained.

[98] The issue as to whether cable diffusion in Belgium constituted a "performance" separate from the broadcast in Germany would have been irrelevant if the common origin principle was being applied.

[99] By Whish, *op. cit.* note 1, *supra*, at p. 382.

[1] Case 144/81, *loc. cit.* note 68, *supra*.

[2] [1982] E.C.R. at p. 2874.

[3] See [1982] E.C.R. at p. 2883. The relevant passage in Mr. Reischl's opinion is rather unclear. The *Sirena* and *Hag* cases are cited but the Advocate General speaks of design owners being "linked by legal or economic ties from which a single origin of the design may be inferred." Does this mean that, as between wholly independent owners, the common origin principle would not apply? In the instant case, the *designs* of the handbags may have had a common origin but the *rights* in those designs did not, since they were derived from registrations effected without the author's licence.

Intellectual property rights and the rules on competition

General principles

The theoretical basis for the application of the rules on competition in respect of national rights of intellectual property is, once again, the distinction between the existence of such rights and their exercise. Indeed, the distinction was first developed by the Court of Justice in competition cases.[4] We have seen that in the *Maize Seeds* case an attempt to place plant breeders' rights beyond the scope of this compromise solution was decisively rejected.[5]

The Court has stressed that an intellectual property right, as a legal entity, does not in itself possess the elements that activate the prohibitions in Article 85(1) or Article 86 EEC.[6] The grant of protection by the authorities of a Member State is not the kind of collusive arrangement (agreement between undertakings, decision of an association of undertakings or concerted practice) to which Article 85(1) refers; nor does it automatically entail the existence of a dominant position within a substantial part of the common market.

The early case of *Parke, Davis* v. *Centrafarm*[7] provides an illustration. The background to the case, like that of *Merck*[8] some years later, was the absence of patent protection in Italy for medicinal drugs. Here, however, the complaint was of the importation, in contravention of patents held in the Netherlands, of a drug manufactured in Italy not by the patent owner himself but by a third party. Two questions were put by the referring court. The first question asked, in effect, whether the holder of a national patent was prevented by Articles 85 and 86 EEC "possibly considered in conjunction with the provisions of Articles 36 and 222" from using it to block imports from a country where they could be lawfully produced without a patent; and the second whether it was significant that the price of the patented product which was manufactured locally was higher than the price of the imported product. The Court replied:

> "1. The existence of rights granted by a Member State to the holder
>   of a patent is not affected by the prohibitions contained in
>   Articles 85(1) and 86 of the Treaty.
> 2. The exercise of such rights cannot of itself fall either under
>   Article 85(1), in the absence of any agreement, decision or con-
>   certed practice prohibited by this provision, or under Article 86,
>   in the absence of any abuse of a dominant position.
> 3. A higher sale price for the patented product as compared with

[4] See Joined Cases 56 and 58/64 *Consten and Grundig* v. *Commission* [1966] E.C.R. 299; [1966] C.M.L.R. 418; Case 24/67 *Parke, Davis* v. *Centrafarm* [1968] *loc. cit.* note 25, *supra*; Case 40/70 *Sirena* v. *Eda*, *loc. cit.* note 81, *supra*. For the view of the Commission on the distinction between the existence of rights and their exercise as applied to competition matters, see Comp. Rep. 1974, p. 20.
[5] Case 258/78 *loc. cit.* note 71, *supra*.
[6] Case 40/70 *Sirena* v. *Eda* [1971] E.C.R. at p. 82; Case 51/75 *EMI* v. *CBS United Kingdom* [1976] E.C.R. at p. 848; Case 258/78 *Maize Seeds* [1982] E.C.R. at p. 2061.
[7] *Loc. cit.* note 25, *supra*.
[8] Case 187/80 *loc. cit.* note 31, *supra*.

that of the unpatented product coming from another Member State does not necessarily constitute an abuse."[9]

The reply acknowledges that Article 85 or Article 86 may, in principle, be invoked to prevent the exercise of intellectual property rights, but only where additional factors, satisfying the criteria of prohibition in those provisions, are present; and of such factors there was no evidence before the Court.

In principle, therefore, the application of the rules on competition to an agreement respecting intellectual property rights should take place in two stages. The first stage involves considering whether particular provisions of the agreement go to the very existence of the property form in question (in other words, are necessary to safeguard its specific subject-matter) or merely regulate its exercise. If the former, the competition rules cannot be applied at all. If the latter, then the second stage—consideration of whether the provision is prohibited under Article 85 or Article 86—commences. In practice, however, the distinction between these two stages is not always clearly marked in the reasoning of the Commission or even of the Court.[10]

Assignment of intellectual property—"spent"[11] agreements

Where rights of intellectual property are assigned outright, as opposed to being licensed, the contract between the assignor and the assignee will be discharged by completion of performance. In such a case, will there by any consensual relationship to which the prohibition in Article 85 may attach? The question was first addressed by the European Court in *Sirena v. Eda*.[12] Under a contract concluded in 1937 the Italian rights to the trade mark PREP had been assigned to Sirena by an American company, Mark Allen. Sirena subsequently re-registered the mark in its own name, together with two other marks incorporating the word PREP. The right to use the mark in Germany had been granted by Mark Allen at some unspecified date to a German company and marked products manufactured by the latter were imported into Italy, where they were sold at much lower prices than Sirena's products. The national proceedings were brought by Sirena to prevent the infringement of its rights by the importer, a company called Novimpex.

In a similar case today the parallel importer would, presumably, rely on the common origin doctrine enunciated in *Van Zuylen v. Hag*.[13] However, the referring court framed its questions in terms of the rules on competition, and the European Court responded accordingly. It was stated by the Court that the exercise of a trade mark right "might fall within the ambit of the prohibitions contained in the Treaty each time it manifests itself as the

---

[9] [1968] E.C.R. at pp. 73–74.
[10] As an illustration of systematic application of the rules, see Case 198/83 *Windsurfing International v. Commission* [1986] 3 C.M.L.R. 489 at pp. 531–540. The case is more fully examined, *infra*.
[11] The term is used by Bellamy and Child, *Common Market Law of Competition*, 3rd ed. 1987 at para. 2–025.
[12] Case 40/70 *loc. cit.* note 81, *supra*.
[13] Case 192/73, *ibid*.

subject, the means or the result of a restrictive practice."[14] The suggestion has been made, and it was evidently the view taken by the national court, that in fact, a concerted practice existed between Mark Allen and its assignees in the common market countries under which each respected the territorial rights of the others.[15] The Court contented itself with the statement that:

> "If the restrictive practices arose before the Treaty entered into force, it is both necessary and sufficient that they continue to produce their effects after that date."[16]

This indicates, mysteriously, that Article 85(1) can somehow be "applied" to a practice which ceased before the Article came into force.

The statement was qualified in *EMI* v. *CBS*,[17] the facts of which have already been given.[18] CBS' second main line of defence in the infringement proceedings brought by EMI was that the agreements for the assignment of the COLUMBIA trade mark were caught by the prohibition in Article 85(1) because they formed part of a complex of agreements the object of which had been to partition the world market. The agreements themselves had been terminated before the EEC Treaty came into force but CBS argued, with the support of the Commission, that the prohibition would apply so long as they continued to produce effects which were felt within the common market.

The Court held that an agreement between Community undertakings and their competitors in third countries which tended to isolate the common market from supplies of products originating in third countries and similar to products protected by trade marks in the Member States may adversely affect the competitive situation on the Community market; and where the proprietor of the disputed mark outside the Community has subsidiaries established in various Member States which would be capable of marketing the goods, trade between Member States may be affected.

On the question of "spent" agreements the Court said:

> "For Article 85 to apply to a case, such as the present one, of agreements which are no longer in force it is sufficient that such agreements continue to produce their effects after they have formally ceased to be in force.
>
> An agreement is only regarded as continuing to produce its effects if from the behaviour of the persons concerned there may be inferred the existence of elements of concerted practice and of coordination peculiar to the agreements and producing the same result as that envisaged by the agreement.
>
> This is not so when the said effects do not exceed those flowing from the mere exercise of the national trade-mark rights."[19]

The meaning of this statement is not entirely clear. Do "elements of con-

---

[14] [1971] E.C.R. at p. 82.
[15] In his Opinion in *Van Zuylen* v. *Hag* Advocate-General Mayras suggested that the European Court may have acted on this assumption: see [1974] E.C.R. 731 at p. 750. For the view of the Tribunale of Milan, see [1975] 1 C.M.L.R. 409 at pp. 430–431.
[16] [1971] E.C.R. at p. 83.
[17] Cases 51, 86 and 96/75 *loc. cit.* note 87, *supra.*
[18] See p. 496, *supra.*
[19] [1976] E.C.R. at pp. 848–849.

certed practice and coordination" amount to something less than a concerted practice *tout court*? It is hard to imagine how they could, given the
exiguous nature of the "practical cooperation" which suffices to establish
the existence of such practices.[20] On the other hand, if a continuing concerted practice is necessary for the application of Article 85, what purpose
is served by harking back to the original agreement? A possible explanation has been suggested.[21] Normally, it is unsafe to infer the existence of
concertation purely from the fact that the parties concerned are conducting
their business in a similar or mutually beneficial way, because this might
represent nothing more than a prudent reaction to the conditions of the
market to which both are subject. However, the objection falls away if the
parties are merely continuing a course of conduct which they embarked
upon as a result of a restrictive agreement now formally terminated. The
pre-existing agreement would raise a presumption of collusion which it
would be for the parties to rebut by showing that, in fact, they had been
acting independently.

Licensing intellectual property

In the field of intellectual property the greatest practical impact of the
EEC competition rules has been upon the terms of licensing agreements.
In its enforcement activity the Commission has been concerned mainly
with patent licensing[22]; but many of the principles it has developed are
capable of being applied to other property forms, while there have been
important decisions of the Court of Justice on the licensing of trade
marks,[23] copyright[24] and plant breeders' rights.[25]

A licensing transaction consists essentially of the granting by the owner
of an intellectual property right of permission for a third party to exploit
the right, in consideration of the payment of a royalty. The possibility of
exploitation through licenses was explicitly recognised by the Court in *Centrafarm* v. *Sterling Drug* as an element in the specific subject-matter of a
patent[26]; and the same is true, it is submitted, of all intellectual property. It
would follow that any terms in a licensing agreement that may be recognised as indispensable to this indirect method of exploitation would enjoy
immunity from the competition rules. These, however, as we shall see, represent a minority of the terms that may be included in such agreements.
The rest, if they fulfil the criteria of Article 85(1), can only escape prohibition through the gateway of Article 85(3); and on occasion a possible
infringement of Article 86 may also have to be considered.

---

[20] See Chap. 14, *supra*.
[21] By Laddie, (1975–76) 1 E.L.Rev. 499 at p. 502.
[22] The Commission's preoccupation with patent licensing goes back to the earliest days of the
competition policy. An Announcement on Patent Licensing Agreements, setting forth its
views on the application of the competition rules to such agreements, was issued on
December 24, 1962. Over the years those views came to be modified in important respects
and the Announcement ceased to be a reliable guide. It was withdrawn, following the
adoption of the Block Exemption Regulation on Patent Licensing Agreements: O.J. 1984,
C220/14.
[23] Joined Cases 56 and 58/64 *Consten and Grundig* v. *Commission*, *loc. cit.* note 4, p. 500,
supra; Case 28/77 *Tepea* v. *Commission* [1978] E.C.R. 1391; [1978] 3 C.M.L.R. 392.
[24] Case 262/81 *Coditel* v. *Ciné Vog Films (No. 2)*, *loc. cit.* note 64, *supra*.
[25] Case 258/78 *Nungesser* v. *Commission (Maize Seeds)*, *loc. cit.* note 71, *supra*.
[26] Case 15/74 [1974] E.C.R. at p. 1162.

In the present section we examine the application of the competition rules, and more particularly of Article 85, to certain terms commonly found in licensing agreements.[27] The following section contains an account of the Block Exemption Regulation on Patent Licensing Agreements which, after a long period of gestation, finally saw the light in 1984.

(i) *Exclusivity.* A licensing agreement may seek to provide for the parties various degrees of protection against competition. A licensor may undertake to appoint no other licensees within the contract territory (a "sole" licence); or he may go further and agree that he will not himself exploit the property within that territory (an "exclusive" licence). The licensee's exclusive right may relate to the manufacture of the protected product or it may extend to marketing the product as well. On his side, the licensee may agree not to exploit the product in any territory the licensor has reserved for himself. Finally, an attempt may be made to give each of the parties absolute territorial protection against parallel importers.

A grant of sole or exclusive rights to a licensee is not regarded by the Commission or, it seems, the Court as coming within the specific subject-matter of patents or other forms of intellectual property. This has been explained by the Commission on the ground that contractual terms which fetter the exercise of an intellectual property right by its owner cannot be regarded as necessary incidents of that right.[28] The explanation would not apply to a licensee's obligation to refrain from exploiting the property in territory reserved for his licensor; and it is submitted that such obligations fall under the heading of specific subject-matter, provided that the property in question is protected in the reserved territory.[29]

The rules on competition thus apply in principle to exclusive manufacturing or marketing licences. Whether a given licence fulfils the criteria in Article 85(1) will depend on the particular circumstances in which the agreement is made. On the one hand, the inability of the licensor to grant further licences in the contract territory means that potential competitors of the licensee will have no opportunity of exploiting the property there.[30] On the other hand, the financial risks of exploitation may be such that, without protection at least against direct competition, no one may be willing to accept a licence: in such a case, the grant of an exclusive right, far from restricting competition, actually enhances it by bringing a new participant into the market. The Commission has often been criticised for giving too little weight to this latter consideration. Its approach has been, broadly, that exclusive licences can normally be expected to have the

---

[27] For a more extensive catalogue and a fuller discussion of specific clauses in licences, see Guy and Leigh, *op. cit.* note 1, p. 477, *supra*, Chap. 11. See also the discussion in Whish, *op. cit.* note 1, p. 477, *supra*, pp. 358–369.

[28] See, in particular, *Re AOIP/Beyrard* O.J. 1976 L6/8; [1976] 1 C.M.L.R. D14. The Court's view is implicit in the approach it adopted in Case 258/78 *Maize Seeds, loc. cit.* note 71, *supra*.

[29] Case 198/83 *Windsurfing International* v. *Commission, loc. cit.* note 10, p. 501, *supra*.

[30] This argument has been repeatedly used by the Commission to justify the application of Art. 85(1) to exclusive licences. See, *e.g. Re Davidson Rubber Co.* [1972] J.O. L143/31; [1972] C.M.L.R. D52; *Re Kabelmetal/Luchaire* O.J. 1975, L222/34; [1975] 2 C.M.L.R. D40; *Re Eisele-INRA Agreement (Maize Seeds)* O.J. 1978 L286/23; [1978] 3 C.M.L.R. 434.

object or effect of restricting competition within the meaning of Article 85(1), though they may well qualify for exemption under Article 85(3).[31] A more nuanced approach is, however, apparent in the Preamble to the Block Exemption Regulation on Patent Licensing Agreements[32] reflecting the judgment in *Maize Seeds*,[33] where a sharp distinction was drawn by the European Court between two kinds of licensing arrangement—"open exclusive licences" and "absolute territorial protection."

Under an "open exclusive licence," the licensor agrees not to allow any other undertaking to exploit his property within the contract territory; and he agrees not to manufacture or market the protected product himself within that territory. Here the exclusivity is a matter between the contracting parties: the market in the contract territory remains open to parellel imports by third parties, including licensees for other territories. Such an arrangement, the Court held, would not infringe Article 85(1) in the circumstances of the *Maize Seeds* case. Those circumstances involved "the cultivation and marketing of hybrid maize seeds which were developed by INRA after years of research and experimentation and were unknown to German farmers at the time when the cooperation between INRA and the applicants was taking shape."[34] The Court concluded that, unless it were able to obtain an open exclusive licence, an undertaking might be deterred from running the risk of introducing the product onto the German market, a result which, it said, "would be damaging to the dissemination of a new technology and would prejudice competition in the Community between the new product and similar existing products."[35] It remains to be seen whether the Court will acknowledge the pro-competitive effects of such licences in the exploitation of less sensitive products.

The notion of "absolute territorial protection" has been encountered in Chapter 14, *supra*, in connection with distribution agreements. In the present context it refers to arrangements under which, by means of export bans or more informal pressure on his other licensees and his customers, a licensor does his best to seal off the contract territory from parallel imports. The Court found in *Maize Seeds* that an undertaking to this effect had been given by the French licensor, INRA[36]; and concrete steps had been taken to prevent third parties who purchased INRA seeds in France from exporting them to Germany. No licensee is entitled to demand such complete protection. The Court affirmed its consistently held view "that absolute territorial protection granted to a licensee in order to enable parallel imports to be controlled and prevented results in the artificial maintenance

---

[31] The Announcement of December 24, 1962 on Patent Licence Agreements stated that, on the basis of the facts then known to it, the Commission did not consider undertakings by a licensor not to authorise anyone else to exploit the invention and not to exploit the invention himself to be covered by Art. 85(1). However, the experience of dealing with the first batch of notified licensing agreements, in the aftermath of the decision in Joined Cases 56 & 58/64, *Consten and Grundig* v. *Commission, loc. cit.* note 4, p. 500, *supra* seems to have brought about a change of mind.

[32] See the 11th recital.

[33] Case 258/78 *Nungesser* v. *Commission, loc. cit.* note 71, *supra*.

[34] [1982] E.C.R. at p. 2069.

[35] *Ibid.*

[36] The initials stand for "Institut National de la Recherche Agronomique."

of separate national markets, contrary to the Treaty."[37] Subject to the *de minimis* rule, any such agreement is bound in practice to be caught by Article 85(1).

Between these two extremes are intermediate forms of exclusivity, *e.g.* a ban on direct sales by other licensees, which the Court did not consider in *Maize Seeds*. However, from the general tenor of the judgment it seems unlikely such arrangements would be found compatible with Article 85(1).[38]

Exclusive licences which are caught by Article 85(1) may qualify for exemption under Article 85(3). In the past, while its treatment of exclusive manufacturing rights has been relatively generous, the Commission has been reluctant to grant exemption in respect of exclusive selling rights.[39] As to the latter, however, the Block Exemption Regulation on Patent Licensing Agreements shows a significant change of attitude[40]; and this seems likely to be reflected in the Commission's treatment of agreements relating to other forms of intellectual property.[41] Any attempt to provide protection against parallel imports remains beyond reasonable hope of exemption.

(ii) *Royalties.* A patentee makes the profit to which he is entitled by "selling" permission to work his patent. An obligation on the licensee to pay a royalty thus clearly belongs to the domain of specific subject-matter.[42] However, Article 85 may be infringed if products not covered by the patent in question are taken into account in calculating the sums payable.[43] In *Windsurfing International* v. *Commission*[44] the Court took the view that the licensor had not been justified in charging royalties on the basis of the net selling-price of complete sailboards when the patent related only to "rigs."[45] A provision for the continuance of royalty payments after the expiry of a patent is similarly liable to fall foul of Article 85,[46] unless the payments relate to secret know-how still being used by the licensee.[47]

---

[37] [1982] E.C.R. at p. 2070. The point has been clear since Joined Cases 56 and 58/64 *Consten and Grundig* v. *Commission, loc. cit.* note 4, p. 500, *supra.* See also Case 28/77 *Tepea* v. *Commission, loc. cit.*, note 23, p. 503, *supra.*

[38] *Cf.* Case 262/81 *Coditel* v. *Ciné Vog Films (No. 2)*, *loc. cit.* note 64, *supra*, where it was held that a contract under which the owner of the copyright in a film grants an exclusive right to exhibit the film for a specific period in a Member State is not, as such, subject to the prohibition in Art. 85. The Court said that the exercise of the exclusive right may fall within the prohibition "where there are economic or legal circumstances the effect of which is to restrict film distribution to an appreciable degree or to distort competition on the cinematographic market, regard being had to the specific characteristics of that market": [1982] E.C.R. at p. 3402.

[39] See, *e.g. Re Davidson Rubber Company, loc. cit.* note 30, p. 504, *supra*; *Re Kabelmetal/Luchaire ibid.*; *Re AOIP/Beyrard, loc. cit.* note 28, p. 504, *supra.*

[40] See Art. 1(1)(5) and (6), discussed *infra.*

[41] The solution in Art. 1(1)(5) of the Reg. was anticipated in *Re Campari* O.J. 1978 L70/69; [1978] 2 C.M.L.R. 397.

[42] See Comp.Rep. 1975, p. 20.

[43] See Block Exemption Reg., Art. 3(4).

[44] Case 198/83, *loc. cit.* note 10, p. 501, *supra.*

[45] The "rig" is defined in the judgment as "an assemblage consisting essentially of a mast, a joint for the mast, a sail and spars." This is distinguished from the "board," defined as "a hull made of synthetic materials equipped with a centreboard." See [1986] 3 C.M.L.R. at p. 524. In the event, the method of calculating the royalties did not result in the infringement of Art. 85, since the sum charged was no higher than it would have been if it had been based solely on the price of the rigs. See [1986] 3 C.M.L.R. at pp. 535–536.

[46] *Re AOIP/Beyrard, loc. cit.* note 28, p. 504, *supra.*

[47] *Re Kabelmetal/Luchaire, loc. cit.* note 30, p. 504, *supra.* See Block Exemption Reg., Art. 3(2).

(iii) *Duration.* The Commission has written that "Article 85(1) does not in principle touch upon the contractually fixed duration of a patent licence agreement, if this is for the life of a single licensed patent or a shorter term"[48]; though it notes that, exceptionally, Article 86 might apply to abusively short contract periods.[49] On the other hand, a clause extending the duration of an agreement beyond the life of the patent to which it relates obviously cannot be regarded as indispensable to the patent's exploitation. Thus in *Re AOIP/Beyrard*[50] the Commission condemned a clause which enabled a licensee to extend indefinitely an agreement with a number of restrictive features by granting successive licences in respect of patented improvements.[51]

(iv) *Quality controls.* An obligation on a licensee to meet prescribed standards of production will come within the specific subject-matter of a patent if it is genuinely necessary to ensure that the technical instructions in the patent are carried out.[52] On the other hand, quality controls are liable to infringe Article 85 if they relate to products not covered by the patent. The criteria to be applied must be agreed in advance and must be objectively verifiable. In *Windsurfing International* v. *Commission*[53] an obligation on licensees to obtain Windsurfing's approval of the boards incorporated into their sailboards was held by the Court to infringe Article 85 because the patent was considered to cover only the rig. Even if the whole sailboard had been covered, the controls in question would still have been outside the specific subject-matter of the patent, owing to their discretionary character, which made it possible for Windsurfing to impose its own selection of models on the licensees.[54]

Quality controls are of particular importance in relation to trade marks because of the licensor's interest in preserving the reputation associated with the mark. Thus in its *Campari* Decision[55] the Commission raised no objection to an obligation on trade mark licensees to observe instructions from the licensor regarding the manufacturing process and ingredients of the famous drink.

(v) *Tying.* A licensee may be put under an obligation to work a patent or sell patented products only in conjunction with other products or services specified in the agreement. Tie-in clauses which are necessary for a technically satisfactory exploitation of the licensed invention are closely allied to quality controls and belong to the specific subject-matter of the licensor's patent.[56] An example from the sphere of trade marks is, again, provided by the *Campari* Decision[57] where the Commission did not object to a

---

[48] Comp.Rep. 1975, p. 23. See Block Exemption Reg., Art. 2(4).
[49] Comp.Rep. 1975, p. 23, note 1.
[50] *Loc. cit.* note 28, p. 504, *supra.*
[51] See the reasoning of the Commission at [1976] 1 C.M.L.R. D23. See also Block Exemption Reg., Art. 3(2).
[52] See Block Exemption Reg., Art. 2(9). Genuine quality controls have been favourably treated by the Commission since its earliest decisions on patent licensing: see *Re Burroughs/Delplanque* J.O. 1972 L13/50; [1972] C.M.L.R. D67.
[53] Case 198/83, *loc. cit.* note 10, p. 501, *supra.*
[54] See [1986] 3 C.M.L.R. at pp. 532–533.
[55] *Re Campari, loc. cit.* note 41, p. 506, *supra.*
[56] See Block Exemption Reg., Art. 2(1).
[57] *Loc. cit., supra.*

requirement that certain secret ingredients be purchased from the licensor.[58] Where, however, tying cannot be justified in any way, it falls within the express terms of Article 85(1)(e) and is likely to prove irredeemable.[59] Such was the fate of the obligation imposed on the licensees of Windsurfing International in Germany to supply the rig covered by the patent only in conjunction with approved varieties of board.

(vi) *Field of use restrictions.* Where a patent is capable of being worked in two or more distinct applications, a right to grant licences limited to a particular field of use will form part of its specific subject-matter.[60] On the other hand, restrictions on the use of a patent which are not technically justified are liable to have the object or effect of dividing up the market between licensees. This was the main burden of the Commission's objection to the requirement that rigs covered by the Windsurfing patent be used only in conjunction with certain boards.[61] The Court agreed with the Commission that "Windsurfing International's real interest lay in ensuring that there was sufficient product differentiation between its licensee's sailboards to cover the widest possible spectrum of market demand."[62]

(vii) *Grant-back clauses.* A clause requiring the licensee to grant back to the licensor a licence in respect of any improvements for which he may obtain patents can hardly be regarded as essential to safeguard the specific subject-matter of the original patent. The Commission takes the view, however, that such clauses are not normally restrictive of competition, provided that the licensor is put under a corresponding obligation, and the licences to be granted by either party are non-exclusive.[63] On the other hand, the Commission will insist on the removal from an agreement of a clause requiring the licensee to cede the property in improvements, or to licence them exclusively, to the licensor.[64]

(viii) *Licensed-by notices.* Some of the licensees in *Windsurfing International* were under an obligation to place on boards manufactured by them a notice which referred to the licence.[65] This, in the Commission's view, gave the erroneous impression that the boards as well as the rigs were covered by the patent. The licensees were thus made to appear less technically independent than they were, and their position on the market was affected. Addressing this point, the Court of Justice said:

" . . . such a clause may be covered by the specific subject-matter of the patent provided that the notice is placed only on components protected by the patent. Should this not be the case, the question arises

[58] [1978] 2 C.M.L.R. at p. 409.
[59] See Block Exemption Reg., Art. 3(9).
[60] Comp.Rep. 1975, p. 22. See Block Exemption Reg., Art. 2(3).
[61] Windsurfing International sought to justify the requirement as a quality control measure, as well as a form of protection for individual licensees against slavish imitation of their products.
[62] [1986] 3 C.M.L.R. at pp. 533–534.
[63] See Block Exemption Reg., Art. 2(1)(10). See also *Re Davidson Rubber Company, loc. cit.*, note 30, p. 504, *supra.*
[64] *Re Raymond/Nagoya* J.O. 1972 L143/39; [1972] C.M.L.R. D45; *Re Kabelmetal/Luchaire, loc. cit.*, note 30, p. 504, *supra.*
[65] [1986] 3 C.M.L.R. at pp. 536–537.

whether the clause has as its object or effect the prevention, restriction or distortion of competition."[66]

In the instant case, it was held, the notice encouraged uncertainty as to the scope of the patent and was therefore likely to diminish consumer confidence in the licensees, allowing Windsurfing to gain a competitive advantage for itself.[67]

(ix) *No-challenge clauses.* Because of his privileged access to information and his experience of working the patent, a licensee is particularly well placed to detect any possible flaws in the patentee's title. Licensors may, accordingly, seek to protect themselves by exacting an undertaking from their licensees not to challenge the validity of the patent. Such "no-challenge" clauses, the Court has held, do not come within the specific subject-matter of a patent "in view of the fact that it is in the public interest to eliminate any obstacle to economic activity which may arise where a patent was granted in error."[68] That being so, a no-challenge clause is virtually certain to be caught by Article 85(1), with no realistic prospect of exemption under Article 85(3).[69]

The Block Exemption Regulation on Patent Licensing Agreements[70]

The Regulation covers patent licensing agreements and agreements combining the licensing of patents and the communication of know-how, to which only two undertakings are party.[71] It entered into force on January 1, 1985 and applies until December 31, 1994.[72]

Article 1(1) of the Regulation lists seven types of clause that benefit from the block exemption. Six of these are concerned with aspects of exclusivity. Although, as we have seen, open exclusive licences do not always require exemption, the terms characteristic of such licences are included in the list. These are: an obligation on the licensor not to appoint other licensees for the contract territory; an obligation on the licensor not to exploit the licensed invention himself within the contract territory; and an obligation on the licensee not to exploit the licensed invention in territories reserved for the licensor. Also exempted is an obligation on the licensee not to manufacture or use the patented product in the territories of other licensees. This reflects the established approach of the Commission to exclusive

---

[66] [1986] 3 C.M.L.R. at p. 537.
[67] See Block Exemption Reg., Art. 2(6). See also *Re Burroughs/Deplanque* J.O. 1972 L13/50; [1972] C.M.L.R. D67; *Re Burroughs/Geha* J.O. 1972 L13/53; [1972] C.M.L.R. D72.
[68] Case 198/83 *Windsurfing International* v. *Commission* [1986] 3 C.M.L.R. at p. 540. The Court struck down no-challenge clauses relating to certain word and design marks and to the patent itself; see [1986] 3 C.M.L.R. at, respectively, pp. 537–538 and 539–540.
[69] See *Re Davidson Rubber Co.*, *loc. cit.*, note 30, p. 504, *supra*, where the parties removed a no-challenge clause from their agreements under pressure from the Commission. See also the reasoning of the Commission in *Re AIOP/Beyrard* [1976] 1 C.M.L.R. at D23. No-challenge clauses are at the top of the black list in the Block Exemption Reg.; see Art. 3(1). On the other hand, such a clause may be acceptable in a "delimitation agreement" between the owners of trade marks that are liable to be confused. See Case 35/83, *BAT* v. *Commission* where the Court took the view that a purported conflict over trade marks was purely "contrived," the real purpose being to exclude the products of one of the parties from the other's market; [1985] E.C.R.; [1985] 2 C.M.L.R. 470.
[70] O.J. 1984 L219/15.
[71] Power to apply Art. 85(3) to, *inter alia*, categories of bilateral patent licensing agreements was conferred on the Commission by Reg. 19/65, O.J. 1965–1966, 35, J.O. 1965, 533.
[72] Art. 14.

manufacturing rights. More surprising, perhaps, is the acceptance in the Regulation of the need for a large measure of protection for licensees against sales into their territories by a licensee for another territory. Exemption is given to an obligation on the licensee not to pursue an active sales policy in other licensees' territory so long as the product is protected there by a parallel patent: he may thus be prevented from advertising or establishing a branch or depot or from canvassing for custom, but not from responding to unsolicited orders.[73] But the Commission has gone further. The block exemption also covers a ban, during the first five years after the launching of the protected product on the common market, against all sales in the territories of other licensees. Where a product is new, full protection may, therefore, be given against competition from fellow licensees, passive as well as active.

The seventh item on the list of exempted clauses in Article 1(1) is a requirement that the licensee use only the licensor's trade mark and get-up to distinguish the protected product. Exemption is conditional on the licensee's being permitted to identify himself as the manufacturer of the product. This is to enable him to retain the goodwill attaching to the product after the expiry of the patent, without being forced to enter into a new trade-mark agreement with the licensor.[74]

Obligations whose inclusion in a licensing agreement does not affect the availability of the block exemption are listed in Article 2(1). The Commission considers that the obligations in question are not generally restrictive of competition. Should they happen, because of particular circumstances, to fall within Article 85(1), the block exemption will apply to them, irrespective of whether they are accompanied by obligations exempted pursuant to Article 1 of the Regulation.[75] The obligations on the list comprise: tying, where this is necessary for a technically satisfactory exploitation of the licensed invention; an obligation on the licensee to pay a minimum royalty or to produce a minimum quantity of the protected product; restriction of the field of use of the licensed invention; an obligation on the licensee not to exploit the patent after the expiry of the agreement; an obligation on the licensee not to grant sub-licences or to assign the licence; an obligation to mark the protected product with an indication of the patent or the patentee; an obligation on the licensee not to divulge know-how communicated by the licensor (this may be made to continue after the agreement has expired); obligations on the licensee connected with the defence of the patentee's interest against third party infringers; quality controls necessary for a technically satisfactory exploitation of the licensed invention; an obligation on the licensor and the licensee to communicate experience gained in exploiting the licensed invention and to grant one another licences in respect of improvements or new applications; in both cases on a non-exclusive basis; finally, an obligation on the licensor to extend to the licensee any more favourable terms it may subsequently grant to other licensees (a "most-favoured licensee clause").

---

[73] *Cf.* Reg. 1983/83, Art. 2(2)(*c*).
[74] See Preamble, 10th recital.
[75] Art. 2(2).

A "black list" of terms that prevent the application of the block exemption is found in Article 3. These consist of: no-challenge clauses (though the licensor may be entitled, in the event of a challenge, to terminate the licence); clauses that allow the agreement to be extended beyond the life of the patents existing at the time it was entered into through the inclusion of new patents obtained by the licensor, except where both parties are given a right at least annually to terminate the agreement once the original patents have expired[76]; no-competition clauses (other than those covered by the provisions on exclusivity in Article 1); the charging of royalties on unpatented products or on know-how that has entered into the public domain; the imposition of an upper limit on the quantity of the protected products the licensee may manufacture; the fixing of prices for the protected products; restrictions on the classes of customers to whom the products may be supplied; an obligation on the licensee to assign to the licensor patents for improvements or for new applications of the licensed patents; tying which is not necessary for a technically satisfactory exploitation of the licensed invention; a ban on marketing the protected product in the territories of other licensees for a period exceeding that permitted under Article 1(1)(5); and, lastly, an obligation on either party to refuse supplies within their respective territories to parallel exporters or to make it difficult for parallel importers to obtain supplies elsewhere in the common market.

Other provisions in the regulation may be described more shortly. An "opposition procedure" is provided by Article 4. Agreements containing obligations restrictive of competition which are not covered by Articles 1 or 2 and which do not figure on the black list in Article 3 may be notified to the Commission and will automatically be exempted if within six months the Commission does not oppose this. Article 5 excludes from the scope of the Regulation licensing agreements relating to patent pools[77] or joint ventures, reciprocal licensing between competing undertakings and licences in respect of plant breeders' rights. Transitional provisions giving exemption retrospectively to existing agreements that fulfil the conditions of the Regulation, or are amended in order to do so, are contained in Articles 6 to 8. Under Article 9 the Commission may withdraw the exemption from agreements which, although they fulfil the conditions of the Regulation, are nevertheless found to have effects incompatible with Article 85(3). Among the factors mentioned in the Article as likely to justify such withdrawal are: the absence of effective competition in the licensee's territory from products identical, or considered by users as equivalent, to the protected product; the refusal by the licensee, for no objectively valid reason, to meet unsolicited orders from the territories of other licensees; or behaviour by either party intended to frustrate the efforts of parallel exporters or importers.

A patent licensing agreement which falls outside the block exemption

---

[76] The licensor has the right to charge royalties for the continuing use by the licensee of know-how which has not entered into the public domain.

[77] Broadly, arrangements under which the leading firms in an industry have access to one another's patents, while denying their use to other firms. See Cornish, *op. cit.* note 1, *supra*, at p. 233.

may still qualify for individual exemption under Regulation 17. In order to do so, the agreement must have been notified to the Commission, unless it falls within the narrow category of non-notifiable agreements defined by Article 4(2)(2)(*b*) of that Regulation.[78]

Intellectual property and the interplay between Article 30 and Articles 85 and 86

From what has already been said, it will be apparent that reliance on intellectual property rights to exclude imports coming from other Member States may fall foul of the EEC Treaty provisions on both freedom of movement and competition. In the *Maize Seeds* case[79] the Government of the United Kingdom argued, *inter alia*, that the licensing agreement in question could not be regarded as incompatible with Article 85 because it would be possible for third parties to invoke Article 30 in order to prevent the enforcement of the terms designed to achieve absolute territorial protection. In other words, even if the parties had anti-competitive intentions, these would inevitably have been frustrated through the operation of the exhaustion of rights principle. Rejecting that argument, the Court of Justice said it failed to take into account:

" . . . the fact that one of the powers of the Commission is to ensure, pursuant to Article 85 of the Treaty and the regulations adopted in implementation thereof, that agreements and concerted practices between undertakings do not have the object or the effect of restricting or distorting competition, and that that power of the Commission is not affected by the fact that persons or undertakings subject to such restrictions are in a position to rely upon the provisions of the Treaty relating to the free movement of goods in order to escape such restrictions."[80]

The prohibitions in Article 30 and in Articles 85 and 86, therefore, apply cumulatively.

What if the application of the two sets of rules to the exercise of an intellectual property right leads to conflicting results? This is unlikely in the case of attempts to exclude parallel imports, since the exhaustion of rights principle seems to be on all fours with the authorities on absolute territorial protection. On the other hand, a ban on direct sales by a licensor in the territory of the licensee, or by a licensee in the territories of the licensor or of other licensees, while it may be allowable under Article 85, offends *prima facie* against the common origin principle. Since the rules on freedom of movement belong to the "Foundations of the Community," in the event of conflict they must, presumably, prevail. However, until the common origin

---

[78] In Case 198/83 *Windsurfing International* v. *Commission* it was held the clauses in question did not fall within the non-notifiable category because they went beyond the subject-matter of the patent: [1986] 3 C.M.L.R. at p. 541. See also *Re Advocaat Zwarte Kip* O.J. 1974 L237/12; [1974] 2 C.M.L.R. D79; *Re Vaessen/Moris* O.J. 1979 L19/32; [1979] 1 C.M.L.R. 511.
[79] Case 258/78, *loc. cit.* note 71, p. 493, *supra*.
[80] [1982] E.C.R. at p. 2070.

principle has been more fully considered by the Court of Justice, the extent of any possible conflict will remain a matter for speculation.[81]

As the Court pointed out in the quoted passage, it is a feature of the competition regime that the Commission enjoys executive powers which can be used against individual undertakings. Anti-competitive exploitation of intellectual property may, for example, be the subject of an order under Article 3(1) of Regulation 17 to terminate an infringement of Article 85 or Article 86; or it may provide grounds for the imposition of a fine under Article 15(2) of the Regulation.[82] No such powers exist in relation to Article 30 (or Article 59). The only action open to the Commission, if national legislation on intellectual property represents an unjustifiable barrier to intra-Community trade, is to bring proceedings under Article 169 against the Member State concerned.

In the definitive phase of the Community both the rules on freedom of movement and the rules on competition are directly effective. However, to make out a case under the competition rules, an individual resisting the exercise of an intellectual property right must be able to show that the right is "the subject, the means or the consequence" of an agreement or concerted practice or that its owner is abusing a dominant position in a substantial part of the common market.[83] Where a choice exists, therefore, Article 30 is likely to be seen by importers as providing a simpler and surer route to success in national proceedings.[84]

---

[81] See the discussion of these issues by Turner, (1983) 8 E.L.Rev. 103.
[82] See Whish, *op. cit.* note 1, p. 477, *supra*, at p. 378.
[83] See the discussion at pp. 500–501 *supra*.
[84] The point was first brought home in the *Deutsche Grammophon* judgment: Case 78/80 *loc. cit.* note 54, p. 489, *supra*.

PART IX: PUBLIC UNDERTAKINGS

CHAPTER 19

PUBLIC UNDERTAKINGS

Public undertakings and the common market

The present chapter is concerned with Article 90 EEC. There is another provision of the Treaty, Article 37, which relates to a particular category of public undertakings, namely State monopolies of a commercial character.[1] However, since Article 37 constitutes a specialised regime for the removal of obstacles to the free movement of goods which may be associated with the arrangements under which such monopolies operate, it has been dealt with in Chapter 7.

An ever more conspicuous part is played in the economic life of the Community by undertakings which are State controlled or which enjoy a privileged legal status, normally in return for carrying out certain tasks deemed to be of public importance. To illustrate the point it is only necessary to mention a few well known names: the State holding company, IRI, in Italy; British Coal and British Steel, where industrial sectors have been taken into public ownership; the nationalised motor manufacturers Renault in France and the Rover Group (formerly British Leyland) in the United Kingdom; broadcasting bodies such as Radio Audizione Italiana (RAI), the BBC and the ITV companies; British Gas and Gaz de France, as examples of public utilities, variously organised in the Member States on a national, regional or local level; finally, British Rail, the SNCF and other railway undertakings.[2]

The general approach of Community law to such undertakings is that, while there can be no objection in principle to their special relationship with the State,[3] whatever legal form this may take, their behaviour as market participants is governed by the same rules as those applicable to purely private undertakings, except where the Treaty itself specifically permits some derogation. The first limb of this proposition depends in part upon Article 222 EEC, preserving intact the systems of property ownership in the Member States, which are therefore free to determine the extent and internal organisation of their public sectors; and in part upon the clear inference to be drawn from Article 90(1) EEC that the conferment of special or exclusive rights upon an undertaking does not, in itself, consti-

---

[1] Arts. 90 and 37 belong to a wider group of "provisions relating to infringements of the normal functioning of the competition system by actions on the part of the States": see Case 94/74 *IGAV* v. *ENCC* [1975] E.C.R. 699, [1976] 2 C.M.L.R. 37. The Court also mentioned in this connection Arts. 92 to 94 and Arts. 101 and 102.

[2] In 1984 public enterprise accounted for about 13 per cent. of employment and 14 per cent. of value added in the non-government sector of the EEC economy, excluding agriculture: Comp.Rep. 1984, point 280. See also Keyser and Windle, *Public Enterprise in the EEC*.

[3] But see Deringer in *Equal Treatment of Public and Private Enterprises*, FIDE (1978), para. 36 to the effect that expansion of the public sector might be inconsistent with the mixed economy foundations of the Community.

tute an infringement of any Treaty rule.[4] Support for the second limb of the proposition can be found in the unqualified reference to "undertakings" in Articles 85 and 86, and in the limited exemption contained in Article 90(2) for the benefit of entrusted undertakings and fiscal monopolies (see below) which would have bee formulated differently if the rules of the Treaty did not normally apply to public undertakings.

At the same time it had to be recognised that the close links existing between the State and certain undertakings entailed dangers for the proper functioning of the common market. For example, the authorities of a Member State would frequently be in a position to influence the appropriations policy of public undertakings, so as to give preference to domestic producers, although positive proof of an infringement of Article 30 might be very difficult to find. It was also necessary to take into account the importance attached by Member States to the use of undertakings as instruments of public policy, in particular for the performance of public service functions. These two considerations explain the inclusion of Article 90 in the Treaty, and its general shape.

Article 90 EEC

The Article provides as follows:

"(1) In the case of public undertakings and undertakings to which Member States grant special or exclusive rights, Member States shall neither enact nor maintain in force any measure contrary to the rules contained in this Treaty, in particular to those rules provided for in Article 7 and Articles 85 to 94.

(2) Undertakings entrusted with the operation of services of general economic interest or having the character of a revenue-producing monopoly shall be subject to the rules contained in this Treaty, in particular to the rules on competition, in so far as the application of such rules does not obstruct the performance, in law or in fact, of the particular task assigned to them. The development of trade must not be affected to such an extent as would be contrary to the interests of the Community.

(3) The Commission shall ensure the application of the provisions of this Article and shall, where necessary, address appropriate directives or decisions to Member States."

It can be seen that Article 90 has a dual function: to ensure that Member States conduct themselves towards public undertakings and undertakings which they have granted "special or exclusive rights" in a manner fully compatible with Community law[5]; and to define the privileged status in Community law of "undertakings entrusted with the operation of services of general economic interest or having the character of a revenue-produc-

---

[4] So held by the Court in case 155/73 *Sacchi* [1974] E.C.R. 409; [1974] 2 C.M.L.R. 177. See also Case 311/84 *Centre Belge d'Etudes du Marché-Télé-marketing* v. *Compagnie Luxembourgeoise de Télédiffusion* [1986] 2 C.M.L.R. 558.

[5] Shindler points out that, since it imposes an obligation exclusively upon Member States, Art. 90 is misplaced in Section 1 of the Treaty chapter on competition, which is headed "Rules applying to undertakings": (1970) C.M.L.Rev. 57 at pp. 57–58.

ing monopoly." Paragraph (3) of the Article established machinery, on the one hand, for the enforcement of the obligation imposed on Member States by paragraph (1) and, on the other hand, for the retention within closely defined limits of the exception created by paragraph (2).

According to the Court of Justice, Article 90:

" . . . concerns only undertakings for whose actions States must take special responsibility by reason of the influence which they may exert over such actions. It emphasises that such undertakings are subject to all the rules laid down in the Treaty, subject to the provisions contained in paragraph (2); it requires the Member States to respect those rules in their relations with those undertakings and in that regard imposes on the Commission a duty of surveillance which may, where necessary, be performed by the adoption of directives and decisions addressed to Member States."[6]

As the developing case-law shows, the Court and the Commission have been concerned to prevent Article 90 from becoming a dangerous loophole in the system envisaged by the Treaty.[7]

Article 90(1): the responsibility of Member States for the conduct of public or privileged undertakings

Article 90(1) constitutes a particular application of the general principle contained in the second paragraph of Article 5 EEC that Member States are required to abstain from measures which are liable to jeopardise the attainment of the objectives of the Treaty.[8] The inclusion of a specific provision concerning the relationship between the State and public and privileged undertakings served both to highlight the particular seriousness of the problems which may arise, and to clarify the very extensive nature of the responsibility imposed upon Member States in this situation. It also enabled provision to be made in Article 90(3) (see below) for a more flexible and effective procedure than that of Article 169 in dealing with such cases.[9]

The categories of undertaking in Article 90(1)

The concept of an undertaking as a body having legal capacity and carrying on economic (not necessarily profit-making) activities was discussed in relation to Articles 85 and 86,[10] but some nuances may be added in the context of Article 90. In the *Sacchi* case,[11] it was held by the European

---

[6] Cases 188–190/80 *France, Italy and the United Kingdom* v. *Commission* [1982] E.C.R. 2545; [1982] 3 C.M.L.R. 144.
[7] See the analyses of Art. 90 by Page (1982) 7 E.L.Rev. 19; and by Marenco (1983) C.M.L.Rev. 495.
[8] Case 13/77 *INNO* v. *ATAB* [1977] E.C.R. 2115 at pp. 2144–2145; [1978] 1 C.M.L.R. 283. Measures in relation to wholly private undertakings are within the scope of the general principle.
[9] The point is fully discussed by Pappalardo in Van Damme, *Regulating the behaviour of monopolies and dominant undertakings in Community law*, pp. 539 *et seq.*
[10] See Chaps. 14 and 15, *supra*.
[11] Case 155/73 *Sacchi, loc. cit.* note 4, *supra*. There are several further references to the case in this chapter, where the facts are presented more fully.

Court that, even where the primary objects of a body are non-economic, it will have the status of an undertaking to the extent that it engages in economic activity. Thus a broadcasting organisation may be entrusted with tasks of a cultural or informative nature; but it behaves as an undertaking, for example, when purchasing programmes or selling advertising time. The State itself and its regional or local subdivisions, it is thought, constitute undertakings when they participate in the production or distribution of goods or in the provision of services, but not when they act in the exercise of sovereignty or purely as consumers.[12] For instance, a local authority which had been empowered to carry on certain forms of retail business, and in the course of doing so had been guilty of predatory market practices, would risk attracting liability under Article 86 for itself and under Article 90(1) for the State to which it belonged. On the other hand, a decision taken by a Minister under statutory powers, fixing maximum prices at a level which interfered with the free movement of goods, or the policy of a government department not to buy imported office equipment, would infringe Article 30, but not Article 90(1) since it would not involve entrepreneurial activity.

There would be no consistency in the application of Article 90(1) if it were necessary to rely upon the widely varying classifications of undertakings as "public" or "private" in the national legal systems. Community law must, therefore, provide its own test of what constitutes a public undertaking, specifically adapted to the aims of Article 90(1). Although the Court of Justice has yet to define the concept exhaustively, in the *Transparency Directive* case[13] it approved the Commission's definition set out in the measure in question.[14] According to the Directive, which was adopted in 1980 and extended in 1985,[15] a public undertaking is:

" . . . any undertaking over which the public authorities may exercise directly or indirectly a dominant influence by virtue of their ownership of it, their financial participation therein, or the rules which govern it."

Article 2 of the Directive creates certain presumptions, so that a "dominant influence" will be taken to exist where the public authorities: hold the major part of the undertaking's subscribed capital; or control the majority of the votes attaching to shares issued by the undertaking; or can appoint more than half of the members of the undertaking's administrative, managerial or supervisory body.

The Court held that this definition of a public undertaking did not amount to an abuse by the Commission of its powers under Article 90(3), since the financial criteria which the Directive adopted reflected the substantial forms of influence exerted by public authorities over the commercial decisions of public undertakings and were thus compatible with the

---

[12] See Deringer, *The Competition Law of the European Economic Community*, pp. 228–229. *Cf.* Shindler *op. cit.* note 6, *supra*, at pp. 62–64.
[13] Joined Cases 188–190/80 *France, Italy and the United Kingdom* v. *Commission*, *loc. cit.* note 6, *supra*.
[14] Dir. 80/723 O.J. 1980 L195/35: see Page (1980) 5 E.L.Rev. 492.
[15] O.J. 1985 L229.

Court's view of Article 90(1). Of course, the Court remains free to provide an extended meaning of public undertaking for the purposes of the latter provision in the future.

"Public undertakings," therefore, include the following: the state and its subdivisions (see above); corporations established under public law, or in the United Kingdom statutory bodies such as British Coal; public services or authorities, *e.g.* a health authority with regard to the provision of private hospital treatment; and State-controlled undertakings operating under private law. With regard to the latter, doubts used to be expressed as to the status of undertakings owned partly by the State and partly by private stockholders, *e.g.* British Petroleum. Applying the criteria of the Transparency Directive, everything turns on whether the State exerts a dominant influence in such situations.

The category of undertakings to which Member States grant special or exclusive rights partially overlaps that of public undertakings. The rationale behind the category is the fact that the state has deliberately intervened to relieve the undertaking concerned either wholly or partially from the discipline of competition, and must bear responsibility for the consequences. A right conferred by national legislation upon those carrying on an economic activity which is open to anyone, who thus form an indefinite class, is unlikely to be regarded as "exclusive."[16] Similarly, undertakings which are licensed to engage in an activity on the basis of their fulfilment of certain objective conditions (*e.g.* the financial safeguards imposed in the public interest upon insurance businesses) would be excluded from the category. The mode of granting the right (whether by an act under public law, *e.g.* a statute, regulation or administrative order, or by a private contract) is immaterial, again because formal differences between the legal systems of the various Member States cannot be allowed to interfere with the operation of Article 90(1).

Examples of undertakings falling within both the categories of Article 90(1) were found in the *Hein*[17] and *Sacchi*[18] cases. The former case raised the question of the compatibility with Community law of arrangements for the operation of river port facilities in Luxembourg by the Société du Port de Mertert. This company has close links with the State (including the right of the State to nominate half the members of the management and supervisory boards) and also enjoys certain privileges, *inter alia*, that of being consulted before permission is given for the development or operation of any other port or loading or unloading wharf on the Luxembourg bank of the Moselle. In *Sacchi* the relevant undertaking was the Italian broadcasting body, RAI, which is controlled by the State holding company, IRI. The State is also represented in its organs, and has powers of intervention in its operations. At the same time RAI enjoys a statutory monopoly in the field of broadcasting. Examples of private undertakings which have been granted special or exclusive rights would be the commercial television com-

---

[16] See Case 13/77 *INNO* v. *ATAB*, *loc. cit.* note 8, *supra*, at p. 2146.
[17] Case 10/71 *Ministère Public of Luxembourg* v. *Hein, née Muller* [1971] E.C.R. 723.
[18] Case 155/73, *loc. cit.* note 4, *supra*.

panies in the United Kingdom or the companies taking part in the French petroleum import system.[19]

The scope of the obligation imposed on Member States

The phrase "shall neither enact nor maintain in force any measure" is wide enough to cover any forms of positive action by a Member State, or the failure to remedy such action previously taken. There is no reason to exclude from the category of "measures" general legislative acts (statutes or regulations): thus Deringer gives the example of a statutory provision requiring public utilities to obtain energy exclusively through a State purchasing agency.[20] However, a distinction must be drawn between legislation specifically relating to public or privileged undertakings, and legislation relating to such undertakings only among others,[21] *e.g.* an aid for nationalised industries, as opposed to a general regional aid system: the latter would not in itself constitute a measure for the purposes of Article 90(1), but its application in a particular case might do so. At the other end of the scale would be the exercise by the State of its rights as a shareholder, and the application to management of wholly informal pressures.

The first decision under Article 90(3) (see below) to challenge specific legislation of the type prohibited by Article 90(1) was issued by the Commission in 1985.[22] This related to a measure requiring all public property in Greece to be insured with a Greek State-owned insurance company, and also obliging State banks to recommend customers seeking a loan to take out associated insurance with a State-owned company. In the Commission's view,[23] the preferential treatment accorded to domestic State-owned companies had the effect of excluding from large sections of the Greek insurance market not only Greek private insurers but also insurance companies from other Member States with subsidiaries or branches in the country. The legislation thus amounted to a restriction on freedom of establishment, enacted by Greece in contravention of Article 90(1).

A literal view of Article 90(1) clearly embraces a standstill obligation upon Member States and the need to take positive action to undo prohibited measures. Additionally, the paragraph impliedly makes Member States accountable for the behaviour of public and privileged undertakings.[24] In other words, responsibility under Article 90(1) does not presuppose positive action by the Member State itself: it suffices merely that a

---

[19] Importation of petroleum products into France was carried out under specific State authorisation by a number of undertakings in competition with each other. See also the French system for the collection and disposal of waste oils which was the subject of Case 172/82 *Syndicat national des fabricants raffineurs d'huile de graissage* v. *Inter Huiles* [1983] E.C.R. 555; [1983] 3 C.M.L.R. 485. The Court, *ibid.*, merely said " . . . even if the approval granted by a Member State must be regarded as the grant of an exclusive right within the meaning of Article 90(1), that would not exempt the Member State from the obligation to respect other provisions of Community law, particularly those relating to the free circulation of goods and those which result from Directive 75/439."

[20] *Op. cit.* note 12, *supra* at p. 240. See also Case 90/76 *Van Ameyde* v. *UCI* [1977] E.C.R. 1091; [1977] 2 C.M.L.R. 478. *Cf.* Case 72/83 *Campus Oil Ltd.* v. *Minister for Industry and Energy* [1984] E.C.R. 2727; [1984] 3 C.M.L.R. 544.

[21] The qualification is also made by Deringer, *op. cit.* note 12, *supra* at p. 240. The example has been slightly adapted.

[22] O.J. L152. See also Bull. EC 6–85, point 2.1.52.

[23] Comp.Rep. 1985, point 258.

[24] See Page, *op. cit.* note 7, *supra.*

public undertaking or an undertaking granted special or exclusive rights has been guilty of conduct which, on the part of the State, would have involved a Treaty violation. In such a situation the Member State is under an obligation to take any remedial steps which may be necessary; and if its existing legal powers are inadequate, it may be required by the Commission to equip itself with additional powers.

Whether the notion of maintaining a measure in force can be given such an interpretation is a question which must await an eventual answer by the Court of Justice. However, the approach is consistent with the obligation to take general and particular measures imposed on Member States by Article 5 and with the policy of Article 90(1).[25] If State responsibility under this paragraph is derived, respectively, from the ability to influence public undertakings and from the assumption of the risk inherent in the deliberate distortion of competition by a grant of special or exclusive rights, it ought to make no difference whether the role of the State has been active, in imposing or encouraging certain behaviour, or passive, in failing to correct it.

Article 90(1) refers, by way of example, to Article 7 (the general prohibition against discrimination) and Articles 85 to 94 (the rules on competition including the machinery for the supervision of aids granted by Member States). Thus in *Van Ameyde* v. *UCI*[26] the European Court held that, in the context of the green card system of motor insurance, a measure giving a national insurance bureau sole responsibility for settling claims in relation to damage caused by foreign vehicles would not constitute an infringement of Article 90(1) in conjunction with Articles 85 and 86. The reservation of the *settlement* of claims to such a body, composed of insurance companies which had been subjected to the checks and guarantees required under national law, complied with one of the objectives of the green card system, namely that the interests of accident victims should be properly safeguarded. However, it is clearly implied that if the *handling and investigation* of claims had been similarly reserved, thereby excluding other types of undertaking, and notably loss adjusters, from this business, there might have been an infringement. Another provision of obvious importance in the present context is Article 30. Thus a government direction to a public undertaking instructing it to purchase its company cars from a nationalised car manufacturer would contravene the prohibition against measures having an equivalent effect to quantitative restrictions; and the discussion above suggests that it would make no difference from the point of view of Article 90(1) if the undertaking adopted such a policy spontaneously. The provisions of acts validly adopted by Community institutions would be covered by the phrase "the rules contained in this Treaty."

The responsibility of a Member State under Article 90(1) is entirely independent of any violation of Community law by the undertaking in question: it is not based upon a theory of imputation, like the joint liability

---

[25] See Comp.Rep. 1976, point 145 and the strong statement by Mathijsen, FIDE 1978, Conference Reports vol. 2, p. 11.4.
[26] Case 90/76, *loc. cit.* note 20, *supra*.

of a parent company for infringements of the competition rules by a sub-sidiary which it controls.[27] For instance, the undertaking need not itself have acted at all, if it is the recipient of an aid contrary to Article 92; or its own conduct may be unimpeachable: *e.g.* it has been compelled by the State to enter a cartel, so that the element of agreement required by Article 85 is missing. And in cases where the undertaking is guilty of infringing a rule, *e.g.* abusing its dominant position on a relevant market by imposing unreasonable conditions on its trading partners, the position of the Member State falls to be determined not under the same provision, in this instance Article 86, but under Article 90(1).

Effect of the obligation

It remains to consider whether the obligation in Article 90(1) is directly effective, enabling individuals to bring appropriate proceedings against Member States before their national courts. The Commission maintained that it was so in its submissions relating to *Hein*,[28] and there is dis-tinguished support for this view in the literature.[29] The argument against direct effect, based upon the fact that special powers are given to the Com-mission under Article 90(3), seems unconvincing: because there is a more than usually effective remedy at Community level, it does not follow that individuals should be deprived of the opportunity of enforcing the obli-gation. The answer, it is submitted, must be sought in the application to Article 90(1) of the three customary tests of direct effect, *i.e.* clarity, unconditionality and the absence of discretion in the course of implemen-tation by the Community institutions or the Member States. These are liable to yield a different result, depending upon the particular rule of Community law which a measure is alleged to contravene. For example, the tests would presumably not be satisfied as regards a government direc-tion to a publicly owned bank to grant low interest loans, since the determi-nation whether this amounted to an illicit aid would be as much a matter for the judgment of the Commission under Article 92 as where a grant is made without the use of an intermediary. On the other hand, a direction to a publicly owned supplier of petroleum products to give preference to domestic customers in the event of a shortage would be readily identifiable as a measure contrary to Article 34 EEC. Thus the obligation in Article 90(1) may be directly effective, but only where it concerns the observance of Community provisions which are so effective.

Article 90(2): the exception relating to entrusted undertakings[30] and fiscal monopolies

Article 90(2) is drafted in terms which first emphasise that "undertakings entrusted with the operation of services of general economic interest or having the character of a revenue-producing monopoly" are normally sub-

---

[27] See the discussion *supra*, Chapter 13. See also Mathijsen *op. cit.* note 27, *supra* p. 11.3 to 4.
[28] Case 10/71, *loc. cit.* note 17, *supra*.
[29] See, *e.g.* Mégret *et al*, *Le droit de la Communauté Economique Européenne*, vol. 4 at pp. 86–87.
[30] This convenient description is used by Deringer, *op. cit.* note 12, *supra*.

ject to the rules of the Treaty and then goes on to exclude the application of the rules, where the performance of the particular tasks assigned to the undertakings is liable to be obstructed.[31] The exception is subject to a proviso designed to ensure that the disruption of the Community system will not be taken too far.

The categories of undertaking in Article 90(2)

There is nothing in the text of the Article that would restrict the categories of undertakings in the second paragraph to those covered by the first. However, in practice it seems unlikely that undertakings would be called upon to perform services of the type envisaged by Article 90(2) unless they were either State controlled or given a *quid pro quo* in the form of special or exclusive rights.

The more important of the two categories in Article 90(2) is that of entrusted undertakings. Because of the possible derogation which may be involved, the European Court has said that the category must be strictly defined.[32]

It is immaterial whether the undertaking concerned is public or private, provided that the service has been entrusted to it "by an act of the public authority."[33] This does not imply that the act need be in any particular form, and references by Advocate General Mayras in *SABAM* to a "legislative" or "unilateral" act seem unduly restrictive.[34] The essential point is that the State must have taken legal steps to secure the provision of the service by the undertaking in question. Thus an undertaking created as a result of private initiative and managing the intellectual property rights of its members on an ordinary contractual basis, could not be an entrusted undertaking, even if it happened to serve public purposes.[35] The same is true where legislation only *authorises* an undertaking to act, even though some supervision of those activities may be exercised by a public agency. Thus, in *GVL* v. *Commission*,[36] the Court held that the relevant German legislation did not confer the management of copyright and related rights on specific undertakings but defined in a general manner the rules applying to the activities of companies which intended to undertake the collective exploitation of such rights.

The phrase "operation of services" seems to have been chosen advisedly to indicate the organisation of some kind of regular performance, *e.g.* a public utility.[37] It is generally agreed that the definition of "services" in

[31] The European Court may at one time have regarded Art. 90(2) as the source of obligations under the EEC Treaty for the categories of undertakings to which it relates. Its present view seems to be that the paragraph merely reaffirms the application of the general rules of the Treaty to such undertakings, while introducing a limited exception. See Page, *op. cit.* note 7, *supra* at pp. 31–35. See also the discussion, *infra*.
[32] Case 127/73 *BRT* v. *SABAM*, [1974] E.C.R. 313; [1974] 2 C.M.L.R. 238.
[33] [1974] E.C.R. at p. 318.
[34] [1974] E.C.R. at p. 327.
[35] SABAM was such an undertaking. See also the Commission's Decision in *GEMA*; J.O. 1971 L134/15; [1971] C.M.L.R. D35.
[36] Case 7/82 [1983] E.C.R. 483; [1983] 3 C.M.L.R. 645.
[37] The relevant phrase in the other official versions of the Treaty has been chosen with equal care to denote the conduct of a service rather than the provision of services; see the discussion in Deringer *op. cit.* note 12, *supra* at p. 246; and Shindler, *op. cit.* note 5, *supra* at p. 70.

Article 60 EEC, as a residual concept relating to types of performance not governed by the provisions on the free movement of goods, persons or capital, does not apply in the context of Article 90(2).

A service will be "of general economic interest" where it involves economic activity (although its *aims* may, *e.g.* be social) and is furnished in what the relevant authority of the Member State concerned believes[38] to be the interest of the general public (although the ultimate benefit of the service may be enjoyed by specific recipients).[39] Not surprisingly, telecommunications undertakings[40] and water supply companies[41] have been treated as serving the general economic interest, although the derogation afforded by Article 90(2) remained inapplicable on other grounds in both cases (see below). In *Campus Oil Ltd.* v. *Minister for Industry and Energy*[42] the Court of Justice apparently did not dispute the Greek Government's contention that a State-owned oil refinery could be an undertaking operating a service of general economic interest.[43] On the other hand, a bank will not perform such a service when transferring customers' funds from one Member State to another.[44] Nor, it seems,[45] would the management company in the *GVL* case have fulfilled the criterion, since the collecting society was only engaged in the furtherance of the interests of private artistes.

Writers have pointed to various other factors which may be helpful in determining whether "general economic interest" is present, notably: the fact that the provider of the service is subjected to positive duties which he may not vary unilaterally (Deringer cites as an example the duty to maintain a regular bus service); the vital character of the service, which means that it would have to be provided by the State, if not entrusted to an undertaking; the granting of certain public law powers or of exclusive rights to an undertaking and, on the other hand, the retention of powers of intervention by the State with regard to the operation of the service; and the fact that the service is required to be available to all users under the same conditions.[46]

In the United Kingdom entrusted undertakings might include British Rail, British Airways, British Gas, regional Electricity Boards, the BBC

---

[38] The arguments are summarised by Page, *op. cit.*, note 7, *supra*, at p. 29.

[39] In Case 90/76 *Van Ameyde* v. *UCI* the Commission argued that the national insurers' bureau responsible for the settlement of claims in relation to damage caused by foreign vehicles in Italy did not qualify as an entrusted undertaking "since its activities do not benefit the whole of the national economy," but this view seems too restrictive: see [1977] E.C.R. 1091 at p. 1117. The Court seems to have taken for granted that the bureau would so qualify: *ibid.* at p. 1126.

[40] *Telespeed Services* v. *United Kingdom Post Office* [1982] O.J. L360/36; [1983] 1 C.M.L.R. 457. The Commission's Decision was unsuccessfully challenged in Case 41/83 *Italy* v. *Commission (British Telecom)* [1985] 2 C.M.L.R. 368.

[41] *The Community* v. *ANSEAU-NAVEWA* [1982] 2 C.M.L.R. 193; challenged on other issues in Joined Cases 96–102, 104–105, 108 and 110/82; *IAZ International Belgium and others* v. *Commission* [1983] E.C.R. 3369; [1984] 3 C.M.L.R. 276.

[42] Case 72/83 *loc. cit.* note 2, *supra*.

[43] *Ibid.* paras. 18–19 of the Judgment. But note the strong statement that "Art. 90(2) does not, however, exempt a Member State which has entrusted such an operation to an undertaking from the prohibition on adopting, in favour of that undertaking and with a view to protecting its activity, measures that restrict imports from other Member States contrary to Article 30 of the Treaty."

[44] Case 172/80 *Zuchner* v. *Bayerische Vereinsbank (Bank Charges)* [1981] E.C.R. 2021; [1982] 1 C.M.L.R. 313. The bank was not viewed as "entrusted," either.

[45] *Per* Advocate General Reischl.

[46] See Deringer *op. cit.* note 12, *supra*, pp. 248–249.

and ITV companies, the Bank of England[47]; but not, it is submitted, British Coal or British Steel which are engaged in the production of commodities, rather than in the operation of services. Until the different emphasis placed upon its activities by a change in Government, the National Enterprise Board[48] could have been viewed as an entrusted undertaking in certain circumstances.[49]

Undertakings "having the character of a revenue-producing monopoly," the second category in Article 90(2), are distinguished by the overriding purpose of raising revenue for the national exchequer through the exploitation of their exclusive right. They are normally combined with commercial monopolies, which causes problems in the application of Article 37 (see below).

In the discussion that follows references to entrusted undertakings should be understood to include fiscal monopolies, unless the context indicates otherwise.

The scope of the exception

The exception is capable of restricting the application of any Community provision, including Article 90(1). It makes no difference whether the rule in question is one designed primarily to influence the conduct of undertakings, e.g. Articles 85 or 86, or that of States, e.g. Articles 30 or 92.[50] Of interest in this connection is Article 37, which lays down certain rules for the adaptation of State monopolies of a commercial character to the requirements of a common market. To the extent that such monopolies perform the function of raising revenue, they fall within the second category of undertakings which may benefit from the exception; thus activities strictly related to this fiscal role would escape the effect of Article 37.[51] However, the protection of Article 90(2) would not extend to any other aspect of their activities, e.g. if maximum prices were fixed in respect of the goods marketed by a State monopoly, which had the effect of discouraging imports from other Community countries.

To benefit from the exception, an undertaking must show that application of the Treaty rules would obstruct the performance of the tasks assigned to it. Descriptions of that standard have varied. In the *British Telecom* case[52] the Court spoke of Italy's failure to prove that condemnation of British Telecom's behaviour as abusive within Article 86 would

[47] The example is given by Lipstein in *The Law of the European Economic Community*, p. 241, note 3.
[48] Since 1981 the NEB and the National Research Development Corporation have been co-operating under the name of British Technology Group. The modification in practice of its activities under a Conservative Government may be seen in the Annual Report and Accounts of the NEB.
[49] See Wyatt & Dashwood, 1st edition p. 371 for the earlier conflicts surrounding the NEB. See also Sharpe, The Industry Act 1975; Dashwood and Sharpe (1978) C.M.L.Rev. 9 at p. 22 *et seq.*
[50] The possibility that Art. 90(2) may restrict the operation of Art. 92 was explicitly recognised by the European Court in Case 78/76 *Firma Steinike und Weinlig* v. *Germany* [1977] E.C.R. 595 at pp. 610–611.
[51] The relationship of Art. 90 and Art. 37 was discussed in some detail by Advocate General Rozés in Case 78/82 *Commission* v. *Italy (Tobacco Margins)* [1983] E.C.R. 1955. The Court found no breach of Art. 37 and did not discuss the exception.
[52] Case 41/83 *Italy* v. *Commission, loc. cit.* note 40, *supra*. Noted by Ross (1985) 10 E.L.Rev. 457.

"prejudice" the accomplishment of the specific tasks assigned to that undertaking. The Decision of the Commission had considered whether application of the EEC's rules on competition would obstruct the performance by British Telecom of its duties "in an efficient and economic way."[53] These formulations may be contrasted with the approach adopted in the *Tobacco Margins* case[54] by Advocate General Rozès, who argued that the undertaking must have no choice but to infringe Treaty rules before the condition of Article 90(2) would be satisfied.[55] Similarly, the Commission in its *ANSEAU-NAVEWA* Decision stated:

> "It is not sufficient . . . that compliance with the provisions of the Treaty makes the performance of the particular task more complicated. A possible limitation of the application of the rules on competition can be envisaged only in the event that the undertaking concerned has no other technically and economically feasible means of performing its particular task."[56]

Finally, the European Court in *CBEM Télé-Marketing* v. *Compagnie Luxembourgeoise de Télédiffusion and Information Publicité Benelux*[57] reiterated the stance it had taken much earlier in *Sacchi*,[58] that rules of the Treaty continue to apply[59] so long as it is not shown that their prohibitions are "incompatible" with the performance of the undertakings' tasks.

In the light of these comments, and the normally strict construction to be given to any derogation from fundamental provisions of the Treaty, it is not easy to see how the "obstruction" condition in Article 90(2) can be satisfied. One example which has been suggested[60] is that of a fiscal monopoly imposing abusively high prices on its customers, but it is very doubtful whether Article 86 would be excluded in this case, unless the undertaking had been specifically charged to maximise revenue. The exception is, perhaps, most likely to be successfully invoked in the field of State aids: *e.g.* operating aids to bus or railway companies may be essential for the continued provision of a public transport service.

The wording of Article 90(2) indicates that recourse may only be had to the exception after the consequences of applying the normal rule to the case in point have become clear. It follows that the paragraph does not permit any relaxation of the procedural requirements connected with the application of the rule. Thus, for example, Member States are obliged to give the Commission advance notice of new or amended aids to entrusted undertakings, in accordance with Article 93(3)[61]: it is only when the Commission has found that the purposes of an aid do not fall within one of the categories in Article 92(2) or (3) and it is consequently liable to prohibi-

[53] *Telespeed Services* v. *Post Office, loc. cit.* note 40, *supra.*
[54] Case 78/82 *Commission* v. *Italy, loc. cit.* note 51, *supra.*
[55] But Madame Rozès herself used a less forceful phrase in Case 172/82 *Inter-Huiles, loc. cit.* note 19, *supra,* where she said that the privilege being claimed was unnecessary to enable the undertakings in question to accomplish their tasks "without compromising their profitability."
[56] *Loc. cit.* note 41, *supra.*
[57] Case 311/84 *loc. cit.* note 4, *supra.*
[58] Case 155/73 *loc. cit. ibid.*
[59] *In casu*, Art. 86.
[60] By Thiesing, cited by Deringer *op. cit.* note 12, *supra* at p. 256, note 93.
[61] See Chap. 17, *supra.*

tion, that Article 90(2) comes into play. Any such aid, prematurely introduced, would be illegal. The only possible qualification is that the application of the rule in Article 93(3) itself might be excluded, if the ability of
the entrusted undertaking to perform its allotted task were dependent on
the *immediate* introduction of the aid. The effect on the notification procedure under Regulation 17[62] may also be illustrated. Thus a notifiable
new agreement, one of the parties of which is an entrusted undertaking,
will not qualify for exemption under Article 85(3) if it has not been notified. Assuming that the agreement is caught by the prohibition in Article
85(1), it would normally be void under Article 85(2). But here the exemption intervenes, preserving the legality of the agreement, provided that it is
essential to the task of the entrusted undertaking.

The proviso in the second sentence of Article 90(2) identifies the point at
which it becomes necessary to apply the relevant provisions of Community
law, even at the cost of preventing an entrusted undertaking or a fiscal
monopoly from performing its allotted task. The phrase "the development
of trade" refers to the process of establishing a common market (*cf.* the
wider concept of affecting trade between Member States, which features in
Articles 85, 86 and 92).[63] When interference with this process threatens the
attainment of the Treaty objectives, the interests of individual Member
States are subordinated to those of the Community. According to the
Court:

" . . . the application of Article 90(2) is not left to the discretion of the
Member State which has entrusted an undertaking with the operation
of a service of general economic interest. In fact, Article 90(3) confers
on the Commission, subject to review by the Court, the task of ensuring application of the Article."[64]

Although made in the context of an argument relating to the *locus standi* of
the Italian Government to challenge a decision addressed to British Telecom, these comments clearly reject the suggestion by Advocate General
Darmon that the judgments to be made under Article 90(2) should be left
in the hands of Member States.

Effect of the exception

A difficult problem is that of the effect Article 90(2) has in proceedings
before national courts. This may be formulated in terms of whether or not
the paragraph is directly effective, but it must be kept firmly in mind that
we are here concerned with a provision under which the scope of obligations imposed by the EEC Treaty is restricted in relation to certain categories of undertakings. The question is how far a claim that a matter falls
within the exceptions of Article 90(2) will intefere with the application by a
national court of Community provisions on which individuals would normally be entitled to rely.

The European Court recognises the competence of national courts to
decide whether an undertaking falls into one of the categories which are

---

[62] See Chap. 16, *supra.*
[63] See Advocate General Rozès in Case 78/82 *Commission* v. *Italy, loc. cit.* note 5, *supra.*
[64] In Case 41/83 *Italy* v. *Commission, loc. cit.* note 40, *supra.*

eligible for exemption. In *SABAM*[65] a musical copyright society enjoying a *de facto* monopoly in Belgium had replied to an allegation of abusive conduct contrary to Article 86, *inter alia*, by claiming to be an entrusted undertaking within Article 90(2). In dealing with this aspect of the case the Court spoke of "the duty of the national court to investigate whether an undertaking which invokes the provisions of Article 90(2) for the purpose of claiming a derogation from the rules of the Treaty has, in fact, been entrusted by a Member State with the operation of a service of general economic interest."[66]

But what if the national court finds that the undertaking in question has been so entrusted? May it go on to apply the exception and, where appropriate, the proviso, to see whether they provide an escape from the consequences of the normal Community rule? The answer that emerges from the case law is tolerably clear, though it should still be treated as a tentative one. The leading cases are *Hein*, *Sacchi* and, more recently, *Inter-Huiles*.

The *Hein*[67] case originated in a prosecution in Luxembourg for the unauthorised use by the defendants of a wharf on the Moselle, in breach of legislation giving special rights and responsibilities in connection with the operation of river port facilities to the Société du Port de Mertert. The legislation was alleged by the defendants to contravene the EEC rules on competition and a reference was made for a preliminary ruling under Article 177, which the Court of Justice treated as a request for an interpretation of Article 90.[68] Having summarised the second paragraph of the Article, the Court went on:

"An undertaking which enjoys certain privileges for the accomplishment of the task entrusted to it by law, maintaining for this purpose close links with the public authorities, and which is responsible for ensuring the navigability of the State's most important waterway, may fall within this provision.

To answer the question referred, therefore, it is necessary to consider whether Article 90(2) is of such a nature as to create individual rights which the national courts must protect.

Article 90(2) does not lay down an unconditional rule.

Its application involves an appraisal of the requirements on the one hand, of the particular task entrusted to the undertaking concerned and, on the other hand, the protection of the interests of the Community.

This appraisal depends on the objectives of general economic policy pursued by the States under the supervision of the Commission.

Consequently, and without prejudice to the exercise by the Commission of the powers conferred by Article 90(3) Article 90(2) cannot at the present stage create individual rights which the national courts must protect."[69]

The tenor of the judgment is very clear. No interpretation is offered of

[65] Case 127/73 *BRT* v. *SABAM*, *loc. cit.* note 32, *supra*.
[66] [1974] E.C.R. at p. 318.
[67] Case 101/71 *loc. cit.* note 17, *supra*. The case is also frequently referred to as *Muller*.
[68] No EEC provisions were specified in the questions.
[69] [1974] E.C.R. at p. 730.

Article 90(1) or of any other provision which might have given grounds for not applying the national legislation in question. The referring court is being advised that, because the legislation relates to an entrusted undertaking, the Community point raised by the defendants cannot affect the outcome of the national proceedings.[70] But why, it might be asked, does the Court say Article 90(2) cannot *create* individual rights, when what the paragraph does is to *deprive* individuals of rights they would otherwise have? Page[71] explains that the Court must have been thinking of the paragraph as a *lex specialis* for undertakings in the privileged categories: it must, in other words, have taken the view that, in so far as the Treaty imposed obligations on entrusted undertakings, this would be by virtue of Article 90(2) and not through its general provisions. And it must have concluded, in view of the exception and the proviso in the paragraph, that such obligations could not be directly effective. So interpreted, *Hein* conveys an uncompromising message: as against entrusted undertakings, Community provisions cannot be invoked by individuals in the national courts.[72]

However, by the time of *Sacchi*,[73] it seems, an evolution in the Court's thinking had taken place. The questions referred by a court in Italy concerned, *inter alia*, the compatibility with the Treaty of a measure extending the national broadcasting monopoly, RAI. Having held that, in so far as they engage in economic activities, broadcasting bodies fall within the provisions of Article 90(1), but that a further grant of exclusive rights to such a body would not, in itself, constitute an infringement of Article 86 taken together with Article 90, the Court continued:

> "Moreover, if certain Member States treat undertakings entrusted with the operations of television, even as regards their commercial activities, in particular advertising, as undertakings entrusted with the operation of services of general economic interest, the same prohibitions apply, as regards their behaviour within the market, by reason of Article 90(2), so long as it is not shown that the said prohibitions are compatible with the performance of their tasks."[74]

As to whether certain practices allegedly entailed in the monopoly amounted to abuses within the meaning of Article 86, the Court said:

> "Such would certainly be the case with an undertaking possessing a monopoly of television advertising, if it imposed unfair charges or conditions on users of its services or if it discriminated between commercial operators or national products on the one hand, and those of other

---

[70] The formal ruling on the questions submitted under Art. 177 contained in the *dispositif* of the case simply reiterates the final paragraph of the quoted passage.

[71] *Op. cit.* note 7, *supra* at pp. 32–33. Strong approval of Page's approach is expressed by Marenco, *op. cit.* note 7, *supra*. *Cf.* the view of Smit that the Court was considering the individual rights not of the defendants in the national proceedings but of the Société du Port de Mertert. On his reading of the case, it is the special privilege created by Art. 90(2) for the benefit of entrusted undertakings which lacks direct effect. See Smit and Herzog, *The Law of the European Economic Community*, 3–361 to 3–363. That seems to us impossible to reconcile with what the Court actually *did* in *Hein*. However, it probably represents the Court's present understanding of the effect of Art. 90(2) (see *infra*).

[72] This is the result attributed to the case by Mégret *et al.*, *op. cit.* note 29, *supra* at p. 88.

[73] Case 155/73 *loc. cit.* note 4, *supra*.

[74] [1974] E.C.R. at p. 430.

Member States on the other, as regards access to television advertising.

The national court has in each case to ascertain the existence of such abuse and the Commission has to remedy it within the limits of its powers.

Even within the framework of Article 90, therefore, the prohibitions of Article 86 have a direct effect and confer on interested parties rights which the national courts must safeguard."[75]

The two quoted passages seem calculated to correct the impression left by the *Hein* judgment that Article 90(2) creates a special set of truncated obligations for undertakings in the privileged categories. The paragraph is presented as reaffirming that the general rules of the Treaty apply to such undertakings, while creating a limited exception in their favour.[76] It is also explicitly stated that within the framework of Article 90(2) individuals enjoy Community rights which are enforceable in the national courts. The distinction rather obscurely drawn between the respective roles of the national courts and the Commission need not be interpreted as denying the competence of the former to remedy an abuse once ascertained. It is probably just intended to underline the Commission's power under Art. 90(3) to take steps against the Member State concerned.[77]

Sacchi showed that Community provisions which are directly effective remain so, even when invoked against entrusted undertakings; but no guidance was given as to how the exception in Article 90(2) interacts with such provisions. The answer may be found in what amounts to hardly more than an aside in the Court's *Inter-Huiles* judgment.[78] The main issue in the case was the compatibility with Community law of a French scheme for the collection and disposal of waste oils which had the effect of preventing their exportation to other Member States. Advocate General Rozés thought the undertakings licensed to operate under the scheme could be regarded as entrusted undertakings within the meaning of Article 90(2) but that a ban on exports was not essential to enable them to carry out their task. For its part, the Court was content to observe, "As regards Article 90(2), the Court has already held that it cannot at this stage create individual rights which the national court must protect."[79] At first sight, this looks like a reversal of *Sacchi*. However, on closer examination it can be seen that, although the Court is repeating what it said in *Hein*, the statement has an opposite connotation here. If the "individual rights" in question had been those of prospective exporters of waste oils from France, the Article 90(2) point would not have been brushed aside as of no concern to the referring court. It would have been dealt with in the formal ruling of the Court as a

---

[75] *Ibid.*

[76] In Case 90/76 *Van Ameyde* v. *UCI, loc. cit.* note 20, *supra* at p. 1126 the Court spoke of "the prohibition contained in Article 90 of the Treaty in conjunction with Article 86." This suggests that Art. 90(2) (the provision which the Court must have in mind, since the passage concerns the behaviour of UCI) may itself impose a prohibition. However, it is submitted that the statement should be understood as a reference to the prohibition in Art. 86, as reaffirmed by Art. 90(2).

[77] See Page, *op. cit.* note 7, *supra* at p. 35.

[78] Case 172/82 *loc. cit.* note 19, *supra*.

[79] [1983] E.C.R. at p. 567.

matter potentially decisive of the national proceedings.[80] What the Court must have had in mind were the rights (in Hohfeldian language, "privileges" or "liberties"[81]) being claimed under Article 90(2) by the licensed disposal firms. The Court is saying, in effect, that national courts are not competent to apply the exception in the paragraph for the benefit of entrusted undertakings. The only way such undertakings can obtain exemption from the normal rules of the Treaty is by a decision of the Commission under Article 90(3). Unless and until such a decision is taken, the rules apply to them with full rigour. Article 90(2), therefore, functions similarly to Article 85(3), though without a formal system of notification to set the exemption process in motion.[82]

The more recent *Télé-marketing* case[83] is consistent with that analysis. The Court repeated its ruling in *Sacchi* that broadcasting monopolies, when entrusted with the operation of services of general economic interest, are subject, as regards their behaviour in the market, to the prohibitions of Article 86, so long as these are not shown to be incompatible with their tasks.

So, it seems, the Court of Justice has achieved, by a feat of legerdemain, a synthesis of its case law that minimises the impact of Article 90(2) on the protection of individual rights under the Treaty.

Article 90(3): the supervisory functions of the Commission

By Article 90(3) the Commission is both placed under an obligation to ensure the application of the Article and equipped with a special power to issue directives or decisions for this purpose. So far the Commission has adopted the Transparency Directive and taken one decision, against discriminatory insurance provisions in Greece.[84]

Directives or decisions under Article 90(3) can only be addressed to Member States. However, where appropriate the Commission may have recourse to other powers, *e.g.* under Regulation 17 against the undertaking concerned. There is, of course, nothing in Article 90 to prevent the Commission, if it so chooses, from issuing non-binding recommendations.

The Commission may act under Article 90(3) not only in response to infringements which have already occurred but also for the taking of preventative measures, whether general or specific. Where it is available, the Article 90(3) procedure has clear advantages over the Article 169 procedure. In the first place, it enables the Commission to adopt legally binding acts, as compared with the reasoned opinion envisaged by Article 169. Secondly, there is the advantage of flexibility. Thus Article 169 is designed

[80] *Cf.* the ruling in *Hein*: [1971] E.C.R. at p. 731.
[81] See Hohfeld, *Fundamental Legal Conceptions*. In Hohfeld's analysis, "privilege" or "liberty" connotes the absence of duty.
[82] Smit, *op. cit.* note 71, *supra* at p. 3–363 points out that the Commission is the most appropriate body to be given the task of ruling on the permissibility of anti-competitive conduct within the Community system.
[83] Case 311/84 *Centre Belge d'Etudes du Marché-Télé-marketing* v. *Compagnie Luxembourgeoise de Télédiffusion*, *loc. cit.* note 4, *supra*. As in *Sacchi*, the Court did not address the question of how the privilege given by Art. 90(2) may be asserted.
[84] See p. 522, *supra*.

purely as a means of dealing with specific cases where a Member State is in breach of a Community obligation.

The Transparency Directive[85]

This Directive, on the transparency of financial relations between Member States and public undertakings, requires Member States to keep available for five years information concerning the financial relations in question and to supply such information to the Commission where it so requests. The preamble to the Directive stresses the Commission's duty to ensure that Member States do not grant undertakings, public or private, aids incompatible with the common market, and the need for equal treatment of public and private enterprises. The complexity of financial relations between Member States and public undertakings hinders the achievement of that equality, and provides the rationale for the measure.

The definition of a public undertaking and the examples of financial relations contained in the Directive have already been discussed. Small undertakings and undertakings which supply services not liable to affect intra-Community trade are excluded from its scope. An amendment in 1985[86] removed the original exclusion of specific sectors, namely public water authorities, energy, posts and telecommunications, transport undertakings and credit institutions.

The first use the Commission made of the Directive was to require Member States to submit annual accounts for the previous three financial years of public undertakings in five industries: motor vehicles (construction, assembly and sale of vehicles, bodies, components, equipment and accessories); man-made fibres (production and sale); textile machinery (building and sale of machinery and accessories); shipbuilding (building, conversion, repair and sale); and tobacco products (manufacture and sale).[87] The Italian Government's refusal to comply with this request in relation to the State tobacco monopoly led to the opening of Article 169 proceedings.[88]

A challenge to the validity of the Directive was made by France, Italy and the United Kingdom in Cases 188–190/80.[89] The European Court rejected the various claims, which principally alleged that the Commission lacked competence to enact the Directive and that the Directive discriminated against public undertakings.

Part of the argument over competence concerned the relationship between Article 90(3) and Article 94.[90] The latter confers upon the Council power to determine the conditions in which Article 93(3), relating to notification of state aids, is to apply. The applicant Member States claimed that the Directive fell within the Council's competence under Article 94, rather than that of the Commission under Article 90(3). The Court replied, after contrasting the objectives of the two provisions:

---

[85] See Brothwood (1981) C.M.L.Rev. 207; Page, *op. cit.* note 14, *supra.*
[86] *Loc. cit.*, note 15, *supra.*
[87] Comp.Rep. 1983, point 283.
[88] Comp.Rep. 1983, point 283; 1984, point 284.
[89] *Loc. cit.* note 6, *supra.* See Brothwood (1983) C.M.L.Rev. 335; Page (1982); E.L.Rev. 496.
[90] As to Article 94, see Chap. 17, *supra.*

"In comparison with the Council's power under Article 94, that which is conferred upon the Commission by Article 90(3) thus operates in a specific field of application and under conditions defined by reference to the particular objective of that Article. It follows that the Commission's power to issue the contested directive depends on the needs inherent in its duty of surveillance provided for in Article 90 and that the possibility that rules might be laid down by the Council, by virtue of its general power under Article 94, containing provisions impinging upon the specific sphere of aids granted to public undertakings does not preclude the exercise of that power by the Commission."[91]

The Commission's competence was thus confirmed, although it would seem that the Directive could have been adopted under either provision.

By upholding the validity of the Transparency Directive, the Court of Justice has underlined the opportunity for the adoption and application of a coherent policy by the Commission towards State aids. Further directives, for example in the context of the criteria used to determine the award of contracts by public undertakings may be forthcoming in the future.

---

[91] [1982] E.C.R. at p. 2575.

INDEX

admiral, accompanied by his alarmingly beautiful secretary Kathy O'Brien, was ready to go. In attendance was the Secretary of State Harcourt Travis, the Chairman of the Joint Chiefs, General Tim Scannell, the Chief of Naval Operations, Admiral Alan Dickson, the Director of the National Security Agency, Rear Admiral George Morris, and his personal assistant Lt. Commander James Ramshawe, American by birth, Australian parents.

As the great man took his leave, they all stood in a small 'family' huddle, veterans in the last half dozen years of some of the most brutal secret operations ever conducted by the United States military. Their devotion to Arnold had grown from the series of great triumphs on the international stage, due, almost entirely, to the strengths of the admiral's intellect.

Like Caesar, Admiral Morgan was not lovable – except to Kathy – but his grasp of international politics, string pulling, poker playing, threats and counter-threats, Machiavellian propaganda, and the conduct of restricted, classified military operations, was second to none. At all of the above he was a virtuoso, driven by an unbending sense of patriotism. During his reign in the West Wing he had intimidated, cajoled, outwitted and bullied some of the most powerful men on earth. His creed was to fight and fight, and never to lower his blade short of victory. General Douglas MacArthur and General George Patton were his heroes. And now the admiral was departing, leaving his Washington confidants devastated, convinced that another heaven and

CHAPTER ONE

Thursday 8 January 2009
The White House, Washington, DC

The brand new Democratic Administration, fresh from a narrow election victory, was moving into the West Wing. With the exception of the President, who knew he was going anyway at the end of his second term, every hour of every day was a trauma for the outgoing Republicans. For the big-hitters of the military and government handing over the reins to what most of them believed to be a bunch of naive, inexperienced, half-assed limousine liberals, led by an idealistic young President from Rhode Island, who would have been pushed to hold down a proper executive job, well, anywhere, was appalling.

And today was probably the worst day of all. Admiral Arnold Morgan, the retiring President's National Security Adviser, was about to leave the White House for the last time. His big nineteenth-century naval desk had already been cleared and removed, and now there were only a few goodbyes left. The door to his office was wide open, and the

15

to boil rapidly, and then expand, like a pressure cooker. That's what will blow the mountain to pieces, and will most certainly collapse the entire southwest section of La Palma into the sea. A landslide on a scale not seen on this earth for a million years.

So, if you fired a missile at the vulnerable spot on the volcano of Cumbre Vieja, which you said tonight was the most active, you'd need it to penetrate the surface and then explode deep below the ground.

It would need to hit hard and pierce the rock strata which guards the lava, before it blew. The released magma surging up from the core of the earth would then erupt into the atmosphere, drawing zillions of tons of incinerating magma right behind it. The underground lakes would boil, and then flash off into steam. That's when the whole mountain range would explode.

The former Major Ray Kerman liked Professor Landon. This was a man who expertly understood explosions, both natural and man-made, and who was consumed by his subject. And he did not dwell upon ramifications. He spoke frankly, as a scientist. Very much to the point. Untroubled by the obvious innuendoes of the equally obvious terrorist who held him prisoner. The science was what mattered to Professor Landon.

Yes, General Rashood liked him. This whole thing was rather a pity.

'Thank you, Professor,' said the HAMAS general. 'Thank you very much. We'll have some breakfast now, and talk more.'

14

Montserrat volcano on the western side of the island. I should think you could bring that one forward with a well-aimed hand grenade. It's never really stopped erupting in the last five years.

How about Mount St Helens?

More difficult. But there have been small explosions and a lot of rumblings in the past several months. And remember. When St Helens blew in 1980 it unleashed forces equal to four Hiroshimas every second. But it's very dangerous now and getting worse. I'd say four big cruise missile explosions bang in the right place on the vulnerable south side would almost certainly unleash its lava again.

And Cumbre Vieja?

You mean to cause the mega-tsunami I was talking about last night? No conventional explosion would prise that huge hunk of rock off the cliffside. The volcano would have to erupt. And you'd need a sizeable nuclear blast to make that happen.

You mean a full-blooded nuclear bomb?

No, no. Not that big. But you mentioned cruise missiles. And if you were thinking short-range, not ballistic, I'd say a medium-sized nuclear warhead would probably blow a big enough hole to release the magma.

And that starts the landslide into the bottom of the ocean?

No. No. Not on its own. You see, that whole line of volcanoes in southern La Palma contains a vast amount of water deep in the mountains. The release of the magma bursting up to the surface creates stupendous heat inside the rock. In turn this causes several cubic miles of water

13

Certainly . . . Montserrat in the West Indies . . .
Karangetang, Indonesia . . . San Cristobal, Nicaragua . . .
Tangkubanparahu in Java . . . at least three on the
Kamchatka Peninsula, Siberia . . . Fuego in Guatemala
. . . Stromboli in Italy . . . Kavachi Seamount, Solomon
Islands . . . Chuckinadak Island, Alaska . . .

How many in the past twelve months?

You mean serious ones, or just rumblings?

How many explosions?

Well, Colima in Mexico . . . Etna in Sicily . . . Fuego,
Guatemala . . . the one in the Solomon Islands, and all
three of the big ones on Kamchatka . . . plus Kilauea in
Hawaii . . . Maman in Papua New Guinea . . . always
the Soufrière Hills in Montserrat . . . with a bit of a shout
from Mount St Helens in Washington State. Also some
dire rumblings in the Canary Islands – the most serious
of all.

Because of the tsunami?

Absolutely.

By 7 a.m. Professor Landon was growing anxious.
One hour from now, he was due in his office in the
splendid white-pillared Benfield Greig building on
Gower Street, near Euston Square. As the senior professor in UCL's Department of Geological Sciences,
his absence from his second-floor lecture room was
sure to be noticed. But the questions continued, and
he had little choice but to answer them.

What would it take to explode an active rumbling
volcano? A big bomb? Maybe a couple of cruise missiles
straight down the crater?

Well, the magma is very close to the surface in the

in London for nearly half a century, since the night gangsters gunned down three policemen in Shepherd's Bush, a couple of miles to the west of the Albert Hall.

But at that time the police had been pretty sure who had committed the crime within about five minutes of the shooting. This time they did not have the remotest idea. They had no clues, no witnesses, and absolutely no motives to work on. And, of course, they had no notion whatsoever that a celebrity kidnap victim was being held in the back of the getaway vehicle.

The interrogation of Professor Landon began at one o'clock in the morning. The black bag had been removed from his head, his wrists were unbound, and he was given coffee at a large dining-room table in a white room with no windows. Flanking the door were two Middle Eastern-looking guards, wearing blue jeans, black boots and short brown leather jackets. Both were holding AK-47s.

Before him sat a broad-shouldered, British Army officer type, more formally dressed, no longer wearing sunglasses. He too was Middle Eastern in appearance, but his voice and tone could have been honed nowhere else on earth but at a leading English public school.

The discussion was about volcanoes.

How many genuine eruptions in the world in recent years?

Probably a hundred since 2002, maybe a few more.

Can you name some?

11

cars and were driving leisurely through west London to a cast-iron 'safe house' owned by a few fellow Muslims in the suburb of Hounslow.

Professor Landon's hands were now bound together with plastic masking tape, and he was still in the bag, in every sense of the phrase. He was sitting between two of the world's most lethal Muslim fundamentalists and in answer to his frightened pleas to know what was going on, since his captors plainly had the wrong man, he was told softly and firmly, *keep quiet, Dr Landon, we wish only to talk to you and then you will be set free.*

The first part was accurate. Almost. The second part was a lie. 'Lava' Landon already knew far too much.

Back at the scene of the crime, two ambulances were transporting the bodies of the murdered officers to St Mary's Hospital, Paddington, an RSPCA van was loading the carcass of Roger into a box and the police were desperately looking for witnesses.

But no one had heard gunshots. No one had actually seen either policeman being attacked. No, it was impossible to identify the exact type of four-wheel-drive wagon, which may have contained the criminals. No one had seen its number plate.

Someone thought it had driven off with no lights. Someone thought it turned right, down Exhibition Road. Someone else thought it turned left. No one could cast a single ray of light on the physical appearance of its occupants.

It was the most brutal slaying of police officers

classic unarmed combat killing blow of the SAS. The London bobby was dead before he slumped back onto the edge of the sidewalk.

The men from HAMAS had practised the 'defensive' operation for weeks, and there had been no mistakes. Only the presence of the big German-bred attack dog had surprised them. But not for long. From the moment they first grabbed the professor, to their quick getaway, only seventeen seconds had passed.

And now the Range Rover made a full turn around, its lights still dark, and headed for Exhibition Road, the back-seat prisoner unaware of the carnage that quickly grew smaller in the rear-view mirror.

It took a full five minutes for two or three people among the pop concert crowd to realise that something had happened. No, Roger was not taking a nap. Yes, that was actual blood. Yes, the policeman lying flat on his back had indeed been shot dead and the holes in his forehead were not birthmarks. And, yes, the other chap in the blue coat slumped face down in the gutter was definitely a policeman. And no, he was not drunk. And yes, like Roger and his colleague, he was also dead.

Two London policemen, and their guard dog, slain at the bottom of the great stone stairway, south of the Albert Hall.

Finally, more than seven minutes after the Range Rover had left, someone dialled London's 999 Emergency Service on a cellphone. Within another five minutes, two patrol cars were on the scene. By that time General Rashood and his men had changed

9

bared, going for the driver's right arm through the open window.

Big mistake, Roger. From the back seat of the Range Rover, Ahmed Sabah almost blew the dog's head off with a burst from a silenced AK-47. The policeman running in front could not believe what he had seen with his own eyes, and he stopped some three yards from the vehicle, the late attack dog Roger in a heap at his feet.

Ahmed's light machine-gun spoke quietly again, three dull muffled thumps, and a short line of bullets through the forehead flung the constable backwards to the ground, dead.

The second policeman, seeing the dog but not yet his fallen colleague, ran instinctively towards the driver. But he was too late. The general was out on the sidewalk and seized the astonished cop's raised right arm, flinging him down in one fluid motion, his head almost on the seat.

He grabbed him by the throat and rammed his head against the door's recess. A split second later Ahmed slammed the door shut with stupendous force, cracking the policeman's skull from the bridge of his nose to the hairline. At that moment, the Range Rover became the most expensive nutcracker since Pyotr Tchaikovsky worked his magic more than one hundred years before.

Ravi spun the police officer around and, with the butt of his gloved right hand, thundered a terrible upward punch into his already bleeding nose. The force rammed the bone clean into the brain, the

die and against his left kidney he could feel the unmistakable push of a large knife.

It's curious how the swarm of preoccupied people could have missed entirely what was happening in their midst. It must have been their single-minded determination to get home – searching for cabs, or late buses, hoping to make the London underground station at South Kensington in time for one of the infrequent late-night trains.

No one paid attention to the incident, certainly not the two London policemen, on patrol with a large German shepherd named Roger, who were swept along by the throng spilling out of the concert hall at the top of the steps, 30 feet above the scene of the kidnap.

True to the modern ethos of the London police they missed the crime but homed in instantly on the illegal parking, fighting their way down the steps to apprehend the Range Rover's driver, their hands already fumbling urgently for their trusty breathalysers.

By the time they arrived, the driver's seat was occupied. Seated behind the wheel, his eyes hidden behind dark glasses, was the former SAS major, Ray Kerman, currently known as General Ravi Rashood, Supreme Commander of the revolutionary forces of HAMAS and quite possibly the most dangerous and wanted terrorist in the world.

Right now he was revving the engine impatiently, causing the policemen to unleash the huge dog, which flew at the car in two bounds, teeth

faces, at the back at the auditorium, a twenty-three-year-old Palestinian freedom fighter, Ahmed Sabah, was taking notes, intent on every word, every graphic.

After the speech, Sabah had slipped out quickly and was now waiting quietly in the dark southern precincts of the Albert Hall, London's spectacular rounded concert hall, situated a few yards from the Royal Geographical Society.

As 'Lava' Landon walked along Kensington Gore, turning into the courtyard of the great hall of music, named for Queen Victoria's consort Prince Albert, several thousand fans began to flood through the doors after a concert celebrating popular bands of the eighties.

It actually took Paul Landon four more minutes to reach the top of the long, wide flight of steps, which lead down from the hall to the notoriously dark rear side road. There were hundreds of fans headed the same way and they almost engulfed the great geophysicist on the steps.

Directly below him he could see a black Range Rover, illegally parked, close to the sidewalk, no lights, facing the wrong way, with no one in the driver's seat.

Ahmed Sabah and his two colleagues chose that moment to strike from behind. They expertly rammed a black canvas bag over Paul Landon's head, holding him in an iron grip, and bundled him down the last two steps and into the back of the waiting vehicle.

There was no time to cry out, no time to fight back. An accented voice kept hissing into his ear, urging him to remain quiet unless he wanted to

6

Professor Paul Landon was one of the world's pre-eminent volcanologists, Benfield Greig Professor of Geophysical Hazards at University College, London, and Director of the university's Hazard Centre.

He had worked on the slopes of dozens of the world's most dangerous volcanoes, often successfully forecasting powerful eruptions. His nickname was well earned. And his skill in assessing the temperature and intent of the magma was matched only by his brilliance at the lectern.

A bearded man of medium height, with pale blue eyes and the inevitable tweed sports jacket, chequered shirt and college tie, he was forty-four years old and at the height of his game, his lectures in demand all over the world.

'Lava' Landon lived outside London in the commuter belt of Buckinghamshire with his wife Valerie, a City lawyer. Their two sons, aged fourteen and fifteen, collectively considered their father to be more or less insane, hearing almost every day of their young lives that the world would probably end next week.

Their scepticism didn't faze Professor Landon in the least; like many of his fellow academics he was quite astonishingly self-absorbed and fireproof to criticism. As he stood now in the hoofprints of the mighty Scott, Shackleton, Hillary and Hunt, he reflected on an evening's work well done.

He knew he had mesmerised the entire audience. What he wasn't aware of, however, was one particular listener. Seated among the sea of spellbound

5

The packed audience of ex-military and naval officers, scientists, academics and scions of ancient landed families which had always shown an interest in such scientific matters, had listened wide-eyed as the professor explained the establishment of a gigantic column of waves, ascending from the seabed to the surface, driving forward to reach speeds of 500 mph, and rising to a height of maybe 200 feet into the air as they arrived in shallow coastal waters.

He described how the monstrous tidal surge would wipe out large hunks of coastal southern England, Spain and West Africa. And then, within nine hours from the moment of the rock's impact on the surface of the Atlantic off southwestern La Palma, the massive wall of water would travel across the Atlantic and obliterate the entire East Coast of the United States.

'If Cumbre Vieja blows, this *will* happen,' he confirmed. 'A rare and terrible mega-*tsunami*. Scientific research has estimated a number of intense waves, still perhaps 150 feet high, crashing into the restricted seaways off Lower Manhattan, and then flattening the Wall Street area of New York with its very first sweep.

'The opening tidal wave would suck the debris out of the streets, and flatten the ground, before the next one of the wave series hit, demolishing buildings up to possibly fifteen blocks from the waterfront. And these giant waves – each one more than 100 feet high – would keep coming, progressively, until all of New York City was levelled.

'The biggest *tsunami* in recorded history. And all because of a single volcano.'

4

the north flank swelled into a massive balloon of lava, before exploding, blowing the mountainside asunder and obliterating nearly 400 square miles of forest.

That happened in 1980, and it led Professor Landon inevitably to the climax of his speech – the possibility of a *tsunami*, a Japanese word describing a series of mountainous waves, generated either by an earthquake or, more likely, a massive volcanic landslide into deep ocean.

Professor Landon's closing focus was on the new potential landslide on the southwest coast of La Palma, the northwesternmost of the Canary Islands. Jutting out from deep Atlantic waters, La Palma stands 375 miles off the coast of southern Morocco.

Fact was, he explained, a gigantic hunk of volcanic rock, several miles long, set on a searing fault line in the earth's crust, had slipped in the last forty or fifty years, maybe 12 feet down the steep cliff, detaching from the west flank. And somewhere behind this colossal, unstable chunk of rock, lay, potentially, the simmering core of the mighty volcano of Cumbre Vieja.

'That lets rip, the lot goes,' Professor Landon asserted, brightly. 'It'd send a staggeringly large rock, several cubic miles of it, crashing off the west flank of the volcano, straight into the Atlantic at more than 200 mph, and surging along the ocean floor, at maybe 400 mph. I'm talking about one of the largest landslides in the past million years. Actually I'm talking about the total collapse of the southwest section of La Palma.'

of the twentieth century and Professor 'Lava' Landon was that of subject. Whereas Scott, Shackleton, Hillary and Hunt had entertained with breathtaking accounts of human survival in freezing conditions, the professor had just explained in dazzling detail the forthcoming end of the world. No firm dates, of course. Like all masters of global geophysics, Professor Landon operated in approximate time-slots of 10,000 years.

The oncoming catastrophe would likely occur in around 7,000 years, he concluded. 'But then again,' he added, 'it could just as easily happen next Friday, shortly after lunch.'

The typical Royal Geographical crowd, the understated, well-heeled, scholarly English elite which occupied the auditorium, had loved the lecture. It had been meticulously planned, and flawlessly delivered, with excellent graphics and film clips.

It illuminated the mighty eruptions of volcanoes around the world, the coast-shuddering effects of tidal waves, the ravages of earthquakes. But mostly it focused on the super-eruptions of the past like the one which split Indonesia's Krakatoa apart in 1883, wiping out 36,000 residents of Java and Sumatra.

He told them of the staggering eruption of Wyoming's Yellowstone National Park volcano, which dumped molten magma and ash onto California, Texas and even onto the seabed of the Caribbean. It actually happened 650,000 years ago but 'Lava' Landon made it seem like last summer.

He produced a graphic study of the pulverising blast of Mount St Helens in Washington State, when

PROLOGUE

10.30 p.m. Thursday 8 May 2008
Kensington, London

Professor Paul Landon, known to an entire generation of university students as 'Lava' Landon, hurried through the lower ground floor doorway of the Royal Geographical Society and out into the darkness of wide, tree-lined Exhibition Road, the capital's highway of enormous museums running south from Hyde Park.

He paused on the broad greystone doorstep, a spot where many another great man had stood before him – the explorers, Captain Scott of the Antarctic and Ernest Shackleton; the first conquerors of Everest, Sir Edmund Hillary, who made the summit, and Lord Hunt, who led the historic 1953 expedition.

Like Professor Landon, they were celebrated Fellows of the Royal Geographical Society, and, like him, they had all delivered a series of stunning Spring Lectures inside the great building, at the lectern of the auditorium. Like him, they had packed the place, and held their audience spellbound.

The prime difference between the great adventurers

1

Mrs Kathy Morgan (wife of Admiral Arnold Morgan, recalled to White House)
His Excellency Mark Vollmer (United States Ambassador to Dubai)

Lt. Commander Shakira Rashood (Special Navigation and Targeting – *Barracuda II*)

Rear Admiral Ben Badr (CO *Barracuda II*)

Ship's Company *Barracuda II*

Captain Ali Akbar Mohtaj (Executive Officer)

Commander Abbas Shafii (senior submariner Iranian Navy and nuclear specialist)

Commander Hamidi Abdolrahim (Chief Nuclear Engineer)

Lt. Ashtari Mohammed (Navigation Officer)

Chief Petty Officer Ali Zahedi (Chief of Boat)

Chief Petty Officer Ardeshir Tikku (nuclear computer controls specialist)

Major Ahmed Sabah (freedom fighter and personal bodyguard to General Rashood)

Foreign Military

Colonel Dae-jung (Commandant Nuclear Operations, Kwanmo–bong Complex, North Korea)

Captain Habib Abdu Camara (Commander-in-Chief Navy of Senegal)

Civilian Connections

Professor Paul Landon (Volcanologist, University College, London)

David Gavron (Israeli Ambassador to Washington, ex-Mossad Chief)

Mr Tony Tilton (Seattle Bank President and star witness)

Admiral Frank Doran (Commander-in-Chief
Atlantic Fleet CINCLANT)
Rear Admiral Freddie Curran (Commander
Submarines Pacific Fleet COMSUBPAC)
General Kenneth Clark (Commandant United
States Marine Corps)
US General Bart Boyce (Supreme Allied Com-
mander NATO)
Rear Admiral John Bergstrom (Commander Special
War Command SPECWARCOM)

Combat Commanders
Admiral George Gillmore (Search Group Com-
mander, Task Group 201.1 – USS *Coronado*)
Captain Joe Wickman (CO USS *Simpson*)
Captain C.J. Smith (CO USS *Elrod*)
Captain Eric Nielsen (CO USS *Nicholas*)
Captain Clint Sammons (CO USS *Klakring*)
Major Blake Gill (Commander, Patriot Missile
Batteries)

US Navy Seahawk Combat Pilots
Lt. Paul Lubrano
Lt. Ian Holman
Lt. Don Brickle

Middle Eastern High Command
Admiral Mohammed Badr (Commander-in-Chief
Iranian Navy)
General Ravi Rashood (HAMAS Supreme
Commander Combat)

CAST OF PRINCIPAL CHARACTERS

Senior Command (Political)

Charles McBride (Democrat, Rhode Island – President of the United States)

Vice President Paul Bedford (Democrat, Virginia)

Cyrus Romney (National Security Adviser)

Senator Edward Kennedy (Senior Member Senate Armed Service Committee)

Bill Hatchard (President McBride's Chief-of-Staff)

Admiral Arnold Morgan (Supreme Commander Operation High Tide)

National Security Agency

Rear Admiral George R. Morris (Director)

Lt. Commander James Ramshawe (Assistant to the Director)

US Naval and Military Senior Command

General Tim Scannell (Chairman of the Joint Chiefs)

Admiral Alan Dickson (Chief of Naval Operations)

Admiral Dick Greening (Commander-in-Chief Pacific Fleet CINCPACFLT)

Published by Arrow Books in 2005

1 3 5 7 9 10 8 6 4 2

Copyright © Patrick Robinson 2004

Patrick Robinson has asserted his right under the Copyright, Designs and Patents Act
1988 to be identified as the author of this work

First published in the United Kingdom in 2004 by William Heinemann

Arrow Books
The Random House Group Limited
20 Vauxhall Bridge Road,
London, SW1V 2SA

Random House Australia (Pty) Limited
20 Alfred Street, Milsons Point, Sydney,
New South Wales 2061, Australia

Random House New Zealand Limited
18 Poland Road, Glenfield,
Auckland 10, New Zealand

Random House (Pty) Limited
Endulini, 5a Jubilee Road,
Parktown 2193, South Africa

The Random House Group Limited Reg. No. 954009

www.randomhouse.co.uk

A CIP catalogue record for this book
is available from the British Library

Papers used by Random House
are natural, recyclable products made from wood grown in
sustainable forests. The manufacturing processes conform to
the environmental regulations of the country of origin

ISBN 0 09 943986 7

Typeset in Bembo by Palimpsest Book Production Limited,
Polmont, Stirlingshire
Printed and bound in Germany by
GGP Media GmbH, Poessneck

SCIMITAR SL-2

Patrick Robinson

arrow books

Also by Patrick Robinson

Nimitz Class
Kilo Class
H.M.S. Unseen
Seawolf
The Shark Mutiny
Barracuda 945
Hunter Killer

Non-fiction
Classic Lines
Decade of Champions
The Golden Post
Born to Win
True Blue
One Hundred Days
Horsetrader

SCIMITAR SL-2

Patrick Robinson is the author of seven international bestsellers, as well as his forthcoming novel, *Hunter Killer*. He is also the author of several non-fiction bestsellers including *True Blue* (with Dan Topolski) and *Born to Win*. He is the co-author with Admiral Sir Sandy Woodward of *One Hundred Days*.

although the murder of London cops was not his business and neither, of course, was the killing of a UCL professor, he nonetheless logged a full notation about the strange and mysterious death of Paul Landon.

He found it hard to dismiss the incident from his mind. And at the end of the day, he was still puzzling over it on the way to the Australian Embassy in Washington, where he was dining with his fiancée Jane Peacock, daughter of the Ambassador. It was almost 8 p.m. before he arrived and he gratefully accepted a tall glass of cold Foster's lager from Miss Peacock before joining her parents in the dining room. Jimmy had always got along very well with Ambassador John Peacock. Their families had been friends for many years, and indeed Jimmy's parents, who lived in New York, were due to stay at the embassy two weeks from now.

He waited until they were well into the main course, a superb rib of beef, cooked to perfection and accompanied by a particularly elegant Australian red wine, Clonakilla Shiraz, made up in the Canberra district in the temperate foothills, a couple of hundred miles south of Sydney. John Peacock was a lifelong collector of good wine and owned an excellent cellar at his home overlooking the harbour in Sydney. As Australian Ambassador to the USA, he was expected to serve vintages from his own country and he rose to the occasion every time.

Jimmy waited until they were all smoothly into

a second glass before broaching the subject which had been on his mind for the past six hours.

'You ever read anything about a volcano professor in London who managed to get murdered last May, John?'

'Maybe. What was his name?'

'Professor Paul Landon.'

'Now wait a minute. I did notice something about that, because he was coming to speak at two or three universities in Australia – and one of 'em was Monash, in Melbourne, where I went. I think that's the same guy. I remember it because the Sydney newspaper ran quite a story on his death. Why d'you ask?'

'Oh, I just ran into some stuff on the internet today. Seemed such a strange murder, no rhyme or reason. No one has ever discovered why he was killed. And no one's ever been charged with anything connected to it.'

'No. I remember that. He wasn't just an expert on volcanoes. He was into the whole range of earthly disasters; you know, earthquakes, tidal waves, asteroid collisions and Christ knows what. As I recall he was coming particularly to lecture on the effect of a major tidal wave, it's got some bloody Chinese name . . . Let me think . . . chop suey, or something. Anyway, it's a lot of water.'

Jimmy chuckled. He really liked his future father-in-law, who'd insisted on being called John since Jimmy was a kid at college. 'The word we're groping for is *tsunami*,' he said. 'Japanese. I've been a bit of an expert since about quarter past two this afternoon.'

'Yes, that's it,' replied the Ambassador. 'It's when a bloody great hunk of rock falls off a mountain and crashes into the sea causing a fantastic upsurge as it rolls along the ocean floor? Right, expert?'

'Yes, I think that's a fair and thoughtful summation,' said Jimmy, frowning and putting on what he thought might be a learned voice. 'Very well put. I think in future I'll address you as "Splash" Peacock, *tsunami* authority.'

Everyone laughed at that. But the Ambassador was not finished. 'I'll tell you something else I remember about that article. The prof. was coming to Australia to talk in particular about these bloody great waves, which have happened on Pacific islands north of us. That's the danger spot, right? Your professor, Jimmy, knew a whole lot about one of 'em on New Britain Island off Papua New Guinea. It fell into the ocean and the 'ole thing developed and drowned about 3,000 people on neighbouring islands.'

'For a bloke who can't say it, you know a hell of a lot about *tsunamis*!' replied Jimmy.

'Gimme a coupla weeks, I'll master the word as well,' chuckled John Peacock.

'So why do you think someone murdered the professor?'

'Who knows? Could have been just mistaken identity, I suppose.'

'Maybe,' replied Jimmy. 'But the police think it looked like an execution.'

29

Friday 9 January 2009
The Pentagon, Washington, DC

The first memorandums were beginning to arrive from the incoming Administration. Clearly, the new President was planning to impose savage defence cuts, particularly on the Navy. He considered the expenditure of billions of dollars on surface warships and submarines to be a lunatic waste of money. And he reasoned, not without just cause, that he had been elected to do precisely that. People did not want to raise armies and battle fleets. They wanted better health care and a better start in life for their kids. The recent election had demonstrated that thoroughly. McBride had not routed the Republicans. In fact, he had only narrowly won the White House, and both Houses of Congress were still held by the GOP.

But the people had spoken. They had heard his message of hope and the chance of a better life for their families. They had listened to him rail against their own country, in which people could be bankrupted, their life's savings extinguished, just for being ill. They had listened to Charles McBride swear to God he was going to change all that. Yes, the people had spoken, no doubt about that.

It all struck home, especially in the headquarters of the veteran Chairman of the Joint Chiefs up on the Pentagon's second floor. General Tim Scannell, in the big office directly below that of the outgoing Secretary of Defense, Robert MacPherson, was not a happy man.

'I don't know how long he's likely to last. Hopefully only four years. But this bastard is probably going to inflict more damage on the US fleet than Yamamoto.'

Among those sitting opposite the Chairman was Admiral Alan Dickson, and the Chief of Naval Operations was not smiling.

'I've been in the middle of these things before,' he said. 'And it's not just the big issues. You guys know as well as I do that severe defence cuts have an effect on everything, because all over the place there are people trying to cut costs. And they usually go a step too far – no one *quite* gets the reality. Until it's too late.

'Especially the Navy. You start decommissioning carriers, mothballing amphibious ships, laying up destroyers and frigates, you're punching a major hole in the US Navy's requirements for really top guys. And when they think you don't need 'em, they don't show up at Annapolis.'

'Left-wing politicians never understand it,' answered Admiral Dick Greening, Commander-in-Chief Pacific Fleet. 'All those goddamned cities which survive on defence contracts. You stop building warships, you're not just seeing cities going broke, you're watching the unique skills of an area start to vanish. Pretty soon you end up like some Third World harbour, buying technology from abroad.'

The room went silent. 'Do you guys know what it is that really brasses me off about governments?'

said Admiral Dickson. 'The stuff no one explains to the people.'

No one spoke.

'The fact that governments don't have any money of their own,' continued Admiral Dickson. 'Only what they take from the American people and from American corporations. So when they tell the people an aircraft carrier is too expensive, they are talking absolute horseshit. They do not *spend*, in the accepted sense of the word. They only distribute. They take it from whatever source they can get it, without causing outright civil war, and then redistribute it into the economy. They don't *spend*. They only push everyone else's money around.

The Navy Chief paused. Then said, 'Half of the money in labour costs goes to the guys building the ships – paychecks to people who *immediately* give a third of it back to the government. They don't tell 'em the rest gets spent in the community, providing other people with jobs, who also hand a third of it back to the government.

'They never mention that a big hunk of the cash goes to US Steel, the electronics companies right here in the USA, the missile systems, shipbuilders in Maine, Connecticut and Virginia – they're all paying corporate taxes. Some of the money goes to US Navy personnel, who pay their taxes back to the government, just like the people at US Steel. The whole thing is just a roundabout. The god-damned aircraft carrier is not expensive, it's *free*. It's

32

not the government's damned money anyway. They are only moving it around.'

'Any clues yet about our cuts?' Rear Admiral Curran asked gravely.

'No one's been specific. But we've been put on a kind of unofficial high alert to start cutting back. I'd say the conversions on those four Ohio Class SSBNs will go on hold.'

Admiral Dickson referred to the programme to remove the Trident missiles from the old 16,600-ton strategic missile boats and turn them into guided missile platforms, each carrying 154 Tomahawks. All four submarines were to be upgraded with Acoustic Rapid COTS insertion sonar.

'I wouldn't be sure we'll keep the green light for two more Nimitz Class carriers either. CVN 77 and 78 will probably get cancelled.'

'Jesus,' said the Commander of the Atlantic Fleet, Vice Admiral Brian Ingram. 'That would be bad. Some of the big guys are just about getting to the end of their tether. We need new, and we need it now – how about the Arleigh Burke destroyer programme?'

'Well, as you know, we're supposed to get thirty-six and we only have twenty-four. I'm just not sure about the final twelve.'

'Jeez. I'd just hate to see us run short of missile ships . . . And I'd sure feel better about everything if the Big Man was still in the White House.'

By anyone's standards, this was a very worried group of US Navy execs and the Pentagon boss.

Not worried for themselves but for the future ability of United States warships to continue safeguarding the world's oceans. Whenever necessary.

And the Big Man was far away.

11.30 a.m. Tuesday 27 January 2009
Tenerife, Canary Islands
Mrs Arnold Morgan had spent the last hour of her honeymoon on her own. Relaxed on a lounger by the lower pool at the imperious Gran Hotel Bahia del Duque, way down on the southern tip of the island, she was reading quietly.

Behind her, a detail of two security agents was playing cards, and at infrequent intervals a waiter appeared to inquire if she needed more orange juice or coffee. About 100 feet above stood her new husband, ensconced in an observatory at the top of a tower; he was staring out to sea through a telescope many times more powerful than most people will ever have used.

The Canaries, with their pure Atlantic skies, attracted astronomers from all over the world, and giant telescopes have been built in observatories on every one of the seven islands. The instrument at Gran Hotel Bahia del Duque was constructed mostly with astronomers in mind, and it was generally focused on the heavens. Today, however, it looked out to the surface of the deep, blue waters to the south of the Costa Adeje, where the seabed swiftly shelves down to depths of almost a mile.

Kathy wished he'd make his way back down

and talk to her. Isolation did not suit the former goddess of the West Wing. She slipped back into her book, occasionally gazing at the magnificent surroundings of the five-star Gran Hotel, a sprawling waterside complex, half-Venetian, half-Victorian in design, set in a semi-tropical botanical garden. Her new husband adored such grandeur and he had sweetly instructed her, with his usual olde worlde charm, to locate a place and book them in for two weeks – *Listen, Kathy, just try to stop boring me sideways with goddamned hotel literature, and get us into some goddamned place, Casa Luxurious. And hasta la vista*, he had added, handing her a credit card. *That's Spanish for on the double.*

He was, of course, utterly beyond redemption and Kathy forgave him only because he treated everyone like that. As his secretary for six years in the White House she had seen diplomats from the world's most powerful countries quake before his onslaught. Especially the Chinese and almost as often the Russians.

The whole idea of this tiny cluster of Spanish islands set in the sparkling Atlantic off the coast of Africa had been hers. She had lived in Europe when she was much younger and her sister-in-law, Gayle, who lived in southern Spain had suggested the Canaries because of the January weather, which was warm, much warmer than mainland Spain, a thousand miles to the northeast. But the most significant reason for Tenerife was that Kathy had wanted to arrange a Catholic blessing for their marriage, which

35

had thus far been only legally formalised by a US Justice of the Peace in Washington.

Gayle had located the perfect little church, in the neighbouring island of Gran Canaria, the Iglesia de San Antonio Abad, down near the waterfront at Las Palmas, the island's main town. She had arranged for the English-speaking priest to meet Arnold and Kathy on Friday morning and conduct a short private service.

Only after their arrival did Kathy plan to tell her husband that San Antonio, unprepossessing, painted white and Romanesque in design, was the very church where Christopher Columbus had prayed for divine help before sailing for the Americas.

The Great Modern American Patriot and the Great European Adventurer: two naval commanding officers somehow united at the same altar, separated by the centuries, but not in spirit. Yes, Kathy thought, Arnold would like that. He'd like that very much, the secret romantic that he ultimately was.

So it was settled. A honeymoon in the Canaries. And even the globally sophisticated Arnold had been taken aback by the sheer opulence of the place, the terra cotta exteriors, five swimming pools, the perfect al fresco dining area on the terraces looking down to the soft sandy beaches.

'And here he is, up the stupid tower, for the fourth day in a row,' thought Kathy. 'With the telescope, presumably looking for the enemy.'

Just at that moment, the former National Security

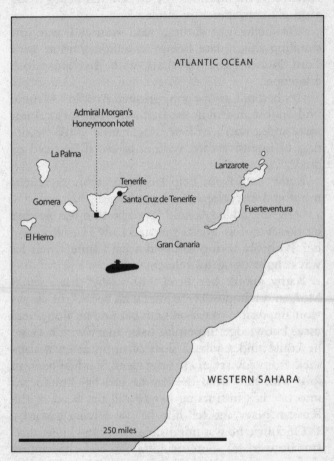

ATLANTIC OCEAN

Admiral Morgan's
Honeymoon hotel

La Palma

Lanzarote

Tenerife
Santa Cruz de Tenerife

Gomera

Fuerteventura

El Hierro

Gran Canaria

WESTERN SAHARA

250 miles

THE CANARY ISLANDS - SEVEN VOLCANIC RISES
OFF THE COAST OF NORTH AFRICA

Adviser to the President of the United States made a timely appearance poolside.

'Oh hello, my darling,' said Kathy. 'I was just thinking this is like being on a honeymoon with Lord Nelson, you up there with that ridiculous telescope.'

'It's better, I assure you,' grunted Arnold. 'Admiral Nelson lost an arm in the Battle of Santa Cruz about forty miles north of here. Right now you'd be sitting in intensive care, waiting to see if he lived or died.'

Kathy could not help laughing at his mercurial mind and encyclopaedic knowledge.

'Anyway,' added Arnold, 'Lord Nelson was not big on honeymoons. Never married Lady Hamilton, did he? Probably trying to avoid a hard time when he was caught using his telescope.'

Kathy shook her head. She knew that Arnold Morgan was impossible to joust with because he always won, impossible to reason with because he always had more knowledge, impossible to be angry with because he could find a joke, a shaft of irony, or even slapstick, from any set of circumstances. She had been in love with him from the day he had first thundered into her life, instructing her to call the head of the Russian Navy and tell him he was a lying bastard.

Of course he was impossible. Everyone knew that. But he was also more exciting, fun and challenging than any man she had ever met. He was more than twenty years older, an inch shorter and the most confident person in the White House. He cared nothing for rank, only for truth. The former President had plainly been afraid of him, afraid of his absolute devotion to the flag, the country and its safety.

To the former Kathy O'Brien, when Arnold Morgan pulled himself up to his full five feet, eight and a half inches, he seemed not one inch short of 10 feet. In her mind, and in the mind of many others, she had married the world's shortest giant.

It seemed incredible that he was gone from the West Wing. Kathy, a veteran of the White House secretarial staff, simply could not imagine what it would be like without the caged lion in the office of the President's National Security Adviser taking the flak, taking the strain and laying down the law about 'what's right for this goddamned country'.

Whoever the new President decided to appoint in the admiral's place, he'd need some kind of a hybrid John Wayne, Henry Kissinger, Douglas MacArthur. And he wasn't going to find one of those. The only one in captivity was, at this moment, sprawled out next to Kathy, holding her hand and telling her he loved her, that she was the most wonderful person he ever had or ever would meet.

And now, he announced, he was going to take a swim. Four days in Tenerife had already seen him acquire a deepening tan, which contrasted strikingly with his steel-grey close-cut hair. Even as he approached senior citizenship Arnold still had tree-trunk legs, heavily muscled arms and a waistline only marginally affected by a lifelong devotion to roast beef sandwiches with mayonnaise and mustard.

He was pretty smooth in the water too. Kathy watched him moving along the pool with a cool, professional-looking crawl, breathing every two strokes, just turning his head slightly into the trough of the slipstream for a steady pull of air. He looked as if he could, if necessary, swim like that for a year.

Kathy decided to join him and dived into the pool as he went past, surfacing alongside him and slipping into a somewhat laboured form of sidestroke. As always, it was difficult to keep up with the admiral.

When finally they came in to rest on the hotel loungers, Arnold made a further announcement. 'I'm taking you to see something tomorrow,' he said. 'The place where scientists predict there will be the greatest natural disaster the earth has ever seen.'

'I thought you said that was due to happen in the White House next month?'

'Well, the second greatest then,' he replied, chuckling at his sassy new wife.

'What is it?' she asked absently, turning back to her book.

'It's a volcano,' he said, darkly.

'Not another,' she murmured. 'I just married one of those.'

'I suppose it would be slightly too much to ask you to pay attention?'

'No, I'm ready. I'm all ears. Go to it, Admiral.'

'Well, just about 60 miles from here, to the northwest, is the active volcanic island of La Palma. It's only about a third of the size of Tenerife, pear-shaped, tapering off narrowly to the south –'

'You sound like a guide book.'

'Well, not quite, but it's an interesting book that I found by the telescope.'

'What book?'

'Honey, please. Kathryn Morgan, please pay attention. I have just been reading, rather carefully, a very fascinating account of the neighbouring island of La Palma and its likely affect on the future of the world. You may have thought I was just goofing off looking through the telescope. But I actually wasn't –'

'You abandoned the telescope! Then it's surprising Tenerife hasn't come under attack in the last couple of hours. That's all I can say.' Mrs Kathy Morgan was now laughing at her own humour. So for that matter was her husband. 'If you're not darn careful you'll come under attack,' he said. 'You want me to tell you about the end of the world or not?'

'Ooh, yes please, my darling. That would be lovely.'

'Right. Now listen up.' He sounded precisely like the old nuclear submarine commanding officer he once had been. A martinet of the deep. Stern, focused, ready to handle any backtalk from anyone. Except Kathy, who always disarmed him.

'The southerly part of La Palma has a kind of backbone,' he said. 'A high ridge, running due south clean down the middle. This volcanic fault line, about three miles long, takes its name from its main volcano, Cumbre Vieja, which rises four miles up from the seabed, with only the top mile and a half

41

visible. It's had seven eruptions in the last 500 years. The fault fissure, which runs right along the crest, developed after the eruption of 1949. Basically the goddamned west side of the range is falling into the goddamned sea, from a great height.'

Kathy giggled at his endlessly colourful way of describing any event, military, financial, historical, or in this case geophysical.

'Pay attention,' said the admiral. 'Now, way to the south is Volcan San Antonio, a giant black crater. They just completed a new visitors centre with amazing close-up views. Then you can drive south to see Volcan Teneguia, that's the last one, which erupted here, back in 1971. You can climb right up there and take a look into the crater if you like.'

'No thanks.'

'But the main one is Cumbre Vieja itself, about eight miles to the north. That's the big one, and it's been rumbling in recent years. According to the book, if that blew it would be the single biggest world disaster for a million years . . .'

'Arnold, you are prone, at times, to exaggeration. And because of this I ask you one simple question. How could a rockfall in this remote and lonely Atlantic island possibly constitute a disaster on the scale you are saying?'

The admiral prepared his sabre, then metaphorically slashed the air with it. '*Tsunami*, Kathryn,' he said. 'Mega-*tsunami*.'

'No kidding?' she said. 'Rye or pumpernickel?'

'Jesus Christ!' said the President's former National

42

Security Adviser. 'Right now, Kathy, I'm at some kind of an intersection, trying to decide whether to leave you here looking sensational in that bikini but overwhelmed by ignorance, or whether to lead you to the sunny uplands of knowledge. Depends a lot on your attitude.'

Kathy leaned over and took his hand. 'Take me to the uplands,' she said. 'You know I'm only teasing you, you want some of that orange juice? It's fabulous.'

She stood up easily, walked three paces and poured him a large glass. The Spanish oranges were every bit as good as the crop from Florida, and the admiral drained the glass before beginning what he called an attempt to educate the unreachable.

'Fresh,' he said, approvingly. 'A lot like yourself.'

The third, and most beautiful, Mrs Arnold Morgan leaned over again and kissed him.

Christ, he thought. *How the hell did I ever get this lucky?*

'*Tsunami*,' he said again. 'Do you know what a *tsunami* is?'

'Not offhand. What is it?'

'It's the biggest tidal wave in the world. A wall of water which comes rolling in from the ocean, and doesn't break in the shallows like a normal wave – just keeps coming, holding its shape, straight across any damn thing that gets in its way. They can be 50 feet high.'

'You mean if one of 'em hit Rehobeth Beach or somewhere near our flat Maryland shore it would just roll straight over the streets and houses?'

'That's what I mean,' he said, pausing. 'But there is something worse. It's called a mega-*tsunami*. And that's what can end life as we know it. Because according to that book up by the telescope, those waves can be 150 feet high. A mega-*tsunami* could wipe out the entire East Coast of the USA.'

Kathy was thoughtful. 'How 'bout that?' she said quietly, feeling somewhat guilty about the lightly frivolous way she had treated Arnold's brand new knowledge. 'I still don't see how a volcano could cause such an uproar – aren't they just big slow old things with a lot of very slow molten rock running down the slopes?'

'Aha. That's where La Palma comes in ... Cumbre Vieja last erupted about forty years ago, and the scientists later discerned a massive slippage on the western, seaward flank. Maybe 12 feet downwards.'

'That's not much.'

'It is if the rock face is eight miles long, and the whole lot is slipping, at a great height above sea level, sending a billion tons of rock at terrific speed, straight down to the ocean floor. That will be the biggest *tsunami* the world has ever seen –'

'Are they sure about that?'

'Dead sure. There's a couple of universities in America and I think Germany with entire departments experimenting with the possible outcomes of a mega-*tsunami* developing in the Canary Islands.'

'Did one of them publish the stuff in the book you read?'

'No. That was done by a couple of English professors at London University. Both of 'em very big deals by the sound of it. One of 'em's called Day, the other one Sarandon, I think. They sounded like guys who knew what they were saying.'

9.30 a.m. the following day
At the insistence of his two armed agents, the admiral and his wife chartered a private plane to take them over to La Palma, an elderly ATR-72 turbo prop which was only slightly more silent and restful than a train crash. They took off from little Reino Sofia Airport, only five miles from their hotel, and shuddered, shook and rumbled their way up the west coast of Tenerife, past the main resort areas and along the spectacular coastline. Before the northwest headland of Punta Teno they veered out to sea, crossing Atlantic waters almost two miles deep. They touched down at the little airport four miles south of Santa Cruz de la Palma at 9.25 in the morning.

A car and chauffeur awaited them. Actually two cars and one chauffeur. The agents, which had accompanied them, would follow in the second automobile. A condition of Admiral Morgan's original appointment to the White House had been that he would be provided with round-the-clock protection for a minimum of five years, effective immediately upon his retirement. In the US he had a detail of four agents, working shifts, twenty-four hours a day. Two of them had been designated to accompany the former NSA on his honeymoon.

The admiral was now a wealthy man. His full vice admiral's pension had been accruing since he had left the Navy, almost ten years previously. He had no children to educate, no alimony to pay, no mortgage. He had sold his house in Maryland, and moved into Kathy's much grander home in Chevy Chase. This too carried no mortgage; Kathy had a liberal trust fund, provided by a rich but unfaithful first husband, and she too had been able to bank most of her salary over the last six years while Admiral Morgan took care of regular expenses. Together, Arnold and Kathy had a net worth of several million dollars. Sufficient for the admiral to have tossed straight into the bin two $5 million offers from New York publishing houses for his memoirs. Neither received even the courtesy of a reply.

Stepping down onto the runway, dressed in a dark blue polo shirt, smartly pressed stone-coloured shorts, no socks, tan Gucci loafers and a white Panama hat, the admiral was unable to avoid looking precisely what he was, ex-government, ex-Navy, a powerful man, not to be trifled with. No bullshit.

'The car's over here, sir,' said Harry, Arnold's longtime secret service agent. 'The front one of those three black Mercedes parked outside the building.'

They walked across the already warm runway under a cloudless blue sky. Harry held open the rear door. The admiral jumped in first and slid across the back seat. Harry continued to hold the door for Kathy, nodded his head curtly and said, 'Mrs Morgan.'

Ten years earlier, Agent Harry had once asked the

svelte newly divorced Kathy O'Brien if she'd care to go out to dinner with him. She had politely declined, and now the memory of that innocent but toe-curling piece of misjudgement actually gave Harry acute chills on the rare occasions he allowed himself to recall the incident.

With Mrs Morgan safely on board, the chauffeur moved slowly out of the airport, while Harry, now at the wheel of the second Mercedes, fell in behind him, line astern, as the admiral insisted on putting it. They drove south, towards the very tip of La Palma, all along the coastal highway for around 10 miles, before arriving at the little town of Los Canarios de Fuencaliente, which used to be a spa, dotted by hot springs. The most recent eruption in 1971 had buried them, to become great lakes deep in the underground caverns of cooled-off lava.

Now, the whitewashed outpost of Fuencaliente served as a kind of volcano mission-control area, with signposts everywhere, pointing the way up to the great line of craters and mountains which patiently guarded the future of planet earth.

The big white board, which proclaimed Volcan St Antonio above a black painted arrow, instantly caught the admiral's eye. 'Straight up there, Pedro,' he told the chauffeur, checking his stern arcs through the rear window to ensure Harry was still in strict convoy.

Kathy, who was fiddling with the digital camera Arnold had just bought her, complete with all bells and whistles, even a telephoto lens, said distractedly, 'How d'you know he's called Pedro?'

'Well, I'm not dead certain. But many people in Spain are called Pedro or Miguel, like Peter or Michael in the States.'

'God help me,' said Kathy. 'Darling, you can't go around making up names for people. It's rude. Like me suddenly calling you Fred.'

'Oh, I agree you couldn't do it with Americans. But the odds are stacked in your favour in Spain. Or anywhere in Arabia. Mohammed, Mustapha or Abdul. Can't miss.'

'Still, it's rude. Just like you shouldn't go around calling every dark-skinned man a towelhead.' Admiral Morgan muttered something and, despite herself, Kathy laughed. And she tapped the chauffeur on the shoulder. 'Excuse me,' she said. 'Could you tell me your name?'

'Oh, sure, *señora*. It's Pedro.'

'How did you know?' she demanded, smelling a rat and turning back to Arnold.

'Harry told me,' replied the admiral.

Kathy rolled her eyes heavenwards.

Which was more or less where they were headed. The Mercedes was now revving its way up a very steep escarpment, through the pines, towards the yawning chasm at the peak of the great black cone on the top of the mountain.

Recent rumblings inside this sixty-year dormant volcano had caused officials to cordon off the rim of the crater to all visitors. But Harry was already out, talking to the guard and explaining the precise identity of the man in the Panama hat.

The guard waved Admiral Morgan and his wife through and they wandered companionably up to the very edge of the crater, staring down into the abyss. Up ahead of them they could see another group of four people, all men, taking photographs of the area, and obviously heading north, along the tourist paths, up the great ridge of the mountains. Two large golf carts were parked nearby.

'Can we get a couple of those?' asked the admiral.

'Lemme check with the guard,' said Harry, who returned three minutes later with the good news that one big cart, a four-seater, was on its way up from the Visitor's Centre.

'Beautiful,' said Arnold. 'That way we can ride right up to Cumbre Vieja and then I'd like to take the car down to the coast road to see the cliffs above the ocean.'

The excursion in the cart revealed some spectacular scenery, all along the lava fields, the Ruta de Los Volcanos, across the rugged range of mountains, sometimes redolent with thick light-green Canary pines, sometimes just a stone wilderness, in which the golf cart bumped and lurched across terrain which had been molten rock less than forty years earlier. In many places on top of the ridge it was possible to see the Atlantic both to the east and the west. But they were not sure the battery on the electric-powered golf cart would make it all the way down to the west coast, and they elected to turn back, pick up the car and drive on down in comfort. Ninety minutes later they found themselves parked at the top of a gigantic cliff of black basalt rock, towering over a strange black sandy beach hundreds of feet below, beaten by the seemingly endless breakers of the Atlantic.

They were parked in a rough, flat clearing, and there was only one other car, another black Mercedes, just beyond them. Photographing the cliff were the same four people they had seen on the rim of Volcan St Antonio. They were all swarthy in appearance, with short, curly black hair, but somehow not Spanish. And despite their phalanx of cameras draped around their necks they were not Japanese either. Arabs, from the looks of them.

'What the hell?' muttered Arnold. 'What are they doing up here photographing the landscape and getting in our way?'

'I can't really help you there, my darling,' said Kathy. 'They never even bothered to leave a copy of their tour plan in the car –'

'Goddamned towelh –,' growled the admiral, but in a gesture of deference to his wife he checked himself, swallowing the rest of his exclamation.

Two minutes later the other Mercedes took off, driving swiftly south. And when Pedro finally began to head back south himself, they spotted the other Mercedes up ahead, parked again, its occupants still photographing fiercely, both with cinecameras and stills.

'Pull over, Pedro,' said the admiral. 'Let's take another look at the view. Park as close to the other car as you can without crowding 'em.'

Sure enough, the photographers had found another prime spot. There was a slight crescent shape to the bay, winding away towards the north, and it offered a spectacular vista, from one of the highest points on the western coast.

Arnold didn't really think much of it; it was simply that his job was so deeply engrained in his personality and mind. By sea, the admiral was paranoid about submarines and on land, since 9/11, he was unable to look at an Arab without thinking, *goddamned terrorist*. Of course many other operatives in US Intelligence thought much the same, but, being Arnold, he had to act upon it in some fashion.

As soon as the car came to a halt Arnold Morgan was out, walking back to Harry and the other agent. His instructions were terse. Get a hold of the camera in the back seat of my car, and then start taking pictures of Kathy and me. Use the telephoto lens, get the guys nice and close.

'Yes, sir.'

There were probably 30 yards between the two groups, and Harry did his job admirably. The Arabs seemed to notice that the other visitors' camera was aimed their way, because they quickly looked away. But not quickly enough. Harry had them all clearly, except for one whom he only managed to catch from the side and back. But in one way or another, all four of them were now sharply recorded in Kathy's digital.

'Could you by any chance tell me what all that was about?' asked Kathy as they began the drive back around the southern headland and on to the airport.

'Well, I don't think those people were really tourists,' replied the admiral. 'No wives, no girlfriends. Very serious. Kinda got the impression they had a purpose. You know, stopping and taking a lot of pictures of the cliff.'

'Well, they could have been compiling a book. *Great Atlantic Coastlines*,' said Kathy. 'Or scouting out a location for a movie. Or working for the Canary Islands tourist board, preparing a new brochure. Or working for a hotel or development corporation, looking at new sights with amazing ocean views, anything. After all, we were standing right on the top of one of the great volcano ranges in the world . . .'

'Yeah. I know,' he replied. 'And I don't think anyone's thinking of building much up there, not with Cumbre Vieja rumbling away beneath our feet. Fast way to lose your hotel, right?

'I don't know,' he mused, slowly. 'I just had a feeling about those guys . . . how they kept showing up. And now I got a little record of 'em. And I just might ask young Ramshawe to have a shot at identifying 'em.'

'Can he do that?'

'Not if they are entirely obscure. But you never know . . .'

'I'll tell you one thing, though,' said Kathy. 'If that whole western side of the ridge suddenly collapsed into the ocean, that sure would make a major splash.'

'Wouldn't it?' answered the admiral. 'The mother of all splashes.'

CHAPTER TWO

1500 Wednesday 27 May 2009
East Coast Highway, North Korea

They were just north of the seaport city of Wonsan and the Chinese-built off-road military juggernaut was rumbling up the strangely deserted road. To the right stretched a long expanse of jagged coastline, guarded from the great rollers off the Sea of Japan only by a few tiny islands, which could be seen in the distance.

This was rugged country, the 'highway' cleaving its way north for 200 miles into the extreme northeast where China, North Korea and Russia converge, some 80 miles south of Vladivostok.

The HAMAS general in the front passenger seat was accompanied by his personal bodyguard, his brother-in-law and veteran HAMAS combat commander Ahmed Sabah, who sat quietly in the rear seat cradling a fully primed AK-47. The general stared through the windshield without speaking. The language was just too damned strange, the people too odd, the country too foreign, for any attempt at social chat with the Korean Army driver.

Ravi Rashood was numb with boredom. Here in what might be the world's most secretive country, a police-state throwback to the dark ages of communism, he felt so out of place, so utterly estranged from anything he had ever known, that he was at a loss for perspective. He looked over at the driver, whose uniform was without military insignia save for a small metal badge showing a portrait of the 'Dear Leader', Kim Jong-il, presumed insane by most of the Western world but a God-like presence to the people of North Korea. A red rim surrounded the driver's badge, signifying his military rank.

Kim Jong-il's father, the late Kim il-Sung, was believed to be The Greatest Leader Ever in the history of the world, including the likes of Genghis Khan, Alexander the Great, Julius Caesar, Washington, Charlemagne, Napoleon, Mao, Gandhi and Churchill. North Korean children had to learn a hymn to Kim – *The Greatest Genius the World Has Ever Known* – and sing it daily. Huge portraits of him adorned cities, towns, villages and parks. His words were still regarded as the Will of Heaven.

Kim's fat little son, Kim Jong-il quickly matched his father's near-immortality, and loudspeakers proclaimed his undisputed family greatness on the streets, in cities and towns throughout the land. Undisputed that is unless you didn't mind jail or even execution. The twenty-first-century regime of Kim Jong-il did not tolerate dissent in any form whatsoever. Which at least simplified the issue – *Love the Dear Leader or else* . . .

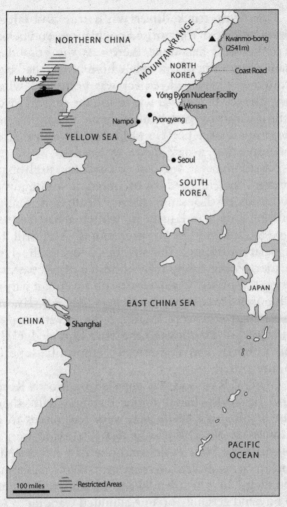

THE 'PRIVATE' NUCLEAR MENACE AROUND THE YELLOW SEA -
NORTH KOREA'S WEAPONS FACTORIES - CHINA'S SUBMARINE BASE

The Army truck driver was a true and faithful representative of a terrorised population. And behind his enigmatic half-smile there was the zombified, blank expression of a people whose morale had been shattered, whose self-respect was gone and whose only chance of survival was to toe the line and worship the earthly god Kim – always making certain there was a large portrait of him in the house, ready for inspection, as laid down by the law.

North Korea was an Orwellian nightmare, forever on the borders of outright famine with hundreds of thousands already dead from malnutrition. This was Russia in winter a half-century ago, Stalinesque in its procedures. And still the populace thronged the streets, cheering the Dear Leader, as the tubby little monster drove past, the living tsar of one of the worst-run sovereign nations since the Dark Ages. And every day, all day, and all night if you were listening, the government of Kim Jong-il broadcasted the 'true knowledge' that this country, was intrinsically, ethnically superior to any other.

General Rashood was appalled by North Korea. And he really hated doing business with them. But in his game there were very few places to do business at all. For part of his job made him an international arms dealer, and one of a rare breed: a nuclear arms dealer, an arena near-silent, clandestine and illegal, in which hardly anyone admitted wanting to buy and certainly no one admitted wanting to sell.

Aside from a somewhat seedy part of Bosnia,

North Korea was very nearly the only game in town. This dastardly, friendless little pariah of a state, trapped between China, Russia and Japan, had been making the components for nuclear weapons for many, many years, and cared not a jot for the International Treaty of Non-Proliferation.

For years, since back in 1974 when they first joined the International Atomic Energy Agency (IAEA), Korea had been a clear and obvious problem to the West, constantly trying to produce plutonium, endlessly trying to produce SCUD missiles for sale to the Middle East.

But in 1985, against everyone's most optimistic forecasts, Kim il-Sung signed the Nuclear Non-Proliferation Treaty (NPT), promising not to produce a bomb and to open all nuclear sites to inspection.

That same year the North Koreans started to build a 200 megawatt reactor which could produce enough plutonium to make seven to ten bombs a year. Separately that same year they started to build large plant to process plutonium into weapon-ready form.

Twelve months later they had a 30 megawatt reactor on line producing plutonium. In 1987 they missed the first eighteen-month deadline for international inspection. A few months later they delivered 100 SCUD-B missiles to Iran.

For the next two years they refused inspections and continued to build reactors, which would create plutonium. They consistently sold SCUD missiles to Syria and Iran.

By 1992 the IAEA concluded the latest nuclear declarations by North Korea – some 90 grams of plutonium! – was fraudulent, and demanded access to Yongbyon, the ultra secretive underground nuclear plant which lies 50 miles north of the capital city of Pyongyang. They did not get it.

A year later, both China and Russia had cut off all aid to the Republic of North Korea. And the US demanded that Kim il-Sung come clean and show his nuclear hand like everyone else. North Korea immediately barred all IAEA inspectors, and threatened to drop out of the NPT altogether.

Finally, in mid-1994, North Korea quit the IAEA. President Clinton, ever eager for compromise, agreed that the US would provide North Korea with two lightwater reactors and 500,000 tonnes of heavy fuel oil per annum if only the new Dear Leader, the hideous Kim Jong-il, would rejoin the IAEA and the NPT, and 'normalise economic relations' between North Korea and the US. It would end up costing the US taxpayer $20 to $30 million per year, and they called it the 'Agreed Framework'.

In 1995, less than one year after the Clinton deal, the head of the CIA, John Deutsch, estimated that North Korea's new No-dong-1 missile would be deployed within a year, and that the North Koreans were continuing under the most secretive circumstances to work on nuclear, chemical and biological warheads. The constant warnings of the US Intelligence community were essentially ignored by the Administration.

By the spring of 1997 the situation had deteriorated. It was obvious that Kim Jong-il was producing plutonium.

Evidence was building. A defector, a high-ranking North Korean general, fled to China and published a paper confirming that his former country did indeed have nuclear weapons, which could be used against South Korea and Japan. The brilliant US satellite Big Bird picked up sensational pictures of heavy activity in the sprawling Yongbyon nuclear facility, much of which is located underground. The warnings of a new defector, Choon Sun Lee, a senior official in North Korea's giant military infrastructure, of top-secret underground plutonium production and weapons development were almost certainly correct.

In June 1998 Kim Jong-il's government declared it would continue to develop and export nuclear-capable missiles. The US Intelligence community, almost beside itself with concern, issued warning after warning that North Korea had built a huge underground facility that might be either a nuclear reactor or reprocessing plant and a report from Bill Richardson's Department of Energy claimed to have evidence that North Korea was undoubtedly working on uranium-enrichment techniques – which meant, broadly, turning that lethal substance into weapons-grade nuclear explosive.

Four months later the National Security Agency in Fort Meade, in the person of the aggressive Admiral Arnold Morgan, practically bellowed down the phone to the President that North Korea had between 25 and 30 kilograms of weapons-grade plutonium, enough to make several nuclear warheads.

By the year 2002, things were on their way from moderate to diabolical. It was now clear that Kim Jong-il had already produced a formidable arsenal of SCUD missiles for sale to anyone who needed them.

The writings of Choon Sun Lee came rushing back to haunt everyone involved. Choon had sworn that the great mountain of Chun-Ma had been hollowed out to house a secret uranium-processing plant. He described a massive tunnel, extending more than a mile into the mountain, opening into underground facilities housed in chambers carved out of the rock. In one of them there was a plant to turn uranium ore into yellowcake, the first step towards enriching it into weapons-grade material.

US Intelligence considered Choon's observations to be too detailed to be false, and it all stacked up accurately with their own satellite observations of the existence of vast, mysterious excavations, twenty-two of them, in the mountains of North Korea. If you believed Choon, the West was staring at a nuclear empire operational under the reign of Kim Jong-il.

And Choon was by no means finished. He described every aspect of the ore's removal by truck and helicopter to an underground facility in a hidden valley. A third major defector came forward, announcing in 2002 that the great mountain of Kwanmo-bong, 270 miles to the northwest of

Pyongyang, and at almost 8,000 feet the second highest peak in the country, had been hollowed out by an army of thousands, at night, sandbag by sandbag, to house yet another secret nuclear plant.

Everything erupted into an icy standoff in December 2002. The Americans located a Korean freighter near Socotra Island off the coast of Yemen and requested a nearby warship from the Spanish Navy to apprehend it. A few hours later the Spaniards fired several broadsides over the ship's bows, forcing it to stop, and then boarded. The *So-San*, which flew no flag, contained fifteen SCUD missiles, large as life, carefully hidden under a cargo of 40,000 sacks of North Korean cement. There were, in addition, 15 conventional warheads, 23 tanks of nitric acid (rocket propellant) and 85 drums of unspecified chemical. Kim's men had finally been caught red-handed.

But before the US could roar its disapproval, North Korea announced it would immediately restart the nuclear reactors at Yongbyon and resume operations producing electricity. A total lie. They'd never ceased operations, and what the reactors really produced was plutonium; plutonium for nuclear warheads. Kim seemed to think he could best operate his country's economy by becoming an illegal nuclear arms dealer, selling weapons-grade plutonium, medium- and short-range missiles and warheads. It was hard to imagine a more antagonistic marketing plan, deliberately designed to infuriate the Americans, especially a Republican Administration which was essentially fed up to the back teeth with rogue states and uncooperative, pain-in-the-ass foreigners.

The international inspectors now claimed they were unable to continue monitoring the North Korean facility. And Kin Jong-il expelled them all within a few more days.

As the first decade of the twenty-first century wore on, the reactors at Yongbyon continued to harvest plutonium, and reports arrived daily at Fort Meade that the big cog in the Korean nuclear wheel had undoubtedly become the great mountain of Kwanmo-bong, in the remote northeast, only 25 miles from the Chinese border.

It was to this hidden underground plant that General Ravi Rashood was now headed. Deep inside that mountain, he hoped, was the one weapon which would drive the hated Americans out of the Middle East forever.

He did not even pretend to understand the oriental mind. All he knew was that North Korea had a reputation for on-time, no-questions-asked delivery. Their product was not cheap, in fact everything carried a risk premium, bumping up the price to compensate the Koreans for any unhappy circumstances which might befall them as a result of their manufacturing policies.

Very few people from the outside world had been permitted to see the North Korean nuclear facilities, certainly not inside the enormous mountain caverns, which housed the plant. But the HAMAS general, whom the Koreans swiftly identified as a major customer, had insisted on stringent terms for his acceptance of the product.

Yes, he would accept the ex-factory terms. As soon as his order left the plant, it became the property, and its journey to a seaport the responsibility, of HAMAS. The Koreans would accept no liability for accident.

General Rashood assumed this meant that if the whole lot accidentally disappeared somewhere on the highway, the Koreans would still be owed the money. He told them he would agree only if he and his men watched and supervised the loading, and travelled with the product trans-North Korea to the waiting ship. In the end he accepted that there would be just one Korean driver for the 300-mile journey to the western seaport of Nampo.

He had been told that North Korea, which is about the size of the state of Mississippi, had a population of twenty-four million, half of whom lived in Pyongyang. But even after driving halfway across the country, miles upon miles through a deserted, rugged landscape, he had no idea where the others lived. Only occasionally were there small fishing villages clustered to his right, on the shores of the Sea of Japan.

Ravi had been allowed no insights or prior knowledge before entering the country. There were no photographs or promotional handouts demonstrating the excellence of Korean manufacturing. He was just given a map of the country, showing the main towns and roads, and a driver to take him to the factory inside Kwanmo-bong.

The only other facts the general knew about North Korea were military – that this ridiculous, backward Third World outcast owned the third largest army in the world, with 1.2 million men under arms – as opposed to 650,000 in the south. One quarter of Korea's GDP was spent annually on their armed forces and yet their Navy was a very modest Navy, their Air Force large but mostly obsolete.

The place gave Ravi the creeps. But he had no time to worry about that. In a couple of hours he would need to be on high alert and he stared straight ahead, thinking, while the big Army truck clattered along the coastal highway.

They came roaring through the towns of Hamhung and Pukchong and followed the north-eastern Korean railroad to Kilju and Chilbosan. Another 20 miles and his driver would veer left off the main road onto what looked like a track – only this one would be a 15-mile track, into the foothills of the mountains, and then cleaving a long upward path through the granite range. Wooden guardhouses would stand sentinel on either side, every half-mile. Almost nowhere along this sinister highway was it possible to be out of sight of the armed patrols. It was, without question, the most secret of all roads, befitting this most secretive of all nations.

For General Rashood it meant the end of a long journey, starting essentially in Moscow, although he had not gone there personally. Here, the formal inquiry from the Iranian Navy, requesting the purchase of a number of RADUGA SS-N-21 cruise missiles, two of them equipped with 200 kiloton nuclear warheads, had been met with a stony silence, and just one question – *Do you intend to have them fitted into your* Barracuda *submarine?*

The Iranians valued their relationship with the Russian Navy and were not about to tell a flagrant lie. Their affirmative reply had led the Russian Navy to inform them they were unable to supply the RADUGAs under any circumstances whatsoever.

Next stop Beijing. The Iranians asked if they could produce a missile precisely copying the RADUGA. It was a question which elicited an immense amount of hemming and hawing from the Chinese, who finally admitted that, after having been so closely involved with the HAMAS mission of *Barracuda I* in the USA, the last thing they needed now was for *Barracuda II*, with a boatload of nuclear-capable Chinese-made missiles, to be discovered by the Americans, in brazen conflict with the Non-Proliferation Treaty.

In general terms, the Chinese were not averse to assisting their friends and clients in the Middle East. They had an extremely serious interest in the oilfields around the Gulf, and were prepared to run certain risks while helping the occasional rogue regime. But that did not include arming the second *Barracuda* for these wild men from the Middle East to cause havoc. Too dangerous. Not good for business. Americans can get cross with Muslims. Not China.

They did not really have a missile which would be readily adaptable to convert to the RADUGA dimensions anyway. They probably had the guidance and tracking software, cunningly acquired from the Americans in the 1990s, but they were less confident in their own hardware, especially for short-range cruises.

Which left General Rashood with few options, the most unlikely of which was the little state of Bosnia, where Jugoimport, a state-owned conglomerate in Belgrade, was reputed to have been working with Iraq to develop a cruise missile. Jugoimport was also reported to be working with the military operation Orao Arms, located in Bijeljina, the second largest city in the Bosnian Serb Republic, up in the northeast.

Orao had claimed only to have helped repair Iraqi warplanes, but the cruise missile evidence was damning, and it was obvious that Orao knew a) how to make a guided missile, and b) how to propel it for fairly long distances. Every arms dealer in the Middle East knew they had considerable expertise in the field of warheads. And for that reason General Rashood had undertaken the journey there from Syria.

But there had been too many gaps. The personnel at Orao were hard working and ambitious. They had scientists working night and day trying to perfect nuclear warheads. But they were not there yet. They were superb in propulsion, and very competent with the guidance software. But General

Rashood wanted precision, guaranteed workmanship, which would work first time, every time.

The general demanded massive penalty clauses should there be a malfunction. The Bosnians thought long and hard about the huge income from the HAMAS operation but the risk was too great. HAMAS would clearly have had problems persuading a court of international law to uphold their delivery contracts. But the Orao executive had an uncanny feeling that if they failed to make reparations for malfunction, this cold-eyed Middle Eastern military chief would not hesitate to have them taken off the map.

They were correct about that, but everyone parted friends. The last words one of the scientists uttered to General Rashood before he flew home to Damascus were: *You must go to North Korea. They can sell you what you want. They have the technology and much more experience than we do.*

And now he was looking for the left turn, the track up through the foothills of the Hamgyong-Sanmaek range, the one which led to the nuclear complex inside Kwanmo-bong.

And General Rashood looked grim as he considered his awesome checklist – dimensions, fuel requirements, software for the detonation. And, above all, cost. He was about to spend close to $500 million on a magazine of missiles, eighteen cruise with a standard warhead. Two with nuclear warheads, 200 kilotons of explosive each.

Barracuda I had been purchased with a full

complement of RAGUDA cruises already aboard, so he knew almost to the inch what they should look like. The big Russian shells were grey in colour with SS-N-21 Sampson (RK-55 Granat) in small Russian letters painted on the underside.

They were 26 feet long, 18 inches wide, with a launch weight of almost one and three-quarter tons. They carried a single nuclear warhead packing a 200-kiloton wallop. RADUGA flies at Mach 0.7, 680 mph, 200 feet above the surface with a range of 1,620 nautical miles. Launched from a standard 21-inch torpedo tube, the RADUGA's wings, mounted towards the stern, unfold immediately it blasts clear of the water. The missile is essentially land-attack, and operates on a terrain-following system, guided by a radar altimeter. It's accurate to about 100 yards. Plenty for General Rashood's purposes.

In a world full of big business, nothing was much bigger than his. Nothing was more ruthless. And nothing was more dangerous. He just hoped the North Korean technicians could now justify their low bows, confident smiles and promises he had seen when last he had been here.

As they approached the first gate along the track, he was not looking forward to any part of this visit. Beyond pondering the ability of the North Korean technologists to replicate faithfully the RADUGA missile he was looking for, right now he was a great deal more concerned with their safety procedures in what was obviously a toxic environment inside Kwanmo-bong.

General Rashood was not a nuclear expert. But he knew the subject, and, above all, the qualities of uranium, its three highly radioactive isotopes, with their nucleus of unstable elements, U-238, U-235 and U-234, with the prevalent U-238 forming more than 99 per cent of the whole, the weapons-precious U-235 only 0.711 of a per cent.

U-235 is the isotope, which mattered. Because it not only had the ability to 'fission' – split into two lighter fragments when bombarded with neutrons – it could also sustain a chain reaction, each 'fission' producing enough neutrons to trigger another, thus eliminating the need for any other source of neutrons. This raging build-up of energy in the bombardment of the neutrons, smashing into and splitting the atoms millions of times over, was, essentially, a nuclear bomb. That U-235 was rare and hard to produce, but it produced an impact, which made regular TNT look childish.

In comparison, though, regular U-238 is no slouch in the weapons industry. It could not produce the deadly chain reaction of U-235 but converted to plutonium-239 it can. This substance, virtually non-existent in nature, was the heart of the atomic bomb which destroyed Nagasaki on 9 August 1945.

The general had spent countless hours studying nuclear energy at his home in Damascus and he understood its production to a tee. The mining of uranium, the 'milling' process, in which the uranium oxide is extracted from the raw ore to form the yellowcake, that yellow or brown powder almost entirely made up of the oxide. Then there's the huge volume of waste, the 'mill tailings', some forms of which are radioactive for 75,000 years.

Ravi had no idea whether any of this stuff had leached into the ground water in the mountain springs around Kwanmo-bong, but he was resolved not to risk it. Any drinkables might be full of radium-226, and heavy metals like manganese and molybdenum. He was pretty certain this miscreant communist state would not have the safety measures in place, which are enforced by law in the West.

Inside this great mountain there was a vast uranium-enrichment plant, which converts the element into a chemical form, uranium hexafluoride, a diabolically toxic and radioactive danger to anyone who gets near it. The 'enrichment plants' have suffered a number of accidents, all of them involving hexafluoride, and Ravi was not looking forward to this close proximity with living death.

Shaking himself out of such grim thoughts, he turned around and, grinning encouragingly at young Ahmed Sabah, his own wife's beloved brother, he concentrated instead on the missiles. Could the North Koreans deliver on their promise to use their own technology to convert their one-stage medium-range No-dong-1 missile into a submarine-launched RADUGA? They were approximately the same size and dimension and had successfully been sold to the Iranians — the Shahab-3 — but it was open to question whether the North Koreans could engineer the more refined rocket motor, the rocket's automatic wings, and the correct components to affix a nuclear warhead.

They had sworn they could and had been sufficiently honest to admit their weakness with regard to the software for the automatic guidance system. But Ravi had successfully bargained with the Chinese, who agreed to fit these anonymous but expensive and critical finishing touches to the missile's pre-programmed navigational computers. Most of the technology was American in origin.

So far as Ravi had been informed, the missiles were complete, ready for shipping to the North Korean seaport of Nampo. All he needed to do was conclude the payments and accept delivery. The Koreans might have been fugitives from the international community but no one had ever questioned their business methods or their reliability.

The sun was sinking fast behind the mountains now, and it was beginning to rain. Up ahead Ravi and Ahmed could see lights and what looked like a long, high chainlink fence. They were bumping over a rough and hilly surface, and they could see the big gates folded right across the track, floodlit, the rain glistening off the metal, armed guards standing directly in front of the high, steel structure. It would have required a full-blown US M-60 tank to smash its way through there and you would not have put your life savings on its success.

Ravi's driver drew the juggernaut to a halt and wound down the window on the driver's side. The guard, who was obviously expecting the big military truck, held out his hand for papers, stuffed them inside his raincoat, and walked to the front and rear of the vehicle, checking the registration number. Then he walked over to the guardhouse and inspected the papers under a light, in the dry, before walking back out and handing back the documents. The big gates were already being swung back by two other guards. The first guard waved them through and the driver continued on up the track in driving rain and pitch dark.

They passed several more guardhouses on either side of the stony, pitted causeway to Kwanmo-bong and stopped again by another set of high metal gates after about seven miles. The inspection procedures were much the same as before, and again they were waved through, grinding their way up the mountain.

The last five miles were easily the most arduous. The track became steeper and the rain, if anything, worsened, slashing down out of the northwest, head-on into the windshield of the lurching Army truck. You didn't hear many compliments about the cars made in the Qingming Automobile Company in the old Chinese capital of Chongqing. But on the way up Kwanmo-bong, Ravi found a new respect for the Chinese car factory.

'Ahmed,' he said in English, 'I guess those guys know how to make a mean automobile in Chongqing. This thing has taken some kind of a pounding, and somehow we're still going.'

'I didn't even know the Chinese made automobiles,' replied Ahmed. 'I thought they bought shiploads of them, second-hand, piled on all decks from the USA.'

'No, that's the Russians. The Chinese have a huge manufacturing plant in Chongqing.'

'Where the hell's that, Ravi?' asked Ahmed.

'It's very deep in the interior. Sichuan. They somehow built this damn great city halfway up a mountain overlooking the valley where the Yangtze and Jialing Rivers meet. It's nowhere near anywhere, 700 miles from Shanghai, 800 from Beijing. More than fifteen million people live there, and they make a lot of cars and trucks.'

'How do you know all that?'

'I've been there.'

'I didn't know you'd been to central China?'

'Neither did the Chinese.'

Ahmed laughed and shook his head. 'You have many surprises no one knows, General Ravi,' he said.

'I'm hanging on to 'em as well,' replied the HAMAS C-in-C. 'Since I plan to go on breathing.'

In Ahmed's humble but youthful opinion, the general was without doubt the cleverest, toughest and most ruthless man he had ever met. He had seen him kill without blinking, destroy without a moment's pity for the dead and suffering. And he had seen him lavish on his own very beautiful Palestinian sister Shakira a devotion and admiration almost unknown in the Arab world.

Ahmed had been best man at their wedding.

73

Ahmed had acted as Ravi's personal bodyguard throughout several missions against the Israelis and the West. And Ahmed had stood almost dumbfounded when a reckless young Palestinian terrorist had attacked the general before a mission, viciously trying to land the butt of an AK-47 on Ravi's jaw.

The speed with which Ravi had dealt with him was blinding. He had broken the young man's arm into two places, and his collarbone, and then rammed his boot into the boy's throat as he lay on the floor, saying quietly, 'I've killed men for a great deal less. Take him to a hospital, Ahmed.'

On the way, young Sabah had explained that the Iranian-born HAMAS C-in-C had been one of the most feared team leaders in the British Army's SAS, and probably the best exponent of unarmed combat in the Regiment. By some miracle, the former Major Ray Kerman had found himself on the wrong side in a bloody battle in the holy city of Hebron, where he had been saved by Shakira.

Shakira had brought him to HAMAS. Changed his name back to that of his birth. Converted him back to his childhood religion of Islam. And in the process provided the organisation with possibly the most important Muslim battle commander since Saladin 800 years earlier. At least that's how the High Command of HAMAS used his name to inspire new recruits.

And now he fought alongside his Arab brothers, with whom he shared forefathers. As the most

74

wanted terrorist in the world, he returned to the Muslim religion and married his adored Shakira.

'Allah himself sent him to us,' Ahmed had said en route to the hospital. The kid with the broken arm and collarbone was inclined to think Satan himself had also had a hand in it.

The Chongqing-built truck faced the most hazardous part of its journey over the last mile. The gradient looked like Mount Everest, and the engine howled in low gear, the four-wheel-drive tyres somehow managing to grip the granite and mud surface, which was slick from a small river gushing out of the mountain.

There were many lights and the final 600 yards were downhill, into a hollow with a tall, steel-topped barbed-wire fence crossing it. 'Impregnable' was the only word General Rashood could find to describe it.

To the left and the right of the main gates were high guard posts, each one built on six stilts the size of telegraph poles. They were set 10 feet above the razor-sharp steel spikes ranged along the top of the structure. Inside the post were two searchlights and two armed guards, each one manning a mounted heavy machine-gun. General Rashood could not quite work out whether they were trying to stop people getting in or out. Either way, his money was on the guards.

Patrolling the outside was a detail of eight men, split into two groups of four, stationed in the open on either side of the gate, rain or shine. Through the gate Ravi could see no additional light, save for that coming through a regular seven-foot high doorway. There were no more lights between the huge outside gates and whatever lay beyond. Ravi and Ahmed just sat still and waited.

The guard chief ordered the main gates open and their driver moved forward, headlights on full beam straight at what seemed like a massive wall of rock. It was not until they were quite close up that Ravi saw that the wall was actually solid steel. A small open doorway was set into the steel, and the whole wall suddenly disappeared completely, sliding to the right into the rock face.

Before him was a yawning dark cavern, without a semblance of light. It was like driving into a gigantic tomb. The truck moved forward, and silently the great steel doors behind them slid back into place. Ravi sensed them shutting firmly and felt the chill of enclosure by forces way beyond his control.

They had sat for just a few seconds before the entire place was lit up by a near explosion of electric power. This was no tomb, no cavern. This was Main Street Kwanmo-bong, street lights, central white lines, and lights from shops, or offices, or laboratories. The street was dead straight, and it stretched through the heart of the mountain as far as he could see.

The general guessed the source of the electricity: nuclear energy gone berserk. North Korea's biggest underground nuclear facility, blasted out of solid rock.

A titanic achievement, to be sure, but at what cost had it been built? Ravi wondered. He stared up at the ceiling, which was still, in places, just bare rock face. But the walls were made of concrete, and even now, through the truck windows, he could feel the soft hum of the generators pervading the entire subterranean structure. Somewhere, behind or beneath this vast reinforced cement cave, there must be a huge nuclear reactor, providing the power.

And if anyone wanted to close it down, sealed as it was from the outside world, beneath the 8,000-foot high peak of Kwanmo-bong, they'd need, well, an atomic bomb. It was, he thought, entirely possible that the only people who could destroy the nuclear facility inside this mountain were the people who had built it.

'Jesus Christ,' whispered Ravi.

They drove forward for about 500 yards, and the truck began an elaborate reverse turn into what appeared to be a loading dock. The driver cut the engine and opened his door, at which point four North Korean officials appeared. Two of them wore white laboratory coats, the others were in that curious military garb of the Far Eastern officer – olive-drab green trousers and open-necked shirt, same colour with a central zipper instead of buttons, epaulettes, rolled cuffs.

General Rashood and Ahmed joined their driver on the smooth concrete floor and were greeted, in English, by the obvious commandant, who was all business despite the late hour in the day.

'You will see your merchandise?' he said, bowing medium-low, twice. Like a Japanese double-domo. Then he extended his hand and said, 'Greetings, General. We welcome you here — hope this first of many visit.'

He introduced himself as Colonel Dae-jung and his colleagues in turn. Then he led the way back around the corner he had come from and into a wide, brightly lit vestibule, where two armed guards and a desk clerk were on duty.

Each man stood to attention and saluted the colonel, who now led the way along a corridor and up a flight of steps into a wide, bright warehouse with overhead cranes, surrounded by cables leading to great, broad upward-sliding, steel doors. Ahead of them were two gleaming stainless-steel cylinders about 15 feet high and six feet in diameter, known as 'flasks' in the trade — heavily constructed Western containers, whose sole task on earth is to transport radioactive nuclear material. They were actually perfected at British Nuclear Fuels in England and are generally considered to be as close to fail-safe as you can get.

Built of one-inch-thick steel, the flasks are heavy with inbuilt shields to reduce radiation, making them at once safer for passers-by, and also less vulnerable to attack by terrorists.

'Inside there, General,' said the Korean commandant, 'are two nuclear warheads you ordered. Each one correctly assembled includes decoys. Both warheads ready for fitting in the new missiles, packed separately – Chinese guidance and navigational engineers may wish work inside the nose cone of missile – this way no encumbrance of nuclear material. Mostly fit warhead at last moment, before missile sealed and loaded into submarine.'

Ravi nodded. 'May I see the warheads?' he asked.

'Certainly. There is small window, glass four inches thick, but you can see inside.' He led Ravi around to the six-inch porthole in the flask and shone a flashlight through it. Ravi peered inside and could just make out the shape of the cone behind the cross-beams and cable, which held it secure.

'I assure you, no one disappointed,' said the commandant. 'That's 200 kiloton warhead. Detonate properly will make all the damage you intend . . .'

The North Koreans were known for their integrity in these matters and Ravi did not doubt him. 'And the regular missiles?' he asked. 'The RADUGA lookalikes.'

'Crated over here,' said the commandant, leading the way. 'One of them not sealed, so you can see –'

Ravi looked at the long, 30-foot crates, each one weighing two tons. 'These conventional warheads are assembled and fitted?' he asked.

'Correct.'

'No problem matching the Russians?'

'Absolutely not. We have two Russian RADUGAs here in plant. Reconstruction very straightforward. We have shell casings for certain SCUDs, and for No-dong-1 – more or less identical.'

'I won't even ask how you got a hold of the RADUGAs,' said the general, grinning.

'No. Perhaps not,' replied the commandant, not grinning. 'But we fit entirely Korean-made engine for the rocket. We think it's marginally superior to Russian motor, and definitely more reliable. Works on regular nitric-acid rocket propellant.'

Ravi nodded. He counted the crates, inspected one of them, leaned over and touched the cold metal casing.

'Are the loading docks at Nampo ready for a heavy cargo like this?'

'Loading docks at Nampo second to none in whole world,' replied the commandant modestly. 'We expert at loading and transporting missile and warhead. Been doing it for very long time now. No mistakes.'

'Made one off the coast of Yemen a few years back,' said Ravi.

'No mistakes in area of northeast Asia,' said the commandant. 'That more important. That's what you need to know.'

'You're right there,' said Ravi. 'That more important.'

'Are you satisfied with the shipment?'

'I am. Would you like to conclude the payment details now?'

'Very good, General. Then we have some dinner and then you go. Three of our trucks travel in convoy. Gas tanker inside plant now. Plenty fuel get you to Nampo.'

'I appreciate that,' said Ravi.

The method of payment had been established several months before – US$150 million advance, the final balance of US$350 million payable upon completion, ex-factory. Arrangements had been made through the Korea Exchange Bank in downtown Seoul, south of the border, and the money had been deposited direct from Tehran several weeks previously.

The bank in Seoul would receive a code-word from General Rashood either by phone, fax or e-mail. Only when the North Pacific Exchange confirmed that with TEHERAN NATIONAL BANK would the funds be released to a North Korean Government account. Tonight everyone was on stand-by awaiting the big-money communiqué from the HAMAS general.

He sat before an open on-line computer in the commandant's office and tapped in the phrase in Persian, *se-panjah bash-e* – which meant, broadly, *three-fifty, it's cool*. Moments later the code was transmitted 5,000 miles west and six hours back in time to the Bank Melli in downtown Tehran, right on the main commercial avenue, Kheyabun-e Ferdosi, opposite the German Embassy.

The reply was back in Seoul in moments . . . *release funds to the North* . . . Thus, in less than five minutes, US$350 million changed hands, and the brutal terrorist High Command of HAMAS took delivery of its first-ever nuclear weapons.

Dinner with the North Koreans surpassed Ravi's

expectations. They provided a superb *sinsollo*, a special national dish of boiled red meat, fish and vegetables, flavoured with *dweonjang* (bean paste) and *gotchu* (red chilli), a bit like Japaneswe *shabu shabu* but tastier, more salty. Ravi's was served with buckwheat noodles and egg rolls.

They drank only mineral water which he sincerely hoped had not come out of the ground anywhere near the radioactive environs of Kwanmo-bong.

He declined a tour of the laboratories but could not help seeing dozens of technicians walking around dressed entirely in white, including low-fitting hats and gloves. He trusted they were staying well clear of the old hexafluoride, and that the executive of this astounding underground complex had rules and regulations about safety and a secure environment for their noxious raw material.

Before he left, the commandant informed him, 'Remember, we conduct the entire nuclear process right here in Kwanmo-bong. Enrichment, harvesting of plutonium, and refinement of U-235. Right into weapons-grade material.

'Down at far end, nearly one mile away, we make rockets and missiles. SCUD-B; Hwasong-5 short-range; Hwasong-6 short-range, like SCUD-C; the No-dong medium range; the Taep'o-dong-1, like Soviet SS-4; the NKSL-1/Taep'o-dong-1 intermediate -range satellite-launch; and the big long-range ballistic missiles, Taep'o-dong-2 and NKSL-X-2/Taep'o-dong-2 – we make Iran's Shahab from that last one – like

Soviet SS-5, satellite launch. We make what you want. Two or three stage missiles. Big payload. No problem. Very good, ha?'

'Excellent,' replied General Rashood. 'Most impressive.'

They walked on and turned into the big-loading bay. The commandant was correct. There were three big North Korean Army trucks in there now, parked between the massive steel girders of the overhead cranes. A team of young soldiers was swarming all over the vehicles, refitting the big waterproof canvas covers over the rear beds into which were now stacked the 30-foot-long missiles.

Ravi noticed that the truck in which he had arrived contained the two stainless steel flasks with the nuclear warheads. The eighteen missiles were stacked nine on each of the other two; three stacks of three, piled slightly apart, separated by timbers and wooden palettes but lashed together with bands of sprung steel.

Ravi considered the weight, probably 18 tons per vehicle, and thought again what he had thought on the long journey to the northeast – *they make a hell of a truck in Chongqing.*

He shook hands with the commandant and he and Ahmed climbed aboard. The young bodyguard had not removed his AK-47 from the rear seat and it had not been touched. It was still loaded.

The three drivers started their engines and in convoy they made their way to the main entrance. The entire place was plunged into darkness immediately before the great doors smoothed their way back into the rock. All three trucks were on dipped headlights now, but no other light came flooding out into the pitch dark of Kwanmo-bong.

They drove straight out, into the rain, and headed for the gates, which were open and held back. The duty guards saluted as they rumbled out onto the southward track and drove noisily away from the underground factory.

Despite the presence of two good-sized, utterly illegal nuclear warheads encased behind him, the general felt quite righteous as they began their journey. He might be planning something diabolical but his people had a just cause and were prepared to fight and die for their beliefs, for the right to self-government for the ancient peoples of Palestine and other oppressed nations in the Middle East, which were currently forced to march to the beat of an American drum. On the other hand the North Koreans were just racketeers. They had had no plans, no loyalties, no morals, no higher creeds or beliefs, no allies. They just wanted cash for arms – arms of the worst possible type for whoever wanted to commit crimes against humanity.

The great Allah had proved to be on the side of the HAMAS warriors. And He had shown it many times. Ravi knew He would accompany them on all of their great missions against the West. Of that he had no doubt.

The three trucks roared and skidded their way downwards, lurching around bends where the track attempted to follow the contours of the mountain. The surface was rough, the gradients uneven and the rain never let up. And nor would it, all the way to the junction where the forbidden track to Kwanmo-bong joined the east coast highway.

But the gates were open ready for them at each checkpoint and they were not stopped by the guards. They just drove straight on through and turned south, at which point the rain stopped almost immediately. Heading to the capital city of Pyongyang, they swerved around south of the metropolis before picking up the new expressway to the seaport of Nampo, twenty-five miles to the southwest. General Rashood was disappointed not to see the urban sprawl of Pyongyang, but he understood there was something bizarre about pulling into the tourist area along the Taedong River, with three trucks filled with nuclear warhead and missiles.

Instead, the little convoy kept going, driving through the night towards the shores of the Yellow Sea. It was almost dawn now, and the sun was fighting its way towards the horizon. Daylight came as they passed through the gates into the dockyard at Nampo, the largest port on the west coast. Ravi and Ahmed, tired and hungry, were astounded at the size of the jetties, all occupied by major container ships, moored beneath great overhead cranes. Most of them flew the flags of countries in South East Asia and Africa, but there were three from the Middle East and one from Europe. Freighters had no difficulty entering and exiting the port of Nampo, regardless of their size, since the construction of the enormous West Sea, Floodgates significantly elevated water levels and dramatically improved berthing capacity.

Ravi's convoy pulled up alongside a much smaller ship, an old 500-tonner, dark blue, with rust marks all over the hull. The numbers 81, just visible beneath the paint, gave little away, but the thirty-six-year-old freighter was in fact a converted ASU Class auxiliary ship originally built for the Japanese Navy, a twin-shafted diesel, which now looked to be on its last legs.

The for'ard superstructure was in dire need of a few coats of paint, as was its one broad funnel. The aft area was flat and carried a hefty looking crane, which had once lifted Japanese naval helicopters. There had also been a small flight deck, now converted for short-haul freight.

The red-painted hull letters on its port bow were barely legible in either Korean script or regular English – *Yongdo*. Ravi had no idea what that meant. But she flew the broad maroon stripe and single star of the North Korean flag on her stern, stretched out hard in the gusty morning breeze.

The jetty was staffed entirely by military personnel and it was not until the three Army trucks came to a halt between carefully painted markings, and they all disembarked the trucks; that General Rashood noticed they were in a sealed area. A large iron gate had already been closed behind them. There was obviously no way out and there sure as hell was no way in.

Awaiting their arrival was the ship's commanding

officer, North Korean Navy captain Cho Joong Kun.

'Welcome to Nampo,' he said in English. 'Please come aboard immediately. I have arranged breakfast and cabins. We sail tonight on the tide around midnight. As you know, it's a two-day voyage.'

Ravi glanced down at the officer's sleeve insignia, two black stripes on gold, with a downward line of three silver stars. In this navy you needed to make commodore to get four stars.

'Good morning, Captain Cho,' he said. 'I'm glad to see you. We've been driving all night.'

'Yes, I was told. You may sleep most of the day if you wish. By the time you awaken we'll be loaded. That crane over there will be ready for us in about three hours. It will take some time. You have a rather delicate cargo.'

'Very delicate,' replied Ravi. 'And expensive.'

1900 Thursday 28 May 2009 (same day)
27.00N 124.20E. Depth 400. Speed 25
Barracuda II moved swiftly north, through 460 fathoms of ocean, 80 miles northwest of Okinawa, and clear now of the long chain of the Ryukyu Islands where the ancient territories of imperial Japan finally come to an end.

They were running up towards the line of the Japan current, which effectively provides China with a frontier for the Pacific end of the East China Sea. The newly promoted Rear Admiral Ben Badr intended to stay out in the deeper water on the

Japan side of the current as long as he could. Like most Middle Eastern and Eastern submariners, he preferred to run deep whenever he could, away from the prying eyes of the American satellites.

It was, of course, unusual for a rear admiral to serve as commanding officer, but Ben would have a full-fledged captain on board for their next mission, and his own authority in this ship was tantamount. Anyway, HAMAS was not hidebound by the traditions of other people's navies. They were in the process of establishing their own.

The *Barracuda* had cleared Zhanjiang, headquarters of China's Southern Fleet, on Tuesday evening, on the surface, in full view of anyone who was interested. They went deep just before the Luzon Strait which separates Taiwan and the Philippines, and were now about halfway through their 2,400-mile journey to the north.

This was the second of the two *Barracuda*s, which the HAMAS organisation had purchased from Russia in utmost secrecy. And while the Americans might have harboured serious suspicions about who actually owned it, they only knew three things. For one, Russia did not admit to selling this particular *Barracuda* to anyone; two, China did not admit to owning it; and three, neither did anyone else.

The fate of the first *Barracuda*, destroyed in Panama, was known to the Americans, but it was a highly classified subject, and Washington was as close-mouthed as Beijing and Moscow.

Admiral Ben Badr knew that the sight of

Barracuda II, steaming cheerfully out of Zhanjiang bound for God knows where, would most certainly have attracted the attention of US Naval Intelligence. And in Fort Meade, the same old question was doubtlessly about to rear its irritating head again: *who the hell owns this goddamned thing?*

The *Barracuda*, an 8,000-ton, 350-foot-long Russian-built hunter-killer, was on its way to its first mission. Its initial destination was the ultra-secret Chinese Navy base of Huludao, way up in the Yellow Sea, the cul-de-sac ocean where China prepared and conducted the trials of its biggest Inter-Continental Ballistic Missile submarines.

'*Come right 10 degrees,*' called the CO. '*Steer course three-zero. Make your speed 25, depth 200.*'

The Yellow Sea was notoriously shallow and the last part of the journey, through China's most forbidden waters, would have to be completed on the surface right below the American satellites.

He wished to conduct the voyage with as little observation as possible, but nonetheless, in the end, so what? A Russian-built submarine, headed for a Chinese base, mostly through international waters – no one was obliged to tell Washington anything. The Pentagon did not, after all, own the oceans of the world. China and Russia were perfectly entitled to move their underwater boats around, visiting each other's ports.

Admiral Badr smiled grimly . . . *just as long as they don't find out where we're going in the end*, he thought.

Generally, he was pleased with the handling of

the big submarine. Her titanium hull, which had originally made her so expensive, helped give her low radiated noise reduction, but she had proved very costly to complete and would be even more so to run.

Essentially she had never been to sea until a year ago. She'd made one long, unhurried and uneventful journey halfway around the world, and been in a long and thorough overhaul in the yards of China's Southern Fleet ever since. She handled like a new ship, her nuclear reactor running smoothly, providing all of her power, enabling her to stay underwater for months at a time if necessary.

When armed, the *Barracuda* could pack a terrific bang. She was a guided missile ship and fired the outstanding Russian 'fire and forget' SSN-21 Granat-type cruises from deep beneath the surface. Right now her missile magazines were empty, a situation which would be rectified as soon as she reached Huludao.

Admiral Badr, Iranian by birth and son of the C-in-C of the Ayatollah's Navy in Bandar Abbas, was an accomplished handler of a nuclear submarine. And he aimed *Barracuda II* north, crossing the line of the Japan current on the 30th parallel, running into waters around 300 feet deep, friendly waters, patrolled by his Chinese buddies.

So far as Ben Badr was concerned, this was a pleasant cruise, among colleagues he knew well, alongside whom he had fought and triumphed, in *Barracuda I*. He looked forward to the coming months with immense anticipation. And the words of his father were always fresh in his mind . . . *stay as deep as possible, as quiet as possible and, when danger threatens, as slow as possible. That way your chances of being detected in that big nuclear boat are close to zero.*

It was almost 2300 hours now on the pitch-dark and rainswept East China Sea, and the *Barracuda* held to course three-five-zero some 300 miles due east of Shanghai. They were headed more or less directly towards the beautiful sub-tropical island of Jejudo, the 13-mile-long remnant of a long-extinct volcano, situated off the southwesternmost tip of South Korea.

Ben Badr intended to leave this sun-kissed tourist paradise, 'Korea's Hawaii', 60 miles off his starboard beam as he continued north into the Yellow Sea, where life would become a great deal more testing and staying alert paramount.

The southern part of the Yellow Sea was a particularly busy spot. A veritable highway for tankers and freighters out of the big westerly ports which serviced Seoul, and the other great seaport of Kunsan, and the heavy tanker and freight traffic in and out of Nampo. In addition there was constant fishing boat traffic, also from South Korea, not to mention the ships of the Chinese Navy from both the Eastern and North fleets. The sonar of any submarine commanding officer had to be permanently on high alert through here.

Now, as the four bells of the watch tolled the midnight hour inside the submarine, the Korean freighter *Yongdo* was just clearing the West Sea

Floodgates outside Nampo harbour 420 miles to the north, her elderly diesel engines driving her twin shafts in a shudder which might easily have been a protest.

It was a stark contrast to the silk-smooth hum of the *Barracuda*'s turbines, driving the submarine swiftly into the Yellow Sea now only 100 feet below the rainswept surface of the ocean.

General Rashood and Ahmed had slept much of the day, dined with the CO and his first officer, and were now on the bridge of the *Yongdo* as honoured guests. You don't sell a shipload of guided missiles and two hugely expensive nuclear warheads every day. Not even in North Korea.

The *Yongdo*'s journey would be a little more than 400 miles, and somewhere in the northern reaches of this forbidden sea she would be passed by the *Barracuda*, which was scheduled to dock in Huludao early on Saturday evening. Ravi wondered if he would see her come by, since she would most certainly be on the surface. It was strange to think of his old shipmate and great friend Ben Badr charging up the same piece of ocean as he and Ahmed.

They could see little in the dark, but there was a considerable swell and the freighter soon began to pitch and yaw. Captain Cho said not to worry, it never got much worse, but General Rashood nevertheless had a fleeting feeling of dread. It would be a real drag if his precious cargo went down. For obvious reasons it could scarcely be insured, and the terms were ex-factory. Those missiles hit the seabed, the losses would be born by the new owners.

They were 240 miles west to the Bohai Haixia – the Yellow Sea Strait – and here navigation was extremely tricky. The narrow seaway between the provinces of Shandong to the south and the seaward headland of Liaodong to the north was guarded by the Chinese much like the White House is protected by the Americans.

This was the choke point, containing two large areas completely prohibited to shipping and the one place where the Chinese Navy can apprehend an intruder with ease. Not even the most daring submarine CO would attempt underwater passage through the middle, where the water was less than 80 feet deep.

The chart looks like an obstacle course: fishing banned, anchoring banned, oil pipelines, naval waters. Endless patrol boats. Rocks, wrecks, sandbars and constant 'forbidden entry' signs. Don't even think about it. The Chinese, with a nuclear shipbuilding programme in full operation on the distant shores to the north, had much to protect from the West, indeed much to hide.

Even the friendly little North Korean freighter *Yongdo* would have a Navy escort in the small hours of Friday morning. As would the *Barracuda* several hours later.

The *Yongdo* was there first, by midnight on Friday, with the *Barracuda* charging along behind, gaining with every hour. Still underwater, in 26 fathoms, Ben Badr knew he would shortly have to come to periscope depth as the sea shelved up into the Strait and then to the dead end section of the Yellow Sea.

With every mile they covered, he was more and more pleased with his crew. Everyone had learned an enormous amount in the previous two years, the training with the Russians in Araguba, the endless courses in nuclear physics, nuclear reactors, turbines, propulsion, engineering, electronics, hydrology, weapons and guidance systems.

And alongside him, there were no longer rookies but seasoned submariners. There was his number two, the Executive Officer, Captain Ali Akbar Mohtaj, the former reactor room engineer who had commanded this very ship halfway around the world.

There was Commander Abbas Shafii, another engineer, nuclear specialist from General Rashood's home province of Kerman. He would take overall command of the control area. There was the Chief of Boat, Chief Petty Officer Ali Zahedi, and CPO Ardeshir Tikku, who would take overall command of the top three computer panels in the reactor control room.

A first-class electronics lt. commander from Tehran, who had three tours of duty in Iran's Kilo Class diesel-electrics, was also on board; and he was highly valued since he had sailed with Captain Mohtaj from Araguba to Zhanjiang the previous year.

In addition to the always comforting presence of General Rashood, there was his cheerful personal bodyguard Ahmed Sabah, who acted as a huge help in crew relations, cheerfully complimenting the men on their work. It was as if his words came from the

HAMAS military boss himself, and Ben Badr knew it served great purpose towards the general morale of people working under stress, spending weeks on end without laying eyes on the world outside.

And then, of course, the beautiful, slender, steely-eyed Shakira, the general's wife, Ahmed's sister, one of the most trusted operatives in the entire HAMAS organisation; the Palestinian freedom fighter who had saved the life of Major Ray Kerman when he was hopelessly trapped in a murderous shootout at the wrong end of Hebron.

In return, General Rashood had allowed free rein to his wife's talent, encouraging her to develop her principal strength, the gathering and ordering of immense detail, mainly in the area of maps, charts and topology. In Ravi's view no one could plot and plan with greater detail than Shakira, especially cruise missile navigation. In the end he had caved in to her demands to be allowed to serve on board the submarine. And a wise decision it had been.

This lovely, black-haired Arab woman, now twenty-seven years old, had a mind like a bear trap. And her performance in *Barracuda I*, in the missile programming area, had been flawless. So flawless Ravi had almost forgotten her final summing up before he permitted her to become the first women ever to serve in a submarine – *Either we both go, or no one goes. You're not dying without me . . .*

And now she awaited them in the port of Huludao, and Admiral Badr greatly looked forward to seeing her, though perhaps not quite as intensely as North Korea's big customer, sharing the bridge with Ahmed Sabah in companionable silence, staring at the endless waters of the Yellow Sea, a couple of hundred miles to the north.

For both ships, the journey passed without incident. Escorted through the Strait, no one hit or even dodged anything. The *Barracuda* docked at around 1900 on Saturday evening. The *Yongdo* came in twelve hours later on Sunday morning.

Chinese customs, all in naval uniform, boarded her before anyone was permitted to leave the ship. And they insisted on inspecting at least two of the new missiles and having them identified with the full paperwork provided by the owner, General Rashood.

Two of the crates were unbolted, one of them containing the missile which would include one of the nuclear warheads sealed in the bright stainless steel flasks, lashed down for'ard of the freight deck.

General Rashood knew they were looking at one of the two nuclear cruises, because he could see the lettering near the stern, in English, denoting it was a Mark-2 Submarine-Launched weapon, custom-built for a designated submarine.

The missile had been named by Shakira in honour of the ancient curved blade of the Muslims; the sword, forged in Damascus, carried by Saladin himself, when he faced the Lionheart's Christians at the gates of Jerusalem in the twelfth century.

The name was clear, painted at Shakira's request in letters of gold. They stood stark against the gun-grey curve of the missile's casing – *SCIMITAR SL-2*.

CHAPTER THREE

1130, 4 June 2009
National Security Agency
Fort Meade, Maryland

The lt. commander's office looked as if it had been ransacked. Sheets of paper covered every square inch of the area – on the desk, on the 'research table', next to the printer, on the printer and all over the floor. There were big piles, little piles and single pieces. There was colored paper and plain. There was stuff in files, stuff wrapped in rubber bands. Stuff crammed between the pages of books. There was *Secret*, *Top Secret*, *Classified*, *Highly Classified*. The last pile was the largest.

Contrary to first impression, however, the place had not been ransacked – merely Ramshawed. Every office space he had ever occupied looked the same. His boss, the National Security Director, Rear Admiral George Morris, put it down to an active mind. Ramshawe mostly operated on around seventeen fronts. Damned efficiently.

'I try,' he once said, 'to keep tabs on important matters, plus a few others which might become significant.'

Right now he was into one highly significant matter, and another, which had elbowed its way forward from the back burner. The 'highly significant' item required attention today as it involved a potential enemy's nuclear submarine. The envelope from the back burner required action yesterday, because it had just arrived from Admiral Arnold Morgan.

The very name of the now retired National Security Adviser still sent a tremor through the entire Fort Meade complex.

Jimmy Ramshawe had just sliced open the envelope with a wide-bladed hunting knife with a bound kangaroo-hide handle that would have raised the pulse of Crocodile Dundee. Inside the outer envelope was a plain white file containing six 8 x 10 black and white photographs. Attached was a brief note from the admiral – *Four towelheads photographed on top of a volcano in the Canary Islands. When you've got a moment, try to identify them. I think it might be useful. AM.*

Jimmy studied the pictures. There were four men in each frame. The pictures had been taken high on a cliff top with the ocean in the background. Three of the men were very clear, one was less so. But even this fourth image was well focused and showed the man in stark profile, from either side. The last one was snapped from his seven o'clock, as the admiral might have said, *right on his portside quarter.*

If the request had come from anywhere else, Jimmy Ramshawe would have put it in the nether regions of all back burners. But requests from

Admiral Morgan, though rare, did not even count as requests. These were orders.

Jimmy picked up the envelope and headed to the office of his immediate boss Admiral Morris, who was alone at his desk reading one of the endless stacks of field reports.

'G'day, chief,' said the lt. commander. 'Just got an envelope from the Big Man; thought you might like to see it . . .'

Admiral Morris was instantly on alert. 'What does he need?' he asked, already pulling the pictures from the file.

'Only the impossible,' replied Jimmy. 'Please identify four towelheads out of a world population of about seven billion, spread through nineteen countries of their own, and about five hundred belonging to other nations.'

'Hmmmm,' said the admiral. 'I guess he thinks they may be prominent, or at least a couple of them may be. He wouldn't ask us to identify a group of camel drivers, would he?'

George Morris studied the pictures for a moment and nodded. 'Well, they're good quality shots, which means that Arnie didn't take 'em himself. With something like a modern camera, he'd have an attention span of about five and a half seconds . . . Right. These would be the work of Harry. Remember the ones from the admiral's farewell party?'

'Yeah. Couldn't forget 'em. There was one Jane said made me look like a bloody swagman, hair floppy, shirt out, holding a pint of Foster's, asking Mrs Morgan for a dance.'

'Yes. I saw that one. And here's four more guys who look like they didn't want to be photographed. Again, in very sharp focus. More dignified than you, of course, but very finely focused.'

They both chuckled. But Admiral Morris was not taking this lightly. 'Okay, Jimmy,' he said. 'Get these copied. Let's have fifty sets. Then draft a note and we'll send them through the regular mail to places we might get some feedback.'

'Like where?' asked Lt. Commander Ramshawe.

'Well, we could start with our embassies in Iran, Iraq, Syria, Egypt, all the Arab Emirates, Saudi Arabia, Jordan, Lebanon, Israel. Then we'll get the Pentagon to make some more copies and check out the commanding officers in all our military and naval bases around the Middle East. We'll get the FBI on the case, and the CIA. We'll ask the Brits, MI5, MI6, Scotland Yard . . .'

'Christ, that's a lot of trouble to go to, sir.'

'Happily, we are assisted by a very large staff. I suggest we avoid putting anything on the networks. No internet, no computers or e-mails, other than internal secure. The pictures are, after all, taken by a private citizen. And there is no suggestion of urgency. Arnold's honeymoon was five months ago. It's taken him that long to send them. But if the Big Man wants a check, we give him that check. As well as we can.'

'Okay, sir. I'll take care of it right away.' And

Jimmy Ramshawe retreated to his paper-strewn lair, muttering, 'Some bloody private citizen. Takes a few holiday snaps, sticks 'em in the mail and half the world goes into free fall.'

He picked his way through the piles of paper and studied the photographs again in a thoroughly Ramshavian way . . . *well, they were taken on top of a volcano, but we can't see it . . . we can only see the top of this cliff . . . a very high one . . . right on the shore line of the Canary Islands . . . so the volcano must be behind the photographer . . . wonder what it looks like . . . suppose it's dormant . . . they wouldn't be standing around on top of it, not if the bastard was chucking molten lava all over the place . . . I didn't even know they had volcanoes in the Canary Islands.*

But he had no time for reveries. He called for someone to come and make copies and for someone else to draw up a list of all the US embassies in the Middle East. He buzzed US Army Captain Scott Wade down in the Military Intelligence Division and asked him how to circulate the pictures to the US Middle East bases. Then he summoned Lt. Jim Perry and asked him to put the whole thing into action.

The letter of request he drafted himself, e-mailed it to Jim and told him to download, print and distribute it, together with the pictures, as soon as they were ready next morning. Then he turned his attention to something he thought might really matter.

Fresh from the National Surveillance Office there was a satellite shot of a Russian-built *Barracuda* nuclear submarine making its way north through the Yellow Sea, presumably to the Chinese naval base at Huludao, on account of there's not much else at the dead end of the Yellow Sea to interest anyone.

Also he had a three-day-old picture of the *Barracuda* clearing the breakwater outside the base at Zhanjiang, headquarters of China's Southern Fleet.

The satellite had taken two shots of the submarine, the second one about 25 miles out of the base, just before she dived. The next snapshots of that stretch of ocean showed absolutely nothing, and Jimmy had wondered where the hell the ship was going.

There was only one operational *Barracuda* in the entire world and the new photograph of the submarine cruising north on the surface meant this one in the Yellow Sea was the same that had cleared Zhanjiang four days earlier.

He still did not know who owned it. The Russians had been evasive, claiming they had sold it to the Chinese, and the Chinese flatly refused to reveal anything about their submarine fleet to a Western power, even the USA, whose money they so coveted.

Thus, there were unlikely to be any definitive answers. Jimmy Ramshawe would write a brief report and keep a sharp eye on the photographs from northeast Asia, ready for the moment the *Barracuda* sailed south again heading for God knows where.

Again, he pondered the mystery of the *Barracuda*. Why the hell's the damn thing going to Huludao anyway . . . *that's their nuclear missile base, where they built their two oversized, primarily useless* Xia Class *ICBM boats. Beats the shit out of me. The ole 'Cuda's too small for an ICBM. Maybe the Russians are really selling her this time.*

But then, they could just as easily have sold her in Zhanjiang. Why take her north for 2,500 miles? What's in Huludao that the Barracuda *might need . . . maybe specialist engineering for her nuclear reactor . . . maybe, and more likely, missiles. The Chinese make cruises up there . . . I don't know . . . but I'd better watch out for her if she leaves port . . .*

He scanned the photographs again, pulling up a close-up of Huludao and its docks and jetties. It was a busy place, full of merchant ships, in a seaport geared to handle well over a million tons of cargo per year. The place was groaning with tankers and merchant freighters.

He tracked the activity at the Huludao Base for the next two days, and was pleased with the NSO's very clear photograph of the *Barracuda* arriving and heading straight into a covered dock.

The next set of prints showed the unusual sight of a civilian freighter, with a longish flat cargo deck parked bang on the submarine jetties. *Must be bringing in spare parts;* he thought, not knowing that the *Yongdo's* lethal illegal cargo had been unloaded in another covered dock, two hours before the satellite passed.

He fired in a request, purely routine, for the CIA to identify that ship, but did not have much luck.

Langley said it was a pretty old vessel, probably Japanese Navy in origin, but converted, like so many old warships in the Far East, for civilian freight. They were uncertain of the owners, but guessed it was either still Japanese, if not, North Korean.

Probably bringing in a couple of fucking atom bombs for onward shipment to the Arabs, he thought, sardonically. *Nothing serious. Only the end of the bloody world.*

Another week went by without event. The *Barracuda* had not been seen since, and no one had been able to identify the Japanese-built freighter in the submarine yards at Huludao. And then something fascinating happened. The United States Ambassador in Dubai, who had previously served in the embassy in Tehran, sent a note to say that he recognised *two* of the four men in Admiral Morgan's photograph.

His Excellency Mark Vollmer, a career diplomat from Marblehead, Massachusetts, was absolutely certain. According to his note: *during my tenure in Iran I was personally asked to process the visa applications from two extremely eminent professors from the Department of Earth Physics at the University of Tehran. One of them was Fatahi Mohammed Reza, the other was Hatami Jamshid, both natives of Tehran.*

Ambassador Vollmer recalled that they had each accepted a one-year degree course at the University of California in Santa Cruz. Both men were specialists in volcanology and in the ensuing landslides which might devastate areas in the immediate vicinity after an eruption. He had thoughtfully marked on the photographs which professor was which. Jimmy Ramshawe guessed from the men's body language that Professor Hatami was the senior man, and the serious, frowning look of Professor Fatahi suggested he too was an expert in his field.

Ambassador Volmer's phone call to the University of Tehran confirmed they were both back in Iran, were members of the faculty and lecturing at the Department of Earth Physics. Both were resident in Tehran and travelled widely, observing and researching the behaviour of the subterranean forces which occasionally change the shape of the planet.

'Wow,' said Jimmy. 'That Volmer ought to be working here, not scratching around in the bloody desert with a bunch of nomads.'

He was both relieved and amazed the matter had been so easily cleared up, and with some slight feeling of pride he drafted a note to the Big Man.

His e-mail ended with a flourish . . . *a couple of volcano professors doing their thing . . . here endeth the mystery of the Arabs on the mountain.*

Kathy picked up the e-mail, as she always did. Her new husband was always threatening to hurl the expensive laptop computer into the Potomac – *it was so goddamned slow.*

Arnold read the note with great interest and thanked Jimmy, asking him to keep a careful watch for any information on the other two anonymous figures in Harry's cliff-top snaps.

'Typical Admiral Arnie,' Jimmy reported to

George Morris later in the day. 'He gets a 10 million to one triumph, and *still* wants to know more. You'da thought the two professors would be plenty. Cleared it all up. Just four volcano academics having a careful look at their subject.'

'You know him nearly as well as I do,' said George. 'It's not his fault. It's his brain. The damn thing is unable to relax while there are questions to be answered. And he wants to know who those other two guys are . . . can't help himself.'

'He'll be lucky,' replied Jimmy.

Prophetic words indeed.

Four days later an encrypted signal from the CIA landed on Lt. Commander Ramshawe's desk. It was the cyber-note heard round the world . . . *MI5 London passed on your request of 5 June to British Army Special Forces. Colonel Russell Makin, Commanding Officer 22 SAS, says the figure on the far right, not facing the camera, is the missing SAS Major Ray Kerman. Four other SAS personnel confirm. Mr and Mrs Richard Kerman driving to Stirling Lines tomorrow. Please forward date, time, and place of photographs soonest.*

Lt. Commander Ramshawe nearly jumped out of his skin.

He strode along the corridor, knocked, and barged into the office of Rear Admiral George Morris. The room was empty, so he stormed out again and found the admiral's secretary.

'He's around somewhere, sir. You want me to have him call you?'

'Tell him to come to my office. I have something

which will shrink his balls to the size of a jackrabbit's . . .' James Ramshawe could hardly contain his excitement, never mind his language.

Ten minutes later George Morris picked his way through the piles of paper on the floor, sat down and read the note.

He nodded sagely. 'Well, Jimmy,' he said, 'we just proved what we already knew. One – Major Kerman was definitely alive five months ago, and two – we all ignore the instincts of Arnold Morgan at our peril. I am sure you have considered the fact that it was he who first felt uneasy about those guys, he who had them photographed, and he who suggested we find out who they were.'

'I have, sir. That's really all I've been doing for the past fifteen minutes.'

'You haven't told him yet?'

'No, sir.'

'Well, don't. I'm gonna give him a call and suggest you and I take a run over there this evening. With a bit of luck Kathy'll ask us to dinner.'

'I agree with all that, sir. I think a chat with the admiral right now would be a very good exercise. He might come up with something else.'

'Meanwhile, find out anything more you can about those two professors. If they're working with Major Kerman, there's got to be a plot. And if he's in it, that plot's likely to be big. And you know Arnie's likely to fire a lot of questions.'

'Okay, sir. I'll get right on it.'

And for the next four hours he scanned the

internet ceaselessly, starting with the University of California. He discovered a substantial Department of Geophysics and, to his surprise, a special area devoted entirely to the phenomenon he'd been discussing with his future father-in-law a few weeks back. *Tsunamis*. There were several world-renowned computer models of great volcano-induced *tsunamis* of the past, and a number of highly detailed research studies of those which could occur in the future.

Several of them pinpointed the hotspots in the South Pacific, especially around the Hawaiian Islands. Interestingly enough, an entire section dealt with what could potentially be one of the biggest landslides in the entire history of the world: the southwest corner of the island of La Palma in the Canaries.

One of the most renowned professors in the United States had published a thesis in which he stated flatly that, because of the initial size and shape of the unstable flank of Cumbre Vieja the waves would most likely retain a significant proportion of their energy as they propagated outwards from the Canaries, heading for the USA, Europe and northern Brazil. The initial wave heights would be approximately one kilometre and as the *tsunami* travelled westwards at high speed – as fast as a passenger jet aircraft – it would slow down and pile up, increasing its height as it entered shallower water. Those waves would be 50 metres high – approximately 160 feet, considering the evidence of massive undersea boulders and other deposits off the coast of the Bahamas, from the last *tsunami* developed in the Canary Islands several thousand years ago.

The irrevocable conclusion of this computer model, perfected over years of study, was the same that Arnold Morgan had outlined for Kathy: some six to nine hours after the initial landslide from La Palma, the collapse of Cumbre Vieja would cause devastation on the eastern seaboard of the United States.

The website provided brilliant modern graphics, particularly in reference to wave heights, red bands, blue bands and yellow dots. Jimmy Ramshawe's eyes were on stalks.

'One hundred and sixty feet,' he breathed. 'Christ, there wouldn't be a coastal city left standing from Boston to Miami. No wonder the bloody Arabs were checking it out. But I dunno what Major Kerman was doing there . . . unless he's planning to wipe out half the USA in one fell swoop –'

But then he gathered himself. *No, he couldn't be doing that . . . he might be all right having a whack at a power station or a refinery which basically blew themselves up . . . but this stuff is different. This is the giant power from the core of the bloody earth. This is God, and Christ knows what. This is a greater power than the human race has ever seen. Right here we're talking the fist of the Almighty, not a bunch of half-assed terrorists . . . I think.*

Other than his find on the University of California website, there was little hard copy on the two Iranian professors, and nothing about Major Kerman, who hadn't been seen in the West since his 'defection' five years previously. There were a few reluctant statements from the Ministry of Defence in London, but nothing casting any light on his whereabouts and certainly not his future plans.

Mrs Kathy Morgan came through in precisely the way Admiral Morris had hoped, and invited them both for dinner at their house in Chevy Chase. And both men looked forward to it, since neither of them had seen the Big Man for several months.

They arrived at eight o'clock sharp in the Morgans' somewhat grand Maryland residence which had been a part of Kathy's divorce settlement. The admiral came to the front door and greeted them with great warmth, hustling them inside and announcing he was personally cooking dinner, outside on the barbecue.

He'd fix drinks and then they could lay the bombshell on him that Admiral Morris had promised earlier in the afternoon. All three of them went for a long Scotch and soda on the rocks, and stepped out into the warm early summer night for the first highlight of the evening.

'Okay, Arnie,' said Admiral Morris. 'Prepare for a shock. The guy on the right-hand side of your photograph, the one Harry never snapped face-on, is Major Ray Kerman, late of the British Army's SAS. How about that?'

'Are you kidding me?' said Arnold. 'That little bastard, standing not 30 feet from me on top of the goddamned cliff. Hell, if I'd known that I'd have killed him with my bare hands!'

'If he'd known who you were he'd probably have killed you first,' said Jimmy, laughing, with no idea how close to home his words were. Then he explained to Morgan how they'd confirmed the identification of the most wanted terrorist in the world.

'Now that, George, is really something,' said Admiral Morgan. 'But, more important, what the hell's he doing on the top of the volcano with the Arabs?'

'Well, I guess that's the question,' said George. 'And it's very tricky because there's no evidence anywhere that these men are actually Islamic fundamentalists . . . they're academics whose life study is volcanoes.'

'If you ask me,' said Jimmy, 'the question is, why La Palma? Of all the volcanoes in the world, why is the most vicious terrorist leader in the world having a fucking powwow with a couple of scientists on the slopes of potentially the most dangerous volcano on earth?'

Arnold Morgan grinned wryly. 'How do you know it is?' he said.

'Oh, I just became a world volcano expert around five o'clock this afternoon . . . checked out the old Cumbre Vieja on the net . . . on the University of California website. That's the school out in Santa Cruz where those Iranian professors went for post-grad. courses.'

'Goddamned internet,' said Arnie. 'I had to travel halfway around the world at vast expense to get my knowledge of the La Palma range. You get the same thing in about five minutes at a cost of about five bucks –'

'Five cents,' replied Jimmy. 'Not including the printout paper.'

Just then Kathy came out of the house with a large serving plate containing four New York sirloin steaks, one-pounders, aged and primed.

'Hello, George,' she said, handing the platter to her husband. 'Jimmy – will these do?'

'Oh, g'day, Mrs Morgan,' replied the lt. commander. 'I'd say they'll do just great.'

Kathy, as always, looked nothing short of stunning. Her red hair was loose, cut shoulder-length, her make-up consisted of lipstick and little else. She wore a ruby-red silk blouse with white matador pants. Around her neck hung a pendant, two golden dolphins, stylised as in Greek mythology, but nonetheless an adapted emblem of the United States Navy's submarine service.

Arnold pronged the steaks with a long fork and placed them on the grill, eliciting four loud, encouraging sizzles – the national anthem of his home state of Texas.

'Git along little doggies,' muttered the old submarine trail boss, manoeuvring the steaks into position, bow, stern, port and starboard. He declined to close the lid, keeping the gas heat on the grill high. 'Way to cook 'em, boy,' he said to Jimmy. 'Just like my daddy taught me. Big heat, keen eye and fast reactions. That's what you need with barbecued steak.'

'And life,' replied Jimmy, grinning. 'Turn your back and you'll probably get burned.'

'Hopefully not by a goddamned volcano,' said Arnold. 'I just wonder what those bastards are up to.'

'Maybe nothing,' said George Morris. 'Maybe this Kerman character just has an interest in the subject. Maybe he just went on a field trip with the two professors. Maybe he's on a world volcano tour.'

'I don't think so,' said Arnold, somewhat predictably. 'Guys like that don't have hobbies. They're fanatics, consumed every waking hour of every day with their own agenda. I just don't trust those bastards . . . especially this Kerman character . . . I mean, if he's done half of what we think he's done, he's getting up there with Attila the Hun and he's a lot worse than Colonel Gaddafi.'

'I was looking at the Cumbre Vieja problem this afternoon,' said Jimmy. 'There's no explosion in this world big enough to blow a four cubic kilometre hunk of mountain into the ocean.'

'I know that, Jimmy,' said the admiral. 'But it's not the eruption of the volcano that's the catalyst. It's the rush of molten lava to the surface, heating the underground lakes and causing a massive steam explosion.'

'I've seen an old picture of a locomotive boiler blowing up,' said Jimmy. 'It knocked down the entire station, and it was a big railroad terminus. But it would surely have to be an unbelievable force to set off that kind of chain reaction?' mused Jimmy. 'One

113

professor said thankfully the entire scenario would have to be an act of God, and the Almighty hasn't bothered with anything that big for centuries.'

'Hope he's right,' gritted Arnold, flipping the steaks deftly. 'Just don't trust any Arabs on the goddamned mountain, that's all. They're up to no good. They always fucking well are.'

They sipped their drinks companionably, but there was a tension in the air that summer night. George Morris knew that Arnold was not happy about the arch terrorist Ray Kerman consorting with the volcano men. And Arnold's roaming mind was scanning the problem, wondering what to do, and what might lie in store in the future.

The man was out of the White House, essentially a civilian. The cares and worries of high office should have been behind him. He and his new wife ought to have been planning vacations, world trips, visiting friends. And indeed they were. But Arnold Morgan had always treated the problems of the United States as if they were his own, and it was an old habit, hard to break.

Kathy was quiet too. She hated it when her husband acted as if he were still the President's National Security Adviser. But she knew that nothing was going to make much of a difference. So she just hoped the mood would pass. She tried to distract him instead, asking solicitously if he felt the wine they were serving was sufficiently close to room temperature.

It was a question which almost always did the

trick. The admiral hurried inside to taste the rich 1998 Pomerol, Château de Valois, and a few moments later he seemed to have forgotten about Major Kerman, briefing his guests instead on the superb red Bordeaux they were about to drink.

'Right bank for the 1998s, eh, Jimmy?' said Arnold.

'What's that?' said Jimmy.

'Nineteen ninety-eight was an excellent year for Bordeaux, but was only reliable on one side of the Gironde Estuary.'

'Where's that?'

'Oh, where the Gironde and Dordogne Rivers flow out into the Bay of Biscay in western France – and on the left-hand side of that estuary are most of the great French châteaux. On the other side you have the other great Bordeaux vineyards, St Emilion and Pomerol. And in 1998 there was a lot of rain, just before the harvest – swept down off the Pyrenees, up the left-hand shores of the estuary and soaked the Médoc. But somehow it missed St-Emilion and Pomerol, which had a wonderful harvest. I've opened a couple of bottles for tonight. After George called, I asked your future father-in-law to join us, but I believe the whole family's out of town?'

'Yes. They're with my folks in New York. Pity John's not here . . . he'd have loved to try the wine.' Jimmy paused. He could see Morgan's mind whirring. 'Sir, I'm not sure when you last read up on the subject, but I gave it a good go this afternoon,' he said. 'I know the scientists do have dire warnings about La Palma, but in fairness, most of 'em think the big bang is about 100,000 years away . . .'

'So they might,' said Admiral Morgan. 'But I'd sure as hell prefer it if this Kerman character were dead.'

0500 (local) Monday 5 July 2009
Submarine Jetties, Huludao
One month in the huge dry dock at the Chinese naval base had the *Barracuda*'s full complement of North Korean guided missiles in perfect order. The Chinese electronics engineers had tested every system in every missile, and fitted the nuclear warheads into two of them.

The guidance and navigation 'brain' in the nose cone of the most deadly of the Danmo–gang cruises was checked and rechecked. It would blast clear of the water, and then set off on the course plotted and preset by Lt. Commander Shakira Rashood.

All eighteen of the missiles were correctly loaded into the magazine of *Barracuda II*. The Chinese would now present an outrageous bill for the work to the Iranian Navy, as agents but not owners – US$8 million. No one ever said the Chinese were confused about making a buck. Of course, their expertise was very nearly priceless in this part of the world. And their scruples were few.

SCIMITAR SL-2 was ready to roll.

They had begun 'pulling the rods' the previous evening and the turbines had been declared ready at 0300 by the chief engineering officer, Commander

Abdolrahim, the top nuclear specialist on board. The veteran Iranian submariner had been on duty all night, monitoring the slim Hafnium shafts being withdrawn in groups from the potentially lethal uranium heart of the reactor. Every few minutes the neutrons were thus given greater freedom to split and cause further fission, heating the system, creating that self-sustaining critical mass, the basis of nuclear energy.

Commander Abdolrahim was in total control, regulating the heat through the pressurised circuit to its phenomenal operational norm of 2,500 pounds per square inch – in contrast to the 15 pounds per square inch that humans are accustomed to living in.

With the water temperature high enough, the 47,000-hp turbines were ready to run, powered from the colossal energy contained inside the impenetrable stainless steel cylinder covering the seething U-235 core, which, when suitably enriched, forms the business end of a nuclear bomb. The dome was essentially sealed inside the reactor room's eight-inch-thick walls of solid lead. Here, Commander Hamidi Abdolrahim headed a five-strong team of fellow Iranian personnel.

Two hours before dawn, the HAMAS underwater boat had been towed out of the covered dock behind two Chinese tugs. The ship's entire company was either ex-Iranian Navy or HAMAS professional, trained in Bandar Abbas, China, and/or Russia.

They had cleared the outer breakwater now and

were operating under their own steam. The Executive Officer, Captain Ali Akbar Mohtaj, had the ship, and Chief Petty Officer Ardeshir Tikku was standing behind his principal operators in the separate reactor control room.

They watched as the *Barracuda* accelerated to eight knots, staring at the three critical computer panels, propulsion, reactor and auxiliary.

The Chief of Boat (COB), CPO Ali Zahedi, was with Captain Mohtaj and the navigation area was occupied by Lt. Ashtari Mohammed, a British-born Iraqi whose family had fled the brutal dictator Saddam Hussein in the 1990s. Ashtari was a revolutionary at heart, and he in turn had fled the UK to join HAMAS and ended up at staff college in Bandar Abbas.

His skills in the navigation room in a nuclear submarine had been honed at the Chinese naval training college at Qingdao, 230 miles to the south along the western shore of the Yellow Sea. He had worked on the *Barracuda I* mission and been commissioned for this operation because of his outstanding work in the past.

Up on the *Barracuda*'s bridge, as they ran fair down the channel in dredged but alarmingly shallow water, Admiral Ben Badr stood with General Rashood and Lt. Commander Shakira Rashood. Dead ahead, the eastern sky was coloured a deep, rosy pink, as the rising sun tried to fight its way over the horizon. The sea was flat, oily, with a distant ruby-red cast in the early minutes of the dawn.

The Chinese tugs, escorting the 8,000-ton nuclear boat out into the Yellow Sea, slowed and turned away to starboard, their officers giving a friendly wave of farewell. The *Barracuda* was entirely alone now. But the men onboard had faced danger together before and each was confident in the task which lay ahead. Only Shakira, clutching Ravi's arm in the warm morning air, shuddered involuntarily as they steered an easterly course, making 12 knots on the surface of waters which were only about 50 feet deep.

They were in the strictly prohibited area of Liaodong Bay, an 80-mile-long by 60-mile-wide cordoned-off zone stringently patrolled by Chinese Navy ships, way up on the northwest corner of the Yellow Sea.

Shortly before 0730 Admiral Badr went below and ordered a course change to the south, back down towards the choke point 120 miles away. It was too shallow even to go to periscope depth out here. And they were constantly under the observation of their protectors in the Chinese Navy.

But the North Sea Fleet of the People's Liberation Army/Navy were not the only eyes upon them. At 0745, almost immediately after they made their turn, Big Bird, the US military satellite, snapped off several shots of the *Barracuda*, noting at once its speed and direction. It was almost 6 p.m. the previous evening in Washington. The photographs from the National Surveillance Office would be on Lt. Commander Ramshawe's desk by 8 a.m. his time.

By then, of course, the *Barracuda* would be well

into the Bohai Haixia, the Chinese obstacle course which guards the business end of the Yellow Sea. And from there she would dive, running free, just below the surface in depths of around 150 feet, not quite invisible but close.

Meanwhile, Ravi and Shakira stayed on the bridge as the day grew warmer. Ahmed Sabah brought them coffee while the rest of the crew carried out their customary daily equipment checks. Admiral Badr huddled in the navigation area with Ashtari Mohammed, poring over the sprawling Navy charts, plotting their way through the myriad islands around the southeast coastline of Japan, their route to the North Pacific.

0800 (local) Monday 5 July 2009
Fort Meade, Maryland
Lt. Commander Ramshawe stared at the photographs of *Barracuda II*, running south down the Yellow Sea. 'And where the fuck do you think you're going?' he muttered to no one in particular.

He was looking at a map reference of 40.42N 121.20E. The NSO had helpfully identified the submarine as the only Barracuda Class boat in existence exiting the Chinese naval base.

'This is unbelievable,' said Jimmy to himself. 'We *still* don't know who actually owns this damn thing. The Russians *refuse* to admit selling it to the Chinese, on account of it's none of our damn business. And the Chinese decline to say anything, presumably for the same reason.'

He pulled up a chart of the Yellow Sea and Japan on his computer and gazed at the screen. Some time in the next couple of days that bloody ship is going to go deep once she's clear of the Bo Hai Strait, and we're not going to see her again for Christ knows how long.

'She could run north up through the Korean Strait and into the Sea of Japan. She could run right around the east of Japan and into the Pacific, where she could run north, south or east. Or she could continue diving back to Zhanjiang where she came from – that would begin to look suspiciously like China was the owner. She could do anything, and we will not know for sure until she resurfaces, which could be six months. Fuck.'

Lt. Commander Ramshawe did not like dead ends. He disliked especially the Yellow Sea and everything to do with it. And here was the *Barracuda* in the West's least accessible waters, running cheerfully along the sunlit surface, plainly with Chinese help and protection, if not actual crew.

He requested blow-ups of the very clearly focused pictures, and an hour later he could see three figures on the bridge. But all of them wore hats, and the photographs were shot mainly from directly overhead, making it impossible to identify any of them, even with regard to rank or nationality.

'There's nothing we can bloody do,' he grumbled. 'I better show them to the boss, but I can't progress this any further except to keep watching the satellite shots until she dives . . . but I still have a feeling that China bought this damn submarine for someone else . . . Middle East, Pakistan, North Korea? Who the hell knows?'

He stood up and walked to the door, stepping out into the corridor, which led along to the Director's office, on the eighth floor of the OPS-2B building, with its massive one-way glass walls, and twenty-four-hour heavily armed guard patrols.

'I just hope,' he murmured, as he walked, 'we haven't inadvertently shot another photograph of Major Ray fucking Kerman, right out there large as life on the bridge of the damned *Barracuda*. Because if we have, that's big trouble, right around the corner, and this new President's going to hate us worse than he does already.'

1400 Wednesday 7 July 2009
32.50N 125.28E Yellow Sea (South)
Speed 12. Course 112
They were due southeast of Jejudo, the big holiday island off the southernmost tip of South Korea. The *Barracuda* was about to run into deeper water, 400 feet in the rough, wide reaches where the Yellow Sea meets the East China Sea. Right here they would dive, making a hard southeast course, straight towards the scattered islands which stretch hundreds of miles off the end of the Japanese mainland at Kyushu.

It was somewhat tricky coming through the archipelago, but there were wide deep-water routes which would permit the *Barracuda* to stay well out of reach of the American satellites. Once those islands had been negotiated it was a straight run into the two-mile deep western Pacific, where they would become invisible.

Selection of this particular route had occupied hours of their time in the week before departure. General Rashood had very much wanted to swerve northeast and up through the tight, shallow Korea Strait into the almost landlocked Sea of Japan. His broad plan was to exit the Sea 600 miles later through the Perouse Strait, then head up through Russia's Sea of Okhotsk, and make a dash through the Kuril Islands into the open waters of the Pacific. Sheltered, protected water all the way.

But Ben Badr had objected, strenuously, on about ten different fronts. Worse, Shakira agreed with him. So did Captain Mohtaj.

The crux of the matter was that Ben Badr had become a very serious submarine officer in the past couple of years, constantly operating under the same sense of danger that affects all submarine commanding officers.

'Just look at this Sea of Japan,' he said. 'I know it's big, and I know it's 480 miles wide and 1,000 miles long and I know it's very deep right across the Yamato Basin. But it's a death trap. If we got in there and ran into an American warship, we simply could not use our speed to get away. They'd pick us up and we'd be like rats in a trap, because we could not get into open ocean. We'd either have to turn around and get back to the Korea Strait, or head for Perouse, a classic choke point, way north of Sapporo at the end of Hokkaido island.

'Ravi, they'd sink us. And if we tried to sink them, they'd send more ships from their base at Okinawa, and we *still* could not get away. We really do not want to go in there.'

'Well, I understand the remote possibility of being detected by the USA,' said the general. 'But if we did creep through quietly and made the Perouse Strait, we could move quietly into the Sea of Okhotsk, which is huge, and slide through one of those gaps between the Kuril Islands on the right, and into open ocean.'

'Ravi, I actually regard the Sea of Okhotsk with even more dread than the Sea of Japan, mostly because it's considered by the Russians as their private ocean. And it's full of their warships and submarines. I don't know if the Americans are in there or not, but if they are, and they picked us up, we'd be in an ocean bound by land, Russian, on three sides, with a line of Russian islands barring our only escape route into the Pacific.

'If the Americans are watching anywhere in this part of the world, it's got to be the passes between the Kuril Islands. In my view it would be potential suicide to try and escape that way. It's a bit longer, but we have time, and I say we head straight for the Pacific. Forget the Sea of Japan and Okhotsk. Let's just get clear of these communist nutcases, into open ocean, and make our own way to our destinations. We're in a very fast boat, and I just hate to see us squander that advantage in land-locked oceans.'

General Rashood saw the sense of the argument but continued to believe that Ben Badr was being somewhat overcautious. Shakira was equally adamant, though.

'Don't we have enough risk?' she said. 'What's the point of taking more when we don't need to. Also, I would not want our operational commanding officer to be making an underwater journey entirely against his will. I know my husband is in overall command, but surely we don't want to put more pressure on Ben. After all, if we do get caught, he's the one who has to get us out.'

'I think the inland seas would be a big mistake, Ravi,' emphasised Admiral Badr. 'But I accept that the final word is yours. And I will abide by your decision.'

The general smiled and said, 'Let's go, Ben, all-ahead . . .'

'Which way, sir?'

'Straight into the North Pacific.'

'Aye, sir.'

And so they accelerated to the southeast, taking a route south of the bigger islands of Yaku Shima and Tanega Shima. They crossed the line which marks the Japan Current and held their depth at 150 feet. They left the ocean rises of Gaja Shima and Yakana Shima to starboard, twice coming to periscope depth just short of the 130-degree line of longitude. They picked up the flashing light on

Gaja and then the more southerly warning off Yakana.

And after that it was much simpler. The ocean shelved down to depths of more than two miles, and there was relief in the voice of Admiral Badr when he made his course change.

Come left 40 degrees, steer course zero-seven-zero . . . bow down 10 and make your depth 600. Make your speed 12 . . .

They held a course inshore, some 60 miles off the jutting headlands of Ahizuri, Stiono and Nojima, the latter of which lies 50 miles south of Tokyo. The seabed rose and fell along here, and the water was famously 'noisy', never less than a mile deep, and full of crisscrossing currents. Captain Mohtaj had the ship where he wanted it, in deep, turbulent sea, full of fish and undersea caverns where the mysterious caverns of the deep echo and re-echo, causing mass confusion to all sonar operators.

The *Barracuda* continued to run northeast, 600 feet below the surface, the sonar room constantly on high alert for fishing boats and their deep trawl nets. Right off Nojima Saki, Admiral Badr ordered another course change:

Come right 70 degrees, steer course three-six-zero, retain 600 feet . . . speed 12.

They were still 60 miles offshore, 1,440 miles and five days out from Huludao when they made their turn up towards Japan's big triangular northern island of Hokkaido, north of the 40th parallel. From here they would begin to edge out to starboard, to the

126

east, away from the Russian patrols along the Kurils. Ravi insisted on ensuring a good distance between themselves and the Kamchatka Peninsula, when eventually they reached that far northern outpost of the old Soviet Navy's Pacific Fleet.

The first landfall they would record would be the Alaskan island of Attu, which sits at the very end of the Aleutians, bang in the middle of the North Pacific, dead opposite, and due east, of the Russian Navy Base of Petropavlovsk, less than 500 miles of ocean between them.

The Aleutians stretched in a narrow 1,000-mile crescent from the seaward tip of the great south-western panhandle of Alaska, more than halfway across the Pacific, dividing the world's largest ocean from the Bering Sea, which lies to the north of the islands. The weather all along the Aleutian chain is mostly diabolical, a freezing, storm-lashed hell for eight months of the year.

Not that this worried General Rashood and his men, who would make the journey past the islands in the warm comfort of their underwater hotel, way below the gales and thunderous ocean.

For 1,500 miles they ran northeast from the Japanese coast south of Tokyo. They stayed deep, leaving the little cluster of Russia's Komandorskiye Islands 120 miles to the north, off their port beam. These remotest of islands stand 140 miles off Kamchatka, with their southeasterly point only 180 miles from the outer Alaskan island of Attu.

The commanding officer of *Barracuda II* elected

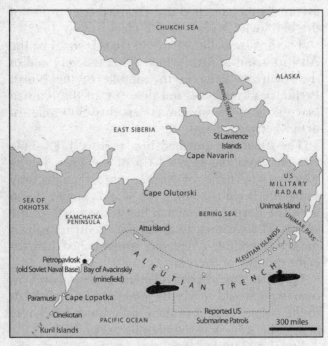

CHUKCHI SEA

ALASKA

BERING STRAIT

EAST SIBERIA

St Lawrence
Islands

Cape Navarin

US
MILITARY
RADAR

SEA OF
OKHOTSK

Cape Olutorski

KAMCHATKA
PENINSULA

BERING SEA

Unimak Island

Attu Island

UNIMAK PASS

ALEUTIAN ISLANDS

Petropavlosk
(old Soviet Naval Base)

Bay of Avacinskiy
(minefield)

A L E U T I A N   T R E N C H

Paramusir   Cape Lopatka

Onekotan

PACIFIC OCEAN

Reported US
Submarine Patrols

300 miles

Kuril Islands

ROUTE OF BARRACUDA II FROM RUSSIA'S NORTHERN
FLEET BASE TO NORTH AMERICA

to take the western side of the freak ocean rise of Stalemate Bank, where the near-bottomless North Pacific steadily rises up from *four miles* deep to a mere 100 feet, no problem for surface ships but a brick wall for a deep submarine. It only just fell short of being the real outermost island of the Aleutians, and perhaps once had been.

Admiral Badr knew the Stalemate required a wide berth, but he considered its eastward side too close to Attu Island. To transit the 230-fathom channel between the two would take them far too close to known American ocean surveillance. Attu was a very sensitive listening station for the US Navy, having stood as the first line of defence against ships from Soviet Russia for many, many years.

In Shakira's opinion they needed to make a slow sweep around to the north and then begin their 1,000-mile journey along the island chain. It was Friday 16 July, shortly after noon, and they were moving very slightly north of the 53rd parallel, heading due east across the two-mile-deep Bowers Basin which lies to the north of Attu.

There is a long near-deserted seaway between the Attu group and the next little cluster of the Rat Islands, and according to all the data Shakira had amassed, the US Navy surveillance, both radar and sonar, was extremely active all through these waters. She had spoken at some length to Admiral Badr and they agreed they should give Attu a wide berth to the north and to stay out there for 540 miles, deep at 600 feet, making no more than seven knots.

That ought to take them past the next major US listening station on Atka Island somewhere to the north of Nazan Bay. Thereafter the Aleutians comprised the much larger, though still long, narrow islands, Umnak, Unalaska and Unimak, all three of which Shakira claimed would have intense US surveillance in place.

They had, of course, accepted Shakira's assessment of the southern route which she had deemed impossible, since she was stone-cold certain there would be at least one, and possibly two, Los Angeles Class nuclear submarines patrolling the Aleutian Trench 24/7, the long, deep 'ditch' which lay between the sensitive US Navy SOSUS wires to the south and the southern shores of the Aleutian Islands.

On the previous mission Lt. Commander Rashood had claimed she would rather see the whole operation abandoned than risk being fired upon in the Aleutian Trench by a US submarine, which would unleash deadly accurate torpedoes, fatal to any intruder.

They crept past Attu Island at slow speed, 600 feet below the surface, the great black titanium hull of the *Barracuda* muffling the revs of their turbines. At the 175th line of longitude east from Greenwich, Ben Badr risked a slight acceleration, not much, just from five knots to eight. At that moment the hydraulic system on the after planes jammed, angled down.

Immediately the bow went down and the *Barracuda* headed on a steep trajectory towards the seabed. Alarms in the control room flashed, the depth was increasing, the angle of the entire boat was wrong, and the aft plane refused to move.

The Chief of Boat, Ali Zahedi, had an instant vision of the submarine heading all the way to the bottom, and shouted . . . *ALL REVERSE . . . ALL REVERSE!*

The 47,000-hp turbines slowed and then churned furiously in the water, pounding the wash over the hull the wrong way and causing the nearest thing to underwater commotion a big, quiet nuclear boat can manage.

The huge prop thrashed, arresting the forward speed, then hauling the 8,000-tonner backwards. But the angle was still wrong.

BLOW FOR'ARD BALLAST TANKS! There was urgency but no panic in the voice of Chief Zahedi. Ben Badr came hurrying into the control room, just in time to hear the propulsion engineer reporting . . . *aft planes still jammed, sir. Hydraulic problem, probably a blown seal . . . switching to secondary system right away, sir. Thirty seconds.*

Everyone heard the for'ard tanks blow their ballast, much more loudly than Admiral Badr would have wished. The submarine righted itself. And moments later the secondary system came on line and the jammed plane moved correctly. There were already two engineers working on the seal change, trying desperately not to make a noise, hanging on carefully to the rubber-coated wrenches, knowing the crash of anything on the metal deck could be heard miles away. Everyone in the boat was aware of the continued, unbreakable rule of silence, the need to tiptoe through the ocean, making certain that no one, anywhere, could hear anything, ever.

Unfortunately, luck was against them. The US listening and processing station at the easternmost point of Attu picked up the sound, at 45 miles. And it was a strong signal, more than just a fleeting 'paint' on the sonar. The young American operator nearly fell off his stool so stark were the marks of the *Barracuda*'s turbines being flung into reverse. Then he saw the near-unmistakable signature of big ballast tanks being blown.

'*Christ!*' he snapped. '*This is a goddamned submarine . . . and it sounds like it's sinking or in collision.*'

The underwater sounds continued on and off for about a minute. The operator had summoned his supervisor in time to see the submarine's ballast. But just as suddenly everything went quiet again. Making only five knots, the *Barracuda* vanished, humming through the pitch-black, ice-cold depths of the Bering Sea.

That was a transient, sir. Don't know who the hell it was, but it was a submarine, and not American. We got nothing up here . . . with luck we'll hear it again.

They did not. The *Barracuda*, holding its five-knot speed as it moved away from Attu Island, was careful not to accelerate.

Nonetheless, the Americans were suspicious, and they posted the information on the nets . . . *161750JUL09 Transient contact north of Attu Island*

132

station western Aleutians approximately 175.01E 53.51N . . . nuclear turbine, possibly Russian Delta. Contact included ballast blowing and high engine revs for one minute. Not regained . . . no submarine correlation on friendly nets.

The signal was relayed through the normal US Navy channels and would be read that afternoon in the National Security Agency in Maryland. Meanwhile, Admiral Badr kept moving slowly east north of the islands towards the mainland of America's largest state.

They were not detected again, all along their 720-mile route to the gateway to the Unimak Pass, through which they would try to make safe passage behind a freighter to the southern side of the Aleutians and then turn left into the Gulf of Alaska. The journey to the Pass took them until midnight on Wednesday night, 21 July, by which time the surface weather was brutal, a northeasterly gale and driving rain plus a blanket of fog, which refused to move despite the wind. They took up the same safe position they had occupied the previous year, 10 miles off the flashing beacon on the northern headland of Akutan Island.

Visibility on the surface was less than 300 yards and they faced a long and frustrating wait, trying to locate a sufficiently large merchant ship or tanker, astern of which they could follow at periscope depth, their mast obscured by the wake of the leading ship, the typical sneaky submarine's trick.

That Wednesday night was quiet. They finally

detected two medium-sized freighters moving towards the pass, but they were not big enough, and they were heavily laden, going slowly, hardly leaving a wake. Ben Badr wanted a major container ship or a giant tanker in a hurry to cross to the Gulf of Alaska.

But traffic remained light all night. The watches slipped by, sailors slept and ate, and the reactor ran smoothly. Ravi and Shakira retired to their little cabin at 0200 after two fruitless hours of waiting. The general ordered the COB, Chief Petty Officer Ali Zahedi, to call him instantly if anything was sighted, but nothing was and the *Barracuda* continued in a slow racetrack pattern, occasionally coming to PD for a GPS check, observation, then back under the surface.

The weather, if anything, worsened. The fog had cleared but the rain was still lashing down, visibility maybe a couple of miles. At 0915, sonar reported a likely contact approaching from the northwest. Taking a swift look through the periscope, Ali Zahedi spotted a serious crude oil tanker churning down into the Pass, the great 10-mile-wide seaway between the islands.

'*Here he is, sir,*' he called. '*A real possible . . . three-zero-zero . . . but it's close . . . only 3,000 yards . . . I'm 35 on his starboard bow . . .*'

PERISCOPE DOWN!

Admiral Badr moved in. 'Let me look, Ali –'
PERISCOPE UP!

'*Three-three-five,*' he called.

'Now bearing that . . . range that on 24 metres . . . what are we, two and a half thousand yards? . . . put me 25 on his starboard bow . . . target course . . . one-two-zero.'

DOWN PERISCOPE!

'Come right to zero-six-zero . . . dead slow . . .'

'Here she comes, sir . . .'

UP PERISCOPE!

And for the next three minutes they worked the mast up and down, finally accelerating in behind the freighter, with a burst of 12-knot speed, before slowing down to the freighter's nine knots and becoming invisible in her wake.

'She's Russian, sir,' called Ali Zahedi. 'Siberian crude, I imagine.'

Over in the US listening station at Cape Sarichet, the seaward northwesterly point of Unimak Island overlooking the approaches to the Pass, the American radar picked up the periscope mast of the accelerating *Barracuda*, 18 miles away to the west.

But just as quickly the 'paint' vanished after only three sweeps, leaving behind a mystery. Had they picked up the periscope of a submarine? Or was it just flotsam in the water? And if it was a periscope, did it belong to the same submarine the Attu Station had heard and reported the previous Friday night?

In the normal course of events, the Unimak Station would not have reported any of the random radar 'paints' picked up on a commercial throughway like the Pass. But there was something about this contact, the stark clarity of the 'paint', its sudden

135

appearance from nowhere, and its equally sudden disappearance. Plus the report from Attu the previous Friday.

They decided to put the information on the nets ...*221127JUL09 Possible transient radar contact detected Unimak Station. Five seconds, three sweeps on screen. Further to Attu Station submarine contact 161750JUL09* . . . Unimak detection consistent with slow five-knot submarine progress from Attu to Unimak Pass.

It was a signal which would, in a very few hours, set off alarm bells inside the head of Lt. Commander Ramshawe in Fort Meade. And it would cause his mind to whirl in hopeless search for the missing *Barracuda*. Though even he would have to admit that he couldn't say even within 10,000 miles where it might be. But it would not be the first time he had wondered about a clandestine submarine passage along the route north of the Aleutian Islands. And right now, he would have given almost anything to know the precise whereabouts of that mysterious underwater ship and who its owners were.

Meanwhile, Admiral Badr had his ship ranged perfectly behind the Russian tanker, the whole operation one of geometry rather than navigation. They were separated by about 100 yards of swirling white water, and they had a beam ranged on the mast light of the merchant ship.

The correct angle was around 13 degrees. If it decreased they were falling behind, out of the wake, which protected them from the US radar. If the angle increased, it meant they were getting too close.

And the tanker, blissful in its ignorance of the nuclear arsenal following in its wake, kept steaming forward. Captain Mohtaj, the XO, personally took the helm during this most intricate part of their journey and steered them dead astern of their leader.

Ninety-five revolutions . . . speed over the ground 9.2 by GPS . . . 8.6 through the water, sir . . .

When they reached the GPS position 54.15N 165.30W they no longer needed to be a shadow. They broke away and went deep to 300 feet, heading for a point 60 miles southeast of Sanak Island, where Ben Badr ordered a course change to due east. They had turned away at last from the long sweeping arc of the Aleutians and were making eight knots along the 54th line of latitude, straight into the Gulf of Alaska.

Down in the navigation area, General Rashood was sharing a pot of coffee with Shakira and Ashtari Mohammed. The Arab lt. commander, and the navigator were poring over the big charts, trying, as always, to second guess the United States' defences.

General Rashood was sitting at a high desk with a pile of notes illuminated by an adjustable reading light. In great detail, sectioned off in colours, numbered and bound, they contained details of geological strata, depths of rock, likely weak points in certain areas of the earth's crust. Lists of volcanic activity. Lists of 'modern' volcanoes likely to erupt. There were detailed maps of great mountains, which could develop interior lava in the next five years. There were estimates of potential damage, endangered areas and a special section on inland volcanoes, plus two entire eighteen-page 'chapters' on seaward volcanoes.

Ravi had compiled the document himself, typed up, filed and catalogued every specific section, cross-referenced each and every volcano which might interest him. It was a precious project, representing the very bedrock of his plan to drive the Great Satan out of the Middle East for ever.

Every aspect, every detail, was gleaned from the personal knowledge and research of the world's foremost authority on geophysical hazards – Professor Paul Landon. Ravi Rashood regretted that their friendship in London had been so very brief.

CHAPTER FOUR

0300, 23 July 2009
53.30N 161.48W. Depth 500
Speed 5. Course zero-eight-zero

The *Barracuda* crept east–nor'east across the steep underwater cliff faces at the eastern end of the Aleutian Trench, where the gigantic Pacific 'ditch' which guards the southern approaches to the islands finally shelves up, close inshore, into the Gulf of Alaska.

Here, despite the colossal depths of more than two miles, the ocean steadily grew shallower, angling up towards the coastal islands of mainland Alaska. In this, the more friendly US end, enemies are just about unknown, unlike its other side, out towards the western Aleutians towards Russia and China, where American submarine COs stay on top of the game at all time.

Ravi and Ben considered their slow expedition into the quiet section of the Trench not much of a risk; it was simply not a place where the US Navy would be looking for trouble, mainly because of the serious difficulties of getting there . . . either straight through the patrolled waters of the Trench (out of the question, unless contemplating suicide); through the Unimak or Samalga Passes (impossible under US radar); or, across the Pacific Basin and through the Gulf itself, passing over the lethal, constant, electronic tripwires of SOSUS, again suicidal.

Both Ravi and Ben considered the *Barracuda* safe in the eastern waters of the Trench, and at this dead-slow speed they would hear any US submarine a long time before it detected them.

At first it had seemed logical to cross the 1,000-mile-wide Gulf of Alaska, straight through the middle, in water never much less than two and a half miles deep. But Ben Badr was nerve-wracked thinking about the US Navy's deadly Sound Surveillance System and in answer to every one of General Rashood's questions weighing the possibilities of the much shorter straight-line route, he just said, 'Forget it, Ravi. They'll hear us.'

And then he added the inevitable, 'We have to stay inshore, along the coast, in noisy water, where there's massive shoals of fish, rough ocean, island surf, changing depths, and that north-running current. That's where we're safe, out there with the commercial traffic, freighters, tankers and fishing boats, all kicking up a hell of a racket while we creep along 500 feet below the surface.'

Ravi had been staring at the chart. 'You mean right up here, through this Shelikof Strait between Kodiak Island and the mainland coast?'

'I wish,' said Ben. 'And I expect you've noticed

we'd have 600 feet almost all the way along that island for about 130 miles. However, you'll see that the Strait ends right at the gateway to the Cook Inlet, which leads up to Anchorage. Afraid that's not for us. Shakira says it's bristling with radar, busier traffic than Tehran, and only a couple of hundred feet deep.'

'That's not for us,' agreed Ravi. 'What do we do? Go outside Kodiak?'

'Absolutely,' said Ben, staring at the chart. 'Even wider than that. We need to get outside the 200-metre line . . . see? Right here . . . we'll get in the Alaska Current and head zero-seven-zero.'

Ravi looked at the chart. 'We stay 50 to 60 miles offshore all the way up that coast, we'll be in water that's two miles deep. As far as Prince William Sound. What does Shakira say about US surveillance up there?'

'She thinks they will have plenty of shore-based radar, which won't affect us because we'll be deep. And she thinks there'll be surface patrols in that big bay beyond the Sound, which also won't affect us. But she has seen no sign of increased submarine patrols up there.

'And knowing the huge expense of mobile underwater surveillance, I'd be surprised if they put a couple of nuclear boats in there to protect essentially foreign tankers. Submarines operating in defensive mode, in a non-war area, like Alaska, really only protect against other submarines. And let's face it, the chances of a foreign strike submarine getting into those waters with intent to attack are zero.'

Ravi smiled. 'Not even us,' he said.

'Not even us,' answered Admiral Badr. 'We're just passing through, very quietly, very unobtrusively. There's no US submarine patrols and a lot of noise. We'll be fine.'

And so they set off up the Gulf, steering a north-easterly course, deep. It took them four days to reach the old Russian colony of Kodiak, and they left it 50 miles to port. They moved slowly past the rugged, mountainous island, home to more than 2,000 three-quarter-ton Kodiak brown bears, the largest bear on earth, on the largest island in Alaska.

The frigid waters which surged around Kodiak were not only home to a 2,000-strong fishing fleet, but also to the giant king crab. Vast legions of these iron-shelled 15-pound monsters, which sometimes have a leg span measuring four feet across, occasionally made the city of Kodiak the top commercial fishing port in the United States.

And the Alaskans guard their precious stocks assiduously. The biggest US coastguard station in the state operates four large cutters, with fully-armed crews, out of the old US naval base on Kodiak. They patrol these waters night and day, ruthlessly seizing any unauthorised fishing boat. As Shakira Rashood warned her commanding officers, *they may not be looking for submarines, but they'd sure as hell blow a very loud whistle if they thought they'd heard one.*

By midnight on Tuesday 28 July, way below the bears but several hundred feet above the clunking armour of the king crabs, the *Barracuda* was dawdling silently northeast at only six knots. Occasionally they heard the deep overhead rumble of a laden tanker moving west towards Anchorage from the new terminal in Takutat; occasionally the state ferry, the *Tustumena*, from Seward on the Kenai Peninsula; less often the growl of the powerful coastguard diesels.

Three hours before dawn, Shakira came into the control room and brought Ben and Ravi hot coffee and toast, announcing they were 90 miles southeast of the port of Kodiak, steaming with the Alaskan Current in 550 fathoms, staying west of the shallow Kodiak Seamount.

She also brought with her a snippet of knowledge to dazzle the two senior officers on board. 'Did either of you know that the port of Kodiak was practically levelled as recently as 1964?'

'Not me,' confessed Ravi.

'Nor me,' said Ben.

'The whole downtown area,' she confirmed, 'the entire fishing fleet, the processing plants and 160 houses. The Good Friday Earthquake, they called it, shook the entire island from end to end.'

'How come an earthquake wrecked the fishing fleet?' asked the ever-probing, practical General Rashood. 'Why didn't they just head out into the bay like every other ship does when an earthquake starts?'

'Because it wasn't the earthquake which got them,' said Shakira. 'It was the *tsunami*, the huge tidal wave which developed when half a mountain fell hundreds of feet into the sea . . . there you are, darling, your very favourite subject, delivered personally.'

Ravi grinned. 'I'm telling you,' he said. 'Those tidal waves, when they get going, they're a real killer –'

'According to my notes on this area,' said Shakira, 'this *tsunami* developed with great speed. When the wave surged into the port of Kodiak, it just picked up all the ships and dumped them from a great height into the streets, flattened every building . . . turned everything, ships, boat sheds and shops into matchwood. Most people luckily had just enough time to get out and drive to high ground. Anyone who didn't was never heard of again.'

'Allah,' said Ben Badr. 'I suppose that's the only good thing about a *tsunami*. It takes just that little bit longer to get organised. There's warning. And the wave inshore is making only 30 or 40 knots. Probably gives everyone a half-hour to get out.'

'In some cases much longer,' said Ravi, thoughtfully. 'Some of those Pacific surges which started with earthquakes or volcanoes in the Hawaiian Islands took hours to reach very distant shores . . . where they inflicted their worst damage.'

'You want to know about *tsunamis*, ask my oh-so-clever husband,' laughed Shakira. 'He knows everything. Or thinks he does.'

'Unlike you two, I have been given expert tuition, instruction and knowledge from a great master,' said Ravi. 'Professor Paul Landon, the world's leading authority on volcanoes, earthquakes and tidal waves took me under his wing for a few days. Brought my knowledge right up to scratch.'

'Excellent,' said Admiral Badr. 'Not too long now.'

They ran on past Kodiak, crossed the sea lanes leading up to the Cook Inlet and to the port of Anchorage. A day later they were creeping through 1,200 fathoms of water, south of Prince William Sound, 500 feet below the surface.

Following the big sweep of the Gulf, they changed course here, making a gradual turn to the south-east, staying in the Alaska Current, outside the 200-metre line, tiptoeing warily past the Yakutat Roads, on down to the Dixon Entrance, north of Graham Island. These were waters where both senior commanders had worked before.

The sheltered, noisy expanse of the Hecate Strait looked tempting, lying as it did between the 160-mile-long Graham Island and the Canadian mainland. But the depths were treacherous. Right here the ocean runs hard south past the great archi-pelago of islands, hundreds of them, on the rough, violent coast where the Rocky Mountains sweep down to the sea. It's noisy, it's damn near paradise, except for the outstanding opportunities to rip the hull wide open in 30 feet of granite-bottomed seabed.

'Outside the island, I'm afraid,' said Ben Badr. 'It's deep, and, according to Shakira, almost certainly shuddering with SOSUS wires. It's our usual story, very slow, very careful, right down 800 miles of Canadian coastline, past the Queen Charlotte Islands, past Vancouver Island, then past the great American state of Washington. Should reach our op area on 6 August. Then it's more or less up to Shakira.'

And no one knew that better than the beautiful lt. commander who worked tirelessly at her desk in the navigation room. Occasionally, Admiral Badr took the *Barracuda* to the surface for a satellite fix and to suck messages swiftly off the comms centre in the sky, reporting course and position to Bandar Abbas via the Chinese Naval Command Centre in Zhanjiang.

They were in the risk reduction business, and their *modus operandi* did not include providing the slightest glimmer of information, even on Chinese military satellites, to sharp-eyed Fort Meade detectives like Lt. Commander Jimmy Ramshawe. Ravi and Ben wouldn't know Jimmy's favourite exclamation – *Christ, here's the ole Shanghai Electrician.*

This somewhat esoteric description had evolved from the more usual phrase of *casting a chink of light* on a problem and George Morris had found Ramshawe's linguistic ingenuity so amusing that he spread it all over the eighth floor of OPS-2B. For most people, it contained a touch more panache than a mere Chink of Light, the same kind of espionage flourish as *The Tailor of Panama.*

Ravi and Ben were not willing to give one thin amp of credibility to the Shanghai Electrician. They accessed the satellite only every four or even five days, averaging twenty-four seconds of mast exposure per twenty-four hours. They stayed deep, and slow, all the way along their southern voyage, past the Canadian coastline. They slipped down to 600 feet depth as they crossed the unseen frontier, west of the Strait of Juan de Fuca, into North American waters off the coast of Washington State.

Out where the *Barracuda* ran, 45 miles offshore, the waters were not officially American, but in the world of international terrorism those great Pacific swells far off the coast of the Evergreen State were about as American as Fifth Avenue; patrolled ruthlessly by US warships, working out of the sprawling Navy bases of Everett and Bremerton, deep in Puget Sound, which guards the great northwestern city of Seattle.

Shakira's view was to stay well clear of the vast seascape, which washes onto the shores of Washington State. She regarded it as the most dangerous part of their long journey, a place where there might well be US submarine patrols, and many more highly sensitive surface warships all carrying state-of-the-art detection and surveillance ASW equipment.

In her opinion they should stay deep until they were well south of the fast and lethal predators from the Bremerton and Everett US Navy Bases. Those predators would show not the slightest mercy to an intruder, especially an unannounced Russian-built nuclear submarine they had been puzzling over for several weeks. And there was no doubt, certainly in the mind of General Rashood, that the Americans were most definitely wondering about them.

Admiral Badr kept in touch with Shakira's heavily marked charts all the way, unfailingly agreeing with her and her sense of caution. They moved slowly on, the big lightly used reactor running steadily, all systems operating flawlessly throughout the submarine. Ravi and Shakira would have liked a bigger cabin, but there was no chance of that. They worked and slept exhausted, welded together by the fire of love and revenge upon the Great Satan and its Israeli devils.

They crossed the 48th parallel, which bisects the northern timberland of Washington State, then the 47th, which took half a day. On 5 August they were due west of the estuary of the mighty Columbia River, the great 1,200-mile-long waterway which rises in a snow- and rain-filled torrent in the mountains of British Columbia, surges south and then swerves west to form much of the border between Washington State and Oregon.

The Columbia was the most powerful river in the United States, generating one-third of all the hydro-electric energy in the entire country. The Chief Joseph, the Grand Coulee, the John Day and the Bonneville were the biggest of eleven massive mainstream dams. And the names of the latter two had been marked carefully on Shakira's charts, circled in red, her personal code for potential danger.

In Shakira's view, these two hydro giants, set upstream from Oregon's commercial hub of Portland, would be heavily protected from terrorist attack and the chances of high radar sweeping the skies above the dam were excellent. What Shakira wished to avoid especially was a missile detection from US radar defences, mainly because she considered that to be an unnecessary hazard, and most certainly avoidable.

The preprogrammed data inside the computer of the SCIMITAR SL-Mark 1s (plain TNT, *not* the nuclear warheads of the Mark 2s) would guide the rockets downstream of the big protected dams, crossing the Columbia in lonely, near-deserted countryside.

But the entire project made her nervous, and she found it difficult to sleep, often pacing the navigation room at all hours of the night, pulling up the charts of coastal Oregon on the screens of the satellite navigation computers.

Ravi too understood the scale of the project they were undertaking, but he was consumed with the minutiae of the target area. He combed through the notes provided by the late Professor Landon and longed each day for the luxury of a satellite communication, which would detail the ever-changing situation among the high volcanoes within the mountain ranges of America's vast northwestern coastal states.

He had pages of data on Mount St Helens, the 'Fuji of the United States', which was almost identical in its symmetrical shape to the legendary Japanese volcano. At least it had been before it finally blew with stupendous force on 18 May 1980, sending a shudder across the entire southwestern corner of the state of Washington, and literally shot a tremor straight through the gigantic Cascade Range of mountains.

The blast flattened fully grown Douglas fir trees up to 14 miles away from the volcano, and obliterated 400 square miles of prime forest. Fifty-seven people died. Raging mudflows thundered into the rivers. Volcanic ash showered from the darkened skies all the way to Montana, 650 miles to the east.

The colossal eruption blew the entire snow-capped glory of the summit clean away from one of the most spectacular mountain peaks in the United States. Before 18 May, Mount St Helens rose thousands of feet above every hill and mountain which surrounded it, dominating the landscape. It stood, serenely peaceful, 9,677 feet high. After the blast it stood less proudly, at only 8,364 feet. Its great shining white crest was entirely missing; it remained now like a spent firework.

A broad, tilted, circular crater, more than two miles across, was embedded into the pinnacle of the mountain. From its lower edge carved into the north side, the crater rim was cut into a giant V, through which had thundered the pyroclastic flow. The molten lava was now set into a grotesque black basalt highway down the mountain, splitting into a wide fork as it reached the six-mile-wide base. The western surge had rumbled into the clear and refreshing waters of Spirit Lake; the rest had barrelled down the beautiful snowy valley of the Toutle River. It was like an open-cast coal mine set in the garden of Santa's Workshop.

Ravi knew the facts verbatim. But the part that captivated him most was one particular detail of the blast. The central 'chimney' of Mount St Helens was blocked with hundreds of tons of lava from the previous eruption and the surging new magma, climbing into the volcano, had nowhere to go. It ultimately forced its way higher into the north flank, pushing outwards and forming a giant swelling, a dome of rock, volcanic ash and general debris.

These great carbuncles are not unique to Mount St Helens. They happen often with active volcanoes. But shortly before the eruption, this one had developed into a fair size – a mile across and probably 120 feet high. And it was not the rising magma which finally smashed the great bulge asunder but a relatively small earthquake, which completely destabilised the north face of the mountain.

The dome, cracking on all sides, blew outwards within minutes of the quake and crashed down the mountainside in a landslide. The mammoth weight of a half-million cubic yards of rock was now removed from the upward flow of the lava and the gasses decompressed instantly, detonating out like a bomb, levelling every tree in sight.

It was the carbuncle that Ravi now focused on. According to Professor Landon another one was forming on the same gutted north face of Mount St Helens, right in the old crater, 46.20N 122.18W on the GPS, to be absolutely precise.

There had been strong, steaming activity inside the volcano for several years, since the early 1990s: occasional eruptions of steam and ash, less frequent pyroclastic flows, with intermittent 'swellings' on the northern rock face of the mountain. A much more violent blast of steam and ash on 1 July 1998 had frightened the life out of the locals before it had seemed to subside again. The new, mile-long carbuncle had begun to develop in 2006, right in the middle of that massive, sinister crater which scarred the once-beautiful north face.

As they crossed the 46.20N line of latitude, Shakira knew they were dead level with their target, dead level with the four-mile-wide estuary of the Columbia River. They were 200 miles offshore, 600 feet below the surface, steering one-eight-zero, straight down the 127 degree line of longitude. Mount St Helens lay 75 miles due east of the estuary. Right now, moving slowly, they were exactly 195 miles from their target, a mere formality for the North Korean-built SCIMITAR SL-1 missiles, currently resting malevolently in the magazine room of *Barracuda II*.

The Pacific was a little less than a mile deep here, the seabed a flat, scarcely undulating plain. On the surface the swells were long, rising to 10 feet, but here, in the quiet depths of the cold, gloomy ocean, there was nothing save for the stark network of the US Navy's SOSUS wires, resting like black, angry cobras in military formation on the ocean floor, ready to spit venomous, fatal betrayal on any unsuspecting intruder.

Admiral Badr recommended running south for another 100 miles, a position which would put them in easy range of the great scarred mountain in southwestern Washington. Shakira's missile course was plotted and agreed. General Rashood had decreed there was no reason to move too far away. His overall strategy had been something of a surprise: he was ordering a daytime firing, rather than using the hours of darkness in which they all felt to be much safer, although cocooned in their boat at 600 feet there was not the slightest difference in night or day, summer or winter, nor the days of the week.

When Shakira wanted to know why, Ravi's explanation was succinct. 'Because a big cruise missile trails a large fiery tail when it leaves the water. It can be seen for miles, especially in the dark. If we do it in the day it will be much, much less visible.'

'But before we fired at night.'

'That was because we did not want the missiles to be seen by security guards at the target end. This is different. We are firing into a void. Into the open wild, where there are no guards, no surveillance, no people.'

'Hmmmm,' mumbled Shakira, irritated that she had not thought of that herself.

'Our only danger on this mission,' said her husband, 'is being detected by a passing warship, out here in the night, with the ocean lit up like a bloody amusement park by our rocket motors.'

'The missile could still be seen during the day,' said Shakira. 'If there were passing ships.'

'There won't be,' replied Ravi.

'How do you know?'

'Because I intend to fire when there is fog on

the ocean surface. And I intend to use passive sonar and my own eyes to ensure there is nothing around.'

'But even you cannot just order fog.'

'No, but this part of northwestern America is well known for the rain which sweeps up the Pacific. And where there's rain and cool temperatures, interrupted by warm air currents, there's fog.'

'But there may not be any, not exactly when we want it,' said Shakira.

'We'll wait.'

Shakira Rashood asked him if he would like some tea, and her husband replied that he considered that an excellent idea, briefly toying with the temptation to remark how thrilled he was that she had decided to return to what she was good at. But he quickly rejected it, not wishing to have the entire contents of the teapot poured over his head.

Instead he looked up and smiled. 'I'm very grateful, my darling,' he said. 'The way you force people to explain themselves.'

'You're too clever,' she said, affecting a pout. 'Always too clever. I like being on your side.'

'You're a good officer, Shakira. Ready to challenge when you do not quite understand. But in the end, respectful of your commanding officer. As we all must be.'

'I am a good officer,' she said seriously, but smiling. 'But I hope you think I'm a better wife. Because I expect to be that for much longer.'

'If you go on doing as I tell you, at least while we're in this ship on Allah's mission, you will be my wife for a long time. I usually know what to do, and how to keep us safe.'

'You see,' she laughed. 'You don't even have a commanding officer. You make your own rules.'

'I have a commanding officer,' he replied. 'And I hope He's watching over both of us.'

Shakira looked at him with undisguised adoration; this powerfully built, ex-British Army major, the toughest man she had ever met, with the polish of a Sandhurst-trained officer and the strategic brilliance of an SAS commander. And yet he was an Arab still, with his dark, tanned skin, the softest brown eyes and the inborn fortitude of his Bedouin forebears.

And she thanked Allah for the day she had fled with him, terrified, through the rubble of shattered Hebron, while all around them there was only the blast of shells and the whine of bullets and the cries of the wounded. She thanked Allah for the strength she had found to take him into hiding with the HAMAS freedom fighters.

Looking back, when she dared, to the devastation of that blasted cement house in the Palestinian district, she could still see her slain children and the blood from the wounds of the dead SAS sergeants, blood pouring down Ravi's combat uniform, blood on her children, on her own hands and dress. And she remembered how her own little Ravi had lain so still in the dust, next to his tiny dead sister, and how Ray had saved her life by committing two savage murders.

There was nothing, she thought, that could have been worth all that. But the former Major Ray Kerman had made it almost so. She could not imagine anyone loving another person more. She would have followed him into the mouth of Hell.

As it happened, Ray followed her into the mouth of the galley, the empty end, where the cooks where not working, and he kissed her longingly behind the shelves of canned fruit.

'You said this is why girls are not allowed on submarines,' she giggled, twisting away in case anyone discovered them.

'People are only required to do as I say,' he said, cheerfully. 'Not as I do.'

'You see – I'm always telling you – you do just as you like, because you have no commanding officer.'

Ravi looked admiringly at his wife, her beauty undiminished even in her standard dark blue Navy sweater, and he said simply, 'I don't think Allah would desert any of us on this mission. He has given us the power of the false gods of the ancient world, and He will guide us to victory. We are doing His work.'

'And to think,' said Shakira, shaking her head in sham disbelief, 'you used to be an infidel . . . one sugar or two?'

General Rashood chuckled, quietly thankful at the talent Shakira had for diminishing the tensions of his great mission, if only for a few moments.

They made their way to the navigation room, Shakira carrying the teapot and three little silver holders containing glasses already with sugar, in case Lt. Ashtari Mohammed was working. It was almost midnight now.

They found Ashtari hunched over the chart of the eastern Pacific plotting their southern course. He stood up and stretched, grateful for the tea. 'Admiral Badr thinks we should run for another day, maybe less, and then turn east towards our target.'

Ravi nodded in agreement and glanced down at Shakira's chart. It contained so many notes it was almost incomprehensible. But the line she had drawn from the 127th western line of longitude had four definite course changes at various points of contact from the 47th parallel to 46.20N at 122.18W.

Ravi had managed only two sips of his hot bitter tea when a quiet voice came down the ship's intercom . . . *General Rashood to the control room . . . General Rashood to the control room . . .*

He took his tea with him and headed for the area directly below the bridge, where Ben Badr was waiting.

'At which point do you want to begin searching the area for surface ships? We're about 100 miles north of the datum right now . . . I was thinking maybe 50 would be right . . . I presume we don't want to surface?'

'No, we don't want to do that. But we should get up as high as we can, maybe to periscope depth every couple of hours, just for an all-around look. Meanwhile, we can use passive sonar as our main lookout. We cannot risk detection. There are no suspects for a mission such as this – it would seem ridiculous to alert *anyone* to our presence –'

'I agree, Ravi, so 50 miles from our firing position is okay?'

'Yes, good. If there's anything around we may want to track it for a couple of days . . . make sure it's well clear. Meanwhile, we'll just hope for fog.'

The *Barracuda* pushed on, running quietly all through the night until mid-afternoon on Thursday 6 August. At 1630 Admiral Badr ordered the planesmen to angle the bow up 10, sending them smoothly to periscope depth. The admiral himself took an all-around look, and Lt. Ashtari Mohammed called out the numbers, 43 north, 127 west.

Lt. Commander Shakira Rashood wrote them onto her chart, marked the spot where the line of latitude bisected the longitude, checked her distances with dividers and wrote in blue marker pen, *290 miles to Target.*

In seconds, Ben Badr ordered them deep, *bow down 10 to 600.* There was no communication on the satellite, no ships anywhere near. Their part of the Pacific was a sunlit wilderness, devoid of engines, lacking in fog. Their only danger was the ever-present black cobras on the seabed, which must not be disturbed. Admiral Badr ordered a racetrack pattern, speed 5, banking on the fact that cobras were deaf to such low revolutions in a boat as quiet as the *Barracuda.*

And so they waited, for two days and two nights, until at 0300 on Sunday morning a gusting summer rain squall swept eastwards across the ocean, right out of the northwest. They picked it up on sonar and moved silently upwards, through the black depths to PD for a first-hand look. They stayed there for only seven seconds, sufficient time for the Chief of Boat, CPO Ali Zahedi, to report a slashing rainstorm on the surface, very low visibility, no more than 100 yards.

General Rashood considered the possibility of firing then and there. But he knew it could still be clear on the shore, and he did not relish sending missiles with fiery tails over inhabited land, even at three o'clock in the morning. No, he would wait for widespread fog, which he was sure would occur as soon as the regular warm summer air currents ran into the cold squally Pacific gusts surrounding the storm.

At dawn they checked again, moving slowly to periscope depth. Ravi had been correct. A great fog bank hung over the ocean, visibility no more than 50 yards. Ravi guessed it would probably extend all the way inshore, with the clammy white blanket hanging heavily against the mountains of Oregon's coastal range.

'This is it, old boy,' he said to Ben Badr.

'Aye, sir,' replied the young Iranian admiral.

Prepare Tubes 1 to 4 . . . missile director and Lt. Commander Shakira to the missile room . . . planesman, bow up 10 to 200 feet . . . put me on course zero-three-zero . . . speed 5 . . . sonar room check no contacts . . . Missile Director final check prefiring routines and settings.

They all felt the submarine angle slightly up, and

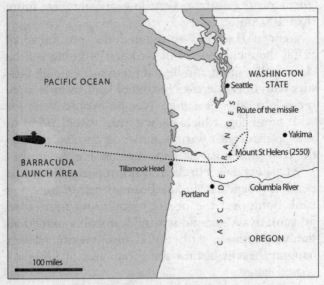

BARRACUDA STANDS OFF THE OREGON/WASHINGTON COAST -
DRAWING A BEAD ON MOUNT ST HELENS

they heard Ravi summon the crew to prayer. Those not hurrying to the missile room knelt on the steel decks in the Muslim fashion. Men clambered out of bunks, engineers laid down their tools and everyone heard the Mission Commander's warning of the coming turmoil, urging them to be prepared to hear the angels sound the trumpet three times. At the sound of the trumpets, he said, only the righteous would cross the bridge into the arms of Allah. They were engaged in the work of Allah, they were His children, and they dwelt today in this great weapon of war on behalf of Allah. It was built for Him and they were born to serve Him.

He read from the Koran —

. . . from Thee alone do we ask help.
Guide us on the straight path,
The path of those upon whom is Thy favour.

General Rashood ended as he often did with undying praise of Allah . . . *I have turned my face only towards the Supreme Being who has created the skies and the earth . . . to You be the glory . . . Yours is the most auspicious name. You are exalted and none other than You is worthy of worship . . .*

They prayed silently for a few seconds and then returned to their tasks. Shakira reported to the Missile Director and checked once more the SCIMITAR's preset guidance programs — *Zero-three-zero from blast-off to latitude 46.05N degrees. Then course change to zero-nine-zero to longitude 127W . . . then course change*

161

to three-six-zero for 30 nautical miles . . . then final course change to two-one-zero 15 miles to the precise position of the target.

It was 0630 when General Rashood gave the order . . . *STAND BY TUBES ONE TO FOUR!*

Then, seconds later, *TUBE ONE LAUNCH!!*

And, at long last, the 26-foot steel guided missile, driven in an Army truck from the bowels of Kwanmo-bong in May, was on its way. *Barracuda II* shuddered gently as it blew out of the launcher, lanced up to the surface and split the Pacific swells asunder, its engines igniting, the searing light of the fiery tail obscured by the fog.

It blasted upwards, crackling into the morning sky, adjusting course and levelling out at 200 metres above the surface. At 600 knots the gas turbines kicked in, removing the giveaway trail in the sky, steady on its northeasterly course, its flawless precision a tribute to the craftsmen of Kwanmo-bong.

As they prepared to launch Tube Two, the senior command felt safe in the knowledge that the Koreans had sworn to make a true and faithful replica of the old Russian RADUGA, and that the SCIMITAR would match its performance in every way. The refined new rocket motor would be no problem, and the automatic rear wings would spread immediately the missile was airborne.

At this very moment, the North Koreans were batting 1,000, and the cruise missile they had created was hurtling diagonally towards the distant northern shores of the American state of Oregon. It was 220 miles to its landfall, and it would cross the coastline in twenty-one minutes. By which time three other identical missiles, already under the control of the *Barracuda*'s launch sequencer, would be streaking, line astern, right behind it. Same course. Through the fog. Destination: the fractured, haunted north face of Mount St Helens.

Missile One screamed in over the high, rugged coast, just north of Tillamook Head, at 1654. It thundered on across the 3,000-foot peak of Saddle Mountain, rising and falling with the contours of the earth. It passed Clatsop State Park and into Columbia County, making 600 knots as it crossed the wide river, then the state frontier, 20 miles downstream of the city of Portland.

This was high country, deep in the towering southern uplands of the Cascade Range. The SCIMITAR's preset computer brain, reading the sonar altimeter, was working overtime dealing with the dramatically changing ground levels. But the Chinese technicians had served General Rashood well.

The big Mark 1 missile ripped across Interstate 5 and shrieked through the peaks of Cowlitz County, heading along the Kalama River Valley to the Swift Creek Dam where it swerved north, right on schedule. By now the mighty tower of Mount St Helens was just a dozen miles to port, and the missile swept right past, still heading north. It flew swiftly over the great forests of the Cascades, and just after the little town of Gifford it made its turn, wheeling left in a great semi-circle.

The wilderness below was silent, but from the high peaks you might have heard the *W-H-O-O-O-O-SHHHHHH!* of disturbed air, as the SCIMITAR turned to the southwest. It held course two-one-zero, drawing a bead on the giant unstable carbuncle, which grew on the floor of the volcano crater, near the pinnacle of the mountain.

It came in fast, gathering speed as it lost height, almost 700 knots as it cleaved through the morning air above the foothills of Mount Hughes, where the Green River rises, east of Coldwater Creek. Moments later it hurtled into the skies high above the fog-shrouded, blue waters of Spirit Lake.

It rocketed through the thick, damp mist and crossed the north shore still making over 600 knots, and then angled up sharply to follow the steep slopes of Mount St Helens. It scythed through the air, taking just under nine seconds to make the one and a half mile ascent to the summit, where it banked, wickedly, downwards, and hammered its way straight into the middle of the crater.

Programmed to detonate two seconds after impact, the missile's sharp, reinforced steel nose lasered into the crater's unstable base of loose rock and ash, burying 15 feet below the surface before exploding with a booming impact. Rock and shale flew 100 feet into the air.

The SCIMITAR's warhead sent cracks like lightning bolts deep into the crust of the earth, splitting open the already shifting strata, way down where the magma seethed and churned, ever seeking an outlet. By itself, the first SCIMITAR could not have caused Mount St Helens to erupt. But there were three more where that came from, and the great volcano, had it known, would have braced itself for the incoming man-made thunder.

As it was, a great belch of steam did shoot skywards, but local residents did not see the warning; not even those driving trucks through the morning mist along local routes, 503, or 90, or south on 25 from Gifford. Even in clear conditions, it was not always easy to see the mountain peak from the tree-lined roads, and almost everyone had seen gouts of steam up there before, even the occasional fiery burst of ash.

Fifty-five seconds later Missile Two hit, in exactly the same spot, 46.20N 122.18W. It drove deep into the brand-new hole, not 10 feet from Missile One. It slammed into the lava rubble, detonating with staggering force into a part of the mountain that was rotten to the core, a shifting, sliding heap of black fragmented rock debris.

The fury of the explosion, though muffled to traffic five miles away, was enough to send long fissures deep into the upper conduit of the lava chimney. White-hot magma now came seething up through the black shale, as yet only eking its way out of the relatively slender gaps, but moving steadily higher.

Less than a minute later, there was a breakthrough. Missile Three came screaming in with sufficient force to knock down three skyscrapers. More burning magma came searing up through the underground channels; not yet a blast but close. The lava began to spill into the crater, steam and fire burst into the foggy skies.

And then came Missile Four, arrowing straight down into the molten lava and exploding instantly, same force as the others, same place, same effect. The metal casing melted, but the warhead's TNT did its work, blew the crevasse wide open, released a zillion cubic feet of compressed gasses. At 0706 on Sunday morning, 9 August 2009, Mount St Helens erupted with savage force for the second time in less than thirty years.

The explosion levelled thousands of Douglas fir trees within roughly a 12-mile half-circle to the north. The crater, which contained the unstable carbuncle, was already tilted that way, and when the eruption came it exploded northwards, leaving the area behind it, to the south and west, more or less unharmed, except for a 'rainstorm' of ash.

Again, as in 1980, the massive pyroclastic flow of molten lava surged down the upper slopes of the mountain, a terrifying nine-foot-high, white-hot river of molten rock from the very core of the earth. It seemed to move slowly, but it was making 40 mph as it crackled and growled its way into Spirit Lake, burning everything in its path, wiping out the lake's vegetation, boiling the water, sending hot steam up into the fog.

Of the campers on the north side of the lake and on the lower slopes of the mountain's pine forest, mostly kids and college students, none had a chance. A handful of burnt dust buried deep in volcanic rock would be all that remained of the soldiers in a cruel and sadistic war no one even knew was being fought.

The fog had cleared now, around the little towns of Glenoma, Morton and Mossyrock up on Routes 12 and 508, and the pinnacle of Mount St Helens could just be seen jutting up through the summit mist, belching fire and spewing thousands of tons of rock and red-hot ash hundreds of feet into the air.

It looked awesome, like many displays of nature too frightening to contemplate. But every man, woman or child in those picturesque little Washington townships knew they were witnessing havoc, pitiless destruction and heart-breaking loss of lives. Everyone who stood helplessly watching knew there would be many, many empty places at dinner tables that night, all over the American Northwest.

The lava rolled over a total of fifteen cars parked around the lake's perimeter, and the burning hot deposits of avalanche debris cascaded into the north fork of the Toutle River, almost damming it in some places. It completely blocked Coldwater Creek. A vast area of lateral blast deposits, thousands of tons of ash, spread over a distance of 200 square miles, choking rivers, burying forest and remote farm-houses.

The warm, sleepy Sunday morning of 9 August would be remembered for ever throughout this lonely rural corner of the 42nd State as Mount St

Helens, the towering snow-capped sentinel of the Gifford Pinchot National Forest, suddenly, without warning, reared and destroyed the very land which gave it grace.

On that Sunday morning, those who had not witnessed the shocking 1980 eruption saw the real nature of the mountain. And it had little to do with grandeur or with the great silent peak, which had dominated this southern part of the Washington State mountains – the bastion of strength, Queen of the Cascades.

This was the real St Helens, a colossal, 8,000-foot-high, black, unstable pile of rotten volcanic rubble, spewing forth dark grey burning ash, white-hot rock, black smoke and lava, vomited up from the basement of Hell. And it was bent on burning everything it could reach.

Within minutes of the first major eruption, right after SCIMITAR Four, the fires began. Great hunks of molten rock and dense showers of red-hot ash were landing in the pine forests. The tinder-dry dead needles on the forest floor practically exploded into flame, and the trees took only moments longer to ignite. The inflammable resin inside the needles, boughs and trunks of the Douglas firs popped and crackled into a giant, highly audible bonfire. From a distance, the blaze sounded like the eerie murmur of a battlefield.

Thousands of acres burned ferociously, spreading with terrifying swiftness before the west wind that billowed gently off the Pacific, dispersing the fog, fanning the flames. Every five minutes there was another grim and furious roar from the summit, and another plume of fire and ash ripped into the powder-blue sky, and another obscene surge of magma rolled over the crater and on down the mountainside.

By 0830 every household, every car full of tourists, every truck-load of outdoor sportsmen inside a 25-mile radius knew that Mount St Helens had erupted. The radio stations were cobbling together news bulletins based on almost nothing except the incontrovertible fact that the damn mountain just blew its goddamned head off. Again.

Volcano experts from all over the area were being rounded up, electronically, and interviewed. All of them confessed absolute bewilderment and by 0900 radio and television newsrooms were desperate for information. The State Police had placed a ban on media helicopters and it was impossible to get near the mountain.

The 'experts' who were permanently monitoring the volcano were impossible to find and the university study groups, collecting data in the foot-hills below the crater, were dead. Most of the observation posts to the north of the mountain were devastated, the building on the high ridges reduced to burned-out hulks, the low ones swept away by the incinerating magma.

Trees smashed by the blast leaned at ridiculous angles against others, which had withstood the explo-sion. These now formed towering enclosed pyramids of volatile, combustible dry pine branches, lit from within as the fire raced across the dead needles on the forest floor.

From above they looked like scattered furnaces, burning to red-hot flashpoints, and instantly setting fire to anything made of wood and resin within spitting distance.

By lunchtime the President had declared south-west Washington State a disaster zone and Federal help was on its way. The trouble with volcanoes, however, was that there were no half-measures, no wounded, no traumatised persons – and no witnesses. The fury of this type of assault on the planet is too formidable.

If you're near enough to cast light on the actual event from a close-up position, your chances of survival are close to zero. It was no different at the base of Mount St Helens on that Sunday morning . . . except for one big four-wheel-drive vehicle which had been parked all night on the northwest shore of Spirit Lake. This contained a selection of sporting rifles, fishing rods and four sportsmen, three of them local, one from Virginia.

Leader of the little expedition was Tony Tilton, a former attorney from Worcester, Massachusetts, currently President of the Seattle National Bank. Accompanying him was the legendary East Coast marine art dealer Alan Granby, who had moved west with his wife Janice after a money-grabbing private corporation threatened to build a massive wind farm opposite their backyard on the shores of Nantucket Sound.

The third member of the party was another East Coast native, the eminent broadcaster and political observer Don McKeag, who had finally abandoned his show on a local Cape Cod radio station for a huge network contract which required him to live and work out of Seattle – the Voice of the Northwest.

The fourth serious sportsman in that accomplished little group was the big-game fisherman, duck hunter and car racer, Jim Mills, from Middleburg, Virginia. They were on a week-long hunting, shooting and fishing trip, and they'd been camped by the lake all night, ready for an assault on the superb trout which made Spirit Lake their home.

There was one prime difference between these four and the rest of the sportsmen scattered around the lake in the warm summer months. Tony Tilton and his wife Martha had been cruising in the eastern Caribbean when the Montserrat volcano had exploded in 1997, burying two towns, wrecking the entire south side of the island and showering everything within 40 miles with thick, choking volcanic ash. Tony Tilton had stood on the foredeck of his chartered yacht and watched the towering inferno belch fire from the Soufrière Hills.

Etched in Tony's memory was the speed with which the mountain unleashed its wrath upon the island. He had seen the blast, watched the roaring plume of burning ash and smoke burst upwards, hundreds of feet into the sky. Almost simultaneously he had seen the great glowing evil of the magma begin its fatal roll down three sides of the mountain.

A trained attorney, he had the lawyer's grasp of facts and the banker's eye for the minutiae. In Tony's opinion you had approximately fourteen minutes to get the hell away from that mountain or perish.

And now, twelve years later, on that early Sunday morning on the shores of Spirit Lake, Tony heard a strange and sudden wind, a *wh-o-o-o-o-sssh* through the dense foggy air above the water. Instinctively he had glanced up but seen nothing.

Less than twelve seconds later he heard a dull muffled roar from way up on the mountain, but again he could see nothing up the slopes through the fog. He heard the wind again, and another shuddering distant thump from the summit of the mountain. It was louder this time, but perhaps only because Tony was already on high alert.

That did it for the Seattle Bank President. He turned to Don McKeag and said sharply, 'Get in the wagon, Donnie. And don't speak. Just get in, then yelled towards the tent '*ALAN, JIMMY . . . GET UP AND GET IN THE WAGON . . . RIGHT NOW . . . WE'RE IN BIG TROUBLE.*

Alan Granby, a big man, but as light on his feet as the late great Jackie Gleason, got it in one. He and Jimmy had slept fully dressed and they both came scrambling out of their tents, alerted by the obvious tension in Tony Tilton's voice.

The engine of the wagon was already running, and they both jumped into the rear seats. Tony hit the gas pedal and they burned rubber on the warm shores of the lake, heading west through the short

172

forest trail which led to Route 504. The trail was straight and relatively smooth and the wagon was moving at almost 70 mph when they heard the third explosion right behind them, followed quickly by another.

'What in the name of hell was that?' asked Don McKeag.

'Nothing much,' said Tony. 'Except I think Mount St Helens just erupted.' By now they were on the country road which would lead north up to the town of Glenoma and the much faster Route 25. And all around them there were strange glowing lights falling into the trees like a meteor shower.

But the brightness had gone out of the day. Alan Granby glanced at the sky. 'If I had to guess,' he said, 'I'd say this was the start of a partial eclipse of the sun.'

At that moment, they felt an earth-shuddering rumble beneath the wheels of the wagon, and a howling wind screamed through the forest, like a hurricane. Tony hammered the wagon up deserted Route 12, heading north and conscious of the burning debris beginning to litter the road.

'Let's hope I don't get into reverse by mistake,' he muttered. 'I got a feeling anyone left back there might not make it.'

The miles whipped away beneath their wheels, and now the sky was darkening into a thick, high, gun-grey cloud above them. Yet through the rear window they could discern a terrible glow in the sky. In eleven minutes they had put 12 miles between themselves and the lower slopes of Mount St Helens. Up ahead it looked slightly brighter, and Don, ever the journalist, suggested they pull over after another couple of miles and take a look back at the mountain, and the fires, and the scorched earth they had somehow escaped.

'Any of you guys fancy a short hunting–fishing trip next year to Indonesia?' asked Tony. 'You know . . . a nice little base camp on the slopes of Krakatoa . . . I'm getting to be a real pro at volcano escape . . .'

Three hours later

Good morning everyone, this is Don McKeag, reporting first-hand from the front-line of our state-wide catastrophe. During the sudden and devastating eruption of Mount St Helens, I was in a hunting camp right in the foothills of the volcano as it was about to detonate.

I think I can say honestly it is nothing short of a miracle that I am here talking to you this morning . . . because I was spared from certain death by the quick thinking of my friend Tony Tilton who somehow drove us to safety . . . through the fires and the volcanic ash . . . out in front of the molten lava . . . away from the cataclysmic explosion.

For my regular weekday morning programme you know I always take calls and discuss the politics of this great state . . . today I'm changing the format . . . I just want to sit here, catch my breath, and try

to explain what it's like, literally, to escape from the
jaws of Hell . . . so far we're getting reports of per-
haps a 100 of our fellow citizens who never made
it . . . to their families I want to express my deepest,
most profound sorrow and sympathy . . . I might
very easily have been one of them . . .

As Don spoke, in measured yet inevitably dramatic tones, every fireman in southwest Washington State was engaged in fighting the fires along the periphery of the central blaze. It was pointless even to think about entering the interior zone below the north face of the mountain or about running a fleet of ambulances into the inferno. There would be no injured.

The only thing that could be done now was to try and stem the blazing forest, to stop it spreading outwards to wreak havoc and misery upon un-suspecting homeowners. Soon they would have crop-sprayers in the skies dumping hundreds of tons of water on the parts of the forests which remained intact. Others were out there pumping and spraying great tracts of forest, trying to stop the searing heat from evaporating the water before the fires even arrived.

By mid-Sunday afternoon, the disaster was big national news. CNN had pictures, as did Fox News and most of the networks. By Sunday evening, all of the twenty-four-hour news channels were strug-gling with the story. They were without any fresh information, new facts or revelatory opinions. Yes,

Mount St Helens had made a titanic eruption early on Sunday morning. Yes, there was a lot of fire and fury, ash, molten rock and lava. And yes, anyone trapped in the immediate vicinity of the mountain was most certainly dead. And yes, there were God-knows-how-many forest fires raging all around the northern territories beyond the volcano. Eyewitnesses from close-up? Zero, except for Don McKeag and his three friends.

Volcanoes traditionally do anything they damn well please, ruling out the possibilities of indignant editorials proclaiming in time-honoured cliché, *WHY THIS MUST NEVER HAPPEN AGAIN.* Or *DID THEY DIE IN VAIN?* Or, *WAS THIS AN ACCIDENT WAITING TO HAPPEN?* Or even, that cringe-making old favourite, *HEADS MUST ROLL!* Instead, the news and feature rooms turned, admittedly with a mixture of reluctance and relief, to The Experts, many of whom had died on the mountain, but some of whom were ready to cast a light on an occurrence about which they had not the remotest clue.

Yes, there had been steam and even some gasses leaking from the crater on the summit in recent weeks. Yes, there had been signs of fire, ashes and black smoke bursting into the atmosphere. And no, it would not have been a tremendous surprise if Mount St Helens had erupted in the next five years. The giant carbuncle was indeed a significant factor.

What baffled the professors was the sheer speed of the eruption; so sudden, so unexpected, so utterly

176

without warning. This was a new concept for volcanologists all over the world. No angry early blasts, no torrents of high sparks and sinister rumbles, not even the sight of molten lava creeping out over the rim of the crater. Nothing. This was The Whispering Death of Mount St Helens. Unseen. Unsuspected. Unannounced.

CNN rustled up a young volcanologist from the University of California in Santa Cruz. He had never even seen Mount St Helens and was not born when it erupted in 1980. His father was not born when Lassen Peak, the only other comparable volcanic eruption in the US, let fly in 1914. But the recently qualified Simon Lyons from Orange County spoke with the unwavering authority of those sufficiently youthful still to know the answers to everything.

'Any halfway decent student of geohazardous situations must have known this volcano could have erupted any time,' he said. 'That carbuncle was growing at a very fast rate, maybe a half-mile across in the last two years. That's the sign we're all looking for. That's the sign of the encroaching magma, surging up from the core of the earth. You see a carbuncle being force-fed with lava from below; right there you're looking at a volcano fixing to blow.'

'Then you blame those study groups based on the mountain, supposedly monitoring it for the benefit of us all . . . using Federal funds?'

'Yes, sir. I most certainly do. Incompetence. Ignorance of the value of the data. Ought to be anathema to a real scientist.'

Professor Charles Delmar, of the University of Colorado, was older, more experienced and more circumspect. For News got a hold of him and he was the first to admit he could throw little light on the eruption.

He said the photographs he had been shown suggested the Sunday morning blowout on the summit of the mountain had been aimed to the north, which suggested the carbuncle itself had given way to the pressure of the magma below. Professor Delmar found that 'most unusual' simply because there were no other reported symptoms of eruptions from that precise location. There had been evidence of steam gouts and some smoke, but that was reportedly emanating from the mountain peak, not from cracks in the carbuncle, which would have been an indication of pressure underneath the dome of lava rock.

Therefore Professor Delmar considered it 'most odd' that it should suddenly have obliterated itself and 'even more odd' that it should have given way so comprehensively, so quickly, that the third biggest volcano eruption in the USA in a hundred years should have happened, literally, within moments.

Barracuda II moved slowly south down the Pacific, following the 127th western line of longitude for another 100 miles. It was almost 0300 when the great submarine moved stealthily to the surface, ran up an ESM mast and transmitted a one-word message to their command headquarters, via the satellite, in faraway Bandar Abbas on the Strait of Hormuz.

SALADIN was the word. And the transmission was forwarded on by e-mail to a computer based on Via Dolorosa, in the Muslim section of Jerusalem, the very street down which Christ is said to have carried his cross en route to Calvary.

Within moments, a sealed letter with air mail stamps already affixed was in the hands of a messenger, running swiftly through the old city to the Central Post Office on Schlomzion Street.

It was addressed to *Admiral Arnold Morgan, The White House, 1600 Pennsylvania Avenue, Washington, DC, USA. PRIVATE AND CONFIDENTIAL.* General Rashood knew the admiral no longer worked in the West Wing, but he was confident the US Administration's gigantic, 50,000-pieces-a-week mail room would find a way to forward the letter to the admiral's private home address.

CHAPTER FIVE

Friday 14 August 2009
Chevy Chase, Maryland

Harry, chief security agent to Admiral Arnold
Morgan, signed for the four letters delivered
by the White House courier. Then he walked to the
mail box especially fitted inside the porch, emptied
it and walked around to the high gate which guarded
the entrance to the swimming pool area of the
house, the large dark-blue, rectangular body of water.

Three of the surrounding high stone walls were
in a light Spanish-style salmon pink; giant terra cotta
pots overflowing with green shrubs were planted all
around. The fourth wall was a high wooden fence
into which was set a small *cabana* with a polished
teakwood bar and four stools.

'*Sir!*' Harry called. 'Would you like me to bring
the mail through?'

'I guess if you must persist in ruining my entire
day with goddamned trivia, then you better do
it,' came the rasping voice over the top of the
fence.

'Yes, sir,' said Harry, let himself in and walked

across to the wide glass-topped table where Admiral Morgan sat in a director's chair, frowning, as he mostly did, at the political views of the *New York Times*. As with many of America's daily publications, the paper was currently enjoying a gleeful period, congratulating the wonderful new Democratic President Charles McBride.

'Jesus Christ,' growled Arnold. 'I didn't realise you could get that many total assholes under one editorial roof. Except possibly in the *Washington Post* . . . which I haven't read yet, since I'm trying to keep my blood pressure steady.'

'Yes, sir,' said Harry, putting the admiral's mail on his table, next to the coffee pot. 'See the Orioles won again last night?'

'I did,' replied the admiral. '*And* they made two errors. Same spot as usual. Straight up the goddamned middle. I'm telling you, they've needed a top short-stop ever since Bordick left. And until they get one, they'll never make the play-offs . . .'

'You watch the game, sir?'

'Just the last coupla innings, after dinner. Missed all the runs, though. Only saw the errors. For a minute, I thought the Yanks might catch us.'

'Yeah. So did I. Good closer though, that kid from Japan. Saved our ass, right, sir?'

'He did too . . . now, what's all this bullshit you've brought me? Hop inside and bring me out a plastic bag, will you? I've a feeling this consignment is about 99 per cent garbage.'

'Okay, sir . . . be right back.'

181

The admiral looked at the top four letters, the ones from the White House. One was from the pensions department, two were invitations, the fourth was from someone in the Middle East, judging from the sheik portrait on the stamp.

Arnold rarely looked at a photograph or painting of an elderly Arab without remembering, automatically, the towers of the World Trade Center eight years earlier. He took the letter and tore open the cream-coloured envelope impatiently. The single sheet of writing paper inside was not headed by a printed address. It was plain. No date. Across the middle were three typed lines, plus a one-word printed signature. Nothing personal.

Admiral Morgan, you do not suppose for
one moment that the eruption of Mount St
Helens was an accident, do you?   *– HAMAS*

Arnold gaped. He turned the sheet over, checked the envelope. There was not another clue, anywhere. Just this barefaced inquiry, full of menace. Could it be a hoax.

In the old days he would have instantly summoned Admiral Morris and then gone straight into the Oval Office, without knocking.

Today, however, sitting by the pool at 11 o'clock on a warm morning, a civilian in every sense of the word, things were very different. What were his duties? What should he decide? Well, nothing was the answer, on both counts. He was not required to decide a damn thing, and he found this almost impossible to accept.

Kathy was out at the hairdresser. He absent-mindedly watched Harry bring out the plastic bag in which he would deposit most of the mail. But the letter from HAMAS was burning his hand like a hot coal. He watched Harry wander out of the pool gate, poured himself a cup of coffee and ruminated.

Finally, he decided the correct thing to do was to take the correspondence, place it in an envelope, tell Harry to whistle up the White House courier, and send the little package around to the man who had replaced him in the office of the President's National Security Adviser.

Let him worry about the damn thing. It was no longer his, Arnold's, concern. So he went inside, carefully made a couple of copies and did exactly what he had decided. After placing the letter into a plastic bag, he added a little note to his successor, Cyrus Romney, former professor of Liberal Arts at Berkeley, and marcher *in almost every misguided, half-assed, goddamned demonstration for peace the West Coast had seen in living memory*.

If Arnold Morgan had had his way, Cyrus Romney would have been instructed to march his way to Outer Mongolia and stay there. Arnold Morgan did not at all believe the California to be an ideal choice to occupy the great Office of State, which, by all accounts, he owed mainly to a lifelong friendship with fellow peacenik, Charles McBride.

Arnold's letter was cool: *Dear Cyrus . . . This came*

to me, mistakenly, today, possibly from people who did not know of the changes in the US Government this year. Make of it what you will. Sincerely, Arnold Morgan.

The personal note from the old Lion of the West Wing, would, Arnold knew, probably get short shrift from both Cyrus and his boss. Did he care what either of them thought? Not a jot.

Did he care what the implied HAMAS threat might mean to the United States of America? On a scale of 1 to 1,000, Admiral Morgan was somewhere in the high fractions above 999. He walked back to the pool, picked up his mobile phone and made a call to the private line of Admiral George Morris at Fort Meade.

'George . . . Arnie . . . got time for a brief private chat?'

A half-hour later he was on his way around the beltway, Harry at the wheel of the admiral's new automobile, General Motors' state-of-the-art four-wheel-drive masterpiece, the 2009 Hummer H2A, a direct descendant of the military's old desert warhorse the Humvee. Admiral Morgan's great friend Jack Smith, the Energy Secretary in the last Republican Administration, and former President of General Motors, had told him: 'This thing is made for you, mainly because Kathy could drive it easily, and you could go to war in it.'

Arnold replied, 'Would General Patton have liked it?'

'General Patton would probably have lived in it!' replied Jack.

Two other armed agents in a private White House car followed hard astern. They too had bullet-proof glass.

They swung north up the parkway, drove quickly through the sprawling countryside surrounding the National Secury Agency. At the main gates, a security guard walked to the driver's side and asked for passes. He was hardly able to finish his sentence.

'*Get in, and escort me immediately to the office of the Director, in OPS-2B.*' The guard recognised the former tsar of Fort Meade, and understood that he might be working out the last three minutes of his career if he was not careful.

'SIR, YES SIR!' snapped the former US Army Master Chief, and hopped right into the back seat. Harry knew the way, and the guard jumped out and hissed to the next guard on the main doors. 'Chuck, it's the Big Man – I'm taking him up to Admiral Morris.'

'Rightaway, sir,' he replied and opened the door while Arnold was disembarking. He and his escort went up to the eighth floor in the Director's private elevator.

'Tell Harry to take you back, then to wait right outside for me . . . and thanks, soldier.'

'You're welcome, sir,' he replied holding the door open and waiting to hear Admiral Morris greet the Big Man, as he knew he would.

'Arnie, great to see you . . . come and sit down. It's been too long.'

Actually it had been about two months. Too long.

For both of the old seafarers. And for the first time Admiral Morgan did not walk around to the big chair, which he had once occupied himself. He accepted an offer of coffee, declined lunch, and parked himself in a large wooden captain's chair in front of the Director's desk.

Solemnly, he reached into his inside jacket pocket and handed over a copy of the letter he had received a couple of hours earlier. George Morris stared at it, his bushy eyebrows raised.

'Jesus,' he said. 'When did this arrive?'

'This morning.'

'How?'

'Regular mail.'

'From where?'

'The Middle East. All the postmarks were very smudged. But I think the stamp was Palestinian, the special ones issued in parts of Israel. Had a picture of some sheik on it.'

'Have you told anyone?'

'Oh, sure. I sent the original over to the White House, to my successor. Told him the letter had come to me by mistake.'

Admiral Morris nodded. 'You did not elaborate about our previous discussions on the subject of Arab terrorists and volcanoes?'

'Hell, no. They would have loved an opportunity to imply that I was a paranoid old relic from the Cold War . . . and anyway I don't have the energy to argue with jerks.'

'Yes, you do.'

'I know. But I don't feel like it.'

George Morris looked again at the message from HAMAS. And he recalled their evening together with Jimmy Ramshawe in Chevy Chase a couple of months earlier.

'Of course I know what you're thinking, Arnie . . . your honeymoon mountain in the Canaries last January, right? One of them almost certainly a HAMAS assault commander? And we have your photograph of him, in company with two volcanologists from Tehran? And now this – eight months later, HAMAS sends a note . . . implies it blew Mount St Helens. Kinda fits together.'

'Well, the coincidence is a little striking. Although I understand you can't just go around blowing up volcanoes. So far as I recall no one's ever done such a thing. Not in all of history, and volcanoes have a lot of that, thousands of years.'

'Yeah, but the last sixty are the only ones that count,' said George. 'No one had a big enough explosive before that.'

'You read anything about nuclear fallout in the Mount St Helens area?'

'Well, I haven't looked. But we would have been informed if there was any such thing. I'd guess that mountain is still a lot too hot for anyone to make any checks.'

'I don't get it,' pondered Admiral Morgan. 'I cannot believe anyone just planted a bomb in the crater. And anyway, a bomb probably would not have done the job. They don't explode downwards. Surely to

187

blow a volcano you'd have to burrow down into the ground, way down and then detonate.'

'Christ,' said George. 'Imagine doing that. Excavating the main lava chimney of a volcano, probably several hundred feet, knowing the damn thing could erupt any moment and fry you.'

'How about a missile?' said Arnold suddenly. 'How about a missile coming in at high speed with a sharp front end, designed to bang its way into the rock on the floor of the crater?'

'Well, who knows? It would take a pretty wide investigation to find out if such a thing was possible – like how thick was the floor of the crater . . . you know, it might have been impenetrable. And anyway, where could the missile have come from – I imagine you're not talking ICBN, are you?'

'Well, not from HAMAS. God help us if they've got one of those. But I'm thinking maybe a cruise aimed at the crater. Or two. Or three. Or more.'

'Fired from?'

'Usual place, George. Possibly that second *Barracuda* which appears to have vanished off the face of the earth.'

'Well, I suppose that's all possible. But with this Administration, we cannot spend a lot of time chasing up theories like that. They're already asking us to downsize every department, there's going to be enormous budget cuts, and they have their own agendas, mostly to do with calling off our world-wide hunt for imaginary terrorists.'

'Hmmmm,' said Arnie. 'Do you think they're

going to react in any way to the letter from HAMAS?

'Romney will dismiss it as a hoax. And the President will agree with him. My guess is, it will never get as far as here. Though they might just forward a copy to the CIA.'

'How about it isn't a hoax. How about they did hit Mount St Helens? How about they are in that fucking nuclear submarine, loaded to the gunwhales with missiles, planning God knows what? How about they really did send a letter of warning?'

'I guess we'll know soon enough,' said George.

'How'dya mean?'

'Well, that letter was unfinished,' said George. '*You don't think Mount St Helens was an accident because it wasn't . . . we did it . . . and what's more . . .*' His voice trailed off. 'That's what it really said, right?'

'Absolutely. And if the letter had any substance whatsoever, we'll hear again, correct?'

'That's my take on it, Arnie old buddy.'

'Okay. But meanwhile I would like you to ask young Ramshawe to do a bit of sleuthing, check a few things up for me . . . I want to show him the letter, if that's okay by you.'

'No problem. I'll walk you down to his office. He's less busy these days. We all are.'

The two admirals finished their coffee and walked down to the office of the Director's assistant. Lt. Commander Ramshawe was hunched over a pile of papers, his office much less like a rubbish tip than usual, the clear and obvious sign of a workload reduction.

189

Everything had changed in the world of international Intelligence. Where once people in the White House and the Pentagon jumped when a single word of warning emanated from Fort Meade, nowadays there was only cynicism. NSA suspicions were dismissed curtly. The new Administration's significant operations staff followed their President's lead – that is, the CIA, the FBI, the military and the National Security Agency were comprised of a group of old-fashioned spooks, out of touch with reality, living in a somewhat murky past of Cold Wars, Hot Wars and random terrorism.

The modern world, at the conclusion of the first decade of the new millennium, was a completely different place. What mattered here was friendship, cooperation, not military build-ups, witch-hunts for allegedly corrupt dictators, and truly ferocious attacks by America's Special Forces against those who displeased or fell foul of the United States.

People like old Arnold Morgan, even General Scannell, Admiral Dickson and certainly Admirals John Bergstrom (SPECWARCOM) and George Morris, were regarded as dinosaurs. Young White House execs had taken to using Jurassic Park as a kind of insider's code-name for the great Fort Meade Intelligence complex. The Pentagon's High Command were The Psychopaths. And President McBride had served notice that he did not like being surrounded by the military, not inside his own White House. And this despite the fact that the Navy practically ran the place, the Army providing the cars and drivers, the Defense Department the communications, the Air Force all aircraft, and the Navy the helicopters.

Yes, a President could marginalise the military. And yes, he could dismiss them as irrelevant to his programmes. But, as Commander-in-Chief, he would upset the admirals and generals at his own peril. No President of the United States had ever gone quite as far as losing the confidence of the Pentagon.

So far, Charles McBride was only tinkering. But he was already having an effect and soon young officers like Lt. Commander Jimmy Ramshawe might decide the civilian world was beckoning. But not yet.

'G'day, gentlemen,' he greeted the two admirals. And he stood up to shake hands with Admiral Morgan. 'Peaceful retirement, sir? Not missing the factory yet?'

Arnold chuckled, amused that Jimmy still remembered he traditionally referred to the White House as 'the factory'.

Admiral Morris took his leave, saying, 'Jimmy, the Admiral wants to have a chat with you. I have to go to that meeting. You needn't bother about it. Stay here and talk to Arnold. He's got some interesting stuff to show you.'

'As ever,' replied the lt. commander, grinning his lopsided Aussie grin. 'See you later, sir. Okay, Admiral, I'm all ears.'

Arnold Morgan took out the copy of the HAMAS

letter and handed it over, watching while Jimmy read.

'Streuth,' he said softly. 'That looks to me like these bastards just blew up Mount St Helens?'

'Maybe,' said Arnold, cautiously.

'Well, if they didn't, what's this then?'

'Good question, James. Good question. Although we shouldn't dismiss the straightforward answer that it's just an ordinary hoax, the kind we get from all manner of fucking lunatics, all the time.'

'Yeah. But this is a bit subtle for a lunatic, sir. They're apt to write more on the lines of . . . *Listen to me, assholes. I just blew up the goddamned volcano, and I'm planning to do it again. God's telling me to clean up the planet. Ha ha ha.*'

'I know. That's true. And I'm glad you're getting a feeling of authenticity from this note. Like I am. It's just the way it's phrased. And George jumped on the fact that it seemed like unfinished business . . . *You thought it was an accident . . . well, it wasn't . . . it was us . . . and we'll be in touch* . . . That's its tone. It doesn't say so, but it might as well have ended by stating . . . *we'll be in touch.*'

'That's my feeling. No doubt,' replied Jimmy.

'Well, to short-circuit a lot of chat,' said Arnold. 'Let's assume they did blow Mount St Helens. A bomb could not have done it. Which leaves a missile, or missiles.

'As ever, they seemed to come from nowhere. As ever, they must have come from a submarine. You know, specially made cruises, big, sharp-pointed nose

192

cones, which would pierce the floor of the crater. So far as I can see, that's the only possibility. So . . . where, Jimmy, is the second *Barracuda*?'

'Hold it, sir. Lemme just jump into the ole computer.' He hit several keys, the screen flashed a few times and settled into the file he requested. 'Sir, I'll read this stuff off, just the important bits . . . you might want to make a couple of notations while I do it. Here's a notepad and a pen . . . ready?'

'Fire at will,' replied the admiral, easing into the spirit of things.

'July the 5th, spotted the *Barracuda* making a southerly passage down the Yellow Sea, out of Huludao, where she'd been for one month in a covered dock. We got her at 40.42 North 121.20 East heading for the Bo Hai Strait. After that it's anyone's guess.

'She could have gone through the Korean Strait, or around the outside of Japan and headed north, south, east or west. Or even back to Zhanjiang where'd she'd been for many months. The satellite shots showed three tiny figures on the bridge. I made a note, hope to Christ one of 'em wasn't Major Ray Kerman, or we're in real trouble!

'She dived as soon as the water was deep enough off South Korea, then vanished. But I have two more notes here . . . on 16 July our SOSUS station on the island of Attu, far west end of the Aleutians, reported a transient contact to the north, 53.51–175.01 East. They thought it was a nuclear turbine. They also thought it was Russian. Heard a lot of noise, ballast blowing, high revs for one minute. Then nothing.

'But we picked up something on 22 July, six days later, precisely consistent with a submarine making a very slow five-knot passage for 720 miles to the Unimak Pass. It was just a radar contact . . . five seconds . . . three sweeps on the screen.

'Then it disappeared. Tell you the truth, sir, I would not have bothered much. It was just the length of passage, 120 miles a day for six days, average five knots, just the exact numbers you would expect from a sneaky little sonofabitch, right?'

'Running north of the Aleutians, eh?' said the admiral. 'How about its passage from the Yellow Sea to Attu? Does that fit a pattern?'

'Hell yes, sir. Ten days, no trouble. I should think they were moving pretty carefully. It could have been the *Barracuda*. Plus, I checked the boards and there's not another bloody submarine within a thousand miles, except our own patrol in the Aleutian Trench.'

'I wonder,' said Arnold Morgan. 'I really wonder. Could these little bastards really have exploded a massive volcano? You've got to doubt that. But with this Ray fucking Kerman, who knows? And he was checking out the most dangerous volcano in the world when I last saw him!

'Jimmy, I think we want to get in touch with a top volcano guy and find out once and for all whether it was *possible* to have exploded Mount St Helens. Then we want to find out if there was anything remotely suspicious about that eruption.

194

Maybe check out the local police and FBI. Then we want to cast a long look over any major volcano story which appeared anywhere in the past year. Anything which might show the guys we seek are active in the field . . .'

'Sir, we'll have to settle for *one of the top* volcanologists, rather than *the top* volcanologist.'

'We will, why's that?'

'Because the top man was found murdered in London last May. He was called Professor Paul Landon. Washed up in the middle of the River Thames, some island halfway along the University Boat Race course according to the London *Daily Telegraph* . . .'

'Christ,' said Arnold. 'That sounds bad. Must have been Chiswick Eyot, just upstream from Hammersmith Bridge – that's really the only island around there.' Arnold chortled, always pleased to have bamboozled the young. 'I know the river pretty well. A long time ago I pulled the bow oar for Annapolis at the Henley Regatta in the Thames Cup. And a few years later I did a couple of stints helping coach the eight.'

'Ah, well, Landon was the main man in his field. I don't believe the police ever did find out who or why. They seemed to write it off as mistaken identity of some kind. I wouldn't have been so sure myself. The professor was executed, two bullets in the back of the head. Doesn't sound much like an accident to me.'

'Jimmy, have another look at that, will you? Talk to someone about the feasibility of blowing Mount

St Helens. And find out if anyone had any suspicion whatsoever about the eruption . . . meanwhile I've gotta go . . . tell George g'bye and keep him well posted.'

'Okay, sir, I'll walk you downstairs.'

'No need, kid. I was finding my way in and out of this place while you were throwing toy tanks across the room.'

They both laughed, shook hands, and Admiral Morgan was gone. Four hours later a copy of the letter from HAMAS arrived on George Morris's desk. It was direct from the White House, headed FYI, and signed by Cyrus Romney. At the bottom was a note scrawled by hand informing the admiral that both Cyrus and the President regarded it as an obvious hoax and no action would be necessary, nor should time be wasted upon investigation.

Admiral Morris, who had been sequestered with Lt. Commander Ramshawe for the past two hours, just muttered, 'Oh, I see, Mr Romney? And that's with the benefit of your entire five months' experience of international terrorism? Asshole.'

Meanwhile, down the corridor Ramshawe was in full cry. He tackled the London murder first, because they were five hours ahead and if he needed to call anyone today, he'd have to be quick.

He keyed into the internet and searched diligently for anything more on the professor. Found nothing after the report of the body being washed up, and an account in the *Telegraph* about the subsequent memorial service in London, attended by Britain's heaviest academics. But he'd read that already in the Court and Society page a couple of months earlier.

He scrolled down into a website, which pulled up front pages of the *Telegraph*, the *Daily Mail*, *The Times* and the *Financial Times*. He'd found it useful before, and he went into each day from 9 May, when Professor Landon first went missing.

Jimmy had checked out the *Mail* and the *Telegraph* before, but that was three months ago when no one else was interested. He was much more thorough now. Whereas last May he had only persisted for a week after the professor's disappearance, now he went further. And he checked those front pages assiduously.

It was the edition of the *Daily Mail* for 18 May which caught his eye. There was a splash front-page strapline, which read:

Scotland Yard Baffled by the Albert Hall Massacre

Beneath this, in three decks of end-of-the-world type, ranged left, it demanded:

WHO KILLED THESE
MEN ON THE NIGHT
OF MAY 8TH?

To the right were three photographs showing Police Constables Peter Higgins and Jack Marlow and then Professor Paul Landon. A photograph of Roger, the dead German shepherd attack dog, was set much smaller in the centre of the page . . . *Gunned Down: a cruel end for brave Roger* was the caption

Lt. Commander Ramshawe almost had a seizure. The *Daily Mail* had skipped over one highly significant fact: that Special Branch had been called in to investigate one of the police murders. Jimmy knew there must have been some suspicion of terrorism.

The *Daily Mail* knew something really important, however, of which James Ramshawe had been utterly unaware so far: all three murders may have been committed within a few yards of each other at precisely the same time.

Jimmy sat back and regained his composure. He poured himself a cup of cold coffee and settled down to read every word of the newspaper account.

And slowly, as he read the story, the indisputable facts became clear. On the night of 8 May, Professor Landon had delivered his speech at London's Royal Geographical Society, and then headed southwest, towards his car. The vehicle was later found nearby, parked in the precincts of Imperial College off Queen's Gate. The professor had been seen by a member of his audience hurrying through to the wide steps at the rear of the Albert Hall.

That was the last time 'Lava' Landon was seen alive. He never returned home that night, and his body was found in the river six days later on the afternoon of 14 May. The police pathologist said he was uncertain of the time or even the day of death, because the body had been in the river for some time.

That same night of the lecture, the two policemen were murdered in the area directly behind the Albert Hall, on the precise route of Professor Landon's walk to his car, at the precise time Professor Landon was there on the wide steps. The *Daily Mail* had shrewdly connected the two, and, taking a leaf out of Roger's book, bounded eagerly into the fray, announcing *The Albert Hall Massacre*. There were, after all, three dead bodies. Plus Roger.

Of course, an Intelligence officer would instantly ask the crucial question: who said the professor was murdered, like the policemen, on the back steps of the Albert Hall? Plainly the professor could have been kidnapped and *taken* anywhere, and in the end, *been shot* anywhere. There was not one lick of evidence to suggest he too had died on the steps of the Albert Hall.

Indeed, if he had, the killers would probably have left his body there, together with the policemen.

In Jimmy's opinion, the *Daily Mail* was essentially on the right track. The devastating coincidence of the place and time of the crimes was simply too great. There must have been a connection of some kind, and the big London newspaper had made it, even though Scotland Yard had not been able to come up with a motive.

But, Jimmy thought, chances were that the professor had been taken alive, and the two cops had been killed for interfering. The question now was: what the hell were Special Branch doing, involved in a civilian crime?

'Well, it wasn't a bloody kidnap as such, was it,' mused Jimmy. 'Otherwise there'd have been a ransom demand. Whoever grabbed Landon wanted him for something else. They took him away alive, then killed him later. I'd be bloody certain of that.'

He pondered the problem, called someone and inquired what precisely one had to do to get a hot cup of coffee around here? And was there anyone in residence who cared one way or another whether he carried on trying to save the world, or, alternatively, died of thirst. The resident eighth-floor manager of the twenty-four-hour-a-day executive kitchen had a very soft spot for the affable Aussie lt. commander, although he secretly believed that Jimmy was becoming more and more like the terrifying Admiral Arnold Morgan every day.

'Be right over, sir . . . want some cookies or anything?'

'Those are the words of a bloody Christian,' replied Jimmy, in his best Aussie accent. 'Ship 'em in.'

And he put the phone down slowly, still wondering what exactly New Scotland Yard's Special Branch was doing in the investigation into the London murders.

Not for the first time he decided to call an old Navy buddy, Rob Hackett, over in the CIA at Langley, just to check if they had anything on the murders. The answer was sharp. Nothing. It was a purely British domestic crime and the CIA had made no inquiries.

Jimmy's pal couldn't help with the question of

Special Branch, but he immediately agreed to make a few calls. Inside forty-five minutes, Rob was back.

'Ve-e-e-e-ry eeeenteresting,' said the CIA man slowly, impersonating Hercule Poirot, or some other European gumshoe. 'Special Branch were in there because of the manner of death inflicted on one of the policeman . . . not the one who was shot, like the woofer. The other one whose skull was split.'

'Yeah?' said Jimmy. 'I didn't even know his skull was split.'

'And how,' said Rob. 'Straight down the middle of his forehead, like he'd been hit with a fucking axe. And then we have the eeeenteresting part. What killed him was a terrific punch under his nose, which drove the bone directly into his brain. It was a blow, according to my guy in London, which could *only* have been delivered by a trained Special Forces expert in unarmed combat. That's why Special Branch was in there. Plus for anti-terrorist guys. Scotland Yard have never announced one word of this.'

Jimmy Ramshawe froze in his chair. 'Have we been here before, Rob?'

'We surely have. Last year. That Member of Parliament, Rupert someone, was killed in exactly the same way. Though with less of a long fracture of the forehead.'

'No wonder the anti-terrorist guys were in there,' said Jimmy. 'Hey, Rob, thanks a million . . .'

'Okay, Jim,' chuckled the CIA man. 'Now don't go rushing in there and adding up two and two to make six.'

'Not me, old mate. I'm about to add things up to at least four hundred, maybe more.' He slowly replaced the receiver, blew out his cheeks and expelled the air noisily, the universal sound of utter amazement.

'Holy shit,' he said to the otherwise empty room. 'That fucking "Lava" Landon was grabbed by Major Ray Kerman. I think. Told him how to blow up a volcano. And he's just bloody done it. And what's more he's just *TOLD* us he's bloody done it. *H-O-L-Y SHI-I-I-T!! . . .*'

He steadied himself, cooled down his excitement. Thoughts rampaged through his mind . . . *what do I do first? Call George? Call Admiral Morgan? Write a report? Stand on my fucking head? Have another cup of coffee? How urgent is this? Hold it, Jim . . . get into control . . .*

He'd been given three tasks by Admiral Morgan, and he'd done two of them – checked out the volcano stories and checked out Special Branch involvement. Scored a bull's-eye both times.

Conclusion: Professor Paul Landon, the world's leading volcanologist, was snatched in London by Major Kerman and his men. In the course of this operation they had to kill two interfering policemen and one attack dog. Kerman then grilled and subsequently executed the professor. Three months later, on behalf of HAMAS, the ex-SAS major calmly informed the US he had blown up Mount St Helens.

The third and only outstanding task Jimmy had left was to check with the Washington State police whether there was anything to suggest a missile had been fired into the bloody crater near the top of the mountain.

With the West Coast three hours back, he picked up the phone and asked the operator to connect him to someone in the State Police HQ who had first-hand knowledge of the Mount St Helens dossier. It took a while to make the call because the highly trained Fort Meade operator went from person to person until he found a trooper likely to satisfy a high-level investigator from the National Security Agency. Then they had to call back to verify the validity of the call from the NSA.

When Jimmy picked up the phone, a voice said, 'Sir, this is Officer Ray Suplee speaking. How can I help?'

'Officer, this is Lt. Commander Jimmy Ramshawe, assistant to the Director of the National Security Agency at Fort Meade, Maryland. May I assume you were involved in the immediate report on the Mount St Helens disaster?'

'Yes, sir. I was on patrol along Route 12 heading south towards the mountain when it erupted. It happened pretty quick, and I could see it from a high point in the road. I heard it too. Huge blast, followed by wind, and the sky seemed full of ashes, blocked the sun right out.'

'Did you get in close?'

'No, sir. No one could. It was too hot. We realised real soon that anyone caught close to the mountain could not have survived the blast, and the heat, and, ten minutes later, the molten lava. Our task became one of containment . . . leading in the fire trucks to douse the forest . . . getting people to evacuate their homes where we though the forest fire was spreading. Almost no one who was anywhere near the actual eruption could possibly have lived to talk about it.'

'I understand, officer. I guess there was more time to get clear in 1980?'

'Oh, definitely. They were working on an evacuation programme for several days before it finally erupted. This time there wasn't a New York minute. Damn thing just blew. Without warning . . .'

'Officer, you said *almost* no one who was in close lived. Did you mean that? Or did you mean *absolutely* no one?'

'Sir, I meant *almost*. Because there was a wagon-load of outdoor sportsmen who somehow did get clear. Four of them, three of them local. But I never heard tell of anyone else.'

'Did you interview them?'

'No, sir. I heard it on the radio, 'bout four hours after the blast. One of them was a well-known broadcaster Don McKeag, Voice of the Northwest. Everyone listens to him, but not usually on Sundays. He's a weekday guy, you know, the eight to eleven a.m. slot, regular news and politics.'

'Did he have much to say?'

'Plenty. Described in big detail how they got away, racing through the burning forest, trying to stay ahead of the fires . . . it was like listening to a thriller.'

'Did these guys actually hear the first eruption?'

'Oh sure. They were camped in the foothills of the summit. They said about a mile and quarter from the peak.'

'Did Don mention how they made such a fast break for safety?'

'He did. One of the four was a pretty well-known Washington State finance guy. Mr Tilton, President of the Seattle National Bank. Tony Tilton. Apparently he'd been on a yacht in the Caribbean when that volcano blew up and damn nearly destroyed the entire island, maybe ten to twelve years ago?'

'Montserrat?'

'That's it, sir. Mr Tilton was watching that from a few miles offshore. Boat got covered in ash, he was washing it down with a hose. Anyway, he knew better than anyone how darned quick you have to be to get away from an erupting volcano.'

'Sounds like a big scoop for Don?'

'Hell, yes. But there was one thing I heard Mr Tilton mention on the programme that I thought was a little offbeat. He said he heard the mountain erupt three times, way up there in the crater. But before the first one he heard a strange gust of wind, above the lake, kinda through the mist.

'I don't know. Didn't seem to connect to me. A high wind doesn't set off a volcano, does it? And he wouldn't have made anything like that up, not Mr Tilton. He's a very well-respected guy in Washington. Some folks say he might run for governor.'

'Officer, could you arrange for me to speak to Mr Tilton?'

'Certainly, sir. I'll get onto the bank right away and get back to you with a time.'

'Thanks for that,' said Jimmy. 'You've been a real help.'

'Okay, sir. I'll be right back on the line.'

Lt. Commander Ramshawe replaced the telephone thoughtfully. Had Tony Tilton actually heard a couple of low-flying cruise missiles heading for the fractured crater of Mount St Helens?

It did not take long to find out. Five minutes later State Trooper Ray Suplee was back. 'Twenty minutes, sir. Mr Tilton will be waiting on this line —'

Jimmy jotted down the number and decided to wait until he had completed his three-part investigation before he told Admiral Morris what he suspected. He took his watch off and propped it up in front of him, a habit he'd copied from his father, then carefully wrote up his notes.

At 6.10 p.m. precisely he punched in the number and was instantly connected to an ivory-coloured telephone 2,800 miles away, in a spacious air-cooled office tower, in downtown Seattle, where it was only 3.10 in the afternoon.

'Tilton,' said a voice at the end of a private line.

'G'day, Mr Tilton. This is Lt. Commander Ramshawe. I'm assistant to the Director of the National Security Agency at Fort Meade, Maryland. I believe you were expecting my call . . .'

'I was. Heard from the State Police about twenty minutes ago. What can I tell you? It has to be about the volcano; there's never been so many people wanting to chat to me, all on the same subject.'

Then the lt. commander got down to the heart of the matter. 'The state trooper told me you'd given a radio interview and you mentioned a high wind just before the blast?'

'Almost. What I heard, in sequence, was this strange, sudden whoosh of air, right above the lake, in the mist. It was the kind of sound you get in an old house in the middle of a rainstorm . . . you know, when a strong wind suddenly rises and makes that kinda creepy wailing noise. Except there was hardly a breath of wind on the lake that morning. Just that sudden rush of air.'

'Anyone else hear it?'

'No. I was the only one who heard it. I actually looked up, out over the water, it was such an unusual noise.'

'Then what?'

'Seconds later, I'm talking maybe ten seconds, there was this dull, muffled thumping sound from way up the mountain. That really got my attention, and Donnie's, as you know I'm jumpy about volcanoes, after Montserrat, and we got the other two out of the tents. Then I heard it again, 'bout a minute later . . . that wind. Followed by another more obvious explosion. Way high up.'

'Did you hear a fourth explosion?'

'No. But we sure felt it. The whole area kinda shuddered. And then the sky became overcast . . . and all this burning stuff was falling into the trees. The first fire we saw, out on the right, was way up ahead, maybe a half-mile. That's how far the debris was being blasted. We were on the road by then . . . I'd say a good six miles away from the mountain . . .'

'Mr Tilton,' Jimmy said, 'I can't thank you enough. You've been a real help.'

'No problem, Lt. Commander,' replied the bank president. 'But tell me, why is the National Security Agency interested in a plain act of God?

'Oh, just a routine checkup. We always take a look at these things. You know earthquakes, major fires, tidal waves . . . Thanks for your help, Mr Tilton.'

1130 Tuesday 18 August 2009
The White House, Washington, DC
President McBride, a lanky, slim man, with receding curly grey-brown hair, was irritated. A few moments earlier he had been looking forward to his salad and now this. A detailed three-page memorandum direct from Jurassic Park – copy to Cyrus Romney – outlining the possibility that a person or persons unknown had blown up Mount St Helens from a submarine apparently parked several hundred miles away, on the bottom of the goddamned Pacific Ocean.

Absurd, and precisely the kind of harebrained quasi-military, scaremongering the President had vowed to eradicate. 'Years and years wasted on lunatic military adventures, billions of dollars of taxpayers' money, chasing shadows, witch-hunting spies, Reagan and Bush, threatening people, bombing people . . . and for what?'

President McBride's views were well known. He considered the prospect of war, any war, unthinkable. He'd been known to say, 'If we've got to fight in order to retain our place in the modern world, we ought to opt out and become isolationist.'

The President held up the memorandum he had just skimmed through, shook his head and resisted the temptation to toss it in the bin. Cyrus had even told Fort Meade to waste no time on it. Of course they'd done the exact opposite, and now this. He hit the button requesting his National Security Adviser to come in and discuss the matter. He always felt better when he was chatting to Cyrus. Old friends, they had marched shoulder to shoulder in Washington protesting Middle Eastern wars. They were both 'enlightened', not stuck in the gloomy, antagonistic past.

Cyrus tapped lightly on the door and entered. 'Hi, Mr President,' he said cheerfully. 'And what awful turmoil has this uncaring world visited upon you today?' Cyrus wrote poetry in his spare time.

'This, old buddy,' replied the man in the Big Chair. 'This deranged bullshit from Jurassic Park. They think there's some kind of monster from *Waterworld* groping about on the bottom of the Pacific Ocean pushing buttons and letting off our American volcanoes. Can you believe this crap?'

'To be honest I've only just got to my mail. I assume they copied me?'

'Yes. They have. It's based on that hoax letter about Mount St Helens. Admiral Morris seems to

209

think that there might be someone out there firing cruise missiles at Washington State.'

'Jesus Christ,' said Cyrus. 'Those guys. They should've been novelists.'

'All I know is there are two gigantic US Navy bases in Washington State and now these clowns at Fort Meade are telling me that despite several trillion dollars of surveillance equipment sweeping Puget Sound and all points west, on the water, above the water and under the water, there's a damn great nuclear submarine prowling around underneath our ships firing stuff at volcanoes. Now am I missing something, or is this a load of horseshit on an almost unprecedented scale?'

'Well, I haven't read it yet, Charlie. But it does sound kind of far-fetched.'

'The gist of the thing is that some terrorist organisation snatched a volcanologist in the street in London last May, and then murdered him. They think he told HAMAS how to erupt dormant volcanoes, and they may have done it a couple of weeks ago, right here in the USA.'

'Did they catch the murderers? Any charges? Evidence?'

'Hell, no. The Brits never caught anyone. But Fort Meade seems to think that there was some Middle East connection.'

'Well, what do they want us to do about it?'

'They want the entire US Navy on high alert, and they want their theories to be taken seriously. They want us to believe these guys are for real, and that they do know how to blow up volcanoes.'

'Those guys at Ford Meade are nuts. You do know that, don't you? You want me to draft a reply to them.'

'That's more or less what I had in mind. And Cy . . . for Christ's sake tell them to avoid these rabble-rousing scare stories. They don't do a lick of good to anyone.'

'Okay, Chief. I'll read this and get it done.'

Cyrus left and, later that afternoon, Admiral George Morris received his sardonic reply to the threatening scenario he'd presented to them that morning.

Dear Admiral Morris – I am sorry you chose to ignore my advice about that hoax HAMAS letter sent to Arnold Morgan. As you know, my judgement was then, and remains now, that it was simply a ludicrous declaration involving the power of God. I expect you have noticed, those who are truly deranged typically invoke the power of the Almighty, especially when laying claim to global disasters.

I have conferred with the President on this matter, and his view reflects mine, mainly that there is not one shred of hard evidence connecting any Middle Eastern terrorist with those London murders. And it is difficult to see how you manage then to conclude that, before he died, Professor Landon wrote out some kind of a world volcano-eruption guide and handed it over to a bunch of Arab freedom fighters.

Certainly there is not enough serious evidence

*here to accept the implications of what is nothing
but a crank letter.*

*Sorry, Admiral. The President is adamant. We are
unconvinced.*

*Remember, always, we are spending the taxpayers'
money, and they voted President McBride in precisely to avoid the obvious financial excesses of the
Armed Services. Today, in the third millennium, people
want a say in how their money is spent.*

Sincerely – Cyrus Romney.

Lt. Commander Ramshawe looked up at his boss
in disbelief.

'We're up against it here, old son,' Admiral Morris
said. 'Right up against it. They're against us before
they start, before they even read our opinions and
advice.'

'Do we let the Big Man know the state of the
battle?'

'Absolutely. We tell him the full details of our
investigation. And we also tell General Scannell. I
don't mind being ridiculed by the President and his
know-nothing National Security Adviser. But if I
happen to believe that President is wilfully putting
our country in danger, then it is my duty to blow
a few whistles. He might be the President, but he's
only a goddamned politician. And he's not here for
long.

'We belong to a permanent organisation which is
here specifically to keep the United States of America
safe. Mostly we do what the President wishes. But

212

there is a line, and he steps across that line only at grave peril to himself.'

'You think he just did?' asked Jimmy.

'I read your report, Lt. Commander. I *know* he just did.'

Admiral Morris and his assistant got lucky again. Jimmy Ramshawe called Arnold Morgan at home and requested a private meeting as soon as possible on a matter which Admiral Morris regarded as a 'supreme priority'.

'Can't it wait until tomorrow?' asked the ex-National Security Adviser.

'Yes. It could. But Admiral Morris believes we should meet NOW, and you know he doesn't get overexcited on a regular basis.'

Admiral Morgan did know that. And he paused for a moment before saying, 'Look, Jimmy, I'm taking Kathy out this evening to her favourite little restaurant in Georgetown. I can't cancel at this late hour, so I suppose you and your boss better join us.'

'Are you sure, sir?' said an utterly delighted Jimmy Ramshawe.

'No, I'm not. But you've cornered me. Le Bec Fin. I expect you know where it is; I've seen John Peacock there a few times.'

'Yes, sir,' replied Jimmy. 'Went there for Jane's birthday. What time would you like to see us?'

'Eight bells. End of the Last Dog Watch, and don't be late.'

'No, sir,' said Jimmy, laughing to himself at the

old submariner's unending sense of humour, so often disguised as a growling commanding officer's impatience.

At 8 p.m. precisely the staff car from Fort Meade pulled up outside the restaurant. They found Arnold and Kathy sitting opposite each other in a wide, comfortable private booth towards the rear of the main dining room. George was placed next to the admiral, Jimmy next to Kathy.

'I'm really sorry about this,' said the young lt. commander, 'but I have to give a short document to Admiral Morgan to read before we can talk. It's about three pages long, and it's not my fault – the culprit for this awkwardness is sitting right opposite me, and he's too big a cheese to argue with.'

That rather skilfully broke any ice which might have been hanging around after the enforced invitation. Arnold and Kathy both laughed, and the admiral poured four glasses of white Burgundy for them. He never was much for asking people what they wanted to drink. As with most things, he felt he knew best. And, as with most things, he was usually right. The pale-gold Burgundy was excellent, from the Domaine Chandon de Briailles, a 1998 Pernand-Vergelesses *blanc*. Jimmy Ramshawe knew what he inelegantly described as a real snorto-deluxe when he tasted it.

'My oath, this is a great glass of wine, sir,' he ventured.

'Silence, Ramshawe. I'm reading.'

'Yes, sir.'

It took the admiral about five minutes to finish the report on the eruption of Mount St Helens. And when he did so, he took a Navy-sized gulp of his wine. 'Mother of God,' he breathed. 'Our old friend Major Kerman again. And by the sound of this he's only just started. The volcano was just a sideshow, or he wouldn't have sent that self-congratulatory letter to me, would he?'

'No, he would not,' said George Morris. 'In my opinion we'll be hearing from him again.'

'And mine,' said Arnold. 'But meantime, where the hell is he? Because I agree with Jimmy; I think we heard that damn creeping *Barracuda*, twice, north of the Aleutians. And a few days later, what sounds like a very reliable man hears a couple of guided missiles bearing down on Mount St Helens, seconds before the entire thing explodes. That'll do for me; it's Kerman, and he's out there, under the water, planning God knows what.'

'That'll do for me as well,' replied George. 'However, it will not do for our President and his main adviser.' At which point he handed Arnold a copy of the letter he had received from Cyrus Romney.

Again Arnold read, in obvious alarm. 'Everything I ever feared about a soft, left-wing President,' he said. 'All on one page, written by one of the greatest assholes on this planet. Jesus Christ. Romney's a goddamned flower-child dressed up in a suit. The *New York Times* published one of his Godawful poems last month. Goddamnit, we've got the

Wordsworth of the White House guiding the defences of the United States against one of the most dangerous terrorists we've ever encountered . . . *a host of golden daffodils . . . season of mists and mellow fruitfulness . . .*'

'Darling, those happen to be the lines of two different poets,' interjected Kathy.

'Excellent,' said the admiral. 'I happen to be dealing with two different assholes.'

Lt. Commander Ramshawe came remarkably close to shooting 1998 Pernand-Vergelesses down his nose but the waiter arrived at that precipitous moment and deflected everyone's attention to the menu.

'I think we need another five minutes,' said Arnold, and immediately returned to the subject at hand. 'George,' he said. 'First, I want to congratulate Jimmy on an outstanding example of detective work. And secondly, I want to tell you that I have never been more nervous of the men who occupy the key Administration seats in the White House.

'The letter to you from this Romney character is, in my view, nothing short of a disgrace. The head of our National Security Agency, an Admiral and former Commander of a United States Navy Carrier Battle Group? I'm absolutely shocked. But all that pales before the real problem. And that's the reluctance of this Administration to act in the true interests of this nation.

'Even if the President does not believe it personally, he has to face up to the truth that these terrorists may already have killed maybe a hundred of our citizens up in Washington State. And that dismissal of the facts may mean that Charles McBride is in serious breach of his oaths of office.'

'So what do we do?'

'For the moment, we keep very quiet. But I do want to alert General Scannell and Admiral Dickson. If something as serious as this is really happening, I want to ensure the proper authorities are up to speed. We probably should tell 'em to keep a weather eye out for a slow Russian nuclear, anywhere along our west coast waters.'

'Arnie, what would you recommend we do if we locate that *Barracuda* somewhere in the Pacific, offshore, but maybe not strictly in our national waters?'

'Sink it, George,' replied the admiral. 'Sink that sonofabitch, hopefully in damn deep water. No questions asked. Deny all knowledge.'

'Right on, sir,' said Jimmy, grinning. 'That's the spirit.' And all three of them, at that moment, wished to high heaven that Admiral Morgan was still in his old office in the West Wing.

Midday (local) Tuesday 18 August
Pacific Ocean 24.30N 113.00W
The *Barracuda* cruised slowly south-sou' west, following the coastline of the USA and then Mexico, about 500 miles offshore, 600 feet below the surface. She had stayed further west while they ran the gauntlet of the huge US naval base in San Diego, then angled left, moving inshore.

There was apparently no one searching for her.

They heard no transmissions and made none themselves. They had not surfaced for more than a week, and were now running parallel with the great 800-mile-long Mexican peninsula of Baja California. Indeed, they were heading for the line latitude of the Tropic of Cancer, just about opposite the most southerly headland of the peninsula.

Ahead of them was an 8,000-mile-long haul, all down the west coast of South America, around Cape Horn and up the Atlantic. At their current speed of only five knots, this would take more than two months. But the ocean ahead of them was lonely, largely unpatrolled by the US Navy, and not heavily photographed by US satellites.

Down there, along the wild and woolly coastline of Peru and then Chile, they could make much better speed. They could wind those big turbines up to perhaps 15 knots, in very, very deep water, where the southern Pacific shelves down steeply west of the colossal mountain range of the high, craggy Andes.

General Rashood spent the day, along with everyone else, in a watchful but relaxed mood. He and Shakira dined together quite late in the evening, while Ben Badr had the ship. And Shakira went to bed at around midnight.

It was almost 2 a.m. when Ravi ordered the *Barracuda* to periscope depth. They came sliding up out of the black depths and immediately raised their ESM mast. They made no report to the satellite. They just sent a fast signal of a couple of words in the six seconds their mast remained visible.

SALADIN TWO

CHAPTER SIX

The satellite signal from General Rashood arrived exactly on time. And Admiral Mohammed Badr received it with some relief. They were still operational. And his beloved son, Ben, was safe.

The sealed documents in the package next to the telephone were almost burning a hole through his desk. The admiral rose swiftly and stepped out into the night. A staff car drove him out of the base on the north road, and then swung sharply west down to the airport, less than two miles from his office.

Already on the runway, its engines howling, was a small private jet from Syrian Arab Airlines. Admiral Badr's car took him right up to the aircraft and he handed the package personally to the pilot.

Then he stood and watched the little jet scream into the dark, hot skies, banking northwest for the 1,200-mile journey across the Gulf, along the Saudi–Iraqi border to Jordan, and then north up to Damascus.

A lt. commander from the Iranian Navy would be awaiting it, and he would drive the package personally to the Saudi Embassy on Al-Jala'a Avenue. From there it would be placed in the Kingdom's Diplomatic Bag to the Syrian Embassy at 2215 Wyoming Avenue NW, Washington, DC.

One way or another, that was a package just about impossible to trace. It would arrive in the White House mail room delivered by the Special Diplomatic Courier Service, addressed to the President of the United States. Official. Very Official. But origins unknown.

Admiral Badr was rather proud, and rightly so, of the circuitous route he had planned for its arrival in the Oval Office.

1100 Friday 21 August 2009
The White House, Washington, DC
President McBride's Chief-of-Staff, Big Bill Hatchard, former underachieving defensive lineman for Yale University, tapped lightly on the door of the Oval Office. The President was on the phone but Bill was used to waiting for the former Rhode Island Congressman, having served him on the Hill, driven him, written for him, protected him and finally headed up his campaign for the Presidency. Charlie McBride treated him like a brother.

Finally he heard the old familiar call, 'C'mon in, Bill, what's going on?'

Bill entered, clutching the package from the Navy base at Bandar Abbas, which he had opened and

222

skipped through. Only packages which the President's aides deemed of unusual importance went directly to the White House Chief-of-Staff. And this one looked highly important, having arrived by diplomatic courier, marked for the specific attention of the President (*PRIVATE AND CONFIDENTIAL*).

Nothing, however, got past Big Bill Hatchard en route to the Chief Executive. As opposed to his fairly disastrous football career, he could stop anything or anyone from his West Wing office. Safe-hands Hatchard, that was Bill.

But this morning a worried frown clouded his big, broad, usually cheery face. It was an expression mightily familiar to all his colleagues on the Yale bench, but it was seen much less in the White House. Part of Bill's Presidential brief was to keep morale high throughout the building, to jolly people along, to play down the stress, to make light of any problems.

'Whatever you've got in your hand, young William, is giving you cause for grave concern,' said the Chief. 'If it's anything less than a direct death threat, I'm going to find it necessary to lighten your mood.'

Bill laughed thinly. 'Sir, it might be a whole lot worse than a death threat. And I would like you at least to read through it – it's only two pages. Mind if I have a splash of this coffee?'

'Help yourself, buddy, and get one for me too, will you? Meanwhile, I'll take a glance at the ill tidings you bring me –'

Mr President:

You will by now have realised that the eruption of Mount St Helens was not an accident. It was indeed perpetrated by the freedom fighters of HAMAS, as I intimated in my communiqué to Admiral Morgan. I am now ready to lay out my demands, which you must obey, in order to prevent us from destroying the entire eastern seaboard of the United States of America, including Boston, New York and Washington.

We intend to do this by causing the greatest tidal wave this world has seen in living memory.

We estimate the wave will be approximately 150 feet high when it rolls through New York Harbour and straight through Wall Street, until it engulfs Manhattan. It will almost certainly keep going for 20 miles inland across New Jersey, before finally breaking and sucking back over the land towards the coast. However, it will be followed by another wave similar in height and then another. Possibly a total of fifteen in all, each of them more than 80 feet in height.

No city could possibly withstand such an impact from the ocean, and I fear there will be little left of your eastern seaboard when this mega–tsunami is finally over.

You may be doubting our capability to cause such havoc. But it is quite simple, it has happened several times in the history of our planet.

There are various places where such an effect on the ocean could be caused, but we have chosen one which could not fail. I am sure you will agree that if we can explode the biggest volcano in the United States, we can probably arrange a large rockfall in the middle of the deserted ocean. Have no doubt, Mr President.

Which brings me to the objective of this letter. In order to prevent us from carrying out this threat, you will undertake the following actions:

1) You will evacuate all US military personnel; and remove all stockpiled artillery, bombs, missiles, ammunitions, and other materiels of war, from your illegal bases in Kuwait, Saudi Arabia, Qatar, Oman, United Arab Emirates and Djibouti. All warships and aircraft will leave Bahrain and the British-owned base at Diego Garcia. All three of your Carrier Battle Groups, and all other naval forces afloat in the Gulf of Iran and neighbouring seas will depart the area immediately. You will remove aircraft and support equipment from the Turkish air base at Incirlik.

Our time frame is not flexible. We expect to see immediate movement of troops, ships and aircraft within seven days. We expect final withdrawal to be complete within six weeks, even if this means abandoning materiel.

2) There will be immediate recognition by the Israeli Government of an Independent, Democratic and Sovereign State of Palestine, based on the territories of the West Bank and the Gaza Strip, occupied by Israeli forces on and since 4 June 1967. There will also be agreement to take immediate steps to withdraw all Israeli troops from the occupied territories. We also require an immediate undertaking from the Government of the United States to MAKE Israel comply with the HAMAS demands without delay.

Failure to comply with the above conditions will

mean the certain destruction of your great cities of Boston, New York and Washington, as well as the remainder of the East Coast of the United States.

We are assuming you receive this document on 21 August. You have until midnight Thursday 8 October to enter the final stages of your total evacuation from the Middle East. Unless we see clear signs that this is happening, we shall cause the tsunami within twenty-four hours of that date.

I am certain your experts will confirm for you the absolute feasibility of our intentions. We are perfectly capable of causing a landslide, sometime on 9 October 2009.

Do not delay. With the great Allah fighting with us, we wish you out of the Middle East for ever. Only He can grant us victory. We will stop at nothing to achieve our objectives.

– HAMAS

President McBride sighed. 'Bill,' he said, 'this letter is from a nutcase. He came up with the bright idea of claiming to have exploded Mount St Helens, after the fact, of course. Which anyone could have done.

'Then he used the absurd notion that someone might have believed him, in order to press home these outrageous demands. But I doubt even he is crazy enough to think we might start evacuating the entire military force of the United States from the most volatile part of the world. Just because he has threatened to drown New York City.'

'I guess so, sir,' replied Hatchard. 'But, Christ . . . you don't suppose this guy *could* be for real, do you?'

'Hell, no. Let me tell you something. Anytime there is a natural disaster, volcano, earthquake, flood, fire or famine, you get a spate of letters from deranged people claiming to have caused it, started it, inspired it or forecast it.

'Billy, no one takes notice of these crank communications. It's not as if someone called the day before and announced, *I'm going to blow Mount St Helens tomorrow at around 7.30 in the morning*. And then did it. Because that might prove pretty difficult. Nutcases like this wait 'til something happens, and then say, *Oh, right, that was me.*'

'Okay, sir. If that's your decision. Meantime, you want me to have this letter copied and sent around to various interested parties in the military and in Intelligence, maybe the Defense Secretary, Secretary of State, perhaps?'

'I don't think that's necessary, Bill.'

'Okay, sir. But a word of caution. In the million to one chance that someone actually did explode Mount St Helens, and is now planning to drown the East Coast, how about I just circulate this document, with a short cover letter? You know, informing people you are inclined to dismiss the entire thing as a hoax? But you are open to guidance? That way, we've covered our asses. I know it's not going to happen, but if it should, well then it won't be your fault. It's the useless military for not taking care of it in the early stages . . . in politics, always cover your ass . . . right, sir? You stick that document in a file, and then it happens, there's no one to blame but you. Why take that chance? Trust me, sir, let's cover our ass . . .'

'Okay, buddy. But if we suddenly have the entire office filled with raging admirals and generals champing at the goddamned bit to attack Arabs, I'll blame you.'

'Fine, sir. You can do that.'

Bill Hatchard retreated and had copies made of Admiral Badr's letter. He dictated a short memo to each recipient which read:

The President believes this to be either a hoax, or from a straightforward crank. He notes the writer's claim to have erupted Mount St Helens did not come until a few days AFTER the event and has asked me to inform you that, at this time, as Commander-in-Chief, he has no intention of evacuating our entire military presence from the Middle East as requested.

Nonetheless, he wanted you to see this, for what it's worth, and he will keep you informed should there be a further communiqué. Sincerely, Bill Hatchard, Chief-of-Staff.

The document was sent to the Defense Secretary and the Secretary of State, who both agreed entirely with their Leader. It was also sent to Admiral Morris, who did not; to General Tim Scannell who had read Lt. Commander Jimmy Ramshawe's brief and to Admiral Alan Dickson, the Chief of Naval Operations who, in agreement with Scannell, most definitely did not go along with the President's assessment.

Admiral Arnold Morgan was not on Bill Hatchard's circulation list, but he received a copy by courier from George Morris. Alan Dickson sent a copy to Admiral Dick Greening (Commander-in-Chief Pacific Fleet CINCPACFLT), to Rear Admiral Freddie Curran (Commander Submarines Pacific Fleet COMSUBPAC) and to Rear Admiral John Bergstrom (Commander Special War Command SPECWARCOM).

By mid-afternoon (EDT), all high-ranking US Navy personnel with major responsibilities in the Pacific operational area had been instructed to read the Ramshawe brief, *before* reading the latest communiqué from HAMAS.

To a man, they considered the coincidences to be too great. There was, no doubt, ample evidence for linking the assumed HAMAS terrorist leader Major Ray Kerman to the current volcano problem. According to Ramshawe, Admiral Morgan had actually photographed Kerman, in company with leading Iranian volcanologists, on top of Cumbre Vieja, which most realised, after reading Ramshawe's brief, was the most likely target for the kind of event threatened in the letter.

Meanwhile it did seem likely that the second *Barracuda* might be creeping at that moment quietly through the eastern Pacific right off America's West Coast. Or, alternatively, beating a rapid path around Cape Horn into the Atlantic making straight for the towering, unstable southwest coast of La Palma in the Canaries. If a collective response had been possible from the concerned military, it would undoubtedly have been along the lines of *H-O-L-Y S-H-I-I-I-T!!!*

President or no President, General Scannell, Chairman of the Joint Chiefs, called an emergency conference in the Pentagon for Monday morning, 24 August, 1030. This was strictly military, highly classified, and the general had also invited Admirals Morgan and Morris, plus the young Sherlock Holmes of Fort Meade, Lt. Commander Jimmy Ramshawe.

The task was fivefold. One, to examine the letter from HAMAS and call in an expert to judge the psychological condition of the writer. Two, to appreciate the situation and discuss a possible plan of defence against an attack on the volcano of Cumbre Vieja. Three, to discuss the possibility of the terrorists going for any target other than Cumbre Vieja. Four, to hold preliminary discussions on the possible evacuation of New York City, Boston and Washington. And five, to make recommendations to the President of the United States for immediate civilian action in those cities.

General Scannell called Admiral Morris and requested he bring data with him that outlined the basic requirements a terrorist might need for knocking down a four-mile-long, high granite cliff. Also it would be useful to have an American expert from one of the universities to explain the ramifications of such a landslide, perhaps to offer expert opinion on the real-time chances of a mega-*tsunami* developing.

He booked lunch the following day, Saturday, with Arnold Morgan, Admiral Dickson and the visiting Rear Admiral Curran to try to assess a Navy operational plan in the eastern Atlantic, almost certainly to surround the west coast of La Palma with a US battle group, with state-of-the-art surface-to-air missile capability.

General Scannell broke with long Pentagon tradition by inviting the retired Admiral Morgan to chair the lunchtime meeting, on the basis of his long experience as a strategist and a commanding officer, and by virtue of his months-long involvement with the terrorist volcano threat.

Admiral Morgan accepted, pretending to be put out, protesting that he was supposed to be retired, enjoying himself hugely.

'Aren't you?' asked Admiral Dickson, handing over a preliminary chart of the deep waters around La Palma.

'You bet I am,' replied Arnold, glaring at the detailed map of the ocean depths. 'Now, where we gonna find these fucking underwater towelheads?'

The great man hadn't lost his touch, no doubt about that, and the three senior officers who sat at the table with him, in General Scannell's private conference room, all felt a stab of nostalgia for the old days of not so long ago, when the world was a simpler place.

As recently as one year earlier this meeting would not have taken place privately, on a Saturday. It would have happened in the West Wing's Situation Room in the White House, with the full backing and probably the attendance of a President who believed in them. This was different. The meeting was on the verge of being subversive. The current President did not trust their judgement.

'I think we all accept that if Mount St Helens was deliberately exploded, it was probably hit by a broadside of cruise missiles coming through the early morning fog? Correct?' Admiral Morgan was swiftly arranging his ducks in a line.

Everyone nodded.

'And those missiles must have been fired from a submarine, which we photographed leaving the Yellow Sea, and picked up twice, north of the Aleutians. No other submarine in the entire world fitted the pattern and every one of them is accounted for. The dates fit. The speed fits. And the possible attack on Mount St Helens fits.

'Also we have the perfect witness – a highly reliable, highly respected Seattle bank president standing at the foot of the mountain. He's a banker and a lawyer, paid to have suspicions, but not reckless imagination.' Admiral Morgan paused. 'Gentlemen, that's not 100 per cent, cast-iron fact. But it is way, way too strong to be dismissed. Agreed?'

Everyone nodded again.

'And therefore,' continued the admiral, 'in light of the letter received from HAMAS, we must face the possibility that there is a boat-load of Middle Eastern terrorists determined to bang a big hole in the cliff face of La Palma. Militarily, any other line of thought is childish. That's what we're for, goddamnit. To keep this country safe. And we have no right to go around making half-assed assumptions that it might not happen. And I think it will happen, unless we can get between their fucking missile and that cliff.'

'Correct,' said General Scannell. 'I hope we are all agreed on that . . . gentlemen?' Once more Admirals Dickson and Curran nodded their agreement.

'And for the purpose of this meeting,' said General Scannell, 'we should concentrate on how we catch 'em. Which is unlikely to be easy. We learned that the hard way.'

'Essentially, we're looking for a submarine-launched cruise missile,' said Admiral Dickson. 'I suspect not a big ICBM which we would pick up a long way out. I'd say it's a cruise, probably to be fired at around 500-mile range. You can fire 'em from 1,000 miles but that would give us too long to locate it. They'll want to be in closer than that, maybe only 250 miles . . . twenty-five minutes uprange from the target. No nearer, Freddie?'

The Pacific Fleet submarine chief was frowning. 'That's likely to add up to one hell of a lot of water, sir,' he said. 'If we take a best-case distance of a 500-mile north–south line-up and down the La Palma coast . . . forming a box, out into the Atlantic from both ends . . . with the Cumbre Vieja volcano in the middle . . . then take a spot 500 miles due west of the mountain, we're talking probably 200,000 square miles of ocean. If the *Barracuda* stands any further offshore, it's a whole lot more. But that way we'd have more time to locate an incoming cruise . . .' He paused for a moment, then added, 'If I were trying to launch and get away, I'd probably go for around 300 miles uprange of my target . . . so if we placed a cordon up to 500 miles out, we'd kind of have him trapped . . . except the little sono-fabitch could creep right out underneath us, dead slow in very deep water, and vanish. As he has done a few times before.'

'How many ships would we need?' asked the Chairman.

'Well, if we had a hundred in all, twenty sub-marines, plus frigates, destroyers and cruisers, they'd each have to look after 2,000 square miles – roughly a 45-mile square each.'

'Jesus, Freddie . . . we didn't have that many ships in the South Pacific in 1944,' said Arnold Morgan.

'And our enemy didn't have nuclear submarines, which could go as deep, stay there indefinitely, and run as quietly as this bastard,' replied COMSUBPAC. 'And I'll tell you something else. Even then, with that big a fleet we still might not catch him. With any fewer than 100 ships I'd say we were almost guaranteed to miss him.'

'Even if we caught him, chances are he'd get one of his missiles away,' pondered Admiral Morgan.

'I'm not too bothered about that,' replied Admiral Curran. 'Because I think we'd nail that missile. But I'm sure, sir, as ever, you'd rather nail the archer than the arrow.'

That was an old favourite policy of Admiral

Morgan's, and Arnold smiled wryly. 'You got that right, Freddie,' he said. 'But hunting submarines in a big pack is very difficult . . .'

'We'd have to use a box system,' said Admiral Curran. 'You know, give each US submarine an area in which he must stick . . . otherwise we'll have 'em shooting at each other . . .'

'And there's always a problem with that,' replied Arnold. 'You pick the enemy up and track him to the edge of your box, then you've either got to break the rules and pursue him into somebody else's box. Otherwise let him go, and hope your nearest colleague will pick him up as well.'

'Actually, sir, I was thinking of a search box only. I suggest our submarine COs will have orders to open fire and sink the enemy instantly.'

'Freddie, I think that's exactly correct,' said Arnold. 'Which means we can't have our guys rampaging all over each other's designated areas. In the final reckoning, the box system is usually best. Though I did once hear the Royal Navy's High Command was somewhat less than thrilled when one of their submarines picked up an Argentinian submarine somewhere north of the Falklands and then let him go because they'd reached the end of the patrol box.'

'I guess that's always the downside,' said Admiral Curran thoughtfully. 'But, generally speaking, the worst-case scenario would be one of our nuclear boats hitting another.'

'Well,' said General Scannell, 'I'd be more than happy for you guys to work on some kind of a fleet plan for Monday's meeting . . . but I would like to know if we have enough ships!'

'No problem,' replied Admiral Dickson. 'Right now we have Carrier Groups patrolling the northern Gulf, the east end of the Strait of Hormuz, the northern Arabian Gulf and one in readiness at Diego Garcia. There's a fifth preparing to leave Pearl Harbor. All of them could be in the mid-Atlantic in well under three weeks. That's fifty-five ships.'

'Okay. The rest, I presume, are already in the Atlantic, or in Norfolk, or New London, or somewhere else on the East Coast?'

'Correct, sir. We do not have a problem getting a full complement of ships into the operational area.'

'As for the *Barracuda*, of course we have no idea where that might be?' asked the CJC.

'Hell, yes, we got a hundred ideas,' said Arnold Morgan. 'None of 'em reliable. But it seems to me, if this bastard unleashed a battery of submarine-launched cruise missiles at Mount St Helens, somewhere off Washington State, or even Oregon, earlier this month, he's got to be on his way to the eastern Atlantic by now.

'He will not want to go the longest way around. Not the way he came, all the way back north of the Aleutians, way down the coast of Asia, and then all the way across the Indian Ocean. That's too far. Twenty thousand miles plus, most of it at slow speed. It'd take him nearly three months.'

Arnold Morgan let that rest for a few moments. And then he continued, speaking quietly to three very senior men who found it impossible to accept he was no longer their spiritual leader.

'And this clever little sonofabitch certainly will not want to take the shorter route across the Pacific Basin,' said the admiral. 'As you know, it's trembling with our SOSUS wires. No sir. He'll know that. And he'll avoid that.

'And he plainly cannot use the Panama Canal. Which means his most likely route will be down the west coast of South America, which is not heavily patrolled, or surveyed, by our ships and satellites.

'It's shorter, safer and much, much quieter, if he's trying to get into the Atlantic . . . remember, he hit Mount St Helens on Sunday morning 9 August. Today's the 22nd. That's thirteen days and he was probably making only seven knots for ten of them, but now he could probably be making fifteen in deserted waters. Which means he's put nearly 3,000 miles between himself and the datum.

'Way down at the southern end of Chile, he'll be moving even quicker. That damned *Barracuda* will be around Cape Horn in a couple of weeks min-imum.'

'Any point putting a submarine trap down there somewhere . . . try and stop him entering the Atlantic?' General Scannell was wracking his brains.

'Sir, it's such a vast, deep seascape,' said Admiral Curran. 'We'd need a lot of ships, and if we missed him, which we probably would, we'd be involved in some kind of race back to the Canary Islands . . . and we might lose that race. And that *Barracuda* could fire its missiles at the cliff face real quick. Sir, I think we'd be much better getting ourselves in line of battle right where it counts, west of La Palma. We *know* he's going there.'

'I'd go with that,' said Admiral Dickson. 'This seems like no place to be taking any chances whatsoever.'

'I understand,' said the CJC. 'And I have one last point to make before I hand over to the Admirals . . . we have just one credibility gap in my view. That's the actual existence of the cruise missiles.

'But we do have one cast-iron witness, and we're not making the most of him. Gentlemen, I recommend we bring Mr Tilton in from Seattle for Monday's meeting. Just so he can demonstrate to every one of us that what he heard was the genuine sound of an incoming missile.'

'I agree with that,' said Arnold Morgan. 'You know the President and his half-witted advisers are going to pour scorn on our missile theory. I would even consider filming Mr Tilton so his evidence can be locked in, and, if necessary, shown to the President.'

'No problem with that either,' replied General Scannell. 'Now we'll go and find some lunch, and decide an approximate formation of ships, and whatever security we need on the southwest side of La Palma. Who's going to track down Mr Tilton on a Saturday morning out in Seattle.'

'I'll take care of that,' said Admiral Morgan. 'Have someone call Fort Meade and get Lt. Commander

Ramshawe to call me on this private line, fast. He'll be on inside ten minutes.'

That was way too big an estimate. The admiral had just embarked on an alarming account of how he had been in the middle of his honeymoon, 'standing on the same volcano as the world's most wanted man and . . .'

The phone rang. General Scannell answered.

'Good morning, sir. This is Lt. Commander Ramshawe of the National Security Agency returning a call . . .'

'Just a moment . . . Arnie . . . it's your man . . .'

'Hi, Jimmy. You remember that bank president you spoke with about the missiles at Mount St Helens?'

'Yes sir, Tony Tilton. Seattle National.'

'That's him. Can you get him on the line? This line. I mean, I'd like to have him at our Monday morning meeting here.'

'Might take a while, sir. The bank's closed this morning, I guess. But I'll find him.'

'You in the office?'

'Yes, sir.'

'Okay. Let's bring him in Sunday night. Leave Seattle around 0900 his time. Straight to Andrews.'

'How's he to travel, sir?'

'Military aircraft, what d'you think? The fucking space shuttle?'

'Er, no, sir.'

The admiral chuckled. 'Jimmy, get him on stand-by, then call us back and we'll give you his travel details. He can stay at our house.'

Okay, sir. I'll get right back.'

Lt. Commander Ramshawe hit what he called the 'obvious buttons' first. Directory assitance. He found a Tony and Martha Tilton in Magnolia, and dialled the number himself, sparing everyone the hang-up of yet another third party tuning in to a classified subject.

No one answered. It was 8.56 on this Saturday morning. Jimmy left a message, knowing the phrase 'National Security Agency, Fort Meade' was likely to put a rocket under anyone's ass.

It was a three-minute rocket. Tony Tilton was instantly on the line, agreeing to travel to Washington the next day for a Monday morning meeting at the Pentagon, but to discuss it with no one. Jimmy told him he'd be right back with travel details, and hit the wire to the office of the Chairman of the Joint Chiefs.

'He's coming, sir. Let me have the travel plans. He's waiting by the phone.'

This took another twenty minutes, but one day later, at 8.30 a.m. on Sunday morning, the bank president drove to work at his regular high-rise off Union Street at 6th Avenue. Waiting in the lobby were two uniformed naval officers who escorted him to the wide flat roof of the building, thirty floors above street level. And there, its rotors running, was a big Navy helicopter, a Bell AH-1Z Super Cobra, which in less peaceful time carries eight Hellfire missiles for regular strike/assault, and in air warfare is equipped with two killer AIM-9L heat-seeking guided missiles.

This morning the air was clear, the helicopter was unarmed and it was already hot. Tony Tilton was the only passenger, aside from the three-man crew. They lifted off almost vertically then clattered their way north up Puget Sound, about 3,000 feet above the water, for the ten-minute journey.

They descended gently through windless skies and put down on the helicopter pad at the Whidbey Island Naval Air Station, around 30 miles north of the Seattle downtown area, same distance from the sprawling US naval base at Everett.

One crew member disembarked immediately and assisted their civilian passenger down the steps to the area beside the runway. Less than 30 yards away stood a Lockheed EP-3E Aries naval jet, its engines running, steps down, ready for Mr Tilton's arrival.

He climbed aboard, a young officer came back to ensure he was strapped in and they moved forward to the takeoff area immediately. Half a minute later they were in the air, screaming off the runway, scything into the hot, muggy air above the calm US Navy waters of the Juan de Fuca Strait.

Fourteen minutes earlier Tony had been standing on the sidewalk on 6th Avenue, right outside the National Bank Building.

'Christ, I've queued up longer than this in Boston . . . just for a shuttle ticket,' remarked Tony, as the aircraft made a steep left-handed turn, and, still climbing, headed resolutely inland, east, making 450 mph over the fast-disappearing ground.

The Navy lieutenant sitting next to him laughed.

241

'Guess so, sir,' he said. 'It's just that in our game we don't usually have a lot of time to fuck about. We're very big on speed. Would you like some coffee?'

The bank president accepted gratefully as they set off over the high peaks of the Cascade Range. Their route would take them southeast across Montana and Wyoming, over the Rockies, along the Nebraska–Kansas border, then due east, south of Cincinnati, into Washington, DC.

During the six-hour journey, the naval lieutenant came up with more coffee and a beef sandwich and they touched down at Andrews Air Base, southeast of the capital, at 6 p.m. local.

A black Navy staff car awaited them, and the driver took Tony's bag, slung it on the front seat and opened the rear door for the man who had escaped the wrath of Mount St Helens.

Moments later they were headed fast up to Route 95, and onto the beltway. They drove all around the north side of the city, off at Exit 33, and into the toney suburb of Chevy Chase. The remainder of the journey took five minutes, and Admiral Morgan's agents met them inside the gateway of the grand colonial-style house where the former National Security Adviser lived with his new(ish) wife, Kathy.

It was just 6.45 on a hot summer evening and the admiral was dressed in white Bermudas with a dark blue polo shirt and a Panama. He greeted Tony Tilton warmly and thanked him for coming. Harry came over and volunteered to take the visitor upstairs to his room, and Arnold told Tony to come back

242

down right away so they could have a couple of drinks.

Tilton changed out of his blazer and tie, put on a dark green polo shirt and headed back out to the wide patio by the pool.

The admiral was sitting in a big, comfortable chair and he motioned for Tony to join him. The drinks were on a table between them, and both men took a man-sized swig at the cool, relaxing Scotch whisky with ice and soda water.

'I expect Lt. Commander Ramshawe filled you in on why we wanted you in Washington?'

'He did . . . the meeting tomorrow morning in the Pentagon, I believe.'

'Correct. But I should give you some more info . . . and first I better know, if you don't mind . . . may I presume you're a Republican?'

'You may.'

'Thought so, West Coast banker. Capitalist. Red in tooth and claw. Would you say you're rightish, or leftish.'

'Rightish. We have a very Republican state these days. Full of independent people, entrepreneurs and dyed-in-the-wool self-sufficient country boys, wary of Washington, paranoid about the present Administration. East Coast liberals don't play well out where I live. No sir.'

'That's awful good to hear,' replied the admiral. 'You can imagine what it must be like in the Pentagon right now?'

'Sure can.'

'Which brings us right back to Mount St Helens. Can I call you Tony?'

'Of course.'

'I'm a civilian now. So that'll be Arnie to you . . . anyway, Lt. Commander Jimmy Ramshawe tells me you understand perfectly well we have the gravest suspicion about that particular eruption?'

'Well, he was on the line from one of the most important government agencies in the country asking me in great detail about those two blasts of wind on that still morning by the lake . . . I mean there must be suspicion . . . it's difficult to arrive at any other conclusion . . .'

'Not if you work in the Oval Office,' growled the admiral.

Tony Tilton chuckled. 'I should tell you, Lt. Commander Ramshawe did not reveal anything else about his investigation. I merely surmised what he was getting at.'

'I understand,' said the admiral. 'But because I believe you're someone we can trust, I'll give you a little more background, and then have you explain to me, all over again, exactly what you observed on that Sunday morning. Then I shall request you tell precisely the same thing to the meeting tomorrow morning.'

'No problem.'

'Okay, Tony Tilton. Have another slug of that Dewar's and pay attention . . .'

'Lay it on me, Admiral . . .'

'Arnie . . .'

'Oh, I'm sorry,' said Tony, shaking his head. 'These habits of formality . . . hard to shake in my trade . . . may I have your account number . . . ?'

This was too much for the admiral who burst into laughter and then had another slug of Dewar's himself. A few minutes later, Morgan finished by concluding, 'A submarine. Do you follow me?'

'I surely do, Arnie. And you think what I heard were those missiles?'

'Yes I do, Tony. That's precisely what I think.'

'Can you launch them from below the surface? More than one at a time?'

'Oh, sure. They're called SLCMs – submarine-launched cruise missiles. You can get 'em away one at a time, but close together, separated by perhaps less than a minute. They make a heck of a speed, well over 600 knots, flying maybe 500 feet above the ground.'

'How come they didn't crash into the mountains up there?'

'They self-adjust to the contours of the earth, rising and falling on the instructions of their own altimeter.'

'And you think I heard them come in?'

'I think you heard the first two . . .'

'If it'd been the last two, I don't think we'd have made it out of there.'

'Can you tell me exactly what you heard?'

'I'm afraid it can't be much more than I told Don McKeag or Lt. Commander Jimmy Ramshawe . . .'

And just then the French doors slid open, and

Mrs Kathy Morgan made her entrance, walking briskly, wearing a pink floral Italian cotton skirt, with a pink summer shirt, no shoes and a gold anchor pendant on a chain around her neck. Her lustrous red hair was worn loosely and she carried a large platter which, still marinating boldly, held a large 'butterflied' leg of lamb.

This was, unaccountably, her husband's favourite – Texans, of course, are supposed to demonstrate the cattleman's traditional devotion to beef, harbouring at all times the cowboy's general derision of the efforts of sheep farmers.

But Arnold loved butterflied leg of lamb, and, much to Tony Tilton's good fortune, liked it especially on Sunday nights, when he gleefully opened a couple of bottles of outstanding château-bottled Bordeaux, as carefully recommended by his chief adviser, the former Secretary of State, Harcourt Travis, now lecturing modern political history, somewhat loftily, to students at Harvard University.

Admiral Morgan introduced his wife to the star witness for the prosecution and poured her a glass of cold white Burgundy. 'Arnold's been telling me, Tony, how you got away from the volcano,' she said. 'That must have been very scary . . . I think I would probably have fainted with terror.'

'Kathy, when you're as scared as I was, it's amazing what you can do,' replied her guest. 'The morning was very quiet. No wind, just a few people camping around the lake, not more than a half-dozen tents. Nearly everyone was asleep. There was a mist across

246

the water, a high mist, not just a sea fret. You could see neither upwards, nor across the lake. It was one of those soft, silent times you can get out in the wilderness in the early morning. So quiet you found yourself talking softly; even my buddy Don, and he's trained to lambaste his opinions upon the world.'

Arnold Morgan chortled and took another sip of Dewar's. 'Keep going, Tony,' he said. 'I'm enjoying this.'

'Anyway, I heard this sudden wind. Not quite a howl, you know, nothing theatrical. But a real creepy, wailing sound, more like that rise in sound you get in an old house when there's a storm outside.

'It was about as weird as a sound can be . . . *wh-o-o-o-o-sh!* On a dead-still morning. And it was not a sound that was static where we were, it was passing us by, as if heading into the mountain. I found myself looking upwards towards the peak and then there was this deep thumping sound from way up there, like an underground explosion . . . Moments later I heard the goddamned noise again.'

'How long, Tony?'

'Not as long as a minute. But close. And I heard it sweep past. Same sound. In a split second I was looking up over the lake, but there was nothing, not even a moment in the mist. But the sound was identical. And ten seconds later there was another explosion from Mount St Helens. This one was a much more open sound, a real crash . . . you know . . . *KERRRR-BAM!* Like you'd imagine a bomb, although I've never heard one.'

'And then?'

'I started up the wagon and we took off. That's when we heard the third explosion. That one was real loud, and suddenly there was fire and ash raining into the forest around us. Trees were on fire and God knows what. We just kept going, driving faster than I've ever driven in my life.

'The fourth explosion was bigger than all the other three put together – we didn't see it, but the road shook. And then it began to get dark . . . tons and tons of ash and debris flung into the atmosphere, I suppose. Kind of blotted out the sun. If I hadn't seen that sucker blow all those years ago, I guess I'd still have been standing gawping at Mount St Helens when the lava started down the mountain. It just swallows everything.'

'Including the half-gallon of Dewar's, according to your man McKeag,' chuckled Arnold.

'Yeah. Just imagine . . . one small section of volcanic rock, amber in colour, in the middle of all that grey . . . Dewar's Rock. Now that's a landmark.'

'According to Don McKeag's programme you might be running for state governor in a couple of years?' said Arnold. 'Could be your first major act on environmental issues . . . renaming the rock at the foot of Mount St Helens.'

1030 Monday 24 August 2009
Second floor, The Pentagon
One by one they filed into the private conference room of the Chairman of the Joint Chiefs. There

was Rear Admiral George Morris and Lt. Commander Jimmy Ramshawe. Admiral Alan Dickson, Rear Admiral Freddie Curran, Admiral Morgan and Tony Tilton. General Scannell had invited the Air Force Chief, General Cale Carter, plus Major Bart Boyce, NATO's Supreme Allied Commander; and General Stanford Hudson (Readiness Command, US Army).

No politicians were present. But as military brainpower goes, this was a solid roomful, deep in the most secretive inner sanctum of Pentagon planning, directly above the office of President McBride's doveish Secretary of State for Defense, Milt Schlemmer, formerly of the International Atomic Energy Agency and the Campaign for Nuclear Disarmament. The man's name alone brought Arnold Morgan out in hives.

There were only two men from outside the US Military's High Command – an Air Force colonel from US Aerospace Command HQ, who waited in the reception area, and Tony Tilton. Positioned outside the office were two Marine Corps guards, with four others on extra duty in Corridor Seven, which leads directly to E-Ring, the great circular outer throughway of the Pentagon.

The ten men sat at the large conference table, and General Scannell called the meeting to order by informing everyone that this was a gathering of the most highly classified nature, and that no one, repeat no one, was to be informed that it had even been convened.

For reasons which would become obvious, he declared that Admiral Morgan would chair the meeting, and he cited Arnold's long and detailed involvement in the subject. He also explained that Admiral George Morris had been 'on the case' for several months, and that Lt. Commander Jimmy Ramshawe, the Fort Meade Director's assistant, had 'essentially made the running throughout the unofficial investigation'.

General Scannell had issued only the most cursory briefing by coded e-mail to the senior officers around the table. But each man knew enough to understand the grave suspicion which now surrounded the eruption of Mount St Helens, and each man had been furnished with a copy of the letter from HAMAS demanding the United States' formal evacuation from the Middle East.

'Each of you understands,' said General Scannell, 'the distinct likelihood that the crater, high on Mount St Helens, was hit by four incoming cruise missiles on the morning of 9 August. Only one man was near enough to bear any kind of witness to this event, at least only one man who survived. And he is with us this morning, Mr Tony Tilton, the President of the Seattle National Bank.

'Now because I would like to fly him home as soon as possible, I am inviting him to speak to us and explain exactly what he witnessed in the foothills of Mount St Helens on that morning. Mr Tilton has already debriefed Admiral Morgan, so I will invited Arnold to steer our visitor through his account of the incident.'

Admiral Morgan introduced Tony formally to the group and then invited him to recount, in precision detail, everything he had told him on the previous evening. And he did so with a lawyer's clarity. At the conclusion of his story, Admiral Morgan asked if anyone wanted to ask Mr Tilton any questions, but there were none. The bank chief and the former National Security Adviser had between them delivered a detailed, virtuoso performance.

They formally thanked him for coming and Admiral Morgan stood up and escorted him from the room. Two young naval officers were waiting to walk him out to the helicopter pad for the five-minute journey to Andrews and the flight back to Puget Sound.

Back on the second floor of the Pentagon, the meeting was listening to the summing up of the Air Force psychiatrist who had been examining the long letter from HAMAS. His conclusions were very clear: 'While the demands of the letter are plainly out-rageous, I detect no sign of hysteria, or dementia of any kind. This letter was not written by a disturbed person. It was written by an educated man, whose natural language was most certainly English.

'I do not detect one instance of difficulty or con-fusion in writing past and present tenses, which is the classic sign of a foreigner trying to write in another language. Nor indeed one instance of a discordant word, nor a colloquialism which we would not use. Or even the slightest distortion of a common colloquialism. Also there is no sign of heightened excitement anywhere in the writing. The language is straightforward even in its demands . . . *immediate steps . . . immediate undertakings*. He talks of *entering the final stage*. He wants to see *clear signs*.

'There is one sentence in which he points out that if he and his men can explode *the biggest volcano in the United States, we can probably arrange a large rockfall, into the deserted ocean*.

'The key word here, gentlemen, is "probably". Because it represents *irony* perhaps the most elusive of thought patterns, the ability to understate yet to have the same effect. People think Americans sometimes lack this subtlety. The educated British seem practically to live on it.

'And I would remind you of the phrase *intimated in my communiqué* – those are the words of a trained military officer or even a diplomat. That sentence could have been written by anyone in this room.

'Gentlemen, this letter was written by a very serious person. Very sane. Very cold-blooded. I suggest we ignore this guy at our peril. And for what it's worth, if the writer of this letter told me he just blew up Mount St Helens, I'd have no reason to disbelieve him.'

The psychiatrist was followed by Lt. Commander Ramshawe who outlined the problem of the missing *Barracuda*, pointed out the most recent sightings and detections, and his conclusion that the boat was probably on its way down the west coast of South America.

General Scannell then steered the meeting towards

the demands of the terrorists, and he requested General Hudson of Readiness Command to outline the deployment of personnel, plus stockpiles of equipment and munitions in the Gulf.

The general immediately issued a single sheet of paper to each man around the table, and read from his own, for everyone's benefit:

'BAHRAIN. Headquarters of the US Fifth Fleet, and 4,500 personnel. This is the nerve centre for all US warships deployed in the Red Sea, the Persian Gulf and the Arabian Sea.

'KUWAIT. US Army Command, approximately 12,000 military personnel. We got a large training base at Camp Doha, which is now our top favoured desert training area. We're building another, near-identical facility at Arifjan. The US Air Force flies from Ali Al-Salem, and Ahmed Al-Jabar air bases.

'SAUDI ARABIA. Reopened. US Air Force Command, approximately 10,000 personnel. Combat aircraft, including fighter and reconnaissance. We got E3 AWACs and air-refuelling aircraft based at Prince Sultan Air Base, protected by two Patriot missiles batteries.

'QATAR. Around 4,000 personnel. Al Udeid Air Base, which has the region's longest runway, is available to us. We've built aircraft shelters there, and we operate the KC10 and KC135 air-to-air refuelling aircraft. Central Command (CENTCOM) of all forces in the Gulf has been established at Camp as Sayliyah.

'OMAN. We use the docks and al-Seeb

International Airport as transit points for onward movement either to Afghanistan or the Gulf. Approximately 3,000 personnel are based there.

'UNITED ARAB EMIRATES. We got 500, mostly Air Force personnel based here.

'DJIBOUTI. Way down there on the Gulf of Aden. Up to 3,000 US Special Forces, Marines and Air Force personnel, all part of the counter-terrorism task force. This is the base for the CIA unmanned Predator aircraft.

'DIEGO GARCIA. There's around 1,500 US personnel here. It's our base for the upgraded B-52 heavy bombers, and the B-2 stealth bombers.

'In addition we've always got three Carrier Battle Groups in the area, on a rotation basis, depending on the political climate.'

General Scannell interjected, 'Which adds up to one hell of a lot of people and equipment to move out of the area on the sole demand of one Middle Eastern freedom fighter.'

'Unless,' added Admiral Morgan, 'that freedom fighter really does have the capability of destroying the entire East Coast of the United States. Then, of course, the evacuation of our military in the Middle East would be a very small price to pay.'

'It cannot be possible. It simply cannot,' said General Boyce.

'*If we can explode the biggest volcano in the United States, we can probably arrange a large rockfall into the deserted ocean*,' intoned Admiral Morgan.

And for just a few seconds the entire table went

silent. Then Admiral Morgan spoke again. 'Gentlemen, let's face it, we have to start from the basis that this guy is not joking. And our options are very limited. Priority number one is to catch and destroy the fucker. Right?'

He glared around the table. No one dissented. 'Therefore number two is to produce a fleet deployment plan. Number three is to appoint a commander-in-chief to that fleet. Number four is to try to get the President, the Commander-in-Chief of all US Armed Forces, to agree to such a deployment. The last one is the most difficult, by a very long way.'

'You want an educated guess?' asked Admiral Morris.

'Always,' replied Arnold Morgan.

'He is not going to agree, now or ever, to put this country, essentially, on a war footing to deal with what he believes is a crank letter. And he will not listen to us. Now or ever.'

A silence enveloped the table. 'Then we may,' said General Scannell, 'have to go without him.'

'Which would be a bit unorthodox,' said Admiral Dickson.

'Maybe,' replied the CJC. 'But we cannot knowingly let down the people of this nation, when we all believe there is a real danger someone could wipe out the East Coast of the United States. I believe Lt. Commander Ramshawe has issued everyone with a short and concise report on the experts' assessment of the volcano on the island of La Palma.'

'I guess there's no stopping the tidal wave once it develops?' asked General Boyce.

'Apparently not,' replied Arnold Morgan. 'Because when that develops, we're looking at probably the greatest force on earth, travelling along the seabed at the speed of a jet aircraft. Less than nine hours to New York, the waves building all the way.'

'Jesus Christ,' replied the general.

'So far as I can see,' said the admiral, 'we have two chances. The first one slim, the second one better, but not foolproof. We set sail for the Canary Islands with a 100-strong fleet and search for the missing *Barracuda*, which we probably won't find. Not if the driver's as smart as I think he is.

'Secondly, we position a defensive screen of surface warships to the west of La Palma, primed to hit and destroy the missile, or missiles, in mid-flight. It would help, of course, if we knew roughly where they're going to fire it from. But we don't.'

'Well, regardless, we'll have to move the entire East Coast fleet the hell out of all our Navy bases,' said Admiral Curran. 'A wave like that would wipe us out. We can't leave any ship in port. We have drafted a rough plan, which I think Admiral Dickson would like everyone to see . . . that is, if we are unanimous about the reality of the threat. And are we unanimously agreed that we must go ahead with a fleet plan to counteract that threat, regardless of the opinions of our political masters? Right hands, please.'

Nine right hands were solemnly raised high.

'No choice,' said General Scannell. 'Absolutely no choice.'

'Okay. Now today's the 24th,' said Arnold Morgan. 'That means we have forty-seven days to get things into line. I suggest we invent some forthcoming fleet exercises in the Atlantic and start getting ships at least on stand-by for deployment. I presume the Middle East is sufficiently quiet for us to move the Carrier Groups into the Atlantic without causing a huge amount of fuss? Alan?'

'No problem.'

'Good. Now perhaps we should hear the preliminary plan I understand Alan and Freddie have been developing for the past couple of days . . .'

Admiral Curran handed out one single sheet of paper to each man. Then he told them, 'As a submariner, I have been asked to explain the first part of the plan, before I hand over to Admiral Dickson. I am sure you know there are innate difficulties in conducting underwater hunts with submarines, on account of how they are apt to shoot each other if we're not damned careful.

'My recommendation is we take a "box" 500 miles north to south, running up and down the La Palma coastline, by 500 miles west out into the Atlantic. That's a colossal area of 250,000 square miles, and from somewhere in there we expect the *Barracuda* to fire her missiles at the cliff.

'It is not impossible that she could fire from even further west, perhaps up to 1,000 miles out from La Palma. But I personally doubt that. Her commanding officer will know we're out there in force looking for her, and will probably be keenly aware of our excellent surface-to-air missiles defence systems and probably will not want to have his birds in the air for too long.

'If I had to guess I'd say he'll launch from under 300 miles from the La Palma coast. But we cannot take that chance. We need to cover the outer limits of his range.'

'How many missiles do you think, Freddie?' asked Arnold Morgan.

'Possibly twenty SLCMs to be sure of knocking the cliff down. Unless he goes nuclear. Then he'll only want two.'

'Can he go nuclear?'

'I don't think so,' interrupted Admiral Morris. 'Simply because I can't imagine where he'd get 'em. They have to be especially fitted for the *Barracuda*, and the Russians are not about to help him to that extent. They won't even admit selling the *Barracuda* to anyone except China. And the Chinese will not even admit to owning it.

'Certainly they are unlikely to admit compliance with a bunch of terrorists trying to wreck the East Coast of the United States of America. The Chinese might be cunning and they might be devious, but they're not stupid.'

'They might be able to buy 'em at that place in Bosnia,' said Arnold Morgan. 'But I'd be surprised if a European country would agree to that, especially one in NATO, or the EU.'

'How about North Korea?' said Admiral Morris.

'Possible. Though I'm not sure if they have developed the sophistication to build a nuclear-headed missile which would fit into a big Russian submarine.'

'Let's hope not,' said Admiral Dickson. 'But I guess in the end it doesn't matter where they got the warhead. We have to stop it, whether it was made in Korea, Belgrade or Macy's.'

'Okay,' said Arnold, 'Let's hear that outline from Freddie on the deployment of the fleet.'

'We'll definitely need to use a "box" system for our submarine force,' said Admiral Curran. 'And my recommendation is we form a screen from the 500-mile mark moving inshore to perhaps 300. Each one of fifteen boats taking a square of around 40 miles by 40 miles, each of them with a towed array, trying to pick up every sound in the water. Altogether that should take care of an area of 24,000 square miles.

'My personal view is that the *Barracuda* will not hang around in the ocean west of La Palma, firstly because he'll guess we're in there, thick and fast, and secondly because he'll be coming in from further south and may have a great distance to cover at a slow speed. Our best chance is to catch him coming in, though I have no real confidence he'll make the kind of mistake we need to detect him.

'I then recommend we take five more submarines and position them in boxes 40 miles long, right inshore. The water's very deep, and there is just a chance the *Barracuda* will move in quietly at night in order to launch with a visual look as well as the GPS.

'I do not say this is any more likely a scenario than any other. But it would be ridiculous to have our defensive screens way offshore, while our enemy creeps underneath us, in two-mile-deep ocean, and opens fire from close range, giving us restricted time to set up for the intercept.'

General Hudson apologised but requested permission to interrupt, reminding the group that there plainly had to be a Patriot missile shield positioned at the top of the cliff and around the rim of the volcanoes. 'We can only hope he launches something which flies high, rather than a sea-skimmer,' he said. 'Just to give us a real shot at it.'

Admiral Curran nodded in agreement. He suggested the submarine force should answer directly to SUBLANT headquarters, wherever that may be. It was becoming ominously certain they were looking at a general evacuation of all naval and military command posts on the East Coast of the USA, as the 9 October deadline approached.

Admiral Alan Dickson very briefly discussed the deployment of the surface fleet, recommending that another eighty ships would be required for the offshore vigil which might save the east coast. 'We're looking at a force of maybe forty frigates, modern missile ships with towed arrays, listening in the water throughout that central area between the two submarine forces.

'We're talking maybe a 200,000-square-mile patrol area with eighty ships, that's 2,500 square miles each, a 50-mile-square box, and they'll search it end to end, night and day, waiting for the intruder. If he's good, we may never hear him. If he's careless, just once, near any of our ships, he's rubble.

'If the meeting agrees, we'll begin work on the defensive layout right away, and we better start moving ships into the area from the Middle and Far East.'

'I agree with that,' said Arnold Morgan. 'But I remain concerned about the time frame, and I remain concerned about HAMAS watching our activities at the bases around the Gulf over the next couple of weeks.

'If they see we are doing absolutely nothing, in response to their evacuation demand, they might just get frustrated and whack the cliff, or somehow up the ante. I'd like to try and avoid that.'

'You mean start moving stuff, as if we're obeying them?'

'So far as I can see,' said Arnold, 'that's the only chance we have of buying time. If they see we're reacting to their threats, they may be happy to give us more time. And we need time. A defensive operation like this needs all the time it can get.'

'Sir,' said Lt. Commander Ramshawe, 'I wonder if I may ask a question?'

'Sure, Jimmy, go right ahead.'

'Do you think these jokers will attempt to bang some high ordnance straight into the cliff and knock it into the sea, or do you think they'll try to bang a couple of big nuclear warheads straight into the Cumbre Vieja volcano, blow it wide open and let nature take its course with the steam blast.'

'Good question,' replied the admiral. 'In the normal way I'd say any terrorist in that situation would want to fire in a missile, hit the cliff and bolt for freedom, from maybe 300 miles offshore.

'But this bastard's different. We believe he's an expert on volcanoes. Option two, hitting the crater, will take much longer to develop, and it is more difficult to execute, but it's also more deadly. Altogether a more awesome and terrifying project. I think he'll go for option two. He's not afraid of difficulty, and he'll try for maximum effect.'

'Just like he did at Mount St Helens,' replied the lt. commander thoughtfully.

'Exactly so,' said Admiral Morgan.

'Which brings us back to the business of time,' said General Scannell. 'Does everyone think we should stage some kind of an unobtrusive departure from the bases in the Gulf?'

'I don't think we can, not so long as President McBride thinks we're all crazy.' General Boyce, the Supreme Allied Commander NATO, was visibly unhappy. He shook his head, and said twice, 'I just don't know.'

General Tim Scannell was braver. 'Bart,' he said, 'I think I mentioned it before. On this one, we may just have to go without him.'

And the eight men sitting around the big table in the CJC's conference room felt the chill of a potential mutiny, led, unthinkably, by the highest command of the United States military.

CHAPTER SEVEN

0800 Friday 4 September 2009
56.18S 67.00W. Speed 15. Depth 300

Admiral Ben Badr held the *Barracuda* steady on course two-seven-zero, 25 miles south of Cape Horn, beneath turbulent seas swept by a force eight gale out of the Antarctic. They were moving through the Drake Passage in 2,500 fathoms of water, having finally concluded their southward journey, down past the hundreds of islands and fjords which guard mainland Chile from the thundering Pacific breakers.

They had made good speed across the Southeast Pacific Basin and the Mornington Abyssal Plain, and were now headed east, running north of the South Shetland Islands in the cold, treacherous waters where the Antarctic Peninsula comes lancing out of the southern ice floes.

Ben Badr was making for the near end of the awesome underwater cliffs of the Scotia Ridge. At the same time he was staying in the eastern flows of the powerful Falkland Islands Current. His next course adjustment would take him past the notoriously shallow Burdwood Bank, and well east of the Falkland Islands themselves.

These were lonely waters, hardly patrolled by the Argentinian Navy, and even more rarely by the Royal Navy which was still obliged to guard the approaches to the islands for which 253 British servicemen had fought and died in 1982.

It was mid-winter this far south, and despite not having seen daylight for almost two months, Ben Badr assured the crew they did not want to break the habit right now. Not with an Antarctic blizzard raging above them, and a mighty southern ocean demonstrating once more that Cape Horn's murderous reputation was well earned.

Submarines dislike the surface of the water in almost any conditions. They are not built to roll around with the ocean's swells. But 300 feet below the waves, the *Barracuda* was in its element, moving swiftly and easily through the depths, a smooth, jet-black, malevolent tube of imminent destruction, but the soul of comfort for all who sailed with her.

That 47,000-hp nuclear system had been running sweetly for eight weeks now, which was not massively demanding for a power source which would run, if necessary, for eight years. The Russian-built VM-5 Pressurised Water Reactor (PWA) would provide every vestige of the submarine's propulsion, heat, fresh water and electronics on an indefinite basis. Barring accident, the only factor which could drive the *Barracuda* to the surface was if they ran out of food.

Their VM-5 reactor was identical to the one the Russians used on their gigantic Typhoon Class ballistic missile boats. The world's biggest underwater warships, which displace 26,000 tons submerged, required two of them, but the reactors were the same state-of-the-art nuclear pressurised water systems.

The *Barracuda*, with its titanium hull, was a submariner's dream. It could strike with missiles, unexpectedly, from a position unknown. It was incredibly quiet, as quiet as the US Navy's latest Los Angeles Class boats, silent under seven knots, undetectable, barring a mistake by her commanding officer. A true phantom of the deep.

General Rashood and Ben Badr stared at the charts which marked the long northward journey ahead of them. It was more than 4,000 miles up to the equator, and they knocked off three parts of that with a brisk, constant 15 knots through the cold, lonely southern seas, devoid of US underwater surveillance and largely devoid of the warships of any nation.

They remained 1,000 miles offshore, running 500 feet below the surface up the long Argentinian coast, across the great South American Basin until they were level with the vast, 140-mile-wide estuary of the River Plate. This is the confluence of the Rivers Parana and Uruguay, and the enormous estuary contains some of the busiest shipping lanes in the world, steaming along the merchant ship roads into the ports of Buenos Aires on the Argentinian side and Montevideo on the Uruguayan.

Ben Badr stayed well offshore here, keeping right

of the shallow Rio Grande Rise and pushing on north, up towards Ascension Island. And long before they arrived in those water, he cut the speed of his submarine, running through the confused seas above the craggy cliffs of the Mid–Atlantic Ridge on his starboard side, while he made his way silently past the US military base on this British-owned moonscape of an island.

This was probably the only spot in the entire mid- and South Altantic in which they might be detected. And they ran past with the utmost care, slowly, slowly, only six knots, deeper than usual, at 700 feet. The *Barracuda* was deathly quiet on all decks, Lt. Commander Rashood huddled in the navigation room, Admiral Badr and the HAMAS general were in the control room listening to the regular pings of the passive sonar.

On Friday 18 September, the *Barracuda* crossed the equator, the unseen divider of north and south in the centre of the earth's navigational grid. This was the zero-degree line which slices in, off the Atlantic, and through Brazil, a few miles north of the Amazon Delta.

Ahead of the HAMAS warship were another 1,000 miles through which they made good speed, covering the distance in a little under three days. By midday on Monday 21 September they were at their rendezvous point, running slowly at periscope depth, eight miles off the port of Dakar in the former French colony of Senegal, right on the outermost seaward bulge of northern Africa.

11.00 a.m. (local)
Monday 21 September 2009
Chevy Chase, Maryland

Arnold Morgan was entertaining an old friend, the new Israeli Ambassador to Washington, sixty-two-year-old General David Gavron, former head of the most feared international Intelligence agency in the world, Mossad.

The two men had met, and cooperated, while David Gavron had served as military attaché at the Israeli Embassy seven years previously. They had, by necessity, stayed in touch during Admiral Morgan's tenure in the White House, when the general had headed up Mossad.

Today's was an unorthodox meeting. David Gavron, like every other high-ranking military Intelligence officer in the world, knew the admiral was no longer on the White House staff. But this certainly had neither diminished his towering reputation nor his encyclopaedic knowledge of the ebb and flow of the world's power struggles.

General Gavron guessed, correctly, that the USA had a serious problem. He had been for years a close friend and confidant not only of Arik Sharon, but also of the former Yom Kippur war tank division commander, General Abraham 'Bren' Adan. General Gavron was possibly the most trusted man in Israel.

He was a pure Israeli of the blood, a true Sabra, born a few miles southwest of the Sea of Galilee near Nazareth. On 8 October 1973, the first day of the Yom Kippur war, as a battalion tank commander

267

he had driven out into the Sinai right alongside 'Bren' Adan himself. On that most terrible day, hundreds of young Israelis, stunned by the suddenness of the onslaught by Egypt's Second Army, fought and died in the desert.

For two days and two nights, David Gavron had served in the front line of the battlefield, as one of 'Bren' Adan's bloodstained young commanders who flung back wave after wave of the Egyptian tank division. Twice wounded, shot in the arm and then blown into the desert sand while trying to save a burning tank crew, David Gavron's personal battle honour was presented to him by Mrs Meir herself. It was inscribed with the same words as Great Britain's coveted Victoria Cross . . . *FOR VALOUR.*

This was precisely the kind of man Admiral Morgan now needed urgently because only someone like David Gavron, a man who had faced the onslaught of an invading army, could ultimately decide whether his beleaguered little country could comply with America's request to vacate the West Bank of the River Jordan.

So far, in unofficial but probing talks, the signs had not been good. From Tel Aviv there had been zero enthusiasm. The big hitters in the Israeli military had almost visibly shuddered at the prospect of a Palestinian State. Hard-eyed men from the Knesset, Mossad and Shin Bet, the interior secret service, had intimated this was too big a favour to ask.

Arnold Morgan stared at the jagged scar on the left side of the Israeli's face. He knew it was a legacy from a far distant tank battle in the desert. And that scar ran deep. David Gavron's reaction to a polite request for an end to hostilities with the Palestinians would have a major bearing on the next approach by the Americans.

Admiral Morgan did not know precisely how much General Gavron knew, but he suspected HAMAS might have informed Mossad directly of their threat to the United States, and their demand that Israel back up and give their Arab enemy some living space.

It was a warm Fall day and they sat outside on the patio surrounding the pool area. Arnold sipped his coffee and gazed into the cool blue eyes of the tall, fit-looking Israeli diplomat, with his close-cropped hair and tanned skin.

'David,' he said, 'I want you to level with me.'

'As always,' smiled the general.

'Are you aware of the threat made upon my nation by the High Command of HAMAS?'

'We are.'

'Do you know of the twofold nature of the demands, that we vacate the Middle East in its entirety, and that we compel you to agree to the formation of a Palestinian State inside the present borders of Israel?'

'Yes, we are aware of precisely what they threaten.'

'Okay. Now, you also know we have begun to make troop and armament movements in our Middle East bases.'

'We do.'

'And do you think HAMAS now believe we intend to comply with their demands?'

'I doubt it.'

'Why not?'

'Because you are probably not doing nearly enough. Just playing for time, while you get ready to obliterate your enemy, in the time-honoured American way.'

'It's damn difficult to obliterate HAMAS. Since we can't see them.'

'I assure you there is no need to tell us that. We can see them a lot better than you. And we can't get rid of them either.'

'Well, David. We can certainly step up our evacuation plans, sufficient to make us look real. But we plainly need your cooperation, just to demonstrate we have persuaded you to make a lasting peace, with redrawn borders for the West Bank and the Gaza Strip.'

David Gavron, somewhat ominously, did not answer.

'So I have two questions to ask you,' said the admiral. 'The first because of your known expertise in dealing with terrorist enemies of your nation . . . do you think we should take the HAMAS threat seriously?'

'You mean their assurance that they will cause this giant landslide and then a tidal wave to flood your East Coast?'

'That's the one, David.'

'My answer is, yes. Because HAMAS have become very dangerous in the past two or three years. You will have noticed several of their spectacular successes – some at our expense, others at yours . . . ?'

'Of course we have. And now they are threatening again. Goddamnit, David, they never used to be *that* dangerous.'

'Not until they found a new Sandhurst-trained military assault leader.'

'You mean the SAS officer who absconded from the Brits?'

'That's the man, Arnold. And I've no doubt you realise he went over the wall in my own country, during the battle of the Jerusalem Road in our holy city of Hebron.'

'Actually, David, my information was that he went around the wall, not over it.'

'Very precise of you,' replied General Gavron, smiling. 'We do, of course, have the same sources. Anyway, he's never been seen since, and HAMAS has never been the same since.'

'Don't I know that. But now we're stuck with this volcano bullshit.'

'I wonder if you also heard,' replied the Israeli, 'that he undoubtedly kidnapped and murdered that professor in London earlier this year, the world authority on volcanoes and earthquakes?'

'We only surmised that very recently.'

'We were perhaps quicker in Tel Aviv. But we knew there was an active cell of the HAMAS High Command in London. Matter of fact, we just missed them. One day earlier might have saved everyone a lot of trouble.'

'Or, alternatively, left you on the short side of a half-dozen assassins . . .'

'Yes, we are always aware of that possibility when dealing with such a man,' said General Gavron. 'Nonetheless, I should definitely take his threats seriously if I were you . . . we can surmise from his London activities that he is now an expert on volcanoes. And I'm told by our field chief in Damascus that they definitely planned to erupt Mount St Helens. We've never had confirmation of that, but the coincidence is a little fierce.'

'Which leaves our East Coast on the verge of extinction,' said Arnold. 'I've read up on the subject, and the truth is obvious. He hits the Cumbre Vieja volcano, that mega-*tsunami* will happen. And that's likely to be *sayonara* New York . . .'

'Of course, I see your problem. You are obliged to buy a little time by making moves in the Middle East to look as if you are leaving. But what you are really doing is getting a great battle fleet into operation in the Atlantic in order to find and destroy the submarine, or intercept the missile as it flies into La Palma?'

'How the hell do you know they're in a submarine?'

'Please, Arnold, give us some credit. We know about the missing *Barracudas*. We know you found one of them, already scuttled. And we know the other one is on the loose. There is plainly no other way to hit the volcano except with a submarine-launched missile. An aircraft is out of the question, so is a surface ship, and a blast from the mainland of black North Africa would be to invite instant detection by US satellites.

'No, Arnold, they have informed you what they plan to do. And quite obviously they are going to launch their missile attack from a submarine creeping around, deep, somewhere in the North Atlantic, somewhere off the coast of Africa. And since that *Barracuda* is the only suspect . . . the rest is academic.'

'Correct. And if I am *not* able to demonstrate the nation of Israel is prepared to acquiesce to our instructions, I guess HAMAS will open fire, and we'll just have to see if we can stop 'em. I should warm you, however, if that little scenario should occur, the Knesset ought not to hold its breath for any more help from the USA . . . finance or weapons.'

'I do realise that,' said General Gavron. 'And, quite honestly, I have tried to stay out of the talks. I know there has been nothing formal yet, but these things get around fast. And we are aware that sooner or later we will have to answer a very serious question from the United States.'

Admiral Morgan poured them both more coffee. He stood up and walked for a few paces, and then retraced his steps. 'David,' he said, 'what is your personal reaction to the HAMAS demand for immediate recognition of the Independent, Democratic and Sovereign State of Palestine based on the territories on the West Bank and the Gaza Strip

. . . as they say, *occupied by the forces of Israel since 4 June 1967*?

'I guess you know they want all Israeli troops out of these territories right away?'

'That's what they always demand, Arnold. But they are asking the rulers of Israel to commit political suicide. And you know what your great hero Sir Winston Churchill said about that?'

'Not offhand. What was it?'

'The trouble with committing political suicide is you usually live to regret it . . .'

Arnold Morgan laughed, despite the seriousness of the conversation. He sat back and sipped his coffee thoughtfully.

'Arnold,' Gavron said. 'There are thousands of families whose relatives died for those new Israeli lands, died defending them against the Arab aggressor. My grandfather was killed in the Sinai in 1967, my beloved and brave grandmother died on a human ammunition line, passing shells up to our tanks on the Golan Heights in 1967. My father's two brothers were killed in the battle for the Sinai in 1967, and my niece, aged eleven, was killed by a Palestinian bomb in a supermarket twelve years ago.

'I'm sorry, Arnold, I could never agree to a Palestinian State within our borders. Not one which caused us to surrender the lands we fought for, against overwhelming aggression from the Arab nations. My government might agree if America were to get very rough with us. But would I? Never.'

Arnold smiled a rueful smile at the old warrior

from the Holy Land. 'But what about us, David?' he said. 'We, who have done so much to keep your nation secure. What about us, in our hour of real need?'

'Well, the East Coast of America is a very long way from Israel. More than 5,000 miles. And just for once, we are not the ones being threatened by an armed enemy.

'In my country, there are vast numbers of young Israelis who were not even born when Egypt split the Bar-Lev line, and attacked us on our most holy day of the year. We'd be asking them to support their government giving away great slabs of the only land they have ever known . . . to the Palestinians. Well, Arnold, that's what civil wars are made of . . .'

'You mean Israel is *never* going to agree to the creation of a Democratic Palestinian State, never going to withdraw from the occupied territories?'

'No, I don't mean that. I don't mean *never*. But probably not in the next five weeks. That's just asking the utterly impossible. For a problem which is not even ours. Remember it's the USA under threat. Not Israel.'

'For an officer and a diplomat that's a rather short-sighted answer,' replied Admiral Morgan.

'Not really. The USA would find it very difficult to get rough with us. No American President is going to risk losing the massive Jewish vote in New York.'

'I was not referring to the USA getting rough,' said Arnold.

'Oh . . . what were you implying . . . ?'

'I was suggesting that if we get jack-hammered by this tidal wave, that will somewhat preoccupy us for a while. And since you did nothing to assist us, you'll probably find us too busy to help you.'

'But we don't need help, Arnold. We're not threatened.'

'If the US Navy and military is effectively disabled on the East Coast for a period of several months, how long do you think it will take HAMAS to turn its thwarted anger on Israel?'

David Gavron was thoughtful. He said nothing for a few moments and then replied, 'They are essentially a hit-and-run organisation. Terrorists. They do not have our training, our combat readiness. They have no answers to heavy artillery. And we can withstand terrorism. We always have. HAMAS is simply not a big enough force to take down a nation like ours.'

'That may have been so three years ago,' said Arnold. 'But it's not so now. They have a general as accomplished in the field as anyone we've seen for years . . .'

'This damn Kerman character?'

'That's the man, David. That's the man.'

1530 (local) Monday 21 September
Atlantic Ocean 14.43N 17.30W
Speed 5. Course unconfirmed. PD
The *Barracuda* cruised in warm waters, out among

the blue-fin tunas, just below the surface, less than 10 miles off the most westerly port in Africa. Dakar was in the middle of its rainy season, and warm tropical rain lashed the calm waters of the deep Atlantic way out to sea.

They had been waiting for almost four hours now and the rain had not let up. Every fifteen minutes Ben Badr ordered his mast up and scanned the surface picture, looking in vain for the patrol boat from the Senegalese Navy which had been due to arrive at around midday.

When it finally did show up, shortly before 1600, both he and Ravi were becoming extremely jumpy. Running this close to the surface, even in waters in which the US Navy had zero interest, it was still unnerving. Just knowing the US satellites, if correctly focused, could pick them up in moments.

The unrelenting rain reduced visibility and the Senegalese were no more than a mile away when Admiral Badr saw them. Immediately he ordered the *Barracuda* to the surface. With a blast of emptying ballast, and an increased hum of the accelerating turbines, the *Barracuda* surged up into the fresh air for the first time for ten weeks. It was the first daylight they had seen since the submarine had gone deep just south of the Japanese island of Yaku Shima and headed out into the North Pacific.

The great underwater warship shouldered aside the blue waters of the eastern Atlantic, and the helmsman brought her almost to a halt on the surface, facing south awaiting the Senegalese patrol ship which would pull alongside.

The seas were otherwise deserted and the *Barracuda*'s deck crew waved the incoming ship into position on the starboard side of the hull. They could already see a special long gangway out on the scruffy looking deck, and they sent over lines to help the two Senegalese crewmen to shove it out between the two ships.

General Rashood, standing on deck with Shakira, gazed with some distaste at the condition of the patrol boat, a US-built Peterson Mark-4 Class 22-tonner, almost twenty years old, black-hulled and in dire need of a coat of paint. The once white deck was rusted, and further rust marks stained the hull. A couple of black tyres were set against the superstructure. As a Navy vessel it looked like a Third World fishing smack, but it was the only way to leave unnoticed and the Senegalese, sharing their Muslim faith, had been willing to help, although Ravi guessed his colleagues in Bandar Abbas had paid expensively for this short inter-Navy 10-mile voyage, probably as much as the boat was worth.

On board were three smiling seamen, jet-black in colour with gleaming white teeth, no uniforms, white T-shirts and jeans. They waved cheerfully and tossed for'ard and aft lines across to the *Barracuda*'s deck crew to make her fast.

'Are we actually going on board this wreck,' whispered Shakira.

''Fraid so,' said Ravi. 'At the moment it's all we've got.'

They stood on the casing in the rain and said their goodbyes to Ben Badr, Shakira's brother Ahmed, and the XO, Captain Ali Akbar Mohtaj. Everyone had known this was as far as the general and his wife were going, but there was a great deal of sadness in their departure.

Now, however, the task of the *Barracuda* was strictly operational. The mission was laid out, her course set, her missiles loaded, their tracks pre-planned. All that was required was a careful command, dead-slow speeds if they were close to any other ships, and a steady run into deep, getaway waters.

There would be satellite signals in and out of Bandar Abbas. There would be possible adjustments in the orders, but the signals coming back to the submarine would be direct from General Rashood. There was comfort in that for all of the *Barracuda*'s executive.

And there was an even greater comfort in knowing that if plans needed to be altered, in any way, they would be schemed by the general, the HAMAS military leader who would now play satellite poker with the Americans in the final stages of the operation to drive them out of the Middle East for ever. On board the *Barracuda* there was nothing more Ravi could do.

Shakira hugged her brother, kissed Ben Badr on both cheeks and shook hands with Captain Ali Akbar Mohtaj. Ravi shook hands with each of them and then steered his wife towards the gangway. She carried with her a long dark blue seaman's duffel bag, in which was stored her make-up, shirts, spare jeans, underwear and Kalashnikov AK-47.

General Rashood watched her traverse the little bridge, holding the rail with one hand, and then he too stepped off the deck of the *Barracuda* for the first time since they had left the Chinese port of Huludao in the Yellow Sea. And he made his way carefully over to the Senegalese Navy's 52-foot-long *Matelot Oumar Ndoye* – whatever the hell that meant.

It took all six of the patrol boat's crew to man-handle the gangway back aboard. The operation was conducted with a great deal of shouting and laughing. Twice it almost went over the side, and by the time they had it safely stowed the *Barracuda* was gone, sliding beneath the great ocean which divides the African and American continents.

It was heading west, for the moment, out towards the burly shoulders of the Mid-Atlantic Ridge, running effortlessly, 600 feet below the surface, in the gloomy depths of its own nether world, far away from the prying eyes of the American photographer high in the sky.

Ravi and Shakira sat in a couple of chairs under an ancient awning on the stern, beneath the machine-gun mountings. The captain, a heavily muscled ex-fisherman had made a sporting attempt to introduce himself, but he spoke only French in the heavy Wolof vernacular. In the end they settled for a laugh and a rough understanding that he was

Captain Rémé and he'd have them moored in the great port of Dakar inside thirty minutes.

So far as he could tell, Captain Rémé was restricted to only two speeds – all-stopped and flat out. Right now they were flat out, in a ship which shuddered from end to end as its aged diesels struggled to drive the twin shafts at their maximum possible revs.

Happily the sea was calm all the way, aside from a long Atlantic swell, and the *Matelot* shuddered along at its top speed of 20 knots towards the great Muslim city of Dakar, where at least one of the towering white mosques rivals the finest in Istanbul and Tehran. Senegal has always had one foot in the Middle East and one in West Africa, similar to Dakar, which is known as the crossroads where black Africa, Islam and Christianity have met for centuries, occasionally clashed, yet ultimately blended. The bedrock of the country's subsistence economy is peanut oil and not much is left over for Senegal's Navy budget. The US Government spent more on the Pentagon's cleaning staff than Senegal spent on its Navy.

Captain Rémé was as good as his word. They pulled alongside in exactly thirty minutes. The elderly diesels had not shaken the ramshackle craft to pieces and Ravi and Shakira stepped ashore into a working naval dockyard. Much of the quayside was stacked with fishing gear and shrimp nets, which made it a somewhat more relaxed operation than the one they had left ten weeks earlier on the shores of the Yellow Sea.

But it was a dockyard, no doubt about that. On two adjoining quays there was a 450-ton French-built Navy patrol craft, twenty-six years old, lightly gunned, named the *Njambuur*. Next to it was a Navy coastal patrol craft, a Canadian-built, Interceptor Class gunboat, thirty years old. No engines were running. It was plain to Ravi that the Senegalese Navy was not planning to go to war with anyone in the near future.

They were greeted by the Head of the Navy, a broad-shouldered black officer aged around forty; Captain Camara's teeth were as white as his short-sleeved uniform shirt. He saluted and said, in impeccable English, how pleased he was to welcome them to his humble headquarters. He had spoken to his friend Admiral Badr in Iran only that morning and everything was ready, as planned.

He would, he said, be driving them personally out to the airport, a distance of just three miles. But first he was sure they would like some tea. Their aircraft expected them at 1800, so they had half an hour to kill.

Thus, in the now hot, late afternoon sun, General and Mrs Rashood were ashore at last, strolling along the peaceful African waterfront, through the very heart of the sleepy Senegalese Navy – just a couple of weeks before they were scheduled to eliminate the entire East Coast of the United States of America. The contrast was not lost on either of them.

Tea with Captain Camara was a cheerful interlude. They sat outside and watched little boats crossing the harbour, sipping tea, with sugar but no milk, from tall glasses in silver holders. The captain asked no questions about the long voyage of the *Barracuda*, though he plainly understood there was a dark, subversive edge to its mission.

He knew his guests were important, and he knew they had arrived in a submarine, which had then vanished. But he did not think it was his place to pry into the business of his fellow Muslims who would shortly be flying home across the Sahara Desert, the vast wilderness of sand lying to the northeast of Dakar.

He had visited this remote, burning landscape only once, and had recoiled from it, as most black Africans do. But he understood that those endless sands represent the very fabric of the Muslim world. He understood, remotely, that his own tiny coastal community was somehow joined by the swirling dunes of the Arabian Desert, to the great Islamic nations of Egypt, Syria, Libya, Iraq, Iran and the Gulf States. And he knew it was timeless. And that it mattered. And he respected his visitors from the far ends of the Muslim kingdoms.

The captain observed that General Rashood had an extremely pronounced English accent, and asked if, like himself, he had attended school in the British Isles.

Ravi, who was desperately tired after a 20,000-mile voyage from communist China, could think of a thousand reasons not to tell anyone of his background. But he smiled and opted for mass confusion. 'No, Captain, I did not,' he said. 'I went to a school in Switzerland. They taught me to speak like this.'

'I see,' he replied. 'But I expect you noticed that I too speak like you, and I did go to school in England. Charterhouse. And from there I went to Oxford University . . . studied engineering at St Edmund Hall, but my main achievement was to play golf for the University against Cambridge. Twice. Once as captain.'

Ravi, who was almost nodding off in the hazy African heat after the rain, jolted himself back into the conversation, and offered, 'You're a Carthusian, and you got a Blue for golf? That's impressive.'

'I did,' said Camara, who was momentarily bewildered by his guest's instant grasp of his elite education, especially the fact that Ravi knew, esoterically, that Old Boys of Charterhouse are known as Carthusians.

But he continued, 'They taught me to play at school, and when I arrived at Oxford I turned out to be one of the best players. I really enjoyed it . . . very jolly people. It was funny, but they never could get a firm grip on my full name, which is Habib Abdu Camara, and when the team list was posted each week, they used to write me in as *The Black Man*.'

'Christ, if they did that these days they'd all be in the slammer,' said Ravi, smiling.

Captain Camara laughed. 'I suppose so, but they meant no harm. And even I thought it was funny. All of them have stayed my good friends.'

'You still see them?' asked Ravi.

'Well, I came down from Oxford seventeen years ago. And we did have a reunion for several years at the public schools' golf . . . you know, the Halford Hewitt Tournament down at Royal Cinque Ports in Deal. Of course, we were all playing for different schools, but at Oxford when we were together, we did beat Cambridge twice, and we're all rather proud of that.'

'You stopped going to the Halford Hewitt?'

'Not entirely. But my Navy career here prevented me from playing for Charterhouse for many years. Matter of fact, I'm going back next year. It's funny, but you see the same chaps, year after year, playing for their old schools. We've been in three semi-finals against Harrow and I don't think either team changed much.'

Ravi stiffened at the mention of his old school, but the chatterbox Captain of the Senegalese Navy had seized the moment to expound on his golfing career to someone who appeared to know what he was talking about.

'Great matches we had against the Harrovians,' he said. 'Chap called Thumper Johnston was their captain. His real name was Richard Trumper-Johnston, but he was a very fine player. He beat me twice, both times 2 and 1, dropped long putts on the 18th . . . he wasn't so good at foursomes.'

Again Ravi found himself nodding off. But he jolted back, trying to sound as if he'd been listening. And uncharacteristically he came out with an unguarded sentence. 'Thumper Johnston? Yes, he went back to Harrow as a housemaster, taught maths.'

'You sure you didn't go to school in England?' asked the captain. 'I know you Middle Eastern officers, very secretive men. Reveal nothing. But many of you went to school in England, especially Harrow . . . Thumper Johnston and King Hussein, eh? Ha ha ha.'

Captain Camara's wide face split into a huge grin. 'I think I catch you, General. But any friend of Thumper's is a very good friend of mine. I keep your secret.'

'I didn't say I knew him,' said Ravi. 'I just know of him. My father knew him.'

'Then your father went to Harrow?' said the captain. '*Someone* must have gone to Harrow . . . to know Thumper. He's never really left the place, except to play golf.'

Ravi smiled and he knew he had to admit something. Anything to shut this idiot up. 'My father was English, and I think he played against Johnston in the Halford Hewitt. I just remember his name.'

'Your father played for Harrow?' asked Captain Camara.

This was a critical moment. 'No, he played for Bradfield,' said Ravi.

The captain pondered that for a moment, doubtless, thought Ravi, assessing the absurd notion that an Englishman named Rashood was sufficiently impressed by the play of an opponent, Thumper Johnston in the Halford Hewitt, to regale his son with the man's career as a schoolmaster.

No, I don't think he's going to buy that, he thought.

And, sure enough, Captain Camara came back laughing. 'Aha,' he said. 'I think I find you out. You are a highly classified Old Harrovian submarine commander . . . you come out of nowhere . . . out of the ocean . . . and I check you out in England next year, maybe with Thumper in person . . . now I give more tea to my friends from deep waters.'

Shakira, who was even more tired than Ravi, had actually fallen asleep and had missed the entire conversation. She awakened just in time to hear Ravi say, 'You should have been a detective, Captain, but you have this case wrong . . .'

'Then how come you know Thumper, the Harrovian maths master!' cried Captain Camara, laughing loudly. 'You are rumbled – by The Black Man from Oxford . . . Ha ha ha!'

Even Ravi laughed, silently cursing himself for his carelessness. He declined more tea, and asked if they might make their way to the airport, since Shakira was so tired she would probably sleep all the way home.

'Of course,' said the captain, jumping energetically to his feet. 'Come . . . I'll call Tomas to carry the bags to the car . . . it's parked just over there.'

They walked across the quay to a black Mercedes-Benz naval staff car which carried small flags fluttering in the evening breeze on both front wings, the green, yellow and red tricolour of Senegal with its single green star in the centre.

Captain Camara drove to the airport in a leisurely manner, out to the Atlantic Peninsula north of the dockyard where a Lockheed Orion P–3F in the livery of the Iranian Air Force awaited them. The captain parked the car and insisted on walking out to the aircraft and carrying Shakira's bag. She climbed up the steps to board and Ravi followed her, now carrying both bags.

They waved goodbye to their escort and watched him stride away towards the car. And, quite suddenly, Ravi moved back to the top of the aircraft steps and called out, 'Captain . . . come back . . . I have a small gift for you in my bag . . . I forgot about it.'

Captain Camara grinned broadly and turned back towards the aircraft, as Ravi knew he would. He ran swiftly up the steps. They were agile, nimble strides, the last he would ever make. They were the strides which would end his life.

He entered the cabin and made his way to the rear of the aircraft where Ravi was fumbling in his bag. And with the speed of light, the HAMAS assault chief whipped around and slammed the hilt of his combat knife with terrific force into the space between the captain's eyes, splintering the lower forehead.

Then he rammed the butt of his right hand straight into the nostril end of The Black Man's nose, driving the bone into the brain. Captain Camara had played his last round. He was dead before he hit the floor. Shakira stood staring in amazement at the departed three-handicapper, spreadeagled in the aisle, presumably already on his way to the Greater Fairways.

The pilot, who had not seen all of this action, was fairly astonished too, and he walked down the centre aisle in company with his first officer.

'General Rashood?' he said, saluting. No questions. Military discipline.

'Sorry for the mess,' said Ravi. 'Put his head and shoulders in a garbage bag, will you? We'll throw him out either over the desert or the Red Sea. I'll let you know.'

'Yes, sir.'

'Oh, Captain. You'll understand this was a classified operation. This man knew too much about us. He was a menace to Iran, and a danger to Islam. Also, he was about to reveal my identity as a HAMAS commanding officer to the British. That was out of the question. Plainly.'

'Yes, sir. I understand. But I'll have to slow down and lose a lot of height if we're going to open the rear door. Just let me know when you're ready. We fly at around 28,000 feet. I have some hot coffee on board, and some sandwiches. We can get something better around 0100 when we refuel at Aswan.'

'Thank you, Captain. I think we better get the hell out of here now. Before someone starts looking for the Head of the local Navy.'

He and Shakira moved back towards the front of the aircraft and strapped themselves into the deep leather seats usually occupied by observers and

289

computer technicians on the Orion's early warning missions over the Arabian and Persian Gulf areas.

The pilot, Captain Fahad Kani, taxied the aircraft swiftly into the takeoff area, scanned the deserted runway in front of him, and shoved open the throttles without even waiting for clearance. The Orion rumbled forward, gained speed and climbed into the early evening skies, out over the Atlantic.

He banked right, to the north towards Mauritania, then banked again to a course a few degrees north of due west, aiming the aircraft at the southern Sahara. It was a course which would take them across the hot, poverty-stricken, landlocked African countries of Mali, Niger and Chad, and then over northern Sudan. Hours later they would drop down into the green and fertile Nile Valley, way upriver from Cairo at Aswan, home of the High Dam.

Ravi was unable to make up his mind whether to deposit the body of Captain Camara in the burning sands of the Sahara, hoping it would either be devoured by buzzards or covered for ever by the first sandstorm; or to go for the sea, where the blood from the captain's shattered nose would ensure the sharks would do his dirty work on a rather more reliable basis.

Trouble was, he was not sure if there *were* sharks in the Red Sea, and the body might wash up on the shore. Also, he knew that timing was critical in a high-speed aircraft, and that heaving a dead body out of the door would not be easy. He did not relish the prospect of a foul-up, whereby the carcass of the former Head of the Senegalese Navy landed in the middle of Jeddah. Ravi opted for the buzzards.

He and Shakira were almost too tired to eat anything. But the coffee was good and they each ate a small chicken sandwich with tomato on pitta bread, before falling asleep.

Two hours later, Ravi, who never slept longer than that, awakened and checked their whereabouts with the pilot. They had just crossed the Mauritania border and were flying over Mali. Ravi had consulted his treasured *Traveller's Atlas*, a small leather-bound pocket edition with pages edged in gold, a gift from Shakira. And he had selected his spot for the Camara heave-ho.

It would take another three and a half hours to get there, and he instructed the first officer to wake him and then prepare to slow the aircraft down, losing height to around 5,000 feet for the ejection.

He went back to the sleeping Shakira and held her hand, but he dozed only fitfully himself as they flew above the mountains of northern Chad. A few minutes later they entered the airspace over the Libyan Desert, one of the loneliest parts of the Sahara, 750,000 square miles, stretching through north-western Sudan, western Egypt and eastern Libya.

Ravi had chosen a 100-mile-wide area of unmapped sand dunes between the oases of Ma'Tan Bishrah and Ma'Tan Sarah. There was not a town for 100 miles in any direction. Down below, in this burning, arid, uninhabitable Al Kufrah region, the temperature hovered around 105 degrees.

Only the GPS could tell the pilot precisely where they were and Captain Kani was watching it carefully. Ravi, with the first officer, dragged the body to the rear door as they came down through 10,000 feet and slowed to a just–sustainable 190 knots.

Ravi and the airman were both standing, strapped in harnesses attached to the fuselage. And as they approached the drop zone they both heard the captain call out . . . '*ONE MINUTE!*'

The first officer unclipped the door and pulled it sideways to swing it open. The noise was deafening, as the wind rushed into the gap. Both men held on and shoved the body into the doorway with their boots.

'NOW!' yelled the captain, and with two more good shoves they rolled the former Oxford University golf captain out into the stratosphere, watched the body fall towards the desert floor and then hauled the big aircraft door shut fast.

'*Okay, Captain . . . as you were!*' called Ravi. And they both felt the surge, as the Orion angled slightly upwards and accelerated towards its cruising height. As a measure of her desperate tiredness, Shakira never stirred. As a measure of his profound relief at having eliminated the talkative Senegalese sailor from all contact with the Harrovian Golf Society, Ravi poured himself another cup of coffee.

Captain Kani pressed on across Africa's fourth largest country all the way to the border with Egypt, about 550 miles shy of the Nile Valley. 'Little more than an hour to Aswan,' called the captain, 'and that'll be the first 3,000 miles behind us.'

'How far's that from home?' asked Ravi.

'It's around 1,500 miles from the Nile to Bandar Abbas. 'Bout another three and a half hours. We'll be on the ground in Aswan for about an hour.'

Ravi slept while the Orion inched its way across the desert, awakening only when they could see Lake Nasser, the 350-mile-long stretch of water which started backing up against the south-side wall of the High Dam when they halted the natural flow of the Nile.

They came in over the 1,600-square-mile artificial lake, dropping down into the flat, barren, brown terrain west of the river, and landing at the little airport which stands 16 miles from Egypt's southernmost city. It was 0100 back in Senegal, but three time zones later it was 0400 in the land of the Pharaohs.

Captain Kani had organised food for his distinguished passengers, the Egyptian dish of *kushari*, which a local Air Force orderly brought out to the aircraft on a golf cart. Ravi and the still-tired Shakira gazed in some alarm at the large plates containing that fabled desert combination of noodles, rice, black lentils, fried onions and tomato sauce. It was, after all, still pitch dark, but they had lost all track of time and the *kushari* turned out to be delicious. They devoured it with hot pitta bread and ice-cold orange juice, and the orderly waited to take everything away, the Iranian Air Force being light on catering in its Lockheed prowlers.

Refuelled and refreshed, they set off again shortly after 0500 (local), flying out towards the Red Sea and the Arabian Peninsula. Their halfway point was the western end of the dreaded Rub Al Khali, the 'Empty Quarter', in the most inhospitable desert on earth. From there they headed up to Dubai, and crossed the Gulf just west of the Strait of Hormuz, landing at Bandar Abbas at ten o'clock on Tuesday morning, 22 September.

A Navy staff car collected General and Mrs Rashood direct from the runway the moment Captain Kani switched off the Orion's engines. They were driven immediately into the base and delivered to the Iranian Navy's suite for visiting dignitaries. It represented the final word in air-conditioned hotel luxury, from its vast green marble-floored bathroom, redolent of soap, shampoo, aftershave and eau-de-Cologne, to its wide four-poster king-sized bed.

There were two naval orderlies dressed immaculately in white uniforms, shirts with epaulettes and shorts with long white socks. They had already filled the bathtub with scented, oiled water and laid out two soft dark green bathrobes. Black silk pyjamas were on the bed.

There was an assortment of clothing in the wardrobe, newly pressed shorts, slacks, navy blue skirts, shirts, socks, underwear and shoes, for male and female personnel. Shakira thought she might look like a freshly bathed deckhand when finally she emerged, and Ravi reminded her it was she who had requested permission to join the Navy.

The orderlies had placed a bowl of local fruit salad on the table in the outer room overlooking the harbour. There was fresh coffee, tea and sweet pastries. The television was tuned to the American news station CNN. Two newspapers, one Arabic, one English, lay on a table set between two big comfortable chairs.

One way and another, it compared very favourably with the general's living quarters in the *Barracuda*.

To Shakira Rashood it looked like paradise and she languished in the bathtub for almost an hour, washing her hair three times 'to stop smelling like a submarine'.

The two Iranian assistants left at midday, taking with them all of the two submariners' laundry. One of them drew down the shades and suggested sleep, since Admiral Badr had convened a meeting in his office at 1630 that afternoon. 'You will be collected from here,' he said. 'The Admiral wishes you both a very pleasant day.'

Outside the door there were four armed naval guards. At the foot of the stairs there were two more. And a four-man detail was on duty outside in the heat. Admiral Badr was keenly aware of the importance of his guests. He was also keenly aware that half the world would have paid a king's ransom to know where the HAMAS assault commander was at this precise moment.

Ravi and Shakira were awakened by telephone at 1600 and informed they would be collected in thirty minutes. They dressed slowly, poured some coffee from the heated pot and headed downstairs to the waiting car.

Admiral Badr greeted them both warmly, and told them how dramatic it had been in the base when news of the eruption of Mount St Helens had come through. 'It was a wonderful moment for us,' he said, 'after all the months of planning. But we have heard no response from the Americans with regard to the new HAMAS threat and demands.'

'I did not really expect any word from them,' said Ravi. 'However, I did expect to see some activity in their Middle Eastern bases. And perhaps a general communiqué from the Israelis to the principal Arab and Gulf nations, of which Iran would be one.'

'That really is the object of this meeting,' replied the admiral. 'We have not been informed of any new initiative with regard to the West Bank. And neither has anyone else. However, I do have a list of movements of US troops and equipment in the bases.'

'Perfect,' said Ravi. 'I would like to consider them, and we can decide immediately what further action to take.'

'I think that's correct,' replied the admiral. 'I have all the information here . . . but, first . . . how is my son? Is he handling the submarine well?'

'Oh, Ben's great,' said Ravi. 'He has plainly developed into a first-class nuclear submarine CO, perfectly in command, and trusted by all of his crew.

The ship is behaving very well. We've had nothing beyond minor problems, and I expect them to carry out successfully the rest of our plans.

'I also expect them all to make it safely home, eventually. Though it may be necessary for them to stay deep for a few weeks, should we be compelled to make our final attack.'

'As we always planned,' said the admiral. 'It is quite apparent to me the *Barracuda* simply cannot be detected during an operation. Even in hostile waters.'

'Not if it's being handled by a master like Ben,' said Ravi. 'And he has become a master, nothing less. We've moved that ship through dangerous waters, when we knew half the US Navy must be looking for us. But, so far as I know, they never got a sniff.'

'Those are presumptuous words for a submariner,' said the admiral, smiling. 'But I'm delighted to hear them . . . shall we look at the American evacuation now?'

'Please go right ahead. I'll just take notes as we go.'

'Right, first, Bahrain. That's the US Fifth Fleet HQ. Two weeks ago the *Constellation* Carrier Battle Group was in there, and three days ago it left. Eleven ships, including two submarines. We tracked them down the Gulf to the Strait. Also we noticed some troop reduction, maybe 500 Navy personnel flying out to Incirlick in Turkey.

'Second. Kuwait. That's a very big US Army Command and training base. They have upwards of 12,000 military personnel in there. We have observed some movement of US Air Force fighter planes leaving there for Diego Garcia, but no substantial troop movement by sea.

'Third. Saudi Arabia. That's the US Air Force Command base they just reopened. They have 10,000 personnel in there, just like old times. Plus a large but shifting number of reconnaissance and fighter aircraft. We have discerned no appreciable change in anything.

'Fourth. Qatar. There's been a substantial movement of troops from there. We are only seeing 2,000 of the original 4,000 US personnel. There was a big evacuation of aircraft too. We could tell that because of the huge empty shelters they recently built. We saw no troop movement by sea, but certainly many hundreds of them left by air.

'Fifth. Oman, The docks have always been heavily used by the US military. So has al–Seeb International Airport. They usually have around 4,000 personnel in the country and we have observed no change whatsoever.

'Sixth. United Arab Emirates. Small USAF garrison here. No change.

'Seventh. Djibouti. Busy US Special Forces training area. We've assessed 3,000 personnel at various times. No change.

'Eighth. Diego Garcia. Navy base and serious air base. They have B–52 heavy bombers and B–2 stealth bombers. No change in the number of aircraft. And it's a very transitional place for warships. No discernible change.'

'They probably think we have a real nerve asking them to vacate Diego Garcia, since it is several thousand miles from the Gulf,' said Ravi. 'But this list is very disappointing. The United States plainly does not take our threat seriously. They're merely trying to buy time.

'By the way, how many carriers do they now have in the area?'

'One in the northern Arabian Sea, none in the Gulf and one heading, I believe, to Diego Garcia.'

'Is that *Constellation*?'

'Correct.'

'They are not really behaving like a nation which is about to have half its business coast obliterated, are they?'

'No, Ravi. They are most certainly not.'

'And do we yet have any information as to the attitude of their President McBride?'

'We've heard nothing. Which may mean he is working behind the scenes to destroy us. But more likely he doesn't believe our threat.'

'I'd go with the latter, Admiral,' said Ravi. 'He's a known liberal and pacifist. And those kind of people usually stick their heads in the sand. The danger to us is when people like Admiral Morgan get into positions of power, because they are likely to lash out. Or at worst, lash back, at any perceived enemy.'

'So where do you think that leaves us.'

'Admiral, I think we're ready to move into the second phase of the plan.'

'I thought you might take that view, General. And I agree with you. We have the power right now to make them do what we want. Or at least we should have. Have you decided on your next communiqué?'

'Absolutely. I know precisely what to do. But first I must send Ben on his way. He is well briefed, and will not personally be heading into any danger zone. This next step is probably the easiest, and certainly the most likely to get major results.'

Admiral Badr smiled. 'Go to it, my son. And may Allah go with you.'

1430 (local) Tuesday 22 September 2009
14.45N 18.00W. Speed 7. Racetrack Pattern
The *Barracuda* cruised slowly 600 feet below the surface of the deep Atlantic, 40 miles west of Senegal. As of 1200 (local), the young Rear Admiral Badr had been awaiting instructions via the Chinese naval satellite. They would be orders direct from Bandar Abbas, where he knew his father and Ravi Rashood were in conference.

Every two hours, out here in these lonely semitropical Atlantic waters, he brought the submarine to periscope depth, put up his ESM mast and accessed the satellite, requesting a signal. The entire operation took him less than seven seconds, by which time he was submerging again. But there had been nothing at 1200, nothing at 1400, which he knew was 1830 on the Strait of Hormuz. And now he was growing anxious.

Another thirty minutes went by and again he ordered the planesman to blow main ballast and take the *Barracuda* to PD once more. Up went the mast and again they accessed. And this time the signal came back from 22,000 miles above the ocean . . . *Proceed west to 57 degrees (16.50N) . . . launch 282400SEPT09.*

At least that's what it meant. What it actually read, coded, was . . . *Proceed east to 157.00–56.50N – launch 300200NOV11.* The time and launch date was plus two all the way. The chart references were coded as agreed – a lunch date in a restaurant on the wrong side of the Kamchatka Peninsula on the shores of the Sea of Okhotsk at end of November 2011.

Ben Badr knew that he had six days for the voyage which was a little over 2,100 miles. That meant his father considered an average speed of 12 or 13 knots to be reasonable in these desolate mid-Atlantic seas. Desolate of warships, that was. He would cross the very centre of the ocean, deep, at maybe 17 knots and then slow down within 1,000 miles of the US naval base in Puerto Rico. He was not going that far anyway.

He went down to the navigation office where Lt. Ashtari Mohammed looked lonely without Shakira. She had left the correct charts on her wide desk, and they quickly checked the spot which would be their holding area for the next strike.

The target numbers 16.45N 62.10W were already in place in the missile room, preprogrammed into the computers in the nose cones of the SCIMITAR

SL–Mark 1s. Ben Badr made a careful note of the holding area, 16.50N 57W, and wrote it down for Lt. Mohammed. The selected area was 380 miles east of the target, approximately a half-hour from launch to impact. No problem.

Ben Badr returned to the control room and issued his orders . . . *steer course two-seven-two . . . make your speed 17 . . . depth 600 . . .*

1130 Thursday 24 September 2009
The Pentagon, Washington, DC
General Tim Scannell knew he had just been given the unmistakeable bum's rush. He had called the President of the United States on the private line between his second-floor Pentagon HQ and the Oval Office, and for the first time in living memory a Chairman of the Joint Chiefs had been put through to a White House Chief-of-Staff instead of the Chief Executive.

Big Bill Hatchard had been polite and accommodating, but that didn't mask the fact that the phone call between the military's executive chief and the C-in-C of all US Armed Forces had been intercepted. And, worse, Bill Hatchard had wanted to know precisely what the call was about, in the opinion of General Scannell an unacceptable intrusion, but Hatchard had made it subtly clear that either he was told the reason for the call or the CJC was not going to speak to President McBride.

And General Scannell, for the only time in a long and distinguished combat career, was forced to surrender. 'Tell him it's in relation to the contact from HAMAS,' he said brusquely, his anger not so far beneath the surface. 'And to call me back after he's done with whatever the fuck he's doing.'

The general slammed down the phone. On the other end, Bill Hatchard experienced no sense of triumph. Instead he felt a rather unnerving sense of apprehension, knowing that he had just made an enemy of America's most senior and most revered military commander, a man who was not in any way afraid of either him or his boss. That was not good.

Bill Hatchard knew the rules. These high-ranking Pentagon guys were extremely powerful, and, more importantly, permanently installed in the White House. General Scannell would be there long after President McBride had departed. So would most of the other gold-braided generals and admirals who surrounded him. Quietly, Bill resolved not to mention the bad blood that had so quickly developed between himself and the CJC, to make light of it, as if all was well.

That was all of forty-five minutes ago. And General Scannell still hadn't heard anything from the Oval Office. He would undoubtedly have been even more furious had he heard the short, sharp conversation between the Chief and Hatchard half an hour earlier. In essence, it proceeded on the following lines:

Sir, I wonder if you could return a call to the CJC's office in the Pentagon?

What does he want?

Something about that HAMAS business?

Have they received something new?

Don't know, sir. He did not really want to talk to me, it was you, he wanted.

Call him back and tell him if it's new to try my line again. If it's not, forget about it. I'm extremely busy.

Yes, sir.

But the mighty nerve which had never deserted the slow-moving, ponderous Yale defensive lineman in a dozen games for the Elis, now folded up on him. He simply could not bring himself to call the Chairman of the Joint Chiefs and make him look small. This was nothing to do with tact and empathy. This was pure and simple dread. Bill Hatchard was not about to engage General Tim Scannell in open combat. And like many would-be executives, operating in waters too deep and too hot, he elected to do . . . nothing.

Which left an extremely angry General Scannell simmering in the Pentagon, currently on the line to Admiral Arnold Morgan — *the only person around here who understands precisely what is going on.*

The two men spoke very seriously. According to Admiral Morgan's guess, the *Barracuda* was probably in the South Atlantic by now, somewhere in a million square miles of ocean off the east coast of Argentina.

He listened with interest to the general's report of the troop movements out of the Middle East, and was pleased to hear that there was no longer a Carrier Battle Group in the Gulf. Both men believed that the HAMAS demand to vacate the US Navy facility in Diego Garcia was insolent in the extreme. DG was, after all, an official British colony, and, in any case, thousands of miles closer to predominantly Hindu India than Muslim Iran or Iraq.

But what occupied them most was the knowledge that the terrorist attack had been threatened for 9 October. And that was a mere fifteen days away. Arnold was seriously worried about the deployment of 100 US warships in the mid–Atlantic, both in terms of logistics and the fact that the C-in-C of all the US Armed Forces knew nothing of the operation. And that he actively refused to know anything about the operation.

At this point, neither General Scannell nor Admiral Morgan cared one jot for the moral rectitude of the mission. As Arnold put it, 'It cannot be right, just because the President says it's right. And it cannot suddenly become wrong, just because the President refuses to consider it. The judgement itself, right or wrong, remains sacrosanct, whatever he thinks.'

The fact was that both men sincerely believed the United States to be under threat; a threat in which a million people or more might die, and several of its greatest cities might be destroyed. Unless, that was, the military moved fast and decisively. In General Scannell's opinion, 'If there is one chance in twenty this tidal wave might actually happen, we must either stop it, or harness all of our considerable defences. Any other course of action represents a gross dereliction of duty.'

Given the evidence, the general put the chances of this attack on the lethal granite cliff face of La Palma not at one in twenty, but even money. They had to get the President on their side.

0100 Monday 28 September 2009
Communications Centre
The Pentagon, Washington, DC

The duty officer stared at the screen, punching the button to download and print. The e-mail signal, unencrypted, was addressed personally to:

> THE CHAIRMAN OF THE JOINT CHIEFS,
> *The Pentagon, Washington, USA.*
> *Sir, you plainly have not taken our last communiqué seriously. Pay attention just after midnight tonight, 28 September, and you will see what we can do, and perhaps change your mind. – HAMAS.*

Major Sam MacLean, a veteran infantry officer in the Second Gulf War, was instantly on full alert. He ordered someone to trace the e-mail immediately and then, checking his watch, fired in a call to the senior officer on duty in the United States Army ops area on the third floor.

Just the word HAMAS, like 'terrorist', caused him to relay the message immediately to the CIA in Langley, Virginia, and the National Security Agency at Fort Meade, Maryland.

It was circulated to the ops area night staff, with a copy to the Director's assistant, Lt. Commander

306

Jimmy Ramshawe, who was still in his office, poring over photographs and signals which might betray the whereabouts of the elusive *Barracuda* submarine.

The Army colonel, holding the fort at 0100 in the Pentagon, did not hesitate. He opened up the hot line to the home of the CJC and reported the message to General Scannell, word for word. Jimmy Ramshawe was already on the wire to Chevy Chase, where Admiral Morgan came out of his sleep like a 4 July mortar shell.

He scribbled a short note and called Tim Scannell who was still on the line to his office. By 0130 all the key players were tuned in to the new threat. General Scannell convened a meeting in the Pentagon for 0700.

Meanwhile, the tracers in the communications centre had come up with a vague solution. The e-mail had originated somewhere in the Middle East. Either Damascus, Jordan, Baghdad or possibly Kuwait. Definitely not to the west of the Red Sea, nor to the south or east of the Arabian Peninsula. The investigation was so sketchy Major MacLean relayed it only to the CIA, for possible further clarification.

By 0700 there was a pervasive sense of unease throughout the Pentagon. Word had inevitably leaked out that there was a new threat from HAMAS. And it had not been specified. It could be anything, even another lunatic driving a passenger aircraft into the building. By the time the meeting began the entire place was moving to red alert.

In the CJC's private conference room, Admiral Morgan again chaired the meeting, and there was no one who believed that the HAMAS writer was not deadly serious.

'I suppose there's nothing on any of the nets which might throw light on the *Barracuda*, is there?' asked Arnold. 'I mean a possible contact anywhere in the world?'

'Nothing, sir,' replied Lt. Commander Ramshawe. 'I've been up all night searching. But there's not a damn squeak. The only item on any naval network of any interest to anyone came from France. They're saying the C-in-C of the Senegalese Navy has gone missing.'

'Probably been eaten by a fucking lion,' growled Admiral Morgan. 'Anyway, we're going to find out what these HAMAS guys are up to seventeen hours from now. If nothing happens, maybe the President's right. Maybe all our evidence is just coincidental.'

'Not a chance, Arnie,' said Admiral Morris. 'Something's going to happen, somewhere. And you know it.'

'Then we better get the President of the United States of America off his ass, right now,' replied Arnold Morgan. 'Somebody tell him we're coming over at 0900 and he better be listening.'

CHAPTER EIGHT

General Tim Scannell and General Bart Boyce, in company with Admirals Dickson and Morris, arrived unannounced in two Pentagon staff cars at the West Wing entrance to the White House. Three of them were in uniform, as instructed by the CJC. Only the retired Navy Battle Group Commander George Morris wore a formal dark grey suit.

Both secret agents on duty were somewhat uncertain whether to detain this illustrious military quartet while visitors' badges were issued, or whether to escort them immediately to the reception area outside the Oval Office.

Like all guards, the secret agents were indoctrinated with a strict code to play every issue by the book. That meant badges. But this was different. The Chairman of the Joint Chiefs, the Supreme Allied Commander NATO – that's two four-star generals, plus the Chief of US Naval Operations and the Director of the National Security Agency. Both agents arrived at the same conclusion. Fast. This was no time for visitors' badges.

They escorted the four officers to the Oval Office holding area, and informed the secretary precisely who was there to see the President. Within one minute Bill Hatchard was on the scene and summoned them to his office down the corridor.

'You would like to see the President?' he asked amiably enough.

'Correct,' replied General Scannell.

'That's going to be extremely difficult this morning,' he said. 'President McBride has a very busy schedule.'

'That's okay. You've got a full five minutes before we either walk into the Oval Office or instruct the Marine guards to search the place until they find him,' said General Scannell. 'So hurry up.'

'Sir?' said Bill Hatchard, looking desperate. 'Is this some kind of a national emergency?'

'Find the President,' said General Scannell. 'Now.'

Bill Hatchard was not an especially clever man but he was long on native cunning. He recognised real trouble when it reared its head. If he continued to defy four of the most senior military figures in the United States, he could very likely be out of a job by lunchtime. Quite frankly, he would not give much for the President's chances either, if this situation was as serious as it looked. *Jesus, guys like this don't just show up en masse unless something very big is happening.*

Bill Hatchard rose. 'I'll be right back with some more information,' he said quickly.

'Forget the information, soldier,' snapped General Scannell, a lifetime of sharp commands to lower ranks suddenly bubbling to the surface. 'Come back with the President.'

Bill Hatchard bolted out of his office. He was back in three minutes. 'The President will see you now,' he said.

'Well done, soldier,' said General Scannell. 'You accomplished that with forty-five seconds to spare, before we relieved you of command.'

'Yes, sir,' said Bill Hatchard. 'Please come this way.'

They walked down to the Oval Office, where President McBride awaited them. 'Gentlemen,' he said. 'What a nice surprise. I have ordered you some coffee. Perhaps you'd like to sit down.'

All four of them sat, in large wooden captain's chairs, and General Scannell immediately produced a copy of the communication from HAMAS.

'May we assume you have read this short letter, Mr President?' asked the CJC.

'You may.'

'And may I inquire as to your views?'

'Of course. I have taken on board the last communication, allegedly from HAMAS, in which someone wrote, one week after the fact, to reveal he had just exploded Mount St Helens. It now looks as if the same person may have written again, to suggest he is going to do something else, somewhere, tonight.'

'That is correct, sir,' replied General Scannell, deferring to the President's rank as Commander-in-

Chief of US Armed Forces. 'And do you have an opinion on what, if any, action, we should take?'

'Yes, I do. Since both letters are plainly the work of a nutcase, my answer is to do nothing. In the great offices of State we can't spend our lives chasing around in pursuit of every damn fool threat that comes our way.'

'Sir, there were in fact three communications, as you know . . . suggesting he blew the volcano, demanding we vacate the Middle East or he would blow another volcano in the eastern Atlantic and wreck our East Coast. And reminding us that we are ignoring him at our peril. And that tonight he will show us precisely how dangerous he is.'

'Well, we do not have one shred of proof that he's ever done anything. So why should you expect me to turn the world upside down, moving half the US armed forces around the world?'

'The answer to that is very simple, Mr President,' replied General Scannell. 'Because he might actually be telling the truth. Maybe he did blow Mount St Helens; maybe he is going to pull off some outrage tonight. And maybe he could cause one of the world's great landslides, and put New York and Washington under 50 feet of water.'

'Well, I don't think so. I think we're dealing with a crank.'

'Sir. In the military we are taught to think precisely the opposite. What if he did? What if New York was underwater?'

'What if, General? What if, what if? The cry of the

civil servant, the cry of the frightened executive. What if . . . I would remind you that I did not get to sit in this chair by running scared. I got here, to use your parlance, by facing down the enemy . . . do you really think that one man could possibly wreak the havoc and destruction you are forecasting?'

'Yes, Mr President, I do. For a start we have incontrovertible evidence that cruise missiles may have been fired at Mount St Helens. And if they were, they came from a submarine.'

'From the documents I have read, you were relying almost entirely on a bank manager who appeared to have drunk a half-gallon of Dewar's Scotch.'

'The bank manager was actually the President of one of the largest financial institutions in the West,' interjected Admiral Dickson. 'He will probably run for state governor at the next election, and the half-gallon of Dewar's was unopened. The proof that he heard what he heard is evidenced by the fact that he escaped from the foothills of the mountain, when no one else did.'

'All he heard was a couple of gusts of wind, and that's not enough hot air to have me redeploy half the US Army, Navy and Air Force.'

'Sir, we have come to see you, to offer advice involving the safety of this country. If our enemy is indeed planning to do something tonight, something quite possibly beyond the scale of 9/11 and Kerman's last attack on our soil, we should be on full alert. I do not need to confirm that the Pentagon is already in a state of readiness. I suggest the White House does the same.

'I also ask your permission to begin deploying the fleet into the eastern Atlantic on a search for the submarine, which might be carrying nuclear missiles, and to begin a substantial troop and aircraft evacuation of our bases in the Middle East. Essentially I'm trying to buy us some time to locate the HAMAS assault ship.'

'I'm certain we'd be chasing our tails, General. Permission denied on both counts. Let's just wait 'til midnight and see what happens.'

'I should warn you, sir, that if anything drastic happens at midnight, either to ourselves, or to someone else, you will have to consider your position very carefully. Remember, unlike politicians, we in the military are not trained to lie.'

'General, I resent that remark . . .'

'Do you? Then I suggest you spend the next fourteen hours wondering what you'll say . . . if you are proven wrong. Good day to you, sir.'

With that the two generals and the two silent admirals stood up and took their leave. Alone in the Oval Office, the President shook his head, muttering to himself . . . *Goddamned paranoid military. Nothing's going to happen . . . these guys are crazy* . . . and he hit the button for Bill Hatchard to come in for a sensible chat about the real issues of the day.

2300 Monday 28 September 2009
56.59W 16.45N. Western Atlantic
Speed 6. Course 270. Depth 500

Admiral Ben Badr's *Barracuda* moved slowly through the outer approaches to the Caribbean. He was due east of the Leeward Islands, and somewhere up ahead, two days running time at this low speed, were the playgrounds of the rich and famous, St Kitts and Nevis, Antigua and Barbuda.

Admiral Badr's target was located 25 miles further into the Caribbean than Antigua. It was much less of a playground than its bigger palm-strewn brothers, since half of it had been obliterated in the ferocious eruption of 1996/97.

Montserrat, battered, dust-choked, grieving, almost wiped out; workaday Montserrat, tonight slumbered peacefully beneath a Caribbean moon. For those who remained in residence on the island there was always the hope that the great steaming, smoke-belching heart of the Soufrière Hills would soon calm down and relapse into its familiar dormant state, beneath which generations of islanders had grown up, safe and sheltered.

At least they had until that fateful hour in 1997 when the south part of the island was bombarded with massive molten rocks and lava, as the mountain exploded like an atom bomb. Nothing was ever the same again and the islanders have lived ever since in the fear that it will happen once more; against the hope that the high-surging magma would finally subside.

Volcanologists had not been so optimistic. People were periodically advised to leave. But too many had nowhere to go. They merely fled to the north, away from the lethal south side of the volcano. And the Soufrière Hills continued to growl, to blast steam, dark smoke, fire and occasionally lava, with uncomfortable regularity.

Below its shimmering peak, set to the west, the town of Plymouth, formerly home to the island's seat of government, lay virtually buried under the ash. Its one tall British red phone box is long gone. The high clock on the war memorial juts out almost at ground level above the grey urban landscape of dust and rocks.

As Professor Paul Landon had said to General Rashood in a house in west London five months earlier . . . *Montserrat! You could probably blow that damn thing sky high with a hand grenade. It could erupt any day.*

Ravi Rashood's master plan to frighten the Pentagon to death, to scare them into obeying HAMAS demands, was within one hour of execution. The launch time of midnight in the eastern Caribbean was one hour in front of Washington. General Rashood had allowed thirty-five minutes running time for the missile, and maybe twenty-five minutes for the news of the eruption to make it to the networks.

Admiral Badr was confident. His orders were to launch four missiles, the SCIMITAR SL-1's (non-nuclear warheads) straight at the high crater in the Soufrière Hills. In 1996, the entire island, roughly the shape of a pyramid if seen from the sea, had looked like an exploding Roman candle in the night.

Like Mount St Helens, the Soufrière Hills volcano was not a proud, towering queen, standing like a sentinel over the lush green island. Instead, like her ugly sister in faraway Washington State, she was an unstable, dangerous bitch, rotten to the core, unable to control herself, a lethal pile of black, shifting rubble, swollen by mammoth carbuncles, which every now and then lanced themselves and released the satanic magma.

Admiral Badr kept the *Barracuda* going forward to the edge of his launch zone. He checked his watch.

In the past hour they had made dozens of checks on the prefiring routines and setting. Lt. Commander Shakira Rashood had personally supervised the numbers which had been punched into the tiny onboard computers in each of the SCIMITAR's nose cones. They had pored over the little screen which displayed the chart references. All four were the same – *16.45N 62.10W*, the very heart of the volcano high in the Soufrière Hills on the island of Montserrat.

With the competence of the North Korean technicians and the electronic engineers of Huludao, the quartet of SCIMITARs could not miss. They would plunge into the crater within 10 feet of each other, each one drilling deeper into the upper layer of rock, all four of them driving substantial fault lines into the flimsy pumice-stone crust which held back the deadly fire.

Shakira had selected a southerly route for the missile attack, on the grounds of her uncertainty about US tracking stations either in or near the old Roosevelt Roads Naval Base in Puerto Rico.

The SCIMITARs would swerve 20 degrees off their due western course and swing through the Guadeloupe Passage, passing five miles to the north of Port Louis on the French island's western headland. They would make their big right-hand turn out over the open water northwest of Guadeloupe, and then come swooping in to Montserrat out of the southwest.

They would flash over the half-buried ghost town of Plymouth, and then follow the infamous route of the 1997 magma, two miles at 600 mph over the rising ground, straight up to Chance's Peak before diving into the crater.

And this time there would be no Tony Tilton below, no observer to hear the eerie swish of the rockets' slipstream through the air. These days, this southern part of Montserrat was deserted. Shakira's plan was for no one to hear or see anything. Until the vicious old mountain exploded again.

Ben Badr checked with the sonar room. Then he ordered the submarine to periscope depth for a lightning fast surface picture check. The seas were deserted and nothing was showing on the radar, critical factors when launching a missile with a fiery red tail as it cleared the ocean, visible for miles.

He ordered the *Barracuda* deep again. Then he made a final check with his missile director. And at

318

one minute to midnight (local) he issued the order to activate the immaculate preprogramming plan. The sequencer was watching his screen. The *Barracuda* was facing west, running slowly, 300 feet below the surface.

'*STAND BY TUBES ONE TO FOUR . . .*'

'*Tubes ready, sir.*'

'*TUBE ONE . . . LAUNCH!*'

The first of the SCIMITARs blew out into the pitch-black water, angled upwards, and came blasting out of the ocean into the warm night air. It left a fiery crackling wake as it roared into the sky, until it reached its preset cruising height of 500 feet and settled onto a firm course for the Guadeloupe Passage. At this point the state-of-the-art gas turbines cut in and eliminated the giveaway trails in the sky.

SCIMITAR SL-1 was on its way, and there was nothing in this lonely part of the western Atlantic which could possibly stop it. And even as it streaked high above the waves, Admiral Badr was ordering the second one into the air, then the third, and then, a mere three minutes after the opening launch, the final missile. The volatile, unstable volcano in the Soufrière Hills was about to awaken the Caribbean once more.

Twenty-five minutes after the opening launch sequence, the lead rocket came swishing past the inshore waters of northern Guadeloupe. Four minutes later it was hammering towards the Plymouth waterfront, deserted now for twelve years, beneath the haunted rockface of Chance's Peak.

319

It ripped over the almost buried war memorial with its high clock tower, now only five feet above ground level. It shot straight above George Street, with its second-storey-only shopping façade, past Government House, over the cricket pitch and on towards the mountain.

At the back of the town it made a course adjustment, veering right to the northeast, following the inland road down from the east coast airport. One mile from the central crater it swung right again for its final approach and came hurtling out of clear skies, straight at Gage's Mountain.

At 0036 on Tuesday 29 September, General Rashood's SCIMITAR SL-1, courtesy of the illegal North Korean arms factory, smashed eight feet deep into the steaming active crater in Montserrat's Soufrière Hills, detonating with barbaric force.

The packed rubble of the volcano gave the blast a dead, muffled, subterranean thumping effect, just as the first missile had done at Mount St Helens. But less than one minute later the second SCIMITAR crashed bang into the middle of the crater and exploded savagely, splitting the already wide bomb cavern almost in two.

That was plenty for the fragile, cantankerous killer mountain, which seemed to take a deep quivering breath before belching fire and ashes a thousand feet into the air. And then, with an earth-shaking rumble, it erupted with mind-blowing force, sending a thousand white-hot rocks and boulders hundreds of feet into the sky, lighting up

320

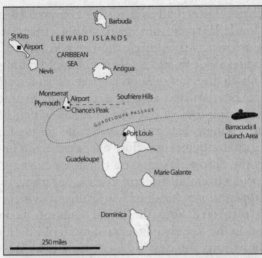

THE VOLCANIC ISLAND OF MONTSERRAT - BLOWN TO
PIECES IN ITS CARIBBEAN PARADISE

the entire eastern stretch of the Leeward Islands.

Admiral Badr did not need Missile Three, which came arrowing in through the fire and fury of the exploding volcano and reached its target before detonating in the immeasurable heat of the magma. Missile Four melted and blew to pieces in midair, in the raging fires of gas-filled magma which lit up the atmosphere half a mile above the mountain.

A gigantic pyroclastic flow now developed on the southwest side of Gage's, and the dense burning ash began to envelope the entire area, cascading down the upper slopes heading for farmland which had never recovered from the initial eruption in 1996, and on to the already half-buried town of Plymouth.

If anything, this was a bigger blast than the one seen on Montserrat thirteen years earlier, when the ash plume had blown itself *40,000 feet* into the air and endangered all nearby commercial aircraft. It was not quite so high this time, but by common consensus the heat and the fire were greater, and the surging lava flow down the mountain was deeper and just as hot.

It took ten minutes for the massive second phase of the explosion. The biggest of the carbuncles to the northeast of Chance's Peak suddenly began to collapse. Later, geological studies surmised that the carbuncle must have shaken and cracked with the upward surge of the magma which was unable to exit from the main crater.

It finally gave way and a new gout of molten rock burst 200 feet into the air in a hurricane of blazing ash, gas and black rubble. Instantly the magma began to flow, and it gushed out from the heart of the mountain, rising up from the fires of Hell.

And it rumbled down the northeastern slopes of the Soufrière Hills, down the ghauts, down the Tar River Valley towards the airport. Anything it touched burned instantly. It melted the blacktop on the roads, set fire to every tree and hedge in its path, incinerated cottages and barns, most of them abandoned.

Moving at 40 mph it rolled towards the sea, surging right to the little town of Spanish Point and then crushing and burning every last vestige of the old airport. The coastal area went completely black as the burning ash cloud blotted out the moon and stars. The ocean boiled along the shores as the white-hot lava rolled into the light Caribbean surf.

Then, nine minutes after the last square foot of blacktop on the airport runway had melted, Chance's Peak erupted again, this time on the south side. It was a second devastating explosion, from the same mountain, and it once more blew rocks and boulders thousands of feet into the air, before they crashed down around the remains of the deserted fishing village of St Patrick's, setting fire to everything within 50 feet of their landing.

Like the other two eruptions, this one broadly followed the lava paths of the 1996/97 blast, the magma pouring south and then splitting near the little village of Great Alps Falls. The main torrent burned its way straight over the road and directly into St Patrick's, the secondary flow veering left, over the same road, a mile to the east and into the sea. There was nothing left to weep for in St Patrick's. The thriving little seaport had been taken off the face of the earth.

By 0100 there was no one asleep on the entire island. Indeed, almost everyone was awake on the north coast of Guadeloupe, the southwest coast of Antigua around the town of Falmouth, and Charlestown on the neighbouring island of Nevis.

The lady who ran the Montserrat radio station was up and broadcasting within seven minutes of the first massive explosion on Gage's Mountain. The transmitter was in a building adjacent to her home on the island's safe area north of the line which demarked the southern exclusion zone since 1997.

From her studio in the Central Hills, the news was hitting the airwaves by 0048. The giant volcano in the Soufrière Hills had erupted, without warning. In the modern observatory built by the international scientific studies group on a hillside near the western town of Salem, they recorded no pre-eruption activity whatsoever, on either the tiltmeters or the seismographs which constantly monitored the state of the petulant mountain of fire.

In fact, the seismographs had given very early and very definite warning of the oncoming catastrophes in 1996/97, their needles almost shaking themselves off the rotating drums as the onrushing magma rumbled and roared below the earth's crust.

But this time there was absolutely nothing; not

one of the observatory's new computer screens registered even the faintest tremor. Nor did the state-of-the-art tiltmeters, which the scientists in permanent residence had set to measure, constantly, any earth movement on the mountain slopes around the developing carbuncles, or, in scientific parlance, the domes.

The Montserrat observatory was the most sought-after study area in the world. Students, professors and specialist volcanologists travelled from all five continents to experience, first-hand, the geophysical hazards of a brooding, threatening mountain which had already destroyed half of its island.

The detection systems were second to none. Every subterranean shudder, every gout of steam or fire, every ton of escaping lava was meticulously recorded. It was said that the volcano in the Soufrière Hills was the most carefully observed square mile in the world, including Wall Street.

And yet, on this moonlit September night, that volcano had blown out with an unprecedented explosion, without so much as a shudder or a ripple to warn of the cataclysmic eruption. The eruption had come from nowhere, and it would, at least temporarily, baffle volcanologists from the finest geohazard departments of the world's most prestigious universities.

On this September night, the troubleshooters of Montserrat, the police, fire departments and ambulances, were not even on high alert until the first convulsion of the mountain almost shook the place to pieces. And even then there was little they could do, although members of the Royal Montserrat Police Force made instantly for the helicopter pads where they ran into scientists already assessing the dangers of flying into an area almost engulfed by smoke and burning ash. The Police Chief himself banned all takeoffs until the air cleared.

This time there were no instances of farming people being swallowed up in their own fields by the onrushing lava. No one was incinerated in their own homes. This was a clinical, no-killing, fiery spectacular in the eastern Caribbean lighting up the Leeward Islands and threatening certain members of the United States military with cardiac arrest.

Shortly before midnight (EST) reports of the eruption on Montserrat were filtering through to the United States networks. The radio station in Antigua was the first to go on air, describing what could be seen. They managed to hook up with Radio Montserrat and their signals were picked up by the eastern Caribbean network, which in turn was monitored by one of the US network offices in Puerto Rico.

Moments later the news was out in Miami, Florida, and three minutes later CNN was on the case in Atlanta. Television pictures from Falmouth, Antigua, were poor and slightly late after the initial blast, but there was truly spectacular footage taken by the scientists' cameras in the Salem observatory.

These were instantly wired electronically to Antigua and Puerto Rico, under the contractual agreement which paid for much of the research undertaken at Salem.

By 12.05 a.m. (EST) thanks to CNN, Atlanta, the sensational pictures of a giant volcano in full cry were on television screens all over the world.

Lt. Commander Jimmy Ramshawe was sitting comfortably in an armchair in the pricey Watergate complex his parents owned in Washington when the erupting volcano jumped onto the screen. His fiancée, the surf-goddess Jane Peacock, was in bed reading, paying no attention whatsoever to Jimmy's grave forecast of a big event around midnight.

The first she knew was when Jimmy leapt to his feet, stark naked, pointing at the screen, and shouting *HOLY SHIT!! HE'S DONE IT . . . THAT MONGREL BASTARD WAS NOT JOKING!*

He grabbed the telephone and dialled Admiral George Morris at home in Fort Meade, as arranged. The Director of the National Security Agency had been to a naval dinner, and was already snoring like a bull elephant. It took him a couple of minutes to hear the phone and answer, but he was visibly shaken by Jimmy's news.

'How long ago, Jimmy?' he asked.

'I'd guess about half an hour,' replied his assistant. 'What do we do?'

'Well, we can't do much now. But we'd better schedule a very early start tomorrow. Say, 0600 in my office.'

'Okay, sir. You want me to call the Big Man? Or will you do it?'

Just then the admiral's other line rang angrily – General Scannell. George Morris told Jimmy to speak to Arnold Morgan while he dealt with the CJC and then Admiral Dickson.

Lt. Commander Ramshawe, still stark naked, dialled Admiral Morgan's number in Chevy Chase, but Arnold had been watching CNN news.

'Well, sir, that's taken a whole bloody lot of the guesswork out of this conundrum, right?'

'You can say that again, kid,' answered the admiral. 'Right now I'm planning to sit here and watch this thing develop . . . maybe see if there was any warning. And I think that's what we all should do. Then we better meet early . . .'

'Admiral Morris has scheduled a meeting in his office at 0600 which is where I'll be. We can take a look at the CIA stuff, if any, then I guess we better all meet up somewhere around 0900. My boss is on the line to General Scannell right now . . . tell you what, sir, I'll leave a message on your machine soon as I knew where we're meeting in the morning . . . I guess the Pentagon, but I'll confirm.'

'Okay, Jimmy. Keep your eyes and ears open. This bastard's serious. He just hit the fucking mountain with missiles, and that mega-*tsunami*'s getting closer by the minute, no doubt in my mind.'

'Nor mine, sir.'

What's happened? Will you please tell me what's going on? Jane Peacock had lost all interest in her magazine.

'Throw me that notebook, would you?' said

328

Jimmy. 'And that pen over there? Now, let me get some pyjamas on. I've got to watch the news for at least the next couple of hours.'

0230 (local) 29 September 2009
The *Barracuda* was steaming swiftly away from the datum, 500 feet below the surface. They had been moving for three and a half hours, since the moment the last of the four SCIMITARs had been launched. They were headed east, making 15 knots through the dark water, a speed that Admiral Badr thought they could sustain for no more than two or three days longer, less because he feared the US Navy hot on their trail, but because Shakira had been uncertain where exactly the US SOSUS system became more dense in the North Atlantic.

The men from HAMAS were now 50 miles away from Admiral Badr's strike zone and a total of almost 400 miles from the stricken south coast of Montserrat. He planned to retain speed and keep running at moderate knots towards the disturbed and somewhat noisier waters over the Mid-Atlantic Ridge where he would be very difficult to trace. Later, when he cut back to six or seven knots, crossing from the Ridge to the Canary Islands, in open water, he would be impossible to trace, anywhere in this vast ocean.

They had eleven days in which to make their next launch zone, and would spend three of them moving as fast as they dared, for thirty-three hours to the Ridge, then forty hours heading north above its rocky underwater cliffs. That would give them eight days to tiptoe over the ultra-sensitive SOSUS wires, traps which, Shakira had warned Ben, were primed to scream the place down if any intruding submarine crossed them. Once they turned east from the Atlantic Ridge, they would be in latitudes around 28–29 degrees, 300 nautical miles north of Miami, similar latitudes to places like Daytona Beach, Jacksonville, Cape Canaveral. Finally, they would take up position somewhere east of La Palma, depending on the US defences that Ben Badr fully expected would be patrolling the area.

In Lt. Commander Rashood's opinion there was no way that the US Navy was going to let foreign submarines go charging around in the Atlantic anywhere north of the 25th parallel without wanting to know a lot about that ship's business.

Admiral Badr, now without his ace precision missile direction officer and assistant navigator, was resolved to be excessively careful. He looked forward to his next satellite communication when someone would doubtlessly tell him whether he had managed to wipe out the island of Montserrat.

0600 29 September 2009
National Security Agency
Fort Meade, Maryland
The CIA had been on the case all night. And, generally speaking, they had drawn a blank as big as that in the newsrooms of the television networks and the American afternoon newspapers: the totally

330

unexplained and unexpected eruption of the most volatile volcano in the western hemisphere. No reasons. No warnings. No theories.

The CIA were well up to speed with the threats and demands of the HAMAS freedom fighters, and even more with the views of the most senior military figures in the nation.

They put twenty different field agents on the project, working through the night, searching and checking for any sign of a missile attack on Montserrat. But, so far, they had turned up nothing except for the absolute bafflement of the local scientists whose equipment had registered zero before the first explosion from Gage's Mountain.

They sent in a preliminary report to the National Security Agency at around 0500, which Lt. Commander Ramshawe read with interest. Particularly the last paragraph, written by the senior case officer: . . . *the complete absence of any warning before the eruption is regarded by the professionals as unprecedented. Every volcano betrays the smallest movement of the earth beneath its mountain, and indeed any upward surge of the magma. This time there was nothing. Which, we think, indicates detonation by a man-made device.*

Jimmy Ramshawe sifted through the reports and the more he read the more it became obvious that the *Barracuda* had struck again. Even small eruptions in relatively harmless volcanoes are signalled on their seismographs. And the equipment stationed in the Soufrière Hills was much more sophisticated than

331

most, hooked up to a brand-new computerised system in the observatory.

There were reports of staggering amounts of ash covering Montserrat's buildings even in the supposedly safe north of the island. Any building with a flat roof seemed to have a minimum 12 to 18 inches of the stuff, thick, heavy ash, more like baking flour than the light airy remnants of a bonfire.

There were reports of ash covering the gardens of Antigua on the southwest coast, especially at Curtain Bluff and Johnsons Point. Guadeloupe awoke to a hot, grey cast over the whole of Port Louis. The southern beaches of Nevis were distinctly off-white. And the southern end of Montserrat was on fire. Miles of green vegetation were still burning from end to end of the exclusion zone. The devastation was almost complete in the south with even the old disused jetties on fire out over the water.

As the morning wore on, the pictures became more and more graphic. The television networks had helicopter crews up and filming at first light. This was the second mammoth volcano explosion in the Americas within four months, and every news editor in every newsroom in the entire country knew that this was a very big story. Not one of them, however, had any idea precisely *how* big.

Admiral Morris had his 48-inch screen tuned to CNN as soon as he arrived at Fort Meade. There were other home news items of some interest, but nothing to rival the live pictures from what looked like the detonation of an atomic bomb in a Caribbean island paradise.

He and Lt. Commander Ramshawe took only ten minutes to scan the incoming reports and a lot less to arrive at the inescapable conclusion that HAMAS had done exactly what they had threatened.

. . . Pay attention . . . you will see what we can do . . . and perhaps change your mind. The words of the letter were stark in the minds of both men. Dead on time, almost to the minute, they had blown another volcano. Now everything was in place. Tony Tilton's missiles were real. They had exploded Mount St Helens. Last night had proved it. And now the USA faced the greatest threat in its long history of wars and battles.

Admiral Morris picked up the telephone and called Arnold Morgan, confirming their meeting in General Scannell's office at 0800. Arnold had been up most of the night, studying charts of the Atlantic, wondering where exactly the *Barracuda* might be, wondering where it was headed, wondering how to catch it. In thirty years, George Morris had never seen him so worried, so utterly anxious.

He and Lt. Commander Ramshawe gathered up all relevant charts and documents and climbed into a staff car at 0700, fighting the traffic and arriving at the Pentagon by 0750. Up in the general's office the pervasive concern of the military had been heightened by the arrival of a new communication from the Middle East. E-mail. Traceable only to either Syria, Jordan or Iraq or Iran. Useless.

It had arrived at 0415, and it was formal in its tone . . . *To the Chairman of the Joint Chiefs, The Pentagon, Washington, DC: We do not, you see, make idle threats. Remove your armed forces from the Middle East now. And bring the Israelis into line. You have exactly eleven days. – HAMAS.*

Admiral Morgan was already in his place at the head of General Scannell's conference table. He was flanked by General Bart Boyce and the CJC himself. General Hudson was also in attendance, with Admiral Dickson and the Atlantic Fleet's Commander-in-Chief Admiral Frank Doran, former commanding officer of the *Lake Erie*, a 10,000-ton guided-missile cruiser out of Norfolk, Virginia.

The other newcomer was General Kenneth Clark, Commandant of the United States Marine Corps, and Admiral Dickson said he had the Commander of Submarine Force (Atlantic Fleet) on stand-by to fly in from Norfolk, if required.

Admiral Morgan opened the discussions. 'Gentlemen, it is perfectly clear now that HAMAS have exploded their second volcano. We were 99 per cent sure they had erupted Mount St Helens, and I think we can now make that 100 per cent.

'Last night, precisely as they had promised, they blew up Montserrat. I guess that's game, set and match to HAMAS. With one match still to play . . . I need hardly remind you of the peril we are all in . . . it's a scenario which once seemed remote, then much more likely . . . now it's a goddamned certainty. Are we broadly agreed on that summation?'

Everyone at the table nodded.

'So that leaves us with three essential tasks – the first of which is to begin the evacuation of Washington, Boston and New York. The second is to nail the *Barracuda*, if and when it shows. Third is to hit and destroy the missile or missiles, if and when they are launched at Cumbre Vieja.'

'Is there no chance of evacuating the military in time to make any difference?' asked Admiral Morris, wanting to explore all options.

'Not in the few days we have left,' answered General Scannell firmly. 'Not enough to convince HAMAS. And in any case, they want the Israeli peace plan signed and settled by then, with the State of Palestine recognised. We simply cannot get that done. For a start, the Israelis have indicated that they will not cooperate so it's out of the question, even if we had more time.'

'Especially with a President who is not involved in the discussions,' said General Scannell.

'And not interested in the defensive measures we must take to avoid this attack taking place on our shores,' added Admiral Morgan. 'I am therefore proposing that we see him today, explain our aims and why we believe he should now face up to the problem.'

'And if he refuses?'

'Then we will have to remove him from office,' replied General Scannell. 'I see no alternative. Under the Constitution of the United States, there is no provision for a state of martial law being declared without the whole rigmarole going through Congress. And we don't have time for that. I did ask Arnold a few days ago to check out our options. And although I sincerely hope we do not need to realise them, I'm sure he would be glad to outline the alternatives.'

Every eye in the room looked towards Admiral Morgan, who said with neither sentiment nor emotion, 'In accordance with Article II, Section I, of the Constitution of the United States of America, the President may be removed from office. It states the reasons for this as his death, resignation, or *inability to discharge the powers and duties of the said office.*

'It also says that his powers and duties shall devolve on the Vice President, it's very clear on that, and if both of them need to be unloaded, Congress has to make a choice.'

Did James Madison actually use the word, *unloaded*? asked Admiral Morris.

'No. He stuck with *removed*,' said Arnold. 'I'm just trying to keep it clear.'

'Thank you, Admiral,' said George Morris. 'Just checking.'

'That's what you're good at, George. Stay with it.'

Even at a moment of such national gravity, Arnold Morgan could still set precisely the tone he wished.

'And, gentlemen,' he said. 'We have no choice but to get this man out of that damned Oval Office.

336

Since it would plainly suit our purposes to have Vice President Paul Bedford onside, and ready to do as we ask, I have asked him to attend this meeting and he'll be here at any moment. You'll understand, I have undertaken this purely because we have only one week to make our moves, effectively to put the East Coast under direct martial law with regard to the evacuation – and we don't have time to sit and wait while those damn Congressmen twitter around like a bunch of schoolgirls.

'It's my view that if these HAMAS guys fire a couple of nuclear-headed missiles at Cumbre Vieja, the mountain will collapse into the sea and the mega-*tsunami* will happen. And that's the view of every darned scientist we have consulted. We have either to destroy our enemy or be ready to cope with whatever he throws at us.

'And remember, he's not asking us to *agree* to anything. He's simply asking us to fulfil their demands, now. We've wasted several weeks thanks to the incumbent in the Oval Office. And right now time's running out in a big hurry. These guys are almost ready.'

Everyone knew that the President had selected a Democratic Senator from the right of the party to help him in the South. It had not done much good all in all, but Paul Bedford still remained a far less radical liberal than any of Charlie McBride's other acolytes. And he had served as an officer in the US Navy for a five-year term which included the First Gulf War.

He was a fairly worldly man and was already being sidelined by the strong liberal mainstream of McBride's White House. In the editorial offices of the *Washington Post* and the *New York Times* the somewhat sardonic Virginian was regarded almost as an outlaw, thanks to his resolute and sincere support in the Senate for the Republican President who had gone to war with Iraq in 2003.

His presence in the Pentagon was announced by a young Marine lieutenant on guard duty outside the CJC's headquarters. And everyone stood up to greet the Vice President when he made his entrance. General Scannell introduced him, then moved back to the antique sideboard which ran half the length of the main table and poured coffee for everyone. There were no lower ranks in this meeting, no one to take care of menial tasks, except, perhaps, for Lt. Commander Ramshawe, who was too busy even to look up from his charts and notes.

When Arnold Morgan inquired exactly how much the VP knew about the problem that faced them, Paul Bedford said flatly, 'Nothing.' It was a tacit admission that this capable former navigation officer in a guided-missile frigate had already slipped out of the Presidential loop.

Admiral Morgan took it upon himself to bring the VP up to speed on the phantom volcano blaster from the Middle East. The men around the table watched Mr Bedford's eyes grow wider with every sentence. Arnold walked him through the voyage of the missing *Barracuda* submarine, the obvious attack on Mount St Helens, the threats and demands, the blasting of Monserrat and the communication which had arrived in the Pentagon a few hours before.

'Are you with us?' asked Admiral Morgan.

'If you mean, do I understand, Admiral, the answer is, plainly, yes. But you have not informed me of the reaction of the President of the United States. Does he know?'

'Of course he knows,' said Arnold, without even cracking a smile. 'He's now rejected each of three pleas by the highest military officers in the country – please to listen, to take some precautions, to make some preparations, or even organise our defences. He says the letters are from a nutcase, and the whole thing is a figment of our imagination. Needless to say, we did not, do not and will not agree with that.'

'Of course not,' replied Vice President Bedford, who was already displaying the inbuilt respect of a former Navy lieutenant in the presence of the mighty.

'Have you yet offered him the opportunity to read the latest communication from HAMAS?'

'No, sir. We have not,' said Arnold. 'He sincerely believes that we are all crazy – and if you would like to step up here next to me, I'll show you just how crazy we are.'

Paul Bedford moved next to the admiral. Arnold traced a circle of about eight inches in radius on the Navy chart in front of him.

'Somewhere in there, Paul,' he said, 'is a big nuclear submarine. Russian-built, with one, or probably two, cruise missiles on board containing nuclear warheads, which as you know pack a wallop one thousand times bigger than any conventional bomb ever dropped on anyone.

'Eleven days from now, they are going to launch those babies at this range of mountains, right here on this next chart . . . here . . . La Palma in the Canary Islands . . . probably from close range. And that will cause, from a great height, the biggest landslide this world has seen for around 10,000 years. Straight into the Atlantic.

'The resulting tidal wave, or, *tsunami*, as it is called, will develop into a succession of waves, 150 foot high, which will hit the East Coast of the United States nine hours later.'

'How big will the waves be at the point of coastal impact?'

'About 120 to 150 feet.'

'You mean straight over New York.'

'Correct.'

'Will the waves break onto the city?'

'No, sir. *Tsunamis* keep right on going. Probably break about 10 to 15 miles inland.'

Paul Bedford drew in his breath sharply. 'Have you asked top scientists their opinion on this likelihood?'

'Of course.'

'How many did you ask?'

'About twenty.'

'And how many of them agreed, conclusively, that this will happen.'

'All of 'em.'

'Jesus Christ,' said the Vice President. 'This is going to happen. Unless we can stop it?'

'Precisely. And we cannot stop it by negotiation, or by compliance, because we have two non-cooperative parties, Israel and the President of the United States. Anyway, we don't have much more time. Which leaves us with two essential tasks, to evacuate the big East Coast cities, and to attempt to destroy either the incoming missiles, or the submarine, or both.'

'And you anticipate having to sideline the President?'

'No. We anticipate the removal of the President?'

Bedford looked up abruptly. 'When?'

'This afternoon. Right after lunch.'

'You realise I am in office as the Vice President and I am sworn to support Charles McBride so long as he shall continue to faithfully execute the office of the President, and to the best of his ability preserve, protect and defend the Constitution.' Paul Bedford was quoting from the President's sworn oath on the day of his inauguration.

'I guess allowing the Constitution of the United States to go under 50 feet of tidal wave might contravene that preserve and protect clause,' replied Admiral Morgan.

'Admiral, the whole scenario adds up to a total dereliction of duty. But you have to give President McBride one last opportunity to take this matter seriously. And you have to remember that I am in no position to play any role in the removal of the President from office.'

'We understand that, sir,' said the CJC. 'However, we may have to put you on notice to stand by to *become* the President of the United States, sometime this afternoon.' General Scannell at times filled the office of Chairman of the Joint Chiefs with immense dignity, and this was surely one of them.

And he added, 'No one in this room wants this to happen. We don't want to be involved in some kind of a Third World junta, removing the President. But this is deadly serious, and only the United States armed forces can avert it, or, in the event of a successful HAMAS attack, prepare the populace to deal with it. Remember the President has already refused, flatly, to grant permission to lay out a Navy submarine trap in the eastern Atlantic.'

'And are you working on that? Moving ships into the area?' Bedford looked from one to the other.

'Of course we are, sir. But we cannot go on like this, operating in defiance of our own Commander-in-Chief.'

'No, you cannot. I understand that.' The Vice President was beginning to look more worried than Arnold Morgan, who was frowning right now like General Custer at the Little Bighorn.

The former National Security Adviser concluded the outline of the massive task which faced the military. 'Paul,' he said, 'we have to evacuate not only millions of citizens, but also the treasures of this nation, our entire systems of government and business. Right here in Washington, we need to move great works of art, much of the contents of the Smithsonian, not to mention historical papers from the Library of Congress, the White House and God knows where.

'In New York, we have to move the art from the great museums. We have to get the entire Stock Exchange, hardware and software, out of range of the ocean. We have to evacuate hospitals, schools, universities, and, most importantly, people. And we need a strong military presence to prevent looting.'

'I understand that,' replied the Vice President.

'This operation will involve the military commandeering railroad trains, the New York subway, buses, maybe trucks and even private cars. This is a national emergency, and we have to be prepared. If this bastard gets those missiles underway, we have to accept the possibility of New York, Boston and Washington being wrecked as comprehensively as Berlin in World War II.'

Paul Bedford was thoughtful and the room fell silent for a few seconds. 'Only the United States military could possibly take care of such a situation,' he said at last. 'Have you thought of a chain of command?'

General Scannell looked up. 'Sir, I am proposing to appoint Admiral Morgan to head up the entire operation. He first alerted us to the problem and, in due course, identified the threat as serious. In company with Admiral Morris and Lt.

Commander Ramshawe, Arnold Morgan has made all the running.

'He is an experienced naval officer, vastly experienced in politics, and capable of masterminding a plan which may allow us to nail the aggressor. I have no hesitation in appointing him Commander-in-Chief of Special Op High Tide. And Special Adviser to the President. Above all, he will be listened to by all branches of the military, the Intelligence community and politicians.

'Any other course of action would be unacceptable.'

'And where do you suggest he works from?' already knowing the answer.

'Oh, the White House, most definitely, since he will have to call the shots. Bear in mind – this situation will probably last for only a couple of weeks, IF we get our act together and catch the *Barracuda*. During that time, speed is of the essence. There can be no arguments, no debates, no reluctance. Everyone must move fast and without hesitation. Admiral Morgan will need instant obedience, and, to tell you the truth, I think he has a better chance of getting it if he's sitting in the Oval Office, as a kind of acting President, before you were to move in once the operation is complete.'

This, more than anything, revealed to Paul Bedford the gravity of the situation – military command in the Oval Office. It couldn't be done any other way. He saw that.

'Will you require me to fulfil any duties during

the transition period early this afternoon,' he asked simply. A general sigh of relief went through the room. The main hurdle had been taken.

'Better not,' said General Scannell. 'We intend to ask just once for the President's cooperation, then remove him from office. At which point we shall have an announcement prepared, to the effect that the President has suffered a serious nervous breakdown and has retired, with his family, temporarily to Camp David. Of course he will be under "house arrest" without contact with the outside world whatsoever.

'Right then we'll have the Judge, appointed by the Supreme Court, in the White House to swear you into office.'

'And the great offices of state? Who will you be getting rid of?'

General Scannell replied. 'That idiot Defense Secretary and the National Security Adviser will have to go immediately, before Arnold throttles them both. And you'll probably want to appoint your own Chief-of-Staff. So that buffoon Hatchard will have to go.'

Paul Bedford said, softly, words he never expected to utter, 'Correct. Romney and Schlemmer must go immediately. I'll explain to Hatchard that, with his boss gone, this is the end of his West Wing tenure.'

Scannell spoke for everyone in the room when he said: 'Sir, everyone at this table is very grateful for your understanding. We cannot sit here and allow this clown in the Oval Office to stand and watch while our cities are destroyed. We cannot. And will not.'

'I understand,' said the Virginian. 'And I, in turn, am grateful for your foresight, and your confidence in me. Especially Admiral Morgan, of whom, I should confess, I have long been terrified.'

'C'mon, Paul,' rasped Arnold. 'You never even met me before today.'

'I assure you, Admiral, your reputation precedes you. And I look forward to working with you . . . er . . . I think.'

Everyone laughed, the kind of restrained laughter born of high tension and trepidation. But it would not be long now. And when the Vice President left the room, to return to the White House, they all instinctively checked the time. 10.04 on Tuesday morning 29 September 2009. It was the moment when Admiral Arnold Morgan became the *de facto* leader of the United States of America.

Same day, same time 1934 (local)
Bandar Abbas Navy HQ
General Rashood and the Commander-in-Chief of the Iranian Navy, Admiral Mohammed Badr, were trying to decide whether another communication to Washington was necessary. Did the Americans think that the HAMAS High Command would not carry out their threat, because world opinion would most likely turn against them?

In which case someone needed to put the Pentagon right. Sometime on 9 October, young Ben

Badr would fire those two SCIMITAR SL-2s straight at Cumbre Vieja, no ifs, ands or buts.

Ravi was working on a draft and he was nearly through with it. The wording was as follows . . . *To: The Chairman of the Joint Chiefs, The Pentagon, Washington, DC: There is nothing you can do to stop us now. We regret that you have ignored our instructions. You will still be underwater when our brothers in Palestine rise again.* They agreed to transmit the letter some-time the following day, Wednesday 30 September.

1005 Tuesday 29 September
The Pentagon, Washington, DC
A minute after Paul Bedford has left the office, General Scannell excused himself from the meeting and returned next door to his own office. He picked up his private line to the White House and asked to be connected to the President.

'I'm sorry, General. The President is extremely tied up right now. Can I have him call you back?'

'No, you may not,' replied the general. 'Put him on the line now.'

One minute later the unmistakeable voice of President McBride said quietly, 'General, I am getting slightly tired of these unannounced inter-ruptions during my working day. However, I under-stand the priority which your position in the military grants you, and I am able to give you five minutes . . .'

'Thank you, Mr President. You will doubtless have noticed that HAMAS have carried out their threat, and that at around midnight they did indeed blow up another volcano?'

'Well, I have been told that there was an eruption on Montserrat, if that's what you're referring to, but so far as I can see it erupts on a kind of monthly basis . . .'

'Not like it did last night, sir. Trust me. That was one of the biggest volcano blasts we've seen for years. Almost as damaging as Mount St Helens –'

The President interrupted him impatiently. 'Well, what do you want me to do about it? It was obviously in no relation to us. It took place 4,000 miles away from here, in a foreign country. I think I advised you when we last spoke on the subject that your theories were a complete waste of time, and there was absolutely no reason to place the Pentagon and the White House on a state of alert –'

Now it was Scannell who broke in. He could see where this conversation was headed and he wasn't about to waste his breath much longer.

'You did indeed, sir. But they did not threaten to attack us directly, only to show us what they could do, in the hope that we would change our minds and get out of the Middle East. I would say, for the second time in too short a time, they have shown us what they are capable of doing.'

'Well, I remain unconvinced. I think that the Mount St Helens eruption gave some crank the idea to write threatening letters to the US military and by some off chance they managed to coincide a threat with a very volatile volcano which erupts on a regular basis somewhere down in the Caribbean.

'That is not reason to ask the President of the United States to activate an oceanwide search by the entire US Navy at vast expense, to withdraw all of our forces from the Middle East at even greater expense, and then tell Israel they must evacuate their settlements in the Holy Land by next week.

'Can't you see, General, that these are the actions of a hysteric? They are issues so great, almost impossible, and without any reasonable grounds – no President could possibly tackle them without becoming a laughing stock.'

'Sir, I must inform you for the final time that your military High Command regards the threat from HAMAS as serious. We think they can, and will, explode that volcano in the Canary Islands, which, not for the first time, will unleash a tidal wave. Only this one will flood our entire East Coast.

'I have not spoken to a single volcanologist who disagrees with the theory. All these guys need to do is to hit the crater of Cumbre Vieja with a big missile, probably nuclear, and it will happen. The ensuing landslide is a certainty. And nothing could then stop the *tsunami* from developing.'

'Please,' the President said scornfully. 'Preserve me from admirals, generals and scientists. Collectively you guys cause more unnecessary trouble than everyone else on this planet combined. You asked me a final question. I give you my final answer. I believe your theories are a fairy tale. I have been proved right so far, and I have no doubt I will continue to be right.'

He was finished with the discussion, his mind clearly already occupied with other, most important, matters of state.

'As for the overwhelming actions you ask me to take, I must say again, no, General. I deny my permission to sweep the Atlantic for a non-existent submarine at a cost of about a billion dollars an hour. I will not evacuate our armed forces from the Middle East. And neither will I call the Prime Minister of Israel and demand the creation of an instant Independent Palestinian State. Do I make myself clear?'

'I'm afraid you do, sir. I'm afraid you do.'

General Scannell replaced his telephone and walked back into the conference room. 'I have spoken to the President again. His position has not altered.'

Admiral Morgan looked grave but unsurprised. 'Then our plan for a transfer of power will have to be put into action. This day,' he said. 'Gentlemen, I know we must prepare for an evacuation of these cities, but what we *really* need to do is to find and destroy that fucking submarine.'

'Arnold,' said Admiral Dickson, 'do you have a preliminary plan for the Atlantic deployment? I mean, this is a huge step involving possibly a hundred ships.'

'Alan, I have been giving this a great amount of thought. If this ship is carrying regular cruise missiles, top-of-the-line, Russian-built, they have a range of

1,200 nautical miles. In my view he stands well off, perhaps launching 500 miles, or maybe even 1,000 miles, from his target.

'So let's assume a missile range of 1,000 nautical miles. Initially I suppose we'd have to use SSNs or TAFFs on an area search/patrol.'

Admiral Morgan, like all senior naval officers, spoke to the entire room as if everyone habitually spoke in service jargon. It never occurred to him that not everyone knew an SSN was an attack submarine, or a TAFF was a towed-array frigate, or that the mysteries of the long, sensitive, electronic listening device trailing out behind the ship might not be clearly comprehended by every single person in Washington. Time was too short for explanations, though.

'And remember,' he added, 'the TA will pick up nothing, unless *Barracuda* makes a mistake or goes unaccountably noisy, which I doubt. But we have to start somewhere. *Something* has to be done, since this is the most serious threat to the United States. *EVER*.

'Now, the naval commanders at this table will know that the towed arrays are highly variable. But working from just one at 10 knots, covering a circular area of 10-nautical-miles radius . . . that's 300 square miles per hour. We have a search area of 3,000,000 square miles, which means that each towed-array unit needs 10,000 hours to sweep the area once. Fifty units would do it in eight days.'

He looked around the room.

'We've got ten days, if we start tomorrow. And that massive sweep would not have covered the inshore areas, which are considerable and extremely difficult. For that we need a fleet of helicopters with dipping sonars, covering all waters with depths of 15 fathoms, or deeper to 50 fathoms.

'I suppose one might hope that active sonars might drive the SSN into deeper water, where the TAs have a better chance. But if you are only searching one given spot every eight days . . . Jesus Christ . . . the chances of success are negligible.'

He got up and turned to the navigational chart on the wall, indicating the vast body of water they were dealing with.

'And any success depends on us getting there before the *Barracuda*. If we do, and if we are certain of this, we could perhaps form an outer ring, through which the fucking *'Cuda* must pass. Total ring length would be 6,000 nautical miles (3.142 X diameter). Fifty TA units would cover 2,000 nautical miles. So, to be effective, you'd need to be pretty damn sure from which direction the SSN was making his approach . . . I mean a sector of less than 120 degrees.

'Gentlemen, not to put too fine a point on it, this is going to be difficult, with the chances of success in the 5 per cent bracket at the most. Which, given the effort, is a depressing thought, to say the least. It means a huge deployment of ASW assets – and even if we had weeks and weeks to continue the search, the likelihood of actually tripping over this little bastard is remote in the extreme. I'm afraid we need to think this out much more carefully.'

He sat back down, the worried look on his face deepening.

'Obviously we have to get our warships out of port regardless, unless we want them all crushed or capsized by the tidal wave. But we can't just send them charging out into the Atlantic into the possible teeth of a *tsunami*.

'I could stand the cost . . . you know in fuel, food and personnel . . . but not if I believe we have almost no chance of success. And the prospect of that massive naval search actually gives me the creeps. Remember, we have not really picked up this damned *Barracuda* in months. Their CO is very good, and we know he's in a very quiet boat. He could creep slowly underneath our frigates and *never* be detected. We've just got to think this out, gentlemen.'

'A rather pessimistic speech, Arnold,' said Admiral Morris, wryly. 'Illuminating, but pessimistic. For Christ's sake don't repeat it in front of the President this afternoon. He'll think you've become some kind of a fellow liberal traveller.'

'George,' chuckled Arnold, 'that day ever comes, I'll step out of this room with my service revolver, and do the honourable thing, like an officer and a gentleman.'

CHAPTER NINE

1330 (local) Tuesday 29 September 2009
Atlantic Ocean, 18.00N 53.00W

The *Barracuda* was making 15 knots through deep waters, east of the Puerto Rican Trench, 600 feet below the surface, with 2,500 fathoms under her keel. Shortly before first light that morning they had come to periscope depth for a seven-second satellite check, and the signal awaiting them, more than 20,000 miles above the planet, confirmed their course and mission . . . *A cruel sea for the songbirds* . . .

General Ravi Rashood, plotting and planning in faraway Bandar Abbas, did not consider the sin of self-congratulation to be among his faults but he did harbour one small vanity – he believed he composed one hell of a military signal . . . and *a cruel sea for the songbirds* was one of his finest, pre-arranged with Ben Badr. It was stuffed with hidden information. *The Cruel Sea*, the famous book by Nicholas Monsarrat, meant that the attack on Montserrat had been a total success, the mention of the songbirds referred to . . . *Onward! My brave boys to the Canary Islands*. Three words to explain that

354

the sensational SCIMITAR missile attack on the Soufrière Hills had been accurate, devastating and world news headlines. Three more to confirm the *Barracuda*'s next mission, and to seal the fate of the arrogant Satan which dominated the Middle East. Not to mention most of the world.

Admiral Ben Badr was ecstatic as he and his cohorts crept along towards the destiny Allah had awarded them. Everything was going according to plan.

The *Barracuda* was now 560 miles from Montserrat, steering zero-eight-three, in open water, approximately halfway between the burning Caribbean island and the relative safety of the Mid-Atlantic Ridge.

Admiral Badr and his Chief of Boat, CPO Ali Zahedi, were down in the missile room sipping coffee and inspecting the arsenal they had left – ten SCIMITAR cruises, eight of them with conventional warheads, plus two Mark 2s, with their 200-kiloton nuclear warheads. Two hundred kilotons, the explosive equivalent of *200,000 tons of TNT*. Ten conventional warheads (500 pounds each) pack a combined wallop of a couple of tons of TNT.

Ben ran his thumb over the sharp, reinforced steel nose cone of the nearest Mark 2, and he trailed his hand lightly, hesitantly, over the casing, as if stroking a dangerous lion. And he bowed to the golden lettering SCIMITAR SL-2 – 'It is the will of Allah,' he said softly, contemplating the coming thrust to the heart of Cumbre Vieja.

1500 Tuesday 29 September 2009
The White House, Washington, DC

President Charles McBride had agreed with undisguised irritation to a short meeting with General Tim Scannell and the Chief of Naval Operations, Admiral Alan Dickson. He agreed because he had no choice. Even his Chief-of-Staff, Bill Hatchard, had managed to shake his massive head when the President tried to evade seeing the Chairman of the Joint Chiefs. 'Forget it, sir,' he had hissed from across the Oval Office. 'You have to see him.'

In the following minutes, big Bill pointed out that no President can avoid his CJC. 'It's simple, sir,' he said, unnecessarily, because if it had not been simple he would have had trouble with the concept himself. 'If he has some really important information for you, and you refuse to see him, and the worst happens, he has it in his power to see you impeached. You *have* to see him, and that's that.'

Charles McBride gave General Scannell and the Chief Executive of the United States Navy ten minutes at 3.05 p.m. They arrived five minutes early, in two staff cars because there were rather more of them than the President was expecting.

In the back seat of the first car sat the CJC in company with Admiral Arnold Morgan. In the front passenger seat was General Kenneth Clark, Commandant of the United States Marines.

In the second car was Admiral Dickson, with Admiral Frank Doran, Commander-in-Chief of the Atlantic Fleet, and General Bart Boyce, NATO's

Supreme Allied Commander. With the exception of Admiral Morgan, the rest were in uniform.

They came in through West Executive Avenue, parked in front of the steps leading up to the Diplomatic driveway, and the 'front' door to the West Wing. Then they strode in tight formation, accompanied by a detail of four Marine guards who had been awaiting their arrival.

They marched to the Marine guard station right on the West Wing door, where a tall, polished guardsman, in full dress red, blue and gold-braided uniform, snapped to attention and said crisply, 'Good afternoon, sir.' The remark was addressed to General Clark, who smiled and nodded as the Marine pulled the brass handle to open the door.

Inside, the White House 'greeter', a six-foot, six-inch-former naval Petty Officer, plus one of the resident secret agents, were plainly ready for this onslaught of military power. The agent ventured to ask the CJC if he could help.

'Two things,' said General Scannell. 'A US Navy helicopter from Andrews will be landing on the lawn in under ten minutes. Make sure the military office knows about it. Inform the main White House telephone executive next to the ops room over in the Old Executive Office Building we are conducting an emergency exercise, strict security. No further calls for one half-hour, incoming or outgoing, as from right now.'

'Right away, sir,' said the agent, a former Army captain himself. 'Oh . . . er . . . Admiral Morgan, sir . . . will you be requiring a visitor's badge?'

'Sit down, Tommy, I'm busy.'

The agent, who had always held an almost hero-worshipping view of the former National Security Adviser, laughed, despite himself. And he utilised the admiral's favourite phrase, one he had heard so many times during his five-year career in the West Wing.

'No bullshit, right, sir?'

'No bullshit, Tommy,' replied Arnold.

And with that, all six of them, plus the Marine guard detail, marched along the corridor towards the office of the President of the United States.

Outside the Oval Office, Bill Hatchard was speaking to the President's secretary, who bade General Scannell a polite 'good afternoon', looking curiously at the little group. She had not realised there were so many people scheduled for the short meeting, she said apologetically.

'Don't worry about it.' General Clark turned to one of the two Marine guards already on duty outside the Oval Office and ordered him to summon at least eight more to the corridor.

'*SIR! YES SIR!*' the guard snapped, obeying quickly and instinctively. The secretary now looked vaguely anxious and her alarm deepened when General Clark said to the other guard, 'Head down to the main telephone switchboard and ensure that there are no incoming or outgoing calls. The order to suspend all service in and out of the White House has already been issued.'

'*SIR! YES SIR!*' he replied to his commandant, and set off instantly for the Old Executive Building where the lines of telephone operators guard the President and his senior people from unwanted calls.

General Scannell now walked straight past the stunned secretary and opened the door to the inner sanctum of the US Government. Charles McBride was at his desk, reading some papers, and he looked up in surprise as five senior military figures strode in behind the general.

'General, this is unacceptable. I agreed to see two people, not six. Please ask four of them to leave.'

The Chairman of the Joint Chiefs simply ignored him. 'Mr President, at 10 a.m. you informed me you would not give permission for the United States military to take steps either to prevent, or otherwise cope with, a threat from the Middle East terrorist organisation HAMAS. May I presume you have not changed your mind?'

'You may. It's just a load of nonsense. Now, if that's all you have to say, I'll thank you to leave.'

'Sir. This is by no means all I have to say. I must confirm that the Head of your Navy, the Head of your Army, the Supreme NATO Commander, the Commander-in-Chief of the Atlantic Fleet, the Commandant of the United States Marine Corps, plus Admiral Morgan, are unanimous in their belief that you are wrong.

'Each one of us believes that the East Coast cities of the United States are in mortal danger from a ruthless enemy. You are not just absolving yourself from the responsibility, you are hindering our efforts to protect the citizens and their property. Not to mention the historical documents and treasures of this country, which are held in those important cities.'

'Listen, General, these decisions are mine to make . . . not yours, nor any other military officers in the Pentagon.'

'Sir, I assure you, that if we consider this nation is threatened, and we have an incompetent President in this office, he will go, not us. We are the permanent guardians of this nation. And I think you'll find that the people of the United States trust us more than a politician.'

The President stared at him, disbelief on his face. 'How dare you speak to me in that manner? I've had enough of it, do you hear? I have had quite enough. Now get out all of you, before I have you escorted out by the guards.'

'Perhaps I should remind you, sir, that the White House is guarded by the Marine Corps, and their Commandant is standing right next to me . . .'

The President brought his fist hard down on the desk. 'We'll see about that . . . ,' he shouted, picking up the telephone. But the line was dead, as were all lines in the White House. And that was the way they would stay for another twenty-five minutes.

He crashed down the phone, his hands shaking. In short angry bursts, slightly disjointed, and too loud, he hissed. *'I've always thought you were all crazy . . . you're asking the impossible . . . I can't just evacuate the East Coast . . . I can't persuade Israel to help . . . I don't even understand deployment of ships . . . why are you doing this? Why the hell can't you leave me alone? To do what I was elected to do . . .'*

'Sir, it is our opinion that you are not competent to lead this nation in the crisis in which we now find ourselves. The President has to talk to the people . . . today . . . and it plainly cannot be you.

'On behalf of the United States Armed Forces, I am relieving you of office. For the next ten minutes this country will be under a self-imposed martial law. By that time we shall have sworn in the new President . . . as you know, under our Constitution that's Vice President Paul Bedford . . .'

'*YOU CAN DO NO SUCH THING!*' yelled Charles McBride.

'Can't I?' replied the Chairman of the Joint Chiefs. 'General Clark, summon a Marine guard of four men . . .'

'Yes, sir.' General Clark walked to the door and ordered four armed Marines into the Oval Office. 'Stand on either side of the President's chair and be prepared for him to do something careless,' said the commandant.

'Sir,' said General Scannell. 'This sheet of paper contains your resignation. You will see it already has the Presidential Seal embossed on it . . . read and sign . . .'

The President read the sentence . . . *I hereby resign the office of President of the United States for reasons of failing health. Signed by my own hand on this 29th day of September, 2009.*

'And if I refuse . . . ?'

'We shall place you under arrest for deliberately and wilfully endangering the citizens of the United States by refusing to take military precautions in the face of an enemy threat. That would mean, of course, your instant impeachment and disgrace. Sign it, sir, and sign it now, or we'll carry you out of here. Time, for us at least, is very short.'

'But you cannot just appoint a new . . .'

'SHUT UP, MCBRIDE!' rasped Admiral Morgan. 'You've said plenty.'

The President was stunned into silence. With the generals glaring, he signed the resignation paper.

'You will now be escorted to a Navy helicopter out on the lawn, and be flown to Camp David, where you will remain under house arrest until we have dealt with the HAMAS threat . . . is the First Lady in residence? Any other members of family?'

'Just the First Lady upstairs in the residence.'

'She will be brought to the helicopter immediately. At Camp David neither of you will be permitted any contact with the outside world whatsoever. No phones will be connected. Mobile phones will be confiscated.' General Scannell glanced at his watch and muttered, 'Have him escorted out right now. We're going straight to the office of the new President. Judge Moore is already in the Old Executive Building, specifically to swear him in.'

The operation had been conducted so far with immense precision.

The High Command of the United States Armed

Forces was trusted implicitly to tell the truth and to operate objectively, free from political or civilian agendas. The members of the Supreme Court understood that perfectly and the two Supreme Court Judges, required to authorise Judge Moore's powers, had complied instantly with the request from the Pentagon.

The only politician who had been informed of the palace coup was Senator Edward Kennedy, the senior member of the Senate Armed Services Committee, whose patriotism was unquestioned and whose personal motives to act on behalf of the United States were always impeccable.

In this instance Admiral Morgan had assured everyone of the Senator's support, since, he said, the entire Kennedy compound was situated on the shores of Nantucket Sound, in the direct path of the ensuing *tsunami*.

'But I know Teddy,' he said. 'If he lived on top of the goddamned Rockies he'd still do the right thing about a threat like this. Also, he knows us, and he knows the Navy. He's head of the Sub-Committee on Sea Power. And he knows we wouldn't be making this up. He'll trust us, and he'll give us his total support. You can count on it.'

And now Charles McBride was on his feet, with a Marine guard on each elbow, being frogmarched to the door of the Oval Office. Upstairs, Mrs McBride was being escorted more gently along the corridor carrying only her purse. Their personal possessions would be ferried up to Camp David in the early part of the evening. The announcement of his retirement, to a shocked nation, would be given in a broadcast within the hour, when President Bedford would cite McBride's nervous breakdown.

The six White House visitors walked behind the Marine escort as far as the portico door to the lawn. One hundred yards away they could see the huge rotors of the helicopter already howling. Mrs McBride emerged from a different door. General Clark remained to watch the US Navy helicopter take off, bearing the President and his First Lady into exile from the seat of government. The others headed directly to the office of Vice President Paul Bedford. They had agreed to ignore the intricacies of the Twenty-Fifth Amendment, which essentially dealt with the transfer of power to the Vice President, if a President was incapacitated and unable to carry out his duties. The Twenty-Fifth has only been used twice, once when President Reagan was shot, and once when President Bush underwent a general anaesthetic in April 1989.

In this instance, it was decided that the VP would be immediately sworn in. There was, after all, no possibility of McBride making any kind of a comeback.

Senator Kennedy had already arrived in the VP's office, and Judge Moore intoned the sacred words that all President must recite: 'I do solemnly swear that I will faithfully execute the Office of the President of the United States, and will to the best of my ability preserve, protect and defend the Constitution of the United States.'

Section 2 of the Constitution made him at that moment Commander-in-Chief of the Army and Navy of the United States.

Within moments he had signed the prepared document which appointed Admiral Arnold Morgan his Special Adviser for the forthcoming crisis with HAMAS. He willingly signed the rider to that document which ensconced the admiral in the Oval Office as Supreme Commander of all US military forces involved in Operation High Tide, 'with civilian powers as far-reaching as may be necessary for safe evacuation of the citizens of the affected areas'.

General Clark, the only person in the room with a working knowledge of a digital camera, photographed the entire scene for the public record, somehow managing to wipe out four pictures taken by Mrs Bedford the previous week at Camp David in the process. But they had to avoid the intrusion of an official photographer and the endless possibilities for this incredible private ceremony to be leaked to the media.

Senator Kennedy observed the formalities and swiftly headed back to the Capitol to brief the heads of Senate Committees on the approaching political bombshell. The remainder of the House would learn of the shift of power at more or less the same time as the media, and indeed the nation. The military chiefs were confident that Teddy would combine his legendary down-home friendliness with the certain tough authority that was his trademark, to convince the elected representatives of the fifty states that the nation stood in mortal danger.

Meanwhile, back in the West Wing of the White House it was plain that staff members had to be informed and then silenced, until the press had been given the news. Admiral Morgan, standing in the Oval Office with General Scannell, decreed that senior staff should report immediately to President Reagan's especially built Situation Room in the basement of the West Wing. There they would be briefed by the admiral himself, and there they would watch the television address to the nation by the new President of the United States. A guard of four Marines outside the door would ensure no one left the room, and all mobile phones would be surrendered to the guards as each senior staffer arrived.

'It's important that Paul tells our story just the way we want it,' emphasised Arnold Morgan. 'We do not want some newsroom rewrite asshole speculating and jumping to conclusions. This White House already has a reputation for press leaks, and we don't want *anyone* releasing information until we're good and ready, and we have the situation under control.'

He glanced at his watch. It showed five minutes before four o'clock. He walked out through the Oval Office door and told the ex-President's secretary to walk around the building and inform all heads of departments to report to the Situation Room. Since internal communications were down, he ordered one of the Marine guards to walk down to the Press Room and inform those present that there would be a Presidential Address in twenty minutes in the White House Briefing Room.

By now Admirals Dickson and Doran, in company with Generals Boyce and Clark, had arrived back in the Oval Office. Arnold Morgan, already sitting behind the only available desk, that of the former President, was writing, fast, on a legal pad, the one on which the former occupant had earlier that afternoon been drafting a personal speech to the Third World Initiative.

Still scribbling, he spoke without looking up. 'Okay, I'll take Frank Doran with me to the situation room, where I'll stress the enormous task of the Navy to the senior White House Staff. I think everyone else should go with President Bedford, and stand behind him on his port and starboard quarter. General Scannell and General Boyce on his four o'clock, Admiral Dickson and General Clark on his eight. That's the Head of the Pentagon, the Head of NATO, the Head of the Navy and the Head of the United States Marine Corps. Solid, right?'

Just then Paul Bedford walked in and Admiral Morgan immediately stood up, nodded, and said, 'Mr President . . . I'm just drafting a few notes for your address . . . they're only notes . . . but we have no time . . . you'll just have to wing the speech, but it'd be a good idea to stick to the outline here . . .

'Stress the nervous collapse and subsequent resignation of the President, who is currently under medical care at Camp David . . . tell 'em how

367

shocked we all are . . . then come clean over the HAMAS threat, tell 'em the whole story, not in detail, but start with Mount St Helens, then the demands of the terrorists . . .' His finger ran down his notes on the legal pad. 'Then the threat which convinced us, when they blew up Montserrat. Explain the terrible danger, the silent terrorist submarine with its nuclear-warhead guided missiles, the vulnerability of Cumbre Vieja, and the certainty of the *tsunami*, IF they hit the volcano.'

Paul Bedford nodded as firmly as he was able to. Right now, in his own mind, he was not so much President of the United States as a naval lieutenant receiving a briefing of the most staggering importance from one of the most senior admirals ever to serve his country.

Arnold ripped the page off the writing pad and handed it to the new Chief Executive. He had printed everything in bold capitals, including the first two sentences, then a clear synopsis of the rest.

'Is that it?' asked President Bedford.

'As best as we can do,' said Arnold agreeably. 'You're on parade in fifteen minutes, and I'm out of here with Frank, right now.'

'Okay, sir,' said Paul. 'I can follow this.'

'You can call me anything you like in this room,' replied Arnold. 'But for Christ's sake don't call me 'sir' in public!'

'No, sir,' said Paul Bedford, laughing despite the gravity of the situation.

'And, Mr President . . . ,' said Arnold, as he headed

for the door, 'remember one other thing . . . when Sir Winston Churchill demanded an entire reorganisation of the Navy fleets in the North Atlantic . . . he told his First Sea Lord if it wouldn't fit on one side of one sheet of paper it hadn't been properly thought out.'

And with that he was gone, the Commander-in-Chief of the Atlantic Fleet, Admiral Frank Doran, somewhere in his wake.

'Jesus,' said President Bedford. 'Is he something, or what?'

And then, to everyone's surprise, Admiral Morgan's head popped back around the door. 'Oh, Paul, I forgot. You'd better fire Defense Secretary Schlemmer, and the NSA Romney right now, and then Hatchard, right after he's released from my briefing. Handwritten notes thanking them for all they have done. One side of one sheet, right?'

'Okay, Arnie, you got it,' replied the President of the United States, slipping into the easy informality enjoyed by men under severe stress. 'Is it okay if I borrow your desk?'

Still chuckling, Admiral Morgan headed for the West Wing basement where he found a scene of extraordinary restlessness. The heads of White House departments had mostly arrived. Protocol, Secret Service, Communications, Catering, the chief Butler, Security, Transportation, the Press Office, the State Department, Speech Writers, Bill Hatchard, and indeed the former President's secretary, were crowding into the room. All requesting information, yearning to know what was going on. The four Marine guards had taken up positions outside the door, and two more guarded the exit from the elevator. With the correct credentials they would let you in, but no one was leaving. Not until the Presidential Address was completed on television. Surrendered cellphones formed a small pile on a desk behind the principal Marine detail.

Arnold Morgan and Admiral Doran made their way into the sound-proof, teak-panelled conference room, which, aside from its central table, was filled with secretarial desks, computers and video-conferencing telephones. None of this was currently active, though staff members were hurriedly claiming the desks since the packed gathering could plainly not fit around the main table.

Admiral Morgan moved into the big chair once occupied by President Reagan. He dragged another seat next to him for the C-in-C Atlantic Fleet, and called the meeting to order by banging his open palm down on the polished surface of the conference table.

'For a very few of you, this may seem a bit like old times. For the rest of you, my name is Arnold Morgan, former Admiral in the United States Navy, former Director of the National Security Agency, former National Security Adviser to the President.

'I'm not precisely sure how fast rumours move around here these days, but I would like you all to know that President Charles McBride resigned within the last hour for health reasons. According to the Constitution, the Vice President has instantly assumed the Oval Office and he was sworn in by the man appointed to do so by the Supreme Court of the United States, Judge Moore. The ceremony took place in the Old Executive Building, and President Paul Bedford swore to uphold the Constitution of the United States.

'The witnesses present were Senator Edward Kennedy . . . the Chairman of the Joint Chiefs, General Scannell . . . the Chief of Naval Operations, Admiral Alan Dickson . . . the Commander-in-Chief of the Atlantic Fleet, Admiral Frank Doran, who is seated here beside me . . . the Supreme Allied Commander of NATO, General Bart Boyce . . . the Commandant of the United States Marine Corps, General Kenneth Clark . . . and myself.

'The press will learn of the change in government inside the next ten minutes, and you will all see President Bedford's Address on the screen in this room shortly.

'There will, of course, be changes in staff, but none where we are able to rely on the old order. The most important thing that I must tell you, though, is that the East Coast of this country is at present under the most terrible terrorist threat in US history. Worse, immeasurably, than 9/11.

'It was this threat which caused Charles McBride to suffer what his doctors consider to be a nervous breakdown. He willingly and selflessly stepped aside as the pressures on him mounted, aware that he has no military experience and that his Vice President Paul Bedford, who served as a navigation officer in

371

a guided-missile frigate during a five-year term in the United States Navy, might be a better leader for the US in this time of crisis.

'The former President is resting under medical supervision at Camp David right now. The First Lady is with him and they will not be returning to the White House.

'As to the threat we face, in the simplest terms there is a Russian-built nuclear submarine loose in the North Atlantic crewed by a group of HAMAS terrorists.'

The Situation Room was absolutely silent as Admiral Morgan delivered his briefing. He shook his head. 'And we know from the events of the last few months,' he said, 'that HAMAS has this capability. They exploded Mount St Helens, and last night they carried out their second threat, accurate to the minute, by exploding Montserrat down in the Caribbean. Their latest communiqué says they will hit La Palma on 9 October.

'We need to find that submarine, most importantly, but we have already started the preliminary stages of an evacuation of the entire East Coast to high ground, just in case we don't find it. By the end of the day, the US Army, National Guard and metropolitan police forces will unobtrusively control the streets to prevent a panic after the President's TV Address. From the moment Cumbre Vieja erupts, it will take nine hours for the *tsunami* to hit New York harbour. And those tidal waves don't break . . . they'll just keep rolling.

372

'Your new President has appointed me Supreme Commander of all the United States forces engaged in this operation for the next two weeks. During this time we will begin evacuating the nation's treasures, its museums, its historic papers, its Stock Exchange in New York and its schools. I shall be working from the Oval Office, closely with President Bedford, and with the five senior commanders who witnessed the inauguration ceremony an hour ago.

'Right now, I will not be taking questions, and I would like someone to turn on the television sets around the walls and tune into one of the networks to hear the Presidential Address . . . Admiral Doran and I will remain here to listen with you.'

The Situation Room remained stunned. No one spoke, but people moved quietly, finding places in front of the television screens.

Meanwhile, upstairs in the Briefing Room, the fifty or sixty members of the White House Press Corps, the journalists Marlin Fitzwater referred to as the Lions, were growing more restless by the minute. None of them had a clue what was taking place, and although a few photographers were plainly bored senseless by the whole procedure, dozing in the fourth row, there was an unmistakable growling at the back of the room, where the wire service reporters operated.

This was a most unusual call to a briefing, issued out of the blue at twenty minutes' notice. The reporters were huddled together, discussing possibilities. The favourite forecast was that President

McBride had recognised the state of emergency on the island of Montserrat and was sending aid. Big deal.

However, journalists of a more thoughtful nature had noticed the *eight* Marine Corps guards in position in front of the dark wood dias. That hinted at something more than aid to Montserrat. But it did not suggest the imminent unleashing of the biggest news story of the year.

A few more minutes slipped by and the level of restlessness grew. It was always the same at feeding time. The Lions began to lose their cool if the keeper was late. Actually, it wasn't his lateness that was relevant. It was the pack's perception of lateness which mattered.

Where the hell is he? . . . Christ, it's getting too late for the evening papers . . . stupid time to call a briefing anyway . . . who the hell cares if he sends the taxpayers' money to Montserrat?

By 1625 the room was buzzing, and the sudden appearance of Lee Mitchell, Vice President Bedford's spokesman, had no effect on the noise level whatsoever. But when he walked up to the dias, turned on the microphone and asked for their attention, they gave it reluctantly.

Mr Mitchell, a tall, young, former political reporter for the *Atlanta Constitution*, came right to the point. 'I am here to announce formally that Charles McBride resigned from the office of President of the United States less than one hour ago. At seven minutes before four o'clock, under the

374

precise requirements of the Constitution, Vice President Paul Bedford was sworn into office.'

The entire room exploded with the shrill, desperate, near panic-stricken sound of fifty odd reporters flailing between the quest for more detail and the overriding desire to speak to their newsrooms.

RESIGNED! Whaddya mean resigned? When? . . . Where? . . . Why . . . ? How? . . . Where is he? Is he still in the White House? What caused it?

It took a full two minutes for the row to subside, and only then because it was obvious that Lee Mitchell had not the slightest intention of uttering a single word until there was once more silence from the Lions he was supposed to be feeding.

'Thank you,' he said, carefully. 'There will be no questions at this briefing. But I will tell you that former President McBride is resting under medical supervision at Camp David. He has suffered an apparent nervous breakdown and may not recover fully for some weeks. The First Lady is with him. Under the circumstances, he felt he had no option but to resign.'

Again, the suppressed pandemonium of the Lions was let loose. Regardless of the 'no questions' edict, they stood and roared . . . *this is a national issue . . . the people have a right to know . . . what do you think I'm gonna tell my readers . . . what kind of a nervous breakdown? . . . has he been ill for long? . . . this is America not tsarist Russia . . . c'mon Mitchell, you're paid to tell us what the hell is happening to the President of the United States . . .*

The journalists did have some power, and some of them had more than a few brains, but nothing to match the shrewd orchestration masterminded by Morgan, Scannell and Bedford. And at this point the scene shifted. Lee Mitchell moved aside to greet formally the Chairman of the Joint Chiefs, then in quick succession the Head of the Navy, the Supreme Allied Commander of NATO and the Commandant of the United States Marine Corps, who all took up the positions allotted to them by Arnold Morgan, port and starboard quarters to the dias.

And as they did so the noise from the Lions subsided, to be replaced by a more dignified sound. Through the loudspeaker system came the unmistakably familiar tones of the band of the US Marines playing *Hail to the Chief*, loudly, robustly, summoning that overwhelming sense of patriotism into the chest of every American in the room.

By now the White House phone lines were back on, and the place was connected to the outside world by a zillion kilowatts. The television cameras were rolling, commentators were speaking, the wire service reporters were filing copy from the back of the room. Everyone else, confined to their personal seats by both protocol and tradition, was scribbling.

And into this media feeding frenzy stepped the heavy-set, balding Virginian, Paul Bedford, making the short walk to the dias in time to the music.

He faced the gathering with outward calm, flanked by the High Command of the US military, standing behind the armed Marine guards. He stared at the phalanx of microphones arrayed before him, and then said firmly, 'It is my honour to inform you that one hour ago I became the 45th President of the United States of America. As I believe you have been told, President McBride was compelled to resign at short notice for reasons of health. It was both unexpected, and unfortunate, and we all wish him a swift and full recovery.

'Meanwhile, the business of government must continue, and it is my most unhappy duty to inform you that today we stand in perhaps the worst danger this nation has ever faced. I will not take questions, but I will endeavour to outline the scale of a forthcoming terrorist attack we believe will happen . . .'

'*Any connection between the attack and the President's resignation . . . ?*' someone yelled.

'I wonder if you'd be kind enough to let my secretary know your native tongue?' replied the President. He was reading off Arnold Morgan's only offering of a riposte to unwanted questions.

The laughter subsided and Paul Bedford never missed a beat. 'Four months ago we received a communiqué from the Middle East that the terrorist organisation HAMAS had been responsible for the eruption of Mount St Helens in Washington State. Our investigations subsequently showed this was true.

'We were then informed that we had just a few weeks to remove completely our military presence in the Middle East and to force Israel to vacate the occupied territories on the West Bank. The Administration, needless to say, was sceptical about the validity of this demand, but cautious. We even moved some troops and ships around.

'However, we received another threatening communiqué, and this one contained a further detail – that if we did not comply, they would do the same to a volcano in the Canary Islands as they did to Mount St Helens.

A deathly hush had fallen over the Briefing Room as the journalists waited for President Bedford's next words.

He paused for a few moments longer, fervently wishing he had either Winston Churchill or Arnold Morgan passing him notes, never mind the one-side-one-sheet decree. He soldiered on, outlining briefly the scientific predictions.

'Well, President McBride remained sceptical. He was quite worried, but the military was *seriously* worried. And then came the final communiqué, which said, a) we will now show you what we can do, at midnight on Tuesday 29 September, and b) we will hit the volcano around 9 October.

Do you have American scientific opinion on this?

'Of course not,' replied the President, trampling all over his 'no questions' ultimatum. 'We never thought of that.'

This time he reduced the Associated Press reporter to a figure of fun. And once more he never missed a beat.

'And so, ladies and gentlemen, we are left with two tasks – to track down and kill the submarine which we believe launched cruise missiles at

378

Montserrat and Mount St Helens, and to begin to evacuate the East Coast. Just in case we are unable to achieve our naval objectives.'

'*Sonar*,' yelled a reporter, displaying a certain in-depth nautical knowledge. '*Can't we catch 'em on sonar?*'

'Well, we'd prefer trained dolphins but we may not have a enough,' shot back President Bedford. 'I have asked you not to interrupt me, particularly if you can only shed a glaring light on the obvious.' This was the sharp, sardonic turn of mind which would make the press more wary of this new President than they had initially expected to be.

'In any event,' Paul Bedford continued, 'this defensive operation is 100 per cent military. And I have appointed the former National Security Adviser Admiral Arnold Morgan to head up both the search-and-kill submarine operation and the evacuation programme. He has the total support of the most senior commanders in the US Armed Forces, who are standing behind me.

'That's all I have to say right now, but I hope you will urge your readers and viewers to cooperate fully at this most difficult time. There is enough time for everyone to leave, but we have to remain calm and organised. Naturally you will be informed of the day-to-day operations in the cities, and everyone is advised to move west to higher ground, to camp out with relatives and friends. If this tidal wave, or *tsunami*, hits, there will be no survivors. Everyone must leave the East Coast, under the guidance of the military . . . Thank you.'

President Bedford turned and walked out of the room, accompanied by Generals Clark and Boyce. Admiral Dickson remained with the Chairman of the Joint Chiefs, who now stepped up to the dias.

'For anyone who does not know, I'm General Tim Scannell, and I'm here to support the President. Right now I will be happy to answer five or six questions regarding the military, so make them pertinent, since we are very busy, as you may well imagine.'

Sir, will there be wholesale changes in key White House positions, Secretary of State etcetera . . . ?

'That's not military, but I do understand President Bedford will appoint a new Defense Secretary tomorrow.'

Can you describe the scale of the search in the Atlantic for the submarine?

'Not really. But we have decided that a wide search area of maybe a thousand miles out from the Canaries would be unlikely to succeed. Admiral Dickson, right here, believes a well-handled nuclear submarine might evade even a hundred US pursuers on an indefinite basis.'

How do you know it's nuclear?

'That's our appreciation of the situation.'

If so, how did the terrorists get it?

'I cannot answer that. But I will say if it's not nuclear we would have caught it by now, and will almost certainly catch it in the next ten days.'

Can't the sonars pick it up? We're always hearing how technically advanced the US Navy thinks it is?

'A modern nuclear submarine is just about silent under eight knots. And if he's running deep, over 500 feet below the surface, he's dead silent . . . anyone wants to ask more about the submarine, Admiral Dickson will answer.'

Sir, how will this tsunami *develop if the volcano erupts?*

'We're looking at a rock face maybe six cubic miles in volume crashing hundreds of feet down into the ocean. It will hit the floor, maybe 2,000 feet below the surface, and roll westwards, building to speeds of over 400 mph, like the ripples on a pond if you drop a big rock into it.'

How long to hit New York?

'According to the scientists – *all of the scientists,* that is – around nine hours from impact.'

Can the terrorists be stopped?

'Maybe.'

Can you outline your plan to find and destroy the submarine?

'No.'

Does that mean you do not yet have a plan?

'No. It does not. But to tell you is to tell the submarine and its masters.'

Will you be providing us with details of the evacuation plans?

'Absolutely. We will be on air again shortly to inform the public of evacuation measures and procedures. Thank you for your time. No more questions.'

General Scannell and Admiral Dickson left the dias and headed back to the Oval Office, leaving the Fourth Estate to tackle one of the biggest political and military stories of modern times.

They were accompanied by four Marine guards, and on the way fell into step with Henry Wolfson, Press Officer to Charles McBride and one of many senior staffers who would retain their positions in the new Administration.

He offered a handshake to the two officers and introduced himself. 'Guess our paths have never crossed before,' he said. 'But I have a feeling that that's going to change as from this moment.'

'Correct, Henry,' replied General Scannell. 'We're counting on you to try and keep this situation under control. The object is to prevent an outbreak of public panic without concealing the seriousness of the situation. We'll do a more detailed briefing on this later, but one thing's for certain. HAMAS did slam a broadside of big cruise missiles into both Mount St Helens last August and Montserrat last night.

'It would take something larger to blow the volcano in the Canaries apart. But a nuclear warhead on a medium-range cruise would probably do it. The bastards are firing from a submarine, submerged launch, and that's real hard to locate. You coming to see the President?'

'Yes, sir. And Admiral Morgan. And that scares the hell out of me.'

'Don't worry. His bite's worse than his bark.

And he scares the hell out of all of us at times. But I'm glad he's on board for this one.'

'That seems to be the general opinion around here, sir,' said Henry Wolfson. 'Makes everyone feel a little more confident.'

'We're supposed to be apolitical in the military,' said the CJC. 'But things are usually easier for us when the GOP are at the helm.'

They reached the Oval Office. Generals Boyce and Clark were just leaving and General Scannell joined them for the return journey to the Pentagon. Meanwhile, Arnold Morgan had turned the most hallowed room in Western government into a naval strategy room. He had charts of the Atlantic Ocean all over a central table that he had ordered to be brought up especially from the office of the National Security Adviser. It had a dark polished teak surface and had been in the same place since Admiral Morgan's own years in that office.

Cyrus Romney, the Liberal Arts professor from Berkeley, had been somewhat irritated by the sudden appearance of White House removal staff, and had demanded to know where his table was going.

'Oval Office, orders of Admiral Morgan,' was the reply.

Cyrus Romney, who had heard the rumours around the offices, had decided wisely not to pursue the matter, on the basis that he was certain he too, in the next couple of hours, would be making a similar but equally sudden exit from his office.

In the next thirty minutes, the table became a far busier place than it had been for many months. It now displayed charts of the western Atlantic and the approaches into the Leeward Islands, of the central Atlantic above the Mid-Atlantic Ridge.

There were maps of the western approaches to the Canary Islands, and three different charts of the Canaries themselves – one showing all five islands from Gran Canaria to Hierro, including Tenerife, Gomera and La Palma. Another showing the other two big islands of Lanzarote and Fuerteventura much further to the east, the latter only 60 nautical miles off Morocco's northwest headland.

The entire seven-island archipelago stretched east to west for 250 miles and Arnold Morgan had made but one mark on the entire nautical layout, a small circle located at 28.37N 17.50W, the main crater of the great Cumbre Vieja fault line.

Right now he was standing with President Bedford, scrutinising the depths of water which surrounded the island of La Palma, almost 10,000 feet 50 miles to the east, 5,000 feet all around the 1,000-metre line, 200 feet close inshore, and almost 100 feet sloping steeply west right below the cliffs – *almost on the goddamned beach.*

He glanced up as Admiral Dickson came in, the President having retreated to the far end of the room to speak with Henry Wolfson. It was clear already that the Oval Office was about to become Admiral Morgan's ops room, and that an army of possibly five cleaners and tidiers would be required twice a day to keep even a semblance of order.

The former President's secretary, Miss Betty-Ann Jones, the very lady who had been ordered to fire Arnold as soon as the result of the Presidential Election was known, was in the process of clearing her desk and preparing to leave for her home in Alabama. She had given herself no more than two hours to remain at her power desk, outside the Oval Office, since it was rumoured that Mrs Arnold Morgan was on her way into the White House, essentially to take charge of her husband's life while he tried to fight off the HAMAS threat.

Betty-Ann need not have worried. Arnold Morgan treated everyone the same, presidents, admirals, generals, ambassadors, emperors and waiters. Usually with impatience, occasionally with irritation, but rarely with malice. He would not have remembered the manner of his removal from office – only that he was leaving his beloved nation in the hands of people whom he judged to be incompetent to handle the task. That almost broke his heart. Phone calls from secretaries did not figure in the equation. But he did want his capable wife close at hand in the hours of duress.

'Where the hell's Kathy?' he growled to Admiral Doran.

'Who's Kathy?' replied the Commander-in-Chief of the Navy's Atlantic Fleet.

Arnold looked up from his charts, surprised. 'Oh Kathy? Sorry, Frank, I was talking to myself . . . pretty familiar phrase in my life – they'll probably inscribe it on my grave . . . *where the hell's Kathy?*'

'Is that Mrs Morgan?'

'That's her. The best secretary I ever had, the best looking lady who ever even spoke to me, and the best of my three wives, by several miles.'

Frank Doran chuckled. 'You expecting her, sir?'

'Damn right. I just gave her back her old job, and told her to get right down here to the West Wing, on the double.'

'Is she coming?'

'Well, she told me she'd give some thought to working again for the rudest man she ever met. But not to hold my breath.'

Admiral Doran laughed out loud at that, and ventured that everyone had to refrain from the impulse to speak to wives and children as if they belonged on the lower deck.

Arnold was about to reply when Kathy Morgan came marching into the office, looking, as ever, radiantly beautiful.

Without looking up, he snapped, ''Bout time. COFFEE! And call the Iranian Ambassador and tell him he's a devious lying sonofabitch.'

Admiral Doran was stunned. Admiral Dickson, who had attended this charade before, just shook his head. And Arnold leapt up from his desk and hugged his wife right in front of everyone.

Throughout all her years as Arnold's secretary she had always been astounded at the commands he gave her . . . call the head of this, the head of that, ambassadors and diplomats, and say the most frightful things to them. To Arnold Morgan a request for speed of reply from a senior Russian admiral translated to *Tell Nikolai whatsiname to get his ass in gear . . .*

The sudden order to lay into the Iranian Ambassador was a mere 'Welcome Home' to Kathy, who had promised to return to work only if it was for a two-week tenure.

Arnold introduced Frank Doran, and then instructed Kathy to tell that lady outside, Betty Something, that she was welcome to work as Kathy's assistant in the smaller office for a couple of weeks. Failing that, to tell her to go now, and get a replacement.

The former Kathy O'Brien knew the White House routines as well as anyone, but she balked at this. 'Darling, I cannot just arrive here and start firing people,' she said.

'Okay,' said Arnold, returning to his charts of the waters on the eastern Atlantic Ocean. 'Get Frank to do it.'

'I'm not firing President McBride's secretary!' said Admiral Doran.

'All right, all right,' said Arnold. 'I'll do it.' And with that he walked out of the door and explained to Betty-Ann that his secretary of many years was now in residence, and that she would be taking over. Betty-Ann should now clear her desk but she was more than welcome to stay as an assistant, in the smaller office, so long as she was sharp and stayed on her toes.

Admiral Morgan did not wait around for a chat. Having established his opening chain of command,

387

he returned to the Oval Office and trusted matters secretarial would somehow sort themselves out.

He sat at the head of his new table and suggested Admirals Dickson and Doran be seated on either side so they could each look at the Atlantic charts. 'We'd better have some coffee, and some cookies,' he told Kathy. 'None of us had any lunch. And can you make sure I have a pair of dividers, a compass, rulers, calculators, notepads and pencils?'

'How about a sextant and a telescope, since you appear to be going back to sea?' Mrs Arnold Morgan had lost none of her edge.

Just then the President himself arrived, and Arnold introduced him to his wife. 'You were very good on television, sir,' she said. 'Very neat the way you kept those reporters in line.'

'From the wife of Admiral Morgan, I'm taking that as a major compliment,' he replied, smiling. 'And you're nothing like so stern as he is – and much better looking.'

Arnold invited Paul Bedford to sit down and join them. 'I'm starting right now with our opening plan to trap that submarine,' he said. 'We'll finalise our evacuation plans tomorrow. But I want to get some heavy warships in the area into which we believe he's heading. We just might get lucky and trip over him, and I don't want to deny us that chance.'

'How many ships, Admiral?'

'I think for the moment we want to send in a dozen frigates. We can use the Oliver Hazard Perry guided-missile ships. Then I guess we want to move an aircraft carrier into the area, and pack its flight deck with helicopters.

'I think Admiral Dickson and I are agreed we're more likely to catch this bastard from the air, rather than in deep water with submarines. As you know, submarine hunts are very difficult. They usually end up with subs under the same flag shooting at each other by mistake.'

'Do we have a CVBG anywhere near?'

'We do. The *Ronald Reagan*, eastern end of the Mediterranean, maybe three days away. The frigates can all be in the area within six days – five of them are halfway there already, and the rest are ready to clear Norfolk tonight, five hours from now.'

'Did our departed President know that?'

'The hell he did. If we'd been listening to him, we would not have been ready.'

'One thing, Arnold. The communiqués from the terrorists. None of them actually mentioned Cumbre Vieja, did they? Are we certain we got the right volcano?'

'Sir, you have to get into deep volcanology to find that out,' chuckled Arnold. 'HAMAS mentioned the eastern Atlantic, and when you're talking tidal waves, that means the Canary Islands. Because of the height of the mountains, and the depth of the ocean.

'There is nowhere else in the Atlantic where such a *tsunami* could develop. And when you express that scenario to any volcanologist, they say before you finish your sentence . . . *Cumbre Vieja. Canary Islands.*

It's happened there before, and it will one day happen there again.

'It's not even the height of the mountains and the deep ocean which makes it unique. It's the enormous volume of underground water, the lakes beneath the volcanic range. That's what will explode the cliffs into the sea . . . if those bastards hit the Cumbre with a nuclear-tipped missile.

'And, Mr President, we have clear photographs of the HAMAS C-in-C standing on top of Cumbre Vieja, this year, with known Iranian volcanologists, studying the terrain. They also kidnapped, interrogated and then murdered the world's top volcano expert, in London, last May.'

President Bedford nodded. 'I guess that's about as decisive as it gets,' he said. Arnold spread out the big chart of the Atlantic in front of them and began a recap on the scale of the problem.

'Taking a point 400 miles from the island of Montserrat . . . puts him around here at midnight . . . twenty-four hours later he's probably here if he's steaming through these unpatrolled waters at around 12 to 15 knots . . . that puts him right here tonight and probably here tomorrow night . . . that ship he's in will have to move very slowly over the SOSUS wires, maybe six knots all the way across here . . . that's only 150 miles a day . . . won't reach the datum until 9 October, right? . . . bang on time, sonofabitch . . .'

'The question is, sir,' said Admiral Dickson, 'will he ever get that far? Maybe he'll just stand off and let fly with his missiles from, maybe 1,000 nautical miles out?'

'We can't let him, Alan,' said Arnold Morgan. 'We cannot let him.'

'Hard to know how to stop him.'

'Hard but not impossible. Question one. How do his missiles get their guidance?'

'They just hook up with the world global navigation system, the GPS,' replied Admiral Dickson. 'Steers them right in. The satellite does the rest. Punch in the numbers and fire 'n' forget.'

'Question two, Alan. Who owns the GPS?'

'Essentially, we do. There's twenty-seven satellites up there orbiting the earth every twelve hours. All American military, made available to all the world's navigators. They'll guide anyone home, friend or foe.'

'Correct. So, question three. How do we stop this bastard tuning his missiles into our satellites and homing in on the volcano's crater?'

'Well, I guess we could switch 'em all off, so nobody could access them.'

'Correct, Alan. And that would do just what I want him to do – drive him inshore. Because, when he comes to the surface to check his GPS, his screen will read, *satellites non-operational at this time*. And that will leave him no option. He'll have to fire visually, and that'll bring him in to around 25 miles from La Palma. Right there he will be forced to loose off his missiles using visual range and bearing only.

'And that's where we have a chance. Because we'll have our frigates and helos combing the area. When he comes to the surface for a visual fix, we might just pick him up him first time. And even if he gets his missiles away, we have two and a half minutes flying time to locate and kill with a SAM. Failing that, we'll have to rely on ground missiles, probably Patriots, set in a steel ring around the volcano . . . take 'em out before they hit.'

'It's going to take a lot of very brave men to man that missile battery, up there on top of the volcano,' said the President.

'We got a lot of very brave men,' replied Arnold Morgan, sharply.

'Will a nuclear warhead detonate if a Patriot slams into it, in midair?' asked the President.

'Probably not, sir,' said Arnold. 'These things do not explode on impact. You have to *make* them explode with split-second timing, crashing the two pieces of U-235 directly into each other with high explosive, and stupendous force, accurate to a hundredth of a second. A couple of hundred pounds of TNT designed to blow the entire rocket to smithereens, on impact, will not fulfil those explicit timing credentials. But it'll sure as hell disable it, and knock the damn thing into the sea.'

'What are our chances?'

'They're very good, once we switch off the GPS.'

'I was coming to that,' replied President Bedford. 'I assume we can't just shut it down and leave it at that, can we? I mean, what about all the navigation, all over the world . . . Christ, there'd be ships running aground all over the place, wouldn't there?'

'Sir, if we just shut off the GPS,' said Arnold, 'I'd

392

say we'd have a couple of dozen supertankers high and dry on various beaches within about five hours. The rest would be turning around in large circles, baffled by that most ancient of skills, or lack of it.'

'You're right there,' said Admiral Dickson. 'Most merchant ship navigators couldn't find their way out of the harbour without GPS. And most of them have grown up with it. We've had military satellites up there since the early 1970s.

'Your average navigator on a big freighter or a tanker knows nothing else. And there are probably 4,000 yachtsmen at any one time groping around the oceans entirely dependent on the GPS to find their way home.'

'Who runs GPS?' asked the President.

'Fiftieth Space Wing's Second Space Ops Squadron, out at Falcon Air Base, Colorado,' said Arnold. 'The full name of the system is NAVSTAR GPS. It's really a constellation of satellites, orbiting the earth, a space-based radio-positioning and time-transfer system. It provides incredibly accurate data – position, velocity and time. That's PVT in the trade.

'Over the years it has become a world-wide common grid, easily converted to other local datums, passive, all-weather operational; real-time and continuous information, and survivability in a hostile environment. It's a twenty-four-hour navigation service. And it's all-American, totally controlled from Colorado. We put all the satellites up there, right on the back of a Delta II expendable launch vehicle, out of Cape Canaveral, Florida.'

'And we can make the system non-operational?'

'We can do anything we damn please,' said Arnold. 'But we will have to give ample warning to the international community, otherwise the consequences might be horrendous.'

'It beats the hell out of me why we ever made this military asset available to everyone else,' said the President. 'Especially since the darn thing is so accurate.'

'Left to the military, it would not have happened. But Clinton's Vice President, the great universal do-gooder, insisted. Of course the military were furious, but Al's boss did not think much of the military, and that's why we got a bunch of deranged Muslims able to fire accurate missiles anywhere they like.'

Even Paul Bedford laughed at this vintage Morganian discourse, despite a certain loyalty to a fellow Democratic President.

'So when do we switch 'em off, Arnold?'

'Well, if the submarine's making 600 miles a day, and he's aiming to arrive and fire instantly, immediately making his getaway, I'd say he'll be within 200 miles of his launch zone by midnight on 7 October. He'll probably take a satellite fix in the small hours of the morning of the 8th, and then keep steaming in to his ops area. I guess we better shut the GPS off at midnight on Wednesday the 7th, and keep it off until either we destroy him or he fires his missiles.'

'That may be forty-eight hours with the world's

navigation system non-operational?' said Paul Bedford.

'Correct,' said Arnold. 'But at least they've got eight days to learn how to use a sextant, and take a look at the stars, and study the positions of the sun, and make their timing from GMT. Do 'em good. Turn 'em into proper sailors.'

'No alternative, is there?' replied the President.

'None that I can see. We have to switch off the GPS. Blind him. Drive him inshore. Force him to periscope depth.'

'Which side of the island,' asked President Bedford, peering at the charts.

'Oh, he'll come east, right Alan? Frank?'

'Not much doubt of that,' said Admiral Doran. 'At least, that's what I'd do. First, because I don't want to get turned over by the *tsunami*, which I would be if I was west of the impact when the mountain collapses. And second, because I could tuck myself right in here . . .'

Frank pointed at the chart with a pencil at the waters to the northwest of the island of Gomera. 'Right there,' he said, 'I'm in 1,000 feet of deep water with the land behind me. Sonars are never as good looking into the land, and that's what I'd be thinking; that I was trying to evade other submarines.

'I'd try to make it hard for the guys who were looking for me. I'd run deep and slow. Then I'd make my run in, right through this deep water, 7,000 feet on the chart, still moving slowly. I'd come to PD, take my mark on the island, one of these mountain peaks, get my range and bearing, then go deep again. Right here, 25 miles out I'd give myself a new visual check, then I'd fire, two missiles, fast. Then head for shelter, probably behind Gomera or even Tenerife – away from the tidal waves.'

'Jesus,' said Paul Bedford. 'I'm glad you're on our side.'

'The only trouble is, Mr President,' said Admiral Morgan, 'we have just one slight glitch.'

'Lay it on me.'

'There is just one other, smaller satellite system up there that we do not control. It's the European GPS, the Galileo project, which is still dwarfed by our own system. But it's there, and it works, and anyone can get into its guidance system. I imagine our HAMAS opponents are aware of this. But they must realise we will pull every trick in the book to screw 'em up. Therefore we must be aware of the problem. They might be navigating close in by the European system only.'

'We have to use everything in our power to blind our enemy,' replied the President.

'Which means, sir, I am about to award you a fairly disagreeable task . . . the central satellite we have to silence is called Helios. It's French and someone has to deal with 'em. And you know how cooperative they're likely to be if they get a call from Washington asking them to switch off their very own GPS . . .

'*Sacré bleu* and all that Gallic bullshit,' added

396

Arnold. 'And there is one other irritation which might actually turn out to be of major significance – when the Europeans began work on Galileo six years ago, they rowed in China for a 10 per cent share. Cost Beijing $400 million. Gave 'em not only the China–Europe Global Navigation Satellite System, they all agreed the Technical Training and Cooperation Centre would be based in Beijing. We now see China as our geostrategic rival of the future.'

'China, always damn China,' said the President. 'And you mean I have to tackle all of that? Because you know darned well the French will immediately say they have to ask Beijing.'

'Well, we'll ask Master Control Station at Falcon Air Base to send a request direct to Paris first,' said Arnold. 'Then we'll try frightening the French to death by telling 'em the *tsunami* will also flood their Brittany coastline, which it will. Then we'll have to go President-to-President.' Arnold Morgan paused, somewhat theatrically, then continued. 'And if none of that works, Mr President, we shall be obliged, on behalf of this great nation, both morally and ethically, under the Laws of Almighty God and Man, to shoot the fucker clean out of the stratosphere.'

CHAPTER TEN

Meanwhile, the evacuation of the East Coast had begun. The Federal Emergency Agency (FEMA) had split the mammoth task into five main categories: the general public; State and Federal Government; Culture and Heritage; Commerce and Industry; and Public and Emergency Services.

President Bedford had already announced a state of national emergency and immediately authorised the FEMA to oversee evacuation operations. They had handed over power to the Eastern Seaboard State Governments to mobilise local National Guard troops in all areas under threat. A principal part of the Guard's duties was to patrol urban areas, and 'maintain control on the ground'.

Plainly, as soon as the gravity of the situation had sunk into the mind of the public, a widespread panic would be inevitable, which the criminal element would most likely be swift to exploit. The President warned that in any cases of looting, particularly of Federal property, the National Guard was fully empowered to open fire.

A strategic review of the situation, and an

assessment of the overall threat, had been underway since earlier that day. Contingency plans were being finalised, and battalions of US Army forces were already rumbling down the highways towards Washington, DC, and the other three major cities of Boston, New York and Philadelphia.

The President's next speech, currently being drafted feverishly by Henry Wolfson, would warn of the specific effects of a 150-foot wall of water racing through the coastal shallows and thundering into the streets. It would be similar, he wrote, to the murderous destruction caused by the exploding island of Krakatoa in 1883: unstoppable, devastating and certain death for anyone who remained in its way.

The chaos would be wholesale, the water would level almost anything which stood in its way, huge waves would continue to pound the coastline after the initial shock. Great tracts of land maybe 15 miles from the beaches would be absolutely wiped out, power supplies damaged, communications severed, and there would be widespread saltwater flooding, fatal to infrastructure equipment and installations, like power stations, and domestic water utilities. Henry Wolfson actually managed to frighten himself.

The essence of this first draft was that every citizen had a duty to his country in the face of the coming onslaught from the deep. Every family should be attempting to find its own point of refuge, driving to friends or relatives who resided inland on higher ground, but some people should remain in the city, for several days if possible, to assist employers with the packing and removal of all items of value, principally from the Federal Government but also from private commerce. A special department was being set up to record when families vacated their homes, and precisely where they would reside during the coming catastrophe.

The evacuation of the poorer areas was an even more pressing dilemma, especially with regard to those under criminal justice supervision. Many did not have their own transportation or a place to go. Local authorities were being instructed to provide both, somehow; buses, trains, and reception areas, utilising schools and community halls beyond a 20-mile radius. They were already contacting towns and cities in nearby counties to the west and northwest, where the Blue Ridge Mountains leave Virginia and cross the border into Maryland.

The President's 7 p.m. speech was dramatic. The East Coast population, already stunned by the res-ignation of President McBride, now had to swallow the enormous significance of the mega-*tsunami*. The entire concept was so outrageous that people seemed unable to grasp this mammoth intrusion – the spectre of the destruction of the entire East Coast of the United States unacceptable and unimaginable.

People sat transfixed before their television screens as he outlined the opening steps everyone had to take in order to survive and to preserve what must be preserved.

The first signs of panic began almost as soon as he concluded the address. The White House switchboard was jammed by thousands of calls. The largest number of viewers in living memory hit the wires to the television networks, demanding more information. There was a late-night run on gasoline, lines quickly forming up and down the east coast as people prepared to fill up and move inland, right now, never mind 9 October.

On the heels of the President's announcement, the Department of Transportation announced that as of Monday morning 5 October, all ports and airports on the East Coast would be closed to incoming ships and aircraft – except for those aircraft specifically designated for evacuation purposes.

The London tabloids, five hours ahead of Washington, set the tone for the media bonanza, ruthlessly joining together the two American news stories, and on the streets by 2 a.m. East Coast time on Wednesday morning, 30 September.

MAC CRACKS UNDER TERRORIST THREAT

shouted the London *Daily Mail*'s headline, in end-of-the-world type, above a sub-head which read:

US President McBride Quits
White House Tyrant Morgan Recalled

One large single photograph of the new President was captioned: *Paul Bedford takes the oath, with Admiral Arnold Morgan at his side.*

It was, in fact, a dazzling front page, and all the twenty-four-hour American television news channels were showing it before 3 a.m. The *Mail* devoted six pages to the story, the lead being written by its star political feature writer, Tony Pina.

On a bright September afternoon of pure political theatre, Charles McBride yesterday resigned as the 44th President of the United States. He left secretly by Navy helicopter from the lawn outside the Oval Office.

Minutes later, Vice President Paul Bedford was sworn into office, before a select group of military chiefs which included the former National Security Adviser Admiral Arnold Morgan, the Chairman of the Joint Chiefs General Tim Scannell and the heads of the United States Navy and Marine Corps.

Senator Edward Kennedy was also in attendance for the ceremony which was conducted by Judge David Moore, who had been especially appointed by the Supreme Court.

Fifteen minutes into his Presidency, Paul Bedford summoned the White House Press Corps to the Briefing Room, where he explained that his predecessor had suffered a nervous breakdown and was under medical supervision at Camp David.

He then revealed that the United States had been under a monumental threat from a Middle Eastern terrorist group, which had already blown up Mount St Helens, the giant volcano in Washington State, and then exploded the simmering Caribbean volcano on the island of Montserrat on Monday night.

The threat to the USA was to erupt Cumbre Vieja on La Palma in the Canary Islands, thus setting off a mega-tsunami across the Atlantic, which would wipe out the American East Coast and greatly harm the shores of Western Europe and North Africa – unless the American President agreed to move its entire military force out of the Persian Gulf area, and strongarm Israel into an Independent State of Palestine, vacating the Left Bank territories.

So far as we know, the United States has made no effort to comply with these demands, and is believed to be conducting a massive search in the Atlantic to find a nuclear submarine, apparently containing the terrorists and submerge-launch cruise missiles with nuclear warheads.

Their threat, that horrendous prospect of a mega-tsunami, is believed to have proved too much for President McBride, who was reported to have collapsed on hearing the news the terrorists had hit Montserrat on Monday, carrying out a previous threat almost to the minute.

President Bedford has vowed to catch the submarine and destroy it and has announced plans to evacuate the cities of Boston, New York and Philadelphia.

Scientists say that from the moment of impact in the seas off La Palma, there would be just nine hours before New York City went under more than 100 feet of water.

On the opposite page was a large picture of Admiral Morgan in naval uniform, beneath the headline – THE RETURN OF THE IRON MAN. The accompanying story began:

Admiral Arnold Morgan, the former nuclear submarine commander who held the last Republican Administration together, was yesterday called out of retirement and summoned to the White House by the new Democratic President.

The White House confirmed the admiral has been appointed Supreme Commander of Operation High Tide, the code-name for the massive submarine hunt currently under way in the Atlantic to locate and take out the terrorist warship . . .

Since the Chairman of the Joint Chiefs had been reluctant to admit there was any connection between the McBride resignation and the threat from HAMAS, the US television networks had been reluctant to join the two stories. The devil–may–care treatment of the situation by the London papers, however, gave them all the Dutch courage they needed, and by breakfast time there was no doubt in the minds of any Americans. Charles McBride had cracked and wimped his way out of the Oval Office, afraid to face the personal torment of ordering his fleet into action to destroy an aggressor. Worse yet, he might not have had the courage to order an evacuation of the big cities and coastal communities. And there were several newspaper and television features on Arnold Morgan, 'The man the US Government apparently cannot do without.'

There were various headlines on the same theme:

ADMIRAL MORGAN – THE LION OF
THE WEST WING

THE DAY ADMIRAL MORGAN FACED-
DOWN CHINA

ARNOLD MORGAN – A MAN FOR
TROUBLED TIMES

ADMIRAL MORGAN – PATRIOT
OR A GLOBAL GAMBLER?

MORGAN – THE MAN WHO
FLEXES AMERICA'S MUSCLE

What no one wrote, anywhere in the world, was
that President McBride had been frogmarched out
of the Oval Office by a detail from the United States
Marine Corps, while the Service Chiefs looked on.

It had been a military coup of the kind that
usually happens in those restless countries around
the world where economic crises, drug wars and
power-hungry dictators had taken their toll. But with
the difference that this was America, Land of the
Free, where the coup, if the term even applied, had
lasted only ten minutes; after which order was
restored and the flag never lowered.

Wednesday morning, 30 September saw a drastic
change of pace in Washington. The entire city was
dominated by the military, the National Guard and
the police. All unnecessary business was halted,

criminal and civil cases were suspended, arrangements were made to evacuate court officials. In two instances it was necessary to isolate the juries, certainly for nine days, possibly for longer. Colleges and schools were preparing to close down at the end of the day. Hospitals were cancelling planned operations, discharging as many patients as possible, and preparing for the evacuation of the seriously ill.

The Army were already in the corridors assisting with the removal of high-value medical equipment. At some of the bigger establishments there were as many as six eighteen-wheelers parked outside emergency room entrances while the troops loaded up and recorded space-age hospital diagnostic machinery, in readiness for journeys to US Air Force bases on higher ground.

Hotels and motels all along the East Coast were refusing all new reservations and guests already in residence were asked to leave as soon as possible. The HAMAS threat was not, after all, from a group of reasonable, educated people. It was from a bunch of Middle Eastern brigands, who would stop at nothing, and who might even panic and blow Cumbre Vieja four or five days early, since it was now obvious the USA could not, or would not, comply with their demands.

If the *tsunamis* of Krakatoa were anything to go by, any heavy, freestanding objects, like automobiles, railroad cars, pleasure boats, even light aircraft, would be swept up and hurled around like toys. This applied also to more permanent structures like telegraph poles, statues, billboards, electric pylons and trees.

Evacuation of the areas was essential for every citizen. The FEMA was already drafting plans for removal and trucking corporations, even from outside the areas, to be sequestered by the government to support the evacuation. Railroad stock, both passenger and freight, would be put on stand-by.

In the meantime, Arnold Morgan pondered the difficult question of how to persuade the awkward and non-cooperative French to shut down the European GPS satellite Helios for a couple of days. The question was kicked back and forth in the Oval Office for three entire hours.

Finally, it was decided to make a formal request via the Master Control Station in Colorado direct to the French Government to close the satellite down for forty-eight hours, in accordance with the US closure. This would be in order to test significant improvements in the system, which would of course be shared, ultimately, with the Europeans.

All three admirals agreed this would receive a resounding '*non*' from their counterparts across the ocean. And at this point the US would come clean about their real reason for the GPS blackout.

Arnold Morgan had scientific data showing the path of the *tsunami* fanning out from the opening landslide all the way to the nine-hour hit zone along the US East Coast. In three hours it would be a wide crescent in the middle of the Atlantic, but also heading north, gigantic tidal waves already in the Bay of Biscay.

According to the scientists, the *tsunami* would likely thunder into the French naval headquarters of Brest three hours and thirty minutes from impact. The tidal waves would not be as great as those crossing the Atlantic, but they would form a 50-foot wall of water which would hammer its way onto the rugged westernmost tip of France.

The Americans knew they would have to explain the terrorist threat in some detail to the French, but that was unavoidable if they were to hunt down the *Barracuda* before it wiped out New York.

The sight of Arnold Morgan's *tsunami* maps was a chilling reminder of the reality of this wave of destruction. Cumbre Vieja represented a rare geological time bomb, one which could ravage countries on the other side of the world. Recent research into the last known mega-*tsunami* caused scientists to look carefully at the seabed around Hawaii, and they were astounded at what they discovered – the gigantic remains of ancient landslides, millions of years old. The *tsunami*'s first landfall to the west would be the northern coastline of Brazil, six hours after impact, waves 120 feet high. One hour later the *tsunami* would swamp the Bahamas and the outer islands of the Caribbean.

Two hours after that, the gigantic wave would roll straight up Massachusetts Bay and Boston would be hit by a 150-foot wave which would probably sweep away the entire city. The *tsunami* would then thunder onto the US coast, hitting New York next, then Philadelphia, then Washington, then the mainly flat coastline of the Carolinas, Georgia and Florida all the way to Miami and the Keys.

Arnold Morgan's dossier of recent studies estimated the first wave could be 2,000 feet high a half-mile west of La Palma, after the mammoth splash caused by maybe half a trillion tons of rock crashing into the water at 200 mph. Travelling at high speed, 160 miles in the first ten minutes, the wave would weaken as it crossed the ocean, but it would definitely still be 150 feet high when it hit the eastern seaboard of the United States.

On the other side of the Atlantic, the shores of Western Sahara would receive waves of 300 feet from crest to trough, although there would be shelter in the eastern lee of the bigger Canary Islands, Fuerteventura and Lanzarote, depending on where you found yourself as the tidal wave developed.

The scientists were also unanimous that a mega-*tsunami* off the Canaries, caused by a sudden volcanic eruption, would be the highest wave in recorded history. Even the south coast of Great Britain, not in its direct path, would be subject to serious flooding.

In world geohazard opinion, right there, laid out on Arnold Morgan's reclaimed office table, Cumbre Vieja was an absolute certainty to be next. Everything was ideal, the towering peaks of the mountain range, the colossal height, the depth of the ocean, the sonorous rumbling of the volcanoes, with the last explosion some sixty years ago in the south crater proving it was all still active, that the molten lava was not so very far below the surface. The underground lakes were ready to boil over at the instant of eruption. And, of course, the enormous fracture line crack in the cliff, which had already caused a 10-foot shift in the rock face high above the ocean.

The newest report pointed out, thoughtfully, that the last time a volcano had erupted with anything like the *tsunami* potential of Cumbre Vieja had been 4,000 years ago on the island of Réunion, a French territory since 1643, situated 420 miles east of Madagascar in the Indian Ocean.

A report from the Swiss Federal Institute of Technology, which had high-tech facilities to model waves created by landslides, said flatly, 'If the Cumbre Vieja were to collapse as one single block, it would lead to a mega-*tsunami*.

So far as the scientists understood, the volcanoes on the southwest flank of La Palma erupted about every 200 years. And there was no evidence that one single eruption would cause the landslide. In fact, it might take five eruptions. There was, of course, no section which dealt with the probable effects of a couple of 200,000-ton nuclear warheads blowing up in the middle of the Cumbre Vieja crater.

Admiral Morgan had another fearsome little aid to his presentation, a two-foot-square, 18-inch-high scale model of the volcanoes on the southwest corner of La Palma. It came from the University of California and had been flown in to Andrews by the US Air Force, arriving at the White House by helicopter.

The model showed the seabed to the top of the peaks, the steeply sloping volcanic cliffs falling away from the mountains, way down below the surface of the water. The shoreline was marked, highlighting the sudden sweep of the land into the depths. It showed the probable zones of the landslide on the seabed, and it illustrated starkly the tremendous impact such an avalanche would create on the water.

On the top of the model were the great peaks of Caldera de Taburiente, Cumbre Nueva, and, just below them, Cumbre Vieja, sitting atop a massive craggy rock wall, 2,000 feet above the ocean, which the model showed shelving down to a depth of 4,000 feet.

'Jesus Christ,' said Admiral Doran. 'That puts a pretty sharp light on it, eh?'

'Just look at the position of Cumbre Vieja, perched up there on top of the wall,' said Arnold. 'Just imagine what a nuclear bomb could do . . . Holy shit! We gotta find this bastard!'

'I've just been reading a damn good book by Simon Winchester about Krakatoa,' said Admiral Dickson. 'Been meaning to read it for years. That was one hell of an explosion . . . goddamned mountain blew itself to pieces, punched a damn great hole in the ocean, wrecked 300 towns and villages and killed 36,000 people. And you know what? Almost

411

all the destruction, and absolutely all of the deaths were caused by the *tsunami*. And the sonofabitch was nothing like as big as the one we're looking at.'

'Jesus, Alan. You're making me nervous,' said Arnold. 'But I guess we have to face reality, otherwise we'll *all* end up under medical supervision at Camp David.'

'Okay,' said Alan Dickson. 'We've sorted out the President. We've sorted out the French. Nearly. Now we're about ready to sort out the ships. Maybe Frank could give us a rundown on the Atlantic Fleet as it stands.'

'Perfect,' said Arnold. 'Lemme just call the President. He'd better sit in on this. Since he has been C-in-C of the Armed Forces for all of four hours.'

He called upstairs to the private residence and within five minutes Paul Bedford was back in the Oval Office, listening to the rundown of the Navy situation. He was a man who had never forgotten his days as a frigate lieutenant, and he often recalled the excitement of being a young officer, racing through the night at the helm of a US warship.

And predictably he asked questions no civilian would ever dream of. 'Frank, these Oliver Hazard Perry frigates. They were brand new when I was serving, and I haven't kept up . . . good ships?'

'Excellent, sir . . . 3,600 tons, 41,000 hp . . . couple of big gas turbines, single shaft, 4,500-mile range at 28 knots, need refuelling when they reach the ops area. But that's no problem. They pack a pretty good wallop too . . . four McDonnell Douglas Harpoon guided missiles, homing to 70 nautical miles at Mach zero-point-nine . . . plus ASW torpedoes.'

'Beautiful,' said President Bedford. And he really meant it. 'That little sonofabitch comes to the surface, he's history, right?'

'Just so long as we can see him,' replied Admiral Doran. 'And we are putting a lot of faith in the helicopters . . . you know each frigate carries two of those excellent Sikorsky SH-60R Seahawks . . . they got state-of-the-art LAMPS Mark III weapons systems. They're just great machines, 100 knots, no sweat, up to 10,000 feet.

'They're exactly what we need . . . airborne platforms for anti-submarine warfare. That *Barracuda* shows up where we think he'll be, we got him. Those helos have outstanding dipping sonar, Hughes AQS-22 low frequency.

'They all have USY-2 acoustic processors, upgraded ESM and Integrated Self-defence. Plus APS-124 search radar . . . and twenty-four sonobuoys. Those helos carry three Mk-50 torpedoes, an AGM-114R/K Hellfire Missile and one Penguin Mark-2.'

'I just hope the French cooperate,' said the President.

'They will ultimately not be a problem,' said Arnold Morgan. 'If they won't shut the damn thing off, we'll shut it off for them. I was not joking when I first said that. We'll shoot it down, because we don't have any choice.'

'This means,' said the President, 'you have entirely

abandoned the idea of a wide search out in the Atlantic, west of the islands?'

'Again, no choice,' replied Arnold. 'With a hundred ships out there in deep water we could still miss him easily. It's too vast an area, hundreds of thousands of square miles of water.'

'So we're sticking to a small force of just twelve frigates, plus the Carrier Group. Perhaps, Frank, you could let the President know where we are with the fleet right now?'

'Sure,' said Admiral Doran, flicking the pages of his notebook. 'We just diverted two ships from the Gulf of Maine on a southwest course to the Canaries, that's USS *Elrod*, under the command of Captain C.J. Smith, and USS *Taylor*, under the command of Captain Brad Willett.

'The *Kauffman* and the *Nicholas* were both in the North Atlantic, and have been heading south for the past three days. Captain Joe Wickman's *Simpson* was off North Carolina, and we sent him east two days ago. Tonight seven more frigates are due to clear Norfolk by midnight.

'That's the old *Samuel B. Roberts* commanded by Captain Clay Timpner – rebuilt of course, since she hit a mine in the First Gulf War; USS *Hawes* under Commander Derek DeCarlo, the *Robert G. Bradley*, under a newly promoted young Commander, John Hardy, from Arizona. Then there's USS *De Wert*, commanded by Captain Jeff Baisley.

'My old ship, the *Klakring*, will be ready next. She's now commanded by Captain Clint Sammons, from Georgia, who'll probably make rear admiral next year. The *Doyle*'s already on her way under Commander Jeff Florentino. And the USS *Underwood*, commanded by Captain Gary Bakker, will be the last away. She only came in yesterday morning.'

'How about the helos for the carrier deck?'

'We're sending the *Harry S. Truman* out from Norfolk with fifty Seahawks on board – they'll transfer to the *Ronald Reagan* flight deck as soon as possible, then bring the fixed wings home.'

'So that'll give us more than seventy Seahawks active over the datum?'

'Correct, sir. We'll be flying a lot of patrols around the islands, as from midnight on 7 October. He sticks that mast up for more than a few seconds any time in the next two days, we'll get him. If he doesn't have any satellites he'll need time to get an accurate range.'

'How accurate does his damn missile have to be?'

'If it's nuclear, which we're sure it will be, he can hit within a half-mile of Cumbre Vieja, and the impact would be terrific. But I think he'll try to bury those babies right in the crater. Remember, he's trying to blow the volcano wide open. He's not trying to knock the cliff down . . . because that won't be enough. He's vowed to erupt Cumbre Vieja, and he'll need time to set up for an accurate fix. And that's our chance . . . while his periscope's jutting out of the water, and we're sweeping the surface with radar.'

'There's a lot riding on this, Frank,' said the

President. 'A whole lot riding on the skill and sharpness of your boys.'

'Yes, sir. But if it can be done, they'll do it. Of that I'm in no doubt.'

President Bedford and Admiral Morgan refused all requests for interviews via the White House Press Office. There was a hot line established between the National Security Agency and the Oval Office. And Lt. Commander Ramshawe was constantly combing the myriad US intercepts for anything which might give a clue to the whereabouts of the phantom *Barracuda*.

At 11 a.m. on that first morning of Paul Bedford's Presidency he got one; vague, coded and not much use to anyone. But the US listening station in the Azores had picked up something which arrived from the satellite of the Chinese Navy's Southern Fleet. A short signal transmitted at 0500 (DST) on Tuesday morning . . . *A cruel sea for the songbirds.*

There was something about it which caught Ramshawe's attention. He stared at it, pondered its possible meaning. *Cruel sea . . . a cruel sea . . . the cruel sea . . . novel about the Navy . . . Nicholas Monsarrat! Holy shit! On the day the island volcano blew.*

Lt. Commander Ramshawe did not have the slightest idea about the difference in spelling. This might have been a message from anyone, to anyone. But it was in English, and it was on the Chinese Navy satellite. And it must have meant something to somebody.

So who's the bloody songbirds? He did not waste any more time thinking. He picked up the phone to his boss, Admiral George Morris, and recounted the signal. George thought slowly. Eventually he spoke. 'Jimmy,' he said, 'that's very interesting. Especially if those songbirds turned out to be canaries.'

'Hey! That's a beaut, sir. You got it. Can't be sure what it means, but it surely suggests the bloody *Barracuda* is on its way to La Palma.'

Neither of them knew that a new signal had just hit the Chinese satellite. Again brief . . . *RAZOR-MOUTH 71.30N 96.00E*. General Rashood, operating from Bandar Abbas, did not yet think that the Americans had already cracked the *Barracuda/ Razormouth* code many months previously. And in any case, the Americans who picked up the new signal would not understand the coded global positions. The numbers 71.30N 96.00E put the submarine somewhere in the landlocked foothills of the North Siberian Plain.

They should have read 21.30N (*minus 50 degrees*) 48.00W (*divided by 2*). Which put the *Barracuda* precisely where Admiral Badr had her . . . steaming at 15 knots hard above the eastern shoulders of the North Atlantic Ridge, right over the Kane Fracture Zone, more than 900 miles east-nor'east of the island of Montserrat. She was making a beeline for the Canary Islands.

When he went deep again after his transmission, Ben Badr would order a reduction in speed, down to nine knots in 600 feet, above the somewhat noisy waters of the Ridge. He would cut it further as they continued eastward, running softly over the quiveringly sensitive underwater wires of SOSUS.

'Well, Admiral,' he said, 'at least we know where the little bugger is headed. You want to call the Big Man, or will I do it?'

'You go ahead, Jimmy . . . I'm just looking over the comms plan for the command ship . . . we're using the *Coronado*, an old warhorse, newly converted.'

He referred to the 17,000-ton Austin Class former Landing Platform Ship which acted as Flagship Middle East Force as from 1980. The *Coronado* was the US Navy's flagship in the First Gulf War, and then flagship to the Third Fleet in Hawaii in the 1980s.

Commissioned in 1970, she had undergone three major conversions in a long life. A massive rebuild in the late 1990s saw her emerge virtually brand new. They turned her well deck into offices, with a three-deck command facility and accommodation for four flag officers.

She was twin-shafted, driven by a couple of turbines which generated 24,000 hp. All her combat data system were state-of-the-art, including an automated planning air control system and wide-band commercial. She used Raytheon SPS-10P plus G-Band for surface search and carried two helicopters.

After the turn of the century the *Coronado* became the US Navy's sea-based battle-lab, to act as a test-bed for new information technology systems.

At 9 o'clock that morning, the CNO Admiral Alan Dickson announced from the Pentagon that Rear Admiral George Gillmore, a former hunter-killer nuclear submarine CO, had been appointed Search Group Commander, Task Group 201.1. He would report only to Admiral Frank Doran (CTF 201 – CINCLANT), who now represented the front line contact, through which Arnold Morgan would remain close to all developments off the Canaries.

Admiral Gillmore had been the outstanding sub-mariner of his year, along with Captain Cale 'Boomer' Dunning, a fellow commanding officer from Cape Cod. When he took his first surface ship command, aboard the frigate *Rodney M. Davis*, George had quickly proved one of the best ASW officers in the Navy, in a class of his own in almost every exercise.

He had all the right qualities, including the ability to concentrate for hours at a time, the sharpness to react instantly to even a sniff of an underwater con-tact and the courage to act decisively when he was sure he'd found one. His long years underwater served him well. Admiral Gillmore could always recollect what he would have done had he been the hunted rather than the hunter. And he had an almost uncanny knack of being correct in his predictions. Bad news for Admiral Badr and his men.

A tall, bearded disciplinarian, George was based in the Atlantic Fleet, and he had already sailed for the Canaries from Norfolk in the small hours of Tuesday morning, two days previously, several hours before President McBride had left the White House.

It was the fact that such an act of open defiance towards a sitting President had been necessary, which had convinced Admiral Morgan and General Scannell that McBride simply had to go.

Admiral Gillmore's overall task would be to coordinate the search frigates, helos and the Carrier Battle Group ships in an intense and complicated operation, which might explode into action at any moment. He would have a staff of more than 100 men and eighteen officers.

Right now, as the announcement was made, Admiral Gillmore was familiarising himself with the new systems on board the *Coronado*. He was assisted by two lt. commanders and three lieutenants as he toured the ship's ops rooms, checking the comms, the sonar room, the radar, the navigation area and the GPS, which he alone knew would go dark at midnight on Wednesday 7 October.

The Navy Press Office issued a release to the media announcing the appointment of Admiral Gillmore, but a few doors down the corridor, in the Office of the CNO, there was a major disturbance. They had just received a communiqué from the French. On no account would they close down the European GPS. They cited the consequences to the world's shipping, the obvious hazards to yachtsmen and the prospect of beached freighters and tankers. They could not, in conscience, agree to such a course of action.

Immediately, Admiral Dickson prepared to go to Plan B, which would entail Admiral Morgan speaking to – or yelling at – the French Foreign Minister on a direct line to Paris.

Admiral Dickson was quite certain that the American admiral was capable of frightening the French into submission, which, under the circumstances, would be a wise course of action. There was no question in Alan Dickson's mind that Arnold would blow the Helios satellite clean out of the stratosphere if there was not immediate cooperation from France.

As the evacuation process continued, it quickly emerged that Washington's treasures posed a huge problem, mainly because the capital city was entrusted with the preservation of the national heritage, and all that the nation holds dear. Of the 750,000 residents of Washington, DC, 70 per cent were employed by the Federal Government, which meant that a broad structure was already in existence for easy dissemination of information and execution of the evacuation plans.

The greatest concern by far, in the city itself, was the vast range of fine art, documents and items of priceless value which record the birth, development and history of the nation.

Across the Potomac, a Special Ops Room was established inside the Pentagon, in the US Navy area. A large computer screen occupied an entire wall and two lt. commanders were marking out the west-nor'westerly direction of the incoming *tsunami*, as it would come driving forward off the Atlantic.

So far as they could tell, the one certainty was that the initial impact would be borne by the peninsula of land stretching south from Salisbury.

The path of the *tsunami* would be straight across the outer islands, onto the eastern shore of Maryland, a 150-foot wave taking out Salisbury completely. From there it would roll clean across the flatlands, drowning the Blackwater National Wildlife Refuge, and into the wide estuary of Chesapeake Bay. Speed: approximately 300 mph, causing massive flooding all the way north up the main channel and causing a tidal surge up the Potomac of 120 feet minimum, *if* the jutting headland of Pautuxet was able to remove some of the sting from the wave. By now it would have levelled probably fifty small towns and communities.

Minutes later, the great city of Washington, DC, would go underwater. Scientists on the line from the University of California were telling the Pentagon Ops Room they could expect a rise of at least 50 feet throughout the course of the Potomac River as far upstream as Bethesda, where it should begin to decrease to maybe 20 feet, up near Brunswick.

The waters would, of course, recede within a few days, but the damage would be inestimable, and on no account should anything be left to chance. Washington itself was particularly low-lying indeed, the Lincoln and Jefferson Memorials were built on land that was formerly a swamp. Some of the great city buildings might survive, but not many, and no human being should risk standing in the way of the tidal wave.

The Treasury, the Supreme Court, the Department of Defense and the FBI were effectively out of action for any new business. The CIA, perilously situated just north of the Georgetown Pike, on the west bank of the Potomac, where the river sweeps downstream to the right, was beginning a massive salvage operation of some of the most sensitive documents in the country, not to mention the kind of high-value equipment and files which could cause a world war should they be washed up in the wrong place.

Like their colleagues in Federal Government offices, they were packing and dispatching computers, hard drives, documents, archive material and valuable records. Department staff were packing the stuff into military cases, all numbered and recorded, before making the journey under armed guard to Andrews Air Base, over in Georges County. From there they would be flown under guard in the giant C-17 transporters to carefully selected US air bases, beyond the reach of the floodwaters. Those cases would be stored in Air Force hangars, closely guarded around the clock by Federal troops with orders to shoot intruders on sight.

Over on Independence Avenue there was a major operation in the Library of Congress. Things had been relatively calm in there since they had moved into their new building as long ago as 1897. But the Library was no stranger to catastrophe, twice having burned down when it was located in the Capitol in the first half of the nineteenth century.

Today the activity was close to frenzied as troops from the air base joined the staff trying to pack up more than eighty-four million items of information, in 470 languages.

This was the world's largest library, its books, pamphlets, microfilm, folios of sheet music and maps were all stored in three great stone centres of learning, named after three of the Founding Fathers, three Presidents: the main Thomas Jefferson Building, lavishly decorated in Italian Renaissance style, the James Madison Memorial Building and the John Adams Building, all located to the rear of the US Supreme Court.

Into the big packing cases the troops and the permanent staff were bundling the first volumes of the most priceless source of information in the entire country, the fountain of knowledge used by Congressmen, Senators and selected researchers from all over the world.

To complicate the task still further, the US Copyright Office, with its unique store of critical business data, is also located there. It would take twenty-four-hour shifts every day until the ocean crushed the city to move even half the contents of the great buildings on Independence Avenue.

Over on Pennsylvania Avenue, behind the giant stone columns of the National Archives, a more delicate operation was under way. Curators and troops were working in the midst of this final repository of all US Government documents, packing up documents beyond price – the Declaration of

Independence, the Constitution, the Bill of Rights, all destined for Andrews Air Base, from where they would be flown to secure US military establishments and guarded night and day.

Up on 14th and C Streets there was a total evacuation from the Bureau of Engraving and Printing, where $35 million of US Government bank notes were printed every day, just to replace the old ones. In here they also printed postage stamps, government bonds, licences and revenue stamps. There was a US Marine guard of more than 100 men forming a cordon around this building while the presses were dismantled and crucial components carried out to the waiting trucks.

All along Washington's imposing Mall area the story was the same. The evacuation was under way. Military trucks lined the avenues, parked two deep outside the Capitol itself, and similarly inside the grounds of the White House. Historic portraits, ornaments, furnishings and furniture were being loaded by Marines along with Presidential papers and records.

Critical offices of government remained open, and inside the Oval Office Admiral Morgan and Admiral Frank Doran wrestled with the problem of the United States Navy's warships. They had to be removed, fast, from all dockyards on the East Coast that would be sure to be smashed to rubble. And they could not head east to assist with the submarine operation around the Canaries, not into the jaws of the *tsunami*. They had to be sent into calmer waters, and the two admirals pored over the charts. Not even the submarine jetties up in New London, Connecticut, were safe.

And certainly it was too great a risk to send several billions of dollars worth of nuclear submarines into deep waters in the hopes that the huge waves of the *tsunami* would simply roll over them. No one knew the depth of the turbulence which accompanied such a wave, sub-surface, and it was clear that the submarines would have to follow the same route as the East Coast-based frigates, destroyers, aircraft carriers and the rest into a sheltered anchorage.

Frank Doran had considered the possibility of running the ships north, into the 30-mile-wide Bay of Funday, which divides southern Nova Scotia from Canadian mainland New Brunswick.

'There's no problems with ice up there at this time of year,' he said. 'We could push the fleet north as far as Chignecto Bay . . . that'd put a hilly hunk of land 60 miles wide between the ships and the Atlantic. They'd be safe in there.'

But Arnold did not like the surge of the waves from the southwest, and he was afraid the *tsunami* might curl around the headland of Funday and then roll up the bay, dumping ships on the beach. There would be no possibility of escape in the shallow confined waters of Chignecto, and, generally speaking, Admiral Morgan preferred to send the fleet south.

'But the Caribbean may be under worse threat than anywhere,' said Frank. 'This document we have here from the University of California says the tidal wave will hit the coast of Mexico, never mind Florida.'

'I know,' said Admiral Morgan. 'But Florida's a very big chunk of land. It's more than 100 miles wide even at its narrowest, and scientists do not expect the tidal wave to last much more than 12 or 15 miles at most, once it hits land. I'm saying we should get the fleet south, around the Keys and then north into the Gulf of Mexico, maybe up as far as Pensacola . . . anywhere there's deep water along that Gulf Coast . . . because there's got to be shelter under the armpit of Florida . . . are you with me?'

'I am,' said Admiral Doran. 'And like all sailors, I'd rather go south than north.'

'You're not going anywhere,' said Arnold Morgan, 'except to your office in Norfolk. And you'll be running the show 'til those missiles come bursting out of the ocean. That is, if your boys don't nail him first. I just wish they were attacking from anywhere else on earth, rather than a nuclear submarine. Anywhere, anything. I'd rather they were attacking from outer space than from a nuclear boat, sub-merged launch.'

'So would I,' replied Admiral Doran. 'Meanwhile I'd better get back down to Norfolk. Every time I look at the place I think tidal wave and the havoc it would cause down there. That thing could pick up a 100,000-ton carrier according to the scientific assessments. And if it didn't do that it would most likely crush the big ships against the jetties.

'I know that the cities are badly threatened, but

a *tsunami* could just about wipe out the Navy on the East Coast. That thing comes in from the southwest, it'll slam straight into Virginia Beach and then take out all three of those bridges/tunnels across the Hampton Roads. And the land's so flat, just a maze of docks, dockyards, creeks, lakes and rivers all the way in from the Atlantic.'

'Don't remind me, Frank. And how about the shipyards, Newport News and Norship, all in the same darned complex. Christ! We got two aircraft carriers half finished in there . . . couldn't hardly move them if we tried – except with tugs . . . not to the west coast of Florida.'

Frank Doran shook his head. 'And we have to get Kings Bay, Georgia, evacuated. We got four Ohio boats in there, and God knows how many of those Trident C4 missiles. Probably enough to blow up most of the goddamned universe, and we're prancing around trying to find a bunch of guys dressed in fucking sheets underwater.'

Admiral Morgan chuckled. He really liked Frank Doran and his unexpected humour. The task that faced them both was truly overwhelming, and they had to fight against letting it take over. They had a chance to nail the *Barracuda*, both men knew that, if it came to periscope depth. And if it didn't, and just fired straight at the volcano, they had a chance to nail its missiles, surface to air. Failing that, there was one final line of defence, the steel ring of Patriot missiles around the rim of Cumbre Vieja, which would hit back. If they had time.

Failing those three options, life would not be the same on the East Coast of the USA for a very long time.

'Okay, sir, I'm out of here. I'll put the evacuation plan for the Gulf of Mexico into operation right away. If it floats, and it steams, that's where every ship is going. I think we better get those ICBMs to sea and headed south as quickly as possible. But we might have to commandeer a few commercial freighters to vacate the submarine support station. There's a million tons of missiles and other materiel in there. And it's absolutely vulnerable, right on the Atlantic coast, protected by nothing more than a couple of sandbanks.'

'Don't tell me, Frank. I used to work there,' said Arnold, shaking his head. 'Is this a goddamned nightmare or what?'

Admiral Doran walked to the door of the Oval Office. 'You coming back tomorrow?' asked Arnold.

'Uhuh. In the morning. We might have some better news by then.'

1930 (local) Friday 2 October 2009
Damascus, Syria
Ravi and Shakira were back in their home on Sharia Bab Touma. Admiral Mohammed Badr had decided that satellite signals between the Iranian naval base at Bandar Abbas and the *Barracuda* were too vulnerable to American interception, so their expertise and advice were not needed right now. All they could do was wait.

429

The Americans could intercept anything, with the National Security Agency's Olympian ability to eavesdrop on anything, anywhere, any time, and very little was transmitted from the Navy bases of potentially troublesome countries without Fort Meade knowing about it, chapter and verse.

So General and Mrs Rashood had evacuated their lush guest quarters in Bandar Abbas and flown home to Damascus. And there, high in the rambling house they had lived in when they first were married, was a state-of-the-art satellite transmitter and a state-of-the-art receiver. But the path of the signals was Damascus–satellite–Tehran–satellite–Zhanjiang–satellite–*Barracuda*.

On the way back it was precisely the same in reverse, all coded. Ravi made his way back down the stairs holding the latest message from Ben Badr, which read simply 72.30N 76.00E. The HAMAS general quickly decoded the true position and marked the spot on his map of the Atlantic.

Ben had made almost 10 knots since Tuesday morning, covering 700 miles across the Mid-Atlantic Ridge. The *Barracuda* was now almost on the line of the Tropic of Cancer, creeping at only five knots over the SOSUS wires. They were roughly 775 miles short of their ops area, which at this speed, 120 miles a day, was six and a half days away. Ravi's fingers whipped over the buttons on his calculator. It was now around midday on Friday where the *Barracuda* steamed, and they should arrive at the Canaries firing zone around midnight next Thursday 8 October.

'Right on time for the hit,' said Ravi to himself. 'Just pray to Allah the SCIMITARs work again.'

'I'm hearing a certain amount of mumbling here,' said Shakira, who had just appeared in the doorway to the kitchen. 'Would you like some tea, to calm your nerves?'

'Thank you. That would be perfect,' said Ravi. 'By the way, I've just received a signal from the *Barracuda*, and it's good news. They report no illness or casualties, they're right on time, right on course, in mid-Atlantic, 775 miles short of La Palma.'

'I was just watching CNN on the television,' said Shakira. 'The Americans are very concerned. The President has broadcast twice, and an evacuation of the East Coast is in full swing. They seem to have accepted the reality of our threat.'

'Are they saying anything specific about their defensive measures . . . you know, a deployment of ships around the islands?'

'Nothing much, only that they'll be starting an extensive search for the *Barracuda* soon.'

'Hmm,' replied Ravi. 'They'll have a lot of search power out there, but I don't think they'll be able to catch Ben. He's firing from 300 miles out, way to the southeast . . . and so far as I can see, there's no way they'll catch him in that deep water . . . not if he stays slow and deep, and launches from two or three hundred feet below the surface.'

'I don't think we've ever missed anything,' said Shakira, thoughtfully. 'You think our luck will hold?'

431

'This isn't luck. It's planning,' said Ravi. 'Planning over a long period of time.'

'You think they know it's definitely a submarine, definitely launching missiles at the volcanoes from below the surface?'

'Hell, yes,' said General Rashood. 'They know that.'

'Well, what would you do, if you were them?'

'Evacuate,' said Ravi. 'As fast as I could.'

'Nothing military or naval – no aggressive action.'

'Well, I'd certainly send ships out to hunt for the submarine, but the Atlantic's a big place. I would not hold my breath.'

Shakira was still thinking. 'You know, my darling,' she said, 'I spent a lot of time plotting and planning with the missile guidance systems. They do work from the satellites, you know.'

'Just on the regular Global Positioning System.'

'How about if the Americans somehow interfered with that. Made it non-operational?'

'Well, I believe there's nearly thirty satellites up there, and I've always thought they were involved in television, telecommunications and all kinds of things. And every ship in the world is entirely dependent on them for navigation. I don't think even the Americans could somehow turn off the entire communications and navigation system for the whole world. They'd be too afraid of the lawsuits that would probably amount to billions of dollars.'

'Let's hope they are,' said Shakira, pouring tea

into two glasses with little silver holders. 'Otherwise, Ben will miss our target.'

The Fort Meade code-breakers had almost completed their job. Admiral Morris had taken the first signal off the Chinese Navy's satellite and drawn a large circle on a chart of the North Atlantic.

'That's where we think the *Barracuda* is,' he said. 'In there somewhere. We are almost certain this signal with the numbers 71.30N 96 00W is reporting her precise position. Try to come up with something, will you?'

Shortly before noon on the previous day, the code-room had come up with a close solution. '*On the first number, we think they just subtracted 50 . . . or maybe 49 or 48. No more. On the second number the W for West, means E for East. And we are nearly certain they just cut the number 96 in half. Which would give us 21.30N 48.00W, and that's right about in the centre of the circle.*'

Admiral Morris and his assistant were delighted with that. And they were waiting anxiously for a new signal. At 12.30 p.m. Lt. Commander Ramshawe located something on the Chinese satellite . . . *OLD RAZORMOUTH 72.30N 76.00E.*

Jimmy whipped fifty off the first number and divided the second one in half. He changed the West to East and came up with 22.30N 38.00W. He checked on his detailed computerised chart of the

433

central Atlantic and recorded the precise spot in which he believed the *Barracuda* had been steaming, probably three hours earlier. He checked back with the previous numbers and plotted the submarine 700 miles further east than it had been on Tuesday morning.

He calculated the speed, and, like faraway General Rashood, assessed it at just below 10 knots. *He keeps that up he'll spring one of those SOSUS wires for sure in the next few hours.* Jimmy Ramshawe's confidence was rising by the minute. The submarine was slightly further north, maybe 60 miles, but the overall difference was definitely 700 miles. That put her on a direct route to the Canary Islands.

He called Admiral Morris, who guessed it might take four hours to get surveillance ASW aircraft into the area, which would mean the *Barracuda* would be possibly 70 miles further on. But they had no further guarantee of her course, which could change at any time. And that presented a large surface area, as much as 5,000 square miles, to search.

George Morris called Admiral Morgan, who followed the conversation on his wall-sized computer chart, which was now in the Oval Office. He said to put the information on the wire immediately to Admiral Doran in Atlantic Fleet Headquarters, Norfolk, and to the CNO in the Pentagon.

'George,' said Arnold. 'This comes down to the same thing as always. A huge area to search, out in the middle of the Atlantic, and almost no chance of catching him if he's deep and quiet. Also we don't know the timing of the signal from the *Barracuda*.

'I think Jimmy's right. It was probably sent three hours before we picked it up. But it could have been yesterday. This bastard is very smart. Note there was no time and date on the signal. I guess they know when he's scheduled to transmit, and so long as he says nothing, they know he's on schedule.

'But I continue to think any kind of a wide search in the remotest areas of the Atlantic is hopeless. We're not going to find this sonofabitch until we can drive him inshore. Then we have an excellent chance.'

Ten minutes later, Admiral Doran was on the line to the Oval Office. His view was the same as Arnold's. 'We could waste an enormous amount of time and effort out there. And it's still only about a 5 per cent chance we'd catch him,' he said. 'The value of that signal is it confirms the existence of the *Barracuda*. And it confirms roughly where he is, or was, plus his course, and obvious destination. We just have to force him inshore . . . any luck with the French?'

'I'm speaking to their Foreign Minister in a half-hour, Frank. At this stage I'm not hopeful. I think it's going to come down to President-to-President. But I'll be doing my best to scare this little sonofabitch in Paris.'

Admiral Doran replaced the receiver. He instructed someone to alert all Atlantic ships as to the perceived whereabouts of the *Barracuda*. And then he returned to the colossal task of evacuating the Norfolk shipyards.

One hour later, thirty minutes late, Kathy put the French Foreign Minister on the telephone. Arnold did not know the man, and decided that politeness was the sensible course to steer. They introduced themselves formally. The Frenchman spoke good English and the admiral decided to come straight to the point.

'Minister,' he said, 'you probably already know why I'm calling. You must have read about the terrorist threat in the newspapers, right?'

The French minister confirmed and impressed his apprehension upon the admiral.

His government had just received a report from the Swiss Federal Institute of Technology about the likely effects of a *tsunami* caused by the explosion of the Cumbre Vieja, and were concerned with the apparent seriousness of the situation. However, his government wasn't yet fully convinced that the threat was actually real; contrary to the States, they had seen no hard evidence that it would take place.

Arnold asked him simply to accept, on trust, the opinion of the United States military on this matter. 'Mind you, we intend to do everything in our power to stop them,' added Arnold. 'And we're not asking for assistance, though there will be damage to the cities and coastlines of many other nations.'

'Yes, the Swiss scientists confirm the damage would be widespread,' was the reply.

'And, of course, your own coast in Brittany may be on the receiving end of a very substantial tidal wave, possibly 80 feet high, straight into your Navy headquarters in Brest. That's almost as much trouble as we'll be in four hours later.'

'I understand,' said the Frenchman hesitantly. 'The issue for us is, firstly, do we believe in the threat? Secondly, do we think it is sufficiently serious for us to dismantle the entire European Global Positioning System? I'm sorry to say that the answer would be no.'

'Well, we are not asking for a complete dismantling,' said Arnold. 'Just a forty-eight-hour shutdown, if we have not already located and destroyed the submarine. You do understand that we will black out our own satellites, which represents a total of 90 per cent of all the Global Positioning Systems in space?'

'I imagine you will, Admiral. Given your history with the Middle Eastern nations, I'm afraid the French Government does not approve of anything you do east of the Suez Canal.'

'Then I am obliged to inform you of the consequences. First, you will lose your Navy on your west coast. The Atlantic peninsula of Brittany will be catastrophically flooded. Secondly, you will forfeit the goodwill of the United States for a very long time. And should the eruption take place on La Palma with all that it entails, we will not hesitate to make public the fact that it was France which essentially caused it, refusing even a modicum of cooperation in the cause of preventing a world disaster.

'Thirdly, the President of the United States will ask Congress to approve a Bill to level a 100 per cent tariff on all French goods entering the United

States. And fourthly, we will lock you out of the oil markets of both Iraq and Saudi Arabia, both of which we effectively control. Which would seem a pity, for the sake of turning the fucking lights out for a couple of days.'

'I will relay your thoughts, and your threats, to my President,' replied the French Foreign Minister.

But Arnold had already slammed down the phone. '*Vive la France*, asshole,' he growled, to the mild surprise of Kathy, who had just come through the door with his roast beef sandwich, mustard, mayonnaise.

'Everyone's late today, the French Foreign Minister, the sandwich . . . I'm being treated like someone who works in the mail room.'

Kathy laughed. 'No luck with Paris?'

'None. Can you get the French Ambassador in here right away. I need to try to get him to understand.'

'Now?'

The level of jocularity between the two was at its lowest in recent memory. Outside the door, removal men were carrying priceless tables and lamps along the corridor. Army trucks were lined up outside. Officers were checking and recording every treasure every step of the way. The Pentagon had taken over the networks on the East Coast, broadcasting twenty-four hours a day from the Press Briefing Room four doors from the office of the Chairman of the Joint Chiefs.

Government spokesmen were already urging families with no commitment to employers in

Washington to leave the city in order to ease congestion. Traffic was being directed to state highways to the north and west, leaving Interstates 66 and 270 in the main for Federal convoys and other official traffic.

It was a little over two miles to the French Embassy, located on Reservoir Road on the northern border of Georgetown University. And Arnold Morgan awaited the arrival of the Ambassador with growing impatience. Finally, Gaston Jobert showed up at 2.20 p.m. and Kathy ushered him into the Oval Office, where he was greeted by both Admiral Morgan and the President.

Kathy brought them coffee, and M. Jobert sat and listened to the chronology of events from beginning to end. Arnold left out nothing, from the missiles identified at Mount St Helens to the blasting of Montserrat. He explained the HAMAS demands, the impossibility of complying with them, and he explained the strategy of the United States Navy. Above all, he specified the critical nature of the GPS satellites.

'Generally speaking,' said Arnold, 'he'll send his missiles in under guidance from our own satellites. If he cannot locate them, he'll search for the European one. And if he locates that, he'll use it.

'If he runs into a blackout situation, he'll have to come inshore, for a visual firing. And that's when we'll get him. Needless to say, I am mystified at the attitude of your government, and I have invited you here essentially in order for you to make them see sense.'

'Does my government know the full history, the submarine, the missiles and everything?'

'Pretty much.'

'Well, I have understood with much . . . er, clarity . . . I see it would be very bad for France . . . if we were seen . . . to, er . . . have stopped you catching this submarine before it destroys your coast, and part of ours as well. That would be absolutely crazy . . .'

'Well, M. Jobert, *we* know that, but I am afraid your Foreign Minister has not understood so well as you have,' said the President.

M. Jobert, a debonair man of around fifty, slim, dark, Gallic in attitude, replied, 'This was M. Jean Crepeau?'

'That's him,' said Arnold. 'A very anti-American little man, actually, which is somewhat absurd in the world today. Can you imagine us refusing to help you in this way if Paris was under threat of a major terrorist attack?'

'No, Admiral Morgan. No. I cannot. But I have lived here for many years. I am very fond of the Americans, and this rather embarrasses me, as it will, in the end, embarrass my government.'

M. Jobert paused for a moment and sipped his coffee. 'For a diplomat, I am going to speak out of turn. But you have been frank with me. M Crepeau is a man whose political ambitions are very much greater than his abilities. And our Prime Minister is not much better. But in the President himself, Pierre Dreyfus, you have a man of far greater stature and far more sense . . . a little too proud for his own good. But a man of intelligence and judgement.

'Most people in my government are afraid of him . . . on the other hand I am not, mainly because he's married to my sister, Janine. I've known him since we were both about fifteen years old.

'I have already discussed this with him. And I think a call direct from President Bedford tomorrow morning will sort this out fairly quickly. In the end, France has no option because in the end you would shoot our satellite down, *n'est ce pas?*'

Admiral Arnold smiled grimly. 'You would leave us very little choice,' he replied. 'The cities of Washington and New York, against your little sputnik Helios? No contest.'

M. Jobert stood up to go. 'You may leave it with me, gentlemen,' he said. 'I will speak to the President at length this evening. I'll tell him it's too much trouble to refuse your request . . . I believe the expression was '*a pity for the sake of turning out the fucking lights for a couple of days . . .*'

'Nicely put,' said Arnold Morgan.

CHAPTER ELEVEN

0800 Saturday 3 October 2009
Mid-Atlantic 23.00N 38.40W
Depth 600. Speed 6

Admiral Ben Badr held course zero–six–zero as they moved across the black depths of the Cape Verde Plain. Young Ahmed Sabah, Shakira's brother and HAMAS officer, had become a trusted confidant of the *Barracuda*'s CO and the two men were studying the charts of the eastern Atlantic with Lt. Ashtari Mohammed, the British-born Iranian navigator.

Nothing is real until it faces you, and what had once looked like a simple run into the Canary Islands now looked fraught with peril. They both understood that the threat which General Rashood had issued to the Pentagon had been made public. Plainly the United States was taking major steps to locate and destroy them, and the nearer they crept towards the Canary Islands, the more dangerous the waters became.

Neither officer had the slightest idea what form the US defence would take, but Admiral Badr, a former submarine and surface CO himself, felt confident that they would not resort to a submarine hunt.

'They won't risk them firing at each other, Ahmed,' he said.' I think it is much more likely that the Americans will go for frigates or destroyers with towed arrays. As long as we stay dead slow and deep we'll be almost impossible to find. The one worry I do have is the satellites. We need them for guidance of the SCIMITARs – and the GPS is just about entirely American.

'If they believe we are going to wipe out their East Coast, they may just shut down the whole system. Which would be pretty bad for us. Because that would leave only the European system and I'm not sure we can log on to it. Whereas everyone has access to the US system.'

'Do you think the Americans could persuade the Europeans to shut down at the same time?'

'Well, the Brits would cooperate. But the French might not. My own view is that they will somehow *not* get both systems to shut down at the same time . . .'

'But what if they do?' Ahmed was wide-eyed and very worried.

'Then we have no alternative. We'll go inshore, take a visual range and bearing, and open fire on Cumbre Vieja. The SL-2 has one advantage . . . its nuclear warhead does not need the critical accuracy of the SL-1 non-nuclear. We bang that thing in there within a half-mile, we'll split that volcano in half. The burning magma will do the rest.'

443

'How close do we need to be?'

'Around 25 miles. So long as we can see enough through the periscope to get a good visual fix on the volcano.'

'Where do we fire from?'

'We'll have to see. If the satellites work we'll launch from range 250 miles . . . from this point here, about 30 miles south of the most easterly island, Fuerteventura. That would put us in very deep water around 30 miles off the coast of Western Sahara.

'The moment we fire, we turn north and make all speed for the eastern coast of Fuerteventura . . . right here, see . . . off the town of Gran Tarajal. That's going to take us one hour from the point of launch. But the missile will take twenty-five minutes to get there, the main explosion causing the landslide will take an estimated ten minutes and then the *tsunami* will take another thirty minutes to reach the west coast of our island . . . not the east coast where we will be sheltering . . . the wave will go right past us. And we'll just hang around under the surface until everything calms down.'

'How about they DO get the satellites shut off? What do we do then?' Ahmed was fast realising the enormous risks they were taking.

'Then we would have to come inshore, from the southwest . . . making for this point here.' Ben Badr pointed to the chart at a spot 20 miles off La Palma, in very deep water, 8,000 feet. 'Right here we take our visual fix, we range these two points here on the chart . . . two lighthouses, Point Fuencaliente, right here on the southernmost headland of the island . . . and then, nine miles to the north, Point de Arenas Blancas. We'll see them both clearly through the periscope, right?'

'Yes sir, Admiral.'

'In between those two points, is Cumbre Vieja. We have all the data we need on its precise spot, satellite photographs. We then take a third point, a mountain peak . . . and we take range and bearing . . . it's a regular three-point fix. And even if the satellites are down, we can come back to that exact spot in the ocean, any time we wish, with just a quick glance through the periscope.

'The next time we come back, we launch the SCIMITAR SL-2 straight at the volcano, and this missile cannot miss . . . because it doesn't have to be accurate . . . even allowing for errors caused by wind direction, wind speed, turning circle, height adjustments . . . it still can't miss . . . The warhead is so enormous, even if it is swept a half-mile off course, it will still blow the volcano.'

'Admiral, have you given any thought about how we get away afterwards?'

'Yes. I have. So has your brother-in-law. Somewhere in the South Atlantic, somewhere lonely, we bail out and board an Iranian freighter. The submarine will blow itself to pieces a half-hour after we all leave. We have to scuttle her in the deepest water we can find. So she'll never be discovered. Then we sail home on the freighter, disembarking a few men at a time, at various ports, all the way to Iran.'

'So right now you want to steer a course more easterly?' interrupted Lt. Mohammed. 'Presumably we're going to our long-range launch position . . . to see if we can still get a fix on the overheads?'

'Exactly. But we don't need to make much of an adjustment . . . two degrees right rudder. I'll speak to Ali Zahedi . . . just so long as he keeps our speed to five knots.'

The *Barracuda* was moving quietly beneath the surface, some 540 miles short of its ops area. Some time in the next three days Ben Badr expected to pick up the beat of a US warship. But so far they had been in deserted waters, way south of the much busier North Atlantic shipping lanes.

On this Saturday morning the nearest US ship to the *Barracuda* was Captain Joe Wickman's guided-missile frigate *Simpson*, currently steaming southeast towards the northwest point of the Canaries, La Palma.

Captain C.J. Smith had his frigate, the *Elrod*, already in the region around the islands, moving east across the Canary current to a position north of Tenerife. There he was awaited by Captain Brad Willett's USS *Taylor*, which had arrived shortly after midnight.

The *Kauffman* and the *Nicholas*, commanded by Captains Josh Deal and Eric Nielsen, were scheduled to arrive on station sometime in the next two hours, in a holding area 20 miles off Tenerife's jagged northern headland of Roque de Anaga.

The seven-frigate fleet out of Norfolk was proceeding in a long convoy across the Atlantic. They were the last to leave and were not expected on station until Sunday night. The *Ronald Reagan* Carrier Battle Group was currently approaching Gibraltar and was expected to arrive at her ops area northeast of Lanzarote by Sunday afternoon.

Admiral George Gillmore, on board the electronic wondership, USS *Coronado*, was already 2,500 miles out from the Norfolk base, and less than 1,000 miles from his ops area. They were expected to arrive around midnight on Sunday.

The last arrival would be the carrier *Harry S. Truman*, laden with helicopters and currently pushing through a storm system out over the Atlantic Ridge, escorted by two destroyers and a nuclear submarine, hull 770, the USS *Tucson*.

They were all to the north of the *Barracuda*, unknown to Admiral Ben Badr and his men, who expected trouble but probably not as much as this. *You'll always be safe if you stay deep and stay slow.* The words of his father rung clearly in Ben's mind. And still, somehow, he felt vulnerable without Ravi and Shakira.

This weekend he was due to open one of the timed safes on board the submarine that held a sealed letter, written, but not signed, to him, as commanding officer from the learned Ayatollah who presently ruled the Islamic Republic of Iran. It had been his father's idea, to give Ben a sense of true purpose. It would provide confirmation that he wielded the curved sword of the Prophet Mohammed when he launched his missiles.

Admiral Mohammed Badr had told his son what the envelope would contain. And he was most anxious to read it. He had tried twice already that morning but the timing device was still locked and Ben planned to give it another try in just a few hours.

Meanwhile, back in the Oval Office, Admiral Morgan had received another setback from Paris. A communiqué from the President had stated that, despite a long conversation with his Ambassador in Washington, he remained undecided about the validity of the HAMAS threat and the need to turn off the GPS.

He wanted to sleep on the problem and would give his decision on Monday morning. He continued, like his Foreign Minister, to believe that the Americans were exaggerating the importance of a terrorist attack on the volcano. He did not particularly wish to join them in alarming the entire world unnecessarily, and being responsible for any death which might occur as a result of closing down the world's global navigation system. He could see no merit in providing further fuel to world anti-American opinion, if the threat turned out to be spurious.

Arnold Morgan was furious at the word 'spurious'. 'How could the damned threat be "spurious".' he raged. 'Who the fuck does this jumped-up fucking despot from some fourth-rate town hall in Normandy think he is? Answer that someone?'

'I guess he does,' said President Bedford, who happened to be the only other person in the room at present. 'Does this mean I have to speak to him?'

'It used to,' said Arnold. 'Not any more . . .

'KATHY! CONNECT THIS OFFICE TO THE PRESIDENT OF FRANCE RIGHT NOW!'

'For President Bedford?' she inquired, standing in the doorway, still not absolutely certain why her husband felt the need to yell through closed wooden doors, rather than pick up the phone.

'Tell him that,' growled Arnold. 'Then put the little sonofabitch through to me.'

Kathy shook her head and instructed the White House switchboard to make the call to the Elysée Palace, in the northwest corner of central Paris, and to stress the urgency of the matter.

Three minutes later, the French President was on the line . . . slightly confused . . . *Mais je pense que le Président Bedford . . . ?*

'Mr President,' said Arnold Morgan. 'I am sitting here in the White House right next to the President of the United States of America . . . and for three days now we have been asking for your cooperation in stopping what might be the worst terrorist threat this world has ever faced. Am I to understand you are not yet ready to give us your help? That, by the way, is a *oui* or a *non*.'

'Well, I have not yet decided as to the merit of the case.'

'Is that a *non*, Mr President?'

'Well, I think we could work something out, possibly in a few days . . .'

'Mr President, this is a highly charged military action. We do not have time for your vacillation. Either you shut down the satellite when we tell you to shut it down, or that satellite will not even exist this time tomorrow morning . . .'

The line between Washington and Paris froze. 'Admiral Morgan, are you threatening me?' asked the President.

'No. I am absolutely promising you. I want that satellite down for forty-eight hours at midnight on Wednesday, your time. And that's what I'm going to have. Either you do it the easy way and have it blacked out. Or you can have it the hard way, and we'll get rid of it for you.

'And, as promised, we'll put an immediate and total ban on French imports into the United States of America. We'll close your embassy and expel your diplomats from Washington. You have ten seconds to answer.'

Morgan felt that the President of France, like so many of his predecessors, was long on posture, short on real principle. He thought of the huge expense of renewing the satellite, his mind flashed on the near-total wreckage of the French wine and cheese industries, the colossal damage to Peugeot, Citroën . . . the lockout of France from the many international councils . . . the appalling international publicity . . . the personal hatred of millions of people aimed at him, the man who had refused to help, when the USA, under dire threat, his fellow United Nations Permanent Council Member, had asked for what seemed like a comparatively very minor favour. He knew true immortality when he faced it.

'Very well, Admiral Morgan. This time your belligerence has won the day. The European GPS will be blacked out at midnight on Wednesday 7 October, for forty-eight hours. I have not liked your methods. But, as always, my country will do the right thing. Please send your emissaries to my government with the appropriate documents early on Monday morning.'

'That's very good of you, Mr President. Two things more – don't let there be any delays or foul-ups, and don't forget . . . but for us, you'd be speaking fucking German . . .'

Arnold crashed down the receiver. 'I'm not altogether certain that last remark was absolutely vital,' said President Bedford, smiling.

'Who gives a damn?' said his C-in-C High Tide. 'The goddamned French satellite is going off, and that's all that matters. We got a GPS total blackout, and that's going to force that *Barracuda* inshore, because his long-range missiles have just gone blind. That's where we want him. That's where we have a real chance.'

President Bedford said, 'You want me to put the agreement with France into operation? I'll just call the State Department . . .'

'Perfect, sir. Will you also call General Scannell

and inform him of the French agreement. He'll get the practical side under control . . . you know, coordinating the satellites, so it all goes blank at the same time.'

The President nodded and left the room. And Arnold returned to his huge computerised charts of the Atlantic. 'East,' he muttered. 'It's gotta be east. Anywhere west of those islands is in the direct path of the *tsunami* as it rolls out. No ship could survive. The *Barracuda*'s CO must have worked that out.'

'What's that?' said Kathy, who was trying to beat her way through the piles of paper on the other office table.

'Come over here,' said the admiral. 'And I'll show you what I mean . . . see this? These are the Canary Islands . . . And the big question is, will the *Barracuda* stay south, if he's coming in from somewhere east of the Caribbean? Or will he make a big circle and run north to surprise us?'

'I'm not really sure.'

'Well, north is best. We got two nuclear boats up there with the carrier . . . he can't go there without getting caught. My guess is he'll stay south, come in towards Western Sahara, and then turn in for his launch. He cannot be more than 250 miles out, when he launches, satellites or not . . . because if he can't get in behind those islands, fast, the *tsunami* will dump him right on the goddamned beach in Long Island, upside down with his prop in the air.'

Kathy laughed at her incorrigible husband, as she always did.

Back out in the dark waters of the Cape Verde Plain, Admiral Ben Badr held his personal letter from the Ayatollah. It read:

Benjamin, you are a priceless soul in the cause of Allah. And soon you will carry His sword into battle. This letter is to remind you of the responsibility you bear in our crusade against the Great Satan.

Perhaps I should remind you that our Islamic faith came originally from the deserts of Arabia. And it always had overtones of war. For the Prophet was also a Conqueror and a statesmen. There was no precedent for the word of the Prophet. It came directly from God, and within 100 years it destroyed the Persian Empire, and conquered great swathes of the Empire of Byzantium

At that time Arab armies swept through North Africa, obliterating Christianity in Egypt and in Tunisia, the home of their St Augustine. Those armies ransacked the Iberian Peninsula, and drove into France. Ah, yes, my son, from the very beginnings, we have been a warlike people.

Remember too that Islamic science and scholarship were ahead of Europe for centuries. We gave them the idea of universities, which the Crusaders took home with them. We conquered Turkey, captured Constantinople which became the Capital of the Ottoman Empire.

Only in the last 300 years did the Unbelievers emerge from defeat and total irrelevance to dominate the Middle East. They redrafted our borders, invented

453

*new states, divided up our land, stole our wealth,
our oil, and divided it up between European
Imperialists, forcing upon us Western ways and what
they think is culture.*

*After we had triumphed for so long, the conquest
of the entire world by our True Faith seemed inevitable.
But it went wrong for us. And now Allah has granted
us a way to make a huge stride to correct those 300
years of Western arrogance and plundering.*

*You must remember always, this is our endless
Jihad, a war both spiritual and violent, and one
which would have been blessed by the Prophet. This
Jihad should be central to the life of every Muslim.
We do not wish to steal what is not ours, but we
dream of a wide Islamic Empire, one which is not
dominated by the United States of America.*

*My son, we want them out of the Middle East,
and with them their degenerate, debauched way of
life. And if we cannot bend them to our wishes, we
will surely make them grow weary of the conflict. I
pray for your Holy Mission, and I pray that you
and your brave warriors will succeed in this great
venture. All Islam will one day understand what you
have done. And we wish Godspeed to the
SCIMITARs, and may Allah go with you.*

The Ayatollah had not signed the letter, but it was
written in his own hand, and Ben Badr folded it
and tucked it into the breast pocket of his shirt.

Ben Badr was a consummate naval professional,
at ease with his crew, with his own abilities as a

454

commanding officer and with the rewards of his long training. He did not see himself as a candidate for a suicide mission, but in the deepest recesses of his own soul, unspoken and rarely considered, he knew he was prepared to die, if necessary, a hero, so long as he was fighting for what he and his people believed in. He was honoured that he should be in the vanguard of those who were chosen. He would bring the submarine within range of the great volcano, and he would blast it with his tailor-made nuclear missiles. Either that, or he would die in the attempt. He neither sought nor expected death. But if death pressed its hot, fiery fist upon the hull of the *Barracuda*, as he drove towards Cumbre Vieja, then he would face it with equanimity, and without fear.

Admiral Badr checked with Chief Petty Officer Ali Zahedi that their course was correct, and the speed still under six knots. He then moved down to the bank of computer screens outside the reactor room and talked for a while with CPO Ardeshir Tikku. Everything was still running sweetly after their long and often slow journey from the far eastern coast of China. This really was the most tremendous ship, Russian engineering at its very best.

The VM-5 PWA, reputed to be Russia's most efficient ever nuclear reactor, was built up on the shores of the White Sea by the renowned engineers in Archangel. So far, deep in the *Barracuda*, it had never faltered, and was still effortlessly providing steam for the GT3A turbine. Ardeshir Tikku could not imagine any ship's propulsion units running with more precision.

The jet-black titanium hull slipped through the water. Every last piece of machinery on board was rubber-mounted, cutting out even the remotest vibration. If you listened carefully you might have heard the soft, distant hum of a computer. But that was no computer. That was the 47,000 hp turbine, driving this 8,000-tonner through the deep waters of the Atlantic.

As each day passed Ben discerned a tightening of nerves among all the key men in the ship. Captain Ali Akbar Mohtaj was very much within himself, spending much of his spare time with Commander Abbas Shafii, the nuclear specialist on board, who would prime the detonators on the SCIMITAR missiles. They had already decided to launch both the SL-2s at the mountain, especially if there was a problem with the satellites.

Two SL-2s rather than one, the equivalent of *400,000 tons* of TNT, would seem to guarantee the savage destruction of the entire southwestern corner of La Palma. Even if they were detected, even if American warships rained depth charges down upon them, even if the US Navy found them, and launched torpedoes, there would *still be time*. Only seconds. But time for the *Barracuda* to launch the two unstoppable missiles which would cause the tidal wave to end all tidal waves. Captain Ali Akbar Mohtaj and Commander Abbas Shafii had thought about that a lot. They'd still have time.

Meanwhile, Washington, DC, prepared to meet its doom. If Ben Badr's missiles hit Cumbre Vieja, the Presidency of Paul Bedford would be flown en masse, at the last possible hour, direct from the White House to the new secret base of the Administration at the northern end of the Shenandoah Mountains, out near Mountain Falls.

The base, with all of its high-tech communication systems and direct lines to the Pentagon and various foreign governments, was constructed inside a heavily patrolled military base. It was a vast complex, built almost entirely underground, fortuitously in the rolling hills to the west of the Shenandoah Valley, several hundred feet above sea level.

Known in Washington circles as Camp Goliath – as opposed to Camp David – it was always envisaged as a refuge for the government *and* military, if the US ever came under nuclear attack, and Washington, DC, was threatened. It took three days to activate all the communications, and it now stood in isolated, secret splendour, a five-star hotel with offices, situation rooms, every secretarial facility, every possible element of twenty-first-century technology required to keep the world moving.

The President, in company with his principal staff members and their assistants, would fly to Camp Goliath in one of the huge US Marine Super Stallions, a three-engined Sikorsky CH-53E helicopter capable of airlifting fifty-five Marines into trouble zones.

Just in case HAMAS proved even more ambitious

than they so far seemed, the helo was equipped with three 12.7mm machine guns. It would rendezvous in the skies above Washington with four cruising F-15 Tomcat fighter bombers to escort it to the American heartland beyond the Shenandoah River.

Camp Goliath was located 15 miles southwest of Winchester, in the wooded hills above the valley where 'Stonewall' Jackson's iron-souled Southern regulars had held sway over the Union Army for so many months in the 1860s and when General Nathaniel Banks and his 8,000 troops were driven right back across the river; Harper's Ferry at the confluence of the Shenandoah and the Potomac, where General Jackson's men captured 13,000 Northern troops; Front Royal, Cedar Ridge, and, a little further north, the bitter, killing fields of Antietam.

Camp Goliath stood above those historic Civil War farmlands on the Virginia–Maryland border, where the great rivers meet. And if the missiles hit the mountain in La Palma, and that great complex was activated, HAMAS would surely feel the wrath of another generation of ruthless American fighting men.

Meanwhile, the Washington evacuation continued. And by Sunday morning the thousands of National Guardsmen who had joined the troops in the city were concentrating on a task equally as important as moving the Federal Government and its possessions out of harm's way. They were now trying to safe-guard the thousands of artefacts, documents, books and pictures which record and illustrate the founding of the nation and its subsequent development.

Much of this priceless hoard is contained within the Smithsonian Institution – another great, sprawling complex which embraces fourteen museums – the collective custodians of millions of priceless exhibits, ranging from centuries-old masterpieces to modern spacecraft. In the gigantic Air and Space Museum alone there are 23 galleries displaying 240 aircraft and 50 missiles, a planetarium and a theatre with a five-storey screen.

Already some of the museums understood they were not going to get this done, with thousands of items packed, in storage, not even on display. All of them had called the White House for guidance. Admiral Morgan was impatient: *Priorities. Establish priorities, hear me? Concentrate on objects of true historic value. Forget all about those special exhibits. Abandon all mock-ups and models. Get photographs, copies of drawings. But concentrate on what's real. And keep it moving over there . . .*

National museum curators are unaccustomed to such brusque and decisive tones. In some of the art galleries, there were so many pictures it was impossible to crate and ship them all. Decisions had to be made to leave some in the upper floors of the buildings, in the hope they might survive the initial force of the *tsunami*, and the subsequent flooding did not reach the top storey.

Chain gangs of troops and employees were moving up and down the massive staircases of the National Gallery of Art, trying to lift masterpieces, some of them from the thirteenth, fourteenth and fifteenth centuries, either down to awaiting trucks or up to the high galleries, please God above the incoming waters.

There were some tasks too onerous even to contemplate. The warships, submarines and aircraft displayed in the 10,000-foot-long Memorial Museum in the Washington Navy Yard would have to take their chances. So would the massive collection of historic machinery, the heavy-duty engines which drove America's industrial past, all located on the first floor of the National Museum of American History.

An even more difficult task was the National Zoological Park. The Madison Bank took a special interest in the animals' safety and set up an ops room in their Du Pont Circle branch. Twenty people spent the day in a frenzy of activity, contacting other zoos inside a 100-mile radius, checking their spare capacity, trying to find temporary homes, and suitable habitat, in the limited time available.

They hired cages from Ringling Brothers, trucks from U-Haul; they even commandeered a couple of freight trains from the Southern Railroad. Everyone wanted to help the animals, though the Baltimore baseball management balked when a young Madison Bank zealot demanded they turn the 48,000 seat Oriole Park at Camden Yards into a bear pit.

By the afternoon, the evacuation of the Zoological Park was well under way. And all over the city there were even more poignant reminders of the horrors to come. The historic statues, by special order of Admiral Morgan, were being removed and shipped out to the Maryland hills.

This had caused the first real friction of the entire operation, because the National Parks official who administers the statues and their upkeep decreed the task to be utterly impossible.

'What do you mean, impossible?' rasped the voice from the Oval Office. 'Get the Army Corps of Engineers in here with heavy lifting gear, cranes and trucks.'

'It simply will not work, sir. The statues in almost every instance are too heavy.'

'Well, somebody put 'em up, didn't they? Someone lifted them.'

'Well, yes, sir. But I imagine those people are all dead. And you can't fax the dead, can you?'

Arnold did not right now have time for 'smart-ass remarks from fucking bureaucrats'.

'Guess not,' he replied. 'You better try e-mail. But get the statues moved at all costs.' At which point he banged down the telephone.

Within hours the Army Corps of Engineers was on its way from Craney Island, at the head of the Norfolk shipyards, up the Potomac with barges full of the necessary hardware. By dusk the great Theodore Roosevelt Memorial was being lifted from its island in the middle of the Potomac.

And the 78-foot-high Iwo Jima Marine Corps Memorial, one of the largest statues ever cast, was being raised by crane, complete with its black marble plinth, 500 yards from the Potomac at the north end of Arlington National Cemetery. The sight of it being removed attracted a large, sorrowful crowd, watching the apparent conclusion of America's most touching tribute to the courage of the US Marines.

'Don't worry about it,' called one young soldier. 'We'll have this baby right back here by the end of the month.'

Officers from the Engineering Corps were already inside the classic domed rotunda of the Jefferson Memorial which houses the 19-foot-high statue of America's third President, gazing out towards the Tidal Basin. It was a difficult task, but not an impossible one. Outside there were four different sized cranes and fifty troops, all experts in their trade.

A young lieutenant, under strict orders, used his mobile phone to call the White House.

'We got it, sir. The Jefferson will be on a truck by midnight.'

'That's my boy . . . how about the oriental cherry trees around the outside?' replied Admiral Morgan.

'Gardeners say not, sir. They'll die if we move 'em.'

'They'll sure as hell die if they get hit by a fucking tidal wave,' said Arnold.

'Yes, sir. I did mention that to the gardeners. Well, words to that effect. But they said the trees could be replaced. It was a waste of time.'

'Glad to see those gardeners are thinking, right, Lieutenant?'

'Right, sir.'

The Lincoln Memorial, Arnold's favourite, presented an even bigger challenge. Another 19-foot statue, this one of solid marble; Abraham Lincoln, the 16th President, seated on a high chair overlooking the Reflecting Pool, surrounded by his own immortal words, carved in stone.

It was considerably heavier than the statue of Thomas Jefferson, but the Engineering Corps was undaunted. As darkness fell, they began moving two cranes between the twelve towering white columns along the front of the building.

There were dozens of others, some of which would be left to take their chances, while others would be lifted and moved, like the Ulyssess Grant Memorial and the bronze casting of Andrew Jackson on horseback, made from British cannons captured at the Battle of Pensacola in 1812.

The eternal flame which burned in a bronze font at the grave of the 35th President, John F. Kennedy, could not be extinguished and Admiral Morgan and Senator Edward Kennedy decreed that a new flame would be lit from the original and transported to another military cemetery.

They ordered the flame, which had burned without interruption since the President was laid to rest in 1963, to be extinguished the moment the new one was relocated in consecrated ground. The entire grave site and memorial was then to be sealed immediately in steel and concrete, in readiness for the relighting when the floodwaters subsided.

Senator Kennedy was uncharacteristically shy and reserved about his late brother's memory, but Arnold said precisely what was on his mind: 'I'm not having some goddamned terrorist snuffing out the Eternal Flame at the grave of a truly great man. If it's going to be extinguished, the Navy will attend to it. And the Navy will relight it at the proper time. Just so its light never dies, right here on American soil. And Teddy's with me on that.'

America was a nation which honoured its heroes, and one of the largest memorials to remove was the solemn 500-foot-long, gleaming black marble wall which immortalises the men who died, or remain missing, in the Vietnam War. Thousands of pilgrims visited here each year, just to reach out and touch the stone, just to see his name. Arnold Morgan ordered it to be removed *by strong men wearing velvet gloves*. 'I do not want to see one scratch on that surface when we return it,' he said.

And there was already a company of Army engineers in Constitution Gardens, carefully wrapping the long line of angular black marble tablets which bear the names of every last one of the 58,156 soldiers who were lost. The memorial was set less than 300 yards from the giant, stern figure of Abraham Lincoln, who, perhaps above all other Americans, would have understood the cruel perversity of that distant battlefield.

Admiral Morgan ordered an evacuation of the Peace Memorial erected to honour Navy personnel lost at sea during the Civil War and he asked someone to remove and store the Benjamin Franklin statue, which depicts the old statesman in his long coat holding the eighteenth-century Treaty of Alliance between the United States and France.

'He probably could've got the goddamned satellite shut down a helluva lot quicker than us,' added Arnold.

Amidst the cranes, the armies of workers, the endless roar of the huge evacuation trucks a steady stream of traffic was bearing its citizens to the high ground of the northwest. The University was now closed and the streets in Georgetown were thinning out.

Fortunately the nation's capital wasn't home to much large-scale commercial business and industry, but at the banks there was intense activity, with customer records, cash and safety deposit boxes being shipped to outlying branches.

On this Sunday the banks were open until 10 p.m. allowing customers, preparing to flee the city at first light Monday morning, to withdraw funds or remove valuables. Many law firms, lobby companies and stockbrokers were moving one large truckload of documents apiece out of the offices and generally heading for the hills.

Almost all other commercial operations not involved in transportation or in assisting the government with emergency procedures were already closed down, having removed as much stock and hardware as possible. Theatres and cinemas, too, had locked their doors.

465

But Washington's local television and radio stations were instructed to keep transmitting for as long as possible, under the control of the Pentagon, and, from time to time, watched beadily by Admiral Morgan. They would turn off the power only upon the certain information that the Cumbre Vieja volcano had blown itself into the Atlantic Ocean. That was the official time to leave. Nine hours.

The evacuation of the hospitals was a long and laborious operation. Every ambulance in the city had been running non-stop since Friday, ferrying not-too-sick patients home so that they could leave the city with their families and driving very sick patients to other hospitals inland, wherever beds could be located. No new patients were being admitted, except for accidents and other emergencies. The situation was getting extremely difficult because so much of the best medical equipment had already gone into military storage for safekeeping.

Any hospital with spare capacity within 100 miles of Washington was accepting patients from the city. No one wanted to move very sick patients any further than was absolutely necessary, but the Pentagon had ordered all patients to be out of all hospitals by Wednesday evening. That would entail every ambulance being well outside the city by the time Ben Badr launched his SL-2s. Admiral Morgan had made it clear he did not intend to lose any ambulances whatsoever, no matter how great the flood.

For the final forty-eight hours the military would

provide reserve medical units out of Fort Belvoir, the gigantic military base south of Alexandria, right on the severely threatened west bank of the Potomac. Emergency treatment centres, staffed by the Army, were already operational in Whitehaven Park, Constitution Gardens and the Washington Hospital Center.

A small fleet of US Marine helicopters was on stand-by to ferry serious cases to a brand new military field hospital set up in a safe area out near Dulles Airport. Treatment centres in the city would remain open until they received the message that the HAMAS missiles had hit home on the faraway island of La Palma, at which point the Marines' Super Stallion helicopters would evacuate everything and everyone directly to the Dulles area.

The Police Department in downtown Washington was possibly the busiest place in the city. All leave was cancelled, officers were working around the clock, mainly on the streets, patrolling in groups of three and four, especially in areas where widespread evacuation had already taken place.

This was not confined just to shops and department stores, the police were vigilantly patrolling and checking on all private homes. The Oval Office had made it clear to the public, backed by the Pentagon – permission to shoot looters if need be had been issued. *Otherwise this whole damn thing could get right out of hand. We've got a bastard of an enemy out there, certainly we do not deserve to fight enemies within. If it comes to that, they can expect no mercy . . .* Arnold Morgan was not joking.

And, of course, the hard-pressed Police Department knew that, as the evacuation gained momentum, the traffic problems would multiply. They were already providing information and advice, and escorts for large convoys. Overhead, police helicopters were constantly reporting, issuing a general overview of traffic movement within the city and helping to direct resources to where they were most needed.

They were already being supported by thousands of National Guardsmen who were out on the streets, not only assisting with logistics, transportation and vehicle recovery but also watching the streets and movements of Washington's citizens closely. This was, one way and another, a bad time to be an American criminal working the nation's capital.

The various Fire Departments were under orders to stay open and active, providing cover until the very last moment, but reducing their manpower wherever possible. All fire-fighting vehicles were already in working order, so the whole fleet could be withdrawn en masse down the specially cleared highway, at the first news that Ben Badr had struck the volcano.

By far the most troublesome point of the Pentagon's evacuation plan was the section which dealt with prisons, and the problem of moving highly dangerous criminals around the country. General Scannell had detailed three companies of National Guardsmen, 300 men, to assist in preparing a disused military base in West Virginia.

Right now, working under newly installed security lights, they were building high perimeter fences and fitting out accommodation huts. This part of the camp was for prisoners judged to be a menace to the public, and they would be under constant surveillance by armed Army personnel.

Other less dangerous prisoners would be moved to normal jails which had spare capacity, but there was little room for brutal, convicted killers and no one had yet taken Admiral Morgan's advice to '*put the whole lot of them in front of a goddamned firing squad and have done with it*'. He'd said it only half-jokingly.

Meanwhile, out in the real battleground, the US warships were arriving on station, and by midnight the USS *Coronado* had steamed into her holding area 40 miles northwest of the coast of Lanzarote. Admiral Gillmore immediately opened communications with the *Elrod* and the *Taylor*, which were positioned north of Tenerife, some 60 miles to the west of the *Coronado*. The first orders issued by the new Task Group Commander were for these two frigates to begin close inshore patrols around the islands at first light; tomorrow, that was. Monday 5 October, four days before H-Hour – H for Hit.

Admiral Gillmore did not expect to stumble across the *Barracuda* by accident. Indeed, he did not believe the HAMAS submarine to be in the area yet. But in the next day or so they needed to familiarise themselves with the local charts. The admiral wanted more reliable underwater fixings. They needed to identify anomalies and problem spots among the permanent characteristics of this part of the eastern Atlantic Basin – water swirl areas, thermal layering, fish concentrations, rocks, reefs and ridges, all the myriad sub-surface elements which can confuse a sonar operator.

Non-submarine contacts do one of two things: vanish completely, if they are, for instance, fish shoals; or, if they are rocks, remain solidly in place. Submarines are apt to get moving, giving strong signals with marked Doppler effects.

The initial task of the inshore group was to conduct a comprehensive search of the whole area, mapping the ocean floor as they went. They would use depth charges if anything suspicious came up, and even if no contact was located their active sonar, sweeping through the depths, would almost certainly drive a marauding submarine out into deeper water, possibly at speed.

And out into that deeper water Admiral Gillmore was sending six towed-array frigates, ultra-sensitive to the slightest movement, the merest hint of an engine. Their task was to prowl the surface, probing the depths, waiting, listening. This offshore group, effectively a second line of attack, would be working in 30 fathoms or more, 25 miles out from the island beaches.

USS *Samuel B. Roberts*; USS *Hawes*; the *Robert G. Bradley*, the *De Wert*, the *Doyle* and the *Underwood*: these were the six submarine hunters designated by Admiral Gillmore to guard the offshore areas, and at the same time watch for the *Barracuda* if it tried to run in from out of the west.

The *Kauffman* and the *Nicholas*, two of the earliest arrivals in the Canary Islands from the North
Atlantic, would take the western half of the inshore
patrol, moving into the waters close to the islands
of Tenerife, Gomera, tiny Hierro, and, to the north,
La Palma itself.

Because Admiral Gillmore believed the *Barracuda*
was most likely to take a southerly route into its ops
area, he felt it was most likely to be detected east
of the big islands closest to the shores of North
Africa, Lanzarote and Fuerteventura. That's where
he wanted his two first-choice ships, the *Elrod* and
the *Taylor*.

These frigates were commanded by two very
senior captains he had known well for many years,
C.J. Smith and Brad Willett, both dedicated ASW
men, sub-hunting specialists like himself, with
months of service in the still suspect Atlantic waters
up by the Griuk Gap.

Like Admiral Morgan, and his immediate boss,
Admiral Frank Doran, George Gillmore had arrived
at an irrevocable conclusion . . . the terrorist submarine would have to launch its missiles from a
point where it could rush for cover from the *tsunami*.
Before the *Barracuda*'s comms room discovered the
satellites were down, they would surely try the area
off Western Sahara for a long-distance launch and
then race for the cover of the eastern shore of
Fuerteventura.

When they did discover there were no GPS satellite coordinates, they would need to creep to the

south of Gran Canaria, in the area of the *Elrod* and the *Taylor*, before running towards the south coast of Tenerife and then into the inshore waters around Gomera. From there they would need to regroup, get a good visual fix and then move in towards La Palma for the launch.

The *Elrod* and the *Taylor* had a chance of detecting the *Barracuda* as it made its way in from the open ocean, running south of all the islands towards the North African coast. They definitely had a shot at an early detection while the men from HAMAS had a mast up, trying to access the GPS. And they would have another if and when it began a move west towards Gomera.

Four ships inshore and six standing off, 25 miles out. Admiral Gillmore had done his geometry. Each TA frigate would need to patrol in a circle radius of 10 to 20 nautical miles . . . the area measured from the volcano itself to cover the entire band out to 25 miles from the work of the inshore group. The distance around such a circle is around 150 nautical miles. And this would allow the six frigates to cover the entire area continuously. If the *Barracuda* somehow strayed into those waters, life could quickly become extremely tense for Ben Badr and his men.

This left Admiral Gillmore with two other frigates, Captain Clint Sammons' *Klakring* and Captain Joe Wickman's *Simpson*. He would use these to extend the search area, whenever it might become necessary, or to prosecute nearby towed-array contacts, or even to thicken up radar coverage inshore. In such a complex operation, George Gillmore knew better than to leave himself without flexibility. At this stage, his task orders were, of course, extremely narrow – sink the *Barracuda*, however, wherever, whenever, but soon.

Situated 20 miles to his east was the *Ronald Reagan* CVBG. The massive aircraft carrier was preparing to rendezvous with the *Harry S. Truman*, and essentially exchange its fixed-wing aircraft for ASW helicopters. The Battle Group arrived with two Los Angeles Class nuclear submarines but Frank Doran was not anxious to use them in any kind of an underwater hunt.

Admiral Gillmore was aware of that and both men felt the destruction of the *Barracuda* would be achieved by the ASW helicopters. The *Harry S. Truman* was expected to arrive on Monday morning and the exchange operation would begin immediately. As the sun came blazing out of the clear African skies to the east there was as yet no sign of the second carrier, but they knew it was less than 100 miles away. And the *Elrod* and the *Taylor* were already on their way to their inshore search areas.

By 0900, the *Harry S. Truman* had made its Atlantic crossing and was 30 miles off the northwest coast of La Palma, steaming east towards the rendezvous with the *Ronald Reagan*. The sea was calm and a brisk, warm southeast wind blew off the coast of Africa. In the next three hours, this was forecast to shift southwest and bring in a succession of rain squalls throughout the afternoon. Which was not perfect for the large-scale carrier-to-carrier transfer of aircraft, scheduled to begin at 1400.

Shortly before 1030, Admiral Gillmore completed his deployment of ships for the offshore operation, and, led by the USS *Hawes*, under Commander Derek DeCarlo, the six frigates set off for their respective search 'circles' in the wide band of ocean between the islands of La Palma and Hierro, and the 25-mile outer limit of their operations area.

The *Kauffman* and the *Nicholas* made their way into the inshore waters of La Palma and Hierro, where they would move slowly around the coast-lines, mapping the ocean bottom, recording the appearance of sudden shoals of fish, or perfectly stationary sea ridges, before moving on to Gomera and Tenerife, always watching the computer screen which would betray a creeping nuclear submarine.

0800 Monday 5 October 2009
Mid-Atlantic 27.30N 24.50W
The *Barracuda* still ran slowly at just under six knots, still 500 feet under the surface, transmitting nothing. Admiral Ben Badr checked their position and noted they were 240 miles out from the most westerly of the Canary Islands, La Palma and Hierro, around 18.50W. They were on a due easterly course which would take them 20 miles south of the seven volcanic islands which jutted up separately from the ocean bed.

So far they had heard no searching submarines,

no warships. They had twice ventured to periscope depth to check the GPS was in sound working order, and found no problems. They had two more days to run before they slid quietly into the area which Admiral Gillmore's ships were currently combing.

As soon as the *Barracuda* slipped by its first landfall, the island of Hierro, it would be within 19 miles of the *Nicholas*, unless Captain Eric Nielsen had already moved on to the southern coast of Tenerife, into the waters once scanned so thoroughly by the honeymooning Admiral Arnold Morgan.

If the *Nicholas* had moved, the chances of the *Barracuda* remaining undetected were doubled, because even the south shore of Tenerife lay 25 miles further north than Hierro. This would put the *Barracuda* 44 miles south of the nearest US warship, but the day, and the game, were both still young.

Three and a half thousand miles away on the US East Coast the sun was battling its way out of the Atlantic into cloudy skies. And it was not just the big cities which were trying to empty themselves; all along the eastern seaboard, rural communities were frantically making their preparations to escape the wrath of the coming tidal wave.

It was cold on the rocky, tree-lined islands off the coast of Maine, and most of the summer people had stored their boats and vanished south to escape the notoriously chilly Maine fall. Inland the cold was, if anything, worse. There's usually snow in the outfield by the first week of November at the University of Maine baseball park in Orono, Maine, home of the Black Bears.

The islands were effectively left to the Maine lobstermen, one of the most intrepid breed of cold-water fishermen in the world. There was not a single safe harbour along this coast.

It was essential either to haul up the lobster boats and get them to higher ground, or, more daringly, anchor them in the western lee of one of the 3,000 islands that guard the downeast coast. These rocky, spruce-dark islands are mostly hilly, great granite rises from the ocean which might not stop a tidal wave but would definitely give it a mild jolt. On the sheltered side it was just about possible that the *tsunami* might roll right by, perhaps leaving a high surge in its wake but not dumping and smashing large boats on beaches 10 miles away.

The seamen of the Maine islands were accustomed more than any other fishermen on the East Coast to terrible weather. And for three days now they had been moving the endless, scattered fleet of lobster boats to anchorages out of harm's way.

Boats from Monhegan, North Haven, Vinalhaven, Port Clyde, Tennants Harbor, Carver's Harbor, Frenchboro, Isleboro and Mount Desert headed inshore, praying that if the giant wave came, the islands, with their huge granite ramparts, would somehow reduce the power of the waves.

Similar prayers on precisely the same subject were

almost certainly being offered by somewhat less robust men – librarians, politicians and accountants – 600 miles south in Washington. The Library of Congress was built out of granite from the Mount Desert area. So was the House of Representatives and the Treasury Building.

Out in the deep water, 15 miles from the coast, the three great seaward guardians of Maine's stern and mighty shoreline – the remote and lonely lighthouses of Matinicus Rock, Mount Desert Rock and Machias Seal Island – were left to face the coming onslaught single-handed. According to local scientists, the mega-*tsunami* would sweep more than 100 feet above them. Whether they would still be there when the water flattened out was anyone's guess.

Meanwhile, the fishermen and their families were being ferried onto the mainland where relatives, friends and volunteers were lined in packed parking lots waiting to drive them to safety. Maine is a tight-knit, insular community off-season, with less than one million residents. At a time like this, they were all brothers and sisters.

In far, far greater danger was Provincetown, the outermost town on Cape Cod, 120 miles to the south across the Gulf of Maine. This small artistic community set in the huge left-hand sweep of the Cape is protected strictly by low sand dunes and grass. By that Monday afternoon it was a ghost town. Those who could towed their boats down the mid-Cape highway and onto the mainland. The rest just hit the road west and hoped their homes and boats would somehow survive. Lloyd's of London were not hugely looking forward to future correspondence with regard to Cape Cod.

All along the narrow land, every resident had to leave. Massachusetts State Police were already supervising the evacuation. All roads leading from all the little Cape towns to Route 6A were designated one-way systems. Wellfleet, Truro, Orleans, Chatham, Brewster, Denisport, Yarmouth, Hyannis, Osterville, Cotuit and Falmouth. No one was to come back until danger had cleared.

The evacuation, all the way down that historic coastline, was total. The whaling port of New Bedford was deserted by Monday evening, and the flat eastern lowlands of Rhode Island, a myriad bay shores and islands, was going to be a write-off if Admiral Badr's missiles made it to the volcano.

In the shadow of the towering edifice of Newport Bridge, the little sailing town was on the verge of a collective nervous breakdown. Some of the most expensive yachts ever built were home here for the fall, and many of them had not yet been hauled or yet departed for the Caribbean or Florida.

The New York Yacht Club's headquarters, gazing out onto the harbour, would probably be the first to go if the tidal wave came rolling in past Brenton Point. Offshore Block Island had been evacuated completely by Sunday night, and whether Newport Bridge itself could survive was touch and go.

Further down the coast there were obvious areas of impending disaster in the long, narrow New

England state of Connecticut. The shoreline was beset by wealthy little seaports, the more plutocratic the nearer they were to New York. Bridgeport, Norwalk, Stamford, Darien and Greenwich – Connecticut's Golden Suburbs, all along the narrowing waters of Long Island Sound. Billions of dollars worth of manicured property and people, all hoping against hope that central Long Island itself, around 15 miles wide, would bear the brunt of the *tsunami*.

But it was the northern seaport of New London which was causing the most concern in the state of Connecticut. This is one of the United States Navy's great submarine bases and home of the Electric Boat Company, which builds them. It is a traditional Navy town and there had been ferocious activity since before the weekend, all along the jetties, preparing the big nuclear boats to make all speed south to the west coast of Florida. Unfinished ships were being towed 10 miles upriver, anywhere which might be beyond the reach of the *tsunami* after it hit the helpless north shore of Long Island Sound.

South of New York the flat sweep of the Jersey shore, with its miles and miles of vacation homes, was defenceless. So was the entire eastern shore of Maryland, which was nothing but a flat coastal plain on both sides of the Chesapeake Estuary with no elevation higher than 100 feet and nothing to stop the thunderous tidal wave but the flimsiest of outer islands, not much higher than sand bars beyond the long waters of Chincoteague Bay.

By Monday afternoon the entire area was almost deserted, hundreds of cars still heading north, joined by another huge convoy from neighbouring Delaware which shared the same long shoreline and was equally defenceless.

South of Virginia, the coastal plain of North Carolina was, if anything, even more vulnerable than Maryland. The Tidewater area was flat, poorly drained and marshy, meandering out to a chain of low barrier islands, the Outer Banks, separated from the mainland by lagoons and salt marshes. Out on the peninsula of Beaufort, Pamlico and Cateret Counties, which lie between the two wide rivers, Neuse and Pamlico, the issue was not whether the giant *tsunami* would hit and flood, but whether the little seaports would ever stick their heads above the Atlantic again.

Myrtle Beach Air Force Station, right on the coast of South Carolina, was playing a huge role in the evacuation of the coastal region, with a fleet of helicopters in the skies assisting the police with traffic. Hundreds of Air Force personnel were helping evacuate the beautiful city of Charleston, one of the most historic ports in the United States and home of Fort Sumter, where the first shots of the Civil War were fired.

Right on the border lies the oldest city in Georgia, the port of Savannah. There were 10,000 troops assisting in the evacuation here, and no one even dared think about the wreckage of the perfect colonial city, so carefully preserved over the centuries yet so unprotected from the ravages of the ocean.

Florida was, of course, another story, with its 400-mile-long east coast, open to the Atlantic, largely devoid of hills and of mountains, all the way south to Miami, Fernandina Beach in the north, then Jacksonville Beach, Daytona and Cocoa Beach, Indian Harbor, Vero Beach, Hobe Sound, Palm Beach, Boca Raton, Fort Lauderdale and Miami.

Stretching out to the south were the low-lying resorts of the Florida Keys, all the way across the Everglades, right down to the yachtsmen's paradise of Key West. Although every one of the Keys had borne the wrath of Atlantic hurricanes before, they had not seen a *tsunami* since long before the Pharoahs ruled Egypt.

The East Coast of the United States was absolutely powerless in the face of such a threat. General Rashood had thought out and prepared his attack with immense skill, giving the US no option but to pack up and run, taking only what little they could carry.

Unless Admiral George Gillmore and his men could find that submarine.

CHAPTER TWELVE

1700 Monday 5 October 2009
Atlantic Ocean 29.48N 13.35W

High Tide was one of the most complex and large cross-decking operations in recent memory. The *Harry S. Truman* stood a half-mile off the port bow of the *Ronald Reagan*, and it was pouring like the devil, a gusting sou'wester that swept sheets of rain across the carriers' flight decks.

On paper, the preparations looked simple: to transfer fifty Sikorsky Seahawk helicopters from the deck of the *Harry S. Truman* onto the deck of the *Ronald Reagan*. Trouble was, the deck of the *Ronald Reagan* was already full with the greater part of its eighty-four embarked aircraft, most of them being flown by four of the most famous fighter squadrons in the United States Air Force.

The new F-14D Tomcat fighter bombers were controlled by the fabled flyers of the VF-2 *Bounty Hunters*. Three large groups of F/A 18C Hornets were flown by the VMFA-323 *Death Rattlers*, the VFA-151 *Vigilantes* and the VFA-137 *Kestrels*. In addition, there were the Prowlers and the Vikings, but these were parked carefully away from the main runways.

And then there were the mighty E-2C Group II Hawkeyes, the biggest and most expensive aircraft on any carrier. The radar early warning and control aircraft, the quarterback of the squadron, first to get in the air and always parked right below the island, wings folded, ready to head for the stern catapult. No US carrier would leave port without at least three onboard.

Aside from the Prowlers, Vikings and Hawkeyes, the rest were ready for takeoff from the rainswept deck of their longtime home, the 100,000-ton Nimitz Class carrier, the *Ronald Reagan*.

Over on the newly-arrived *Harry S. Truman,* fifty Sikorsky Seahawk helicopters, the latest in modern submarine hunting, were lined up alongside the main runway, blades folded, with six just preparing to leave. The US Navy had 300 of these hovering state-of-the-art ASW specialists, but not one of them had ever been under more steel-edged orders than those received in the Norfolk yards the week before.

Admiral Gillmore had left it to the carrier COs to carry out the aircraft exchange, and both captains had decided on six at a time as the safest method, especially in this weather.

The helicopter maintenance crews were ferried across separately, in a Sikorsky CH-53D Sea Stallion assault and support helicopter, transported from Norfolk especially for this phase of the operation. The Sea Stallion was designed to carry thirty-eight

Marines but today it was to move back and forth between the carriers, laden with spare parts for the Seahawks plus the Navy experts who knew how to fit them. They would also be ferrying the fixed-wing maintenance crews which were returning to the US with the Tomcats and Hornets.

And now the Seahawks were ready. The *Harry S. Truman*'s flight-deck controller signalled them away, and one by one their screaming rotors bore them almost vertically into the sky, banking out over the port side of the carrier to form a long convoy making a wide, slow circular route towards the *Ronald Reagan*.

With six airborne, there was now an open deck for the first of the *Ronald Reagan*'s Tomcats to land. And over on the Battle Group's flagship there was intense activity. The red light on the island signalled . . . *Four minutes to launch*.

The first Tomcat was in position at the head of the runway, the visual checks completed. Two minutes later the light flicked to amber and a crewman moved forward to the catapult and attached it to the launch bar. The light turned green, Lt. Jack Snyder, the 'shooter', raised his right hand and pointed it directly at the pilot. Then he raised his left hand and pointed two fingers . . . *Go to full power* . . . Then he extended his palm straight out . . . *Hit the afterburners* . . . Immediately, the pilot saluted and leaned slightly forward, tensing for the impact of the catapult shot.

Lt. Snyder, still staring directly at the cockpit,

saluted, then bent his knees, extended two fingers on his left hand and touched the deck. He gestured *FORWARD!* And a crewman, kneeling on the narrow catwalk next to the fighter jet, hit the button on catapult one and ducked low as the stupendous force of the hydraulic mechanism hurled the jet on its way.

Engines howling flat out, it left a blast of hot air in its wake. And, as always, every heart on that deck, every heart in the island control centres, stopped beating. For just a couple of seconds no one breathed as the Tomcat hurtled towards the bow, up the ramp and out over the water, climbing away, dead ahead, ready to start its 25-mile circle to the flight deck of the *Harry S. Truman*, which would bear it home to the United States.

Five more times the flight-deck crew of the *Ronald Reagan* sent the Tomcats away, up into the lashing rain, before the flight controller, in his fluorescent waterproof yellow gear, signalled that the Seahawks were on their way in.

Back on the *Harry S. Truman*, the flight-deck crew anticipated the first of the F-14 Tomcats, which had broken off from the stack of six and circled at 8,000 feet, 20 miles out, heading their way.

It was a 22-ton brute of an aircraft which didn't just glide in, flaring out elegantly just above a mile-long runway like a big passenger jet, but came bucking in, lurching along in all weathers, at 160 knots, damn near out of gas, and then slamming down onto the deck, the pilot praying for the arresting wire to grab and hold.

485

If it missed, he would have approximately one-twentieth of a second to ram the throttles wide open and thunder off the flight deck . . . before $40 million worth of aircraft hurtled over the side and punched a hole in the ocean's choppy surface. And there was always the possibility of an outright catastrophe, the hook missing, the pilot's reaction a shade slow and the aircraft slewing around, piling into forty others, all within yards of millions of gallons of jet fuel.

However many times a pilot had done it, the exercise of landing a fighter bomber on the heaving deck of a carrier would remain a life or death test of nerve and skill.

Right now, on the rain-lashed stern of the *Harry S. Truman*, the Landing Signals Officer, tall, lanky Texan Eugene 'Geeno' Espineli, was in contact with the incoming Tomcat's pilot, Lt. J.R. Crowell from West Virginia. Espineli's binoculars were focused as well as they could be in the weather, trying to track the aircraft's incoming path.

Ensign Junior Grade Taylor Cobb, the Arresting Gear Officer, was calling the shots, bellowing down the phone, above the howl of the wind, to the hydraulics team working below. He was out on the stern in his bright yellow waterproofs, earphones on, his eyes scanning the deck, checking for even the slightest speck of litter which could be sucked into the Tomcat's engine and blow it right out. He was checking for the fourth or fifth time for a broken arrester wire, which could lash back and kill a dozen people, not to mention the absolute certainty of sending the aircraft straight over the bow.

'STAND BY FOR THE TOMCAT . . . TWO MINUTES!'

The massive hydraulic piston was set to withstand the controlled collision between fighter jet and deck. And now everyone could see J.R. Crowell fighting to hold the Tomcat steady, two degrees above the horizontal against the driving rain and unpredictable gusts.

The *Harry S. Truman* was pitching through three degrees in the long swells, dead into the wind, at 18 knots. She was rising and falling one and a half degrees either side of the horizontal, which put the bow and stern through 60 feet every thirty seconds. Conditions to challenge the deftness and fortitude of any pilot.

'*GROOVE!*' bawled Ensign Cobb, code for, '*She's close, stand by . . .*'

Then, twenty seconds later, '*SHORT!*' – the critical command, everyone away from the machinery.

Out on the deck all LSOs edged towards the big padded pit into which they would jump if young J.R. misjudged and piled into the stern. They could see the aircraft now, screaming in through the rain, engines howling.

'*RAMP!*' bellowed Ensign Cobb. And with every eye upon it, J.R. slammed the Tomcat down on the landing surface, and the flight-deck crew breathed again as the cable grabbed the hook, then rose up from the deck into a V. One second later the Tomcat stopped dead in its tracks, almost invisible in the swirling mist of rain and spray in its wake.

The deck crews came out of the starting blocks like Olympic sprinters, racing towards the aircraft to haul it into its designated parking spot. And out there on the stern, Ensign Cobb, the rain beating off his hood, had already made contact with the second incoming Tomcat . . . *Okay one-zero-eight . . . wind gusting at 38 . . . check your approach line . . . looking good from here . . . flaps down . . . hook down . . . gotcha visual . . . you're all set . . . c'mon in . . .*

One by one they repeated the procedure. Then six more Seahawks took off in the failing light. Then six more Tomcats blasted off the deck of the *Ronald Reagan*, and headed for the stack 20 miles astern of the *Harry S. Truman*. Six at a time. Then the Hornets, six more groups, all going through the same death-defying combat procedures, slamming the jets down on the deck, the aces of the *Death Rattler* squadron, the *Vigilantes* and the *Kestrels*.

These unsung heroes of the US Navy displayed the lunatic, rarefied skills of their profession almost always in private, out here in the Atlantic, away from the celebrity-obsessed society they were trying to protect.

It took six hours to complete the transfer of the aircraft, and it was almost midnight when the final Hornet made its landing. By now the rain had stopped and the weary flight-deck crews were heading for their bunks. The fighter pilots were going home with the *Harry S. Truman* and their aircraft.

The Seahawk crews, now safely on board the *Ronald Reagan*, were mostly asleep. Their task, their intensive ceaseless mission, to find the *Barracuda*, would begin at first light on Tuesday morning, 6 October. And there would be little rest until the submarine was detected. If it was.

Another twenty-four-hour-a-day operation had been taking place simultaneously 2,700 miles away to the west in the concrete canyons of New York City.

Ten times more vulnerable than Washington, DC, New York would take the full might of the tidal wave head-on, straight off the ocean. And although the great towers of Wall Street would probably be the most resolute barrier the tidal wave would hit, they could not possibly stop a force that would probably have swept the Verrazano Narrows Bridge clean off its foundations seven miles earlier, planted the Coney Island fairground on top of Brooklyn Heights and dumped the Statue of Liberty into the bottom of Upper New York Bay.

Whether the skyscrapers of Downtown Manhattan would still be standing after the opening surge was a subject currently being assessed by a team of eighteen scientists working everywhere from basements to the city's skies. Opinion raged high and the only thing they could agree on was that none of them thought more than a half-dozen buildings at best could survive in any shape whatsoever.

Midtown, with its close, tight grid of towers, densely crowded and stretching high into the sky, was an even worse prospect. The breakwater of Wall Street would have reduced the first two waves significantly but nonetheless, like a house of cards, Midtown would fall. Several of the scientists believed that if two or three high-rises crumbled before the onslaught of the ocean, they would cause a chain reaction, bring down others until the city was levelled.

The most dangerous part was the two wide rivers which flowed past, east and west of Manhattan – the Hudson and the East River. The *tsunami* would have lost none of its power when it rampaged up these ship-going seaways, and both rivers could rise, initially, by around 100 feet, with millions of tons of ocean water crashing through the city's cross streets. The tides of east and west would probably collide somewhere in the middle, around Park Avenue, moments before the main surge smashed with mind-blowing force into the old Pan-American building somewhere around the fifteenth floor.

New York City was no place to be these two weeks. And the same went for Staten Island and Brooklyn, Queens and the Bronx. The flatlands of New Jersey were even more exposed and places like Bayonne, Jersey City, Hoboken and Union City were utterly defenceless. So was Newark, with its wide, flat, sea-level airport, right where the Passaic

River widens into Newark Bay. That was *tsunami* country, with a vengeance.

New York City's evacuation operation had begun the previous Wednesday, but the city's biggest problem wasn't so much historic documents, books and artefacts. It was people. New York City received more visitors every day than the combined permanent population of Washington, DC, and its environs. In addition to the eight million residents, living and working in the crowded urban sprawl of New York and its greater area, 800,000 visitors took in the sights below the world's most famous skyline every day.

It was a colourful, vibrant melee of races, religions and nationalities, a volatile mix in a time of crisis. Immigrants from the Far East, India and Mexico had been pouring in for years, and most of them had few contacts outside their ethnic neighbourhoods. Now they had no way of moving themselves, their families and few possessions out of the city to higher ground. A couple of days after the President's TV Address, Tammany Hall had accepted the responsibility of evacuating two million residents of New York City, providing shelter and food for those who had nothing and those who would most likely have nothing to go back to.

The exodus from New York had already begun, and thus far there had been monumental problems due to the sheer volume of people who had to be moved westward. Most of them were terrified, panicked and shocked. Rumours coursed wildly, crowds were alternately lining up for cars and gas masks or hitting the highway in a rush, sitting for hours on congested roads. Everyone was up in arms and the Army and National Guard could just barely control the mobbed streets, anxiety and fear flaring on every corner, spreading slowly across the city, simmering. Hundreds of National Guardsmen were drafted in from all over New York State to try to prevent riots breaking out.

The Police Department had by now issued instructions for the more affluent members of society to drive out of the area. They designated highways as strictly one-way systems and decreed which roads could be used to get away, no matter who you were. If you lived in Brooklyn or Long Island the way out was across the Verrazano Bridge to Staten Island, and then through the Outerbridge toll, wide open now, crossing onto highways running west and southwest.

Residents of Queens and Manhattan were ordered to use the Lincoln and Holland Tunnels and then pick up the westward highways. The great span of the George Washington Bridge was off limits, both ways, for use of the police, Army and government officials only. The great convoys of trucks evacuating the city were non-stop, both ways, twenty-four hours a day.

During the weekend a brand new worry cropped up. Thousands of people, many of whom hardly spoke English, were too afraid to wait for their transportation slots from the Army, the National

Guard or the New York Police Dept; some were more afraid of those than of the incoming tidal wave. Many took matters into their own hands, buying and temporarily fixing up an entire armada of ancient car wrecks, not only unfit to be on the road but a danger to anyone in or near them.

This clapped-out procession of backfiring, brakeless rattletraps was moving like a mobile junkyard out into the mainstream of the traffic, which was now already crowding the roads and highways.

By Sunday evening the traffic jams had escalated, the like of which had rarely, if ever, been seen in the free world. People were sitting on the roadside beside vehicles which were filled to overflowing with humanity and possessions. Cars edged slowly towards the west, coming to a complete standstill as soon as an ordinarily harmless flat battery felled a vehicle in front. On the Triboro Bridge, the 59th Street Bridge, both levels were throbbing with cars; cars jammed the Whitestone, clogged the Throg's Neck, brought the West Side highway to a standstill. The Lincoln and Holland Tunnels and Harlem River Drive were parking lots.

By Monday morning, the Mayor had signed an edict giving the New York Police Department emergency powers to sequester every breakdown truck in the city and hand it over to the National Guard. The authorities designated instant scrapyards, under raised highways and under bridges; they beat down wire fencing to free up space on outdoor basketball courts. They dragged vehicles off the bridges and out of the tunnels and dumped them in the nearest available space.

The Mayor had already named New York City as a potential disaster area, and now he had the Army move in and take over the subway and all of its trains, plus Amtrac and the entire Long Island Railroad.

The trains were for transport out of Manhattan and Long Island only. But the going was slow. Vast lines of travellers had been forming along Seventh and Eighth Avenues around 33rd Street waiting for hours to enter Penn Station.

The trains were efficient and available to move people out of the city on a continuing basis with executives from Amtrac and the major New York bus corporations summoned to City Hall to coord-inate and manage the operation.

A massive complex, a refugee camp of sorts, was being set up in the hills of New Jersey, west of the horse country around Far Hills. It was a former Army base and the huts were still waterproof. By Monday evening 100,000 National Guardsmen and troops were on duty, assisting with the evacuation from New York City.

The nearest New York came to full-blooded riots was, curiously, at truck-hire corporations, which were attempting to quadruple the regular price structure. They had no way of knowing if they would ever see their trucks again in the face of the incoming disaster, but locals saw it as naked price gouging, a cynical exercise in ripping off frightened citizens.

Three tearaways actually set fire to one rental operation in the Lower East Side, torching the office and three trucks. The Fire Department didn't make it in time to salvage them, and the National Guardsmen who were on the spot quickly had little sympathy with the owners.

The Police Chief and the Mayor moved in immediately and made price increases illegal, adding that if truck-hire corporations no longer wished to rent, that was fine too, empowering in the same breath the National Guard to sequester all trucks in the city.

They came a few hours too late for a more serious riot on the Lower West Side when hundreds of fleeing people became enraged at the asking price of $1,000 a day for a compact-sized truck. They stormed the office, overpowered the four assistants, smashed the windows, seized the keys hanging on a cork board at the rear of the counter and made off with twenty-six trucks.

Again, there was nothing much the police could – or would – do. They were working in squadrons with the Army, systematically clearing out residential blocks, helping people with their possessions, issuing exit instructions from the city. More and more National Guardsmen were being ferried in from upstate New York to help with the compulsory evacuation.

And their task was mammoth, especially on the Middle and Upper East Side where so many residential apartment blocks crowded close together, on all streets from 57th Street, north to Sutton Place, First, Second and Third Avenues. Not so much the more commercial strips of Lexington and Madison, but again on densely residential Park Avenue, and, of course, the east side of Fifth Avenue.

Almost all visitors to the city were either gone or on their way, having been advised at the end of the previous week to leave without delay. The Mayor ordered the police and the Army to seize the bus corporations in order to ferry thousands of tourists out to the airports.

They alerted foreign governments to the imminent disaster and informed every US embassy, world-wide, that all visitors were banned forthwith from flying to any airport on the East Coast. They requested foreign airlines to bring in extra aircraft, empty, to assist with the transportation of tourists out of JFK, Newark and LaGuardia. Inbound aircraft with passengers were diverted to Toronto to refuel and return home.

The Port of New York was closed except to outgoing shipping, which was redirected south, unless you particularly wanted your big cruise liner or freighter to end up in Times Square.

All businesses not directly involved in transportation were closed; commercial or retail, the service industry, tourist attractions and places of entertainment. Schools, colleges and universities also shut down.

The objective was partly to reduce drastically the amount of daily routine traffic on the streets of the city in order to provide space for the Army and police, dispatching truck-loads of important government and commercial documents stored in Manhattan by the big corporations.

The closing of shops and stores caused another spectre to rear its snarling head in the planning offices of Tammany Hall: the chilling recollection of the Big Blackout in the summer of 1977 when a massive power failure plunged the city into almost total darkness. It had taken the criminal element about ten minutes to realise all the lights were out and the burglar alarms silenced, sending several thousand looters and rioters into immediate action. By first light they had broken into stores city-wide and stolen millions of dollars worth of merchandise.

The situation at hand was not quite that serious. There was plenty of electric power and many extra thousands of police and National Guard on duty. And looters themselves had to fear for their lives. Nonetheless, the great silent neighbourhoods of New York City and stores full of merchandise were standing unattended, tempting nefarious characters far and wide.

The police presence tended to gather in full force in certain areas moving as one large unit from block to block, leaving desolate areas in their wake. Two serious break-ins along West 34th Street near Macy's department store alerted the authorities, and the armed National Guard were moved into the silent areas the moment they arrived in the city.

Police cars drove slowly along the streets, loudly

informing anyone who cared to listen that this was now a designated no-go area, closed to pedestrians and private cars unless on official business. The cold-blooded warning was loud and clear: *LOOTERS WILL BE SHOT*. This was as close to martial law as it was possible to get, but the Service Chiefs had been adamant – there was only one way to run an operation like this . . . *rigid rules, and ruthless application of those rules. Citizens must learn to do precisely as they are told. Instantly. And not to step out of line. That's the only way we can get this done.*

The guidelines on the desk of the New York Mayor had come directly from the White House, from the all-powerful Admiral Arnold Morgan, refined by the Chiefs of Army Staff in the Pentagon. There was to be no arguing, no discussion, no inter-ruptions, no alternative plan. This was strictly mili-tary. These were orders, not suggestions . . . *DO IT! AND DO IT NOW*!

Generally speaking, it was working. There had been some dissent and attempted robberies at first, but the sight of the perpetrators who were caught, bundled into the back of an Army truck and driven off to God knows where, had a steadying effect on anyone else with similar ambitions.

The police worked around the clock, aiding, protecting, urging people along the way. On the Upper East Side, elderly former chief executives and various New York dowagers found it was too much to be asked to be separated from a precious painting or valuable items of furniture and refused to leave without them. Most New York cops were understanding, the more so since these people usually had two or three automobiles at their disposal plus chauffeurs and were more than happy to make them available to help with the evacuation.

An acute problem was the number of prisoners and guards under the supervision of the New York City Department of Correction, which was currently holding 19,000 inmates, plus a staff of just over 10,000 uniformed officers and 1,500 civilians. The City Department ran ten holding facilities on Rikers Island, a building about the size of the Kremlin which sat in the middle of the East River, including two floating detention centres docked off the northern tip of Rikers in an old converted Staten Island ferry. This was, of course, a site unlikely to have much of a long-term future once Admiral Badr drew a bead on Cumbre Vieja – it stood an outstanding chance of being flattened and simply swept away by the tidal wave.

There were six additional jails run by the Department, one in Manhattan and one in Queens, two in Brooklyn and two more in the Bronx, one of which was an 800-bed barge, moored on the south side. The New York City Police Chief had immediately decided on early release of those detainees that he judged unlikely to represent much of a future danger to the public and those unable to post bail. The rest were being transferred to jails in upstate New York, New Jersey, Pennsylvania, Connecticut and Massachusetts, under armed guard, on trains, where security was somehow more manageable than on the open highway.

Back in Manhattan, the trenches of Wall Street had been in a state of near-pandemonium for five days. After 9/11, many corporations, headquarters of multi-nationals, general commerce, manufacturing, service industries and financial institutions, had been jolted into reviewing and updating their crisis management procedures. They had already put into operation disaster recovery strategies, to get the businesses back up and running in the event of a catastrophe and thought of back-up facilities and systems, which could be activated fast if the head office were struck or disabled.

But not many of them had thought it through nearly well enough and many of the same old problems that had haunted so many US corporations in the aftermath of 9/11 were still present.

Several corporations, devastated by the fall of the twin towers, did have back-up systems, but in neighbouring streets of Manhattan, which obviously rendered them utterly useless in this case.

There were other corporations which had tried to save money by sharing facilities through third-party providers, outfits that had reasonable storage for IT facilities, but almost no desk space for employees, who were trying to salvage the business from calamity.

The *tsunami* suddenly highlighted the looming potential for a systematic failure, which might put several of the world's largest financial institutions out of operation for a significant time. On this early October Monday, the financial capital of New York City was staring down the gun barrel of the most terrible domino effect, which could very easily lead to the total collapse of the world's financial system.

A stern warning, in the aftermath of 9/11, had been issued by the regulatory body, the Security and Exchange Commission. In one section of the consultative document the SEC had imposed specific requirements on major financial institutions – stipulating precisely the acceptable recovery periods and minimum distances between back-up facilities.

Some corporations, like IBM, had put these hugely expensive plans onto a fast track, probably fast enough to stay ahead of the *tsunami*. IBM had scoured the Kittatinny Mountain area out in western New Jersey, looking for a site to install a complete new complex, which would enable them to pro-vide, in corporate parlance, 'full IT resilience' plus duplicate live data centres.

Finally, they had settled on Sterling Hill and invested heavily in setting up their Business and Continuity Recovery Center in a maze of great office complexes 35 miles northwest of Wall Street, some of them underground, in disused mines, others in the hills and forests. And there, many of their clients had paid a monthly rental for several years, in return for secure office space with computers and desks, plus entire computer back-up if ever required.

IBM's foresight caused several other Manhattan

corporations to head for the New Jersey hills as well. For five days now there had been a steady stream of executives, bankers, financial officers and an army of back-up operators, moving out to New Jersey. A gigantic electronic surge in the local power stations signalled their arrival, as the alternative offices came on stream, operating parallel to their headquarters in nerve-wracked Manhattan.

Still battling away in the almost deserted ops rooms of Wall Street was a battalion of computer technicians, retrieving hard-drive material, main servers and ancillary equipment, sending truck load after truck load of high-tech data out to the crowded highways towards the mountain ranges east of the Poconos.

Morgan Stanley, the securities giant, had been forced to relocate 3,700 employees when the World Trade Center was destroyed. In the ensuing years that corporation had been committed, more than most, to building a state-of-the-art back-up trading facility. They selected their site and were up and running, 18 miles outside Manhattan, by 2007. The only problem: the complex was located in Harrison, less than two miles from Mamaroneck Harbor, along the flat northern shore of Long Island Sound, where the tidal surge was estimated at about 80 feet. Not ideal for Morgan Stanley.

Alas, very few stockbrokers were among the exodus. The New York Stock Exchange had made a strategic misjudgement. In response to the edict laid down by the SEC they had built an alternative trading facility to serve as back-up in the event of a disaster in Lower Manhattan. It could be fully operational inside twenty-four hours, a turnaround time superior even to that laid down by the SEC. Problem here: the NYSE's back-up facility was in New York City. Its unfortunate location was causing anxieties from Wall Street to the White House. The sudden closure of the main world market, possibly for several weeks, would likely have catastrophic effects.

The NYSE listed more than 2,800 companies (both foreign and multinationals) which have a global market capitalisation of around $15 trillion between them. Its daily functioning was absolutely fundamental to the continued stability of the world markets. Almost all stock exchanges, major and regional, had been agonising in recent years over disaster recovery facilities. Three thousand business personnel supported trading on the NYSE floor every day, using 8,000 telephone lines and 5,500 hand-held electronic devices. A back-up trading floor, with full equipment, was a $50 million project.

And it's not as if everything was neatly kept together. The NYSE has, historically, spread itself all over the place. They had started enlarging and remodelling as long ago as 1870, beginning with their original five-storey building at 10 Broad Street. Over the years, more buildings opened, finishing with a fifth trading room, located at 30 Broad Street in 2000, featuring the most up-to-date display technology on earth.

All of this was no easy operation to pack up, and

it was almost impossible to imagine duplicating everything somewhere else, under one roof. The exodus of the Stock Exchange was a permanent preoccupation for many high-ranking government officials, the irony being that the *tsunami* would most likely rub out the back-up before it even hit the main Exchange. It looked like they would have to head for Chicago. Philadelphia was out of question, since the City of Brotherly Love was sited on a peninsula, where the broad Schuykill River ran into the even broader Delaware. The Philadelphia Navy Base had already evacuated both ships and personnel, since scientists from the University of Pennsylvania thought the rivers could rise up to 25 feet.

The third and biggest issue, after the evacuation of big businesses, was the removal of the city's art treasures. As one of the world centres of art and culture, New York City contained seventy-five notable museums, plus scores and scores of art galleries. The Metropolitan Museum of Art, the Museum of Modern Art, the Guggenheim, the Whitney and the Museum of Natural History, known locally as the Big Five, were world-class institutions. The dozens of others, if located in a smaller city, would have been star attractions in their own right.

The Metropolitan, for example, or the 'Met' as they call it in the Big Apple, is tantamount to a universal culture zone all on its own, with wing after wing, labyrinths of corridors and galleries, three millions objects in all − paintings and sculpture, ceramics, glass, furniture, Medieval armour, statues, bronzes and the rarest musical instruments. Each item historic, genuine, and coveted by curators the world over.

For days now, a great convoy of military trucks had been evacuating the building, designated by the US a National Historical Landmark. Already they had removed 36,000 treasures of Ancient Egypt, from dynastic and pre-dynastic times. Everything was on its way to a US Air Force base in upstate New York where it would be guarded 24/7 by upwards of 300 military personnel.

Statues, carvings, sculpture from the land of the pharaohs were packed and shipped, each truck occupied by museum staff, plus a minimum of a dozen armed soldiers. An absolutely priceless, life-sized, enthroned, limestone sculpture of Queen Hatshepsut who ruled during the fabled 18th Dynasty (1570–1342 BC) was transported in an Air Force truck all on its own, save for the stern attendance of twelve unsmiling bodyguards from the National Guard. It must have been like old times for the Queen as she roared over the Triboro Bridge, not even considering the possibility of the tolls. The entire Temple of Dendur, a gift from the people of Egypt, had been dismantled and trucked out. The massive stones dating from the Roman period and depicting Caesar Augustus making offerings to the Egyptian and Nubian gods had been presented to the US for helping to save ancient monuments during the 1960s, after the construction of the High

Dam at Aswan which flooded the Nile and formed Lake Nasser.

Roman and Greek statues and sculpture, some up to 5,000 years old, even a bronze chariot worth millions, had been packed and sent north to the enormous Fort Drum military base, way upstate in the Watertown area where the St Lawrence River runs into Lake Ontario.

The paintings were in the process of being removed by a special detachment of United States Marines, an entire battalion, 600 men, working around the clock. By special order of the Pentagon, one of the greatest collections the world has ever seen was being removed to West Point Military Academy, 50 miles up the Hudson. Thus, from the moment they were taken down from the walls, the paintings were under guard, in the hands of some of the most trusted men in the United States.

During the weekend they had packed and trucked away almost the entire collection of Florentine and Venetian masters, works by Raphael, Tintoretto, Titian, Veronese and Tiepolo, plus some of El Greco's greatest work. The $100 million *Juan de Pareja*, painted by Diego Velazquez in the mid-seventeenth century, was already being guarded at the US Army's stronghold on the Hudson.

And one of the most famous paintings in the world, *Aristotle with a Bust of Homer* by Rembrandt, was due to leave at the end of the afternoon, in company with the artist's several other works owned by the Met. The shimmering waters of Claude

Monet, Van Gogh's cypresses, the dancers of Degas, the works of Paul Gauguin, Auguste Renoir, Manet, Rodin and every other renowned artist who has ever lived, were also on their way north.

The Met's collection of drawings alone, by Leonardo da Vinci, Michelangelo, Rembrandt, Dürer, Rubens and Goya, were worth enough money on the world market to operate the annual budgets of every African country south of the Blue Nile.

Master sergeants prowled the corridors of the museums, while privates and corporals sweated and heaved the huge wooden packing cases. Officers supervised the convoys. Inside the Met there were two US Marine brigadier generals.

Two hundred miles to the north, the city of Boston, though less than a quarter the size of Brooklyn, was in as great a danger as New York, its downtown district being surrounded by open water. The *tsunami* would roll in from the southeast, heading northwest, and although the island of Nantucket, the shoals of Nantucket Sound and the narrow sandy land of Cape Cod might just offer some kind of shield, expert opinion nonetheless forecast that the wave that would come seething up Massachusetts Bay and smash into the downtown area would still be over 100 feet high.

There were only 550,000 people resident in the city, 250,000 of them students at sixty different colleges and universities, all of which had been closed, as had the 3,000 software and internet corporations which had sprouted around the city during the high-tech revolution of the 1980s and 1990s.

Of greatest concern were the famous education centres: the Harvard Business School situated three miles upstream, right on the west bank of the Charles River; and Massachusetts Institute of Technology (MIT), sprawled across 150 acres downstream near Harvard Bridge, one mile on the Cambridge side of the wide Charles River Basin, right on the water.

Boston University, the third largest university in the United States, had a vast waterfront campus west of downtown Boston, on the opposite bank of the river from MIT. Dr Martin Luther King's old Alma Mater had 30,000 students from fifty states and 135 other countries, most of whom had returned home or to friends for the week.

The evacuation of the universities and the museums was identical in procedure to the other great East Coast cities, but little Boston was somehow more vulnerable than the others. It lacked the granite muscle of New York, and Washington's shelter from the ocean. There was a feeling of genuine terror all around the historic New England seaport.

0600 Tuesday 6 October 2009
La Palma Airport, Canary Islands
The runway of La Palma Airport, newly extended, was now a mile long, almost as if the arrival of the four giant US Air Force C-17 Globemaster III freighters which were now making their approach from the west, six miles apart, line astern, had been anticipated. The cargo leviathans with their 170-

foot wingspans stood 55 feet high on the ground, with a cargo compartment three times longer than a Greyhound bus and more than 12 feet high.

Right now, all four were full as they came in over the Atlantic, circled around to the north and headed directly into the southwest wind gusting over the runway. One by one they touched down at the little airport seven miles south of the main town of Santa Cruz, 20 miles northeast of the yawning crater of the Cumbre Vieja volcano.

Each aircraft taxied to a special holding area where their massive rear doors were opened and lowered. There, over the next two hours, they were unloaded by US Army personnel who had travelled all the way from Air Mobility Command, Charleston Air Force Base, South Carolina, 437th Airlift Wing.

The first Globemaster contained the front ends of four Army trucks, which were driven out and then backed up the ramps of the other three. When they drove back down onto the blacktop, they looked more complete, with the long bed of the truck now attached.

And fitted to those flatbeds were the mobile, truck-loaded Patriot missile launchers, eight of them, the super-high-tech platform for the state-of-the-art MIM-104E guidance enhanced missiles, the only SAM which has ever intercepted ballistic missiles in combat.

Each launcher came complete with four of these MIM-104E Patriots, the sensational long-range, all-altitude, all-weather defence system, designed to counter tactical ballistic missiles, cruise missiles and advanced aircraft. The thirty-two already fitted inside the launchers on La Palma were built by Raytheon in Massachusetts, and by Lockheed Martin Missiles and Fire Control in Florida.

Their theoretical objective was relatively simple – to seek out and destroy incoming missiles. The reality, though, was rather more complicated. These things travelled at Mach 5, close to 4,000 mph, which pretty much guaranteed that whatever enemy missile might be on its way in would have zero time to get out of the way.

The US military spent all of the 1990s trying to perfect the Patriot after it missed too many of Saddam's SCUDs over Israel in the First Gulf War. They spent months and months in the Pacific, ironing out the problems. The new, updated, improved Patriot had an uplink from its ground-radar control unit, to feed it final course-correction, target-acquisition orders, and a downlink to feed back information on the target's position. These had to be transmitted pretty sharply since the Patriot was travelling as close to the speed of light as possible.

The system is known as TVM – track-via-missile guidance system – and is fitted to the new low-noise front end, which had dramatically increased seeker sensitivity to low radar cross-section targets. The Patriot MIM-104E was a completely new missile, a variant of the Lockheed Martin ERINT (Extended Range Interceptor). It is the last word in advanced hit-to-kill technology, carrying a warhead consisting of 200 pounds of TNT, enough to knock down New York's Yankee Stadium.

Admiral Badr's SCIMITAR missiles were fast, reliable and accurate. But in the devastating new Patriot they had a ferocious opponent. The main asset of the HAMAS attack was the element of surprise enjoyed by all submerged launched missiles. No one would know where it was coming from. You had to see it, and you had to move very fast. Your Patriot would nail it, but you'd have to get it away in seconds. Not minutes. The soldiers working on the La Palma airfield knew that. The first four launch trucks moved off now, down towards Atlantic Highway 1. They were heading south to begin with, but would soon swing up the west coast of the island towards the volcanoes, and the rugged rim of Cumbre Vieja, where they would set up their missile battery in readiness, perhaps for their last stand, against a lethal enemy.

There were sixteen young soldiers in this first group, four of them officers. Each of them knew that if the system acquired, and they missed their 600-mph incoming target, it would be their last act on this earth. It would spear in at them from a high trajectory, and the SCIMITAR would blast the great mountain peak to smithereens, sounding a violent death knell not only for them but for the whole of the East Coast.

Major Blake Gill was in overall command. Aged thirty-five, he was a career officer, trained at West Point. Back home, in Clarksville, Tennessee, his wife and two sons, aged five and eight, were waiting. As one of the US Army's top missile experts, he was stationed, along with the 101st Air Assault Division, at one of the biggest military bases in the country, Fort Campbell, Kentucky, hard on the Tennessee border.

Blake Gill had been in an Army missile team seconded to the US Navy's cruisers, during the Patriot testing programmes off Hawaii. He was an acknowledged aficionado of the Patriot system, and a glittering career awaited him either with Raytheon or Lockheed Martin, if and when he ever finished with the Army.

But Blake Gill was, like his missile, a patriot. He was a man cut from the mould of Admiral Arnold Morgan himself, a sworn enemy of his country's foes, a man to whom personal gain was a total stranger. The heavy-set Southerner, with his scorched-earth haircut, was plainly headed for the highest possible rank his branch of the service had to offer. If anyone was going to slam the SCIMITAR it was Blake Gill, husband of Louisa, father of Charlie and Harry. Missile man.

He rode in the lead truck in front of the launcher, the four hunter-killer Patriots towering behind him. He carried with him three different ground elevations of the Cumbre Vieja site – one a satellite photograph of the entire area taking in the coast-lines, another a map drawn from much closer in, and the last one a detailed map of the undulating terrain immediately around the crater.

Since no one had a precise idea from which direction the incoming missiles were to be fired, Blake Gill was relying on the facts presented to him at the Pentagon on his way to the Charleston Air Force Base. He knew he must cover the westerly approach and the more unlikely north, but he had been carefully briefed by both Admiral Frank Doran and the Chairman of the Joint Chiefs himself, General Tim Scannell, that the biggest threat was from the east and southeast.

The *Barracuda* ultimately had to get out of the way of the *tsunami* or it too would be destroyed. And that meant it had to seek cover on the eastern side of La Palma or Gomera if he launched close range.

Major Gill had pencilled in one of his mobile launchers to face outwards from the eight principal points of the compass. Any preprogrammed cruise missile could be directed on the most circuitous route into any target, but not without GPS. Therefore a major detour around the volcano, and then a route in from the north or west, seemed utterly unlikely.

Yes, the Pentagon was nearly certain that the missiles would come straight in, out of the east or southeast, simply to give the submarine a chance to save itself. He knew he must place launcher number five to the southeast. The problem of the northeast occupied him, however. There would be no course correction to the incoming weapons, and no cover out there in open water, nor any place the submarine could reach to find shelter before the tidal wave slung it straight onto the sandy beaches of Western Sahara.

And yet . . . he knew these suicide bastards from the Middle East . . . maybe sacrificing themselves was the master plan . . . maybe they just did not care . . . they would fire and forget from any spot they pleased and let Allah do his worst. Paradise, perhaps, beckoned. It was not, after all, particularly unusual for the young men of HAMAS to terminate their lives willingly in the Jihad against the West.

Major Gill was thoughtful. Clearly, the *Barracuda* was on its final mission. They were never going to take it home. To where? It could never again come to the surface, never again fire a missile. The forthcoming launch would betray its position, and the odds of it evading a strike force like the US Navy currently had at sea were close to zero.

No, the HAMAS terrorists almost certainly knew the game was up, the moment they opened fire within a very few miles of ASW warships and heli-copters. So they just might launch from anywhere. And he, Blake Gill, had to be ready for a threat from any direction with plenty of overlap.

He would position his mobile launchers, evenly spaced around the compass, facing out from the crater, in all directions. His maps showed the ground to be extremely rough and uneven, once the end of the road had been reached, and he was grateful for the huge US Marine Chinook helicopter awaiting him up at the summit, which he knew would place the launchers with effortless efficiency precisely where he wanted them.

They drove on down to the town of Los Canarios de Fuencaliente, where once hot springs had bubbled but, long buried by the eruptions of various volcanoes, now formed part of the deadly, roughly 10-mile-long cauldron beneath the mountain.

Major Gill studied his maps. To the south he knew was Volcan San Antonio. A signpost directed visitors to a pathway and a visitors' centre around its gaping black crater. Even further south was Volcan Teneguia, which is off the beaten track, where only a few adventurers could struggle up its slopes and peer in over the shattered rim.

The convoy of launchers was headed the other way, north, up towards Cumbre Vieja, glowering under the crystal-blue arc of the sky above the islands. As they drove on, in a cloud of black dust, the major could see the Chinook parked up ahead, about 200 yards off the main road.

It took about twenty minutes to secure the cables which would take the weight of the launcher. Major Gill and the missile crew climbed aboard for the short ride to the summit, and, under his direction, the Navy pilot put the launch truck exactly into position, facing due east, overlooking the Atlantic and the distant shores of Gomera and Tenerife.

The giant helo had already deposited all the equipment needed for the Engagement Control Centre further up the escarpment, to a slightly higher peak to the north. Twelve more technicians, who had travelled across the Atlantic in the *Harry S. Truman*, had already began to erect the station, ensuring it had views in all directions, overlooking the Atlantic to the east and west, where the frigates were patrolling. And, of course, overlooking the Patriot batteries around the crater to the south, with clear radar range at every point of the compass.

The Engagement Control Centre was the only manned station in a Patriot Fire Unit. It could communicate with any M901 launching stations and with other Patriot batteries, and it also had direct communications to the higher command facilities, in this case Admiral Gillmore's *Coronado*.

Three operators had two consoles and a communication station with three radio relay terminals. The digital weapons control computer was located next to the VHF Data Link terminals.

One of the C-17 Globemasters had brought in the trailer-mounted Raytheon MPQ-53 phased Army radar unit, a band-tracking radar capable of identifying 100 targets at a time. It was a superb component of any top-of-the-line shore missile battery, and it would carry out search, target detection, track and identification, missile tracking and guidance, plus electronic counter-countermeasures (ECCM) functions.

Its radar was automatically controlled, via a cable link, by the digital weapons control computer in the Engagement Control Centre sited further up the hill. The radar had a range of up to 55 miles, and could provide guidance data for up to nine missiles at any one time. Its wideband capability provided target discrimination never before achieved.

In normal circumstances, this overwhelming piece of electronic equipment might have been considered overkill in the search for one or possibly two incoming 'birds'. However, in this case, by express orders of Admiral Morgan, there was no such thing as overkill.

As the Patriot missile came flashing into its target, the TVM guidance system would be activated and the weapon could scarcely miss. And it would not require a midair collision to blow Admiral Badr's SCIMITAR clean out of the sky. The Patriot just needed to be close enough for a proximity fuse to detonate the high-explosive warhead, in this case an M248 91 kilogram – 200 pound – TNT blast fragmentation.

The MIM-104E was over 17 feet long, 16 inches in diameter, weighing 2,000 pounds. At Mach 5, its range was 43 miles and, if necessary, it could fly to a ceiling of 80,000 feet. Arnold Morgan had estimated a very high trajectory from the *Barracuda*'s missiles, which he thought would aim to lance down very steeply at the crater of Cumbre Vieja.

Major Gill had a copy of that shrewd assessment from the Supreme Commander folded neatly in his breast pocket as he prepared the US Army's ring of steel around the volcano's black heart. As he watched the mighty Chinook flying the Patriot launcher trucks right over the crater and into position, he knew that if the frigate's batteries were not in time, out in the open ocean, his own guided missiles would be the United States' last line of defence.

Five hundred feet below the surface, the *Barracuda* had cut its speed from six knots to five, after a very slight swing to the south. Its course would take it 14 miles south of the flashing light on Point Restinga, the southernmost headland of the Canary island of Hierro. Right now they were a little under 40 miles to the west and several days out of satellite contact with General Rashood.

Ben Badr was in the submarine's control room with his XO, Captain Ali Akbar Mohtaj, who was coming to the end of the First Watch. The admiral ordered the submarine to periscope depth for a swift GPS check and a visual look at the surface picture.

In the clear autumn night skies they could see that the ocean around them was devoid of shipping. The GPS numbers were accurate, according to their own navigation charts meticulously kept by Lt. Ashtari Mohammed, Shakira's old colleague.

DOWN PERISCOPE . . . MAKE YOUR DEPTH 500 . . . SPEED FIVE . . . Admiral Badr wore a soft smile as he felt the ship go bow down 10 degrees. He felt safe – so far as he could see no US Navy dragnet was trying to hunt him down.

The time was 11.30 and 15 seconds. What he didn't know as the *Barracuda* glided back towards the ocean floor was that in precisely 24 hours, 29

518

minutes and 45 seconds the world's GPS systems, US and European, would be shutting down. Ben Badr was proceeding to a long-range launching, which could not work. First blood to the United States.

He and Captain Mohtaj sipped hot tea with sugar and lemon and stared meditatively at the charts. They would be inside the grid of the seven islands shortly after dawn, and he would now head east, according to their original plan, to launch 30 miles south of Fuerteventura, 30 miles off the coast of Western Sahara.

'If we can launch long-range,' said Ben, 'we're bound to hit. The missile takes longer to get there. We have longer to get into shelter, and our chances of being detected are close to zero. So far I like it very much.'

By the time they finished their tea, and Captain Mohtaj had retired to his bunk, the GPS was still transmitting. But in twenty-four hours there would be a mind-blowing change to their plan.

Worse yet, the US guided missile frigate *Nicholas* was still in the area and Captain Nielsen's ops room had very nearly picked them up when they put up a mast for that last GPS check. The US frigate was less than 20 miles away and caught a slight 'paint' on two sweeps of the radar. It had disappeared on the third, but the ops room of the *Nicholas* was very sharp and the young seaman watching the screen had called it immediately. His supervisor had logged and given it a numbered track. It was now on the nets, circulating to the rest of the fleet. Of course, it could have been anything, a flock of birds, a rain squall, a breaching whale or a dolphin. But the operator was not so sure, and the *Nicholas* hung around for an hour, wondering if the 'paint' would return.

But nothing unusual occurred and Captain Nielsen proceeded on slowly through the night down the coast of Hierro, before making for Tenerife. He was steaming only a little faster than the *Barracuda*, which was travelling in the same direction, 20 miles off their starboard quarter, deep beneath the waves.

CHAPTER THIRTEEN

Wednesday 7 October 2009
Eastern Atlantic

The *Barracuda*, still making only six knots, steamed quietly past the flashing light on the stark southern headland of Hierro's Point Restingo shortly after 0700. They remained 500 feet below the surface, 14 miles south of the lighthouse, on a bright sunlit morning.

Twenty miles to the north, moving slowly south, four miles off the rust-red volcanic eastern coastline of the island, was the gun-grey 3,600-ton US frigate *Nicholas*. She was on a near-interception course with the *Barracuda* but Captain Eric Nielsen would turn east for Tenerife 10 miles north of the submarine.

On the west coast of the island, Captain Josh Deal's *Kauffman* was combing the Atlantic depths electronically, searching, searching for the telltale whispers which may betray the presence of the lethal underwater marauder.

If Captain Deal held his course, he too would eventually reach the submarine's track, but he also was under orders to swing east for Tenerife. Both

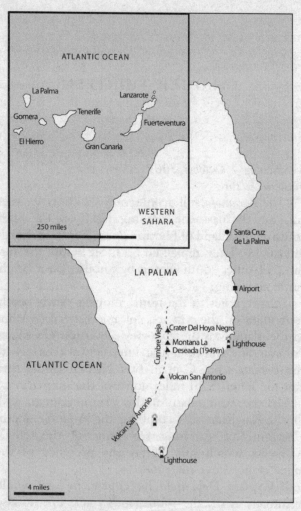

THE LINE OF VOLCANOES IN THE CUMBRE VIEJA RANGES
MAKES LA PALMA'S SOUTH A THREATENING PLACE

ships were proceeding with caution, not too fast to miss anything but with enough speed to cover the wide patch of ocean allotted them by Admiral Gillmore.

The tiny island of Hierro, only 15 miles wide, was once about three times the size. But a massive eruption around 50,000 years ago had blown it asunder, and, according to modern volcanologists, dumped about 100 square miles of solid rock onto the bottom of the Atlantic.

The shape of the island conformed precisely to the geological pattern of a great volcano rising up from the seabed. It shoaled down steeply to 850 feet right off the rock-strewn beach, then, in less then seven miles, plummeted to a narrow plateau 5,000 feet below the surface. From there, the ocean floor dived steeply for a mile and a half, straight down to a depth of more than 12,000 feet – almost identical ocean statistics to those of La Palma, 50 miles to the north.

At 0800 Admiral Ben Badr ordered the *Barracuda* to creep up slowly from these massive depths, to access the satellite, check the GPS and to report course and position to the private satellite receiver above the house on Sharia Bab Touma in Damascus, the command headquarters of the operation where the former Major Ray Kerman, awaited the signal.

Admiral Badr's Executive Officer, Captain Ali Akbar Mohtaj, ordered the periscope and the ESM mast up. There was no threat radar on the surface, and the comms room instantly retrieved a message off the Chinese Navy satellite. It revealed the wave-band numbers of the French GPS should the US take the precaution of blacking out the main access channels. General Rashood had received intelligence of possible 'limited GPS interruption', but the Pentagon had been cagey, releasing the news only on the restricted shipping and airline channels. The Arab newspapers hardly mentioned it and it would be several hours before the general could access the *Wall Street Journal*, since he was operating eight hours ahead of the US East Coast.

The *Barracuda*'s comms staff checked French and American GPS wavebands. Both were on-stream. Suddenly they heard US Navy radar. Captain Mohtaj quickly ordered mast and periscope down and the submarine back to depth 500 feet. Too late. Eric Nielsen's *Nicholas* had picked up a suspect at extreme range with three sweeps, 12 miles north of the jutting periscope.

The frigate's computers flashed into action, bringing up the previous 'paint', seven hours earlier at 40 miles to the west, and, if the same ship had caused both sightings, they were looking at a transient contact, making around six knots, bearing zero-nine-zero, due east, along latitude 27.25N.

Within seconds, the computerised deductions hit the comms room in the *Coronado*, up to the northwest of Lanzarote, and Admiral Gillmore immediately appreciated the situation. For the moment the *Elrod* and the *Nicholas* were slightly behind the eight-ball, but on stand-by, right off the northeast headland of Tenerife, he had Captain Clint Sammons' *Klakring* and Captain Joe Wickman's

Simpson. He ordered them to make good speed south for 100 miles, and to began their search as they crossed latitude 27.30N. ETA *Barracuda*: 2200 hours.

So far as Admiral Gillmore could see he had the submarine trapped between his four frigates. But he also knew that the *Barracuda* was so quiet it could creep 500 feet beneath them, at a silent five to six knots, and not to be detected by passive sonar, though it might be on 'active'.

He fired off a signal to Admiral Frank Doran, who was still in the command centre at Atlantic Fleet Headquarters in Norfolk . . . *070800OCT09 Possible detection Barracuda course zero-nine-zero 14 miles south of Hierro island. Course and speed correlates possible six-knot transient submarine detected 070100OCT09. Elrod and Nicholas tracking, Klakring and Simpson running south to intercept. Gillmore.*

Eight minutes later, Arnold Morgan leapt to his feet from his desk in the sparsely furnished Oval Office, punched the air, and gritted '*Come on, guys . . . let's tighten the fucking screws, put that little bastard on the seabed . . .*'

'You're not beginning to take this personally by any chance, are you, Arnold?' asked President Bedford, disarmingly.

'Christ no, sir. I just love chasing boatloads of underwater terrorists around the oceans – I just get a little edgy after the first year . . .'

Meanwhile, back in the eastern Atlantic Admiral Gillmore ordered the carrier *Ronald Reagan* southwest towards the coast of Gran Canaria, from its holding position 15 miles north of Lanzarote.

The US Navy's dragnet was closing in, but Admiral Gillmore was taking a calculated risk that the transient contacts were indeed the *Barracuda*. If they were not, and the HAMAS terrorists were coming in from further north, he would be heavily dependent on the steel cordon of guided-missile frigates out of Norfolk, which currently circled La Palma, inshore and offshore.

Right now a carrier was flying two continuous patrols, between the west coast of La Palma and the towering coast of the island of Gomera, where the precipitous cliffs plunge headlong into the ocean, just 35 miles northeast of Hierro.

All the Navy's assessments claimed that the submarine, if it was to fire its missiles visually, *must* come in towards Cumbre Vieja from either Gomera's southwest or northeast coast. The *Barracuda* might ultimately duck back behind this rocky fortress for shelter, in the moments before the mega-*tsunami* surged outwards into its horrifying reality.

Oblivious of the bear trap closing around them, the *Barracuda* had somewhat carelessly failed to detect the closeness of USS *Nicholas*, and now the Russian-built nuclear boat proceeded deep along her easterly course, slowly and quietly.

Down in the navigation area, Lt. Ashtari Mohammed estimated that by midnight they would reach a point 24 miles southwest of Playa de Inglés, the seething gay mecca of the island of Gran Canaria, winter headquarters of Sodomites International and a place likely to be crushed beneath a 50-foot tidal wave one hour after impact. Still, death by drowning would probably arrive on fleet wings, which would doubtless beat the hell out of being turned to stone.

That particular point on the chart would be critical for the submarine, because they would arrive there just as the world GPS was scheduled to crash. And the precise moment that Admiral Badr ordered his ship to the surface would determine how swiftly he would know that a long-range launch was out of the question.

And they ran quietly and silently all day, without the US frigates locating them. At 0030 on that moonlit Thursday morning, Admiral Badr ordered the *Barracuda* to PD, and her periscope came thrusting out of the water, alongside her mighty ESM mast, which was almost as thick as a telegraph pole. The two steel poles jutted right into the path of the radar sweeping across the water from all four of the trailing US frigates.

The *Barracuda* sucked down a signal from General Rashood in the couple of seconds before the submarine's ops room picked up the frigates on their ESM. Continuous sweeps. Captain Mohtaj said simply, 'We're surrounded, sir.'

'I understand that,' replied Ben Badr. 'But they're six miles away and we're not finished by any means . . . *10 BOW DOWN 600 . . . MAKE YOUR SPEED TEN . . . COME RIGHT TWENTY DEGREES . . .*'

At that moment young Ahmed Sabah came bursting out of the comms room with the communication from Damascus . . . *US GPS satellite communications crashed at midnight . . . Zhanjiang naval base making no contact with French version . . . world GPS black. Abort long-range launch. Repeat abort long-range launch . . . change course northwest and proceed to coast of Gomera . . . then head into La Palma launch zone 25 miles off the East Coast, for visual set-up. Allah goes with you. Rashood.*

All four US frigates picked up the radar contact and all four had solid contact. Both previous detections had been along the 27.25 line of latitude, and so was this third one. Each of the four commanding officers, Eric Nielsen, C.J. Smith, Clint Sammons and Joe Wickman, was now certain that they had their quarry under surveillance. And they all knew, of course, that the GPS was down and that the *Barracuda* was almost certain to change course right here at 27.25N 16.06W.

Admiral Badr's navigation room had not immediately understood the extent of the GPS blackout. Lt. Ashtari Mohammed had observed that they were receiving nothing from the satellites on their screens, but he was looking for a technical fault at first. It was not until Ahmed Sabah read out the signal from General Ravi that Ashtari fully realised the implications of his blank screen. There was no GPS, and there was not going to be any. The US Air Force's 50th Space Wing, out in Colorado, had placed a four-minute transmission delay on their formal announcement: *No GPS signal before 0100 Saturday 10 October.*

That had been Admiral Morgan's order, on the grounds that four minutes would be too long for the *Barracuda* to leave a mast up, and it might just run on for several more miles before they realised the GPS was down permanently.

General Rashood had dealt with that, however, and now Ben Badr ordered an immediate course change . . . *COME RIGHT ONE HUNDRED NINETY DEGREES . . . STEER COURSE THREE-ZERO-ZERO . . . MAKE YOUR SPEED FIVE . . . DEPTH 600.*

Captain Mohtaj, at the helm of the *Barracuda* now making course west-nor'west, handed the ship over to the COB, Ali Zahedi, at 0100. There was a 90-mile deep-water run to the shelter of the eastern shore of Gomera, and there was no problem staying 'below the layer', 600 feet under the surface, since the Atlantic all around the Canary Islands was nearly two miles deep.

But the sudden course change had unnerved the crew. Even though just a few of the senior command were aware that they were surrounded by US warships and their long-range launch plan had been scuppered, everyone quickly knew there was something amiss.

They were headed into the jaws of the United States Navy, which was not a great place to be. But General Rashood had made no mention of aborting the mission; rather, he had urged them forward, as soldiers of Allah, to strike the fateful blow against the Great Satan.

Admiral Badr called a briefing meeting in his small private office. In attendance were Captain Mohtaj, Commander Abbas Shafii, the nuclear specialist, Commander Hamidi Abdolrahim, the chief nuclear engineer, Lt. Ashtari Mohammed, the navigator, and Ahmed Sabah.

'Gentlemen,' said Ben Badr. 'I am no longer able to say with any certainty that any of us will survive this mission. However, my orders are that it must be completed, and it will be completed.'

He poured tea for them all from a silver pot into the little glasses with their silver holders. And he paused carefully, to allow his words to sink in. It was the first time in two underwater missions that anyone had ever suggested martyrdom. The anticipation of death is not so very far from the minds of any Islamic freedom fighter, and the fear of imminent death was in the minds of these men less than it might have been among those of another religious persuasion. Nonetheless, Ben Badr was surrounded by grave faces, and he was aware of the need to hold their attention.

'In many ways,' he said, 'nothing very much has altered. Of course, it would have been preferable to fire our missiles from two or three hundred miles out, but, as we now know, that will no longer be possible. However, our target has not moved, and we are perfectly capable of creeping in to a 25-mile range, taking our visual bearings and launching our SCIMITAR missiles straight at the volcano.

'The only change in our attack pattern is a need to be nearer the target, but the computerised missile will still obey our command. We just have to aim it straight and true. A nuclear missile doesn't need to be dead accurate, as long as it hits within a couple of hundred yards of the target. The blast will do the rest.'

'But there are two changes, Admiral,' said Ahmed Sabah. 'One is the length of time we shall be on the surface, the other is our departure.'

'Of course,' said Ben Badr. 'We will most certainly be detected by the American warships, but I believe we will have a few precious minutes to get deep after the two launches. And no matter how good they are, it remains extremely difficult to locate and attack a quiet submarine which is running very slow hundreds of feet below the surface.'

'How deep, sir?' asked Commander Shafii.

'One thousand feet, minimum. If they are using depth charges we will go to twelve hundred. It's blind chance, and terrible bad luck to get hit at that depth. Especially if we have a five- or 10-minute start on them. And we'll try to make our missile launch at least two miles from the nearest warship.'

'Will they launch missiles at us, the moment they catch a sight of it?' asked Ahmed.

'I'm hoping they'll concentrate their energies on trying to shoot down the SCIMITAR,' replied Admiral Badr. 'They may get a couple of ASROC away, but even then we still have a few minutes to get deep. They'd be very lucky to hit us, especially if they were hellbent on shooting down the SCIMITAR at the same time.'

'I think we've got a serious chance of escape,' said Ahmed Sabah.

'Yes,' replied the HAMAS admiral. 'An excellent chance.'

'Sir, how about an attack from the air? I mean torpedoes launched from helicopters?' said Commander Abdolrahim.

'That, Hamidi, is a game of cat and mouse. We will put up a mast for our fix. Then go deep again, and stay there, before we run up to our ranged launch point, take our bearings and fire, twice. The helicopter may be close, but it is unlikely to be close enough in my view. And again, all US energies will be concentrated on the SCIMITARs. We still have a great chance, believe me. And we have one other huge advantage . . . Allah goes with us; not with the infidels.'

And with that Ben Badr called the entire ship's company to prayer, using expertly the words of the muezzins which echoed from a thousand Middle Eastern mosques four times a day:

Allahu Akbar . . . God is most great.

Ashhadu an la ilaha Allah . . . I bear witness that there is none worthy of worship but God.

Ashhadu ann Muhammaden Rasoolullah . . . I bear witness that Mohammed is the Prophet of God.

La illah ill Allah . . . There is no Deity but God.

Each man, with the exception of the helmsman and the sonar chief, made his Declaration of Intent and followed through the twelve positions of prayer, making two prostrations in which their foreheads touched the steel of the deck.

The second salaam signified *Peace and Mercy to You*, and Admiral Badr, aware of the men's fear of the next few hours, began by quoting from the Koran: *Never think those slain in the cause of God are dead. They are alive and well provided for by the Lord.*

And he reminded them that the Prophet Mohammed, close to despair, once cried out to God: *O Lord, I make my complaint upon Thee of my helplessness and my insignificance before mankind. But Thou art the Lord of the poor and the feeble. And Thou art my Lord. Into whose hands wilt Thou abandon me?*

And Ban Badr, summoning all of the emotion of the 1,400-year-old world-wide brotherhood of Muslims, quoted again from the Koran, from God: *Remember me. I shall remember you! Thank me. Do not be ungrateful to me. You who believe, seek help through patience and prayer.*

Each member of the crew, now standing, palms outstretched to God, now wiped them across his face to symbolise the receipt of God's blessing.

Admiral Badr prayed silently, then he too wiped his face and indicated that prayers were concluded. He once more confirmed to the helmsman the course of west-nor'west and ordered his senior staff to the missile room, where they would begin the task of checking the nuclear warheads on the two great SCIMITARs.

By this time, Admiral Gillmore was in receipt of the data from all four of the tracking frigates. Their data showed the precise position of the submarine's periscope, which all four of the US radars had swept, at 0030, twenty-four miles off the most promiscuous area in the North Atlantic, apart, that is, from the area populated by rutting stags in the Isle of Skye off the coast of northern Scotland.

US Navy commanders are accustomed to keeping accurate charts and would cope with the downed world GPS system better than anyone else. And George Gillmore studied his screen carefully ... *now this character understands he can't fire long range ... therefore he'll turn in towards his target ... maybe west-nor'west ... maybe due west back along his old course ... but no other direction is any good to him ...*

He immediately ordered the *Elrod* and the *Nicholas* to take the west-nor'west track, with the *Klakring* and the *Simpson* proceeding more westerly. He also ordered the carrier to alter course, bringing its formidable air power, from the northwest coastline of Tenerife westward into the 80-mile-wide open seaway which divides that island from La Palma.

But the *Barracuda* kept moving forward, slowly, softly, through the dark ocean depths, unseen, unheard, her transmissions shut down. She made no sound through the water. Her great turbines were doing little more than idling, betraying no vibration lines. The Russians had spent years and years building their two state-of-the-art underwater hunter-killers, and thus far no one had detected either of the HAMAS *Barracuda*s with any real certainty or accuracy.

Admiral Gillmore thought he knew damn well where the *Barracuda* was, and so did his four front-line frigate commanders. At least they had known one hour earlier. But no one could prove the submarine's direction, and until the Americans locked on to a new surface radar 'paint', or obtained an active radar contact, that submarine was going to remain elusive.

And all through the next fifteen hours it ran on undetected. Despite the constant Seahawk helicopter patrols across every yard of water between the seven islands, despite the probing searches of the ASW specialist S-3B Viking aircraft. Despite the quivering sensitivity of the frigates' electronic towed arrays, and the high-powered blasts of their active sonars. And despite two serious attempts to trap the submarine between highly alert electronic sonobuoys, dropped into the water from the helos.

Not all the probing of the low-frequency dipping sonars could locate the *Barracuda*, as it steamed silently west-nor'west, way below the thunder of the noise above the surface, where the distinctive howl of the Vikings' GE turbofans were sufficient to awaken the dead.

Only twice, towards the end of the long journey up to the coast of Gomera, did Ben Badr risk a fleeting five-second thrust of his ESM mast, and both times they picked up radar transmissions from the Vikings which were operating out beyond the 25-mile circle around the volcano. Each time the ESM computerised accurate bearing and classification. By the time they reached the inshore waters, 'behind' the east coast of Gomera, Admiral Badr privately thought that this had rapidly begun to turn into a suicide mission.

Again he called his most trusted men into his office, Mohtaj, Shafii, Ali Zahedi and Ahmed Sabah.

Did they still have a chance? At getting away that is, not firing the SCIMITARs? Answer, probably not. They were driving forward into the very teeth of the US Navy's steel ring of defence. And right now they each understood that they would need several separate sorties to periscope depth. To try to achieve their mission with just one, or even two, extended visits to the waters right below the surface would be tantamount to blowing out their own brains.

Their only chance of success and escape was to come to PD fleetingly, to make their visual set-up, to get a fix on the land and the high peaks of the Cumbre Vieja mountains. And then to vanish, to return for a final fleeting range check, then to fire the two missiles in quick succession. At no time should they spend more than seven seconds above the surface. Not if they hoped to stay alive.

By 1600 on that Thursday afternoon they were in relatively shallow water, 2,500 feet, running 600 feet below the surface, four miles off the east coast of Gomera. Captain Mohtaj was in the navigation room assisting Lt. Ashtari Mohammed as he plotted a northerly course to a point six miles off Point del Organo. From there it was a straight 16-mile run-in to the proposed launch zone, 25 miles off the volcanic coast of La Palma. Subject to enemy intervention, they aimed to fire from 28.22N 17.28W.

Every man in the ship knew that the US defences would grow tighter and tighter with every mile they travelled. But no one had ever put a firm fix on the *Barracuda* as far as they knew. The crew were now generally aware of the prospect of imminent death, but they also felt a sense of security in their deepwater environment. They had just journeyed several hundred miles under the brutal surveillance of the US Navy, and no one had located them yet. They still had a chance.

By 1800 it was still broad daylight as they crept along the Gomera coast, and Lt. Mohammed advised that they now had a clear range in front of them straight to La Palma. Admiral Badr had already rolled the dice in his own mind. He was determined to accomplish the mission, determined to get a correct fix on Cumbre Vieja, determined to fire his two missiles straight into the crater, or as near as he possibly could. For the escape, everything was in the hands of Allah. But Admiral Badr knew that the odds heavily favoured the Americans.

Lt. Mohammed checked the ship's inertial navigation system (SINS), a device beyond the purse of most commercial shipping lines, and, in the end, way beyond that of Russia's cash-strapped Navy. But the

Barracuda had one, and it had measured course, speed and direction every yard of the way since they had left the submarine jetties in Huludao in the northern Yellow Sea three months earlier.

The system was developed especially for submarines in the 1950s and had been progressively refined in the years that followed. It had one objective: to inform navigators precisely where they were in the earth's oceans even after not having seen the sun, moon or stars for weeks on end. Both US nuclear boats the *Nautilus* and the *Skate* had used the system when they navigated under the polar ice cap in 1958.

The *Barracuda*'s SINS was vastly improved from those days, and phenomenally accurate, calculating regular accelerations but discarding those caused by gravitational attraction, pitching and rolling. All the way across the North Pacific, all the way down the endless West Coast of Canada and the USA, around South America and up the Atlantic, the SINS had provided a continuous picture of the submarine's precise position. Given the pinpoint certainty of their starting point, the system would be accurate to between 100 and 200 yards at the completion of a round-the-world voyage.

In recent years, the ease and brilliance of the GPS had somewhat overshadowed the old inertial navigation processes, but every submarine navigation officer kept one quietly on-stream. Indeed, most senior Navy navigators instinctively checked one against the other at all times.

Lt. Ashtari Mohammed knew precisely where he was, despite the best efforts of the US Air Force in Colorado to confuse the life out of him. The SINS screen now put him at 26.17N 17.12W. They were off the north coast of Gomera in 125 fathoms, still 500 feet below the surface.

This would be the final visual fix before they headed into the firing zone, and Lt. Mohammed requested a seven–second look through the periscope to take a range and bearing on the towering basalt cliffs of Les Organos, just over five miles to their southwest, and still visible in the late afternoon light, now a little after 1830.

Ben Badr agreed to head for the surface at slow speed, and he did so knowing their target above the coast of La Palma was dead ahead, 41 miles, west–nor'west. The periscope of the *Barracuda* slid onto the azure surface of the water on a calm afternoon. The admiral was staring at a stopwatch, ticking off the seconds. He heard them call out the fix on two points of Gomera's coastline – Les Organos and the great curved headland north of the village of Agula.

'*UP PERISCOPE!*'

'*All round look . . .*'

'*DOWN!*'

'*UP! Right-hand edge – MARK! DOWN!*'

'*Two-four-zero.*'

'*UP PERISCOPE! Left-hand edge – MARK! DOWN!*'

'*One-eight-zero.*'

'*UP!*'

'*Organo anchorage light . . . two-two-zero . . .*'

'*DOWN!* How does that look, Captain Mohtaj?'

'Excellent fix, sir. Course for launch position . . . two–nine–zero . . . distance 16 miles.'

Admiral Badr heard the comms room accept a signal from the Chinese naval satellite, and then he snapped: *Okay, that's it, five down . . . 600 feet . . . make your speed seven knots. Make a racetrack pattern when you're on depth . . .*

Ben Badr knew there was little point making a three-hour low-speed run through the night into the launch zone, and then hanging around until daybreak right on the 25-mile line from La Palma's east coast. The place would be jumping with US warships, helicopters and fixed–wing aircraft.

Right here off Gomera no one was looking quite so intensely. Generally speaking, Ben Badr preferred to run in silently, arriving at first light and setting up his visual fix with the sun rising to the east directly behind him. That way he could come to PD essentially out of nowhere, and he'd surely be able nail down his fix without detection, seven seconds at a time.

He called for the satellite message, which he knew was from General Rashood. *Ben, the thoughts of both Shakira and myself are with you at this time. If Allah is listening, as He surely must, His humble warriors will be safe. The prayers of all Muslims right now are only for you . . . to wish you the safest journey home after the SCIMITARs have done their holy work. Ravi.*

2300 Thursday 8 October 2009
The White House, Washington, DC

Admiral Morgan and President Bedford were gathered with senior naval commanders in the Situation Room in the lower floor of the West Wing. A huge, back-lit computer screen showed a chart of the Canary islands, a sharp red cross in a circle signifying the last two sightings which the Navy believed to be the *Barracuda*. A brighter white cross in a circle showed the spot Admiral Frank Doran, on the Norfolk link, believed the *Barracuda* now to be.

He had it already on the 25-mile radius line from the La Palma coast. Which was slightly jumping the gun. Admiral Badr had not yet made his final commitment to the run-in to the launch zone. And would not do so for another half-hour. The US admirals' estimates were about 16 miles ahead of themselves, which is a fair long way in a remote and deserted ocean.

Admiral Morgan was personally bracing himself to read a report from a hastily convened meeting in London of the International Convention for the Safety of Life at Sea. This august gathering meets only around every twelve to fifteen years specifically to draw up the International Regulations for the Prevention of Collisions at Sea, more generally known as the Rules of the Road.

Before him was the Convention's first report of a day without GPS. And the opening instance of disaster, the very first serious wreck, astounded him.

A Liberian-registered crude carrier of some 300,000 tons had somehow mistaken the southern shores of the entrance to the Magellan Strait for the Isla de la Estada, turned sharp right making 20 knots, and driven the tanker straight onto the beach at Punta Delgada.

'Five hundred miles off course! In a calm, near-landlocked bay, and he thought he was on his way through the roughest goddamned ocean waters in the world, on his way to Cape Horn!'

'Jesus Christ!' said Arnold. 'Jesus H. Christ.'

The second item did even less to restore his equilibrium. A Panama-registered freighter out of Indonesia had completely missed Japan's huge southern island of Kyushu, never mind the port of Kagoshima, her final destination. The freighter headed straight for the tip of the South Korean peninsula, but never made that either; charged straight into the seaport of Seowipo on the lush sub-tropical island of Jejudo and rammed the evening ferry from Busan.

Arnold could hardly believe his eyes. The third item was equally appalling. The master of a 200,000-tonner, carrying crude oil to Rotterdam, slammed into the Goodwin Sands at low tide, six miles off the coast of Kent at the north end of the English Channel, and was still jammed tight in about four feet of water.

There was a another huge tanker on the beach in northern Nigeria, a chartered yacht parked 300 miles adrift off the wrong island in the West Indies, and the captain of a large cruise ship out of Naples wondering why no one was speaking Italian on the island of Corsica.

Lloyd's of London were apoplectic. Every fifteen minutes there was another report from some remote corner of the globe where an expensive ship had lost its way and floundered ashore. Admiral Morgan was just beginning to see a glimmer of humour in all this, but the consequences of massive lawsuits directed at the United States for switching off the GPS prevented him from actually laughing out loud.

'The legal ramifications are clearly a nightmare,' offered Admiral Alan Dickson. 'Lloyd's might see it as an opportunity to get back at us after all these years – you know, that nutcase US judge who nearly bankrupted them twenty years ago, holding Lloyd's responsible for all those asbestos cases which happened years before anyone even dreamed the stuff was a health hazard.'

'They might at that,' said Arnold. 'But they'll have to do it here. And since it was essentially the military which switched the GPS off for military reasons, we'll probably refuse to submit to the judgement of civilians.'

'Good idea,' replied Admiral Dickson. 'Meanwhile, the world's beaches are filling up with shipwrecks.'

'Driven and piloted by incompetents,' said Arnold. 'Guys who should not hold licences to navigate in open waters. And we gave all shipping corporations ample warnings of a forty-eight-hour break in GPS service. They put monkeys at the helm of their own ships, that's their goddamned problem, right?'

'Absolutely, sir,' said the CNO. 'Guess there's no change in the eastern Atlantic. No sight nor sound of the submarine, for what? Almost a day?'

'Almost,' replied Arnold. 'And right now we're coming up to midnight. Just a few minutes and it's 9 October. D-Day. I just hope the little bastard comes to the surface real soon. George Gillmore's got the entire area surrounded.'

'Well, the only good thing about not seeing him is that he can't fire without coming to PD. Just as long as he stays submerged he ain't firing. And that pleases me no end.'

'And me,' said Arnold.

Lt. Commander Jimmy Ramshawe, sitting thoughtfully in the corner with his laptop, suddenly spoke. 'You know, sir. I wouldn't be the least surprised if we were way off in our assessment of the *Barracuda*'s position right now. I can't imagine why he'd run right up to the heaviest patrolled spot in the area and then hang around. If you ask me, he's still lurking off Gomera. And he won't close in 'til he's good and ready to launch.'

'As a matter of fact, that's what I'd do,' said Arnold. 'I'd stay somewhere quiet and then run in at first light.'

'How long's that, Arnold?' asked the President.

'Well, they're four hours in front of us, so I'd say another couple of hours.'

'Not me, sir,' said Lt. Commander Ramshawe. 'I'd

go while it was still bloody dark. And I'd go damn slow, so the minute I got there, I could get the periscope up and make my visual fix.'

'Have you ever been in a submarine, Ramshawe?' said Admiral Morgan, sternly.

'No, sir.'

'Well, you shoulda been. Got the right instincts. And I think you might be correct. Let's get Frank on the line in Norfolk. See what he thinks. Then we'll get a signal on the satellite to George Gillmore.'

Meanwhile, beyond the White House, the East Coast prepared for the final stages of the evacuation, which, by Presidential decree would begin at midnight. The streets were busier now than they had been for several hours. The lights were beginning to go out in several government buildings as skeleton staffs headed for the cars and the roads to the northwest.

The police were scheduled to make the beltway around the city one way, anti-clockwise, and designate the main Highway 279 'north only', starting at midnight. This would enable all members of government to head for the Camp Goliath area, fast.

President Bedford insisted on being among the very last to leave the deserted capital city. 'Not until we know that the volcano has been blown,' he said. 'Not until the *tsunami* is within 500 miles of our shores. That's when we go.'

Over at the Pentagon, the Special Ops Room staff intended to remain functional until the very last moment before flying up to Goliath. The US Marines had two Super Stallions ready to take off from the Pentagon, and two more on the White House lawn. Between them they could airlift 220 key personnel from the jaws of danger.

As the clocks ticked into the small hours of the morning, the vast evacuation of the East Coast was almost complete. It was now 9 October, and all the small towns from Maine to south Florida were very nearly depleted.

Places like Boston, Newport and Providence, Rhode Island, the Long Island suburbs, New Jersey and the Carolina coastal plains were all but deserted. The one city still writhing in desperate last-minute agonies was the Big Apple – New York City, where the traffic snarls were still appalling and the railroads were still packed with thousands of people trying to make it to safety, west of the city. But their journeys were so much longer than those of the short-haul Washington evacuees, and the New Englanders fleeing Boston for the relative closeness of the Massachusetts hills.

Trains took twice as long to return to New York, across the vast New Jersey flatlands, most of which were about six inches above sea level. And there were so many more thousands of people with nowhere to go. The Army was coping valiantly, bringing in hundreds upon hundreds of trucks, and commandeering just about every gallon of gas in the state. But the evacuation was just swamped with the massive throng of people trying to get out of the city and the Army commanders began to think that there were not enough trucks, buses and trains in the entire world to sort them all out, before the whole goddamned place went underwater.

The Ops Room in the Pentagon received a new and heartfelt request from New York every hour. More transportation, more manpower, more helicopters. The last one read by General Tim Scannell was from a Gulf War veteran, a high-ranking colonel, and it ended thus: '*Sir, you have absolutely no idea what it's like up here. I never saw so many frightened people. Terrified people, that is. They don't know what's going to happen to them. I implore you to get another hundred trucks into Midtown Manhattan. Or I'm afraid we'll just go under.*'

Admiral Morgan was well aware of the crisis facing the Big Apple, and he conferred with General Scannell on an hourly basis. They banned any form of crisis coverage by the media, shut down the New York newspapers and took over the television networks, using them strictly to broadcast military information and instructions to the population. Coverage of any kind of confusion, or 'human interest' stories, which might spread panic, was absolutely banned.

Admiral Morgan told all corporate media managements that if one of them dared to transgress his guidelines, their building would be instantly shut down and then barred by the heavy guns of the tanks which roamed the New York City streets.

General Scannell actually appeared on the screen in a closed-circuit television link-up to all broadcasting stations on the East Coast to confirm the martial law threat made by the Supreme Commander of Operation High Tide. 'We can cope with damn near anything,' he said, 'except for mass panic. Do not even consider stepping out of line.'

So far no one had.

And now it was 0100 on the morning of 9 October, D-Day for the HAMAS hit men. With the exception of the churning cauldron of New York City, the East Coast evacuation was winding down. Millions of people had made their way to higher ground and now waited in the western hills from Maine to the Carolinas and beyond.

Military spokesmen occupied every television and radio channel and their words were professionally calming, assuring the population that the front line of the United States Navy still stood between the terrorists and the execution of their attack on the great volcano in the eastern Atlantic.

Admiral Morgan had instructed the military broadcasters to sign off each one-hour bulletin after midnight with the reassuring morale-boosting words, 'We have the power, the technology and the bravest of men to carry out the Pentagon's defensive plan — and always remember the words of the great American sports writer Damon Runyon, *the race is not always to the swift, nor the battle to the strong — but that's the way to bet!*

090500OCT09. Eastern Atlantic
Barracuda *28.21N 17.24W*
Speed 5. Depth 600. Course 290

The waters were still dark above the *Barracuda* as it ran silently along its west-nor'west course. They were three miles short of their launch position, running well below the layers, transmitting nothing, still undetected.

At 0530 local time Admiral Badr slid up to periscope depth, and inside his seven-second exposure limit he was immediately aware the entire area was lousy with anti-submarine units, active and therefore probably passive too. But the 'layers' had protected him well, and he threaded his way deep again, into the great underwater caverns which so distort and confuse probing sonars from the surface.

Ben had enough time to assess that there were almost certainly Viking aircraft combing the surface above him but few ships. As they continued forward, however, he could hear active transmissions from helicopters and frigates inshore of him. All in all, he concluded, there was a highly active layer of US defence from about 12 miles off the towering eastern shores of La Palma.

For the fifth time in the early morning journey he ordered a major course change, just to check that there was no one trailing behind him. Then he corrected it back to two-nine-zero, and slowly, making scarcely a ripple, he once more brought the ship to periscope depth for his final fix. And as the submarine slid gently into the now brightening surface waters, he made one single order:

'*PREPARE MISSILES FOR LAUNCH!*'

They detected no active transmissions close to, and Admiral Badr nodded curtly to the helmsman, Chief Ali Zahedi, who cut their speed to just three knots.

'*UP PERISCOPE, ALL ROUND LOOK!*'

Twenty seconds later '*DOWN!*'

Ahmed Sabah, keenly aware of the seven-second rule drummed into him by Admiral Badr, knew the mast had been up too long. And he stared at the CO, trying to read either 'rattled', 'desperate' or 'confused' into his leader's expression. But he saw nothing, apart from a certain bland acceptance. And he did not like what he saw. Not one bit.

'*Allah!*' thought the brother of Mrs Ravi Rashood. '*He's given up, he thinks we're trapped.*'

'Sir?' he said, questioningly.

And Ben Badr, apparently unhearing, said mechanically, 'The place is swarming with helicopters. And I thought I saw a frigate inshore.' And then:

'*STAND BY FOR FINAL FIX AND LAUNCH! UP!*'

'*Point Fuencaliente Lighthouse. Bearing. MARK! DOWN!*'

'*Two-eight-six.*'

'*UP! Point de Arenas Blancas Lighthouse. Bearing MARK! DOWN!*'

'*Three-zero-seven.*'

The planesmen held the submarine at PD. And

the seconds ticked away before Ben Badr again ordered:

'UP! *High Peak, Cumbre Vieja Mountains. Bearing.* MARK! DOWN!'

Lt. Ashtari Mohammed, drawing swift, straight pencil lines on his chart, connected the final X which marked the High Peak and the launch point, then called clearly:

'TWO-NINE-SEVEN . . . *range 26.2 miles.*'

'Plot that pilot – and get the positions into the computer right away – for launch.'

0556 (local) US Army Patriot Station
Cumbre Vieja Volcano Summit

To the east, the American guided–missile men manning the ring of Patriot rockets had a sensational view of the Atlantic Ocean, beyond which the sun was shimmering dark red as it eased its way above the horizon. The rose curtain of dawn reflected the burning west coast of Africa, and it seemed to illuminate their battleground.

The Americans stared down–range towards the waters which shielded their enemy. They were out there somewhere, but hidden, an unseen force waiting to strike at them from out of the blue. But the men of the Patriot batteries were ready, and many of them stood, fists clenched tight, watching the tireless Navy helicopters and Vikings clatter over the distant ocean wilderness, sonars probing.

Major Blake Gill had snatched some sleep late the previous afternoon, but had been wide awake ever since, patrolling his eight missile batteries ranged around the crater. He made his patrols on foot, accompanied by four Special Forces bodyguards. At each one he stopped and stared at the looming launch platforms above his head, as if probing for a mistake, a wrong angle, a wrong electronic connection. But he found nothing.

The MIM-104E enhanced guidance Patriots, the only SAM which had ever knocked a ballistic missile out of the sky in combat, were immaculately deployed on all points of the compass. All thirty-two of them were in place, ready to go at a split-second's notice. Blake knew he was looking at the greatest interceptor ever built, a steel hit-to-kill weapon.

He had towering pride in the equipment he controlled, and he told each and every team as they gathered around him up there in the dark, on the summit of the volcano, 'I been in the ole missile game a long time. And I seen a lot of guys come and go. But if I had to name the one team I ever met who would damn and for sure knock this bastard out of the sky, it would be you guys. And hot damn! I mean that with all of my heart.'

He left them all feeling 10 feet tall, ready to operate at the absolute top of their game. And now he was watching the screens inside the Engagement Control Centre, just a little higher up the hill from the eight batteries, and he was demanding a last-minute check on communications, ensuring they were in constant touch with the missile launch and tracking stations on the four frigates in the immediate area, the *Elrod*, *Nicholas*, *Klakring* and the *Simpson*.

He opened up the lines and checked with Admiral Gillmore's ops room on the *Coronado*. He checked the computer lines, and the comms to the patrolling airborne helicopters. Blake left nothing to chance – any one of those guys out on the water, radar men, lookouts, sonar rooms, pilots or navigators; anyone who saw anything was just two touches of a button from instant contact with the Patriot Engagement Control Centre.

They needed to move fast, but they still had time. In Major Gill's opinion, the US defence forces were heavy odds-on to win. Just as long as everyone stayed on top of their game.

The big 17-foot Patriots would do the rest. At least, the 200 pounds of TNT jammed inside the warheads would, as they streaked in towards the SCIMITARs at Mach 5. The HAMAS missiles had the element of surprise in their favour, but the US Patriot was six times as fast, and well-proven over the course.

Major Gill spoke to Admiral Gillmore and the two men once more checked their entire comms systems. The new Patriot could cope with bad weather, a long, 40-mile-plus range, any altitude, and it did not need to collide with the incoming missile. The Patriot's state-of-the art proximity fuse would detonate when one came close, and would blast the SCIMITAR to bits without even hitting it.

0635 (local) Barracuda
28.22N 17.28W Launch zone
'UP! Better all-round look . . .'

Ben Badr looked and felt relaxed. He marked a helo in the dip three miles to the west, and another in transit two miles to the north. He noted the class of the Oliver Hazard Perry frigate inshore of him, and its bearing.

It was a rather leisurely survey of the waters around the submarine, conducted by a man who believed he had all the time in the world but knew, in his heart, that there would be no escape in the end. They couldn't stop him firing, and they probably would not have time to stop the SCIMITARs. But whatever happened, they would not let him out of the waters around the Canary Islands. This had become, most definitely, a suicide mission.

The *Barracuda*'s periscope was jutting out of the water for all of sixty seconds, too long, too hopelessly long. And the US helicopter in transit, piloted by Lt. Don Brickle caught it on radar, at 0635.

He swerved towards it, for a dip on the last known position, and instantly alerted the ops room in the *Nicholas*, plus any other helicopter in the vicinity.

Three minutes later the *Barracuda* sonar room reported the helo's hydrophone effect (HE) and sonar transmissions from close astern.

Simultaneously Lt. Ashtari Mohammed called out the positions inserted into the SCIMITAR's fire-control computer.

554

'MISSILES READY TO LAUNCH!'

Lt. Brickle banked his Seahawk hard to starboard and spotted the great black shadow of the *Barracuda* just below the surface as he overflew. It was holding its two-nine-seven course and over his right shoulder he saw the *Nicholas's* second helo, piloted by Lt. Ian Holman, hurtling in from the southeast.

And at that precise moment, Ben Badr ordered his missiles away.

'STAND BY!'

'READY!'

'FIRE!'

The big Russian submarine shuddered gently as the first of the mighty SCIMITARs ripped out of its tube and broke the surface, roaring skyward in a cloud of fire and spray. Its rear wings snapped out sharply and it cleaved its way up through the clear early morning air, growling and echoing with malevolence, just as it had been programmed to do by the secret rocket engineers beneath the North Korean mountain of Kwanmo-Bong.

Admiral Badr watched it through the periscope. He stood staring at the lenses as the Mark-2 nuclear-headed weapon made a high, steep trajectory, 600 mph on an unswerving course, straight at the crater of Cumbre Vieja, 26 miles away. Two minutes and thirty-six seconds flying time. It was headed straight into the path of the USS *Elrod*, under the command of Captain C.J. Smith.

Ben Badr wished with all of his heart that Ravi and Shakira could have been with him to share the moment. He would not, however, have wished the next half-hour on his worst enemy.

And he stepped away to give what he believed correctly might be his last command.

'*STAND BY MISSILE TWO!*'

High above them Lt. Brickle was hard at work vectoring Lt. Holman onto their target.

'*Firm contact active. Classified CERTSUB bearing two-nine-seven — range 600 yards, opening slow. Vectoring Dipper Delta Three into immediate attack, using light-weight torpedo.*'

'*Delta Three this is Bravo Two, vector 225, stand by weapon launch . . .*'

'*Delta Three, roger — out.*'

'*STAND BY — STAND BY! MARK DROP! Now! Now! NOW!*'

Lt. Holman hit the button with his right hand and the Mark-50 torpedo flashed away from his undercarriage, diving steeply towards the water.

Bravo Two — this is Delta Three. Weapon in water. I can see his periscope still headed west-nor'west. Intend taking dip station three miles ahead.

'*Roger that, Delta Three. Target speeding up — Jesus Christ! He's launched another missile!*'

On board the *Barracuda* everyone heard the explosion and they felt the massive impact of the torpedo as it slammed into their starboard quarter 30 feet astern of the fin. The blast almost spun the submarine over, rolling it onto its port side.

Aft in the reactor control, Commander Abbas Shafii and Commander Hamidi Abdolrahim were

556

hurled with terrific force into the bulkhead. But the roll was too great for the reactor, which automatically 'scrammed', the rods dropping in and shutting it down completely.

The main lights went out instantly and water cascaded onto the decks, but the compartments were sealed, and though Admiral Badr knew that the ship was damaged, probably severely, it wasn't sinking. He ordered the crew to reduce speed, down to five knots, on battery power only. And he made a course change to the south, bow down 10, trying to get deep.

The battered commanders in the reactor control room regained their feet. Chief Ardeshir Tikku came away from the screens and tried to assist. Every alarm in the ship was sounding, and Captain Mohtaj took over the conn while Ben Badr and Chief Ali Zahedi made their way for'ard.

'SHAFII . . . we need to get that reactor up and running fast . . . start pulling the rods, otherwise we're beaten.'

Chief Ardeshir Tikku's fingers flew over the keyboard, unaware that, high above, Lt. Ian Holman and Lt. Don Brickle were preparing to strike again. The two Seahawks were clattering directly above the wallowing *Barracuda*, communicating calmly with a new arrival, *Delta Four*, the helicopter from *Elrod* piloted by Lt. Paul Lubrano.

'*This is Bravo Two. Explosion on bearing two-nine-six. Delta Four stand by second weapon drop. Delta Three interrogative hot?*'

'*Delta Three Hot, bearing three-five-six, range two*

557

thousand five hundred yards. Explosion on bearing, still closing. Explosion on bearing. Delta Four standby.'

'*Delta Four.*'

'*Delta Four, Delta Three, vector 065, stand by.*'

'*Delta Four, this is Delta Three, MARK DROP! Now, now, NOW!*'

'*Delta Four, weapon away!*'

The second torpedo dropped away from the pursuing Seahawk and split the waves with its impact, powering hard towards the stricken *Barracuda*, which now limped along 50 feet below the surface. It smashed into the casing for'ard of the fin and blew a hole almost 30 feet wide. Water thundered into the submarine.

No one knew exactly what had hit them. In precisely thirty-two seconds the submarine had been slammed twice and now she made her last dive. Through the sonars the US Navy operators heard the strange metallic, tinkling sound that signifies a big warship breaking up on its way to the ocean floor.

The reactor control room staff managed to seal off their section of the boat with seconds to spare. And they might have lived one minute longer than the rest of the ship's company. But at 2,000 feet the pressure could not but crush the remnants of the hull. And now it sliced down in several large pieces, still clanking, like the bells of hell.

Meanwhile on board the *Elrod* the lookouts saw the missile launch and watched it climb to the west. Inside the ops room the McDonnell Douglas Harpoon radar system acquired the target immediately and locked on.

The Officer of the Deck reported to the CO, 'Captain, sir, sub-surface missile-launch green 65, four miles opening arcs for SAM.'

'*Very well, Missile Control . . . you have permission to shoot – WEAPONS FREE!*'

The first ASROC lanced into the air in a huge cloud of smoke, making Mach O.9, straight at the SCIMITAR hurtling upwards, high overhead. Seconds later there was a huge puff of smoke, way up in the stratosphere as the heat-seeking US missile smacked into North Korea's finest, reducing it to high-altitude rubble.

In the same split second the next Harpoon was launched at the same target, but in the absence of a SCIMITAR it locked onto the nearest Seahawk, *Bravo Two*, swerved towards it and it was just 'cut down' in time by the *Elrod*'s fire-control centre.

Bravo Two's pilot, Lt. Don Brickle, nearly had a heart attack when he saw the Harpoon scything through the sky, coming straight at him. And even when it blew apart a mile and a half out, he was still aggrieved.

'Jesus, you guys. Are you out of control? I'm on your side . . . you think I was wearing a fucking turban!'

There was a semblance of mass confusion and a slight amount of shaky laughter, interspersed with one report stating that the second Harpoon had been 'cut down' and splashed into the water, another confirming the hit on the first SCIMITAR. A third confirmed two major explosions from the submarine. Yet another announced the second of the *Barracuda*'s missiles was on its way.

The high-octane chatter on the helicopter frequencies was now baffling the life out of everyone. Captain C.J. Smith ordered, *WEAPONS TIGHT!* before someone else tried to shoot down a Seahawk.

And then it became crystal-clear. The second SCIMITAR was well on its way, making a steep trajectory straight down the bearing towards Cumbre Vieja. It had been running a full forty seconds. It was still climbing after six miles, and C.J. Smith himself snapped out the critical order:

'*Patriot Boss – frigate Foxtrot Charlie. Missile inbound one-one-three. All yours, over.*'

Major Gill, up on the heights in the Engagement Control Centre, watched the automatic system instantly activate the band-tracking radar, the radar beams which could locate and track 100 targets at a time if necessary.

The search, target detection, track and identification, missile tracking and guidance, took four and a half seconds to lock on . . . *Got it, sir!*

'*This is Patriot Boss. We have it. Are you expecting more?*'

'*Unknown, Patriot Boss. We have problems out here, but launch vehicle is under heavy attack. Further launches possible but unlikely.*'

'*Patriot Boss, roger that.*'

At which moment the first of the most sophisticated guided missiles ever built howled into the sky above the crater, its radar being controlled automatically from the digital weapons control computer right next to Major Gill in the ECC.

The Patriot thundered up its course, bearing 113, seeking its target, which was now headed downwards from an altitude of 30,000 feet, about 10 miles out from the crater.

Major Gill ordered missiles two, three and four to launch. But there was scarcely a need. Patriot One, making over 3,000 miles an hour, screamed through the air towards the SCIMITAR. Twelve seconds from launch, it blasted with staggering force less than 50 feet from the HAMAS missile. Two hundred pounds of TNT, almost enough to make a dent in the island of Gomera, cast a bright but smoky glow in the azure skies.

The second SCIMITAR was blown apart, its burning fuel falling colourfully over a wide area, nine miles out from the volcano. Its nuclear warhead never ignited; it simply dropped into the Atlantic. And the cheer that went up from Major Gill's missile men would not have disgraced Yankee Stadium.

'*Foxtrot Charlie. This is Patriot Boss. Missile splashed.*'

'*Foxtrot Charlie. Thank Christ for that.*'

Admiral George Gillmore sent in the official report to the Pentagon: *090652OCT09. Barracuda submarine fired two submerged-launch guided missiles at the Cumbre Vieja volcano east of La Palma from 25-mile range. Submarine destroyed and sunk by two helo-launched torpedoes. Both missiles splashed. Harpoon from USS Elrod. Patriot from the summit. God Bless America. Gillmore.*

EPILOGUE

Operation High Tide was declared at an end in the small hours of 9 October. Americans awakened to learn that the danger had passed. The threat had been real, the US military had destroyed it, and it was a weary Admiral and Mrs Arnold Morgan who left the Oval Office at four o'clock that morning.

They climbed aboard the new Hummer 2A, with its bullet-proof, darkened windows, and were driven out through the northern suburbs of Washington to the big colonial house in Chevy Chase, followed by a Secret Service detail of four guards.

It was almost 5.45 when Kathy produced poached eggs, English muffins, grilled bacon and sausage. It may have seemed like a banquet, but neither the Supreme Commander of High Tide nor his wife had eaten anything since the previous Wednesday's breakfast of fruit salad.

Admiral Morgan, calling the shots from the Oval Office, may have looked what the media called him – the Consummate Military Hardman – but the HAMAS threat to the USA had taken a seven-week toll on him.

Personally, Kathy blamed Charles McBride. 'If that

damn fool had listened,' she said, sipping her coffee. 'If he'd just taken the advice of his Intelligence officers and the military, half the pressure would have been removed from this operation. The people who knew how to handle things could have just got on with it.'

'You're right there,' muttered Arnold. 'We've got to keep our guard up. Always. Because there's a lot of enemies out there. But the biggest danger to the United States of America is when you get some comedian in short pants in the Oval Office.'

'Do you think it will all come out – the military coup in the White House, the removal of the President, and . . . everything?' asked Kathy.

'I sure as hell hope not,' replied Arnold. 'I hate to see the country tearing itself apart. And I'm just hoping that that jackass McBride feels suitably ashamed. At least too ashamed to write his god-damned memoirs.'

'Did Alan Dickson tell you how close that last missile was when the Patriot blew it up?'

'Oh, that wasn't a problem. The guys had a ton of time once they got the bird away.'

'Yes, but how long would it have been before it hit the crater?'

'Forty seconds.'

'Mother of God.'

President Paul Bedford broadcast to the nation at 7 a.m. He announced an end to the emergency, and an end to the effective martial law which had been in place for the past ten days.

He appealed for a calm return to normal life and assured everyone that the armed forces would do everything in their power to help restore order in the big cities.

He congratulated the media on their restraint and cooperation, without ever referring to the fact that Admiral Morgan had threatened to blow up their buildings if they stepped out of line.

He regretted all of the inconvenience and huge amount of Federal money which had been expended on the civilian and government operations.

'However,' said President Bedford, 'I was sworn into this great office, not just to protect the Constitution, but to protect the citizens of the United States of America. Each and every one of you. It was an unwritten promise, but one which I took most seriously.'

He outlined with brevity and a certain coolness the scale of the threat from a group of Middle Eastern terrorists.

'I could take no chances,' he said. 'Five hours ago, the United States armed forces destroyed the terrorists and their missiles, and their submarine. The danger is passed.

'However, we have opened up consultations with the Government of Spain to place a US missile shield on permanent guard on the summit of Cumbre Vieja. We have also begun negotiations to form a coalition of interested parties to build an engineering system which will drain the underground lakes beneath the volcano.

'And with these initiatives, we issue a warning to

HAMAS, and to other organisations like them – *WE ARE NOT YET FINISHED WITH THIS – WE WILL COME AFTER YOU WHEREVER YOU MAY BE HIDING.'*

Same day. Damascus, Syria

Ravi and Shakira Rashood, watching the CNN satellite news broadcast in the big house on Sharia Bab Touma, were stunned at the announcement, slowly grasping the fact that Ben Badr and Ahmed Sabah, together with the rest of the crew, were dead.

They had believed their mission to be impregnable, that even the mighty USA was powerless to locate a marauding nuclear boat.

Still in shock, they walked to the great Umayyad Mosque before the Citadel and prayed for their fallen comrades. Each of them had known of the massive danger. And each of them had realised that Allah might call their companions to Paradise at any moment.

However, when close friends, comrades and relatives are involved, death always comes on ravens' wings. And the general and his wife were unable to speak for a long time.

White House. Same time

Meanwhile, President Bedford concluded his address to the nation. 'Once again,' he said, 'the men of the United States Army and Navy have come through for all of us with their customary bravery and efficiency. And I thank them all, in particular their outstanding commanders.

'I thank also the Supreme Commander of this operation, both civilian and military, Admiral Arnold Morgan, who most of you will remember from the last Administration. The admiral, as ever, stepped up to the plate when the nation was threatened.

He has scarcely left the White House for the past eight days, and yet, when our combat troops fought that short and vicious engagement out there in the eastern Atlantic this morning . . . well . . . I guess we had an extra man on every missile battery, at sea and on land . . . in every helicopter . . . in every ops room . . . A man who was, in a sense, with them, every yard of the way.

'Admiral Morgan is just that kind of guy, and every man in the armed services knows it. And I do not quite know how we would have got along without him.

'And I am sure you will join with me in now wishing him a long and happy retirement.'

Chevy Chase. Same time
Arnold took another king-sized bite of sausage, and Kathy blew him a kiss from across the room.

'Hear that, my darling?' she said. 'Retirement.'

'That's right,' said Arnold, munching away cheerfully. 'That's what I'm doing.'

'Right,' replied Kathy Morgan, a little uneasily. 'It's just that I darn well know when something diabolical happens, they'll summon you again. And when the bugle sounds, you'll still come out fighting.'

ACKNOWLEDGEMENTS

My long transglobal journey in a Russian-built nuclear submarine was masterminded by Admiral Sir John 'Sandy' Woodward, former nuclear boat commander, former Flag Officer Submarines, Royal Navy. The admiral is the last man to fight a full-scale modern naval action at sea – as Task Force Commander, Royal Navy, in the battle for the Falkland Islands, 1982.

He also advised me with endless patience on the complexities of nuclear propulsion, without demonstrating even a glimmer of frustration. Well, not that many. In the decisive naval action of the book it was his decision to strike from the air rather than underwater. He also helped me plan the US Navy's search-and-kill strategy in the eastern Atlantic. And, as ever, he has my gratitude.

The former Special Forces officers, who tend to be in constant attendance while I write these 'techno-thrillers', never wish to be identified for obvious reasons. But I thank them all the same. And they each know how grateful I am.

I consulted on both sides of the Atlantic with

three eminent scientists on the cause and effects of *tsunamis*. On two or three critical issues there was a slight variance of opinion. I thus name none of them, since to do so might cause a certain amount of friction in the geophysical community. Worse yet, I should almost certainly get the blame for tampering, albeit lightly, with sincerely held opinions!

AUTHOR'S NOTE

January 2005

Scimitar SL-2 – that's a medium-range guided missile, submerged launch from a submarine, Mark 2 nuclear warhead. Generally speaking, one of these could knock down a town the size of Brighton.

It ended up the title for this novel. But it was not my first choice. That was 'Tsunami', which had, at the time, raised a near-unanimous objection from my agent and publishers on both sides of the Atlantic: *Japanese word, no one knows what it means.*

Well, everyone knows only too well what that word means now. The horrific events of December 26 2004, which have devastated literally millions of lives, brought the word 'tsunami' into the world's vocabulary. Its literal meaning is 'harbour wave', but that doesn't seem an adequate description for what is possibly the greatest geophysical catastrophe which can befall the planet Earth, short of a direct hit by a comet.

And words could barely describe the monstrous events that early morning when a colossal earthquake below the floor of the Indian Ocean caused great waters to rise up and drown, at the time of writing, an estimated 178,000 people on coastlines near and far from the epicentre of the waves' formation.

My research for *Scimitar SL-2* means that for months I had been researching the cause and effect of such mammoth waves.

The causes are relatively simple. You need a mighty splash in the ocean, and essentially there are only three ways to get one big enough: landslide, volcanic eruption or earthquake. A tsunami can develop a speed of up to 400 knots as it rolls across the ocean floor; a blast in the Hawaiian islands started a tsunami which swept huge rocks thousands of miles, to end up in Sydney Harbour. When the volcanic island of Krakatoa blew off its entire summit in the Sunda Strait in 1883 it was one of the biggest blasts ever witnessed, or heard, for thousands of years. But it was not the blast that killed 36,000 people along the coasts of both Java and Sumatra. Most of them drowned beneath the mega-tsunami which engulfed the entire coastal area. This was the direct result of the splash in the ocean.

For over a year, I metaphorically lived tsunamis, trying to work out what would happen if the world's most dangerous geohazard – the glowering volcano of Cumbre Vieja in the Canary Islands – should erupt and cause the Atlantic mega-tsunami everyone in the trade believes to be a certainty. The one which would wipe out America's east coast, including Boston, New York, Philadelphia and Washington.

So when the first person walked up to me on Sunday morning, December 26th 2004 and said 'How about that tsunami then?' I experienced one of those cold shudders you're supposed to feel when someone's walking on your grave.

'The Atlantic?' I asked, horrified.

'No, somewhere in the Indian Ocean . . . but a lot of people are feared drowned.'

And as the day drew to a close, and I spoke with friends and family and watched on television the devastating effects of this geophysical disaster on the villages and tourist resorts along the coast of the Indian ocean, devastation that reached as far away as the coast of Somalia, I couldn't help but think of my novel *Scimitar SL-2*, and the imaginary tsunami I had unleashed on a different part of the world: the Eastern seaboard of the United States. I am in the fiction business. My imaginary scenario is set several years into the future where a group of high-tech terrorists succeed in exploding a volcano with guided missiles. I hadn't counted on the natural world providing the scenario for me. Fiction didn't prepare me for the tragic sight of families torn apart, nor the scenes of destruction of homes and businesses in neighbourhoods that were already poverty stricken. And I watched with horror as the death toll rose exponentially hour upon hour.

Thanks to my extensive research for *Scimitar SL-2*, I had a good idea about what had happened. Deep in the Indian Ocean the tectonic plates had shifted opening up a giant chasm into which the water had cascaded. When the chasm closed again the water was forced back upwards with stupendous

571

force and caused the massive waves of the mega-tsunami, rolling out in an ever-widening circle.

I went back to my charts of the Indian Ocean and the Bay of Bengal, not used since I wrote *The Shark Mutiny* in the year 2000, and looked at the surrounding coastlines. I knew from these charts that the initial estimate of 15,000 dead was set to rise. There is land at every point of the circle. The tsunami could not miss every town and village along the shore for hundreds of miles.

Of course, the terrible irony was, I had been trying to cause a fictional tsunami, trying to find out whether a man-made attack on a volcano could blast sufficient rock from a great height into the ocean and trigger the giant waves.

In the years between 2002 and 2010 it is estimated over 200 major eruptions will occur. But not many would cause a tsunami. Mount St. Helens in Washington State keeps letting out a smoky shout of warning, but the rumble that is the most worrying is the one beneath the Cumbre Vieja.

The world's foremost authority on volcanoes, Bill McGuire, is professor of Geophysical Hazards at University College, London. Bill McGuire is King of All Disasters, the author of hundreds of papers and books, broadcaster and acknowledged world authority on tsunamis and all that they stand for. He has studied Cumbre Vieja extensively and knows the devastation it could unleash should the worst case scenario happen. Professor McGuire finds an endless frustration with the refusal of governments to heed the warnings of him and his team, and all the other worldwide geo-hazard reports. And I understand that. For he has the inner sadness of a man who has been crying out for early warnings on tsunamis for many years.

I too have a similar sadness, because I have studied thousands of his words. And, from a plainly removed standpoint, I feel his pain at the apparent sudden-ness of the Asian tsunami, the absolute shock with which it descended into all our television sets and all of our newspapers.

But I have also been moved by the incredible generosity of people around the world who have contributed to the charities that have been set up to help those people directly affected by the tsunami. In a world where headlines are dominated by the escalating conflict in the Middle East it is this sort of generosity which shows the compassion of the human spirit. Yet the people in the region are going to need help not just in the weeks following the disaster, but in the months and years beyond that while they struggle to rebuild their lives.

You can contribute by donating to the Merlin Tsunami Appeal in the following ways:

By calling: 0870 199 6308
By post: Merlin
                Freepost Lon15423
                London
                EC2B 2BR
Please make the cheque payable to 'Merlin'.
Or online at www.merlin.org.uk
If you would like to increase the value of your gift,

please complete a <u>Gift Aid declaration form</u>, available from the website. It will enable Merlin to reclaim 28% of your donation from the taxman at no extra cost to you.

Thank you.

Patrick Robinson
January 2005

Coming in May 2005 from William Heinemann
Patrick Robinson's next thrilling bestseller **. . .**
HUNTER KILLER

Saudi Arabia, the world's leading oil nation, is on the brink of revolution. The Royal Family is ransacking the country's dwindling coffers while the desert kingdom seethes with unrest. Appalled at his family's extravagant lifestyle, Crown Prince Mohammed vows to end the careless and destructive rule and sets in motion a top-secret operation to destroy the Saudi oil industry and bankrupt the monarch. Mohammed turns to France. Her lethal Hunter Killer submarines can inflict devastating damage on the massive oil installations on the shores of the Red Sea and the Persian Gulf.

Under the command of Colonel Gamoudi, joined by Admiral Morgan's arch enemy HAMAS, the ferocious battle for the desert kingdom begins. As the world's oil markets plunge into chaos, who can capture Gamoudi first, the American Special Forces or French assassins?

Read on for an exclusive extract . . .

PROLOGUE

Prince Khalid bin Mohammed al-Saud, aged twenty-six, was enduring a night of fluctuating fortunes. On the credit side, he had just befriended a spectacular looking blonde named Adele who was just now clinging on to his left arm. On the debit side, he had just dropped $247,000 playing blackjack in one of the private gaming rooms.

The Casino in Monte Carlo was currently costing Khalid's great-great uncle, the King, around the same amount every month as the first-line combat air strength of the Royal Saudi Air Force. There were currently almost 35,000 Saudi royal princes giving new meaning to the word hedonism.

Like young Prince Khalid, many of them loved Monte Carlo, especially the Casino. And blackjack. And baccarat. And craps. And roulette. And expensive women. And champagne. And caviar. And high-speed motor yachts. Oh, boy; did those princes ever love motor yachts!

Prince Khalid pushed another $10,000-worth of chips towards his new princess and contemplated the sexual delights which most certainly awaited him. 'I think we shall seek further pleasures elsewhere,' he smiled. He caught the eye of a champagne waitress and requested a floor manager to settle his evening's account.

Prince Khalid was a direct descendant of the mighty Bedouin warrior Abdul Aziz, 'Ibn Saud', founder of modern Saudi Arabia, progenitor of more than 40 sons before his death in 1953. The young Prince Khalid was of the ruling line of the House of Saud, but there were thousands of cousins, uncles, brothers and close relatives. The King treated them all with unquestioning generosity.

With such generosity, in fact, that now, towards the end of the first decade of the twenty-first century, the great oil kingdom of the Arabian Peninsula now stood teetering on the brink of a financial precipice, because millions of barrels of oil needed to be pumped out of the desert purely to feed the colossal financial requirements of young spendthrifts like Khalid bin Mohammed al-Saud.

He was one of dozens who owned huge motor yachts moored in the harbours the length of the French Riviera. His boat, *Shades of Arabia*, a growling 107-foot long, sleek white Godzilla of a powerboat, was built in Florida by the renowned West Bay SonShip Corporation. Boasting five staterooms it was just about the last word in luxury yachts for its size.

Slipping his hand deftly around Adele's waist, Prince Khalid nodded to the members of his entourage who were crowded around the roulette wheel. They included his two minders Rashid and Ahmed, both Saudis, three friends from Riyadh, and five young women.

Outside the imposing white portals of the Casino, two Rolls-Royces and a Bentley slid into the forecourt. Prince Khalid slipped into the back seat of the lead car with Adele. Rashid and Ahmed, also boarded the gleaming dark-blue Silver Cloud, both of them in the wide front side.

The other eight were spread evenly between the other two cars and Prince Khalid instructed his driver to take them down to the boat.

'Of course, Your Highness,' replied Sultan, and moved off towards the harbour, followed by the other two cars. Three minutes later they pulled alongside *Shades of Arabia*, which rode gently on her lines in a flat calm harbour.

'Good evening, Your Highness,' called the watchman, turning on the gangway light. 'Will we be sailing tonight?'

'Just a short trip, two or three miles offshore to see the lights of Monaco, then back in by 1 a.m.,' replied the Prince.

'Very good, sir,' said the watchman, a young Saudi naval officer who had navigated one of the King's Corvettes in the Gulf Fleet headquarters in Al Jubayl. His name was Bandar and he had been specifically selected by the C-in-C to serve as first officer on *Shades of Arabia*.

Captain Hank Reynolds, out of Seattle Washington,

liked Bandar and they worked well together, which was just as well for Captain Reynolds because one word of criticism from young Bandar would have ended his career. The Saudis paid exorbitantly for top personnel from the West, but tolerated no insubordination directed at the royal presence.

Gathered in the magnificent stateroom Prince Khalid's party drank more vintage Reynolds from dewy magnums which cost around $250 each. On the dining room table there were two large crystal bowls, one containing prime Beluga caviar from Iran, at $100 an ounce.

The other contained white powder and was placed next to a polished teak stand upon which were set a dozen small, hand-blown, crystal tubes, four and a half inches long. The content of the second bowl was approximately twice as expensive as the Beluga. It was also in equal demand among the party.

Right now Prince Khalid was blasting the white powder up his nostrils with his regular abandon. He really liked cocaine. It made him feel that he was the right-hand man of the King of Saudi Arabia, the only country in the world that bore the name of the family which ruled it. His name.

Prince Khalid did his best not to confront the undeniable truth that he was as close to useless as made no difference. His Bachelor of Arts degree from a vastly expensive California university was, so far, his only true achievement. But in order for that degree to be awarded his father had had to persuade the King to build a huge new library for the university *and* stock it with thousands of books.

These days it was only when he took his nightly snort of cocaine that he felt he could face the world on equal terms. Indeed, on some evenings, with exactly the right combination of Krug and coke, Prince Khalid felt he could do anything. Tonight was one of those evenings.

The moment his head cleared from the initial rush he ordered Bandar to the bridge to inform Captain Hank that he, Khalid, would be taking the helm as soon as the great motor yacht had cast her lines. 'Have the Captain call me as soon as we're ready,' he added, making absolutely certain that Adele could hear his stern words of command.

Ten minutes later he took Adele up to the enclosed bridge area with its panoramic views of the harbour and assumed command of the yacht.

'She's ready, sir,' said Hank, a worried frown already on his face. 'Steer zero-eight-five, straight past the harbour wall up ahead, then come right to one-three-five for the run offshore . . . and watch your speed, *please*, Your Highness . . . that's a harbour-master's patrol boat right off your starboard bow . . .'

'No problem, Hank,' replied the prince. 'I feel good tonight; we'll have a nice run.'

And with that he rammed open both throttles, driving the twin 1800hp DDC-MTU 16V2000s to maximum revs, and thundered off the starting blocks. Adele squealed with delight. Hank Reynolds, as usual, nearly went into cardiac arrest.

Shades of Arabia, now with a great white bow wave